501
MUST-VISIT ISLANDS

501
MUST-VISIT ISLANDS

Bounty Books

Publisher: Polly Manguel

Project Editor: Emma Beare

Publishing Assistant: Sarah Marling

Designer: Ron Callow/Design 23

Picture Researchers: Janet Johnson and Mel Watson

Production Manager: Neil Randles

Production Assistant: Gemma Seddon

This paperback edition first published in Great Britain in 2008 by
Bounty Books, a division of Octopus Publishing Group Limited
2-4 Heron Quays, London E14 4JP
www.octopusbooks.co.uk

An Hachette Livre UK Company

A CIP catalogue record is available from the British Library

ISBN: 978-0-753717-64-6

Printed and bound in China

Please note: We now know that political situations arise very quickly and a country that was quite safe a short time ago can suddenly become a 'no-go' area. Please check with the relevant authorities before booking tickets and travelling if you think there could be a problem.

The seasons given in this book relate to the relevant hemisphere. Be sure to check that you visit at the correct time.

Contents

Introduction

There is a magical quality about the word 'island' that sends an endorphin rush to the head and the heart. It can conjure up visions of a tiny speck of land in the midst of turquoise seas, complete with white sand and coconut palms, or perhaps of a larger island swathed in dark green forest, with neat, wooden houses and clear water washing over granite boulders. It's wonderful that there are so many islands all over this planet of ours, which is made up of 70 per cent water, that there must be one that suits you perfectly. One dictionary definition of an island is 'a mass of land that is surrounded by water and is smaller than a continent'. Some islands, like Madagascar or Borneo, are huge landmasses, home to indigenous peoples and unique flora and fauna, while others are just dots in the ocean.

Perhaps living on an island makes people feel secure – surrounded and protected by the sea as they are. Islanders tend to be proud of their homeland, and somewhat insular in nature; for example, there are people on the Isle of Wight who have never felt the need to visit mainland Britain (also an island of course), just a short boat ride away. Most people in Corfu have never set foot upon Albanian soil, despite being so close to it geographically. There are Italians in Sicily and Sardinia who have never been to the mainland of their own country. Traditionally, islanders often feel slightly superior to their nearest – and usually bigger – neighbour.

We are curious about islands and are drawn to visit them, whether they are situated in an ocean, a lake, or a river or even man-made, as in the case of Dubai's Palm Islands. For their part, islanders themselves wonder how others can bear to live in the middle of a landmass, far from the sea.

Unique cultures arise on islands, where everything – the religion, the arts, the interaction between the sexes, and even the language – may be different from the mainland. It is a real tribute to the ingenuity and variety of mankind. There are island peoples who have no desire whatever to meet foreigners or join the 21st century, and whose governments wisely leave them to get on with their lives. For example, in

2004 a group of Andaman islanders attacked a helicopter with bows and arrows when it flew over after the tsunami, to check whether or not there were survivors. On the other hand, the Dani, a tribe in the interior of New Guinea, live extremely traditionally but they accept the tourist dollar for allowing outsiders to see how they do it.

Today, some islands are becoming more politically important and find themselves at the centre of geo-political wrangles – not so much because of the land itself but because of the oil and gas that lie beneath the surrounding seas; the Antarctic islands and East Timor come instantly to mind. Often several major political heavyweights make attempts to grab these resources, and the islands' populations have to fight to keep a realistic share of the profits.

While some islands are dedicated to religion, others embrace Mammon: there are islands in the Caribbean that are such wealthy tax havens that they are almost sinking under the weight of their banks, with one per cent of the population living in luxury and the rest living on virtually nothing. The island of Manhattan is a showcase for the world's richest and most technologically advanced country, but New York City is home to some of America's most deprived and dysfunctional areas. Bali, a Hindu island with its own language, culture and local laws is located in the middle of the world's largest (in terms of population) Muslim country, Indonesia. There are islands in the world's frozen north whose inhabitants have proved incredibly ingenious at finding ways to live harmoniously with the elements despite their inhospitable nature. The world is a wonderful place, and its islands are diverse and extraordinary.

This book attempts to give you a flavour of 501 of the world's most interesting islands, but there are thousands more out there. Some are incredibly difficult to reach; others are just a short trip away from the mainland by boat or plane. Some are littered with remarkable historical ruins and echoes of ancient cultures; others are no more than sandy beaches and a few palm trees. Why not go mad and visit an island you have never been to – maybe one you had never even heard of before? If the world is your oyster, then you can surely find the island that is your pearl.

AMERICAS AND THE CARIBBEAN

The rocky coast near Cape Knud

Baffin Island

POPULATION:
11,000 (2005)
WHEN TO GO:
June to August
HOW TO GET THERE:
By air from Montreal, Ottawa or Yellowknife.
HIGHLIGHTS:
Kimmirut – famous for its aboriginal stone-carving industry.
Auyittuq National Park: a pristine wilderness within the Arctic Circle.
Pond Inlet: a stunning mix of mountains, icebergs and glaciers.
The Pangnirtung Pass – a spectacular 100 km (62 mi) hike around fjords.
YOU SHOULD KNOW:
In the summer the inhabitants of Iqaluit leave their homes to live in tents and visitors are invited too. There is no better way to plan a trip than to sit around a campfire, under the midnight sun and discuss it with the people who know the landscape best.

Baffin Island is in the eastern Canadian Arctic, lying between Greenland and the Canadian mainland. Covering 507,451 sq km (195,928 sq mi), it is the largest island in North America and the fifth largest in the world. It was named after the British explorer William Baffin but the overwhelmingly Inuit population know it as Qikiqtaaluk.

Made up of a dozen or so sparsely populated communities, Baffin lives up to its reputation for being unspoiled, untamed and undiscovered. With 60 per cent of the island lying above the Arctic Circle and summer temperatures struggling to reach even 5° C (41° F), this rugged ice-covered landscape is not for the fainthearted. However the rewards for any visitor are great, with unrivalled scenery and the chance to see the rich and diverse Arctic wildlife, including polar bears and whales in their natural environment.

Getting to Baffin Island is only feasible by air. The island has only one airport (Iqaluit) which deals with external flights and another six which handle internal transfers. Arriving at Iqaluit you will find a thriving First Nations community. This capital of the newly-formed state of Nunavut can provide all you need for a kayaking, canoeing or trekking holiday.

Most of the finest mountains are located on the Cumberland Peninsula, at the head of the South Pangnirtung Fjord. Much of the area is included within Auyuittuq National Park, and is accessible from Pangnirtung, a small coastal Inuit settlement. From here, access to the peaks is by boat, dog sled, float-plane or ski-plane, depending on ice and weather conditions.

The sheer vastness of the island is difficult to take in and any traveller should plan ahead, not be too ambitious and allow extra time for weather related delays, even in summer.

Quadra Island

At 35 km (22 mi) long and covering 310 sq km (120 sq mi), Quadra Island is the largest and most populous of the Discovery Islands, which lie between Vancouver Island and the mainland of British Columbia. A short ferry ride from Campbell River takes you through whale- and dolphin- rich waters to this island of ancient temperate rainforest.

Human activity on the island dates back over 2,000 years and is thriving. Salish and Kwagiulth First Nations communities still exist here today. A misguided search for the fabled Northwest Passage brought Spanish and British ships to these treacherous waters in the late 18th century and contact began. Today most of the descendants of the native bands live at Cape Mudge on the south of the island, where visitors can experience a flourishing artistic community. Quadra is also home to many well-known contemporary artists, writers, potters and other artisans, and a growing community of alternative health practitioners.

With its rich woodland, diverse topography, and plentiful wildlife, Quadra Island has become a huge draw for outdoor enthusiasts. There is an extensive system of lakes and rivers for kayaking and canoeing and many paths and trails for hiking and mountain biking. Guided bird watching and fishing charters run in the summer months, as do seaborne whale and bear watching trips. Its sheltered coves and inland lakes are home to an incredible variety of wildlife, including black-tailed deer, river otters, harbour seals, sea-lions, cormorants, snowy owls, the great blue heron and the rarely seen peregrine falcon.

Its relative remoteness at the top of the Strait of Georgia helps this island community retain an idyllic charm. Aboriginal and European people live side by side, and whilst tourism is growing it is not overwhelming.

POPULATION:
2,650 (2006)
WHEN TO GO:
All year round although the ferries can get crowded in the May to August period.
HOW TO GET THERE:
By ferry from Campbell River or Cortes Island.
HIGHLIGHTS:
The Kwagiulth Museum in the Village of Cape Mudge, which houses an unrivalled collection of old totem poles.
Any of the studios of the 120 or so artists who live on the island.
Nature watching and rambling.
YOU SHOULD KNOW:
Several operators offer whale and wildlife watching tours around the island. Recent research has shown the faster zodiac style boats to have an injurious effect on whale populations, so if you are booking a tour, a slow boat may seem less thrilling but you will be doing less damage to this fragile environment.

Totem poles in the village of Cape Mudge

Victoria Island

POPULATION:
2,050 (2006)
WHEN TO GO:
June to August
HOW TO GET THERE:
The only year-round direct flights are from Yellowknife.
HIGHLIGHTS:
Bird watching on the Diamond Jenness Peninsula.
Watching the fantastic migrations of oxen and caribou.
Camping out in the midnight sun in July and August.
Seeing grizzly bears feasting on salmon in September/October.
YOU SHOULD KNOW:
Hunting and culling are a big part of the local culture. If this is not to your taste, check with guides before joining any expedition.

Victoria Island is part of the Canadian Arctic Archipelago that straddles the boundary between Nunavut and the Northwest Territories. Covering an area of 217,290 sq km (83,890 sq mi) it ranks as the ninth largest island in the world. Only just smaller than Britain and with a total population of little more than 2,000, it rates as one of the most sparsely populated regions on earth.

It is an island of peninsulas, craggy coastlines and innumerable inlets. Glaciers have carved the scenery into a series of moraines and glacial lakes, and though the landscape is relatively flat the Shaler Mountains in the north rise to 655 m (2,550 ft) above sea level. Though seemingly bleak, this habitat supports over two hundred species of plants and breeding populations of 50 species of bird and nine species of mammal.

This hostile environment supports only two communities of note. Located on the island's south east coast, Iqaluktuutiak (Cambridge Bay) serves as the administrative centre for Canada's Arctic region. Originally named after the Duke of Cambridge by fur trappers in 1839, the area was used by Copper Indians as a summer camp until the 1950s and given a more descriptive name, which means 'good place to fish', reflecting the local diet. Holman, situated on the island's west coast, is the best place to view the seasonal migration of caribou, musk ox and grizzly bear that use the year-round ice to move to and from the island.

This is a place where tourism feels like exploration and, whilst human activity has left some scars on the landscape, Victoria Island is still a near pristine wilderness. You will need the guidance of local experts to travel safely and to understand this magical Arctic landscape.

A snow laden church in the icy wilderness of Iqaluktuutiak (Cambridge Bay)

The beautiful colours of the forest in autumn

Manitoulin Island

Situated just off the Ontario coast in Lake Huron, Manitoulin Island, at 2,800 sq km (1,100 sq mi), is the largest freshwater island in the world. A tranquil place of small villages, gently rolling pasture, forest and lakes, its edges are fringed with long beaches and white cliffs.

The First Nations Ojibwa people, the island's original inhabitants, believed that when the Great Spirit, Gitchi Manitou, created the Earth he kept the best bits and made Manitoulin his home. In 1648 a group of French Jesuits became the first Europeans to settle on Manitoulin Island, which they named Isle de Ste. Marie. Unfortunately they brought with them new diseases that rapidly devastated the Ojibwa population. Marauding Iroquois bands then drove out those who remained, leaving the island uninhabited for over a hundred years. During the 19th century, the island's beauty attracted the attention of white settlers who, after first giving Manitoulin to other native bands, then revoked all treaties and claimed it for themselves. To this day the Ojibwa have refused to sign any treaty, and some 3,000 of them live on an 'unceded reserve' in the east of the island.

Today Manitoulin and the waters around it serve as Ontario's summer playground with boats of all kinds weaving in and out of its many bays and filling its large inland lakes. Hiking is popular and the island has a well signposted system of trails. Every August the Ojibwa Band holds one of Canada's biggest powwows (Wikwemikong or Wiky) a celebration of life through dance, storytelling and displays of arts and crafts.

POPULATION:
12,500 (2004)
WHEN TO GO:
May to October
HOW TO GET THERE:
by road-bridge from Highway 17 or by car ferry from Tobermory.
HIGHLIGHTS:
Ten Mile Point Lookout with its stunning views of Georgian Bay.
Little Current-Howland Museum – with 10,000-year-old artefacts.
Bridal Veil Falls – a popular place for a summertime swim.
Mississagi Lighthouse – now a museum celebrating the pioneer spirit.
YOU SHOULD KNOW:
Manitoulin's alkaline soil precludes the growth of North American staples like blueberries, but allows the growth of the island's trademark hawberries – celebrated in an annual festival each August and earning the islanders the epithet of Haweaters.

Sunset over St Joseph Island and Lake Huron

St Joseph Island

POPULATION:
1,960 (2005)
HOW TO GET THERE:
By road bridge via Highway 17 or by snowmobile when the river freezes in winter.
WHEN TO GO:
There is something for everyone all year round although many attractions are open only from May to October.
HIGHLIGHTS:
St Joseph Island Museum – a four building complex housing local artefacts.
Fort St Joseph – for an insight into early island life.
The view of the busy channel from Sailors Encampment.
The Artisans Gallery, Richards Landing – famous for its native craftwork.
YOU SHOULD KNOW:
The island's population swells to over 10,000 in summer so booking accommodation in advance is strongly recommended.

Many colourful stories, some legend, some historical fact, are told about St Joseph Island. It is the westernmost of the Manitoulin chain of islands, situated in the channel between Lakes Huron and Superior. It's 45 km (28 mi) long and 24 km (15 mi) wide and covers 365 sq km (141 sq mi). Originally named Anipich, the Ojibway word for 'place of the hardwood trees,' the island was given its present name by Jesuit missionaries to honour the patron saint of a new Indian church they erected. It is linked to the mainland by a toll-free bridge, opened in 1972.

St Joseph's location was of strategic importance to the British who fortified it as a bulwark against the Americans during the war of 1812. Fort St Joseph itself was abandoned when peace broke out, though it has now been restored as a National Historic Site.

Today St Joseph Island is noted for its peaceful beauty, its friendly residents and its recreational activities. It is a place of undisturbed bays, rocky inlets and the undulating hills, mixed forests, marshes and meadows that lend themselves to scenic drives, bike tours or leisurely walks. Most of the population live in the pretty villages of Richards Landing and Hilton Beach. The main industries are tourism, logging and agriculture.

Water sports are very popular here in summer and good fishing is to be found. In winter you can cross-country ski on 160 km (100 mi) of prepared trails.This is an island of festivals, from the winter Flurryfest and the Maple Syrup Festival in the spring, to Community Nights in the summer through to the Jocelyn Harvest Festival in the autumn.

Pelee Island

Pelee Island is a haven of green, encircled by the blue waters of Lake Erie. Sitting just above 42° North, it marks Canada's most southerly inhabited point (the uninhabited Middle Island, located just to the south, is the country's southernmost point). Measuring 14.5 km (9 mi) long and 5 km (3 mi) wide and located in the western half of the lake, it lies close to the Ohio boundary and on the same latitude as Northern California. Pelee's position gives it the best year-round climate in Eastern Canada.

Originally a marshland, little used by First Nations people, the island was leased by white settlers in the 19th century. Its mild climate lent Pelee to the growing of grapes, and the wine industry flourished until the Great War only to die out and then be revived again in the 1980s. The marshland was dredged in the late 19th century and tobacco was planted. Today the main crops are soybean and wheat.

Pelee Island is an important stopover for migrating birds and even non-twitchers will be impressed by the array of blue herons, cormorants, ducks and eagles on display. In 1984 the Lighthouse Point Nature Reserve was established, with trails that meander through wetland and marshes on to sandy beaches.

This is an ever-changing landscape where the coastline is easily eroded, dunes come and go, lagoons appear and new bays are formed. Its isolation makes for a gentle pace of life and the island only really springs to life during the pheasant-shooting season in autumn. It is a perfect place to walk, cycle or sail in a largely manufactured, but surprising unspoilt, nature reserve.

POPULATION:
260 (2003)
HOW TO GET THERE:
By ferry from Leamington, Ontario or from Sandusky, Ohio (USA)
WHEN TO GO:
All year round, but unless you are a pheasant shooter, it is best to avoid the autumn when the island becomes crowded and expensive.
HIGHLIGHTS:
Memorial Park, which features a giant aboriginal grinding stone.
The Pelee Island Lighthouse – built in 1833.
Birdwatching – particularly in the west of the island.
A winery tour at one of the island's vineyards.
YOU SHOULD KNOW:
Visible on a clear day, Hulda's Rock marks the spot where, according to legend, an Indian maiden jumped to her death after an ill-fated liaison with an Englishman.

An aerial view of Pelee Island

Ile d'Orléans

POPULATION:
6,860 (2006)
HOW TO GET THERE:
Across the Taschereau suspension bridge on Highway 440 from Quebec City
WHEN TO GO:
Popular all year round, but most facilities are only open from June to October.
HIGHLIGHTS:
The Maison Drouin – the oldest building on the island.
Chocolaterie de l'Ile d'Orléans – a treat for all those with a sweet tooth.
The Cidrerie Verger Bilodeau – take a guided tour and sample everything you can make with an apple.
The Île d'Orléans churches – a tour along the Chemin Royale, taking in the island's six churches.
YOU SHOULD KNOW:
During the height of winter the river freezes, allowing people to cross to and from the island on snowmobiles via an ice bridge.

Covering 193 sq km (75 sq mi), Ile d'Orléans plugs the narrowing St Lawrence River like a champagne cork, just 8 km (5 mi) east of Quebec City. Cut off from the mainland until a bridge was built in 1935, the island is a living museum of French Canadian life. This is a land of gentle terraces, rolling pasture, orchards, stone churches, quaint cottages and majestic manor houses, a place where food and wine are plentiful and café society is central.

The First Nations Algonquin people named the island Windingo, meaning 'bewitched corner,' until the French arrived in 1535 and gave it its present name, after the Duke of Orléans. The six villages of the island are connected by a perimeter road (Chemin Royale) and it is via this that most visitors explore the island and take in the wonderful mountain views across the St Lawrence.

Each village has its own church and its own atmosphere, ranging from Sainte-Pétronille, the preserve of wealthy Quebecois, to Saint-Francois, a more modest farming community where the river is widest and the views of the surrounding mountains most stunning. Sainte-Pierre boasts one of the oldest churches in Canada and is home to the island's most vibrant community. The island is home to over 600 listed buildings in all, and its close proximity to Quebec City makes it one of the most desirable places to live in Eastern Canada.

Whilst most people take their cars, the best way to absorb this wonderful island is to cycle the 67 km (42 mi) of the Chemin Royal. Any visitor to Quebec should take a day or two to sample what the island has to offer – a place where tradition is the watchword, where old farming methods combine well with fine French cuisine and the three hour lunch is king.

A traditional house overlooks a frozen St Lawrence River

Cape Breton Island

The Cabot Trail Scenic Highway

Nova Scotia's Cape Breton has an untamed beauty that makes for some of the most impressive scenery in North America. Covering 10,311 sq km (3,981 sq mi), the island is a wonderful mixture of rocky shores, rolling pasture, barren headlands, woodland, mountains and plateaux.

The Cape Breton Highlands, an extension of the Appalachian Mountain chain and a national park since 1936, dominate the north part of the island. The famous Cabot Trail Scenic Highway, one of the most spectacular scenic drives in Canada, winds through nearly 300 km (185 mi) of this ruggedly beautiful countryside.

Comprehension of the people of Cape Breton Island is not possible without some knowledge of its earliest settlers. Cape Bretoners today reflect the resolve of those pioneers – whether their roots are Mi'kmaq, Acadian, Scottish, Irish or Black Loyalist. The Island has shaped them just as they struggled to shape the island. Since then settlers have arrived from all over the world and have made their own distinct contributions.

The largest town, Sydney, still bears the scars of a failed industrial past but outside of the immediate area, the theme of the island is heritage mixed with outstanding natural beauty. Fortress Louisbourg faithfully recreates the French military might of the early 18th century, pioneer cottages line the north shore of the imposing Bras d'Or Lake and the island's most northerly point, Meat Cove offers spectacular, unspoilt ocean views.

Accommodation on Cape Breton is limited, so booking in advance is recommended, and as the public transport is poor, driving is your only real option to explore this wonderful land.

POPULATION:
150,000 (2004)

WHEN TO GO:
June to August is the best time but even then the weather is notoriously unpredictable. Though colder, September to early November offers a spectacular vista of flaming leaf colours.

HOW TO GET THERE:
By road-bridge from mainland Nova Scotia or by air to Sydney which has an international airport.

HIGHLIGHTS:
Hiking around Fortress Louisbourg.
Nature watching on Lake Ainslee.
Driving around the Cabot Trail Highway.
Fishing for salmon on the Margaree River.
Cheticamp – the largest Acadian community in Nova Scotia.
The Celtic Colours Festival in early October – a celebration of fiddle playing.

YOU SHOULD KNOW:
Much beloved by the inventor of the telephone, Alexander Graham Bell, Cape Breton was at the centre of a communications mix-up when an English couple made an online booking to go to Sydney, Australia only to find themselves flown to Sydney, Canada.

Roosevelt's Cottage

Campobello and Grand Manan

Campobello and Grand Manan are the principal islands of the Fundy Archipelago, situated in the south-western corner of New Brunswick, in Passamaquoddy Bay.

Campobello, at 14 km (9 mi) long and about 5 km (3 mi) wide, is easy to see in a day. The north of the island bustles with second home owners and day trippers, while in the South the protected area of the Roosevelt Campobello International Park covers 1,135 hectares, (2,800 acres). Here you will find the famous Roosevelt Cottage, the elegant summer home of Franklin D. Roosevelt's family, along with wooded coves, mixed forests, marshes and tidal flats.

Grand Manan, 34 km (16 mi) long, with a maximum width of 18 km (11 mi), is a bird watchers' paradise, with summer nesting sites for a wide variety of sea birds. Its coastal scenery is stunning – towering cliffs up to 90 m (295 ft) high and potentially dangerous surrounding waters. Despite its three picturesque lighthouses, the island was the site of many shipwrecks during the years of sailing vessel and commercial steam traffic.

The Passamaquoddy Nation, the original inhabitants of Campobello, called it Ebaghuit, which literally means 'lying parallel with the land'. Waves of European explorers brought first French and then British rule. In 1866, a Fenian Brotherhood war party attempted to seize the island, but was dispersed by a US military force. This scare prompted New Brunswick to join with the other British North American Colonies, when the Dominion of Canada was formed. Grand Manan was also home to the Passamaquoddy Nation prior to its discovery by Europeans, who first settled on the island in the late 18th century with the arrival of Loyalist refugees from the American Revolutionary War.

The area's popularity can mean long delays for the car ferry in July and August and you are advised to book accommodation in advance in high summer.

POPULATION:
Campobello 1,195; Grand Manan 2,500 (2001)

HOW TO GET THERE:
Both islands can be reached by ferry from Blacks Harbour and Campobello is connected with Lubec in the US state of Maine by the Franklin Delano Roosevelt Bridge.

WHEN TO GO:
Bird watching in spring, summer and autumn; hiking and aquatic sports from mid-June to September.

HIGHLIGHTS:
On Campobello – the Dutch Colonial style, 34-room Roosevelt Cottage, packed with memorabilia – open to the public from late-May to mid-October.
Family-friendly gentle hikes in the Roosevelt Campobello International Park.
On Grand Manan – the thousands of puffins, gannets, guillemots, stormy petrels and kittiwakes which visit the island; best times to see them are during the spring and autumn migrations and the summer nesting season.
The Grand Manan Museum – housing the largest collections of shipwreck-recovered items in the Maritime provinces.

YOU SHOULD KNOW:
It was while on holiday with his family on Campobello in 1921 that Roosevelt contracted the polio that left him permanently paralysed from the waist down.

Newfoundland

With lofty peaks, immense landscapes and nearly 10,000 km (6,250 mi) of rocky coastline, Newfoundland is the sixteenth largest island in the world, covering 109,000 sq km (41,700 sq mi). It is an entrancing land where giant icebergs drift along the coast, whales swim in huge bays and large herds of moose graze on flat open marshes.

The rich fishing grounds off the coast first attracted the Vikings and then the British, in the form of Henry VII's agent John Cabot, in whose name the daunting Cabot Tower was built to mark the 400th anniversary of his landing in 1497. The island has a brutal history, with constant disputes largely between the British and the French. In 1713 the French gave up any claims to the island and it was run as a lawless outpost of the British Empire, which by 1829 lead to the extinction of the indiginous Beothuk people.

Newfoundland is home to two national parks. Gros Morne National Park, located on the west coast, was named a UNESCO World Heritage Site in 1987 due to its complex geology and remarkable scenery. It is the largest national park in Antlantic Canada at 1,805 sq km (697 sq mi). Terra Nova on the island's east side, preserves the rugged geography of the Bonavista Bay region and allows visitors to explore the historic interplay of land, sea and man.

The island also offers a major hiking trail running along the eastern edge of the Avalon Peninsula. The East Coast Trail extends for 220 km (137 mi), beginning near Fort Amhurst in St John's and ending in Cappahayden, with an additional 320 km (200 mi) of trail under construction. The trail winds along the coast, taking hikers through many small fishing villages and along miles of rocky, uninhabited coastline.

POPULATION:
475,000 (2004)

WHEN TO GO:
All year round but it's less cold from May to September

HOW TO GET THERE:
By air to St John's, Newfoundland's capital.

HIGHLIGHTS:
Pippy Park in the city of St John's which features an underwater lookout.
Cape Spear Lighthouse – the most easterly point in North America.
The colourful village of Trinity with a museum housing over 2,000 artefacts.
Viewing icebergs close up on a boat trip from Notre Dame Bay.
L'Anse aux Meadows National Historic Site – including a reconstruction of an early Viking settlement.

YOU SHOULD KNOW:
For an authentic depiction of life on Newfoundland read Annie Proulx's *The Shipping News*, later made into a film starring Kevin Spacey.

The village of Trinity

Fogo Island

POPULATION:
2,560 (2005)
HOW TO GET THERE:
By ferry from Musgrave Harbour or by floatplane from St John's.
WHEN TO GO:
May to October has the better weather.
HIGHLIGHTS:
The Brimstone Head Folk Festival each August.
Whale watching from Snug Cove.
Fogo Wireless Relay Interpretation Centre – a recently renovated living museum of communication.
The Bleak House Museum – a preserved 19th century family mansion.
Brimstone Head - a unique geographical rock formation, which juts out into the Atlantic Ocean.
YOU SHOULD KNOW:
Between October and January each year the annual Eider Duck Hunt takes place. Hunters travel out by boat and are advised to bring their own guns and ammunition. Participation will make for an interesting tale when you are asked 'Where did you get that beautiful Eiderdown in the guest bedroom?'

Fogo Island, the largest of Newfoundland's offshore islands, is separated from the mainland by Hamilton Sound. The island is about 25 km long and 14 km wide and has a total area of 235 sq km (90 sq mi). Originally used by the First Nations Beothuks as a summer campground, it was taken over by Europeans in the early 16th century and given the name Fogo from the Portuguese word Fuego for fire, after the Beothuks' campfires.

Until the late 18th century Fogo Island was on an area off the coast called the 'French Shore'. However the British and the Irish came to settle here, thus ignoring various treaty obligations, and by the end of the century it had become a thriving hub for the British North Atlantic fleet. Evidence of this can be found today in the names, accents and culture of the local population. Fogo's location has long made the island a centre for transatlantic communications, with Marconi setting up a wireless station in the early 20th century.

This is an island where everything points to the sea. Red and white buildings line its craggy shoreline, while behind them muddy green pasture tells the story of the island's harsh environment, where the growing season lasts only a few months of the year. Fogo also boasts an extensive system of boardwalk trails making its North Atlantic wilderness accessible to all.

In the 1960s the islanders turned down the chance to be resettled on mainland Canada and they chose instead to preserve their unique cultural identity. Fishing still plays a central role in the islanders' day-to-day lives, but it is tourism that is increasing in importance to the area. There are now many operators offering guided nature tours to watch whales and the island's rich and varied bird life.

One of Fogo's traditional white buildings

A colourful harbour on the North Shore

Prince Edward Island

The crescent-shaped Prince Edward Island (PEI) is the smallest Canadian province. Its area of 5,520 sq km (2,184 sq mi) makes it even smaller than some of Canada's National Parks, but also allows it to be explored in less than a week. The island lies in the Gulf of St Lawrence, separated from the northern coasts of the Maritime Provinces of New Brunswick and Nova Scotia by the narrow Northumberland Strait.

The Mi'kmaq people, original inhabitants of PEI called the island Abegweit, meaning 'Land Cradled on the Waves'; they believed that it was formed by the Great Spirit throwing some red clay into the sea. In 1534 the French explorer Jacques Cartier laid claim to the island but by the end of the eighteenth century the British were in control. They expelled the Acadians and named the island after Queen Victoria's father, Prince Edward. The islanders maintained a sense of independence until the Charlottetown Conference of 1864 when Canada was born, earning PEI the epithet 'Cradle of the Confederation'.

PEI is a well-known haven of peace and tranquillity for those seeking a place to get away from it all. The islanders are warm and welcoming. The nature here seems to possess a serene quality, with expansive undulating hills where rich green and ruddy farmland offer up a pleasant patchwork of colour. Dotting this gentle landscape are little hamlets, where the tempo has remained unchanged by the rigours of modern life. Like their Mi'kmaq predecessors, many of today's islanders draw their livelihood from agriculture and fishing.

This is a land of plenty with bountiful harvests from land and sea, famous for its oysters, mussels and above all lobsters. It boasts beautiful lighthouses, tree-lined streets and 19th century terraces, as well as coves, parks, rocky headlands and long sandy beaches.

POPULATION:
137,000 (2006)
WHEN TO GO:
Most attractions open from Victoria Day (in May) to Thanksgiving (early October). The island is less crowded and more spectacular in the autumn months.
HOW TO GET THERE:
Fly to Charlottetown, ferry to Wood Islands from Nova Scotia or across the Confederation Bridge.
HIGHLIGHTS:
The July Lobster Carnival in Summerside.
Green Gables House near Cavendish – the setting for the famous book.
Hiking up and down the craggy coastline in Brundenell River Provincial Park.
The view from Panmure Island Lighthouse (open May to September).
Orwell Corners Historic Village – a recreation of 19th century island life.
The visitor centre at the PEI National Park – a must for those interested in marine wildlife.
YOU SHOULD KNOW:
For that unique holiday experience check out the perennial musical adaptation of *Anne of Green Gables* during the Charlottetown Festival (June to October).

The Gulf Islands

POPULATION:
16,500 (2004)
WHEN TO GO:
All year round, although the islands are often crowded in summer
HOW TO GET THERE:
Ferry from Vancouver (Twawwassen) or Victoria (Swartz Bay). Float plane from downtown Seattle or Vancouver.
HIGHLIGHTS:
The Market in the Park (Ganges, Salt Spring) held on Saturdays (April to October) 'The Mother of all Markets'
Montague Harbour Park (Galiano) – a wonderful preserve of beach and forest.

The Gulf Islands are a group of a hundred or so mountainous islands scattered across the Strait of Georgia between Vancouver Island and the mainland of southern British Columbia. In geological terms they are part of a larger archipelago that includes the San Juan Islands just to the south in Washington State (USA). The ferry journey from Vancouver to Vancouver Island winds between this myriad of islands that boast the best climate in Canada. Of the whole group only six support any population of note.

By far the easiest to get to and therefore the most popular and populous is Saltspring Island – Canada's arts and crafts island. Its mellow pace, beautiful landscapes and isolation have drawn artists and crafts people from all over the world. It has recently become the haunt of several Hollywood film stars.

Bucolic Mayne Island is a medley of rock bays, forested hills and pasture. Once the agricultural hub of the area, it retains the rural lived-in charm of yesteryear.

Saturna Island is tucked away at the southern end of the island chain. Rural, sparsely populated and difficult to reach, it is easily the least spoilt of the group.

The Pender Islands, also known as the 'Friendly Islands' and the 'Islands of Hidden Coves', have over 20 public ocean access spots to visit along its beaches and coves. Pristine wilderness makes the Penders a hotbed for outdoor activities. Galiano Island has always enjoyed a reputation for being the most welcoming to visitors. With little land suitable for farming, the early settlers here opened their homes to tourists as a way of earning a living.

As a group the Gulf Islands are still underdeveloped and many of the best lodges and restaurants are hidden away down forest tracks. There is little in the way of organized activities – just magnificent scenery to enjoy.

The view from the grounds of Georgina Point Lighthouse (Mayne).
The Brown Ridge Nature Trail (Saturna) – with great views of Washington State's Mt Baker – officially the snowiest mountain in the world.
Cycling around the unspoilt beauty of South Pender.

YOU SHOULD KNOW:
You should plan and book in advance. The BC ferry schedule can be confusing and it is not always possible to get from one island to the next. Families should also note that many resorts do not cater for children.

Boats sailing around Tumbo and Cabbage Islands

The Thousand Islands

POPULATION:
22,450 (2002)
WHEN TO GO:
The shoulder seasons of late April to May and September to early October are less crowded and can have surprisingly good weather.
HOW TO GET THERE:
Via the Thousand Islands Bridge from New York State or tour the area by boat from Gananoque. Canada's Via Rail also offers great views of the islands on the line from Kingston to Montreal.
HIGHLIGHTS:

The views of the folly Boldt Castle on Heart Island.
Clayton Boat Museum where you can view or even rent out antique wooden boats.
The beautiful and secluded Lake of the Isles between Wellesley and Canadian Hill Islands.
Singer Castle on Dark Island – open to the public in summer.
The Thousand Islands Parkway – a popular hiking trail that runs from Gananoque to Mallorytown Landing.
YOU SHOULD KNOW:
'Thousand Islands Dressing' was invented by the actress May Irwin and not, as is popularly believed, by the head Chef at the Waldorf Astoria Hotel in New York.

The Thousand Islands are a network of in fact nearly 1,800 islands that span the American-Canadian border in the Saint Lawrence River. Some, like Wolfe Island, the largest at 124 sq km (48 sq mi), have significant year-round populations, while others are merely rocky outcrops visited by migrating birds. The whole area is enormously popular as a holiday destination, particularly for sailing – so much so that it's sometimes called the 'fresh water boating capital of the world'.

Around twenty of these islands form the Saint Lawrence Islands National Park, the smallest of Canada's national parks. The Thousand Islands Frontenac Arch region was designated a World Biosphere Reserve by UNESCO in 2002. The US islands include numerous New York State parks, most notably Robert Moses State Park.

The area is frequently traversed by large freighters on their way into and out of the Great Lakes shipping lanes, but is so dotted with barely concealed rocks that local navigators are hired to help the vessels travel through the hazardous waterway. Because of this it is unwise to travel the waters at night, except in the main channels and with good charts. It's a popular place for experienced divers as the waters are mostly so clear and the sea bed is littered with many shipwrecks for them to explore.

The area has long been popular with wealthy up state New Yorkers and many of the islands are privately owned. A plethora of 'No Landing' signs reminds potential visitors that they can look but not touch, so perhaps the best way to enjoy the area is from a boat.

Boldt Castle on Heart Island

Queen Charlotte Islands

Ancient Haida totems in South Moresby National Park

In the Pacific Ocean west of Prince Rupert in British Columbia, the Queen Charlotte Islands are the peaks of a submerged mountain chain. The seven largest islands of the 1,884 islands and islets in the archipelago are Langara, Graham, Moresby, Louise, Lyell, Burnaby and Kunghit. Graham Island in the north and Moresby Island in the south make up most of the landmass of the archipelago. Just 2 km (1.2 mi) into the sea, the continental shelf falls away dramatically to the immense depths of the ocean, and this is Canada's most active earthquake area.

The islands are known as Haida Gwaii (islands of the people), or Xhaaidlagha Gwaayaai (islands at the boundary of the world) to the Haida people who have lived here for at least 7,000 years. The first European contact was in 1774 when Juan Perez discovered what is perhaps one of the most beautiful landscapes in the world. Fur traders followed to exploit the extraordinarily rich fauna here, creating a major impact on the Haida. In 1787, the islands were named by the British in honour of Queen Charlotte, the wife of King George III.

Despite European interference, the islands have kept their natural tranquillity and have a rich cultural history. The Haida earn their living through mining, logging and commercial fishing, and nowadays tourism is also a good source of income. Most Haida communities can be found on Graham Island. At Skidegate there is a cultural centre with Haida artefacts and local art, at Tlell there is an artistic collective, and Old Masset is home to traditional native carvers.

Naikoon Provincial Park, in the north-east of Graham Island, covers a range of diverse environments including sandy beaches and dunes, sphagnum bogs, ancient forests and rivers. The landscape was formed during the last ice age out of the deposits left by retreating glaciers. The main attraction here are the endless stretches of broad sandy beaches. On the North Beach is Tow Hill, a 100 m outcrop of basalt columns which make a dramatic landmark. Also worth exploring is Rose Spit, an ecological reserve where you can spot migrating birds travelling over the Pacific.

The Gwaii Haanas National Park Reserve and Haida Heritage Site is in the south of the archipelago. This wilderness area of 138 islands stretching 90 km from north to south is only accessible by boat or chartered aircraft. Mountains rise steeply to the west, and the coastline is dotted with picturesque inlets, bays and islands. Rainforest and upland bog, salmon streams, estuaries and kelp beds sustain a rich diversity of life here. This is a great place to observe whales, bald eagles, nesting seabirds, black bears, river otters and sea lions.

POPULATION:
4,935 (2001)

WHEN TO GO:
April to November.

HOW TO GET THERE:
Fly from Vancouver or Prince Rupert to Sandspit, or take a ferry from Prince Rupert.

HIGHLIGHTS:
Naikoon Provincial Park – explore the gorgeous sandy beaches and dunes.
Gwaii Haanas National Park Reserve and Haida Heritage Site – this remote area is blessed with immense natural beauty. Discover the close relationship between the Haida and their natural environment.
Langara Island – in the north-west of the archipelago, this rugged island has ancient rainforests, an impressive seabird colony and an interesting lighthouse.
Port Clements – a traditional logging and fishing village where you can see the giant trees of the temperate rainforest.
Rennell Sound, bordered by the snow-capped Queen Charlotte Mountains – this is a great place for kayaking, hiking and fishing.
Louise Island – see one of the largest displays of ancient totem poles in the archipelago.

YOU SHOULD KNOW:
This is a remote area with little development, so do not expect busy resort hotels with all the tourist comforts.

St-Pierre et Miquelon

The tiny archipelago of Saint-Pierre et Miquelon sits 25 km (16 mi) off the coast of Newfoundland in the north west Atlantic Ocean, at the opening of the Gulf of St Lawrence. However it owes more to France some 6,400 km (4,000 mi) away than it does to Canada or even to Quebec. French is spoken almost exclusively, the Euro is its currency and the morning air is filled with the smell of freshly baked baguettes.

When France finally surrendered her North American colonies, she was allowed to keep these islands and they quickly became a base for French Atlantic fishing. Fiercely loyal to their motherland in spite of some shoddy treatment, particularly from De Gaulle who sent in the navy to break a dockers' strike, the islanders saw heavy losses in both World Wars.

The islands are bare and rocky, with only a thin layer of peat to alleviate the harsh landscape. The coasts are generally steep, and there is only one good harbour – in the port of St-Pierre, where over 80 per cent of the islanders live. Adding to its importance, the town of St-Pierre is also the administrative centre and the site of the principal airport. The harbour, which originally could accommodate only small vessels, has been improved with artificial breakwaters.

Once there were three main islands: St-Pierre, Miquelon and Langlade, but since the 18th century, Miquelon and Langlade have been permanently joined by a giant sand bar. Miquelon and St-Pierre are separated by a 6-km (4-mi) long strait, whose fierce currents inspired fishermen to name it the 'Mouth of Hell'.

Today the islanders rely on fishing and, increasingly, on tourism for their income. In addition, the islands receive generous grants from the French government, determined to maintain France's last remnant of its once extensive empire in North America.

The ghost village of Ile aux Marins

POPULATION:
6,400 (2005)
HOW TO GET THERE:
By air from Sydney, Nova Scotia or St John's. By ferry from Fortune.
WHEN TO GO:
The summer (June to August) is best but even then the weather can be unpredictable, with heavy fogs and cool temperatures.
HIGHLIGHTS:
A boat trip to the ghost village of Ile aux Marins, abandoned in the 1960s.
Dune of Langdale – a sweeping 10 km (6 mi) long sandbar.
The imposing 20th century Cathedral of St-Pierre.
The St-Pierre Museum – with its emphasis on the islands' nautical past.
YOU SHOULD KNOW:
The prohibition of the 1920s and 30s gave the islands a short-term economic boost when the islanders more or less abandoned fishing for a more lucrative trade in illicit alcohol. Many of the warehouses built to house this trade lie empty on the waterfront to this day.

Vancouver Island

Vancouver Island is a large island in British Columbia, just off Canada's Pacific coast, separated from the mainland by the Strait of Georgia. It is 460 km (286 mi) long and up to 80 km (50 mi) wide, a magnificent landscape of emerald forests, snow-capped mountains, flower-filled meadows, crystal-clear ice-cold lakes and rivers, and pristine coastline pounded by the Pacific Ocean. The island is paradise for outdoor pursuits enthusiasts, and it is one of the few places in the world where you can play golf and go skiing on the same day.

There are mountains down the centre of the island, the Vancouver Island Ranges, dividing it into the rugged and wet west coast and the drier east coast with a more rolling landscape. The highest point on the island is the Golden Hinde at 2,195 m (7,200 ft), lying within the Strathcona Provincial Park, and there are a few glaciers here, the largest of which is the Comox Glacier. The west coast is rocky and mountainous, characterized by fjords, bays and inlets, while the interior has many rivers and lakes, of which Kennedy Lake, northeast of Ucluelet, is the largest.

At the southern tip of the island is the elegant capital, Victoria, with its historic parliament, narrow streets dotted with cafés, pubs and colourful gardens, and boats floating lazily in the sparkling harbour. There is an abundance of sights to experience here, including the world-famous Butchart Botanical Gardens, with over a million plants. The gardens are divided into themed areas, such as Japanese or Italian, and each is a beautiful garden in its own right.

Activities available in this big outdoors include skiing, white-water rafting, caving, mountain biking, surfing, sailing, diving and snorkelling, bungy jumping and many other exciting pursuits. There are deep-sea fishing trips for halibut, salmon and chinook, whale-watching excursions or kayaking in the inlets of the Pacific Rim National Park. Trekking and hiking through the wilderness is also popular here, and can be done on horse or on foot along the trails in the fir-lined woods. Wildlife viewing is becoming more and more popular, with black bears high on the wish-list, and ecotours by boat can offer sightings of bald eagles, sea lions and sea otters.

POPULATION:
656,312 (2001)
WHEN TO GO:
April to November.
HOW TO GET THERE:
By ferry from the mainland, or by plane to Victoria International Airport.
HIGHLIGHTS:
Whale watching – visit between March and May when 21,000 whales, including the grey whale, migrate from California to Alaska.
Butchart Botanical Gardens – among the best, and most imaginatively planted in the world. Come on a summer evening to attend an outdoor concert while enjoying the gardens illuminated by coloured lights.
The fishing village of Tolfino – located on Clayoquot Sound, the village is a centre for ecotourism, with lovely sandy beaches to the south and opportunities for whale-watching and surfing.
Trekking on horseback across this magnificent landscape.
YOU SHOULD KNOW:
It is also known as 'The Island'.

Clayoquot Sound on the west coast

Isle Royale

POPULATION:
Uninhabited
HOW TO GET THERE:
By ferry from Copper Harbour, Michigan, a journey of 90 km (56 mi) or by floatplane from Houghton, Michigan.
WHEN TO GO:
Only really accessible in the summer (June to August)
HIGHLIGHTS:
The 6-hour ferry ride across Lake Superior.
Nature watching – seeing beavers, foxes and seabirds in their natural environment.
Hiking across the island's well-preserved trail system.
Just being there – cut off from the stress of modern-day life.
YOU SHOULD KNOW:
The island is rich in mineral deposits: US law prohibits the collection of any materials from the area. Souvenir hunters should satisfy themselves with photographs and memories alone.

At 74 km (45 mi) long and 14 km (9 mi) wide, with an area of 535 sq km (206 sq mi), Isle Royale is Lake Superior's largest natural island, as well as being the second largest in the Great Lakes. Although it is far closer to Canada, it was ceded to the United States in 1843. The island's history is one of extinction and renewal, of ventures tried and failed, leaving what is now an almost pristine wilderness to be enjoyed by hikers and nature lovers alike. The island, together with the surrounding smaller islands and waters, now make up Isle Royale National Park.

For over 2000 years First Nations people visited, hunted and fished, picked up copper nuggets, and later mined copper on the island they knew as Isle Minong. By the mid-19th century white settlers tried their hands at mining, logging and fishing but the isolation of the island made this economically unviable.

On arrival at Rock Harbour, the island's only working dock, the rudimentary welcoming sign lets you know that you are going back to nature. There are no motorcars and only a couple of basic lodges. A good pair of walking boots, a tent and a rucksack is all you need to soak up this amazing landscape.

Isle Royale's animal life also expresses its island nature. In the recent past, both wolf and moose have come in search of better hunting and browsing grounds. Other animals found nearby, like the black bear or the white tail dear, are missing; cut off from a good source of food, they simply died out. This is an ever-changing environment. Every so often, Lake Superior freezes at its northern edges, forming an ice bridge to the mainland that allows in new species of grazers and predators, and so another cycle begins.

Lake Superior

Aleutian Islands

A remote and sparsely populated chain of some 300 islands in the North Pacific, the Aleutians extend westwards in a 1,900 km (1,200 mi) arc from the Alaska Peninsula. By crossing longitude 180°, this rugged chain is the westernmost part of the USA and also, technically, the easternmost. The islands have 57 volcanoes and are part of the 'Pacific Ring of Fire', the area of frequent earthquakes and volcanic eruption that stretches in a huge inverted 'U' from South America to New Zealand. There are five groups within the Aleutians: The Fox Islands, nearest the mainland; Islands of Four Mountains; Andreanof Islands; Rat Islands; and the paradoxically named Near Islands, furthest from the mainland. There are few natural harbours in the chain and navigation is treacherous.

The indigenous inhabitants are the Unangan people, generally known as the Aleut. Originally exploited by Russia for the fur of seals and sea otters, the Aleutians formed part of the USA's Alaska purchase in 1867. Today, the principal commercial activity is fishing, though there is a strong (and rather secretive) US military presence.

A number of islands are inhabited, but the main centre of population is the settlement of Unalaska on the island of the same name, overlooking Dutch Harbour. Most of the rather exclusive (for which read 'expensive') tourist activity in the Aleutians is centred here, with cruise ships making it a regular port of call and the island serving as a base for tours by boat and plane.

The Aleutians are a dream destination for adventurous travellers, with a natural wilderness to explore and sensational wildlife to be found – brown bear, wolves, caribou, whales, sea lions, sea otters, porpoises, the ancient murrelet, eagles, the rare whiskered auklet, puffins and much, much more.

POPULATION:
8,200 (2000)

WHEN TO GO:
During the growing season (May to September), though winters are not always especially harsh.

HOW TO GET THERE:
With difficulty! The State Ferry operates bi-monthly from Kodiak Island to Unalaska (between May and October only), which also has regular flights from Anchorage. Beyond that, island-hopping involves custom trips with experienced guides.

HIGHLIGHTS:
The oldest Russian Orthodox cruciform church in North America, an endangered national historic monument in Unalaska.
Gently steaming Makushin Volcano, also on Unalaska Island.
The Aleutian World War II National Historic Area, Fort Schwatka on Mount Ballyhoo overlooking Dutch Harbour.

YOU SHOULD KNOW:
A small number of Aleutian Islands were occupied by Japanese forces in World War II – as close as they got to invading the USA.

Snow covered mountains along the coast of Adak Island

Kodiak Island

POPULATION:
14,000 (2000)
WHEN TO GO:
Visit in June, July or August when the salmon are running and the bears are feeding.
HOW TO GET THERE:
There is a passenger and vehicle ferry service to Kodiak and Port Lions from Seward or Homer. Commercial carriers fly into Kodiak from Anchorage.
HIGHLIGHTS:
The Baranov Museum in Kodiak, located in 200-year-old Erskine House, an old fur warehouse. It features artefacts, documents and photographs relevant to the Kodiak and Aleutian Islands.
Fort Abercrombie State Historical Park with its rugged coastline and military remains from World War II, including the Kodiak Military History Museum at Miller Point.
The Russian Orthodox Church in Kodiak, an atmospheric reminder of Alaska's Russian heritage.
YOU SHOULD KNOW:
Kodiak is home to the largest US Coastguard base in America, on the site of a US Navy air station established in 1941.

By far the largest of the Kodiak Archipelago's 30 islands off Alaska's south coast, Kodiak is also the second-largest island in the USA, weighing in at a hefty 160 km (100 mi) long and 16 km (10 mi) to 96 km (60 mi) in width. It is the ancestral home of the Koniag people, but the Russians arrived in the 18th century and the island was part of the USA's 19th century Alaska purchase.

Alaska's 'Emerald Isle' is aptly named for the vivid green that characterizes its summer appearance. The main town is Kodiak, with minor settlements at Akhiok, Old Harbor, Karluk, Larsen Bay, Port Lyons and Ouzinkie. The island is mountainous and heavily forested to the north, with few trees in the southern part. The main economic activity is fishing, with associated canning factories, though tourism is becoming increasingly important.

The Kodiak National Wildlife Refuge occupies a large portion of the island, and its most famous inhabitants are the huge Kodiak brown bears (estimated population 2,300). However, the Refuge is also home to native species such as red fox, river otter, ermine and tundra vole, plus incomers such as reindeer, beaver and red squirrel. Wildlife watching is a major leisure activity, as is sea kayaking. Hunting and fishing also draw many visitors in season, with amazing Pacific salmon runs up rivers like the Karluk.

Kodiak Island is one of the most unspoiled yet easily accessible wilderness areas on the planet. It's spectacular, but not for the faint-hearted. Whilst many worthwhile sights may be seen by travelling the island's relatively small number of paved roads, the truly wild experiences can only be enjoyed by employing the services of specialized guides or staying at one of many back-country lodges that offer outdoor adventures.

A brown Kodiak bear wades through the O' Malley River on Kodiak Island.

Little Diomede Island

Ice sheets around Little Diomede

POPULATION:
140 (2000)
WHEN TO GO:
Wrap up well and try winter for reasons of access (see below).
HOW TO GET THERE:
Almost impossible. Try landing by chartered ski plane on sea ice in winter, but remember that a good Alaskan light plane touchdown is one you walk away from!
HIGHLIGHTS:
Seeing into the future – because the dateline runs between them, you can look across from Little Diomede and see what's happening on Big Diomede tomorrow.
The water treatment plant and newly built rubbish incinerator.
Splendid Eskimo carvings in sea ivory.
YOU SHOULD KNOW:
Be patient. One day getting there may be easy – the Diomede Islands are a certain stop on the oft-proposed 'Intercontinental Peace Bridge' across the Bering Strait.

Slap-bang in the middle of the Bering Strait between Alaska and Russia, the USA's Little Diomede Island and Russia's Big Diomede Island separate the former sworn adversaries by just 3 km (2 mi). The border and international dateline is equidistant from each, and the former was established to delineate the USA's Alaska purchase of 1867.

Little Diomede Island is an inhospitable, flat-topped, steep-sided rock that is just 7.4 sq km (2.8 sq mi) in size. The small Inuit population operates a subsistence economy, harvesting crab, fish, beluga whales, walrus, seals and polar bears. Almost every part of this hard-won bounty is used for some purpose. Diomede, crouching at the base of the island's western face, is actually classified as a city, proudly boasting one church, one school and a store. The entire island falls within city limits.

It is isolated by persistently rough seas and summer fog. In 1995 BBC television presenter Michael Palin arrived on Little Diomede to begin filming *Full Circle*, his epic circumnavigation of the Pacific Rim. He intended to close the circle back on the island eight months later, but unfortunately the winter seas were so rough that even the doughty US Coast Guard cutter *Munro* was unable to put Palin and his crew ashore.

Weather permitting, there is a weekly mail drop by helicopter, general supplies are landed once a year by barge and there are occasional visits by passing fishermen. Scientists are sometimes choppered in by the Alaska Air National Guard (there is an Arctic Environmental Observatory on the island).

Pribilof Islands

POPULATION:
684 (2000)
WHEN TO GO:
June to August, when the flowers are out, birds are nesting, seals are on shore and it's merely chilly.
HOW TO GET THERE:
Commercial carrier to Anchorage, from whence smaller aircraft serve the islands.
HIGHLIGHTS:
The Ridge Wall on St Paul – a spectacular sheer cliff above the Bering Sea that is birdwatching heaven.
Community-owned TDX Power's advanced wind/diesel generation facility on St Paul, with its 37 m (120 ft) wind turbine.
Seals, seals, seals and . . . more seals.
YOU SHOULD KNOW:
St Paul Island is the setting for the Rudyard Kipling tale 'The White Seal' and poem 'Lukannon' in *The Jungle Book*.

Named after a Russian navigator who visited in the 1780s, this group of four volcanic islands (five if you count Sea Lion Rock) in the Bering Sea is 320 km (200 mi) north of Unalaska Island in the Aleutians and the same distance south of Cape Newenham on the mainland. The rocky Pribilof Islands have a collective land mass of just 195 sq km (75 sq mi) and are largely covered by tundra and meadowland which produces a spectacular display of wild flowers.

The main islands are St Paul and St George, each with a settlement of the same name, whilst Otter and Walrus Islands are near St Paul. Seal hunting ended in 1966 and the main attraction is now the annual opilio (snow crab) fishery, as featured in the dramatic TV series 'Deadliest Catch'. Marine support services make an important contribution to the economy, as does US Government activity – there is a US Coast Guard base, the National Weather Service has a station and the National Oceanic and Atmospheric Administration is present.

The indigenous Alaskan Aleut people's largest community is here. They were transported from the Aleutians to the Pribilofs in the 18th century by Russian fur traders and have remained ever since. They still go subsistence hunting and are permitted to pursue their traditional quarry.

For intrepid visitors the main attraction is birdwatching, as the Pribilofs host some 240 species, including many rarities. Over two million seabirds nest annually, alongside up to one million fur seals. Various companies offer tours and this is the best way to see the islands, which are a naturalist's paradise sometimes called the 'Galapagos of the North' for their abundant wildlife, which may be observed at close quarters with the necessary permits from tribal governments.

Resting Northern fur seals

Pieces of iceberg from nearby South Sawyer Glacier in the Tracy Arm Fjiord

Alexander Archipelago

You need lots of fingers to count the islands in the rugged Alexander Archipelago, which stretches for 485 km (200 mi), hugging the southeastern coast of Alaska – there are about 1,100 of them. They are the tops of submerged mountains rising steeply from the Pacific Ocean. Deep fjords and channels separate mainland and islands, which have inhospitable, irregular coasts. The whole area is densely forested with fir woods and temperate rain forests. Much of the archipelago is protected from development and teems with wildlife.

The main economic activities are tourism, fishing and logging. The largest islands are Admiralty, Baranof, Chichagof, Dall, Kupreanof, Revillagigedo, Prince of Wales and Wrangell. Alaska's period of Russian domination is reflected in the names of several islands and the archipelago itself, which is called after Alexander Baranof, who ran the Russian-American Fur Company in the early 19th century – or Tsar Alexander II, depending on who you listen to.

People are thinly scattered throughout this vast area, with the main centres of population being Ketchikan on Revillagigedo and Sitka on Baranov, each with some 8,000 souls – the latter was once the capital of Russian America. The archipelago is traversed by heavy boat traffic along the Inside Passage, a sheltered route that follows a path between the mainland and coastal islands of British Columbia and the Alaska Panhandle.

There's no point in pretending that Alaska is a conventional tourist destination. The Alexander Archipelago perfectly illustrates this, offering both the challenges and rewards that make a visit to the 49th state an unforgettable expedition. There is no road access, so the only ways in are by sea or air, but those who make the effort will be rewarded by the ultimate wilderness experience.

POPULATION:
39,000 (2007 estimate)

WHEN TO GO:
Unless you want to risk being marooned, go between mid-May and mid-September.

HOW TO GET THERE:
Fly Alaska Airlines to the state capital of Juneau on the mainland, which offers a good ferry service to main islands. There are bush carriers who will undertake floatplane charters.

HIGHLIGHTS:
The out-of-season Alaska Day Festival in October, offering a series of events in Sitka, where the USA's Alaska purchase was signed in 1867 on the city's Castle Hill.
The Pack Creek Brown Bear Viewing Area on Admiralty Island (permit required from the US Forest Service).
A scenic ride on Prince of Wales Island's Inter-Island ferry service.
The Russian Orthodox Cathedral of St Michael (completed 1848) in Sitka.
Spectacular Glacier Bay National Park, with headquarters at Bartlett Cove, 105 km (65 m) from state capital Juneau (fly in to nearby Gustavus).

YOU SHOULD KNOW:
The entire island of Annette is a reservation, the only one in Alaska, and is home to the Tsimshian, Tlingit and Haida Native peoples.

Waves from Lake Erie break on the shore of Kelleys Island

Kelleys Island

POPULATION:
380 (2000)
WHEN TO GO:
May to August – almost everything closes in September. The island is icebound in winter.
HOW TO GET THERE:
There is a regular ferry service from Marblehead. Another runs from Sandusky to South Bass Island and Kelleys in summer only.
HIGHLIGHTS:
Inscription Rock – with (now barely visible) pictographs drawn by the Native American Eries tribe in the 16th century.
The Kelleys Island Winery, established in the 1980s at the site one of the island's oldest houses, built in 1865.
Kelleys Island Historical Association in the Old Stone Church on Division Street.
YOU SHOULD KNOW:
The Lake Erie Islands are known as the 'Vacationland of the Midwest' – so don't expect to have Kelleys all to yourself!

Though it is the largest of Ohio's Lake Erie Islands, Kelleys is still not big, with an area of just 9 sq km (4.6 sq mi). The other islands in the group are North, Middle and South Bass Islands, Sugar Island and Rattlesnake Island, located in the lake's western basin. It's not hard to read the island's history – there is evidence of lime production everywhere, and the Kelley Island Lime & Transport Company was once the world's largest producer of limestone products, operating from 1886 until the 1960s. A small quarrying operation still exists, but is a shadow of its former self. There was once one of the USA's largest wineries here, too, but it closed in the 1930s as a result of fires and Prohibition. The ruins may still be seen.

Now, however, the mainstay of the island's economy is tourism. The principal establishments are all pubs and restaurants, the most famous of which is the old Village Pump. But the real attraction is the island's natural beauty and fascinating remains of its industrial heritage, plus the fact that it's a perfect setting for outdoor pursuits.

Kelleys Island is heavily forested, with several sparsely populated residential areas that fill out in summer when the owners of vacation homes arrive. It is home to the Kelleys Island State Park, that occupies the northern third of the island and offers hiking trails, a sandy beach and campground. The adjoining Glacial Grooves State Memorial features this tiny island's second world 'first' – glacial striations containing the world's largest remains of glacial grooves. The North Shore also has a preserved limestone pavement (alvar) and a nature reserve.

Drummond Island

This is the largest island among many in St Mary's River where it ends its journey from Lake Superior by flowing into northern Lake Huron in Upper Michigan. It is also the second-largest freshwater island in the USA. Drummond Island extends to 335 sq km (130 sq mi) in area and is within touching distance of the Canadian border. The island is largely forested, with cliffs at the eastern end, and over two-thirds of the land is owned by the state of Michigan. Its economic mainstay is tourism and, whilst that has traditionally meant summer visitors, Drummond – in common with many Great Lakes islands – is trying to promote all-year-round activities to keep the tills ringing, with some success.

Drummond Island is a natural paradise, described by its proud inhabitants as the 'Gem of the Huron'. Diverse topography ranges from rocky ledges to cedar swamps, prairie meadowland to hardwood groves, rugged shores to sandy beaches. The summer wild flowers can be spectacular, as are the trees from September. It is a wildlife haven, with numerous deer the most visible animals. But there are plenty of raccoons, skunks, rabbits, squirrels, chipmunks, woodchucks and weasels. Rarer sightings include bears, moose, bobcats, coyotes and wolves. There is also a variety of reptile life, including snakes and turtles, plus many species of bird.

Vacation activities on Drummond Island include boating, camping, hunting and fishing, hiking, biking, wildlife watching, photography, stargazing (no light pollution here), off-road vehicle activity or simply exploring the island's varied terrain.

Beautiful Big Shoal Bay

POPULATION:
1,200 (2007 estimate)

WHEN TO GO:
May to September is the best time to visit, except for those interested in specialist winter pastimes like snowmobiling. Many facilities close out of season.

HOW TO GET THERE:
The M-134 highway on the mainland continues for 13 km (8 mi) on the island via the Drummond Island Ferry from DeTour Village. There is a small airport.

HIGHLIGHTS:
The new Drummond Island Museum, built after the old one (be warned!) collapsed under the weight of snow.
Big Shoal Bay, a beautiful natural enclave on the island's southern edge.
De Tour Reef Light, a preserved lighthouse in the passage between Drummond Island and the mainland.
The Heritage Trail, a hiking route created to show off the island's habitat and wildlife.

YOU SHOULD KNOW:
The British were reluctant to surrender the island, only abandoning Fort Collier in 1823, thus finally ending their military presence in the USA.

Mackinac Island

POPULATION:
523 (2000)
WHEN TO GO:
June to August sees a huge visitor influx, so why not be completely different and make a winter visit across the frozen lake by snowmobile?
HOW TO GET THERE:
High-speed ferry (from Mackinaw City or St Ignace), private boat or light aircraft.
HIGHLIGHTS:
Fort Mackinac – closed in 1895, now a museum in Mackinac Island State Park and designated a National Monument.
The view from the world's largest porch – a 200 m (660 ft) monster on the Victorian Grand Hotel (fee payable by non-residents).
The view from the island's highest point, Fort Holmes (originally called Fort George by its British builders).
Michigan's oldest surviving church – Mission Church, built in 1829 – and the adjacent Mission House.
Striking limestone formations like Arch Rock, Sugar Loaf and Skull Cave.
YOU SHOULD KNOW:
A sweet tooth is required – no visit is complete without sampling the nationally famous Mackinac Island Fudge, so popular that visitors are nicknamed 'fudgies'.

Traditional houses on the shores of Lake Huron

Showing remarkable advanced sensitivity to global warming, the inhabitants of Mackinac Island banned motorized vehicles in 1898 – a prohibition that exists to this day with limited exception for emergency and service vehicles. But there are still plenty of eco-friendly horse-drawn carriages to be seen.

The island covers 9.8 sq km (3.8 sq mi) and belongs to the US state of Michigan. It is located in Lake Huron's Straits of Mackinac, commanding the passage between Lake Michigan and Lake Huron. As such, it was of strategic importance to the Great Lakes fur trade in the 18th century and the British built a fort during the American Revolutionary War. The island, then garrisoned by the Americans, was the scene of two battles during the War of 1812. After the twice-victorious British relinquished the place in 1815, Fort Mackinac served as an outpost for the US Army.

By the end of the 19th century Mackinac Island had become a popular summer colony, and extensive preservation has ensured that much of the original character remains – to such good effect that the entire island is now a National Historic Landmark, with 80 per cent also conserved as the Mackinac Island State Park. In short, it continues to provide a civilized holiday destination for tourists generally and the people of Michigan in particular, as it has for well over a century – up to 15,000 a day now arrive in high season. They are drawn by the island's natural beauty and powerful old-fashioned charm, with little or no building in intrusive modern styles.

The island is the home of several galleries and many cultural events, including an annual show of 19th century American art from the Masco Collection. The Mackinac Arts Council organizes an outstanding programme each summer.

Beaver Island

The Great Lakes' most remote inhabited island has a great harbour, pristine woods, isolated beaches, trails for biking and trails for hiking. Beaver Island in its 14-island archipelago is the largest island in Lake Michigan, lying 51 km (32 mi) from the small mainland town of Charlevoix. It is 21 km (13 mi) long and up to 9.5 km (6 mi) wide, mostly flat with poor sandy soil. There are extensive tracts of forest.

The island has a fascinating history. It attracted white frontiersmen from the early 1800s, who made a living from trapping, fishing and, later, cutting wood for passing steamers. But the most extraordinary chapter in the island's history came when a Mormon splinter group led by James Strang evicted the previous inhabitants in the early 1850s. Strang had himself crowned king in a bizarre coronation ceremony, married several queens and encouraged his subjects to build roads, clear land and start cultivating. Unfortunately, they were not to enjoy the fruits of their labour – Strang was killed by disgruntled followers in 1856 and a land-hungry mob arrived from Mackinac Island to evict the Mormons.

The next wave of incomers was mostly Irish and Gaelic was widely spoken. The community flourished until the prolific Lake Michigan fishery declined drastically in the 1890s, after which there was a period of intense logging. When that finished the community steadily dwindled until fewer than 200 souls remained. Tourism came to the rescue from the 1970s, since when the resident population has more than doubled.

Once dependent on fishing, logging and farming, Beaver Island now relies on government services, tourism and the construction of vacation homes. It prides itself on a serene, relaxed lifestyle that attracts visitors back time and time again.

POPULATION:
600 (2007 estimate)

WHEN TO GO:
This is an open-air sort of place, which, this far north, means visiting between May and October.

HOW TO GET THERE:
There is a ferry from Charlevoix. The island may be reached by regular air taxi.

HIGHLIGHTS:
The only Mormon-era building left – their old print house, now a museum of island history.
Dr Protar's home – the simple house where a revered island character lived from 1893 to his death in 1925 (open by appointment).
Two lighthouses – Beaver Harbour Light on Whiskey Point where the island's lifesaving station was once located, and Beaver Head Light.
Guided island tours – various options, including an eco-tour.

YOU SHOULD KNOW:
Beaver Island is still known as 'America's Emerald Isle' after it was so nicknamed by the large number of islanders of Irish descent in the late 19th century.

St James Township on Beaver Island

Manitou Islands

POPULATION:
Uninhabited
WHEN TO GO:
The Sleeping Bear National Lakeshore is open all year round, but the islands are really a May to September destination.
HOW TO GET THERE:
There is a ferry service from Leland, Michigan.
HIGHLIGHTS:
Birdlife, including eagles and the endangered piping plover that nests on North Manitou.
A stand of northern white cedar trees in the Valley of the Giants on South Manitou, said to be among the largest and oldest in the world.
The redundant lighthouse (built 1871) that marks the deep bay harbour on South Manitou.
Spectacular sand dunes on North Manitou and the 'perched' dunes of South Manitou, so called because they sit atop limestone bluffs.
YOU SHOULD KNOW:
The Manitous are surrounded by numerous shipwrecks, which are popular with recreational divers.

The two Manitou Islands in Lake Michigan were once settled, but are now uninhabited. That doesn't mean they are abandoned, as both are part of the Sleeping Bear National Lakeshore. Each has a ranger station and the islands are a popular destination for day trips and adventure holidays – note that visitors who stay require park and camping permits.

North Manitou is the larger at 13 km (8 mi) long and 6.5 km (4 mi) wide, with some 32 km (20 mi) of shoreline. By the mid-1800s there were piers at which passing steamships refuelled, but the island has few exploitable resources and never had a thriving settlement. Ruined homesteads, logging roads, a few wild orchards and the old cemetery are all that remain of that era, and the principal activities are wilderness camping and deer hunting in season.

South Manitou, though just 5 km (3 mi) by 5 km (3 mi), was always more populous than its larger sibling. It had some fertile ground and the only natural harbour between the Manitous and Chicago, making the island a regular stopping-off point for lake mariners from the late 1700s into the 20th century. The hardy inhabitants have long gone, but they have left buildings and evocative ruins as evidence of their presence. This island has a system of trails and three campsites, and guided tours are available in open-top vehicles.

Chippewa Indian legend has it that a mother bear and her two cubs tried to swim across the lake to escape a fire on the Wisconsin shore. She made it and climbed a steep bluff to await her cubs. She waited and waited, but they never came. Eventually she died, and the Great Spirit Manitou marked her resting place with the Sleeping Bear Dunes and raised North and South Manitou Islands where the cubs drowned.

Sleeping Bear Dunes

Antelope Island

Utah's Great Salt Lake is the largest lake in the western United States and Antelope is the largest of ten islands in that lake. In fact, when the water level is low it ceases to be an island, becoming a peninsula. From the mainland the island appears barren and deserted, but there is abundant flora and wildlife, including the pronghorn antelope that give the island its name. Other larger species include mule deer, bobcats, coyotes, elk and bighorn sheep, whilst there is also an abundance of waterfowl. But the most striking animals are undoubtedly the American bison, a free-roaming herd of around 600 animals. They were introduced in 1893 and have played an important role in the conservation of this once-abundant species that was hunted almost to the point of extinction in the 19th century.

The island has an area of 68 sq km (42 sq mi) and is mostly flat around the outside (except on the rocky western side) with beaches and plains that stretch to the central mountains, which rise steeply to an elevation of some 760 m (2,500 ft) above the level of the lake. It was once in private ownership and included a working ranch, but was purchased by the state and Antelope Island State Park is now part of the Utah State Parks system.

This is the perfect place to see the Great Salt Lake and appreciate the vast solitude of the Great Basin it occupies. The island offers beaches, paved roads, campgrounds, a sailboat marina, hiking trails, biking, horse-riding and an excellent visitor centre.

POPULATION:
Uninhabited
WHEN TO GO:
This is an all-year-round destination, though winter activities are limited.
HOW TO GET THERE:
Via an 11 km (7 mi) causeway from West Point in Davis County. In periods when the lake is high (most recently 1981-1991) there is boat access only.
HIGHLIGHTS:
Floating effortlessly in the Great Salt Lake (nearly as buoyant as the Dead Sea!).
The buffalo corral and management facility run by the Utah Division of Parks and Recreation – annual roundup in late October.
The incredible sunsets over the western part of the Great Salt Lake.
YOU SHOULD KNOW:
Brine flies abound around the lake and are, in the local lingo, 'darn pesky'.

Antelope Island sits in the Great Salt Lake.

Boss Harbour Marsh with Western Mountain in the background

POPULATION:
Varying populations up to 10,000. Many of the islands are uninhabited.
WHEN TO GO:
Travel the Maine Marine Island Trail between July and September.
HOW TO GET THERE:
By kayak, sailboat or small motorboat only (boat hire generally available all along the coast).
HIGHLIGHTS:
A stop-off on the mainland to see Harriet Beecher Stowe's house in Brunswick, where she wrote *Uncle Tom's Cabin*.
A visit to one of the 49 islands that comprise the Maine Coastal Islands National Wildlife Refuge.
For those who prefer driving to paddling their own canoe – a visit to Georgetown Island with a wonderful shoreline and abundant wildlife.
YOU SHOULD KNOW:
As a crow flies the Maine coast is just 367 km (228 mi) long, but it has 5,597 km (3,478 mi) of shoreline – more than California.

Maine Islands

The Maine Island Trail – a member organization – organizes access to a stunning coastline. The trail runs for 565 km (350 mi) from Cape Porpoise Harbour, northeast to Machias Bay. There are over 150 designated island and mainland stops along the route, which can be travelled only by private craft. Interesting calling points are Monhegan Island, Mount Desert Island, Warren Island and Isle au Haut, though all or any part of the Trail should appeal to lovers of unspoiled places and adventurous holidays.

Tiny Monhegan is off Lincoln County. It is sustained by a winter lobster fishery and by summer visitors who come for breathtaking scenery and abundant bird life. The island has a long-established art colony that has attracted prominent painters, including Edward Hopper. Most of the island, with a resident population of less than 100, is uninhabited and may be freely explored.

Mount Desert is Maine's largest coastal island. It lies off Hancock County and is by far the most heavily populated of the Maine Islands, with some 10,000 inhabitants. It is a major tourist destination with up to four million people visiting its rugged Acadia National Park each year.

Uninhabited Warren Island is a State Park representing a typical wild stop-over on the Trail – this 70-acre spruce-covered island in Penobscot Bay offers safe mooring, campsites and fresh water for those who like to make their own way in life. A ferry goes to the neighbouring island of Islesboro, but no closer.

Isle au Haut is also in Penobscot Bay, but is inhabited by some 80 full-timers. Most of the island's 191.8 sq km (74 sq mi) area falls within the Acadia National Park, and that's what attracts visitors. It is a working island with few amenities.

Peaks Island

Once known as 'Maine's Coney Island', Peaks Island is in Casco Bay some 5 km (3 mi) from Portland. The close-knit community recently tried to secede from the city so Peaks Island could become a town in its own right, but it seems that might is right and Portland got to keep its island jewel. Peaks is one of over 200 islands in the bay and the most populous, though only 3.2 km (2 mi) long and 1.6 km (1 mi) across at the widest point. Casco Bay is where the spectacular Maine coast really begins, offering a world of rocky shorelines, wooded islands, abundant wild flowers, secluded beaches and hidden coves.

By contrast with the other bay islands, Peaks Island became a developed resort towards the end of the 19th century, with a small resident population swelled by thousands of summer visitors ever since. It was once a place of organized summer entertainment with a particularly strong theatrical tradition, its three theatres playing host to many already or subsequently famous types over the years, including D. W. Griffith and the Barrymores. Almost all the original hotels, theatres and amusement parks have been lost over the years, though the island retains many quaint cottages from the Victorian era.

As tastes changed, the island traded on its traditional small-town atmosphere and has become popular with those who like natural beauty, scrambling over a rocky seashore, bike riding, horse-riding, kayaking or simply loafing on the beach.

POPULATION:
840 (2000)

WHEN TO GO:
As with most East Coast resorts, May to September is when it all happens, but various hotels offer cosy winter breaks.

HOW TO GET THERE:
By regular ferry sailing from Portland – it's a perfect day trip.

HIGHLIGHTS:
A scenic bay cruise with Casco Bay Lines that not only takes in Peaks Island, but also Little Diamond, Great Diamond, Long, Chebeague and Cliff Islands.
The Gem Gallery on Island Avenue, featuring the work of local artists.
The annual Peaks Fest event held at the end of June to celebrate the island's unique community.
Abandoned World War II military installations including Battery Steele, whose big guns broke windows all over the island when first tested.

YOU SHOULD KNOW:
The great Portland-born Hollywood director John Ford was nicknamed 'Mayor of Peaks Island' – he worked the ferry, ushered in the Gem Theatre as a young man and vacationed on the island all his life.

The shoreline on Peaks Island shows its winter face!

Ellis Island

POPULATION:
Uninhabited
WHEN TO GO:
March to June, or September to November
HOW TO GET THERE:
Fly to New York City, then take a ferry from Battery Park at the southern tip of Manhattan or from Liberty State Park in New Jersey.
HIGHLIGHTS:
The Statue of Liberty – the ferry to Ellis Island will take you right past.
The Ellis Island Immigration Museum – three floors of audio/visual displays and exhibits detailing the history of immigration processing on the island. The museum attracts more than two million visitors a year.
YOU SHOULD KNOW:
Ellis Island is part of the Statue of Liberty National Monument.

Ellis Island has played an integral role in the shaping of America. Lying at the mouth of the Hudson River in New York Harbour, the island is an icon of America itself, a reminder of the American ideals of freedom, liberty and justice for all. In the shadow of the Statue of Liberty, this largely artificial island was the main portal for immigrants entering the United States from 1 January 1892 until 12 November 1954. Annie Moore, a 15 year-old Irish girl, was the first immigrant to be processed here, and over the next 62 years more than 12 million people followed her.

Up until 1890, the individual states regulated immigration, rather than the federal government. Castle Garden, or Castle Clinton, in the Battery served as the New York State immigration station and processed eight million immigrants between 1855 and 1890. Most of these early immigrants were from northern and western Europe, including Britain, Ireland, Germany and Scandinavia. Throughout the 19th century, political instability, famine and deteriorating economic conditions in Europe caused the largest mass migration in human history. In 1890 President Benjamin Harrison designated Ellis Island the first federal immigration station to handle the growing numbers of immigrants.

In the early years of the 20th century, officials thought the peak of immigration had passed, but it was actually on the increase and in 1907 alone around 1.25 million were processed at Ellis Island. As World War I approached, emigration to the United States slowed. During and just after the war, the island was used to detain thousands of suspected alien radicals from across the United States. Hundreds were deported simply because they were loosely associated with an organization advocating revolt against the federal government. In 1920, the immigration processing facility reopened on the island and dealt with a further 225,000 immigrants until it closed in 1954. In 1965, it was declared part of the Statue of Liberty National Monument. Today it is wholly in the possession of the federal government, but under the jurisdiction of the US National Park Service.

An aerial view of Ellis Island

Fire Island

Ocean Beach

This elongated, thin barrier island in Suffolk County, New York, protects much of the southern shoreline of Long Island from the worst excesses of the Atlantic Ocean. At the last count Fire Island was 49.5 km (31 mi) long and 0.8 km (0.5 mi) across at the widest point. But the shape is constantly changing – at one point it stretched for 95 km (60 mi) from adjacent Jones Island in the east to Southampton at the New York end and was as wide as 8 km (5 mi). In 1931 a northeasterly gale broke through to Moriches Inlet, dividing Fire Island from Southampton.

Fire Island is separated from Long Island by a series of bays – Great South Bay, Patchogue Bay, Bellport Bay, Narrow Bay and Moriches Bay. The western 7.5 km (4.5 mi) is made up of Robert Moses State Park, a hugely popular summer destination for New Yorkers. Since 1964 the rest of the island has been protected as the Fire Island National Seashore. There is no road along the island's length and vehicular traffic is banned during the summer season (June to August). Even out of season only a limited number of driving permits are available for residents.

The main resorts are Ocean Beach on the South Shore, reached by water taxi or a walk along the sand from Robert Moses Park, nearby Saltaire and Davis Park on Moriches Inlet. Among various hamlets on the island, Cherry Grove and The Pines are popular with the gay community. The year-round population is small, but thousands flock to their vacation homes or rentals in high summer, joined by many thousands more who come out from New York for the day to enjoy Fire Island's miles of boardwalk and laid-back beach life.

POPULATION:
300 (2000)

WHEN TO GO:
Join the summer crowds – this is definitely no place to be in winter.

HOW TO GET THERE:
Limited road access via Robert Moses Causeway (western end) and William Floyd Parkway (eastern end). Numerous resort ferries from Long Island in season.

HIGHLIGHTS:
The Fire Island Lighthouse, that replaced an earlier light in 1858. Now privately operated by a preservation society and open to the public.
Smith Point County Park to the east end of the island – it has a large car park with tunnel access to the seashore.
A rare survivor – the Sunken Forest on Sailor's Haven, one of the few remaining maritime forests on the eastern seaboard, featuring gnarled trees twisted by wind and salt spray.

YOU SHOULD KNOW:
In 1966, avant-garde American poet Frank O'Hara was struck by a beach buggy on the Fire Island shore. He died the next day.

Manhattan Island

At New York City's heart, Manhattan consists of Manhattan Island, a long, thin strip bounded by the Hudson River (west), East River and Harlem River (north), plus various smaller islands and a section on the mainland (Marble Hill, adjacent to The Bronx). The island is 21.6 km (13.4 mi) long and 3.7 km (2.3 mi) wide at 14th Street, the widest point, and is connected to the other four boroughs by bridges, tunnels and the (free) Staten Island Ferry. This is the commercial, financial and cultural centre of the city and therefore (New Yorkers would argue) of the world.

The frantic pace of Manhattan life generates an energy that invariably excites (but sometimes alarms) first-time visitors. A 'New York Minute' is very short, referring to the impatient character of the city in general and Manhattan in particular – once amusingly defined as 'from the lights turning green to the guy behind honking his horn'.

Manhattan Island seems familiar to people who have never been there, with a cityscape and skyline that have appeared in countless films and television series, many of which featured the twin towers of the World Trade Centre in Lower Manhattan, tragically destroyed on 9/11/2001. Manhattan is full of names that seem equally familiar – Greenwich Village, Wall Street, Broadway, the Upper East Side, Fifth Avenue, Harlem, SoHo, Times Square, Madison Square Garden... the list could go on and on. But everyone should visit Manhattan at least once for shopping and the sights, because seeing is believing.

Orientation isn't as easy as the regular grid layout of streets would suggest, partly because there are exceptions to the rule (one of the most notable is Broadway), but one of those famous yellow cabs will get you where you want to go.

POPULATION:
1,537,000 (Manhattan Borough, 2000)

WHEN TO GO:
If inclement weather bothers you, the months to avoid are December to March (often very cold, sometimes with heavy snowfall).

HOW TO GET THERE:
By air from practically anywhere in the world to one of New York's three airports (Newark, JFK and La Guardia). La Guardia is closest to Manhattan, but all have excellent links to the island.

HIGHLIGHTS:
Central Park, Manhattan's 'green lung' – the USA's first public park and the country's most-visited (currently by some 25 million people each year).
The breathtaking view from the top of the Empire State Building by day or night (buy tickets on line in advance, or be prepared to queue in line for a while).
Some of the world's finest museums – the Metropolitan Museum of Art, the Guggenheim, MoMA (Museum of Modern Art) and Whitney Museum of American Art (allow at least a day each to do them any sort of justice).
A Broadway show – there really is no business like show business, New-York style.

YOU SHOULD KNOW:
One derivation of the name 'Manhattan' is from 'Manahachtanienk' in the native Lenape language, meaning 'place of general inebriation'. Surely not!

An aerial view of Manhattan

Staten Island

POPULATION:
465,000 (2006)
WHEN TO GO:
Any time between May and October for the best of the weather.
HOW TO GET THERE:
The island is served by four bridges and a rapid transit line, but the only way to go is the famous Staten Island Ferry from Lower Manhattan, for incomparable harbour views.
HIGHLIGHTS:
Historic Richmond Town – an open-air museum site containing old commercial and government buildings (including the former Richmond County Courthouse), plus homes and farm buildings moved from elsewhere on the island.
North America's best collection of rattlesnakes (and other reptiles) at the small Staten Island Zoo in Barret Park.
Snug Harbor Cultural Centre – 26 buildings in various classic styles that are home to a wealth of activities, with grounds that include the Staten Island Botanical Garden and Newhouse Centre for Contemporary Art.
YOU SHOULD KNOW:
Following the 9/11 attack, debris from Ground Zero was taken to the unfortunately named Fresh Kills landfill site on Staten Island – for years the repository of New York's trash (now closed).

This is one of New York's five boroughs (the others being Manhattan, Brooklyn, Queens and The Bronx). It is the most geographically isolated and the least densely populated of the five. Until the 1970s Staten Island was known as the Borough of Richmond, reflecting its proximity to Richmond County, the most southerly in New York State. It is the third-largest borough at 153 sq km (59 sq mi).

The island's modern history goes back to the arrival of European settlers. Dutch attempts to settle the place in the early 17th century foundered in the face of stiff opposition from the indigenous tribes, but in 1670 they gave up their claim and English and Dutch settlers took over. It was on Staten Island in 1776 that massed British forces under William Howe learned of the Declaration of Independence, shortly before routing George Washington at the Battle of Long Island and capturing New York.

Compared to the rest of New York, the island remained relatively undeveloped until the completion of the Verrazano Narrows Bridge in 1964, which opened the place to rapid development by providing direct road access to Brooklyn. The bridge also provided a better way for traffic from New Jersey to reach the other boroughs and Long Island, and a network of new roads soon changed the island's hitherto relaxed pace of life. The North Shore is heavily urbanized, whilst the South Shore is more suburban. However, the conservationists didn't give in without a fight, and the 1960s saw the establishment of New York's largest area of parkland and preservation of large tracts of woodland for public use. Staten Island also has New York's highest (natural) point – the summit of Todt Hill at 125 m (410 ft).

The famous Staten Island Ferry

Long Island

Yes, it is long – 190 km (118 mi) to be precise. And it's quite wide too – up to 37 km (23 mi) across. And populous – heading steadily towards the 8-million mark, though well over half of those live in New York. Two of the city's five boroughs – Queens and Brooklyn – occupy the western end of the island, but this is a mere geographical fact. They consider themselves part of New York City rather than Long Island and in colloquial use 'Long Island' means the suburban communities of Nassau and Suffolk Counties beyond city limits.

Long Island is a very affluent area, with enclaves of real wealth such as the Hamptons and the North Shore's cliff-top Gold Coast overlooking Long Island Sound, or South Shore communities along now-protected Atlantic beaches and wetlands. But the island's real prosperity is built on the city workers who commute into New York. Summer tourism is also important as the island has numerous parks, beaches and great scenery, tending to act as New York's playground.

The two suburban counties have roughly similar populations, but Nassau County in the centre of the island is the most heavily urbanized. By the time a determined traveller reaches the Twin Forks area in Suffolk County at the eastern extremity there is a more rural feel. It sometimes seems that the whole place is just a sprawling extension of New York, but there is more to Long Island than that. Actually, the place is something of a metaphor for the American Dream – start with nothing in the mean streets of Brooklyn, move out to an apple-pie suburb and finish up with a multi-millionaire's beach-front retreat in the Hamptons. Lots of Long Islanders have made it half way.

Beach house on East Hampton Beach

POPULATION:
7,559,000 (2006)

WHEN TO GO:
This is a summer tourist destination, with many facilities closed out of season.

HOW TO GET THERE:
From New York City by road or bus (MTA Long Island Bus) and rail (the busy Long Island Rail Road).

HIGHLIGHTS:
Coney Island in Brooklyn, that faded beachfront icon of yesteryear, now undergoing a renaissance.
Rural Long Island: Typified by the North Fork resort area with its quaint fishing villages, old-fashioned towns and famous wineries.
Unspoiled Long Island: Try the Sweetbriar Nature Centre in Central Suffolk, with hiking trails along the Nissequogue River and a summer butterfly house.
Maritime Long Island: Represented by lighthouses – lots of them, often in stunning coastal settings, many now preserved and open to the public.

YOU SHOULD KNOW:
In 1927, Charles Lindbergh's historic solo flight across the Atlantic began at Roosevelt Airfield in Nassau County.

Tangier Island

POPULATION:
600 (2000)
WHEN TO GO:
Access is easiest in the summer months and winters can be very hard.
HOW TO GET THERE:
There is a landing strip for air taxis, ferry services from the mainland (Crisfied, Maryland and two Virginia ports, Onancock and Reedville), plus island boat cruises.
HIGHLIGHTS:
Spanky's 1950s-style ice-cream parlour on Main Ridge.
Birds – thousands of pelicans, blue herons, egrets, rails, osprey, ducks and geese attracted by rich marshland.
An island speciality – Christmas decorations made from sea shells.
YOU SHOULD KNOW:
Tangier islanders only abandoned the practice of burying their dead beneath the family lawn in the early 20th century, when most of the small yards became fully occupied.

This isolated island in Chesapeake Bay is part of Accomack County, Virginia, and is separated from the Bay's eastern shore by Pocomoke Sound. It is tiny, with an area of just 0.6 sq km (0.2 sq mi). Its first known explorer was Captain John Smith of Pocahontas fame, and the island passed through various hands in the 1600s.

In fact, Tangier Island is a series of long islets divided by marsh and small tidal streams. These are all connected by narrow wooden bridges that do not permit the passage of motor vehicles, so the main modes of transport are golf cart, boat, moped, bike and foot. There are three significant ridges – Main Ridge, Canton and West Ridge. The northern part of Main Ridge is quaintly named Me at Soup. Other island districts are Black Dye, Sheep's Head and Hog Ridge.

The two words that best describe the island are 'old' and 'fashioned'. The tough and independent inhabitants speak a unique dialect thought to be unchanged since its first occupation by English colonists. There is one payphone, no ATM and the few tourist facilities have only recently started accepting credit cards. That said, the island is modernizing fast with the arrival of cable TV – a process not to everyone's liking. Tourism supplements the island's main economic activity – soft shell crabbing and oyster fishing. Men tend to focus on the latter, leaving the women to deal with tourists.

There are bed-and-breakfast establishments offering overnight stays, but most visitors come as part of an organized tour, or take a day-trip to the island by regular ferry. Upon arrival, they find a few gift shops, eateries (crab cakes a speciality), one general store... and an island with unique character.

Chesapeake Bay at sunset

Fenwick Island

A barrier island between Little Assawoman Bay and the Atlantic Ocean, Fenwick Island is part of Delaware's fast-growing beach resort area, along with Bethany Beach, South Bethany, Dewey Beach, Lewes and Rehoboth Beach. It is the southernmost of the so-called 'Quiet Resorts', though in truth the area is not always that quiet, partly because it is just across the state line from Ocean City, Maryland, which definitely is a wild place with a buzzing boardwalk and notorious nightlife. Fenwick Island, however, still claims to be a relatively peaceful enclave.

The island is named after an English planter who acquired the place in 1692, but never lived there. Until then it was known as Fishing Harbor. Its southern extremity is now marked by the Transpeninsular Line. This was surveyed in 1750-51 and runs due west to Taylor's Island and meets the 'tangent line' section of the famous Mason-Dixon line that divides the USA's old northern and southern states, the Union and Dixie. Both lines had marker stones every five miles, with the arms of Maryland's founding family (the Calverts) on one side and the arms of Pennsylvania's Penn family on the other. Many of these survive, and the marker at Fenwick is said to be 'the oldest standing man-made object on the coast between Indian River and Ocean City'.

Separated from the mainland by a narrow channel, Fenwick Island is tiny, with a landmass of just 0.9 sq km (0.3 sq mi), and is all about one of the best beaches in southern Delaware. It is partly occupied by the town of Fenwick Island, incorporated in 1953 to prevent the advance of Ocean City, with the rest considered to be part of Sussex County. The resident population is swelled by several thousand each summer, who come for the renowned fishing and the simple pleasures of a perfect beach holiday – loafing, sunbathing, swimming, sandcastle building and watching the sensational sunrises and sunsets over the sea. For the more active there is wind surfing, body surfing and jet skiing.

POPULATION:
340 (2000)

WHEN TO GO:
Although claiming to appeal to year-round visitors, out of season is reserved for those who like wild seas and deserted beaches.

HOW TO GET THERE:
Fenwick Island is reached by a bridge built in 1958 – the fourth to occupy the site.

HIGHLIGHTS:
Fenwick Island State Park, part of the larger Delaware Seashore State Park that offers an accessible expanse of beach, dunes and Atlantic scenery.
Fenwick Lighthouse, completed in 1869, which sits upon the Transpeninsular Line and the Delaware-Maryland state border.

YOU SHOULD KNOW:
According to local lore, Cedar Island in Little Assawoman Bay was used to bury pirate treasure. True or false, pirates did hide out along the Delaware coast in the mid-17th century.

Fenwick Lighthouse

Traditional gingerbread houses

Martha's Vineyard

Few placenames in the USA contain a possessive apostrophe, and that says something about the exclusive character of Martha's Vineyard. In the late 19th century the US Board of Geographical Names ordered the apostrophe to be dropped, but the decision was soon reversed after high-level lobbying. This prosperous island off Cape Cod in Massachusetts is a thriving summer colony, with some 100,000 vacation homers joining year-round inhabitants and thousands more casual visitors who arrive each day.

The place was named by English explorer Bartholomew Gosnold (his daughter was called Martha), who arrived in 1602 and found a triangular-shaped island some 33 km (20.5 mi) in length. It flourished as a whaling centre in the 19th century, but when that industry declined it became a resort for tourists, especially wealthy ones, and the island still serves as a magnet for the rich and famous. It has six townships: Tisbury, including the main village of Vineyard Haven and West Chop peninsula; Edgartown, the old whaling port; Oak Bluffs with its famous 'gingerbread' cottages; agricultural West Tisbury; rural Chilmark with its hilly terrain and the fishing village of Menemsha; and Aquinnah, home to the indigenous Wampanoag tribe and spectacular Gay Cliffs.

A history of peaceful coexistence with the Wampanoags established the island's reputation for tolerance, and it has long been a place where the African-American elite has felt able to summer, mainly around Oak Bluffs. Many prominent Jewish families also have homes on the island, after being subtly discouraged from buying on nearby Nantucket Island in more prejudiced times.

Unlike Nantucket, the rapid growth of Martha's Vineyard from the 1950s was not well controlled, and some parts of the island suffered visually as a result of haphazard development.

POPULATION:
15,000 (2007 estimate)
WHEN TO GO:
June to August for the full experience, out of season to avoid crowds and explore the island's delights at leisure.
HOW TO GET THERE:
Regular ferry services from mainland ports including Woods Hole, Falmouth, New Bedford, Hyannis and Quonset Point (Rhode Island). Scheduled air services in season.
HIGHLIGHTS:
The On Time ferry trip to adjacent Chappaquiddick Island, scene of Senator Edward Kennedy's infamous plunge off Dike Bridge that killed Mary Jo Kopechne in 1969.
The USA's oldest operating Flying Horses Carousel at Oak Bluffs, built in 1876 and brought to its present site in 1886 – now a National Historic Landmark.
The Felix Neck Wildlife Sanctuary in Edgartown, principally for birdwatching.
Vineyard Haven Harbor and Marine Railway, a traditional boatyard.
YOU SHOULD KNOW:
If you go down to the sea today... Steven Spielberg filmed *Jaws* here in 1975.

Nantucket Island

The English explorer Bartholomew Gosnold was here too – putting Nantucket Island on the map in 1602 when he passed by on the Dartmouth bark *Concord*. This Massachusetts island off Cape Cod is nicknamed the 'Grey Lady' (it often rains). Nantucket was settled by the English from the 1660s, going on to become the world's leading whaling port. The industry faded throughout the 19th century and the community declined, a process hastened by a destructive whale oil fire in 1846 that destroyed much of the town.

This ultimately proved to be the island's salvation, as a hundred years of isolation and stagnation meant that very little changed on Nantucket after the Civil War era. When enterprising developers moved in after World War II, they had the vision to see that the USA's largest concentration of ante-bellum buildings was an asset to be restored rather than something to be swept away and replaced with modern development. Strict controls have maintained this policy ever since, with a result that there's little tackiness evident on this up-market summer resort island. The Nantucket Historical Association maintains six wonderful properties that represent the island's preserved heritage, including the oldest house (built 1686), the Old Gaol and Quaker Meeting house built in 1838 to serve the island's most prominent religion.

The island has an area of just 124 sq km (48 sq mi). The main settlement is also called Nantucket which lies beside the harbour at the western end. Other notable localities are Madaket, Miacomet, Polpis, Siasconset, Surfside and Wauwinet.

Much of the northeastern seaboard aims to offer the sort of idealized, laid-back beach holidays amidst traditional New England architecture that have almost become part of the American Dream (summer section). Inexorable commercial pressures have made such simple pleasures harder to find, but Nantucket delivers in spades.

POPULATION:
10,200 (2006 estimate)

WHEN TO GO:
Most attractions are open in summer season only (June-October), though the island is beautiful all year round.

HOW TO GET THERE:
A choice of three ferry services from the mainland or light aircraft to the busy Nantucket Memorial Airport.

HIGHLIGHTS:
Historic Nantucket Town and harbor, for a real sense of a long-vanished New England way of life.
The new Whaling Museum, run by the Nantucket Historical Association.
Seal Encounter Cruises from Nantucket Harbor to remote Tuckernuck and Muskeget Islands.
The Nantucket Life Saving Museum, providing a fascinating tribute to the early islanders who saved countless lives in the treacherous waters around Nantucket.
Beaches – Nantucket has lots of them, all sandy, all pristine.

YOU SHOULD KNOW:
A key acronym on Nantucket and neighbouring Martha's Vineyard is BYOB. If you want to eat out (or drink in), bring your own bottle – no booze for sale here!

Houses and dinghies in Nantucket Harbor

Rhode Island

POPULATION:
60,900 (2000)
WHEN TO GO:
September or October for sensational foliage – the locals even run 'leaf peeper' tours.
HOW TO GET THERE:
By road bridge. There is no scheduled airline service to Newport State Airport.
HIGHLIGHTS:
The Newport Cliff Walk from Easton's Beach to Bailey's Beach – wonderful ocean views.
Fort Adams State Park (music lovers note that the Newport Folk and Jazz Festivals are held here).
The amazing Green Animals Topiary Gardens in Portsmouth.
Sachuest Point US Fish & Wildlife Preserve in Middleton.
Wine tasting at Newport Vineyards in Middleton or Greenvale Vineyards in Portsmouth.
YOU SHOULD KNOW:
Polo playing has long been an island tradition and matches can still be seen at the Glen, Portsmouth.

Everyone knows that Rhode Island – actually the State of Rhode Island and Providence Plantations – is the smallest in the USA. But not everyone knows that the state and island that gives it a colloquially abbreviated name are not one and the same. Indeed, the Rhode Island part of the longest state name in America is unofficially called Aquidneck Island to distinguish from the state as a whole.

Now that's cleared up, what of Rhode/Aquidneck Island? It is the largest of several in Narragansett Bay, with its southern shore facing the Atlantic Ocean. The area of this well-developed island is 117 sq km (45 sq mi) and it is connected to the mainland by three bridges. The Newport Bridge goes to Jamestown on nearby Conanicut Island, and thence to the mainland on the western side of the bay. The Mount Hope Bridge in Portsmouth connects the northern side of the island with Bristol. The same area is served by the Sakonnet River Bridge over a narrow saltwater channel to Tiverton. The nearby Stone Bridge was destroyed by Hurricane Carol in 1954. The island is divided into three municipalities – Newport, Middleton and Portsmouth.

The island's population shrank by a fifth in the ten years after the US Navy reorganized its major base at Newport in 1973 but is growing again, with over half its area now built over as housing demand increases. But wetland and woodland still occupy a third of the island and there is an active preservation society trying to keep it that way.

After the naval base, the island's principal revenue generator is tourism. Narragansett Bay is a magnet for visitors and they come to Rhode/Aquidneck Island principally for the beaches and coastline, enjoying related activities like sailing, kayaking, sailboarding, diving and fishing.

Mansions dot the coast of Cliff Walk in Newport, with Newport Pell Bridge in the background.

Golden Isles

The Sea Islands are a chain of barrier islands along the coasts of South Carolina, Georgia and Florida. They were colonised by Spanish missionaries seeking to save the souls of indigenous Indians, though both groups were violently ejected by the mid-1700s. The islands featured in the American Revolution and became a haven for fleeing slaves during the Civil War, since when many have been intensively developed as resorts. The middle section of Georgia's islands is known as the Golden Isles, and consists of St Simons, Sea, Jekyll and Little St Simons Islands. Since the 1870s, all but Little St Simons have been up-market places frequented by some of the USA's wealthiest families.

The largest is St Simons Island (population 13,400). The resident resort community includes many well-heeled retirees and is swelled by seasonal residents and vacationers.

Sea Island is an exclusive resort created from the late 1920s. The name was changed from Long Island and a plush hotel and golf course constructed. Together, they catered for many of America's richest industrialists. Sea Island is privately owned, a gated community reserved for homeowners, club members and hotel guests. Permanent entry doesn't come cheap – a property recently sold for $12 million.

Jekyll Island (population 900) has a number of interesting buildings from the late 19th and early 20th centuries, earning a Landmark Historic District listing, and is a wildlife haven. A wide variety of mammals and reptiles may be found on the inland marshes.

In stark contrast to the other three, Little St Simons Island is virtually unchanged since it was purchased from King George III in 1760. It is the most remote of the Golden Isles, an uninhabited 10,000-acre wildlife paradise. There is public access for no more than thirty visitors at a time, who pay handsomely to explore this unique island.

The uninhabited Plum Orchard Mansion on Cumberland Island

POPULATION:
70,000 (2000)

WHEN TO GO:
The temperate climate allows comfortable year-round visiting.

HOW TO GET THERE:
Road access to all but Little St Simons Island (boat only).

HIGHLIGHTS:
Fort Frederica National Monument, the remains of a fort and settlement completed in 1748 by British General James Ogelthorpe on St Simons Island.
The St Simons Island Light – a lighthouse still used as a navigational aid but also a museum run by the Coastal Georgia Historical Society.
An excursion from Jekyll Island to the uninhabited Cumberland Island National Seashore, that is preserved in its natural state.

YOU SHOULD KNOW:
Before leaving the Anglican Church John Wesley, founder of the Methodist Church, was a missionary in the Golden Isles, along with his brother Charles.

Dauphin Island

POPULATION:
1,400 (2000)
WHEN TO GO:
High summer for laid-back resort attractions, other seasons for bird watching. Be aware that access is sometimes restricted in Hurricane Season (June-November).
HOW TO GET THERE:
Across the high-level bridge that replaced an earlier structure destroyed by Hurricane Frederic in 1979. There is also a public ferry from Fort Morgan.
HIGHLIGHTS:
Fort Gaines, a remarkably well-preserved fortification begun in 1853 and finally completed in 1898. There are regular tours and historic re-enactments.
Audubon Bird Sanctuary, the main site of protected maritime habitat on the island.
The Estuarium and public aquarium at the Dauphin Island Sea Lab, a resource centre featuring the key habitats of coastal Alabama.
St Agnes Church – one of the oldest in Alabama, rebuilt from salvage in 1740 after being destroyed by a hurricane.
YOU SHOULD KNOW:
The French initially called the place 'Massacre Island', as they found a gruesome litter of human bones upon arrival – actually graves laid bare by a hurricane.

This barrier island is 5 km (3 mi) off the mouth of Mobile Bay in the Gulf of Mexico and falls within Mobile County, Alabama. With a landmass of 16 sq km (6 sq mi), Dauphin Island is 22.5 km (14 mi) long and 2.8 km (1.75 mi) across at the widest point. The eastern end is developed, whilst the long western 'tail' is uninhabited.

The island was named after the heir to the French throne, in this case the great-grandson of the Sun King, Louis XIV, serving as a reminder that there was once considerable Gallic influence in these parts. Indeed, Dauphin Island was effectively the capital of the French Louisiana Territories for many years.

The first European visitor was Spanish explorer Alonzo Pineda in 1517. The French arrived in 1699. Pirates raided in 1711. The British captured the island in 1766, losing it to the Spanish in 1780. The Americans arrived in 1813 and built Fort Gaines, which was occupied by Confederate forces in 1861. In 1864, the island was taken by the Union during the Battle of Mobile Bay, when Admiral David Farragut entered the list of famously gung-ho naval commanders with the order 'Damn the torpedoes! Full speed ahead!' after the USS *Tecumseh* was sunk by a torpedo (then a naval mine).

Today, the town that shares the island's name is a popular resort, offering laid-back attractions like beaches, golf courses, parks, sailing and water sports. However, its main claim to fame is ornithology. The whole island is a designated bird sanctuary, and over 340 species have been recorded. There are spring and autumn migrations from the Yucatan Peninsula and South America, with Dauphin Island often the first landfall for thousands of exhausted birds.

The devastating Hurricane Katrina destroyed a third of the island's structures in 2005.

Boathouses along the shore

Channel Islands

This island chain lies off the coast of Southern California. Officially they are the Channel Islands of California, but are often called the Santa Barbara Islands. Indeed, the smallest in the chain is Santa Barbara which, unlike the nearby mainland metropolis bearing the same name, is uninhabited.

From north to south, the islands are: San Miguel; Santa Cruz; Santa Rosa; Anacapa; Santa Barbara; Santa Catalina; San Nicholas; San Clemente. They fall into two groups of four, the Northern and Southern Channel Islands. The archipelago extends for 258 km (160 mi) with a combined land area of 895 sq km (346 sq mi).

The only island with a significant resident population is Santa Catalina, largely developed by chewing gum heir William Wrigley II from the 1920s. It has the resort city of Avalon and small town of Two Harbours. Around one million visitors a year are attracted by a wilderness of sage, cactus and oak, plus a wonderful marine environment and genteel resort comforts.

The Channel Islands were under military control in World War II, and the US Navy retains a significant presence. In 1980 five islands (San Miguel, Santa Cruz, Santa Rosa, Anacapa and Santa Barbara) became the Channel Islands National Park. In addition, the waters six nautical miles (11 km, 7 mi) off San Miguel, Santa Cruz, Anacapa and Santa Barbara are protected as the Channel Islands Marine Sanctuary.

The National Park aims to restore and nurture an incredibly rich and diverse biosphere. No more than 250,000 people a year are encouraged to visit, protecting the Park's fragile ecology. Getting there can be an effort, with a trip by small boat or light aircraft the only options, but the effort is certainly worthwhile, allowing visitors to see what mainland California's coast was once like.

Cuylers Harbor on San Miguel Island

POPULATION:
4,000 (2007 estimate)

WHEN TO GO:
The islands have a Mediterranean climate allowing comfortable year-round visiting.

HOW TO GET THERE:
Santa Catalina can be reached by helicopter or ferry from various starting points in Orange and Los Angeles Counties.

HIGHLIGHTS:
Avalon's spectacular Art Deco Casino, a huge circular dance-hall and entertainment palace completed in 1929.
The Catalina Island Museum (in the Casino), with over 100,000 items including Native American artefacts and island-made pottery and tile.
Catalina's bison herd, descended from beasts brought to appear in the 1925 silent movie of Zane Grey's Western novel *The Vanishing American*.
The Wrigley Memorial and Botanical Garden atop Avalon Canyon on Catalina, featuring desert plants from around the world – including eight island natives found nowhere else.

YOU SHOULD KNOW:
In the early 1940s Marilyn Monroe lived on Santa Catalina with first husband James Dougherty, a Merchant Marine officer.

The Florida Keys

The Florida Keys are one of America's biggest tourist attractions. This subtropical archipelago is made up of 1,700 islands which begin at the south-eastern tip of Florida and extend in a gentle arc south-west and then west to Key West, the furthest of the inhabited islands, and on to the uninhabited Dry Tortugas, only 145km (90 mi) from Cuba.

'Key' is a corruption of the Spanish *cayo*, meaning small island. For many years, Key West was the largest town in Florida, grown wealthy on plundering the many ships wrecked on the nearby rocks and reefs. This isolated outpost was well placed for trade with Cuba, and was on the main trade route from New Orleans. Eventually, better navigation led to fewer shipwrecks, and Key West went into a decline in the late 19th century.

The Keys were long accessible only by water. This changed when Henry Flagler built his Overseas Railway in the early 20th century. Flagler extended his Florida East Coast Railway down to Key West using a series of over-sea railroad trestles, a bold and ambitious project for the time it was built. The Labor Day hurricane hit the Keys in 1935, however, with wind speeds of up to 200 miles per hour, and put paid to the Overseas Railway. The damaged tracks were never rebuilt, but the Overseas Highway (an extension of US Highway 1) replaced the railway as the main transportation route from Miami to Key West. This largely two-lane road consists mostly of bridges which connect the islands along the chain.

The Keys are known for their wildlife, with many endemic plant and animal species including the Key deer and the American crocodile. There are many different species of dolphin and porpoise in the warm water surrounding the islands, and the Keys are home to the endangered manatee (sea cow), which is always a delight to observe. The Key lime is not an endemic plant but a naturalized species introduced from Mexico. The Keys have, however, made it their own in the form of the world-famous Key Lime Pie. Each of the Keys has its own personality, but they all share a laid-back approach to life. Key West is the most popular of the islands with tourists, and from here many cruises and boat trips can be arranged to appreciate the natural beauty of this place. The island has an Old Town with charming colonial architecture, bars, cafés, restaurants and shops on its palm-fringed streets, and don't miss the Key West Botanical Forest and Garden for a relaxing stroll.

POPULATION:
79,535 (2000)
WHEN TO GO:
November to May.
HOW TO GET THERE:
Fly to Key West or Marathon airports, or drive via the scenic Overseas Highway.
HIGHLIGHTS:
Conch fritters followed by Key Lime Pie.
The lovely guest houses with wrap-around porches in Key West.
The tropical hospitality of Jimmy Buffet's famed 'Margaritaville' – located on Duval Street, Key West, this laid-back bar serves fine local food and drinks to the sound of live music.
Relax on one of the fabulous beaches, go sport fishing, have a romantic seaside meal, swim with dolphins, look for manatees.
The Ernest Hemmingway Home and Museum – visit the house in Old Town, Key West, where the famous author lived and wrote for ten years. Relive Hemmingway's lifestyle at one of his favourite watering holes after your visit.
PrideFest – this week-long festival takes place in early June to celebrate Key West's Gay and Lesbian community.
YOU SHOULD KNOW:
Key West has long been noted as a gay vacation destination, and is home to the United States' first Gay and Lesbian Chamber of Commerce.

Aerial view of Ohio Key

A rainbow and spring rain clouds at sunset

Angel Island

POPULATION:
60 (2000)
WHEN TO GO:
June to September is definitely the best time to enjoy the open-air delights of Angel Island.
HOW TO GET THERE:
By private boat or public ferry from San Francisco, Tiburon or Vallejo. Be aware that ferry services are scaled back considerably from November to mid-May.
HIGHLIGHTS:
A visitor centre and museum at Ayala Cove (formerly Hospital Cove) where there was once a quarantine station for foreign ships and immigrants suspected of carrying infectious diseases.
Island tours on a Segway, the strange self-balancing personal transportation device.
The island tram tour, an hour-long guided trip that covers all the key sights.
Spectacular views of San Francisco Bay and the Golden Gate Bridge.
YOU SHOULD KNOW:
At the end of World War II, the first thing many troops returning from the Pacific Theatre saw was a 20 m (65 ft) illuminated sign on Angel Island that read 'WELCOME HOME, WELL DONE'.

The small resident population of San Francisco Bay's largest island is regularly swelled by summer visitors who flock to Angel Island State Park, with its spectacular views of Mount Tamalpais, Marin County Headlands and the iconic San Francisco skyline. These are best enjoyed from the island's central high point, Mount Livermore which reaches 240 m (788 ft).

Angel Island has served many purposes over time. It was once a hunting and fishing ground for Miwok Indians, and used as a refuge by early Spanish explorer Juan Manuel de Ayala. The place supported cattle ranching in the 19th century, and was extensively used by the military from the Civil War until a Nike missile base was decommissioned in the early 1960s. At one point the whole island was designated as Fort McDowell. There are two lighthouses on the island, but perhaps it will be best remembered as the 'West Coast Ellis Island' – the Angel Island Immigration Station processed hundreds of thousands of Asian migrants between 1910 and 1940.

This is not a destination for sedentary visitors in search of ready-made attractions. There are good beaches for sunbathing, but swimming is dangerous, as there are no lifeguards to rescue swimmers who get into difficulty in fast-running tides. These do make beachcombing a worthwhile occupation, and there are numerous scenic waterside walks. Hiking trails and fire roads provide good walking or bicycle access to the unspoiled interior (these may be taken to the island or hired on site). Vehicles, dogs, roller skates, roller blades, skateboards, wood fires and some night travel are all banned on the island.

Alcatraz Island

If one word caused a chill to run down the collective spines of America's toughest public enemies, hoodlums, gangsters and career criminals from the 1930s to the 1960s, that word was 'Alcatraz'. Appropriately known as 'The Rock', this craggy island in San Francisco Bay was indeed a hard place, becoming the USA's most notorious federal prison.

Surrounded by strong currents, Alcatraz was considered to be escape proof. Of 34 prisoners involved in 14 attempts during the prison's 29-year life, seven were shot and killed, two drowned, five were unaccounted for and the rest were recaptured. Two made it off the island only to be returned. The most famous attempt – immortalized in the movie *Escape from Alcatraz* – saw three men vanish. They were listed 'presumed drowned', but there has been persistent speculation that they got away.

In fact, the federal prison was a short-lived if notorious part of the island's history, operating from 1934 to 1963. Alcatraz Island was first used to site a lighthouse in the 1850s, but the US Army quickly moved in to fortify the place and protect the seaward approach to San Francisco. In 1868 Alcatraz became a military prison, a role that eventually saw the completion of a huge new cell block in 1912, which was used by the military until handed over to the US Government on cost grounds.

Now a hugely popular visitor attraction dotted with buildings dating back to the Civil War era and supporting a variety of wildlife, the uninhabited island has appeared in many movies. Apart from those featuring prison life, several have used the abandoned prison as a location, including Lee Marvin's *Point Blank*, Clint Eastwood's *The Enforcer* and Sean Connery's *The Rock*. Strangely, the hundreds of tourists who visit Alcatraz every day were nowhere to be seen in any of these films!

POPULATION:
Uninhabited
WHEN TO GO:
Summer for the best weather, off season to avoid the worst of the crowds. Be prepared to book tours in advance during peak times.
HOW TO GET THERE:
There are various organized tours from San Francisco and a ferry service from Pier 33 close to Fisherman's Wharf.
HIGHLIGHTS:
The memorable audio-visual tour of the old prison – Doing Time; The Alcatraz Cellhouse Tour.
The even-more-memorable Alcatraz Night Tour, voted 'Best Tour of the Bay Area'.
Various other themed tours featuring island buildings and wildlife.
The old parade ground, now covered with rubble and an excellent wildlife haven.
Agave Path, a good walk located along a shorefront bulkhead on the south side of the island.
YOU SHOULD KNOW:
Native Americans occupied the island in 1969. Although quickly evicted, the event marked a step forward for the American Indian self-determination campaign.

Alcatraz Island and the Golden Gate Bridge

A Washington State ferry passes through the San Juan Islands.

San Juan Islands

POPULATION:
14,000 (2007 estimate)
WHEN TO GO:
Although the islands boast an average of 247 annual days of sunshine and low rainfall, winters can be windy and chilly, so they are an ideal May-September destination.
HOW TO GET THERE:
Lopez, Shaw, Orcas and San Juan (usually in that order) are reached by ferry from Anacortes. Guemes Island also has a ferry service from Anacortes. Fly to San Juan by light aircraft from Seattle.
HIGHLIGHTS:
Orca-watching from Lime Kiln Point State Park on San Juan Island (May to September).
The panorama seen from the highest point in the San Juan Islands, Mount Constitution on Orcas Island – said to be the most impressive view in Puget Sound.
Shark Reef Sanctuary on Lopez Island, a completely natural park with sensational cliff-top sea views.
Total tranquillity on Shaw Island, where the only commercial operation is the general store run by the Franciscan Sisters of the Eucharist.
YOU SHOULD KNOW:
Some lesser San Juan Islands can tell their own story – for example Barren Island, Cemetery Island, Justice Island, Picnic Island, Skull Island, South Finger Island or the Wasp Islands (named after a ship rather than the insect).

The San Juan Archipelago in the northwestern corner of the continental United States is divided. The San Juan Islands are part of Washington State, whilst a second group belonging to Canada is known as the Gulf Islands. The archipelago has more than 450 islands but fewer than one-sixth are occupied and only a handful may be reached by public ferry.

The islands were initially named by the Spanish explorer Francisco de Eliza in the 1790s, but subsequent American and British expeditions in the 19th century changed many of the original Spanish names, though not that of the archipelago itself. Most of the islands are hilly, with valleys or flat areas in between. Coastlines vary enormously, with sandy and stony beaches, inlets, coves, bays and harbours. Many shorelines are characterized by the presence of gnarled madrona trees, with pine forests often covering inland areas.

The four main San Juan Islands are San Juan itself, Orcas (the largest), Shaw and Lopez. Nearby Guemes is small, with limited facilities. The islands serve as an important tourist destination, easily reached from booming Seattle, much appreciated by those who love the sea, unspoiled nature and the great outdoors. Principal activities are hiking, sailing, kayaking and orca-watching.

But the islands are well organized to serve all the needs of visitors with numerous facilities such as museums, galleries, boutiques and restaurants to be found, especially on San Juan and Orcas. The towns are small but welcoming – historic Friday Harbor on San Juan and Eastsound on Orcas head the line-up, supported by numerous villages and hamlets full of character.

For those who can afford it, the very best way to visit the San Juan Islands is by seaplane, with views to die for all the way (be sure to get a window seat).

Bermuda & its islands

Bermuda's 180 coral islands and islets sit 1,050 km (650 mi) off Cape Hatteras, North Carolina, in the middle of the Atlantic. Effectively, they form a single island unified by the causeways, bridges, and other developments of 350 years of continuously stable history and government. First 'discovered' by the Spaniard Juan de Bermúdez in 1511, it was settled by English colonists shipwrecked on their way to Virginia in 1609 – and it remains a British Dependent Territory by local choice.

British customs and culture govern everything, though Bermuda's jacket-and-tie formality and decorum is a version of British gentility that the motherland never actually experienced outside literature and the colonies. Most visitors find afternoon tea, 'bobbies', and the manners of a bygone age quaint. They mask a steely form of rule that protects the wealth and privacy of the business institutions and many world-famous people who call tax-friendly Bermuda home.

Play the game – as you must – and you'll find one of the world's most enchanting, beautiful and historically captivating places. Bermuda's beaches are white or coral pink, a series of 30 coves and strands backed by rocky cliffs or groves of olivewood, casuarina and Bermuda cedars as well as palms. Its towns and hamlets set their white colonial and pastel neatness against the manicured green of gardens and golf courses, and huge sprays of hibiscus, oleander and morning glory mark the course of roads.

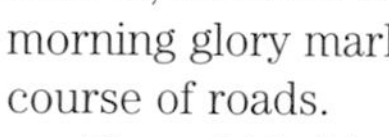

The cobbled lanes of St George, the capital until 1815, wind through a dozen military and naval fortifications preserved, like all the houses and shops, as they were built from 1615 to the mid-19th century. The authenticity of the entire area has earned it UNESCO World Heritage status. Bermuda is an island of living history, modern pleasures, and balmy climatic perfection.

POPULATION:
66,163 (2007)

WHEN TO GO:
April to October is busier and best for watersports, people and entertainment; from November to March many boat and diving services are suspended, but it's comfortably warm, more tranquil, and 40 per cent cheaper.

HOW TO GET THERE:
By air on scheduled flights; or by private yacht or cruise liner to Hamilton or St George.

HIGHLIGHTS:
The Keep on Ireland Island North, one of Bermuda's biggest forts, and home to the Maritime Museum at the Royal Naval Dockyard.
The heavenly scent of the 14.5-hectare (36-acre) Botanical Gardens in Paget Parish, where the Double Fantasy Flower inspired John Lennon.
The sprawling underground system and tidal pools of the Crystal Caves, Hamilton Parish.
The 17th and 18th century forts around the cedar woods, the perfect cove, and rocky cliffs of Achilles Bay.
The 18th century Ducking Stool on Ordnance Island, next to the replica of the 1610 wooden sailing ship *Deliverance*.
The Confederate Museum, describes Bermuda's role in smuggling European arms and supplies in exchange for cotton from the southern States during the American Civil War.

YOU SHOULD KNOW:
Shakespeare wrote *The Tempest* after reading the original colonists' account of their 1609 shipwreck. In the play, he refers to 'the still-vex'd Bermoothes', but relocates them to Italy.

The village of Flatts

An aerial view of the Bimini Cays

POPULATION:
1,800 (2005)
WHEN TO GO:
Year-round. The fishing tournament season runs from March to September.
HOW TO GET THERE:
By scheduled air to S Bimini, from Nassau or Florida; by weekly mailboat to Alice Town (N) or Cat Cay (S), from Nassau.
HIGHLIGHTS:
Bottom fishing in the marshes and mangroves of South Bimini.
The dockside scales where the big game fish get publicly weighed.
Diving/snorkelling at Little Caverns.
The heritage bar-crawl known as 'Hemingway's Hideaways'.
The Bimini Museum in Alice Town, with mementos of the town's notoriety as a liquor depot for Prohibition-era rum-runners.
YOU SHOULD KNOW:
Visitors may rent only mopeds, bicycles, or golf carts – and you must drive on the left, because British rules apply.

North Bimini & Bimini Cays

The Bimini Cays, 75 km (45 mi) east of Miami and Florida, mark the highest point of a submarine ridge that emerges from the turquoise water at North Bimini, and runs the length of the island along the Gulf Stream. Here, in complete contrast to the sandy slopes of the bay side where most people live, there's only a narrow coastal ledge before the ocean floor drops into a sudden deep. This is the fishing capital of the Bahamas, the site of world record catches of marlin, sailfish, giant tuna, swordfish, wahoo and bonefish.

The big game fish bring divers as well as hunters to Alice Town, the commercial centre of North Bimini and the cays. It's bisected by the King's Highway, the main drag lined by Government buildings, hotels, restaurants, stop-at-nothing bars, shops, tattoo parlours, the Straw Market, resorts and marinas. This concentration of amenities leaves Bimini's most beautiful beach empty: Queen's Highway, on the island's west, stretches past the endless sands of Radio Beach, Blister Beach and Spook Hill. Divers head for the bonanza of colourful fish on Rainbow Reef or the Bimini Barge wreck in 28 m (90 ft) of crystal-clear water; and the shallows of North Bimini's enclosed bay also provide a rare opportunity to explore the extraordinary marine life of proliferating Red Mangroves.

Bimini's reputation for fishing and adventure was cemented by the American laureate Ernest Hemingway. The combination of lush tropical mangroves and the crashing spume of the open ocean proved an irresistible lure – and inspired both 'The Old Man and The Sea' and 'Islands In The Stream'. You'll feel the same visceral attraction to Bimini's primal appeal.

An idyllic beach on Eleuthera

Eleuthera

Eleuthera is the Greek word for freedom; and it was in search of religious freedom that the island was accidentally colonised in 1648 by Captain William Sayles and a group of Puritans from Bermuda. The shipwrecked adventurers found a haven of peace, cleared of its original Lucayan Indian inhabitants by Spanish slavers, and rapidly developed their settlements along its 145 km (90 mi) of curving bays, offshore cays and natural harbours.

Here are the oldest, and still the prettiest townships in the Bahamas. Pastel green, blue, pink and yellow houses with white picket fences and gingerbread fretwork crowd stone quays; miles of pink and white sand beaches glisten into the distance; and the lush plantations of pineapple, and smallholdings of fruit and vegetable farms stretch for miles behind the fringe of coastal palms. Yet for all its length, Eleuthera is never more than 3.5 km (2 mi) wide – and at the Glass Window Bridge, which replaced an earlier natural rock archway, it narrows to less than 32 m (100 ft) between the turbulent Atlantic and Exuma Sound.

Tortuous geology has given Eleuthera some of the world's best dive sites like the Blue Hole, the Train Wreck, the Devil's Backbone and the famous Current Cut. You might prefer the bonefishing along miles of wadeable flats, or braving fishable surf for snapper, jacks and barracuda – but whatever your particular indulgence, you'll return to Eleuthera for its natural beauty and serenity. It is blessedly free of gambling, shopping and amusement parks. Even Dunmore Town, on Harbour Island off the east coast and the heart of celebrity-dripping, upscale Bahamian chic (Versace's personal architect recently re-designed what was already called 'the most luxurious beach in the world') is full of the calm and grace that form Eleuthera's greatest asset.

POPULATION:
9,000 (2005)

WHEN TO GO:
October to June. Come for the 4-day Pineapple Festival and Junkanoo party over the first weekend in June.

HOW TO GET THERE:
By air via Miami or Nassau; by excursion ferry from Fort Lauderdale; or by the weekly Out Islands mailboat service.

HIGHLIGHTS:
The fishing village of Spanish Wells off the north coast, where Spanish galleons watered, and the locals are direct descendants of the original Eleutheran colonists.
Hill Steps in Dunmore Town, an underground tunnel cut by 18th century prisoners from the cove to a nearby house; and re-used for rum-running during the US Prohibition years.
The 1.5 km (1 mi) long, vaulted magnificence of Hatchet Bay Cave.
Fishing for wahoo in 'the pocket' between Chub Cay and The Joulters.

YOU SHOULD KNOW:
The island is called 'Citagoo' in the rural patois.

Exuma Cays

POPULATION:
3,600 (2004)
WHEN TO GO:
December to May.
HOW TO GET THERE:
Fly from Fort Lauderdale, or Nassau on New Providence, or ferry from Nassau to George Town.
HIGHLIGHTS:
Iguanas on Allen's Cay – one of the few places you can still see these prehistoric-looking but harmless creatures.
Thunderball Cave on Staniel Cay – this beautiful grotto was a location in the film *Thunderball*.
The Family Island Regatta – this is held every year in George Town, Great Exuma, in the third week in April.
Mount Thompson Packing House, Exuma – where island produce is prepared for shipping to Nassau. Watch heaps of brightly coloured peppers, bananas, tomatoes and other produce being loaded for export.
YOU SHOULD KNOW:
The Tropic of Cancer runs through George Town.

Forty kilometres (25 mi) south-east of the Bahamian capital Nassau is Beacon Cay, the first of 365 cays belonging to the Exuma chain. The Exuma archipelago continues 150 km (90 mi) southwards in a gentle curve, ending with the two main islands of Great Exuma and Little Exuma. The islands are sparsely populated, mainly by conch fishermen, but offer a wonderful environment for yachting, sailing, diving, and coral reef and cave exploring.

Some of the cays are just barren chunks of reef, others are islands with densely vegetated rolling hills, caves and grottos to explore. The Exumas are famous for their pristine beauty, outstanding anchorages and breathtaking marine environment. Under the clear turquoise waters are beautiful natural gardens of coral teeming with fish and lobster. With the excellent water visibility and abundant marine life, the cays are popular with divers and underwater photographers.

Much of the area, including large tracts of offshore reefs, are protected as part of the Exuma Cays Land and Sea Park, the first national marine park in the world. There are many endemic species within the park, including the Hutia, the only terrestrial mammal native to the Bahamas. Iguanas forage unmolested and sea turtles lay their eggs on undisturbed beaches without interference. The no-fishing policy means there are plenty of species to discover in the sea, but perhaps the most intriguing are the stromatolites, blue-green, reef-forming algae. Stromatolites are the oldest living creatures on earth, with some fossil reefs dating back 3.5 billion years.

Exuma was settled in 1783 by American loyalists fleeing the Revolutionary War who established a number of cotton plantations in the cays. George Town, the biggest settlement in the chain, was named in honour of George III, to whom the settlers maintained their sovereignty. One Loyalist settler, Lord John Rolle, was a major figure in the islands' heritage. On his death in 1835, he left all of his Exuma lands to his slaves. This led to a number of towns on Great Exuma being named after him (such as Rolleville and Rolletown).

Today, George Town is a quaint village surrounding Lake Victoria, boasting a safe natural harbour. The harbour attracts boats from all round the world, and hosts the Family Island Regatta each year. The population of George Town grows from about 1,000 to more than 20,000 as teams from all over the Bahamas arrive to race around the harbour in traditional wooden boats.

An aerial view of Exuma Cays and its reefs

Cat Island

Located between Eleuthera and Long Island, Cat Island is the sixth largest island in the Bahamas at 77 km (48 mi) long and 2–7 km (1–4 mi) wide. Unlike many other islands in the chain, Cat Island is definitely low key when it comes to tourism, despite the 97 km (60 mi) of deserted pink and white sand beaches which surround it. This is one of the most beautiful and lush of the islands. From its high cliffs there's a stunning view of the densely forested foothills of Mount Alvernia. This is the highest point on Cat Island, and the highest point in the Bahamas, albeit at just 63 m (206 ft) above sea level. At the summit of Mount Alvernia is a medieval monastery called The Hermitage, hewn from the limestone cliffs by Father Jerome, a penitent hermit, as a place for meditation.

There are two theories on the naming of the island. Some believe it was named after Arthur Catt, the famous British sea captain, others that it got is name from the hordes of feral cats the English discovered when they arrived in the 17th century. The cats were said to be descendants of those left behind by early Spanish colonists as they passed through on their way to find the gold of South America.

The first permanent settlement at Cat Island was made in 1783 by cotton planters who brought wealth to the island. Now the crumbling remains of their mansions, as well as the associated slave villages, stand among the wild tropical flowers and grasses. One such plantation is at Port Howe, a pretty village said to have been built by the intrepid Colonel Andrew Deveaux who recaptured Nassau from the Spanish in 1783. Many descendants of the original early settlers remain on the island today, including actor Sidney Poitier who spent his youth in Arthur's Town and later returned to settle here.

The island may have gained wealth from cotton plantations in the past, but slash and burn farming is now the main way of life for Cat Islanders. Many grow cascarilla bark as a cash crop, which is gathered and shipped to Italy where it becomes a main ingredient in medicines, perfumes and Campari.

Much of the folklore of the Bahamas originates on Cat Island. Traditionally, when the last remaining person of a generation dies, his or her house is left empty for the spirit to live in. The person's relatives gather stones from the site to make a new house. In the north of the island, some people still place spindles on top of their houses to ward off harm.

POPULATION:
1,647 (2000)
WHEN TO GO:
Any time of year.
HOW TO GET THERE:
Fly from Fort Lauderdale or the other islands in the Bahamas, or mailboat from Nassau on New Providence Island.
HIGHLIGHTS:
The Hermitage – a medieval monastery on Mount Alvernia, the highest point in the Bahamas.
The glorious stretches of pink and white sandy beaches.
Snorkelling and diving in the clear waters.
The crumbling mansions on the old cotton plantations as a reminder of the past.
YOU SHOULD KNOW:
This is said to be Columbus' original landing site in the New World.

A pink sand beach at Conch Bay

The Cayman Islands

POPULATION:
Grand Cayman 49,792 (2006); Cayman Brac 2,000 (2006); Little Cayman 200 (2006)
WHEN TO GO:
Come between late April and early December, when it's 40 per cent cheaper, and 70 per cent less crowded in George Town.
HOW TO GET THERE:
By air from London, Chicago, Miami or Havana
HIGHLIGHTS:
The endangered blue iguanas and hickatees at Queen Elizabeth II Botanic Park on Grand Cayman.
The birds on Little Cayman – including the Antilles grackle, ani, snowy egret, green-backed and yellow-crowned herons, bananaquit, green parrot and red-footed booby.
Ten Sails Park, East End, Grand Cayman, where ten ships were wrecked on the reefs on the same night in 1794.
House of Miss Lassie (Gladwyn K. Bush, b.1914) – the artist's landmark house is completely covered in brilliantly coloured paintings of her religious visions since 1984.
YOU SHOULD KNOW:
Going topless anywhere is illegal – and don't wear a swimsuit away from the beach! On the other hand, there are no beach-hawkers to annoy you.

South of Cuba in the heart of the western Caribbean, the three Cayman Islands are the visible summits of the Cayman Ridge, an underwater mountain range which drops suddenly into the 7,100 m (22,000 ft) Cayman Trench, separating them from Jamaica.

Grand Cayman is by far the largest. The 'Sister Islands' of Cayman Brac and Little Cayman are mostly a wilderness of fruit trees, orchids and cacti; where tranquility and an authentic West Indian culture are the main attractions. Just 145 km (90 mi) to the southwest, Grand Cayman at first resembles nothing so much as a transplanted American urban nightmare.

The capital, George Town, and Seven Mile Beach, its renowned local playground, are full of condos, resorts, satellite dishes and mini-malls. The streets teem with bankers and the faceless suits of the institutions that have made it the world's fifth largest financial centre. Five days a week, cruise liners decant up to 22,000 tourists, joining the millions each year whose holidays have given the Cayman Islands the eighth highest GDP per capita in the world. George Town is so busy, loud, and determinedly up for it, you feel the privateers and pirates of former times have merely put on modern dress in their eagerness to empty your wallet.

In the small towns and villages outside George Town, the atmosphere changes immediately. Grand Cayman's true self is African-European, deeply Christian, conservative and church-going (there are lots of churches); and also West Indian – openly friendly and well-mannered, laughing and hospitable. Isolated by the central mangrove wetlands – 3,440 hectares (8,500 acres) of lush forests, emerald green parrots and bright orange frogfish, the mainspring of the complex ecology that maintains both the turtle grass and shrimp mounds of North Sound Marine Reserve – Rum Point typifies Grand Cayman at its best.

Sunrise in the Caymans

Looking down on Parrot Cay

The Turks & Caicos

Just 900 km (550 mi) south east of Miami, at the very bottom of the Bahamian Archipelago, lies a British Crown Colony which uses the US Dollar as its official currency. The Turks & Caicos (TCI) 40 islands and cays, eight of them inhabited – are full of major contradictions. They are set round the edge of two limestone plateaus, in shallow waters that merge into mangrove swamps and refresh the salt pans on which their prosperity has depended since the late 17th century. But at either end of the group, the surrounding coral reefs give way to seriously deep water channels, and the combination has given TCI the richest ecological variety of any island group in the area.

On land you can see iguanas, blue herons, osprey, pelicans, frigates, boobies and huge flocks of flamingoes. You can share the warm water, either fishing for tuna, wahoo, blue marlin or barracuda, or diving among the turtles, spotted eagle and manta rays, octopus, sharks and humpback whales for whom (from December to April) the offshore deeps are major transit points. Underwater, the reefs of Northwest Point, the historic wrecks of Salt Cay, and the waving coral formations descending the legendary 'walls' (some 2,100 m, 7,000 ft) of Grand Turk and West Caicos are as staggeringly beautiful as the onshore natural world.

The contradiction is that TCI is much more famous for its pursuit of material rather than natural wealth. Providenciales (aka Provo), at the western end, is the most developed island, with the international airport, wall-to-wall hotels, resorts, condos and 'entertainments'. To the east, Grand Turk, the TCI capital, is now a horrific service depot for the big cruise ships. Unless you come by yacht, you'll have to pass through Provo or Grand Turk. Grin and bear it – paradise lies beyond.

POPULATION:
30,000 (2007 estimate) – of which some 28,000 live in Provo and Grand Turk

WHEN TO GO:
Year round, but whale watching is only possible from December to April.

HOW TO GET THERE:
By air to Providenciales or by cruise ship to Grand Turk; then by private boat or plane charter to the other islands.

HIGHLIGHTS:
The 18th and 19th century architectural styles of TCI's original Bermudan salt merchants, along Duke St and Font St in Cockburn Town, Grand Turk.
The Molasses Reef Wreck exhibit at the TCI National Museum – it tells of the oldest European shipwreck in the western hemisphere, in 1505.
Salt Cay, proposed as a UNESCO World Heritage Site for its historic integrity.
Any of 33 protected island and marine sites totalling 842 sq km (325 sq mi).

YOU SHOULD KNOW:
Columbus first set foot on Grand Turk in 1492 – most of TCI has remained untouched since then.

The coastline of Port Anegada

Anegada

POPULATION:
200 (2001)
WHEN TO GO:
December to August
HOW TO GET THERE:
Fly to the small Auguste George Airport, or by ferry or private boat.
HIGHLIGHTS:
Relax on a pristine white sand beach.
Flyfishing – there are good populations of bonefish here.
See the flamingoes – they are being reintroduced into the salt ponds at the west end of the island.
Scuba diving – the many shipwrecks on the reef make this an interesting place for diving.
YOU SHOULD KNOW:
If you intend to do any fishing, you must buy a recreational fishing permit.

Lying in a remote corner of the Caribbean to the east of Puerto Rico, Anegada is the second largest of the British Virgin Islands (BVI). With a population of just 200, the remoteness of Anegada is one of its main attractions. Most visitors come to the island to simply unwind and relax on the beautiful but relatively deserted white sandy beaches. The clear warm waters around the island are home to a large population of bonefish, making Anegada a popular destination for flyfishing. In fact, the marine life is so plentiful here that local fishermen provide the majority of the fresh fish and lobster catch for the British Virgin Islands.

Anegada is also known for the large salt ponds that cover the west end of the island, or more particularly, the creatures that live there. In the 1830s, thousands of roseate flamingoes inhabited these ponds, but after decades of being hunted for their feathers and meat, the population had all but been wiped out by the 1950s. The flamingoes are currently being reintroduced, which offers a great draw for tourists. Too great a draw, in fact, as scientists are trying to reduce the impact of tourism on the bird population.

Anegada is the only island in the chain which has formed from coral and limestone, rather than volcanic rock. While the other islands are steeply mountainous, Anegada is flat, rising to just 8.5 m (28 ft) above sea level at its highest point; its name translates as 'the drowned land'. Extending south-east from the end of the island is the Horseshoe Reef. At 29-km (18-mi) long, it is the largest barrier reef in the Caribbean and the third largest on earth.

Many tourists hire charter boats while visiting the Virgin Islands, but some yacht-hire companies forbid clients to sail to Anegada because of the dangers of running aground on its shallow reefs. Many vessels have come unstuck here, including the HMS *Astrea* which ran aground in 1808. There are many shipwrecks on the reefs, which make this the perfect spot for scuba diving.

Virgin Gorda

The British Virgin Islands are where Caribbean dreams are made real. They are the paradigm of tropical island beach perfection, and the most popular cruising area in the Caribbean. Virgin Gorda combines the best features of all of them, packing enormous variety into its 21 sq km (8.5 sq mi). Dramatic mahogany forests crown the volcanic Gorda Peak, the island's centre and highest point. The Peak is one of several National Parks on Gorda and its neighbouring cays of Fallen Jerusalem, Prickly Pear and Saba Rock, and in its gorgeous offshore waters. They are sanctuaries for the endangered red-billed tropic bird and important sites for brown boobies, noddies, royal terns and pelicans.

On Gorda's southern tip is The Baths, the most iconic geological wonder in all the BVIs: huge granite boulders are piled haphazardly on a curving beach, some of them forming natural pools which require a ladder to reach. They have also arranged themselves into secret coves that can only be entered on all fours, and into a series of eye-popping 'caves' and chambers, where shafts of tropic sun pierce waist-deep water to create the most romantic tableaux in the West Indies. A lot of visitors come to Gorda just to see The Baths: go early or late, before or after the cruise ships land their extra clientele.

Few islands have as many secluded, luxury resorts as Virgin Gorda, and with the degree of protection offered by the Parks and marine reserves, the island doesn't even have a complete road system, so you can reach some beaches and coves only by boat. It means you can always find something idyllic and completely deserted – although there's always a bar of some kind within minutes. The area around North Sound is brilliant for getting lost among darting shoals of fish, or flocks of colourful birds, in the lap of affordable luxury rarely available to Caribbean visitors.

POPULATION:
4,100 (2002)
WHEN TO GO:
Mid-December to mid-April
HOW TO GET THERE:
Flights from Antigua via Tortola or from San Juan (Puerto Rico), St Thomas or St Croix (US Virgin Islands)
HIGHLIGHTS:
The wildlife sanctuary around the 17th century Spanish ruins at Little Fort National Park.
Diving at the BVIs most celebrated site – the wreck of the *Rhone*, a 94-m (310-ft) long Royal Mail steamer sunk in the 1867 hurricane – between Salt Island and Dead Man's Chest Island.
The exquisite beaches of Prickly Pear National Park, North Sound.
Hiking Gorda's more rugged trails, like those to the Copper Mine National Park, worked by Cornish miners between 1838 – 67.
Snorkelling or diving among the many spectacular coral reefs of the nearby Dog Islands.
YOU SHOULD KNOW:
Anchoring your boat is forbidden in most places – use the official mooring buoys or jetties instead.

The beautiful harbour of Virgin Gorda

Anguilla

POPULATION:
11,797 (2006)
WHEN TO GO:
Mid-December to mid-April (beware Christmas & New Year, when already high prices can more than double)
HOW TO GET THERE:
By air to Puerto Rico, Sint Maarten or Antigua; then by boat to Blowing Point, the ferry terminal for The Valley, Anguilla's capital.
HIGHLIGHTS:
The magnificent cliffs and panorama of the cays from Crocus Bay beach – from which you can swim among the reef fish and corals to Anguilla's hidden secret, Little Bay.
Shoal Bay East, voted one of the Caribbean's ten Best Beaches. It is, and a short way offshore is a live reef of magical colour and movement.
The stone beach 'sculptures' created by wind and tide at Rendezvous Bay.
Swimming with turtles, and looking for spiny lobsters on the spectacular reefs of Anguilla's cays like Dog Island, Seal Island, Scrub Island and Prickly Pear Cays.
Playing dominos in a village bar. Day and night, the loud slap of crashing dominos is the sound track of the island.
YOU SHOULD KNOW:
Anguilla is the only former British island in the Caribbean not to list cricket as its national sport. Anguilla lists 'boat racing'.

Anguilla got lucky. Since the 1650s it has been more or less bypassed by major development of any kind. At 28 km (16 mi) long by 5 km (3 mi) at its widest, its scrubby hinterland was too arid for big plantations; and early efforts to export cotton, salt and tobacco faded in the early 1800s with the demise of slavery. Even the explosion of Caribbean tourism made little impact – so as the island has finally awoken to its potential, it has been able to take advantage of mistakes in other islands' development strategies.

It has kept its laid-back atmosphere and the sleepy charm of letting goats wander in the restricted traffic. Its 33 white sand beaches are free of ribbon-built hotels and amenities to cope with mass culture. Instead, Anguilla is gaining a reputation as a centre for six-star luxury, with a series of highly individual resorts designed to modify the land and seascape as little as possible. It offers visitors the dreamworld Caribbean of crystal, limpid waters and horizons merging in a hundred shades of blue – along with a degree of 21st century comfort, pampering, mouth-watering food, and the most up-to-date electronic gadgetry, that puts other places to shame. Anguilla appears to have learned that real sophistication means disguising world-class consumption behind ecological authenticity.

You might go there on business. You don't go there for shopping, or for getting raucous (unless it's to impromptu reggae beats on the beach). You go to bask in the sun in perfect conditions, to swim or snorkel or dive, or stroll or ride. You escape the rest of the world when you come. Anguilla is a purist's island, where the wind brings the scent of sea, salt, coral sand and fragrant shrubs of which it is made. Visitors are encouraged to merge with the landscape.

Wind-blown palms on one of Anguilla's beautiful beaches

A typically perfect beach in Barbuda

Barbuda

In the eastern Caribbean just north of Antigua, Barbuda is one of the Leeward Islands. On one side of the island the Atlantic Ocean ravages the wild beaches, strewing them with driftwood and shells, while on the other the calm Caribbean Sea creates endless stretches of perfect white and pink sandy beaches. The island is much less developed than many of its Caribbean neighbours, offering the perfect place to unwind. Popular activities include swimming and snorkelling, as the clear waters abound with turtles and tropical fish, as well as some interesting shipwrecks that lie undisturbed in the turquoise water.

At just 24 km (15 mi) long and 13 km (8 mi) wide, Barbuda is largely rocky and flat. Most of the island is covered in bush, home to deer and boar, land turtles and guinea fowl as well as the occasional wild cat. The island is famous for its colony of more than 5,000 frigate birds which gather on the north-western lagoon at the bird sanctuary.

There are many caves on the island. One of them, Indian Cave, contains ancient Amerindian petroglyphs carved into the rock. In others it is possible to climb right through to the top of the Highlands from where you can see for miles. Other caves go underground and underwater and should only be explored by experienced cavers.

The Ciboney were the first to inhabit the island in 2400 BC, but when Christopher Columbus landed on Barbuda in 1493, Arawak and Carib Indians were living here. Early settlements by the Spanish and French were succeeded by the English, who formed a colony in 1666. In 1685, the island was leased to brothers Christopher and John Codrington. The Codrington family produced sugar on their land in Barbuda, and also transported slaves as labour for their sugar plantations on Antigua. For much of the 18th century, the sugar plantations proved a successful and prosperous industry.

The Codrington family influence can still be seen in the street names and architectural remains on the island. The ruins of the Codringtons' Highland House stand on the highest point of the island, and on the south coast can be found the enormous Martello tower, a fort built both for defence of the island and as a vantage point from which to spot valuable shipwrecks on the outlying reefs.

POPULATION:
2000 (2003)
WHEN TO GO:
November to April
HOW TO GET THERE:
Fly or take a ferry from Antigua.
HIGHLIGHTS:
Beachcombing on the Atlantic coast.
Snorkelling the shipwrecks in the shallow waters and reefs.
Indian cave – see the ancient cave carvings.
The frigate bird sanctuary at Codrington Lagoon – this is one of the best places in the world to see these birds.
YOU SHOULD KNOW:
Book accommodation in advance as there are only a few boutique-style resorts on the island.

A vibrant street in Speightstown

POPULATION:
280,000 (2006)
WHEN TO GO:
November to August. Come for 'Crop Over', the festival of music competitions and traditional activities from July to the costumed parade of Kadooment Day, the first Monday of August.
HOW TO GET THERE:
By air from almost everywhere – Barbados is the international hub for the eastern Caribbean.
HIGHLIGHTS:
The underwater flora waving in the currents inside Animal Flower Cave (St Lucy).
The immaculate, blue-painted 1660 Jacobean manor of St Nicholas Abbey (St Peter).
The 'green flash' of a tropical sunset, seen from any of the fabulous west coast beaches.
The Mount Gay Rum Tour, Bridgetown – home of the 300-year-old maker (the world's oldest).
The monkeys in the tropical rain forest of Welchman Hall Gully (St Thomas).
A cricket match – on a beach or at the Kensington Oval, Bridgetown.
YOU SHOULD KNOW:
It is an offence for anyone, even a child, to wear camouflage clothing. It's not unknown for someone to arrive at the airport from, say, Antigua, trailing three or four live crayfish on a string.

Barbados

Set apart in the Atlantic, Barbados sits 160 km (100 mi) east of its nearest neighbour, distanced from the brutal colonial rivalries of Caribbean history, but subject to 350 years of unbroken British rule. Even so, its nickname of 'Little England' derives from a superficial gloss of customs and mannerisms that barely disguise Barbados' West Indian core. Get past the trappings of mass tourism and you find a culture of classic calypso and soca-samba, breadfruit and flying fish, and 1,600 rum shops in which Barbadian ('Bajan') quirks and characteristics can best be appreciated. The comfortable mix of the familiar and exotic local flavour has made Barbados the most popular destination in the eastern Caribbean.

Barbados is densely populated and heavily developed. So making the most of the island requires a bit of effort – but the rewards are proportionately stupefying. Of course, you can buy your fun at any number of resorts of every standard, but strike up a conversation in a rural rum shop (usually a brightly-painted, semi-derelict shack), and you plunge into Bajan oral histories that connect you to centuries of buccaneering, colonial adventure, slavery and the sugar trade, and local predictions of the island's future in offshore banking. You might easily end by 'workin' up' (dancing). Hang out in Holetown or Speightstown, or the villages in the Scotland District, where 300 year-old mahogany woods stand on crags looking down on the rocky wilds of Bathsheba Beach, and the Atlantic thrills and terrifies surfers. You can do anything at all on Barbados, but the best thing to do is talk to the Bajans: it is they who will make you want to return.

Guadeloupe

It's called the 'Butterfly' after the shape of its two main islands, but Guadeloupe is a mini-archipelago of wide geographical contrasts. The outlying islands of Marie-Galante, La Desirade and Les Saintes are undeveloped, full of old and crumbling reminders of their historic importance as sugar plantations. Their tranquil coves are especially valued for their privacy and proximity to spectacular reefs, popularized by Jacques Cousteau himself.

Grande-Terre, the eastern wing of the 'Butterfly', is a mostly flat, dry limestone plateau perfect for the huge sugar plantations that make it so prosperous. At its extreme eastern point, St Francois, you'll come to the Pte des Chateaux, an arrangement of cliff and tumbled rock that looks like a series of castles, and carefully hides the only nudist beach in Guadeloupe. In the south, St Anne's beauty is veiled by the mind-numbing throb of salsa classes during the day. At night the beats and the action transfer to the clubs and bars of Gosier, Abymes and Pointe-à-Pitre, Guadeloupe's economic capital, and as suburban a provincial city as anything in France itself.

Guadeloupe is proud that it offers visitors a genuinely West Indian take on its metropolitan motherland, and this is most evident in Basse-Terre, the biggest island, with the administrative capital of the same name. The island's heart is a national park of mountains covered in orchid-filled tropical rainforest. The Rte de la Traversée winds through vast stands of bamboo, tall mahoganies and gums, heliconia and ginger, to the dormant summit of la Soufriere volcano. On one side you can trek your way through jungle to the Cascade des Ecrevisses, one of many waterfalls. Then go back to the terrific nightlife on the coast – if the backbeat of Zouk doesn't get you, then the Biguine, a West African/Creole form of clarinet and trombone jump-up – will. Celebrate it.

POPULATION:
453,000 (2006 estimate)

HOW TO GET THERE:
By air from Paris or Miami to Pointe-à-Pitre; or via San Juan, Martinique or Barbados. By inter-island ferry, or by private boat-taxi, from all neighbouring islands.

WHEN TO GO:
Year-round. Come for the Fete des Cuisinières in August, a culinary nirvana of French Creole celebration, with music and parades and spectacular food.

HIGHLIGHTS:
The Porte d'Enfer, an extraordinary vista of sea between coral reefs at Anse Bertrand, where the cliffs erupt with *Souffleurs* – geysers powered by sea pressure.
Snorkelling/diving in the marine Reserve Cousteau around the Ilets Pigeon.
The three Chutes du Carbet, the highest waterfalls in the Caribbean, on Basse-Terre.
The gossip, the music, and changing vistas of a local bus ride, if you have the stomach.
Guadeloupean local clubs and bars, where the combination of 'ti' punch' and salsa, meringue, RnB, and Zouk will cure all the ills of urban malaise.

YOU SHOULD KNOW:
Rum is considered an art form, and integral to Guadeloupean life. As one of France's overseas departments, Guadeloupe's currency is the euro.

Terre-de-Haut on Les Saintes

Martinique

POPULATION:
400,000 (2006)
WHEN TO GO:
Year-round. Come for a really spirited 5-day Mardi Gras in February/March.
HOW TO GET THERE:
By air from Miami, Puerto Rico or Paris; or from New York or London via Antigua, St Lucia or Barbados.
HIGHLIGHTS:
La Pagerie, (Trois-Ilets) 1763 birthplace of Josephine, Napoleon's Empress. The garden is a riot of frangipani and hibiscus. The museum includes notoriously passionate letters.
The ruins of St Pierre, once called the 'Paris of the West Indies'; the former capital holds a jazz festival each May to mark its obliteration by the eruption of Mt Pelée in 1902.
Diamond Rock, the 180 m (600 ft) high offshore pinnacle manned by the British in 1804, and for 18 months registered by the Royal Navy as an 'armed warship'.
The Musée Gauguin at Le Carbet, where the painter lived, and where Columbus landed in 1502.
Les Gorges de la Falaise – follow the floral route of 'Les Ombrages' to the waterfalls.
The perfect beach at Salines on the island's southern tip.
YOU SHOULD KNOW:
At Fonds St Jacques in 1658, Dominican priests built what is now the best-preserved plantation on Martinique. Here Pere Labat (explorer, polymath, soldier and priest) revolutionized the rum distilling process between 1693 and 1705.

Martinique's Creole chic is a Caribbean wonder. As a Department of France, the island gets all the benefits of the north European Euro-zone, allied to the technicolour brilliance of West Indian music and culture. It's a heady and glamorous mix.
The downside of the French umbilical is overdevelopment and overcrowding, which can be dismaying if you arrive from another island; but after a day or so, the infectious ambience and sheer *élan* of the island will captivate you.

Martinique is big enough to have mountains, rivers, forests and flower-filled wolds – all of which have more than 350 years of history every bit as powerful as the buccaneering tales of its reefs, coves and white sandbars. Fort de France is itself set on one of the world's loveliest bays. Head north on the Route de la Trace, a floral glory of a road rising from the central Lamentin Plain through the legendary tropical rainforest on the flanks of the dormant volcano Mt Pelée at 1,400 m (4,586 ft) and its twin Mt Carbet. Nearby at Case-Pilote is a 17th century rococo Jesuit church, the island's oldest, and the best-preserved working plantation, where the Master's House is now the Musée de la Banane, and the Creole shanties are now little craft shops. Here too, at St Marie et Macouba, perched on a cliff over the Atlantic, are some of Martinique's most famous rum distilleries – but remember local rum is often twice the strength of the other islands.

The Caravelle Peninsula is especially beautiful at Baie du Trésor and Château Dubuc. Further south, you can watch the fishing fleet come home from the hills above Le Vauclin, among the hundred secluded coves and offshore sandbars that make south Martinique so attractive to yachties.

The church of St Henri Anse d'Arlet overlooks an idyllic beach on Martinique.

St Lucia

Every inch of St Lucia tells a story. Lovely Marigot Bay in Castries is where a British Admiral ambushed the French by camouflaging his fleet with palm fronds. Forty-acre Pigeon Island, a nature reserve connected by a causeway to St Lucia's west coast, is crossed by trails linking 1,000 year-old Carib artefacts with 18th century remains like Fort Rodney and a museum highlighting Admiral Rodney's Fleet victory at the Battle of the Saintes. Incidentally, it's also where St Lucia holds its annual Jazz Festival.

One of the Caribbean's most dramatically beautiful islands, St Lucia is a mix of French and British influences, completely subsumed into a distinct West Indian culture, unique among the islands. It's a working country where tourism is just one of several industries – and although St Lucians are glad of your dollars (of course!), they welcome you primarily as visitors to their way of life.

Luckily for St Lucia, the age of big resorts is ending. The island has already recast itself, with an environmental policy designed to protect its outstanding reefs as well as a topography and ecology unmatched anywhere else. The spires of the Pitons in the south are the most famous of its volcanic mountains; the 7,689 hectares (19,000 acres) of National Rain Forest include deep valleys of giant ferns, bromeliads, birds-of-paradise and a riot of orchids, and lakes and waterfalls criss-crossed by swooping parrots, orioles, white-breasted thrashers and peewees; the Mankote Mangrove, the Bois d'Orange swamp and Boriel's Pond provide the best of many birdwatching opportunities; and from March to July you can stargaze on the beach at Grand Anse in the north, while leatherback turtles rise from the sea.

Between its natural splendour, relic-studded history, charming (and hospitable) villages, and graceful town squares, St Lucia is inexhaustibly intriguing and full of wonderful surprises.

One of St Lucia's many breathtaking scenic hideaways

POPULATION:
160,765 (2005)

WHEN TO GO:
Year-round. St Lucia's topography means that every season offers fresh novelties.

HOW TO GET THERE:
By air to Vieux Fort (international) or Castries (local/inter-island).

HIGHLIGHTS:
'Jump-up' (dancing in the streets), to soca and reggae on Friday nights at the fishing village of Gros Islet.
The colourful murals and gingerbread trim of the marketplace at Soufriere, the oldest town in St Lucia, founded by the French in 1746.
Morne Fortune (Hill of Good Luck), Castries, the 17th century French fortress completed by the British in 1796, that was the key strategic point in the wars of colonial possession.
A shower beneath the cascades of Diamond Falls, where Louis XVI built bathhouses for the French garrison troops.
A walk through Latille Gardens – a hidden treasure of tropical fruits, flowers, trees and waterfalls. Enjoy the lush colours as afternoon turns to dusk – and return by moonlight.

YOU SHOULD KNOW:
St Lucia does get a lot of visitors – but you can always find a sandy cove or a country village where you can leave the crowd behind.

The lush vegetation of Dominica's oceanic rainforest

Dominica

POPULATION:
69,625 (2001)
WHEN TO GO:
There's six times more rain in the interior than on the coast, so come for the (generally) dry season between January and June. August to October is the wettest time – but the World Creole Music Festival is from late October to November.
HOW TO GET THERE:
By air, via San Juan, Antigua, Barbados or St Lucia, to Melville Hall in the northeast (international); or to Canefield/Roseau (local islands). By boat, L'Express Des Iles ferry to/from Guadeloupe, Martinique and St Lucia.
HIGHLIGHTS:
The Roseau Museum in the old post office – and behind it the Old Market where slaves were once sold, and which is now a Carib crafts market.
The 'crushed bus' in the Botanical Gardens – testimony to the force of 1979 Hurricane David, and to nature's regenerative power (the tree is still growing on top of the bus).
Champagne – a large area near the fishing village of Pointe Michel, where volcanic activity causes thousands of bubbles to rise from beneath the sea.
The 6,880-hectare (17,000-acre) Morne Trois Pitons National Park – example of Dominica's surpassing oceanic rainforest.
The Boiling Lake: a huge 63 m (200 ft) fumarole crater, a swirling bubbling grey cauldron set high in the green mountains. The world's biggest of its kind.
YOU SHOULD KNOW:
Buying and selling coral is illegal. Please resist the temptation.

At 45 km (29 mi) long and 25 km (16 mi) wide, Dominica is the most mountainous of the volcanic Antilles. The 1,447 m (4,747 ft) Morne Diablotin and Morne Trois Pitons at 1,400 m (4,600 ft) are the highest of several peaks whose proximity attracts much more rain than most islands. The result is Dominica's famously fabulous tropical rainforest, full of rushing torrents, cascades and stepped waterfalls. It's a dark-green world slashed by ribbons of bright sunshine striking into the pretty valleys, catching the riotous colours of 18 m (60 ft) trails of orchids, bougainvillea and hibiscus, and populated by vivid blue, red and yellow signature splashes of the island's astonishing birds – including the rare sisserou parrot. Dominica's extraordinary wildlife is enhanced by its unusual geography: cool, freshwater crater lakes like the Emerald Pool, 24 km (15 mi) from Roseau, the capital, co-exist with steaming fumaroles and naturally hot-water baths.

The island is culturally different from its neighbours, too. It was French, then British, then both – but its original inhabitants, the Caribs, always tried to co-exist with their colonial overlords; and in 1903 gained title to a 1,497-hectare (3,700-acre) Territory in the northeast where 3,000 Caribs still live. They call the island Waitikubuli, and many villages still have Carib names. Away from the coast, you'll hear their Creole patois more than English, the official language.

As high as it rises, so does Dominica dive deep into the ocean. The same adventurous spirit that makes the island beloved of extreme sports enthusiasts (river-tubing, rapid-running, para-gliding off the peaks) brings divers to Dominica's reefs – great walls of colour and life, rich in great and small marine rarities. It's even a prime site for whale watching, especially in the marine reserve around Scott's Head and Soufriere at the southwestern tip. Factor in its reputation for night-life and all you need for Dominica is energy.

Grenada

The ruins of Brimstone Hill Fortress overlooking the Caribbean Sea.

With a royal flush of rainforests, rugged mountains, fragrant spice trees, rare tropical flowers, kaleidoscopes of birds, cascading rivers, waterfalls, sugar-fine white sand beaches, secluded coves, crystal-clear mountain lakes, picturesque villages, living history and unique local culture, Grenada is both the most beautiful of all Caribbean islands and the most charming. It is a cornucopia of natural wealth and human warmth – and therefore a very rare treasure.

St George's, the capital, is wrapped around a natural harbour, its traditional pastel-coloured buildings and red-tiled roofs reminiscent of a French town. It's dominated by the Gothic tower of the 1818 Cathedral, which with the Georgian public buildings (built by the British between 1780-1801) of Church Street confirm the city's rather European physical character. But its soul is in the bustle and colour and noise of Market Square, for 200 years the crucible of Grenada's post-colonial, post-slavery, Afro-Caribbean and definitively self-respecting West Indian culture of open-handed politesse. Only recently (since the USA invaded in defence of free markets [sic], in 1983), has Grenada's traditional preference for quality over quantity been threatened by new developments of the kind that have already wrecked Barbados. Grand Anse, the island's famous two-mile beach risks being over-run. Luckily, easy-going, tolerant Grenadans have a parallel tradition of repelling unwanted people and schemes – and half the island is now national park, and new schemes are to be rigorously controlled.

Don't get the idea that Grenada wants to preserve its glories in aspic. Historical chance made it the Spice Island of nutmeg, cloves, ginger, cinnamon and cocoa, instead of another giant sugar plantation. These 'industries' make aromatic additions to the sum of the island's existing perfection. Grenadans' most charming feature is the way they welcome you as an honoured guest to share their lives and lifestyle.

POPULATION:
90,000 (2007)

WHEN TO GO:
Year-round. Carnival, Grenada's biggest event, is in August; the Spice Island Billfish Tournament is in January; and the Grenada Sailing Festival is in February.

HOW TO GET THERE:
By air via Barbados, Puerto Rico or Trinidad. Or by cruise ship to St George's 300 year-old harbour of Carenage.

HIGHLIGHTS:
The panorama from the rambling fortifications of Fort George (1710), whose Napoleonic-era cannons are still used to fire salutes.
The rainbow of bird-life, tropical fauna, and rare orchids of the rainforest (ferns, mahogany and giant gommier trees) of the Grand Etang Lake Reserve.
The triple cascades of Concord Falls, near the teak groves of Fedon's Mountain, the former base of Julien Fedon, who led a slave uprising against the British in 1765.
Levera National Park – Grenada's most scenic coastal area, including coral reefs, mangrove swamp, lagoon wildfowl reserve, picture-perfect beaches, and turtle hatcheries.
The Saturday morning markets of St George's and Grenville; and any local fair, festival or market where you can talk and share a glass of rum with the islanders.

YOU SHOULD KNOW:
Undeveloped Carriacou, famous for its completely traditional West Indian villages and pristine reefs, is one of several small islands forming Grenada.

Nevis

POPULATION:
10,000 (2007)
WHEN TO GO:
Year-round. It's much, much cheaper from May to November, outside the northern winter 'season'.
HOW TO GET THERE:
By air, via Antigua or St Kitts; or by 6-times a day boat ferry from St Kitts.
HIGHLIGHTS:
The pelicans and fishermen along 3-mile Pinney's Beach, on the leeward (west) coast.
The hot spring baths at the 1778 Bath Hotel & Spring House (recently restored after hurricane damage and re-opened as a hotel with public access to the 'healing waters').
The New River Estate – the last to produce rum commercially, and you can see the massive machinery and sugar boiling wall, as well as the great house and chimneys.
The windmill tower (one of Nevis's finest), works, kitchen and house of the early 18th century sugar mill at Coconut Walk Estate.
A carriage ride through the island's historic Gingerland area. You see authentic West Indian life from an authentic mid-19th century, Creole, mahogany carriage. Great cliché – but great fun.
YOU SHOULD KNOW:
The only actual flurries of activity on Nevis are at the Saturday market, or when a cargo boat docks from a neighbouring island.

Small, unhurried and serenely beautiful, dominated by a massive volcanic cone whose graceful curves slope down to luminous green flatlands fringed by ranks of tall palms, Nevis is full of old stone buildings and plantation houses that hint at the West Indies' historic grace and finery. Prettier and more difficult to reach than its sister island of St Kitts, Nevis's claim to represent the romance of the West Indies' age of elegance is quite justified.

From the 17th century, the opulent mansions of its sugar plantation owners were the haunt of high society from Europe as well as the other islands. In Charlestown you can wander among the churches, bridges, fortifications and houses with their wooden balconies and gingerbread trimmings – still much the same as when Horatio Nelson met and married Fanny Nisbet from the Montpelier Plantation, here in 1787 (their signatures are in the register at Fig Tree Church).

Nevis has everything you could dream of in the way of beaches, forests, and exuberant flora and fauna, albeit on a small scale. Follow the road that links the Golden Rock Plantation on the windward side to the northern tip. You pass a troop of African Green (Vervet) monkeys in the exotic foliage, and work your way up the ridge and ravine beds through fields of fruit and flowers set in the rainforest. A shifting panorama of nearby islands sits in a huge sea- and skyscape; inland, you realize that Nevis simply has no mass tourism. Even at the one real hotel, there are no buzzing jet skis; and visitors stay in pretty villas or the old plantations, listening to the island breathing instead of tannoy calls. But with fewer electronics and less delirium, Nevis can party just as hard as anywhere – it just does so with stress-busting charm and intensely enjoyable finesse.

The remains of an old sugar mill at Montpelier Plantation Inn

Boats moored off the beautiful island of Tobago.

Tobago

Tobago is the beautiful, reserved, soul-sister of jump-jiving Trinidad, its partner in the Republic. The contrast is awesome. Tobago is small. It has no major industry to impinge on its lush fertility. It has one main town, Scarborough, and dozens of hamlets and villages with names that reflect the Spanish, French, Dutch, and English colonial powers which coveted it for centuries.

Outside the smallholdings of its sparse population, it's full of nature reserves harbouring wildlife otherwise found only on the South American mainland of which it was once part. At its highland heart, among the many waterfalls splashing down into idyllic bathing pools among the rocks and ferns, Tobago protects the oldest untouched tropical rainforest in the hemisphere. The 'rainy' season between June and December (short, sharp bursts, and a brilliant time to take a swim) freshens the landscape, which erupts into a natural carnival of colourful flowers; and this is matched underwater, where the myriad flashing shoals play lethal hide-and-seek among the cup coral in the canyons and deep caves where barracuda, dolphin and manta rays cruise. You can dig for chip-chip (a kind of shell fish) in the warm clear water of Manzanilla Bay, or hunt the big game fish like marlin, wahoo and yellow-fin tuna. You can have double fun in the knowledge that there's nothing in Tobago – in the water or on land – to kill you: no man-eating sharks, box jelly fish, bird-eating spiders, or poisonous snakes!

Undeveloped (no house, hotel or resort is allowed to build anything higher than a palm tree grows) and peaceful, Tobago does however know how to party. Carnival here is homespun, but just as colourful, rum-fuelled and demoniacally energetic as anywhere. What's more, you can practise every week throughout the year at the open air dance they call 'Sunday School'.

POPULATION:
52,000 (2006)

WHEN TO GO:
Year-round. In mid-July, the 2-week Tobago Heritage Festival is an island-wide celebration of music, dance, food and song which you follow from village to village.

HOW TO GET THERE:
By air, from London, Atlanta and Miami; or via Port of Spain.

HIGHLIGHTS:
The tiered pools of the Argyle Waterfall, one of Tobago's loveliest rainforest cascades.
Fort King George (1779), commanding the heights over Scarborough, the capital, and its harbour.
Surfing the breaks at Mt Irvine beach; then meeting the locals at next-door Buccoo Beach for 'Sunday School', Tobago's hottest weekend event, where visitors are encouraged to join in the islanders' live music, dance and beach barbecue.
The 'Nylon Pool' – way out to sea, you jump out of the boat and walk waist-deep among the fish on the sandbar just below the surface. A truly weird sensation.
The spectacular coast drive to Speyside in the north, where offshore Goat Island is home to Tobago's famous manta rays.
Goat racing and crab racing - in villages, fields, or on the beach, at any time of day.

YOU SHOULD KNOW:
Nobody is pretending it's perfect, but Tobago makes you feel good about the world again.

Trinidad

At its closest, Trinidad is just 12 km (7 mi) from Venezuela, and it has a more South American feel than any other Caribbean island. In fact, forget any Caribbean preconceptions: Trinidad is a highly developed industrial society, densely populated and cosmopolitan. It's fascinating because it's the only island wealthy enough not to depend on tourism. You will be welcomed as a visitor – but in much of the island, your visit will be permitted rather than encouraged, because of unusually strong regional influences that stem directly from Trinidad's history. Competing claims of former Spanish (still spoken in the south), sub-continental Indian, African and English interest groups still provoke political and social discord, and with the huge wealth of its oil, gas and manufacturing industries at stake, Trinidadians are apt to approach business with the same colour, flair, and violent enthusiasm that they put into carnival, music and dancing.

Port of Spain, the north-west and most of the west coast are in the grip of heavy industry. Agribusiness and crowded suburbia fills most of the central flatlands. But in every bar or roadside foodshack, you rock to irresistible Soca, Calypso, Steelpan, Indian Classical, Chutney and Limbo beats. 'Liming' – sociable talking – and laughter underpin every Trinidadian transaction. Theatre gets improvised on the street. The urge to celebrate is central to the multi-ethnic character of Trinidad, and it doesn't matter whether the inspiration is religious or secular. If you're present, you're part of the community – so join in.

Of course there are terrific beaches, too, in the northeast and southwest; tropical rainforests in the northern mountains around 940 m (3,200ft) Cerro del Aripe; and the flora and fauna of reef and swamp. But you go to Trinidad to join the dance for as long as you can keep up with the fun.

A fruit stall in the lively market at St James

POPULATION:
1, 248,000 (2006)

WHEN TO GO:
Year-round. Come for the best Carnival in the world, two weeks in February/March.

HOW TO GET THERE:
By air to Port of Spain.

HIGHLIGHTS:
A night with the Patrol guarding the leatherback turtle breeding sites on the east coast.
Getting down with Parang (Venezuelan-influenced Christmas music), Chutney-Soca, Rapso and Pichakaree (Indo-Trinidadian fusion) – music indigenous to Trinidad.
The scarlet ibis and other exotic species of the Caroni swamp in central Trinidad.
Pointe-à-Pierre Wild Fowl Trust, near San Fernando on the west coast – a nature reserve of mango trees, myrtle and soursop, against a skyscape of flames spouting from the nearby oil refinery flare stacks!
Dunston Cave, home to a colony of the elusive nocturnal guacharo (oilbird), at the Asa Wright Nature Reserve, a former coffee plantation in the northern rainforest.
Pitch Lake, near San Fernando – the natural phenomenon of a 36-hectare (90-acre) lake of asphalt which constantly replenishes itself.

YOU SHOULD KNOW:
Trinidad still sanctions the use of the Cat o' Nine Tails to flog convicted law-breakers.

St Barths

St Barths (St Barthelemy/St Barts) is very small, hilly and arid. Compared to other islands, it doesn't have a lot going for it – yet, aside from privately owned islands, it is the most chic, glamorous and swanky place in the entire Caribbean. It's where the rich, famous, and beautiful go to de-stress, gossip on their mobiles to their friends on the other side of the pool, and very, very carefully reduce the pallor of their northern skins to the lightest of sun-kissed tans.

St Barths was 'discovered' in the 1950s by Rockefellers and Rothschilds looking for privacy. Unsuitable for any kind of plantation, it had only ever been a trading post run by the French, and for 100 years the Swedes, who left only some street names in Gustavia, and a large number of descendants to intermarry with the returning French. So the island has no Creole influence, and though it has pockets of apparently Caribbean bijou prettiness, it has more of a French provincial ambience perfectly adapted to pretentious and world-class posers. In season, the really lovely stone harbour of Gustavia is literally overshadowed by the ranks of mile-high prows of superyachts. The comings-and-goings on the gangplanks during the day, and the competing buzz of ten parties taking place two inches apart at night, makes for the best 'beach TV' in the world – you'll see body language justifying not only your entire visit, but a complimentary PhD as well.

The food is legendary, like every other amenity in St Barths. Its exclusivity has attracted many of the world's great chefs, masseuses and skilled practitioners of other crafts. You can take the beaches for granted: staff will deal with whatever nature can't already provide. It is total, glorious, over-the-top fun.

Gustavia Harbour

POPULATION:
7,000 (2007 estimate)

WHEN TO GO:
It's packed in high season, December to April, with the Music Festival in January and Carnival in February. The islanders hold their Fêtes Patronales in August, along with Boubou's Festival and Pitea Day – in all of which the chic is authenticity.

HOW TO GET THERE:
By air via St Maarten, Antigua or Guadeloupe (NB. Owing to the short runway, pilots require a special licence to land at St Barths); by boat from St Maarten (NB. Owing to strong currents, this is a notoriously rocky crossing), or by private yacht.

HIGHLIGHTS:
Pelicans disporting on the many offshore rocks and islets; hummingbirds and yellow-breasted bananquits; frigate-birds and waders in the salt ponds and on the beaches.
Cocktails on the quay at Gustavia when the superyachts are parked up.
The white sand perfection of Grande Saline, the naturists' beach where everybody goes.
The tortoises, rays and lobsters on the rich sea bed at Anse du Grand Colombier, a horseshoe cove on the 'wild' coast of the Marine Reserve, relatively undeveloped by hotels.
Next month's copy of *Vogue*/*Vanity Fair* before it/they go to press.

YOU SHOULD KNOW:
Traditional manners are important on St Barths, however little you are wearing. You shake hands on the first encounter of the day; kissing cheeks is customary (right cheek first) for men and women greeting women; and honking car horns to attract attention is very rude.

Traditional pastel coloured houses

St Vincent and the Grenadines

POPULATION:
120,519 (2005)
WHEN TO GO:
January to May. Come for the Maroon Festival on Union Island in May, when the whole island stops for the Big Drums to ring in the planting season.
HOW TO GET THERE:
By air via Barbados, Martinique, St Lucia or Trinidad to St Vincent (international); via St Vincent to Bequia, Mustique, Canouan and Union Is (local). By regular ferry to/from St Vincent around the islands to/from Grenada.
HIGHLIGHTS:
The oldest (1763) Botanic Garden in the West Indies, St Vincent – including one of Captain Bligh's original breadfruit trees, and a rare Soufriere Tree not seen in the wild since 1812.
Model boatbuilding in Port Elizabeth, Bequia – in the tradition of the real schooners for which the island's whalers were famous.
The illustrations of Black Carib history in the Officers' Mess of the 18th century Fort Charlotte, with a panoramic view of Kingstown and the islands from its 201m (660 ft) ridge.
The Owia Salt Pond, St Vincent – you swim in a huge natural pool enclosed by lava peaks and ridges. The Atlantic waves pound into the rocks, and gently cascade over the edge.
YOU SHOULD KNOW:
The Grenadines are where reality beggars the most exuberant imagination.

It's easy to feel something of an intruder in the Grenadines. These islands epitomize the classic image of the West Indies – of green fertility and turquoise shallows merging into an aquamarine horizon notched by ever more dreamy coastlines, where everything appears to sparkle, and people greet each other with an open smile. You sail (you always sail in the dream) on the infectious buoyancy of easy-going happiness that characterizes the Caribbean's almost forgotten, tranquil corner. And for visitors, it's all true – with the difference that regular ferries and cheaply-available air and water-taxis mean you don't actually have to have your own boat.

Pockets of world-class luxury exist, notably in Mustique (home to Mick Jagger, David Bowie and a handful of other celebrities with a legitimate desire for privacy), Palm Island and Bequia (pronounced 'Beck-way'); but the soft trade winds will draw you south with the smell of spices from Canouan, Mayreau, and the Union Islands, and the fabulous Tobago Cays where *Pirates of the Caribbean* was filmed. You travel through a weave of French, Carib, Creole and British cultures. You find village rum shops full of animated cheer and crashing domino slates; monkeys foraging by forest lakes in the high mountains; fish markets on stone quays; 18th century cannon amid giant ferns on the walls of once-important forts or whaling stations; deserted crescents of pure-white or volcanic black sand; rocky bays that explode with the chatter of parrots – rainbows arcing across the blue. Dolphins ride your bow-wave (even in the ferry!), and at anchor, in the clear water, yellow and blue-striped sargeant-major fish flip somersaults in the passing shadow-triangle of rays.

You don't have to be rich to fall in love with St Vincent and the Grenadines, but what Grenadinians call "ri-thinkin' frame of min".

Saba

The smallest island of the Netherlands Antilles, Saba is an unspoilt island paradise in the West Indies. The rocky island is the cone of an extinct volcano rising out of the sea to 850 m (2,800 ft). The peak of the volcano, Mount Scenery, is the highest point in the Kingdom of the Netherlands. Despite being Dutch, the island's main language is English, which has been used in the school system here since 1986.

The first European to discover Saba was Christopher Columbus in 1493, though he did not go ashore due to the steep rocky cliffs which surround the island. In 1632 a group of British sailors landed on Saba after they were shipwrecked nearby. They said the island was uninhabited, but it seems likely that Carib or Arawak Indians may have been living there at the time. The island then passed variously between French, Dutch and British hands until the Netherlands finally took possession in 1816.

During the 17th century, the island was used as a hideout for local pirates. England also deported its undesirables to the area and many of them, too, became pirates taking refuge on Saba. The most famous was Hiram Breakes who coined the phrase 'Dead men tell no tales'. Through the 17th and 18th centuries, the major industries on the island were sugar, rum and lobster fishing. Legitimate trade soon became important and the islanders exported Saba lace, made by the island's women.

Today there are four charming villages on the island – Hell's Gate, Windwardside, St John's and The Bottom. The verdant forests, punctuated by the red roofs of the villages, offer a stunning contrast to the brilliant blue sea surrounding the island. The waters here are clear and the island is renowned as an excellent dive site.

Unlike many places in the world, Saba's shallow reefs are still pristine. When dive tourism began here, local fishermen agreed not to fish on the best diving reefs, so the reefs were protected before any damage could be done. The area is now more formally protected under the Saba National Marine Park. Although the shallow reefs and walls are excellent here, the island is best known for its underwater pinnacles, the rocky summit of underwater mountains. These pinnacles are home to incredible numbers of large fish and pelagics, and populations are actually increasing, making shark sightings more frequent.

POPULATION:
1,349 (2001)
WHEN TO GO:
September to February
HOW TO GET THERE:
By plane or ferry from the nearby island of St Martin.
HIGHLIGHTS:
Diving around Saba's famous pinnacles – there are numerous large fish species here, and shark sightings are becoming more frequent.
Mount Scenery – the peak of this ancient volcano can be climbed via a series of over 1,000 steps. Alternatively, take a car up the narrow roadwhich spirals to the top through the lush vegetation.
The quaint villages on the island are old-fashioned and delightful, and the local people very friendly. Take the time to look for some lovely Saba lace to take home as a souvenir.
Saba Spice – the local Saba Island rum is masterfully blended with Canadian rum to achieve a smooth, distinctive, complex taste.
YOU SHOULD KNOW:
The Saban Government has its own hyperbaric chamber to treat those suffering from decompression sickness, so you will be well looked after if you over-do it.

Red roofs of The Bottom, Saba's capital, sit in the bowl of an extinct volcanic crater.

Aruba, Bonaire & Curaçao

POPULATION:
Curaçao 133,644; Aruba 103,484; Bonaire 14,006 (2007)

WHEN TO GO:
April to September, when it's much quieter without the three million-plus visitors escaping the North American winter months.

HOW TO GET THERE:
By cruise liner – like 600,000 others each year – or by air (international or inter-island). There are no ferries.

HIGHLIGHTS:
The early 19th century red gold mines at Bushiribana and the gold mill at Balashi, Aruba.
The bone ceremonial 'vomiting stick' and Arawak artefacts at the Oranjestad Archaeological Museum, Aruba.
The flamingoes, parrots, cacti and green iguanas at Washington-Slaagbai National Park, near Rincon, Bonaire.
The swan park at the former slave holding camp (late 17th – early 19th century) and lavish plantation house of Landhuis Zuurzak, Den Dunki National Park, Curaçao.

YOU SHOULD KNOW:
Despite their willingness to encourage visitors, the island people take real offence at topless sunbathing or swimming outside hotels.

Known as the ABCs, these are the biggest of the former (disbanded Dec 1996) Netherlands Antilles, and lie off the western coast of Venezuela. They share a thriving culture evolved from their Arawak, Dutch, Spanish, West Indian, Latin and African heritage; a common geography of starkly arid, cactus-strewn interior hills, surrounded by countless bays of white sands and ridiculously opal seas where wrecks and coral reefs promise world-class diving; the prosperity of refining Venezuela's huge oil reserves and of their huge tourist industry – while still retaining the benefits of being part of the Netherlands. They are outside the hurricane belt and there's a year-round tropical climate of 28 °C (82 °F) with guaranteed sun and balmy breezes. Though each island has unique features, they are collectively distinct in every way from all other Caribbean islands.

Aruba lies closest to Venezuela, only 30 km (19 mi) away and its version of Papamiento, the polyglot patois of the Netherlands Antilles has much greater Spanish influence. You might go there for its grand, high-rise resorts, but it's the Arawak petroglyphs in Arikok National Park, which covers 20 per cent of Aruba, that will capture your imagination. So will 'socarengue', Aruba's own, super-sexy, bump'n'grind party music.

Curaçao, the nexus of Dutch Caribbean history and culture, has 'tumba', identified by its primal, undiluted African beats. Curaçao is for partying, duty-free shopping, casinos and the World Heritage capital of Willemstad, beautifully restored to its 300 year-old Dutch colonial magnificence. The northwest of the island, where former slave plantations give way to the wildlife in rugged Mt Christoffel National Park, is much less developed. Bonaire lacks the crazed sophistication of its neighbours, but it has flamingoes and a marine park of deserved world fame among divers. It also has the marvellous Simadan Festival, held between February and April just after the sorghum harvest.

The colourful harbour-front buildings of Curaçao

The coastline of Saint Maarten

Saint Maarten

Famous as the smallest island ever to have been partitioned, St Maarten/St Martin has been shared by the Dutch and French since 1630, when they united to repulse the Spanish. Until 1817 nobody bothered with boundaries, and you can still move freely about the island; but despite the inextricably mixed Dutch, French and African heritage, you can't fail to distinguish the contrasting styles of the island's French and Dutch communities.

St Maarten welcomes cruise liners, commerce, gambling, reggae, hard rock and rijsttafel restaurants. It's the only place in the Caribbean where shopping is 100 per cent duty-free, and in Philipsburg you'll find 500 of the smartest luxury shops in the world. Despite heavy tourist development, it's still a treasure-trove of old world Dutch architecture and military relics, often next to the white beaches that guarantee St Maarten's popularity. The French emphasize comfort and elegance on their side, with secluded, luxury resorts and the best food in the Caribbean. Euros will pay for your croissants in the cafés and typically Gallic, charming bistros which are as relaxed as they are cosmopolitan (though French or Dutch, you must factor in the spicy aromas of West Indian cooking). Marigot, the capital, is the most French in spirit of all Caribbean cities, a luxury colonial version of a Mediterranean market town. But on the beaches you can always tell where you are by the dress code – modest on the Dutch side, topless or nude chic on the French. Orient-Plage is officially 'clothing-optional', but on the French side no-one is looking and no-one cares. With steel bands and firelit dancing, it makes for heady beach barbecues. The combination of cultures means you can do just about anything here on some of the Caribbean's prettiest and liveliest beaches and in the towns.

POPULATION:
Sint Maarten 35,000 (2007); Saint Martin 34,800 (2007)

WHEN TO GO:
October to June. In March, the Heineken Regatta attracts world-class yachting enthusiasts.

HOW TO GET THERE:
By air from Miami, San Juan (Puerto Rico), or Caracas.

HIGHLIGHTS:
The tropic green valley of Colombier between Marigot and Grand Case.
The spectacular vista from Pic Paradis, the highest point on the island at 450 m (1,400 ft) .
Tuesday night festivities on the Blvd de Grand-Case, during high season.
The beautifully-preserved 17th century fishing village of Orléans on the east side.
The pre-Colombian and colonial treasures at the St Martin Museum in Marigot.
Fort St Louis, built in 1767 and overlooking Marigot.

YOU SHOULD KNOW:
St Maarten/St Martin operates a joint nature and marine reserve, which includes 40 km (25 mi) of trails through mountains, forests and along the shore – where you walk through groves of 200 year-old mango and mahogany trees.

The perfect volcanic cone of Mount Mazinga

POPULATION:
3,183 (2006)
WHEN TO GO:
October to June
HOW TO GET THERE:
By air, from Miami, Antigua, or Curaçao.
HIGHLIGHTS:
Diving with the spectacular flying gurnards – rare in the Caribbean, common in Statia.
Exploring the archaeological shipwrecks, of which Statia has many.
The Historic Museum in Oranjestad, where divers bring all their archaeological finds.
The true Eden of The Quill crater: its flora and fauna are pristine.
YOU SHOULD KNOW:
Peter Stuyvesant bought Nieuwe Amsterdam (New York) from Native Americans for 30 blue beads from Statia. Blue beads were once used in Statia as currency for slave wages.

Saint Eustatius

Saint Eustatius is always called Statia, and pronounced 'Stay-sha'. Everything about it – history, geography, culture and amenities – defies its tiny 21 sq km (8 sq mi). Now a Dutch overseas province, it once changed hands 20 times between the Spanish, French, English and Dutch. During the English blockade of the American Revolutionary War it reached its zenith, when a population of 20,000 serviced hundreds of merchant ships at Oranjestad, the island capital. Now, after two centuries as a slumbering backwater, Statia's buccaneering past – the stone quays, ancient buildings and forts, plantation houses and offshore wrecks – is bringing it new prosperity as one of the Caribbean's most fascinating but unspoiled islands.

At its north end, a series of hills creates pockets of banana and fig groves, where overgrown lanes twist between neat, clapboard hamlets and idyllic coves. The big plantations (many now resorts), of the central plain give way in the south to the lush rainforest of the National Park, which includes the perfect volcanic cone of the 602 m (1,968 ft) Mt Mazinga. From the top, you descend 329 m (1,080 ft) into a tropical paradise called The Quill. The huge crater is filled with a magnificent array of trees, fauna and flora, most notably 17 different kinds of orchid and 55 exotic species of birds.

Underwater, Statia's volcanic origins have left fissures, pinnacles and canyons covered in corals and sponges that attract a huge variety of fish like black rip sharks, eagle rays and rarities including flying gurnards, high-hats and jack-knife fish. A single dive site consists of tangled wrecks where barracuda patrol huge schools of snappers and goat fish, and spotted morays and stingrays commonly lurk below. Statia may be small, but it has the natural wealth of a marine Serengeti.

Cuba

Cuba's history is as shocking as it is lurid. After four centuries of genocide, slavery and savage exploitation, in 1898 Spain lost control of the biggest island in the Caribbean and world's largest sugar producer to its covetous neighbour, the United States. Prevented by its own laws from annexing Cuba (as it had the Philippines, Guam and Puerto Rico), the US instead institutionalized racism, economic slavery, and tourism based on drinking, gambling and prostitution. When Castro's popular revolution stopped them, the US retaliated by wrecking Cuba's economy, but retaining 'rights' it had assigned to itself like the notorious Guantanamo naval base. For 50 years, the US blockade and trade embargos have hurt Cuba – but by delaying the island's fundamental modernization and development, they are proving to have been an even greater blessing in disguise.

Even under Castro's cyclical Puritanism, Cubans never forgot how to party, big-time. Havana, especially Old Havana, has been restored, not rebuilt as a high-rise mall – and it throbs to the happy syncopations of rumba, sound-splashed on bright colours. Havana is loaded with easy-going character that belies the true vigour and energy driving Cuban culture. You find it everywhere. As the US position becomes increasingly silly, more visitors are discovering the real thrill of vibrant beach-life, fabulous nightclubs, ecstatic rhythms, dance and laughter; plus an astounding repository of natural wealth, with all mod cons, but without the paraphernalia of dedicated consumerism that has spoiled up so much of the Caribbean. Twenty-two per cent of Cuba has recently been dedicated to protected reserves, including a 70,000 strong flamingo colony in the Río Máximo-Cagüey wetlands, winding 'mogote' caves, and the 3,000 rare Cuban crocodiles in the Zapata swamps. These, and the wrought-iron grills, dilapidated mansions, heavenly cigars and mojitos are the things others have built over or excised. Not Cuba. It's got the best of the past, and the future. Go now.

POPULATION:
11, 275,000 (2005)
WHEN TO GO:
December to March is the prime beach season but it's brilliant all year-round.
HOW TO GET THERE:
By air to Havana, from everywhere except the United States. The US also prevents all passenger ships, and most cruise ships, from calling. US visitors generally come by air, via Cancun, Nassau or Toronto.
HIGHLIGHTS:
High jinks in Old Havana – rumba/salsa/ritmo-ritmo in the winding streets of resplendent colonial buildings, an atmosphere of spiritually uplifting, world-class hedonism.
Santiago, Cuba's second city, more Caribbean than Havana, with a Creole influence in the palaces, mansions and museums that make it Cuba's historic heart.
The 1795 Tower of the Manaca Iznaga Estate, the manor of a wealthy slaver, and one of the 'ingenios' (19th century sugar mills) set among the Royal palms, waving cane and rolling hills of the Valle de los Ingenios.
UNESCO World Heritage city of Trinidad – a smuggler's backwater from 1514 to the late 18th century, when a brief sugar boom bought it the marble-floored mansions you see today.
The 235 pictographs at Cueva de Punta del Este – called 'the Sistine Chapel of Caribbean Indian art', created circa 800 AD, and the most important of their kind.

The Cathedral of Havana

Hispaniola

POPULATION:
17.71 million: Haiti 8,490,200 ; DR 9,219,800 (2000)

WHEN TO GO:
Haiti has two rainy seasons, April to May and September to October. But there's no peak tourist season to raise prices, so come from November to March. The DR is lovely from November to July.

HOW TO GET THERE:
By air to Port-au-Prince (Haiti) or Santo Domingo (S) or Puerto Plata (N) (Dominican Republic).

HIGHLIGHTS:
The 19th century Marché de Fer (Iron Market), noisy, chaotic centre of activity in Port-au-Prince's rundown buildings, huge coloured murals and 'taptaps' (public buses covered in crazy art and Creole proverbs).
The Spanish architecture of Cap Haitien, the former capital once called the 'Paris of the Antilles', where the aroma of orange speaks of making Grand Marnier and Cointreau.
The Samana Peninsula, DR, where from January to March, 10,000 humpback whales return from the North Atlantic to breed and nurse their calves.
The 16th century cathedrals, fort and cobbled streets of Santo Domingo's Ciudad Colonial; beautifully preserved, and now set with cafés, lively bars and restaurants.
The lowest point on the Caribbean (40 m, 131 ft below sea level), Lago Enriquillo in the SW of DR – salty, full of crocodiles, it's where tropical rainforest meets cactus-strewn desert.

The second-largest island in the Caribbean, claimed by Columbus in 1492, and Spain's launch pad for its South American conquests, Hispaniola has long been divided into French-speaking Haiti and Spanish-speaking Dominican Republic. Europeans brought disease to wipe out the indigenous Arawak, then imported slaves to do their bidding and work the fertile island into the most profitable 'farm' in the world – which Spain, France, Britain and the United States quarrelled over for 200 years while Hispaniola's two halves developed distinct cultures characterized by rapacious dictatorships that suppressed whole populations in the name of personal profit. Trujillo in DR used an army of bruisers; in Haiti 'Papa Doc' Duvalier had the Tonton Macoute secret police to create two-tier societies which have gone, but are not yet replaced by democratic reform.

All of which leaves visitors with a political choice. Hispaniola is geographically and ecologically astounding, in addition to having all the first-class attributes of sub-tropical hedonism demanded by northern snowbirds in search of a parasol-shaded daiquiri. The island's scale means that its flora and fauna are richer, matching higher mountains and more varied ecologies; but both Haiti and DR are poverty-stricken and over-populated, and still suffering the consequences of civil strife and exploitation. So the choice is between taking your pleasures in the confines of resorts, and taking an interest in the wildly different cultures beyond them. Hispaniolans share fantastic forms of music; vibrant colour in their art, clothes and dance; and deep spirituality expressed in every way from denominational churches to voodoo to animism. But Haiti is Afro-Caribbean, its European influences submerged since Toussaint l'Ouverture led the first slave rebellion; while DR, in just a decade or so, is on its way to becoming West Indian-American, another Puerto Rico. On Hispaniola, culture is way more intriguing than the admittedly marvellous beach life.

Palm trees line Playa Punta Cana on DR

Colourful huts line Saona's beaches

Saona

Off the southeast tip of the Dominican Republic, where the Atlantic and the Caribbean go head to head, lies the incarnation of the tropical island idyll. Its curves of white sand fringed by swaying palm trees, green against the azure sea, combine in a single image celebrated by millions of Europeans as the setting for the Bounty (chocolate) Bar TV commercial. Saona is the notion of paradise made manifest – and it looks even better than on film.

There are just two tiny settlements on the 25 km (15 mi) by 5 km (3 mi) island. Punta Gorda and the picturesque fishing village of Mano Juan are sleepy relics of the trading stations established after 1493 by Colombus, who bullied the Taino chieftain Cotubanama into an unequal partnership. Cotubanama's descendants now appear to be exacting an exquisite revenge. After centuries of subsistence fishing, in just ten years they have become unofficial beachmasters to the fleet of speedboats and catamarans that each day bring over hundreds of day-trippers from every major resort on the mainland, to bear witness to the existence in fact of a television dream. But Saona is part of a National Park and Marine Reserve with no amenities except in the tiny, restricted areas allotted to each resort group – where the islanders ply the by now rum-happy tourists with trinkets, curios, 'personalized' photos or video clips and 'massages' to the thumping beats of a beach boom-box.

You can walk away along equally fabulous but empty beaches, to lagoons full of flamingoes and mangroves stirred by pelicans, red-footed boobies, and Hispaniolan lizard-cuckoos and parrots. You can snorkel or dive among giant sponges and teeming fish on the reefs where manatees float in languor and dolphins somersault. The serenity of wonderland is still there – if you want to find it.

POPULATION:
300 (2007)

WHEN TO GO:
November to June

HOW TO GET THERE:
By catamaran or speedboat from the beach at Bayahibe or Dominicus on the mainland. Most of the boats are pre-booked to resort groups, but there are some independent excursion sellers.

HIGHLIGHTS:
Getting there – with or without the rum-fuelled party boats, the speedboat/catamaran trip across the currents of the Paso de Catuano, from the limestone cliffs of the mainland to island romance on the horizon, is huge fun.
Laguna de los Flamencos near the mangroves in the southwest.
The amazing Arawak and Taino rock art in the Cueva Cotubanamá – the cave in the island's west where the Chief hid before his capture by the Spanish.
'La Piscina Natural' – underwater sandbars hundreds of metres out to sea, where you jump into waist-deep water to drink, party, and frighten the lovely fish. Or just swim.
The photo you take home showing you at the Bounty Bar beach, yes, really!

YOU SHOULD KNOW:
On the big catamarans, someone will come round putting a little hat on your head. They are not being kind – unless you reject it immediately, you will be charged at least US$4 for it on leaving the boat.

The beach at Ochio Rios

Jamaica

POPULATION:
2,780,132 (2007 estimate)
WHEN TO GO:
Year-round, but much more expensive from December to April. Come for a festival – Carnival in March/April is huge, aimed at Jamaica's booty-shakers rather than tourists; Reggae Sunsplash in Ocho Rios, and Reggae Sunfest in Montego Bay come a week apart in July/August; and in January Kingston celebrates cultural roots in the Rebel Salute Music Festival, and the traditional Accompong Maroon Festival. Jonkanoo is a Christmas masquerade revel, and cricket, in the street or stadium or on the beach, always involves music and dancing.
HOW TO GET THERE:
By air, to Kingston, Montego Bay or Ocho Rios.
HIGHLIGHTS:
The Blue Lagoon, Fairy Hill.
Negril, on Jamaica's western tip, is stunningly beautiful, and the vortex of anything-goes, fun-in-the-sun, up-for-it beach life.
Dunn's River Falls – the archetype of the perfect West Indian landscape. There's white-water tubing nearby on the White River.
Night swimming in the Luminous Lagoon of Martha Brae River, near Falmouth – the bio-luminescent glow where the river meets the sea is one of the rarest sights on earth.
YOU SHOULD KNOW:
The Rastafari religion, founded in Jamaica, reveres the late Emperor Haile Selassie I of Ethiopia.

Jamaica is the great cultural boom-box of the Caribbean, constantly advertising an identity already so strong that it is recognized anywhere in the world. It's not at all typical of the West Indies, but by asserting itself so vigorously, this one island has come to epitomize them all.

After Columbus, who tried to make it his personal fief in 1494, Jamaica was always an English/British colony after Admiral William Penn (father of William Penn of Pennsylvania) seized it in 1655; and centuries of aggressive control by sugar oligarchs and naval and military commanders created a style still apparent in the gangs and societies that make the unofficial rules in Jamaica today. Parts of Kingston and other towns are plain dangerous for visitors, and you go warily almost everywhere outside resorts and tourist destinations. Happily, the resorts are themselves set in such beautiful places that visitors don't mind their self-imposed restrictions; but if you want to explore outside the envelope the best way is to join in one of the many festivals all over the island, in which Jamaicans celebrate their countryside, religions, planting, harvest, towns, rivers, and history, with the intense joie-de-vivre that infects the island's brilliant music, dance and theatre. On these occasions you'll see an open-hearted, deeply spiritual, carefree and generous people intent on pleasure rather than your tourist bucks, and you'll love it.

There's much to love in Jamaica, especially reggae, street markets, genteel towns like Mandeville (laid out in 1816, and still serves tea around 4 pm), Jamaican rum in its many light and dark forms, Blue Mountain coffee and the mountains themselves, the aura of elegance and celebrity inherent in Ocho Rios and Montego Bay, limpid peach sunsets silhouetting palms on Negril's 11 km (7 mi) nudist-happy beach, and – insistent and everywhere - more reggae. Grab some goat jerky and get stuck in to the fun.

Puerto Rico

Just 1,600 km (1,000 mi) southeast of Miami, the freeways, skyscrapers, malls and parking lots of the United States crash into four centuries of Spanish colonial culture. Puerto Rico sounds like the most uncomfortable kind of shotgun alliance – but being Caribbean, it gets away with it. It became American in 1898 after the Spanish-American War, and you'd think a century was enough for two fundamentally opposed cultural styles to assimilate. It isn't, even in San Juan, and even though all Puerto Ricans are US citizens. When you explore the island's mountainous interior, you feel that the infrastructure of roads and amenities is extraordinarily misplaced, like gleaming chrome set in the middle of fine old porcelain. What Puerto Rico has given so successfully to New York and other US cities, doesn't travel back the other way. The island's delights are all in its colonial history, in its Taino (Amerindian) origins, and its Caribbean present.

The best of these is Old San Juan, the island heart of the capital, and the site of its colonial government since 1509. Massive ramparts and fortifications guard its oldest sections, a maze of palatial homes, tree-shaded plazas and public buildings that demonstrate Puerto Rico's colossal wealth. The dramatic panorama from the Santa Barbara Bastion on the 42 m (140 ft) heights of Morro Fort, of towers, tunnels and 5m (16ft) thick bulwarks guarding the headland where the Atlantic is restrained by San Juan Bay, is an inspirational image of bygone power; and Old San Juan's historic splendour (now enlivened by little bars and quietly sizzling music) ranks with the world's best historical areas.

Like Honolulu, San Juan has sugar-soft white beaches; and like Hawaii generally, Puerto Rico is a unique version of the United States. Weirdly Caribbean, horribly crowded and brash, but fun.

POPULATION:
3, 927,776 (2006 estimate)

WHEN TO GO:
Puerto Rico is 'full' from December to April. Come for the Salsa Congress in July, when thousands participate in dance competitions, at Isla Verde, San Juan.

HOW TO GET THERE:
By air to San Juan, which is also the hub for domestic flights.

HIGHLIGHTS:
The trompe l'oeil painting in the cathedral dome, and the 17th century splendour of the colonial homes, plazas, fountains and churches of colourful Ponce, Puerto Rico's second city.
The stunning cavern systems, weird rock formations, world's largest underground river and blue-eyed river crabs at Parque de las Cavernas del Rio Camuy, SW of San Juan.
El Yunque, the only tropical rainforest in the US, and rich in flora and fauna
Eating 'alcapurria', a plantain fritter stuffed with seafood, from a roadside kiosk at the Balneario (public beach) de Luquillo, one of the prettiest beaches near San Juan.

YOU SHOULD KNOW:
1. There is a board game called 'Puerto Rico'. This witty game of colonial domination was ranked the No.1 Internet Game 2007. 2. Puerto Ricans who live in New York City are called 'Nuyoricans'.

The vibrant houses lining Recinto Sur Street in Old San Juan.

Isla Carmen

POPULATION:
Uninhabited
WHEN TO GO:
October to May; but you'll see whales by the score between January and March.
HOW TO GET THERE:
By air from San Diego or Los Angeles to Loreto on the Baja side of the Gulf; then by private yacht or boat charter (hiring a zodiac or skiff is recommended – anchoring is forbidden to prevent reef damage, and they are easier to beach and to swim from).
HIGHLIGHTS:
Getting close-up and personal to the big, barking sea lion community at Punta Lobos, a dome-shaped islet at the northern tip, connected to Carmen by a sand causeway.
Sitting low in the water in a dinghy in the company of dozens of dolphins and whales who bring their young to inspect and possibly play with you. You just laugh with happiness.
Star-gazing by the embers of your campfire; and waking to a fiery sunrise of molten bronze and gold – here, at least, nature is as it should be.
Kayaking in the caves, and between the rock formations and reefs below the cliffs.
The view of Carmen – like an offshore stegosaurus – from Loreto, itself a historical delight dating back to 1697. Loreto was the first Spanish mission in the Californias.
YOU SHOULD KNOW:
In 'The Log from the Sea of Cortez' (1951), John Steinbeck delivers a close study of marine life around Isla Carmen. He also describes breaching swordfish and 4 m (12 ft) manta rays

The Gulf of California (aka Sea of Cortez), between Baja and the Mexican mainland, is one of the world's marine marvels. Baja's 1,000 km (650 mi) spine of mountainous cactus scrub and sea pine forest guards a milk-warm oceanic playground from the violence of the Pacific. It's the southern nursery of fin, blue, sperm and orca whales, and home to countless family pods of bottlenose and common dolphins, sea lions, manta rays, and rainbow shoals of angelfish, guitarfish, redtail tigerfish and some 600 other species. Red-billed tropicbirds, blue-footed boobies, pelicans, frigatebirds and rare Heerman's gulls nesting by the thousand help to emphasize the great wildlife spectacle. And half way down the Gulf, where the temperate merges with the tropic zone, bringing together all kinds of species at their seasonal ranges in a cacophony of seabirds and harmony of underwater song, is Isla Carmen, the biggest island in Loreto Bay National Marine Park.

Carmen used to be famous for the purity of its salt deposits, discovered in the early 16th century. Now, Salinas, its only settlement, is a ghost town among the 60 m (100 ft) cliffs, sand dunes and white beaches. Shale and gravel slope sharply to high ridges veined with dry arroyos. From any of Carmen's isolated coves, you lose sight of the sea in minutes, and walk in a windswept desert of giant cacti and hummingbirds. Nobody lives here, and there are no amenities. You can camp for a few days but you need prior permission (from the park authority at Loreto on the mainland) even to be there. Since commercial and big game sport fishing were banned in 1996, the ecological chain has been fully restored both on the island and in the sea: Isla Carmen's natural wealth has never been greater than in its present, splendid isolation.

A rare whale shark in the Sea of Cortez

Revillagigedo Islands

The dramatic coastline of San Benedicto Island

Most maps don't show them. Roughly 400 km (250 mi) southwest of Cabo San Lucas at the tip of Baja California, and 720-970 km (450-605 mi) west of Manzanillo on the Mexican mainland, and beyond the continental shelf, lie the four volcanic Revillagigedo Islands. Clarion, San Benedicto, Roca Partida and the biggest, Socorro, are often called 'little Galapagos', because they developed in similar isolation – to the extent that nearly half their flora, and almost all their fauna and avifauna, occur nowhere else in the world. The percentage might be higher but for the predation and damage caused by plant and animal introductions by the few travellers that ever reached the islands following their discovery in 1533, when they were uninhabited and untouched. Still, their ecology is unique. They are dominated by dry forests of cactus and sage, but in the denser and more humid areas high in the mountains (Socorro's Mt Evermann reaches 1,130 m (3,550 ft), lichens, giant ferns and endemic ilex and bumelia are abundant. Scarred by deep ravines, the terrain has a wild beauty. It also provides cover for the invasive domestic sheep and goats who have degraded much of it, and the now feral descendants of cats, who have hunted the Socorro dove to extinction in the wild, and now threaten the Socorro mockingbird.

Walking on the islands is a weird sensation. Earth, sky, plants, birds, lizards – all familiar, but you recognize none of them. You're in someone else's version of the world, and it's a privilege, if unsettling. It makes perfect sense that the Revillagigedo Islands are one of the world's most important nesting, breeding and foraging sites for no less than four critically endangered marine turtle species – the leatherback, Pacific olive ridley, green and hawksbill. Learn from them. Turtles know a good place when they see it.

POPULATION:
250 on Socorro (staff and families at the naval station); 9 on Clarion (the naval garrison).

WHEN TO GO:
Any time you can get permission. For scuba-divers, November to May, when the weather and seas are calmer.

HOW TO GET THERE:
By boat, usually live-aboard dive vessels from Cabo San Lucas. You need permission from the Mexican Navy to land anywhere on the islands other than the naval station on Socorro. The naval airstrip at Socorro is not open to the public.

HIGHLIGHTS:
Scuba-diving with dolphins, sharks, manta rays and other pelagics.
The awesome, perpendicular cliffs – 24-183 m (75-560 ft) – of Clarion Island, broken only at Bahia Azufre (Sulphur Bay).
The lava domes, flows and cinder cones that mark Mount Evermann on Socorro as a shield volcano.

YOU SHOULD KNOW:
The islands are named after Don Juan Vicente de Guemes Padilla Horcasitas y Aguayo, 2nd Count of Revillagigedo, the 53rd Viceroy of New Spain, even though they were visited by Alexander von Humboldt, of Current fame, in 1811.

Isla Holbox

POPULATION:
1,600 (2007)
WHEN TO GO:
May to September, for the whale sharks and the breeding dolphins who like to play with them.
HOW TO GET THERE:
By air to Cancun, then by bus from Cancun City to Chiquila on the north coast of Quintana Roo, then by regular ferry or water taxi from Chiquila. There is a small air-strip for light aircraft on Holbox.
HIGHLIGHTS:
The Yalahau Cenote, a sweet water spring surrounded by the salt-water mangroves of the Yalahau Lagoon, accessible only by boat. The combination attracts crocodiles, pink flamingoes, white ibiss, spoonbills, cranes and 130 species to Isla de los Pajaros in the lagoon – and two watchtowers on stilts in the water enable you to enjoy them in safety.
Big game fishing at Cabo Catoche, where the Gulf currents meet the Caribbean.
Punta Mosquitos, where turtles come by the thousand to lay their eggs, from May to July.
Passion Island – tiny, uninhabited, and perfect.
YOU SHOULD KNOW:
Alas! In late 2007, plans for massive development (10,000 rooms in hotels, condos and villas; two golf courses; airport) on Holbox, and on the mainland facing it, were accepted. It will take some time – go before it happens.

Tucked in behind the northern tip of Mexico's Yucatan Peninsula, separated from the mainland by a shallow lagoon teeming with flamingoes, pelicans, and over 130 other rainbow-hued bird species, Holbox is the new kid on the tropical island block. It's only 12 km (7 mi) long and up to 1.5 km (1 mi) wide, but with 32 km (20 mi) of white sand beaches, and huge, endless sunsets to silhouette its ranks of nodding coconut palms, it's something of a cartoon image. Holbox (pronounced 'hole-bosh') was originally settled by pirates who intermarried with the Mayan residents, and the descendants of the original eight families still live in the island's single fishing village. Centuries of isolation have brought man and place into symbiotic tranquility, recently shared by a handful of discerning Europeans and North Americans who quietly live there. But with the neon glitz of Cancun and other high-rise resorts beginning to pall, it's inevitable that Holbox's perfection should become better known.

Its eco-credentials are impeccable, so far unthreatened even by the small hotels beginning to proliferate. The village streets are sand, bordered by quaint wooden houses in lively colours and thatched with steeply-raked palm. You can join the fishermen in pursuit of barracuda, swordfish, red snapper, speckled trout, grouper, and octopus; dive for lobster; or just wander the beaches for mother-of-pearl shells. Transport is by bicycle or golf buggy, but there are no golf courses (or cars). If you come between May and September, you can swim or snorkel within touching distance of the world's biggest fish, the whale shark. Holbox sits exactly where the turquoise Caribbean meets the nutrient-rich, emerald Gulf of Mexico, and the upwellings attract the highest concentration of the gentle, plankton-feeding monsters (typically around 14 m, 45 ft long) in the world. Holbox is a terrestrial and marine Eden.

A traditional Holbox village

The colourful boats of Cozumel

Cozumel

One of Mexico's largest islands, Cozumel lies 20 km (12 mi) from the mainland, and 60 km (36 mi) south of Cancun. It's a flat, limestone formation shaped like a holster, and pierced by dozens of *cenotes* (water-filled sinkholes), many with their own marine forms, which are an extra attraction for swimmers and snorkellers who come to explore the island's fantastic offshore reefs.

Jacques Cousteau first popularized Cozumel in 1960, when he identified Palancar at the island's southern tip as one of the world's best scuba-diving sites. He triggered an explosion of tourist development, only reined in with the establishment of the National Marine Park in 1996; but the reefs were badly damaged by the deepwater piers built for cruise ships to bring new clientele. Attitudes changed quickly. Cozumel's new islanders (the 40,000 Maya who welcomed Hernan ('Stout') Cortes in 1519 were reduced to 30 by 1570, and Cozumel became uninhabited) realized the value not just of their spectacular marine wealth, but of the island's undeveloped centre.

You'll never get a better chance to appreciate Mayan culture so close to good beaches. The biggest Mayan site, San Gervasio (named much later), was for centuries sacred to Ix Chel, the goddess of fertility, and one of the Yucatan's most important sanctuaries. There are several others, recovered from jungle and swampy mangrove lagoons now teeming with cormorants, pelicans, primary-coloured tree frogs, iguanas and crocodiles.

These days, the duty of collective care is replacing brash mistakes of the 1970s. You can see 250 species in its clear waters, including the bright blue-and-yellow queen angelfish, the toad fish (unique to Cozumel), and enormous sponges like the barrel and elephant ear, which grows to 3.6 m (12 ft) across. Cozumel is fabulously pretty and exotic, and you should go there with someone you love and watch the sunsets.

POPULATION:
73,193 (2005)

WHEN TO GO:
Year-round. Temperatures average 32 °C (90 °F) in July and August, and 24 °C (75 °F) in December and January. Come for the traditional feasting, rodeos, bullfights, music and fairs of the 5-day Festival of El Cedral in late April or May.

HOW TO GET THERE:
By air to San Miguel from Houston, New York, Miami or Mexico City; or by air to Cancun, then scheduled boat ferry from Playa del Carmen.

HIGHLIGHTS:
The Mayan lighthouse at Punta Celarain, part of the huge Punta Sur Ecological Reserve of mangrove, jungles and reefs – you can see crocodiles (safely), 220 bird species, iguanas, and from June to August, giant turtles beaching to lay their eggs.
The only inland reef formation in the world, with its own species of fish, crustaceans, and corals, at the Chankanaab Lagoon, south of San Miguel.
The underwater 'Maya City' – one of dozens of attractions for children, including lots of imaginative water games, at the noisy (!) Playa Mia Grand Beach Park.

YOU SHOULD KNOW:
A plaque at the Museo Cozumel commemorates US President Lincoln's decision to buy Cozumel as a place to send freed US slaves. The Caste War of Yucatan (started 1848) forced him to change his mind.

Ambergris Caye

POPULATION:
8,000 (2007)
WHEN TO GO:
November to June
HOW TO GET THERE:
By air, via Belize City, to San Pedro; by boat (fast ferry) from Belize City to San Pedro.
HIGHLIGHTS:
The toucans, crocodiles and howler monkeys, among many marvels at the Crooked Tree Wildlife Sanctuary in the jungle.
Cave tubing, one of several adventures on jungle river expeditions on the mainland.
The major Mayan sites of Tikal, Lamanai, and Altun Ha among others near San Pedro.
Birds like the scarlet tanager, laughing falcon, white-collared seed-eater, flaming parakeet, chachalaca and green-breasted mango hummingbird. The birds are astonishing.
Swimming/snorkelling among the unique aquatic life of the Zaak Ba Ajo Lagoon – with its own, small 'blue hole', at San Juan, north of San Pedro.
YOU SHOULD KNOW:
With its abundance of first-class seafood, huge variety of seasonal tropical fruits, and combination of influences from many different cultures, the food in Ambergris Caye is justifiably famous – and it's all local.

In Mayan times, Ambergris Caye was a trading post supporting 10,000 people. At 40 km (25 mi) long, and up to 1.5 km (1 mi) wide, it's the largest of 200 cayes studding the coastline of Belize, and lies off the southernmost tip of Mexico's Yucatan Peninsula. In fact, the Mayans created the island by digging a channel to provide a trade route from the bay of Chetumal to the Caribbean – and it is now the border between Belize and Mexico. Then and now, there is only one major settlement, San Pedro, built over Mayan ruins and home to most of the population of Mestizos (Maya-Spanish), Creoles, Central American refugees and Americans, all of whom have merged into a one-off community with its own extraordinary 'Sanpedrano' dialect – much of which is recognizable to visitors from various languages, but usually means something quite different. It's that kind of place: quirky, fun, easy-going and very welcoming.

Visitors flock to Ambergris Caye (pronounced 'Am-BER-grease') because the 310 km (190 mi) Belize Barrier Reef, second only to Australia's Great Barrier Reef, runs parallel to the island only 370 m (0.25 mi) from the beach. It's one of the world's greatest dive sites, with every feature of caves, walls, columns, cathedrals and bridges that fantasy can dream up. Even better, the reef's proximity to shore means that swimmers and snorkellers can enjoy its delights almost as much as certified scuba-divers.

The island itself is a wildlife bonanza of white, red and black mangrove and buttonwood trees; littoral forest plants like gumbo limbo, sapodilla, fig, coco plum and palmetto; egrets, orioles, kiskadees, cinnamon hummingbirds, blue herons and rose-throated becards among some 300 species; and forests full of deer, peccaries, raccoons and occasional jaguar. And the night life in San Pedro is excellent, too – especially the 'punta', a hip-swivelling local dance.

The shallows of Ambergris Caye

Bay Islands

A glorious whale shark

Columbus found the Bay Islands on his fourth voyage in 1502, and Britain held them from 1643 until they were ceded to Honduras in 1860. On the three principal islands – Utila, Roatan and Guanaja – English is the first language, but the true lingua franca is scuba diving. They sit on the Bonacca Ridge, surrounded by reefs which form part of the biggest system in the world after the Great Barrier Reef. Furthermore, the Cayman Trench flanks the islands, creating spectacular drop offs from the coral walls, some just 100 m (328 ft) from the shore. Typically amazing is 'Spooky Channel', one of 50 major dive sites on Roatan's 62 km (40 mi) length – you navigate from a dock on the beach through huge coral formations that open to cathedral size before narrowing over your head in a long channel that emerges the other side of the wall. Adventurers go back and swim it at night.

Utila is smallest and flattest, wonderfully safe for children to learn watercraft. Roatan, the biggest, has a lush green mountainous backbone and the most developed infrastructure for visitors to its staggering coves (called 'bights') and beaches. Guanaja's mountains go higher still, and are covered with Caribbean pine trees; it has no roads, and its development appears to favour super-luxury resorts at odds with its largest community, Bonacca, which is a tiny, crowded cay next to the main island, criss-crossed with canals full of colourful boats and canoes and nicknamed 'Little Venice of the Caribbean'. You pay more to stay closer to Guanaja's forests, rivers and miles of unspoiled beaches, but Bonacca itself, like Roatan and Utila, is where backpackers and billionaires can meet on the equal terms of enthusiasm for crystal waters, marine menagerie and the blossoming corals of the living reefs.

POPULATION:
43,000 (2005) (Total for all 8 inhabited Bay Islands)

WHEN TO GO.
Year-round. Come for the Sun Jam, two days of music and dancing on Water Cay, the definitive deserted tropical island near Utila, in August.

HOW TO GET THERE:
By air to Coxen Hole, Roatan, from Houston or Miami, or via Tegucigalpa or San Pedro Sula; by air to Utila and Guanaja from Roatan or Ceiba; by ferry boat to all three from La Ceiba on the mainland.

HIGHLIGHTS:
Conch fritters and coconut bread at Punta Gorda, the only Garifuna settlement on Roatan, with a dynamic culture unchanged since the late 1700s.
12-18 m (39-59 ft) long whale sharks, eagle rays, Creole wrasses, groupers, octopus and reef crabs – among the pillar corals, seafans and barrel sponges on the spectacular precipice of West End Wall.
The forest waterfalls of Guanaja, 90 per cent of which is protected reserve.
Dropping in to exclusive hotels on private beaches for a drink and a dive – it's the accepted culture for meeting new people and creating parties.

YOU SHOULD KNOW:
It was from Roatan that 17th century buccaneers and pirates launched their famous collective raids on Porto Bello and Cartagena.

An aerial view of Corn Island surrounded by pristine coral reefs

POPULATION:
8,000 (2007)
WHEN TO GO:
Any time except mid-May to mid-September, when almost daily rain creates an awful lot of mud. If you come during Semana Santa (Holy Week) at Easter, book in advance because Nicaragua heads for the beaches. Or come for the Fiesta del Cangrejo (Crab Festival) at the end of August.
HOW TO GET THERE:
By air from Managua to Big Corn; by bus from Managua to El Rama on the Escondido River, then ferry to Big Corn. Little Corn can only be reached by boat from Big Corn.
HIGHLIGHTS:
The local Sunday baseball match.
Lying in your hammock between two palm trees within finger-raising distance of a bar.
Letting yourself enjoy doing nothing much – without guilt.
YOU SHOULD KNOW:
Places like the Corn Islands are very, very rare. So rare, that a sculptural project called 'The Soul of the World' has designated the Corn Islands as one of only eight places in the world where the vertices of a giant imaginary cube emerge. Which, if you're stuck, is something to contemplate in your hammock.

Islas de Maiz

Lying 70 km (45 mi) off the Caribbean coast of Nicaragua, east of Bluefields Island, Big Corn and Little Corn Islands are temples to tropical tranquility. Tourism is still in its infancy, and though there are lots of hotels and houses where rooms are for rent, local charm and generosity of spirit are a terrific substitute for electricity and other amenities associated with fluffy white towels. The only certainty is that if things temporarily don't work, you won't care, because you'll be swimming or diving or walking or lying in a hammock or drinking at one of the bars (music optional, and seldom of noxious boom-box magnitude). You might even take a book and read it while waiting for the green flash of sunset – the litmus test of tropical island perfection.

Both islands have reefs on their doorstep, and Big Corn's Sally Peaches (a beach, not a misprint) is absolutely stunning. You step off a long curve of glittering white sand, take a few strokes, and enter the first of a series of crazy-castle coral formations all of which are accessible to snorkellers. You might need scuba qualification for the furthest formations, like Blowing Rock where it feels like swimming through a model of Manhattan, but in the company of spotted eagle rays, green turtles and angelfish instead of a Hill Street squad car. Around Little Corn there are spectacular underwater caves, patrolled by barracuda, nurse sharks and scuttling lobsters among the darting rainbow shoals which no degree of familiarity could take for granted. There are several ship wrecks, including a bona fide Spanish Galleon – and if you haven't already done it, there's no better place to get PADI certification so you can get the most out of the adventure. Or indeed, a better place to regroup and recharge your natural soul.

Solentiname Islands

There are no roads, no cars, telephones or electricity. The Solentiname Archipelago of 36 volcanic islands is a true wilderness, uninhabited save for some 800 people spread amongst the four largest – Mancarroncito, Mancarron, San Fernando and La Venada. At the most remote, southern end of Lake Nicaragua (aka Lake Cocibolca), near the Costa Rican border where the San Juan River connects it to the Caribbean, the Solentiname are definitive tropical islands: they are covered with tropical tree species, transitional between wet and tropical dry, and attract a super-spectrum of brilliantly-coloured flora and fauna within both ranges. It's incredible that authentic natural wealth of this calibre is accessible, a couple of hours from urban catatonia.

The marks of history are faint. Museums in Mancarron and San Fernando show pre-Columbian artefacts and tell of older Chichan petroglyphs. Once, the islands protected a strategic route to the Pacific. A young Horatio Nelson lead a bloody expedition to San Carlos, built in 1527 at the San Juan River mouth, but regularly sacked by pirates like Henry Morgan. In the 19th century, until Panama did it first, the Solentiname's virgin plenty was threatened by the proposal to build a canal across the Nicaraguan isthmus. For now, the islands are held in a rhapsody of immense silence and tranquility that heightens your every sense. The pure white of an egret is sharp against robin egg blue sky; brilliant red hibiscus deepens the green forest. A streak of yellow-and-red and a sudden shriek is a toucan; and howler monkeys send parrots clattering in a stream of firework sparks. A swirl of water is momentarily shocking – and in the hot, humid, earthy-damp air, you merge with all four elements in their fecund equilibrium. The Solentiname Islands represent eco-tourism at its classiest – a natural world you feel as well as look at.

A native Keel-billed Toucan

POPULATION:
800 (2006 estimate)

WHEN TO GO:
Year-round.

HOW TO GET THERE:
By air via Managua to San Carlos; then by slow public boat or fast private water-taxi to Mancarron or San Fernando (where you can stay in eco-friendly comfort, but don't expect resort-style amenities).

HIGHLIGHTS:
The world's only known freshwater sharks, plus tarpon, swordfish, sawfish and 40 other species in the teeming waters.
La Pajarera ('the Birdcage') and Mancarroncito Islands, especially favoured by toucans and parrots and at least 75 other species of local and migratory birds.
The swamps of Los Guatuzos Wildlife Reserve – 40,000 hectares (74,000 acres) of tropical wetlands and rainforest, home to commonly-seen caimans, crocodiles, jaguars, monkeys and feral boar; to over 389 resident bird species and thousands of migratory visitors; turtles, butterflies and extraordinary crabs; and 130 kinds of orchids – a RAMSAR-protected Wetland, and part of the Solentiname Biosphere Reserve, on the shore opposite the islands.
The lively primitivism of the wood carvings and paintings of the Solentiname artists' community, introduced by the poet-priest Ernesto Cardenal in the 1960s.

YOU SHOULD KNOW:
The canal proposal was revived in 2007, when someone realized that ships over 130,000 tons won't fit through the newly-enlarged Panama Canal – yet by 2017, there will be 3,000 ships of close to 300,000 tons all wanting to go to and from the Pacific. The threat is extremely real.

Ometepe

POPULATION:
35,000 (2006)
WHEN TO GO:
Year-round, so come for the *fiestas patronales* (patron saints' days) like Moyogalpa's Santa Ana in July, when the *Baile de las Inditas* dance celebrates both Spanish and indigenous culture; or Altagracia's all-dancing, all-drinking feast of San Diego in November. Ometepe holds more folk and religious festivals than anywhere else in Nicaragua.
HOW TO GET THERE:
By boat (car/passenger ferry or basic 'lancha' (small boat)) from San Jorge on the lake shore near Rivas; or the big boat ferry to/from Granada – San Carlos, which stops at Ometepe, and which you must book in advance.
HIGHLIGHTS:
Sunset at Punta Jesus Maria, the western tip, where a 5 m (16 ft) wide sandbar projects 1 km (0.6 mi) into the lake, with water splashing you from both sides. Magic.
The Sompopo dances at Altagracia – the line of dancers carry green leaves on their hands, and sway to the drumming like a line of red insects going to and from their nests – these insects are called Sompopos.
Troops of howler, white-faced and spider monkeys en route to swimming at the jungle San Ramon waterfall, along with the hummingbirds and urraca (blue-tailed magpies).
Staying quite still, looking at and listening to the living fairytale.
YOU SHOULD KNOW:
Ometepe is still getting used to the idea of eco-tourism. A lack of hotels means many islanders are opening their homes to (low) paying guests. The offers are genuine, and you will make new friends.

The perfect twin cones of Concepción and Maderas, two volcanoes linked by a rainforested isthmus, rise majestically from the 'sweet' (ie 'fresh') water of vast Lake Nicaragua. These are the 'two hills' of the island's Náhuatl name, Ometepe, and for many centuries they have been held in reverential awe by succeeding cultures, as the repository of myth and legend as well as an island of exceptional fertility and beauty.

Ometepe's unique, double-breasted shape was foretold in a vision to Nahuas and Chorotegas who came from Mexico and made it their sanctuary; and Chibchas came north from South America. Their petroglyphs are all over the island, greeting you on rock faces and prominent boulders, giving what is already a natural paradise another-worldly mystique. It's tempting for visitors to take cultural myths fairly lightly – but Ometepinos, though as sophisticated in modern ways as anyone, still integrate their combined history into their daily lives. The island's volcanic fertility and biodiversity is in their view a consequence of their respect for the legends associated with it. In 1957, when Concepción erupted, everyone refused a government order to evacuate: not one was killed. And Ometepe was bypassed in the revolution and the war with the Contras, which damaged so much of Nicaragua.

The friendly Ometepinos are always willing to show you some fresh delight on the island. You can sample its phenomenal riches on an easy hike on Maderas, the extinct and smaller volcano. Its crater is a slightly spooky cold lagoon, set in thick tropical jungle which really is full of howler monkeys, boas, jaguars and thousands of birds. The jungle runs down to the Charco Verde Reserve, where you find the best beaches – and an ancient witch called Chico Largo, who may offer you a life of luxury in return for transmuting your soul into one of the island's cows. It adds a dimension to eco-tourism.

Smoke drifts from the crater of Concepción.

Cocos Island

The primeval landscape of Cocos Island

Once described as the most beautiful island in the world, Cocos lies in the eastern Pacific, 550 km (344 mi) off the coast of Costa Rica. The island formed around two million years ago from cooling lava and today the mountainous and irregular slopes are covered with misty primeval rainforest, and scored with ravines and waterfalls. Cerro Iglesias, the summit, is 671 m (2,201 ft) high and rises in the southwestern part of the island. Because the island is so remote, much of its flora and fauna is endemic, which has led it to be designated a national park and a UNESCO World Heritage Site. The only inhabitants are the park rangers.

The sheer 600 m (1,970 ft) high cliffs that surround much of the island plunge deep underwater, and are riddled with secret caves. The coastline is so precipitous that there are only two safe landing places. The island was discovered in 1526, and soon became legendary as a hiding place for pirate gold.

In 1820 when the revolt of Peru seemed imminent, the Spanish Governor in Lima arranged for the Spanish treasure there to be shipped to Mexico. The loot, which included two life-sized statues in pure gold from the church, along with countless other treasures, was entrusted to a Captain Thompson of the *Mary Deare*. Thompson could not resist the temptation and, killing all the other passengers on board his ship, buried the treasure on Cocos. He died before he could return to recover it, and over the years at least 300 expeditions have been mounted to find the gold from the *Mary Deare*, or any of the other pirate treasure buried on the island. Even now people have not given up hope of stumbling across a hoard of bullion in one of the innumerable coastal caves or jungle ravines.

Nowadays most visitors come here for the diving. Cocos Island offers the perfect environment for every sort of fish, from tiny baitfish to huge whale sharks: a pollution-free, no-fishing zone at a crossing point of currents and counter-currents. The area has one of the richest concentrations of pelagic species in the world, literally hundreds of hammerhead and white-tip sharks, mantas, rays, tuna, bottlenose dolphins, green sea turtles, whale sharks and even humpback whales. Ten-day boat tours can be arranged in San José.

POPULATION:
Park rangers only.
WHEN TO GO:
Diving is best between March and December.
HOW TO GET THERE:
Fly to San José, Costa Rica, then by pre-arranged tour boat.
HIGHLIGHTS:
Diving in the waters around the island – it is literally like falling into a fish tank.
Birdwatching – despite the lack of vegetation, many species of birds visit and nest on the island.
Hire a bike and explore the many tracks that lead to the lagoon.
Atoll walking at low-tide to reach the more remote islands.
YOU SHOULD KNOW:
You can only go on an organized seasonal diving trip and with the permission of the island rangers. You are not permitted to camp or sleep on the island.

Isla Colon

Bocas del Toro Islands

POPULATION:
9,000 (2007)
WHEN TO GO:
The rain never entirely stops, but the islands are driest in September/October and February/March. Happily, at these times the islands are both cheaper and less crowded.
HOW TO GET THERE:
By air, from Panama City, David or Changuinola, to Bocas Town; by bus/car from Chiriqui Grande (S) or Changuinola (N) to Almirante, then by water-taxi or car ferry to Bocas Town.
HIGHLIGHTS:
Toucans in the pristine rainforest of Isla Popa – where the ancient Ngöbe culture predominates in the five main villages.
Laguna Bocatorita, on the east of Isla Cristobal, where a labyrinth of mangroves forms a giant natural aquarium 6 km (4 mi) across, drawing in fish, manatees and bottle-nose dolphins.
The only Panamanian nesting site of red-billed tropic-birds, on Swan's Cay.
Snorkelling among the mangrove channels of Cayo Crawl, en route to the magnificent coral gardens on the southeast coast of Isla Bastimentos.
The candy-coloured houses of Bocas Town, heritage of the banana boom, when 25,000 people lived here.
YOU SHOULD KNOW:
The rocks and fossils around Bocas hold the key to understanding the formation of the Isthmus of Panama, the separation of the Atlantic and the Pacific – and the triggering of the Gulf Stream.

The Caribbean coast of Costa Rica and Panama merges in a seamless sequence of barely-explored mountains and rivers, dense forests opening onto turquoise waters and pristine white beaches, mysterious mangrove channels, coral gardens and exotically-coloured wildlife. This is the Panamanian province of Bocas del Toro. Its capital, Bocas Town, is on Colon, one of the 68 Bocas del Toro Islands that fill the Laguna de Chiriqui for 100 km (60 mi). Collectively, they are one of the Caribbean's richest, unspoiled eco-surprises.

Columbus careened his boats here in 1502, on Isla Carinero, as he named it. For 300 years the Bocas Islands' remote bays were shared between the indigenous Ngöbe-Bugle people and a variety of official and unofficial pirates, until in the early 1800s the bananas and cacao business attracted immigrant Jamaicans, and turned the archipelago into an English-speaking part of a Hispanic nation.

Island culture is much more Afro-Caribbean than Latin-American. Towns and villages have a bright but dilapidated air, and the residents are perfectly matched to the young, hip crowd of international visitors. The high funk factor of thatched bars on stilts and infinite versions of incomers' fantasy tropical getaways, is driven by residents' own appreciation for the natural paradise in which they live. However hard they party, people respect the marvels of the Marine Park surrounding Isla Bastimentos, where one beach is the world's only home to the black polka-dotted, scarlet frog, and another to scores of rare sea-turtles; and to the 350 bird species, sloths, caimans, dolphins, and monkeys that you see throughout the islands.

Only on Isla Colon is uncontrolled tourist development beginning to threaten the very high diversity of marine and terrestrial ecosystems that – along with its delightful, quirky, retro-culture – has made Bocas del Toro famous.

Isla Grande

Isla Grande is where Panamanians go for the weekend to get the city out of their system. You jump in the car or bus, and in two hours you swap Panama City for snorkelling in the Caribbean, on the maze of coral reefs that mark the edge of the Portobelo National Park.

La Isla (everyone calls it just 'La Isla') is in fact only 166 m (550 ft) from the mainland. Although it's thick with tropical flowers, coconut palms and greenery, the largest of the islands in the area and the easiest and cheapest to get to, nobody went until the potholes in the road from Portobelo were repaired. By the time that happened, La Isla was safe from either ribbon development or high-end exclusivity. There are still no roads on the island – just a walkway that ambles past the bars, markets, street vendors, small restaurants, few hotels and lots of basic but comfortable, rental cabanas that have sprung up along the beachfront. Most of the island isn't even accessible, because it's carved up into half a dozen private estates, and apart from the path across its centre, you enjoy its charms from the waterline on three sides.

Isla Grande is your chance to do a full-on tropical Caribbean island, with excellent reefs, fluffy clouds and shimmering turquoise waters, at almost no expense, and with no hassle getting there. It's so lovely, and people are so happy to be there that every weekend, as you stroll, you encounter impromptu parties on the public beach and on the main walkway. You're expected to join in; and often you'll find one or more of the small community that has always lived here, fishing and growing coconuts, and now making sure you've got food, drink, music and good fellowship to help your day go well.

POPULATION:
200 (2007 estimate)

WHEN TO GO:
Any day of the week, any time of year. Weekends are obviously much more crowded, but with people who contribute to the happy, carefree atmosphere of release from quotidian stress.

HOW TO GET THERE:
By car or bus from Sabanitas or Portobelo, to La Guaira; then by water-taxi for a five-minute ride to the island.

HIGHLIGHTS:
The Spanish Forts and ruins at Portobelo, once (16th and 17th centuries) one of the world's most important cities.
La Punta, the sweeping curve of sandy beach at the island's western end.
Walking around the island on its rocky waterline: even at weekends, you can feel like Robinson Crusoe.
Climbing up to the lighthouse.The original lens was designed by Gustave Eiffel, famous for the Eiffel Tower in Paris.
The flowers, butterflies and hummingbirds everywhere.

YOU SHOULD KNOW:
When Sir Francis Drake died of dysentery in 1596 at sea, he was buried in a lead coffin near Portobelo Bay.

Part of the Spanish Forts and ruins at Portobelo

Pearl Islands

POPULATION:
300 (2007) (full-time residents, but generally occupied by many more).
WHEN TO GO:
Year-round
HOW TO GET THERE:
By air, from Panama City; by sea, if you can hitch a ride on a yacht leaving the Canal, to Contadora, Del Rey, or any island en route. Inter-island services are irregular at best.
HIGHLIGHTS:
The hour-long walk round Isla Contadora, marvelling at some of the villas.
Diving the reefs off Contadora, more closely related to South Pacific corals than those of the Caribbean. Playa Larga takes you to the best place for sharks and turtles.
Sitting on a hotel terrace with a drink, enjoying the white tip sharks circling Playa Sueca.
Snorkelling at Playas Cacique, Galeon and Canoa on Contadora – but with a twice-daily tide of up to 5 m (17 ft), you need to time your plunge for low tide.
YOU SHOULD KNOW:
The Pearl Islands are (perhaps without viewers knowing) internationally famous for having featured in three seasons of the reality TV programme *Survivor*, shown in many countries.

Heading south from the Canal, 50 km (30 mi) into the Gulf of Panama, the first thing you see are the Pearl Islands. There are more than 200, most of them tiny, and few even inhabited. Some are hardly more than rocky islets, but most are outcrops of thick jungle fringed with sand, set in clear waters teeming with whales, dolphins, sea turtles and major game fish. By far the biggest island in the archipelago is Isla del Rey, 30,000 hectares (74,000 acres) of thickly-forested hills, natural springs, rivers and waterfalls that power lush vegetation which feels like it might at any time overwhelm the cultivated estates and fruit farms surrounding its main town San Miguel. Its charm lies in its slow pace, matched to the tranquillity of its coves and beautiful valleys.

Much smaller and of hugely greater significance is Isla Contadora, its neighbour. It got its name (it means 'book-keeper') in the era of the Spanish Conquistadors, when Spanish ships from Peru, Ecuador and Chile paused there to take inventory of their massive booty before transhipment across the isthmus, and it has never looked back. It's still a hub, if only for the Pearl Islands, but the yachts stop here to brace up before heading for the South Pacific, and because it is unquestionably the centre of island chic for the region. It's only 304 hectares (750 acres), but it is second home to many wealthy Panamanians, and to several exclusive resorts which trim the rampant orchids and vines to create the kind of Pacific terraces on which you expect to find Maurice Chevalier singing 'Some Enchanted Evening'.

Amenities on Isla Contadora include prolific reefs immediately off the beaches, and a nudist beach at Playa Sueca. It's a wonderful island.

The Pearl Islands Archipelago

San Blas Archipelago

A traditional bright and intricate design as seen on a mola, *a garment worn by females.*

Like so many cartoons, the majority of the 378 islands in the San Blas Archipelago are blobs of white sand with a cluster of coconut palms in the middle, strewn in an arc across the hundreds of miles between the Gulfs of San Blas and Darien, where Panama's eastern Caribbean coast meets Colombia.

Only 49 are inhabited – by the fiercely independent Kuna Indians. These islands (and the whole mainland coastal area of virgin forest opposite) are their territory, Kuna Yala, a semi-autonomous homeland that the Kuna run according to their own economics, language, dress, music and culture. Men still fish from canoes and shin up palm trees for coconuts. Picasso himself would have envied Kuna women their famous skill in creating *mola*, the rainbow-coloured fabrics crowded with geometric fish, birds and jungle animals inspired by tribal legend. You'll see it at its finest in the tidy huts of Isla Maquina, the quietest and most purely traditional settlement in the area. On many islands, the thatch roofs of the Kuna huts almost touch, so walking around is challenging, but the intimacy gives you a glimpse of the mythology and ritual of Kuna daily life, and you'll always be welcomed.

Most visitors just want to hit the tropical perfection of the islands. The most idyllic, inhabited or not, are east and north east of the busy hub, El Porvenir. Achutupu, Kagantapu and Coco Blanco are the most interesting, but the area is surrounded by some of the world's oldest reefs. In an ideal world, of course, we'd all have sleek yachts to reach the truly gorgeous *Cayos* like Holandeses, Chichime and Limones – but provided you don't expect more than a hammock and fresh fish by way of amenities, these remote, uninhabited tropical jewels are well worth the effort of getting there by lesser means.

POPULATION:
40,000 (2007 estimate)

WHEN TO GO:
Year-round, but April to June for the best snorkelling and diving.

HOW TO GET THERE:
By air from Panama City or Colon, to several of the islands; by water-bus or hired boat from Colon (you can often catch a ride with small Kuna merchant ships out of Colon – and let the crew find you your perfect Pleasure Island).

HIGHLIGHTS:
Snorkelling among the brilliant corals of the overgrown shipwreck in the shallow waters off the south side of Achutupu, a 5-star beautiful emerald island set in sapphire sea.
The thatched Kuna museum of culture (mythology, history and rituals at Carti Suitupu, where the existence of electricity from 6pm to midnight enables two dozen bars to attract more foreigners than anywhere in the archipelago, and cruise ships have begun to call.
The hypnotic charm of watching a Kuna woman sewing mola, from a swaying hammock.

YOU SHOULD KNOW:
Once you've been there and met them, you'll always call the area Kuna Yala – 'San Blas Archipelago' is for maps and tourists.

Isla Coiba National Park

Coiba

POPULATION:
Uninhabited
WHEN TO GO:
January to April, the dry season, is the best time to see monkeys and onshore fauna; diving is superb year-round, but subject to unpredictable visibility.
HOW TO GET THERE:
By air, via Panama City, and then charter flight from various points on the mainland (the Coiba airstrip is only open to charter flights); by boat from the beach at Santa Catalina and other mainland points.
HIGHLIGHTS:
Barco Quebrado – where scarlet macaws gather in the largest concentrations on the planet, the most glamorous among Coiba's 150 amazing bird species.
Diving off Bahia Damas, on Coiba's east side – the biggest – 135 hectares (334 acres) – coral reef in Central America.
The mantled howler monkeys, capuchins, fiddler and hermit crabs, Coiba agoutis, and boa constrictors and fer-de-lance on the Sendero de los Monos (Monkey Trail).
Snorkelling among the extensive fields of brain and fan coral, off Granito de Oro's sandy beach.
The jungle river – the Rio Negro.
YOU SHOULD KNOW:
Because of the fragility of Coiba's ecosystem, and the necessity of knowing its waters well, diving and fishing trips should be arranged through local professionals. Local advice has it that 'anyone found tossing an anchor onto the reef will likely get an anchor tossed at his head'.

The largest – 493 sq km (310 sq mi) – island in Central America, Coiba lies 50 km (30 mi) off the Pacific coast of the Panamanian province of Veraguas. Roughly 80 per cent of it is virgin tropical rainforest, home to trees and a profusion of plants no longer found on the mainland. Throughout its hilly centre and network of rivers, thick jungle supports an unusual number of howler and white-faced capuchin monkeys, amphibians, reptiles and commonly seen, rare birds. This is where you go to see the Coiba spinetail, crested eagle, and whole flocks of gorgeous, scarlet macaws. The macaws are the most dramatic visible evidence of the island's hitherto miraculous escape from development.

From 1919 to 2004 it was a prison colony, and even now visitors' access is restricted. In fact, in the interests of protecting Coiba's pristine ecosystem, organized tours currently offer the lowest-impact form of tourism – and help to frustrate opportunities for poaching, illegal logging and other encroachments.

Although visiting Coiba isn't easy, the rewards are stupendous. The island is now the heart of a National Park covering 38 islands and a huge chunk of the Gulf of Chiriqui. Its ecological and marine importance is acknowledged by its designation (2005) as a UNESCO World Heritage Site. The Indo-Pacific current swirls its warmth through the Gulf and around Coiba, bringing with it coral, much of the Pacific tropical underwater life you just don't expect in the usually cold coastal waters of the Pacific Americas, and the larger fish/mammals like humpback whales, white tip, hammerhead, tiger and whale sharks, manta rays, barracuda, amberjack, big snappers, three kinds of marlin, and four kinds of sea turtle. The variety and numbers make for world-class diving – an obvious pedigree once you know that Coiba is the beginning of the underwater cordillera that includes both the Cocos Islands and the Galapagos.

Taboga

Established in 1524 as a deepwater harbour for Panama City, visible at night 18 km (12 mi) away on the horizon, Taboga was the very first Spanish port in the Pacific. Through it passed the gold, pearls and treasures of the Incas, in transit to Madrid, while the trinkets to buy them, and the soldiers to enforce the sale, passed the other way. In 1671 the buccaneer Henry Morgan sacked city and port, initiating Taboga's heyday as a rip-roaring pirates' lair.

The new, deep-draught steamships, and French efforts to build the canal, restored the island's prosperity in the 1870s; incidentally bringing the French painter Paul Gauguin to the area, at the start of his search for the epitome of colourful tropical exotica. He can only have been inspired – Taboga is famous as the 'Island of Flowers'.

Ever since, the island has been Panama City's favourite day or weekend out. It's so close – and so very distant in lifestyle and atmosphere. There are no cars in the maze of paths around the 300 or so houses and Spanish colonial buildings of San Pedro, and just three little trucks to carry cargo and visitors' baggage. Ruins are draped in climbing bougainvillea and hibiscus; roses and huge trumpets of morning glory fill the gardens and walkways. Around the flourishing fields of fruits such as pineapple, orange, red and yellow orchids compete for attention.

Little cafés and bars surround the plaza and beach, and you look up to where you walked, in the thickly forested wildlife reserve that covers the hills encircling the town, and the whole of the steep south shoreline. Nothing much happens these days: to do nothing, on a lovely tropical island a few minutes from the stress of the city, that's why people come.

POPULATION:
850 (2006 estimate)

WHEN TO GO:
Mid-December to mid-May is the dry season – but urban Panamanians come year-round to the highly sociable festivals that take place all the time.

HOW TO GET THERE:
By boat ferry, from the left side of the pier just before the entrance to the Smithsonian Institute building, on the northern side of Isla Noas.

HIGHLIGHTS:
Game fishing – the relatively deep waters round Taboga are full of blue and black marlin, yellowfin tuna, roosterfish, cubera snapper, amberjack, wahoo and Pacific sailfish.
Hanging out, playing games, or chilling over a drink in the 16th century plaza of San Pedro. The church is the second oldest in the hemisphere.
The 17th century fort on El Morro, the rocky islet linked at low tide by a sandbar to the rest of Taboga.
The orchids, lianas, ferns, roses, nisperos, mameyes, nance, mangoes, tamarinds and pineapples that pierce the core of your five senses, often simultaneously.

YOU SHOULD KNOW:
Pissaro used wood from Isla Taboga to build the ships he used to conquer the Incas in 1539.

Playa Honda

Islas los Roques Atoll National Park

POPULATION:
1,500 (2007)
WHEN TO GO:
Year-round. Between July and September the possibility of storms muddying the water makes that period less suitable for scuba-diving.
HOW TO GET THERE:
By light aircraft from Caracas to El Gran Roque (NB. Inbound flights from all points to El Gran Roque come, or remain, under flight control from Maiquetia airport on the mainland); or by boat from Isla Margarita.
HIGHLIGHTS:
Getting a close look at the complex interaction between mangrove species and the degree of water salinity – time and the conditions are on your side.
Sunset from the lighthouse (built 1870-80) on El Gran Roque – the archipelago dotted into the horizon, and on a clear day you can see Mt Avila (about 1,600 m, 5,000 ft) near Caracas.
All the marvels to be seen and done on, in and under water next to one of the biggest and best coral reefs in the Caribbean.
The archaeological remains of Amerindian activities that tell of surviving much more hostile conditions than you'll find today.
YOU SHOULD KNOW:
There are no superlatives to describe the sense of peace you get in the Los Roques Archipelago.

The Los Roques Archipelago is one of the world's biggest National Marine Parks, and lies 145 km (80 mi) due north of La Guaira, the mainland port for Caracas. About 50 coral cays and sand bars are arranged in a huge oval around a lagoon, but it's only from the air you get a true idea of its scale – it covers the same area as the whole of the Virgin Islands.

The fragility of the islands and their ecosystem is all too obvious. Luckily they are shielded from eastern currents by a 24 km (15 mi) coral reef running from north to south, and a second barrier running 32 km (20 mi) from east to west. Protected since 1972, they represent a pristine environment that attracts only the most discerning visitors, who come either in their own boats or yachts in search of solitude and untrammelled tranquillity, or in small groups by light aircraft, often just for the day, from Caracas or elsewhere on the Venezuelan mainland. The island residents, who are descendants of the 110 families who originally came from Isla Margarita in the early 19th century, to make a living as fishermen, all live on El Gran Roque ('The Big Rock').

They will welcome you as temporary family members, and you'll find that, along with the old style of manners and hospitality, they still use the old ways of fishing to catch lobsters, king conch and Spanish mackerel. If you're not staying on a boat, you'll probably eat the catch at one of the 66 posadas (small family lodges) scattered throughout the island, but all of which are within 100 m (328 ft) of the beach. Los Roques is about countless transmutations of blue and green beauty, and sharing the natural rhythms of a completely unspoiled, discrete ecosystem.

The stunning Los Roques Archipelago

Isla de Margarita

Margarita is mostly as brash as it is beautiful, Caribbean in looks and climate but completely South American by temperament. With 170 km (106 mi) of coastline, mainly endless white beaches, breathtaking coves and picturesque, rocky headlands, and a lush interior where the

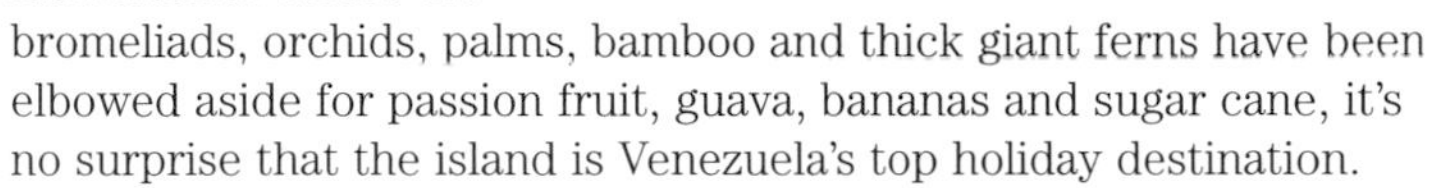

bromeliads, orchids, palms, bamboo and thick giant ferns have been elbowed aside for passion fruit, guava, bananas and sugar cane, it's no surprise that the island is Venezuela's top holiday destination.

It's just 60 km (40 mi) from the mainland, and big enough at 78 km (49 mi) long to get lost in, despite the highly developed agglomeration of malls, high-rise housing, traffic and colossal duty-free warehouses on the Paraguachoan (east-side) Peninsula. This intense urbanization, creeping out from the main coastal cities of Porlamar, Pampatar and Juan Griego towards the much smaller inland capital Asuncion, is made palatable by the determinedly carefree, pervading atmosphere. The casinos and night-life are really good, throbbing with 24-hour merengue and salsa in the crowded streets and on popular beaches like Parguito, Caribe and Puerto Cruz, next to huge tourist complexes. Constant balmy trade winds make Playa El Yaque in the south an international Mecca for windsurfers.

For solitude, tranquillity and romance, you go west, to the Macanao mountains and dozens of small, deep valleys blazing with hibiscus and morning glory against the jigsaw of tropic green, sky and sea. To get there, you cross Margarita's central isthmus, a 10, 000 hectare (25,000 acre) wetland maze called La Restinga National Park. Oysters cling to mangrove-roots along the canals that thread this wilderness paradise of yellow-shouldered parrots and blue-crowned parakeets, and you might see ocelots in the dappled shadows. Eventually, the dozens of lagoons lead you to a 60 km (40 mi) sandbar of crushed coral and seashells.

The impressive Isla de Margarita

POPULATION:
420,000 (2007)

WHEN TO GO:
Year-round. Venezuelans crowd the island at Christmas, Easter, and from July to September.

HOW TO GET THERE:
By air, direct from Europe and N America, or via Caracas, to Porlamar; by boat (car/passenger ferry) from Puerto La Cruz, Cumana, and La Guaira, to Punta de Piedra.

HIGHLIGHTS:
Isla Margarita's five-star history: discovered 1498 by Columbus; site of Spain's very first New World settlement 1500; seized for its pearl industry by the notorious Lope de Aguirre ('God of Wrath') 1561; first territory to fight Spain and achieve independence 1814; and the place where Simon Bolivar was confirmed as leader, and successfully launched the liberation of Venezuela, Colombia, Peru, Ecuador and Bolivia in 1818. Every fort and cannon you see on the island is a tribute to Margarita's indomitable spirit.
Diving for pearl oysters on Isla Cubagua, just offshore – its pearls were worn in the crowns and clothing of 16th century European royalty – and possibly still are.

YOU SHOULD KNOW:
Beer is cheaper than bottled water on Margarita. The island has the reputation of being 'the Caribbean on the cheap' in every way. It's true, but only because the islanders prefer to encourage visitors to enjoy themselves, rather than to fleece them.

San Andres & Providencia

POPULATION:
106,000 (2007) (San Andres 100,000; Providencia 6,000)
WHEN TO GO:
August to May. Every couple should spend one night of a full moon on Providencia's Manchineel Beach – it's the most romantic, quietly Dionysian party of them all. Or come for San Andres' Reina del Coco Festival in November.
HOW TO GET THERE:
By air, from Bogota, Cartagena, Panama City, etc to San Andres; to Providencia, by twice-daily small plane from San Andres. By cruise ship from Cartagena or Panama to San Andres; by water-taxi from San Andres to Providencia.
HIGHLIGHTS:
Johnny Cay, just off San Andres Town (there are water-taxis always waiting on the beach), where you sip your 'coco loco' in the bars lining the beach while the most lissom parade and frolic in the perfect waves.
Eating the delicious local crab – unlike most places, a big, black land crab; you see them all over the islands, where they live in burrows.
Playing Robinson Crusoe on Haynes Cay, which has just enough amenities (food and drink) to keep the game comfortable.
Morgan's Cave on Providencia – spectacular, and you might find the pirate's treasure...
YOU SHOULD KNOW:
On Providencia, meeting people on dive boats is the best way to make new friends.

Only 220 km (140 mi) from the coast of Nicaragua, San Andres and Providencia are the two significant islands of a scattered Caribbean archipelago of cays that in fact belongs to Colombia, 775 km (480 mi) to the southwest.

Providencia was named by its first settlers, English Puritans who in 1627 split from their contemporaries in Massachusetts, USA, in search of somewhere warmer to practise their religion. On arrival, they turned to slavery, then piracy; and from 1670-89, the island was Henry Morgan's HQ until the Spanish regained control and lost interest. Now, the descendants of former slaves and Europeans still speak their own Creole English, and still fish and farm an island barely brushed by tourism. Blessed by copious fresh water running off its three central peaks, it's a fertile eco-paradise, part of a biosphere reserve including most of the archipelago and its 'seven-shades-of-blue' and turquoise waters.

San Andres is coral, not volcanic like Providencia, and though it's equally lovely, it's bigger and much more developed. It's where the young and energetic from the mainland go for excursions – and San Andres' 'spring break' ambience is non-stop and infectious. In between the glamorous parades, people hone their lithe forms swimming or diving in some of the fifty sites in 5,000 sq km (1,930 sq mi) of shallow reefs, wrecks, caves, tunnels, walls, multilevels and night-dive sites that surround the two islands. Their isolation has enabled the huge reef complex to grow astounding sizes of fan, finger and brain corals, with proportionately bigger and colourful shoals of fish darting among them.

In the constant excitement – either about the islands' ecology or the partying – you notice the unusual absence of Americans. It may be wise to be wary, but Colombia's mainland conflicts are pretty well ignored by the islanders. Obviously, paradise is considered neutral.

A balconied wooden building in the local Caribbean style

Islas Rosario

The 23 islands, cays and islets of the Rosario National Park are a geologically infant 5,000 years old, formed when the sea level dropped, revealing areas of coral reef, which were gradually colonized by mangroves and other accretions. Eventually, the islands consolidated into three distinct ecosystems – coastal lagoons, the mangroves surrounding them, and the very dry tropical forests of the interior. On Isla Grande, you can follow an environmental interpretation path that explains the inter-dependence of the systems and their importance to the breeding cycles of the hundreds of marine and bird species you can see all around you.

Along with the islands, the National Park protects the sea floor, and one of the most important coral reefs on the Caribbean's southern shore. Diving, snorkelling and swimming are actually encouraged, but the most beautiful underwater sites are guided, to lessen the risk of physical contact with the spectacular fans and finger-towers waving gently in the slow swirl of the currents. You see giant turtles, dolphins, sea horses and the occasional shark, and in the sea meadows, tiny shrimp hide from scuttling crabs, and fish dart from the translucent fronds to the nearest crevice of coral safety. An open-water Oceanarium gives non-divers the chance to get close to some of the 1,300 species of plants and animals native to the Islas Rosario.

The most extraordinary feature of the Rosario National Park is its proximity to Cartagena, 40 km (25 mi) away. So close to a major port, city and industrial centre, and closer still to the big merchant shipping lanes, the archipelago is a miracle of healthy productivity and abundance. You wouldn't even know it's there except for the crowds of day-trippers, for many of whom visiting a wildlife and nature park might not otherwise be possible. It's a priceless asset to Colombia and the southern Caribbean.

POPULATION:
Uninhabited
WHEN TO GO:
Year-round
HOW TO GET THERE:
By water-taxi from Muelle de la Bodeguita, across the street from the Walled City, El Centro, Cartagena.
HIGHLIGHTS:
The mangrove forests – 5 of 7 American Atlantic species of mangrove thrive in the National Park.
The rarified tree species of the dry forest, like the Higuito, Majagua and Guasimo. Some, like the Matarraton and Totumo have medical significance; all shed their leaves in summer to conserve water.
Migrating birds like the tanga and barraquete duck; and residents like the gavilan pollero, crown pigeon and outrageously colourful parakeets.
The 17th century Spanish fortifications at Isla Boca Chica, built to protect Cartagena harbour from pirates and buccaneers. Now they overlook lovely beaches with great beach-shack restaurants and bars.
YOU SHOULD KNOW:
If you want to visit and/or camp on one of the smaller cays in the National Park, you need to get permission from Park authorities.

A jetty stretches out into the glorious Caribbean.

Isla de Malpelo

POPULATION:
Uninhabited
WHEN TO GO:
December to May: northern winds bring calm cold water and clear skies. May to November: the Equatorial counter-current brings rain and warmer water rich in plankton.
HOW TO GET THERE:
Fly to Bogota, then to Buenaventura. Eight-day tours are run from Buenaventura.
HIGHLIGHTS:
The diving – this is one of the top diving spots in the world due to the clear waters, sheer underwater cliffs, caverns and tunnels.
YOU SHOULD KNOW:
You must have an open-water diving pass and obtain a permit from the Colombian Ministry for Ecology to go on an organized tour.

Around 500 km (314 mi) off Colombia's Pacific coast, a towering barren rock rises from the ocean floor with sheer precipitous cliffs. The island of Malpelo has a slightly sinister air, perhaps because it is the peak of a huge submarine ridge rising straight up from the ocean floor from depths of 4,000 m (13,120 ft). At 376 m (1,233 ft) above sea level, the island is high enough to create its own weather system and it is often wreathed in cloud, however clear the sky. At first glance, the island seems to be a barren rock without vegetation, but deposits of bird guano have helped to establish colonies of algae, lichens, mosses and a few shrubs and ferns.

However, it is not really the island but rather the waters around it that attract visitors. This is one of the most revered diving sites in the world due to its steep underwater cliffs and caves of outstanding beauty, and the amazing visibility. Powerful warm and cold ocean currents interact to create a unique habitat for a huge variety of marine life at all levels of the food chain. These deep unpolluted waters are home to important populations of large predators and pelagic species. Schools of over 200 hammerhead sharks and over a thousand silky sharks, whale sharks and tuna have been recorded here, as well as a newly discovered deepwater shark – the Short-nosed Ragged-toothed shark.

The Malpelo Nature Reserve was set up to protect the rich flora and fauna here, and covers an area with a six-mile radius around the island. In 2006, Malpelo was also declared by UNESCO as a natural World Heritage Site. The sheer granite cliffs plunge into deep water, and on one of these, known as the Altar of the Virgin, you can see countless moray eels, snappers and groupers, dolphin and mantas. At the northern end of Malpelo there is a group of three pinnacles, known as the Three Musketeers, poking out of the sea. Here there is a series of underwater tunnels, caverns and cathedrals crawling with lobsters, groupers, goat fish, silvery bait fish and white-tipped reef sharks. At La Gringa, a sheer granite wall, divers can experience hundreds of female hammerhead sharks swimming in the strong currents. This vast marine park, the largest no-fishing zone in the Eastern Tropical Pacific, provides a critical habitat for internationally threatened marine species, and a wonderful place to view them in their natural surroundings.

A school of Hammerhead sharks

Galápagos Islands

In the Pacific Ocean, some 965 km (600 mi) off the coast of Ecuador, lie the Galápagos Islands. The name comes from the Spanish *galápago*, or saddle, after the saddlebacked tortoises found on the islands. This volcanic archipelago comprises 13 main islands, six smaller islands and 107 rocks and islets. The oldest island is thought to have formed between five and ten million years ago. The youngest islands, Isabela and Fernandina, are still being formed. In 2005, an ash and water vapour cloud rose 7 km (4.4 mi) above Fernandina and lava flows descended the slopes of the volcano and into the sea.

The islands first became part of scientific history when the survey ship HMS *Beagle* under captain Robert Fitzroy visited the Galápagos on September 15, 1835 to chart the navigable waters around the islands. The captain, with his companion the young naturalist Charles Darwin, spent a month making a scientific study of geology and biology on four of the islands before they continued on their round-the-world expedition. Darwin noticed that the finches differed between the islands, and he was told by the governor of the prison colony on Charles Island that the tortoises also showed some small difference between islands. These observations were crucial in the development of Darwin's theory of natural selection which was presented in *The Origin of Species*.

Today, thousands of visitors flock to the islands each year to see the same species Darwin recorded, many of which are endemic to the islands and found only here. They include land iguanas and giant tortoises, blue- and red-footed boobies, albatrosses, flightless cormorants, Galápagos flamingoes, magnificent frigatebirds, Galápagos penguins and the buntings now better known as Darwin's finches. The islands themselves have been designated a UNESCO World Heritage Site, and even the waters around the islands have been made a marine national park to protect the marine animals here, which include Galápagos sea lions, otters and marine iguanas.

Despite these protections, the biggest threat to the islands is the rapidly increasing human population, which was estimated at around 30,000 on 2006, a massive jump from the 2001 census which recorded 18,000 inhabitants. The huge numbers of tourists are also a problem, and may end up destroying the very islands and wildlife that they come to see. In a bid to control the problem, the government is now restricting access and a tour guide certified by the national park authority must accompany each group.

POPULATION:
30,000 (2006)
WHEN TO GO:
Any time of year.
HOW TO GET THERE:
By air from Quito or Guayaquil to San Cristobal Island or Baltra.
HIGHLIGHTS:
Punta Suarez on the island of Española – see the Marine iguanas, Española Lava lizards, Hood mockingbirds, Swallow-tailed gulls, Blue-footed boobies and Nazca boobies, Galápagos hawks, a selection of finches and the Waved albatross.
Punta Espinosa on Fernandina – a narrow stretch of land where hundreds of marine iguanas gather on the black lava rocks. The famous Flightless cormorant can also be seen on this island, as well as Galápagos penguins, pelicans and sea lions.
North Seymour – an extraordinary place for breeding birds, home to a large colony of blue-footed boobies and magnificent frigatebirds.
YOU SHOULD KNOW:
Visitors to the islands must be accompanied by an accredited guide.

Red Marine Iguanas on Espanola Island in the Galápagos archipelago

Ilha Grande

South-east of Rio de Janeiro in the Agra dos Reis district of Brazil lies Ilha Grande, a long mountainous ridge emerging from the turquoise sea. There are over 360 islands in the bay, their forested slopes leading down to some of the most pristine beaches in the world. Much of the area is designated as the Ilha Grande State Park to protect its natural beauty. There was once a penal colony here, the infamous Cândido Mendes, set up to hold the country's most notorious criminals, but today people come here to enjoy themselves in the glorious natural surroundings.

Between the 16th and 18th centuries, the bay saw countless battles between corsairs, imperial invaders and pirates. This has resulted in one of the greatest concentrations of shipwrecks in the world, and a wonderful place for diving and snorkelling. Among the best sites are Lage do Guriri (Ponta de Castelhanos), Jorge Grego Island, Meros and Naufragios Islands. There is even the wreck of a helicopter 8 m (26 ft) below the surface. The ocean floor also offers a fascinating selection of caves and caverns 10–20 m (32-65 ft) high, home to a great variety of fish and corals. The excellent visibility and calm seas make diving here a memorable experience.

But if you prefer less active pursuits, take a stroll around Abraão, a pretty village with whitewashed churches and low buildings in soft hues of yellow, blue and pink. There are restaurants, cafés and craft shops here, and a lovely soft sand beach. This tropical paradise offers many other beautiful beaches, many of them acessible only by boat or kayak. Lopes Mendes is excellent for surfing, windsurfing and other water sports, as are Freguesia de Santana and Saco do Ceu. The calm, shallow, azure waters of Lagoa Azul (Blue Lagoon) on Macaco's Island are home to millions of yellow and black fish and make this a lovely place to spend the day.

Also worth a look is the cave at Acaiá. Inside the cave the intensity of the sun makes the water change from light blue to emerald green. The foam on the water catches the light and twinkles like diamonds, making this an enchanting experience.

Trekking is also a popular activity here. The forested hills are dotted with exotic, colourful blooms, and give way to coastal plains and mangroves. Wildflife includes many bird species, such as parrots and saracuras, in addition to a variety of monkeys, iguanas and snakes. Most of the trekking trails pass through tropical forest and end on a pristine beach, perfect for a picnic lunch.

The rocky coastline of Ilha Grande

POPULATION:
2000 (2007)
WHEN TO GO:
March to June
HOW TO GET THERE:
Ferry from Angra dos Reis or Mangaratiba on the mainland.
HIGHLIGHTS:
Diving and snorkelling around the many shipwrecks in the bay.
Hire a kayak to explore the beautiful coastlines and find deserted, pristine beaches for a swim.
The Praia do Sul biological reserve – explore the abundant flora and fauna of the island.
Abraão – the unofficial capital of Ilha Grande with pretty architecture and interesting churches. Here are the best bars, restaurants and hotels.
YOU SHOULD KNOW:
Most of the bay and islands are designated a State Park to preserve this tropical paradise.

Fernando de Noronha

From the warm clear waters of the Atlantic Ocean, 350 km (220 mi) off the coast of Brazil, the lush green mountains and sheer cliffs of Fernando de Noronha rise in all their tropical perfection. There are 21 islands in the archipelago, all uninhabited apart from Fernando de Noronha itself. The waters surrounding the islands are a National Marine Reserve and home to countless species of fish, rays, sharks and spinner dolphins. Considered to be one of the most important ecological sanctuaries in the world and designated a UNESCO World Heritage Site, the area attracts keen divers and wildlife enthusiasts for the trip of a lifetime.

To prevent damage to the natural landscape, only 420 visitors are allowed on the island at a time. Accommodation is in sustainable tourist lodges which are designed to have minimum impact on their surroundings. The island is nearly always fully booked, particularly in the busiest months of December and January.

First discovered by an Italian merchant and cartographer in 1503, the archipelago is 4 degrees south of the Equator. During its 500 years of history, Fernando de Noronha has been temporarily occupied by the Dutch, French, British and Portuguese, who held it from 1737 onwards and built a series of nine forts on the island to defend their territory.

Fernando de Noronha is known for its beaches, which offer crystal clear blue water perfect for swimming. The Praia do Leão and Baía do Sancho are widely considered to be the best in Brazil. With underwater visibility up to 50 metres, the island is a Mecca for divers and snorkellers, with more than two hundred species of fish, five shark species, sea turtles and dolphins. Snorkelling in the tidal pool of Praia da Atalaia is now restricted to 100 people per day, but well worth the effort for its remarkable diversity of sea life. Lobsters, octopus and numerous fish species inhabit the pool and you may even see a baby shark.

Another memorable sight is the Baia dos Golfinhos (Bay of Dolphins), where every morning more than 1,000 spinner dolphins gather to frolic and dance in the early sunshine. Sea turtles are also prolific here, using many of the wide, secluded beaches as ground on which to lay their eggs.

POPULATION:
2,100 (2000)

WHEN TO GO:
Any time of year; even in the rainy season (April–August) there are only intermittent showers.

HOW TO GET THERE:
Fly from Recife or Natal in Brazil, or take a cruise ship between October and February.

HIGHLIGHTS:
Praia do Leão and Baía do Sancho – these pristine beaches are the best on the island and widely considered to to be the best in Brazil.
Praia da Atalaia – a beautiful tidal pool just 45–60 cm (18–24 in) deep with an enormous diversity of marine life to explore with a snorkel.
Diving in the crystal clear waters to view spinner dolphins, turtles, lemon sharks and other marine life.

YOU SHOULD KNOW:
The smaller islands can only be visited with an official license from the Brazilian Environmental Institute.

Fernando de Noronha at sunset

Florianopolis

POPULATION:
406,564 (2006)
WHEN TO GO:
June to November to see Right whales migrating along the coast.
HOW TO GET THERE:
Fly to Florianopolis International Airport.
HIGHLIGHTS:
Enjoy diving, snorkelling, sailing, surfing, fishing or just relaxing by the sea on one of the many gorgeous beaches.
Catedral Metropolitana – one of the most beautiful buildings in the city, located at Praça XV de Novembro.
Ribeirã da Ilha – this pretty area is famous for its well-preserved fishing villages built by Azorean and Portuguese immigrants.
Lagoa da Conceição – try your hand at wind-surfing, then treat yourself to a seafood meal at one of the good restaurants nearby.
YOU SHOULD KNOW:
Florianopolis is known as Floripa for short.

Florianopolis, the capital city of the Brazilian state of Santa Catarina, lies mainly on the beautiful island of Santa Catarina, which is itself widely referred to as Florianopolis. This vibrant city has the best standard of living of any in Brazil, and the inhabitants know how to enjoy themselves. The island is famous for its long stretches of sugar-soft sandy beaches, excellent seafood and traditional Azorean hospitality. The tropical climate, exotic landscapes and incredibly relaxed way of life make the island a firm favourite with holidaying Brazilians, but it is also becoming more and more popular with the international crowd.

Most of the population lives on the northern end of the island. Although originally settled by the Portuguese who came from the Azores, the city has strong German and Italian influences. In the high season, from December to February, the population of the city trebles and the beaches closest to the city centre – Canasvieiras, Jururê and Praia dos Ingleses – are packed. But there are plenty more not far away.

To the east the lush green hills give way to the wide, sandy beaches of Galheta, Mole and Joaquina. Here the big, exciting waves attract surfers looking for that perfect ride. In the south-east of the island looking out into the Atlantic are the rugged, deserted beaches of Campeche, Armaçao, Lagoinha do Leste and Naufragios, which can only be reached by trail.

Ribeirão da Ilha, on the west side of the island, bears testament to Azorean immigration. The beautifully preserved Azorean and Portuguese fishing villages boast colourful architecture and friendly inhabitants. The historic centre, in Frequesia, has an attractive plaza with the Igreja Nossa Senhora da Lapa do Ribeirão church, and an interesting Ethnological Museum. The area is accessible only via a narrow, winding and picturesque seaside road affording scenic views of Baia Sul and the lush hills of the mainland across the bay.

The Lagoa da Conceição is a famous natural attraction in the centre of the island. The large lagoon is partially surrounded by sand dunes and its shallow waters and high winds make it perfect for wind-surfing. Here are also some of the best restaurants and nightlife on the island.

Florianopolis and the Lagoa da Conceição

Ilha de Marajo

Bigger than Switzerland, Marajo is one of the world's great, fluvial islands. Even though it's open to the Atlantic on one side, it's completely surrounded by fresh water: the force of the Amazon outflow on its north, and the Tocantins/Para estuary on its south side, keep the salty ocean at bay.

Marajo's western half, the Regiao da Mata, is mainly thick forest and jungle. The Regiao dos Campos in the east is an area of low lying fields; and the coast is a spectacular combination of dense mangroves and lovely beaches, flanked by arcades of miritzeiros (Amazon royal palms). Despite seasonal flooding, the east is home to most of the population, and the preferred habitat of the herds of wild buffalo that provide Marajo's sustenance. In the main town of Soure, a few miles up the Rio Paracauari, buffaloes have priority rights of way, but they can still end up as food, transport, or leather goods.

During 3,000 years, Marajo nurtured successive Indian civilizations, who initiated a tradition of ceramic art, brought together at the Marajo Museum in the pretty, rustic town of Cachoeira do Arari. This area is famous for its caboclo culture, waterways and lagoons: it's where you drift in a canoe or small boat to see blue macaws and egrets, giant storks, scarlet ibis and a scandal of colourful, noisy species breaking from the green canopy. Marajo teems with caimans, sloths, monkeys, deer, turtles, boas and countless fish including pirarucus, tucunares, tambaquis and piranhas. It is an entrancing equatorial water-world, its jungle forest constantly renewed and enriched by the Amazon. If you can get past the rudimentary service culture of the island's east coast, you'll find that Marajo is as secretively different from Brazil as Switzerland is from Europe; and in its own way, just as rich.

An Amazon estuary runs through Ilha de Marajo

POPULATION:
250,000 (2007)

WHEN TO GO:
The 'dry' (less rainy) season from June to December/January. Come for the Festivals of Quadrilhas and Boi-Bumba at the end of June; September's AgroPecuária Fair of all things buffalo; or the November regional celebration in Soure of Cirio de Nazaré.

HOW TO GET THERE:
By air taxi from Belem to Soure; by passenger boat, from Pier Escadinha, Belem, to Soure; by car/bus ferry from Icoroaci 13 km (8 mi) from Belem) to Salvaterra.

HIGHLIGHTS:
Getting involved at a fazenda (working buffalo farm) in the jungle.
Witnessing the pororoca – the offshore collision between the Amazon and the incoming Atlantic tide, a phenomenon best seen at the full or new moon between January and April.
Dancing the carimbo and the lundu at rural celebrations.
Praia Pesqueiro and Praia Araruna – two of several beautiful beaches near Soure, where the tide rises and falls a mighty 3 m (10 ft).

YOU SHOULD KNOW:
Wear shoes in and around towns/villages: among the nasty parasites found here are jigger bugs that burrow into human feet.

Ilha do Papagaio

POPULATION:
100 (2007 estimate)
WHEN TO GO:
July to November, when the whales and penguins are on show.
HOW TO GET THERE:
By air to Florianopolis from Sao Paolo, Curitiba or Buenos Aires, then by helicopter, or take the launch from the Veleiros Yacht Club in Floripa; by car, from Highway 101 to Praia do Sonho on the mainland.
HIGHLIGHTS:
Bathing in the crystal magic of the 15 m (50 ft) Zanella waterfall in the heart of the Serra do Tabuleiro Atlantic Rainforest Park, on a trail lit up by colourful tropical birds.
Pondering the meaning of 'God's Eye' and other petroglyphs on Papagaio.
Playing chess on the waterfront of Ribeirao da Ilha, one of the oldest villages, just across the water from Papagaio.
The stone bungalows, bleached boats, and women riding donkeys on cobbled streets past 250-year-old churches in San Antonio de Lisboa – a direct link with the Azorean fishermen who settled Santa Caterina from 1752.
YOU SHOULD KNOW:
Ilha do Papagaio was recently acclaimed in *The Guardian* newspaper as 'the stuff of fantasy'.

Properly speaking, Papagaio is a private island with just 20 stand-alone bungalows set in a forest of palms and fruit trees. It lies at the southern tip of Santa Caterina Island, some 30 km (18 mi) from Florianopolis, the island capital of Santa Caterina State in southern Brazil.

Two things make Papagaio really special. Firstly, most of it is a protected nature reserve, like the 145 km (90 mi) of adjoining coastline that constitutes, onshore, the Atlantic Rainforest State Park of Serra do Tabuleiro; and, offshore, Brazil's Right whale sanctuary. Less than ten years ago, Southern Right whales had been hunted almost to extinction. Now, between July and November, you can see scores of them frolicking with their calves in the area – and because they hug the shore to avoid predators, they regularly come very close to Papagaio's beaches, which protrude into their safety zone.

Secondly, besides having all the delights of a super-tranquil tropic sanctuary, including its own delicious oysters, Papagaio has its own petroglyphs. Geometric rock-carvings of some complexity found recently in and around the island's caves show that this particular paradise once belonged to a sophisticated society that extended right across Santa Caterina Island.

Papagaio also has a third attribute: its ready access to the history and the very different kind of sophistication of nearby Florianopolis, with its 17th century fishing villages, jungle-covered hills, emerald lagoons and 40 sugar-soft beaches, full of bijou clubs and glamorous people. From Papagaio, you get the best of every world laid at your feet.

A sailing boat moored in one of Papagaio's emerald lagoons.

Tinhare Archipelago

Bahia is one of the oldest regions of Brazil, settled by the first Portuguese in the early 16th century; and its atmosphere is famously laid-back. Just to the south of Salvador itself, at the heart of the Costa do Dende (named after the African oil-palms which grow everywhere) is the Tinhare Archipelago. Its small islands dot the deep blue sea, divided by rivers, lush virgin rainforests, mangroves and beautiful hidden bays with picturesque fishing villages untouched by tourism – and a handful of resorts popularized by some of the world's most famous and fashionable people.

Tinhare is the largest at 22 km (13 mi) long and 15 km (9 mi) wide, and Morro de Sao Paolo village at its northern tip is the focal point of most of what happens in the archipelago. Morro is historic – you land beneath the ruins of forts, built in 1630 to defend the bay from pirates, and the main street is a sandy path between old stone buildings now converted to little shops, restaurants and bars.

There are no cars. For transport, you use horses, donkeys or the occasional tractor for long distances, and wheelbarrows to carry your bags. It's a genuinely eco-responsible place but most people come to Morro to party, not to take in the local culture. They soak up the natural splendour, not just because it is so beautiful but also to work off the hangovers they get from the beach parties that explode spontaneously every single night of the summer. Morro is so off-the-wall that its beaches have numbers, not names. It's difficult to imagine anywhere more attractive than Tinhare Island.

WHEN TO GO:
Year-round. Go immediately after Carnival, when Tinhare is still charged with atmosphere and party-people get their second wind.

HOW TO GET THERE:
By air, via Salvador, from Rio or Recife to Morro; by boat, from Mercado Modelo in downtown Salvador or Valenca on the mainland.

HIGHLIGHTS:
The monkeys, birds and orchids you find on the Fonte do Ceu trail through Tinhare's forests.
Praia Segunda (Second Beach), for just one night of your life.
The sensational panorama from the Ruinas da Fortaleza, especially at sunset, when dolphins come out to play.
Moqueca – Bahia's signature dish, a rich stew of palm oil, coconut milk and fish or prawns, with rice, and spiced up with chilli sauce.

YOU SHOULD KNOW:
Pau Brasil (*Caesalpinia echinata*), Brazil's national tree, now an endangered species confined to Brazil's Atlantic rainforest, is still considered the only wood suitable for making violin bows.

Sao Paolo beach

One of the beautiful bays of Isla del Sol

Isla del Sol

POPULATION:
5,000 (2007 estimate)
WHEN TO GO:
October to March, when the days are warmer. Nights are always cold.
HOW TO GET THERE:
By the principal ferry boat, via several of Titicaca's islands, to/from Puno (Peru) from/to Guiaqui (Bolivia). Backpackers can reach the small Bolivian lakeside village of Copacabana by bus or car, then take an open boat for the 1-hour ride to Isla del Sol.
HIGHLIGHTS:
The settlement of Challapampa, set among Inca ruins in the 'V' of two beaches narrowing into an isthmus at the island's northern tip. Jacques Cousteau used a mini-submarine to search the offshore area for the two-ton gold chain of Inca Huascar, part of the legendary Inca treasure sunk in Titicaca when the Spanish reached Cuzco.
The imaginings triggered by the breath-sapping climb straight up 200 ancient Inca stairs, leading from the port to Yumani, the only real 'town'.
The Bolivian 'beach town' of Copacabana, site of the Fiesta de la Virgen de la Candelaria ('The Dark Virgin of the Lake'), carved by Inca Tito Yupanqui in 1592.
YOU SHOULD KNOW:
The Aymara and Quechua of Lake Titicaca, and of Isla del Sol in particular, drive hard bargains in their dealings with the urban world of their visitors – but they are not of that world; and we trespass on their sacred sites.

The biggest lake in South America, and the highest navigable lake in the world, lies at 3,810 m (12,507 ft), its 196 km (122 mi) length spanning the Andean border between Peru and Bolivia. Lake Titicaca is the cradle of Inca civilization – and Isla del Sol is the Incas' holiest site. Here, Inti's (the Sun God's) children, Manco Tupac and Mama Ocllo, burst from a prominent sandstone crag called Titikala (the Sacred Rock), banishing darkness and bathing the world in the brilliance of the re-born Sun. The Incas built a temple on the rock, later expanded by the 10th Inca Tupac, Inca Yupanqui. He also built a convent for the 'mamaconas' (chosen women) and a 'tambo' (inn) for visiting pilgrims, and these are among 180, mainly Inca, ruins on the island. But the excavations at Ch'uxuqulla, above the small Bay of Challa, also show that Isla del Sol had been a sacred place for at least 5,000 years before the Incas.

Even today, most things about Lake Titicaca are at odds with the modern, technological and political world. The Aymara people who farm Isla del Sol grow barley, quinoa wheat, potatoes and maize on the stepped terraces hacked into every available surface of the harsh, rocky terrain – just as their ancestors did for millennia, while the Incas came and went from power. Today, the island is part of Bolivia, but power and ownership simply don't matter when you are actually there. It's the resident Aymara who guard the spiritual continuum of the place. Their fishing, fields and alpaca herds allow no development of conventional tourist amenities or roads (though local families will happily rent you a cabin or room), and the way of life is utterly indifferent to visitors who pace and race. Coming from cities, take the time to pause and drink in the harsh geography, made beautiful by an innate and transcendent sense of peace.

Isla de Chiloé

Chiloé is big, 190 km (118 mi) long and 55-65 km (35-40 mi) wide, with a central spine of mountains that divides the wild, rain-swept, Pacific west coast from its warmer, drier east coast, deeply indented with natural harbours and lots of small islands.

Long before 1608, when the Spanish brought the Jesuits to drive spiritual bargains with the Huilliche, Cuncos and Chonos, the Indians settled and fished these sheltered bays; now they are full of industrial salmon pens. Colonial occupation left a highly colourful architectural mark. In towns like Castro and Chonchi, *palafitos* (stilt-houses) became fashionable in the 19th century – and they, like most other houses and buildings, are painted in a dazzling assortment of bright colours. Chiloé's truly eye-popping heritage, though, is its wooden churches. The Jesuits built hundreds in the 17th and 18th centuries, in each case incorporating local whimsy in a bid to win souls. Imaginations soared in pinnacles, towers, arches and galleries of wood, shaped by folklore and layered by mythology into hymns of colour. They marry native and Christian faiths with such unique beauty that UNESCO has listed them as World Heritage Monuments.

Meanwhile, the Pacific rages against Chiloé's west coast, and even before you reach the Chiloé National Park you'll realize that little has changed since Darwin came in 1834. Riding or hiking through pristine evergreen forest (the Valdivian temperate rainforest is extremely rare world-wide) of myrtle, luma, coigue, tepu and larch, you'll see an unusual amount of wildlife, much of it endemic like the Chiloé fox or Patagonian woodpecker. Reach Quellon in the south and you can watch blue whales close inshore. In Ahuenco, in the Park's northern (Chepu) sector, you can walk across coastal dunes and wild beaches to the only penguin colony shared by Humboldt and Magellan penguins. Chiloé, after all, is famously friendly.

POPULATION:
155,000 (2005 estimate)

WHEN TO GO:
December to March – but you can experience all four seasons within a few hours on Chiloe. In December, flowers bloom everywhere, and there are many local festivals; or come for February's Festival Costumbrista Chilote.

HOW TO GET THERE:
By air, from Santiago to the small airports of Castro or Quellon; by bus and boat, via Pargua (mainland) and Chacao (island) from Puerto Montt to Ancud (N); by boat, from Chaiten or Puerto Chacabuco to Quellon (S)

HIGHLIGHTS:
The waterfront *palafitos, tejuelas* (roof shingles) of Alerce wood, and other colourful architecture around the Plaza de Armas in Castro, founded in 1567.
The wildlife havens on the islands between Chiloé and the mainland – you can reach lots on foot at low tide, or with a small boat.
The winding forest trail of the Sendero El Tepual, and the traditional reed-built Chilote house and Huilliche artefacts of the Museo Artesanal at the National Park.
The 3-storey tower and multiple arches of 19th century Iglesia San Carlos de Chonchi, centrepiece of picturesque Chonchi, (aka 'the three-floored city') built into a hillside.
The ponchos, woollens, wooden crafts and basketry at the Sunday Feria Artesanal, Chiloé's best craft market, in Dalcahue.
Standing among the birds on the wilderness Pacific coast in the streaming rain, beginning to understand Darwin and much else.

YOU SHOULD KNOW:
Chiloé's Huilliche traditional culture is one of South America's most remarkable and relatively complete survival stories – including its folklore and erotic mythology.

Saint-María Church in the town of Colo

SOUTH AMERICA/CHILE

Kerguelen

POPULATION:
70 in winter, 120 in summer (estimates)

WHEN TO GO:
November to March – but year-round the wind speed averages 100 kph (63 mph), the (ice-free) wave heights are commonly 12-15 m (40-50 ft), and it rains violently, or snows, 300 days a year including summer.

HOW TO GET THERE:
By (occasional) cruise ship; or licensed by the French Government in Paris or Réunion, by sea, either accompanying a supply vessel, or with one of the small fleet of fishing boats from Réunion allowed to fish in the archipelago.

HIGHLIGHTS:
Port-au-Francais – the 'capital' and main base, with bar, gym, hospital, library and the well-named chapel of Notre Dame des Vents.
The partly restored 1908 whaling station of Port Jeanne d'Arc, in the NW corner of the Presqu'ile Jeanne d'Arc, across the Buenos Aires Passage from Ile Longue.
Port Christmas, one of the historic geo-magnetic stations, at Baie de l'Oiseau, NW Loranchet Peninsula. It's also the place where Captain Cook anchored on Christmas Day 1776, and coined the nickname of Desolation Islands.
The 'strombolic' volcano of Mt Ross – Grande Terre's highest point at 1,850 m (6,068 ft).
Ile Foch, N of Grande Terre – the largest island with no introduced species (rabbits, cats, rats etc), and used as a reference for the archipelago's original ecosystem.
The enormous number of penguins, seals, albatrosses, petrels, Kerguelen terns and other magnificent bird species.

YOU SHOULD KNOW:
Kerguelen lies on the Antarctic Convergence, where upwelling cold currents mix with the warmer water from the Indian Ocean, thus encouraging the huge number of birds and marine mammals.

Midway between Africa, Australia and Antarctica lies the French territory of Kerguelen, also known as Desolation Island. Officially it's called the Kerguelen Archipelago, but Grande Terre, the main island, covers 6,675 sq km (2,577 sq mi), and the other 300 just 540 sq km (208 sq mi). Grande Terre looks a bit like a spiny lobster on the map, with several peninsulas and promontories, and is deeply indented with fjords, bays, and inlets. Its core is the 550 sq km (344 sq mi) Cook Glacier on the western side: the island's landscape is the result of extreme glacial and fluvial erosion, and one typical effect is the huge, flat and fertile plain of the Courbet Peninsula on the eastern side, formed by the detritus swept from the steep interior valleys.

Kerguelen is the visible part of a giant, volcanic plateau, a micro-continent that sank 10 million years ago. Today, volcanic activity is limited to a few fumaroles – but after discovering sedimentary rocks similar to ones in Australia and India, which point to Kerguelen having once been covered in tropical flora, scientists hope that the archipelago's textbook volcanic formations will explain the break-up of the once-unified super-continent of Australia, India and Antarctica.

Since its modern discovery in 1772, Kerguelen became legendary among sailors firstly for its large numbers of whales and seals, which were rapidly hunted to near-extinction, and secondly for its indigenous cabbage, rich in vitamin C, which saved countless thousands from scurvy during the 18th and 19th centuries. Now, it supports only a satellite tracking station, and a research base for earth scientists and biologists. The marine wildlife and the bird populations have recovered. Captain Cook thought it looked sterile, and named it 'Desolation'. With its restored natural wealth, and at the centre of cutting-edge geological discovery, Kerguelen confounds its nickname.

Cormorant at sunset on Kerguelen

Heard Island

Young bull elephant seals on Heard Island

Heard Island is Australia's only active volcano complex, a roughly 25 km (15.5 mi) cone thrusting 2,745 m (9,006 ft) out of the southern Indian Ocean. From Mt Mawson, the highest point, the Big Ben volcanic massif is linked by a narrow ridge to the 10 km (6 mi) long Laurens Peninsula, a mountainous headland riddled with lava tunnels. Big Ben's shape makes the already vicious weather patterns so bad that Heard Island is reputed to be the wildest place on earth. Even so, it's one of the few places in the sub-Antarctic where continuous weather observation has been possible.

Significantly, no plants or animals have ever been introduced, and since 1972 all forms of human intervention have stopped – so there's no better site to monitor the effects of climate change on permanent glaciation in an undisturbed environment. For example, there are 12 glaciers on Big Ben, contributing to the 80 per cent ice cover of the island, and forming most of the sheer, 100 m (328 ft) ice cliffs that make landing on the island so difficult. Glaciers that used to terminate only in the sea now terminate far inland.

This retreat has benefited flora and fauna. As mosses, lichens, herbs and grasses colonize greater areas, they become habitat for ever-larger colonies of indigenous birds and marine mammals. Heard is a classic example of a sub-Antarctic island with low species diversity but huge populations. There are well over a million macaroni penguins, and tens of thousands of king, emperor, and gentoo penguins; 3,000 pairs of southern giant petrels, 700 pairs of black-browed and 500 pairs of light-mantled albatross, and 31 other species. Heard Island now belongs to them and it has been declared a UNESCO World Heritage Site.

POPULATION:
Uninhabited

WHEN TO GO:
November to March – but summer is no guarantee of better weather conditions.

HOW TO GET THERE:
By arrangement with ANARE (Australian National Antarctic Research Expedition), who monitor all boat movements within the island and offshore Heritage area. NB there is no natural or built harbour or port.

HIGHLIGHTS:
Wedell, Ross and crabeater seals, at the extreme northern limit of their pelagic ranges.
The trypots (used to process seal blubber into oil), cooping iron, gun parts, hut ruins, graves and workshops, among other remnants of the sealing industry at Atlas Cove.
The Heard Island cormorant – an endemic sub-species of only 100 pairs.
The wandering albatross – reported to be breeding for the first time in 1980.
The formations of volcanic extrusion on karst along the Laurens Peninsula.

YOU SHOULD KNOW:
Before decreeing that 'artefacts should not be moved, souvenired or relocated by tourists', ANARE repatriated (to Australia) a 'blubber press and the only known carving on basalt rock from the Antarctic or sub-Antarctic'.

LACE
IRON

EUROPE

Åland Islands

POPULATION:
26,711 (2005)
WHEN TO GO:
May to August for sunshine, December to February for winter sports.
HOW TO GET THERE:
By boat from Grisslehamn or Kapellskär in Sweden, or from Turku in Finland. Fly from Helsinki, Turku or Stockholm.
HIGHLIGHTS:
Exploring the islands and islets in a rowing boat, and discovering the beautiful deserted beaches.
The *Pommern* – an historic sailing ship built in Glasgow at the beginning of the last century, now on display at Mariehamn.
The Bomarsund – the great Russian fortress destroyed by French and British marines during the Crimean War.
Sunrise and sunset over the archipelago – be sure to have your camera handy.
YOU SHOULD KNOW:
Despite being under Finnish sovereignty, the language spoken here is Swedish.

Islands in the tranquil Åland archipelago

In the clear blue waters of the Baltic at the mouth of the Gulf of Bothnia, Åland is an archipelago consisting of around 80 inhabited emerald islands plus 6000 smaller islets and rocks. Officially belonging to Finland, the islands were awarded a wide degree of autonomy by the League of Nations in 1921 to settle a long-running dispute between Sweden and Finland. Åland has its own government, its own flag, its own stamps and its own vehicle licence plates.

Most visitors come here for the slow pace of life and the tranquil beauty of the archipelago. The best way to explore the islands is by rowing boat. You'll soon find a beach all to yourself – perhaps even a whole island.

Fasta Åland is the largest island in the archipelago, with an area of around 1,000 sq km (600 sq mi). Here can be found Mariehamn, the only town in the archipelago, where just under half of the population of the islands live. Founded in 1861, Mariehamn is the centre of the shipping and tourist industries and home to the Landskapsregering – the local seat of government.

In the summer months, from May to August, the Åland Islands receive more sunshine than any of their Nordic neighbours, making them a popular holiday destination. In winter, visitors come for the long-distance skating or to experience ice-boating through the ice-

sheets that form around the smaller islands and skerries.

At any time of the year there are various cultural highlights to entertain visitors, including the Kastelholm. This medieval castle, mostly a ruin today, was home to many Swedish kings who ruled the combined kingdom of Sweden and Finland. The great fortress of Bomarsund was built by the Russians in 1832, but later destroyed by British and French warships in 1854 as part of the campaign in the Baltic during the Crimean War. On the other side of the channel there is a small museum with pictures and objects from the Bomarsund.

Mariehamn's Maritime Quarter is also worth a visit, where you can see traditional boat-building, a smithy and other local handicrafts. The marina accommodates small ships and traditional wooden boats. The Maritime Museum contains exhibitions of historic and contemporary boat-building.

Kvarken Archipelago

This outstanding conservation area in the Gulf of Bothnia consists of around 5,600 islands off the coast of Finland, stretching about 70 km (45 mi) east-west and 60 km (40 mi) north-south. The archipelago is continuously rising out of the sea as a result of glacio-isostatic uplift (see 'You Should Know'); islands are constantly changing and merging, peninsulas expand, reefs and rocks emerge from the sea, and bays evolve into lakes, marshes and peat fens. The rate of land rise is so fast that there are noticeable changes to the landscape within a generation.

Small clusters of low-lying wilderness islands dot the sea. Beaches of stones and boulders are bordered by alder trees, the fens abound with blueberries and rowan trees, and the open heathland merges into forests of pine and spruce. The unique charm of the Kvarken lies in its dynamic scenery, stark natural beauty, outstandingly rich bird life, and picturesque villages.

The landscape was formed under the ice sheet 10,000 – 24,000 years ago by glaciers scraping away vast amounts of clay, gravel, sand and boulders in their path. As the ice melted, this mass was deposited in various geological forms known as moraine. An unusual feature of the Kvarken Islands is the rare "de Greer" ridged moraine, as well as the more usual humps and drumlins of post Ice Age scenery.

The first written evidence of permanent villages dates from the early 15th century, but the archipelago was probably settled much earlier. The inhabitants made their living as fishermen and by small-scale sheep and cattle farming, trading fish and sealskins for grain. Today the Kvarken is sparsely populated, and its World Heritage status ensures that it will remain a protected natural region.

POPULATION:
2,500 (2005)

WHEN TO GO:
April, May, September and October for the bird migrations. June to August for boating, cycling and walking holidays. In January and February you can walk across the iced-over sea.

HOW TO GET THERE:
From Vaasa on the coast of mainland Finland, you can drive to one of the inner islands with a bridge connection, where you can either rent your own boat or take guided cruises.

HIGHLIGHTS:
Valsörarna – the 36 m (118 ft) high lighthouse built in 1885 at Eiffel's workshop in Paris.
Björköby and Raippoluoto – for canoeing through the maze of inlets and a hiking trail to Panike through incredibly varied scenery.

YOU SHOULD KNOW:
Glacio-isostasis is the reaction of a landmass that has been squashed under the massive weight of layers of ice, often kilometres thick. When the ice finally melts, the land "bounces back" as a result of the release of pressure on it and gradually rises up. At the present rate of land-rise the islands of the Kvarken archipelago will, in around 2,000 years, time form a continuous stretch of land between Finland and Sweden, turning the Bothnian Bay into a huge lake.

Stockholm Archipelago

POPULATION:
Highly variable depending on season
WHEN TO GO:
Mid May to early September
HOW TO GET THERE:
From Stockholm, take scheduled or charter boats from outside the Grand Hotel; or get a boat pass from Waxholmsbolaget boat company, which enables you to travel anywhere in their timetable; or rent your own boat if you want to sail independently.
HIGHLIGHTS:
Dalarö Schweizerdalen, – beautiful white beaches.
Dalarö – 15th century Church.
Utö – 200-year-old windmill with amazing view over the archipelago.
Kymmendö – a privately owned island where daytrippers are welcome to stroll through the fields and woods and see the cabin where August Strindberg stayed for seven summers. He described it as paradise.
Sandhamn Pine forest – a beautiful place for walks.
YOU SHOULD KNOW:
By far the best way to explore the Stockholm archipelago is in your own boat – to live out a Robinson Crusoe dream. Many of the islands are uninhabited and Swedish Public Rights of Access permit you to land almost anywhere and pitch a tent. It takes two days sailing to reach the outermost islands.

The Skärgården (skerry garden) stretches 60 km (40 mi) seawards from the city of Stockholm running some 150 km (95 mi) from north to south. It is an amazing labyrinth of some 24,000 forested granite islands, many of them less than 100 m (300 ft) apart. In the evening light especially, this maze of pine-covered rock floating in the sea is heartbreakingly beautiful. Here you can sail for miles, weaving your way past empty forested shores without seeing a soul. For hundreds of years the islands were sparsely populated by seafarers. Only in the 19th century did they start to become fashionable as a weekend retreat for wealthy Stockholmers.

Today, although the central archipelago is virtually a suburb of Stockholm, there are still some outstandingly beautiful places to visit. The outermost island of Sandhamn is renowned for its splendid 18th and 19th century architecture, natural landscapes, and wonderful beaches; and Grinda, one of the tiny inner islands, is a famously romantic place for an overnight stay.

In the southern part of the archipelago, Dalarö is an old customs island with a picturesque charm; the surrounding islands are brilliant for camping and kayaking. Utö, one of the outermost islands, has superb swimming while Nåttarö is noted for its fauna, fishing and pretty country lanes. Nynäshamn is a bustling port with a charming harbour from where you catch the island-hopping ferry.

To the north, Tjockö is the main island of an archipelago of about 350 islands that have a long history as a base for piracy and smuggling. Arholma, the northernmost island of the Skärgården, has a charming old fishing village and amazing views.

Although it is one of the world's largest archipelagos, the Skärgården is relatively unknown outside Sweden. Its hauntingly beautiful atmosphere, an almost spiritual quality, is an extraordinary experience.

Picturesque red huts on the Stora Nassa Island group

Holmöarna

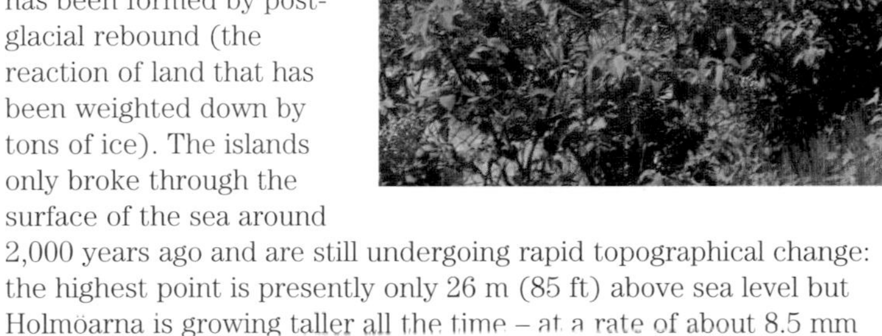

This scenically beautiful island group lies 10 km (6 mi) off the coast in the Gulf of Bothnia. It is Sweden's largest maritime nature reserve – a strange wetland of peat bog and lakes interspersed with heath, woodland and spruce forest. Holmöarna has been formed by post-glacial rebound (the reaction of land that has been weighted down by tons of ice). The islands only broke through the surface of the sea around 2,000 years ago and are still undergoing rapid topographical change: the highest point is presently only 26 m (85 ft) above sea level but Holmöarna is growing taller all the time – at a rate of about 8.5 mm (0.03 in) per year.

The islands appear to have first been settled around 1,300 and by the 16th century there were seven farms in the north of Holmön, the main island. Today this is still the only part that is inhabited – where the ferry comes in at Byviken and the nearby houses alongside a ridge of centuries old farmland, a charming patchwork of small fields that is the only area of cultivated land on the islands.

Nature lovers will be in their element exploring the magical lakes and forest and wandering along the bemusing eastern coast of inlets and skerries, peat bogs and pools, coastal birch woods and rocky shores. From Byviken you can take a boat to the islet of Stora Fjäderägg, an ancient fishing and sealing base that is now a well-known ornithology centre. The only island road runs the full length of Holmön and crosses a narrow strait, the Gäddbäckssundet, to the uninhabited island of Ängesön. To the south, the island of Grossgrunden is open heath that is difficult to access but if you do manage it there is superb fishing in the stretch of water that separates it from Holmögadd, a protected military zone famous for its old stone lighthouse.

POPULATION:
90 (estimate)

WHEN TO GO:
May to September unless you're seriously hardy.

HOW TO GET THERE:
From Stockholm, fly/drive/rail to Umeå, the largest town in northern Sweden. Take the ferry from Norrfjärden, 30 km (19 mi) NE of Umeå. It is free of charge and runs three times daily in the summer and twice daily the rest of the year. When the sea gets iced-up the ferry service is replaced with a hydrocopter service.

HIGHLIGHTS:
Boat Museum, Byviken.
Berguddens Fyr – lighthouse. An especially good spot for bird watching.
Trappudden – cliffs and post-glacial rock fields.
The beach at Jebäckssundet, 5 km (3 mi) south of Byviken.

YOU SHOULD KNOW:
Holmöarna is at the westernmost end of the Kvarken Archipelago – designated a UNESCO World Heritage Site for its extraordinary moraine scenery, formed around 10,000 years ago at the end of the Ice Age.

Lilac bushes on Grinda Island

Bohuslän Islands

POPULATION:
Variable. Many of the islands are uninhabited or only populated during the summer months. You are guaranteed an escape from the crowds.
WHEN TO GO:
June to September
HOW TO GET THERE:
Fly to Gothenburg. Ferries go to the islands from mainland ports such as Uddevalla, Strömstad, Hamburgsund and Smögen, depending on which one you are heading to. During the high season of July and August there is also an inter-island ferry service.
HIGHLIGHTS:
Marstrand – a beautiful wooden town with a 17th century fortress.
Käringön – enjoy fresh oysters and Champagne while having a seawater sauna.
Hållö – an uninhabited, wildly beautiful nature reserve where guillemots breed and where you can plunge into the Marmorbassängen (Marble Pool), a natural pool of deep turquoise seawater enclosed by smooth rock. The archipelago's oldest lighthouse is located here.
Valfjäll, North Koster – a beautiful spot with a little wooden church and wonderful views across the islands.
YOU SHOULD KNOW:
There is not much accommodation on the Bohuslän Islands. If you want to have a real island holiday experience rather than restricting yourself to day trips, you need to do some thorough research and book well in advance.

Wild, rugged and bleak, some 3,000 granite islands and skerries stretch for roughly 150 km (95 mi) along the coast of the province of Bohuslän, west Sweden. They are renowned for their desolate treeless beauty. "...Huge skies, immense seas...everything so bright and shining...such a feeling of isolation" is how Ingrid Bergman described them. She holidayed here for years and her ashes were scattered off the island of Danholmen. These are islands for nature lovers, sailors and divers, with few villages, virtually no nightlife, and hardly any cars.

Although some of the settlements date back to medieval times, the islands were mostly uninhabited until the 18th century herring boom made it viable to earn a living here. Little seems to have changed, apart from the fact that tourists rather than herrings now support the local economy: picturesque fishing villages of pastel painted cottages cling to the rocks; the salt smell of the sea mingles with the scent of dill, allspice, seaweed and smokehouses; seagulls whirl and scream in the vast open sky.

Marstrand is by far the most sophisticated island. It is a popular yachting resort with superb swimming and diving, wonderful seafood restaurants and even the odd late-night bar. The Koster Islands are the other extreme. These, the westernmost islands, are a nature reserve of beautiful beaches and rocky Ice Age landscapes – a paradise of rare plants and Nordic light. The village on Gullholmen is a famously picturesque settlement of quaint wooden houses huddled together, using every inch of space. A footbridge leads to the neighbouring island of Härmanö, one of Bohuslän's largest nature reserves. Väderöarna is a cluster of windswept skerries, home to Sweden's largest seal colony; and a trip to Stora Kornö, perhaps the least touched of all by the 21st century, is a must.

Bohuslän harbour

Gotland

The whole atmosphere of this wonderful island is redolent of the Viking Age – ruins and runestones, cairns, medieval churches, windmills and trolls. According to some historians the original home of the Goths, Gotland lies 90 km (56 mi) east of the mainland and is Sweden's largest island, covering an area of 3,140 sq km (1,225 sq mi). The island is renowned for its natural beauty – a craggy limestone and shale landscape with rugged shores, mainly given over to farmland.

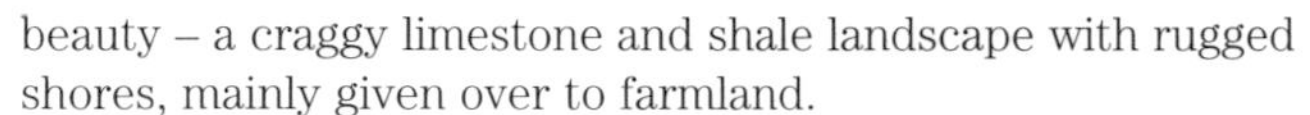

Gotland was once an important independent Baltic nation, eventually integrated into Sweden in 1645. The picturesque medieval city of Visby, a UNESCO World Heritage Site on the west coast, was once the main port of the Baltic with trading links as far away as Arabia. Its massive city walls are 11 m (36 ft) high and 3.4 km (over 2 mi) long; as you walk along its cobbled streets, past rose garlanded stone and wood houses, to the medieval harbour, you can't help being blown away by its Viking charm.

The bleak north coast has a peculiar Nordic beauty with its stony shoreline and breathtaking clifftop views. Most of the island is rich pastoral scenery of fields, woods and moors with drystone walls, whitewashed churches and windmills – perfect for horse riding and cycling. You can always find a secluded spot around the 800 km (500 mi) coast of rocky crags enclosing shingle and sand beaches. All along the east coast spectacular *raukar* – limestone columns up to 6 m (20 ft) high, weathered into extraordinary shapes – stick out of the sea like mysterious trolls. The most famous *rauk* is the island's landmark of Hoburgsgubben (Old Man's Rock) on the south coast which is a magnet for birds.

Part of the city wall of Visby, Gotland

POPULATION:
57,317 (2006)

WHEN TO GO:
Late May to early September

HOW TO GET THERE:
Daily flights from Stockholm. Ferry several times a day from Nynäshamn or Oskarshamn on the mainland, takes about three hours. In the summer season there is also a boat connection with the island of Oland.

HIGHLIGHTS:
Day or overnight trips to beautiful islets of Stora Karlsö and Lilla Karlsö.
Källungen's Kyrka – a 13th century church with 12th century artefacts and pictures.
Lojsta Hed – lovely moorland area.
Bunge Open Air Museum – more than 50 buildings and runestones.

YOU SHOULD KNOW:
This is an excellent place for an outdoor family holiday of biking, boating or camping. Children will be thrilled by the Viking atmosphere and the chance to visit the home of Swedish super-heroine, Pippi Longstocking.

Gotska Sandön

POPULATION:
4 (National Park staff)
WHEN TO GO:
Late May to early September unless you are a serious endurance enthusiast.
HOW TO GET THERE:
By boat from Nynäshamn on the mainland or the island of Faro.
HIGHLIGHTS:
Gamla Gården – an old farm where there are Viking artefacts.
Tarnüdden – the beach on the south coast.
Madame Souderland's homestead – the 18th century house of the first woman to live on the island.
Borgström's – a fishing cottage built out of driftwood and shipwreckage in 1900.
YOU SHOULD KNOW:
Visitor numbers are strictly regulated and you have to obtain a permit. You can stay either in the camping site, a simple cottage or sleeping hut.

Sand dunes at Bredsand

This giant sand dune is the most remote island in the Baltic – isolated in the middle of the sea 38 km (24 mi) to the north of Gotland. It is just 9 km (6 mi) long by 6 km (4 mi) across, part of the crest of an undersea ridge formed by glaciation, almost entirely composed of sand with a few odd areas of moraine and rocky beach. From a distance Gotska Sandon looks completely flat but when you walk around you soon realize how hilly sand dunes can be. The highest point is 42 m (138 ft) above sea level.

Despite its distance from the mainland, there are signs of human activity from the Stone Age onwards. It was used as a seal hunting and fishing base by the Faro islanders, who also grazed their sheep here, but there were no permanent inhabitants until the 18th century. From 1783-1859 the island was privately owned. It eventually became Swedish Crown territory and is now a National Park.

The island is mainly pine woods with ground cover of heather, cowberries (lingon) and moss. In places the forest is incredibly dense and contains many rare insects and plants. The entire coast is bordered by a sand ridge 10-15 m (33-50 ft) high and 100-300 m (330-985 ft) wide where there are shifting sand dunes which move up to 6 m (20 ft) a year.

There is no harbour so landing is a tricky exercise – leaping straight from the ferry onto the shore or, in bad weather, beaching by rubber dinghy. There are few concessions to the 21st century on Gotska Sandon: it is perfectly possible to be stranded for several days, the only transport on the entire island is a single tractor, there are no shops or restaurants, and hardly any inhabitants. If you want an adventure in self-sufficiency this is the place to come.

Faro

Off the northern tip of Gotland, this magical little island is famous for its beautiful sandy beaches, moody landscapes, and dramatically beautiful raukar (limestone rock formations). For years it was a restricted military zone and has only recently been opened up to foreign tourists, although it has long been popular among the Swedes.

The island has a barren, spooky beauty. The west coast is windswept and rocky, the waves beating against the bizarre limestone monoliths, while the east is long drifts of fine white sand. At Ullahau, on the north coast, the shifting sand dunes have been planted with pine trees to stabilise the soil – a perfect children's playground that makes a brilliant winter sledging track. There are hardly any roads on the island. Dirt tracks overgrown with long grass cut through the pine forests and rocky green pastureland where sheep and cows graze. There are fields full of wildflowers, old agricultural landscapes with small fields and disused windmills, dotted with ancient farm buildings more often than not roofed with sedge.

The acclaimed film director, Ingmar Bergman lived and died here. He used the island as a location for several of his films as well as making two documentaries about its people. Visitors to Faro were never able to discover the whereabouts of his house; and the locals still remain determinedly tight-lipped. One wonders for how much longer such admirable resistance to external pressure will endure, for the day that Faro gives up this secret must surely be the day that it starts to lose its mysterious aura. Until that time comes there can be no doubt that everyone who comes here will be bewitched.

POPULATION:
571 (2005)

WHEN TO GO:
The magical atmosphere of Faro is best experienced out of season. Although the weather may be a lot bleaker in April or October than in July and August, the island is at its most beautiful in terms of landscape and light, and you can be certain that it won't be packed with tourists.

HOW TO GET THERE:
From Stockholm either fly to Visby in Gotland or take a train or bus to Nynäshamn and then a ferry to Visby. From Visby go by road to Farosund where you can get the free car ferry to Faro once an hour.

HIGHLIGHTS:
The superb beaches of Sudersandsviken, Ekeviken and Norsta Auren.
Langhammars – a rocky beach with Ice Age monoliths, used as the backdrop in Bergman's film *Through a Glass Darkly*.
Faro Fyr – the 19th century island lighthouse, 30 m (98 ft) high.
Digerhuvud – a nature reserve with huge raukars (sea stacks), diving area and fishing village of Helgumannen.
Ryssnäset – a stark coastal landscape.

YOU SHOULD KNOW:
Faro has no bank, medical services or police and the natives speak their own dialect.

Raukar on one of Faro's beaches

Oland

POPULATION:
25,000 (2005)
WHEN TO GO:
To see this beautiful island at its best, avoid the high season of July and August when it is packed with holidaymakers. It is well worth sacrificing a bit of sunshine for the sake of experiencing the Alvaret landscape in the famous Nordic light and tranquillity of April-May and September-October.
HOW TO GET THERE:
Fly/drive/train to Kalmar via Stockholm then cross over one of the longest bridges in Europe, built in the 1970s.
HIGHLIGHTS:
Borgholm Castle – 'the most beautiful ruin in Scandinavia' and one of Sweden's most famous buildings, reflecting more than 800 years of architecture and history.
The 17th century wooden windmill at Gettlinge. medieval drystone bridge, Alby. Böda Crown Park – woods in North Oland where you can see elk.
Lange Erik – the tallest lighthouse in Sweden, on the northernmost point of the island.
YOU SHOULD KNOW:
Oland is by far the best swimming spot in the whole of Sweden and a favourite place for Swedish holidaymakers. It's a great place for a family holiday with plenty to see and do.

Once the private Royal Game Park of the Swedish monarchy and now one of the most popular Swedish holiday resorts, Oland is a 137 km (86 mi) long, narrow strip of land running along the southeast coast. It is renowned for its superb beaches, unique World Heritage limestone landscape, four hundred windmills, and ancient history.

Oland was first inhabited around 10,000 years ago when settlers from the mainland crossed the iced-over sea. There are traces of ancient cultures all around the island, including the remains of nineteen Iron Age ring forts, an incredibly well preserved Viking burial ground at Gettlinge, and a completely preserved fort at Eketorp dating from 400 AD. The city of Borgholm is the island's historic capital; the Swedish royal family have their summer residence at Solliden Palace nearby.

Böda Bay at the northern end of the island is 20 km (12 mi) of soft white sand, windswept dunes and pine forest. As you go south, the forest gradually gives way to fields and meadowland. Suddenly this pastoral scene comes to an abrupt end; spreading endlessly in front of you is an apparently barren steppe; you have reached the Stora Alvaret – a bizarre limestone shelf, scraped bare by glacial movement and almost bereft of soil. It covers 260 sq km (100 sq mi), more than a quarter of the island's surface. Although it appears to be treeless, if you look closely you will see a stunted forest. The trees are unable to grow any taller because they are water-starved – rain simply seeps straight through the limestone. A huge variety of rare grasses and wild flowers grows here and the ground contains thousands of fossils – an invaluable resource for botanists and the study of prehistory, and one of the strangest and most fascinating landscapes of Europe.

A row of post mills on Oland

Tjörn

Sunrise over Tjörn

Just north of Gothenburg on the west coast, Sweden's sixth largest island covers an area of 167 sq km (65 sq mi) and is the gateway to the beautiful islands of the Bohuslän archipelago. The coastline is extraordinarily complex and varied – rocky shores, sandy stretches of beach, winding inlets and sheltered bays that are natural harbours for yachts and small boats. The island has a stark beauty and liberating sense of space about it. At its highest point, 116 m (380 ft) above sea level, you feel on top of the world as you stand on one of the craggy granite outcrops gazing across the rough treeless pasture and ancient drystone walled meadows full of wild flowers, with breathtaking views of open skies and the sea.

There are traces of human habitation on Tjörn from the Stone Age onwards and you can see Bronze Age pictures carved into the rocks and the remains of Iron Age burial cairns. For many hundreds of years the islanders have depended on the fishing and boat building industries for their livelihoods. There are pretty little villages and hamlets of red and white painted houses dotted around the coast where people still work at these traditional activities. In recent years the island has also become well known as an artists' colony; it is home to the Nordic Watercolour Museum, opened in 2000 – a centre for contemporary art, research, and training in watercolour techniques. This is the only centre of its kind in Europe, in an inspiring setting in the historic main village of Skärhamn. There are also private galleries and exhibitions all over the island.

Although Tjörn is a popular resort among the Swedes, its economy is not reliant on tourists; it is mercifully free of the rampant commercialism that is so often found at holiday destinations.

POPULATION:
15,022 (2005)
WHEN TO GO:
Mid-May to early September
HOW TO GET THERE:
Fly to Gothenburg. Tjörn is only 50 km (30 mi) away and, since 1960, has had a bridge connection to the mainland.
HIGHLIGHTS:
Sundsby – 18th century wooden stately home with a history dating from 1338.
Rörestrand beach – watch the sunset over the water.
Sandhölmen – bathing island off the pretty fishing village of Skärhamn, reached by boat.
Tjörne Huvud – wonderful view for miles across the sea.
Mjörn – a nearby island to the northeast with wild landscape and shell banks.
Walking the trail at Toftenäs through beautiful scenery.
YOU SHOULD KNOW:
Tjörn is a great place for cycling, walking, boating, and nature holidays, and an ideal base from which to explore the beautiful islands of the Bohuslän Archipelago.

Lake Mälaren Islands

POPULATION:
24, 000 (estimate)
WHEN TO GO:
late May to early September
HOW TO GET THERE:
On Stockholm's doorstep; some of the islands are connected by bridge. Two-hour ferry ride from Stockholm to Bjorkö.
HIGHLIGHTS:
Lovö kyrka – a parish church dating back to the 12th century.
Svartsö Slott, Faringsö – a rococo castle and park.
Stenhamra, Färingsö – a beautiful rugged area with old stone quarry.
Hantverksstallet, Gällstäo Gård – ancient oak trees in historic grounds.
Ekebyhovs Slott, Ekerö – one of the oldest wooden castles in Europe.
Luruddon, Helgö – ancient ruins with dwellings dating back to 200 AD, where a 6th century Buddha from India has been found.
YOU SHOULD KNOW:
Although there are ferries to the islands, the best way of visiting them is by yacht so that you have the freedom to explore at will. Most of the islands have guest harbours for mooring.

Lake Mälaren is the third largest lake in Sweden, adjoining the city of Stockholm. Its many islands contain an incredibly rich heritage, a breathtakingly lush historical landscape with palaces, old churches, runestones, forty castles, and two World Heritage Sites – the Palace of Drottningholm on the island of Lovö and the Viking sites of Birka on Bjorkö and Hovgården on Adelsö.

The Royal domain of Drottningholm with its Chinese pavilion, wooden theatre, and Baroque gardens is a stunning 17th century palace complex, modelled on Versailles and set in the pastoral landscape of Lovö. Birka, Sweden's oldest city, and one of its most famous ancient monuments, is situated on Bjorkö – an island that today has a romantic, desolate air about it. Birka was founded at the end of the 8th century and for nearly 200 years was at the centre of European trade. In the late 10th century the build up of sediment made the lake too shallow for ships to negotiate and the city was abandoned. Hovgården, the king's farm on the neighbouring island of Adelsö, remained in use until the late Middle Ages. Today these lovely islands are beautiful places in which to walk and cycle as well as see the incredibly well preserved Viking ruins.

The landscape of Lake Mälaren was formed at the end of the Ice Age when the land started to rise as a result of the gradual melting of the ice-cap lifting the tons of pressure that had been bearing down on it. Quite apart from the cultural heritage contained in these islands, the moraine ridges and lush valleys are scenically lovely – rolling farmland dotted with oak trees, pine forest on rocky hills, and trees and grasses growing right down to the waterline.

The stunning interior of Drottningholm Palace

Visingsö

Legend has it that a giant called Vist threw a lump of turf into Lake Vättern so that his wife could cross it without getting her feet wet; and so Visingsö came into being – a 14 km (9 mi) long, skinny island in the southern part of the second largest lake in Sweden. It is famous for its lovely countryside, historical sights, spotlessly clean beaches, and views of the lake from almost anywhere.

Visingsö has probably been inhabited since the Stone Age; the number of burial mounds attests to a sizeable prehistoric population. There are also a large number of graves from the Viking era.

In the 12th and 13th Centuries Näs Castle, on the southern tip of the island, was the seat of the king of Sweden. The castle was burned down in 1318 and most of it is now submerged in the lake but what remains is well worth a visit. At the turn of the 16th and 17th century the aristocratic Brahe family built the castle of Visingsborg. After 1680 it remained empty for some years, before being used to hold Russian prisoners of war who, it is said, burned it down in 1718; today one wing remains – an impressive sight. In the 1830s, a farsighted plan on the part of the Swedish navy for future ship building material led to the planting of the Elkskogen – 360 hectares (890 acres) of oak trees. However, by the time they reached maturity, their wood was no longer needed. Consequently, today you can lose yourself in a magnificent mature oak forest, the largest in Sweden.

Walking and cycling trails lead you through a rural idyll of open meadows, berry fields and, of course, the woods. Visingsö has an atmosphere pervaded with history, myth and legend in one of the most scenic regions of Sweden.

POPULATION:
800 (2007)
WHEN TO GO:
May to August
HOW TO GET THERE:
From Stockholm fly/drive/rail to Jönköping. Road to Gränna, 30 km (19 mi) to the north. Car ferry service from Gränna to Visingsö, twice hourly in the summer.
HIGHLIGHTS:
Kumlaby Church – a 12th century building with 15th century frescoes and a tower you can climb.
Tempelgården – gallery and outdoor art centre with a temple built by the theosophists, who had their European centre here in the early 20th century.
A horse-drawn carriage ride around the island.
Visingsborg Örtagård – a 17th century Baroque style herb garden, with 900 species of herb and spice plants.
Erstad Kärr – nature reserve marshland in the north of the island, a breeding ground for wading birds.
YOU SHOULD KNOW:
Lake Vättern is the fifth largest lake in Europe, covering an area of 1912 sq km (746 sq mi). Its deepest point, just south of Visingsö is 128 m (420 ft). The water is so pure that it can be safely drunk untreated from almost any place in the lake.

Sheep grazing by Lake Vättern.

Ven

POPULATION:
371 (2005)
WHEN TO GO:
May to September
HOW TO GET THERE:
Ferry from Landskrona on the Swedish mainland several times a day; and from Helsingborg and Copenhagen in the summer only.
HIGHLIGHTS:
Brahe Observatory and Museum – dedicated to Tycho Brahe.
The distillery and whisky bar at Backafallsbyn – the largest collection of single malts in Sweden.
St Ibbs Church – dating back to the 13th century in a lovely spot above Kyrkbacken village.
Nämndemansgården farm – the oldest farmstead on the island; now a heritage museum.
Eating the island's pasta – a Ven speciality made from locally produced durum wheat.
YOU SHOULD KNOW:
The cliffs are heavily eroded in some places and you should be careful when walking along them. Bikes and tandems can be hired on the island so there is no need to travel with one.

The Pearl of Oresund is a tiny dot in the strait between Sweden and Denmark, 8 km (5 mi) off the Danish coast and just 4.3 km (under 3 mi) from Sweden. It is only 7.5 sq km (3 sq mi), a shelf that slopes downward south to north from its highest point at 45 m (150 ft) to just 5 m (16 ft) above sea level. The island is incredibly fertile farmland with rich clay topsoil on layers of shifting sand and clay.

Ven belonged to Denmark until 1660 when it fell into Swedish hands. During the 16th century, Tycho Brahe, a famous Danish astronomer, persuaded the king of Denmark to give him the island so that he could study the stars from here. He built a Baroque castle, now in ruins, and for the next 20 years took measurements of the night skies, incredibly precisely considering his primitive equipment.

When you go ashore from the ferry at Bäckviken, the grassy slopes of the celebrated Backafall cliffs rise straight out of the sea 40 m (130 ft) high, giving amazing views over the Oresund to the Danish and Swedish coasts. Kyrkbacken, the oldest and largest harbour with a yachting marina, is a pretty village with a fish smokery. There are sand beaches near both harbours.

Ven is a lovely island for camping and cycling holidays. Paths cut through the fields and copses so that you can wander freely everywhere. Coastal walks take you along some hair-raising cliff tops where you will see dramatic landslips and down to curious rocky shores full of marine life. Artists and craftsmen have been attracted here by the inspiring tranquillity and you can visit their studios and workshops. The bucolic surroundings, sea views, lively harbours, and sense of history make it an ideal place for anyone seeking a relaxing island break.

A marina on Ven Island

Svalbard Archipelago

Further north than Alaska and all but a few of Canada's Arctic islands, the Svalbard Archipelago is the northernmost part of the kingdom of Norway, lying about half way to the North Pole. The Gulf Stream current sinks close to the archipelago, and were it not for its moderating influence, the islands would be locked in ice throughout the year and totally uninhabitable.

There are three large islands in the Svalbard Archipelago – Spitzbergen, Nordaustlandet and Edgeøya – and many islets. The islands are barren, rugged and desolate, with around 60 per cent of the land covered with glaciation. The mountains look like steep piles of rubble, with peaks jutting out at all angles. Some are covered in snow all year round and many valleys are filled with glaciers. Vegetation is very sparse and there are no trees on the islands. However, the warm season brings many Arctic flowers into bloom, transforming parts of the islands into colourful meadows.

The islands were probably first discovered in the 12th century by the Vikings, but the earliest recorded landing here was by William Barents in 1596. Spitzbergen, the largest of the islands, became an important whaling station in the 17th and 18th centuries, and many animal trappers also arrived to exploit the archipelago's natural resources. By the 20th century, whale stocks had become so depleted that coal mining replaced whaling, an activity which still goes on today. The main settlement on the island is Longyearbyen where most of the population lives. The other islands in the archipelago are largely uninhabited, except for research scientists.

Being so far north, Svalbard gets the midnight sun from 20 April to 23 August, although the sun itself may be hidden by fog. The polar night, where the sun does not rise above the horizon at all, runs from 26 October to 15 February, and most visitors stay away during this time unless they are here to see the Northern Lights.

Most tourists come here to experience the raw climate, see the midnight sun, and try their hand at some of the exciting activities on offer here, including snowmobile trips, kayaking, ice cave exploration, dog-sleding, skiing and horse riding. The tourist board organizes many activities and tours, some of which include one or more nights of wilderness camping. Although it is possible to arrange your own activities, most visitors choose to go on an organized tour with a professional guide because of the number of polar bears on the island. Anyone straying outside the main settlement is required to carry a rifle, and know how to use it.

POPULATION:
2,400 (2005)
WHEN TO GO:
April to August
HOW TO GET THERE:
Fly from Oslo or Tromsø to Longyearbyen, or go on an organized cruise.
HIGHLIGHTS:
Try dog-sleding or driving a snowmobile.
Wildlife watching – the islands have as many polar bears as people so you are bound to see some. There are also Arctic foxes, reindeer, walruses and seals here.
Boat trips – join a boat to see whales, dolphins and seals, plus the breeding colonies of seabirds, including puffins, on the cliffs.
The intricate maze of raised stone 'doughnuts' at Kvadehuksletta on the west coast of Spitzbergen, caused by an extraordinary natural phenomenon called frost heave.
Svalbard Museum – the museum in Longyearbyen tells the story of Svalbard, from the discovery of the archipelago, 17th century whaling history, expeditions, winter trapping techniques, flora, fauna, geology and mining history.
YOU SHOULD KNOW:
In most of Svalbard's buildings, including some hotels and shops, you are expected to take off your shoes before entering.

A snow field and mountain on Spitzbergen

Greenland

POPULATION:
57,100 (2006)

WHEN TO GO:
May to July for 24-hour daylight; November to February for polar darkness. The Northern Lights are usually most impressive in the months of September and March.

HOW TO GET THERE:
By air, from Copenhagen or Baltimore, to Kangerlussuaq (W); from Reykjavik to Nuuk (SW) or Kusuluk (E); from Copenhagen to Narsarsuaq (S). Kangerlussuaq is the hub for domestic flights within Greenland. Visitors also use scheduled ferries on the west coast, or helicopters. Cruise ships call at Ittoqqortoormiit.

HIGHLIGHTS:
Whale safaris from Nuuk – in summer humpback and minke whales congregate just offshore; and you might also see fin, blue, sperm and pilot whales, and narwhals.
The Viking longhouse, Tjodhilde's Church and extensive Brattahlid ruins at Qassiarsuk, near Narsarsuaq – from where Leif Eriksson set sail, and 'discovered' Newfoundland.
A sailing trip among the icebergs calved by the Ilulissat Icefjord – when the low-lying midnight sun bathes 100 m (330 ft) column icebergs in golden light.
A trip by zodiac or snowmobile on the edge of the sea ice, in the National Park that occupies the whole of northeast Greenland – your best chance of seeing a polar bear.
Bathing in the hot springs on Uunartoq Island in southern Greenland – the stone-dammed pool is surrounded by wild flowers, and a panorama of mountain peaks and drifting icebergs.
The white-tailed eagle, peregrine and gerfalcon, fulmar petrel, aavooq (eider) and aqisseq (ptarmigan) – among 60 breeding and 170 migratory bird species.

YOU SHOULD KNOW:
The Icelandic Sagas describe the arrival in Greenland of Norse settlers in 982. The last word concerning the Viking population is an account of a wedding in Hvalsey Church, Qaqortoq (still standing) in 1408, found in the annals of the Vatican, in Rome.

A self-governing province of Denmark, Greenland is the world's biggest island. An ice sheet up to 3 km (1.9 mi) thick, 2,500 km (1,553 mi) long, and up to 1,000 km (600 mi) wide covers 81 per cent of it. That represents 10 per cent of the world's fresh water, and it's so heavy that it has caused the central land mass to subside more than 300 m (1,000 ft) below the surrounding sea level.

Constant movement recycles the ice sheet, and in places it's 100,000 years old at its edge. Enormous glaciers are forced outwards to the coast, where they break off into icebergs. The Sermeq Kujalleq glacier on the west coast reaches the sea through the Ilulissat Icefjord, advancing at 19 m (65 ft) per day and calving over 35 cubic km of ice per year. Now in dramatic retreat – 15 km (9 mi) in four years – the World Heritage Site of Illulissat is a spectacular demonstration of climate change.

Ice defines Greenland's culture and ecology as well as its weather. People have lived on its ice-free margins for 4,500 years, and in the south and west you can see hundreds of major ruins demonstrating the fusion of Inuit, Viking and recent Danish cultures. You can participate in modern Inuit culture in Qaanaaq in the north. Besides the traditional drum dancing, singing and kayak demonstrations, you can hunt or fish on a dog sled trip among walrus, seal, musk oxen and huge bird colonies. In season, it's one of the best places to revel in both the midnight sun and the Northern Lights (Aurora Borealis).

Ice here locks both land and sea, and culture belongs to the hunter/gatherer and the polar bear. Yet global warming means that the fate of hundreds of millions of us depends on the future of the Greenland ice sheet.

Nuuk, the snowy capital of Greenland

Clare Island

POPULATION:
150 (2005)
WHEN TO GO:
May to September
HOW TO GET THERE:
Ferries run from the mainland throughout the year, weather permitting.
HIGHLIGHTS:
The square tower, which served as Grace O'Malley's Castle, on a rocky headland at the harbour.
The ruins at Tuar Mor of a signal tower, built in 1804, as an answer to the impending threat of a Napoleonic invasion.
A visit to the neighbouring island of Inishbofin with its ruined Cromwellian castle.
YOU SHOULD KNOW:
Grace O'Malley was a notorious pirate for 50 years. At the age of 37 she gave birth on board ship whilst being attacked by Moorish pirates, and after a brief rest, joined the battle, and of course, triumphed.

Just 5 km (3 mi) from County Mayo, off the north west of Ireland, Clare Island stands guard over the entrance to Clew Bay. Only 8 km (5 mi) by 5 km (3 mi), the island is dominated by two hills, Knockaven to the east, and Knockmore to the west. Clare is fertile, green, undulating and treeless, with hundreds of sheep dotted over the landscape, their wool providing yarns which are dyed and worked into beautiful, individual scarves, bags and other woven items.

Inhabited for 5,000 years, Clare Island has many ancient sites. These include the remnants of ten promontory forts, Bronze Age cooking sites, Iron Age huts and field systems, and a megalithic tomb. The charming, white painted lighthouse on the western side has been in private hands since 1965, first as a B&B but now as a rarely used second home. Fantastic views can be enjoyed from the 19th century Napoleonic signal tower.

Clare Island is home to a 12th century Cistercian Abbey in which can be seen the remains of some of Ireland's best murals, depicting mythical figures, warriors and animals. It also contains the tomb of the island's most famous resident, Grace O'Malley, the 16th century pirate queen. During her colourful life she headed 20 pirate ships, fought – and met – Elizabeth I, and lived here in Granuaille Castle, which is due to be renovated.

Clare is also well known for the *craic*, and many wedding parties take place here as a result. There is no resident policeman here, so the opening hours of the island's bar is a moveable feast. Should a policeman be travelling from the mainland, that fact will be known in good time, since the ferry is owned by the O'Malleys, who also own the hotel…

A rain storm over Clare Island

Aranmore

Aranmore, sometimes known as Aran, lies off the indented west coast of Donegal, and is the largest of the little group of islands to be found there. At 5 km (3 mi) long by 4 km (2.5 mi) wide, and only a 5-minute, fast ferry ride away from the mainland, Aran is rapidly becoming a holiday island.

Most of the permanent population live around the southern and eastern coasts – and evidence that Aranmore has been inhabited since at least 800 BC is visible in the shell middens (mounds) found on the southern beaches. To the west, spectacular cliffs rise from the sea, and from Glen Head there are splendid views across to the mainland. Hills rise in Aranmore's centre, but most of the landscape is rocky, with many small lakes. The country roads are peaceful and the island is terrific for walking and mountain biking.

At the end of the 17th century, Aranmore was a centre of the herring fisheries, with over 1,000 people employed in the industry. However, in the mid-1800s a combination of clearance by the landowner, and famine, hit the population hard and many families left for the New World. Subsequently, the landowner's house became the island's first hotel and, where fishing was once the crux of the economy, now people fish for pleasure. Cowan's Lake, the island's reservoir, is one of the few European lakes in which rainbow trout breed naturally, while two other lakes contain brown trout.

The lighthouse at Rinawros Point was first built in 1798, but was rebuilt in 1865. The Old Coastguard Station gently decays nearby, but there are rock arches and sea caves to be seen. Enjoy the sweeping, golden, sandy beaches at Aphort and Leabgarrow, and later – perhaps best of all – visit the six or seven pubs on the island, one of which will surely tick all your boxes…

The craggy cliffs of Aranmore Island

POPULATION:
522 (2006) growing to 1,500 during summer when ex-pat families return and tourists arrive.

WHEN TO GO:
May to September

HOW TO GET THERE:
By ferry from Burtonport.

HIGHLIGHTS:
The Cave of Slaughter, where a Cromwellian captain committed a massacre in 1641.
A walk to the island's highest point at Cnoc an Iolair (hill of the eagle), where sea eagles once bred, and from which there are fine views.

YOU SHOULD KNOW:
Aranmore is twinned with Beaver Island, Lake Michigan, where many emigrants settled in the 1850s. The two communities exchange visits, and a memorial was erected at Loch an Chomhanaigh in 2000. It is rainbow trout brought from North America in 1900 that have colonized Cowan's Lake.

The ruins of O' Brien's castle on the site of a ring fort near the village of Ballyhees on Inisheer Island. The 15th century castle was destroyed by Cromwell's invading army in 1652.

Aran Islands

POPULATION:
Inishmore: 900; Inishman: 200; Inisheer: 300 (2005)
WHEN TO GO:
At any time, but the weather is best during summer.
HOW TO GET THERE:
By ferry from Connemara and Clare, or by air.
HIGHLIGHTS:
Inishmore
Dun Eochla, the smallest but well preserved fort.Arkin's Castle, built in 1587.
Teampall Bheanain, the ruins of one of the smallest churches in the world.
Inishman
Dun Chonchuir, a large, 5th century, oval fort, with spectacular views.
Teach Synge, the beautifully restored house lived in by dramatist John Millington Synge when he was on the island.
Inisheer
Take part in the festival at Caomhain Caomhan's ruined church, each 14th June.
The 1934 Robert Flaherty film *Man of Aran*, for a superb depiction of life as it was lived on the islands.

Lying across the mouth of Galway Bay are the Aran Islands, Inishmore, Inisheer and Inishman. This popular group has inspired many artists and writers, as well as archaeologists and tourists.

First inhabited around 3,000 BC, the Arans were occupied by Stone, Bronze and Iron Age man, and they contain many early Christian monuments. Persecution of Catholics in the mid 17th century brought many more people, who, finding the islands rocky and inhospitable, devised a brilliant method of producing the topsoil needed for agriculture. Seaweed and sand spread on the rocks created fertile soil and grassland, and a totally self-sufficient way of life evolved.

Inishmore is the largest, most populated and developed island, and the good sized harbour is a hive of activity, particularly during summer, with people coming and going on ferries and yachts, and small boats busying about. Often referred to as an outdoor museum, Inishmore contains over 50 pre-Christian, Christian and Celtic monuments, as well as the extraordinary stone fort of Dun Aonghasa.

Inishman, the middle island, is the least populated and least developed of the three. There are two stone forts to visit, one of which, unusually, is square rather than circular. Inishman is also home to a collapsed Neolithic wedge tomb, Dermot and Grainne's Bed, named after the tragic lovers of Irish mythology. For more worldly interests, this is a good place to purchase some gorgeous Aran knitwear – don't confuse it with the knitwear from Scotland's Arran Islands.

Inisheer is the smallest of the Arans, but it too has a great deal to offer. Here you will find a large, 16th century castle, a 12th century church and a revered holy well. On the rocks is the wreck of the cargo ship *Plassey* which foundered here in the 1960s. The islanders rescued the entire crew safely, during storm force winds.

Valentia

Valentia Island lies at the north west end of the Iveragh Peninsula, at the entrance to Dingle Bay in County Kerry. The island is within the reach of the Gulf Stream, and has an unusually mild climate. Famous today to listeners to the BBC Shipping Forecast, Valentia was the European terminal of the first communications link with America with the laying of the transatlantic telegraph cable in 1866.

At 11 km (7 mi) long and 3 km (2 mi) wide, Valentia has a great deal to offer visitors throughout the year, including early Celtic sites, standing stones, crosses and holy wells. The lighthouse, which was once a Cromwellian fort, gives an unparalleled view over the Atlantic.

Inhabited since 6,000 BC, there are many ancient remnants of man's activities here, but signs of a much older inhabitant came to light in 1993. An undergraduate geology student discovered the fossilized footprints of a tetrapod, Acanthostega, which climbed out of the water and walked here some 365 million years ago. This is now an internationally important site, as it is the only one of its kind in Europe.

Valentia is a lovely place, with wonderful walks, beautiful views, beaches, bogs and cliffs. Knightstown, the island's hub, is a Georgian village, though the red clock tower overseeing the harbour is Victorian. In the north east of Valentia stands Glenleam House. In the 1830s its owner, the 19th Earl of Kerry, planted a unique sub-tropical garden here. Renowned amongst gardeners, it is now possible to stay in the house as well as walk amongst the gardens and woods. Valentia's climate turns the entire island into a delight. Wild flowers grow abundantly, honeysuckle tumbles over stone walls, and every road is lined with hedges bursting with brilliantly colourful monbretia and fuschia, an experience which is best enjoyed on foot or by bicycle.

POPULATION:
650 (2005)

WHEN TO GO:
Any time, though April to October is probably best.

HOW TO GET THERE:
The island is accessible via the bridge from Portmagee on the mainland. However, it's much prettier to arrive in the harbour at Knightstown by boat from Reenard Point.

HIGHLIGHTS:
Listening to traditional Irish musicians playing in the pubs in the evenings.
Deep sea angling or shore fishing.
The Skellig Experience Visitor Centre, which will fill you with enthusiasm for a trip to the nearby Skellig Islands.
Diving – there are two dive centres on Valentia.
The memorial at Foilhommerum Cliff to mark the laying of the transatlantic cable to Heart's Content, Newfoundland.

YOU SHOULD KNOW:
Valentia's famous slate quarry, opened in 1816, was an important employer here, and it is Valentia slate that you see when admiring the roof of the House of Commons in London. Above the quarry entrance is a statue of the Madonna, and just inside is a grotto, with water tumbling into pools.

Cromwell Point Lighthouse on Valentia Island

Skellig Islands

POPULATION:
Uninhabited
WHEN TO GO:
From April to late September, weather permitting.
HOW TO GET THERE:
Only 10 boats are licensed to land on Skellig Michael, each carrying a maximum of 12 people, so book ahead. Fitness is essential as there are almost 700 steep steps to negotiate before reaching the monastery.
HIGHLIGHTS:
The bird life: gannets, fulmars, storm petrels, Manx shearwaters, kittiwakes, guillemots and many more. Puffins – 4,000 on Skellig Michael alone, are always popular.
In the seas around you may see grey seals, minke whales, dolphins and possibly even a basking shark.
The Skellig Experience Visitor Centre on nearby Valentia Island.
YOU SHOULD KNOW:
By the end of the 18th century, the pilgrims who came here were all young men and women, who came to party, not to pray. Their exploits are documented in amusing poems known as 'The Skelligs List'.

Situated about 13 km (8 mi) west of the coast of Kerry rise two extraordinary, rocky islands known collectively as The Skelligs, that, because of their history and ecological significance, are one of Kerry's most special attractions – though they are not for the faint-hearted.

Skellig Michael, the larger of the two rocky outcrops, rises sharply to some 212 m (700 ft), and near the summit, sited precariously on a ledge, are the remains of an early Christian monastery. Its foundation remains shrouded in mystery, but it is known that a small community of about a dozen monks and an Abbott was based here continuously between the 6th and 12th centuries before finally de-camping to an Augustinian monastery on the mainland.

The community lived an amazingly austere life. Six beehive-shaped huts and two boat-shaped oratories remain in a moving testament to the Christian faith. The huts are made of drystone, circular in shape and mortar free, with rectangular interiors having corbelled roofs, and sleeping platforms and shelves built into the structure. The island continued to be a place of pilgrimage until the 1700s and today, after all these centuries of being lashed by storms, the buildings remain intact. On visiting, one can only be astounded that people spent their lives here.

During the 1800s, George Halpin Sr – one of Ireland's greatest lighthouse designers – built two lighthouses here, manned by keepers working on a rota system. Today only one still beams out its warning, and it is fully automated.

Both islands are notable for their bird life, and Little Skellig, where there is no landing point at all, is Ireland's largest and the world's second largest Northern gannet colony, with almost 30,000 pairs. The scale and diversity of the seabird population makes The Skelligs one of Ireland's most important seabird sites.

The monastery on Skellig Michael

Great Blasket

A beautiful bay and the remains of an old stone dwelling on Great Blasket

Great Blasket is the largest of six islands that lie to the west of the Dingle Peninsula. The islands are uninhabited, except during the summer months, when three people live on Great Blasket; one is a weaver and the other two run the café and the youth hostel. The island is hilly, about 6 km (4 mi) by 0.8 km (0.5 mi) wide, and is home to donkeys, rabbits and seabirds.

During the 13th century the islands were leased by the Ferriter family, who built a castle here. Sadly there are no ruins to be seen, as the stones were removed in 1840 and used to build a Protestant soup school, which closed after the Great Famine in 1879. At the same time, all but 100 of the islanders left. Until the early 1800s the islanders survived by growing crops, hunting, and fishing from the shore. The arrival of the seine boat turned them away from the land and into fishermen, catching great numbers of mackerel and pilchard. Later they took up lobster and crayfish fishing and for some years had a successful system running where they exchanged shellfish for tobacco and alcohol.

What is left of Great Blasket's village is situated on the north east of the island. In the 1920s and 30s the young people could bear the privations of life here no longer, and they began to leave for the mainland and further afield. Those who remained struggled on, growing a few vegetables and living their traditional life. By 1953/54 even these few people had to admit defeat. In the last few years, some of the stone cottages on the island have been renovated, and visitors can come to explore the place and stay here for a night or two.

POPULATION:
Uninhabited except in summer
WHEN TO GO:
April to October
HOW TO GET THERE:
Ferries run from the mainland every two hours.
HIGHLIGHTS:
The peace and tranquillity of Great Blasket can be enjoyed while exploring this lovely island. The views are superb.
Diving over the wrecks of several ships from the Spanish Armada.
YOU SHOULD KNOW:
During the 1920s and 30s some remarkable literature was produced in Great Blasket. Autobiographies describing the extraordinary every day life that was led here, all written in the Irish language, have become classics of Irish literature.

Holy Island

POPULATION:
Uninhabited
WHEN TO GO:
June to September
HOW TO GET THERE:
Organized boat trips leave from Tuamgraney, a village on the mainland where the novelist Edna O'Brien was born in 1932.
HIGHLIGHTS:
The10th century Round Tower, in which St Cosgrath, an anchorite, lived and died.
The Saints Graveyard, with its 11th century grave markers.
The 13th century St Mary's Church, the largest building on Holy Island.
Visit some of the other islands in Lough Derg – itself the third largest lake in Ireland.
YOU SHOULD KNOW:
During the 17th and 18th centuries, hundreds of pilgrims came here to do penance by walking around the island seven times, and thereby being cleansed of sin. Gradually the pilgrimage turned into a time of excess rather than piety, as it was believed to be impossible to commit a sin whilst on holy ground. In 1846 the fun was brought to an end.

A place of pilgrimage for hundreds of years, Inis Cealtra – or Holy Island – has been a home to pre-Christian and Christian communities since the year dot. Covering a mere 20 hectares (50 acres), it is a repository of churches, monastic cells, and pre-1,000 AD crosses. The famous bullaun stones, (rocks or stones with deep cups carved into them), dating from the Bronze Age or earlier, lie mainly in the central and eastern part of the island, where most of the religious sites stand.

During the 6th century, St Colum founded a Benedictine monastery on Holy Island, but it was St Caimin, the 5th Abbott, whom people still revere, and many people still bear his name. After his death, the monastery continued to flourish, and was renowned for its learning. Frequent Viking raids over the next few centuries caused the monks much hardship, but in the 10th century, the warrior and chieftain, Brian Boru, who was born nearby, helped re-establish the church here, which continued to thrive until the dissolution of the monasteries and the arrival of Protestantism in the 1500s. At this point all the churches were de-roofed and left to rot – indeed today St Caimin's Church is the only one of six churches on the island that has been fully restored.

Lying at the mouth of Scarrif Bay, Lough Derg, County Clare, Holy Island is fairly hilly, with open fields grazed by animals brought over by boat. There are trees and shrubs, particularly around the edges, while the interior is covered with wild flowers during spring and summer, in particular narcissi, innumerable amounts of which cover the ground. It continues to be a place of burial, with local boat owners providing transport over to the island, where family plots in St Michael's churchyard are still used.

St Caimin's Church

Cape Clear Island

Cape Clear Island is an absolute gem, deserving of all the superlatives you can think of, the pot of gold at the end of the rainbow. Only 5 km (3 mi) long by 2 km (1.5 mi) wide, it is Ireland's most southerly inhabited point, and because of its position, its climate is more benign than that of the mainland.

Cape Clear is one of Ireland's last remaining *gaeltacht*, (Irish language speaking), islands, and during the summer months the small, permanent population swells considerably with an influx of students, anxious to brush up their language skills. This was the birthplace of St Ciaran, supposedly the earliest of Ireland's pre-Patrician saints, and the ruins of his 12th century church stands near the harbour.

The island has several ancient remains, including Megalithic standing stones and a 5,000 year-old passage grave. The ruin of the 14th century O'Driscoll Castle stills hugs its headland overlooking the harbour, which is the island's commercial centre. The castle itself is very hard to reach, a feat only to be attempted on a fine weather day.

Cape Clear's physical position off the coast of County Cork puts it firmly in the path of thousands of migrating birds – indeed it is one of the country's foremost bird watching sites. As long ago as 1959 an Observatory was established near the harbour, manned by enthusiastic and knowledgeable ornithologists.

This is a hilly, fertile place, with soaring cliffs, gentle hills, bogs, a reed swamp, a lake, lovely beaches, remote coves, heathland and farmland – just the ticket, in other words. Undeveloped and unspoilt, heather and gorse cover the hills, which in spring and summer are bright with wild flowers, while in autumn the bracken turns a deep russet red, lending a rich, mellow glow. Winter brings fierce gales, and the locals amuse themselves with storytelling and musical evenings around roaring fires.

POPULATION:
140 (2004)
WHEN TO GO:
June to September for festivities, April, May and October for tranquillity and bird watching.
HOW TO GET THERE:
By ferry from Baltimore on the mainland, all year round.
HIGHLIGHTS:
Spotting dolphins, whales, leatherback turtles, sunfish and basking shark in the surrounding waters.
The Old Lighthouse.
Learn a little more history by visiting the Cape Clear Museum.
Admire the surreally beautiful wind turbines.
Dive, windsurf, sail, canoe and fish off the island.
Enjoy the *craic* of an evening in one of the island's pubs.
YOU SHOULD KNOW:
That the first weekend of September is the time for Cape Clear's International Storytelling Festival, when professional storytellers from around the world keep you spellbound for hours.

A stone cottage overlooking Roaring Water Bay

Dursey Island and Sound

Dursey Island

POPULATION:
12 (2003)
WHEN TO GO:
April to October
HOW TO GET THERE:
By cable car from Garinish, on the mainland.
HIGHLIGHTS:
Walk the well-signed Beara Way, which extends onto the island.
Birdwatching – Dursey Island is renowned amongst birders, receiving thousands of seabirds as well as hawks and falcons. Rare species from America and the Arctic can be spotted here.
Visit the island's antiquities – the O'Sullivan Beara family vault in the old graveyard, the ruined castle, St Mary's Abbey, the standing stones and the Napoleonic signal tower.
Enjoy spectacular views of the off-shore islands and the West Cork coastline.
YOU SHOULD KNOW:
In the 1970s Charles Haughey, then Taoiseach, Prime Minister, of Eire, got caught up in the tricky waters of the Dursey Sound, and sailed his boat into the rocks, requiring rescue by the local lifeboat. Remember, if you are visiting Dursey, there's nowhere to stay and you must bring your own food and water.

Off the south-western tip of the Beara Peninsula, lies the island of Dursey, separated from the mainland by the narrow Dursey Sound, a stretch of water with a very strong tidal race. The most westerly of Cork's inhabited islands, Dursey is home to only three families, although its numbers swell during the summer months with visitors looking for the tranquility that the island can guarantee.

Dursey Island has a long history, as evidenced by the bullaun stones here. The ruined church was built by the monks of Skellig Michael, and during the worst excesses of the Vikings, Irish slaves were held on the island to await ships to remove them. During the early 1600s, Queen Elizabeth's forces sacked O' Sullivan Beara's castle here, and all the captives were thrown to their deaths from the cliffs. Much more recently, a mere 30 years ago, the government decided to relocate the islanders to the mainland, following the collapse of the fishing industry, and almost everyone left.

Dursey is the only island in Europe connected to the mainland by cable car. Riding high above the swirling waters, it can carry six passengers or one cow, and takes about six minutes to complete its journey. Regulars describe it as being 'like travelling in a big biscuit tin', and locals and animals are always given precedence over tourists.

Dursey has only partial electricity, and no running water, shop or pub; its inhabitants live simple, almost spartan, lives. However, the island is beautiful, with high cliffs rising over an indented, rocky coastline, its interior a patchwork of fields divided by old, drystone walls and ditches, sheep dotted here and there. Scarlet fuchsias bloom beside small waterfalls that tumble over the rocks, and aside from various ancient remains, there are also three deserted villages waiting to be discovered.

Achill Island

Off the west coast of County Mayo lies Ireland's largest island, Achill, a picturesque place that boasts the highest sea cliffs in Europe on its northern coast. A popular tourist destination, Achill is connected to the mainland by a swing bridge that enables cars to cross as well as boats to pass. Two large, bleak mountains, Slievemore and Croughan, both rising over 650 m (2,100 ft), loom impressively over the island, 87 per cent of which is formed of peat bog, home to unique communities of plants.

Believed to have been inhabited since 3,000 BC, Achill's megalithic tombs and promontory forts are evidence of its long history. Kildamhnait Castle, built during the 15th century, is also known as Grace O'Malley's Castle, as it once belonged to Achill's ruling family, the O'Malley clan, of whom Grace was the most famous, or infamous, member.

There are several pretty villages on the island, and plenty of choice as to where to stay. Most of the island's architecture is modern, and less attractive than the traditional whitewashed, raised gable cottages of yore, but the building boom of the last 30 years gave much needed work to the islanders, as well as providing many holiday homes. At the base of Slievemore mountain lies the fascinating Deserted Village, thought to have been abandoned during the Great Famine. Almost 100 roofless stone houses stretch out along the road, a strange, slightly eerie sight.

Around the southern tip of Achill runs a 40 km (25 mi) stretch of road, Atlantic Drive. Best travelled by bicycle, this takes you past a ruined 18th century church, a holy well and provides spectacular coastal views. The island boasts five Blue Flag beaches, including the lovely Keem Bay in the west, and Annagh, only accessible on foot or by sea.

POPULATION:
2,700 (2004)

WHEN TO GO:
Accessible all year round, Achill is at its best during the summer months.

HOW TO GET THERE:
By air to Knock, train to Westport, and then bus or car.

HIGHLIGHTS:
Achill Mission at Dugort. Known as The Colony and founded in 1831, this Protestant mission and surrounding buildings is an important historical site.
The Valley House near Dugort, where a notorious attack on an English female landowner occurred in 1894.
The lovely villages of Dooagh and Dooega.
The Achill Seafood Festival, held each July.

YOU SHOULD KNOW:
An ancient prophecy by Brian Rua O'Cearbhain foretold that 'carts on iron wheels' would carry bodies into Achill on both their first and last journeys. In 1894, the Westport – Newport railway was extended to Achill Sound. Amazingly, on its first journey, the train carried the victims of the Clew Bay Drowning and on its last, in 1937, it carried the victims of the Kirkintilloch Burning disaster.

The beautiful sandy beach of Keem Bay

Tory Island

POPULATION:
170 (2001)
WHEN TO GO:
June to September for the best weather.
HOW TO GET THERE:
Ferries run from four ports on mainland Donegal from June to September, weather permitting.
HIGHLIGHTS:
An Cloigtheach, the Bell Tower, built in the 6th or 7th century and the last remnant of the monastery that dominated the island until the 16th century.
Leac an Leannan, the Wishing Stone. This is a flat-topped rock that visitors are advised not to try to stand on – instead you can still make a wish if you manage to throw three stones onto it.
The Tory Lighthouse, built in 1828 by George Halpin Sr, a famous designer of Irish lighthouses.
YOU SHOULD KNOW:
During the 1970s, conditions were so poor that it was thought the population would have to move to the mainland. However, with the help of a semi-retired priest from Dublin, who lobbied relentlessly on their behalf, that plan was dropped and help was forthcoming.

The prehistoric Balor's Fort looks out over Tory Island

Tory Island is tiny, only 5 km (3 mi) long and 1 km (0.75 mi) wide, but with four towns and a number of historical sites, it remains a strong community. Rugged, treeless, bleak and buffeted by wind, Tory Island is also remarkably beautiful in its way. Both mystical and remote, this granite rock rises from the sea off the north-west coast of Donegal.

In the past, the island's economy relied on fishing and farming, but today it is reliant on governmental support. Few people visit Tory Island, and most of those who do, come to see the group of artists who work here. In 1956 the painter Derek Hill arrived on the island. A local man, James Dixon, looked at Hill's painting and said he thought he could do better himself. This led to the birth of the Tory Island school of painting, and today not only does the island have its own gallery, but its artists have been shown internationally. Patsy Dan Rodgers, one of the artists, has been designated Tory's 'King' and representative. He is an honorary member of New York University where an exhibition of these depictions of a fast disappearing way of life was shown to great acclaim.

The islanders are very traditional, Gaelic-speaking, and they live simply. Tory Island is an extraordinary place to visit and to enjoy the various sights, such as the 12th century Tau Cross, one of only two in Ireland, or Dun Bhaloir, Balor's Fort, situated on a peninsula with high cliffs on three sides, it is reached by crossing a narrow isthmus. Otherwise why not just watch the seabirds, marvel at the shifting light on the cliffs and sea, and socialize with the locals?

Rathlin

The island of Rathlin lies about 9 km (6 mi) off the north east coast of County Antrim in Northern Ireland and less than 25 km (16 mi) from Scotland's Mull of Kintyre. Only 7 km (4 mi) long by 1.6 km (1 mi) wide, and shaped like a boot with its toe pointing towards Ballycastle Bay, it's a small island with a big history.

First inhabited in 6,000 BC, Rathlin became a source of flint implements. St Columba is said to have stayed here en route to Scotland in the 6th century and in 735 AD the island suffered the first of the many Viking raids on Ireland. Robert the Bruce is said to have stayed in Bruce's Cave, gaining inspiration from a spider weaving its web across the entrance, although this is one of several places said to own that distinction. In 1575 hundreds of women and children, refugees of the MacDonnell Clan, were slaughtered here by men led by Francis Drake. Rathlin was fought over by both Scotland and Ireland, and was finally agreed to be Irish in 1617.

These days Rathlin is one of Northern Ireland's Special Areas of Conservation, and is an RSPB Reserve. A viewing platform has been spectacularly sited over two great basalt crags named the 'Stags of Bull Point', where thousands of sea birds, over 30 species, wheel and fly. Rathlin is, most importantly, home to the largest colony of Atlantic puffins in Europe. Thousands of birders visit each year, though its permanent population is tiny.

Around the island, the waters are treacherous and rough, and despite the presence of three lighthouses rising amongst impressive cliffs, forty shipwrecks lie beneath them. In 1898 Marconi transmitted the first commercial radio signals from the East Lighthouse to Ballycastle. In spite of – or perhaps because of – the dangerous seas, Rathlin has always been known as a smuggler's haven.

Rathlin Island

POPULATION:
75 (2001)

HOW TO GET THERE:
By ferry from Ballycastle to Church Bay.

WHEN TO GO:
April to August for the puffin breeding season.

HIGHLIGHTS:
The West Lighthouse.
Exploring the sea caves and watching the seal population.
Diving over some of the 40 shipwrecks.
The standing stones, Iron Age fort and the remains of Bruce's Castle.

YOU SHOULD KNOW:
In 1987 Richard Branson crashed his hot air balloon into the sea a few kilometres off Bull Point after a record-breaking flight from Maine, USA. He and fellow balloonist Per Lindstrom were rescued by a fishing boat; they later returned to the island with a £25,000 cheque for the Rathlin Island Trust, towards the renovation of the old Manor House.

Isle of Man

POPULATION:
80,058 (2006)
WHEN TO GO:
Any time of year, but June to early October for beach holidays.
HOW TO GET THERE:
By air or sea from the UK and Ireland.
HIGHLIGHTS:
The Laxey Wheel, the largest working water wheel in the world.
The House of Manannan, with its replica Norse longship.
Castle Rushen in Castletown and nearby Rushen Abbey.
Ballaheannagh Gardens.
Moore's Traditional Museum, with its working demonstrations of Manx kipper curing.
The inscribed Celtic and Viking stone crosses in the churchyards of Maughold and Brannan.
YOU SHOULD KNOW:
One of the island's main attractions is the annual TT race, an international motorcycle race run over the mountain course at Snaefell, the highest peak on the island at 621 m (2,036 ft).

A British Crown dependency, though not actually part of the UK, the Isle of Man lies smack in the middle of the Irish Sea, in the centre of the British Isles. Relying on the UK for its foreign policy, defence and trade, the islanders are fiercely independent and proud of their heritage. Its parliament, Tynwald, is widely considered to be the world's oldest continuous parliament.

Inhabited since Neolithic times, settled by Celts and Vikings, the island only came under the control of the Crown in 1765. Ferries from England brought tourism during the Victorian era, an industry of continuing importance, but the island's success story has been its low taxation economy, and the development of off-shore banking and other financial services.

A central valley bisects hills to the north and south of the island and much of the interior is moorland, with deep valleys and pockets of woodland. Most of the towns and villages are set in protected bays around the coast. Douglas, the capital, has a marvellous Victorian promenade. Peel, in the west, is the island's only city, its harbour busy with fishing boats, once the mainstay of the economy. Linked to Peel by a causeway is St Patrick's Isle, with its 14th century castle walls enclosing ruins that encompass the island's ancient history. In the 1980s the burial site of an important Viking woman was found here, and her jewellery and other effects reside in the Manx Museum.

The Isle of Man is a treasure trove – here you will find endless prehistoric and early Christian sites, stone crosses and promontory forts. Take a trip to Cregneash in the southwest where traditional village life continues as it has for hundreds of years. If history is not for you, hike through the beautiful countryside, get around by steam or electric train, or enjoy a simple seaside holiday.

Rows of bay-fronted hotels and guesthouses line the Victorian promenade in Douglas.

The Isle of Wight

The sweeping bays of the Isle of Wight

Possibly the best known of England's islands, the Isle of Wight lies in the English Channel, separated from the mainland by the Solent. A ridge of chalk, one of the thickest in the British Isles, runs across the centre of the island, ending dramatically in the three white sea stacks known as the Needles, from the last of which rises a red and white banded lighthouse that was built in 1859.

The island's history goes back 10,000 years – and before that, dinosaurs roamed the countryside. The Romans called it Vectis; they arrived here in 50 AD, stayed for 400 years and left a legacy of two well-preserved Roman villas for us to enjoy today. The Normans built Carisbrooke Castle and further fortifications were built by the Tudors. By the 19th century, the island had become a tourist destination, and Queen Victoria bought Osborne House in Cowes as a summertime retreat, returning there to die in 1901.

About half of the island is designated as an Area of Outstanding Natural Beauty, and there are some 40 Sites of Special Scientific Interest, with habitats supporting the now rare red squirrel, and the Glanville fritillary, an endemic orangey-red butterfly. The coastal path and seven long distance trails enable the visitor to enjoy the island's downs and woodlands as well as its long sandy beaches, dramatic cliffs and coastline.

Sandown, Shanklin, Ryde, Ventnor and Yarmouth are all family holiday destinations, but it is Cowes that is internationally known as a yachting centre, and Cowes Week brings thousands of visitors for its highly competitive races. Another draw is the unexpected annual Garlic Festival, and, for the young, the music festival. First organized in 1968, and featuring stars such as Bob Dylan and Jimi Hendrix, the Isle of Wight Festival was revived in 2002 to instant, enormous success.

POPULATION:
132,731 (2001)
WHEN TO GO:
Any time, but May to early October for summer holidays.
HOW TO GET THERE:
By sea from the mainland.
HIGHLIGHTS:
The Needles Battery.
Brading Roman Villa.
Mottistone Manor.
Tennyson Down and monument.
Appuldurcombe House, near Wroxhall. Ryde Pier.
YOU SHOULD KNOW:
A number of famous people have loved and lived on the Isle of Wight. These include the painter J.M.W. Turner, the poets Keats and Tennyson – who wrote 'The Charge of the Light Brigade' in his house at Farringford: the architect John Nash, the author J.B. Priestly and the film-maker Anthony Minghella.

The Abbey Gardens in Tresco

The Isles of Scilly

POPULATION:
2,153 (2001)
WHEN TO GO:
Anytime but best between April and November.
HOW TO GET THERE:
By plane, helicopter or boat from the mainland.
HIGHLIGHTS:
St Warna's Well, St Agnes.
Turks's Head, the most south-westerly pub in the land, St Agnes.
Cromwell's Castle, Tresco.
Valhalla Museum, Tresco.
Megaliths on the island of Gugh, connected to St Agnes at low tide.
The chambered tomb in Samson Hill, Bryher.
YOU SHOULD KNOW:
Myths and legends are integral to the Scillies' heritage, and the islands are said to be the last visible areas of the drowned land of Lyonnesse, the birthplace of the Arthurian knight, Tristram, and the site of King Arthur's final showdown with Mordred.

The Isles of Scilly are the most westerly part of Britain. An archipelago of 140 islands, with nothing between them and the USA, they are blessed with a benign climate, despite receiving gale force winds during winter.

There are five main inhabited islands; St Mary's being the most developed. Although tourism accounts for 85 per cent of their economy, St Mary's is intensively cultivated. Clement weather produces early flowers, and flower growing remains a considerable industry. The Scillies were designated an Area of Outstanding Natural Beauty in 1975.

Tresco, the second largest island, is also much visited, thanks in large part to the fabulous Abbey Gardens. Acquired in 1834 by Augustus Smith, a keen botanist and Lord Proprietor of the Scillies, the gardens, full of exotic tropical and sub-tropical plants, were designed and terraced around the ruins of the 10th century Abbey.

St Martin's, the third largest island, is very unspoilt. Here you can find Bronze Age burial chambers and the remains of a 5th century chapel. Daffodils and Amaryllis Belladonna are grown commercially, but it's the gorgeous beaches and crystalline waters that most people come for.

St Agnes, the most southwesterly island, is known for its lovely coastline, white sand beaches, coves and rock pools. Granite boulders are strewn over parts of the interior and great granite outcrops guard the western shore. Famed for its wildlife, twitchers arrive en masse each October hoping to spot rare birds blown off course during their migration.

Small and quiet, Bryher is peppered with pre-historic sites. Covered in a blaze of gorse and wild flowers in spring and summer, it's another twitcher's paradise. Bryher makes a perfect getaway from the stresses of modern life, its coastal path offering fabulous views of the rocky shoreline and across the water to Tresco. All in all, the Scilly Isles offer something for everyone.

Jersey

Just 22.5 km (12 mi) north of France's Cotentin Peninsula, in the English Channel, lies Jersey, a self governing British Crown Dependency. A well-populated and attractive island, its low taxation has transformed the economy into a centre for off-shore banking and other financial services. Despite this side of island life, tourism and agriculture remain the backbone for most of the inhabitants.

Occupied since the Stone Age, Jersey has had a turbulent history, with Romans, early Christians, Vikings and Normans all making their mark here, the island came under English rule in 1204. Six hundred years of French attacks followed, but peace finally reigned following the defeat of France in 1815. Invaded and occupied by Germany in 1940, Jersey was forced to reinvent itself, which it did successfully, at the end of World War II.

St Helier, the administrative capital, is an attractive town set around a large bay, but its pretty, narrow streets and prosperous atmosphere hide Jersey's bitter past. During World War II an enormous underground hospital was hacked and tunnelled into a rocky hill, mainly by Russian and Polish slave labour, at the cost of many lives. The complex, at St Lawrence, has been restored as a reminder of what might have been, and the hardship suffered by the islanders during those years may explain their desire for financial success.

Jersey's landscape is delightful and very varied. St Ouen's Bay, in the west, is a magnificent expanse of sandy beach, protected by headlands at either end. The north coast is quite different, its rugged cliffs and sheltered coves attracting thousands of nesting seabirds. Four of the island's coastal wetlands have been designated Ramsar Wetland Sites. The interior contains freshwater ponds and reservoirs, lovely wooded valleys, and agricultural land. This is the home of a favourite British delicacy, Jersey potatoes, and Jersey cattle provide superb dairy produce and beef.

POPULATION:
91,321 (2007 estimate)

WHEN TO GO:
Jersey's climate is mild, but visit between April and November for the best weather.

HOW TO GET THERE:
By air or sea from England and France.

HIGHLIGHTS:
L'Islet and Elizabeth Castle, accessible by causeway at low tide.
The Durrell Wildlife Conservation Trust.
Grosnez Castle.
Samares Manor.
Corbiere Lighthouse.
The annual Battle of Flowers carnival, held during the second week of August.

YOU SHOULD KNOW:
Like the rest of the Channel Islands and the Isle of Man, Jersey is not part of the United Kingdom or the European Union.

Mont Orgueil Castle overlooks the small town of Gorey.

Guernsey

POPULATION:
65,031 (2004)
WHEN TO GO:
Any time of year, but April to October for the best of the weather.
HOW TO GET THERE:
By air or sea from England and Europe.
HIGHLIGHTS:
Sausmarez Manor.
The German Occupation Museum.
The Little Chapel.
Rousse Headland and the Napoleonic Loopholed Tower.
La Claire Mare, including Colin Best Nature Reserve and Les Anguillieres Marine Nature Reserve.
Lihou Island, an uninhabited bird sanctuary, reached by a tidal causeway and containing the ruins of a 12th century abbey.
YOU SHOULD KNOW:
Victor Hugo lived in exile on Guernsey for 14 years from 1855, writing *Les Misérables* and other works here. His house, owned by the city of Paris and in which the French Consulate is based, is now a fascinating museum of his life and work.

Guernsey lies in the English Channel, and at about 48 km (30 mi) west of the Normandy coast it is considerably closer to France than to England. It is a self-governing British Crown Dependency, with several other islands in its bailiwick. It has a successful economy based on tourism, off-shore banking, insurance and agriculture, and thanks to low taxation is known as a refuge for the wealthy.

Inhabited since around 6,000 BC, Guernsey became part of England in 1066, and gained its self-governance as a reward for loyalty from King John in 1204. Used by pirates in the Middle Ages, Guernsey became prosperous during the 19th century, and apart from suffering severely during World War II, during its 5-year occupation by Germany, it remains so today. If the island has a problem, it is that too many people want to settle here.

Mainly flat and low-lying, Guernsey is cultivated intensively, and much of its 63 sq km (25 sq mi) is covered with greenhouses sheltering tomatoes and flowers. It is also home to the island's icon, the Guernsey cow, today being raised for beef as well as milk. However, there's still enough room for several nature reserves, and the variety of habitat is extensive, ranging from wooded valleys, marshland and reed beds to heathland and dunes. The southern coastal path offers 44 km (28 mi) of coastal scenery, and broad sandy bays provide happy seaside summer holidays.

If beach holidays are not your thing, or you hit a spell of poor weather, Guernsey has plenty of other attractions on offer. Castle Cornet, which guards St Peter Port harbour, dates from the 13th century and was built by King John. Connected by causeway to mainland Guernsey in 1860, the castle contains six museums. Another fascinating part of the island's history, the Nazi occupation, is well observed and documented in a number of different locations.

Sailboats moored by Castle Cornet.

Sark

Sark is the smallest of the four main Channel Islands. It lies in the English Channel, about 128 km (80 mi) from England and about 32 km (20 mi) from the coast of Normandy. It is as well that it is small, as there are no cars on the island, and transport other than on foot consists of horse-drawn carriages, tractors and bicycles.

Sark's history is long, and complex. Until the mid 16th century it was a place of pirates, frequently invaded by the French. In 1563, Helier de Carteret, the Seigneur of St Ouen in Jersey, received a charter from Elizabeth I to settle on Sark. Many of the island's laws date back to this period, and the feudal head of Sark is still known as the Seigneur.

The island is formed of steep, rocky cliffs, averaging about 90 m (330 ft) above sea level, rising to a central plateau. At its highest point a windmill can be found, dated 1571. In order to reach this plateau, passengers disembarking in the miniscule harbour must travel upwards through a rock-hewn tunnel made in 1866.

Greater Sark is connected to Little Sark by a narrow, paved isthmus known as La Coupée. Just 2.7 m (9 ft) wide, it has dizzying 90 m (300 ft) drops to either side. La Seigneurie, de Carteret's manor house built in 1565, is believed to stand on the site of an early Christian monastery. Although privately owned, its gardens, some of the finest in the Channel Islands, are open to the public.

This is a delightful island, with gorgeous sandy beaches and coves around the coast, ensuring shelter from winds of any direction. There are woods filled with springtime bluebells, and over 600 different plants and wildflowers grow here. Seabirds nest on the cliffs, and birds of prey, songbirds and migrants enjoy its unspoilt landscape.

POPULATION:
610 (2002)

WHEN TO GO:
Any time, but April to October may provide the best weather.

HOW TO GET THERE:
By ferry from Guernsey, Jersey and Normandy.

HIGHLIGHTS:
St Peter's Church (1820).
Sark Prison – built in 1856 and capable of accommodating only two people, this is the smallest prison in the world.
La Grande Greve, perhaps Sark's most special bay.
A walk through Dixcart valley to the ancient cannon at Hogs Back.
The Boutique and Gouliot Caves.
Swimming at low tide in the Venus Pool on Little Sark.

YOU SHOULD KNOW:
Amongst the curious laws on Sark – no income tax; 'Clameur de Haro', whereby the immediate cessation of any action seen to be an infringement of one's rights can be claimed and gained and then heard at Sark's court; the Seigneur is the only person on the island with the right to own doves, as well as the only one allowed to have an unspayed female dog!

La Coupée connects Sark with Little Sark.

Eel Pie Island is one of London's most sought after locations.

Eel Pie Island

Lying in the River Thames, opposite Twickenham – one of London's more sought after locations, is Eel Pie Island. Tiny in size but huge in reputation, Eel Pie is a legend in the lifetime of the baby boom generation. A mere 181 m (600 ft) from end to end, the island is mainly residential, with a few small businesses and a miniscule nature reserve at each end.

As long ago as the early 1600s, Eel Pie was somewhere to have fun – a map from 1635 shows a bowling green, and there were public houses here by the 1700s. One of these, rebuilt in the 1830s, became a much grander establishment called the Eel Pie Island Hotel, which soon became extremely popular. The Twickenham Rowing Club, one of the Thames's oldest, built its headquarters here in 1880, and today the Richmond Yacht Club is also located on the island.

The hotel contained a sprung dance floor. Used first for ballroom dancing, the 1920s and 30s saw well attended tea dances. However, during the 1950s its owner turned it into a major British jazz venue and by the 1960s jazz was overtaken by rhythm and blues music. All the seminal bands of the era played the Eel Pie Hotel: Long John Baldry, John Mayall's Bluesbreakers, Pink Floyd, The Who, and most famously, The Rolling Stones. It was party time, and hundreds of young Londoners made their way here to make merry. Closed in 1967, briefly re-opened in 1969, the hotel became a hippie commune. In 1971, it was mysteriously burnt to the ground whilst being demolished.

In 1996 another fire damaged Eel Pie, and today boat building is in decline, and new developments loom. However, the inhabitants remain a wonderfully eclectic mix of rich and poor, all brought together by the lure of art, music and a bohemian lifestyle, and all determined to keep the island's unique atmosphere intact.

POPULATION:
120 (2007)
WHEN TO GO:
Any time
HOW TO GET THERE:
By footbridge or boat.
HIGHLIGHTS:
Exploring the island and, for some, remembering times past.
Boating on the River Thames.
A trip to Hampton Court.
YOU SHOULD KNOW:
Eel Pie Island was named for its famous eel pies. King Henry VIII loved them and insisted that the first pie of the season was delivered to Hampton Court by the Waterman of Twickenham. Sadly, pollution has put paid to the eels, and the pies are no longer made here.

The Farne Islands and Lindisfarne

Just off the coast of Northumberland, lies a group of some 20 tidal islands. Divided into inner and outer groups, these are colloquially known as the 'Farnes'. Apart from a few seasonal National Trust bird wardens, they are uninhabited. Rugged and bleak, the smallest islands are just bare, rocky peaks, while the largest support vegetation on peaty soil.

Inner Farne is closely connected to St Cuthbert, who lived alone here for some years. Further hermits followed the saint, who died in 687, many of whom came from the monastery at Durham. In 1255 a small Benedictine monastery was established here, with two separate chapels.

Always dangerous to shipping because of hidden rocks and sea stacks, a warning beacon was first lit in 1673, since when the islands have seen the construction and destruction of many lighthouses. Two fully automated lighthouses stand today on Inner Farne and Longstone and lighthouses ruins can be seen. The islands are known as one of Britain's major seabird sanctuaries as well as being home to several thousand Atlantic grey seals.

To the north of the Farnes lies mystical Lindisfarne, or Holy Island. Connected by a tidal causeway to the mainland, much of both it and its surrounding tidal area is a National Nature Reserve, protecting internationally important winter populations and rare migrant birds.

Lindisfarne's famous monastery was founded by St Aidan in 635 AD, and St Cuthbert was both Abbott and Bishop here for two years. This is one of the most important early Christian sites in England. The remarkable illuminated manuscript, the Lindisfarne Gospels, was made on the island in the early 700s, and is now protected in the British Library. Also on the island is a Tudor castle. Owned by the National Trust, it was built in the 1570s and restored by Edwin Lutyens in 1901, with a garden designed by Gertrude Jekyll.

Lindisfarne monastery

POPULATION:
The Farne Islands are uninhabited; Lindisfarne 162 (2007)

WHEN TO GO:
The best time for birds is during autumn and winter, but Lindisfarne is at its best during spring and summer.

HOW TO GET THERE:
By boat to the Farnes, foot or car to Lindisfarne, depending on the tides.

HIGHLIGHTS:
Scuba diving over the many wrecks surrounding the Farne Islands.
St Cuthbert's Chapel, Inner Farne.
The Pele tower, a small 16th century defensive fort, Inner Farne.
The ruined Lindisfarne monastery, its museum and visitor centre.
The old lime kilns on Lindisfarne.
Lindisfarne Mead – its recipe passed down from medieval times is still a closely guarded secret of the family who still produce it at St Aidan's Winery.

YOU SHOULD KNOW:
Longstone Lighthouse was the home of keeper William Darling. In 1838 his 22 year-old daughter, Grace, saw a shipwreck on a nearby rock. In their rowing boat, she and her father achieved the extraordinarily courageous rescue of nine people in terrible weather conditions, and she became a national heroine.

Foulness

POPULATION:
212 (2001)
HOW TO GET THERE:
By road bridge from Shoebury, having first obtained permission.
WHEN TO GO:
Any time of year, but it is best on a hot summer's day.
HIGHLIGHTS:
The villages of Churchend and Courtsend.
Birdwatching.
YOU SHOULD KNOW:
Bridges to the island were only built in 1926; prior to that access was by boat or on foot. No-one knows when the sea walls were first built, but several of the marshes had sea walls by the beginning of the 13th century. Foulness has been flooded on a number of occasions, the last in 1953, during the Great Tide, when two people lost their lives.

Foulness is the largest of the Essex islands, indeed it is the fourth largest island off England's coast, and yet because of its unique situation, it is one of the least known. There are only three freeholders on Foulness – the Parish Council, the Church of England and, by far the most important, the Ministry of Defence, who bought these 2,550 hectares (6,300 acres) in 1915. It is here that the MoD tests military ordnance.

Physically, Foulness is in the Thames delta, bounded by the rivers Crouch in the north, the Roach and Shelford Creek in the west, with the River Thames to the south and east. The island is made of fertile alluvial marshland, and almost all of it is below high tide level, necessitating its enclosure by a sea wall. Some of the land is farmed, cattle and sheep can be seen grazing and the surrounding Foulness and Maplin Sands are a haven for wading birds, including the second largest population of avocets in the country. Herons can frequently be seen in the many creeks and backwaters. No wonder this was once a favourite destination of smugglers.

You need to make an effort to visit Foulness – by invitation by a resident, or by booking lunch at the 17th century George and Dragon, the island's only pub. Either way, a pass has to be obtained, or you will find yourself turned away from the MoD checkpoint at the start of the series of bridges that connect Foulness to the mainland. Once on the island, you'll find most of the residents living in two villages at the northern end. The atmosphere of Foulness is of a place apart, and for the visitor it is quite an experience, if you can cope with occasional loud explosions.

Brownsea Island

POPULATION:
No permanent population.
WHEN TO GO:
Any time, but booked groups only between November and April.
HOW TO GET THERE:
By boat from Sandbanks or North Haven and Poole Quay, or on a day trip from local resorts, or by privately owned boat.
HIGHLIGHTS:
The mid-19th century St Mary's Church.
The site of Baden-Powell's first Scout camp.
The annual Brownsea open air Shakespeare theatre.

In the mouth of Poole harbour, opposite the town of Poole in Dorset, lies Brownsea Island. The largest of a group of small islands, Brownsea is wholly owned by the National Trust, and as such may be visited by the public. All of Brownsea is designated a Site of Special Scientific Interest, and the northern end of this small, 2.4 km (1.5 mi) long by 1.2 km (0.75 mi) wide, island is leased to the Dorset Wildlife Trust as a Nature Reserve.

Brownsea's lengthy history includes early Christianity, the Vikings, and Henry VIIIth's fortification programme, designed to protect Poole harbour. The island passed through many hands. During World War II it was used as a decoy for the port – so successfully that it received several bombs. In 1961 the owner, who was reclusive and had allowed Brownsea to revert to nature, died,

Brownsea Castle

and the National Trust was able to acquire it.

However, Brownsea is best known as the seat of the Scouting movement. At the turn of the 20th century, Robert Baden-Powell was a guest on the island, and in 1907 he hosted the first Scout Camp for twenty Dorset boys, and thus began a worldwide movement. Brownsea castle and its grounds are now leased by the John Lewis Partnership as a summer holiday destination for its staff.

Brownsea is a place of many habitats, and is home to a wealth of wildlife and plants. It contains saltmarsh, reed beds, freshwater lakes, heathland, peaceful pinewoods and a brackish lagoon. It is one of the last havens of the indigenous red squirrel – probably due to having no competition from the grey variety – and there are many non-native sika deer and rabbits. The island has wonderful birds: herons, little egrets, terns in summer and avocets in winter.

YOU SHOULD KNOW:
2007 was the Scouts' 100th anniversary, and several events were held. The highlight was the Sunrise Camp, which brought together 310 young people from 155 countries to celebrate the occasion. At the exact moment that Scouting had begun 100 years previously, every Scout in the world, all 28 million of them, renewed their Scouting promise.

Mersea Island

POPULATION:
6,500 (2007)
WHEN TO GO:
At its best between April and October.
HOW TO GET THERE:
Via The Strood, the main Colchester to Mersea road (B1025)
HIGHLIGHTS:
Cudmore Grove Country Park.
The Mersea Island Museum.
Colchester Oyster Fishery.
West Mersea Barrow.
Mersea Week and Regatta, annually in August.
Mersea Seafood Festival, annually in September.
YOU SHOULD KNOW:
The author Sabine Baring-Gould (1834-1924) was the rector of East Mersea's St Edmunds Church for a decade. He is best known for the hymn 'Onward Christian Soldiers'.

Derived from the Old English *meresig*, meaning island of the pool, Mersea Island lies just off the Essex coast in the estuary of the Blackwater and Colne rivers. At 14 km (9 mi) southeast of Colchester, Mersea is Britain's most easterly inhabited island. It is small at 8 sq km (3 sq mi), but despite its sizeable population it still has salt marshes and plenty of space for farmland. Here too are beaches, beach huts, and restaurants at the water's edge where you can eat locally caught fish and even drink wine from the local vineyard.

Inhabited since about 3,000 BC, it was under Roman rule when a causeway was first built, connecting Mersea to the mainland. Known as The Strood, the causeway floods whenever the tide is particularly high. Mersea has been a holiday retreat since Roman soldiers first retired here, and once Britain had been pacified, wealthy Romans settled here too. In 1898 archaeologists uncovered the foundations of a villa, together with mosaic flooring and pavement. The Romans left a legacy that is still valuable today – oyster farming, and Mersea Native oysters are still an important (and seriously delicious) part of the local economy.

Most people live in the small town of West Mersea, others in the village of East Mersea with a scattering elsewhere. Farming, fishing, boat making and the tourism industry are the major occupations of this tightly knit community, which has two newspapers and every facility needed in terms of shops, schools and so on. During the summer the population swells dramatically, and the waters are full of colourful sailing boats, wind and kite surfers. The harbour at West Mersea is a bustling mass of boats and boatyards, and is home to the West Mersea Yacht Club, making Mersea one of the east coast's main sailing centres.

A row of colourful beach huts on West Mersea Beach

Lundy

Some 19 km (12 mi) out in the Bristol Channel, where the Atlantic Ocean meets the Severn River, lies the island of Lundy. Protected by its high, granite cliffs and remote location, the island has a colourful past. Today it belongs to the National Trust, is leased to the Landmark Trust, and its solitary and beautiful nature brings visitors back here over and over again.

Lundy has been inhabited since pre-historic times, and has suffered endless disputes over its ownership. In 1242, Henry III built a castle here to consolidate his control – instead Lundy became anarchic and chaos reigned until William Hudson Heaven bought the island in 1834. He erected many of the buildings, including St Helena's Church but sold the island to Martin Harman, a naturalist, in 1925. Harman transformed Lundy, and the National Trust acquired the island from his children in 1969.

The island consists of open moorland in the north, some farmland and a village to the south. Some 20,000 visitors come here each year, for the day or to stay in one of the 23 beautifully restored buildings that include a lighthouse and the castle. Those spending longer here can walk the glorious 11 km (7 mi) coastal path, admiring the surrounding waters that form Britain's first Marine Nature Reserve. Marine life is exceedingly rich – in particular there are rare species of seaweed, corals and fans. Grey seals are much in evidence, and basking sharks can also be spotted.

Much of Lundy is an area of Special Scientific Interest, and the flora and fauna are rich and varied. It has its own endemic species of cabbage, and its own, distinct breed of Lundy pony. It is also, naturally, bliss for birders. Although puffins are now few, the cliffs are home to thousands of seabirds, and in spring and autumn rare visitors occasionally appear, having been blown off course during migration.

POPULATION:
18 (2007 estimate)
WHEN TO GO:
Any time, but April to November is probably best.
HOW TO GET THERE:
By ferry from Bideford or Ilfracombe, or (November to March) helicopter from Hartland Point.
HIGHLIGHTS:
The disused granite quarries.
The Devil's Slide – great for rock climbing.
The three lighthouses – one of which you can stay in, the other two are functioning.
Diving over the wrecks and enjoying other water sports such as surfing.
The Soay sheep and feral goats.
YOU SHOULD KNOW:
In 1929 Martin Harman issued his own Lundy postage stamps, their value expressed in 'puffins'. These stamps are still printed today, but must be stuck on an envelope's left hand corner, their cost including Royal Mail's charges. Known as 'local carriage labels' in the world of philately, some of Lundy's stamps are now highly prized.

The ferry calls at Lundy Island.

Anglesey

POPULATION:
68,900 (2006 estimate)
WHEN TO GO:
Any time of year, but from May to October for the best of the weather.
HOW TO GET THERE:
By road (A5 or A55), by rail or boat.
HIGHLIGHTS:
Holyhead and the 13th century church of St Cybi.
Plas Newydd, an elegant 18th century mansion on the banks of the Menai Strait.
Llanbadrig Church, founded in 440 AD by StPatrick.
Holy Island, off the west coast of Anglesey, packed with ancient religious sites.
The Great Little Trains of Wales – a day out on a steam train.
YOU SHOULD KNOW:
The first Women's Institute was started in the Anglesey village with the longest name in Britain– Llanfairpwllgwyngyllgoger ychwyrndrobwllllantysiliogogogoch!

Separated from the north west coast of Wales by the Menai Strait, lies the island of Anglesey, the largest of the English and Welsh islands. Low lying – the highest point, Holyhead Mountain is only 218 m (720 ft) – the island is mainly agricultural. Its coastline, however, is superb, with sandy beaches, caves, rocky coves and sheer cliff faces, and 95 per cent of which is a designated an Area of Outstanding Natural Beauty.

This is an ancient island, inhabited for some 9,000 years. Its history dates back to the Mesolithic era, and it was home to Druids, Romans, Celts, Vikings, Saxons and Normans before being conquered by Edward I in the 13th century. All these peoples left their mark here, and Anglesey contains a treasure trove of ancient monuments, from standing stones and Stone Age burial sites to historic churches and castles.

Beaumaris Castle, a 13th century masterpiece, is a UNESCO World Heritage Site. Unfinished, it was the last of Edward I's 'iron ring' of castles built around the Welsh coast. This magnificent moated fortress is widely regarded as the finest of Edward's castles. Overlooking the Menai Strait, it commands fabulous views.

Anglesey is connected to the mainland by two bridges. The first, the Menai Suspension Bridge was designed by Thomas Telford in 1826, and the second, newer bridge, is a reconstruction of Robert Stephenson's original. There are many small towns on the island, and 70 per cent of the population here are Welsh speakers.

Most of Anglesey's two million visitors each year come for the coastline, enjoying the beaches, sailing, wind surfing and other outdoor activities. These include the splendid Coastal Path, the circular route of which connects 36 villages and passes through glorious scenery, including Newborough Forest on the south-eastern tip of the island.

The famous sign outside the railway station in the village that boasts the longest name in Britain.

A view out to the Atlantic Ocean from the shores of the serene Caldey Island.

Caldey Island

Caldey Island, which lies 5 km (3 mi) off the south coast of Pembrokeshire, is one of Britain's holy islands. Only 2.4 km (1.5 mi) long and 1.6 km (1 mi) wide, it has been inhabited since the Stone Age, and since Celtic times it has been inhabited by monks.

A Celtic monastery was founded here by Pyro, in the 6th century, and the Old Priory is believed to have been built on that original site. During the 10th century, Viking raids are thought to have put an end to the monastic settlement, but 200 years later Benedictines from St Dogmaels in Pembrokeshire built a Priory here, where they remained until the Dissolution of the Monasteries in 1536. In 1906 Anglican Benedictines bought Caldey and the Abbott, Aelred Carlyle, commissioned the beautiful Italianate Abbey from architect John Coates-Carter. Unable to make ends meet, the Benedictines sold the Abbey to Cistercian monks, Trappists, in 1926, where they remain peacefully ensconced in what is now a Grade II* listed building.

Although Caldey is best known for its monastery, it has a pretty village, too. Here one can buy a number of things made on the island, which provide an income for the monks. Farming produces milk, butter and cream and the monks produce yoghurt, ice-cream, shortbread and chocolate, which are on sale in the village. Their most famous product, however, is a range of perfumes and skin creams, made from Caldey's flowers, herbs and gorse.

This is a wonderful place to visit, with a uniquely serene and tranquil atmosphere. Quiet and unpolluted, with no traffic to disturb the peace, Caldey can be explored on foot. From the gorgeous Priory Beach to the lighthouse at the summit of the island, magnificent views over the south coast of Pembrokeshire can be enjoyed.

POPULATION:
50 (2003 estimate)
WHEN TO GO:
From Easter to the end of October.
HOW TO GET THERE:
Boats run from Tenby Harbour at high tide, and Castle Beach landing stage at low tide. Boats don't sail on Sundays.
HIGHLIGHTS:
St Illtyd's Church and the Old Priory.
Attending Mass in the Abbott's Chapel and touring the monastery (men only).
A guided walk to discover more about Caldey.
The Caldey Stone, inscribed in both Celtic and Latin.
St Margarets, Caldey's sister island (joined at low tide) – a seal and bird sanctuary.
Visiting the Post Office and Museum, and having a postcard franked with Caldey's unique imprint.
YOU SHOULD KNOW:
The Caldey Island monastery provides spiritual retreats throughout the year for both men and women (though only men are permitted to enter the main building), and it is possible to stay on the island.

Bardsey Island

POPULATION:
8-13 including ornithologists (2007)
WHEN TO GO:
April to October
HOW TO GET THERE:
By ferry from Porth Meudwy or Pwllheli.
HIGHLIGHTS:
Celtic crosses.
The 13th century bell tower.
The Bardsey Bird and Field Observatory.
Bardsey lighthouse – 30 m (99 ft) high, this is the only square lighthouse maintained by Trinity House.
The ancient Bardsey Apple Tree, a descendant of apple trees tended by monks 1,000 years ago, and declared 'unique' by experts at the National Fruit Collection in Brogdale, Kent. Cuttings have been planted in order to raise money for the Bardsey Trust.
YOU SHOULD KNOW:
Both Merlin and King Arthur are said to be buried in a glass coffin in a cave within Mynydd Enlii. A 12th century historian claimed that Avalon was an island of apples, and its name was derived from the Welsh word, *afal*. Perhaps the Round Table will be discovered here one day…

About 3.2 km (2 mi) off the tip of the Llyen Peninsula in north Wales lies another holy island. Bardsey, or Ynys Enlli in Welsh, meaning 'island of the great current' is only 2.5 km (1.5 mi) long, but traces of hut circles attest to it having been inhabited since Neolithic times.

During the 5th century, persecuted Christians began to take refuge here, and by the next century a monastery had been built by St Cadfan. Bardsey soon became a major place of pilgrimage, as well known as Iona or Lindisfarne, and it was said that three pilgrimages to Bardsey equalled one to Rome. Many of the faithful remained on Bardsey until they died, and yet more were brought for burial. This led to it becoming known as 'the isle of 20,000 saints'. The ruins that can be seen today are those of the 13th century Augustinian Abbey of St Mary, which was deserted during the Dissolution of the Monasteries in 1537. Bardsey then became a refuge of pirates and ne'er-do-wells until the owner, Lord Newborough, established a farming and fishing community during the 19th century. In 1979 the island was bought by the Bardsey Island Trust, and it is now an Area of Outstanding Natural Beauty, attracting both Christians and those interested in natural history and archaeology.

Most of Bardsey is flat and low lying, and from the slopes of Mynydd Enlli, which rises to 167 m (551 ft), a pattern of fields, divided by old stone walls, can be seen. The coastal margins are home to many rare plants, including over 350 species of lichen, and during spring and autumn many rare and migratory birds can be seen, including a large colony of Manx shearwaters, and, recently, puffins.

Bardsey Island seen through the morning mist

Lewis and Harris

Lewis and Harris, curiously, is one single island, the largest and most northerly of the Western Isles, otherwise known as the Outer Hebrides. By far the largest portion is Lewis, in the north, which becomes Harris at the point where two sea lochs, Resort and Seaforth, cut deeply into the land, itself a natural barrier of bleak, treeless mountains and moorland. Harris, in turn, is also split between north and south by a narrow isthmus, again formed by two sea lochs.

This is an ancient place, with fabulously dramatic landscapes, and a fascinating history and culture. Unlike many of the Scottish islands, it is not dependant in any way on tourism. If you are interested in Gaelic culture, this is its heartland: the majority of the population speak Gaelic as their first language, and keep to their traditional way of life. One third of Scotland's crofts are found here, and a string of settlements run up the west coast from Calanais to the Butt of Lewis in the far north. This is, of course, the home of the world famous Harris tweed, although today most of the weaving is done in Lewis, as that is where most of the island's population live.

The main town, Stornaway, in the east, lies on an impressive harbour, but its main point of architectural interest is the grandiose Lews Castle, built in the 1850s. The interior of the northern part of Lewis is rich in peat moors, while the south and Harris have spectacular mountain scenery, and stunningly beautiful beaches. All the most notable sites are on the west coast of Lewis, while the south, and Harris, offer stunning views over lochs, rivers, and the sea. The Uig peninsula has some of the most spectacular coastal scenery imaginable.

POPULATION:
20,000 (2006)
WHEN TO GO:
May to October
HOW TO GET THERE:
By air from Glasgow, Edinburgh and Inverness, or by ferry from Ullapool or Skye.
HIGHLIGHTS:
The 5,000-year-old Calanais (or Callanish) standing stones.
The village of Garenin with its restored thatched 'blackhouses' and museum.
The Butt of Lewis and its lighthouse overlooking the wild, crashing sea.
The Hebridean Celtic Festival at Lews Castle – a fabulous Celtic music festival held each July.
YOU SHOULD KNOW:
This is the heartland of the 'Wee Frees', the Free Presbyterian Church of Scotland, who rule with an iron hand. Almost everything closes on Sundays, which are reserved for church going and bible reading. Devotees observe many strange religious decrees, most of which appear to have been made to keep women in their place – they are forbidden to attend burials, for example, even that of their husbands or children.

The 5,000-year-old Calanais standing stones

North and South Uist, and Benbecula

POPULATION:
North Uist: 1,386; Benbecula: 1,883; South Uist: 2,064.
WHEN TO GO:
May to September for the machair in flower. Brown trout fishing: 15th March to 30th September; salmon: 25th February to 15th October; sea trout: 15th February to 31st. October.
HOW TO GET THERE:
By car over Scalpay Bridge or car ferry from Harris or Skye, or by air to Benbecula from Glasgow, Barra and Stornaway.
HIGHLIGHTS:
Buy and enjoy lobsters and other seafood at Grimsay, North Uist.
Taigh Chearsabhagh arts centre and museum in Lochmaddy, North Uist.
Try your hand at deerstalking on the North Uist Estate.
Visit the lovely islands of Eriskay and Barra.
Explore the important and ancient religious site at Howmore, South Uist.
Loch Druidibeg Nature Reserve, South Uist.
YOU SHOULD KNOW:
Flora MacDonald was born on South Uist. In 1746 she helped Bonnie Prince Charlie, dressed up as her maid, to escape to Skye where she lived with her husband. This romantic episode lives on in the well-known song that begins 'Speed bonnie boat like a bird on the wing'...

North Uist lies just across the sound from Harris. In sharp contrast, however, it is flat and low-lying. The eastern half of the island, which is 27 km (17 mi) long and 21 km (13 mi) wide, is covered with freshwater and sea water lochs – sheer heaven for trout and salmon fishermen. The Balranald RSPB reserve is a sanctuary for rare corncrakes, and has an extraordinary concentration of breeding waders, as well as raptors, songbirds and terns.

Lochmaddy, the ferry port, makes a good base from which to explore, being close to various curious prehistoric sites, such as the stone circle of Pobull Fhinn. The north and west coasts consist of vast, empty sandy beaches.

Between North and South Uist, and joined by a causeway, lies Benbecula, an unimpressive island of small lochs and peat bogs, and home to an army base. It does, however, have an airport, and its main claim to fame is a cave on its only hill, in which Bonnie Prince Charlie hid whilst waiting to escape to Skye.

South Uist is something of a gem. Its west coast has some of the finest beaches and swathes of machair (sandy, coastal grasslands), covered in heavenly wildflowers during the spring in the Western Isles. A ridge of mountains, broken by lochs, runs down the eastern side, while the crofting settlements are in the west. Rueval is home to a missile tracking station which, juxtaposed with the hundreds of archaeological sites in the area, looks completely surreal. Another nature reserve here is also worth a visit – made up of several types of habitat, you might even get to see a glorious golden eagle.

If you are keen on the great outdoors, North and South Uist are terrific for angling, bird watching or simply enjoying beaches and moorland that you seem to have all to yourself.

Loch Olavat on Benbecula

St Kilda Archipelago

Way out in the Atlantic Ocean, some 66 km (41 mi) to the west of the Outer Hebrides, rises the St Kilda Archipelago, with the exception of Rockall, the westernmost of British islands. St Kilda belongs to the National Trust for Scotland, and is a UNESCO World Heritage Site.

The archipelago consists of four main islands – Hirta, Soay, Boreray and Dun, which is almost an extension of Hirta, and several magnificent sea stacks. Hirta has the highest sea cliff in the British Isles, and Stac an Armin, just north of Boreray, is Britain's highest sea stack. In 2,000, marine scientists found that they are all peaks of the same, drowned mountain. Hirta was inhabited from about 5,000 years ago until 1930, when the last 36 inhabitants asked to be evacuated as conditions there had become untenable. In 1957 a missile tracking station was set up which today is manned by a civilian.

Hirta's sheer cliffs jut starkly from the sea on three sides, while the fourth has Village Bay, the only possible landing place and the site of the main settlement. Here there are Victorian cottages and many *cleits* – turf roofed, drystone structures – that were used to store the smoked or wind-dried seabirds, the basis of the islanders' diet. Nearby are numerous archaeological sites from which Neolithic stone tools, Iron Age pottery and Viking artefacts have been recovered.

But it's the birds of St Kilda that are the thing: these are the largest colonies of fulmars, gannets and puffins in Britain. Visually enthralling, the islands are green but treeless, having no plants growing higher than grass level. Great clouds of birds, unbelievable numbers of them, wheel and shriek in the sky, and clownish puffins whizz up and down the cliffs and grassy slopes like clockwork toys.

The rocky islands of Dun and Hirta, part of the St Kilda group

POPULATION:
There are small numbers of civilians working on the MOD base, otherwise just a few National Trust volunteers work on Hirta during the summer.

WHEN TO GO:
Mid-May to mid-August

HOW TO GET THERE:
Unless you have your own boat, the best way is to join a National Trust for Scotland working party. Contact the NTS first whichever way you want to visit.

HIGHLIGHTS:
Spot the petrels, Manx shearwaters, kittiwakes, guillemots, razorbills, gulls and great skuas that also breed here. Watch for grey seals, basking sharks, killer and minke whales in the waters nearby.
See primitive Soay sheep, which look rather like goats and which may have been here since Neolithic times.
Visit the excellent museum in Cottage No. 3.

YOU SHOULD KNOW:
Stac an Armin was regularly climbed by the St Kildans in order to collect eggs and catch birds to eat. Unfortunately, in 1840, the last great auk in Britain was beaten to death at the top of the stack by two men who believed it to be a witch.

Portree – the pretty main town of the island

Skye

POPULATION:
8,847 (2007)
WHEN TO GO:
The summer months are likely to have the best weather, but the spring and autumn will be less busy.
HOW TO GET THERE:
By road, or ferry from the mainland.
HIGHLIGHTS:
The extraordinary peaks of Quiraing, near Staffin.
The haunted ruin of Duntulm Castle.
The 13th century Dunvegan Castle, stronghold of the MacLeods.
Armadale Castle and the Museum of the Isles.
The Bright Water Visitor Centre, once the home of naturalist Gavin Maxwell, at Kyleakin, and the Forestry Commission otter hide at nearby Kylerhea.
YOU SHOULD KNOW:
In 1891 Sir Hugh Munro published his famous book, *Table of Heights over 3,000 Feet*, giving his name to all Scottish peaks over 914 m (3,016 ft), of which there are 284. In 1901, the Reverend Robertson invented a sport which becomes ever more popular – that of 'bagging the Munroes'. He bagged, or climbed, them all except for the Inaccessible Pinnacle in the Cuillins, which are home to 12 of the Munroes.

No doubt the best known of all the Scottish islands, Skye, which is about 80 km (50 mi) from top to bottom, has a great many things going for it, not least the most achingly beautiful scenery. Ever since the Victorians discovered the joys of climbing the spectacular Cuillin Ridge, the island has attracted more and more tourists, and this, in the summer months, together with its notoriously changeable climate, is its only downside.

Visited by St Columba in 585 AD, Skye was in the hands of the Norsemen for 300 years before being divided by three Scots clans, who fought over it constantly. Its most famous resident, Flora MacDonald, achieved lasting fame for her help in the escape to France of Bonnie Prince Charlie in 1745, and her grave can be visited at Kilmuir. During the 1800s many families were forced to leave the island due to the disastrous Jacobite rebellion and the clearances. Today, tourism is the backbone of the economy, and a bridge has been built to link the island to the mainland.

The biggest draw is the Cuillin Ridge, which is a fantastic area for climbing and hill-walking, but the northern Trotternish Peninsula is equally inspiring, with amazing coastal views and weird and wonderful rock formations such as Kilt Rock and the 50 m (165 ft) high rock needle, the Old Man of Storr. This last is only a few miles from Skye's main town, Portree – a pretty little place on a deep sea loch.

On the west coast, the Minginish Peninsula is worthy of a visit. If the weather is inclement, or you have had enough walking, drop into the famous Talisker Distillery. Founded in 1830, its single malt whisky was a favourite of Robert Louis Stevenson, and since then it has become the favourite of a great many more people too!

Iona

The island of Iona lies just to the southwest of Mull and is small at 5 km (3 mi) long and about 1.6 km (1 mi) wide. Known as the 'Cradle of Christianity', this may have been a Druidic centre even before the arrival, in 563 AD, of St Columba, an Irish prince, who landed with 12 disciples at what is known today as St Columba's Bay. Until his death in 597 AD, he converted the Scots to Christianity, founding a monastery here and forming a centre of Christian learning and pilgrimage. Centuries later, in 1203, a Benedictine abbey and an Augustinian convent were built, followed by another abbey in the 1500s. During the Reformation Iona was ransacked, and 357 of 360 Celtic crosses were smashed to smithereens. Today, the abbey complex is restored and the National Trust of Scotland maintains the rest.

The main village and ferry port, Baile Mor, is a moment away from the pink granite ruins of the convent, while a little further on stands the 15th century Maclean's Cross. The Street of the Dead, leading to the abbey itself, is a 13th century, red granite street, along which Scottish kings were carried for burial. Here stands the 9th century St Martin's Cross, the finest example of a Celtic cross in the British Isles.

Despite the hordes of visitors – 250,000 annually – Iona is worth exploring. With its fantastic white shell beaches to the north and east, the machair and shingle containing semi-precious stones to the west, and the cliffs and bays of the south with their rounded rocks and green pebbled beaches, there's a particular quality about it, an inexplicable atmosphere. Treeless and austere, the pin sharp light picks out the subtle colours of the rocks, the sands and the sea, which varies from brilliant turquoise to deep purple. Stay for a day or two and let Iona's magic capture you.

POPULATION:
85 (2007)
WHEN TO GO:
At its best from May to September
HOW TO GET THERE:
By ferry from Mull.
HIGHLIGHTS:
The Iona Heritage Centre.
Iona abbey, and the related monastic buildings.
St Oran's Chapel.
Oran's Cemetery, containing the graves of 48 Scottish kings, eight Norwegian kings and four Irish kings.
The views of Mull from the top of Dun I.
YOU SHOULD KNOW:
The former Labour Party leader, John Smith, is buried in Oran's Cemetery. He loved Iona, and his favourite walk was to the Bay at the Back of the Ocean, one of Scotland's loveliest beaches.

Iona Abbey

Islay

POPULATION:
3,700 (2007)
WHEN TO GO:
Any time
HOW TO GET THERE:
By ferry from Kennacraig in West Loch Tarbert, or by air from Glasgow.
HIGHLIGHTS:
The National Nature Reserve at Duich Moss.
The Islay Festival of Malt and Music, held each late May/early June.
The Museum of Islay Life at Port Charlotte.
The ancient burial grounds at Nerabus, containing wonderful medieval gravestones.
The island of Jura, a five-minute ferry journey from Islay, this wild, mountainous island is fantastic for hill walking.
YOU SHOULD KNOW:
Portnahaven, a charming fishing village 11 km (7 mi) south of Port Charlotte, is home to the world's first commercial wave-powered generating station. Known as 'Limpet', it powers 200 homes on the island.

The green, hilly island of Islay was, in medieval times, the capital of the Western Isles. Today, Islay is synonymous with its unique, peaty, single malt whisky, and the island is home to eight separate distilleries. Between them they produce some four million gallons of whisky per year, much of which is exported. Most visitors come for the whiskey trail, leaving the rest of the island relatively unknown. The remainder come for the birds because, between October and April, Islay is a destination on the migration route of thousands of white fronted and barnacle geese, flying south from Greenland for the winter.

Islay is always windy, but fairly mild, and the land is fertile. There is moorland, woods, machair, sea lochs and a rugged coastline with great expanses of beach. Inhabited since Neolithic times, there is much here to interest archaeologists, for example the Kildalton

High Cross, often considered to be the finest in Scotland, which was carved from bluestone in 800 AD. Close to the cross are some remarkably carved, 15th century gravestones, and further on, at Trudernish Point are standing stones.

The island's main centre of population and ferry port is Port Ellen, which was planned and laid out in the 1820s. An attractive town, its own distillery dominates the skyline, though it is no longer operational. Nearby, however, are three very well-known distilleries: Laphroig, Lagavulin and Ardbeg, beautifully situated and fun to visit. At Laphroig you not only see the malting but also the peat kilns. Bowmore, on the east side of Loch Indaal, is Islay's current 'capital,' and home to its eponymous oldest distillery, started in 1779. Port Charlotte, on the west of Loch Indaal is probably Islay's prettiest village, and makes a good base for a few days.

The Paps of Jura mountains seen from a cottage on the north coast of Islay.

Coll and Tiree

Coll and Tiree are situated out in the Atlantic Ocean, to the west of Mull. Low lying and pretty remote, they were once one. Both much the same size, about 19 km (12 mi) by 5 km (3 mi), treeless and windswept, they boast the record number of sunny days in Scotland. These days Tiree attracts numerous windsurfers each October for the Tiree Wave Classic event.

If Coll is shaped like a fish, its village, Arinagour, is situated on the west of the gill that is Loch Eatharna, a sheltered anchorage. A village of little, whitewashed cottages, this is where half the island's population lives, and where the shops and post office are. Two 'castles' both called Breachacha, stand on the southwest coast, one dates from the 15th century, while the other is from 1750. To the west of the castles is a huge area of vast sand dunes, and two golden sandy bays. Coll's highest point is Ben Hogh, on the summit of which is an enormous boulder, balanced precipitously on three small boulders, and said to have been placed there by a giant.

Tiree's expanse of fertile machair was once known as 'the breadbasket of the Inner Hebrides'. Today the population survive on crofting and tourism. The island is known for its 'black' and 'white' houses – the black ones have drystone walls, rounded corners and thatched roofs set with the walls for wind protection. The white houses have had their walls cemented and whitewashed and the thatch replaced with corrugated iron. There are also 'spotty' houses, where only the mortar has been painted white.

The Ringing Stone, to the west of Vaul Bay on the north coast, is a large boulder covered with ancient markings. When struck by a stone, it produces a strange, metallic tone. Legend has it that if it ever breaks in two, Tiree will disappear forever beneath the waves.

POPULATION:
Coll: 172; Tiree: 750 (2002)
WHEN TO GO:
Best between April and November
HOW TO GET THERE:
By ferry from Oban, or by air from Glasgow to Tiree.
HIGHLIGHTS:
The RSPB Reserve at Calgary Point, Coll.
Walk the beach at Crossapol Bay, Coll.
Visit Dun an Achaidh an ancient fort, and see the standing stones and cairns near the road running west from Arinagour, Coll.
Dun Mor Vaul, the remains of an ancient broch (a circular stone fort) near Vaul Bay, Tiree.
The Island Life museum at Sandaig, Tiree.
The Skerryvore Lighthouse Museum – tribute to the building of the magnificent Skerryvore Rock lighthouse that stands in the ocean some 16 km (10 mi) southwest of Tiree.

Stones hold the thatched roof in place on this Tiree cottage.

Arran

Cosily nestled in the Firth of Clyde between Ayrshire and Kintyre, is the island of Arran. This is the largest,(at roughly 32 km (20 mi) long by 16 km (10 mi) wide) and southernmost island in Scotland, and the most accessible of them all. People have been holidaying here since the early 1700s, and tourism is still Arran's most important source of income.

Arran, however, is not just a convenient holiday island - it also mimics Scotland as a whole. The north has harsh, high mountains, deep, lonely glens and a small, scattered population, like the Highlands, whilst the warmer, gentler south has moors, forests, some agricultural land and several sandy beaches. The island contains a wealth of archaeological remains, not surprisingly since people have lived here for thousands of years – Britons, Romans, Norsemen, they all left their mark.

Situated on the east coast, on a broad bay backed by hills is Brodrick, Arran's main town and ferry port. To the north of the bay, beneath the highest hill, Goat Fell, stands Brodrick Castle, with notable gardens that include one of Europe's finest collections of rhododendrons. At the northern tip of the island is Lochranza, a charming village with the ruins of a 13th century castle standing on a promontory. The northern half of Arran is visually stunning golden eagle territory. The bare granite peaks and fabulous, wild scenery provide terrific hill walks and climbing.

In the west, Machrie Moor is known for its neolithic sites – there are six stone circles on Arran. Lamlash and Whiting Bay on the south east coast are both resorts, but the best beaches are further south and quite difficult to reach. Arran has many outdoor attractions, not least a road that runs all around it – a siren's call to cyclists.

A mountain stream flows through North Glen Sannox.

POPULATION:
5,000 (2007)

WHEN TO GO:
Any time, but it's probably best from April to October

HOW TO GET THERE:
By ferry from Ardrossan.

HIGHLIGHTS:
The week-long Arran Folk Festival, held every June.
The Machrie Moor Standing Stones and Fingal's Cauldron.
Torrylinn Cairn, a 4,000-year-old tomb.
Torrylinn Creamery, where you can see the cheese-making process and buy Arran cheese.

YOU SHOULD KNOW:
Just north of Whiting Bay, a ten-minute boat trip away, is Holy Island, the 7th century home of St Molias. Bought by the Samye Ling Tibetan Buddhist order in 1991, the plan is to create Europe's largest spiritual sanctuary on the island. Visitors are welcome but are asked to abide by the Five Golden Rules of Buddhism.

The Orkneys

POPULATION:
Just under 20,000, with 85 per cent living on Mainland (2006)
WHEN TO GO:
Spring and summer, when the islands are carpeted with wild flowers and the moors and cliffs are alive with birds.
HOW TO GET THERE:
By ferry from the mainland, or by air.
HIGHLIGHTS:
Mainland's Maes Howe, Europe's most impressive Neolithic burial chambers.
Mainland's Skara Brae, the extensive remains of a Neolithic village.
Dive the shipwrecks at Scapa Flow, Mainland.
North Ronaldsay's New Lighthouse – designed by Alan Stevenson in 1854, this is the tallest land based lighthouse in Britain.
The remarkable and moving Italian Chapel on Lamb Holm, built out of Nissan huts, scrap metal and driftwood by Italian prisoners of war during World War II. Masses are still regularly held here.
Mainland's Standing Stones of Stenness and the extraordinary Ring of Brodgar.
YOU SHOULD KNOW:
Scapa Flow is a great natural harbour with an extraordinary naval history. For the first half of the 20th century it was the Royal Navy's main base, with up to 100 warships at anchor at any one time. At the end of World War I the entire German fleet was interned here, and scuttled by its commanding officer. Between the wars the largest salvage operation in history took place, but there are still 15 German ships and one U-boat on the seabed.

The Orkneys consist of some 70 islands and islets lying a hop, skip and a jump to the north of John o' Groats, where the North Sea and the Atlantic meet and clash in the Pentland Firth. Apart from Hoy, the islands are low, fertile and surprisingly green, with barely a tree to be seen, and the coastal scenery is spectacular. Despite benefiting from the Gulf Stream's warming influence the islands are windy, and in autumn and winter suffer from incredibly violent storms.

Splitting naturally into the North Isles, the South Isles and, between them the major island, known as Mainland, only 16 islands are inhabited. Historically, the Orkneys have been inhabited since the Stone Age, as the many fascinating relics clearly show. Closely linked with Norway for centuries, they only became part of Scotland in 1471.

Mainland has two main towns, Kirkwall, the capital, which stands at the narrowest point of the island, and Stromness, on the south-western shore. This is a truly picturesque port, its many sandstone jetties a visible reminder of the time when it was a base for first the Hudson Bay Company ships and then the Davies Strait whaling fleet. Kirkwall is both larger and less immediately attractive, though it does have a spectacular medieval, sandstone cathedral.

To the southeast, Mainland is joined by causeway to several smaller islands, including Burray and South Ronaldsay. To the southwest, Hoy juts from the sea, its famous sea stack, the Old Man of Hoy, a draw for rock climbers from around the world.

Orkneys' North Isles include Shapinsay, Rousay and Westray, each with its own attractions. North Ronaldsay is the most northerly and isolated of all, and has a unique, almost pioneering atmosphere. On the migration route of many rare birds, a permanent Bird Observatory was established here in 1987.

Waves crash against Yesnaby Castle Stack.

Fair Isle

Lying halfway between the Orkneys and The Shetlands, Fair Isle is a tiny, isolated island, with a population of about 70 souls. Just 4.8 km (3 mi) long and 2.4 km (1.5 mi) wide, it is probably the windiest of the British Isles.

In the first half of the 20th century, evacuation of the island was considered, but the ornithologist, George Waterson managed to buy it and founded the Bird Observatory there in 1948, effectively saving it. In 1954, he passed Fair Isle to the National Trust for Scotland. This is a paradise for birds, ornithologists and twitchers, and each year hundreds of birders flock here when some particularly rare species makes an appearance.

The majority of the population inhabit the southern end of the island, as this is where the only crofting land is available. Fair Isle Crafts, an island cooperative, produces the famous Fair Isle knitwear, the profits from which have funded the island's wind and diesel electricity generators. Other crafts such as ship building and fiddle making are thriving.

The north and west of the island have the finest and most dramatic of scenery. Steep, red sandstone cliffs rising from the water have been pounded by the waves and battered by the wind into convoluted shapes cut by narrow inlets and caves, while rock arches and sea stacks litter the coastline. On the east coast, the 135 m (446 ft) promontory of Sheep Rock thrusts its way into the sea.

As for the birds, some 345 different species have been recorded here, the highest number in Britain. Any number of sea birds can be seen, great colonies of them, including puffins and skuas, and the sound of thousands of birds communicating with each other is just amazing. Fair Isle is on several migration routes, and the Bird Observatory is one of Europe's most important ornithological centres.

Skroo Lighthouse

POPULATION:
About 70 (2004)
WHEN TO GO:
April, late June to early September and late October for bird watching, and late October for rare migrating birds.
HOW TO GET THERE:
By air or by ferry from May to September.
HIGHLIGHTS:
The George Waterson Memorial Centre, May to mid-September.
The North and South lighthouses.
YOU SHOULD KNOW:
The two lighthouses were built in 1892 by the Stevensons. Both were automated in 1998; the South Lighthouse was the last manned lighthouse in Scotland.

Mainland

POPULATION:
17,550 (2001)
WHEN TO GO:
The best months are probably April to September – and don't forget that during the summer months the Shetlands never really get dark.
HOW TO GET THERE:
By air or ferry
HIGHLIGHTS:
The Folk Festival, every April/May.
The Fiddle and Accordion Festival, every October.
Stanydale Temple, an impressive Neolithic roundhouse.
The island of Mousa and the wonderfully preserved Mousa Broch, a 2,000-year-old defensive tower.
The Shetland Library and Museum in Lerwick.
YOU SHOULD KNOW:
The festival of Up-Helly-Aa is held on the last Tuesday in January, and a version of it has been held since Norse times. Celebrating the rebirth of the sun, this is a fire festival, and hundreds of people in fancy dress ritually burn a replica Viking longship.

Physically closer to Norway than to the Scottish mainland, and reflected in the history and many of the place names, Mainland is the largest of the Shetland Islands, and is connected by bridges to the small, narrow fingers of Trondra, West Burra and East Burra. The Shetlands have been inhabited since forever, and were an essential base for the Vikings from which to strike at Ireland, Scotland or the Isle of Man. Mentioned in many Icelandic sagas, they were first mortgaged to King James III of Scotland, then annexed by him in 1472.

Lerwick, the Shetlands' capital, is a thriving, grey stone town, set on a protected natural harbour. At one time the largest herring port in northern Europe, Lerwick languished for decades during the 20th century, until the discovery of off-shore oil during the 1970s raised its profile once again. Nearby, a mile west of town, is the ancient, fortified site of Clickimin Broch, a Bronze Age settlement that was occupied from the 7th century BC to the 6th century AD.

The former capital, Scalloway, only 10 km (6 mi) from Lerwick, is dominated by Scalloway Castle, built in 1600. The town's museum tells the story of the Shetland Bus, the name given to the Norwegian resistance operation of World War II that brought refugees to safety and returned with weapons and fighters.

Mainland has some spectacular scenery, wild moorland ending in dramatic cliffs that plunge into the sea beneath, beautiful lochs and inlets – this is a great place for walking or cycling. The far southwest is close to the RSPB Reserve and an unusual shell and sand isthmus, the largest in Britain and popular with land-yachters. The southern tip of the island has another bird reserve, another Stevenson lighthouse and Jarlshof, the most impressive archaeological site in the archipelago, inhabited continuously from the Bronze Age to the 17th century.

Waves break against the rocky coastline around Sumburgh Head.

Foula

If you find yourself tipping up at Foula, then you are probably either the owner of a boat, or an island 'collector', for this wee speck in the ocean is the most remote of inhabited British islands. Foula rises 22 km (14 mi) west of Mainland, in the midst of the turbulent waters of the Atlantic.

Foula has long been inhabited – recently, the remains of a stone circle was found at Da Heights, in the north, with an alignment to the midwinter sunrise. Conquered by Norsemen in 800 AD, they settled on the reasonably fertile, eastern coastal strip. People here are proud of their Norse heritage, as their culture and traditions bear witness. The last person here who spoke Norn, the old Norse dialect, died in 1926 and a local tradition is the observance of the Julian calendar, meaning that Christmas is on January 6th and New Year on January 13th.

To the west of the two main settlements, Ham, where the ferry docks, and Hametoun, further south, moorland rises to five great peaks, running most of the length of the island. In the west, the Kame is a magnificent cliff, the second highest in Britain, which rears straight up from the waves beneath, and from which, on a good day, you can see all the way from Unst to Fair Isle. Further south is the sinister vertical chimney, Sneck o'da Smallie, that drops right down into the sea – some say all the way down to Hell.

Foula is a great place for birds – 250,000 of them, including the largest colony of great skuas in Britain. Artic terns wheel and screech in the sky, and the cliffs are alive with puffins, guillemots, razorbills and fulmars. Red-throated divers inhabit every small loch on the island, and many rare birds have been spotted here, especially during the spring and autumn migrations.

POPULATION:
31 (2007)

WHEN TO GO:
The summer months are best, but spring and autumn bring migratory birds. Travel to Foula depends on the weather – and even if you arrive on the right day, you might not be able to leave as planned.

HOW TO GET THERE:
By air or sea from Mainland.

HIGHLIGHTS:
The panoramic view from the top of The Sneug.
Spot pods of killer whales, porpoises and seals.

YOU SHOULD KNOW:
There are fearful reefs around Foula, and many ships have foundered here, including *Titanic*'s sister ship, *Oceanic*, which was stranded in 1914, and disappeared completely within 14 days. The 'smiddy' at Ham sells objects made from copper salvaged from her.

Wild Shetland ponies

Unst

POPULATION:
1,067 (2007)
WHEN TO GO:
April to September
HOW TO GET THERE:
By ferry from Mainland via Yell.
HIGHLIGHTS:
The ruins of Muness Castle.
Unst Boat Haven and Heritage Centre
The Valhalla Brewery.
Bobby's bus shelter – a most eccentric, fully furnished bus shelter on the outskirts of Baltasound.
YOU SHOULD KNOW:
In 1700 a sea eagle stole a baby girl from her home on the hill above Nor Wick Bay, and took her to the island of Fetlar. A young boy saw her being deposited in the eagle's nest and was able to rescue and return her to her family. They later married and lived on Yell. This is believed to be a true story.

Unst is the most northerly inhabited British island and third largest of the Shetlands. At 19 km (12 mi) long and 8 km (5 mi) wide it contains diverse terrain due largely to its complex geology. Large swathes of serpentine and metagabbro broken with schists form the eastern side, while the west is gneiss, studded with occasional garnets, underlying the peat moorland. To the south there is limestone and to the north east talc – the only talc mine in Britain.

Unst, like others of the northern islands, has spectacular cliffs, cut by inlets and guarded by sea stacks and sea arches, and beautiful, lonely sandy beaches. It also has rolling, grassy, heather-clad hills, peat moors, freshwater lochs and fertile land, and has been inhabited since the Iron Age, as can be seen in the many ancient archaeological sites. One of its two standing stones, Bordastubble, is the highest in the Shetlands.

There are two National Nature Reserves here. The most unusual, Keen of Havar, is a sub-Arctic stony desert, composed of serpentine scree, a greeny-greyish blue stone that is home to a number of minute rare plants, including frog orchids and mouse-eared Edmondston's chickweed, which grows nowhere else the world.

To the west of Burra Firth, a deep inlet on the north coast, is Hermaness, a bleak, rugged headland that is home to about 140,000 nesting seabirds – huge colonies of fumars, guillemots, kittiwakes, gannets and even great skuas. From the headland you can see the amazing rock lighthouse of Mukkle Flugga, a heroic feat of construction performed by David Stevenson in 1858. Here too is Britain's most northerly golf course. In Baltasound, the main town on Unst, you can send postcards from the most northerly post office as well as enjoy the beer from the most northerly brewery.

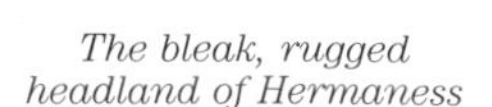

The bleak, rugged headland of Hermaness

Fejø

POPULATION:
611 (2005)
WHEN TO GO:
May to September – particularly beautiful in mid-May when the island erupts into a huge cloud of scented blossom.
HOW TO GET THERE:
The hourly ferry service from Kragenas on Lolland takes 15 minutes.
HIGHLIGHTS:
Fejø kirke – late 12th century church, one of the oldest in Denmark.
Dybvig Vavn – harbour and boatyard where you can see traditional fishing boats being built.
Østerby forge – old blacksmith's, looking just as it has done for hundreds of years.
Fejø Museum – to find out more about the island history.
A plate of local lamb salami washed down with a glass of Fejø cider.
Ferry trip to the neighbouring islands – you will find yourself charmed by the swallows. Every spring they migrate from Africa to travel to and fro with the island ferry, making a living by begging titbits from the passengers.
YOU SHOULD KNOW:
There is not much accommodation on Fejø – a village inn, a farmhouse B&B, and six rental cottages; or you can camp.

One of several tiny islands off the north coast of Lolland, Fejø is an idyllic rural backwater of fruit trees, sand and sea that has, so far, managed to escape the scars of mass tourism. The island is just 16 sq km (6 sq mi) of low-lying, rich clay with a 30 km (19 mi) coastline of gently sloping sand beaches – perfect for swimming, kayaking and windsurfing. It is inhabited by warm-hearted people who live from the produce of their smallholdings and the proceeds of their apple and pear orchards. Fejø apples are the best in Denmark and every year boxes from the latest harvest are sent to the Danish Royal Family.

The first written records of Fejø's history are 13th century, although there is plenty of archeological evidence of human habitation from 10,000 BC onwards. In the 17th century, while under Swedish occupation, the last bit of forest was cleared to make way for agricultural land. The islanders eventually acquired their own freehold, liberating themselves from the dominance of the large landowners of Lolland, and by the early 19th century the island population had reached its height of 1,500 inhabitants – sufficiently large to maintain a doctor and midwife.

Although most of the island is given over to fruit farming, there is some lovely wild walking and riding country at Skobnakken, on the north coast, and Skalo, a 100 hectare (250 acre) salt-meadow islet approached by a causeway where wading birds roost and cattle roam free. There are two charming villages of traditional thatched cottages – Vesterby, where the ferry comes in, and Østerby with its old boatyard – each with a picturesque harbour and jetty. Despite its tiny size, Fejø is a wonderful place for farm and beach holidays, with plenty of activities to suit children and adults alike.

The harbour at Fejø

Funen

The third largest Danish island, lying between Jutland and Zealand, Funen has 1,125 km (700 mi) of varied coast – broad, sandy beaches interspersed with grassland reaching to the sea line and stretches of steep cliff with magnificent views over the Baltic. The low-lying, undulating countryside is dotted with more than a hundred fairytale castles, sumptuous manor houses, historic churches and windmills. It is one of the loveliest regions of Denmark.

The island's cultural centre is Odense – a city with a thousand years of history, nowadays best known for being the birthplace of Hans Christian Andersen. Wandering around the ancient town centre, you can easily conjure yourself into a fairytale. In the summer, the city buzzes with lively, round-the-clock street life and a warm, friendly atmosphere emanates from the many bars, cafés and music venues round the main square.

The historic coastal towns are well worth seeing. The east coast port of Nyborg, one of the oldest towns in Denmark and former capital, has a magnificent medieval castle near the marketplace. Faaborg, on the south coast, is particularly beautiful with its 17th century half-timbered, pastel coloured merchants' houses. There is also a wonderful art museum and some of the island's best beaches. The southern port of Svendborg is the gateway to the cluster of small islands off the coast. Just to the west is Skovsbo Strand where the famous playwright, Bertolt Brecht lived and worked for some years.

Funen is a relaxed rural paradise where the pace of life is slow and nothing seems to have changed for centuries. It is little wonder that it is called the 'Garden of Denmark'.

POPULATION:
447,000 (2006)
WHEN TO GO:
May to September
HOW TO GET THERE:
From Copenhagen – the Great Belt Bridge, a combination bridge and tunnel, connects Funen with Zealand by road and rail. A staggering feat of engineering, it is worth crossing just for the sake of it.
HIGHLIGHTS:
Egeskov Castle and Gardens – a Renaissance castle built on oak pillars in the middle of a lake.
Valdemars Slot – a 17th century Baroque castle.
Mads Lerches Gard, Nyborg – built in 1601, this mayor's house gives a wonderful insight into 17th century life.
H.C. Andersen's Hus – a museum dedicated to the fairytale writer's life and works.
Odense City Museum – a genuinely interesting city museum tracing Odense's history back to its Viking past.
YOU SHOULD KNOW:
The famous 'time warp' island of Aero is just off the south coast of Funen and is well worth a visit. Its capital Aeroskobing is an 18th century town preserved intact and the entire island is a picture-book cliché – but none the less charming for that.

Egeskov Castle

Bornholm

POPULATION:
43,040 (2006)
WHEN TO GO:
May to September
HOW TO GET THERE:
Fly or take the overnight ferry from Copenhagen. Alternatively, take a ferry or catamaran from Ystad (Sweden).
HIGHLIGHTS:
Rundkirkes – four medieval round churches.
Ertholmene (Christiansoe) – Denmark's easternmost point, a 17th century island fortress with fewer than 100 inhabitants, 20 km (13 mi) to the northeast.
Bornholm Art Museum, near Gudhjem.
Gronbechs Gard, Hasle – historic merchant's house transformed into an exhibition and cultural centre.
NaturBornholm, Aakirkeby – cultural and natural history centre designed by visionary Danish architect, Henning Larsen.
Eating warm smoked herring from the fish smokehouses of Aarsdale or Hasle.
YOU SHOULD KNOW:
If you want to visit Bornholm in June or July be sure to book accommodation well in advance. Although the island is a little-known international tourist destination, it is extremely popular among the Danes.

In the middle of the Baltic, some 100 km (60 mi) off the coast of Zealand, a solitary granite outcrop suddenly rises out of the sea. Bornholm is one of the oldest visible rocks in the world, formed by volcanic activity more than a thousand million years ago.

This idyllic little island is 588 sq km (227 sq mi) of rolling hills covered in a patchwork of farms, forests and heathland criss-crossed by more than 200 km (125 mi) of paths – a paradise for cyclists and hikers. Sandy beaches stretch all along the southern shore while towards the north the coastline grows increasingly rugged with small sheltered coves nestling between dramatic rock formations.

Bornholm appears to have been inhabited since at least 3600 BC and everywhere on the island there are reminders from the past – traces of Neolithic and Bronze Age settlements, strategically placed medieval runic stones and churches, picturesque old fishing villages and hamlets. The island's history is a turbulent one, attested to by the fact that the largest fortress in Northern Europe has been standing here since the 13th century. The massive Hammerhus was erected on the northern tip of the island, affording a sweeping view of the surrounding seas and Swedish coast whilst protected from a land attack by a deep wooded valley.

The unusual quality of light here, with only four hours of darkness in summer, has long attracted Danish artists to the island. There is also a thriving music scene – in the summer months the island comes alive with village fêtes and a jazz festival. The main town of Ronne, on the west coast, is a lively 700-year-old port with cobbled streets and a beautiful church. Whether you are seeking natural beauty, culture or entertainment, this beautiful island provides them all.

One of four medieval round churches to be found on Bornholm. These churches were also used as fortresses – probably to ward off Slavic pirates.

Samsø

Once a Viking assembly ground and site of a legendary battle against the 'Berserkers', a terrifying warrior cult, Samsø lies 15 km (9mi) off the east coast of Jutland. It is only 28 km (18 mi) long with a complex, indented coastline linking its two distinct parts, North Island and South Island. These ancient islands were joined at the end of the Ice Age, when the melting glacier waters washed up deposits that created the landscape around Stavns Fjord – a strikingly beautiful conservation area of more than 1,500 hectares (3,700 acres) of low-lying heathland, meadows and reefs. The highest point at 64 m (210 ft) is Ballebjerg in North Island, a region of rolling countryside ideal for cycling and walking, while South Island is open farming land gently sloping to the coast, dotted with picturesque villages, manor houses, and harbours with lovely views over the Baltic.

Samsø is renowned as an ecological 'green dream' island. The entire community has pulled together to demonstrate that it is perfectly possible to be carbon neutral. Electricity is produced by the island's windmills and an offshore wind farm, which between them are able to generate more than enough energy to supply the inhabitants and offset the fuel used by the island ferry service; any excess is sent to the mainland. The islanders heat their water by means of solar panels at community heating plants as well as individual straw-burning central heating systems. All the island's vehicles are run on home-grown biofuel.

Apart from a few days every July, when visitors pour in for the annual Music Festival, Samsø is a remarkably uncrowded, eco-tourist haven in which to unwind, admire the scenery, and experience the hospitable tranquillity and relaxed pace of Danish island life.

Timber-frame houses on Samsø

POPULATION:
4,124 (2006)

WHEN TO GO:
Early May to early September

HOW TO GET THERE:
Ferry from Hov, near Aarhus, Jutland to Saelvig, Samsø or from Kalundborg, Zealand to Kolby Kaas, Samsø.

HIGHLIGHTS:
The Samsø Labyrinth – officially the biggest maze in the world with a path 5,130 m (16,830 ft) long, was opened here in 2000.
Ballen fishing village.
Nordby – the prettiest village on the island with timbered houses and distinctive church belfry.
The harbour at Langor.

YOU SHOULD KNOW:
The island is famous for its early new potato and strawberry crops. In June and July young people come from all over the EU for strawberry-picking holidays.

The Faroes

Battered by the North Atlantic seas between Iceland and Norway, the Faroes are a group of 18 hauntingly beautiful islands. The archipelago covers a total area of 1,399 sq km (545 sq mi) and has a relatively benign climate, warmed by the Gulf Stream. The scenery is breathtaking: rugged basalt mountains up to 880 m (2,880 ft) high are thickly carpeted with impossibly green grass, incised everywhere by waterfalls, rivers and fjords. Sheer cliffs soar upward, ledges teeming with colonies of puffins, gannets and storm petrels. Extraordinary skies constantly transform the landscape, playing kaleidoscopic tricks of light and shade; sea mists descend suddenly, only to give way moments later to streams of sunshine.

Little is known of the islands' early history. Irish hermits settled in the 7th century, introducing sheep and oats, and by the 9th century Vikings had landed. The islands fell under Norwegian control but, from the 14th century, increasingly fell under the sway of Denmark. Today, although still Danish territory, the islanders take pride in their independence of spirit and inimitable forms of Viking language, singing and dance.

The Faroes are still mercifully tourist-free. Many of the inhabitants still live by sheep farming and fishing, in isolated crofts and old fishing villages of brightly painted houses with turf roofs. The charming port of Torshavn, Europe's smallest capital, is on Streymoy, the largest island. A bridge and tunnel connect Streymoy to nearby Eysturoy and regular ferries ply between all the islands. The westernmost island of Vágar has the best tourist facilities and Sudoroy, two hours to the far south, is perhaps the most beautiful of all.

It is impossible not to succumb to the eerie enchantment of these captivating islands, where the only sounds are of birds calling, water trickling over rocks, wind lashing across the headlands, and the breakers dashing the cliffs at the outer edges of the world.

POPULATION:
48,317 (2006)

WHEN TO GO:
May to September, unless you're an exceptionally hardy type.

HOW TO GET THERE:
Regular year-round car ferries from Denmark, Norway, Scotland and the Shetlands. Alternatively, fly to Vágar – the only island flat enough for an airport.

HIGHLIGHTS:
Historic villages – Sandavágur on Vágar and Gjógv on Eysturoy.
Rinkusteinar – 'rocking stones' near village of Oyndarfjordur on Eysturoy.
Lakes of Vágar – Fjallavatn and Hviltkinnavatn.
14th century Magnus Cathedral and the oldest inhabited wooden house in Europe, both to be found at the lovely village of Kirkjubour on Streymoy.
Vestmanna on Streymoy – Boat trip through gorges to spectacular bird cliffs.
Beinisvøro Mountain on Suduroy.

YOU SHOULD KNOW:
Although the Faroes are part of the Kingdom of Denmark, they are moving towards full self-government – they already have their own parliament, flag and language, and are not part of the EU.

A typical fjord village on the Faroe Islands

Terschelling

POPULATION:
4,702 (2007)
WHEN TO GO:
June to September
HOW TO GET THERE:
Ferry from Harlingen (The Netherlands) to West-Terschelling.
HIGHLIGHTS:
Oerol Festival – 10 days every June when around 50,000 people suddenly descend on the island for this incredible cultural event. The whole island becomes an open-air venue for inspired drama, music, art and dance. The villages, dunes, woods, barns and boathouses are used as improvised stages and galleries.
The 16th and 17th century Commodore Houses built for the commanders of the whaling fleets, near Brandaris lighthouse – a 16th century firehouse, 54 m (177 ft) high – in West Terschelling.
The historic village of Midsland.
De Boschplaat Nature Reserve – though there is restricted access during breeding season, from mid-March to mid-August.
YOU SHOULD KNOW:
Don't bother to bring a car here. There are plenty of buses and taxis but the best way of getting around is by bike.

The Dutch island of Terschelling snakes its way along the Dutch coast for 29 km (18 mi) creating a barrier between the North and Wadden Seas. It is the most accessible of the West Frisian Islands, with miles of unspoiled shoreline and a wonderfully varied landscape for its size – only 4 km (2.5 mi) across at its broadest point.

The north coast is a white-sand beach, up to 1 km (over 0.5 mi) wide, backed by windswept dunes with a hinterland of pine forest. To the south is salt marsh – lush meadowland where cattle graze and cranberries grow. The entire eastern end of the island is a nature reserve for migratory birds. From all over the island there are beautiful views – southwards across the mottled earthy shades of the marshes and light-reflecting shallows, northwards over the seemingly endless expanse of the North Sea to a distant horizon.

The main town, West-Terschelling, is a charming port on the south coast, steeped in maritime history. The islanders are renowned for their seamanship, resilience and resourcefulness, and for hundreds of years made fortunes in the whaling industry as well as playing a major role in the 17th century Anglo-Dutch naval trade wars. Only in the 19th century, with the re-routing of shipping, did they turn to farming and, more recently, tourism for their livelihood.

There are walks, cycle paths and bridleways that take you all over the island, superb beaches for sand yachting and surfing, and plenty of opportunities for sailing or just mucking around on a boat. Although Terschelling can be busy in the summer, the island rarely feels crowded. There is a real sense of being at one with nature here – a wonderful sense of freedom and space under vast, ever-changing skies.

One of Terschelling's superb beaches

Heligoland

The tiny island of Heligoland, 70 km (44 mi) off the German coast, towers up unexpectedly, its dramatic rust-coloured cliffs rising up to 61 m (200 ft) high out of the grey emptiness of the North Sea. It is a geological mystery – although its bedrock is limestone, like the White Cliffs of Dover, the island itself is composed of layers of sandstone, unlike any other rock form in the region.

In the 19th century, this 1 sq km (0.4 sq mi) wedge of land was considered the healthiest place in Germany and attracted the attention of artists and writers, Kafka and Goethe among them. The invigorating sea air has an exceptionally low pollen count and the climate is mild, with more sunshine than the mainland and long balmy autumns. Even in winter the weather is rarely cold – fig and mulberry trees flourish here. A ten-minute boat ride to the north-west is a low-lying islet known as The Düne, part of the main island until 1720, when a violent storm caused a huge surge that permanently separated it. It is uninhabited apart from a seal colony, and there are two idyllic, long sandy beaches for bathing and camping.

Amazingly, considering its remoteness, there are signs of prehistoric habitation here. From the 7th century it was populated by Frisians, who named it "Helgyeland" (Holy Land). Although the islanders were semi-autonomous, surviving by fishing, smuggling and wrecking ships, sovereignty alternated between Denmark, Britain and Germany. In 1890, the British swapped it with Germany in return for Zanzibar, but after World War II, the Royal Navy evicted all the inhabitants and tried to bomb it to bits. Although they failed, the force of the explosions left a huge dent in the landscape – a permanent reminder of Heligoland's turbulent past.

POPULATION:
1,650 (2006)

WHEN TO GO:
The best weather is from May to October but the island is interesting at any time of year.

HOW TO GET THERE:
The ferry from Cuxhaven takes two hours. Passengers are met by fishing boats which take them to land.

HIGHLIGHTS:
Lange Anna – a freestanding rock stack 47 m (135 ft) high, Heligoland's symbol.
Lummenfelsen (Guillemots' Rock) – the smallest nature conservation area in the world, where you can watch seabirds and seals.
Unterland heated open-air seawater swimming pool.
Heligoland Historical Museum – to find out more about the history, culture and traditions of this island.
Marine Biology Institute Aquarium – for a close-up look at plants and creatures lurking in the North Sea.
Eating Heligoland lobster – expensive but worth every penny.

YOU SHOULD KNOW:
Heligoland is a tax-free zone so all goods you buy there are at bargain prices, but check your allowances – you may be stopped at customs on re-entering mainland Europe.

An aerial view of Heligoland

A narrow guage railway runs from Hallig Langeness to Oland.

Wadden Sea Hallig Islands

POPULATION:
About 290 (Langeness 100, Hooge 120) (2004)

WHEN TO GO:
The tourist season is May to September but nature lovers and endurance enthusiasts will find the Halligen fascinating at any time of year.

HOW TO GET THERE:
Ferry from Schlüttsiel or Dagebüll, or from the North Frisian Islands of Amrum, Föhr or Sylt.

HIGHLIGHTS:
The lighthouse on Hallig Oland – the only lighthouse in Europe with a thatched roof has a lantern painted red on one side and green on the other to show ships at which point they must change course.
The Königspesel, Hooge – a richly ornamented room with all its original fixtures and fittings in a traditional house showing how people lived on the Halligs.
View from Nordemarsch Lighthouse, Langeness.
Museums, Langeness.

YOU SHOULD KNOW:
The seasonal migrations (spring and autumn) in this globally significant birding region are amazing to experience – the skies are choked with wild duck, crane and geese – more than 3 million birds whirling overhead. Be warned – the tides are notoriously tricky and you should never wander around the mudflats without local guidance.

The Halligen (salt lands) are not strictly islands; they are patches of raised saltmarsh created by tides and floods, without any sea defences. There is huge tidal variation in this part of the North Sea and in winter, at high tide, the islands virtually disappear, while at low tide you can walk across the mudflats to adjacent Halligen. Of the hundreds that once existed only ten remain, scattered over an area 20 x 30 km (12 x 19 sq mi) in the Waddenmeer National Park of Schleswig-Holstein. They are part of the same extraordinary tidal ecosystem that has effected the creation of the North Frisian Islands.

The surreal scenery of these 'dreams floating on the sea' is unforgettable – eerie mirages often appear to be hanging in thin air as land, sea and sky all merge. It is a testament to human ingenuity that the islanders have found a way of inhabiting the continually shifting marshlands. For centuries, they have protected their buildings and livestock against the ravages of the *landunder* (storm tides) by building their houses on *warften* (raised dwelling mounds). Throughout the 17th and 18th centuries they grew enormously wealthy through seafaring, whaling and cattle-rearing. However, the region never recovered after a devastating flood in 1825 destroyed 90 per cent of the old farmsteads and drowned hundreds of the islanders.

Hallig Langeness is the largest at 9.5 sq km (3.7 sq mi) but Hooge at 5.7 sq km (2.2 sq mi) with its church and ten *warften*, is considered the 'Queen of the Halligen'. The other Halligen are bird sanctuaries. The solitude and tranquillity you will find on these strange islands confronts you with a stunning sense of the forces of nature as you immerse yourself in the power of the sea and revel in the scarcely believable sunrises and sunsets.

North Frisian Islands

The North Frisian Islands were once part of the mainland 'geest' – a sandy heathland ridge stretching along the North Sea coast of Germany. Centuries of battering by powerful tides have created the islands of Sylt, Amrum and Föhr, all still in a continual process of changing size and shape. They are part of the unique ecosystem of tidal flats, beaches, sandbanks and saltmarsh along the low-lying coastal region of Schleswig-Holstein.

Sylt is still linked to the mainland by a causeway at low tide. This 'island with a thousand faces' is the largest at 100 sq km (62 sq mi) and most sophisticated of the North Frisians. The west coast is a dramatic landscape of cliffs, dunes and crashing waves, renowned for its 40 km (25 mi) of sandy beaches; to the east, open heathland gives way to stark, wild saltmarsh. There are excellent sports facilities, beautiful walks and cycle paths here and the island is a fashionable holiday retreat for German celebrities.

The least populated island is Amrum – only 20 sq km (12 sq mi) – a remote paradise to immerse yourself in nature. You will find the widest sandy beach in Europe here, with spectacular dunes up to 32 m (105 ft) high. Föhr at 82 sq km (50 sq mi) is the greenest of the three islands, a mecca for birdwatchers, with a single seaside resort, the town of Wyk, and sixteen tiny hamlets.

A visit to the North Frisians is a step into another world with its own distinctive folk culture. The inhabitants still speak their own Frisian dialect, wear traditional costume, and live in picturesque villages of neatly thatched houses with immaculate, brightly coloured cottage gardens. The islands are a fascinating, relatively little-known region of Northern Europe resonating with the unique history of these hardy but hospitable, seafaring people.

POPULATION:
Amrum 2,300; Sylt 21,000; Föhr 8,800 (2005)

WHEN TO GO:
The tourist season is May to September but nature lovers and hardy souls will find the islands interesting throughout the year.

HOW TO GET THERE:
Ferry from Schlüttsiel or Dagebüll and ferries running between the islands.

HIGHLIGHTS:
Bronze monument to poet Heinrich Heine by Arno Breker – City Hall, Sylt.
Historic houses in Westerland, Sylt.
Frisian Cathedral of St Johannis and 12th and 13th century churches, Föhr.
Frisian Museum, Föhr.
Frisian village of Nevel, Amrum.

YOU SHOULD KNOW:
Only walk across the mudflats if accompanied by a local expert guide. The tides are notoriously tricky and on even the sunniest day sea mist can descend without warning.

Reichenau

POPULATION:
5,113 (2006)
WHEN TO GO:
May to September
HOW TO GET THERE:
By road or railway to Konstanz.
HIGHLIGHTS:
The abbey – this was an important spiritual centre for over 1,000 years. Some of what remains today dates from the 9th century.
The Reichenau Museum – housed in the former bailiff's house (one of the oldest half-timbered buildings in southern Germany), the museum tells the story of life in the monastery.
The Ottonian murals in the church of St George, showing the miracles of Christ.
The treasure vaults in the abbey, still housing some of the precious relics given to the monks.
Wander through the pastoral landscape and breathe in the history of this charming island.
YOU SHOULD KNOW:
The island is connected to the mainland by a causeway.

Reichenau Island lies in Lake Constance in southern Germany. For more than 1,000 years, the Benedictine complex here was one of the most important religious centres in Europe. It has been listed by UNESCO as a World Heritage Site because it is the best-preserved ancient monastery north of the Alps and played an influential role in the development of Christian art.

The monastery was founded by St Pirmin in 724, who settled there with 40 of his followers. The abbey soon became a flourishing concern, one of the most important religious and cultural centres in Europe. It was here that the famous monastery plan of St Gall was drafted, an influential set of rules for monastery construction and one of the most important documents of Western monasticism. The monastery's abbots were government officials at the Court, educators of the royal princes, diplomats and envoys of the Emperor.

In the 10th and 11th centuries, the Abbey was home to a famous scriptorium, where the monks produced magnificent illuminated manuscripts for influential customers such as Emperor Otto III and Heinrich II. They used gold, silver and purple inks, and precious metals and ivory for the bindings. Many of these beautiful works can still be found in some of the most revered libraries in the world.

During its heyday, the Reichenau abbey collected many precious relics which remain to this day in their splendid shrines in the treasure vault. On certain holy days they are carried across the island in festive processions. The most important relics include those of the evangelist Mark, the jug from the wedding at Cana, and the relic of the Holy Blood.

The abbey's bailiff lived in a two-storey stone building which was raised by two more storeys of half-timbered construction in the 14th century. Today housing the island's museum, this is one of the oldest half-timbered buildings in southern Germany. As well as telling the story of the monastery, it has exhibits about life on this tranquil island and the surrounding area.

The religious sites on Reichenau

Island are not just limited to the monastery. In the 9th century, Abbot Hatto built a church devoted to St George on the island. The nave still displays some beautiful Ottonian murals showing the miracles of Christ, the only remaining murals of their kind painted before the year 1,000 north of the Alps. Above the entrance to the crypt lies a tomb in which the relics of St George are kept.

The church of St Peter and Paul, a three-nave basilica, was built in the 12th century in Reichenau-Niederzell. Its east towers were added in the 15th century, and the western porch in the 16th or 17th century. The semi-circular apse features a painting from the 12th century, depicting Christ with the Apostles. Other murals were added over the following years, and today there remain scenes from the Passion in the southern side chapel and the porch, and scenes of St Peter in the chancel. In 1756 the church of St Peter and Paul was renovated in the Baroque style, with flat ceilings and Rococco stucco, a style which is still evident today.

Vineyards on Reichenau

Traditional deckchairs on the beach at Usedom

POPULATION:
76,500 (2005)
WHEN TO GO:
May to September
HOW TO GET THERE:
Fly to Usedom. Road/rail from Szczecin, Poland or Zussöw, Germany.
HIGHLIGHTS:
Wasserschloss, Mellenthin – Renaissance castle.
medieval churches in the villages of Benz, Morgenitz, Zirchow and Liepe.
Kamminke – a small fishing port.
Coastal views from the villages of Ziemitz and Neeberg.
Stolpe Castle.
Swinemünde outdoor market in the Polish part of the island.
YOU SHOULD KNOW:
In World War II the island was used as a forced labour and prisoner of war camp. The small village of Peenemünde, renowned as the 'cradle of space travel', was the centre for the V2 missile tests that formed the basis of all modern rocket technology.

Usedom

Germany's second largest island, Usedom is a picturesque, low-lying landscape of rolling meadows, woods and lakes dotted with thatched cottages, windmills and medieval churches. The island, 445 sq km (175 sq mi) in area, lies to the northeast of the lagoon of Stettin at the mouth of the River Oder, the border between Germany and Poland. Inhabited since the Stone Age, first by Slavic tribes then Viking pirates, Usedom was German territory until 1945, when Poland was granted sovereignty over the eastern end and the entire German population were expelled to the west of the island.

The sunniest spot on the North German coast, Usedom is perfect for seaside holidays, with over 100 km (60 mi) of cycle paths, 400 km (250 mi) of walking trails and 40 km (25 mi) of flawless sandy beaches. The northwestern hinterland is one of the most beautiful parts, where the woodland descends steeply to the coast and you are likely to spot sea eagles circling overhead. In the south east of the island there are some lovely stretches of gently undulating scenery enclosing lakes and sleepy villages.

The island's historic spa towns exude an unmistakeable air of culture and luxury. There are rows of magnificent 19th century mansions, elegant Art Nouveau villas, and stately piers more than 300 m (985 ft) long. Ahlbeck, Heringsdorf and Bansin, three former fishing villages on the north coast, are amongst the oldest of the Baltic 'bathtub of Berlin' seaside holiday resorts. They are popularly known as The Dreikaiserbäder (The Emperor's Three Baths), the haunt of the cream of 19th century society and international names like Johann Strauss, Tolstoy and Maxim Gorki. Today, strolling along the promenades, it takes little imagination to transport oneself back into the glamour of the past, retracing the footsteps of European nobility.

Mainau

Emerald water and snowy mountain peaks provide a scenic backdrop to this glorious 45 hectare (111 acre) 'island of flowers', one of three very different but equally interesting islands in Lake Constance. The lake, which is Central Europe's third largest, lies on the Rhine between Germany, Switzerland and Austria.

Visitors to Mainau invariably have all their expectations surpassed when they find themselves landing in one of the most beautiful parks of Europe with a fairytale Baroque palace at its heart. The island gardens are an implausible jungle of exotic vegetation, citrus trees and orchids, made possible by the mild microclimate of the lake. The overwhelming variety of different species, colours and fragrances is an incredible sensory experience – you can relax under palm and sequoia trees, explore winding side paths, catch the scent of orange blossom in the air mingled with all sorts of less familiar fragrances, and dazzle your eye with a kaleidoscope of colour before wandering through parkland to an incredible view over the lake itself.

For 500 years Mainau belonged to the Order of the Teutonic Knights, a Roman Catholic military religious order formed at the end of the 12th century to fight in the Crusades. In 1853 it was bought by the Grand Duke of Baden, who built the palace as a summer holiday residence. The island passed through his heirs until 1932, when it was inherited by Count Lennart Bernadotte, a philanthropist who had a philosophy of environmentally friendly gardening for the benefit of humanity. He initiated the idea of the garden in its present form, set up the Bernadotte Foundation to run it, and opened Mainau to the public.

Count Bernadotte died in 2004, but the island is still run by the Countess on behalf of the Foundation according to his principles; the garden of Mainau is not only breathtakingly beautiful but a model of sound ecological practice.

POPULATION:
Family and retainers
WHEN TO GO:
April to September
HOW TO GET THERE:
Regular boat services from Konstanz or the island of Lindau.
HIGHLIGHTS:
Butterfly House – the largest in Germany.
Palm tree glasshouse.
Schlosskirche.
Mainau Children's Land – Waterworld.
Lake Constance Natural History Museum.
Rhine Falls, Neuhausen – the largest waterfall in Europe, 60 km (38 mi) away.
YOU SHOULD KNOW:
The head gardener or one of his team is always available to dispense gardening tips and ecology advice to visitors.

Tulips on Mainau Island

Hiiumaa

POPULATION:
11,900 (2003)
WHEN TO GO:
May to September, although hardy eco-tourists will be prepared to brave the icy Russian winds for the sake of the winter scenery and wildlife.
HOW TO GET THERE:
Ferry from Rohuküla, mainland Estonia, takes 90 minutes; or from Triigi, on the neighbouring island of Saaremaa, takes 60 minutes. (No boats in winter when the sea is iced up). Twice-daily flights from Tallin to Kärdla airport, takes 45 minutes.
HIGHLIGHTS:
Kopu lighthouse – more than 500 years old, this is the third oldest working lighthouse in the world; 36 m (120 ft) high, it was built as a seamark to prevent the local wreckers and pirates from leading ships aground on the reefs.
Sääre Tirp – a 3 km (2 mi) long tongue of land stretching into the sea, one of the most beautiful places on the island.
Pühalepa Church – one of the oldest on the island, with a stone pulpit dating from the 13th century.
Rebastemäe Nature Trail – passes through highest point of Hiiumaa.
Ristimägi – Hill of Crosses – a sandy hillock where traditionally any passer-by leaves a cross made out of any material at hand.
Kassari Peninsula – wooded landscape with secluded beaches, thatched chapel, windmill and orchard.
YOU SHOULD KNOW:
Estonians regard the island as a sort of national nirvana. Many artists and musicians have retreats here.

Hiiumaa is a bleak but breathtakingly beautiful island in the Eastern Baltic, a nature reserve that covers an area of just under 1,000 sq km (390 sq mi). It is Estonia's second largest island, separated from the mainland by a 22 km (14 mi) wide strait and surrounded by some 200 deserted islets and reefs where, over the centuries, hundreds of ships have come to grief; today there are seal colonies, a rarity in the Baltic.

More than half the island is covered in pine, birch, and spruce forest with many rare plant species – a haven for wildlife; elks, deer, wild boar, and even lynxes may be spotted. The 320 km (200 mi) coastline of meadowland, peat moor, juniper shrubbery, and dunes is highly indented with long stretches of isolated sandy beach. Amongst the hundreds of bird species that nest and migrate here are black storks, golden eagles, cranes and avocets. Less than a quarter of the island is farmland and there is only one sizeable settlement, the town of Kärdla.

Kopu lighthouse is the third oldest working lighthouse in the world.

Human settlement on Hiiumaa dates back to around 4000 BC. It was inhabited by nomadic Germanic tribes until the Swedes discovered it around 1300 AD. Eventually the island became Swedish territory until, at the beginning of the 18th century, it was integrated into the Russian Empire. After enduring turmoil in both World Wars, it became part of independent Estonia in 1991. Although little of the island's history has been recorded, there is a strong sense of its seafaring tradition that continues to be handed down from one generation to the next.

For eco-tourists, Hiiumaa is as unspoiled as it gets – a perfect place to commune with nature, explore unusual scenery and escape from the mainstream tourist routes.

Kihnu

Kihnu lies 12 km (7 mi) off the coast of Estonia and is the largest of more than a dozen islands in the reefs and shallows of the Gulf of Riga. It is 16 sq km (6 sq mi) in area with a low ridge running down the middle and only 9 m (30 ft) above sea level at its highest point. The island farmsteads are enclosed by forest, which prevents soil erosion as well as protecting the islanders from the bitter northeast winds. Huge broadleaf trees stand like sentinels in the coastal meadowlands that lead to a 36 km (22 mi) long shoreline of dunes and shifting sands where the scent of juniper is everywhere in the air. The island is a nesting place for hundreds of bird species and the coastal reef is home to the last grey seal colony in the Baltic.

The first historical documents relating to Kihnu date from the late 14th century but excavations show that the island was inhabited – at least, during the summer months – from around 1500 BC. It has at various times been under Danish, Swedish, Estonian, Polish and Russian rule, reflecting the turbulent history of the Baltic. Since time immemorial the men here have been seafarers and fishermen, skilled at woodwork and shipbuilding, while the women are wholly responsible for working the land and keeping alive the rich island culture of music, dance and poetry.

A trip to Kihnu transports you back in time into a fascinating folk culture. The inhabitants speak their own language and wear traditional homespun costume. Each woman makes her family's clothes with intricately knitted, woven and embroidered patterns symbolizing ancient legends. The islanders are symbiotically bound up with their harsh environment, their survival entirely dependent upon cultural loyalty and community sharing. Against all odds, they have managed to hang onto their heritage at the same time as welcoming strangers to their shores.

POPULATION:
639 (2004)
WHEN TO GO:
May to September unless you want a cold weather experience. In winter the island is ice-bound and covered in snow.
HOW TO GET THERE:
Fly or ferry from Parnü on the Estonian coast; in winter, drive across the iced-up sea for an unusual experience.
HIGHLIGHTS:
Lemsi – a fishing village and port.
Kihnu Local Lore Museum – Kihnu's history and cultural centre with an art collection including paintings by acclaimed Estonian artist, Jaan Oad.
Kihnu Orthodox Church – containing the grave of legendary seafarer, Kihnu Jonn.
Kihnu lighthouse.
Juanipäe – St John's Day, summer solstice ritual celebrations on the shortest night of the year, 23 June, with dancing and singing until sunrise.
A trip to the nearby island of Manija to see the huge Kokakivi boulder.
YOU SHOULD KNOW:
The rich cultural heritage and fragile eco-structure of Kihnu are incredibly vulnerable. The island has been declared a UNESCO Masterpiece of the Oral & Intangible Heritage of Humanity in an attempt to minimize the negative impact of mass tourism and assist the islanders in preserving their way of life without selling out to the tourist trade.

Severnaya Zemlya

POPULATION:
Uninhabited apart from scientific observatories.
WHEN TO GO:
June to August
HOW TO GET THERE:
On an icebreaker ship as part of an Arctic North-East Passage adventure cruise.
HIGHLIGHTS:
Polar bears on Golomyanny Island – where two families of polar scientists have been living and working for the past 16 years.Icebergs in the Red Army Strait. Weird ice formations of the Arctic desert.
YOU SHOULD KNOW:
Global warming is causing the Arctic Sea ice to melt at an extraordinary rate. Over the past two winters the total amount of ice has shrunk by 6 per cent compared to 1.5 per cent over the entire previous decade.

This Arctic archipelago covers a total land area of some 38,000 sq km (15,000 sq mi) nearly half of which is permanently iced over – a frozen wonderland of 17 distinct glacier systems containing ice domes, ice shelves, ice flows and the largest ice cap of the Russian Arctic, 819 m (2,686 ft) thick.

There are four major islands and some 70 small ones with dramatic mountainous scenery, rising to a height of 965 m (3,165 ft) containing lowland areas of arctic desert, tundra and coastal plains. Despite the severe conditions – a mean annual temperature of -16 °C (3.2°F) and six months of the year in total darkness – there is a remarkable variety of plant and animal life. In the short summers the ice-free areas suddenly sprout a strange patchwork of red and green lichens, velvety mosses and bright purple saxifrage. Polar bears trek across the ice floes, and wolves, reindeer, arctic foxes, collared lemmings and arctic hares all manage to survive here, as well as 32 bird species including snowy owls, little auks, and kittiwakes.

The existence of Severnaya Zemlya (North Land) was unknown until 1913. It was the last archipelago in the world to be discovered and is the least accessible group of islands in the Arctic, surrounded by iced-up seas. Boris Vilkitsky, a Russian surveyor exploring the region in an ice-breaker, unexpectedly found himself in the 55 km (34 mi) wide strait (later named after him) that separates the islands from mainland Siberia. This was a momentous discovery: ever since the 16th century explorers had been attempting to shorten the trade route to Asia by finding a North-East Passage from the Barents Sea to the Bering Strait. Today, the journey into one of the least explored and most extreme regions on earth is still an arduous one – a once in a lifetime adventure.

Solovetsky Islands

Less than 160 km (100 mi) from the Arctic Circle in the western part of the White Sea, the Solovetsky archipelago is an ancient place of pilgrimage with a historic UNESCO World Heritage fortified monastery. There are six large islands and countless skerries covering a total land area of 300 sq km (120 sq mi). The climate is relatively mild, benefiting from the Gulf Stream current, and the scenery is extraordinarily varied – hills and pine forests, fens, lakes and birch trees, sandbanks covered in boulders, rocky ridges and sand dunes – a haven for an abundance of flora and fauna.

Solovetsky has a memorable history of both intense spirituality and indescribable suffering. The first permanent settlers were two hermits, Sabbatius and Herman, who arrived on Greater Solovetsky, the largest of the islands, around 1430. They were soon joined by like-minded searchers after solitude and a monastery was founded in 1436. The island gradually grew into an influential religious and political centre, attracting the attention of the Tsar who gave orders for fortifications to be built and a garrison to be stationed here.

The hermits' spiritual dream was beginning to turn into a worldly nightmare. Their monastery became one of the largest and most powerful of the Russian kremlins (fortresses) and by the end of the 17th century it was one of the largest monasteries in the world. Later, as its strategic importance declined, the island became a place of exile and death for political and religious troublemakers, a practice that grew to apocalyptic proportions under Stalin.

Despite the bleakness of its past, there is a hypnotic spiritual quality in the atmosphere of Solovetsky. There are spectacular natural as well as manmade wonders and you cannot help but fall under the spell of the Russian north.

POPULATION:
1,000 (2002)
WHEN TO GO:
June to September
HOW TO GET THERE:
Sea boats from Karelian towns of Kem and Belomorsk. Cruise ship from Moscow and Arkhangelsk. By helicopter from Petrozavodsk or Arkhangelsk, twice weekly plane from Arkhangelsk.
HIGHLIGHTS:
Solovetsky Kremlin – massive walls up to 6 m (20 ft) thick – built of boulders from the beaches, complete with monastic buildings and churches.
The Botanical Garden – wide variety of plants.
Zayatsky Islands – prehistoric sacred labyrinths, burial mounds, medieval church, and bird colonies.
Exploring the intricate canal and lake system in a rowing boat – the canals were dug out by the monks over the centuries.
Belugas Cape – where you can see whales. Muksalma Island Dam – 19th century monks used Muksalma to graze their cattle; to make transportation easier they erected a huge boulder dam about 1 km (0.62 mi) long and 6.5 m (21 ft) wide, an incredible feat of engineering.
YOU SHOULD KNOW:
Under Stalin, the island was made into a gulag (forced labour camp) and hundreds of thousands of prisoners died here. In 1980, when the Orthodox Church was re-established, Solovetsky instantly became a place of pilgrimage. At the 19th century Church of Ascension on Sekirnaya Hill, you can see the Commemoration Cross erected to honour the people executed here.

A view of Solovetsky monastery

Olkhon is one of the largest lake islands in the world.

POPULATION:
1,500 (2006)
WHEN TO GO:
The peak of the tourist season is from mid-June to mid-August when the weather is warm and dry. The end of May to the beginning of June is cooler but less crowded. For a winter experience, the best month is March. The weather is terrible in October, November and April – to be avoided!
HOW TO GET THERE:
A bus runs five days a week between Irkutsk and Kuzhir, Olkhon, an 8-hour trip including the ferry crossing.
HIGHLIGHTS:
Cape Burkhan – Shamanka Rock, the most sacred site on Lake Baikal with Buddhist inscriptions.
Peschanaya Bay – moving trees in shifting sand dunes.
Museum of Nature and History, Kuzhir.
Lake Khankhoy – the largest of Olkhon's salt lakes, where you can swin and fish.
Cape Sagan Khushun – a dramatic white marble promontory covered in red lichen.
YOU SHOULD KNOW:
Lake Baikal is a UNESCO World Heritage Site. The lake contains as much water as all the Great Lakes of North America combined. Despite its great depth, the water is well-oxygenated providing a unique biological habitat. It is one of the deepest active rifts on earth with sediment on the lake floor more than 7 km (4 mi) thick.

Olkhon Island

The great watery abyss of Lake Baikal is a huge rift valley in the heart of Siberia formed some 25 million years ago. It is both the oldest and the deepest lake in the world, containing around 20 per cent of the planet's fresh surface water. Olkhon, one of the largest lake islands in the world, is the geographical, historical and spiritual heart of Baikal, separated from the southwestern shore by a treacherous narrow strait near the lake's deepest point of 1,637 m (5,370 ft).

There are plentiful traces of human habitation on Olkhon from as long as 13,000 years ago; 143 archaeological sites have been discovered – rock paintings, burial mounds, settlements, defensive walls and sacred places. The Buryat inhabitants of the island are an indigenous people of Mongolian descent, yurt (tent) dwellers with a rich oral tradition and shamanic religious practices. The island is steeped in native myth and legend.

This beautiful island is 730 sq km (285 sq mi) in area and 72 km (45 mi) long, a wild prehistoric landscape of taiga (primeval fir forest), steppe, salt lakes and sand dunes, formed by the earth's shifting tectonic plates. All along the east coast, craggy mountains rear straight out of the lake up to 818 m (2,680 ft) high, in striking contrast to the rolling southern plain carpeted in wild grasses and aromatic herbs that seems to stretch forever – perfect for horse-riding and cycling. There is one proper village, Kuzhir, and a single main road run the length of the island. The rocky promontories along the western shore enclose deep bays with sandy beaches where you can camp in a yurt and go kayaking and fishing. You really are in the wilderness here: there are no power or telephone lines, no cell-phone reception, and the only electricity is from domestic generators.

Vasilyevsky

When Peter the Great decided to build his capital city at the mouth of the River Neva in 1703 he chose the largest and westernmost of the islands at the river's delta to be at its heart – the 'window by which the Russians might look out into a civilized Europe'. Vasilyevsky was a marshy uninhabited wasteland which the Tsar was determined to transform into his administrative centre, with streets of grand houses running alongside broad canals, modelled on Amsterdam. However, it proved impossible to transport materials, drive piles into the boggy ground and erect buildings at the speed required; the city continued to develop on the mainland and the canal plan was eventually scrapped.

Today, Vasilyevsky forms the northwestern corner of central St Petersburg, just across the river from the Winter Palace. The island is saturated in the city's past, containing many of the oldest buildings, dating from the early 18th century. The southern part is built on a grid with 30 'lines' going from south to north across three main avenues – the only traces that remain of Peter's grandiose canal scheme.

The eastern point where the Neva divides, known as the Strelka (Arrow), is a grassy crescent that was engineered by raising and lengthening the ragged, marshy end of the island and re-shaping it into a perfect semi-circle. Here are some of the grandest historical buildings, including the majestic Stock Exchange, reminiscent of a Greek temple. The Strelka is dominated by the Rostral Columns, 30 m (100 ft) tall red pillars decorated with ships' rostra, built in the early 19th century as a symbol of the naval supremacy of the Russian Empire.

From the Strelka there is a superb vista across the arc of the River Neva to the centre of one of the most beautiful cities in the world.

POPULATION:
1 million (2006)
WHEN TO GO:
Any time.
HOW TO GET THERE:
Fly to St Petersburg.
HIGHLIGHTS:
The historic buildings along the quay, including the Academy of Arts – late 18th century waterfront buildings.
Picturesque cobblestone lanes of terraced cottages washed in pale yellows and ochres.
The Institute of Russian Literature (Pushkin House) and Museum of Literature with manuscripts dating back to the 13th century – originally the Customs House.
Twelve Colleges – a long narrow early 18th century building originally intended to house government offices but taken over by the University.
Lieutenant Schmidt Bridge – the first bridge across the Neva.
The interior of Andreyevsky Cathedral
YOU SHOULD KNOW:
Vasilyevsky is traditionally a student and workers district – a convenient area of the city in which to find relatively cheap accommodation.

The Neva River divides at the Strelka into two channels.

Margaret Island

WHEN TO GO:
All year
HOW TO GET THERE:
Bus and tram.
HIGHLIGHTS:
The water tower near the theatre – there are stunning views from the cupola terrace high (153 steps) above the city and changing exhibitions in the Lookout Gallery.
Walking – the island is covered in chestnut trees; around the medieval monastery the paths are lined with statues of Hungarian writers and artists.
The Japanese Garden at the northern end with rocks, pools, waterfalls and exotic plants.
The Fountain towards the southern end – this is the country's highest fountain, with leaps of 25 m (82 ft).
The Centenary Monument, completed in 1973 to mark the union of Buda, Pest and Obuda, it displays nationalist and socialist symbols and is illuminated at night.
YOU SHOULD KNOW:
One of Hungary's most popular mineral waters is found and bottled here. The Romans drank and bathed in water from the same source.

Lying in the Danube anchored to the mainland by the Arpad and Margaret Bridges, Margaret Island is a wonderful green space between Buda and Pest. This tiny island – 2.5 km (1.4 mi) by 500 m (1,640 ft) has been used for various purposes over the years – a place of religious retreat, stabling for the horses of the Turks (and a home for their women of ill repute), a landscape garden for the royal family of Buda and, since 1869, a public park.

King Bela IV had a convent built here on what then was called Rabbit Island; his 11-year-old daughter Margit became a resident in 1251 (she was canonized in 1943) and now the island is named after her. The north of Margaret Island still has several old religious buildings – the cloister and church of the Dominican nuns, a 13 to 14th century Franciscan church, and the reconstructed Premonstratensian chapel whose tower houses the oldest bell in Hungary. Cast in the 15th century, it was found in 1914 in the roots of a storm-damaged tree, having been hidden from the Turks.

As in mainland Budapest, therapeutic springs make bathing here

a popular activity. The modern Hotel Thermal offers medical treatment facilities, and the Platinus Outdoor Baths in their lovely garden setting are filled with spa water. The Alfred Hajos sports swimming complex was designed by and named after the Olympic gold medalist. An open-air theatre and cinema occupy the south of the island.

Margaret Island is a peaceful, green place; it is car-free, though cycles and horse drawn vehicles are available. It also offers tennis, roller-skating and there are plenty of cafés.

The National Parliament on the Danube, looking towards Margaret Island.

Donauinsel

Donauinsel, which lies within the city area of Vienna, is a man-made island that divides the Danube from the New Danube. It stretches 21 km (13 mi) along the river, but has a maximum width of only 210 m (689 ft). It is used nowadays as a recreational area, but its main purpose is as a part of Vienna's sophisticated flood prevention scheme.

The enormous flow of water down the Danube had always resulted in serious flooding and, in 1870 to 75, work was undertaken to create a managed flood plain. A century later, a revised plan resulted in the dredging of a new river bed; the scheme included plans for the strip of land produced from the material excavated by digging out the 'New Danube' to be used as a leisure facility. This

Fireworks during Donauinselfest

ambitious project was carried out from 1972 to 88 and city dwellers are now able to enjoy sunbathing and swimming on their own beaches – including nudist areas to the north and south of the island.

There is provision for various other forms of exercise including cycling, canoeing and rollerblading, as well as a range of bars, restaurants and nightclubs. There is, in addition, an important ecological aspect to Donauinsel. The northern and southern extremities resemble a wilderness, whilst small areas of water meadow and a mature poplar forest enable a variety of plants, birds and animals to survive in the heart of the city.

HOW TO GET THERE:
U-Bahn station; weekend night buses.
WHEN TO GO:
All year
HIGHLIGHTS:
Copa Kagrana – The Viennese found the beach opptsite the district of Kagran so exotic they nicknamed it after its Brazilian counterpart.
Donauinselfest – the annual June party, the largest of its kind in Europe, with up to 3 million visitors.
YOU SHOULD KNOW:
Donauinsel has the world's longest waterslide.

Zitny Ostrov

Extending from Bratislava to Kormano – 84 km (52 mi) – Zitny Ostrov (Rye Island) is Europe's largest river island – so large that most visitors are unaware of being on one. It lies between the Danube and its slower flowing tributary the Little Danube, in the Danubian Plain. Several rivers flow across it and the rich alluvial deposits make it the most fertile land in Slovakia. The island also contains central Europe's largest reservoir of high quality drinking water and it has the warmest and driest climate in Slovakia. A beautiful area of marshes, natural and man-made lakes and rich farmland, the south has been designated a Protected Landscape. The calm waters of the Little Danube provide excellent boating through the alluvial forests; the controversial hydroelectric dam at Gabcikovo may be visited.

Zitny Ostrov has two main towns, both of which have strong Hungarian influences. Dunajská Streda has a majority Hungarian population, though the only reminder of a significant Jewish minority is a 1991 memorial. There is evidence of Bronze Age settlement here. In the late 1990s the town centre was rebuilt with distinctive white buildings topped by towers and elaborate tiled roofs. A large thermal park offers year-round bathing in naturally heated water. Komarno, Slovakia's principal port, lies on the Hungarian border – a bridge leads into Hungarian Komarom, which used to be part of Komarno. Here two thirds of the population speak Hungarian and the street signs are bi-lingual. Europe Place is a large shopping and leisure centre built in a variety of European architectural styles. A native son of Komarno, Franz Lehar is honoured with a biennial music festival, whilst the annual Komarno Days Festival celebrates Slovak and Hungarian culture.

HOW TO GET THERE:
From the capital Bratislava there is a good transport network.
WHEN TO GO:
May to September
HIGHLIGHTS:
The museum of Zitny Ostrov in Dunajská Streda, housed in an 18th century mansion. The exhibits include an excellent presentation of island life.
The fort at Komarno (still in military occupation) offers occasional tours.
Komarno Orthodox Church is the legacy of Serbs who fled the Turks and settled here in the early 18th century.
The watermills on the Little Danube – these wooden pan mills along the riverside have been used for centuries.
YOU SHOULD KNOW:
The former Romantic Officers Casino in Komarno is now the Public Library.

The lighthouse and fort

Chausey Archipelago

In the sea there lies a giant elephant, you can stroke him, he is very quiet and not dangerous at all, because he is made of stone – a local fable

Due to their French jurisdiction, the Chausey Islands, located in the English Channel south of Jersey are not generally included in the geographical definition of the Channel Islands, though geologically they join with them to form a larger archipelago. The islands are popular with French tourists but are almost ignored by the English – there is no ferry link between Chausey and the other islands.

Myth and legend surround this island chain, which in spite of being Europe's largest archipelago, is little more than a cluster of grey granite lumps just above the surface of the sea. Subject to one of the highest tidal variation in the world (14 m, 46 ft), it is said that there are 365 islands at low tide and 52 when the tide is in. Fierce sea currents create a multitude of rocky inlets linked by vast sandy stretches. The stark beauty of the area has attracted the attention of marine artists from around the world.

Only one island, Grande Ile, supports any population. Cars and even bicycles are banned, so the pace of life is pedestrian in the best sense of the word. Even in summertime the facilities on the island are limited, so the best way to enjoy the ever-changing landscape is with the aid of a good pair of walking boots and an ample packed lunch. A coastal path encircles the island and affords good beach access.

This is a fragile environment and there are restrictions on landing boats during the bird-nesting season (April to July). It has few permanent residents, save for a lighthouse keeper and a handful of fishermen and there is even talk of banning tourism altogether.

POPULATION:
Winter 10, Summer 100 (2005)

HOW TO GET THERE:
By ferry (summer only) from Saint-Malo or Granville.

WHEN TO GO:
June to September, although accessible by private boat all year round – weather permitting.

HIGHLIGHTS:
The Chausey Regatta every August.
The local seafood – lobster, mussels and oysters.
Watching the ebb and flow of the spectacular tides.
Sailing in and out of the islands' many inlets.

YOU SHOULD KNOW:
Granite from the Chausey Islands was shipped to Paris, sculpted and then used in the building of the nearby Mont Saint Michel.

Ile de Noirmoutier

Immortalized in a painting by Renoir, Ile de Noirmoutier, which is located off the west coast of France, has long been a summer playground. Stretching 20 km (12 mi) out into the Bay of Biscay, the island caters well for visitors, although tourism does not dominate. Salt marshes continue to be worked and there are still thriving farming and fishing communities.

The island can be accessed by bridge but it's more romantic to approach it via the Passage de Gois, a causeway passable only at low tides. The island town of Noirmoutier-en-l'Ile, located to the north east, is an unassuming place. It houses a 12th century castle, a church with a Romanesque crypt and an excellent market. To the north of the town the Chaize Forest of oaks and mimosas is also worth exploring.

In high summer the west coast is a magnet for sunbathers, with its long sandy beaches resembling those of the mainland. Inland, were it not for the presence of a system of Dutch polders and saltwater dykes, you could be forgiven for thinking that you were far from the sea. In the south of the island the winding roads take you through traditional villages of whitewashed cottages.

Today the theme of the island is recreation, far removed from its monastic origins. The island's restaurants are plentiful and of high quality. There are eight sailing clubs and a well laid out cycling route. For younger visitors there is Sealand, a well-stocked aquarium and Oceanile, a swimming pool complex complete with waterslides and the like. It is an island for the French day-tripper who first checks the weather forecast and then decides to go out and have some fun.

POPULATION:
10,000 (2005)
HOW TO GET THERE:
Across the bridge from Fromentine or via the Passage de Gois.
WHEN TO GO:
Spring to autumn – although a thriving mosquito population in the summer makes wearing insect repellent essential.
HIGHLIGHTS:
The castle at Noirmoutier-en-l'Ile, complete with its 11th century dungeon.
A tour of any of the island's world famous salt works.
The village of Barbatre – as pretty a settlement as you will see in all Atlantic France.
The food – the island is famous for its oysters, lobster and potatoes.
Any of the three regattas that take place each August.
YOU SHOULD KNOW:
Highly prized throughout Europe, a kilo (2.2 lb) of Noirmoutier potatoes once fetched over 200 euros at auction.

Salt pans on the island

Belle Ile

POPULATION:
5,250 (2005)
HOW TO GET THERE:
By ferry from Quiberon (year round) or from Vannes (summer only).
WHEN TO GO:
Spring and autumn are less busy.
HIGHLIGHTS:
Musée Historique – housed in the citadel at Le Palais, it records the island's often turbulent history.
Grotte de l'Apothicairerie – a spectacular coastal cavern.
Storm-watching at Pointe des Poulains – the island's most northerly point.
The cave system at Aiguilles de Port-Coton
YOU SHOULD KNOW:
The British navy captured Belle Ile in 1761, but two years later swapped it for the Mediterranean island of Menorca.

As the name suggests this is a truly beautiful island. A combination of a rugged coastline, attractive fishing villages and white sandy beaches, has made it a magnet for summer tourists. In July and August the population can increase ten-fold, all crammed into 84 sq km (36 sq mi). However, even in peak times, it is possible to lose oneself on this island of contrasts. The deeply eroded south-west is a true Côte Sauvage (wild coast), while the sheltered eastern side can feel positively Mediterranean in spite of its Atlantic location.

Belle Ile's history is closely linked both to the English, who occupied the island for two years, from 1761 to 1763, during the Seven Years War, and the Acadians, who took refuge on the island when the English got the upper hand in France's Canadian colonies.

Now the island is known for the more traditional pleasures of any vacation on the Brittany coast: swimming, boating, fishing, cycling and hiking. It also houses a collection of attractive lighthouses, most notably Le Grand Phare on the west coast, and La Citadelle Vauban, one of a series of substantial 17th century military fortresses built for Louis XIV by Marshal Vauban and now turned into a historical museum.

The island has long attracted the attentions of the world's best artists. Inspired by its natural splendour, Monet, Van Gogh and Henri Matisse amongst others produced some of their finest work here. The island is also said to have inspired the Op Art movement of the 1950s when the Hungarian-born artist Victor Vasarely visited and was inspired by the shapes of the pebbles on the beach at Sauzon.

Belle Ile boasts one of the best hiking routes in Europe. The spectacular 95 km (60 mi) coastal path takes about a week to complete and there are ample *gites d'ètape* (walkers' hostels) and campsites en route.

The picturesque port of Sauzon

Boats moored by the tranquil island of Ste-Marguerite

Iles de Lérins

These two tiny islands, a 20-minute ferry ride from the hustle of Cannes, offer respite for jaded souls and depleted credit cards. Ste-Marguerite is 3.25 km (2 mi) long by 1 km (0.6 mi) wide and St-Honorat even smaller, at just 1.5 km (0.9 mi) by 0.4 km (0.25 mi). Ste-Marguerite is more touristy than its monastic neighbour, but outside its busy port, well-kept trails lead through one of Europe's oldest eucalyptus and evergreen oak forests. St-Honorat's pine and eucalyptus forests are edged with the colour and fragrance of wild flowers and herbs.

Both are blessed with unspoilt beaches, decorated by nature with driftwood and said to be the least crowded on the French Riviera. Neither island allows cars, bicycles or camping, though a forest of motorized yachts clogs the narrow channel between them.

Ste-Marguerite is dominated by its fort and has been occupied at different times in its history by waves of invaders – Barbary pirates, Genoan pirates and the Spanish, twice.

St-Honorat was owned by Benedictine monks from the founding of its first monastery in 410 AD, and was taken over by Cistercian monks in 1869. Remnants of the original abbey remain, but the majority of the building dates from the nineteenth century. The monastery itself is open to the public for spiritual retreat only, but the church and small chapels dotted about the island welcome a more worldly appreciation. The conversion of Ireland to Christianity owes much to St-Honorat, as it was here that St Patrick studied before embarking on his most famous project.

Carrying along a picnic is recommended, as St-Honorat has only one small restaurant, while the few restaurants on Ste-Marguerite keep pace in price with the glitzy mainland.

POPULATION:
Ste-Marguerite 20 (permanent winter population); St-Honorat 28 Cistercian monks.

HOW TO GET THERE:
Ferry from Cannes.

WHEN TO GO:
April to October, but best to avoid the fortnight of the Cannes Film Festival in May.

HIGHLIGHTS:
Forte Ste-Marguerite – which dates from the early 17th century.
Ste-Marguerite's Musée de la Mer – with local Roman artefacts and the remains of a 10th century Arab ship.
Cuvée St-Honorat – in time-honoured tradition of monastic communities, the Cistercian brothers produce a highly prized wine from the island's vines. The monks also produce beer and essential oils, which they sell along with CDs of their chants.
Son et Lumière show – in summer; this portrays the history of the islands and includes an after-dark ferry trip.

YOU SHOULD KNOW:
The cell in which Dumas' Man in the Iron Mask was incarcerated is one of a number that can be explored in the Forte Ste-Marguerite.

Ile d'Oléron

POPULATION:
19,000 (2005)
HOW TO GET THERE:
By road bridge from near Marennes.
WHEN TO GO:
All year round, but it is advisable to book in advance in summer.
HIGHLIGHTS:
Le Marais aux Oiseaux (Bird Park) – originally a sanctuary for injured birds, but it now breeds rare and endangered species.
The view from the Forêt des Saumonards – look out across the sea to the fortress island, Fort Boyard.
The sunset over the Atlantic – sublime views from the western beaches.
A dozen oysters washed down with a glass or two of local white wine.
YOU SHOULD KNOW:
You can enjoy nature's bountiful harvest of shellfish, by gathering your own along the beaches. But beware, the oyster claires and mussel bouchots are private property and fiercely protected by their owners.

At first glance, there is nothing particularly spectacular about flat and wooded Oléron, in spite of the fact that it is, at 175 sq km (68 sq mi), France's second largest island. It sits in the Bay of Biscay, due west of Rochefort and is linked to the mainland by what was France's longest road bridge, when it was built in 1966. However, take your time to explore the island and you will understand why so many holidaymakers flock here in the summer months. Its beaches are long, sandy and clean and, if you venture away from the main towns, not overcrowded even in high summer. Its sumptuous temperate forests of pine and evergreen oak keep the island green all year long, decorated in spring with swathes of frothy pink tamarisk blossom.

Waterways criss-cross the island, leading into the interior, which is pretty and largely unspoilt. The coastal villages are somewhat blighted by a proliferation of holiday homes, but even here many retain their traditional charm. For example, Le Chateau, in the south, where the original citadel still stands and St Pierre in the north are both well worth a visit.

Like other islands in the region, Oléron has changed hands many times over the centuries. In the 7th and 8th centuries, it was under Basque control, while in the 14th century, it was granted to Edward II of England by his father.

Above all, this is an island of settled communities. The islanders extend a warm welcome to tourists, but also continue with their traditional occupations of fishing, oyster farming and boat building. The waterways shimmer with oyster *claires* (ponds) and most towns have excellent markets selling local produce.

Diners enjoy the view from the pier on Ile d'Oléron.

Ile de Bréhat

The beautiful Ile de Bréhat is surrounded by reefs and islets.

Not so much an island as a small archipelago composed of two main islands, Ile de Bréhat, just 3.5 km (2.2 mi) long and 1.5 km (0.9 mi) wide, is surrounded by a wash of reefs and islets stretched across Paimpol Bay off the coast of Brittany. This car-free island with its mild microclimate is a haven for flora and fauna. In summer the smell of ripening figs, eucalyptus, honeysuckle and mimosa fills the air, while the local ornithological survey has noted over 300 species of marine birds.

All boats to the island arrive at the tiny harbour of Port-Clos. From there it is a ten-minute walk to the pretty village of Le Bourg, full of character with a plane tree-shaded square. Be warned though that at low tide the ferries dock some distance from the harbour, requiring a five-minute hike up the beach. Now deemed a conservation area, no new building is allowed on the island and existing buildings are subject to very strict planning regulations. Civic pride is central to the islanders' way of life.

The Pont ar Prat bridge takes you to the wilder north of the island which has the feel of the open sea, with its tiny, whitewashed lighthouse overlooking craggy pink rocks and tidal races at the tip of the island. A network of well signposted, paved roads and dirt paths meander amongst large granite houses concealed by high walls and gardens awash with geraniums, agapanthus and maritime pines.

In the past, Bréhat's vivid colours and tranquil pace drew artists such as Henri Matisse and JD Fergusson – today, the idyllic island is a smart resort drawing in young, trendy Parisians.

POPULATION:
420 (2005)
HOW TO GET THERE:
By ferry from Pointe de l'Arcoust (year round) or from Erquy (summer only).
WHEN TO GO:
May, June and late September to early November are the less busy times.
HIGHLIGHTS:
Verreries de Bréhat – a glass works housed in the citadel in the southwest of the island.
La Chapelle Saint-Michel
Le Phare du Paon – the lighthouse of the 'Peacock'.
Le Moulin à Marée du Birlot – the recently restored tidal grain mill.
YOU SHOULD KNOW:
Most day-trippers miss the island's most spectacular feature by leaving too early. The sunset over the Atlantic combined with the pink colour of the island's bedrock makes for a truly wonderful sight.

Les Iles d'Or

POPULATION:
450 (excluding military personnel) (2006)
HOW TO GET THERE:
By ferry from Hyères (year round) or from Toulon (summer only).
WHEN TO GO:
April to June, late September to early November.
HIGHLIGHTS:
La Hameau – a Mediterranean botanical garden (Porquerolles).
14th century Fort Ste Agathe, housing an underwater archaeological exhibition (Porquerolles).
Fort Napoléon – built in 1813 and now faithfully restored (Levant). The Eminence and Estissac Forts – with free exhibitions in the summer (Port-Cros).
Aquascope boat – a glass-bottomed boat tour of the local seascape (Port-Cros).
YOU SHOULD KNOW:
In order to protect this fragile environment visitor numbers are limited to 5,000 per day on Porquerolles and 1,500 on Port-Cros.

Situated off the Cote d'Azur in southern France, the three islands that make up les Iles d'Or, also known as Les Îles d'Hyères, have a history littered with destruction and lifted by preservation. Forts have been successively destroyed and rebuilt from the time of Francis I through to the present day, with both Porquerolles and Levant still having a strong military presence. The island group is blessed with an exceptionally mild climate, which makes it popular – some would say over-popular – with tourists. The heat of summer is usually tempered by a delightfully cool sea breeze.

Porquerolles is the most accessible of the trio. Formerly in private hands, most of the island was acquired by the state in 1971 and the land is now protected and conserved. The port, which shares the island's name, is a hive of activity. As soon as you arrive, you will be captivated. Behind the boats tied up to the quay, the first houses can be seen, surrounded by lush vegetation. After leaving the port you arrive in the village with its large square and beautiful church, a cluster of shops and alfresco eateries.

Port-Cros, the middle of the three islands, was afforded National Park status in 1963. Uniquely for Europe this park extends some 600 m (2,000 ft) in to the remarkably clear waters that surround the island, providing an underwater haven for both marine life and divers alike. Inland, Port-Cros is the hilliest and wildest of the three islands, with a well-marked nature trail system.

Levant is an oddity: similarly covered in lush vegetation and blessed with fine sandy beaches, 90 per cent of the island is given over to the French military. The remaining 10 per cent has become a Mecca for naturists.

A view down to the crystal clear waters at Porquerolles

Elegant mansions line the streets of Ile Saint-Louis.

POPULATION:
Permanent winter population 1,750 (2003)
WHEN TO GO:
Though less crowded than Ile de la Cité, it can be busy in the summer months, June to August. Be prepared for some shops and cafés to be closed in August.
HIGHLIGHTS:
St-Louis en l'Ile Church – first built in 1622, with a magnificent wooden door decorated with angels.
The island's main street, rue de Saint Louis-en-l'Ile, with wonderful speciality boutiques and shops.
The performers at Pont Saint-Louis
Dining at one of the island's many fine restaurants.
Walking from Ile St-Louis to Notre Dame Cathedral, where an ascent of the spiral staircase affords a wonderful view of the city.
YOU SHOULD KNOW:
The Haschischins Club used to meet monthly at Hôtel Lauzun (17 quai d'Anjou); hashish jelly was consumed there by such notable club members as Manet and Baudelaire.

Ile Saint-Louis

As you enter the Island, past the street entertainers on Pont St-Louis you leave behind the hustle and bustle of its more illustrious sister, Ile de la Cité. With Notre Dame behind you, you could be forgiven for thinking that someone had transported a village and placed it in the centre of Paris. For centuries the Ile St-Louis was nothing more than a swamp, until in the 17th century the developer, Christophe Marie, filled it with elegant mansions along narrow streets, so that by 1660 the island was completely transformed.

In the 1840s the Ile gained popularity as a Bohemian hangout. Residents of this small boat-shaped island have always included wealthy intellectuals, artists and politicians. Voltaire, Cézanne, Baudelaire and Chagall, as well as Racine, Marie Curie, Ernest Hemingway and President Pompidou all lived there at one time.

As you travel eastwards along rue St-Louis-en-l'Ile you enter the heart of the island where Louisiens, as the locals are known, enjoy cafés, art galleries and unique shops. It is a great place to grab a famous Berthillon sorbet and people watch, although anything more than window-shopping could prove expensive. Quai D'Orleans is home to the area's most imposing buildings – of particular note are the 17th century Moorish influenced Hotel Rolland and the former Polish Library, now home to a museum.

Since the island is at the very centre of Paris, views of the River Seine are stunning and particularly atmospheric in the evening. If you're looking for absolute seclusion, head for the southern quais and you'll reach the finest sunbathing spot in Paris.

Corsica

'Get away from here before you are completely bewitched and enslaved'; such was the advice given to Dorothy Carrington by a fisherman in her classic 1971 portrait of Corsica, *Granite Island*.

Corsica is essentially a mountain range that rises from the sea bed. Its craggy coastline is washed on all sides by the Mediterranean Sea. It is 184 km (115 mi) long and 83 km (52 mi) wide covering an area of 8,772 sq km (5,980 sq mi), with Monte Cinto as its highest point at 2,707m (8,798 ft). The mountains are divided by deep valleys carved out by fast flowing rivers – which makes for spectacular scenery, reminiscent of the Dolomites.

The earliest known settlements on Corsica can be traced back over 10,000 years, and traditionally most inhabitants lived in the rugged mountain interior to avoid attack. The shoreline was the preserve of fishermen though much of this is now given over to the tourist trade. At various times through history the island has been governed by Vandals, Romans, Greeks, Genoese and even briefly by the British. Though it became part of France in 1768, the island with its Baroque churches, Genoese fortresses and Tuscan based indigenous language (Corsu) feels more Italian than French.

Aside from the spectacular countryside the towns of Corsica also merit exploration. Often described as 'little Marseilles', Bastia has a vast seafront esplanade and an old quarter of haphazard streets, striking Baroque churches and lofty tenements. The true Corsican experience can be found at Corte, the spiritual and cultural heart of the island situated at the confluence of two rivers; it's a good base for the best hiking on the island. For a more villagey feel head for Piana, which offers spectacular views of Les Calanques without the crowds of Porto.

Be prepared to be bewitched if not enslaved.

POPULATION:
280,000 (2005)

WHEN TO GO:
During the summer months (June-August) the island can get crowded, whilst off-season some facilities close down so check before travelling.

HOW TO GET THERE:
By air from Paris or Nice to Bastia, Calvi or Ajaccio, or by boat from Marseilles, Nice or Toulon to Ajaccio or Bastia.

HIGHLIGHTS:
The megaliths and menhirs at Filitosa – the island's greatest archaeological treasure.
The GR20 – a clumsily named but spectacular 16-stage hike (allow 12 days to complete, but only attempt it if you are fit).
Museu di a Corsica in the Genoese citadel at Corte – explore the island's history from ancient times to the present.
Les Calanques de Piana – weird and wonderful cliff formations; the best way to see them is from a boat.
The town of Sartène – a reminder of what Corsica used to be like, perpetuating traditions that go back to the Middle Ages.
The clifftop citadel at Bonifacio, with marvellous views of Sardinia.

YOU SHOULD KNOW:
Wild herbs grow almost everywhere on Corsica and greatly influence the local diet. *Stufatu*, a fragrant mutton stew, is a must for anyone dining out.

The town of Calvi

Ibiza

POPULATION:
113,908 (2006)
WHEN TO GO:
June to September for the most riotous club scene in Europe; October to May if you want a calmer but rainier experience.
HOW TO GET THERE:
Direct flights to Ibiza. Boat from Palma, Majorca.
HIGHLIGHTS:
Portal de Ses Taules – a massive gateway in the city wall, entrance to Dalt Vila.
Santa Eularia des Riu – a 16th century hilltop church.
Santa Agnes de Corona – inland from the east coast, a picturesque village on top of a hill surrounded by almond trees.
Cala Mastella – a peaceful cove with tiny beach on the east coast.
Es Vedra – a mystical rock off the west coast, said to be one of the earth's most magnetic points.
Benirras Beach – to watch the ageing hippie islanders drumming in the sunset every Sunday.
YOU SHOULD KNOW:
If you are not interested in the club scene, you still should not rule out Ibiza as a holiday destination. It is an amazingly beautiful place with some wonderful historic sites and traditional rural culture. Increasingly on offer are agrotourist holidays in the beautiful inland regions of the island, well away from the clubs and developments.

Renowned as the clubbing capital of the world, hedonists have been flocking to Ibiza in droves ever since the 1960s, when the first hippies, in pursuit of nirvana, were drawn to the island's Mediterranean beauty. The islanders were incredibly poor and welcomed strangers to their shores with open arms, absorbing newcomers into the local culture with such ease that they soon became part of Ibiza's intrinsic character. Despite half a century of particularly boisterous mass tourism and the inevitable charmless coastal developments that accompany it, the island has still somehow managed to retain much of its original attraction.

Ibiza is part of the Balearic archipelago, about 100 km (60 mi) southwest of Majorca. It is scenically incredibly beautiful – 571 sq km (222 sq mi) of pine forested hills and terraced fields, dotted with whitewashed hamlets and solitary churches. The coastline is rugged with stretches of sandy beach and sheltered coves. From the cliffs there are beautiful views of the sea, and you can walk inland through untouched Mediterranean countryside where the scent of pine trees lingers in the air.

The historic Balearic port of Ibiza is a UNESCO World Heritage Site. The old town, Dalt Vila is exceptionally picturesque, built on the side of a cliff with medieval city walls and a maze of narrow streets winding uphill to the 14th century cathedral and the castle. There are two beautiful beaches nearby – Ses Salines and Es Cavallet.

Sant Antoni de Portmany on the west coast is the most developed part of the island, where clubbers congregate for a non-stop party. If the Bacchanalian atmosphere here gets too much, you can head for the unspoilt north coast where you can always find a quiet *cala* (cove) to relax in with only the sea, the cliffs and the sky for company.

A view of the harbour and picturesque old town

Formentera

The town square at Sant Francesca

Less than 6 km (4 miles) south of the party island of Ibiza, Formentera is its complete antithesis – an island with very little coastal development, and not a club in sight. Its relative inaccessibility and lack of water has protected it from the ravages of tourism and it is one of the least spoilt spots in the Mediterranean with only one proper tourist resort, Es Pujols.

The smallest and southernmost of the Balearics, as well as the hottest and driest, Formentera is famous for its peaceful, laid-back atmosphere and incredible stretches of white sand beach, often deserted, where nobody turns a hair at nudity. The scenery is dramatic – an arid, windswept landscape, wild and wooded, with a varied, indented 80 km (50 mi) long coastline which includes dunes, salt flats and innumerable sandy coves. The 19 km (12 mi) long, relatively flat island is best explored by bike. Country lanes lead past *fincas* (farmhouses) festooned with bougainvillea, stone-walled vineyards, and small pastures where sheep and goats shelter in the shade of contorted fig trees. Wherever you are, the sea air is heady with the scent of rosemary, wild thyme, juniper and pine.

Life has always been hard on Formentera. Although there are signs of human habitation from more than 4,000 years ago, it was deserted for nearly 300 years between the early 16th and late 18th centuries for fear of pirates, until a few resourceful farmers resettled here, determined to eke out a living despite the lack of water. The island's fortune changed dramatically in the 1960s when hippies who had had their fill of Ibiza started to move here. It only took Bob Dylan to stay in a windmill on the island for it to acquire a reputation as the hippest spot in Europe – a reputation that has stuck fast and still stands today.

POPULATION:
7,461 (2002)

WHEN TO GO:
May to September for the perfect dream Mediterranean holiday experience.

HOW TO GET THERE:
A high-speed ferry departs from Ibiza approximately every hour.

HIGHLIGHTS:
The Blue Bar – one of the best beach cafés in the Balearics, in the middle of the famous Platja de Migjorn, a beautiful 5 km (3 mi) stretch of beach that runs along the south coast.
Faro de La Mola – a lighthouse standing on the highest point of the island, described by Jules Verne as a magical place in his novel *Hector Servadac*. The nearby town of El Pilar de la Mola has a beautiful church and Sunday hippie market.
Es Cap de Barbaria – walk along the cape to the lighthouse to watch the sun go down.
Estany des Peix – a lagoon with a narrow opening to the sea.

YOU SHOULD KNOW:
The strip of water between Formentera and Ibiza is a marine reserve dotted with islets, part of which is a UNESCO World Heritage Site. In order to dive in the reserve area, you must obtain a permit.

Majorca

POPULATION:
790,763 (2006)
WHEN TO GO:
April, May, September and October are lovely times of year for walking, cycling, climbing and sightseeing – the weather is not too hot and the island is far less crowded than in the high season of June to August when tourists flock to the island for its beaches by day and club scene by night.
HOW TO GET THERE:
Fly to Palma or take a ferry from the ports of Barcelona or Valencia in mainland Spain.
HIGHLIGHTS:
Cathedral, Palma – a masterpiece of 13th and 14th century Gothic architecture.
Deia – a charming village where the English writer Robert Graves lived, with spectacular sea views.
Narrow gauge railway from Palma to the picturesque mountain town of Soller – an unforgettable train ride through incredible scenery and a scarily long tunnel.
The huge market at Inca.
Jardins d'Alfàbia – Arabic gardens.
Alcudia – a walled medieval city, with remains of Roman houses.
YOU SHOULD KNOW:
The first 'tourist' to visit Majorca was Chopin. He came to stay here in 1838, accompanied by his French mistress, Amantine Dudevant (better known as the feminist writer George Sand) in a vain attempt to escape the gossip about their relationship and restore his health, broken by tuberculosis. They rented a monk's cell at the Carthusian Monastery – one of the great historical sights of the island, set in the lovely mountain town of Valldemossa.

The unspoilt mountain town of Valldemossa

Package holidays to Majorca started in 1952 so it is unsurprising that this island is practically synonymous with mass tourism. Do not let this put you off – despite the ugly blot made by the holiday industry, parts of Majorca are still amongst the loveliest places in the world. The historic sights, mountain villages, perfect Mediterranean climate, wonderful beaches, and sublime scenery are what originally attracted tourists here. No less today than then, a holiday here lifts the spirits of even the most jaded traveller.

Majorca is the largest – 3,640 sq km, (1,405 sq mi) – of the Balearic Islands, 88 km (55 mi) off the southeastern coast of Spain. The island's turbulent history had, by the 19th century, led to a bleak existence for its inhabitants many of whom were forced to emigrate – little wonder that they grabbed the opportunity to turn their island into a holiday resort. Amazingly, although Palma Bay has been sadly disfigured by high-rise hotels, nightclubs and overcrowded beaches, Palma itself is an outstandingly beautiful, atmospheric capital city with a historic town centre and wonderful local market, the Mercat Olivar.

To reach the island's northernmost point, Cap Formentor, you take perilous, winding roads through breathtaking mountain scenery, soaring 1,445 m (4,740 ft) to the northwest of a fertile central plain of vineyards, orange and almond groves, windmills and sleepy market towns. The headland is a sheer cliff 384 m (1,260 ft) high, known as the 'meeting point of the winds'. The sight of the beach way below as you are buffeted from all directions is enough to make the strongest head spin.

It is not hard to escape from the tourist trap parts of the island. As soon as you do, Majorca shows you her other face – the idyllic Mediterranean island she still is at heart.

Menorca

The smaller sister island of Majorca, Menorca is only a fifth of the size – 700 sq km (270 sq mi) in area, and less than 50 km (32 mi) long. The island has a beautiful hilly landscape and pine-fringed coast with more beaches than all the other Balearic Islands combined – ranging from long stretches of silver or golden sand to tiny *calas* (sandy coves). It is blissfully free of tourist development and was designated a UNESCO Biosphere Reserve in 1993.

Menorca is renowned for its stone megaliths, some 1,600 of them dotted all over the island, attesting to a prehistoric civilization dating from 2000 BC. From Monte Toro – the highest point at 355 m (1164 ft) – there are panoramic views of the rolling countryside, increasingly wild and rugged to the north and carpeted with a patchwork of fields to the south. The isolated *calas* around the coast are best explored by renting a boat. Many of them are only accessible by sea and even in high season you can always find one to yourself to while away an idyllic day of sand and sea.

Mahón, the island's capital on the east coast is a sleepy, elegant city of Georgian architecture built during a period of British colonial rule in the 18th century. It has one of the world's largest natural harbours, cause of a centuries-long squabble between the English, French and Spanish, and is surrounded by breathtaking scenery. But the architectural jewel in the island's crown is the medieval Moorish town of Ciutadella, with its narrow maze of streets, old walls and beautiful Baroque 17th century palaces – a cultural gem.

POPULATION:
88,434 (2006)

WHEN TO GO:
May to early July and September to October if you want to avoid the worst of the holiday season yet still take advantage of the Mediterranean climate.

HOW TO GET THERE:
Boat from Palma, Majorca, Barcelona or Valencia; direct international flights to Mahón.

HIGHLIGHTS:
Church of Santa Maria, Mahón – with one of Europe's most famous pipe organs on which daily concerts are performed.
Plaça d'es Born, Ciutadella – one of the finest squares in Europe.
Caves at Cala Morell – incredible prehistoric caves.
Naveta des Tudons – the most famous megalithic monument in the Balearics 4 km (2.5 mi) from Ciutadella Fornells – an attractive former fishing village famous for its lobster, set in a lovely bay close to the northernmost tip of the island – Cap de Cavalleria – from where there are stunning views. There is a wonderful beach nearby – Platja Binimella.

YOU SHOULD KNOW:
The British introduced the art of gin distilling to Menorca in the 18th century and it is still produced here today in more or less the original manner. You can take a tour round the Xoriguer Distillery in Mahón.

Boats moored alongside the restaurants in Ciutadella.

The Canaries

POPULATION:
1,995,833 (2006)
WHEN TO GO:
All year. The Canaries have a sub-tropical climate with very little variation in temperature and warm seas whatever the season.
HOW TO GET THERE:
International flights to Tenerife, Lanzarote and Gran Canaria. Ferry to any of the five larger islands from Cadiz, mainland Spain. Local flights or ferries between the islands.
HIGHLIGHTS:
Barrio de la Vegueta, Las Palmas – the historic district of Las Palmas with beautiful colonial architecture, a UNESCO World Heritage Site.
Telde, Gran Canaria – a village in a beautiful setting with traces of the Guanches, the original inhabitants of the Canaries.
Betancuria, Fuerteventura – the oldest village of the Canaries with a cathedral dating from 1410.
Montaña de Fuego, National Park of Timanfaya, Lanzarote – active craters in sensational volcanic moonscape.
Valle de la Orotava, Tenerife – a beautiful valley with the lovely town of Orotava where you can see the Casas de los Balcones, traditional 17th century buildings.
Santa Cruz de la Palma – an incredibly picturesque port town with steep alleys, backed by a huge volcanic crater, the Caldereta.
YOU SHOULD KNOW:
The Canaries are a self-governing region of Spain. Although they were one of the original package tour destinations, the tourist developments are generally well-contained and do not interfere with the enjoyment of the islands' rich heritage and sublime scenery. The fact that four of Spain's National Parks are to be found here – on the islands of La Palma, La Gomera, Tenerife and Lanzarote – and no less than five UNESCO sites gives some indication of the staggering natural and cultural beauty of the Canaries.

The Canaries are a group of seven volcanic islands off the Atlantic coast of North Africa. They cover a total area of 7,450 sq km (2,900 sq mi) containing some of the world's most dramatic scenery. Each island has its own unique landscape and endemic flora and fauna, ranging from the desert of Fuerteventura to the lush mountainous forest of La Gomera. Las Palmas de Gran Canaria is the cosmopolitan capital of the archipelago, reputed to have the best climate in the world.

The Spanish first invaded the Canaries in 1402 but it took the better part of a century to gain complete control of this strategic point on the Atlantic trade route. For the next 300 years, the islands grew increasingly wealthy from trading profits until, in the 19th century, a recession led to mass emigration to America. The development of the tourist industry eventually turned the tide and today, around 10 million tourists visit every year.

Tenerife, the largest island, has the most varied scenery – a landscape of fertile valleys, steep cliffs and wide sandy beaches dominated by the towering outline of El Teide, the third largest volcano on earth at 3,718 m (12,195 ft) high. La Palma, the 'green island', has the world's largest volcanic crater, La Caldera del Taburiente with a diameter of 9 km (6 mi) and a depth of 770 m (2,525 ft).

The smallest island, Hierro is also the rockiest with a dramatic coastline plunging straight into the sea. Lanzarote is the most extraordinary of all – a surreal volcanic landscape of petrified lava from 18th and 19th century eruptions. The stark beauty of its eerily empty scenery, dotted with ancient vineyards, brilliant coloured flowers and sparkling white houses is unlike anywhere else on the planet – a truly memorable experience.

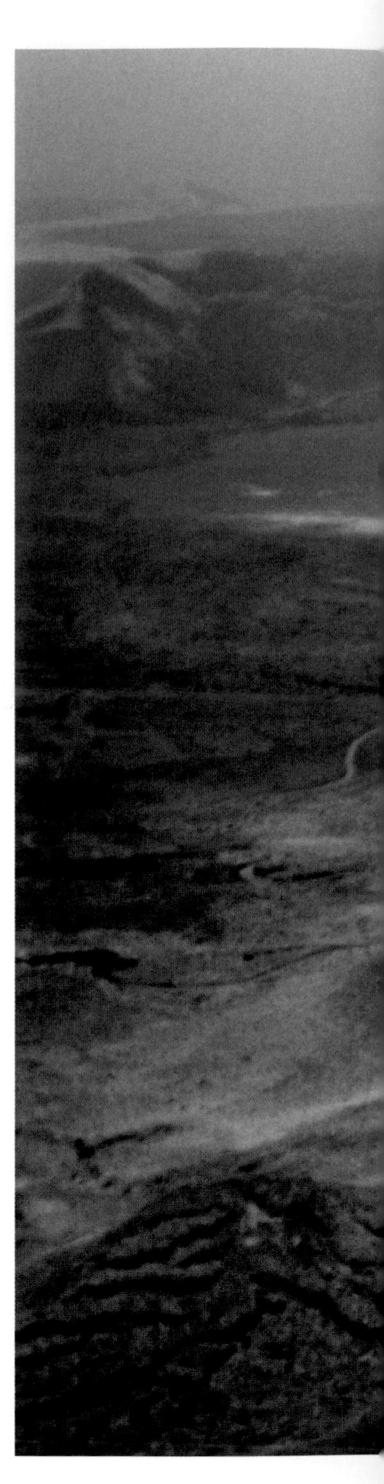

The stunning volcanic landscape of Montaña de Fuego, National Park of Timanfaya

The Azores

POPULATION:
238,767 (2002)
WHEN TO GO:
June to October are the warmest and driest months. November to January is pleasant but rather cooler. February to May tends to be rainy but the azaleas are in bloom in April, which more than makes up for the showers.
HOW TO GET THERE:
International flights from Portugal to São Miguel, Terceira, Faial, or Pico.
HIGHLIGHTS:
Furna do Exofre – sulphur grotto with underground crater lake (Graciosa)
Convento de Esperança – with magnificent statue of Christ (Sao Miguel).
Fajazinha – picturesque village and waterfall of Ribeira Grande (Flores).
Horta – important 19th century whaling port with historic sights (Faial)
Maia and Sao Lourenço – most beautiful bays in the Azores (Santa Maria)
Angra do Heroisme – historic city, UNESCO World Patrimony (Terceira).
YOU SHOULD KNOW:
The Azores are an ideal place for whale watching and swimming with dolphins. The seas around the islands are a natural sanctuary with more than 20 species of marine mammals.

An archipelago of nine volcanic islands approximately 1,500 km (940 mi) from mainland Portugal, the Azores are the remote western tip of Europe. They are the tops of some of the biggest mountains on the planet, mostly hidden under the Atlantic Ocean but rising to a spectacular 2,351 m (7,711 ft) above sea level.

All the islands are wildly beautiful with coastlines of cavernous cliffs, rocky outcrops, black sand beaches and sheltered bays. Traces of massive volcanic eruptions can be seen everywhere in the incredible scenery. Rugged mountains with deep ravines, crater lakes and curious rock formations contrast with verdant plains – the 'terras do pão' (lands of bread) – where fields are bordered with thousands of wild flowers and boundaries are marked with hedging of hydrangeas, azaleas and camellias. The islands vary in size from Corvo, just 17 sq km (7 sq mi) to São Miguel, 759 sq km (295 sq mi), each with its own unique characteristics, history and old island architecture.

The Azores were uninhabited when the Portuguese arrived in 1439. São Miguel and Santa Maria, the most easterly islands, were the first to be settled and there are some magnificent period buildings in Ponta Delgada, the largest city of the islands. During the 16th and 17th Centuries, Terceira, the third island to be colonized, became an important port for the Spanish galleons raiding Mexico and Peru. Later, in the 1820s, it became the base for the liberal struggle against absolutist rule in the Portuguese civil war.

Rural life in the Azores is much as it must have been for centuries and there is a calm, unhurried atmosphere even in the main towns. As you explore the different islands, you become increasingly aware of the striking individuality and unique charms of each one – the pearls of the Atlantic.

The town of Terceira

Madeira

Best known for its cake and wine, Madeira is a sub-tropical island of prolific beauty. The wild volcanic scenery of mountains, forest, streams and waterfalls provides a spectacular backdrop to luxuriant, terraced slopes where vines are cultivated, tropical fruits drip from the trees and roses grow as big as your fist – a truly breathtaking co-operation between nature and man.

This 740 sq km (290 sq mi) island is the top of a 5 million-year-old mid-Atlantic volcano that last erupted 6,500 years ago. A 1,220 m (4,000 ft) high mountain ridge, incised with deep ravines, runs east-west and one of the tallest cliffs in Europe, Cabo Girão, soars up to 589 m (1,932 ft) on the south coast. Ponta de São Lourenço, a 9 km (6 mi) long peninsula of weird rock formations, juts out at the eastern end of the island, attracting hundreds of seabirds.

Originally known to the Romans as the Purple Island, a chance landing by the navigator, João Gonçalves Zarco at the nearby island of Santo Porto in 1418 led to the arrival of the Portuguese. The capital city, Funchal was founded in 1421 and became an important stopping point between Europe and the New World. Today it is a bustling, historic town with old architecture and beautiful views.

The name Ihla da Madeira (Island of Wood) derives from the island's dense primeval laurisilva forest. What remains of it, still covering a fifth of the land, is now under UNESCO World Heritage protection. There are more than 2,150 km (1,350 mi) of *levadas* (irrigation channels) criss-crossing the mountains to divert water from the northwest to the dry south-eastern slopes; they serve a secondary purpose as footpaths for accessing the interior – a great way to explore the incredible scenery of this 'floating garden'.

POPULATION:
241,400 (2006 estimate)
WHEN TO GO:
All year – very pleasant sub-tropical climate, warmed by the Gulf Stream.
HOW TO GET THERE:
Direct flights to Madeira from most cities in Europe.
HIGHLIGHTS:
Monte Palace Tropical Gardens – contains one of the most important tile collections in Portugal; the beautiful town of Monte is often compared to Sintra in mainland Portugal.
São Vicente Caves and Volcano Centre – on north coast; take a trip into the earth following the lava channels.
São João do Pico Fortress – worth the steep climb to get a magnificent view.
Sé Cathedral – early 16th century Gothic/Moorish design with ten arches.
Capela das Almas Pobres – small chapel dug out of the mountainside.
Markets of Porto Moniz, Ponta Delgada and Santo da Serra.
YOU SHOULD KNOW:
The Madeira Mardi Gras Carnival and Spring Flower Festival are both major tourist attractions; New Year celebrations feature a spectacular firework display.

The view from Lombo do Mouro

An aerial view of Porto Santo

Porto Santo

POPULATION:
4,474 (2001)
WHEN TO GO:
February to October but unless you are taking children avoid July and August when the island is invaded by families.
HOW TO GET THERE:
Daily car ferry or fly from Madeira.
HIGHLIGHTS:
Taking a taxi, minibus or bike tour round the island.
Christopher Columbus's house and museum.
Pico do Castelo – island fortress.
Portela – lookout point with spectacular views of the ocean and over the island.
Nossa Senhora da Piedade – town church.
Camacha – village on the north coast with fig trees and windmills.
YOU SHOULD KNOW:
The golden sand of Porto Santo is said to have therapeutic properties.

In the sunshine, as you approach Porto Santo by air, the whole island seems to glow a glorious golden-yellow against the glistening cobalt blue sea, broken only by odd strips of green pine trees and purple mountain folds. Known to locals as a 'painting made by god', this idyllic island, 46 km (29 mi) to the northeast of Madeira in the Atlantic Ocean, is more reminiscent of North Africa than Europe – a starkly beautiful desert landscape of palm trees and cacti, dotted with pine groves, stone-walled vineyards, and small wheatfields. Porto Santo is only 14 km (9 mi) long and 5 km (3 mi) wide with an incredible golden sand beach stretching 9 km (5 mi) along the south coast; to the north there are mountains, rising to the Pico do Facho at 500 m (1670 ft), with a steep, rocky coastline.

Porto Santo was the first island of the Madeira archipelago to be discovered. In 1418 the Portuguese navigator, João Gonçalves Zarco was blown off course from the African coast and found a safe harbour here; he named it Porto Santo (Holy Port) in gratitude. Christopher Columbus came here in 1486 and married the governor's daughter before moving to Madeira to study navigation. The harsh existence and frequent pirate attacks persuaded many of the settlers here to decamp for an easier life in Madeira.

The islanders survive largely by fishing, subsistence farming and goat-herding, using donkeys for transport and oxen to thresh the grain. The main town, Vila Baleira on the south coast is a picturesque cluster of whitewashed houses with a cobbled square, medieval monuments, and small cafés where you can dawdle in the shade of palm trees watching the fishing boats. This is one of the least developed beach resorts in Europe – an unspoilt island paradise.

Capraia, covered in pristine Mediterranean flora and fauna.

Capraia

Wild, hilly and barely inhabited, Capraia is the only volcanic island in the Tuscan Archipelago. A 300 to 400 m (984 to 1,312 ft) ridge divides it into two unequal slopes. On the west, sheer walls of rock are cracked into ravines and riddled with caves; to the east the terrain slopes in a series of shallow valleys down to the sea.

People live either in the port, round a little bay, or in the village that sits on top of the nearby promontory. The rest of the 19 sq km (7.7 sq mi) island is covered in brush, with a few small villas and old farm buildings used briefly in summer. Humming insects follow the scent of wild herbs and flowers, but the ragged shrubs and trees can't hide the many poignant reminders of Capraia's turbulent past. A Roman fortress overlooks the town, crumbling watchtowers dot the landscape, and ruined villas recall the Romans' long romance with the island. The network of trails that hikers use today are 2,000 year-old Etruscan logging trails that often peter out in some rocky outcrop. For centuries after they left, Capraia was a sanctuary for hermits and anchorites – their peace interrupted (bizarrely) in 1796 when the island was seized by England's Admiral Nelson. Otherwise, the anchovy fishermen stayed near the port, and the island became an agricultural penal colony, closed in 1986.

Nature has largely reclaimed Capraia, and most of the island, and the sea for miles around it, is part of a huge National Park and Marine Reserve. There's no nightlife, no neon and no marketing scam to exploit the pristine Mediterranean flora and fauna. For visitors, the symbiosis of land, sea and people is like stumbling on a blueprint of how you want the Mediterranean to be: itself.

POPULATION:
366 (2004)

WHEN TO GO:
April to October – but July and August are both the hottest months and the most (relatively) crowded.

HOW TO GET THERE:
By ferry from Livorno, or by private yacht.

HIGHLIGHTS:
The spectacular, fire-red rock of Cala Rossa (Red Cove), at the southern tip of the island; it used to be one of the craters of the volcano.
Il Laghetto, once the volcano's main crater and now a *stagnone* (small pond), where migratory birds rest on their flight to Africa.
The Roman fort overlooking the port and torre al Bagno, the tower standing on the naturally levelled rocks where islanders come to sunbathe and swim.
Snorkelling or diving in the protected waters of the Marine Reserve at Cala della Mortola, Capraia's only real beach and approachable only by water.

YOU SHOULD KNOW:
If you come by boat, make sure you don't land within the environmental reserve, or use a drag anchor.

Elba

POPULATION:
30,000 (2007)
WHEN TO GO:
Year-round
HOW TO GET THERE:
By ferry/car ferry from Piombino on the west coast of Italy.
HIGHLIGHTS:
The stunning views from Napoleon's principal house, the Palazzo Mulini, above Portoferraio.
The castle at Volterraio.
The ancient hilltop village of Marciana.
The pebbled strand of Capo Branco, where Jason is said to have paused in his quest for the Golden Fleece.
The museum at Napoleon's summer house, Villa San Martino.
The panorama from Mt. Capanne, 1,019 m (3,343 ft), Elba's highest point.
YOU SHOULD KNOW:
The most famous palindrome in the English language runs: 'Able was I ere I saw Elba'!

On the map Elba looks like a fish, swimming placidly some 20 km (12 mi) off the Italian mainland at Piombino. It's the biggest of the volcanic Tuscan islands, easily accessible, and one of the favourite destinations of Italians themselves. Phoenicians and Greeks traded with the Etruscans who first brought it prosperity; and the Romans built a naval base there to defend the original iron mines lying below Elba's characteristic green cloak of holm oak and chestnut forests. The combination of mountains, meadows and woods was irresistible to the ruling Florentines of the Renaissance, and the Medici took it as a family fief from 1548. The Medici fortified Portoferraio, Elba's principal town, against the corsairs of North Africa's Barbary Coast; and established the culture that still makes the island so enchantingly different. It's even why Napoleon chose Elba for his retirement in exile in 1814 – and as its sovereign (for just ten months!), he created the system of government that is still in use today.

There are dozens of secluded coves, backed by rocky cliffs and topped by lavender and perfumed grass along the lanes between olive groves and vineyards. Etruscan hamlets top the hills, and elegant villas sit among cypress gardens. The cafés in every cobbled square and the flag fringed harbour still share their sophisticated glamour. Elba is often busy, but it's still a place to laze. The longest of many beaches lies on the Gulf of Lancona at the island's southernmost point; and you can see the day's catch of anchovies, tuna and sardines at fishing villages like centuries-old Cotone. Elba remains as seductive today as it was 2,000 years ago.

Portoferraio at sunset

Porto Isola del Giglio

Isola del Giglio

Only 16 km (9.5 mi) off the Argentario promontory, Giglio's granite hills rise 496 m (1,634 ft) to their central peak above the Tyrhennian Sea. From Poggio della Pagana you can see almost the entire 28 km- (17 mi-) coastline of the 8 km- (5 mi-) long island. To the west, steep slopes drop to majestic cliffs sheer above the sea; but to the east is a slightly gentler landscape, shelving to long sandy bays divided by rocky headlands. Aleppo pinewoods crown its higher ridges, and the lower slopes are vineyards; the rest is a characteristic Mediterranean mixture of scrub, wild flowers and herbs, broom, thorn trees, chestnuts and cypresses.

Giglio's history is written in its three small towns. The oldest is Giglio Castello, a walled and turreted medieval hilltop maze of arches, dark under-passages and steep alleys of stone houses. Its 13th century appearance hides a much older occupation. First the Etruscans, then the Romans made Giglio a significant military base; and the Romans built Giglio Porto on the east coast as a commercial junction for its maritime trade. Both Pliny and Julius Caesar wrote about it, and numerous Roman wrecks offshore show how busy it was. Visitors still arrive here, and stroll among the colourful restaurants and bars that line the quay between the two piers. The Torre Saraceno, built by Ferdinand I in 1596, stands by the south pier, a reminder of the terrible raids by Barbary corsairs from the 16th century until 1799. On Giglio's opposite side, in what is now the chief tourist resort of Campese, the early 18th century Medici built another imposing watchtower for the same reason. Since those days, Giglio has thrived on its wine production and its granite quarries; they were closed in 1962 to allow the island to revert as much as possible to nature.

POPULATION:
1,406 (2007)

WHEN TO GO:
April to September. Go in spring when the island explodes with colourful wild flowers.

HOW TO GET THERE:
By ferry from Porto Santo Stéfano on Argentario, or by private yacht.

HIGHLIGHTS:
The ruins of the sumptuous patrician Roman villa at Giglio Porto, built by the Domizi Enobarbi family in the 1st and 2nd centuries.
The early 14th century gate and fortifications of the Rocca Pisana at Giglio Castello.
The ivory crucifix (by Giambologna) and other relics in the church of S. Pietro Apostolo in Giglio Castello.
Diving in the many caves below the sheer cliffs on the west coast of the island – Giglio has at least 12 major dive sites.
The birds – cormorants, red partridges, shags, kestrels, hawks, blackcaps, goldcrests, nightingales, redpolls and rare Corsican seagulls are among many resident and migratory species.

YOU SHOULD KNOW:
Giglio granite forms the columns that support many churches and basilicas all over Italy.

Ruins of Villa Domizia on Giannutri

Giannutri

The smallest and most southerly inhabited island of the Tuscan Archipelago, Giannutri is a half moon of just 3 sq km (1.16 sq mi). From the sea it appears inaccessible, even forbidding; but the black volcanic boulders that form an unbroken barrier around it are more blessing than bane. Centuries of shifting rock falls have made it one of the finest diving sites in the Mediterranean, with no sand to cloud the lapis waters; and since there are no beaches at all to attract conventional tourism, the circlet of rocks has preserved the island's wild beauty from all modern depredations. Patrician Romans loved it. They built the small port, and dotted their villas among the vines, olive trees and myriad wild flowers of the interior. Long abandoned, one of them was restored in the late 19th century by one of Garibaldi's naval captains, Gualtiero Adami. He cultivated some of the land, becoming known as Giannutri's own Robinson Crusoe. Local legend has it that the wind is the howling of his lover, Marietta, perpetually desolate after his death in 1922.

There are no cars, and few people. You walk in the cacophonous 'silence' of the purely natural world, senses sharpened by intense colours and heady perfumes of herb and flower. Offshore it gets even better. Dolphins, turtles and sea horses patrol huge meadows of ravishing underwater Poseidonia, set with waving sea fans of coral and sea roses. Ghosts of 2,000 year-old wrecks are shrouded in fronds and guarded by darting fish. Large areas of the Marine Park are set aside for swimming and diving, to the exclusion of boats either in transit or moored, and of fishing. You can do those in many other places. Giannutri's utopian charm provides an opportunity to escape all forms of modern hurly-burly, on land or underwater.

POPULATION:
102 (2005)
WHEN TO GO:
May to September
HOW TO GET THERE:
By ferry from Porto Santo Stéfano on Argentario.
HIGHLIGHTS:
The Roman seaside Villa Domizia.
The lighthouse at Punto Rosso, built in 1861.
The rare Mediterranean corals and underwater meadows of the Marine Park.
YOU SHOULD KNOW:
The exact zoning of the Marine Park; there are heavy fines for breaking the rules.

Ischia

Ischia is the largest of the islands in the Bay of Naples, and many people consider it to be more beautiful even than Capri to its southeast. Ischia is a volcanic island 10 km (6 mi) long and 7 km (4.5 mi) wide that rises to 788 m (2,500 ft) at Monte Epomeo, which divides the island into two zones. The south and west takes the brunt of hot dry winds from Africa, and cacti, agave and palms thrive in the sub-tropical landscape. In the northern shadow of Monte Epomeo, chestnuts flourish among typical Mediterranean trees like holm oak, cypress, cork, almond and olive as well as the vines that fill the terraces. Citrus groves scent the whole island, and flowers run riot in the richly fertile volcanic soil. Even more extraordinary is that despite its high population and millions of visitors, Ischia still has dozens of deserted beaches and coves, and much of its interior is an empty pastoral idyll.

People come for its thermal springs and volcanic mud treatments – Ischia's prime attraction (alongside its excellent strategic position) for a succession of historical overlords from the Greeks in 800 BC, via the Romans, Saracens, Normans, Sicilians, Aragonese, Austrians, pirates, Bourbons, Britons and French, to the wealthy Europeans who now make its coastal strip a sophisticated playground and magnet for the young and beautiful.

Ischia has lost its jet-set exclusivity since the 1960s when it epitomized the fashionable notion of 'La Dolce Vita', but that has been replaced by a new kind of participatory glamour that draws in visitors. Just as it matches thermal springs and hot muds to different therapeutic treatments, Ischia matches its towns and resorts to a wide variety of visitors' expectations. Tranquil countryside walks, café-crawling, beach promenading, or 24-hour fashionable clubbing co-exist without tears. Ischia really is a holiday paradise.

POPULATION:
60,335 (2007) (and six million visitors each year)

WHEN TO GO:
March to November. Come at the end of summer for the Settembre Sul Sagarato in the village of Piazzale Battistessa – two weeks of parades, concerts and general carousing.

HOW TO GET THERE:
By hydrofoil from Naples Beverello or Sorrento to Ischia Porto (E), Casamicciola (N) and Forio (W); or by ferry from Naples Beverello or Pozzuoli, to Ischia Porto.

HIGHLIGHTS:
San Montano bay near Lacco Ameno – where the thermal activity makes the shallow seawater very hot for swimming on Negombo beach.
The spectacular Castello Aragonese, high on a rock connected to Ischia Porto by a stone bridge, rebuilt in 1441 on fortifications begun in 474 BC, along with the Guevara Tower.
Il Torrione, the watchtower at Forio built in 1480, and restored as part museum and part artist's studio.
The stunning southern Mediterranean gardens of Villa la Mortella in Forio, planned by the English composer William Walton in 1946 to include only authentic local flora, and now reaching magnificent maturity.
Concerts at Villa la Colombaia, Forio – formerly the home of film director Luchino Visconti, with a lovely park.
The white façade, decorated with 700 majolicas of saints and scenes from the Passion, of Santa Maria della Neve at Forio (aka the Church of the Soccorso, because of its world-famous location on the promontory square), and its unique and harmonious blend of Greek-Byzantine, Moorish and Mediterranean architecture.
Cooking dinner in the thermally heated sand of Fumarole beach near Sant' Angelo, Ischia's most chic resort.

YOU SHOULD KNOW:
The most ancient springs on Ischia were consecrated to Apollo (Casamicciola), Hercules (Lacco Ameno), Venus Citaerea (Citara in Forio) and the Nitrodi Nymphs (Barano).

The spectacular Castello Aragonese, connected to Ischia Porto by a long stone bridge.

Capri

POPULATION:
13,100 (2001)
WHEN TO GO:
May, June, September or October.
HOW TO GET THERE:
By ferry or hydrofoil from Naples, Sorrento, Salerno, Positano or Amalfi.
HIGHLIGHTS:
Villa San Michele – built by Swedish doctor Axel Munthe, the villa has stunning gardens with views across the sea.
Villa Jovis – Tiberius' magnificent villa, one of the best-preserved Roman villas in Italy.
Grotta Azzurra – the Blue Grotto on Capri's north-west corner is accessible by boat. Book a trip with one of the many operators in the area.
The chairlift from Anacapri up to Monte Solaro takes 12 minutes and provides you with breathtaking views of the island.
YOU SHOULD KNOW:
Book accommodation before you go in the busy summer months.

On the south side of the Gulf of Naples, the beautiful island of Capri has been a celebrated beauty spot for centuries. Today this small island is a popular resort catering for well-heeled Italians and international celebrities, as well as day trippers from nearby Sorrento and the Amalfi Coast. The island rises sharply from the sea and is a beautiful jumble of tumbling purple, pink and white bougainvillea, lemon trees, narrow, winding lanes and pastel houses.

Capri's natural beauty was appreciated as far back as Roman times. The emperor Augustus came here to unwind, supposedly creating the world's first paleontological museum in the Villa Augustus, to display the Stone-Age artefacts found by his builders. Augustus' successor Tiberius built a series of villas on Capri, the most famous of which is the Villa Jovis, one of the best preserved Roman villas in Italy. The eight levels of walls and staircases which remain today only hint at the grandeur the villa must have had in its heyday. Recent reconstructions have shown the building to be a remarkable testament to 1st-century Roman architecture. In 27 AD, Tiberius permanently moved to Capri, running the Roman Empire from here until his death in 37 AD. Both Tiberius and his grand-nephew Caligula were reported to indulge in orgies and torture, even to throw women off the cliff next to the villa, although these may be rumours put about by their detractors.

Today Capri town and Anacapri, the two towns on the island, are crowded with tourists, but the rest of the island is hilly, beautiful and much quieter. Visit the gardens of Caesar Augustus and admire the astonishing views across to the Faraglioni, impressive rock stacks in the sea. At Anacapri don't miss the wonderful gardens of Villa San Michele, built by Axel Munthe on the ruins of one of Tiberius' villas.

Perhaps the most enchanting sight on the island is the Grotta Azzurra, or Blue Grotto, a magnificent sea cave on the rocky coast. Roman emperors reportedly used the Blue Grotto as a private bath. In modern times, it has become a popular tourist attraction visited by boat. Passengers lie down while the guides pull the boat through the low entrance into the cave. Inside, the sea seems to be lit from underwater, making it an astonishing, iridescent blue.

The beautiful island of Capri

Sardinia

Like Sicily, Sardinia belongs to Italy, but has its own distinct history, culture and language. Today it may be famous for its beautiful beaches and mysterious hinterland, but over 3,500 years Sardinia has survived countless invasions by Greeks, Phoenicians, Carthaginians, Romans, Arabs, Byzantine Turks and even Catalans. All these communities still exist in some form, and hundreds of local festivals reflect their indomitable cultural impact. You can see prehistoric castles, villages, temples and tombs all over the countryside – staging posts in the fascinating evolution of one of the Mediterranean's least-known people.

The island has two faces. Its coastline is unequalled in Europe for dramatic beauty coupled with prodigious fertility. Mimosa, oleander and the butterscotch scent of St John's wort waft past the discreet villas of the Costa Smeralda. Elsewhere you'll find huge rock formations eroded into fantastic animal shapes, ancient fishing villages and huge sand dunes concealing colonies of flamingoes. From the coastal plains you ascend a series of green valleys rising to Punta la Marmora at 1,834 m, (6,017 ft) on the mountainous plateau of the Barbagia region. It's an imposing wilderness of oak forests and spectacular canyons, and prehistoric rock villages are the only human habitations.

To the north, around Nuoro, each valley, and each traditional hill town like Desulo or Sorgono, seems to be the province of a different clan. A world away from the sophistication of some of Sardinia's cities and resorts, these places are the collective soul of the island. Their dialects and daily routines provide a direct link with the earliest Sardinians, who built the 7,000 (of 30,000) surviving circular fortifications and dwellings called *nuraghe*. Big and complex, these megalithic structures are spread across the island, and are found nowhere else in the world. Just like all the rest of Sardinia's potent attractions.

POPULATION:
1.66 million (2006 estimate)

WHEN TO GO:
Year-round – but Sardinia can be a place of extreme summer heat and vicious winter winds. Come in early May for the Festival of Sant' Efisio in the ancient town of Nora; since 1656, the guilds and confraternities of all the island's villages wear traditional costume, sing and dance in the most colourful and important of events.

HOW TO GET THERE:
By air to Cagliari (S), Alghero (W) or Olbia (N & E); by ferry from Naples or Civitavecchia to Cagliari (S) or Porto Torres (N).

HIGHLIGHTS:
The best and most complete of Sardinia's prehistoric structures, the Nuraghe Su Naraxi complex in Barumini – with the others, a UNESCO World Heritage Site. The 12th century battlements and medieval town of Alghero, where Catalan is still spoken.
The Maddalena archipelago opposite the Costa Smeralda in the north – especially the rose-coloured beaches of Budelli. The Nuragic village, and Roman and Carthaginian ruins of Nora, where the amphitheatre, forum, baths, temple and casbah are set picturesquely by the sea.
La Pelosa, one of Sardinia's finest beaches, at the small fishing village of Stintino on the northwestern tip.
The 'palios' (horse races) and votive-candle racing, typical of the many village festivals around the middle of August.

YOU SHOULD KNOW:
'Fil'e ferru' ('iron wire') is an alcoholic local speciality. In the 19th century its distillation was illegal: when the bottles were buried, a small iron wire was stuck in the earth to mark the spot.

The picturesque harbour at Alghero

The town of Lipari at dusk

The Aeolian Islands

Named after Aeolus, god of the winds, the Aeolian Islands are a volcanic archipelago not far from Sicily's northern coast in the Tyrrhenian Sea. Also known as the Lipari Islands and Isole Eolie, the principal islands of this chain are Lipari, Salina, Filicudi, Alicudi, Stromboli, Panarea and Vulcano. Between them, the islands boast some beautiful scenery, great beaches, castles, thermal resorts, water sports, good fishing and, of course, some live volcanic activity.

These beautiful islands are quite rugged, with deep caverns, extraordinary rock formations, steep cliffs and splendid views. The volcanoes of Stromboli erupt fairly frequently. Rossellini's 1950 film,

Stromboli, was inspired by this volcano, which still regularly sends molten lava down its scarred rocks. This, however, hasn't prevented these islands from becoming popular smart resorts for well-heeled Italians, so expect crowds in summer.

Lipari is perhaps the most interesting of the islands from a historical point of view, with its citadel and archaeological remains. It is from here that most of the boat trips to the beaches and the other islands start out. Buoyant pumice and smooth black obsidian litter the beaches, and Lipari is well-served by restaurants and cafés. Filicudi, with its basalt shoreline, is much less developed as a tourist resort – the water is magnificently clear, you can hire a boat or scuba dive, and the beaches are often empty.

Panarea offers a lovely scene of rocky hills, ancient settlements, green slopes and pretty buildings characterized by columns and arches. Here can be found the Hotel Raya, opened in the 1960s by artist Paolo Tilche, which has given Panarea the reputation as a party island.

The garden island of Salina offers tranquillity, perfect if you are looking for a hideaway. It is one of the greenest of the islands, producing capers, delicious fish and octopus and a golden dessert wine, Malvasia. It was here that the film *Il Postino* was shot in the 1990s. There is a museum in Lingua, an interesting church in the port town of Santa Marina and spectacular rock formations at Pollara. The stone beaches are clean and rarely crowded, and the views over to Lipari and Stromboli are beautiful.

Stromboli has become the island of choice for a select fashionable crowd. The vulcano is still the main attraction, and is best viewed from an evening boat trip from where you can see the fiery show. Vulcano is fast becoming the most visited of the Aeolians. Volcanic activity ceased long ago but you can still climb the vulcano and peer down into the plugged core and appreciate the views to Lipari and Filicudi. Vulcano's other great attraction is the open-air pool of volcanic mud, which attracts bathers looking for a cure for skin complaints and other ailments.

POPULATION:
13,431 (2002)
WHEN TO GO:
May, June or September.
HOW TO GET THERE:
By boat, ferry or hydrofoil from Milazzo, Palermo or Naples.
HIGHLIGHTS:
The archeological museum in Lipari – artefacts from archaeological sites on the islands and shipwrecks.
The lighthouse with the horses's head on Strombolicchio.
Stromboli at night from a boat trip in the bay.
The ancient citadel (castello) of Lipari, with its acropolis.
The extraordinary red, ochre and yellow shoreline of Vulcano.
Laghetto di Fanghi – the volcanic mud baths on Vulcano are reputed to have therapeutic properties. Wash off the mud in the sea, warmed by the hot springs.
YOU SHOULD KNOW:
The archipelago is a UNESCO World Heritage Site due to its geology and vulcanology.

San Pietro

POPULATION:
6,500 (2007 estimate)
WHEN TO GO:
April to October. Come for the couscous festival in April, or the 4-day 'Girotonno' in early June celebrating the end of the 6-week spawning run of red tuna, for which San Pietro's fishermen are famous.
HOW TO GET THERE:
By ferry, from Porto Vesme (a tiny harbour south of Portoscuro) or Calasetta (on the neighbouring island of Sant' Antioco, which is connected by a Roman causeway to Sardinia itself), to Carloforte.
HIGHLIGHTS:
The dramatic cliffs of Mezzaluna in the south, and the amazing 'Colonne' ('Columns') – offshore pinnacle stacks formed from the same deep rose-coloured trachyte.
The wooden statue of the Black Madonna, symbol of the islanders' release from slavery, in the 19th century Chiesa della Madonna dello Schiavo in Carloforte. The lighthouse on the crags of Capo Sandolo, where enticing grottoes are cut into the cliffs, and you can see individual pebbles on the sea floor 20 m (66 ft) underwater.
The Festival 'Dall' isola dell' isola una penisola' ('The island [San Pietro] of a promontory of an island [Sardinia]) which celebrates San Pietro's Ligurian 'apartness' in street theatre, dance, music, stilt-walking, and communal feasting, at the end of summer.
Freshly caught red tuna, prepared with an extraordinary blend of Genoese (Ligurian) and North African influences.
YOU SHOULD KNOW:
San Pietro is unashamedly introverted, and much more likely to welcome the smaller number of visitors who come in May or September, than the August crowds.

Just 7 km (4.3 mi) from its southwest coast, San Pietro typifies the amalgamation of cultures so characteristic of Sardinia. Though sparsely inhabited for centuries, it was only fully settled in 1736, when King Charles Emmanuel III of Savoy granted it to the descendants of Ligurian coral fishermen from the Genoese suburb of Pegli, who had been enslaved by corsairs and held on the Tunisian island of Tabarka. In gratitude, they named their new town in the King's honour, and today the island itself is often known as Carloforte. Dominated by the belltower of San Carlo, Carloforte is one of the most characteristic fishing villages on the 53 sq km (32 sq mi) island. Its bastions, defense walls and ramparts recall the ever-present pirate threat of the time – though they have been replaced on the seaward side by the lovely 'Lungomare', an elegant, late 19th century promenade. With the smell of pesto – a Genoese speciality – everywhere and the heavily Ligurian local accent, San Pietro feels weirdly dislocated from the normal world.

Its geography helps. Inland it's mountainous and green, full of pine groves, junipers and strawberry trees. In one remote valley near the west coast, lush with wild rosemary, orchids and succulents unique to the island, there's a sanctuary for a very rare breed of (notoriously stubborn) miniature donkey, the 'asinello sardo'. Resident on San Pietro for 5,000 years, they faced extinction by road-kill and human appetite. Now they, and all the island's wildlife, are protected and recovering in numbers – especially the birds. Once, Phoenicians called it 'sparrow hawk island', and with their prey (hares and small animals) again thriving, the sparrow hawks are back. Like the flamingoes which have chosen it as their refuge, they demonstrate San Pietro's unspoiled environmental purity.

The crystal clear waters around San Pietro

Ponza Harbour

Ponza

The largest of the Pontine Islands between Rome and Naples, Ponza is a volcanic remnant lying 33 km (20 mi) south of Cape Circeo, in the Tyrrhenian Sea. It's an irregular crescent of vividly coloured cliffs and crags 12 km (7 mi) long and never more than 2 km (1.4 mi) wide. The kaolin and tufa rock has eroded into fantastic shapes, inspiring names like 'the monk' and 'the giant pair of pants'; and there are giant 'faraglioni' – rock stacks that appear to march out of the sea and across the beach. Long ago, the Etruscans enhanced Ponza's natural charms by hollowing out luminescent sea-grottoes in the cliffs, and the Romans dug through solid rock to create galleries that gave access to the best beaches. In that era, Ponza was covered by primeval forest – and on Monte Guardia, its highest hill, you can still see the rotting stumps of giant trees with a diameter of 2.5 m (8 ft). Now you look down on stepped terraces of vines, cactus pears and fig trees, engulfing the wealth of ruins, ancient and modern, left by a dozen occupying powers.

Ponza was once a Roman penal colony for unwanted Christians. Its isolation also served for the Roman Emperor Nero's exile, and again for Mussolini in 1943. Today the clusters of domed pastel cubes that are the hallmark of Ponsese architecture are exclusive in a different way. What little room there is on the island to expand is protected from development, and existing residents have curtailed neon bars and discos. You don't have to be rich to enjoy its tranquillity, beauty, and terrific diving, but Ponza's style certainly favours the wealthy Italians who holiday here. It's a discreet, clubby kind of place – but most visitors agree that it's a club they'd be only too happy to join.

POPULATION:
3,315 (2000)

WHEN TO GO:
April to October. Come for the Festival of San Silverio, Ponza's patron saint, around 20 June.

HOW TO GET THERE:
By hydrofoil from Anzio or Naples; by ferry from Formia, Anzio and Terracina, to Ponza.

HIGHLIGHTS:
The long crescent of dark volcanic sand under the high cliffs of Chiaia di Luna, accessible on foot from the port via a gallery drilled through the rock by the Romans.
The Grotte di Pilato, three caves near Le Forna where the Romans dug out fishponds to harvest their favourite muranea fish.
Swimming among the arches and grottoes of the Piscine Naturali at Le Forna, an enchanting place to relax.
Hiring a boat to explore the dramatic coastline of Ponza, and to dive among the shoals of colourful fish that congregate in its exotic underwater rock formations.
The nature reserve and ruins of the 1213 Benedictine monastery on the nearby island of Zannone.

YOU SHOULD KNOW:
Lucia Rosa is a local heroine who threw herself into the sea rather than marry against her wishes. To many people round the world, she is a martyr for women's rights, and a symbol of human rights.

San Giulio

POPULATION:
110 (2006 estimate)
WHEN TO GO:
Year-round. It's equally lovely wreathed in the mists of February, and exactly mirrored in the glass-like lake of a summer's evening. Come for the Festival of Ancient Music at the Villa Tallone during June, or the piano recitals on Sundays in September.
HOW TO GET THERE:
By ferry from Orta San Giulio, Omegna, Pella or any of the other lakeside villages; by private water-taxi from Orta; or you can row yourself in a boat hired on the waterfront at Orta.
HIGHLIGHTS:
The intricate carvings on the pulpit in the Basilica, made from grey-green marble from the Oira quarry.
The exuberance of the frescoes in the Basilica. Painted and re-painted over four centuries (the oldest surviving is from 1420), expect to find a Renaissance foot attached to a Mannerist leg, among other interesting anomalies.
The island in the very early morning, in summer, seen from the lake shore. It exudes its centuries of mysticism, and you'd believe any of the legends associated with it.
The 15th century wooden panels showing the life of St Giulio, including his dismissal of the dragon from the island, in the Basilica crypt.
The astonishingly high quality of the Mannerist and Baroque artworks in the 20 chapels dedicated to St Francis of Assisi and built between1583 and 1788, in the devotional complex – and UNESCO World Heritage Site – of Sacro Monte, the hill rising behind Orta town. From Sacro Monte you also get the best view of the island.
YOU SHOULD KNOW:
Very local menus feature 'minced donkey meat' – but that correct translation never appears on the menus handed to visitors!

Close to Lake Maggiore in the foothills of the Alps, Lake Orta is a tranquil, often misty vision of scenic charm. Of the villages and tiny market towns that sit comfortably on its green, wooded hillside banks, Orta town is the prettiest and one of the oldest. It lies on the end of a promontory opposite the intriguing island 400 m (1,300 ft) offshore on which much of its reputation rests.

Isola San Giulio is tiny – only 275m (825 ft) long and 140m (420 ft) wide, but crowded with buildings, towers and terraces positioned with casual elegance among lofty trees. Dominating them all is the great cruciform of the Benedictine monastery and seminary that in 1842 replaced the castle and Bishop's Palace that had stood there for over 1,000 years. But the largest building on the island is in fact the Basilica of St Giulio, founded in 390 by Julius of Novara, whose remains still lie in its crypt. Not much was left after Otto I destroyed the original in 962; but Otto deeded the land to the Basilica's canons and the present Romanesque building, begun at that time, has been extended ever since.

When you actually step onto the island, San Giulio's haunting beauty is magnified by the unexpected quiet. The short circular lane between the monastery and the sumptuous 18th century private villas lining the shore is even called 'The Way of Silence', and dotted with signs admonishing you to 'Listen to the water, the wind, your steps' or advising 'If you can be yourself, you are everything'. Perhaps in reaction to the self-conscious spirituality, one of the private villas carries a Venetian proverb instead – 'Protect this house; so never may a lawyer or a doctor set foot here'.

Isola San Giulio in Lake Orta

Isola Tiberina sits in the Tiber in the centre of Rome.

Tiber Island

Where the Tiber flows through Rome, there is a single island in its southern bend. Technically, Tiber Island is an eyot, measuring a mere 270 km (900 ft) long and 66 m (205 ft) wide it is an agglomeration of ancient fluvial silt and detritus. To Romans, it is the site of the oldest human settlement in the area, only abandoned by their city fathers in the 9th-8th centuries BC when improved archery techniques forced them to move to the Capitoline Hill for safety.

As Rome grew across its seven hills, the island became first an isolation ward for the chronically sick, and then a place of healing and even cure. As early as 290 BC, it was associated with the cult of Aesculepius, the Greek god of healing; remains of the temple dedicated to him, and artefacts of the cult, were discovered at the downstream end in the 19th century underneath the 10th century church of St Adalbert. Today this church is called St Bartholomew's after its primary relics, and is enclosed by a massive basilica. The island's medical traditions are continued at the upstream (eastern) end, where since 1548 hospitaller monks have run one of Rome's most significant hospitals.

The more you investigate tiny Tiber Island, the more you will be intrigued by small details. The pedestrian Ponte Fabricio, Rome's oldest (62 BC) surviving bridge, connects it to the Campo Martio. Two four-faced Janus herms are mounted on its parapet – Janus is usually two-faced, looking both ways, and four-faced images guarded only the most important intersections. Look under the perimeter stairway at the downstream end to see the 1st century travertine marble decoration of the island as a trireme warship, with Aesculepius' snake visibly slithering aboard. We take the snake-entwined Caduceus for granted as the symbol of medicine – Tiber Island reminds us of once widespread commitment to its real meaning.

POPULATION:
1 (officially – the resident priest of St Bartholomew's)

WHEN TO GO:
Year-round. Come for the All Souls' Day (November 2) procession of Sacconi Rossi (Red Hoods), when the Devoti di Gesu Crocifisso al Calvario e di SS Maria Addolorata, for centuries specialists in hauling bodies out of the river for Christian burial, commemorate the dead by walking the island perimeter in costume and with a service at the Church of S Giovanni Calibita. It's not a tourist ceremony – it is linked directly to fundamental Roman mythology and belief.

HOW TO GET THERE:
By car, from Trastevere (left bank), via the restored 46 BC Ponte Cestio, to one of about 30 parking spaces near the piazza; or on foot, from the Piazza Monte Savello near the Ghetto, via Ponte Fabricio.

HIGHLIGHTS:
The view from the downstream end of the Ponte Rotto (Broken Bridge), the only remaining arch of the 179 BC Ponte Aemilius. To one side you can see the circular hole in the embankment of the Cloaca Maxima, Rome's main sewer since 300 BC.
The carved stone wellhead in the Basilica of St Bartholomew, according to legend on the same spot that Aesculepius' snake nested by a freshwater spring.
The 17th century church of S Giovani Calibata. The spire, commissioned in 1867 by Pope Pius IX to replace the destroyed ancient Roman obelisk that made the island look more like a ship, and designed by Ignazio Giacometti with the statues of SS Bartholomew, Paulinus of Nola, Francis and John.
The 11th century tower and fortress of the Pierleoni, the only Jewish family to produce a Pope (Anacletus II 1130-38). Now the HQ of the Sacconi Rossi.

YOU SHOULD KNOW:
Rahere, medieval playboy and court jester to King Henry I of England, was cured of malaria at the hospital of St Bartholomew. He reformed, became a monk, and in 1123 founded the world famous hospital of St Bartholomew ('Bart's') in London.

Colourful boats and homes line one of Burano's canals.

Burano

POPULATION:
3,000 (2007)
WHEN TO GO:
Year-round. The sound of lapping water, and the colours of the houses reflected in the canals, are just as striking in winter mists as in the intensity of the sun.
HOW TO GET THERE:
By vaporetto (water-bus) No. LN (Laguna Norte) from the Fondamento Nuove on Venice's north shore; or by water-taxi from Marco Polo airport.
HIGHLIGHTS:
The impressive tilt of the 53 m (170 ft) high Campanile Storto ('Drunken Tower'), built in Renaissance style in the 17th century and restored with neo-classical elements between 1703-14. You can see it best from the Ponte di Terranova.
The wonderful paintwork – amazing even by Burano's rainbow standard – of Casa Bepi Sua, the archetype of Buranese buildings.
The Wednesday morning market.
Tiepolo's 'Crucifixion', painted in 1725, in the Chiesa di San Martino Vescovo.
The Museo del Merletto, the lacemaking museum of masterpieces including wedding dresses and parasols, some as old as the 15th century.
YOU SHOULD KNOW:
Philippe Starck, the interior designer known for his minimalist work, owns three houses on Burano.

One of the few islands in the Venetian lagoon with sufficient character to emerge from the shadow of its illustrious neighbour, Burano lies 7 km (4 mi) north of Venice. It was settled by people from the Altino region on the mainland, escaping from the carnage of barbarian invasion in the 5-6th centuries. Like Venice, the flimsy wattle-and-daub houses were gradually replaced by stone houses for the fishing community that evolved there; and the tradition of brightly-painted houses for which it is now famous grew with the community.

Burano's isolation was reinforced by Venice's power: the Doges used it as a dumping-ground for victims of plague, malaria and madness. It became, and still is, self-sufficient, with a strong sense of workaday identity that makes it an authentic link in the fabric of Venetian social history. It has no airs or graces, and its ambience is the opposite of that inspired by the grandeur of the Grand Canal. It contains no major 'sights', and there's no space to facilitate a tourist industry, though the Buranese welcome visitors.

Burano is world-famous for its lace. Lacemaking developed over the centuries in the nimble fingers of the fishermen's wives, waiting for the boats to return, and from the 16th century to the end of the Venetian Republic in 1797 it enjoyed royal patronage. It was revived in the desperate winter of 1872, when ice prevented fishing, and Burano faced starvation. The ancient patterns and the delicacy of execution were immediately successful; but now there are no new apprentices to learn, and 'Burano' lace on sale is invariably machine-made and imported. Otherwise, Burano is physically unchanged, except for the covering of one canal to make its only piazza. If Venice demands a series of superlatives, Burano is superlatively ordinary – and that is its beauty.

Torcello

Lying at the northern end of the Venetian Lagoon, Torcello is a quiet, haunting, deserted place, with a handful of old buildings and just a few dozen inhabitants, who grow vegetables. A thousand years ago it was more important than Venice and had a population of over ten thousand.

The islands in the lagoon were first settled in the 5th and 6th centuries. In 452 AD, Attila the Hun destroyed the beautiful coastal city of Altinum and its inhabitants sought refuge in this marshy region using rafts of wooden posts as foundations. Germanic attacks continued on this isolated corner of Byzantium, and in 638 Torcello became the see of the Bishop of Altinum. It became a very important centre of trade and was more or less autonomous. However the lagoon around the island gradually became a swamp; navigation became impossible and malaria was a serious danger. Most of the island's population departed and Venice began its ascendancy.

In its heyday, Torcello had palaces, monasteries and churches, but with its decline, nearly all of its buildings were dismantled and used in the construction of Venice. The Cathedral of Santa Maria Assunta, founded in 639, still stands however – its 11th century campanile can be seen right across the lagoon. There are a few cafés, a museum and another church on the island, as well as the Locanda Cipriani inn and restaurant, where famous figures from the arts and European royalty have enjoyed the peace and the captivating views. From the landing stage you reach the centre of Torcello by following a brick path and crossing the old stone bridge.

POPULATION:
60 (2005)
WHEN TO GO:
All year
HOW TO GET THERE:
Ferry from Venice
HIGHLIGHTS:
The Cathedral, which has many untouched Veneto-Byzantine features.
The Madonna and Child mosaic with its stunning gold background – one of the great works of Byzantine art.
The mosaic of the Last Judgment, covering the whole of the Cathedral's west wall. Santa Fosca – 11th century church in the form of a Greek cross.
The museum – housing art, archaeology and historical exhibits in the 13th century Palazzo del Consiglio.
Attila's Throne – an ancient stone seat outside Santa Fosca.
YOU SHOULD KNOW:
The Locanda Cipriani has works produced by Chagall and Max Ernst during their visits to the island.

The pretty houses of Torcello

Malta

POPULATION:
401,880 (2007 estimate)
WHEN TO GO:
March to December
HOW TO GET THERE:
Direct flights from many European cities; ferries from Sicily.
HIGHLIGHTS:
Valletta, the capital – a glorious city with important buildings and museums, steep streets, sea views and, even in summer, sea breezes.
The Archaeological Museum, which puts the Neolithic sites in context.
St John's Co-Cathedral – awe-inspiring and opulent: the works of art include a fine painting by Caravaggio
Mdina Rabat – high above central Malta, Mdina, the Arab capital, is now a beautiful, silent Baroque town. Lively Rabat has Roman remains and a cave where St Paul is said to have preached.
The Neolithic temples of Hagar Qim and Mnajdra – two large complexes set on a beautiful clifftop on the south coast.
The temples of Hypogeum and Tarxien – of great archaeological importance, these are located in a suburb of Valletta; visits are limited.
YOU SHOULD KNOW:
The Knights of the Order of St John paid a token of a falcon to the Holy Roman Emperor for the island.

Malta lies in the middle of the Mediterranean; its closest neighbour is Sicily but it looks very North African. The landscape is sun-bleached, rocky and waterless; where the thin soil can be farmed it is intensively worked.The tawny fields are criss-crossed by dry-stone walls – the soft golden limestone is used for all construction here. Though relatively small, Malta is one of the most densely populated places in Europe; yet somehow does not feel it.

Civilization came very early – the Neolithic temples date to 3500 BC. Later Malta's strategic position made it very important and it was colonized by a succession of powers from the Phoenicians to the British. Christianity arrived during Roman rule with St Paul, who was shipwrecked here and then sheltered by the islanders. The Arabs had impact on the language – Malti has Arabic grammar but uses words from many languages and is written in the Roman alphabet. The Knights of St John arrived in 1530, held the fortified island against the Turks and handed it to Napoleon in 1789; they left the greatest architectural legacy. In 1942 Malta endured five months of intensive German bombing. It became independent in 1964 and is now part of the E.U. English is universally spoken.

This is a holiday island, with a good climate and excellent swimming and diving, but the unique historical sights are the real highlights. The Knights' fortified cities that surround the magnificent Grand Harbour are unforgettable. Ancient temples and other fascinating archaeological sites dot the island. Hundreds of churches, many flamboyant, domed Baroque structures, dominate town, village and landscape. Despite mass tourism, Malta retains the feel of an older world. The people are well mannered, friendly and devout – though they enjoy the summer-long fiestas, when the night explodes with fireworks.

A narrow street in the beautiful Baroque town of Mdina

Gozo

Tiny Gozo – 14 km (9 mi) at its widest, lies close to north-west Malta, but it has a strong identity of its own. The island is much more fertile than its neighbour, producing grapes, fruit and vegetables on its terraced slopes. There are flat-topped hills, steep green valleys and some lovely undeveloped beaches ranging from rocky coves to long sandy sweeps. More conservative than Malta, Gozo has a relaxed, rural atmosphere. It was settled around 5000 BC, and it was here that the earliest of the great temples was built. Its fortified city, high in the centre of the island, was not proof against the Arabs or later Turkish invaders who almost depopulated the island, but it remained self-reliant and during World War II could offer refuge to evacuees from Valletta and provisions for beleaguered Malta.

There are only two real resorts – busy Marsalform on its wide bay, and popular Xlendi, squeezed into a narrow fjord. Inland Gozo is sprinkled with sleepy villages and little towns, all with their huge domed churches – like the Maltese, Gozitans are very devout.

Rabat, the principal town, was renamed Victoria for the British Queen's Jubilee. It is built on a cluster of steep conical hills which feature on the coat of arms. It is a handsome town of shady squares, churches and Baroque buildings, two splendid theatres and quiet lanes where women sit making lace. Day-trippers flood over from Malta, but, with its slow pace and peaceful walks and its reserved but friendly natives, Gozo is a rewarding place to stay.

POPULATION:
31,053 (2005)
WHEN TO GO:
April to November
HOW TO GET THERE:
Ferry from Malta.
HIGHLIGHTS:
Ggantija Temples, in Xaghra – the most impressive temples in the Maltese islands, and the oldest, dating from around 3600 BC.
Calypso's Cave and Ramla Bay. Gozo is said to be the isle of Calypso and the cave above the glorious red-sand bay is where she supposedly kept Odysseus prisoner.
The Citadel in Rabat, built high above the town. The fortifications offer fine views over the whole island.
The Cathedral – with a trompe l'oeil painted ceiling; money ran out before the dome could be built but the painting is very effective!
The modern church at Xewkija, with one of the largest domes in the world.
The salt pans along the coast from Marsalforn – a web of old rock pans where seawater evaporates into crystals.
YOU SHOULD KNOW:
In the 1970s, a bridge was begun from Malta to Gozo, but work was halted after Gozitan protests.

Gozo Cathedral

Some of the 147 islands of the Kornati Archipelego

POPULATION:
No permanent inhabitants.
WHEN TO GO:
May to September
HOW TO GET THERE:
There are no ferries between the islands. Rent a boat, sail your own, or take an excursion from the island of Murter (headquarters of the National Park and connected to the mainland by bridge at Tisno). The nearest sizeable town is Sibenik, within 50 km (30 mi) of both Split and Zadar airports.
HIGHLIGHTS:
Island of Mana – longest 'crown', 1,350 m (4,428 ft).
Klobucar – the islet with the highest 'crown', 82 m (269 ft).
The geological phenomenon of magazinova skrila, a peculiar limestone rockslide at Kravjacica, Striznja, or Vruje on Kornat.
The breathtaking view of the archipelago from Otocevak on the island of Piskera.
YOU SHOULD KNOW:
You must buy entrance, fishing and scuba diving passes at the National Park Office in Murter or at one of the reception centres in the Park. Apart from a few areas prohibited for conservation purposes, you can sail freely throughout the archipelago. Camping on the islands is not allowed but you can moor your boat for an overnight stay in any of the sixteen specifically designated coves. It is also possible to rent a cottage.

Kornati Archipelago

According to Irish playwright George Bernard Shaw, the Kornati Islands were made by God as his final act of Creation out of 'his tears, the stars, and his breath. The sublime beauty of this labyrinth of 147 islands, islets and reefs is overwhelming: dazzling white limestone cones punctuated by daubs of deep green erupt like magic from the contrasting blues of sea and sky. In the evening light the white rock is suffused in rosy pink and orange hues, and at night there is so little light pollution that an infinity of stars is visible, awe-inspiring in number and intensity.

The geomorphology of the region is extraordinary. The Kornati are the 'crowns' of a tectonic rift that runs underwater from Istria, partially emerging above sea level along a 35 km (22 mi) stretch of the central Croatian coast. The white limestone terrain is largely barren, apart from sparse patches of aromatic shrubs and scattered vineyards or small citrus groves. The islands end abruptly at their south-west faces where jagged cliffs, indented with caves, crevices, and inlets, plunge into a sea trench that is the richest fishing ground in the Adriatic.

Eighty-nine of the islands and their surrounding waters are a National Park covering an area of 220 sq km (86 sq mi). Less than a quarter of the ark is land, the largest island being Kornat at 33 sq km (13 sq mi). Day excursions can be made to the islands but it is worth trying to spend at least one night. 'Robinson Crusoe' holidays can be arranged: a weekly boat drops you off to stay in a hut without electricity or running water – until the next boat passes by to 'rescue' you from this magical otherworld.

Dugi Otok

This curious island in the northern Dalmatian Archipelago gets its name (Long Island)from its distinctive skinny shape, 43 km (27 mi) long and under 5 km (3 mi) wide. The karst limestone rock here has formed into an extraordinarily varied morphology with a height range of more than 300 m (1,000 ft). The landscape is dry and rugged, with regions of completely bare rock giving way to sparse grazing pastures of thorny shrubs and aromatic herbs, interspersed with copses of maritime pine and olive trees.

On the northern tip of the island, Saharun is an immaculate beach of pure white sand – a breathtaking contrast to the intense blue of the Adriatic. The west coast has steep cliffs rising to 338 m (1,109 ft), while the east coast is a low-lying intricate shoreline of rocky coves and shingle beaches culminating in the fantastic Telascica Bay at its south-eastern tip – one of the largest bays in the Adriatic, protected by steep cliffs up to 166 m (545 ft) high. It is a 10 km (6 mi) long conservation area of complex inlets, an extraordinary salt lake, and offshore islets that seem to hover surreally on the still waters of the bay. To its northeast you find yourself in a parched, barren moonscape – turn to the southwest and you are suddenly surrounded by pine, fig and olive trees.

Dugi Otok is a fascinating place to explore on foot, with traces of Illyrian and Roman settlements as well as early Croatian remains, picturesque old villages and the attractive fishing town of Sali. The island is all the more charming for being one of the less frequented of the Croatian coast with a slow pace of life and relaxed, friendly atmosphere.

POPULATION:
1,772 (2001)
WHEN TO GO:
April to October
HOW TO GET THERE:
From Zagreb, fly or drive to Zadar. The ferry from Zadar to Dugi Otok takes 1½ hours.
HIGHLIGHTS:
Strasna Pec – a cave with amazing stalactites and stalagmites.
Saljsko Polje – 'Olive forest' with olive trees up to 700 years old.
The lighthouse of Veli Rat – climb to the top for an amazing view.
National Park of Kornati – 147 islets off the south east coast.
The village of Dragove – with a 15th century church and fine views.
Snorkelling in Pantera Bay – sunken boat wrecks.
YOU SHOULD KNOW:
The underwater caves and offshore waters of Dugi Otok are among the best places for scuba diving in the region.

The tranquil bay around Luka

The beautiful medieval walled town of Korcula

Korcula Island

In Central Dalmatia rising out of the Adriatic off the southern coast of Croatia is the island of Korcula, with its low mountains, pine forests, olive groves and scent of wild herbs. At 47 km (29 mi) long and 6 to 7 km (3.7 to 4.3 mi) wide, it is one of the larger of Croatia's thousand islands. The island is hilly, the highest peak being Klupca just above village of Pupnat at 568 m (1,864 ft). The southern coast of the island is steep and eroded, while the northern shores, facing the mainland, are tamer and boast little pebble beaches. In the far north-east of Korcula, near the village of Lumbarda, there are some lovely sandy beaches.

The main draw on this enchanting island is the town of Korcula, a beautiful medieval walled town on a promontory of land protruding out into the Peljesac Channel. The city was surrounded in the 14th century by thick defensive stone walls punctuated by 12 imposing towers, many of which remain today. The island has changed hands several times over the centuries, but the architectural legacy left by the Venetians between 1420 and 1779 is second to none, and is most apparent in the town. Inside the walls the narrow lanes branch off the main street like the bones of a fish, planned in this way to reduce the effects of wind and sun and make life more comforatble for the inabitants.

Built in the 15th century, Revelin Tower forms the present-day Land Gate which is the main entrance into the Old Town. There was once a drawbridge here, but it was replaced by stairs when the threat of invasion was reduced. The symbol of Venice, the winged lion of St Mark, can be seen above the arch. The view from the top of the tower is lovely, and offers a 360° panorama of the town and its attractive rooftops.

Probably the most important building in the Old Town, the Sveti Marko Cathedral (Cathedral of St Mark) was built in the 15th century in the Gothic-Renaissance style. The main portal, built by Bonino of Milan in 1412, features Adam and Eve on either side, and St Mark above. There is a beautiful fluted rose window in the centre of the façade. The Renaissance interior was carved by a famous local stonemason, Marko Andijic, and contains treasures such as an early Tintoretto.

The Venetian architecture is most obvious in the streets around the Cathedral of St Mark, where there are various Gothic, Renaissance and Baroque palaces built for Korcula aristocrats. Opposite the cathedral is Arneri Palace, with its lovely Gothic facade and Renaissance-Baroque cloister. Next to it is Ismaeli Gabrielli's Palace, built in the Renaissance style in the 16th century, currently housing an art gallery and the Town Museum with exhibits relating to shipbuilding, seafaring and stone-masonry. Also close-by is the 17th-century Bishop's Palace, which holds the town's treasury with a collection of paintings including works by Raphael, Leonardo da Vinci, Carpaccio, Bassano and Tiepolo.

The town of Korcula is famous for Moreska, a traditional sword dance which was common throughout the Mediterranean in the 12th and 13th centuries and became popular in Korcula in the 16th century. The dance probably originated in Spain, inspired by the conflict between Moors and Christians. In Korcula its popularity was probably linked with the struggles against the Ottoman Empire. Through the centuries Moreska vanished from the Mediterranean and now it is only performed in Korcula.

POPULATION:
16,182 (2001)

WHEN TO GO:
April to July, or September to October.

HOW TO GET THERE:
Fly to Dubrovnik or Split, then take a ferry to the island.

HIGHLIGHTS:
Views from the top of Revelin Tower (the Land Gate) over the rooftops of the town to the sea.
The Venetian Palaces in the Old Town – the Baroque, Gothic and Renaissance architecture is beautiful. Some of the palaces now house museums and galleries, which offer a great way for visitors to see inside.
The Cathedral of St Mark – a lovely Gothic-Renaissance cathedral with lots of art treasures.
Moreska – a medieval sword dance performed only in the town of Korcula. Performances take place close to the Land Gate in the summer months.

YOU SHOULD KNOW:
There is only a handful of hotels on the island so make sure you book before you go.

Ciovo

POPULATION:
6,071 (2001)
WHEN TO GO:
Early June to early September
HOW TO GET THERE:
Fly to Split, then by road to Trogir.
HIGHLIGHTS:
The medieval church of St Maurice in the village of Zedno.
The 15th century church and Dominican Monastery of the Holy Cross near the village of Arbanija.
Mavarskika – a beautiful cove surrounded by pine forest.
Renting a boat to tour the small islands of Drvenik Mali and Drvenik Veli.
The magnificent town of Trogir on your doorstep.
YOU SHOULD KNOW:
Ciovo is an ideal place for a family holiday, with houses to rent, safe shallow water, plenty of seaside activities, and lots of sights and entertainments in the historic town of Trogir nearby.

The island of Ciovo is an extension of the magnificent medieval UNESCO World Heritage coastal town of Trogir to which it is connected by a drawbridge. In the past Ciovo was known as 'the barn of Trogir' because so much of the town's food was grown in the island's fertile soil. Today, it has become a popular summer retreat for residents of the nearby city of Split as well as being Trogir's beach.

The island has a hilly landscape, just less than 30 sq km (12 sq mi) in area, with lush and varied scenery. The northern coast is covered in a profusion of pine and cypress forest and, along the south, there are cliffs up to 150 m (490 ft) high. Here, near the church of Prizidnice, there is a famous 460 year-old hermit's sanctuary built into the rocky cliffside. It is an extraordinarily atmospheric pilgrimage site with wonderful views over the startlingly blue waters of the Adriatic. The inland scenery is a picturesque cultivated landscape of olives, figs, almonds and vines, dotted with villages and hamlets. There are innumerable secluded coves along the coasts, with sand or shingle beaches.

There are signs of habitation on the island dating from prehistoric times. In the Middle Ages it was used only as a leper colony but in the 15th century, when the Dalmatian coast was menaced by attacks from Turkish pirates, the citizens of Trogir retreated here for safety and eventually the island became an integral part of the town.

Ciovo is a rare combination of unspoilt seashore side by side with stunning historic urban architecture, with the added bonus that the island has not yet been overrun by mass tourism.

A view of Ciovo from the Adriatic

The village of Baska on Krk Island in the Kvarner Gulf

Krk

Krk vies with neighbouring Cres as the largest island of the Adriatic, covering an area of 409 sq km (160 sq mi). The island is famous for its beaches and ancient cultural heritage as well as its olive oil, white wine and honey. Known as the 'golden island', it is a lively tourist destination with excellent entertainment, sports and sailing facilities in a beautiful natural setting.

The limestone terrain is varied with more vegetation than many of the Croatian islands. The rugged north-west is wild and barren with a high point of 569 m (1,866 ft). The terrain here is difficult and can be dangerous when the fierce Bora north wind is blowing. Towards the south the landscape grows gentler with fertile cultivated valleys and wooded hills. About a third of the island is forested and there are two lakes that provide the fresh water supply. The coastline is ragged with numerous sand or shingle coves reached by steep paths down the cliffs, often sheltered by pine trees.

Krk is rich in animal and bird life and there are wonderful walks and cycle paths that meander through the woods, between picturesque villages, and along the rocky shores. The old towns and villages have some outstanding historic sights including the magnificent 12th century cathedral, medieval city walls and castle of Krk town. In the south, Punat, a picturesque coastal resort of narrow streets and old stone houses, has the largest marina in Croatia, and Baska Bay is renowned for its magnificent beach, nearly 2 km (over 1 mi) long. Despite the popularity of Krk, you can still find traditional folk culture amongst the trendy tourist attractions. There is something for everyone here – sports, sightseeing, drinking, dancing or simply lounging around by the sea.

POPULATION:
17,860 (2001)
WHEN TO GO:
May to September
HOW TO GET THERE:
Krk has an international airport, which serves as the airport for Rijeka, the nearest mainland town, only 30 km (20 mi) away and linked to the island by a 1,400 m (4,590 ft) long causeway. There is a regular bus service between Krk and Rijeka. Ferries from the islands of Rab or Cres.
HIGHLIGHTS:
Vbrnik – a picturesque village, clinging to the cliffside, that produces Vbrnicka zlahtina, a golden white wine known as the island's best.
Soline Bay – a former salt pan with water at a maximum depth of 1 m (3 ft), rich in mineral deposits and known for its health-giving properties.
Omisalj – the oldest settlement on the island on a 90 m (295 ft) high cliff on the north-west coast.
YOU SHOULD KNOW:
Krk is an important Croatian heritage centre. The Baska Tablet (now in the Croatian Academy in Zagreb) was found here. It is a stone slab dating from 1100 on which the name 'Croatia' appears for the first time. It is considered the 'birth certificate' of Croatian culture.

Hvar Town – one of the best-loved resorts on the Dalmatian coast

Hvar

POPULATION:
11,459 (2001)
WHEN TO GO:
April to June, or September to October
HOW TO GET THERE:
By ferry from Split.
HIGHLIGHTS:
The church of St Lawrence at Vrboska – the church houses some valuable works of art and cultural treasures.
Stari Grad – ancient Greek Pharos set in a deep bay on the coast.
Jelsa – a small town and important port in the north of the island known for the wonderful red wine produced there.
The vineyard of Zlatan Otok at Sveta Nedjelja – sample the wines.
The islets of Paklenski Otoci and Scedro – these lovely islets offer great opportunities for walking, swimming and sailing, with wonderful views of Hvar.
YOU SHOULD KNOW:
Hvar was voted one of the ten most beautiful islands in the world in 1997 by *Traveller* magazine.

Just off the Dalmatian coast rising out of the clear waters of the Adriatic Sea lies the Croatian island of Hvar. Around 80 km (50 mi) long, this narrow island is a gentle tapestry of lavender fields, vineyards, olive groves and pretty Venetian villages. The main centre of population on the island is the town of Hvar, one of the best-loved resorts on the Dalmatian coast. The Venetians based their Adriatic fleet here in the 15th and 16th centuries, which brought great prosperity to the island. In 1571, however, the Turks invaded and laid waste to Hvar, so the buildings which make up the town today were built from the late 16th century onwards. The medieval walls and fort in such a beautiful setting by the sea make Hvar well worth exploring.

At the heart of the town is St Stephen's Square, with the magnificent 16th century cathedral at one end and the harbour at the other. Also close by is the theatre of Hvar, the oldest communal theatre in Europe built in 1612. South of the square, there is an impressive 15th-century Franciscan monastery, now a museum, where concerts are performed during summer.

One of the prettiest villages on the island is Vrboska, lying in a picturesque cove at the end of a long bay, surrounded by pine forests and lovely beaches. Its compact stone buildings line the waterways, crossed by charming bridges. The churches in Vrboska house a number of very valuable works of art, some of the greatest cultural treasures of the island.

Along the southern coast of the island are several smaller islands, including Paklenski Otoci in the west and Scedro in the south. Paklenski Otoci is known for its beautiful beaches, clear sea and natural beauty. The island of Scedro offers a safe anchorage for boats and a pleasant place for swimming and walking. The western side of the island offers lovely views of Hvar's mountain ridge, particularly memorable at sunset.

Lastovo

One of the remotest islands of the Adriatic, Lastovo is the largest island in a nature reserve archipelago of 46 islands and islets. It is 56 sq km (22 sq mi) in area, a lush limestone karst landscape of wooded hill slopes pitted with caves and fertile cultivated valleys. The highest point at Hum is 417 m (1,368 ft) and there are three hills that are over 400 m (1,300 ft) high. The island has a dramatic coastline of craggy cliffs with unusually picturesque coves on the west coast.

Inhabited by the Illyrians and then the Romans, who named it Augusta Insula (Emperor's Island), the islanders have always had an independent spirit. For a long time Lastovo was a pirate haven – the Venetians eventually tired of having their ships raided and they razed the port to the ground. As a result, the inhabitants, unbowed, took the precaution of re-building on the slopes of a hill facing inland, which is where Lastovo's main town (Lastovo Town) still stands today. It is a picturesque village of stone houses with narrow stepped streets and a Renaissance church. The island is noted for its 15th and 16th century architecture with more than thirty churches and chapels dotted around.

Lastovo is a peculiarly enticing destination for travellers who want to head off the beaten track. There are no hotels on the island and it is a five-hour ferry ride from the mainland, which means that despite its outstanding natural beauty, all but the most determined tourists will find themselves landing on Korkula or Hvar, equally beautiful but a lot more frequented. On Lastovo you can find a solitary paradise with only the sounds of the sea and the birds as you bask in the warm sunshine and immerse yourself in the breathtaking scenery of green forest and deep blue sea.

POPULATION:
835 (2001)
WHEN TO GO:
May to September or February to see the Poklad, a 3-day traditional carnival that has been celebrated every year from at least the 16th century.
HOW TO GET THERE:
Ferry or high-speed boat from Split via Korkula and Hvar.
HIGHLIGHTS:
Zaklopatika Bay.
Skrivena Luka (Hidden Harbour) – a low sandy bay completely invisible from the sea.
The Church of Saint Cosmos and Damien.
Exploring the island's coastline and surrounding islets by boat
The lagoons of Malo Lago and Velo Lago.
YOU SHOULD KNOW:
The last recorded outbreak of vampirism occurred on Lastovo. A diarrhoea epidemic that caused many deaths on the island in 1737 was blamed on vampires and led to a court case.

One of the many churches and chapels on the island

Brac

POPULATION:
13,824 (2006)
WHEN TO GO:
April to October. May and June are probably the best months for a combination of good weather and few crowds. Avoid July and August when it is difficult to find accommodation.
HOW TO GET THERE:
Hourly car ferry or regular hydrofoil from Split to Supetar, the island's main town. Weekly flights from Zagreb.
HIGHLIGHTS:
The beautiful views from St Vid Church – on Mount Vidova Gora, highest point of all the Croatian islands.
Radojkovic Tower – in Skrip, the oldest village on the island.
The 15th century Dominican Monastery and church, Bol.
Dragon's Cave – an extraordinary hermits' cave temple with mystical pre-Christian carvings.
The Hermitage of Blaca – built into the side of a steep cliff, now a museum.
YOU SHOULD KNOW:
Dolomite stone from the quarries of Brac was used in building the White House, Washington DC.

The third largest island in the Adriatic at 396 sq km (144 sq mi), Brac is also the highest of the central Dalmatian islands, rising to 778 m (2,552 ft). Rugged, pine-forested hills are interspersed with scenic green valleys of vineyards, olive groves and cherry and almond orchards. Brac is famous for its beautiful white limestone and dolomite rock, quarried here for centuries and used in decorative stonework since Roman times.

The greatest tourist draw of the island is undoubtedly Zlatni Rat (Golden Horn), arguably the most beautiful beach in the Adriatic, and certainly the most unusual. It is a 0.5 km (0.3 mi) long tongue of pristine golden sand that juts straight out into the translucent blue water of the Adriatic. A parasol of pine trees runs down its spine and its tip visibly shifts with the tide. This is by far the largest and best-known beach of the island, but all around the coast there are small rocky coves and sandy beaches sheltered by pine trees.

Brac is steeped in history. Inhabited since Neolithic times, the island was first colonized by the Illyrians of the Balkan Peninsula, before becoming part of the Roman and Byzantine Empires. It was annexed to Croatia in the 9th century then fell under Venetian control from 1420 to 1797. Throughout the 19th century it was mainly under Austro-Hungarian rule. This motley heritage is richly reflected in its architecture. All over the island there are beautiful sacral and secular buildings dating as far back as the 10th century. There are also several quaint villages where the old terracotta-tiled stone houses are huddled in narrow cobbled lanes. The combination of natural beauty, superb beaches and cultural heritage in a wonderful Mediterranean climate makes Brac a perfect holiday island.

Supetar is the largest town on Brac.

Cres

One of the largest of the 1,200 islands along the Croatian coast, Cres is situated in the Gulf of Kvarner to the east of Istria. It is long, narrow and mountainous, stretching 68 km (43 mi) from north to south and 12 km (8 mi) across at its widest point. The inaccessible sheer rock face of the spectacular east coast cliffs are a habitat for the griffon vulture, the largest bird in Europe. The northern hills are cloaked in woodland of oak, hornbeam, elm and chestnut, in stunning contrast to the grazing pastures, olive groves and pine thickets further south. In the middle of the island there is the mysterious natural phenomenon of Lake Vrana. It is the main source of fresh water for both Cres and the neighbouring islands, but geologists cannot explain where its 220 million cu m (7,766 million cu ft) of water comes from.

There is evidence of Neolithic habitation: traces of cave dwellings and Bronze and Iron Age hill-forts and tumuli. The Romans conquered the island during the reign of the Emperor Augustus and later it became part of the Byzantine Empire. For several hundred years it was ruled by Venice before falling under the sway of the Austro-Hungarian Empire, eventually becoming integrated into Croatia in 1945. The island's cultural heritage can be seen in the picturesque villages and the charming main town of Cres where there are plenty of remnants of the island's Venetian era.

Surrounded by a tranquil, clear blue sea, with isolated bays and rocky coves, this wild, sparsely populated island is scenically dotted with old ruins, cemeteries and chapels; crumbling dry-stone walls follow the contours of hills on which a huge diversity of native plants can be found. Cres is an ecotourist delight.

POPULATION:
3,184 (2001)
WHEN TO GO:
April to October.
HOW TO GET THERE:
The nearest international airports are Trieste, Pula and Zagreb. Cres can only be reached by boat, either directly on the 12 times daily ferry from Brestova, on the Istrian peninsula, or via the islands of Losinj or Krk.
HIGHLIGHTS:
The 16th century Venetian clock tower in Cres town.
Valun – with a picturesque harbour and 11th century Valun Tablet.
The walk from Stivan to Ustrine – takes 2½ hours, or turn it into a full day.
Lubenice – an ancient village with a beautiful view.
Beli – one of the oldest settlements on the island with an Eco-Centre.
The view from Gorice – the highest point of the island at 650 m (2,130 ft).
YOU SHOULD KNOW:
The shores of Cres are pebble, which is probably the reason why the island has managed to avoid the full glare of the holiday industry and to retain its pristine natural environment. Don't let the lack of sand put you off. The beaches are clean, uncrowded and excellent for swimming and scuba diving.

A view of Cres and other islands in the Predoscica and Kvarner Gulf

Neo-classical buildings line the elegant port of Vis.

POPULATION:
5,000 (2004 estimate)
WHEN TO GO:
Mid-June to mid-September
HOW TO GET THERE:
Fly to Split, then ferry or hydrofoil from Split or the islands of Korcula or Hvar.
HIGHLIGHTS:
The Archaeological Museum.
Zelena Spilja – an emerald cave near Rukavak Bay.
The 16th century St Cyprian Church.
Uvala Stoncica and Uvala Stiniva – delightful small coves.
Blue Cave on the islet of Bisevo.
Gradac Cliff.
YOU SHOULD KNOW:
For centuries Vis has been famous for its viticulture, producing both red and white wines. Opol is an outstandingly good light red wine.

Vis

The furthest out to sea of the inhabited Dalmatian islands, 45 km (28 mi) from the mainland and separated from Hvar by an 8 km (5 mi) wide channel, Vis is an island of wild, windswept beauty. It is just over 90 sq km (35 sq mi) in area with a landscape of rugged cliffs and hidden caves, limestone hills and fertile valleys. After World War II, when it was a partisan hideout, the island became a Yugoslav army base, closed to tourists until 1989. It is therefore refreshingly undeveloped in comparison with the better-known holiday islands in the area and has preserved a genuine island culture dependent on fishing and agriculture.

The town of Vis (Issa) on the north-eastern coast of the island is the oldest urban settlement on the Adriatic. Inhabited since 3000 BC, the island was colonized by Greeks from Sicily who established a *polis* (democratic city-state). It is estimated that the city had 12,000 to 14,000 inhabitants and was therefore a place of enormous significance. You can still see Greek and Roman ruins here as well as some lovely 16th and 17th century churches and villas. On the west coast, the 17th century fishing village of Komiza, with its Renaissance citadel and monastery is in a huge sandy-bottomed bay. This picturesque village is a motley jumble of houses huddled round a harbour at the foot of Hum, the highest hill on the island at 587 m (1,925 ft).

As well as its beautiful wild mountain scenery and unspoiled cultural heritage there are some beautiful beaches, the best known being Zaglav, 10 km (6 mi) south of Vis Town. There is also superb paragliding here and some great diving sites, with six sunken wrecks dating from ancient times to World War II.

Ilovik

The 'island of flowers' is the southernmost inhabited island of the Losinj archipelago. It is 5.8 sq km (2 sq mi) of gentle hills with a high point of only 91 m (298 ft). There are underground wells all over the island that sustain a lush tangle of Mediterranean thickets and vineyards as well as oleanders and roses, palms and eucalyptus trees. The 15.4 km (9.5 mi) long shoreline is easily accessible with lots of secluded bays. The largest is Parzine on the southeast coast, popular for its sandy beach.

The tiny uninhabited islet of Sv. Petras lies just to the north. It is covered in olive trees with the remains of a Benedictine Abbey and the island cemetery. The monks who once lived here used to graze their sheep and grow vines on Ilovik, which was their property for centuries. Sv. Petras protects Ilovik from the harsh northerly winds and the narrow 1.5 km (1 mi) long channel between the islands has served as a safe anchorage since ancient times. It is used by local fishermen and in recent years has become a popular central stopping point for yachts touring the Adriatic.

Ilovik's tiny village, with two shops, a post office and a bar, has only existed since the 18th century when farmers from the nearby island of Losinj made a deal with the church to buy the island and started to settle here. Around almost every house there are colourful flowers and the islanders are justly proud of their carefully tended vegetable patches. Ilovik is an island where you can enjoy uncrowded beaches and a peaceful atmosphere as you immerse yourself in a profusion of unspoilt nature.

POPULATION:
100 (2006 estimate)
WHEN TO GO:
May to September
HOW TO GET THERE:
By boat from Losinj or Rijecka.
HIGHLIGHTS:
Sicadriga – an archaeological site with ruins of a medieval church.
Straza Hill – prehistoric and Byzantine remains.
The ruins of a Venetian castle and the 11th century Abbey walls on the islet of Sveti Petar.
The Golubinka Cave and rock formation on Sveti Petar.
Eating freshly caught fish on the waterfront.
The underwater shipwreck, with a cargo of amphorae.
YOU SHOULD KNOW:
The Ilovik islanders have one of the highest life expectancies – 95 years!

A fisherman returns to Ilovik at dawn.

Losinj

POPULATION:
7,771 (2001)
WHEN TO GO:
May to September
HOW TO GET THERE:
Direct flights to Losinj from major airports in Croatia, Italy, Germany and Austria; or ferry from Venice or Zadar to Mali Losinj; or drive to Losinj from the island of Cres by crossing the road bridge at Osor.
HIGHLIGHTS:
In Mali Losinj – The graveyard around St Martin's Church, where the tombstones give a rundown of the island's history.
In Mali Losinj – the Church of the Nativity of the Virgin, with some fine art works. In Veli Losinj – the 15th century Venetian tower, built to protect the town from pirates.
In Veli Losinj – St Anthony's Church.
Losinj Dolphin Reserve – a trip on a boat to watch the dolphins.
YOU SHOULD KNOW:
In classical mythology the islands of Losinj and Cres were known as The Apsyrtides and were joined together at the bottleneck of Osor. The Romans dug a narrow canal, only 11 m (36 ft) wide to separate them for navigational purposes. A bridge at Osor now connects the two islands.

In the Gulf of Kvarner, nestling alongside the southwest coast of the neighbouring island of Cres, Losinj is a 31 km (19 mi) long narrow island of dolomite covered in lush greenery. The east coast is low-lying, with coves and islets towards the south, while the steep rocky hills of the northwest rise to a high point of 588 m (1,930 ft). Most of the island's 75 sq km (29 sq mi) is evergreen woodland of holm oak, myrtle and laurel.

The heart of the island is Mali Losinj on the southwest coast. This charming amphitheatre of a town is built in tiers around the concave curve of a hill called the Umpiljak and has a harbour said to be the most beautiful in the whole of the Adriatic. There is a wonderful view northwards across the blue waters of Cikat Bay, a long stretch of beach enclosed by sweet scented Aleppo pinewoods. On the opposite coast, only 4 km (2.5 mi) away, the picturesque former fishing town of Veli Losinj is notable for its narrow cobbled streets, fine Baroque houses and beautiful gardens full of exotic plants.

Under Venetian rule, Losinj developed into an important centre for trade, seafaring and the shipbuilding industry, reaching its height in the 18th century. In 1797 the island was subsumed into the Austro-Hungarian Empire and during the 19th century it grew increasingly popular as a health resort. The clear blue sea and uplifting pine-scented air imparts a sense of wellbeing and energy that will appeal to anyone wanting a recuperative holiday of walking, water and sport. There is great windsurfing and scuba diving, cycle tracks through the woods, hill climbs with superb views, and interesting towns where you can stroll past sumptuous 18th and 19th century villas soaking up the island's history.

Boats alongside the harbour restaurants in Veli Losinj

Krapanj

Krapanj is the smallest and lowest of the inhabited Adriatic islands.

It is worth taking a detour off the conventional tourist route to visit this quaint island just 300 m (330 yd) offshore from the mainland town of Brodarica. Krapanj is the smallest and lowest inhabited island of the Adriatic at 36 hectares (89 acres) and only 7 m (23 ft) above sea level at its highest point.

A nobleman by the name of Juric purchased the uninhabited island in 1436 and donated it to the Franciscans who built a monastery here. When the Turks started plundering the coastline, the monks sheltered refugees from the mainland and eventually allowed them to build a settlement. The settlers were originally farmers who had to turn to fishing to scrape a living. Their fortune changed at the beginning of the 18th century when a visiting friar from Crete taught them the art of sponge harvesting and processing. Individual sponges were painstakingly harpooned from a boat and a skilled operator could spear one at a depth of 15 m (50 ft). The market for sponges proved a highly lucrative one – the Venetians couldn't get enough of them and by the mid 19th century there were 40 boats operating from Krapanj exporting sponges to Venice. In 1893 the first diving equipment was introduced, which enabled the spongers to harvest at much greater depths and soon earned them a reputation as skilled divers.

Krapanj has an utterly unspoilt, authentic atmosphere – you can dawdle in one of the waterside coffee houses chatting to the locals, visit a monastery stuffed with antiquities and works of art or wander through the picturesque streets of the town. Above all, this is a terrific little place to learn about the underwater world and improve your diving skills under the guidance of friendly locals who are happy to share their generations of experience.

POPULATION:
2,500 (2004 estimate)
WHEN TO GO:
May to September
HOW TO GET THERE:
Boat from Brodarica, 8 km (5 mi) south of Sibenik, which is well connected by bus or train with Split, Zagreb and Zadar.
HIGHLIGHTS:
The sponge museum.
The 16th century painting 'The Last Supper' by Francesco da Santecroce.
The Renaissance cloister of the monastery.
Tasting the locally produced rakia and eating fresh fish.
YOU SHOULD KNOW:
Of all the Croatian islands, Krapanj is the most densely populated. Almost all the islanders live in the town and no cars are allowed.

Mjlet

POPULATION:
1,111 (2001)
WHEN TO GO:
May to September
HOW TO GET THERE:
Ferries from Dubrovnik or Peljesac peninsula.
HIGHLIGHTS:
Odysseus' Cave – accessed by a 30 m (100 ft) long tunnel and used as a harbour by local fishermen, supposedly where Odysseus fell in love with Calypso and stayed for seven years.
Govedari – a hill village dating from the early 18th century.
The sandy beaches and pinewoods at Saplunara on the east coast.
Polace – the 5th century Roman palace and other ancient ruins.
Swimming in the salt lakes.
YOU SHOULD KNOW:
There is a wide diversity of flora and fauna (including the monk seal – an endangered species) but no snakes on Mljet. The Benedictines introduced mongooses to the island to get rid of them, which upset the natural ecological balance of the island but did do the trick.

Arguably the most beautiful and greenest of all the Croatian islands, Mljet is situated some 30 km (19 mi) from Dubrovnik. The island is a 37 km (23 mi) long sliver of limestone with a gorge splitting its entire length from north to south and a landscape of dramatic, heavily forested peaks and chasms. An area of about 30 sq km (12 sq mi) to the west of the island is a National Park with two salt lakes interconnected by a narrow channel set in idyllic scenery of mountain and forest. In the larger lake there is a tiny island with a picturesque 12th century Benedictine monastery.

Legend has it that St Paul the Apostle landed at Mljet after his ship was wrecked on his way to Rome in 61 AD. In the 12th century the Benedictines acquired the island and built their monastery. Eventually, in the early 15th century, they handed control to Dubrovnik but the monastery still retained its material and spiritual influence, gradually sliding into decline in the 18th century; it finally collapsed under the rule of Napoleon in 1809. Today, Mljet is justly famous for not only its astounding natural beauty but also its distinctive cultural heritage. Village life continues much as it has done for hundreds of years with traditional folk costume, music and dance.

For nature lovers and ecotourists, Mjlet is a paradise. You can cycle, walk and climb without restriction throughout the breathtaking scenery of the National Park, swim in the lakes, or take a kayak out onto the calm Adriatic to explore the complexities of the coastline and watch the marine life in the crystal clear sea. There are charming villages, medieval churches, and historic ruins to wander around, beautiful beaches to relax on, and wonderful local wine and goat cheese to sample. A perfect island dream?

Rab

Renowned for its mountains, pine forests, sandy beaches and fairytale main town, Rab is one of the most bewitching islands of the Adriatic. It is situated just off the coast between the islands of Krk and Pag, only 2 km (1.25 mi) from the mainland at its south-eastern tip. It is 22 km (14 mi) long and about half as wide, covering an area of 93.6 sq km (36.5 sq mi) and surrounded by islets and rocky reefs. It is well known for being one of the sunniest places in Europe with a gentle climate, sheltered by its mountains from the effects of the Bora (the harsh north wind of this region).

The island's scenery is outstandingly beautiful: from the dramatic cliffs of the windswept east coast, a progression of hills and plateaux rises to a 400 m (1,300 ft) mountain ridge that runs down the middle of the island, providing shelter for the verdant slopes of vineyards and forests to the west. Paradise Beach, one of the most famous beaches in Croatia, is on the north-eastern Lopar peninsula. It is nearly 2 km (1 mi) long in a setting of pinewoods with fine golden sand and crystal clear shallow water – perfect for children.

Plenty of traces of Rab's stormy past and rich cultural heritage can be found in the island's magnificent architecture. Rab Town is a picture-book fantasy – built on a steep west coast promontory overlooking a deep blue sea, it is an enchanting Venetian extravaganza of bell towers, palaces, squares and churches in a maze of quaint twisting lanes.

This magical island has become famous for its summer concerts, art exhibitions, and tolerant attitude to naturism. If you want to absorb some culture at the same time as acquiring an all-over tan, Rab is definitely where it's at.

POPULATION:
9,480 (2001)

WHEN TO GO:
End of May to September. The island is really bustling in July and August – with a great holiday atmosphere for those who enjoy the buzz. June and September are much quieter.

HOW TO GET THERE:
12-minute ferry ride from Jablanac on the mainland to Misnjak on Rab throughout the year; or ferry from Krk or Pag to Lopar or catamaran from Rijeka. There is a bus from Zagreb to Rijeka. By plane – the easiest way is to fly to Rijeka airport (on Krk) with pre-booked ferry transfer to Rab.

HIGHLIGHTS:
Belfry of St Mary's Church – an extraordinarily impressive 12th to 13th century bell tower 26 m (85 ft) high.
The Monastery of St Euphemia – with two churches, a beautiful sarcophagus and art works.
Dominis-Nimira Palace – a 15th century Venetian palace.
The 13th century Duke's Palace.
Komrcar Park – an area of pasture turned into a beautiful parkland about 80 years ago.
Kampor – an old fishing village with a peaceful atmosphere and lovely walks nearby.

YOU SHOULD KNOW:
Tourism on Rab started at the end of the 19th century but it made its mark on the international tourist map when Edward VIII and Wallis Simpson had a holiday here. Supposedly, it was they who started the habit of naturism here by swimming in the nude.

The view from St John the Baptist Church in Rab Town

Elaphiti Islands

POPULATION:
850 (2006)
WHEN TO GO:
May to September
HOW TO GET THERE:
Ferry from Dubrovnik to each of the three major islands, or you can take a day-excursion boat trip visiting all three.
HIGHLIGHTS:
The late Gothic Rector's Palace – Sipan.
The remains of the 11th century Church of St Peter – Sipan.
The 16th century Holy Trinity Church – Lopud.
The 15th century Monasteries – Lopud.
The ruins of old basilicas and summerhouses – Kolocep.
The Witches Cave and Blue Cave – Kolocep
YOU SHOULD KNOW:
There are naturist beach areas on all the islands.

These thirteen tiny islands stand out like enticing green jewels in the brilliant blue sea off the coast of Dubrovnik. They have breathtakingly beautiful scenery – outstanding seashore landscapes, verdant wooded hills, and lush valleys of citrus and olive groves. Villages of traditional pantiled stone cottages nestle in the picturesque bays where the inhabitants maintain their traditional way of life as farmers and fishermen.

The Elaphiti cover a land area of less than 30 sq km (12 sq mi) and only three of the islands are inhabited. Kolocep, a favourite local swimming spot, is the closest to Dubrovnik – a mere 20-minute boat ride. The island is only 2.5 sq km (1 sq mi), covered in lush vegetation with paths through fragrant pine woods and olive groves. There are two charming hamlets where exotic flowers, palm trees, aloe and cacti grow in the islanders' gardens. Lopud is the most popular of the islands, renowned for its magnificent fine white sand beach backed by green-forested hills. Sipan, the largest island at 16.5 sq km (6 sq mi), is famous for its wine.

The islands are first mentioned by the Ancient Greek historian Pliny the Elder and their name is derived from the Greek for 'deer'. During the 10th century they became part of the territory of the city of Dubrovnik and churches and monasteries began to spring up. By the 15th century, Sipan had become a favourite summer retreat for

The pretty harbour on Lopud Island

the local aristocracy and you can still see the remains of magnificent mansions secreted among the woods of the coastal bays. Today, the Elaphiti are a favourite getaway from the summer heat of the city – an idyllic place to swim, sunbathe, walk and relax.

Silba

One of the smaller northern Dalmatian islands, only 15 sq km (6 sq mi) in area, Silba has a gentle terrain of low hills covered in richly varied Mediterranean vegetation of trees, shrubs and flowers interspersed with vineyards. Country footpaths lead through wooded valleys to the shore, where there are a number of lovely secluded coves and small harbours. There are no cars on this delightful island – the locals use two-wheeled handcarts as transport. There is a single village at the island's narrowest point – only 700 m (2,295 ft) wide – by the beautiful beach of Sotorisce, renowned for its exceptionally clear turquoise water and shallow sandy seabed.

Silba was colonized by Croatians as early as the 8th century and became church property in 1091– the religiosity of the inhabitants is attested to by the six island churches. Over the centuries the islanders developed an extremely profitable trade transporting cattle from the mainland town of Zadar to Venice and established themselves as the leading seafarers and shipbuilders of the region. The island became known as the 'door to Dalmatia' and reached a height of prosperity during the 18th century when it had a fleet of almost 100 ships. For many years the island was privately owned by a Venetian noble family who extracted a hefty tithe on all the inhabitants' earnings. Eventually, after a lengthy land dispute, the Silbans acquired the rights to their island on St Joseph's Day, 19 March 1852, a date that is still the most important holiday of the year here.

One of the sunniest of the Adriatic islands, with a gentle westerly breeze in the summer that prevents the heat from ever becoming oppressive, Silba is a charming island for peaceful beach, boating and fishing holidays.

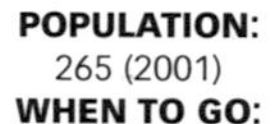

POPULATION:
265 (2001)
WHEN TO GO:
Late May to early September
HOW TO GET THERE:
Boats daily from Zadar and twice weekly from Rijeka or Pula on the mainland, or the island of Losinj.
HIGHLIGHTS:
The 17th century Church of St Mark and its cemetery.
Dobre Verde and Nozdre – small secluded bays backed by woods.
Pernastica – one of the ten most beautiful sand bays in Croatia.
Toreta – a 15 m (50 ft) hexagonal tower with amazing view from the top.
Vele Stene – the only place on the island where the shore is steep. Varh – the highest point of the island at 80 m (260 ft).
YOU SHOULD KNOW:
There are no hotels on Silba but there are plenty of rooms and apartments to rent.

The only village on Susak

Susak

POPULATION:
Under 200
WHEN TO GO:
May to September
HOW TO GET THERE:
Daily boat connection from Losinj. Losinj can be reached by air or boat from the mainland.
HIGHLIGHTS:
Merina Chapel of the Mournful Lady graveyard.
The lighthouse on the Garba, highest point of the island.
The village church with a 12th century cross.
Bok Bay naturist beach.
Tasting the island wine.
YOU SHOULD KNOW:
Susak is famous for diving – it's considered to be one of the best spots in Croatia for the less experienced with an underwater reef, canyon and wreck.

This tiny island of only 3.8 sq km (1.5 sq mi), in the open sea to the west of Losinj, is one of the lowest islands in the Gulf of Kvarner with a high point of 98 m (320 ft). Susak is geologically unique in the region: its terrain is entirely composed of sand, in thick layers up to 100 m (330 ft) deep resting on a bedrock of limestone. This is one of the few places in Croatia where you will have no problem at all finding a proper sandy beach. There is a coastal path around the entire 11 km (7 mi) shore, all of which is fine golden sand with safe swimming.

Like so many of the Dalmatian islands, Susak has a tumultuous history of plunder and conquest. The island was an important western navigational point on the sea route from Istria to Dalmatia and it is marked on nautical charts dating from the 13th century. The islanders have lived in such isolation that even today they have preserved their own centuries-old dialect, customs and wedding rites as well as an extraordinary female folk costume featuring a very full, very short, brightly patterned skirt reminiscent of a ballet tutu.

Susak has always been renowned for the exceptional quality of its wine, considered the best in Croatia. Sadly, after World War II the political and economic climate precipitated a mass exodus to the USA leading to the abandonment of most of the land. However, the fifteen vineyards that are still under cultivation continue to produce superb wine. Today Susak is still a peculiarly quaint place with just one village, built round a small sheltered bay used for mooring yachts. It is the perfect place for a relaxed beach holiday far from the madding tourist crowds.

Brijuni Archipelago

Once a pestilential hellhole, turned into a folly for the aristocracy, commandeered as Communist leader Marshall Tito's summer retreat, and now a National Park, these tiny islands have a bizarre fairytale quality to them – a surreal juxtaposition of verdant woodland, landscaped meadows, wild animals and Roman ruins, surrounded by the intense blue of the Adriatic Sea.

This tiny low-lying archipelago of two islands and 12 islets, only 7.42 sq km (3 sq mi) of land altogether, lies 3 km (2 mi) off the west coast of the Istrian peninsula. The bedrock is white limestone with a topsoil of exceptionally fertile red clay that supports a wide variety of lush vegetation. The islands' shores are indented with secluded coves and the surrounding waters are a conservation area rich in sponges and crustaceans as well as all sorts of fish, and even turtles and dolphins.

Veliki Brijun and Mali Brijun have been inhabited since prehistoric times and there are valuable historical remains, particularly from the Roman and Byzantine eras. Over the centuries the islands were ravaged by piracy and war but it was a malaria epidemic that caused their eventual depopulation. In 1893 an Austrian industrialist, Paul Kupelweiser acquired them to develop an exclusive summer playground for European aristocracy. He drained the fetid pools that were a breeding ground for mosquitoes, imported exotic tropical plants, and transformed the overgrown thickets of Veliki Brijun into a sublime parkland. After World War II Marshall Tito commandeered the islands. He established a safari park and made it known that he expected his guests to donate an animal to his collection – hence the zebras, camels, elephant, ostriches and deer that still roam freely.

The curious history, amazing scenery, and unexpected wildlife of the Brijuni Islands are an experience not to be missed – one of the most extraordinary and romantic places along the Croatian coast.

POPULATION:
Uninhabited – apart from park and hotel staff

WHEN TO GO:
May to September

HOW TO GET THERE:
Daily ferry from Fazana, a town on the Istrian coast, to Veliki Brijun. To get to Fazana, fly to Venice, Trieste or Pula. From Venice there is a boat/bus connection to Fazana and from Trieste or Pula there are buses. Fazana is only 8 km (5 mi) from Pula.

HIGHLIGHTS:
Gradina Hill – a prehistoric settlement.
Verige Gulf – a Roman palace with temples and outbuildings, an outstanding example of Roman architecture.
The 15th century Church of St Germain with a collection of frescoes. Dobrik Bay – Byzantine Castrum and 5th century basilica and 6th century church.
Mali Brijun – 19th century fort.
A ride round Veliki Brijun on the tourist train.

YOU SHOULD KNOW:
Tito entertained an eclectic selection of celebrity guests on the Brijuni islands, including Elizabeth Taylor and Fidel Castro.

The ruins of the Byzantine Castrum in Dobrik Bay

Crete

POPULATION:
540,045 (2001)
WHEN TO GO:
April, May, June, September and October
HOW TO GET THERE:
Direct and domestic flights to Iraklion and Hania; domestic flights to Sitia. Ferries from the mainland and inter-island ferries.
HIGHLIGHTS:
Knossos – Arthur Evans's reconstruction is unmissable; Malia, Phaestos and Zakros are fascinating; they have not been rebuilt.
The Archaeological Museum in Iraklion – for an overview of Minoan civilization.
The Samaria Gorge – Europe's largest gorge, home to golden eagles and Cretan ibexes.
Rethymnon – the back streets of the old town with wooden Ottoman houses, leaning balconies and old mosques.
The Lasithi Plateau – the windmills may not be working but this is a lovely green plateau with pretty villages and the birthplace of Zeus.
YOU SHOULD KNOW:
A real escapist spot, the small island of Gavdos, some 50 km (31 mi), off Crete's south coast, is the most southerly landmass in Europe. A few fishermen live there, and it is possible to stay.

The largest – over 250 km (160 mi) long – and most southerly of the Greek islands, Crete joined independent Greece in the early 20th century, and it retains strong cultural traditions. Its spine of impressive mountains – the highest, Psiloritis, is 2,456 m (8,060 ft) – is snow-covered in winter. The south-west is barren and impenetrably rocky, though the east and south are very fertile – Crete exports a range of agricultural produce to mainland Greece.

The extraordinary Minoan civilization which flourished from 2800 until 1450 BC, was followed by a succession of great powers including Greece, Rome, Byzantium, Venice and the Ottoman Empire. Now the island's archaeological and architectural heritage sums up its history, for here are Minoan sites – Knossos is one of many – and villas and towns, churches and forts, mosques, ghost villages, ancient harbours and cities with fascinating old quarters. Modern invasions too have left their mark – atmospheric spots redolent of the German occupation during World War II and the almost continuous resort development of the north coast which mass tourism has brought.

But Crete offers more than package holidays and archaeology. Inland, for the serious walker there are the challenging mountains and gorges, for the rambler, marked tracks through verdant valleys and spacious uplands, passing a less-visited site or a traditional hill village. In spring the island blazes with wildflowers and hundreds of migrating bird species pass through.

Beaches are not all packed. The far west has remote, empty sands, the south coast small resorts often reached by a spectacular road journey, sometimes by boat.

Crete's cities, Iraklion, Rethymnon and Hania, provide museums, markets, nightlife; they buzz with life and character.

The harbour at Rethymnon

Egina

Egina's geographical position at the mouth of the Saronic Gulf made it an important maritime power in classical times. Athens, concerned by its strength and the huge fortunes amassed from trade with Egypt and Phoenicia, attacked. After two sea battles the islanders were forced to pull down the city walls, destroy the fleet and leave. Egina achieved importance again in 1827-9 as temporary capital of partly-liberated Greece. Now its fame is as Greece's leading pistachio producer, and a weekend beach resort for Athenians.

Egina Town is a bustling, attractive place, with coloured fishing boats bobbing alongside yachts in a harbour that is lined with handsome buildings, cafés and restaurants, an ideal place to sit for a while and soak up the atmosphere. A single column marks the site of the Temple of Apollo, and there is a well-presented archaeological museum.

The island's major resort, busy Ayia Marina, lies, with several smaller resorts, on the east coast. Inland, the pleasant countryside is mountainous. There are several isolated monasteries and churches, including the enormous church dedicated to the first Greek Orthodox saint of the 20th century, Saint Sophia. On the road to Mount Ormos lies the Hellenic Wildlife Rehabilitation centre, which welcomes visits and help with its work for injured birds and animals. Central and western Egina is green and rolling, carpeted with pistachio orchards. Along the west coast lie further beaches, including the pretty harbour village of Perdhika. From here it is a short boat trip to the uninhabited islet of Moni with its lovely beach and excellent swimming.

The Temple of Aphaea

POPULATION:
13,552 (2001)

WHEN TO GO:
May and June, September and October

HOW TO GET THERE:
Ferry/hydrofoil from Piraeus.

HIGHLIGHTS:
The Temple of Aphaea, 112 km (70 mi) east of Egina Town. Built in the 5th century BC, at the height of Egina's power, this beautiful and complex Doric temple is the major ancient site in the Saronic Gulf islands.
Paleohora – a fascinating 'ghost town' which was built as the island's capital in the 9th century. It was abandoned in 1827. Deserted, scattered with ruined churches and homes, it has a melancholy attraction.
Fish supper - the tavernas along the waterfront at Perdhika are considered to offer the best seafood in the area.

YOU SHOULD KNOW:
Minted on the island in its heyday, the silver 'turtle' coins were the first in Greece.

Fully-laden mules come to market.

POPULATION:
2,719 (2001)
WHEN TO GO:
May and June, September and October
HOW TO GET THERE:
Ferry/hydrofoil from Piraeus.
HIGHLIGHTS:
The Koundouriotis Historical Mansion – a splendid 18th century building, home of a hero of the Greek independence struggle and later a president of republican Greece, which has been restored to its former glory, and is now a museum.
The mansions in Idhra town – the homes of the merchant families, many designed by Venetian or Genoese architects. A map of the mansions is available.
Profiti Ilias Monastery, which lies in the hills above Idhra town; the stiff climb rewards with marvellous views.
YOU SHOULD KNOW:
The Miaoulia Festival in June celebrates Idhra's contribution to the independence struggle with feasting, fireworks and a mock battle in the harbour.

Idhra

Tiny, rocky Idhra lies close to the Peloponnese in the Gulf of Hydra. Its only town, and port, rises in tiers of fine buildings from a horseshoe harbour. Its beauty has made it a favourite with artists and film-makers – and with tourists, who come in hordes: cruise-ships, day-trippers and Athenian weekenders. Despite the visitors, Idhra remains alluring. Greek law protects the island from over-development, and from the blight of traffic – everything except building materials and garbage is carried by donkeys.

Because of its infertility, the island was not much settled in ancient times. When Greeks and Albanians arrived from the Ottoman-controlled mainland, they perforce took up ship-building, and by the 18th century, Idhra was extremely wealthy and possessed a large merchant fleet. Nineteenth century Idhra had a population approaching 20,000; its ships formed a large part of the fleet that fought the Greek War of Independence, and the town became a fashionable resort for Greek socialites.

Now the lovely town with its superb grey stone mansions continues to charm. Away from the waterfront bars, shops and tourists, the streets are quieter; higher up, smaller white houses with brightly painted doorways, steps and balconies crowd the steep deserted lanes. Away from the town on the way-marked tracks or the paved path to the town beaches the walker will find peace and solitude.

Spetses

The most distant of the Argo-Saronic islands from Piraeus, Spetses offers a coastline dotted with pine shaded coves and beaches and a hilly interior which, despite forest fires, is still well wooded. It has long been a favourite with holidaymakers, although responsible planning has allowed the island to retain its charm.

Like Idhra, Spetses was largely settled by refugees from the mainland, and became wealthy through ship-building. Spetses' most colourful character was Laskarina Bouboulina, heroine of the War of Independence. Twice widowed and very wealthy, she commissioned her own fighting ship and led the blockade of Nauplion in 1821. She died at home – shot in a family dispute. Her mansion has been made into a museum by her descendents. A later son of the island, philanthropist Sotirios Anargyrios, replanted the pines and financed roads and several buildings, including a boarding-school based on the English pattern. Writer John Fowles taught here – he later used the island as a setting for his novel *The Magus*.

Dapia harbour is lined with old Venetian houses. Ship-building still flourishes on Spetses, and the walk along the shore passes boatyards with traditionally constructed wooden craft.

Cars are restricted on the island; the more distant coves and seasonal tavernas may be reached by bus, scooter, bicycle – or even horse-drawn carriage.

POPULATION:
3,916 (2001)
WHEN TO GO:
May and June, September and early October
HOW TO GET THERE:
Ferry/hydrofoil from Piraeus.
HIGHLIGHTS:
The old fortified harbour, where bright fishing boats jostle with luxury yachts; the harbour wall still bristles with cannons.
The Museum – housed in the splendid Mexis mansion, home of the island's first governor. It contains paintings, relics of the War of Independence and a collection of ships' figureheads.
YOU SHOULD KNOW:
Boubalina, heroically directing cannon fire, featured on the old 50-Drachma note.

Agia Paraskevi beach

The Terrace of the Lions

Delos

POPULATION:
14 (2001)
WHEN TO GO:
April to June, September and October
HOW TO GET THERE:
Day trips from Mykonos; trips from more distant Naxos, Paros and Tinos may allow less time ashore.
HIGHLIGHTS:
The Museum – with some fascinating exhibits, though the significant finds are in Athens.
The Terrace of the Lions: sculpted and given by the Naxians. Five of the nine remain, one is in Venice and the others disappeared.
The outstanding mosaics in the House of the Tridents and the House of the Masks.
The Sanctuary of the Foreign Gods – this area contains temples and shrines built by resident merchants.
Mount Kynthos – the walk to the top is rewarded with fabulous views of the site and the surrounding islands.
YOU SHOULD KNOW:
The island is home to ruins from as far back as 3 BC.

Just south of Mykonos, tiny Delos is a site of great archaeological importance. This was, in legend, the birthplace of Apollo and his sister Artemis, and in the 8th century BC a four-yearly festival in his honour was established, followed in the early 7th century BC by the building of the Sanctuary of Apollo. The island grew in religious and commercial importance. Athens formed the Delian League against the Persian threat, and its treasury was sited here. In Hellenistic times Delos was one of the most important religious centres in Greece, with pilgrims from all over the Mediterranean. Merchants, bankers and mariners also settled here. Rome declared Delos a free port in 167 BC and trade overtook religion – Delos was the largest slave market in the Mediterranean.

But the island was sacked in 88 and 69 BC and stripped of its treasure; ancient religions lost significance and trade routes changed. Delos's long decline began. Almost deserted, it was part of the Ottoman Empire, then a pirate base.

Now, visitors are not allowed to stay on Delos. The Romans decreed that no-one should die or be born here; the only hotel has been ruined for 1600 years. Starting from two separate harbours, the Sacred and Commercial, the site divides into two corresponding areas. In the huge expanse of rubble that is the Sanctuary, there are temples to Apollo and Artemis, a sanctuary of Dionysus, the dry Sacred Lake and much more. In the Theatre Quarter are streets of the remains of artisans' houses and merchants' mansions and a large but fragmentary theatre. The Slave Market lay in the partly excavated Maritime Quarter.

A visit should be carefully planned; many of the day-trips allow too little time in this extraordinary place.

Paros and Antiparos

Central to the Cycladic group, these islands are separated by a shallow channel, which was formed by an earthquake around 550 BC. Paros was important in antiquity; it is large, fertile and produced the famous marble beloved by sculptors and used to make Early Cycladic figures, the Venus de Milo and Napoleon's tomb. Like its neighbours it was part of the Duchy of Naxos and later the Ottoman Empire – though the Russians held it briefly in the 18th century.

Paros is an attractive island with gentle landscapes, peaceful beaches, and, outside a very busy tourist season, an unspoilt feel. Parikia is a bright, bustling port, the hub of inter-island ferry traffic. Away from the waterfront the old town is a tangle of narrow white lanes. It has several museums and a handful of archaeological sites, and the town beaches are reasonable.

Naoussa still has its pretty harbour full of bright fishing boats and its whitewashed old quarter, though now tourist development encircles the village. Around the large bay are some lovely beaches.

The east coast too has excellent beaches and a few attractive villages, though south and westwards small settlements have been swamped by concrete. Inland, traditional white villages and timeless monasteries are scattered around the slopes of Mount Profitis Ilias.

Antiparos, though so close, has its own identity. The delightful little harbour settlement with its lively waterfront and old quarter now spreads into newly built accommodation. Around the coast lie beaches of fine gold sand and, away from the town, some peaceful walks.

POPULATION:
Paros, 12,853; Antiparos, 1,057 (2001)

WHEN TO GO:
May, June, September and October

HOW TO GET THERE:
Domestic flights. Ferry from mainland – Piraeus and Thessaloniki. Inter-island ferry.

HIGHLIGHTS:
The One Hundred Gated Church in Parikia – designed by Isidore of Miletus in the 6th century and still essentially Byzantine.
The Valley of the Butterflies – a cool, refreshing spot. Jersey tiger moths arrive in early summer.
Lefkes – this beautiful old capital with its handsome buildings is a popular spot.
The Cave of Antiparos – now with concrete steps and lighting, but it remains mysterious and awe inspiring.
Watersports – windsurfing, kiteboarding, sailing and diving can be found at various beaches.

YOU SHOULD KNOW:
The cave of Antiparos has long attracted vandals – Russian sailors broke off stalagmites and took them home and Lord Byron apparently left graffiti.

A typical stone-paved street in Parikia

Naxos

POPULATION:
18,188 (2001)
WHEN TO GO:
May to early July, September and October
HOW TO GET THERE:
Domestic flights; flights to Mykonos and connecting ferry. Ferry from Piraeus, Crete or Thessaloniki. Inter-island ferries.
HIGHLIGHTS:
The portera – a huge stone doorframe to a never-completed temple to Apollo on an islet just by the harbour.
The Temple to Demeter, south of Sangri – fascinating ruins on a hilltop location.
Flerio – the marble quarry here is home to two large and very finely detailed 6th century BC Kouroi left lying unfinished because of faults in the stone.
The Domus Della-Rocca-Barozzi in Naxos Town – a home of the old Venetian nobility.
YOU SHOULD KNOW:
After Ariadne died, Dionysus threw her wedding crown of seven stars into the night sky where it became the Corona Borealis.

Largest and most fertile of the Cyclades, and often described as the most beautiful, Naxos is green and mountainous with distinctive architecture and sandy beaches. It is a prosperous agricultural area, growing olives, potatoes, fruit and the citrus – a large fruit used to make preserves and a sweet liqueur, which Naxos exported worldwide in the 19th century. Recently, tourism has become important.

Legendary Theseus abandoned Ariadne here, despite her aid in the Cretan Labyrinth. Dionysus was on hand to comfort her – the god of wine and ecstasy belongs to Naxos and many boys are still named after him. The island has been inhabited since Neolithic times. During the Classical era, its fine white marble was famously used for sculpture and architecture. In 1207 Marco Sanudi founded the Venetian Duchy of Naxos (towers and mansions all over the island date from this period). Later, Cretan refugees colonized the east.

Naxos Town is the bustling and enjoyable port capital. Up from the waterfront, steep alleys wind under archways to the Kastro, the Venetian capital. Many houses still bear the insignia of the original residents; during siesta the atmosphere is hushed, timeless.

The town beach is pleasant but busy; further south, resorts are smaller and the sands emptier. Inland Naxos is scenic and fascinating. The Tragea, the central high plain around Mount Zeus, is a lovely region of olive groves, little churches and traditional villages. Apiranthos, a hilly collection of fine stone houses, is an excellent base for walkers. It has several small museums. The villagers are descendants of the Cretans.

Bustling and enjoyable Naxos town

Milos and Kimolos

The most westerly of the Cyclades, Milos is a joy for the geologist. It is volcanic, with a dramatic coast, strange rock formations, hot springs and fertile lowlands. However, much of the landscape is disfigured by mining – it produces bentonite, perlite and china clay. But industry has brought prosperity; tourism is low-key here, despite some lovely beaches.

Ancient Milos was important for obsidian (used to make sharp tools) and for its sheltered harbour; it was settled by Minoans and Mycenaeans. In 416 BC, Milos paid dearly for refusing to join the alliance against Sparta – Athens executed the men and enslaved the women and children. Under Venetian and Turkish rule, Milos remained undistinguished.

Adhamas, the main port, is a pleasant, lively place. The north-west, inhabited since early times, has a cluster of pretty villages. Plaka, the island capital, an unspoilt whitewashed maze, has the remains of a Venetian kastro and glorious views. Tripity is built downhill near early Christian catacombs. At the bottom of the green valley the fishing village of Klima was the port for ancient Milos, whose remains straggle down the hill.

There are good beaches on the south coast, some with accommodation, others difficult to reach. Most of the south-west around Mount Profitis Ilias is bleak and deserted. The windswept north has hamlets and beaches; Pollonia in the far north-east has a diving centre and is popular with windsurfers.

Kimolos used to export chalk (*kimolia*) and still extracts Fullers earth. The craggy interior is barren, the south fertile, with a string of fishing villages and beaches. In the centre, the ruins of Venetian Paleokastro crown a cliff. This is a peaceful and friendly place.

The fishing village of Firopotamus on Milos

POPULATION:
Milos 4,771, Kimolos 769 (2001)
WHEN TO GO:
May, June, early July and September
HOW TO GET THERE:
Milos: domestic flights; ferry from Piraeus and Crete. Inter-island ferries. Kimolos: boats from Pollonia on Milos; inter-island ferries.
HIGHLIGHTS:
Boat trips round the island visit the inaccessible beaches and view the geological oddities.
Tiny, photogenic Klima, with brightly painted boathouses lining the shore.
The museum in Plaka – containing a copy of the 'Venus de Milo'.
Dazzling white Hora above the bay in Kimolos – with a well-preserved 16th century stockade-type Kastro.
YOU SHOULD KNOW:
The 'Venus de Milo' now in the Louvre Museum in Paris was found by a farmer in 1820; her arms were knocked off in the scramble of her hand-over to the French for 'safe keeping' from the Turks.

Mykonos

POPULATION:
9,306 (2001)
WHEN TO GO:
May and October
HOW TO GET THERE:
Charter and domestic flights; ferries from Piraeus
HIGHLIGHTS:
Little Venice, where multi-coloured balconies hang over the sea facing the setting sun.
The windmills – one working mill is also a museum.
The museums – there are several interesting museums including a folklore collection in an 18th century mansion.
Scuba diving – legal here, and most beaches have a dive centre.
The nightlife – there are plenty of stylish and romantic places to eat and drink.
YOU SHOULD KNOW:
Le Corbusier is thought to have exclaimed about Mykonos: 'Whatever architecture has to say, it is said here'.

This small, rocky island has no ancient sites – it was eclipsed by its tiny neighbour Delos – and little history. It is battered all summer by the Meltemi (winds from the north). It is the most popular and most expensive of the Cyclades. Long before *Shirley Valentine*, Mykonos was an international favourite – with bohemians in the 1960s, then the European jet setters and latterly its beaches have become a destination for gay travellers. With its square white houses, blue domed churches and golden sands, it is, for many, the image of Greece; outside the long season, when sun beds cram the beaches and the town throbs with music, the magic is still strong.

Mykonos Town demands a photo at every turn. Sugar-cube houses are heaped around the harbour where tourists feed the pelican. (The original, christened Petros, arrived in a storm in 1956 and soon became a star.) The old town was designed as a maze to confuse marauding pirates; the little alleyways still bewilder visitors. The whitewashed houses, highlighted with blue painted woodwork, are wreathed with scarlet and magenta flowers.

Inland, the only sizeable town is Ano Maro, a pleasant place, rather self-consciously traditional, and a good base for walks in the rolling countryside. Here the bare brown hills are sprinkled with hundreds of little churches and the snowy cubes of farms.

Mykonos's beaches are justly famed. The tourist industry works to keep them clean, and has banned over-large development. The most popular sands run along the south coast; overcrowded, noisy stretches are interspersed with quieter nudist areas and, for those prepared to walk, there are still some relatively uncommercialized spots. The north is very windy, though Panormos Bay provides shelter.

The sugar-cube houses in Mykonos Town

The Minor Cyclades

This chain of tiny islands lies between Naxos and Amorgos. Only four of the islands are inhabited year-round. In antiquity, all were populated – large numbers of ancient graves have been found. For centuries simply the haunts of pirates, they now attract Greeks in search of their roots and travellers looking for an uncommercialized spot to get away from it all.

Dhonoussa is the least accessible of the islands, lying off Naxos's empty east coast, while the others form a group to the south, en route to Amorgos. Stavros, the port settlement, is backed by low hills. A walk through cultivated land reaches dramatic scenery, remote beaches and pleasant hamlets. Only Kalotaritsas on the north coast has amenities.

Ano Koufonissi is tiny, though more populous, with a sizeable fishing fleet. (Larger Kato Koufonissi is almost uninhabited). The main settlement, Hora, spreads around the harbour. The beaches here are outstanding; some of the golden crescents along the south coast have tavernas and rooms. This island is becoming popular and is busy in season.

The ferry for Skhinoussa docks at Mersini; Hora, the town, in the hills above the minute harbour, has fine views, trails lead from here through low hills and pastures to numerous beaches. Only two, Tsigouri and Almyros, have facilities.

Iraklia, the first stop for the boat from Naxos, gets its fair share of visitors, though, with few amenities, it retains its unspoilt atmosphere. Ayios Yeorgios straggles behind the harbour and a shaded beach. A pleasant walk leads to Panayia, an unspoilt village at the foot of Mount Papas.

POPULATION:
Dhonoussa 110; Koufonissi 366; Skhinoussa 206; Iraklia 151 (2001)

WHEN TO GO:
May to early July and September

HOW TO GET THERE:
Inter-island ferries from Amorgos or Naxos.

HIGHLIGHTS:
Koufonissi – noted for its good fish tavernas.
Keros – a day-trip from Koufonissia, there is the site of an important Neolithic village on uninhabited Keros.
Livadhi – the best beach on Iraklia: among the remains of the deserted villages are remnants of Hellenistic and Venetian architecture.
The Cave of Ayios Ioannis on Iraklia – in this large cave an icon of the saint was found by a shepherd in the 19th century.

YOU SHOULD KNOW:
Over 100 Early Cycladic (3000-2000 BC) figures have been found on Keros; the finest are on display in Athens.

A church in Panayia

The church of Panayia Evangelistria

Tinos

POPULATION:
8,574 (2001)
WHEN TO GO:
May to early July and September
HOW TO GET THERE:
Ferry from mainland (Rafina and Thessaloniki); inter-island ferries.
HIGHLIGHTS:
The dovecotes – these sturdy structures are surmounted by symbolic patterns of open work slate. They are fine examples of vernacular architecture.
Pyrgos – a marble-working village with a museum and school of sculpture.
In pretty Volax, elderly Catholics weave beautiful baskets.
Kolymbithra, a double bay on the north coast – the wilder half is home to visiting flamingoes in spring.
YOU SHOULD KNOW:
Doves were introduced to Tinos by the Venetians; they provided meat, feathers for bedding and droppings for fertilizer.

A large island in the north-eastern Cyclades, Tinos is lovely. It is mountainous, with terraced hillsides, unspoilt remote hill villages and a coastline dotted with good, largely undeveloped beaches. Its landscape is characterized by hundreds of ornate, whitewashed dovecotes, and tall belfries. The Venetians controlled Tinos for 500 years, holding out against the Turks longer than anywhere else in the Aegean. During this time, Catholic and Orthodox churches competed in building these belfries. Several of its many villages are still Catholic.

Although Tinos receives few foreign visitors, thousands of Greeks come as pilgrims, particularly on 25 March and 15 August. Since the 19th century, when a nun had a vision directing her to a miraculous icon of the Virgin, Tinos has been the Lourdes of Greece. Tinos Town, which is modern and functional but relaxed, is packed with shops selling religious paraphernalia; the icon, in the church of Panayia Evangelistria is almost invisible beneath gold, silver and jewels. A thick pad running up the processional street is for pilgrims approaching the church on their knees.

At Kionia, a beach resort outside town, the Sanctuary of Poseidon and Amphitrite has the remains of hostels for ancient pilgrims – Poseidon delivered the island from a plague of snakes. On a rocky crag inland are the ruins of the Venetian capital, Exobourgo. Clustered around the foothills lie dozens of lovely villages and hamlets, each distinctive, and well worth exploring. Tinos enjoys a strong tradition of crafts.

The islanders are open and welcoming – pay them a visit!

Santorini

In the southern Aegean Sea, about 200 km south of mainland Greece, lies Santorini, a spectacular volcanic island in the Cyclades group known for its dramatic views, brilliant sunsets and fine beaches. The beauty of the island and its dynamic nightlife have made this a popular tourist destination.

From above it is obvious that the island, shaped like a ring with a huge bay of sea in the centre, is what remains of a giant volcano which erupted in around 1650 BC, one of the biggest volcanic explosions the earth has ever seen. The walls of the caldera surrounding the bay in the centre rise a sheer 300 m out of the sea. The traces of previous eruptions can be seen in the coloured bands of rock on the island's cliffs: each one is a layer of compressed ash ejected in one eruption. The small island in the middle of the bay is another volcanic cone forming.

Evidence suggests that the massive eruption caused a tsunami which led indirectly to the decline of the Minoan civilization centred on nearby Crete. The Minoan settlement on Santorini itself was engulfed in lava and the stunning remains, at Akrotiri, make a fascinating day out. There are three-storey houses with magnificent frescos, ceramics and staircases, and the hot and cold running water system suggests this was a prosperous and refined town.

Thira is the island's capital, perched high up on the cliffs 300 m above its port below. Its architecture is an attractive mix of Venetian and traditional Cycladic and the white cobblestone streets are lined with shops and cafés. Thira can get busy in summer as cruise ships dock here while the passengers explore the town. There are three main means of getting from the port up to the town – by cablecar, by donkey, or by walking up the 300-odd zigzagging steps.

The town of Ia (sometimes spelled Oia), with its pretty whitewashed buildings and blue domes, is one of the most charming places on the island, albeit rather busy with tourists. The town offers views of the open sea to the east, as well as the bay to the west, and many people congregate here in the late afternoon to watch the sunset over the bay, a really memorable experience.

POPULATION:
13,670 (2001)
WHEN TO GO:
April to October
HOW TO GET THERE:
By ferry from the Greek mainland or other Greek islands, or by plane from Athens, Thessaloniki and a few other European cities.
HIGHLIGHTS:
The excavations at Akrotiri – this Minoan town was buried by lava during the volcanic eruption, and the excavations have revealed multi-level buildings and beautiful frescoes.
The Archaeological Museum at Thira – the story of Akrotiri and other ancient settlements on the island is told through Neolithic and Bronze Age artefacts.
The beaches – the best beach is probably that at Perissa, but the black sand beach in the charming town of Kamari also makes a nice day out.
Mesa Gonia – a small village with lovely traditional architecture, some ruins from the 1956 earthquake, restored villas and a winery.
Pyrgos – an inland village with some grand houses, a ruined Venetian castle and some Byzantine churches.
YOU SHOULD KNOW:
The island is also sometimes referred to as Thira.

The pretty town of Ia overlooks the Aegean Sea.

Alonissos

POPULATION:
2,700 (2001)
WHEN TO GO:
June and early July, September and early October
HOW TO GET THERE:
Charter/domestic flights to Skiathos and hydrofoil connections.
Ferry/hydrofoil from Thessaloniki and Volos via Skiathos.
HIGHLIGHTS:
Old Alonissos – otherwise known as Hora – this beautiful old town is being sensitively renovated by returning islanders and foreigners and has several good tavernas, perfect spots to recover from the energetic walk up the hill and watch the sunset.
A boat trip excursion takes in the numerous small islands, landing on some.
The Monk seal information centre in Patitiri and the Monk seal rehabilitation centre in Steni Vala provide insight into these rare mammals.
YOU SHOULD KNOW:
Evidence has been unearthed of the oldest prehistoric habitation in the Aegean – near the site of ancient Ikos at Kokkinokastro.

The furthest of the Sporades from mainland Greece, Alonissos has not been overwhelmed by tourism. It is a serene place, heavily wooded with pine and oak, an island whose numerous good beaches are reached by rocky donkey paths, whose residents are careful of the area's ecology. In 1992 the seas around the island were designated a National Marine Park and several of the many small islets are off limits. The park is for the protection not only of the endangered European Monk seal, but also of rare sea birds and a unique species of wild goat. Here all homes have cesspit drainage; no sewage enters the brilliantly clean sea. Many islanders fetch fine drinking water from mountain springs, using the piped variety only for washing. Visitors who come to Alonissos are attracted by the tranquility and beauty and by the charmingly hospitable islanders.

Alonissos has rebuilt itself from disaster. In 1950, phylloxera wiped out the flourishing wine-making industry, after which many islanders left for the mainland to make a living. In 1965 Hora, the old capital, was destroyed by earthquake. The residents were re-housed down by the harbour in rapidly constructed accommodation. Patitiri still has a rather thrown-together look, though the waterfront is undergoing a facelift and the port has a lively and friendly atmosphere.

Little traffic on the one real road makes it a perfect place for walkers. Tracks lead into the woods and hills from which paths run down to one of the many small shingle beaches. Swim in the crystalline water and enjoy a lazy meal of freshly caught fish in one of the beachside tavernas.

One of the secluded bays on Alonissos

Skyros

The largest and most sparsely populated of the group, Skyros lies far south of the other Sporades, closer to Evvia than to mainland Thessaly. The north of the island is rolling, cultivated and forested, while the barren, mountainous south is home to an ancient breed of half-wild ponies. Skyros has many beaches, some only accessible on foot; the finest lie on the north-east coast. Until quite recently, few tourists made the journey apart from those attending courses at a long-established centre for alternative lifestyles. Now, more independent travellers visit Skyros.

In mythology, Theseus met his death here, and the young Achilles, disguised as a girl, was hidden. In Byzantine times the island was again a hiding place – for wrongdoers exiled from the mainland. The trade and collaboration by these men with seafarers and pirates resulted in a wealthy élite who filled their mansions with treasures – some looted. The Skyrians' extraordinary traditional homes, like tiny family museums, have their roots in this period. On display among skilful modern needlework and painted pottery are old embroideries, copperware and porcelain. The furniture may have been intricately carved 200 years ago – or last week.

In the far south, at Tris Boukes, is the grave of poet Rupert Brooke, who died offshore en route to Gallipoli in 1915.

Skyros Town is a glorious tumble of Cycladic-style white cube houses on a rocky bluff, high above the lovely, long sand beaches of Magazia and Molos. The maze of little lanes is a real joy; you may see old Skyrians in traditional dress – the men wearing heavy, laced sandals which resemble medieval footwear – sitting outside doors, open to reveal their precious inheritance.

POPULATION:
2,602 (2001)
WHEN TO GO:
June, early July and September
HOW TO GET THERE:
Domestic flight from Athens or Thessaloniki,or ferry from Kymi on Evvia and connecting bus from Athens.
HIGHLIGHTS:
The Faltaits Museum - housed in the family's mansion in Skyros Town, this is an outstanding collection of Skyrian folk art, rare books and photographs and treasures.
The Kastro - this mainly Byzantine fortress above Skyros Town is reached through a tunnel in the walls and a monastery courtyard. The views are outstanding and the walk up through the quieter back lanes enjoyable.
The Brooke monument – a classical bronze, 'Immortal Poetry' faces the sea at the edge of Skyros Town. When it was unveiled in the 1930s its nakedness caused a stir.
YOU SHOULD KNOW:
The pre-Lenten Carnival surely has its roots in pre-Christian ritual – transvestite 'maidens' dance around town with young men in goat costumes, garlands and sheep bells.

Skyros Town

Nyssiros

POPULATION:
948 (2001)
WHEN TO GO:
May, June, early July and September
HOW TO GET THERE:
Flight to Kos and ferry. Inter-island ferries from Rhodes and Piraeus.
HIGHLIGHTS:
The crater – the air stinks of sulphur, blow-holes emit jets of steam, brilliant yellow sulphur crystals. The ground is spongy and hot. From under it comes hissing and bubbling. Paleokastro is a fine 7th century BC Doric defensive bastion south of Mandhraki.
YOU SHOULD KNOW:
Poseidon was annoyed by a Titan, and crushed him under a huge rock, which became Nyssiros. Poor Polyvotis still struggles to escape, and groans. His name is used by the locals for the volcano.

Compared with its large northerly neighbour Kos, Nyssiros is surprisingly green, although its scant water is sulphur-tainted. Its slopes are covered in volcanic-soil-loving oaks. This is not just a small, round island with volcanic soil – it is a volcano. The craggy hill-tops form a circle round a volcanic caldera created by an eruption in 1422. The first great eruptions happened thirty or forty thousand years ago; the most recent in 1933. Contented livestock wander in the woods, though the fertile terraces are largely uncultivated, for the islanders now derive much of their income from pumice extraction – another legacy of early volcanic activity.

The port and island capital, Mandhraki, is a cheerful, charming place with its Knights' castle, closely packed, brightly-painted houses, narrow lanes and sea views. Pali, a pleasant fishing village to the east, has accommodation and a good beach, with long walks to more isolated spots. A trek through the hills reaches the volcano via Emborios, an almost deserted village, which offers sustenance and a public steam bath (volcano heated!) in a grotto. Nikea, a lovely, lively village further round the rim, has a pretty pebble-mosaic square and views over the sea and volcano. A bus stops here and a steep path down into the caldera starts.

From mid-morning till early afternoon, day-trippers from Kos pour into the blighted lunar landscape of the caldera, where there are five craters, with a path into the largest. Few visitors stay on Nyssiros; after the boats depart, a somnolent peace descends.

The lovely village of Nikea with the volcanic crater in the background

Symi

Lying just 41 km (25 mi) north-west of Rhodes close the the Turkish mainland, the little island of Symi is part of the Dodecanese Islands. The interior of this lovely mountainous island is divided by beautiful valleys and its coast is characterized by rocky outcrops and lovely bays, many only accessible by boat.

The island belonged to the Roman Empire, then the Byzantines, until its conquest in 1373 by the Knights of St John whose skills in shipping and commerce brought several centuries of wealth, mainly through boat-building and sponge-diving. The Ottoman Empire took Symi in 1522 but its prosperity continued and its export of sponges still provided much of its wealth. The island's heyday was in the mid-19th century when its population numbered around 30,000, and many of the neoclassical mansions on the island date from that period. Symi was passed between the Turks, Italians, Nazis and British until it finally joined Greece in 1948.

The main settlement, in the north-east of the island, is also called Symi, but locals usually refer to it as Yialos. The town is divided into an upper and lower part. The upper part is known as Chorio and is dominated by the fortress of the Knights of St John. The castle was built in the early 15th century on the site of a much older fortification. It survived until World War II when it was used as a munitions store. This was blown up, destroying the castle and the church within its walls. Parts of the walls remain and there are lovely views from the site. The lower part of town around the port area is stunning, surrounded as it is by green hills making a natural amphitheatre. The two halves of the town are linked by the Kali Strata, 350 steps lined with pastel-coloured neoclassical houses with flower-filled courtyards.

There are many lovely churches and monasteries on the island, some of which can be explored on foot, others that are only accessible by boat. The church of Constantinos and Eleni on the southern slopes of Vigla has lovely gardens and terraces. Set in a bay to the south-west of the island is the monastery of the Archangel Michael at Panormitis, an important pilgrimage site visited by people from all over Greece. Built in the early eighteenth century on the site of a much older monastery, it contains a wonderful iconostasis, fine Byzantine frescoes and two museums with a fascinating library.

Every year from July to September, the famous Symi Festival takes place on the island. The festival features dance and theatre events, as well as a host of open-air concerts by many leading Greek musicians.

POPULATION:
2,606 (2001)

WHEN TO GO:
May to October.

HOW TO GET THERE:
By boat or hydrofoil from Rhodes or Piraeus.

HIGHLIGHTS:
Hire a boat and explore the lovely coastline to find a secluded beach for a picnic.
Hiking – the island lends itself to exploration on foot, and the beautiful countryside is peppered with isolated chapels and wonderful views.
The monastery of Megalos Sotiris – a picturesque monastery with spectacular views. A lovely walk to an old vineyard and the ruins of old wine presses is sign-posted from here.
The Archaeological and Folklore Museum in Chorio – open mornings only, the museum has some interesting exhibits and artefacts.
Chatziagapitos Mansion in Chorio – a restored 18th-century mansion open to the public.

YOU SHOULD KNOW:
Although the island used to be famous for its sponges, those now on sale on the island are imported.

The beautiful harbour at Symi

Rhodes

POPULATION:
117,007 (2001)
WHEN TO GO:
April to June, September and October
HOW TO GET THERE:
Charter and domestic flights. Ferry from Piraeus. Inter-island ferries, catamarans and hydrofoils. International ferry from Marmaris, Turkey.
HIGHLIGHTS:
The Palace of the Grandmasters – heavily reconstructed by the Italians, it is attached to two fascinating collections, the medieval Exhibit and Ancient Rhodes.
The Acropolis of Lindhos – gloriously photogenic Hellenistic and Doric remains in a spectacular setting high above the town.
Thermes Kallitheas, south of Rhodes town. A partly restored orientalized Art Deco complex of pools and domes set in a palm grove.
YOU SHOULD KNOW:
The Colossus of Rhodes, one of the Seven Wonders of the World, was built after the siege in 305 BC; it collapsed after an earthquake in 227 BC. The story has it that it was sold as scrap hundreds of years later, only to return in the form of Ottoman cannonballs.

Large, beautiful and fertile, lying on trade routes close to Asia Minor, Rhodes is now one of the major tourist destinations in the Mediterranean. It has a long history of invasion. The first Siege of Rhodes was laid in 305 BC, a century after the city-states of Lindos, Kameiros and Ialyssos united. After almost a year Demetrius Poliorketes and his superior forces sailed, leaving a powerful and wealthy independent city-state which eclipsed even Athens in the arts. The Knights of St John held it as their main base from 1309 till Suleyman the Magnificent laid the second Siege of Rhodes in 1522, and the whole Dodecanese became part of the Ottoman Empire. The Italians seized the island in 1912, the Germans in 1943; after British administration it joined unified Greece in 1948.

Lindos and the Acropolis

The Old Town of Rhodes, which seethes with tourists all day, is a remarkably preserved and exquisite medieval city. The massive walls, the bustling squares, the palaces and the rather stern, straight streets, all built of glowing golden stone, are a legacy of the crusading Knights. The Ottomans left mosques, Turkish baths and a very oriental-feeling bazaar area. In Mandhraki, the ancient harbour, the Colossos of Rhodes once stood. Some fine Italian Art Deco buildings remain in the New Town. There are several museums and a rousing Sound and Light presentation.

South of the city, big resorts have swallowed most of the coastal area. Heavily commercialized Lindos with its steep lanes, frescoed church and sheltered harbour (supposedly St Paul's landing place) is still beautiful. The wooded, hilly countryside, unspoilt villages and lonely churches of the interior are best explored by car. Tour buses visit the Valley of the Butterflies. The far south is almost undeveloped, though the southernmost point, Prassonissi, is a Mecca for windsurfers.

The Vlacherna Monastery in Kanoni

Corfu

The most northerly and, with Greece's highest rainfall, the greenest of the Ionian Islands, Corfu lies close to the mainland and the Albanian coast. Described by Homer as 'beautiful and rich', it is mountainous, lushly fertile and fringed by fine beaches with lovely aquamarine waters.

From the 8th century BC, Corfu was subject to a succession of powers, though it never became part of the Ottoman Empire. Venice held it for 200 years, then Napoleon seized it, and for some years it was a British Protectorate. Long a favourite with travellers, its quiet, idiosyncratic life is lovingly recorded in the books of Lawrence and Gerald Durrell. Now, despite some indiscriminate tourist development, it remains bewitching.

Corfu Town is a lovely place, a blend of splendid Italianate buildings, narrow alleyways and grand, French-influenced arcades. There are museums and fine churches, including the Church of Ayios Spyridhon, where the mummified body of the island's patron saint lies in a glass-fronted coffin. (It is paraded through the town several times a year.) A popular excursion is to the photogenic islets of Vlaherna and Pondikonissi.

North from Corfu Town, brash or prestigious resorts are interspersed with fishing harbours and backed by magnificent scenery. Southwards lie the site of the ancient capital, Corcyra, and some large resorts. Then a winding coastal road reaches some quieter beaches. The west coast boasts long stretches of glorious sand, a backdrop of green mountains – and some of the largest hotel conglomerations. Even here, more peaceful coves can be reached by boat, or a scramble on foot.

Inland, traditional villages offer shade and good food. Corfiot cuisine, unusually, has no Turkish influence, and often seems more Italian than Greek. A stroll and a climb in scented mountain air amid ancient olive trees rewards with views over ethereal greenness towards the heavenly blue sea.

POPULATION:
109,540 (2001)
WHEN TO GO:
May, June, September and October
HOW TO GET THERE:
Direct charter flights; domestic flights. Ferry from the mainland (Igoumenitsa); international ferry from Italy.
HIGHLIGHTS:
The excellent Archaeological Museum in Corfu Town.
The Asiatic Museum, housed in the former residence of the British High Commissioner.
Mon Repos, the birthplace of Prince Philip, now an interesting museum with lovely grounds, south of Corfu Town.
Watching the sunset from Kaiser's Throne, an observation tower above Pelekas village on the west coast.
The 'ghost village' of Ano Perithia in the north of the island with its several thriving tavernas.
YOU SHOULD KNOW:
A wide green esplanade, the Spianada, in Corfu Town, is home to Greece's only cricket pitch.

Paxi and Andipaxi

Paxi is a tiny island, and has no spectacular sandy beaches or historical sites; its limited accommodation is block-booked in season, and its popularity with yacht flotillas has pushed prices up. However, visitors fall in love with it. Largely unspoilt – its tourism is run by small, discriminating companies – it is beautiful, friendly and charming.

The east coast is characterized by low hills and shingly coves, the west by precipitous cliffs above inaccessible caves and beaches. There are three coastal settlements. Gaios, the capital and main port, is a pleasant, attractive town of old, red-roofed, pastel-washed buildings around a seafront square, with views of two islets. Longos to the northwest is a pretty fishing village and a quieter resort. Picturesque Lakka sits on a beautiful horseshoe bay at the north of the island. It has a couple of beaches and some good walks. Inland Paxi, with its ancient olives and scattering of farms and villages, is perfect walking country. The one main road runs down the spine of the island.

Andipaxi, with its gorgeous sandy coves and dazzlingly blue water, can be reached by excursion boat from any of the resorts. The beaches do get busy, but it is possible to walk across the islet (it is covered in vines, and produces good wine) to quieter bays.

POPULATION:
2,500 (2001)
WHEN TO GO:
May, June, September and October
HOW TO GET THERE:
Ferry from the mainland (Igoumenitsa); hydrofoil from Corfu.
HIGHLIGHTS:
Walking is the best way to get to know the island; good maps and guides are available.
Boat trips – the boat from Paxi to Andipaxi may visit some of the most dramatic caves in the region.
YOU SHOULD KNOW:
The statue on Gaios waterfront commemorates a Paxiot sailor who tried to set fire to the Turkish fleet.

The Trypitos Arch on the south coast of Paxi

Ithaki

POPULATION:
3,080 (2001)
WHEN TO GO:
May, June and September.
HOW TO GET THERE:
Ferry from the mainland (Astakos and Patras); inter-island ferry.
HIGHLIGHTS:
Walking – with its small scale, quiet lanes, paths over gorse covered hills and wonderful views, this is a walkers' island.
Anoyi – once an important settlement, this sleepy village has some fine old buildings.
Afales Bay – a little-visited sweep of pebble and sand below the supposed School of Homer at Platrithies.
YOU SHOULD KNOW:
Ithaca (Ithaki) has long been the symbolic image for the end of a journey.

Two narrowly connected mountain tops rising from the sea, little Ithaki nestles close to north-eastern Kefallonia. With its wooded valleys, vineyards, forested hills and small pebble beaches, it is an excellent place for a quiet stay. Though day-trippers do visit, tourism is low-key here.

Legendary Odysseus returned to his home on Ithaca after years of wandering and much of the detailed geographical description of his island matches features on modern Ithaki. Various sites have been linked to those in the Odyssey, but there is little real evidence. Historically, Ithaki was almost uninhabited till the Venetians re-settled it, and it is hard to imagine this peaceful place the splendid hub of a maritime kingdom.

The harbour town of Vathy, set on a deep bay within a bay, was sympathetically restored after the 1953 earthquake; it has a lovely waterfront and provides a taste of old island life. Within walking distances are a couple of small beaches and the Odysseus' sites of the Arethoussa Spring and the Cave of the Nymphs. Alalkomenae, the site Schliemann claimed as the castle of Odysseus, consists of foundations – the artefacts found are in the museum. There is a good beach at Pisaetos, below the site.

A spectacular bus ride across the isthmus to northern Ithaki reaches Stavros, a busy little town set in fine hilly countryside. An alternative location for the castle is at Pelikata Hill. On the east coast, the tiny harbour settlements of Frikes and Kioni are popular with visitors. Kioni has pretty old buildings and a busy yacht anchorage; Frikes, hidden in a deep wooded valley, is, with its sheltered mooring, a year-round port. It has some pleasant waterfront tavernas.

The pretty harbour at Kioni

Lefkada

Lefkada was attached to the mainland until a canal was cut in the 7th century BC. Now it is reached by road over a pontoon swivel bridge. The heavy Venetian fortification of the north coast, some of which remains, was not enough to prevent the Ottomans taking it in 1479; their tenure lasted about two centuries.

The island is mountainous and very fertile, lush with olive groves and vineyards and traditional villages. The west coast is rugged, the east sheltered, with calm beaches. Some of the low-lying areas are marshy.

The main town, Lefkada, in the far north, was badly hit by earthquakes. Now it is an attractive working town, rebuilt with low-rise buildings, narrow lanes and arcaded streets. Southwards, past a few small fishing ports and pebble beaches, lies Nydhri, the most highly developed resort town. It has good beaches and a lovely setting overlooking small satellite islands. Boat trips tour these – some are privately owned. Further south, several fine bays enclose quieter resorts or fishing villages. Vassiliki is situated on a huge, windy bay: the charming little harbour is lined with shade trees and tavernas. The breezy beach at Pondi, a little west, is visited by vast numbers of windsurfers.

The rocky west coast is dotted with lovely beaches. Most accommodation here is in village rooms or campsites. The southernmost point, Cape Lefkatas, is also known as Sappho's Leap – here the lovelorn lyric poet reputedly threw herself into the sea.

POPULATION:
22,500 (2001)
WHEN TO GO:
May, June and September
HOW TO GET THERE:
By road from the mainland; inter-island ferries.
HIGHLIGHTS:
Meganissi, the largest of the satellite islands. Green and peaceful with pretty beaches and deep bays, it has accommodation.
Windsurfing – Vassiliki is home to some of Europe's best windsurfing.
The beaches – the most southerly beaches on the west coast are, with their dramatic white cliffs and turquoise water, among the loveliest in the Ionian.
YOU SHOULD KNOW:
The German archaeologist Wilhelm Dorpfeld believed that Nydhri, not Ithaki, was Odysseus' capital. He lived there and is honoured by a statue on the quay.

The stunning beach at Port Katsiki

Kefalonia

POPULATION:
31,800 (2001)
WHEN TO GO:
May, June, September and October
HOW TO GET THERE:
Direct charter and domestic flights. Ferry from the mainland – Patras to Sami, Kyllini to Poros. Inter-island ferries.
HIGHLIGHTS:
Mount Enos – the highest peak in the Ionian Islands at 1,632 m (5,304 ft). A road runs almost to the top.
Ayios Yeoryios – the ruins of the medieval Venetian capital, destroyed by earthquake in the 17th century.
Assos, a lovely west coast village at the bottom of a zigzagging road; it clings to a narrow isthmus under a ruined fort.
The caves of Drogharati and Melissani, inland from Sami.
YOU SHOULD KNOW:
The water in the Melissani cave is salt; it flows through an underground channel all the way from Katavothres (swallow-hole) near Argostoli.

Like other Ionian islands, Kefalonia was never taken by the Ottomans – it was too important to the Venetian maritime empire. Also like its neighbours, it was occupied by Italian and then by German forces during World War II; during the Italian 'capitulation', over 5,000 troops were massacred. Louis de Berniere's book *Captain Corelli's Mandolin* covers this tragedy. A flood of tourists came to the island after the film in 2000, though they found none of the elegant Venetian architecture; this was destroyed in the 1953 earthquake.

The largest of the Ionian Islands, with a mountainous interior and magnificent beaches, it absorbs the crowds, and its towns and villages retain traditional independence. After the earthquake, Kefalonia re-housed rather than re-constructed; Argostoli, the capital, is a beautifully situated, functional concrete town. The south of the island is rugged and barren; along the coast are the biggest package resorts and the best beaches. Poros and Skala on the south-east coast are older resorts.

Sami, a large working port built and rebuilt on the site of the ancient capital offers a couple of decent beaches and tavernas which, after the location filming, have now been appropriately re-named. Ayia Efimia, north of Sami, is a friendly fishing village and low-key resort. On the northernmost point of the island stands Fiskardho, the only town to survive the earthquake. Its pretty harbour front curls round a bay bobbing with yachts. Crowded but charming, it has pleasant walks to pebble beaches. The west coast is spectacular – the road runs along dizzying cliffs above dramatic beaches. The landscape of the rather remote Lixouri peninsula has been strangely moulded by the earthquakes; it has some good, quieter, red-sand beaches.

The stunning view down to the sea from a coastal road between Skala and Poros

Zakynthos

The most southern of the Ionian chain, Zakynthos, also called Zante, shares the history of invasion, freedom from Ottoman rule, and devastation by earthquakes. Much of the island is still green and unspoilt. The north and west is barren and mountainous, the centre very fertile, with farms, vineyards and lovely old villages set in beautiful countryside where life is more or less untouched by tourism.

Zakynthos Town was rebuilt on the old plan, an attempt to recreate the atmosphere of the pre-earthquake 'Flower of the Levant'. It is a handsome place, with arcaded streets, grand public buildings, museums and a busy working port. Round-the–island boat trips to sea caves and beaches start here. The ruined Venetian Kastro high above the town makes a pleasant walk.

On the east coast, the resorts close to Zakynthos Town are overcrowded. However, the Vassilikos Peninsula to the south still has small resorts and beaches, and travelling northwards the parade of fishing villages and beach resorts become less developed. The north coast is rocky and inaccessible, with dizzying views. There are one or two spots along the wild and remote west coast where the sea can be reached.

Major package tourism has taken over the south. Kalamaki and Laganas offer round-the-clock entertainment, English pubs and water sports on a fine but over-subscribed beach, which was once a major breeding ground of the loggerhead turtle. Marine biologists are in dispute with tourist bosses over the protection of this endangered creature.

Smugglers Cove – the most famous beach on Zakynthos

POPULATION:
38,600 (2001)
WHEN TO GO:
May, June, September and October
HOW TO GET THERE:
Direct charter and domestic flights. Ferry from the mainland (Kylini); inter-island ferries.
HIGHLIGHTS:
Yerakas – this splendid beach at the tip of the Vassilikos Peninsula is a protected breeding ground for the loggerhead turtle. There is a Turtle Information Centre here.
Boat trips – shorter, less crowded trips to the Blue Cave and Shipwreck Beach run from Ayios Nikolaos in the north-east.
The Byzantine Museum, Zakynthos Town, with artwork and treasures from pre-earthquake buildings.
YOU SHOULD KNOW:
The Virgin of the church in Keri, a village in the south-west, is said to have saved the island from marauding pirates by wrapping it in sea mist.

Kekova

In one of the most attractive spots on Turkey's Turquoise Coast is the lovely Mediterranean island of Kekova. At just 4.5 sq km (1.7 sq mi), the island is uninhabited but lies in a bay close to the mainland. On the north shore of the island are the ruins of ancient Apollonia, dating back to the 5th century BC. The reason these unassuming ruins attract so many visitors is that they lie partially submerged beneath the waves, an amazing sunken city in the clear blue waters of the bay.

The city was submerged by a series of earthquakes over the centuries. Today, marble columns and aches rise into the water, and stone steps lead down into the ocean floor. You can explore the sunken ruins by kayak, or take a ferry trip to view them as swimming is no longer allowed here. Further west on the shore of the Bay of Tersane, where the remains of a frescoed Byzantine church lie, swimming is permitted and this is an evocative and lovely place for a picnic.

Apollonia was part of Lycia, an important kingdom in this region. The Lycian capital was at Xanthos, west of Kekova, where King Sarpedon was born before he went on to fight in the Trojan Wars. The Lycians traded with the Ancient Greeks and as trade increased, so did piracy. For this reason, many harbours and ports, including Kekova, were fortified. As you glide over the calm waters, you can see the remains of buildings and walls beneath your boat, a rather unsettling experience!

On the mainland close to Kekova are some more beautiful ruins, those of ancient Simena, dating back to the 4th century BC. Today the fishing village of Kale stands on the site. A medieval castle sits atop the little hill and from here you get a good view of the ruins, once a thriving city which did not begin to decline until the 9th century AD, when an earthquake damaged the city. The ruined fortress, Simena Castle, features the pointed arches of the Lycian

The ancient city of Lycia

POPULATION:
Uninhabited
WHEN TO GO:
April to November.
HOW TO GET THERE:
By boat from Kas or Kalkan.
HIGHLIGHTS:
Kayaking above the ruins of ancient Apollonia.
The village of Kale with its lovely fish restaurants.
The Lycian tombs in the water below ancient Simena, an enchanting place for a barbecue on the beach and a swim in the turquoise bay.
The amphitheatre at Simena, the smallest in Lycia with seats for just 400 in the audience.
YOU SHOULD KNOW:
Due to visitors taking home souvenirs from the ruins, it is no longer permitted to swim among the ruins of Apollonia. However, there are other ruins close by which can be explored from the water.

period and the walls show signs of having been repaired during the Byzantine era. Look out for the unusual ogival-shaped Lycian tombs which rise from the shallow bay below. Just inside the castle is the smallest amphitheatre in all Lycia, with just seven rows of seats, an orchestra pit and a changing room for the performers.

Outside the castle are the ruins of the Temple of Poseidon, from where you get a wonderful view across the sea of the whole area and its bays, islands and inlets. Farther down towards the sea there are the remains of houses, tombs and a bath house, all of which are well worth exploring.

Gökçeada

The westernmost point of Turkey and its largest island, Gökçeada lies at the entrance to the Bay of Saros in the northern Aegean, 53 km (33 mi) from Çannakale on the Dardanelles Strait. It is one of the least frequented islands of the Aegean despite being renowned for its outstanding natural beauty – nearly 290 sq km (113 sq mi) of volcanic landscape clothed in pine, olives and vineyards, steep hilly sheep pastures dotted with whitewashed houses, a ragged coastline of strange rock formations and sandy beaches surrounded by the intense blue waters of the Aegean.

The reason for Gökçeada's relative lack of tourism is historical. In classical times the island was a colony of Athens known as Imbros, established around 450 BC and lasting for the next six centuries. After the collapse of Athens as a major power, the island was at the mercy of every Mediterranean empire builder and constantly threatened by pirates. At various times it has been Persian, Roman, Byzantine, Venetian, Ottoman and Greek. Throughout the 20th century, tensions between Greece and Turkey eventually led to most of the ethnic Greeks leaving the island and, until recently, kept it out of bounds for tourists.

Gökçeada's inhabitants survive much as they always have done – from fishing, olive oil, wine and honey production and sheep rearing. As well as the main town of Çinarli (Panayia), there are nine villages, mostly up steep hills reached with some difficulty along the notoriously treacherous island roads. The island has some superb beaches, although you need some determination to access the best ones along the south coast.

There is no doubt that the holiday industry will soon ensure that Gökçeada becomes as well known as the rest of the Aegean. Now is the time to visit this undiscovered, distinctive island before the inevitable happens and it turns into a tourist trap.

POPULATION:
8,875 (2000)
WHEN TO GO:
April to October
HOW TO GET THERE:
Fly or drive to Çannakale and take the ferry, which sails past the dramatic coastline of the Gallipoli National Park. You can take a shorter route from Kabatepe on the Gallipoli Peninsula, but you will miss the spectacular views.
HIGHLIGHTS:
Aydincik (Kefalos) Beach – a brilliant spot for windsurfing with a nearby sulphur salt lake spa to wallow in.
Kaleköy Kastro – old castle ruins on a hill with spectacular views.
Zeytinli and Tepeköy – atmospheric villages.
The beautiful valley near the village of Sahinkaya where there is a crater pool.
National Underwater Park – the coastline between Kaleköy and Kuzulimam, where among the marine life there are old wrecks, artefacts and ancient ruins.
The historic village of Derekoyu – a fascinating abandoned village, said to have once been the largest and wealthiest in the whole of Turkey.
YOU SHOULD KNOW:
Of all the islands in the world, Gökçeada has the fourth largest number of natural fresh water sources.

Avsa

POPULATION:
2,000 (estimate)
WHEN TO GO:
May to October
HOW TO GET THERE:
By ferry from Istanbul.
HIGHLIGHTS:
The Byzantine monastery.
Eating freshly caught fish of every conceivable variety.
Walking up into the vineyards to taste the wine.
Taking a boat trip to the neighbouring islands of Ekinlik and Marmara.
YOU SHOULD KNOW:
Turkey is a conservative country and although the island's nightlife may appear liberal, there are much stricter boundaries than the average westerner is used to. It is worth remembering that excessively sexual or drunken behaviour is likely to shock and won't do wonders for your reputation.

Only 40 years ago Avsa was a quiet backwater known only to a privileged few. Although its clean air, sparkling sea, golden sand, island wine and fresh fish has made it ever more popular as a Turkish holiday resort it is still relatively unknown among foreign tourists and remains off the beaten track.

The island lies in the Sea of Marmara, the small inland sea between the Black Sea and the Mediterranean. It joins the Black Sea at the Bosphorus, the strait along which the city of Istanbul is built, so it is no surprise that the lovely islands of Marmara should be holiday resorts for stressed Turkish city-dwellers desperate to escape the stifling summer heat of Istanbul.

Avsa is in one of the main wine-producing regions of Turkey. It is 21 sq km (8 sq mi) of gentle granite hills covered with olives and vineyards that in places run all the way down to the sandy beach. Oleander trees and flowers grow all around the coast and long bays of gloriously soft sand alternate with stone outcrops where the granite has been worn smooth by the sea to create extraordinary shapes. These rocky areas are wonderful for clambering among, or just finding a quiet spot to sit with a bottle of local wine gazing out across the sparkling sea.

The island's town,Avsa, is a typical Turkish seaside resort with holiday homes, restaurants, and scrawny cats hanging around the harbour hoping to snatch a morsel from the fishing boats as they unload their catch. In the summer months the island is a hive of activity and has a vibrant nightlife. In the evenings the air is filled with music and laughter from the bars and clubs as well as the scent of flowers and the smell of the sea.

Bozcaada

There are so many idyllic islands in the Aegean – more than 3,000 of them – that it can be hard to distinguish between them. But Bozcaada really is different – it is one of the only two islands in the region that is Turkish. In Greek mythology it was called Tenedos and because of its strategic position, just south of the Dardanelles Strait, it has been occupied and fought over since time immemorial. For centuries the population was ethnically Greek; today, although it is almost entirely Turkish, the island's distinctive culture bears many traces of its Greek inheritance.

Bozcaada is a roughly triangular shape of just under 38 sq km (15 sq mi) and has relatively flat terrain. From the highest point, Göztepe at 192 m (630 ft) there is a panoramic view across the whole island and on a clear day you can see as far as Levkos. About a third of the land is covered in vineyards, the remainder being scattered trees and scrubland containing an unusually diverse range of plants – 437 species in all. The sea is remarkably clear and seaweed-free, so Bozcaada's waters are superb for diving. There are plenty of pure sand beaches; Ayazma Bay is the longest and most accessible stretch, consequently the most crowded, but there are eleven other sizeable bays, as well as innumerable coves and inlets for anyone seeking solitude.

An impressive Venetian fortress that attests to Bozcaada's turbulent past guards the island's harbour. The stone and wood town architecture is a charming mixture of Turkish and Greek houses – stylistically quite different from each other. The food, too, is a fusion between both cultures, giving it a distinct edge over the usual fare of the Aegean Islands. Red poppy syrup, a local speciality, is an interesting alternative to the island wine.

POPULATION:
2,427 (2000)
WHEN TO GO:
May to September
HOW TO GET THERE:
There are four main ways to get to Yükyeri wharf at Geyikli to catch the ferry for the half-hour trip to Bozcaada:
Fly to Çanakkale from where there are frequent bus connections to take you to Geyikli, 56 km (35 mi) away.
Bus from Istanbul, an 8-hour journey to Geyikli.
By car from Istanbul a) drive either to Gelibolu or Eceabat and take the car ferry across the Dardanelles to Lapseki or Çanakkale then drive down the coast to Geyikli; or b) take the express car ferry from Istanbul to Bandirma and drive a further 3 hours to Geyikli.
HIGHLIGHTS:
Aleybey Mosque probably built in 1700.
Aya Paraskevi Ayazma – a monastery with a small chapel shaded by eight old plane trees where a traditional saint's day festival is held every July.
A tour of one of the island's four wineries.
The wind farm – wind turbines behind the old lighthouse in the west of the island are an impressive sight.
A boat tour of the island – enabling you to explore coves inaccessible from land.
YOU SHOULD KNOW:
The sea is substantially colder here than in other parts of the Aegean because of the cold water springs around Bozcaada. In the sweltering months of July and August it is a welcome, refreshing contrast to the beach.

Fishing boats line Tenedos harbour at dusk

Büyükada

POPULATION:
6,000 (estimate); the population of the Princes' Islands is 17,738 (2000)
WHEN TO GO:
April to October. The Princes' Islands do get very crowded with Istanbullu holidaymakers at the peak of the season but it is still well worth making a day trip if you are in Istanbul in July or August to get some respite from the heat and see the magnificent architecture.
HOW TO GET THERE:
Regular ferry service from all Istanbul's main docks or high-speed sea bus from Kabatas docks.
HIGHLIGHTS:
Ayios Nikolaos Monastery – a romantically rundown old building.
Splendid Palace Hotel – built in 1911 and visited by Edward VIII and Wallis Simpson.
Ayia Yorgi Church – dating back to the 6th century.
YOU SHOULD KNOW:
Leon Trotsky lived on Büyükada for four years after he was banished from the Soviet Union by Stalin in 1929. He wrote most of his *History of the Russian Revolution* during his stay here.

A short ferry ride from the centre of Istanbul transports you into another world – of pine trees, monasteries, and 19th century grandeur. Büyükada (Big Island) is, at just 5.4 sq km (2 sq mi), the largest of the Princes' Islands, an archipelago of nine islands in the Sea of Marmara, on Istanbul's doorstep.

As soon as you step off the ferry at the ornate Ottoman terminal building, you are greeted by the sound of horses' hooves, the sight of contented island dogs lazing on doorsteps in the sun, and the mouth-watering smells of freshly cooked fish and grilled meat wafting from the harbour restaurants. The town's cobbled streets are lined with magnificent 19th century wooden houses whose elaborate balconies and shutters are wreathed in honeysuckle, jasmine and mimosa. In the summer, the lively town is heaving with crowds but you can easily retreat into the hills and woods or to one of the innumerable sandy coves around the coast.

The Emperor Justinian II built a palace here in AD 569 and the islands were later used as a place of exile for unruly Byzantine princes (hence the name). For hundreds of years Büyükada was inhabited only by a few monks and nuns, farmers and fishermen. The 19th century development of a ferry service enabled wealthy city dwellers to travel here with relative ease and, attracted by the Princes' pastoral charm, they began to build summer houses on the islands. Today, in the summer months Istanbullus flock here to escape from the stifling heat and clamour of the city.

Mercifully, cars are banned here. You can go everywhere in a phaeton (horse and carriage), by bike, or on foot. The silence, fresh sea breeze, wonderful swimming, and heart stopping views are in blissful contrast to the stressed-out streets of Istanbul.

The Monastery of St George is nestled between Büyükada's highest hills.

Akdamar

Lake Van is a salt lake – a mysterious inland sea 1,670 m (5,480 ft) above sea level in the heart of the Anatolian Mountains. Nobody can explain the salinity of the water, nor the fresh-water spring on the island of Akdamar. On this tiny island, less than 1 sq km (0.25 sq mi) in area, there is an incredible monument – the Cathedral Church of the Holy Cross, an extraordinarily beautiful example of Armenian architecture.

The Church was built in the 10th century and was the seat of the Armenian Catholicos (prelate) for nearly 700 years, from 1116 until 1895. It is the only remaining building of the Palace of Aght'Amar, built for the Armenian king between 915 and 922 – a magnificent complex of buildings, complete with streets and gardens, entirely built out of a lovely pinkish-red tufa (volcanic rock) which must have been transported from miles away. The Church, which contains 34 rooms, is set in an almond grove. Its exterior walls are carved with exquisitely fine reliefs of biblical, harvesting and hunting scenes that are unique – nothing remotely comparable has been found anywhere else in the world.

The overwhelming beauty of the scene is awe-inspiring. Reddish stone contrasts with blue water against the backdrop of the snow capped Anatolian Mountains towering over the lake. Of all the islands in Lake Van, Akdamar becomes green earliest in the spring, and when the almond trees come into blossom the island is a truly sublime experience. There is a wonderful swimming spot where you can plunge off the rocks into the deep salty water of the lake or just gaze around you absorbing the serene beauty of your surroundings.

The Cathedral Church of the Holy Cross

POPULATION:
Maybe a museum keeper or two.

WHEN TO GO:
March to April, to catch the almond blossom in full bloom.

HOW TO GET THERE:
Fly/train/bus from Ankara to Van. From Van by road to Gevas 45 km (28 mi) to the southwest. Boats leave from Gevas wharf and take about 20 minutes to get to Akdamar.

HIGHLIGHTS:
Çarpanak – a nearby island with a 12th century church.
The medieval citadel at Van.
Muradiye Waterfalls.
Look out for Van cats – famous for having one blue and one yellow eye.

YOU SHOULD KNOW:
The church was extensively restored by the Turkish government and only re-opened for viewing in April 2007. It has caused some controversy between Turks and Armenians, between whom feeling historically runs extremely high. Many Armenians still regard the island as a holy site and they not only object to the name change of the island from Agh'tamar but to the secularisation of this important religious building.

Cyprus

POPULATION:
762,900 (2001)
WHEN TO GO:
April to June and September to November
HOW TO GET THERE:
Direct flights to South Cyprus. Flights to North Cyprus via Turkey. Ferries from Turkey to North Cyprus.
HIGHLIGHTS:
Ancient Kourion, near Limassol – performances take place in the huge amphitheatre.
The frescoed churches in the Troodos – a World Heritage Site.
The Tombs of the Kings in Pafos – these unique tombs show Egyptian influence.
Bellapais, North Cyprus – the lovely mountain village, home to Lawrence Durrell, with its impressive Augustinian monastery.
Ancient Salamis, north of Famagusta – the extensive site of a city first mentioned in 709 BC.
The Karpas Peninsula, North Cyprus. A nature reserve protects the island's best beaches and the green and loggerhead turtles that nest here.
YOU SHOULD KNOW:
Cyprus's national cocktail the Brandy Sour was invented in the 1930s for young King Farouk of Egypt. He asked for a drink that looked like iced tea!

Cyprus, probably named for its copper, smelted since Neolithic times, is the legendary birthplace of Aphrodite. Two impressive mountain ranges surround a huge fertile plain and lovely beaches circle the coastline. Its climate has long attracted visitors – it is now renowned as a place for retirement – or partying.

Lying close to the Middle East and always strategically important, it was taken by many great powers including Greece, Rome and Egypt. The long reign of the French Lusignan dynasty brought prosperity and Roman Catholicism. In 1570 the Turks took the island. It became a UK Crown Colony after World War I. Independence came in 1960, but intercommunal strife increased and in 1974 an unsuccessful Greek coup prompted a Turkish invasion. The island was divided. It is now possible to cross the border, but violence and negotiation alternate and rules can change overnight.

However, north or south, the islanders are warmly welcoming and Cyprus has many attractions. The southeast with its raucous resorts also has archaeological sites and sunsets from Aphrodite's 'birthplace' at the Rock of Remios. Pafos, though surrounded by development, remains a charming town. To the northwest is the remote Akanas Peninsula, with further isolated regions along the coast. Inland, the magnificent Troodos region has forested mountains, lost villages, painted churches, unique wildlife and winegrowing.

In the North, small resorts cluster around the beautiful harbour town of Kyrenia. Famagusta is full of ruined Gothic churches inside

its golden stone walls; outside lies a haunted, wired-off modern town. The rocky coast and bristling Kyrenia range hold unspoilt beaches and villages, classical sites, monasteries and Crusader castles.

Lefkosia (Nicosia) is the world's only divided capital. Inside the massive Venetian fortifications, both sides – the cosmopolitan south and the north with its dusty lanes – are fascinating. Both have streets which end in a wall fluttering with defiant flags.

The Makheras Monastery in the Troodos

AFRICA & ARABIAN GULF

Palm Jumeirah

POPULATION:
Dubai 1,241,000 (2006). Palm Jumeirah yet to be assessed (8,000 residential units are planned).

WHEN TO GO:
The weather is more manageable and cooler from November to April. In the Muslim month of Ramadan hotel prices may drop, but it's illegal to eat, drink or smoke in public between sunrise and sunset.

HOW TO GET THERE:
Flights to Dubai.

HIGHLIGHTS:
Wandering the island – the sheer scale and glamour of the development, and some of its celebrity-type residents (including David Beckham).
Al-Ahmadiya School – Dubai's oldest school and stunning courtyard house.
Dubai's skyscrapers and souks – the gold souk, perfume souk and spice souk.
The old Bastakiya Quarter.
The world's only seven-star hotel – Burj Al Arab in Dubai. Shaped like a sail and with its own helipad. Jumeirah Beach Park – walkways, barbeque pits, clean sands and a women-only day.

YOU SHOULD KNOW:
Camel racing is a major spectator sport in the United Arab Emirates, and Dubai.

Self-declared 'eighth wonder of the world', Palm Jumeirah is an audacious feat of human engineering. Fashioned on the date palm, with its roots on the Dubai coastline and its 17 fronds fanning out into blue waters, this is the first of the planned 'Palm' islands and, though it's the smallest of the three, it is already the world's largest man-made island.

Extravagant boutique hotels and villas are built and residents moving in, with the project aiming for completion in 2009. Measuring 5 x 5 km (3 x 3 mi), the crown is connected to the mainland by a 300 m (98 ft) bridge, and the very top of the palm is reached by a sub-sea tunnel. Ninety four million cubic metres of sand and seven million tons of rock have gone into the formation of this premier resort. Beaches, marinas, cafés and restaurants of every conceivable nature are planned.

Dubai is purported to be the fastest growing city in the world, and the shortage of beaches and hotels seems to have given rise to the three Palm Island resorts which will together increase Dubai's coastline by 520 km (323 mi). Created using land reclamation by the government-owned Al Nakheel Properties, this striking palm blueprint allows for far more beach, and residences, than a plain old circular island. In 2007, the Cunard Line sold the *Queen Elizabeth II* liner to Dubai World – to be permanently anchored at Palm Jumeirah as a hotel and tourist destination.

Once a peaceful town frequented by Bedouin fishermen and pearl divers, Dubai is now rich and racy, and somewhat surreal. Shiny skyscrapers overshadow the surviving and still buzzing souks, and shopping is the major pastime.

Here you are not escaping from people but maybe from reality, and in terms of sheer scale and daring there really is nowhere like it on earth.

An aerial view of Palm Jumeirah

Socotra

The blue lagoon of Qalansiya

In the Indian Ocean off the Horn of Africa lies a small archipelago of four islands and islets. Although closer to Africa, the islands are part of the Republic of Yemen. The archipelago consists of the main island of Socotra and three smaller islands known collectively as The Brothers – Abd al Kuri, Samhah and Darsa. The islands were separated from the mainland so long ago that much of their flora and fauna has evolved here, making the islands of great ecological importance. Due to their geographical isolation, the islanders have also had little outside influence, and arriving on Socotra is like stepping back in time.

The culture on Socotra is very different from the ways of the modern world. Until the airport was built in 1999, the only way to get here was by boat, and during the monsoon season the strong winds and high seas made the island inaccessible. Most Socotris still live without electricity, running water or a paved road. Until 1990 the island still had a barter economy, and even today most people in the mountainous areas still live in caves.

The main island is a little over 130 km (80 mi) long and around 35 km (21 mi) wide. Socotra is a place of contrasting landscapes, with the turquoise lagoon at Qalansiya and the white sand dunes at Ras Momi, the flower-filled alpine meadows of the Haghier Mountains and the desolate cave-riddled plateaux of the interior. Rising to over 1,500 m (4,921 ft), the Haghier Mountains loom over Hadibo, the island's capital, and dominate the skyline. The red granite peaks are peppered with silver lichens which grow thickly on the bare rocks above the tree line. Streams bubble down from the misty heights, teeming with lively fish and freshwater crabs. Limestone plateaux spread east and west, providing alkaline soils for the iconic Dragon's Blood Tree for which the islands are famous. The locals collect the blood-red resin, known as cinnabar, from the tree by making incisions in the bark. In the ancient world, it was used to enhance the colour of precious stones and glass, and as a pigment in paints, and had various medicinal qualities.

The long isolation of the Socotra archipelago and its fierce heat and drought have combined to create a unique endemic flora and fauna. There are no fewer than 300 plant species, 113 insect species, 24 reptile species and six bird species that can be found nowhere else in the world. Botanists rank the flora of Socotra among the ten most endangered island flora in the world, and steps are being taken by the government to protect this unique and spectacular habitat.

POPULATION:
43,000 (2004)
WHEN TO GO:
October to February.
HOW TO GET THERE:
Fly from Sana'a or Al-Mukalla.
HIGHLIGHTS:
The enormous cave at Huq – the eastern end of the island has a vast system of caves and underground pools lying below the Momi plateau. Huq cave, particularly, has wonderful stalactites and stalagmites.
The souq in Hadibo – look out for the local pottery, made by women on the islands, particularly *gisfa*, large ornamental water pots.
Birdwatching – the island group has a rich bird fauna, including endemic species such as the Socotra Starling, the Socotra Sunbird, the Socotra Sparrow and the Socotra Golden-winged Grosbeak.
The white sandy beaches – the best are probably at Ras Ersel and Ras Momi.
YOU SHOULD KNOW:
The island's tourist infrastructure is a pioneering example of ecotourism and In order to protect the island's unique heritage, visitor numbers are limited.

Elephantine Island

POPULATION:
2,000 (2006 estimate)
WHEN TO GO:
Very hot between June and August (daytime temperatures around 40°C (104°F). So December to February is great if you hate the heat, but March to May and September to November gives warm days and fewer crowds.
HOW TO GET THERE:
Motor launch or felucca from Aswan: plane, train or boat from Cairo or further afield.
HIGHLIGHTS:
The Aswan Museum at the southern end of the island.
The botanical garden on nearby Kitchener Island.
The Aswan High Dam and Lake Nasser.
Afternoon tea at the Old Cataract Hotel, Aswan.
A trip on a felucca on the Nile at sunset.
A short flight to Abu Simbel, the stunning temple of Ramses II.
YOU SHOULD KNOW:
A rare calendar, known as the Elephantine Calendar, dating to the reign of Thutmose III, was found here in fragments. The island is equally famous because the Well of Eratosthenes is located here, and was where Eratosthenes made the first measurement of the circumference of the earth in around 240 BC.

Known to the Ancient Egyptians as Abu or Yabu – meaning elephant – Elephantine Island is a truly ancient site resting as it does at the First Cataract of the Nile, and creating a natural boundary between Egypt and Nubia. Being the largest island at Aswan, it was easily defensible and at one time was thought to be a major ivory trading centre – possibly giving rise to its name. But rumour has it the name may also arise from the elephant-shaped granite boulders lying around its shores.

It is said that Khnum, the ram-headed god of the cataracts, dwelled in caves beneath the island and controlled the waters of the Nile. Nowadays, the southern tip of the island holds the ruins of the Temple of Khnum, which was rebuilt in the 30th dynasty. Up until 1822, there were also temples to Thutmose III and Amenhotep III here, but the Ottoman government in their 'wisdom' destroyed them.

Elephantine is an exquisite island, steeped in ancient history and blessed with significant artefacts. Transported instantly back in time, you wander under banana trees and date palms through colourful Nubian villages with narrow, dusty alleyways and mud houses painted or carved with crocodiles and fish.

On the edge of the island is one of the oldest Nilometers in Egypt – a stone 'yardstick' used to measure the height of the River Nile. It was last reconstructed in Roman times and was still in use as late as the 19th century. Its 90 steps, leading down to the river, are marked with Hindu-Arabic, Roman and hieroglyphic numerals, and inscriptions carved deep into the rock during the 17th century can be seen at the water's edge.

Elephantine Island is a green, flower-festooned oasis of calm – lapped by the turquoise waters of the Nile and clinging quietly to its exotic past.

A boat cruises along the Nile alongside Elephantine Island.

Jerba Island

Traditional rugs and pottery for sale at Midoun

Located in the Gulf of Gabès off the coast of Tunisia, the island of Jerba is a simple place with palm-fringed beaches, olive groves, date plantations and white-washed buildings, but it is said to have an enchanting history. Jerbans claim that the Land of the Lotus Eaters Homer described in *The Odyssey* is theirs. The local legend goes that after Odysseus' ship had been blown off course around Greece, he and his men found themselves in a strange land in the south of the Mediterranean where the islanders ate the honeyed fruit of the lotus flower. Odysseus and his crew stayed here enjoying the soothingly narcotic fruits as they recovered from battle.

Today the beautiful island is noted as a centre for the Islamic sect al-Ibadhiyah, and also for its Jewish population which has lived on the island since 586 BC, just after the destruction of King Solomon's temple in Jerusalem. Populations have declined in recent years due to emigration to Israel and France, but the present synagogue, El Ghriba, is a place of pilgrimage for Jewish people worldwide and tourists of all religions. This is thought to be the oldest synagogue in Africa and one of the oldest in the world, built by Jewish priests who came to Jerba after the destruction of the temple in Jerusalem. The present building dates from the 19th century, and inside is a rich mix of blue tiles and coloured glass windows.

One of the nicest ways to explore Jerba is by bicycle. The island is characterized by pretty, but busy, beaches lined with palms, and a gentle rural interior. Here farmers grow olives and dates in the brilliant sunshine. The architecture is clean and simple, with white-washed fortified mosques which are unusual in Tunisia. Fishing is a major industry here but it is still done by traditional methods. See the terracotta pots stacked on the dockside at Houmt Souk which are used to catch octopus, a method perfected by the Phoenicians 3,000 years ago.

If you get the chance, stay in one of the *funduqs* in Houmt Souk. Usually set around a leafy courtyard with a trickling fountain and colourful tiles, these evocative buildings have been receiving guests for hundreds of years. The accommodation is sometimes basic, but the atmosphere is fantastic. The souk on Jerba is a great place to buy souvenirs including rugs, tiles, lamps, leatherwork, hands of Fatima, sculptures made of crystallized desert gypsum and carved pipes. Just be sure to haggle.

POPULATION:
116,300 (2004)
WHEN TO GO:
April to June.
HOW TO GET THERE:
Mellita International Airport has daily services from Tunis and western Europe.
HIGHLIGHTS:
Boukha – the locally brewed fermented drink made from figs or dates is said to mimic the fabled response to imbibing lotus juice.
El Ghriba synagogue – in the village of Er Riadh, this is said to be the oldest synagogue in Africa and has biblical significance.
Er Riadh – a charming village steeped in history, with its winding cobbled streets and courtyards full of bougainvillea and cacti.
Guellala – this village is renowned for its pottery. Many white-washed shops line the streets selling local, handmade wares.
YOU SHOULD KNOW:
Book accommodation well in advance in the summer months as the island can be very busy.

São Tomé and Principe

POPULATION:
137,500 (2005)
WHEN TO GO:
Avoid the rainy season from October to May. The driest and coolest months are from June to September. The rest of the year is hot and muggy.
HOW TO GET THERE:
Flights from Lisbon.
HIGHLIGHTS:
Manta rays and sea turtles.
A picnic at Boca do Inferno – a blowhole south of the capital.
Ascent of ancient Pico São Tomé (2 days with overnight stop).
The rare birdlife.
The family-run chocolate factory on Principe.
YOU SHOULD KNOW:
Divers are in their element here – it is sometimes possible to become a member of the 'Equator Diving Club'.

Part of an extinct volcanic mountain range, São Tomé was named after Saint Thomas by Portuguese explorers, who discovered the island on his feast day. Together with neighbouring Principe, it forms an island nation in the Gulf of Guinea, 250 km (155 mi) off the coast of Gabon that is the smallest Portuguese-speaking country in the world.

For centuries both São Tomé and Principe were important centres for the organized slave trade. Fronted by the Portuguese colonialists, in the 1500s the sugar cane trade here once led the world, and later large-scale coffee and cocoa plantations emerged and engulfed the island. Then in 1975 a national freedom movement led to the collapse of the Portuguese empire and finally brought independence to the islands. With this came the decline of plantations and the mass exodus of Europeans.

On this seriously undiscovered island just above the equator, you can sip some of the best coffee in the world – and, caffeine-charged – sway to the rhythms of *ússua* and *socopé*. Culturally, the people of São Tomé are African but they have been hugely influenced by the Portuguese rulers of their land.

The rich diving in these crystalline waters is yet to be fully appreciated and inland, deep in tropical forests, are some of the rarest birds in Africa. After years of unrest only now is this tiny island state recovering and beginning to feel stable. For the dedicated traveller it's an untapped, untouched haven – life here is sweet and waiting to be shared.

The monument that marks the equator passing through the Ilhéu das Rolhos at the southern tip of São Tomé and Principe.

Bioko

Tropical rainforest covers the island of Bioko.

Lying in the Gulf of Guinea, Bioko is an acutely mountainous, volcanic island still inhabited by the indigenous Bubi people, who speak a Bantu language brought over from mainland Africa. Swathed in tropical rainforest, this boot-shaped island is 70 km (43 mi) long and 32 km (20 mi) off the coast of Cameroon. Bioko has more species of rare monkeys than any other place in Africa; of the seven monkey species living on the island, four are among the continent's most-endangered. This is the place for the adventurous at heart, happy to head well off the beaten track and into deep mud.

The Bubi clans still account for most of the human population, but given Bioko's colourful past this is now mixed with Spaniards, Fernandinos and immigrants from Rio Muni, Nigeria and Cameroon. First named 'Formosa Flora' – Beautiful Flower – by the Portuguese navigator Fernão do Pó in 1472, it then fell into the hands of the Dutch India Company who quickly established trade bases on the island in the 1600s without Portuguese consent – centralizing the trade of slaves in the Gulf of Guinea.

In colonial times it was known as Fernando Pó, and under the Africanization policy of dictator Masie Nguema Biyogo it was renamed Masie Ngueme Biyogo Island. When he was overthrown in 1979 it was renamed Bioko.

Rare primates once thrived in the deep rainforests – the Bioko drill, black and red colobus monkeys – but the luxury bushmeat market in the capital city of Malabo is taking a dangerously heavy toll. Malabo sits at the northern end of the island on the rim of a sunken volcano. Despite being the capital of Equatorial Guinea, this is a pretty poorly developed place with limited paved roads. There are few tourist attractions, but on the densely forested slopes a new world awaits.

POPULATION:
130,000 (2007)

WHEN TO GO:
Average temperatures of 25°C (77°F) and annual rainfall of 2,900 mm (75 in) make this an onerous climate. To avoid the rainy season go between November and April.

HOW TO GET THERE:
Flights to Malabo. Ferries to Malabo from Douala and Bata.

HIGHLIGHTS:
Trekking through the rainforest, searching for primates.
Hiring a boat out of Bata (on the mainland) to spot migrating whales.
The neighbouring paradise island of Corisco.
Malabo Cathedral.
The Moka Valley with its crater lake, between Malabo and Riaba.

YOU SHOULD KNOW:
Travel on any internal carriers should be considered carefully as air traffic control in Equatorial Guinea is marginal at best.

Cape Verde Islands

POPULATION:
420,979 (2006)
WHEN TO GO:
October and November when the land is green after the rains, and before the winds pick up in December.
HOW TO GET THERE:
International flights to Sal and Santiago.
Sporadic ferry services from Dakar and Las Palmas.
HIGHLIGHTS:
Mindelo Carnaval on São Vicente in February – with Rio-style floats and costumes.
Taking in the lively port city of Mindelo on São Vicente.
The lovely town of Vila Nova Sintra on Brava.
Vila de Ribeira Grande on Santo Antao – the first European town in the tropics.
Breakfast on *cachupa* – a delicious bean dish.
Island hopping by ferry – discovering the islands' delights for yourself.
YOU SHOULD KNOW:
The easiest place to get a visa is in Lisbon, or by going through a specialist travel company. In West Africa, the only consulate is in Dakar, Senegal – once you have found it, getting a visa should be easy.

Tipping off the African map, the Cape Verde islands would appear to sit more happily with the Azores, or even the Canary Islands. Composed of nine main islands in two groups – the Windwards and the Leewards – six are volcanic and shapely, while three are sandy and flat. This is no tropical paradise, yet despite the hassle of getting here the islands are well worth the trek.

The Portuguese arrived here in 1460 and made the islands part of the Portuguese empire. Cape Verde became an important watering station for passing ships, then a sugar cane plantation site, and later a major hub of the transatlantic slave trade. In 1975, Cape Verde gained independence from Portugal.

With jumbled African and Portuguese roots, Cape Verdeans certainly know how to make music and dance – samba and salsa sprinkled with African tribal sounds. The soft *morna* lament gives way to the sensual, upbeat *coladeira* and *batuque* dance, and love songs unfurl in Cape Verdean Creole. The official language may be Portuguese, but Creole is favoured colloquially.

The first port of call is often Praia on Santiago Island – Cape Verde's capital. The beaches are fine and white and the mountains impressive, but more importantly it forms the perfect springboard for island hopping. Brava is the smallest inhabited island, the hardest to reach but also the most beautiful. On brooding Fogo there is fine walking, and hikes up into the old volcano crater. There is a good deal of rivalry and many cultural differences between islands – right down to the way the women tie their headscarves.

This small nation lacks resources and has suffered severe droughts. Over the centuries, disastrous famines have continually rocked the lives of the islanders, yet their spirit remains alive and contagious.

The beach and village of Tarrafal on Santiago Island

Saint-Louis

A fisherman passes by Saint-Louis at dawn.

In the north-west of Senegal, near the mouth of the Senegal River, lies the town of Saint-Louis, capital of French Senegal from 1673 until independence in 1960. The centre of the old colonial city lies on a narrow island in the river, measuring just 2 km (1.2 mi) long by about 400 m (1,312 ft) wide, although the modern city now sprawls on the mainland either side.

The first permanent French settlement in Senegal, Saint-Louis was founded in 1659 by French traders on an uninhabited island. Named after the French king Louis XIV, the town commanded trade along the Senegal River, exporting slaves, animal hides, beeswax and gum arabic. Between 1659 and 1779, the city was administered by nine different chartered companies. A Métis (Franco-African Creole) community soon developed, characterized by the famous *signares*. These bourgeois women entrepreneurs dominated the economic, social, cultural and political life of the city, creating an elegant urban culture with time for refined entertainments. They controlled most of the river trade and financed the principal Catholic institutions.

Louis Faidherbe became the Governor of French Senegal in 1854, and spent a great deal of money modernizing the town, including bridge building, setting up a drinking water supply, and providing an overland telegraph line to Dakar. The fortunes of the town began to dwindle as Dakar became an ever more important city. Saint-Louis' port proved difficult for steam ships to access, and a railway between Saint-Louis and Dakar, opened in 1855, took most of its up-country trade.

Today Saint-Louis is a sleepy backwater which retains its lovely colonial architecture. In 2000 it was added to the World Heritage List, and many of its beautiful buildings are being renovated. Among the sites and monuments to see on the island are the Governor's Palace, a fortress built in the 18th century across from Place Faidherbe, the Gouvernance which comprises the town's administrative offices and Parc Faidherbe in the centre of town, named for the French governor. The museum at the southern end of the island tells the story of Senegal's history and peoples, with displays of traditional clothes and musical instruments, and there are various mosques and catholic churches to visit.

The heritage of the *signares* lives on in Saint-Louis today, with the festivals for which the town is famous. *Fanals*, a night-time procession of giant paper lanterns, takes place at Christmas, usually coinciding with the Saint-Louis Jazz Festival, the most important jazz festival in Africa. The annual pirogue race, organized by teams of fishermen from Guet-Ndar, takes place on the river and makes a vibrant spectacle.

POPULATION:
176,000 (2005)
WHEN TO GO:
November to May
HOW TO GET THERE:
Fly to Dakar-Bango airport.
HIGHLIGHTS:
Pont Faidherbe – designed by Gustav Eiffel and originally built to cross the Danube, the bridge was brought to St-Louis in 1897. It is 507 m (1,663 ft) long and offers wonderful views of the town.
The wonderful colonial architecture – stroll around the island and appreciate the lovely buildings, many now with a faded elegance.
National Park of the Langue de Barbarie – in the estuary of the Senegal River, the park is home to thousands of water birds, including cormorants, brushes, pink flamingos, pelicans, herons and ducks.
Fauna Reserve of Guembeul – around 12 km (7.5 mi) south of the city, the reserve shelters birds and endangered species including the Dama gazelle, the Patas monkey and the African spurred tortoise.
YOU SHOULD KNOW:
The town is known as Ndar in the local Wolof language.

The island lies in the River Gambia.

James Island

POPULATION:
Uninhabited
WHEN TO GO:
Best time to visit is between November and February when it's dry and relatively cool. During the wet season (June to October) it's less crowded and cheaper but roads may be inaccessible and malaria is more widespread.
Migratory birds visit between October and April – peak tourist season.
HOW TO GET THERE:
Pirogue (dugout wooden canoe) from the shore.
HIGHLIGHTS:
The history of the island and the River Gambia, and their part in the slave trade.
River fishing.
Bird watching.
Gambia's unspoilt beaches.
Abuko Nature Reserve and Bijilo Forest Park.
Fort Bullen in Barra, at the mouth of the river.
YOU SHOULD KNOW:
Around November to February dry, dusty 'harmattan' winds do blow off the Sahara.

Gambia is a mere sliver of a country with a generous heart, and James Island is a constant reminder of its more turbulent past. This minute island bears witness to the dark days of the slave trade, and sitting as it does in the middle of the River Gambia, about 2 km (1.2 mi) south of Jufureh and Albreda, it was once at the centre of struggles between Africa and Europe. As the river formed the first trade route into the African interior, it also became an early corridor for the slave trade.

On the island are the remains of Fort James – a Dutch nobleman, Jacob Duke of Courland, built the fort in about 1651. The English captured it in 1661 and the island became known as Fort James or James Island, after James, Duke of York. The fort was used as a trading base, first for gold and ivory then for slaves such as Kunta Kinte, who was portrayed in the film *Roots*. The English and French fought over the fort for more than a century.

The fort remained a slave collection point right up until slaving was abolished. Over time it was completely destroyed, then rebuilt at least three times. Now only ruins remain. The island was so small that it had to be 'extended' to accommodate other buildings, which was achieved by creating embankments supported by stakes. Even these are being slowly eroded – and the river is encroaching on the ruins. Now only groves of hefty baobab trees stand to attention beside the old walls.

James Island is a stop-off for enthusiasts. Continuing up-river by boat you are drawn into mangrove creeks and mud-hut villages. The Gambia is a vivid, laidback country and James Island is a small yet stark reminder of another life and times.

Isle of Gorée

The Isle of Gorée lies just 4 km (2.5 mi) from Dakar on the Senegalese coast in the middle of the natural harbour formed by the Cap Vert Peninsula. The protection of the bay explains why the island has been ruled over the years by the Portuguese, Dutch, English and French, each of whom wanted to profit from the safe anchorage there and use the island as a stopover point for ships sailing the trade route between the Gold Coast of Ghana and the West Indies.

At first sight, the island is a peaceful, beautiful place with its imposing forts and pretty pink houses, in harmony with the blue of the sea and the green of the lush gardens. Yet this tranquillity masks a darker past as many of these lovely buildings played an important role in the slave trade. Between the 15th and 19th centuries, Gorée served as the largest centre of the slave trade on the African coast. An estimated 40 million Africans were held for weeks in the houses' dark and dank basements, waiting for ships to take them to the Americas. There were even torture chambers for the slaves who rebelled.

By the end of the 18th century, Gorée was a wealthy place where tradesmen, soldiers and officials lived in sumptuous luxury amid the beautiful scenery. Yet it was also a gateway to hell for thousands of African slaves. Among the most poignant sights on the island is the Slave House, or Maison des Esclaves, built by the Dutch in 1776. It has been preserved in its original state and is now a UNESCO World Heritage Site. The 'door of no return' is an emotional shrine and continues to serve as a reminder of human exploitation. Some believe Gorée was not the site of transportation of such immense numbers of slaves, but no one can disagree with the awe and contemplation that the imposing, silent walls of the Slave House inspire.

Also worth visiting on the island are the Church of Saint Charles on the Place de l'Eglise, with its French provincial architecture, the picturesque ruins of Fort Nassau, the Castle of Saint Michel, which was originally built on the steep basalt hill by the Dutch in the 17th century, and the Historical Museum in the old Fort d'Estrées.

POPULATION:
1,056 (2005)
WHEN TO GO:
March to June, or September to November
HOW TO GET THERE:
By ferry from Dakar.
HIGHLIGHTS:
Visit the Maison des Esclaves, or Slave House, with its 'door of no return'.
The Botanical Gardens on rue du Port – see the famous baobab trees which are prevalent here. The scientific name of the baobab (*Adansonia*) comes from French botanist Michel Adanson, who visited Gorée in the mid-1700s. The gardens are dedicated to Adanson.
The small swimming beach near the ferry slip, perfect for a quick dip.
YOU SHOULD KNOW:
The name Gorée comes from the Dutch *Goeree* meaning island or possibly *Goode Reede* meaning 'good harbour' for its sheltered bay

Colourful pirogues – dugout canoes – on the beach

Dahlak Kebir

POPULATION:
1,500-2,000 (2007)
WHEN TO GO:
Best between October and March
HOW TO GET THERE:
Ferries from Massawa, Eritrea – also linking with other islands.
HIGHLIGHTS:
Snorkelling and diving.
The pre-historic Islamic ruins at Adel.
The Afar fishing villages.
On the mainland – travelling on the steam train from Asmara down to Nefasit.
YOU SHOULD KNOW:
On the island there are 365 cisterns carved from coral limestone, used to collect rainwater – one for each day of the year to accommodate the arid climate, and providing the inhabitants of Dahlak Kebir with a reliable source of drinking water.

Clustered in the Red Sea, off the Eritrean coast, only four islands in the Dahlak Archipelago are inhabited – Dahlak Kebir being the largest. Charter a yacht out of Massawa and cruise the islands – snorkelling, diving and fishing along the way. The waters here have been nicknamed 'fish-soup', as a thousand or so species of fish dart around the reefs.

The Dahlak people still converse in Dahlak and follow a traditional way of life, fishing and herding goats and camels. Off the white sands, around submerged coral reefs, lurks an underwater wonderland of dolphins and dugongs, turtles and hermit crabs, shipwrecks and pumice stones spewed from submarine volcanoes.

The village of Dahlak Kebir lies on the west of the island and is renowned for its ancient cisterns and necropolis, dating from at least AD 912 and holding 800 tombs with coral gravestones that carry Kufic (ancient Arabic) inscriptions. In Roman times there were pearl fisheries here, and even today the occasional pearl is still found.

Under past Ethiopian rule, the archipelago was designated as a national park, and now you can't go there alone and without permission. During the war of independence a group of Eritrean freedom fighters carried out diving operations against the Ethiopian armed forces. Now these same freedom fighters make up the core of Eritrean diving tourism.

In a bizarre twist of fate, the war-torn years have made this a very different sort of diving spot from the rest of the Red Sea. During the fighting, fishing came to a halt and this led to a spectacular increase in the numbers of fish. Another advantage of this forced isolation is their relative lack of shyness. Here the fish swim right up to you.

Lake Tana Islands

Here lies the source of the famous Blue Nile. From Lake Tana, this mega-river sets out on its endless journey via Khartoum to the Mediterranean. Cradled in the Ethiopian highlands, this is the country's largest and most important lake. It holds many scattered islands and their actual numbers depends entirely on the level of the lake at any given time – the water has fallen by about 1.8 m (6 ft) in the last 400 years, and currently there seem to be 37 islands – of which 19 have, or have had, monasteries on them.

The joy of these mysterious and isolated islands is that they shelter well-hidden churches and monasteries of immense historical and cultural interest – decorated with ludicrously beautiful paintings and housing innumerable treasures. Hire a boat from the enchanting town of Bahir Dar to the south of the lake and chug out to the monasteries, where monks proudly display their treasures.

Remains of ancient Ethiopian emperors and treasures of the Ethiopian Church are stowed away here. On the island of Tana Qirqos is a rock on which the monks believe the Virgin Mary rested on her journey back from Egypt. The body of Emperor Yekuno Amlak is interred in the monastery of St Stephen on Daga, and others are also entombed here. The monasteries are believed to rest on even earlier religious sites and include Tana Qirqos, which is said to have housed the Ark of the Covenant before it was moved to Axum.

On a more practical level, Lake Tana is a vital source of water and hydroelectricity for Ethiopia, and supports a massive fishing industry. Attracted by both the water and wild food, local and migrating birds flock to the shoreline – as do many less brightly plumed birdwatchers. Lake Tana and its extraordinary islands are a lure for both their wildlife and rich, forgotten treasures.

POPULATION:
15,000 (2005 estimate)
WHEN TO GO:
Avoid the rainy season, especially in October and November
HOW TO GET THERE:
Boat trips from Bahir Dar. A ferry service links Bahir Dar with Gorgora, via Dek Island.
HIGHLIGHTS:
The monasteries and their treasures.
Eating fish from the lake in one of Bahir Dar's restaurants.
Boat trips on the lake.
Tis Issat, the Blue Nile Falls – about 30 km (19 mi) downstream from Bahir Dar.
Birdwatching around the lake.
YOU SHOULD KNOW:
Some of the island monasteries, particularly in the central part of the lake, do not allow women – it's worth checking before you make the trip.

The calm waters of Lake Tana

Lamu Island

Part of the Lamu Archipelago in the Indian Ocean close to the northern coast of Kenya, Lamu Island is surrounded by long, white sandy beaches framed by rolling dunes, as unspoiled today as they were when the island was first settled in the 14th century.

A port was founded on the island by Arab traders, who built the Pwani Mosque. The port prospered on the export of timber, ivory and amber, and soon became a major centre for the slave trade. After defeating nearby Pate Island in the 19th century, Lamu became a major local power. After the abolition of slavery in 1873, however, the island's economy suffered and has never made a come back. Today, tourism is an important source of income here.

Lamu town, the largest settlement on the island, was founded in the 14th century and contains many fine examples of Swahili architecture. The old town is designated a World Heritage Site as the oldest and best-preserved Swahili settlement in East Africa. With the simple lines of its architecture, built in coral and mangrove wood and featuring porches and rooftop patios, the town has managed to retain its distinctive character and charm. Donkeys wander through the narrow labyrinthine streets as there are no motorized vehicles on this idyllic island.

There are several museums in town, including the Lamu Museum which displays the island's ceremonial horn, and another museum dedicated to Swahili culture. Also worth a visit is Lamu Fort, built on the seafront by the Sultan of Pate in the early 17th century to protect members of his unpopular government. The Riyadha Mosque was built in 1900 and soon became one of the most prestigious centres for Islamic studies in Eastern Africa. The mosque is the centre for the annual Maulidi Festival which attracts pilgrims from all over Africa.

The most spectacular beaches on the island are those around Shela, a village about 3.2 km (2 mi) from Lamu town, with their clean white sand and traditional dhows. The area was unfortunately damaged in 2004 during the tsunami caused by the Indian Ocean earthquake, but it is still a lovely place to while away the day.

The Riyadha Mosque, built in 1900, is an important centre for Islamic studies.

POPULATION:
75,106 (1999)
WHEN TO GO:
December to January.
HOW TO GET THERE:
Fly from Mombasa or Nairobi, or take a ferry from Mokowe on the mainland or Manda Island.
HIGHLIGHTS:
Just chilling out – as there are no cars, this is a very peaceful place with just the sound of braying donkeys and palm trees rustling in the breeze. Leave the mobile phone and laptop at home and enjoy the tranquillity.
The Lamu Museum – housed in a building once occupied by Jack Haggard, Queen Victoria's consul. There are displays on Swahili culture, including a reconstructed Swahili house and relics from Takwa. Here the ceremonial horn of the island is on display.
The seafront restaurants in Lamu town – enjoy very fresh seafood at reasonable prices.
The donkey sanctuary in northern Lamu – set up to protect the 2,200 working donkeys on the island and ensure their well-being.
YOU SHOULD KNOW:
Lamu is strictly Islamic so be sensitive as to how you dress.

Mombasa

In south-eastern Kenya, on an island separated from the mainland by two rivers, Mombasa is the largest port in Eastern Africa. It is Kenya's second largest city and plays an important role in the country's economy, both as a major hub for imports and exports, and as a draw for tourism.

In 1498, Vasco da Gama visited the then-Arab city on his crusade to spread the Christian faith and to improve Portugal's trade links. Although he met with much hostility, he made an alliance with the King of Malindi. When the Portuguese forces arrived two years later, they appointed the King to be the Sultan of Mombasa and he used his influence to tame the local population and rule on behalf of the Portuguese. Mombasa became an important trading station for the Portuguese, and in the 1590s they built a great stronghold, Fort Jesus, to protect themselves against attack and act as a trading centre. The main goods which passed through the port were spices, coffee, cotton and slaves, who were imprisoned in the fort before they were sent away on ships.

The Portuguese ruled Mombasa for around 200 years until they were overthrown by the Omani Arabs, who themselves gave up the city to the British in 1888. In 1963, Mombasa became part of the newly independent Kenya.

Apart from the excellent beaches to the north and south of the city, Mombasa's greatest attraction is its lovely Old Town, with its narrow alleyways and Arabic architecture, featuring carved doorways and fretworked balconies. Bright colours and exotic scents abound, making this a real sensory experience. Don't miss the Old Harbour where traditional dhows come and go delivering fish and other goods from along the coast. The hot, steamy climate dictates the pace of life in Mombasa – slow and easy going. The overall atmosphere is friendly and vibrant, and the nightlife good – bars and restaurants are lively and stay open late.

POPULATION:
700,000 (2004)
WHEN TO GO:
June to March
HOW TO GET THERE:
Fly to Moi International Airport
HIGHLIGHTS:
A dhow cruise around the harbour – no trip is complete without a magical cruise on a traditional Mombasan boat.
Fort Jesus – this stronghold overlooking the sea, built by the Portuguese in the 1590s, now houses a museum displaying artefacts from the time the fort was built. It was here that slaves were imprisoned before being shipped abroad and you can visit the torture chambers and holding rooms.
The beaches to the north and south of the city are lovely, with white sand and coral reefs, and make a great day out.
The famous elephant tusks on Moi Avenue – the arches made out of intersecting tusks form a letter 'M' for Mombasa. They were built to commemorate the visit of Queen Elizabeth II in 1952.
Wandering around the labyrinth of narrow lanes and quaint shops in the Old Town.
YOU SHOULD KNOW:
Mombasa Island is joined to the mainland to the north by the Nyali Bridge, to the south by the Likoni Ferry and to the west by the Makupa Causeway and the railway line.

The varied rooftops of the Old Town

Kiwayu

POPULATION:
800 (2004 estimate)
WHEN TO GO:
January and February are hot and dry and the most popular. From June to September the weather is still dry. March to May are much quieter and cheaper, but wetter.
HOW TO GET THERE:
Flights from Nairobi or Mombasa to Kiwayu (via Lamu). From Lamu by motor boat (2 hrs) or dhow (7 hrs).
HIGHLIGHTS:
Picnics at Turtle Bay.
Canoeing up mangrove channels.
Fishing for your supper.
Hiring a dhow and crew to explore the islands.
On neighbouring Lamu Island – the centuries-old Maulidi Festival.
YOU SHOULD KNOW:
Crews from local villages may look slightly scruffier but are better sailors than most, and they know these somewhat tricky waters well.

Step barefoot from the boat and sink into the warm, soft sands of this pencil-thin paradise island in the Indian Ocean, just off the Kenyan coast. Just 48 km (30 mi) south of Kiwayu sits Lamu – that equally other-worldly yet thoroughly discovered island, packed with visitors and hotels. Fortunately, this 'honeypot' destination manages to steer the crowds away from its less known sister island and only the more intrepid travellers, including the odd mega-celebrity, are tempted to the secluded shores of Kiwayu.

Kiwayu may be remote and undiscovered but for those in the know it's relatively easy to reach. Hiring a dhow out of Lamu is the most pleasurable, slow way to arrive. You can spend days just kicking up the sand and patrolling the shores. On the east side of the island are tidal pools for snorkelling and dipping; and if you can drag yourself away from the beach there are game drives into the bush – alive with lions, giraffes, buffaloes and elephants.

The sea provides the main exercise of the day – snorkelling, diving off coral cliffs, water-skiing or just dipping a toe in the cooling, crystal waters. Offshore, manatees and dugongs float by and for keen fishermen it is apparently easy to land marlin, barracuda and swordfish.

Accommodation runs from plush safari lodges to cheaper guest-houses and camping areas. Wherever you stay, the simple pleasures remain the best. At the end of the day walk to Kiwayu's highest point and watch the crimson sun sinking over the sea.

Local fisherman carry their catch ashore.

A dusty road on Bugala Island

Ssese Islands

In the northwest corner of Lake Victoria, on the Ugandan side, are the 84 Ssese Islands. Just over half of these islands are inhabited and the largest of these, at 40 km (25 mi) long, is Bugala on which is located the islands' main town of Kalangala. Other islands to visit include Bubeke, Bukasa, Banda and Bufumira. The Bantu-speaking Bassese tribe inhabit the islands, and in ancient times this was one of the most important spiritual centres in the region.

Lake Victoria itself was once a huge swamp, but is now the largest lake in Africa, the world's third largest freshwater lake and the source of the White Nile. The huge Nile perch is one of the key catches in the lake, but its over-fishing is at last beginning to sound alarm bells.

These islands have empty, palm-fringed white beaches and virgin rainforest.

People tend to come to the Ssese Islands either to fish or to chill out, read books, relax and hang about the camps on the beach. Walking is one of the main activities, and for birding enthusiasts, the islands are home to a huge diversity of colourful birdlife – turacos and native paradise flycatchers are common. People do swim in the calm waters of the lake but be warned, there is a bilharzia risk.

POPULATION:
35,000 (2006)
WHEN TO GO:
Late December to late February – dry and hot. June through to September is a pleasant alternative.
HOW TO GET THERE:
Ferries from Bukakata on the mainland to Luku on Bugala Island, and from Kampala to Banda and Bukasa. Also there is now a large ferry from Entebbe and Kalangala. Fishing boats take slightly longer.
HIGHLIGHTS:
Camping in a patch of tropical rainforest.
Sun-seeking in the Bay of Lutobaka, on Bugala.
Sailing tours on Lake Victoria.
Island hopping by canoe.
Fishing for Nile perch and tilapia.
YOU SHOULD KNOW:
There are very few vehicles on Bugala Island, so do not expect garage facilities, although there is a fuel station in Kalangala where fishermen come to purchase petrol.

POPULATION:
1,070,000 (2004)
WHEN TO GO:
June to October.
HOW TO GET THERE:
Fly to Zanzibar International Airport or by ferry from Dar es Salaam.
HIGHLIGHTS:
The beaches – the island has many lovely beaches for sunbathing and swimming. The East Beaches are popular as the sand is brilliant white, and the warm waters are deep blue. The scuba diving is good here, with plentiful corals and rich marine life. Swim with the dolphins or arrange a ride in a local's dhow.
Stone Town – explore the lovely buildings, like the House of Wonders and the Arab Fort. Arrange a walking tour with a local guide who can explain some of the fascinating history.
Jozani Park – this beautiful forest has excellent nature trails, featuring some very exotic (and large) trees. See the Red Colobus Monkeys which are native to the island but now nearly extinct. They are curious and playful and will pose for a photograph.
Spice tours – these enjoyable organized tours explain how the different spices grow, allowing you to tour the beautiful plantations of cardamom, ginger, cloves, nutmeg and saffron, and sample some luscious tropical fruits.
YOU SHOULD KNOW:
Zanzibar was the last place to abolish the slave trade.

Zanzibar

Located 35 km (22 miles) from the coast of Tanzania in the Indian Ocean is Zanzibar, boasting white sand beaches lined with palm trees, native forests and an abundance of coral reefs perfect for snorkelling and diving. Today it offers a tropical paradise for holidaymakers, but this low-lying coral island has a chequered history of foreign occupation, intensive commerce and slavery.

The island was first inhabited by the Hadimu and Tumbatu tribes who came here from Africa. In the 10th century, Persian merchants arrived, brought to the island by monsoon winds as they sailed through the Indian Ocean. As they needed the monsoon winds to take them home again, they had to stay on the island for months at a time. They eventually decided to build permanent settlements on Zanzibar, and it soon became a centre for trade in its own right. This busy hub was influenced by the merchants who passed through, with Arabs, Indians, Chinese, Portuguese, Dutch and British leaving their mark here and blending together to create a unique culture.

Shirazi Persians and Omani Arabs settled on the island and ruled the Sultanate, which is why there is such a strong Arab influence evident today. Stone Town, the centre of the old city, has changed little in the last 200 years with its mosques, busy bazaars and grand Arab houses with their ornamental carved wooden doors studded with brass. The Indian influence can be found in the coloured glasswork and decorative balconies of many of the buildings, while the British left some staid colonial houses in the wealthier parts of town.

Today the economy is based on tourism, although fishing is still a major occupation. The island also exports many different types of spices, as well as cocoa and coconuts.

As well as the beaches and beautiful architecture, the island is also home to abundant wildlife, including red colobus and blue monkeys, which can be observed in Jozani Park, a large area of mature native forest which is now protected. There are also many other types of mammals here, including red-bellied squirrels and sun squirrels, and over 200 species of birds. Zanzibar is also a good place to see turtles, including the green turtle and the hawksbill turtle, which can be seen laying their eggs on the beaches near the lighthouse at Ras Ngunwi. Whale watching is also popular here, with humpback whales migrating through the channel in spring and then again in September. Long-snouted spinner dolphins and bottlenose dolphins are also favourites in these waters and it is possible to swim with them if you join an organized tour.

A van loaded with bananas leaves Stone Town market.

Mafia

Mafia is a sleepy, untouched retreat from the real world, and a slice of the old Swahili Coast where people go about their lives simply and traditionally. It may be part of the Spice Islands, alongside Zanzibar and Pemba, but is governed from the mainland. In reality it's a cluster of one main island – 48 km (30 mi) long – and numerous tiny ones, and is now the site of the largest marine park in the Indian Ocean, supporting fine unbleached corals.

For a small island such as this the sea rules. Every conceivable form of boat is crafted locally – from large ocean-going dhows to smaller *masha* or fishing boats and canoes. Crabs are scooped up from the shoreline and seaweed cultivated for sale. The main way of life is fishing, and the waters are rich for both fishermen and divers. Coconuts and cashews are key cash crops, but the price of coconuts on the world markets has fallen in recent years and fishing has become more commercially viable. Mafia is also famous for the striking raffia mats that the women of the island weave, often plaiting as they stroll along. This is an under-developed place, and the infrastructure is poor – there is only electricity around the main tourist areas and very few houses have running water. Most locals get around on foot or bicycle on bumpy tracks.

Mafia's rich history dates back to the 8th century when it was a regular stop-off for Persian boats, and trade routes stretched between the Far East and mainland Tanzania. Mafia has seen Portuguese, German and British occupation and this chequered history has resulted in a shifting, mixed population.

POPULATION:
40,801 (2002)
WHEN TO GO:
July to October and December to March
HOW TO GET THERE:
Small aircraft from Dar es Salaam or by road from Dar es Salaam to Kisiju and then boat to Mafia.
HIGHLIGHTS:
The ruins of 10th/11th century mosques at Kisimani Mafia near the capital Kilindoni.
Diving and snorkelling.
Exploring the deserted beaches.
The world-class deep-sea fishing.
A trip round the island on a traditional sailing dhow.
YOU SHOULD KNOW:
The name Mafia derives from the Kiswahili *mahali pa afya* meaning 'a healthy dwelling-place'.

The crystal-clear waters between Mafia Island and Chole Island

Pemba

POPULATION:
265,000 (2004)
WHEN TO GO:
Tropical climate with high humidity. December to March is the hottest – 25-29°C (77-84°F). Avoid the longer rains of mid-March to May/June and shorter rains (showers) in November to January. Diving is good throughout the year, except May to June.
HOW TO GET THERE:
Flights from Zanzibar Island or from Dar es Salaam or Tanga on the mainland. Dhows from Tanga – erratic service.
HIGHLIGHTS:
Mtambwe Mkuu – by dhow or canoe out of Wete harbour.
Ras Mkumbuu ruins – the site of a Swahili settlement dating back to the 11th century.
Ngezi Forest – home to Pemba flying foxes.
Ras Kiuyu Forest Reserve. Fishing for striped marlin and sailfish.
YOU SHOULD KNOW:
The Portuguese introduced bullfighting here in the 16th century – and they are still held in a few places such as Pujini between August and February.

The pungent aroma of cloves pervades the air. One of the legendary Spice Islands, Pemba has more cloves growing on it than its big sister Zanzibar, just 50 km (31 mi) to the south. On this verdant, hilly island there are over three million clove trees, and this valuable spice is the main export of the Zanzibar Archipelago. Pemba is also renowned for its voodoo and traditional healers, and many are still drawn here to seek cures and learn ancient skills.

In the past political unrest kept visitors away, but now more adventurous spirits are making their way here and avoiding the growing crowds on Zanzibar. Many come to dive – the reefs are unspoilt and for experienced divers the drop-offs are vertiginous. Overhangs, caverns and coral gardens litter the sheer walls and reefs; titan triggerfish, wrasse and Spanish dancers ride the currents. The diving on Pemba is some of the best in the world.

Tourism is still in its infancy and accommodation a little sparse, but resorts are springing up and life is changing. The main town of Chake-Chake sits high on a hill overlooking the bay and Misali Island, and about 10 km (6 mi) southeast stand the ruins of a fortified palace dating back to the 15th century. This was the seat of the infamous Mohammed bin Abdul Rahman who ruled Pemba before the arrival of the Portuguese. These are the only known early fortifications along the whole coast of Eastern Africa.

Chake-Chake is the administrative centre of Pemba.

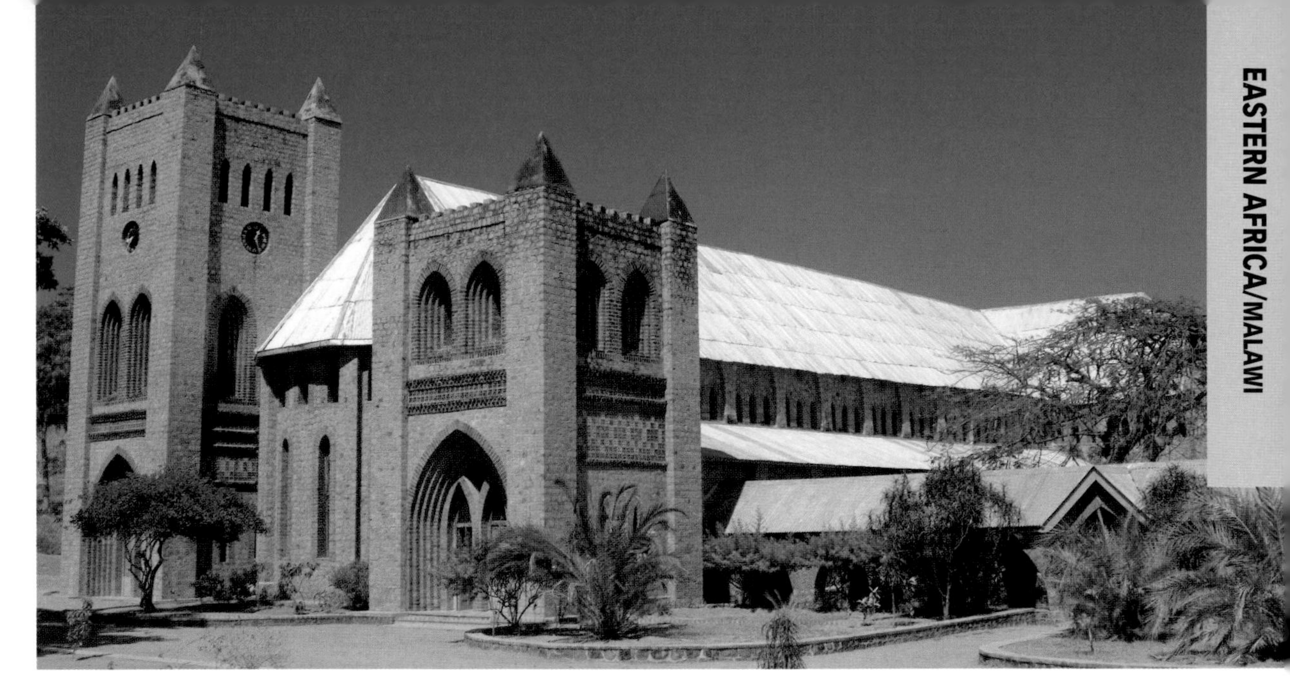

St Peter's Anglican Cathedral

Likoma

Off the eastern shores of Lake Malawi lies Likoma Island and its smaller neighbour Chizumulu, making up a tiny piece of Malawian territory in Mozambican waters. Likoma has remained largely untouched since Scottish missionaries discovered it in the 1880s and it became the headquarters of the University Mission to Central Africa – Livingstone's mission. This led to the islands being retained by Malawi when the lake was divided politically after World War II.

North Malawi as a whole has been long forgotten. Here the massive undulating Nyika plateau collides with the very edge of the Great Rift Valley. In perfect isolation, Likoma commands breathtaking views of the mountains and wilderness of Mozambique, just kilometres away.

Likoma's main town is overshadowed by the mighty Cathedral of St Peter, built in 1903 with elegant stained glass and carved soapstone. The rest of the island is simpler – mainly grassland scattered with mango and baobab trees.

Lake Malawi covers a fifth of the country's total area – about 590 km (365 mi) long and 85 km (52 mi) wide – hence its popular name of 'Calendar Island'. Usually gentle by nature, winds from the north or south can whip the lake up into a frenzy. Below the surface, the lake bubbles with fish and fishing villages along its shores reap the benefits.

The best and easiest way to get around Likoma is on foot. At the southern tip of the island, beyond the baobab plains, lies a crescent-shaped beach of the finest golden sand, framed by mango trees. This island is rich in history and also in silence.

POPULATION:
9,000 (2007)

WHEN TO GO:
Best to visit in the dry season from late April to November. May to August are cooler and dry, but September and October can get hot and humid.

HOW TO GET THERE:
Flights from Lilongwe or boats from the port of Nkhata Bay. Dhows cross between the two islands.

HIGHLIGHTS:
The Anglican cathedral in the main town.
Boat safaris to Mozambique and to other islands.
Snorkelling and scuba diving.

YOU SHOULD KNOW:
Electricity on the island is usually switched off after 10 pm to save generator fuel.

Bazaruto Archipelago

POPULATION:
3,500 (2007)
WHEN TO GO:
Year round, but avoid the cyclone season in February. Little rainfall between April and November.
HOW TO GET THERE:
Flights into Viklankulo (sometimes via Maputo) with connections on to the archipelago.
HIGHLIGHTS:
Marlin fishing from mid-September to the end of December. Sailfish fishing from April to August, and fishing for smaller game fish such as king mackerel, bonito and travelli all year round.

Halfway up the Mozambique coast lies a chain of five islands making up the Bazaruto Archipelago. Formed from sand deposited by the Limpopo River, fine beaches and coral reefs come naturally; and having long been a national park, so does the wildlife. Bazaruto, Benguerra and Magaruque are the largest islands, with Santa Carolina and finally Bangué coming in on the small side.

Thanks to their protected status and relative isolation from the ravages of war, nature has been free to flourish here; and bizarre yet endearing dugongs or sea cows spend their days grazing among sea-grass meadows offshore. Bazurato Island itself is 37 km (23 mi) long, and here gaudy pink flamingoes strut the tidal flats, while large Nile crocodiles lurk in the inland freshwater lakes. The west is cloaked in grassland and thicket while the east coast is built entirely of impressive sand dunes. Benguerra is about 11 km (7 mi) long and its blend of forest, savannah and wetlands provides rich pickings for local wildlife. Cashew nuts are native to the island and grow mainly on the seaward side.

Wild orange trees and sisal trees abound, as do mlala palms – the leaves of which are used in the weaving of mats, baskets and hats. Nature lovers, sun worshippers and water sports enthusiasts alike are drawn here. It may be said of other places, but this is as close as it gets to a true tropical paradise. With clear turquoise waters and endless palm-dotted beaches, this is the place to escape from the pressures of everyday life – to snorkel and surf, and run coral pink sand through your fingers. There are no roads, no shops and no tourist attractions to divert you from the serious business of relaxing.

Birdwatching – sunbirds, bee-eaters, paradise flycatchers and crab plovers.
Shell-seeking for the famous 'Pansy Shells' at North Point, Pansy Island and various sand dunes.
Dining out on freshly caught fish, cooked in the Portuguese style.

YOU SHOULD KNOW:
The locals use the husks from the harvested cashews to make very intoxicating liquor.

The Island of Mozambique

POPULATION:
14,000 (2006)
WHEN TO GO:
May to October
HOW TO GET THERE:
Fly from Nampula. By traditional dhow from the mainland, or cross the bridge by car.
HIGHLIGHTS:
The port area and its fascinating mixture of architectural styles.
The Chapel of Nossa Senhora de Baluarte – this church was built by the Portuguese in 1522 and is believed to be the oldest European building in the southern hemisphere.
Other churches worth a visit include the Church of Santo Antonio and the Church of Misericordia.
YOU SHOULD KNOW:
A 3-km bridge connects the island to the mainland.

The tiny coral island of Mozambique lies in the Nampula Province of Northern Mozambique and has a unique historical heritage unmatched in the rest of Mozambique, and perhaps the rest of Africa. It was the capital of Mozambique for nearly four centuries under Portuguese rule, and had been used as a major base for Arab traders long before that. Today much of the island has been designated a UNESCO World Heritage Site.

The island was a major Arab port and centre of boat building when Vasco da Gama arrived in 1498. By 1507, the Portuguese had established a port and naval base on the island, and went on to build the Fort of São Sebastião. The settlement, now known as Stone Town, became the capital of Portuguese East Africa. It withstood Dutch attacks in 1607 and 1608 and remained a major trading post for the Portuguese on the sea route from Europe to the East Indies, trading in slaves, spices and gold. With the opening of the Suez Canal in 1869, however, the island's fortunes waned.

A study in architectural contrasts, the island's port is resplendent in Arab, Indian and Portuguese influences, a reminder of its glory days. The limestone houses around the port lie on winding, tangled streets surrounding a central square, their facades featuring cornices, high rectangular windows and rows of pilasters. The Chapel of Nossa Senhora de Baluarte, built in 1522, is thought to be the oldest European building in the southern hemisphere, and the finest example of Manueline vaulted architecture in Mozambique.

Other interesting buildings on the island include the Palace and Chapel of São Paulo, which was built in 1610 and is now a museum; and the Museum of Sacred Art with an excellent example of a Makonde crucifix, housed in the former hospital of the Holy House of Mercy.

Mozambique Castle

Quirimbas Archipelago National Park

This sprawling, stunning archipelago is made up of 32 coral islands peppered along the Mozambique coast from Pemba to the Rovuma River – which forms a natural barrier with Tanzania. The southern-most eleven islands and a vast area of mainland forest now make up the Quirimbas National Park. Here elephants pluck mangoes off the trees just metres from the Indian Ocean, and inland four of Africa's 'Big Five' animals still roam.

The archipelago has some of the finest coral reefs in East Africa. The fish here are big – parrotfish, angelfish, cave bass and morays all seem to be oversized. Kingfish will come for a snorkel along the shores, and manta rays and hammerhead sharks can also make an appearance. Matemo Island has countless coves and beaches and is brilliant for diving. On the other hand Medjumbe is a tiny castaway of an island and an idyllic romantic retreat. Quilalea is uninhabited and it feels like you have the whole place to yourself – along with the teeming marine life, of course. Vimizi is rated one of the world's top ten dive sites, and along the shoreline are tracks made by turtles as they scoop and heave their hefty frames up the beach.

In contrast and for a little culture, Ibo Island has beautiful old buildings and a long, dark history dating from well before the arrival of the Portuguese. Once a fashionable town, many of the 18th and 19th century Portuguese-built homes have been abandoned and are now crumbling. Given its history, Ibo is also one of the most visited islands.

When it emerged from a bloody civil war in 1992 no-one expected Mozambique to become Africa's hidden jewel and conservation champion – a safe haven for dugongs, sea turtles and for those fortunate enough to visit its multi-faceted shores.

POPULATION:
Ibo 5,000; Vimizi 1,000; Matemo 500 (2005 estimate). Many of the islands are uninhabited.

WHEN TO GO:
Tropical climate – the rainy season is from December to April, but most days are sunny and the rain is usually in short, sharp showers. It's a little cooler from May to September, and diving is fine all year round.

HOW TO GET THERE:
Flights from Dar es Salaam or Johannesburg to Pemba Island, then on to islands such as Ibo or Matemo. Boats between islands.

HIGHLIGHTS:
Humpback whale watch from June to September.
Going fishing with the locals in their dhows.
Tracking elephants at night.
The island of Ibo – once a trading port for slaves and ivory, and with a magnificent old fortress.

YOU SHOULD KNOW:
Mozambique is a malaria zone so take care and cover up. Quilalea Island is the only malaria-free island in the whole archipelago.

Portuguese colonial buildings line the harbour of Ibo Island.

INDIAN OCEAN

Madagascar Island

POPULATION:
19,449,000 (2007 estimate)
WHEN TO GO:
The cooler dry season (May to October)
HOW TO GET THERE:
By air, with various international carriers serving the island. There is also a ferry service from Mauritius. Air Madagascar operates a network of internal flights.
HIGHLIGHTS:
Ranomafana National Park – lush rainforest teeming with wildlife, including lots of lemurs (permit required).
A ride on the train from Fianarantsoa to Manakara (if it's running!) for a really scenic trip.
The quiet coastal area around the villages of Ifaty, Mangilly and Mandio Rano, for beautiful beaches, coral reefs and whale watching in season (July and August).
The Royal Hill of Ambohimanga, an important historic complex that includes a royal city and burial ground, now a UNESCO World Heritage Site.
Isalo National Park near Ranohira, where the central plateaux explode into spectacular sandstone bluffs and plunging gorges (a local guide and permit required).
The resort island of Nosy Be for those wanting a conventional tropical beach holiday and/or exceptional diving opportunities.
The Pangalanes Canal, a fabulous series of natural and artificial lakes parallel to the sea in the 'Garden of Madagascar' (the east coast).
YOU SHOULD KNOW:
In rural areas be aware of numerous *fady* (taboos) which vary from region to region and can include the forbidding of certain foods, clothes of a certain colour or bathing in a particular lake or river.

The Republic of Madagascar occupies the island of the same name, the world's fourth largest, located in the Indian Ocean off the south-east coast of Africa. Madagascar has a mountainous heart and central plateaux, with rain forests to the east and dry forests and deserts to the west and south. The capital is Antananarivo (Tana for short), and the other major cities are Antsirabe, Mahajanga and Toamasina. The island was violently annexed by France in the late 19th century, attaining independence in 1960. A period of political instability seems to be over and this intriguing nation is at last finding its feet.

Madagascar's long isolation from outside influences has resulted in unique flora and fauna, with many plants and animals that are found nowhere else. Unfortunately, this special ecosystem is under threat from extensive logging and slash-and-burn agriculture. Belated realization of the irreversible damage this is doing has seen a new emphasis on conservation, so there is hope for the island's ecological future. This also has an important economic dimension, with ecotourism a growing trend and Madagascar possessing more potential than most. Unique attractions include lemurs, the mongoose-like fossa and three endemic bird families, but there's plenty more to look at – the island is home to five per cent of the world's plant and animal species.

Tourism has not been a priority in a country that largely depends on agriculture, fishing and forestry. The infrastructure is poor, with only one main road from Tana to the south-west coast. Adventurous visitors tour by bicycle, or charter a yacht with local guide for a memorable exploration of the coastline. Otherwise it's a case of taking an internal flight to the town or city of your choice, finding a hotel and sallying forth from there by bus or taxi.

Village houses in the morning mist near Perinet

Local boys walking cattle along a pristine beach.

Nosy Boraha Island

Also known, rather more romantically, by its French name of Ile Sainte Marie, Nosy Boraha is situated off Madagascar's north-east coast and is a former haunt of pirates, who lived on an island in the bay of Nosy Boraha's main town, Ambodifotatra. Their cemetery still exists and a number of sunken wooden ships from the 17th and 18th centuries, said to be pirate vessels, may be seen below the surface. The island is 60 km (38 mi) long by less than 10 km (6 mi) wide, surrounded by sandy beaches that are fringed with palm trees and protected by coral reefs. The island has a verdant, hilly interior.

These attributes have made Nosy Boraha Madagascar's leading holiday destination, though happily it has yet to be spoiled by excessive commercialism. Holidaymakers can enjoy the essential ingredients of any Indian Ocean resort holiday – sultry tropical weather, low-profile waterside accommodation, wonderful beaches and the usual water sports – swimming, snorkelling and diving within the reef are excellent. But here there is the added bonus of an accessible interior where the rainforest offers fascinating opportunities to observe the rich variety of local flora and fauna. Best of all, this is one of the best places in the world to whale-watch, with humpback whales cavorting in the channel between the Nosy Boraha and the Malagasy mainland during the busy breeding season (July to September).

Those who hire cycles can not only enjoy Nosy Boraha's natural beauty, but can also see how the relaxed islanders enrich their lives with traditional family and social events that invoke the revered spirits of their ancestors – it's the authentic Madagascar experience!

POPULATION:
60,000 (2007 estimate)

WHEN TO GO:
Outside high summer (December to February), when it's uncomfortably hot and very humid.

HOW TO GET THERE:
Internal flights serve the island from most Malagasy cities. By boat from Manompana or Soanierana-Ivongo on the mainland.

HIGHLIGHTS:
Ambodena Forest, alive with wildlife – including lemurs, a huge variety of birds, geckos, chameleons and arboreal frogs.
Marine turtles nesting on the beach at Cocoteraie, where villagers now make an income from guarding the nests and showing them to visitors, rather than eating the turtles and their eggs.
The primeval forest at Ikalalao, remarkable for its many orchid species including the large variety known as the 'Queen of Madagascar'.
A stay in one of the lodges in wildlife sanctuaries, where the focus is on guided animal viewing activities.

YOU SHOULD KNOW:
Nosy Boraha's nickname is 'the scented island', because aromatic coffee, cocoa, cinnamon and vanilla grow in profusion.

Waves break against the outer sandbars of Aldabra Atoll.

Aldabra Atoll

POPULATION:
Uninhabited
WHEN TO GO:
May to September
HOW TO GET THERE:
Virtually the only way is to join a cruise ship, embarking at Victoria, on Mahé Island.
HIGHLIGHTS:
The Aldabran giant tortoises – there are ten times the number of giant tortoises on Aldabra than on Galapagos.
The colonies of breeding birds on the islets in the lagoon – see frigate birds, red-tailed tropic birds and boobies.
The Aldabra flightless rail – the only flightless bird left on any Indian Ocean island.
YOU SHOULD KNOW:
Aldabra Atoll is uninhabited and very isolated. Astove Atoll, part of the Aldabra Atoll, used to be occupied by African slaves who escaped from a Portuguese ship in 1760.

Aldabra Atoll is part of the Aldabra Group, one of the archipelagos of the Outer Islands of the Seychelles. The second largest atoll in the world after Kiritimati, Aldabra is the coraline tip of a volcanic seamount, rising from depths of 4,000 to 4,500m (13,120 to 14,760 ft). At 34 km (21 mi) long, 14.5 km (9 mi) wide and just 8 m (26 ft) above sea level, the atoll consists of four coral limestone islands forming a circle around a lagoon of 224 sq km (86 sq mi). The lagoon is tidal and loses two-thirds of its waters at low tide. Aldabra was given World Heritage status in 1982 to protect its delicate natural environment.

Because the atoll is so remote, many of its species of flora and fauna are found only here. The islets and rocky outcrops in the lagoon provide nesting areas for thousands of birds. It has possibly the largest population of red-tailed tropic birds and the second largest colony of frigate birds in the world. Many other birds are found here too, including the Aldabra flightless rail, the only flightless bird found on any Indian Ocean island.

The Aldabran giant tortoises are, however, the atoll's most renowned residents, being the last of the giant tortoises which were once spread across the entire region. Commercial exploitation is believed to have rendered all other giant tortoises in the area extinct by the mid-19th century, and very nearly exterminated the Aldabran population. Two species of marine turtle also nest on beaches on Aldabra: the green turtle and hawksbill turtle.

Unlike the nearby Seychelles, the atoll is inhospitable to humans as the limestone has been eroded into sharp spikes and water-filled pits. However, the mangroves support fish nurseries, and the lagoon is home to a wealth of marine life, from black-tipped reef sharks to eagle rays and parrot fish. For almost a century, scientists have been studying the flora and fauna of the atoll, which is uninhabited other than by those working at the scientific research station.

Mahé Island

Africa's least-populous sovereign state is the Republic of Seychelles, another of the Indian Ocean's fairly numerous island nations. Officially, there are over 150 islands in the Seychelles, consisting of a mix of granite and coral islands located 1,500 km (930 mi) to the east of the African mainland and 1,600 km (994 mi) to the north east of Madagascar. Other neighbours include Mauritius, Réunion, Zanzibar, Comoros, Mayotte and the Maldives. The Seychellois make good neighbours – they are often described as the world's friendliest people.

Mahé is the largest island, in the north of the archipelago. It contains the capital city of Victoria (no prizes for guessing that this was once a British colony) and has 90 per cent of the country's population. Settlement is concentrated in the north and east, while the south and west are largely occupied by the Baie Ternay Marine National Park and Port Launay Marine National Park. The island's high point, Morne Seychellois, is also a National Park that offers striking scenery and rewarding hiking opportunities. Visitors who merely pass through Mahé on the way to resort islands are missing something – the place is spectacular, with towering mountains, abundant tropical vegetation and beautiful beaches, mostly uncrowded...or, better still, empty.

Victoria is the world's smallest capital city, and its quaint streets and old harbour can easily be explored on foot. The clock tower is a replica of that housing Big Ben at London's Houses of Parliament. The market is open six days a week (excluding Sunday) and local crafts are on sale alongside a wide range of fruit, vegetables and fish. It's possible to take a boat tour of the St Anne Marine Park from Victoria Harbour, covering six offshore islands that include an important nesting site for hawksbill turtles.

POPULATION:
72,000 (2005 estimate)
WHEN TO GO:
All year round – the climate is evenly hot and humid. Even during the rainy season (January and February) there is plenty of sunshine.
HOW TO GET THERE:
Various international carriers fly to Mahé, including Air Seychelles – which also operates internal inter-island services.
HIGHLIGHTS:
The National Botanical Gardens on the outskirts of Victoria – a shady green oasis with a lovely orchid display.
Beau Vallon beach, the most popular on the island, where the action continues with good nightlife after dark.
The annual Creole Festival – a colourful (and noisy) event that takes place during the last week of October.
Victoria's Museum of History, full of exhibits and historic artefacts relating to the cultural and natural history of the Seychelles.
YOU SHOULD KNOW:
Although predominately Catholic, the Seychellois are a superstitious lot and many believe in old magic known as *gris*. But don't worry if you forget to tip – sorcery was officially outlawed in 1958!

Local children playing in the sea.

Praslin Island

Despite being the second-largest island in the Seychelles, Praslin still isn't all that big, with an area of just 38 sq km (15 sq mi). It is 45 km (28 mi) north of Mahé, and in the 18th century was the haunt of Arab merchants and a notorious pirate hideaway. There is obviously some modern development, but those old-time visitors would still recognize the place.

Nowadays the incomers are mostly holidaymakers, honeymooners or cruise passengers. They are all drawn by fabulous beaches, sculptural granite rocks, coral reefs swarming with colourful fish and the lush interior vegetation of the archipelago's most popular tourist destination. There are numerous hotels, resorts and self-catering units, though the island never seems overcrowded. Its two villages are Baie St Anne in the east and Grand Anse in the south and both are worth visiting. Bicycles may be hired, and provide an excellent way of exploring the island.

This is the ultra-tranquil place that thinks Mahé's slow way of doing things is a touch hectic, so life on Praslin is virtually laid back to the horizontal. But those who do stir themselves and leave the beach can visit the fabulous Vallée de Mai, a primeval forest complete with the soaring Coco de Mer palm trees that produce the world's largest nut – just one example of flora unique to Praslin – and also rare endemic bird species like the Seychelles bulbul, fruit pigeon and black parrot. This fascinating place is a UNESCO World Heritage Site, and well deserves the accolade.

POPULATION:
6,500 (2007 estimate)
WHEN TO GO:
Any time – the hot climate hardly varies and the sea remains warm all year round.
HOW TO GET THERE:
By air taxi or fast catamaran from Mahé.
HIGHLIGHTS:
A souvenir that can be obtained nowhere else – an expensive, rare, numbered Coco de Mer nut, once reserved for sultans and said to have magical sexual powers (you'll know why when you see one).
One of the world's most beautiful beaches – Anse Lazio on the east coast, which must be seen to be believed.
The black pearl farm – cultured black pearls at the Indian Ocean's only oyster farm, and also giant clams.
YOU SHOULD KNOW:
General Gordon of Khartoum was convinced that the Biblical Garden of Eden was on Praslin.

Sunrise over Praslin Island

La Digue Island

If it were for sale, La Digue would attract keen competition from the world's billionaires – this is an enchanting tropical paradise. The fourth-largest island in the Seychelles, La Digue extends to an area of 10 sq km (6 sq mi) and lies to the east of Praslin Island. It supports a population that used to survive on fishing, copra and vanilla production but nowadays tourism is the name of the game and the whole island is geared to providing a memorable holiday experience. There are several hotels and guest-houses that offer simpler accommodation and it's also possible to see this magical place by making a day trip from nearby Praslin.

The beaches – especially Anse Source d'Argent and Anse Pierrot – are fabulous, often set off by tumbled rock formations that seem like dramatic granite sculptures. There are plenty of hidden coves to discover, too. Getting around is a matter of foot or pedal power, as there are few vehicles and the locals use ox-drawn carts, which perfectly match the unchanging pace of island life. Focal points are the harbour at La Passe on the west coast and L'Union Estate where traditional activities like copra production and boat building are still practised. A working vanilla plantation welcomes visitors.

La Digue's interior rises to Eagle's Nest Mountain (also known as Belle Vue), a peak that is 300 m (985 ft) above sea level and rewards the active visitor with wonderful views. The densely forested Veuve Nature Reserve occupies much of the interior, and there are picturesque swamps, pools and inlets.

POPULATION:
2,100 (2007 estimate)

WHEN TO GO:
This is a year-round destination, with the hot, humid climate tempered by cooling winds.

HOW TO GET THERE:
By fast ferry from Praslin or Mahé. An expensive helicopter transfer is also available.

HIGHLIGHTS:
A day trip to Praslin's small offshore islands – Félicité, Ile Cocos, Grand Soeur and Petite Soeur.
A famous island sight – giant tortoises in their rocky enclosure.
The lovingly maintained church of Our Lady of Assumption, with an impressive stone-built calvaire by the entrance.

YOU SHOULD KNOW:
La Digue is home to the critically endangered Black Paradise Flycatcher, known locally as 'the widow' – a bird thought to be extinct but now rediscovered.

The striking coastline of La Digue

Silhouette Island

POPULATION:
135 (2007)
WHEN TO GO:
May to September
HOW TO GET THERE:
By helicopter or boat from Mahé.
HIGHLIGHTS:
The deserted sandy beaches set in scenic coves.
The giant tortoises – visit the breeding centre out near the Dauban Coconut Plantation.
Snorkelling above the undamaged coral reefs.
They have a cast-iron neoclassical mausoleum here that is supposedly the most remarkable piece of eccentricity in all of the Seychelles islands.
YOU SHOULD KNOW:
The island is situated within a Marine National Park.

The island of Silhouette lies 20 km (12 mi) north-west of Mahé and with an area of 20 sq km (7 sq mi), it is the third largest island in the Seychelles. Unlike many of the other islands in the chain, Silhouette is formed of granite, but the rocks are softened by the dense, lush rainforest which covers this round island. With a tiny population, and just one small hotel on the island, this untouched paradise is the ultimate get-away.

Named after Etienne de Silhouette (1709–1767), the French minister of finances under Louis XV, the island has five peaks over 500 m (1,640 ft), making the scenery rather dramatic. The summit of Mount Dauban at 740 m (2,428 ft), the highest point on the island, looms above the idyllic, unexplored rainforest thick with rare hardwoods, incense trees and pitcher-plant orchids endemic to Silhouette.

The island supports one of the richest biodiversities in the western Indian Ocean, with many endemic and endangered plants and animals. The large areas of primeval forest are untouched by modern man and are home to, among other species, the last known Seychelles sheath-tailed bats in the wild.

Among the more famous inhabitants are the giant tortoises. The Seychelles tortoise was almost completely eradicated by sailors who used them for food as they were able to survive aboard ships for up to six months without food and water. This activity lasted until 1840 when the last of the animals was taken into captivity. A handful of them were found in captivity in the 1990s, as were a few Arnold's giant tortoises, also previously thought to be extinct. The Seychelles Giant Tortoise Conservation Project aims to keep these two species from extinction. You can see giant tortoises at the breeding centre near the old Dauban Coconut Plantation.

The island's marine environment is just as rich as that on land, and there are coral reefs and granite cliffs to explore. The huge, colourful coral reefs are home to exotic fish of all shapes and sizes, making the island appealing to snorkelling and diving fans. The coral habitats are exceptionally healthy, though the strong currents can be a problem for swimmers. There are also some pristine beaches on the island, set in pretty coves and secluded bays, and it is likely you can find one all to yourself. This island is heaven for honeymooners, or those who simply want to unwind in an island paradise.

Silhouette Island at sunrise

Mauritius

Part of the Mascarene Islands, the Republic of Mauritius is off the coast of Africa in the Indian Ocean, 900 km (560 mi) east of Madagascar. The republic consists of five islands – St Brandon, Rodrigues, two Agalegas Islands and Mauritius itself. The latter was originally uninhabited, but the Dutch named the island and established a colony that was seized by the French in 1715. They renamed the place Ile de France and built a prosperous economy based on sugar. But the British took the island in 1810 and it reverted to the original name.

Independence was granted in 1968 and this Commonwealth country is a stable democracy with one of Africa's highest per capita incomes. This might be guessed by a visitor to Port Louis, who finds a sophisticated place with a cluster of high- and medium-rise buildings that might be mistaken from afar as the downtown area of a small American city...were it not for its location beside the azure Indian Ocean, surrounded by lush tropical vegetation. Tourism has become an increasingly important sector of the economy, which had hitherto been based on sugar plantations and off-shore financial services.

The effort to attract visitors is proving successful, and might not even need the boost of a move to duty-free status. Mauritius is the most accessible island in the Indian Ocean, with wonderful beaches and crystal-clear waters. Important though these essential ingredients of every tropical holiday destination may be, Mauritius has something extra – friendly people and a vibrant cultural mix that will leave an indelible impression. There is a festival or fiesta practically every week and a tempting variety of ethnic cuisines. The place must be good – author Mark Twain remarked that Mauritius was made before heaven, and heaven modelled on Mauritius.

POPULATION:
1,157,000 (2000)
WHEN TO GO:
Temperature is high all year round, though trade winds keep down humidity. May to November are peak months, January and February are cyclone-prone.
HOW TO GET THERE:
By air from several departure points in Europe (especially France) and Africa.
HIGHLIGHTS:
Black River Gorges National Park – an area of outstanding natural beauty reached by the island's only mountain road.
Curepipe – in the centre of a lovely upland area, the place resembles an old English market town.
The Grand Bay Resort, for those who like some lively nightlife after a day on the beach.
The colourful Flacq Market in the east of the island for the best local produce and handicrafts.
Dutch ruins at Vieux Grand Port, the oldest settlement on the island, dating from the 17th century.
Chamarel – an extraordinary multi-coloured landscape made up of different volcanic ashes, culminating in a waterfall complex.
YOU SHOULD KNOW:
Mauritius was the only known habitat of that famous non-flying bird immortalized in the oh-so-sadly-true phrase 'dead as a dodo'.

An aerial view of Blue Bay and its sandbanks

Rodrigues Island

POPULATION:
38,000 (2006 estimate)
WHEN TO GO:
Any time – the temperature is pretty even all year round.
HOW TO GET THERE:
Fly in from Mauritius or Réunion. By boat from Mauritius (36 hours).
HIGHLIGHTS:
The Grand Montagne Nature Reserve, where restoration of indigenous forest is taking place.
A visit to the delightful stone-built, Gothic-style St Gabriel Cathedral.
The bustling Saturday market in Port Mathurin.
A selection of caves with amazing stalactites and stalagmites.
YOU SHOULD KNOW:
Arabs visited Rodrigues as long ago as the 10th century – their name for the island was Dina Moraze.

The smallest of the Mascarene Islands, Rodrigues is an autonomous region of the Republic of Mauritius, though it aspires to independence. It is 560 km (350 mi) east of the main island, extends to 110 sq km (42 sq mi) and is surrounded by a coral reef and various islets. This isolated volcanic island has developed an environment that contains many unique species of flora and fauna. Originally a stopping point for passing mariners, who used to restock their larders with endemic Rodrigues giant tortoises (to such an extent that they soon became extinct), the island was a French possession until the British captured it in 1809. The capital is Port Mathurin on the north coast.

The landscape is a memorable mix of towering central massif, craggy hillsides, windswept pastures, a rocky shoreline punctuated by white beaches and an extensive lagoon that comes complete with tiny 'desert islands'. For more active visitors, this is a haven for hikers and nature lovers, whilst those who simply want to laze around in the sun or enjoy water sports will not be disappointed.

However, the true strength of Rodrigues is that the island is a tranquil place where time seems to have stood still. Residents live an unhurried traditional life, far from the pressures of the modern world, cultivating fruit and vegetables, raising animals, fishing in the lagoon (especially for octopus) and creating wonderful handicrafts. Their friendly character and warm welcome will be long remembered by visitors. Those who want to get away from it all and experience the magic of Rodrigues will find a selection of accommodation ranging from 5-star hotels through to comfortable cottages. It's a long way from anywhere, but the necessary effort is definitely worthwhile.

The windswept pastures of Rodrigues Island

Réunion Island

Not everyone knows this, but Réunion is part of the European Union, being one of France's fully incorporated overseas *départements*. As such, it is one of the French Republic's 26 regions, with the same status as those on the European mainland. Because Réunion is in a time zone to the east of Europe, the first-ever purchase with the EU's new currency was made here in 2002 – a 1-euro bag of lichees in Saint-Denis market.

This tropical island is in the Indian Ocean, 200 km (130 mi) to the south west of Mauritius. The British seized the Mascarene Islands early in the 19th century, but Réunion was later returned to France. It was uninhabited when the first Europeans visited – Portuguese explorers in 1513 – but the Réunion of today is well populated and economically successful. It is 63 km (39 mi) long by 45 km (28 mi) wide.

Réunion's claim to vulcanological fame is that – like Hawaii – it is located on a hotspot above the earth's crust. The Piton de la Fournaise is a shield volcano that has erupted more than one hundred times since the 17th century and is still erupting, most recently in 2007. The higher Piton de Neige is an extinct volcano. The island has a great variety of landscapes – volcanic peaks and lava beds, heavily forested slopes, coastal lowlands, rocky shores and a few sandy beaches (black and white).

Tourism is an important economic activity and a typically French range of accommodation may be found – hotels, pensions, gîtes and the occasional resort. Getting around isn't hard – there is a good public bus service on paved roads, though traffic can jam up at peak times – and Réunion offers a really excellent and varied range of interesting visitor attractions.

A waterfall in the Marsouins River plunges down a heavily forested slope.

POPULATION:
785,000 (2007 estimate)
WHEN TO GO:
The very rainy season (December to March) is best avoided.
HOW TO GET THERE:
By air, ideally (for cost reasons) from Paris or Mauritius. By boat from Mauritius.
HIGHLIGHTS:
The Aquarium de la Réunion, for a wonderful presentation of the island's marine life.
Three impressive volcanic calderas – Cirque de Salazie, Cirque de Cilaos and Cirque de Mafate.
Croc Park – over 150 snappy crocodiles occupying pools in a forest setting.
In the beautiful old Colonial Council building at Saint-Denis – the island's Natural History Museum.
The Cooperative de Vanille de Bras-Panon, for a fascinating insight into the traditional production of vanilla.
YOU SHOULD KNOW:
Back in 1952, the greatest 24-hour precipitation ever recorded took place on Réunion – 1,869.9 mm (73.6 in). And 3,929 mm (154.7 in) once fell in 72 hours.

The Comoro Islands

This archipelago lies in the Mozambique Channel between Madagascar and the African mainland. The former French possession divided into two entities in 1976 – the Union of the Comoros and Mayotte, which chose to remain a French overseas collective. Both have a largely Muslim population. The political situation remains unstable – each of the Union's smaller islands has made a unilateral declaration of independence (since rescinded) and there have been numerous coup attempts in the Union, which claims Mayotte.

Be that as it may, the Union (population 798,000 in 2005) and Mayotte (population 186,000 in 2007) have a lot to offer the intrepid traveller who does, however, have to get used to the variety of alternative names used to describe these fascinating islands. The Union is made up of Grand Comore (Ngazidja), Anjouan (Nzwani) and Mohéli (Mwali). Mayotte consists of the two islands of Grand-Terre (Mahoré) and Petite-Terre (Pamanzi).

Grand Comore is the largest island, an irregular plateau anchored by two volcanoes and shaped by lava flow. Anjouan is a similar lava plateau with three mountain chains. Mohéli is the smallest, with valleys and forests running down from the central mountain chain. Together, they extend to 2,235 sq km (863 sq mi). Mayotte has an area of 375 sq km (145 sq mi) and the gently rolling land rises to volcanic mountains.

The economy of the Comeros is based on small-scale farming, animal husbandry and fishing, augmented by financial support from France. Tourism is not highly developed in the islands, but those who make the journey find good accommodation and an unspoiled place whose colourful and friendly people live as they always have. The beaches rank alongside the world's best – there are splendid reefs, beautiful lagoons, lush forests, volcanic lakes, tumbling waterfalls and picturesque former colonial towns.

POPULATION:
985,000 (estimate)

WHEN TO GO:
Choose your preferred weather – hot, wet and humid from November to April; hot, dry, windy, cool at night between May and October.

HOW TO GET THERE:
The Union is served by Hahaya Airport at Moroni on Grand Comore, which accepts international flights and is also the base for island-hoppers. Fly to Mayotte from Paris via Réunion or Moroni.

HIGHLIGHTS:
The capital of Anjouan, with its bustling streets and alleys, old Sultan's Palace and Friday Mosque.
An area of outstanding natural beauty on Anjouan – the Dziancoundre Waterfall.
An expedition to Karthala, an active volcano on Grand Comore.
Mohéli Marine Park off the island's south coast, where humpback whales breed and green turtles nest.
The bustling market at Dzaoudzi on Mayotte's Petite-Terre for an authentic slice of island life.

YOU SHOULD KNOW:
Two-thirds of the world's natural perfume essence comes from the Comoros, after being processed from orange, jasmine and ylang-ylang blossoms.

Local boys take the plunge!

The Maldives

The Republic of Maldives is an island nation that consists of 26 main atolls encompassing some 1,200 islets, 200 of which are inhabited. They are scattered in the Indian Ocean 700 km (435 mi) to the south-west of Sri Lanka. With a maximum natural height of 2.6 m (7.5 ft), the Maldives are threatened by global warming, as a comparatively modest rise in sea level would make them uninhabitable. Havoc caused by the tsunami in 2004 serves as a stark reminder of the sea's destructive power.

Tourism is the major money-spinner. Visitors are wooed with the slogan 'the last paradise on earth' and they do indeed enjoy relaxed resort holidays in an idyllic setting, with a pleasant climate that encourages water sports such as fishing, swimming, snorkelling, scuba diving, water skiing and windsurfing. A typical resort in the Maldives will consist of an island occupied only by the workforce and visitors, with no local inhabitants, which will be up to 1,000 m (3,300 ft) by 250 m (800 ft) in size. There will be swaying palm trees and a beautiful beach encircling the island, protected by a house reef that encloses a safe lagoon. They come in three varieties – luxury for honeymooners and the jet set, family resorts and dive resorts.

The capital is Malé, an extraordinary city that occupies an entire island – a place of contrasts where high-rise buildings rub shoulders with the narrow streets, lanes and alleys of the old bazaar area. This crowded place houses a quarter of the country's population and is about as close as tourists get to the 'real life' of the Maldives – most of the other islands with local communities are off the tourist map. But if sun, sea and sand are your idea of bliss, the Maldives will delight.

POPULATION:
299,000 (2006)

WHEN TO GO:
High season (December to April) gets the best weather but is expensive (if you fancy Christmas, start entering the nearest lottery now). Low season has higher humidity and occasional squalls.

HOW TO GET THERE:
Fly in to Malé International Airport on Hulhulé Island right next to the capital. Onward transfer to resorts by float plane or boat.

HIGHLIGHTS:
A stay on Seenu (Addu Atoll) for a chance to meet and mix with local people in traditional island communities.
The 450-year-old Friday Mosque (Hukuru Miskiiy) in Malé – it has a superb interior. The nearby minaret dates from 1675.
For divers – the internationally famous Banana Reef dive site, against a backdrop of dramatic cliffs and caves.
The National Museum in Malé, containing many treasures once owned by local sultans, together with pre-Islamic stone carvings.

YOU SHOULD KNOW:
Don't expect a bargain – there is no budget accommodation or travel, resorts are expensive and innumerable 'extras' are charged.

An aerial view of the breathtaking islands and lagoon

Sri Lanka

POPULATION:
20,000,000 (2003)
WHEN TO GO:
December to March on the S and W coasts, and the hill-country; May to September on the E coast. But any other time, the rain isn't constant, and there's always a beach fit for purpose. Come for August's Kandy Esala Perahera, a brilliant 10-day festival in honour of the sacred tooth relic of the Buddha, or the Kataragama Festival.
HOW TO GET THERE:
By air, to Colombo.
HIGHLIGHTS:
The Festival of Kataragama in the SE hills during August, when tens of thousands of Hindus, Buddhists and Muslims unite in pilgrimage to one of Sri Lanka's most important and holiest sites.
The water gardens and royal palace of the 5th century rock fortress of Sigiriya – and the nearby 19 km (12 mi) 1st century, 200 m (560 ft) high cave temple of Dambulla, where the gilded caves shelter 6,000 sq m (20,000 sq ft) of Buddhist murals.
Sunrise at World's End, a 700 m (2,400 ft) vertical drop at the edge of Horton Plains National Park, a 2,000 m (6,500ft) high grassland plateau full of birds and wildlife.
The Pinnewala Elephant Orphanage and Hakgala Natural Reserve, set among the dense forests and oceans of tea in the plantations around Nuwara Eliya, famous as a hill station favoured by the colonial British.
Anuradhapura, Sri Lanka's capital for 1,300 years until the 10th century, and home to the world's oldest authenticated tree – the 2,000 year-old sacred Bodhi tree brought by the sister of Mahinda, who brought Buddhism to the island. One of seven UNESCO World Heritage Sites on the island.
YOU SHOULD KNOW:
The Rabana is a huge circular drum used (usually by women in the villages) on holidays and during festivals for long-distance gossip – it's fundamental to the blazing colour and sound characteristic of Sri Lanka's ancient folk culture.

The Pearl of the Indian Ocean lies only 31 km (19 mi) off India's south coast. Its modern name is taken from the Sanskrit ancient Indian epics *Mahabharata* and the *Ramayana*, and means 'resplendent land'.

Sri Lanka's chief characteristic is intensity – of colour, of beauty, of religious belief, of sectarian commitment, and of affection it inspires in everyone who goes there. The first to stay became the stuff of legend: the 2,500 year-old *Mahawamsa* chronicle describes the arrival of the 'Sinhala' ('lion race'), and the island's history since has been a series of shifting kingdoms, each leaving a treasury of ruins and literature, and a tangle of relationships that are still being decoded in its modern political life. When you go to Sri Lanka's cultural triangle of Anuradhapura, Polonnaruwa and Dambulla/Sigiriya, you see the architectural glories of the past, but they are living history. They are active religious sites, not floodlit movie sets.

The island has the perfect set-up. At any time of year you can lounge on immaculate beaches, and cool off in the hills when you get hot. Colombo, the capital, is a chaotic modern city, and an appropriate synthesis both of Sri Lanka's indigenous cultures and its Portuguese, Dutch and British influences. Tropical beaches stretch north to the bustle of Negambo, a characteristic fishing community; and south in a chain of pink and white arcs, past turtle hatcheries (Indurwa), masked carvers (Ambalangoda), and the coral reefs of Hikkaduwa. Go to Yala West National Park, a teeming rainforest of elephants, leopards, buffaloes, monkeys, crocodiles, deer, sloth bears and a galaxy of birds, on your way to the lush, lakeside hill resort of Kandy. It's Sri Lanka's exotic spiritual centre, and its spectacular parades of frenetic dancers, firewalkers and pounding drummers are, in fact, often a signal to prayer.

Buddhist monks watch elephants in the river at the Pinnewala Sanctuary

A pristine white beach – so typical of the beautiful Cocos Islands

Cocos Islands

Stick a pin in a globe through the Cocos (Keeling) Islands, and it emerges almost exactly through the Cocos in Costa Rica! Discovered in 1609, they were settled and owned by a single family from 1827 until the Australian Government acquired them in 1978.

Lying 2,770 km (1,732 mi) northwest of Perth, the 27 coral islands are formed into two large, heavily vegetated atolls. Not only are they the only atolls that Darwin ever visited, but the coral ecosystem remains intact – and you can still see in their pristine condition exactly why they played such an important part in his theory of evolution. North Keeling, set apart from the other islands, isn't even inhabited; but you can see extreme rarities like the Cocos buff-banded rail, robber land crabs, and both green and hawksbill turtles among other wonders, under its protection as Pulu Keeling National Park, covering both North Keeling and its surrounding waters.

The Cocos (Keeling) islanders live on Home and West Islands, both given over to copra and coconut plantations that only add to their tropical glamour. There is no tourist industry at all. Instead, there are facilities for visitors, sponsored by islanders who take an almost personal interest in everyone who comes. If you happen to be there, you're genuinely welcome to participate in the school fête, sports day, or concert night; and you'd be an idiot not to join in quiz night at the Cocos Club, or not to watch the annual Ardmona Cup Aussie Rules football match. The tradition of hospitality is both Australian and Malay, representing the origins of the tight-knit community. The islanders, as much as the islands themselves, have retained a form of unpolluted innocence, and share a mutual respect that visitors immediately respond to. These islands are a dreamscape worthy of Gauguin.

POPULATION:
546 (2007)

WHEN TO GO:
Year-round. The trade winds last from April to September, and the calmer doldrum season from November to April. Rain is more intense between March and July, but it usually falls in the evening after long, sunny days.

HOW TO GET THERE:
By air, from Perth, to West Island, Cocos (Keeling) Islands

HIGHLIGHTS:
Swimming and snorkelling among the wrasse, parrotfish and reef sharks of the 'Rip' on Direction Island.
The details of Australia's first naval victory, the sinking of the SMS *Emden*, the World War I German raider, among many unusual documents and exhibits at the Museum on Home Island.
Cycling the tracks through the exuberant hibiscus and foliage to the majestic Alexandrian laurels (*Calophyllum* trees) of Bob's Folly, on your way to Trannies Beach, West Island.
Heading up to Northpoint or the West Island jetty at the full moon – when hundreds of land crabs make their way to the water to spawn.

YOU SHOULD KNOW:
Unless the front door of a house is wide open, it is considered more polite to go around to the back door than to knock on the front.

Majuli Island

POPULATION:
140,000 (2001)
WHEN TO GO:
November to April
HOW TO GET THERE:
Ferry from Jorhat
HIGHLIGHTS:
Visiting the *satras* – some of the specializations are dance and arts at Bengenaati, jewellery and handicrafts at Auniati and mask making at Shamaguri.
Ras Purnima, the three-day festival that takes place in October/November.
Angammi Tribal Museum at Auniati – containing old manuscripts and artefacts.
Bird watching.
Studying neo-Vaishavite philosophy at one of the satras. You might be able to stay there if you show real interest.
The spectacular sunsets over the Brahmaputra River.
YOU SHOULD KNOW:
As many as a hundred varieties of rice are grown on Majuli Island.

Majuli Island lies in the Brahmaputra River in Assam. Once it was the largest riverine island in the world, but every year the monsoon erodes more of its shore, and though it is still large – about 1,440 sq km (555 sq mi) – the island is shrinking at an alarming rate. Formed after a flood in 1750 when the river divided, it is a tranquil, flat, watery area, mostly consisting of paddy fields, water meadows, rivers and lakes and it's home to many rare and migratory birds.

Traditionally, the islanders – who comprise several tribal groups – cheerfully rebuild their bamboo and mud houses after each monsoon season, but recently several villages have been entirely lost. It is to be hoped that the government honour its undertakings to prevent this unique location from disappearing completely.

Majuli is famous for its *satras* – Hindu monasteries set up in the 15th century by the philosopher Srimanta Sankardeva, who frowned on the caste system and idolatry. Now villagers meet in the large prayer halls to praise Vishnu in music, dance and poetry. Around 20 of the original 65 *satras* survive; as well as serving as places of worship, they are important as treasuries of the area's culture, each one specializing in a different branch of the arts. The main settlements and *satras* are Kamalabari, with its centre for learning, and Garamur, which specialises in ancient weaponry.

The hospitable islanders tend dairy herds, fish and build boats. The women are famous for their exquisite weaving and their fine pottery. Majuli itself is renowned for the many different types of rice that are grown there.

Waiting for the ferry on the banks of the Brahmaputra River.

Diu Island

Diu is a former Portuguese possession that was taken over by India in 1961 and is now governed from Delhi. It is a small island – only 42 sq km (18 sq mi) – lying off the southern coast of Gujarat's Kathiawar Peninsula and it's joined to the mainland by two bridges.

Diu has preserved a distinctive Portuguese atmosphere and within the Old Town are narrow streets and many public and private buildings in Lusitanian style. Of the churches only one, St Paul's is still used for daily mass, whilst that of St Francis is now a hospital and St Thomas doubles as a museum and guest-house.

The Muslim, Hindu and Christian populations manage to co-exist with few problems, but as cheap alcohol is readily available and Gujarat is a dry state, Diu has something of a reputation for being a rather lively destination for Indian tourists.

The north and south coasts are very different with the former mainly comprising marshland and saltpans (flamingo and other water birds may be seen here in early spring) whilst the latter has limestone cliffs, inlets and sandy beaches. The most popular beach is at Nagoa, which is a favourite venue for Indian day-trippers and those interested in water sports, whilst further west lies the more western orientated resort of Sunset Point. For those interested in the more traditional aspects of Indian life the small fishing village of Vanakbori at the western end of the island has much to offer.

In general Diu is a laid-back and leisurely kind of spot and consequently walking, cycling and swimming tend to be the most popular activities for the tourist.

POPULATION:
21,576 (2001)
WHEN TO GO:
May to September
HOW TO GET THERE:
Flights from Mumbai to Diu airport or via road and rail links nearby on the mainland.
HIGHLIGHTS:
The Shell Museum near Nagoa beach – with over 2,500 shells collected by Captain Fulbaria over a period of 42 years.
The Portuguese fort – mostly dating from 1546-1650, this is now derelict but there is a good collection of cannons, cannonballs and parrots.
Fortim-do-Mar – a former jail just off the island. It's off limits to tourists, but you can circumnavigate it by hiring a fishing boat.
YOU SHOULD KNOW:
The spiky palm-like trees around Nagoa beach are Hoka trees imported from Africa 400 years ago; they don't exist anywhere else in India.

The bustling marketplace in the fishing village of Vanakbori

Kochi

POPULATION:
596,473 (2001)
WHEN TO GO:
March to October.
HOW TO GET THERE:
Fly to Kochi International Airport.
HIGHLIGHTS:
Kalady – on the banks of the River Periyar, this is the birthplace of Sri Adi Sankaracharya, the Hindu philosopher. The Adi Sankara shrine and eight-storey painted Adi Sankara Keerthi Sthambam.
The elephant sanctuary – just north of Guruvayur at Punnathur Kotta, this former rajahs' palace is home to 50 elephants.
Mattancherry Palace – built by the Portuguese, then modified by the Dutch in the 17th century and presented to the Rajah of Cochin. It has fine murals depicting scenes from the Mahabharatha and Ramayana.
Jew Town – the rajah gave the area known as 'Jew Town' to the Jewish community to protect them from persecution. The Paradisi Synagogue, built in 1568, is magnificently decorated with Chinese tiles and Belgian chandeliers.
YOU SHOULD KNOW:
The city is also known as Cochin.

Built on a series of islands and peninsulas, between the western ghats in the east and the Arabian Sea in the west, Kochi is the capital city of the enchanting southern Indian state of Kerala. During its long and fascinating history, the city has been occupied by the Arabs, British, Chinese, Dutch and Portuguese, all of whom have left their mark on the culture and architecture of this vibrant place. When you see fishermen plying the coastal waters with massive Chinese fishing nets as you stroll down Fort Kochi beach against a backdrop of European-style residences, you will realize what a mixture of cultures exists here.

The city became a major player in world trade when Kodungallur (Cranganore) was destroyed by flooding in 1341 and a natural harbour formed at Kochi. Kochi became a prosperous port trading in pepper, cardamom, cinnamon, cloves and other products native to the area's lush soils.

Kochi is still an important trading port today. The modern port is sited on Willingdon Island, a man-made island created from the materials dredged while deepening Kochi Port. The island is named after Lord Willingdon, a former governor of Madras who was involved in the project. Willingdon Island soon became the commercial heart of the city. It is connected to the mainland by Venduruthy Bridge and today houses some of the district's best hotels.

Bolghatty Island, also known as Ponjikara, is popular with tourists and houses the Bolghatty palace. The palace was built by the Dutch during their occupation and is today a heritage hotel. The island also

Fishermen at Fort Kochi

has a golf course. Vypin Island was formed after the flood in 1341. Today it has one of the highest population densities in the world. It is connected to Kochi by a bridge and ferry.

Kochi boasts plenty of historical and cultural gems for the visitor. These include St Francis' Church, the oldest European church in India and burial place of Vasco da Gama. Vasco House, on Rose Street, with its glass paned windows and sweeping verandahs, is one of the oldest Portuguese homes in the country.

Sited on a pretty island on Vembanad Lake, Vallarpadam Church has a serene and calm atmosphere. The church was built by Portuguese missionaries in 1524. It is said that the missionaries discovered a painting of the Lady of Ransom and, later in a dream, were asked to establish a church in Vallarpadam. Mattancherry Palace was built by the Portuguese, then later modified by the Dutch and presented to the Rajah of Cochin. The beautiful palace has served as the location for many coronations throughout history.

Chorao Island

Up-river from Panaji and close to historic Old Goa, Chorao lies between the wide, slow Mandovi and Mapusa rivers. Its Sanskrit name, Chuddamani, means 'Most Beautiful Diamond'. It is a peaceful, lush area of mangroves and fertile fields, with navigable waterways and some protective banking. The Mandovi River is partly tidal and the mixture of fresh and salt water makes the island a prime site for water birds, some migratory, and the southwest region is an important bird sanctuary. Sadly, river traffic is eroding the fragile shores. To some extent, Chorao has been protected by the stop-go construction work on a hugely expensive bridge project – while the island had only its ferry links it was shielded from destructive development. It is to be hoped that awareness of the delicate ecological balance will continue to keep this place unspoilt.

It is said that centuries before the Portuguese arrived, this was a place of learning, with a university of Sanskrit. In the 16th century, the Portuguese re-named the island, and Christianized it. It was such a pleasant place to live that many fine mansions with lovely gardens were built for the gentlemen who were ferried down river to work in crowded Panaji and it became known as the 'Island of Noblemen'. But, like Old Goa, it was depopulated by epidemics, and now all that remains of the Portuguese are a couple of churches and views of the skyline of Old Goa over the river.

Hindu temples were rebuilt in the 20th century and Hindus are now the majority here. The islanders fish, grow cashews and produce a liquor called Fenny. Most of the colonial buildings lie in moss and creeper-covered ruins.

POPULATION:
18,500 (2004)
WHEN TO GO:
November to March
HOW TO GET THERE:
Ferry from Ribander or Pomburpa. By bridge from Bicholim.
HIGHLIGHTS:
Dr Salim Ali Bird Sanctuary – many species, including grey and purple herons and the migrating Siberian crane, may be spotted from a boat trip through the mangroves.
The 16th century church of St Bartholemew.
The adjoining island, Divar – an important place of Hindu pilgrimage.
YOU SHOULD KNOW:
A large Jesuit seminary, now in ruins, was once the home of the Patriarch of Ethiopia.

Lakshadweep Archipelago

POPULATION:
60,595 (2001)
WHEN TO GO:
October to April
HOW TO GET THERE:
Flights from Kochi and Bangalore to Agatti or ferryboat from Kochi.
HIGHLIGHTS:
Seeing India's only true coral atolls, often barely 1.83 m (6 ft) above sea level.
Diving – there are packages for beginners and experienced divers (health certificate required).
Minicoy Island's lighthouse, dating from 1885.
The aquarium on Kavaratti Island.
The unusual walking sticks made of tortoise shells and coconut shells by craftsmen on Amini Island.
YOU SHOULD KNOW:
Marco Polo referred to Minicoy as 'the island of females'.

Though the name means 'hundred thousand islands', there are about 36 islands and islets in this archipelago, which is the smallest union territory of India. Eleven of the group, which lies 200-300 km (125-186 mi) off the coast of Kerala in the Arabian Sea, are inhabited. The total land area is just 32 sq km (12 sq mi) and none of the islands exceeds 1.6 km (1 mi) in width. The islands are coral atolls and reefs, inhabited on the eastern sides and protected by lagoons on the west. Like all 'coral islands', they offer superlative swimming and diving.

The islanders are related to the people of Kerala and the language is Malayalam, except on Minicoy, where both the ethnicity and the language (Mahl) are related to the Maldives. Almost the whole population is Muslim; in the 7th century missionary work and contact with Arab traders persuaded the islanders to convert. From the 12th to the 18th century, when the British took control, the islands were ruled by successive *bibis* ('female rulers') and their husbands, and now it is a matrilinear society where women enjoy unusual economic independence.

The islanders cultivate bananas and vegetables in the rich coral soil, but the mainstay is the coconut. The fibre products, coir and copra, have always been in great demand. Fishing is important, and Minicoy has a tuna-processing plant. The government is now promoting tourism to bolster the economy and Lakshadweep is becoming a popular destination for Indians. Though western visitors – notably Vasco da Gama and Ibn Batuta – explored extensively in the past, today there are very strict limits for foreign tourists and alcohol is prohibited. The easiest way to see Lakshadweep is by organized tour.

An aerial view of the islands and reefs

Andaman and Nicobar Islands

This large group of over 570 islands – of which around 30 are inhabited – lies in the Bay of Bengal quite close to the Indonesian island of Sumatra, but more than 1,000 km (625 mi) from India, of which it is part. It is thought that the name Andaman derives from the name of the Hindu monkey god Hanuman, as most of the islands' inhabitants are Hindu, though there is a sizeable Christian minority. At present the Nicobars may not be visited and access to some of the Andamans is restricted.

The penal colony at the capital Port Blair on South Andaman became notorious in 1872 after the murder of the Viceroy. It lasted until Independence in 1947. Since then, mass immigration from India and developing tourism have effected change. Though the high rainfall and humidity make malaria a risk, and the best beaches are on islands remote from Port Blair, the crystal clear waters and abundance of natural life make a visit worthwhile. A high percentage of the hundreds of bird, animal and plant species are unique to the islands and the butterflies and moths are among the most spectacular in the world. Beaches are rich in shells and corals.

Some of the many islands that can be visited from Port Blair are Interview Isle with its population of feral elephants (left there by loggers), Havelock Isle, settled by Bengalis after Partition, with mangrove swamps and superb snorkelling and Viper Isle, which was once home to several prominent political prisoners, including Subhar Chandra Bose. India's only active volcano can be seen on Barren Isle. On Ross Island the buildings and gardens of the old British administration are deserted.

POPULATION:
356,265 (2005)
WHEN TO GO:
November to May
HOW TO GET THERE:
Flights or ferry boats from Kolkata and Chennai to Port Blair.
HIGHLIGHTS:
The Cellular Jail National Memorial at Port Blair, which now has a museum and a Sound and Light show describing its grim history.
Samudrika Naval Maritime Museum – with displays of marine biology and of the flora and fauna as well as information on tribal communities.
Viewing the marine life from glass bottomed boats.
Scuba diving and snorkelling in the Mahatma Gandhi National Maritime Park, which covers 15 islands.
The Mount Harriet nature trail – for the birds, animals, butterflies.
The Island Tourism Festival in January – with lots of music and dancing.
YOU SHOULD KNOW:
Part of the Sherlock Holmes story 'The Sign of Four' is set in the British penal colony; later in the story, an islander, complete with blowpipe and poisoned darts, appears in London.

Elephants enjoying the cooling effects of the sea.

ASIA

Tioman Island

POPULATION:
3,000 (2005)
WHEN TO GO:
April to December.
HOW TO GET THERE:
By ferry from Mersing or Tanjung Gemuk on the mainland, or by plane from Kuala Lumpur or Singapore.
HIGHLIGHTS:
Snorkelling and diving – there are some lovely reefs with colourful corals and plenty of fish. The best are at Paya, Pulau Tulai, Renggis Island and Air Batang.
Monkey Beach and Monkey Bay – lovely yellow-sand beaches perfect for relaxing. Rainforest walks – explore the dense forest and spot some of the varied wildlife here. Be sure to take water, insect repellent and a hat.
YOU SHOULD KNOW:
The beaches of Tioman appeared in the 1958 film *South Pacific* as Bali Hai.

Tioman Island (Pulau Tioman) is a small island around 32 km (19 mi) from Malaysia, one of about 60 volcanic islands situated off the southern shores of Malaysia's east coast. The island, 39 km (24 mi) long and 12 km (7 mi) wide, is densely forested and surrounded by some spectacular beaches and coral reefs, making it a great place for rainforest treks, relaxing on the beach and snorkelling. The island is sparsely inhabited, with eight main villages, the largest being Kampung Tekek in the north.

The island was used by Arabian merchants in the 10th century, as well as merchants from India, Persia and China who came to export betelnut, sandalwood and camphor. In 1830, pirates landed here and took 70 of its inhabitants away as slaves, leaving the island deserted for 15 years. In the 1920s the island was again deserted after a devastating outbreak of malaria swept through the population.

The most popular activity for visitors to Tioman Island today is snorkelling, and some of the best sites include Paya, which offers a variety of colourful corals and fish, Pulau Tulai (Coral Island) and Renggis Island where the water is pristine. At Air Batang there is a vast garden of yellow coral, and turtles can be spotted here.

Already the most developed of Malaysia's eastern islands, Tioman is the site of a $10 million marina project, complete with cargo jetty extending 175 m (574 ft)into the sea at Kampung Tekek. The Malaysian Nature Society and WWF Malaysia have described the project as a disaster for the environment. Construction has already caused the widespread death of corals and much of the marine life around the site, so be sure to choose one of the other beaches for snorkelling and diving.

At Juara, a lovely quiet beach on the east coast of Tioman, three rivers flow down from the mountains and onto the beach, offering a refreshing alternative to swimming in the sea. A path leads from the beach to a series of waterfalls in the jungle where you can swim and climb over the large rocks.

The interior of the island, around 12,000 hectares (29,652 acres) of dense verdant rainforest, is a strictly enforced nature reserve. There are many endemic species here, and among the protected species of mammals are the mouse deer, binturong, black giant squirrel, long-tailed macaque, slow loris, brush-tailed porcupine, red giant flying squirrel and common palm civet. If you are lucky you may spot a soft-shelled turtle or a Tioman walking catfish while in the rainforest.

Verdant rainforest covers the interior of the island.

The beach at Pantai Cenang

Langkawi

Langkawi is the collective name for an archipelago of around 100 islands in the Andaman Sea, close to the north Malaysian coast. Only two are inhabited – Pulau Langkawi, the main island, and Pulau Tuba, and these are islands of rocky mountains, lush jungle and white sandy beaches lapped by green water.

'Langkawi' is sometimes translated as 'Land of Eagles', and you can still see white-bellied fish eagles here. However, the group is more popularly known as the 'Isles of Legends', and the best known of these is of Mahshiri, a beautiful woman falsely accused of adultery. It is said that when executed for this crime, she bled white blood, and cursed the islands for seven generations. Her tomb remains a major tourist attraction.

Curses notwithstanding, Langkawi has seen dramatic economic development in recent years: in 1987 it was designated a tax-free zone and later gained recognition as a UNESCO World Geopark. This combination has resulted in over two million visitors every year. Some of the best hotels in Malaysia are now situated here (this is not a budget destination!), mostly on the western side at Pantai Tenghah and Pantai Cenang, though the north coast is also developed. Despite this growth in tourism, the main town of Kuah retains its fishing heritage and relaxed lifestyle.

Government policy prohibiting beachfront development over coconut-tree-height is both commendable and in keeping with the up-market approach. Tax-free shopping aside, water sports are the major attraction here. Scuba diving and snorkelling are best within the Pulau Payar Marine Park. The interior of the island offers jungle trekking in one of the world's oldest rainforests, which is home to more than 200 bird species.

POPULATION:
60,000 (2005 estimate)

WHEN TO GO:
Year round

HOW TO GET THERE:
Boats from Penang, Kuala Perlis, Kuala Kedah and south Thailand. Flights from Kuala Lumpur, Georgetown, Ipoh, Singapore and Japan.

HIGHLIGHTS:
The cable car ride to the top of Gunung Mat Cinang.
Lagend Lankawi Dalan Taman in Kuah – a 20-hectare (49-acre) theme park with giant sculptures illustrating some of the islands' many legends.
Crocodile Adventure on the north coast – Malaysia's largest crocodile farm, with over 1,500 saltwater crocs.
Telaga Tujuh – the 'Seven Pools' which you can slide down over the moss, preferably stopping before the water cascades over a cliff to form a 90 m (295 ft) waterfall.
The palace built in 1999 for the film *Anna and the King* which you may visit whilst it still stands.

YOU SHOULD KNOW:
The Galeria Perdaria contains a strange collection of over 10,000 items presented to the former Malaysian Prime Minister Dr Mahathir, who has been very influential in promoting Langkawi.

A street trader in Penang

Penang

Situated on the north-western coast of the Malay Peninsula at the entrance to the Straits of Malacca, Penang Island covers an area of 292 sq km (112 sq mi). The island is separated from mainland Malaysia by a channel of sea varying between 3 km (1.9 mi) and 13 km (8 mi) wide, and they are linked by the 13.5 km (8.4 mi) Penang Bridge, one of the longest bridges in the world.

The island has the oldest British settlement in Malaysia, which was founded by Captain Francis Light in 1786 while he was searching for a docking place for ships of the East India Company. Captain Light made a treaty with the Sultan of Kedah who gave him permission to colonize the sparsely populated island.

Penang today is a fine mixture of old and new: bustling, industrial port meets historic Old Town. In the capital, Georgetown, modern skyscrapers tower above one of the largest collections of pre-war buildings in south-east Asia. Colourful produce markets compete for space with high-tech electronics manufacturers. There is also a fascinating mixture of cultures here. Hundred-year-old churches, Chinese temples, Indian temples and mosques stand side by side.

In the middle of the bustling modern city is Penang Hill (Bukit Bendera), at almost 900 m (2,953 ft) high, with its cool, clean air. From its summit there are amazing views of the town, the island, and even the mountains on the mainland when the sky is clear. There is a Swiss-built funicular railway to take visitors to the summit, which creaks its way up through the beautiful tropical forest. At the top of the hill there is a café, a Hindu temple and a mosque.

If you want to escape the busy city, there are other attractions on the island, including plenty of lovely beaches, some quaint fishing villages, beautiful stretches of forest and cascading waterfalls. Among the less crowded beaches are Muka Head, Pantai Keracut, Monkey Beach, Pantai Acheh and Gertak Sanggul.

Penang Island is enriched by its numerous ethnic communities, among them Malays, Chinese and Indians, which live side by side in harmony to create a multi-faceted culture. Each community maintains its cultural identity through religious festivals and cultural shows, including angsawan, Boria, flag processions, the Chingay Parade, the Nine Emperor Gods Festival, the Hungry Ghosts Festival and Thaipusam. This succession of colourful festivals unravels throughout the year and when one big celebration is finished, another begins.

POPULATION:
678,000 (2000)
WHEN TO GO:
December to July
HOW TO GET THERE:
Fly to Penang International Airport, or cross the bridge from the mainland.
HIGHLIGHTS:
Penang Hill – trek up the hill or take the funicular railway to experience amazing views of the whole island.
Beaches – among the nicest beaches are Muka Head, Monkey Beach and Pantai Acheh.
Pantai Acheh Forest Reserve – this lowland forest covers most of the north-western tip of Penang Island and hosts a diverse eco-system of forest vegetation, mangrove swamps, rock coast and sandy beaches.
Snake Temple – built in 1850 to commemorate the Chinese monk Chor Soo Kong, the temple is situated in the small town of Bayan Lepas and is famous for the pit vipers which live in the temple.
YOU SHOULD KNOW:
The official religion is Islam, so avoid revealing clothing or displays of affection in public.

Labuan

Labuan consists of a main island and six smaller islands 8 km (5 mi) off the northwest coast of Borneo, north of Brunei Bay. Its name derives from the Malay for 'anchorage' and it is in fact Malaysia's only deep-water port. Once a part of the Sultanate of Brunei, it was ceded to Britain in 1846. During World War II it was occupied by the Japanese, and was finally handed to the Federal Government of Malaysia in 1984.

The ethnic composition is predominantly Malay, with a sizeable Chinese minority and some Indian immigrants and it feels quite cosmopolitan, especially in Bandar Labuan, the main town and port. Its position in the middle of the Asia-Pacific region and close to shipping routes and offshore gas and oil fields prompted the Government to encourage foreign investment, and today Labuan is a free port and International Offshore Financial Centre. As a result, duty free shopping is a great attraction for the many tourists who come from Brunei – there is even a month-long, end of year 'shopping carnival'.

The main island covers 75 sq km (50 sq m) and is essentially flat – the highest point is just 85 m (280 ft) above sea level – and mostly covered in vegetation. There is little agriculture – the best land is used for residential or tourist development or, in the southwest, shipbuilding, manufacturing and oil and gas production.

In addition to shopping, Labuan has some good beaches, notably Pohon Batu and Pancur Hitam. The clear blue waters around the islands are perfect for diving, and also offer marvellous fishing, both deep-sea and around the coasts.

POPULATION:
78,000 (2000 estimate)
WHEN TO GO:
January to March, July and August
HOW TO GET THERE:
By air from Kuala Lumpur and Brunei or by ferry from Sabah, Sarawak and Brunei.
HIGHLIGHTS:
The War Memorial, Allied Landing Point and Japanese Surrender Park.
The landscaped cemetery for 3,900 Allied soldiers, maintained by the Commonwealth War Commission, with a special section for the Punjab Regiment.
An Nur Jamek Mosque – an exciting work of modern architecture that cost US $11 million.
Wreck diving – one of the best sites in Asia, with World War II (including USS *Salute*) and post-war wrecks.
Sea sports – each May, the International Sea Challenge comprises an underwater treasure hunt, cross-channel swim, jet sport challenge and big-game fishing tournament.
YOU SHOULD KNOW:
The first Labuan postage stamps (1879) have the usual profile of Queen Victoria, but are highly unusual in incorporating Chinese and Arabic scripts.

Perhentian Islands

POPULATION:
1,100 (2000 estimate)
WHEN TO GO:
March to mid-November
HOW TO GET THERE:
Boats from two fishing villages on the northern Terenggam coast (Air-Kota Bharu airport has taxi desks where transport to the above and boat tickets are available).
HIGHLIGHTS:
Sunbathing, snorkelling, scuba diving and sea kayaking.
Shark and turtle watching (turtles nest on both islands).
Walking the jungle trails that cross both islands.
YOU SHOULD KNOW:
Accommodation is limited and advance booking strongly advised.

This small group of islands lying just 20 km (12.5 mi) off the northeastern Malaysian peninsula, consists of two inhabited islands, Perhentian Besar and Perhentian Kecil (large and small Perhentian), separated by a fast flowing channel, and a few uninhabited ones. The name in Malay means 'stopping point', though British translation had them marked on maps as 'Station Islands'. Sparsely populated by fishermen in the past, tourism is now the islands' mainstay.

These days the local government is keen to preserve the natural beauty of the area – the coral round the islands is some of the best on the east coast and the fine sandy beaches plus crystal clear water have proved a major attraction. In consequence, strict planning restrictions are enforced and a marine park conservation charge levied on all visitors. The three main beaches on the west coast of Perhentian Besar are divided by rocky outcrops. Perhentian Kecil, rapidly losing its previous backpacker image, has prime resorts at Long Beach and Coral Bay.

Apart from the village of Pasir Hantu ('Sand of Ghosts') on Kecil, where medical and police aid may be sought, the only island buildings are resorts. There is no mains electricity or main telephone network connection and the water is from local wells. The wearing of revealing clothing and the consumption of alcohol are not encouraged and the only available means of transport, other than walking, is by boat. The interiors reach a maximum of 100 m (328 ft) above sea level and are covered in dense tropical jungle with no roads and few footpaths. However, intrepid walkers may see flying foxes, macaques and monitor lizards.

The fine sandy beach at Pulauin

Pangkor Island

Pangkor is situated off the west coast of peninsular Malaysia, about halfway between Kuala Lumpur and Penang and only 7 km (4.4 mi) across from Lumut. It is a small island being only 8 sq km (3.2 sq mi) but it has an interesting history, having been a major tin producer in the 19th century. Problems within the local Malay/Chinese communities led to the 1874 Pankor Treaty, which ushered in British control in Malaya.

The island has some of the best beaches on this side of the Malay Peninsula and these are situated on the west coast. The east coast mainly consists of fishing villages, whilst apart from a few trails, the interior is largely inaccessible, despite there being a coast-to-coast road.

Fishing, boatbuilding and allied industries employ the majority of the population, with cuttlefish and anchovy being the most common type of catch – their early morning landing at Pangkor town is a bustling, colourful sight. The island is one of Malaysia's largest dry fish suppliers and in addition it is credited with the invention of 'Fish Satay'.

The main beaches are at Teluk Nipah, Pasir Bogak and Teluk Belanga, whilst at Teluk Ketapang ('Turtle Bay') if you are lucky, you might spot the increasingly rare giant leatherback turtles, which lay their eggs here from May to July. Jungle trekking in the interior offers the opportunity to see many rare orchids and butterflies – there is a four-hour trail that crosses the island. For the less energetic, it is possible to follow the road around the island in a day.

The main cultural event is the two-day Hindu festival of Thaipusam, which takes place between mid-February and early March. This begins on the west coast beach of Pasir Bogak and ends at the Pathirakaliaman Temple on the east coast and is worth catching if you can.

POPULATION:
25,000 (2005 estimate)
WHEN TO GO:
Year round
HOW TO GET THERE:
Direct flights from Kuala Lumpur or ferries from Lumut on the mainland.
HIGHLIGHTS:
The remains of the 17th century Dutch fort – situated in a pretty village, which still retains traditional stilted wooden houses.
Batu Bersrat – the Tiger or Written Rock – scene of an old legend, with the symbol of the Dutch East India Company and a depiction of a tiger stealing a child carved upon it.
Foo Lin Kong Temple – containing not only a shrine with shrunken heads but also a mini version of the Great Wall of China behind it.
YOU SHOULD KNOW:
The private island of Pangkor Laut just off the main island is Malaysia's most exclusive hotel, and a favourite with the late Luciano Pavarotti, after whom a suite is named.

The remains of the 17th century Dutch fort

Redang Islands

POPULATION:
2,500 (2006 estimate)
WHEN TO GO:
March to October
HOW TO GET THERE:
Flights from Kuala Lumpur or Singapore or ferries from Merang.
HIGHLIGHTS:
Learning to dive – Redang offers diving courses as well as dives for the experienced.
Turtles – the island is a conservation site for sea turtles; both the green and hawksbill nest here.
Forest geckoes – the large spotted Tokay gecko can grow to over 0.3 m (1 ft) long.
YOU SHOULD KNOW:
The festival of Candat Sotong in April involves using hand-held lines to catch squid.

There are nine islands in the Redang Archipelago, which is close to Merang on the coast of Terengganu State. Pulau Redang is popular with Malaysian tourists and those from further afield, and much of the east coast is now taken up with tourist development – even the forest has been cleared to make way for a golf course. Kampung Air ('Water Village') was built by the government in 1976 to rehouse the fishing families displaced by hotel building. Like the old village, it is built on stilts over the water; it houses around 1,200 people. Most of the east coast is now lined with up-market resorts.

The coral reefs around Redang and its satellite islands make up one of Malaysia's marine parks, whose management involves the protection of sensitive ecosystems from the impact of human activity.

Tourists are required to pay a conservation fee on arrival. Jet-skiing and water-skiing are banned to protect the coral, and the only fishing allowed in the park area is by the residents, but Redang offers exceptional diving and snorkelling. Outside the monsoon season, diving visibility is at least 20 m (66 ft) though corals and fish can be clearly seen a few metres from the beach. The reefs, composed of corals of a variety of colours and formations, teem with an extraordinary diversity of marine life, including angelfish, reef shark, squid, lionfish, butterflyfish and batfish. Most diving sites lie off the eastern shore, but it is also possible to snorkel off the southern coast and around the islets of Pulau Piriang and Pulau Ekor Tibu.

Banggi

Malaysia's largest island, with an area of 440 sq km (264 sq mi), Pulau Banggi is off the northeast coast of Sabah. It was finally recognized as belonging to Malaysia, after years of dispute with the Philippine Government. The inhabitants are comprised of Bonngi, who speak a unique form of Bornean dialect, and the Orang Sama, or Sea Gypsies.

Banggi is sparsely populated – there are just fifteen villages, renowned for their traditional tribal tree houses. Visitors may stay at a small Government Rest House, but in other respects there are few concessions to tourism here – there are no shops, TV or Internet access, and travel around the island is difficult.

Banggi is positioned where the Pacific and Indian Ocean biospheres meet and its great ecological significance is enhanced by the fact that the reefs are still undamaged by the destructive fishing methods that have despoiled many other southeast Asian sites. Fortunately, this is recognized, and Banngi is now part of a conservation area that covers a rich mix of habitat – reefs, sea grass, open sea and mangroves – where endangered species such as sea turtle and dugongs live.

Diving from these reefs is particularly rewarding – the water is warm and clear and, as well as many coral-dwelling fish, octopus, giant clams, sponges, crinoids and marine algae can be seen. Projects to improve the living standards of the islanders are also underway; the establishment of a commercial rubber plantation, and 'seaplant farming', an initiative by the University of Malaysia at Sabah for seaweed cultivation, will offer alternative livelihoods to the people of Banggi.

POPULATION:
20,000 (2003 estimate)
WHEN TO GO:
Year round
HOW TO GET THERE:
Ferries from Kudat – but departures are unpredictable
HIGHLIGHTS:
Tun Mustapha Marine Park – the site of the second largest coral reef in Malaysia.
Banggi Environmental Awareness Centre – an educational and information resource situated in the largest settlement at Karakit.

Singapore

POPULATION:
4,550,000 (2007)
WHEN TO GO:
January to May.
HOW TO GET THERE:
Fly to Changi Airport.
HIGHLIGHTS:
The Singapore Art Museum – located on Bras Basah Road in a renovated school house, the museum has 13 galleries and is home to the national art collection of Singapore. It was opened in 1996 and holds over 4,000 works of art.
Walking along the waterfront to Merlion Park – the park offers great views of the city's skyline, and an opportunity to see the famous merlion sculpture, a landmark of the city.
The Jurong Bird Park – one of the biggest bird parks in the world, with over 8,000 birds. See the parrot

On the southern tip of the Malay Peninsula, Singapore is one of the few city-states left in the world. The nation comprises one main island and 62 smaller islands in the mouth of the Singapore River. Since independence in 1965, it has become one of the world's wealthiest countries. Combining skyscrapers and subways, with traditional Chinese, Indian and Malay influences, it is a fascinating melting pot of different cultures, all adding their own distinct character to this bustling city. Add in a tropical climate, world-class food, excellent shopping and vibrant nightlife, and you have a very attractive destination.

In 1819, Sir Thomas Stamford Raffles landed on the island, at the time inhabited by just a few fishermen. He recognized its potential as a strategic trading post on the Spice Route and signed a treaty with Sultan Hussein Shah on behalf of the British East India Company to develop the island. Raffles declared Singapore a free port, with no duties or taxes, so the trading post soon grew into one of Asia's busiest, drawing traders from far and wide. It quickly became a great economic success and a jewel in the British colonial crown. William Farquhar, Raffles'

deputy, oversaw a time of rapid growth and immigration, fuelled by a no-restrictions immigration policy. Singapore was made a British crown colony in 1867, answering directly to the Crown. Just 50 years after Raffles arrived on the island, Singapore had a population of 100,000.

The island was taken by the Japanese during World War II but reverted back to British rule in 1945. In 1963 it joined with Malaya, Sabah and Sarawak to form Malaysia, but split again after two years to be an independent republic. Since then the state has seen a dramatic economic boom, owing to both foreign investment and government-led industrialization, which has created a modern economy based on electronics and manufacturing.

Shopping is a national pastime in Singapore, and there is an abundance of shopping malls in the city, particularly around Orchard Road. The low taxes on imports make prices competitive here. With its clean streets and anonymous architecture, Singapore can at first feel blandly modern. But beneath the glitzy surface there is a wealth of multi-cultural diversity as a walk around Chinatown, Little India or Geylang Serai will demonstrate.

circus, the penguin parade and demonstrations with birds of prey. The bird shows are great fun and a perfect way to entertain children.
Sri Mariamman Temple – the oldest Hindu temple in Singapore, the current structure was built in 1862. This colourful and decorative temple has been designated a National Monument by the government.
The food stalls in the hawker centres – here prices are low, hygiene standards are high and the food can be excellent.
The Botanic Gardens – the gardens cover 67 hectares (166 acres) and include the National Orchid Garden, with a collection of more than 3,000 species of orchid.

YOU SHOULD KNOW:
Singlish is commonly spoken on the streets of Singapore, a local dialect which mixes English, Chinese, Malay and Indian words and grammar.

Phuket

POPULATION:
313,835 (2007)
WHEN TO GO:
All year round, but best between November and May.
HOW TO GET THERE:
By air, bus or rail to Surat Thani and then bus, or by sea. Phuket is attached to the mainland by a bridge.
HIGHLIGHTS:
Diving and snorkelling off Phuket.
Yachting and sea canoeing around the island.
The Sino-Portuguese architecture in Phuket City.
Ko Sire with its sea gypsy village and reclining Buddha.
Sirinath National Park.
YOU SHOULD KNOW:
In 1785 Phuket was attacked by Burmese troops, in part of an attempt to take control of the country. The governor died and the island would have been taken but for his widow and her sister, who disguised Phuket's women as men and attacked the Burmese. Thinking that Phuket had received reinforcements, the Burmese withdrew. King Rama 1 bestowed royal titles on the sisters and their action is remembered by the Heroine's Monument, located at a roundabout on the main highway.

Thailand's largest and arguably most popular island, Phuket, lies in the Andaman Sea, off the west coast of southern Thailand, and is a province in its own right. In December 2004 the island was devastated by the tsunami that hit so much of Asia, and many coastal resorts and villages suffered terribly. Fortunately, Phuket is a wealthy province, and today, thanks to a major re-building programme, the island is back in business, and visitors are unlikely to see any noticeable damage.

Phuket is largely mountainous, its highest point being Mai Thao Sip Song at 529 m (1,745 ft), and much of it is forested. From the 16th century until relatively recently, tin mining was important to the economy, and the culture of the Chinese workers has informed that of Phuket. Other influences include Portuguese and Islam – some 35 per cent of the population are Muslims.

Phuket has been known as a holiday island since the 1980s, and its beaches sprout new resorts, restaurants and dive operations with every passing year. Most of the best beaches – huge swathes of white sand, or little sheltered coves – are on the west coast, but those towards the northern tip are much less visited. Patong, the most popular, is very highly developed, and Phuket City is awash with tourists shopping and partying the night away.

The island's interior is worth exploring, with rubber plantations, rice fields and fruit groves providing employment for islanders who live traditionally, a world away from the international tourism scene. Khao Phra Thaeo National Park, just 20 km (12.5 mi) from Phuket City, is a must – its hills and valleys are covered with tropical rainforest, and it contains a Lar gibbon rehabilitation centre. These charming creatures are endangered, and this project is important to their survival.

One of the many fabulous beaches on Phuket

Ko Phi Phi

Some 40 km (25 mi) from Krabi, off Thailand's south western coast, Ko Phi Phi is a group of limestone islands that jut sharply from the surrounding turquoise sea. Phi Phi Don is both the largest and the only one with a permanent population. Phi Phi Leh is much visited but uninhabited. The remaining islets are little more than limestone rocks.

Phi Phi Don divides into two sections joined by a narrow isthmus, on either side of which are two superb sweeps of white sand. It is startlingly beautiful with green hills culminating in astonishing cliffs plunging down to the water, many glorious beaches and unparalleled views. The islands are part of a National Marine Park, which should, though does not, protect them from the worst excesses of the developers.

During the 1940s, Phi Phi Don was populated by Muslim fishermen, and even now a good 80 per cent of the inhabitants are Muslims. Later, coconut plantations were introduced, but by the 1970s travellers had got wind of this remote and delicious paradise, and a fledgling tourist industry grew up. The good news is that as diving and snorkelling are so popular, the fishermen no longer use dynamite, and the surrounding coral is in better shape than it might be. Conversely, attempts to limit the numbers of tourists and tourist facilities, to better preserve the nature of the place, have failed due to greed.

Phi Phi Leh is all towering cliffs, caves and a sea lake. Tourists visit for the day to swim, but it is also famed as a centre of the birds' nest soup industry. Swiftlets nest high up in rocky hollows, and licenced collectors climb rickety-looking scaffolding three times a year to harvest these nests, made of saliva, which are as desirable and valuable to the Chinese as white truffles are to Europeans.

A beach on Ko Phi Phi Don

POPULATION:
1,500 (2006)

WHEN TO GO:
November to April

HOW TO GET THERE:
By boat from Phuket or Krabi.

HIGHLIGHTS:
On Phi Phi Don: Rock climbing. Sea kayaking. Game fishing. Snorkelling with sharks.
Viking Bird Nest Cave, with pre-historic wall paintings and nests on Phi Phi Leh.
The Beach – the actual beach made famous by the eponymous film starring Leonardo di Caprio.

YOU SHOULD KNOW:
Phi Phi Don was shattered by the 2004 tsunami. Over 70 per cent of the buildings were destroyed, about 4,000 people were drowned, survivors were evacuated and the island was closed. Help International Phi Phi was set up by a former (Dutch) resident and with the help of both Thais and back-packing volunteers cleared 23,000 tons of debris, 7,000 tons of it by hand. A second organization cleared debris from the bays and reefs and one year later 1,500 hotel rooms were back in action.

Ang Thong Archipelago

POPULATION:
100,000 (2004) over the 6 inhabited islands
WHEN TO GO:
December to February, August and September
HOW TO GET THERE:
Boat from Ko Samui
HIGHLIGHTS:
Ko Pha-Ngan and Ko Tao are two of the most beautiful islands. Take a sea-kayaking trip or snorkel around the coral reefs.
The salt water lake on Ko Mae Ko – its well worth the walk up to view the lake.
The views from the top of Wua Talap Island of the whole archipelago and across to the mainland.
YOU SHOULD KNOW:
Access to the National Park is controlled. Several boat rental companies in Ko Samui are licenced to hire boats to visit the islands.

Bathed in the aquamarine waters of the Gulf of Thailand about 30 km (20 mi) from Ko Samui, the Ang Thong Archipelago is a collection of 42 uninhabited islands famed for their natural beauty. The islands have been designated a National Marine Park to save them from development and excessive tourism, making them a pleasant and relaxing place to visit. The best way to explore is by boat as most of the islands are close together. Each island is different, but they are characterized by limestone cliffs, tropical forest, caves and secret lagoons, pristine white sand beaches, coral reefs and aquamarine waters.

Ko Mae Ko (Mother Island) is a must-see. Encircled on all sides by limestone cliffs, the emerald lake in the middle of the island is linked to the sea by an underground tunnel. It's a strenuous climb to view the lake but well worth the effort as you gaze down on the stunningly beautiful water and are rewarded by a spectacular view across the whole park.

Other popular islands are Ko Sam Sao (Tripod Island) with its extensive coral reef and Wua Talap Island (Sleeping Cow Island), the summit of which offers magnificent views across the entire archipelago and the mainland. The headquarters of the national park are situated here, and there is bungalow-style accommodation for visitors. There are caves in many of the islands with intriguing rock formations to discover. The lovely white sandy beaches, many of them deserted, are surrounded by coral reefs and the warm shallow waters are ideal for swimming. Other popular island activities include sea-kayaking and snorkelling around the coral reefs.

Ang Thong National Marine Park

Ko Lanta Yai

Situated off the coast of south-west Thailand, between the mainland and the Phi Phi islands, is another, less well known archipelago, Ko Lanta. Made up of 52 islands, 12 of which are inhabited, with only three of them easily accessible. Of these, Ko Lanta Yai is the largest, at 30 km (19 mi) long by 6 km (4 mi) wide. There are two main towns – Ban Sala Dan on the northern tip and Ban Ko Lanta, the district capital, in the east. This has bars, restaurants and shops, but remains a laid back, friendly place. Situated around the coast are several other villages and small resorts linked by a cement road.

Some of the archipelago is part of a National Marine Park; however Ko Lanta Yai is only partially protected, as much of the island belongs to the Chao Naam (sea gypsies) who settled here long ago. Fishing and tourism are mainstays of the economy and in the hilly interior, rubber trees, cashews and bananas are grown. Towards the south, pockets of forest still exist, though not for long if the developers have their way. For now, though, tourism is still less developed than it might be.

Visitors come for sun and sea, and the best beaches run all the way down the west coast of the island, virtually uninterrupted. Offshore there are coral reefs to marvel at and there is good diving just a boat ride away. The atmosphere on Ko Lanta Yai is less frenetic than that of Ko Phi Phi or Phuket, and development is slower. The joys of this place are simple – long walks on the beach, lazy days spent swimming, eating delicious seafood, reading, or snoozing in a comfortable hammock.

POPULATION:
20,000 over the 12 inhabited islands (2006)

WHEN TO GO:
November to March to avoid the monsoon.

HOW TO GET THERE:
By ferry from the mainland, Phuket or Ko Phi Phi.

HIGHLIGHTS:
Ban Sangka-U, a traditional Muslim fishing village.
Tham Mai Kaew, a series of limestone caverns.
A boat trip to Ko Rok Nok and Ko Rok Nai.
A night on tiny Ko Bubu.

YOU SHOULD KNOW:
Ko Lanta Yai escaped relatively lightly from the 2004 tsunami, losing 11 people. Tourists on the island at the time set about helping with the clean up, and most businesses were fully operational within just a few days.

A plantation of coconut palms alongside Klong Khong Beach

The Full Moon Party

Ko Pha Ngan

POPULATION:
11,846 (2004)
WHEN TO GO:
Any time, but December to June is probably best.
HOW TO GET THERE:
By boat from the mainland via Ko Samui, or from the outer islands.
HIGHLIGHTS:
A herbal sauna at Wat Pho.
Learning to meditate at Wat Khao Tham.
Laem Son Lake, a cool oasis.
A trek up Khao Ra, the island's highest point at 630 m (2,100 ft).
Taking a trip to Ko Tao, one of Thailand's major diving centres.
YOU SHOULD KNOW:
Plain-clothes policemen are always around at the Full Moon Party. Be careful, wear shoes to avoid dancing on broken glass, don't accept drinks from strangers – there are many reports of spiked drinks, picked pockets, attempted rapes, muggings and worse, so stay with your friends, and leave the scene if any trouble breaks out. There are also Half Moon and Dark Moon parties to attend if you haven't had enough.

The now notorious Ko Pha Ngan is an island in the Gulf of Thailand, about halfway between Ko Samui, to the south, and Ko Tao, to the north. Twenty years ago the island received just a tiny trickle of backpackers looking for escape from Ko Samui, which already appeared overcooked from a hippy point of view. Today the island is the home of the Full Moon Party, a monthly event that brings thousands of young travellers here to dance the night away.

The island's economy is almost entirely based on tourism, and almost all its beaches are home to little groups of inexpensive bungalows, and ever more trendy resorts, but it is the Hat Rin peninsula at the southeast of Ko Pha Ngan, with beaches to either side, that draws the crowds. The eastern side, Hat Rin Nok, is a long stretch of golden sand beach, backed by coconut trees. Once the site of a few cheap bamboo huts, a couple of cafés and no electricity, it is now lined with restaurants, shops and travel agents, as well as accommodation, and it's become 'traveller town'.

On full moon night everyone takes to the beach, many decorated in UV body paint, to drink and dance to sound systems playing booming house and trance music. And then there are the drugs – despite the heavy penalties that can be incurred, not to mention potential danger to health, drugs are still ubiquitous at this party, as the hospitals can attest.

Ko Pha Ngan is pretty, its hilly, forested interior includes a National Park. Trek up to great look-out points, or cool off under waterfalls if you need a rest. The main town, Thong Sala, is on the west of the island. However, you can choose to stay on a distant, secluded beach, accessible only by boat, and there you may still find a little peace.

Chalok Baan Kao Beach

Ko Tao

Ko Tao is situated a couple of hours boat ride from the mainland, in the Gulf of Thailand. Twenty years ago only the most intrepid of backpackers made it to the island, due to its relative remoteness. Today all that has changed, and Ko Tao has become a major dive centre.

This is a lovely place, all 21 sq km (8 sq mi) of it, and its rocky green interior is bursting with coconut groves. Those not involved with coconuts are either fishermen or in the rapidly expanding tourist trade. There are gorgeous little coves and beaches around the island, some of which are only accessible by boat, but it is the surrounding shallow coral reefs and marine life that are the main attraction here.

Of course you don't have to be a diver to enjoy Ko Tao, but if you are, or have ever wanted to be, this is a great place, and still reasonable, price-wise. The water is clear, the visibility excellent, and you will see a wealth of multi-hued fish and coral even if you stick to snorkelling. Less developed than neighbouring islands, there is still a variety of places in which to stay – everything from basic bamboo beach huts to boutique resorts.

One of the best dive sites is Sail Rock. Shaped like an iceberg, it rises from the sea floor at 40 m (132 ft) and reaches 15 m (50 ft) above the surface, providing fabulous dives for all levels of experience. At certain times of year, you might even get to see a whale shark...

Back on land, there are other activities to occupy your time – elephant rides, rock climbing, yoga, massage and cookery courses. Rent a bike and tour the island using the single existing road, walk, or just find a peaceful spot and laze the days away.

POPULATION:
5,000 (2006)
WHEN TO GO:
December to May
HOW TO GET THERE:
By boat from the mainland, Ko Samui or Ko Pha-Ngan.
HIGHLIGHTS:
Snorkelling at the Japanese Gardens.
Diving at Shark Island.
Diving at Southwest Pinnacle.
Spa treatments at one of the spa resorts.
Learning the martial art of qi gong.
YOU SHOULD KNOW:
Ko Tao literally means Turtle Island – it is thought that the island is shaped like a turtle diving south towards Ko Pha-Ngan.

Ko Samui

Ko Samui, in the Gulf of Thailand, lies some 80 km (50 mi) from the mainland town of Surat Thani. This was the first of the Gulf's islands to receive tourists – backpackers began arriving here about 30 years ago, moving on to Ko Pha Ngan and Ko Tao as the island became more developed. The building of an airport placed Samui firmly into the package holiday niche, leaving Pha Ngan to the partygoers and Tao to the divers.

Apart from tourism, the island is a huge coconut producer, harvesting some three million nuts per month, and palm trees and golden, sandy beaches are the hallmark of the place. At 15 km (9 mi) long and about the same in width, it's impossible not to notice that some of the development back from the beach is pretty nasty. Fortunately new construction cannot be higher than a coconut tree, although large hotel groups seem to get away with it.

Samui tries to cater for everyone, and the individual beaches that lie off the main coastal road do have their different atmospheres. Chaweng and Lamai are the most developed – some would say ruined! Maenam and Bophut are quieter while Choeng Mon, in the north east, is really the classiest, with a few smart hotels round a pretty, tranquil bay.

This is a classic Thai holiday island. People come to swim, snorkel, and wander along the beaches in the daytime, stopping for a bite to eat, a massage, or to have beads braided into their hair. At night there are endless restaurants, bars and clubs to visit, some of which are home to Thai sex trade workers. Ko Samui really does go out of its way to provide tourists with whatever they fancy.

POPULATION:
48,000 (2007)
WHEN TO GO:
Anytime, but it rains most in November.
HOW TO GET THERE:
By ferry from Surat Thani, Ko Pha Ngan or Ko Tao, or by plane from Bangkok, Phuket, Pattaya, Singapore, Hong Kong or Kuala Lumpur.
HIGHLIGHTS:
Bungy jumping at Chaweng beach.
Buffalo fighting.
Thai boxing.
The Butterfly Garden.
A day trip (at least) to the exquisite Ang Thong National Marine Park.
YOU SHOULD KNOW:
The first people to settle here were Chinese from Hainan Island, a mere 150 years ago. They were responsible for setting up the first coconut palm plantations.

Wat Plai Leam

The Islands of Phang-Nga Bay

Phang-Nga Bay is one of Thailand's most jaw-droppingly beautiful seascapes. Covering some 400 sq km (154 sq mi) tucked in between Phuket and Krabi, the bay, edged with mangrove forests, is home to hundreds of limestone karst formations. Some of these are tiny spires, some are large and bizarrely shaped, reaching up to 300 m (1,000 ft) in height, and all covered in tangled rain forest vegetation.

Formed some 12,000 years ago when the sea rose dramatically, flooding a limestone range that had already been eroded, some of the islands have been hollowed out by the forces of nature, leaving hidden, magical lagoons known as *hongs* in their centres. Invisible from the outside, the *hongs* are accessible by sea canoe, but it's only during certain tides that the channels beneath the seemingly impenetrable rock face are navigable. These secret lagoons are tidal, supporting their own ecosystems, while the enclosing circle of cliff walls are covered with extraordinary vegetation, reminiscent of a prehistoric world.

The central area of the bay boasts fantastically sculpted karst islands, including the famous 'James Bond' island, where *The Man with the Golden Gun* was filmed. A stop here, of course, is part of every itinerary and the souvenir sellers are all there, waiting to pounce. Very few of these islands are inhabited, and even fewer have anywhere to stay.

Ko Panyi is an exception – a Muslim fishing village, mainly built on stilts, it teems with visitors during the daytime, but after they have gone it reverts to relative normality. Here you can rent your own sea canoe, and explore the bay at your leisure. It really is quite something – the cliffs are coloured with red and orange sponges close to the water line, and the scenery is awe-inspiring. Apart from rock climbing, most people come here for water-based activities – sea kayaking, sailing and, above all, fishing.

POPULATION:
700 (2006 estimate)
WHEN TO GO:
December to May for the best weather.
HOW TO GET THERE:
By boat from Phang-Nga town, Phuket or Krabi.
HIGHLIGHTS:
Ko Panak, with its five hidden *hongs*.
Khao Kien, with its ancient rock paintings.
Ban Bor Tor, a long tunnel filled with stalactites and stalagmites.
YOU SHOULD KNOW:
These karst islands are the perfect environment for reptiles, in particular water snakes. Watch out for the water monitor, up to 2.2 m (7 ft) long – they look like crocodiles and haunt the mangrove swamps.

Some of the limestone spires of the islands of Phang-Nga Bay

Ko Chang

POPULATION:
5,000 (2007)
WHEN TO GO:
November to May for the best weather.
HOW TO GET THERE:
By boat from Laem Ngop, usually via Trat, which also has a small airport with flights from Bangkok and Ko Samui.
HIGHLIGHTS:
The waterfall at Klong Nueng.
The hornbills, sunbirds, parrots and other birds among the 61 resident species.
Visit Ko Kut, Ko Maak and Ko Wai, islands accessible from Ko Chang.
Travel to Cambodia, only 91 km (57 mi) north west of Trat.
YOU SHOULD KNOW:
Ko Chang was the site of a naval battle between the Royal Thai Navy and the Vichy French in January 1941, during which the Thais were trounced. There is a memorial on Hat Sai Yao (Long beach) marking this battle that gave rise to today's naval presence on Ko Chang.

Ko Chang is the largest of the 52-island archipelago that makes up the Mu Ko Chang National Marine Park. It is also Thailand's second largest island, after Phuket. At 30 km (19 mi) long and 14 km (9 mi) wide, it is no surprise that it is developing into a premier tourist destination, drawing both Thais and foreigners.

Less than a decade ago the island was well off the beaten track, but all that has changed, and today the west coast, strung with sandy beaches, is also strung with beach resorts and bungalows. A coastal road runs around the island, which is mountainous and densely forested in the interior – the highest point, Khao Salak Phet, reaches 743 m (2,500 ft) in height. Treks can be arranged, on foot or by elephant (Ko Chang means Elephant Island), and there are waterfalls in which to swim and magnificent scenery to enjoy.

The island's east coast has been saved from development by its lack of sandy beaches, and here life goes on in its traditional form, with tiny fishing villages, rubber and palm plantations, and fruit orchards. The National Park office can be found at Than Mayom, and the villages of Bang Bao and Salak Phet, on the south coast are both reasonably calm spots in which to stay – the former being the jumping off point for the archipelago's other islands.

Many visitors come to Ko Chang for diving and snorkelling, both of which are very rewarding here, although not as spectacular as the dive sites in the Andaman Sea. If you're looking for a fun, active, beach holiday, with plenty of nightlife, you needn't look further than Hat Sai Khao (White Sand Beach). Fringed by palms and casuarinas, this is Ko Chang's longest and most commercialized beach. For the other extreme, try Hat Sai Yao in the far south.

Hat Sai Khao

Ko Samet

Ko Samet, in the Gulf of Thailand, some 200 km (125 mi) south east of Bangkok, is a favourite holiday island for both Thais and foreigners alike. A mere 30-minute boat trip from the mainland, Ko Samet is quite easily reached from Bangkok, and its famous, white powder sand beaches have made it popular with everyone – families, backpackers, package holiday tourists, even working girls from Pattaya in need of a rest.

Declared a National Park in 1981, the island should have been protected from development, but in reality all the accessible beaches around this 6 km (4 mi) long island have resorts, beach bungalow operations, restaurants and bars lining the sand. Most of the development is on the east and north eastern side, while the most up-market resorts are at the northern tip, the west and the south. Outside the park, the only village, Na Dan, where the boats arrive, is where most of the population live.

The island's interior is quite different – mountainous and covered with dense rainforest, it shelters gibbons, long tailed macaques, monitor lizards, fruit bats, hornbills and many gorgeous butterflies. There are a few tracks cross the central ridge from east to west, but otherwise this at least is left in its natural state. It's worth trekking across though, for great cliff-top views and, of course, magnificent sunsets.

Hat Sai Kaew, or Diamond Beach, is the closest beach to the ferry pier, and at 780 m (2,600 ft) long, is an amazing swathe of sand. Soft and white, its high silicon content makes it squeak underfoot and obviously, it is extremely popular. If you walk south you'll find a mermaid statue, placed here in recognition of the 19th century epic poem written by one of Thailand's greatest poets, Sunthorn Phu, and partly set on Ko Samet.

POPULATION:
1,000 (2005 estimate)
WHEN TO GO:
Pleasant at almost any time of year, September and October bring the most rain.
HOW TO GET THERE:
By road to Ban Phe, then boat to Ko Samet.
HIGHLIGHTS:
Swimming, snorkelling and fishing off the island.
Watch a fire show at Ao Phai beach.
YOU SHOULD KNOW:
Don't buy anything from the touts at Ban Phe pier. Buy single ferry tickets to the beach you're aiming for and find accommodation once you have arrived – easiest on a weekday. Beware mosquitoes and petty theft.

Hat Sai Kaew

Surin Islands

POPULATION:
150 (2007 estimate)
WHEN TO GO:
The Park is only open from November to April, due to the difficult seas.
HOW TO GET THERE:
By pre-booked, live-aboard boat trip from Phuket or Ranong, or ferry from Khuraburi. Don't forget there is a fee to enter all of Thailand's National Parks.
HIGHLIGHTS:
The Visitor Centre and interpretive trail.
The turtle hatchery.
The Chao Leh village.
YOU SHOULD KNOW:
The Andaman Sea Chao Leh number about 5,000 altogether, divided into five groups with different dialects and customs. They have been around for hundreds of years, possibly originating in the Nicobar Islands. The Surin group are Moken, extremely traditional people who live mainly in houseboats called *kabang*, and collect shells and sea slugs, which they trade for food staples. Animist and musical, the Surin Moken are suffering horribly since the 2004 tsunami ruined their boats, and interference from outsiders has hindered more than it helped.

The Surin Islands are one of Thailand's least visited destinations. A group of five islands, both they and the surrounding waters form the Mu Ko Surin National Marine Park. Situated in the Andaman Sea, they lie some 55 km (34 mi) from the mainland, just south of the marine border with Myanmar.

The two main islands, Ko Surin Nua and Ko Surin Tai are separated by a narrow – 200 m (660 ft) – strait, which you can walk across at low tide. The other islands are simply rocky crags, with sparse vegetation. Until World War II they were uninhabited, and by 1981, when they became a national park, only a few hundred people lived here and therefore easy to relocate. Today, a few officials man the park office on Surin Nua, and a small community of Chao Leh (sea gypsies) live semi-permanently on Surin Tai.

The Surins are almost completely unspoilt. There are a few places to stay, (or you can hire a tent) and one, park-operated restaurant which rents out diving and snorkelling gear. There are glorious bays, full of marine life and pristine corals, and the islands themselves are spectacular, their summits rising from the sea, several hundred metres high. There are areas of mangrove, beach forest and dense tropical rainforest, all of which provide habitat for some 80 different species, including flying foxes, lesser mousedeer, reticulated pythons and the rare Nicobar pigeon.

Most visitors come on 'live-aboard' boat trips – the Surin Islands are marvellous for snorkelling and diving, and the coral-covered pinnacle of Richelieu Rock is a big draw, with whale sharks occasionally in evidence. If you can cope with the lack of five star facilities, arrange to stay on Surin Nua and relish the sense of remoteness, closeness to nature, and perfect peace broken only by the sound of the sea, the wind, bird and animal calls.

The Surin Moken are a nomadic tribe of sea gypsies who live in huts built on stilts.

Similan Archipelago

The reefs around the island contain some of the most stunning underwater scenery in the world.

Around 70 km from Phang Nga in southern Thailand, an archipelago of nine granite islands rises out of the Andaman Sea. The reefs around the islands, with some of the most stunning underwater scenery in the world, constitute one of the most famous dive sites in Thailand. The Similan Islands – Ko Bon, Ko Bayu, Ko Similan, Ko Payu, Ko Miang (two adjoining islands), Ko Payan, Ko Payang, and Ko Huyong – all fall within the Similan Islands National Park which was created in 1982. The park was recently expanded to include the two more remote islands of Ko Bon and Ko Tachai. Similan is a Malay word meaning nine.

The islands themselves are virtually uninhabited, apart from park rangers and tourists coming here for the diving. In fact, it is forbidden for tourists to land on several of them due to reef conservation efforts, and to protect the beaches where turtles come to lay their eggs. The island of Ko Pa Yan is owned by HM the Thai Princess who has a house there.

The islands offer two sorts of diving. On the eastern sides, which are protected from the monsoon storms, the white sandy beaches and gently sloping reefs provide safe and enjoyable snorkelling territory. The western shores of the islands get the full force of the waves, and here there are craggy granite boulders in amongst the reefs, with lots of swim-throughs, arches and caves up to 30 m (98 ft) deep. Probably the most famous dive site on the western side is Elephant Head rock, a maze of swim-throughs and sudden strong currents running in all directions.

The beautiful corals, sea fans and anemones make this an underwater paradise, which is teeming with marine life in all shapes and sizes. Shoals of vividly coloured fish such as angel fish, butterfly fish and many more swirl around the submerged landscape. The relatively strong currents around the islands keep the reefs clear of sand, making the water clear and visibilty good.

The islands are also an interesting place for keen birdwatchers. pied imperial pigeons, Nicobar pigeons, forest wagtails and white sea eagles are commonly sighted here, and as few species have been officially recorded on the islands, there is potential to add to the list. All the accommodation is on Ko Miang, and consists of small beach-side bungalows and ready-pitched tents, so expect basic facilities in this glorious location.

POPULATION:
Uninhabited
WHEN TO GO:
December to May
HOW TO GET THERE:
By boat from Phuket, Thap Lamu or Hat Khao Lak.
HIGHLIGHTS:
Diving and snorkelling the clear waters around the islands in one of Thailand's most glorious natural landscapes.
Hiking to the top of Ko Similan for breathtaking panoramic views across the archipelago.
The sea turtles at Ko Huyong – they come here to lay their eggs between January and July.
YOU SHOULD KNOW:
An entry fee is payable in cash when you enter the park.

Koh Rong

POPULATION:
50 (estimate)
WHEN TO GO:
Anytime, but the sea is more difficult to navigate between November and February.
HOW TO GET THERE:
By boat from Sihanoukville or Koh Sdach.
HIGHLIGHTS:
Koh Rong Samloen, with its beautiful beaches and heart-shaped bay.
A boat trip around the island.
Ream National Park on the mainland.

The Kampong Som Islands are another small group lying off Sihanoukville on the Cambodian coast, and Koh Rong, 44 km (27.5 mi) out to sea, is not only the largest of these, but also the second largest of Cambodia's islands. It does see a handful of visitors, mainly day-trippers from the mainland, but occasionally somebody stays and camps on one of the pristine beaches. This happy state of affairs is going to change over the next few years, as plans are afoot to turn both Koh Rong and its neighbouring island into major resorts.

In the meantime, this is pure Robinson Crusoe territory. Shaped like a dumbbell, the narrow 'waist' is flat, but both ends are mountainous and covered in thick, impenetrable jungle. On the southwest of the island is one of the world's most staggeringly beautiful beaches. Some 8 km (5 mi) of almost painfully bright

white sand curves gently into the distance, sand so fine that it lies in drifts and crunches underfoot, and fresh water streams down from the steeply forested hills. At one end is a fishing village, where basic supplies can be bought and a small, wooden temple stands on the southwestern point. The first set of beach bungalows for visitors are going up near here.

The abundance of fresh water feeds several mangrove forests around the coastline, but take a boat and you will find other empty coves and beaches to explore. Apart from the fantastic swimming and snorkelling, there are a couple of dive sites nearby – trips to these can be arranged on the mainland. If you are camping, come with friends if you like being sociable. Alternatively you can lie on the sand, looking up at the spectacular night sky, and muse on our wonderful world.

YOU SHOULD KNOW:
Don't attempt to venture inland – not only does illegal logging take place, but the jungle is home to cobras and other poisonous snakes. There are unfriendly rottweilers at the fishing village, but the villagers themselves are perfectly friendly.

One of Koh Rong's staggeringly beautiful beaches

Si Phan Don

POPULATION:
1,800 (estimate)
WHEN TO GO:
November to February
HOW TO GET THERE:
By air to Pakse, then by road, or by boat down river from Pakse or Champasak, or overland from Cambodia.
HIGHLIGHTS:
Don Khon's boat racing festival, each December.
Tat Somphamit rapids off Don Khon.
Kon Phapheng waterfall.
Taking a boat trip around the islands and seeing if you can spot an Irrawaddy dolphin.
YOU SHOULD KNOW:
Your best chance to see one of the white Irrawaddy dolphins is in April/May, but they are extremely rare now; in fact they may not be there at all any more. If you see one, you should report it.

Deep down in the far south of Laos, the Mekong River fans out to a maximum width of 14 km (9 mi), within which area is the archipelago of rocks, sandbars, islets and islands known as Si Phan Don, or Four Thousand Islands.

Three of the islands not only have a permanent population but also a trickle of tourists. Though it remains a largely unspoilt and unchanged part of Laos, the border crossing with Cambodia will doubtless bring more and more visitors this way, and other islands will become available to stay on. The Mekong is all-important of course, both as the main source of protein, fish, and because its silt-rich waters fertilize the land.

Don Khon is the largest and most developed of the three, with two main villages and several small settlements clinging to the riverbanks, all connected by a coastal road. The interior of the island is agricultural, mainly rice paddies, but it is also home to several ancient Buddhist temples, dating back to around the 7th century. The most interesting of these is probably Wat Phou Khao Kaew, with its carved wooden Burmese sculptures and lovely, gently disintegrating brick stupa. Don Khon and Don Det are joined by a bridge, and are small enough to explore on foot. The former has

Si Phan Don

more genuine village life to enjoy while the latter is becoming a favourite haunt of the backpacking fraternity.

Scenically, these are all utterly delicious islands, picture postcard perfect. Sugar and coconut palm fronds shade the paths; once in a while you'll stumble upon a picturesque, down-at-heel, old French colonial villa, garlanded with plumeria trees and you might see a canoe carrying saffron-robed monks, umbrellas raised against the sun. Swim in the river, splash in the waterfalls, stay in simple but charming guesthouses, and recharge your batteries before moving on.

Whale Island

At the point where Vietnam bulges furthest east into the aquamarine South China Sea, the Hon Gom peninsula of virgin sand dunes and wild grasses curls round Van Phong Bay. Between April and July, the ocean currents make it a natural trap for huge masses of krill and plankton, and an invitation to migrating sperm and blue whales, and whale sharks, to pause and feed. Whale Island, in the middle, is the best place from which to see them.

Most of the time, Whale Island is an ordinary tropical paradise. Uninhabited until 1997, it still has no cars or motorbikes, ordinary mobile phones don't work, and the only buildings are the 23 traditional bungalows set into the dense foliage between the palm trees fringing the perfect beach. The facilities are basic, but visitors come here in the hope of merging seamlessly with the natural, marine world all around.

It's perfect for children, hopeless romantics, and experienced divers. Snorkelling and diving from the beach opens the door on an amazing marine landscape: the corals begin less than 30 m (100 ft) from the bungalows, and are heavily populated by seahorses, morays, frogfish, devil, stone, pipe and leaf scorpionfish among many others in the exceptionally clear waters. In fact Van Phong Bay is so protected that diving is possible from January to October, and from Whale Island the dive sites can be really spectacular. Hon Trau Nam (Three Kings) is named for three rock pinnacles that break the surface of the sea. At a depth of 20 to 35 m (70 to 120 ft) you discover a fantasy of yellow, white and purple soft corals and gorgonians, camouflage for shoals of outrageously patterned fish.

Or you can stroll, swim, or laze in a hammock watching parrots and fish eagles – until the day's catch is ready to eat as the sun sets in glory.

POPULATION:
Uninhabited (apart from resort staff)
WHEN TO GO:
January to October
HOW TO GET THERE:
By car/mini bus, from Nha Trang airport or rail station, to Vangia wharf at Dam Mon; then by boat to Whale Island.
HIGHLIGHTS:
White Rock dive site – sheer walls drop 40 m (135 ft) from the surface, with several massive pinnacles of soft corals and nudibranchs. The bottom is covered in gorgonians and black coral trees, and black rays rest on the open sandy patches.
The rare fire urchin shrimps (among other unusual invertebrates and fish species) at the 18 m (50 ft) level of Bai Su dive site – and at the upper level (up to 10 m, 34 ft), a pure coral garden of many hard and soft species is ideal for snorkelling.
Birdwatching.
The amazing sunsets.

Cat Ba, Ha Long Bay

POPULATION:
13,500 (2007)
WHEN TO GO:
Year-round
HOW TO GET THERE:
By bus/car from Hanoi or Haiphong to Ha Long City, then by water-taxi or tour boat to Cat Ba town.
HIGHLIGHTS:
Getting there – wind and sea have carved Ha Long Bay's karst stacks into fantastic shapes, evoked by names like Kissing Rocks, Wallowing Buffalo, and Fighting Cock.
Exploring the tunnels and grottoes of Khe Sau and Gia Luan cave systems.
The floating village of Cua Van – a fishing community of over 700 people in 176 floating households, including schools and shops.
Contemplating the visual haiku of a red-sailed junk in the deep blue of Lan Ha Bay.
Hiring a small boat to swim in any of the deserted sandy coves and marine grottoes of Cat Ba and its immediate islets.
YOU SHOULD KNOW:
In 1288 General Tran Hung Dao prevented a Mongol invasion by placing steel-tipped wooden stakes at high tide in the nearby Bach Dang River, and sinking the Mongol Dubhai Khan's fleet.

Ha Long Bay translates as 'Bay of the Descending Dragon'.

Ha Long Bay, 170 km (103 mi) from Hanoi, blends earth, sea and sky into one of the world's most iconic beauty spots. Cat Ba, the biggest of a mini archipelago of 366 islands, typifies the spectacular rock relief and bizarre rock formations of the Ha Long World Natural Heritage Reserve: 2,000 large and small islands with cliffs towering a sheer 50-100 m (170-340 ft) from the shallow sea.

Cat Ba's mountainous interior is covered by tropical moist limestone forest, but its spectacular scenery also includes coral terraces, sandy beaches, freshwater wetlands, tidal flats, mangrove forests and willow swamp. Archaeological evidence shows farmers and fishermen have lived here for 6,000 years, but have only recently discovered that the island's dramatic biodiversity is itself a major source of income. Cat Ba's 1986 designation as a UNESCO Man and Biosphere Reserve – the first in Vietnam to include both terrestrial and marine ecosystems – includes them as well as the many rare species of plant, mammal and bird for which it is a refuge.

Cat Ba is an immensely popular destination for short breaks, but most visitors remain near the hotels and bars lining Cat Ba town's waterfront strip, the lively beaches of Cat Co and Cat Dua, or the floating hotel boats moored in Cai Beo Bay. The wooded limestone hills beyond, riddled with jungle caves and stalactite-filled grottoes, and dozens of deserted coves, gateways to a marine wonder-world, promise much greater mystery and adventure. Besides the golden-headed or Cat Ba langur, for which the island is the last sanctuary on earth, you might see the rhesus macacque, the southern serow, leopard cat, oriental giant squirrel, sea-eagle and massed formations of butterflies. And every time you raise your eyes, you can gaze at the marvel of Ha Long Bay, a natural sculpture on a gigantic scale.

Phu Quoc

Phu Quoc is a showcase of the complex forces challenging Vietnam's most precious, pristine environments. Despite being Vietnam's biggest island, its proximity to Cambodia, only 15 km (9 mi) away, has restricted almost all development of its wild beauty. There's still a military presence, but its beaches and mountain forests are completely unspoiled. Phu Quoc is shaped like a long teardrop, and lies deep in the Gulf of Thailand. Though most of it, and its offshore waters, is protected as a National Park, its remoteness and tranquillity, and above all its long strands of perfect beach have now attracted sufficient attention to interest big money developers.

There is very little infrastructure for visitors, even in the main towns. Duong Dong, halfway up the western coast, is a pleasant, unremarkable seaport with several 'nuoc mam' (fish sauce) factories (and Dinh Cau, a temple to the Whale God, full of skeletons of whales and other marine mammals used by cult devotees). An Thoi, a fishing town in the south, is noisier and fishier. Between are beaches like Bai Kem (Ice Cream Beach), a stretch of dazzling white coral sand comparable with the Seychelles, or the coconut palm-fringed infinity of Long Beach, on the west coast and the only place in Vietnam you can see the sun set on an ocean horizon. Inland you can follow the paths through pepper and cashew plantations until the dense rainforest closes in. Along the east coast, it's so thick that it's difficult to reach the empty beaches. The islanders want to open it all up, with a target of two million visitors by 2020. They have discontinued using dynamite for fishing, but so far don't agree that wholesale tourism could be equally damaging to what still is, ecologically and economically, a priceless virgin slice of Vietnam.

POPULATION:
70,000 (2007)
WHEN TO GO:
November to May (the daily short, intense showers from June to October are more refreshing than irritating)
HOW TO GET THERE:
By air, from Ho Chi Minh City or Rach Gia, to Duong Dong; by hydrofoil from Rach Gia to An Thoi, or by cruise ship to Duong Dong.
HIGHLIGHTS:
Diving at Turtle Island off the NW coast – one of Vietnam's best dive sites.
The otherworldly atmosphere of Ganh Dau, the unspoiled fishing village on the NE coast.
The natural sounds and sights of the beautiful Suoi Tranh waterfall on the Da Ban River, deep in the emerald forest.
The iridescence of local pearls grown at the pearl farms – they used to be gathered from the Phu Quoc sea-bed.
Snorkelling/diving on the coral reefs around the islets grouped at Phu Quoc's southern tip.
The tropical flavour of the pastoral idyll of Xa Cua Can – all rivers, flowered green banks and stands of trees.
YOU SHOULD KNOW:
Phu Quoc fish sauce is particularly esteemed for its smell, which comes from the small, protein-rich fish called ca com. The island produces six million litres of fish sauce each year.

Fishing boats on Phu Quoc

An aerial view of Con Dao

POPULATION:
5,000 (2007 estimate)
WHEN TO GO:
Con Dao's climate is governed by the convergence of warm and cool ocean currents. Frequent, violent squalls hit the archipelago's western side from June to September, then reverse to hit the eastern side from October to December. Come between March and early June when the sea is at its most calm.
HOW TO GET THERE:
By air from Ho Chi Minh City or by boat from Vung Tau, to Con Son.
HIGHLIGHTS:
The paper weapons and costumes made as props for prison inmates' New Year 'celebrations', and other artefacts and memorabilia on the guided tour of the prison complex.
Dam Trau, a beautiful, tranquil beach shaded by evergreen trees.
Tropical almond trees swaying in a cool sea breeze.
Dolphins jumping and playing round the boat when you visit Con Dao's smaller islands.
YOU SHOULD KNOW:
When people describe Con Dao's exotic fruits as 'abundant', don't be misled. Apart from bananas and coconuts, everything genuinely edible comes from the mainland.

Con Dao

The Con Dao Archipelago lies 180 km (110 mi) south of Vung Tau, exposed in the South China Sea. Its isolation makes it unsurprising that Con Son, its main island, was a penal colony until 1975. The Portuguese called it Poulo Condor in 1702, and it was under that name that it became notorious as a colonial French prison, from 1861 until the South Vietnamese took it over in 1954. Conditions became so brutal that tiny punishment cells were known globally as 'tiger cages', shaming the USA and its puppet South Vietnamese administration, when they were revealed after reunification in 1975. Today, in what used to be the French Governor's residence, the room housing illustrations of the inhuman torture meted out is labelled 'Hell On Earth'. The small town that has developed round the remains of the penal colony is friendly and attractive – but it's easy to see the poignant distinction between the administrators' comfort and the inmates' squalor.

With potential infrastructure already in place, major tourist development is inevitable unless Con Dao as a whole is elevated from its present National Park to full-blooded UNESCO World Heritage status. The dense forest cover – especially the humid forest growing above 500 m (1,700 ft) – is pristine. Over 1,000 hectares (2,471 acres) of Con Dao's living coral reefs survive in shallow waters, recovering from decades of French harvesting (for lime), and subsequent damage by fishermen using underwater explosives. The terrestrial and marine biodiversity is colossal: Con Dao's habitats attract hawksbill and green turtles, and dugong, among 1,300 species of sea animals. Seagrass meadow and mangrove ecosystems provide nursery space for the 300,000 baby turtles released in a decade. Nature is back in flourishing abundance, gradually obliterating the traces of human suffering that have, in the end, created the opportunity for the rest of us to celebrate.

Cu Lao Cham

In their haste to get from north to south Vietnam, or vice-versa, most people pass by the little archipelago of the Cham Islands Marine Park. Cu Lao, often called Cham Island, is the biggest of seven islands lying 15 km (9 mi) off the ancient trading port of Hoi An, with which it shares considerable history. Cu Lao is where the Indonesian Cham people first came to trade in the 4th century, and it became one of the Champa kingdom's principal ports until Hoi An took over in the 15th century. The significance of both lasted to the 20th century, when the Thu Bon River silted up, and trade moved from Hoi An to Tourane (now Da Nang). Seventeenth century pagodas in its two villages, small temples and monuments, and the rice terrace systems themselves, hidden in the dense forest, recall Cu Lao's historic importance. Now it's better known for its ecological purity, and as one of Vietnam's best reef dive sites.

Cu Lao is 7 km (5 mi) long and 1.5 km (1 mi) wide, with a 517m (1,750 ft) mountain in its centre. Tropical forest covers everything; and the seven white beaches on its western side are empty and untouched. Only on Bai Chong are there a few very friendly fishing families who are happy to offer rudimentary but stunning food and drink. In April monkeys come here to gorge on newly-ripe durian fruits and wild pineapples; freshwater streams run from the coconut palms across the sand; and the parrot, clown, angel, lion, damsel and pipefish, hollyqueen sweetlips, barracudas, moray eels, pink jellyfish and occasional dugong among the lustrous corals offshore complete the picture of paradise. Other reefs are even more spectacular, and there are several known Japanese, Portuguese and US wrecks still waiting to be located.

POPULATION:
3,000 (2007)

WHEN TO GO:
Come from the beginning of March to August, when the water visibility is likely to be much better.

HOW TO GET THERE:
By air to Da Nang, then by car/taxi to Hoi An, then by water-taxi or speedboat from Hoi An (boats wait at the waterside by the market place) to Cu Lao. Da Nang and Hoi An are also served by the Reunification Train and long-haul bus.

HIGHLIGHTS:
The swifts' nests clinging to the high cliffs – a rare chance to see the origin of the delicious bird's nest soup.
The courtly titillation of naming beauty spots, like Suoi Tinh (Love Stream), Hon Chong (Piled-Up Rocks), Suoi Ong (The Gentleman's Stream) and Hang Ba (The Lady's Cave).
Talking to the monks, who practise traditional medicine based on local plants, at the 1753 Hai Tang Pagoda on the western hillside of Hon Lao.
The Rang Manh Pinnacles, a superb series of coral canyons, arches and caves filled with diffused sunlight, each section and depth attracting different groups of species; the range of projecting pinnacles prevents damage to the luxuriant flora and fauna from nets or fishing lines.
The artistic atmosphere of Hoi An, almost car-free, full of brightly-coloured wooden buildings reflecting 300 years of Portuguese, Dutch, Japanese, French and Chinese influences, and an oasis of quiet, intelligent café life.

YOU SHOULD KNOW:
With just one road connecting its only two villages, Bai Lang and Bai Huong, Cu Lao Cham is a fragile gem of authentic history and impeccable ecology.

One of Cu Lao Cham's untouched beaches

Palawan Island

POPULATION:
737,000 (2000)
WHEN TO GO:
March to June
HOW TO GET THERE:
Fly from Manila to Puerto Princesa, or take a ferry which will take about 20 hours.
HIGHLIGHTS:
Tabon Caves – a series of chambers where anthropologists discovered the remains of 22,000-year-old Tabon Man, with various tools and other artefacts. The caves are located at Lipuua Point, Quezon.
Ursula Island Game Refuge and Bird Sanctuary – a haven for birds at Bataraza. Arrive here two hours before sunset, to see them congregate and roost for the night.
Coron Reefs, Northern Palawan – the seven enchanting lakes are surrounded by craggy limestone cliffs and attract hundreds of nature lovers.
Tabon Museum – Devoted to Palawan pre-history, the museum displays artefacts from the Tabon Caves, and gives information on the different tribes of Palawan.
Palawan Museum in Puerto Princesa – this interesting museum showcases the history, culture, music and crafts of Palawan.
The Taytay Fort – built in 1667 under the Augustinian Recollect Fathers, this historic fort was first used as a military station. The fort's small chapel and cannon are still intact.
YOU SHOULD KNOW:
Around 12 hours by boat from Puerto Princesa are the Tubbattaha Reefs, a UNESCO World Heritage Site and a wonderful place to dive.

The beautiful Bascuit Bay

In the northern Phillipines, between the South China Sea and the Sulu Sea, lies Palawan Island, blessed with immense natural beauty and plentiful marine life. With nearly 2,000 km (1,243 mi) of irregular coastline dotted with 1,780 islets, rocky coves, protected coral reefs and white sandy beaches, the island is renowned for having one of the most beautiful seascapes in the world.

A chain of mountains runs down the spine of this long narrow stretch of land, carpeted by vast areas of virgin rainforest. The island also boasts lush green hills and plains, leading down to pristine beaches. Palawan Island has a stunning array of flora and fauna, including the highly endangered dugong, a type of seacow. It is also home to many species of African and endangered Palawan animals, including monkeys, parrots, bear cats and peacocks, as well as mongoose, scaly anteaters, porcupine and mouse deer.

Palawan Island is full of natural wonders. Puerto-Princesa Subterranean River offers 8.2 km (5 mi) of navigable underground river, believed to be the longest in the world. The river winds through a deep cavern under rugged limestone and marble cliffs, and through an underground lagoon with crystalline waters before emptying out in to the South China Sea. There are impressive stalactites, rock formations and domed theatres to explore.

The El Nido Marine Reserve comprises 96,000 hectares (237,221 acres) of diverse ecosystems, including rainforest, mangroves, white sand beaches, coral reefs and limestone cliffs. It is one of the country's main tourist destinations, a haven for wildlife enthusiasts. Countless varieties of fish are found here, including manta rays and the elusive dugong.

Palawan is considered to be one of the top dive sites in the world, partly due to the twelve World War II Japanese shipwrecks off the islet of Busuanga, ranging in depth from surface level down to 40 m (131 ft). Honda Bay is popular with locals and tourists alike who come here to snorkel, swim and dive around the many islets in the bay, with their shallow reefs and fabulous beaches.

Luzon Island

This is the largest island in the Philippines Archipelago, giving its name to one of the country's three island groups (the others being Visayas and Mindanao). Luzon itself is the world's 15th-largest island, with an area of 105,000 sq km (40,550 sq mi), and the fifth most populous. The country's capital, Manila, is located here, along with the largest city, Quezon, making Luzon the centre of political and economic influence in the Philippines.

The area was claimed by Spanish conquistadors in 1571, and the Philippines were only freed from Spain's harsh control after a revolution in the 1890s. Even that came at a price – the revolutionaries were assisted by the Americans, then at war with Spain, but the USA soon annexed the country after waging a short war that destroyed the First Philippine Republic. The United States did not grant independence to the island nation until 1946, after the Philippines had been the scene of bitter fighting in World War II.

Mountainous Luzon is home to the country's second-highest peak (Mount Pulag) and most famous volcano (Mayon). Another natural highlight (stand by for a tongue twister) is the world's largest lake on an island in a lake on an island – Crater Lake on Vulcano Island in Lake Taal on Luzon. This amazing feature was once a vast inlet of the sea. As a result, it has many saltwater species that have adapted to fresh water – there were even bull sharks until the locals eliminated them in the 1930s.

Luzon has the best infrastructure of the Philippines' main islands, facilitating exploration, but still offers a breathtaking contrast between the hustle and bustle of its modern cities, a stunning variety of scenery, spectacular coastline and a rural way of life that has hardly changed for centuries.

POPULATION:
39,500,000 (2000)

WHEN TO GO:
The climate is temperate, allowing year-round visiting, but April to June is the peak tourist season.

HOW TO GET THERE:
There are commercial flights into Luzon's international airports, including cheap flights from Hong Kong.

HIGHLIGHTS:
The mountain haven of Baguio, north of Manila, the island's refreshingly cool summer capital.
Splendid rice terraces at Banaue, dubbed 'the eighth wonder of the world' by locals.
Waterfalls and hot springs on the fertile plain surrounding Laguna de Bay, Southeast Asia's largest freshwater lake.
St Paul's Underground River National Park near Barangay Sabang, a remote wonder consisting of a subterranean river and maze of caverns – now a UNESCO World Heritage Site. Another World Heritage Site – the well-preserved Spanish colonial town of Vigan on the west coast.

YOU SHOULD KNOW:
Vulcan Point on Vulcano Island in Lake Taal is the world's smallest (and the Philippines' second most active) volcano.

The rice terraces of Banaue

Alaminos Hundred Island National Park

POPULATION:
Uninhabited
WHEN TO GO:
All year round, though the rainy season (June-October) can see heavy showers and be quite chilly. April and May are the busiest months with the best weather.
HOW TO GET THERE:
Alaminos City is served by public buses from Manila, Baguio, Dagupan, Subic, Tarlac and Zambales.
HIGHLIGHTS:
Snorkeling to see the giant clam and coral garden on Quezon.
Shell Island for...its amazing shells, especially after the rainy season.
A superb cave on Milagrosa – one of the best among many in the Park.
YOU SHOULD KNOW:
Carry cash – the majority of suppliers (for example, of boat hire) do not accept credit cards.

Actually, it should be 123-Island Park (high tide) or 124-Island Park (low tide), but who's counting? With a total land area of just 18.5 sq km (7 sq mi), most islands are no more than rocky outcrops (some tiny) covered with dense vegetation, though there are plenty of hidden coves and sandy beaches. They are scattered like jewels in the azure waters of the Lingayen Gulf off the northern coast of Luzon. The Hundred Island National Park is now under the jurisdiction of Alaminos City, six hours from Manila by bus.

Most visitors to the Park stay in Alaminos City and set off by boat from the nearby Lucap Wharf where various options are on offer, including boat rental and island-hopping day tours. These tend to feature the major islands of Quezon, Govenor's and Children's plus one other, but customized trips are easily arranged. For those who enjoy the simple life, there is basic overnight accommodation in huts, cottages and shelters on the three main islands (no electricity, public rest rooms only) and camping is permitted (tents can be rented locally). Those are the only islands with tourist facilities, though the authorities – whilst determined to maintain the park's fragile eco-system – do not impose restrictive access rules to the other islands.

There are activities like parasailing, snorkeling or kayaking within the park, but most people simply enjoy island hopping or banana boat tours that allow them to appreciate the natural beauty of these pristine islands...with not a single resort to be seen. The park provides encouraging testament to growing awareness that original and unspoiled places can ultimately be worth far more economically than tacky developments that destroy the very things that most attract visitors.

Over a hundred islands are scattered like jewels across the Alaminos Hundred Island National Park.

Mindanao Island

Islands, islands everywhere – hundreds of them in the Mindanao Island group, of which the largest by far is 'big daddy' Mindanao at 97,500 sq km (37,500 sq mi). Once the seat of the Sultanate of Sulu, a Muslim state founded in the 15th century, Mindanao remains the centre of Islam in the Philippines, though it is now the island's minority religion. Even so, the struggle to secure an independent Muslim state on the island has been taking place for centuries and continues to this day. The Autonomous Region in Muslim Mindanao (ARMM) is a special self-governing area where most of the Islamic population lives, consisting of the Sulu Archipelago and two provinces on the mainland.

Mindanao is at once the most southerly and easterly point in the Philippines. The island has a unique character that makes it seem very different from the rest of the Philippines, resulting from its Muslim heritage and the dramatic mix of ethnic groups. It is also a land of stark contrast between the modern and the traditional.

The thriving industrial centre that is Davao City certainly belongs to the 21st century, as do the many intensive agri-businesses producing commodities like pineapples and meat. But once away from centres of population in the largely unspoiled back country, adventurous visitors will find themselves in a nature-lovers' paradise and be fascinated by the timeless way of life. Rich flora and fauna, outstanding natural attractions, stunning coastline and islands, different ethnic communities with colourful festivals – all combine to make Mindanao a destination that is attracting a rapidly increasing number of tourists. There is more than enough of Mindanao to go round, but despite awareness of the importance of eco-tourism, some of the new facilities will seem intrusive to those who prefer things just the way they were.

POPULATION:
18,134,000 (2000)

WHEN TO GO:
Any time – there is no significant wet or dry season and the climate is pleasant all year round.

HOW TO GET THERE:
Fly in to the recently upgraded Davao City international airport, or take an island-hopping flight if Mindanao isn't your first destination in the Philippines.

HIGHLIGHTS:
Mount Apo, the country's highest mountain, an inactive volcano in a range containing waterfalls, rapids, steaming lakes, geysers, sulphur pillars and primeval trees.
The 17th century Spanish Fort del Pilar in Zambonga, said by many to be the most romantic city in the Philippines.
Rio Hondo and Taluksangay, villages where members of the Samal tribe still dwell in stilt houses – representatives of the many ethnic groups that still live a traditional way of life on Mindanao.
The impressive hydroelectric complex at Iligan City, driven by the Maria Cristina Falls.
Orchids – in the wild or at public gardens like Puentespina (Davao City) or Yuhico (Greenhills).

YOU SHOULD KNOW:
Davao City is the world's largest by area, at the last count sprawling out over 2,450 sq km (940 sq mi)...and still growing.

A view from Mindanao Island

Mount Hibok-Hibok overlooks the beach.

Camiguin Island

POPULATION:
74,000 (2000)
WHEN TO GO:
Any time of year (the island is rarely visited by typhoons). April to June is the prime period, November to January the coolest.
HOW TO GET THERE:
Limited trips available from Cebu by air and sea. Or fly to Cagayan de Oro City, take a bus to Balingoan and boat to the island.
HIGHLIGHTS:
Binangawan Falls in Sagay – an unspoiled series of cascades into a single pool.
The Sunken Cemetery (scuba gear required) – immersed beneath the sea after the volcanic eruption of 1871, marked by a large cross.
Wonderfully elegant ancestral homes full of character that may be seen all over the island.
Old churches – Santo Rosario in Sagay (built 1882), the ruined San Roque in Barangay Bonbon and the Miracle Church in Baylao that saved many lives during a volcanic eruption.
Tangun Hot Spring at Naasag – an unusual natural seashore pool that is hot at low tide, changing to cool as the tide comes in.
YOU SHOULD KNOW:
If this is for you, be careful when you book – there is another Camiguin Island in the Philippines, part of the Babuyan Islands north of Luzon.

The independently minded Camiguin islanders have always fought their corner – unsuccessfully. The Spanish established a settlement in the early 1600s, the Americans invaded in 1901 and proved that bullets were better than *bolos* and spears and the Japanese ruthlessly crushed guerrilla activities in World War II. There was, however, a happy ending in 1946 when the Philippines gained independence.

The pear-shaped island is not large – 230 sq km (90 sq mi) – and is evidently of volcanic origin, as its nickname 'The Island Born of Fire' confirms. There are several large peaks, plus numerous domes and cones. Mount Hibok-Hibok, the largest, is still active, last erupting in 1953. It has hot springs, crater lakes and Taguines Lagoon, a volcanic maar. Hibok-Hibok is a popular destination for hikers, though a permit is required.

This is an island of contrasts, with traditional coastal villages, coconut plantations, lush forests, hot and cold springs, waterfalls, dramatic volcanic landscapes, abundant marine life and pristine beaches. Indeed, Camiguin has one of the world's finest beaches, as voted for by travel journalists – White Island Beach, a bleached sandbar in the turquoise Bohol Sea reached by boat, with great views of Mounts Vulcan and Hibok-Hibok.

Despite national efforts to encourage only sustainable eco-tourism, Camiguin's experience suggests this isn't easy. The newly discovered Camiguin hanging parrot, a handsome green, blue and red bird endemic to this island only, is already under threat as its habitat is eroded by increased economic activity and visitor-friendly development. And the rural tranquility and slow pace of life that makes this enchanted island so appealing is hardly helped by its designation as one of the 'Top 25 Tourist Destinations' in the Philippines.

Cebu Island

This is the main island of the Visayas group in the Central Philippines. It is a long, narrow sliver in the middle of the group, stretching for 225 km (140 mi) from north to south with an area of 4,500 sq km (1,750 sq mi). The capital, Cebu City, is half way down the east coast at the island's widest point. Its deep-water harbour was an important trading centre before the first Spanish settlement in the Philippines was established there in 1565. As a result, Cebu City has the country's first and smallest fort (Fort San Pedro), oldest church (Basilica of Santa Niño), oldest street (Colon) and oldest school (San Carlos). Its historical importance is confirmed by the fact that it was even incorporated as a city before Manila.

Cebu City has developed into an international container port that also acts as a hub for most of the country's domestic shipping, whilst also serving as a major commercial centre for island industries such as agriculture, fishing, copper mining, shipbuilding, steel and cement. Despite this intense industrial activity and the well-developed infrastructure that goes with it, Cebu is still an island that can delight the visitor. It has a rugged mountainous spine separating east and west coasts, rolling hills, limestone plateaux and coastal plains. There are excellent beaches and numerous coral atolls, with many first-class resorts. Principal leisure activities are diving, fishing, parasailing, boating, hiking and mountain biking. Cebu is the diving capital of the Philippines.

Over 150 islands surround Cebu, so it not only has a lot to offer in its own right but also serves as a popular base for day trips to offshore islands, or a jumping-off point for a longer stay.

POPULATION:
3,350,000 (2000)

WHEN TO GO:
Cebu is warm all year round, though the temperature is hottest in the dry season (March to May).

HOW TO GET THERE:
By air direct to Cebu's Mactan international airport, domestic flight from Manila or by sea on a choice of inter-island ferry services.

HIGHLIGHTS:
The Magellan Cross, a newer cross containing remains of the cross planted by the great Portuguese explorer Ferdinand Magellan when he reached the island in 1521 – see it in a small building with a richly painted ceiling in front of Cebu city hall.
Kawasan Falls at Matutinao near the southern town of Badian – the best waterfalls on the island, great for swimming and rafting.
Carcar, a town just south of Cebu with many preserved Castilian houses, gardens and churches.
The National Museum in Fort San Pedro, Cebu, providing insight into the island's colonial past.
A drive along the Cebu Transcentral highway for cool air and sensational mountain views.

YOU SHOULD KNOW:
Ferdinand Magellan was killed soon after arriving here, at the Battle of Mactan, fighting with the Spanish against local Visayan chief Lapu-Lapu.

Samal Island

POPULATION:
83,000 (2000)
WHEN TO GO:
The best months to visit are November to May, especially if intending to dive.
HOW TO GET THERE:
By vehicle ferry or small boat – any number to choose from along the Gulf shore or Santa Ana Pier in Davao.
HIGHLIGHTS:
The Paradise Island resort, complete with palms, mangroves and a small zoo featuring island birds, turtles, snakes, monkeys and deer.
Hagimit Falls – a series of low-drop falls above beautiful pools in a forest setting close to Peñaplata.
A beach-hopping, round-the-island tour by pumpboat, lasting around four hours (depending on stops).
Vanishing Island, a spit of mangrove-covered land that is submerged at high tide.
Pindawon and Aundanao marine sanctuaries on the east coast, where there is every chance of seeing turtles.
YOU SHOULD KNOW:
Samal's renowned bat cave houses the world's largest colony of Geoffroy's rousette fruit bats (all 1.8 million of them).

The island is now known as the Island Garden City of Samal (aka IGaCOS), officially a third-class city. Don't be fooled – this is a delightful holiday destination for those who love a white-sand, blue-sea beach holiday, though it is situated in Davao Gulf within sight of the city of the same name. There are many resorts packed into the island's 300 sq km (115 sq mi) area, but the idea of eco-tourism is taken seriously in the Philippines and considerable effort has gone into ensuring that such facilities don't destroy the island's essential character. For those who like to get away from it all, there are plenty of hiking and biking trails in the forested interior, but you need to be fit as many of them are quite steep.

One of Samal's principal attractions is the wonderful variety of marine habitats and sea life. There is a profusion of small, colourful fish, occasional dolphins and sharks, turtles, a variety of coral reefs, underwater caves and dramatic rock formations. This water wonderland attracts both snorkelers and divers, with instant tuition available for beginners, though caution is advised as currents can be treacherous. Kayaking and (more intrusively) jet skiing are also popular activities.

The Philippines have more to offer than any one person could see in two lifetimes, but the resorts of Samal Island are typical of low-impact tourist developments found along many parts of the country's extensive shoreline – and they are exactly what the majority of visitors come for. If that's your idea of heaven too, Samal could be perfect!

Boracay Island

A typical tropical paradise in the Central Philippines, Boracay is just off the northwestern corner of the large island of Panay in the Visayas group. It rates as one of the country's top tourist destinations, but was a late starter – until the 1970s only the most clued-up of backpackers even knew the place existed.

The island is some 7 km (4 mi) long and extends to an area of some 10 sq km (4 sq mi). The reasons for coming are simple – sand and sea. The long main beach is on the west coast – and White Beach doesn't misrepresent itself. The sand is dazzling and the beach is sheltered from the prevailing wind in high season. This is the place for lazy loafing, with numerous beachfront facilities to cater for après-swim. Bulabog Beach on the east side is more athletically orientated, with kiteboarding and windsurfing on the menu. There are several other beaches for those who want to be different.

There are two distinct seasons on Boracay Island – Habagat and Amihan. They are associated respectively with, and vary in duration depending on the whims of, the global La Niña and El Niño weather patterns. Habagat (generally June to September) is hot and muggy with frequent heavy rain and unpredictable tropical storms. Amihan (usually October to May) sees little rainfall and moderate temperatures, with only the very occasional storm. The latter is very definitely high season.

Make no mistake – with nearly 400 beach resorts and the associated eating and drinking places, Boracay is an out-and-out tourist haven. But if you want to be marooned on a desert island for a week, 21st-century style, they don't come much better than this.

POPULATION:
12,000 (2000)
WHEN TO GO:
Amihan season (October to May) – more expensive, but worth it.
HOW TO GET THERE:
By internal fight to Godofredo P. Ramos Airport in nearby Caticlan, then boat from Caticlan Jetty to Cagban Beach on Boracay.
HIGHLIGHTS:
Traditional dragon-boat races featuring teams from all over the Philippines, held annually in April or May.
A self-sail tour of island waters in a hired *paraw* (canoe with two outriggers), or motorized *banca*.
Pitch and putt – actually a leisurely round on the world-class 18-hole par-72 course designed by top Aussie golfer Graham Marsh.
YOU SHOULD KNOW:
This isn't the ideal place to find peace and quiet – restaurants, clubs, bars and pubs sometimes keep going all night long.

One of the many beautiful beaches on Boracay

Sunrise over the Chocolate Hills

Bohol Island

POPULATION:
1,137,000 (2000)
WHEN TO GO:
Take your pick – November to April is mild, May to July hot and humid, August to October mild but rainy.
HOW TO GET THERE:
By sea to the Tagbilaran City Tourist Pier from Cebu, Manila and various other islands. By air to the recently enlarged city airport.
HIGHLIGHTS:
Antequera's beautiful Mag-Aso Falls – Mag-Aso translates as 'smoke' for reasons that will become apparent upon arrival.
Spelunking – not for everyone, but there are over 100 caves in the eastern part of the island to delight the subterranean adventurer.
A fabulous cruise up the Loboc River from the sea to its source in the centre of the island.
Rajah Sikatuna National Park near Bilar, the largest remaining natural forest on the island.
The tarzier, a delightful bug-eyed creature said to be the world's smallest primate – shy in the wild, but often seen in captivity.
YOU SHOULD KNOW:
During the American-Philippines War of 1901, US troops burned up to 20 villages on Bohol as a punishment for local resistance.

In common with the rest of the Philippines, Bohol came under Spanish influence in the 16th century. The island saw the conclusion of an historic treaty of friendship between the locals and Spain in 1565, when native chieftain Datu Sikatanu made a blood pact with the Spanish conquistador Miguel López de Legazpi. The event is celebrated to this day at the annual Sandugo Festival, and evidence of Bohol's colonial past is everywhere.

This oval-shaped island province lies to the southeast of Cebu Island and due north from Mindanao Island. Bohol is the 10th-largest island in the Philippines, with an area of 3,300 sq km (1,275 sq mi) and a coastline that is 260 km (160 mi) in length. It has gently rolling terrain and a mountainous interior with a central plateau.

One must see are the famous Chocolate Hills near Carmen, described as 'The Jewel of the Philippines'. That description may have been thought up by an astute tourist chief, but this certainly is an amazing natural wonder – some 1,200 uniform cone-shaped limestone hills. They are grass-covered and turn brown in summer, which is where the chocolate comes in. There is a good road system on the island, giving access to both the interior and coastal villages.

The capital city Tagbilaran is located on the south coast, popular with those who like beach holidays on sand that's whiter than white. Bohol is surrounded by 70 smaller islands. Many of these can easily be reached from the mainland, and some offer unusual experiences like whale and dolphin watching. This activity is conducted by former fishermen who now serve as 'stewards of the sea', showing how eagerly the concept of eco-tourism is being embraced in the Philippines.

Panglao Island

Located in the central Visayas Island group, just off the southwestern corner of Bohol Island, this is one of the top visitor attractions in the Philippines. Panglao Island is divided into two municipalities – Dauis town (nearest the mainland) and Panglao town. There are numerous tourist resorts, many clustered around the world-famous Alona Beach. Other notable beaches are Doljo (fronting interesting coral reefs) and Momo.

This small island is tourism in the Philippines personified. There are literally hundreds of assorted resorts along the sandy beaches, with investment money pouring in and many more under construction. There's even talk of a new international airport to make the going easier still. Apart from the obvious attractions of sand and sea, the night-life consists of good food and cold drinks, in the amiable company of fellow visitors and friendly locals.

However, with marine biodiversity said to exceed that of Japan and the Mediterranean Sea put together, Panglao does have one claim to fame that sets it apart. The island is a world-renowned diving location, so many visitors bring flippers and snorkels, or aim to do (or try) some diving.

Scuba dive sites are everywhere, best explored with the help of a local dive master who will know the best places and steer clear of dangerous currents. Apart from sensational corals thronged with small tropical fish, the main sights are hammerhead sharks, massive schools of jackfish and barracudas – even whale sharks in season.

In late August, the island fiesta – Hudyaka sa Panglao – takes place in the grounds of Panglao's San Agustin Church. The local *barangays* compete fiercely for top honours, serving as a reminder of the important place that music and dance have in the culture of the Philippines.

POPULATION:
48,000 (2000)
WHEN TO GO:
The temperate climate encourages any-time visiting.
HOW TO GET THERE:
Manila to Tagbilaran City on the main island of Bohol by air or fast ferry, from there by bridge or causeway to Panglao Island.
HIGHLIGHTS:
Out Lady of Assumption Church at Dauis, built by the Spaniards. It has attractive wall paintings and a holy well said to cure all ills.
Hinagdanan Cave in Bingag, with a passage leading down to a natural swimming pool.
An exploration of the interior on a (cheaply!) rented scooter – there's more to this delightful island than sand and sea.
Panglao Market, a tin-roofed area used by the locals, with all sorts of goodies on offer.
YOU SHOULD KNOW:
If you're considering a maiden dive, be aware that you're not allowed to drink alcohol in the previous 24 hours.

Fishing boats moored off Panglao Island

Borneo

POPULATION:
The population has jumped from 9 million in 1990 to 16 million in 2000.
WHEN TO GO:
It is always rainy and humid in Borneo, but May to September is the best time to go.
HOW TO GET THERE:
It is possible to fly to all three parts of the island from Malaysia, Singapore and Indonesia, and ferries run from Java and Sulawesi.
HIGHLIGHTS:
Gunung Palung National Park.
Tanjung Puting National Park.
Trek through Pegunungan Meratus primary forest.
Chill out, dive and snorkel the glorious marine reserve at tiny, unspoiled Derawan Island.
YOU SHOULD KNOW:
Since 1971, Dr Birute Galdikas has run the orangutan rescue centre, Camp Leakey. Her research is essential to the fight to save the species from extinction. There are other research camps here too that one can visit, as well as a reforestation camp, where rangers are replanting hardwood saplings in an attempt to replace trees lost to logging and forest fires.

The name 'Borneo' conjures up visions of a vast, unknown territory, shrouded in mystery and cloaked in deep, dense, dark rainforest sheltering fearsome tribesmen decked out in feathers and warpaint. Thirty years ago, this would have been largely correct, but Borneo has changed.

Borneo's largest part by far is Indonesian Kalimantan, but it also includes Sarawak and Sabah, (East Malaysia), and Brunei, a small, independent country on the northwest coast. Brunei is wealthy, thanks to crude oil and natural gas. East Malaysia has similar resources as well as logging, palm oil production and some tourism. Kalimantan has it all - oil, gas, minerals, gold, diamonds, timber and palm oil, but its Dayaks, various tribal peoples, are desperate. Their culture is being devastated by deforestation, and their future looks bleak.

Borneo is blessed with natural wonders. Mount Kinabalu, at 4095 m (13,435 ft) is its highest mountain, and there are wonderful National Parks and World Heritage Sites. Hundreds of rivers traverse Borneo and there are extensive, extraordinary cave systems.

The rainforest contains extremely high endemism. Since 1996, 513 new plants and animals have been discovered here. Local shamans have introduced scientists to medicinal plants that are now used in western medicines. However, with unprecedented logging laying waste to the rainforest, the endless palm oil plantations and the arrival of thousands of transmigrants from Java and Madura, who also need land, all this could vanish.

Come to Borneo as soon as you can – in a few more years it may be damaged beyond repair. Meet some of the Dayak tribes living in longhouses on the riverbanks. Gaze in awe at some of the world's last, luxuriant primary rainforest. Take a motorized canoe through Tanjung Puting National Park, seeing and hearing chattering macaques, perhaps spotting the beautiful Giant Bornean butterfly flitting past, and watching the fireflies light up the night.

A river runs through the lowland rainforest of the Danum Valley.

The crystal clear waters around the Maluku Islands provide great snorkelling opportunities.

The Islands of Maluku

The Islands of Maluku, formerly known as the Moluccas, are a group of islands that lie between Sulawesi and Papua, with Ambon at their heart. Stretched out from north to south across 1,000 km (625 mi) of water, Ambon is the gateway to the fabulous Spice Islands.

Until the 16th century these islands were the sole source of nutmeg and cloves, which were in great demand in India, Arabia and China, and which finally attracted explorers from Europe, thus beginning the colonization of the region. Ruled by sultanates until 1512, the Portuguese and the Dutch struggled over the islands for decades, but by 1660 the Dutch had won a monopoly for the trade, making themselves a fortune over the following century. In 1797 the British briefly occupied Maluku, and brought about its downfall by taking away precious seedlings to plant in other tropical British colonies. Within a generation, Maluku sank into the obscurity from which it is just emerging today.

Ambon's tropical flowers, shrubs, bamboo, fruit trees and weeds grow so fast you can almost see it happen. It's a beautiful island, with rolling hills, gentle mountains and beaches, lined with waving palms giving on to limpid, aquamarine seas. Kota Ambon, the region's capital, lost much of its colonial architecture during World War II, but it is gloriously situated on a perfect bay, hills rising behind it.

As befits its status, Kota Ambon is a busy, commercial city, though still small and undemanding in comparison to many. You can easily escape and explore the rest of the island peacefully – take a short 'live aboard' diving trip from popular Namalatu Beach, see the splendid 17th century Dutch fort at Hila on the north coast, or sit on the empty beach at Honimua and plan trips to some of the other remote islands in the area.

POPULATION:
368,000 (2007)

WHEN TO GO:
November to March

HOW TO GET THERE:
By air from Java, or by sea from Java, Sulawesi or Papua.

HIGHLIGHTS:
The sacred eel pool at Waai.
The market at Paso.
The Siwa Lima Museum in Kota Ambon.
Exploring the National Park of Pombo Island and snorkelling in its waters.

YOU SHOULD KNOW:
From 1999 to 2002 there was some serious inter-communal violence in Ambon and several other islands. The population is fairly equally divided between Christians in the south and Muslims in the north. Today, however, the troubles seem to be over and both the economy and tourism are on the rise.

Banda Islands

The Bandas are a remote archipelago of ten tiny, enchanting islands lying in the Banda Sea, well to the south east of Ambon. These specks in the ocean were the greatest source of the best quality nutmeg and mace in the world, which not only brought them wealth and fame but also terrible misery and punishment at the hands of their Dutch oppressors. Today the Bandas are becoming revitalized, for the first time since the early 1800s, by a nascent tourist industry, which it is hoped will ensure both a stable economy and prevent further depopulation of the islands.

The main island is Banda Neira, and its capital shares the same name. Bandaneira was historically the administrative centre, and the ruling Dutch administrators seem to have vied with each other by building bigger and better villas. Fortunately many of these have survived more or less intact, making the town a delight to wander around. There are fortresses to visit as well as churches and several important colonial era buildings. The town is stunningly located on a lagoon, opposite which rises the perfect, 666-m (2,198-ft) high cone of Gunung Api, an active volcano which is a permanent threat to Banda Neira's inhabitants.

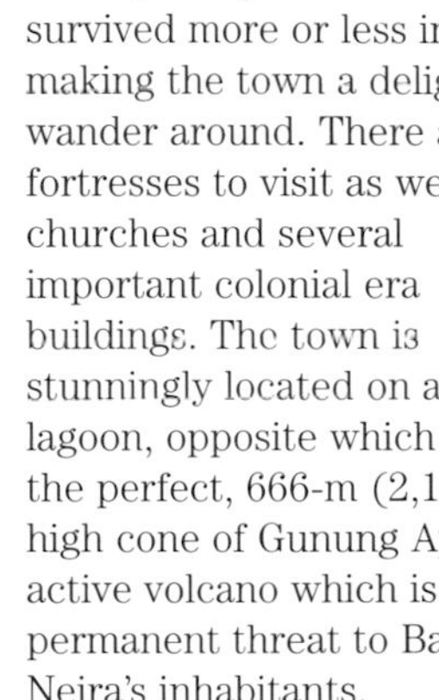

Banda Besar is the largest island in the group, and produced the best and largest quantity of nutmeg of them all. Banda Besar and the other islands all have beaches, diving and snorkelling to die for – this is their strength. Ai and Hatta both have superb underwater drop-offs, with marvellous corals and fish. Run has impressive dive sites, and Neilaka, which you can walk around in just a few minutes, is the epitome of a perfect tropical island, surrounded by pristine, deserted, white sand beaches.

POPULATION:
15,000 (2001)
WHEN TO GO:
October to March
HOW TO GET THERE:
By air from Ambon or Seram, or by sea from Ambon, Sulawesi, Kei Islands, Papua, Timor and Java.
HIGHLIGHTS:
The 17th century forts, Benteng Nassau and Benteng Belgica in Bandaneira.
Bandaneira's museum in Rumah Budaya.
Climbing Gunung Api at sunrise for stupendous views.
The December boat races at Pulau Ai.
The Groot Waling plantation house and estate on Banda Besar.
YOU SHOULD KNOW:
In 1667 Britain offered to give back New Netherland, which included Manhattan Island, to the Dutch in exchange for sugar factories in Surinam. Declining this offer, the Dutch actually forced Britain to give up Pulau Run, thus achieving a nutmeg monopoly. After recapturing New Netherland in 1673, the Dutch were finally forced to cede it back to Britain, this time forever. In retrospect, the Dutch made a serious error…

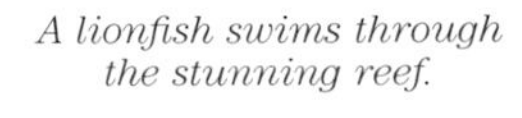

A lionfish swims through the stunning reef.

Nusa Lembongan

POPULATION:
55,000 (2006)
WHEN TO GO:
Anytime, but it is driest from May to September.
HOW TO GET THERE:
By sea from Bali.
HIGHLIGHTS:
The Goa Karangsari caves on Nusa Penida.
The waterfall at Batukandik, Nusa Penida.
The spooky temple of Pura Dalem Penetaran Ped, Nusa Penida.
Mushroom Bay, Nusa Lembongan.
The dive sites of Blue Corner, Jackfish Point and Ceningan Point around Lembongan and Ceningan.

Just off the coast of south east Bali, in the Lombok Strait, lie Nusa Lembongan, Nusa Penida and the tiny Nusa Ceningan. Of these, Nusa Lembongan is generally the island of choice. Easy to cycle or walk around as it is only 4 km (2.5 mi) by 2 km (1.25 mi), Lembongan is a charming, relaxed and peaceful place – ideal for a few days R & R. There are no cars, and few motorcycles here and, apart from income derived from tourism, most of the inhabitants make their living from fishing and seaweed cultivation.

Circled by white sand beaches, Lembongan has attracted backpackers for years. Today however, the island has been 'discovered' and more upmarket facilities are beginning to appear. Lembongan has two villages, and a number of beautiful little bays and beaches. The north shore has good surfing, and there are still plenty of healthy coral reefs for snorkellers to enjoy.

Across a narrow suspension bridge at the south east of the island is Nusa Ceningan. This hilly little place has no roads, just tracks, and lovely views. There is only one village here, but lots of seaweed farming, and at low tide the frames in the lagoon are interesting to visit.

Nusa Penida is an arid, harshly beautiful, limestone island, with a hilly interior. Much less touristy, possibly due to the Balinese belief that it is cursed, it's an interesting place to visit. In the south, steep limestone cliffs drop directly into the sea, while the north coast has sandy beaches.

The big attraction of all three islands is their dive sites, and several dive operators have set up shop here, offering dives that range from shallow and easy, to serious drift dives. Diving off these shores you will probably see several large marine creatures, including sharks, turtles and sometimes sunfish.

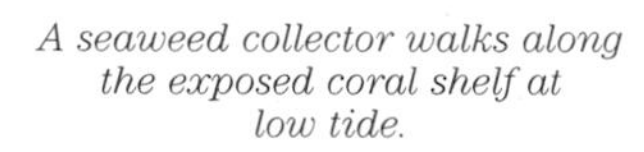

A seaweed collector walks along the exposed coral shelf at low tide.

Bali

Terraced rice paddies with Mount Agung in the background

Bali, the magical island of the gods, lives up to and beyond its reputation. Just 153 km (95 mi) wide and 112 km (69 mi) long, it is small enough to be driven around within a day. This is Indonesia's Hindu island, though like the other islands, animism exists beneath the surface, where art and beauty reign supreme. Three sacred volcanoes dominate the range straddling the north and east, providing bounteous soil – local people say that if you put a bare stick in the earth, it will take root.

When Java's Islamic empire arose in the 16th century, the vanquished Hindus fled to Bali, reinforcing its culture but making an enemy. Over time Bali has been invaded by Java, Lombok, the Netherlands and Japan. In the 1960s thousands died when Mount Agung erupted, and 100,000 more were killed in retaliation for an unsuccessful communist coup against the government in Java. In 2002 and 2005, terrorist bombs killed and injured hundreds of both tourists and locals, but despite these tragedies Bali always recovers.

Beauty touches every aspect of daily life. The island is bursting with artists, wood carvers, musicians and dancers, with Ubud, in central Bali, the artistic heartland, having been home to many European artists since the 1920s. Tourism took off in the 1970s, but is contained in particular areas, leaving much of the island undisturbed. Here you can see classic scenes of brilliant green, terraced rice paddies, stone temples intricately carved with fabulous creatures, and gamelan orchestras accompanying gorgeously costumed dancers performing the Ramayana in the moonlight.

You can climb volcanoes, swim with dolphins, walk along near empty beaches, admire exquisite offerings to the gods and watch colourful religious processions. Currently tourism is down, but Bali and its people are enchanting and completely irresistible.

POPULATION:
3.2 million (2006)

WHEN TO GO:
Anytime, but the driest season is from May to September.

HOW TO GET THERE:
International or domestic flights to Denpasar or ferry from other Indonesian islands.

HIGHLIGHTS:
The beaches and beach life around the island.
The galleries and performance art in Ubud.
Tanah Lot, Bali's most picturesque temple.
Trekking round Tirta Gangga and the water palace.
Shopping – you will be sorely tempted.
The Kecak (Monkey) Dance at sunset in Ulu Watu temple.

YOU SHOULD KNOW:
Negara, in south-west Bali, is famous for its bull races. Water buffalo, pulling small, decorative chariots and carrying elegantly dressed riders, dash hell for leather down the beach in front of a large, hugely appreciative audience.

The coast near Labuhanbajo

Flores

Flores gained its name from the Portuguese, who named it Cabo das Flores, Cape of Flowers. It is a long, narrow island, lying to the east of Komodo and the Rinca Islands and stretching some 350 km (218 mi) from end to end, though only 70 km (44 mi) at its widest. A volcanic chain rises along its length like the jagged spikes on the back of a stegosaurus – this is a landscape of green mountains and steep sided valleys, rushing rivers, savannah, beaches and coral gardens.

Prior to the 16th century, Flores was animist, trading sandalwood, cinnamon and fabric with passing mariners. Sandalwood brought the Portuguese and Catholicism soon took root, leading eventually to Muslim invasions to halt the spread of Christianity. In1859 the Dutch took over, but spent nearly 50 years gaining full control, and departing when Indonesia achieved independence. Today Flores is 90 per cent Catholic, though traditional beliefs are held as well.

In 2003 archaeologists discovered the skeleton of a tiny adult human, a mere 1 m (3.3 ft) high and since then several more have been found. *Homo floresiensis*, nicknamed Hobbit, lived only12,000 years ago, and scientists are still arguing about his precise classification.

This lovely island receives far fewer visitors than the more popular Indonesian islands, but it contains some spectacular natural wonders, in particular the crater lakes at Keli Mutu. Here three lakes at the volcano's summit, separated only by low, rocky ridges display astonishingly different, vivid colours. These change on a regular basis, from turquoise, chocolate brown and dark green through maroon, pale green and café au lait, caused by dissolving minerals in the waters. This is a sacred place, to which the souls of the departed go, and it is impossible not to find it deeply impressive.

POPULATION:
1.8 million (2006)
WHEN TO GO:
April to September
HOW TO GET THERE:
By air from Bali or West Timor, or by ferry.
HIGHLIGHTS:
The Manggarai hill people's penti ceremony, held in August.
Bajawa and the Ngada people and their culture.
The ikat weaving villages of Nggela and Wolojita.
Diving, snorkelling and relaxing at Ahuwair and Waiterang beaches.
The cathedral at Larantuka and the Good Friday and Easter Sunday ceremonies.
YOU SHOULD KNOW:
The area around the fishing village of Riung is the only place to see Komodo dragons outside Komodo and the Rinca Islands.

Gili Islands

Lying in pristine waters off the north western coast of Lombok are three idyllic tropical islands, the Gilis. Fringed with golden, sandy beaches, and ringed with coral reefs that teem with a myriad of fish, the Gilis make a wonderful getaway if you need a break from Bali's cultural wonders, or have exhausted yourself by trekking up Lombok's Mount Rinjani. Come here for the quiet life – there is little traffic, and nothing to do except swim, snorkel, or lie in your hammock with a good book.

Gili Air, the closest to Lombok, is flat and rural. The government has helped the local population by donating coconut and mango saplings to keep the island green and attractive. The coastal path that encircles Gili Air can be walked in about an hour. The atmosphere here is relaxed, although in the high season things can get pretty busy.

Gili Meno, in the middle, is the smallest, quietest and least developed of the three, though it is thought to have the best beaches. To the northwest there is a lake, watch out for mosquitoes, though during the dry season it is used for salt production. Inland are many coconut plantations and few homes: the population here is tiny.

Gili Trawangan is the largest Gili, and a serious party island. Many tourists come here, not only backpackers and gap-year youth but also trendy Singaporeans and Indonesians too, and this is reflected in the number of facilities.

What is great about the Gilis is hopping from one to another, thus quickly discovering where you want to stay, which could be quite different from where you want to swim. Diving and snorkelling is terrific wherever you go, and care is being taken of the reefs themselves. On a clear day, fabulous views can be had across the water to Mount Rinjani, and the sunsets are legendary.

POPULATION:
Gili Air: 1,800; Gili Meno: 300; Gili Trawangan: 1,800 (2004)
WHEN TO GO:
April to September
HOW TO GET THERE:
By ferry or speedboat from Lombok or Bali.
HIGHLIGHTS:
The Taman Burung Bird Park on Gili Meno.
A snorkelling trip in a glass bottomed boat.
Seeing the islands from a horse and trap.
Learn to scuba dive and enjoy some of the Gilis' excellent dive sites.
YOU SHOULD KNOW:
Don't forget that people here are Muslim, and can be deeply offended by the sight of too much flesh.

A woman collects shellfish on Gili Air.

Ternate, Tidore and Halmahera

POPULATION:
Halmahera 162,728 (1995); Ternate 56,000 (1980); Tidore 40,000 (2000 estimate)
HOW TO GET THERE:
Flights from Java, Sulawesi and Ambon to the main airport in Ternate or by sea from Sulawesi, Papua and Ambon. Travel between the islands by boat.
WHEN TO GO:
November to March
HIGHLIGHTS:
The Sultan's Mosque and the Sultan's Palace and Museum in Ternate town.
The Afo clove tree on Mt Gamalama, said to be over 400 years old, and the mother of all clove trees in existence today.
Morotai Island, off north eastern Halmahera, site of an important victory by the Allies over the Japanese during World War II. In 1973, Private Nakamura emerged from the rainforest here, to surrender. He was unaware that the war had been over for almost 30 years.
YOU SHOULD KNOW:
Halmahera now has two gold mines and a copper and cobalt mine in active production.

Ternate, Tidore and Halmahera lie in the Molucca Sea between north east Sulawesi and north west Papua, in a thread of other small, volcanic islands with little or no population. Halmahera is the largest island of Maluku, and is reminiscent of Sulawesi in shape. Ternate and Tidore lie to its west, and are small and circular, boasting larger populations than Halmahera despite the latter's size.

Ternate and Tidore are, historically speaking, enemies, and both have a violent past. They were clove islands, ruled by wealthy and powerful Islamic sultans. In the early 1500s the Portuguese settled in Ternate, and the Spanish were quickly invited to Tidore. By the beginning of the following century, the Dutch took control, building the fort of Oranje on Ternate, and continued to play politics with other interested European powers and to foment trouble between the various sultans.

Pulau Ternate is really just a volcanic cone. Rising to a height of 1,721 m (5,679 ft), Gunung Api Gamalama had its last major eruption in 1840, destroying virtually everything on the island. Small eruptions occurred during the 1980s and 1990s, but currently it is not considered a danger. Ternate town is the administrative centre for the north Maluku region, and there are several interesting buildings to visit here.

Tidore is a much calmer, quieter island, with a local language that is still spoken. Dominated by its own volcano, Gunung Kiematubu, much of it is steeply and lushly forested. The remains of a Spanish fort can be seen in the sleepy main town, Soasio, and there are two smaller islands off the coast, Maitara and Mare, to visit.

Halmahera is mountainous, with several volcanoes and very few roads. The main town, Tobelo, is on the north east coast, and there are various uninhabited, picturesque islands just off-shore upon which you can play Robinson Crusoe to your heart's content.

Gunung Api Gamalama volcano

Nias

Nias, the largest island off the west coast of Sumatra, is roughly 100 km (60 mi) long and 50 km (30 mi) wide, and is the home to a most unusual and ancient megalithic stone culture. The Niha people are farmers, growing many different crops, as well as rice. In the past they were ferocious warriors; fighting between different villages was commonplace, and head hunting was rife long after most other tribal people had stopped the practice.

The Niha divided themselves into three castes – aristocrats, commoners and slaves, who were traded, and until the early 1800s they had virtually no contact with the wider world other than via this trade. Nias itself divides into three parts – southern, central and northern – each having their own style, and the traditional villages are unique, often built defensively on high ground approached by stone steps and enclosed by a stone wall.

In the south, the houses are built along either side of a long courtyard. Made of teak and bamboo, their steep thatched roofs are constructed without nails, each beam slotting into the next. The Niha's wood carving skills are highly regarded throughout South-East Asia. Stone benches, occasionally with human skulls beneath them, and bathing pools, carvings and standing stones can readily be seen, as can the ancient ritual of stone jumping – now practised for important guests and tourists – where young men leap over stone columns some 2 m (6 ft 6 in) high, feet first.

This megalithic culture is not the only attraction here – another is the waves. Internationally famous amongst the surfing fraternity, they attract as many surfers to the south as visitors to the island as a whole. Nias is suffering from the after effects of natural disasters. Travelling is tough and people are needy, but the island is extraordinary and won't disappoint you.

POPULATION:
650,000 (2006)
WHEN TO GO:
June to October
HOW TO GET THERE:
By air or ferry from Sumatra.
HIGHLIGHTS:
The stone carvings and standing stones around Gomo.
The Chieftain's house at Hilinawalo Mazingo.
Stone jumping and war dances at Bawomataluo.
The architecture in Hilismaetano.
Surfing.
YOU SHOULD KNOW:
The surf break at Pantai Sorake is reputed to be the best right-hander in the world – even better since the height of the reef was raised by the 2005 earthquake. Take precautions against malaria and cholera.

Stone carvings on Nias

Samosir Island

POPULATION:
120,000 (2000)
WHEN TO GO:
June to September
HOW TO GET THERE:
By road over the bridge, or by ferry from Parapat.
HIGHLIGHTS:
Batak Museum – in the village of Simanindo, the museum sheds light on the Batak way of life with displays of handicrafts and traditional puppets used in ceremonies and dances. There are also displays of traditional dance performed daily.
Batak handicrafts and musical instruments – these are on sale in many of the villages on the island.
The hot springs on the mainland just over the bridge from Pangururan.
Tomok – in the village can be found impressive stone sarcophagi and other artefacts from the reign of King Sidabutar.
Ambarita – see the traditional Batak houses, and King Siallagan's execution block.
YOU SHOULD KNOW:
Samosir is also known as 'Island of the Dead'.

The largest island within an island, and the fourth largest lake island in the world, Samosir is around 630 sq km (243 sq mi) and sits in Lake Toba in the north of Sumatra. The lake and island were formed after the eruption of a supervolcano around 75, 000 years ago, which is believed to have been severe enough to cause climatic change. Probably the largest and deepest caldera lake in the world, Lake Toba sits high amid treeless mountains. The island of Samosir was originally connected to the surrounding caldera wall by a small isthmus, which was cut through to allow ships to pass.

The eastern side of the island rises steeply towards a central plateau with an altitude of 780 m (2,559 ft), and the land gradually descends towards the southern and western coasts, which are scattered with small villages. The Samosir plateau consists mainly of rock, some scattered forests and swamps and a small lake. From Pangururan on the western side, a bridge connects the island with mainland Sumatra.

The island is best known as the home of the Toba Batak people, an ethnic group whose heartland centres around the lake. Toba Batak are known traditionally for their weaving, wood carving and particularly their ornate stone tombs, many of which can be seen on Samosir. Their burial and marriage traditions are very rich and complex, and in the past they had a reputation for being fierce warriors.

In the village of Tomok, under the sacred Hariara tree, you can see the 200-year-old royal stone sarcophagus of King Sidabutar's clan. Although they resemble coffins, the sarcophagi normally contain the collected skulls of an entire family. Stone sarcophagi have been found in 26 villages around the island.

The island's traditional wooden houses are interesting and may be decorated with clan symbols. In Tomok there are some good examples, as well as at Ambarita, where there are rows of traditional Batak houses. There are also artefacts dating from King Siallagan's reign here, including stone chairs and the execution block. The small museum offers a luridly graphic description of past executions.

The island has some nice sandy beaches, particularly around Ambarita. Or if you prefer your water hot, head over the bridge from Pangururan to the thermal springs on the mainland just 3 km (1.86 mi) away. There are several swimming pools to enjoy, or climb up the hill to where the springs emerge from the ground.

A typical home of the Toba Batak

Riau Islands

Between Sumatra's swampy east coast, Singapore and the South China Sea lie the Riau Islands – some 3,000 of them altogether. Many are nameless, hundreds are uninhabited, and so far just a very few are being transformed under an economic development plan devised between Sumatra and Singapore.

The history of the Riau Islands is interesting. Situated in a strategically important position on the shortest sea route between China and India, they were ruled by various Malaysian sultans, who were dominated first by the Portuguese and then the Dutch. The last sultanate of Riau was established on the now neglected Lingga Island, and it was the British who were responsible for the islands becoming part of Indonesia rather than Malaysia.

Bintan Island is the islands' administrative centre, the largest island of the archipelago and a major weekend getaway for Singaporeans. While its north shore consists of upmarket Singaporean resort hotels and golf courses, the east coast is much less organized; though the beaches are not as good, they provide fine swimming, and there are a few deserted offshore islands that are worth a visit. Apart from the beaches there are several places of interest to see here, and even a small mountain, Bintan Besar, to climb.

Batam Island is very different. The transport hub for the region, it has become an overspill for Singaporean industry. There is a wealth of factories and production plants on the island, and virtually everyone working here comes from somewhere else. There are resorts and golf courses, but most of their clients are businessmen and corporate visitors.

Should you want a quick break from either Singapore or Pekanbaru, Penuba Island might be the place for you. It has some beautiful beaches, is undeveloped and is perfect for relaxing and doing very little.

Bintan Island

POPULATION:
Batam 714,000 (2006)
WHEN TO GO:
March to September
HOW TO GET THERE:
By sea to Batam or Bintan from Singapore or Sumatra.
HIGHLIGHTS:
Penyengat Island, across the harbour from Tanjung Pinang, Bintan's main port town, once the capital of the Riau rajahs.
The Chinese temple in Senggarang, Bintan. Trikora Beach, Bintan.
The ruins of the last Rajah's palace, and royal tombs on Lingga.
YOU SHOULD KNOW:
The first book of Malay grammar was published on Penyengat Island in 1857, and classical Malay is still spoken on the island.

Seram

POPULATION:
247,375 (1993)
WHEN TO GO:
November to March
HOW TO GET THERE:
By air or sea from Ambon.
HIGHLIGHTS:
Snorkel the coral gardens off shore from Sawai.
Look out for some of the island's huge butterflies, in particular the spectacular Blue Mountain Swallowtail (*Papilio Ulysses*), with its 11.4 cm (4.5 in) wingspan.
YOU SHOULD KNOW:
An earthquake of 6.7 on the Richter scale was recorded on Seram in March 2006.

The mysterious island of Seram lies to the north east of Ambon. A wild, mountainous place, rich with rainforest and wildlife, in particular fabulous, colourful birds and some 2,000 species of butterflies and moths, Seram is replete with myths and legends. One of Maluku's largest and least known islands, it is held in awe by the Ambonese, who believe that all life originated here.

Seram is home to numerous indigenous peoples, largely still living their traditional ways of life. Some 75 per cent of the population are animists, and one remote tribe, the Nuaulu, were still head hunting in the 1940s. This is a difficult island to get around, with few roads. Instead, people hop on boats to take them from village to village up and down the coast. Masohi is the island's main town, but most people come here to take guided treks into Manusela National Park, or to visit the dramatically beautiful Teluk Sawai Bay.

Sadly, the Indonesian government have leased logging concessions on Seram, one consequence of which is the loss of birdlife. In the national park, however, the forest is alive with screaming cockatoos and multi-coloured parrots. At Saleman, on Teluk Sawai Bay, great flocks of Lusiala birds, believed to be carrying the souls of their human ancestors, fly from a cave at dusk. Seram is also home to the salmon crested cockatoo, endemic to only four places in Indonesia, but there are other endemic species too – honeyeaters, lories and white-eyes for example. Mount Binaiya at 3,019 m (10,000 ft) is the island's highest peak, and the fabulous, rushing rivers and plunging waterfalls combined with exotic peoples and wonderful wildlife make Seram an adventure not to be undertaken lightly.

The spectacular Blue Mountain Swallowtail butterfly

Siberut

The largest island of the Mentawai group, Siberut is believed to have broken off from Sumatra some 500,000 years ago. Hence the indigenous people remained isolated and evolved their own culture. Siberut's flora and fauna is also unique, and therefore it was listed as a UNESCO Man and Biosphere Reserve in 1981. Additionally a large part of the island is a National Park, as extra protection against predatory loggers.

Until missionaries arrived in the early 1900s, Mentawaians were hunter/gatherers, highly skilled at boat building. They looked exotic: the Sakkudei, for example, wore bark loin cloths or skirts, red rattan bands, beads, tattoos, and filed their teeth to points. Today these customs have largely died out, but many cling to their old beliefs despite the missionaries' best efforts.

Mentawaians live mainly in riverside villages, with a communal longhouse in which to make important decisions. Houses contain several families and there are separate buildings for unmarried men and widows. Some cultivation occurs and hunting (with bows and poisoned arrows) and fishing are important social activities.

The flora and fauna here are extraordinary – 60 per cent of the mammals are endemic, including the Kloss gibbon, one of the 25 most endangered animals. As there are no facilities in the interior, most visitors arrive as part of a group, with local hosts organized in advance. The coast, however, is another story. Highly thought of by the surfing fraternity, small resorts have begun popping up on the best beaches.

Hilly, startlingly green and always humid, luxuriant plant life still smothers large parts of Siberut. As one travels by river, not road, seeing rainforest in every direction and hearing the calls of birds and monkeys rather than the rumble of traffic, it's hard to believe that the city of Padang is a mere 100 km (60 mi) away. Siberut is another world.

POPULATION:
35,000 (2005)
WHEN TO GO:
It is always rainy here, but the driest month is May. The highest rainfall occurs from September to December.
HOW TO GET THERE:
By sea from Sumatra.
HIGHLIGHTS:
Trekking in the interior.
Surfing between April and October.
YOU SHOULD KNOW:
Beware of chloroquine-resistant malaria. Take things with which to barter, and gifts for your village hosts.

Mentawai men in a dugout canoe set out down the Rereiket River.

Sulawesi

POPULATION:
15,500,000 (2006)
WHEN TO GO:
Almost always wet, the driest months are probably July and August.
HOW TO GET THERE:
By international or internal flight to Makassar, Manado or Pula, or by ferry.
HIGHLIGHTS:
Tana Beru – watch Bugis schooners being fashioned by hand.
Lore Lindu National Park, a UNESCO Man and Biosphere Reserve.
Ancient megalithic stone statues in the Napu, Besoa and Bada valleys.
Diving and snorkelling in Tukang Besi National Marine Park.
Chill out in the glorious Togean Islands.
Sungguminasa's Ballompoa Museum.
YOU SHOULD KNOW:
Sulawesi's complicated coastline is longer than that of the whole of continental USA.

Sulawesi lies to the east of Borneo. It's a bizarrely shaped island – the four 'arms' radiating from its mountainous centre make it look like some weird sea creature. Marginally smaller than Britain, nowhere in Sulawesi is more than 100 km (60 mi) from the ocean. Many different ethnic groups and cultures survive here, the most famous of which are the Toraja and the Bugis. The latter are a proud, seafaring people, whose elegant schooners still ply their trade around Indonesia's waters.

Most visitors to the island go to see the extraordinary Torajan people, who live in the fertile valleys of the mountains in the north of South Sulawesi. Their culture is fascinating – living in large, traditionally built family houses with high roofs that rear up at both ends, resembling either the ships in which their ancestors arrived here, or buffalo horns, depending on who you ask.

Buffaloes are essential to the Toraja, a sign of wealth and status and a necessary sacrificial animal in many ceremonies, particularly the Torajans' elaborate funeral rituals. The dead often remain in the house for months or years before the funeral festivities occur, a process lasting several days, involving the slaughter of many animals, with parades, dances and feasting. The dead and their valuables are placed in tombs carved into sheer limestone cliffs, closed with a wooden door and, if they were highly respected, a life sized wooden effigy, dressed appropriately, is placed on a gallery carved into the cliff face.

Sulawesi's largely upland landscape is dramatically spectacular. Its isolation has produced vast numbers of endemic species – some two thirds of its mammals and a quarter of its birds, reptiles and insects. Sadly, this incredible fauna is threatened by habitat loss. Whilst visiting Toraja-land is a unique experience, all the rest of the island deserves your attention as well.

A traditional Torajan house

Sumatra

The island of Sumatra is the sixth largest in the world, stretching almost 2,000 km (1,250 mi) from north to south. To the west, the Bukit Barisan Mountains run almost the entire length of the island, rising from a narrow coastal strip. The highest of the 93 volcanic peaks, 15 of which are still active, is Mount Kerinci, at 3,805 m (12,556 ft). To the east, mountains slope down to swamps and marshes, cut by seething, silt-laden rivers.

Islam reached Sumatra in the 14th century, by which time several fabulous empires had come and gone, and Europeans were ogling the island's natural wealth. Several powers vied for it, with the Dutch emerging victorious in 1824. Sumatrans, however, were not subdued, and they continued fighting until independence in 1949. The Acehnese people still cause headaches for the current Indonesian government.

This is a wild and glorious island. Mainly covered with dense jungle, it contains some of the world's greatest biodiversity. Endemic species such as the Sumatran tiger and the two-horned rhino still survive here, as do orang-utans. Here, too, are both the world's largest and tallest flowers. The island encompasses many different ethnic groups, languages and cultures such as the matrilineal Minangkabau of West Sumatra, the Christian Bataks around gorgeous Lake Toba, and the fiercely Muslim Acehnese.

Sumatra is an adventure. Now largely forgotten by tourists, it can be hard work – the roads are dreadful and the transport worse – but the landscape is fabulous and the traditional architecture, such as the Minankabau longhouses with their buffalo-horn style roofs, breathtaking.

A string of natural disasters has hit Sumatra in the recent past, drastically curtailing tourism, but if you want to explore off the beaten track, amidst fabulous natural wonders, meeting people who will welcome your arrival with open arms, Sumatra is the place for you.

POPULATION:
40,000,000 (2005)
WHEN TO GO:
Always hot and always wet, the driest months are June and July.
HOW TO GET THERE:
By international flights to Medan, domestic flight, or ferry from Malaysia, Singapore or other Indonesian islands.
HIGHLIGHTS:
The orang-utan rehabilitation centre in Bukit Lawang.
Lake Toba for Batak culture.
Climbing the Sibayak volcano.
Trekking in Kerinci Seblat National Park.
The Hindu-Buddhist temple complex at Muara Jambi.
YOU SHOULD KNOW:
The famous World War 1 French spy, Mata Hari, lived in Sumatra for some years. In the Bahasa Indonesian language 'mata hari', literally 'the eye of the day' means 'the sun'.

A Minankabau rice barn, with traditional buffalo-horn style roofs

Sumba

POPULATION:
540,000 (2007)
WHEN TO GO:
April to December
HOW TO GET THERE:
By air from Bali or West Timor, or by ferry.
HIGHLIGHTS:
The Resi Moni megalith, one of the largest on Sumba.
The Purunga Ta Kadonga ceremony at Lai Tarung.
Sodan village and its annual October New Year ceremony.
Ikat weaving at Ngallu and Kaliuda.
Waikabubak and the villages of Anakalang district.
The white sand beach of Pantai Marosi.
YOU SHOULD KNOW:
Betel nut, or *sirih pinang* is widely chewed on Sumba, and it is offered to visitors as a welcoming gesture. It is impolite to refuse it, but if you can't face chewing it, put it away as though to enjoy later.

To the south of Komodo and Flores is the island of Sumba, the arid backwater of the Nusa Tenggara. Some 300 km (180 mi) long and 80 km (50 mi) wide, west Sumba is fairly isolated, but because it receives more rain and is more fertile it is home to 65 per cent of the population. This is a land of low, undulating hills, cassava and maize crops and open grasslands grazed by cattle, buffalo and horses.

Most of the religious influences that affected other islands passed Sumba by, and until Dutch rule in the early 1900s, it was never colonized by outsiders. Instead it was formed of various separate, warring kingdoms. Besides Bahasa Indonesia there are nine other languages spoken on Sumba, eight of which are used in the west, whilst the ninth is exclusive to the east.

Historically known for its horses, slaves and sandalwood, Sumba is now famous for its extraordinary annual Pasola festivals. Held after the full moon in February and March, these are ritual battles between spear-carrying, bareback, tribal horsemen. Although the spears are blunted, this tradition reflects those early kingdoms, and occasionally genuine fighting and deaths occur. The start of the Pasolas is determined by the arrival of thousands of seaworms on the shoreline. Fulfilling their reproductive cycle, the worms are thought to predict the abundance of the coming harvest.

Geographically very different from the west, east Sumba is a barren, rocky place. The 250,000 inhabitants live, for the most part, near the coast, and are renowned for their ikat weaving. The motifs used are often animals such as horses, crocodiles and cockatoos, each deeply symbolic. Despite being largely Protestant, animism is still strongly rooted here.

This island is off the tourist trail, but those who visit will find fascinating traditional villages, extraordinary megalithic tombs, exotic tribespeople and remarkable death ceremonies.

A rider battles it out in a traditional Pasola festival.

Sumbawa

Most of Sumbawa's visitors come for the world-class surfing.

Sumbawa, which lies to the east of Lombok, is larger than Bali and Lombok put together. It is a poor, rugged island, which, thanks to an enormous gold and copper mining project that has recently begun operations, may well become more developed and much wealthier in future. Meanwhile, most of the inhabitants are farmers or fishermen, while some breed and export the island's tough little horses.

Sumbawa naturally divides into two parts, west and east, separated by the Tambora volcano. In 1815 Gunung Tambora erupted, killing thousands and reducing the peak from 4,200 m (13,900 ft) to the 2,850 m (9,400 ft) it is today. The western Sumbawans lean towards Lombok in both looks and language, whilst the easterners lean towards Flores. Everyone, however, is strongly Muslim, and has been since the early 1600s, although traditional animism still plays its part.

The island's attractions are mainly natural: the volcano can be climbed, although it is a hard, two-day trek to the top. Once there, on a clear day, the views are spectacular, and the caldera, which is some 6 km (3.7 mi) wide, contains a two-coloured lake. Most of the visitors to the island, however, come for the world-class surfing at Hu'u and Lakey Beach, which is at its best between June and August.

The island's main town, Sumbawa Besar, is small, dusty and provincial – easy to explore on foot or by horse and cart. People are friendly and hospitable and it makes a good base from which to visit nearby Poto, where the songket (silver or gold threads woven into cloth) sarongs are highly thought of. Also within visiting distance are some fascinating megalithic, carved tombs, believed to be 2,000 years old. Sumbawa may be a fairly low-key island, but it is well worth a few days of your time.

POPULATION:
1,000,000 (2007)
WHEN TO GO:
May to October
HOW TO GET THERE:
By air to Sumbawa Besar or to Bima from Bali, Sumba or Flores. By ferry from many other Indonesian islands.
HIGHLIGHTS:
The wooden Sultan's Palace and the Art Deco Yellow House in Sumbawa Besar.
Surfing at Maluk and Sekongkang.
A trip to Pulao Moyo, an island nature reserve surrounded by excellent coral reefs.
Hire a horse to trek through the forest near Tegel.
Horse racing on a Sunday at the Desa Panda stadium near Bima.
The museum in the Sultan's Palace in Bima.
YOU SHOULD KNOW:
Don't dress skimpily unless you're at the beach – this is a strongly Muslim island and you will cause unnecessary offence.

Java

POPULATION:
120,000,000 (2006)
WHEN TO GO:
May to September
HOW TO GET THERE:
International flight to Jakarta, domestic flight or ferry from Malaysia, Singapore and the other Indonesian islands.
HIGHLIGHTS:
Jakarta's Sunda Kelapa harbour, with its superb traditional schooners.
Ujung Kulong National Park.
The Waicak festival in May at Borobudur.
The Ramayana, danced at full moon at Prambanan.
The Dieng Plateau and its temples.
The hill towns of Malang and Tretes.
YOU SHOULD KNOW:
Some of the best and most expensive coffee in the world comes from Java. Kopi Luwak comes from coffee berries that have been previously digested by palm civets, a type of wild cat.

Indonesia's heartland, Java, has twice the population of Britain in roughly half the area, and is naturally the political and economic hub of Indonesia. Jakarta, the capital, is a city of at least 15 million, where extremes of wealth and poverty sit awkwardly side by side. There are several other large cities, but once outside them, one is unaware of the crowded nature of the island. Some 50 per cent of the population are farmers, tending land which is fantastically fertile, thanks to the residue from the active volcanoes that form the island's spine.

Java Man proves that history here reaches back for a million years. Wonderful Buddhist and Hindu temples, particularly Borobudur and Prambanan, built in the 8th and 9th centuries show cultural depths rarely achieved elsewhere, although the island's golden age came during the 16th century. The three main ethnic groups are the Javanese, Sundanese and Madurese, each speaking their own language, the Javanese being the main group, famous for all things artistic.

Java is beautiful; the landscape soars and swoops, crops growing at every level. Fruit such as apples and strawberries grow around the hill towns, while rice, tobacco, tea, coffee, vegetables and spices seem to grow everywhere else.

This is a fascinating island, where performance arts such as *wayang kulit* – shadow puppet plays – and traditional dance can be seen in tiny villages or a Sultan's palace, and artists and galleries abound. Whether you climb Mount Bromo to stand by the smoking crater as the sun rises, swim or surf in the crashing Indian Ocean on the southern coast, learn batik-making, cookery or massage in vibrant university towns such as Solo or Yogyakarta, or exchange laughter and ideas with students over several 'Bintang' beers, amidst clouds of pungent clove cigarette smoke, Java's exotic, ancient culture is show-stopping.

The smoking crater of Mount Bromo in Bromo Tengger Semeru National Park

Komodo

A Komodo dragon

Part of the Lesser Sunda chain and lying between the neighbouring islands of Sumbawa to the west and Flores to the east, Komodo is one of the many islands which make up the Republic of Indonesia. The inhabitants of this barren volcanic land are descendants of former convicts who were exiled to the island and who have mixed themselves with the Bugis from nearby Sulawesi. However, the island is most famous not for its heritage of convicts, but for the unique fauna which inhabit it. The Komodo dragon, the world's largest living lizard, takes its name from the island. A type of monitor lizard, the dragon inhabits Komodo and some of the smaller surrounding islands, attracting thousands of tourists every year.

The lizards are active during the morning and late afternoon, but burrow into dry stream beds during the heat of the day to keep cool. Guided tours take visitors to see the lizards and this is a good bet if you want to guarantee spotting one. They can grow up to 3 m (10 ft) in length and, despite their short legs, they can run as fast as a dog. Visitors are advised not to wear red and to keep an eye out for their footprints while visiting the island as they can bite. They can also swim from island to island so even the sea is not necessarily a safe place.

Komodo dragons were only discovered by Western scientists in 1910 when a Dutch officer, Van Steyn van Hensbroek, heard rumours of giant crocodiles and went to investigate. Today their range has contracted due to human activities, and they are listed as vulnerable by the World Conservation Union.

The Komodo National Park was set up in 1980 to protect the Komodo dragon, and the area is also now on the UNESCO World Heritage list. The national park includes the three large islands of Komodo, Rinca and Padar, as well as numerous smaller ones. Later it was dedicated to protecting other species as the three islands have a high marine biodiversity, including whale sharks, ocean sunfish, manta rays, eagle rays, pygmy seahorses, false pipefish, clown frogfish, nudibranchs, blue-ringed octopus, sponges, tunicates, and coral. The coral reefs, seamounts, seagrass beds and mangroves make the islands a popular place for diving.

POPULATION:
2,000 (2005)
WHEN TO GO:
April to October
HOW TO GET THERE:
By air to Labuanbajo from Bali, then by boat.
HIGHLIGHTS:
The Komodo dragons – consider joining a guided tour to get a good look at these prehistoric beasts.
YOU SHOULD KNOW:
All visitors to the Komodo National Park now have to pay a contribution to protect wildlife in the park, help support local communities and promote ecotourism.

Anak Krakatau still smoulders on!

Krakatau

POPULATION:
Uninhabited
WHEN TO GO:
April to June and September to October
HOW TO GET THERE:
Join a guided tour, or charter the best, most seaworthy boat you can find.
HIGHLIGHTS:
If you are in west Java to visit Krakatau, make time for a trip to the UNESCO World Heritage Site of Ujung Kulon National Park, home to several rare and endangered mammals.
YOU SHOULD KNOW:
Although the Krakatau explosion is a world famous event, the eruption of Sumbawa Island's Gunung Tambora was roughly equivalent. Tens of thousands were killed, and the island was devastated when the volcano exploded, losing 1,350 m (4,500 ft) of its height, and causing 1815 to be known globally as 'the year without a summer'.

The volcano of Krakatau is probably the most famous in the world. It lies between Sumatra and western Java, quite the reverse of the famous film entitled *Krakatoa, East of Java*. Krakatau earned its notoriety in 1883, when it erupted so violently that it almost completely disintegrated. Great columns of ash rose from the explosion to a height of 80 km (50 mi), which triggered a tsunami that crashed across the nearby Sumatran and Javan shorelines, wiping out over 160 villages and killing some 36,000 people. The noise of the explosion is thought to have been the loudest ever recorded, and the waves' passage was even measurable in the English Channel.

Most noticeable of all were the ash clouds, which travelled around the world for three years, causing extraordinarily vivid, colourful sunsets. It is thought that the background to Edvard Munch's famous painting, 'The Scream', was painted from the sunsets at that time.

In 1928, Anak Krakatau, or 'Child of Krakatau', made its appearance, and has been growing steadily ever since. This is an active, volatile 'child', and as you pass by on the night ferry, rivulets of molten lava are sometimes visible on its flanks. Anak Krakatau lies amongst several other small islands. At its birth, no life existed here, but today, some 80 years later, vegetation has returned, as have snakes, rats, insects, bats and birds.

It is possible to visit and trek on Anak Krakatau with a guided tour, though you cannot go to the caldera as it is potentially dangerous. A trip like this also enables you to visit some of the neighbouring islands, and to snorkel or dive nearby. Underwater, life is thriving – the thermal springs bring abundant plants as well as fish. A visit to Krakatau is truly a once-in-a-lifetime experience.

Lombok

The string of islands lying to the east of Bali are known collectively as Nusa Tenggara, and of them, Lombok is the main destination. Roughly 80 km (50 mi) from north to south, and about the same from east to west, Lombok's landscape is dominated by its northern mountains, their slopes covered in protected forest, from which rises Mount Rinjani, the second highest volcano in Indonesia. The western side is green and lush, but the east and south of the island are noticeably drier and less populated.

Indigenous Sasak people make up 90 per cent of the population, alongside Balinese and others. Sasaks have their own language and culture and although the predominant religion is Islam, they also have their own religion, Wektu Telu, a mixture of Islam, Hindu and animist beliefs. Invasions during the early 1600s led to Lombok being in Balinese hands by 1750, and under Dutch control from the late 1800s until independence. Like Bali, the island suffered massacres after the attempted coup in Java, and in the 1960s and 70s suffered famine conditions. Tourism began in the 1980s but has suffered with the rest of the country. Today there are high hopes for tourism potential in the future.

Lombok has something for everyone: landscapes as lush as Bali, empty white sand beaches, good snorkelling and surfing, hot springs, waterfalls, palaces, temples, and trekking on mighty Rinjani. You can watch traditional dances and ceremonies that follow the seasons, and listen to a remarkable musical style in which voices imitate the sounds of the Gamelan orchestra. There are also unique Sasak contests – Peresehan involves two men fighting with staves and shields, and Lanca, where men fight with their knees. Much less crowded than the better-known islands, Lombok is a great place for a getaway.

POPULATION:
3,100,000 (2007)
WHEN TO GO:
April to September is the driest time.
HOW TO GET THERE:
By air from Kuala Lumpur, Singapore, Java, Bali or Sumbawa, or by ferry between the islands.
HIGHLIGHTS:
The temple of Pura Meru.
The temple compound of Pura Lingsar.
The pottery making villages of Banyumulek and Penujak.
The craft villages south of Tetebatu.
The Sasak Nyale festival, held on the beach at Kuta in February/March.
The Mayura Water Palace and gardens.
YOU SHOULD KNOW:
The Wallace Line, imagined by naturalist Sir Alfred Wallace in the 1800s, separates Bali and Borneo from Lombok and Sulawesi. Theoretically Eurasian plants and animals exist on the western side while Australian species live on the east. In fact, this is a transition area between the two.

Clouds drift over the crater rim of Mount Rinjani.

Madura

POPULATION:
3,300,000 million (2006)
WHEN TO GO:
May to October
HOW TO GET THERE:
Ferry from Surabaya, Java.
HIGHLIGHTS:
The bull racing championship finals in Pamekasan, held every September/October.
The tombs of the royal family at Asta Tinggi, outside Sumenep.
The tombs of the Cakraningrat royal family at Air Mata, near Arosbaya.
Tanjungbumi village – for Madurese batik.
YOU SHOULD KNOW:
Before a big race, the bulls are given honey and herbs and up to 50 raw eggs per day to eat. Music is played to them, and they are given massages. Just before they race, they are given the local firewater, arak, to drink.

Separated from Surabaya in northwest Java by a 3 km (1.8 mi) channel of water, the island of Madura is a world of its own. Little visited either by tourists from overseas or Java itself, except from late August to October, the islanders are proud of their heritage and their reputation as a warrior people.

Madura is some 160 km (100 mi) long and 35 km (22 mi) wide. The south is well-cultivated and lined with shallow beaches, the interior mainly rock and sand, whilst such hills as there are to the north culminate in steep cliffs, with breakers relentlessly pounding on the shore below.

Most Madurese are farmers, fishermen, salt producers or cattle breeders. Cattle are extremely important, not only to the economy but also because of the famous bull races that take place each year. This exciting and colourful sport involves pairs of the finest bulls harnessed to a small sled upon which stands the 'jockey'. The bulls, lovingly nurtured for these events, are decked out in finery and, to the accompaniment of gamelan orchestras and cheering spectators, race down a course of some 120 m (396 ft).

A decent road links the three main towns on the island. Bangkalan, in the west, is the main base from which to go bull racing, Pamekasan is the sleepy capital in central Madura, with Sumenep, in the east, the most attractive of the three. Sumenep's sights are all closely situated around a large, central square, where there is a splendid 18th century mosque, and a *kraton*, a Javanese royal palace. Here you can visit some of the rooms, which contain a curious collection of weapons, ceramics and other assorted items. Beside it is a small, enclosed water garden – *taman sari* – with a clear pool full of fish.

Water buffaloes race at Pamekasan.

Rote

Rote, or Roti Island, is Indonesia's southern-most inhabited island and the southernmost point of Eurasia. Even if it were not both remote and beautiful, those facts alone would give it a certain romantic appeal. As it is, Rote, one fifth of the size of Bali, is full of hills and valleys, cultivated terraces, acacia palms, savannah and forested areas, and its exotic people belong to some 18 different ethnic groups. Rote lies off the southwestern tip of West Timor and, because it is so arid, relies on the extremely useful, drought-resistant Lontar palm to fuel its economy.

In the late 17th century, the ruling Dutch took many slaves from Rote, but as the Rotenese adopted Christianity – today 90 per cent of the islanders are Christians – they were rewarded with an educational system that grew and prospered, turning out many administrators and nationalist leaders. Rotenese men are known throughout the archipelago for their debating skill, although today's standards of education and health are both falling behind the Indonesian average.

The Lontar palm leaf can be made into shoes, bags and the traditional wide-banded hat, with its unusual frontal spike. It provides roofing and interior walls and is also turned into a unique, stringed instrument, the sasando. The wood is made into furniture and planks, and the sap into a nutritious fresh drink that, if left to ferment, makes alcoholic palm wine. Distilled, it becomes the local firewater. Crafts are practised, too – silver jewellery making and ikat weaving.

Rote has some interesting local architecture, boasting carved and thatched roofs, but is best known for its empty, white beaches, translucent waters, surfing, diving and snorkelling in a superbly lush marine environment, complete with spectacular underwater caverns.

POPULATION:
100,000 (2001)
WHEN TO GO:
April to November
HOW TO GET THERE:
By plane or ferry from West Timor.
HIGHLIGHTS:
The island's capital, Ba'a.
The Saturday market at Papela.
Nemberala Beach, with its famous 'left break' surf – best from June to October.
N'dana Island, a tiny, uninhabited nature reserve, with turtle nesting sites.
Ndao Island, and its renowned gold- and silversmiths.
YOU SHOULD KNOW:
There is a red lake on N'dana Island, which is said to be stained with the blood of the inhabitants who were all massacred in an act of vengeance during the 17th century.

Fishing boats at low tide on Rote Island

Weh

Lying a mere 350 m (1,150 ft) off northern Sumatra is the tiny, volcanic island of Weh, surrounded by the Andaman Sea. Weh is the northernmost point of Indonesia's archipelago, and was formed during the Pleistocene age by an eruption that separated it from the mainland. The highest point is a fumarolic volcano reaching 617 m (2,024 ft) in height, but there is also a volcanic cone in the rainforest, three boiling mud fields, hot springs and underwater fumaroles. During the 2004 tsunami Weh received some damage. However, thousands of replacement mangrove seedlings have since been planted, houses rebuilt and the island has recovered.

Sabang harbour, which is both deep and sheltered, was used as a re-fuelling station, first for Dutch naval steamships in the 1880s, and later for merchant vessels. It was a Free Port for a time, though the government withdrew that status during the 1980s, since when both the economy and the population have declined. Today the island's economy is based upon cloves, coconuts, fishing, rattan furniture production and a little tourism.

For those who make the trip, Weh is charming. Scenically lovely, with hills, rocks, caves and secluded beaches, its significant ecosystem has been recognized with a nature reserve, covering both sea and land. The spectacular coral gardens have suffered somewhat, but there are still magnificent underwater walls and canyons to explore, and a multitude of both small, colourful reef fish and large species such as lion fish, manta rays, sharks and turtles. During the winter monsoon, whale sharks can be seen. In 2004 a megamouth shark was found here, thought to be only the twenty-first sighting since 1976.

Weh is a tranquil spot, as yet undeveloped. The locals don't see many foreigners, just a few NGOs from Aceh, and the occasional intrepid diver – simplicity and natural beauty are its strengths.

A giant sea fan in the spectacular coral gardens that surround the island of Weh.

POPULATION:
25,000 (2007)
WHEN TO GO:
It can always rain on Weh, but the wettest months are from November to February
HOW TO GET THERE:
By ferry from Uleh-leh in north Sumatra.
HIGHLIGHTS:
The fresh-water lake near Sabang.
The diving and snorkelling around the island.
The Iboih Forest Nature Reserve.
The Sea Garden coral reefs.
YOU SHOULD KNOW:
Northern Sumatra is very strongly Muslim, so be careful not to offend people by dressing or behaving inappropriately.

Timor

The island of Timor lies to the east of Sumba, and north west of Australia. Like its neighbours, it is an arid place, with a mountain range stretching right across it, from end to end. Timor is divided into West Timor, which is part of Indonesia, and the independent state of East Timor. Divided for centuries, the Portuguese began colonization during the early 16th century, but Timor, which was rich with valuable sandalwood trees, was also desirable to the Dutch. After years of conflict, the Portuguese were relegated to the eastern part of the island.

West Timor became Indonesian when that country gained independence in1945, whilst East Timor remained Portuguese until 1975. Years of civil war, and brutal annexation by Indonesia followed, but in 1999 East Timor became independent, though sadly there are still serious internal problems.

West Timor is a good jumping off point for the eastern Indonesian islands. Kupang, a busy, noisy city, is the capital of East Nusa Tenggara province. Beyond it, starkly beautiful, rugged countryside sweeps away, sprinkled with traditional villages of neat, beehive shaped, grass and bamboo huts. While West Timor is, of course, Muslim, East Timor is about 90 per cent Christian, mainly Catholic, and churches, some well worth visiting, can be found across the whole island. Naturally, however, pockets of animism still occur here.

Timor is ringed with unspoiled beaches, most of which are completely undeveloped. In the hills, maize, sweet potatoes and coffee are grown, while rubber, coconuts, tobacco and rice grow nearer the coast. The island has lots of potential: in time, East Timor will enjoy the financial benefits of having off-shore oil and gas fields, which are being developed with Australia and which are needed to rebuild infrastructure and other war damage. Meanwhile, West Timor will no doubt see tourism increasing, now that hostilities are over.

POPULATION:
2,220,000 (2002)
WHEN TO GO:
The driest months are from May to November.
HOW TO GET THERE:
By air from Indonesia and Australia, or by sea from Indonesia.
HIGHLIGHTS:
Bird watching trips around the island.
The Tuesday market in Oinlasi, W. Timor.
The animist village of Boti, W. Timor.
The ikat weaving village of Temkassi, W. Timor.
YOU SHOULD KNOW:
In 1789 Captain William Bligh reached Timor after having been cast adrift from his ship, HMS *Bounty*, by mutineers. He self-navigated an extraordinary 6,701 km (3,618 miles) from near Tahiti to Timor in 47 days, losing only one seaman of the 18 who were with him.

Timor is ringed with unspoiled beaches.

New Guinea

POPULATION:
7,100,000 (2007)
WHEN TO GO:
New Guinea is always wet and humid, but the driest months are from June to September.
HOW TO GET THERE:
To Papua: by air from Java or Sulawesi, or by boat.
To PNG: Fly from Australia.
HIGHLIGHTS:
Explore Biak Island and swim and dive from its white sand beaches.
Hike around or cruise Lake Sentani on a longboat.
Visit Wasur National Park.
Trek The Kokoda Trail, scene of Australia's hard-fought victory over the Japanese in WWII.
Visit the Huli tribe in the Tari Valley.
YOU SHOULD KNOW:
Thousands of endemic species of flora and fauna exisit in New Guinea, including thousands as yet unknown to the West. Of 284 species of mammal, including tree kangaroos and wallabies, 195 are endemic. Of 578 species of breeding bird, including most Birds of Paradise, 324 are endemic. There are 200,000 species of insect, 400 amphibians, 455 butterflies and 1,200 species of fish. New Guinea is home to 75% of the world's coral.

New Guinea is the world's second largest island, and is also one of the world's last, vast and remote wildernesses. With a complex political history, this great island is divided. The western half, is now known as Papua, a region of Indonesia, while the eastern half, Papua New Guinea or PNG, has been an independent country since 1975.

New Guinea is part of the Pacific Ring of Fire, and endures sporadic volcanic eruptions, earthquakes and occasional tsunamis. A mountain range rises across the length of New Guinea and deep rainforest is all enveloping. The island contains an astonishing wealth of natural features, some protected by National Parks and UNESCO Man and Biosphere Reserves, but huge swathes of it are unmapped and virtually unreachable. The main towns of both countries are, naturally, on the coast, but there is little in the way of roads or infrastructure. Travel is mainly by boat – rivers criss-cross the whole region – on foot, or by plane

New Guinea is inhabited by about 1,000 different tribes, speaking a similar number of languages. Tourists are few, mainly visiting the extraordinary Dani culture, in Papua's beautiful Baliem Valley. Despite being nominally Christians, the Dani live traditionally. Men wear penis sheaths, women wear short skirts, made of orchid fibres, worn beneath the buttocks. This high valley, surrounded by mountain peaks, is a vision of incredibly fertile cultivated fields. The Baliem River provides fish, and pigs are essential, being eaten at every ceremony.

In PNG the major attraction is the tribal hunter/gatherers who live along the banks of the island's longest river, the Sepik. This culture is intrinsically entwined with crocodiles, and the men's extensive scarification reflects the animal's scales. Living in communal longhouses, Sepik River people are famous for their wood-carvings. Varying in style from village to village, many of these find their way into the great museums of the world.

Huli warriors taking part in a 'sing sing' feast.

New Britain

New Britain is the largest island in Papua New Guinea's eastern Bismark Archipelago – in fact, it is the 38th largest island in the world. Mountainous and volcanic, much of the island is covered with a lush tangle of rainforest, the high rainfall feeding several large rivers.

In 1700, William Dampier, the first European visitor, named the island. In 1884 New Britain became part of German New Guinea but in 1914 the Australians took the island from Germany, and it remained Australian, apart from being conquered by Japan in WWII, until New Guinea's independence in 1975. Today, while East New Britain is a tourist destination, West New Britain is largely untouched and undiscovered.

Today's capital, Kokopo, superceded Rabaul in 1994, when a huge eruption destroyed most of the town, covering it with ash and lava. Prior warning enabled all the inhabitants to escape with their lives. The economy here is mixed – palm oil, copra, cotton, coffee and rubber plantations are extensive, while copper, coal and gold are mined. Unfortunately the interior and some of the south coast is now being logged.

The people and cultures that exist here are fascinating. The Kove people in the west were documented for *National Geographic* magazine in the 1960s, and within Papua New Guinea they are known for their practice of superincision of the penis. In the east there are several tribal groups who are matrilineal, and who use threaded shells as currency, not only for dowries and ceremonies but also for buying land and food.

This is a gorgeous island, flowers and plants thrive on the rich, volcanic soil, and scrumptious fruit and vegetables abound. Apart from the fabulous diving and snorkelling there are other attractions such as hot springs and caves, and above all, charming friendly people who are pleased to meet you.

Ulauan volcano

POPULATION:
404,873 (2000)

WHEN TO GO:
It's always hot and wet, but probably receives most rain between December and March.

HOW TO GET THERE:
By air to Tokua from Papua New Guinea.

HIGHLIGHTS:
Bitapaka War Cemetery – a moving memorial to the fallen, maintained by the Commonwealth War Graves Commission.
The Japanese War Tunnels.
Night diving the Cathedral, at Kimbe Bay
Kokopo market.

YOU SHOULD KNOW:
A French caving team believes that not only is the Muruk cave system in West New Britain the deepest recorded in the southern hemisphere, but also that there is a canyon 1,200 m (3,960 ft) below the cave's entrance.

New Ireland

With the Bismark Sea to the southwest and the Pacific Ocean to the northeast, New Ireland is some 320 km (200 mi) long but never much more than 10 km (6 mi) wide. This narrow island contains a range of sharp, rugged mountains – the highest, Mount Lambel, rises to 2,150 m (7,054 ft) – and dense rainforest.

Thought to have been inhabited for 30,000 years, it was not until 1900 that Franz Boluminski, the German administrator for the region, arrived. Until then New Ireland's people were known as ferocious cannibals who cheerfully slaughtered foreign sailors arriving on their shores. Boluminski set up highly successful copra plantations, building a long road of coral in order to utilize the good harbour at Kavieng, the island's capital. After the Japanese invasion of WWII, New Ireland was ceded to Australia, and is now part of Papua New Guinea.

The Melanesian islanders have three distinct cultures, and 22 languages between them. Unique are their splendidly carved Malagan funerary figures, many of which have found their way into European museums. Sculptors can still be found in a couple of villages, but sadly this seems to be a dying art. Shark calling is another tradition. Some islanders can 'call' sharks, which come to the caller's boat where they are speared.

Kavieng is a pleasant town, the road around the bay shaded by beautiful, old trees. While large ships still come for copra and oil, tourists come as well, to enjoy this 'typical Somerset Maugham south-sea-island port', as it has been described. Diving here is exciting – wrecks lie scattered over the seabed, even in the harbour itself. Hire a canoe and paddle out to the islets in the bay, or visit Karu Bay to see where sea turtles come to lay their eggs.

POPULATION:
10,600 (2000)

WHEN TO GO:
The south is always hot and quite wet, while the centre and north is always hot and have a dry season between May and October.

HOW TO GET THERE:
Fly from Port Moresby, Lae or Rabaul, or boat from Rabaul.

HIGHLIGHTS:
The Luka Barok festival held each June/July.
The Malangan Show and Independence Day Festival, held during four days each September.
The Tabar Islands, with their wood carvers and shark callers.
Lihir Island – said to have the second largest gold deposit in the world.

YOU SHOULD KNOW:
During the 1870s and 80s, the Marquis de Raye sold hundreds of hectares of land at Cape Breton, which he described as a thriving settlement, to gullible settlers who were left in the jungle with just 3 weeks' food and little else. Most people died before they could be rescued, and the Marquis ended his days in an asylum in France.

A striking blue starfish on the coral reef

Samarai and Kwato

Lying just 5 km (3 mi) off the south-eastern tip of Papua New Guinea, is the tiny, pretty island of Samarai. Once the bustling administrative centre and port town for Papua, today, a shadow of its former self, the current government has declared it a National Historical Heritage Island.

Discovered by Captain John Moresby in 1873, a mission station was established here five years later. By then a small trading post had been set up, and under British rule it had become a large, successful port. By 1927 Samarai had electricity and street lighting, and the European settlers lived here in fine style – so much so that it was named the 'Pearl of the Pacific'. During WWII, much of the infrastructure was destroyed by the Australians, fearful of a Japanese invasion, and although this never occurred, the Japanese did bomb what was left of the town.

Somewhat restored after the war, Samarai never really recovered, and the administrative centre was relocated to Alotau. Today, visitors to the island, which can be walked in about 30 minutes, can see the remnants of its colonial past, including a church, a school and several small shops as well as an almost surreal cricket oval which is still in use. The inhabitants live simply, mainly doing a little farming and fishing – there is no industry here, although there is talk of setting up a cultured pearl business.

The quiet, forested island of Kwato, just five minutes away, was once a boat-building centre. Settled by a missionary, Charles Able and his family in 1891, the open walled church, built from Scottish limestone and with fine views over Samarai and the China Strait, is still active, and the boat- and house-building tradition lives on.

POPULATION:
Unknown
WHEN TO GO:
October to December
HOW TO GET THERE:
By air from Port Moresby to Alotau and by boat from Alotau, or as part of a cruise.
HIGHLIGHTS:
The Memorial Hall and the District Commissioner's residence on Samarai.
Exploring the islands of Milne Bay.
Diving around the undisturbed coral atolls and island reef systems.
Attending a church service, after taking advice on which has the best choir.
YOU SHOULD KNOW:
The wreckage in Samarai's harbour not only shelters a wide variety of fish but also unusual encrusting corals, including the second of only two colonies of *Acanthastrea minuta* ever to have been recorded. These waters are also home to a rare – possibly endemic – Black velvet angelfish, with a pale head rather than the normal pale back.

Milne Bay on Samarai Island

POPULATION:
12,000 (2003)
WHEN TO GO:
April to November
HOW TO GET THERE:
By air from Port Moresby.
HIGHLIGHTS:
Sit on a deserted beach at night, with local friends, and watch for sea turtles coming to lay their eggs.
Watch local artisans carve walking sticks, huge bowls and figures – these are possibly the best carvers in PNG.
Swim and snorkel beautiful reefs in the impossibly blue sea.
Explore freshwater holes, limestone caves, hot springs, mudpools and geysers.
YOU SHOULD KNOW:
The Trobriand Kiss is described thus: couples lie together on a mat, hugging, then tear out handfuls of each other's hair and nibble off each other's eyelashes. It's considered really cool to have short eyelashes! A note of warning, though, it is not considered appropriate for foreigners to form liaisons with the locals.

The yam feast in Yalumugwa village

Trobriand Islands

Otherwise known as the 'islands of love', the Trobriands are a remote group of low lying coral islands to the north east of Papua New Guinea. There are four main islands, Kiriwina, Kaileuna, Vakuta and Kitava, as well as several islets, most of which are fringed with utterly pristine reefs.

Not much is known about their early history, but the Trobriands were 'discovered' by a French ship in 1793 and named after its first lieutenant. In the early part of the 20th century the culture, curiously more closely linked to Polynesia than to Melanesia, was studied at length by the anthropologist Bronislaw Malinowski.

Malinowski was fascinated by the islanders' matriarchal society, their yam culture and gift exchange systems, but he was utterly seduced by their colourful sexual behaviour, hence the islands' nickname. Sexual experimentation begins in childhood, and by the time adolescence is reached, a fully active sexual life is encouraged, with multiple partners. During this period the lucky adolescents live a life devoted to pleasure; working duties and taboos are not yet binding. Eventually young couples begin to cohabit, a situation that can be withdrawn from without repercussion or, alternatively, made permanent through marriage.

The islands are fertile, and the economy based on yam growing – people take huge pride in their yam gardens, even having yam growing competitions. More exciting for the visitor are the fabulous fish and shellfish that are available – imagine swimming on the reef on a moonless night, watching the local youth dive for crayfish which will be cooked on the beach and eaten with a splash of lime juice – sublime.

The flora and fauna here is also unusual, and endemism is high. The Trobriands are covered in lowland rainforest, and the birds are fabulous – you might just see two endemic species of bird of paradise – appropriate really, since these islands remain little, lost specks of heaven.

Umboi Island

Umboi Island lies between mainland Papua New Guinea and the western tip of New Britain and, at 50 km (31 mi) long, it is the largest of the islands just off New Guinea's northern coast. Formed of several volcanoes, some of which have satellite cones on their flanks, its highest point rises to 1,548 m (5,100 ft). To the north-east it is cut by a large, deep caldera. Breached by the sea, this contains three cones, each with a summit crater lake. However there is no history of eruptions on the island.

Despite its remote location, steamy, mountainous and jungle-clad terrain, missionary activity has led to schools and churches being built, not only in the coastal villages, but also deep in the interior, and some English is spoken. However, Umboi is best known as the home of the ropen, a large, nocturnal creature, said to closely resemble a pterosaur.

Since 1994, American researchers have been exploring the island in an attempt to discover more about the ropen. Hundreds of eyewitnesses describe this creature as having a large wingspan, a long tailed, scaly body and a crocodile-like mouthful of teeth. Some mention a crested head and a flange on the tail. Hunting for fish at night, the ropen is bio-luminescent, apparently glowing for short bursts, attracting fish towards the light.

As yet, no-one has managed to photograph the ropen, which has also been seen on the Papua New Guinea mainland. Lending some credence to this tale are indigenous carvings on display in Port Moresby showing a shaman sitting beneath a lizard like creature with a long neck, scaly wings and a beak. Though there is some doubt about the existence of the ropen, what is certain is that Umboi is home to no less than eight species of fruit bat – all of which are very large.

POPULATION:
4,500 (1997 estimate)

WHEN TO GO:
April to November, although Umboi Island is always hot and wet.

HOW TO GET THERE:
By boat from PNG.

HIGHLIGHTS:
Exploring the island and attempting to become the first person to film or even capture the ropen.

YOU SHOULD KNOW:
Umboi is also one of only two places where Matschie's tree kangaroos are found. Nut brown in colour, with a golden tail and lower limbs, they can hop, but their limbs are slightly shortened to enable them to climb trees successfully.

A traditional Chinese temple set in beautiful gardens.

POPULATION:
560,000 (2004)
WHEN TO GO:
Come for the penguin swimming contest in winter, cherry blossom festival in spring, midsummer night's beach festival, or the festival of horses in autumn when the maples turn brilliant reds and yellows.
HOW TO GET THERE:
By air to Jeju's international airport or by boat, from ports all round the South Korean mainland, to Jeju Port.
HIGHLIGHTS:
Watching the *haenyo* ('sea women'), Jeju's iconic free-divers for abalone and conch, in action. The women – archetypes of Jeju's culture of matriarchy – pass their skills down the generations.
Chonjiyon waterfall, near Seogwipo: the cascades plummet 22m (73 ft) into a basin known as 'Pond of the Heavens' Emperor' among dense subtropical foliage.
Elvis Teddy, Mona Lisa Teddy and the whole of the Last Supper in Teddy Bears at the Teddy Bear Museum.
Loveland – a sexually explicit open-air theme park full of graphic, hands-on exhibits and working models designed to inspire and perhaps instruct bashful but willing newlyweds.
YOU SHOULD KNOW:
Jeju was an independent country called Tamna until 662, and though it has been governed by several powers since then, its isolation has helped it preserve a unique culture incorporating a form of shamanism. You feel it everywhere as an underlying current.

Jeju

Jeju/Cheju is a volcanic island, 73 km (46 mi) long, and 41 km (25 mi) wide, some 60 km (40 mi) southwest of the Korean peninsula. It is a lush, semi-tropical oval with Korea's highest mountain, 1,950 m (6,300 ft) Hallasan, at its centre – and it gets 4 million visitors each year. Most of them are Korean newlyweds: 60 per cent of Korean weddings are followed by a honeymoon on the 'Emerald Island of Asia', or 'Love Island'.

Jeju's cultural and ecological attractions make it a massive tourist magnet in any circumstances. For Korean couples, many of whom don't even meet each other before their wedding, the sheer variety of beautiful, romantic and interesting places to go and things to do gives them a chance to face down their shyness and discover each other. Being Korea, these opportunities are not so much organized as regimented. Everything in Jeju is geared to whisking honeymooners at speed through as many different photo opportunities as possible to fill their official wedding albums. Other visitors can tag along, or muddle through.

Much of the Jeju pleasure production line is seasonal. In spring forsythia turns the island yellow, and cherry blossoms, pineapples, bananas and tangerines are everywhere. By May Hallasan's crater lake reflects a sea of azaleas. Couples explore ancient lava columns and catacombs like the Manjanggul, the longest lava tube on earth at 13 km (8.4 mi) and part of a UNESCO World Biosphere Reserve; or pose at one of the scores of scenic waterfalls in the green countryside and forests. Jeju is awash with a sense of mystery and old legends, and everywhere you see *dol hareubangs* ('stone grandfathers'), cult phallic figures carved from basalt. But the real mystery is when honeymooners get any time to themselves.

Ogasawara Islands

Administratively part of the Tokyo Prefecture, despite lying 1,000km (600 mi) south of the city, the Ogasawara Islands are scattered over the Pacific Ocean south of the Izu Islands. The 30 islands in the group are arranged in three distinct blocks. The Ogasawara Archipelago consists of Muko-jima Island, Chichi-jima Island and Haha-jima Island. The Iwo Islands (Volcano Islands) form the second blocks, while Nishi-no-shima Island, Minani-tori-shima Island, and Oki-no-shima Island belong to the last block. The whole area falls within the Ogasawara National Park.

The islands were claimed by the Japanese in the 14th or 15th century, but in 1827 a British warship came across the uninhabited islands and claimed possession until 1876 when they were handed back to Japan. During World War II, most of the inhabitants were evacuated to the mainland, and a Japanese military base was established there. The Battle of Iwo-jima, one of the fiercest battles of the war, was fought here in 1945. The islands were taken by the US Navy, who allowed the inhabitants of Western descent to return. The islands were given back to Japan in 1968, and the Japanese evacuees were finally allowed home. Nowadays, nearly all of the inhabitants, including those of Western ancestry, are Japanese citizens.

The islands are the highest points of an ancient underwater volcano, so sheer cliffs of up to 100 m (328 ft) characterize their magnificent coastlines. The islands are fringed with beautiful coral reefs, and many have lovely beaches. The highest peak is on South Iwo-jima, at 916 m (3,005 ft).

As the Ogasawara Islands have always been remote and have never been part of a continent, much of the flora and fauna is unique, with species varying between islands as they do in the Galapagos. For this reason, the islands are being considered by UNESCO to be added to the World Heritage List. Unspoilt and unpolluted, the waters surrounding the Ogasawara Archipelago are part of the Ogasawara Sea Park, and diving and snorkelling are very popular here as the visibiltity is very good and there are plentiful coral reefs and colourful tropical fish.

This is also a great place for whale watching – sperm whales can be spotted all year, while humpback whales and their calves are around from February to April. Many different types of dolphin inhabit the waters too, and it is sometimes possible to swim with bottlenose and spinner dolphins.

POPULATION:
2,300 (2005)
WHEN TO GO:
Any time of year.
HOW TO GET THERE:
By ship from Tokyo to Chichi-jima. The ship leaves once a week and the journey takes 25 hours.
HIGHLIGHTS:
Swimming with dolphins – both bottleose and spinner dolphins can be found in the clear waters around the islands.
Whale watching – see sperm whales and humpback whales in their natural habitat. An organized tour will lead you to where the whales are most plentiful and increase your chances of seeing them.
Snorkelling and diving among the coral reefs. Marine life is plentiful, and this is where the first-ever filming of a giant squid took place in 2004. At around 8 m (25 ft) long, these creatures are, luckily, only to be found deep in the ocean.
YOU SHOULD KNOW.
In English, the islands are called the Bonin Islands.

A whale's giant tailfin breaks through the waves.

Rebun and Rishiri Islands

POPULATION:
Rebun 3,400; Rishiri 6,200 (2005)
WHEN TO GO:
June to August when the wild flowers are in bloom.
HOW TO GET THERE:
Travel by air or ferry from Wakkanai to Rebun and Rishiri.
HIGHLIGHTS:
The Hachi-jikan hiking trail – the trail runs down the whole of the west coast of Rebun, from Sukoton Misaki in the north, through woods and across flower-filled meadows, to Motochi in the south.
Rishirifuji Onsen – a hot spring with indoor and outdoor baths in the town of Oshidomari on Rishiri.
Otatomari Pond – a beautiful pond in the south of Rishiri Island. The views of Mount Rishiri reflected in the still water are fantastic.
Garota Beach – a sandy beach on the western coast of Rebun, popular with wind surfers. The section of hiking trail between Cape Sukoton and Garota Beach on the island of Rebun.
YOU SHOULD KNOW:
The islands are known as Rishirito and Rebunto in Japanese.

In the far north of Japan off the north-west coast of the island of Hokkaido, lie two smaller islands famed for their natural beauty, abundant wild flowers and hiking trails. The islands of Rebun and Rishiri form part of a national park, along with the island of Sarobetsu and part of Hokkaido.

Rishiri Island is dominated by Mount Rishiri a 1,721-m (4,170-ft) dormant volcano. Most visitors come here to climb the volcano, an arduous but enjoyable hike which takes about 12 hours. There is a small shrine at the summit, and the views of the neighbouring islands are fantastic. There are many other hiking routes on the island from which you can appreciate the wonderful scenery, including a lovely three-hour trail from the lake at Himenuma, crossing the lower slopes of two smaller peaks.

Another way to take in the scenery is to explore by bicycle. A 20-km cycle track follows the northern coast of Rishiri from Hime Pond to Kutsugata, a lovely route offering stunning views of the volcano. Bicycles can be hired or borrowed from your hotel.

The coast of Rishiri is peppered with small fishing villages and the island is famous for its sea urchins (*uni*) and konbu seaweed. Near the port of Oshidomari, Rishiri's largest town, is the picturesque headland of Cape Peshi. There is a walking trail to the top of the headland, from which there are stunning views of Oshidomari and Mount Rishiri.

In contrast, Rebun is a low-lying island. It is most famous for its rich flora, particularly its alpine flowers, some of which are not found anywhere else in the world. The flowers bloom between June and August, so this is a good time to visit. Look out particularly for the Rebun Usuyukiso, rather like an Edelweiss. It is one of several protected, rare plants found on the island and can be seen in the Rebun Usuyukiso Area, a place

with a relatively high number of them.

With its breathtaking scenery and views of nearby Rishiri, the island of Rebun is best enjoyed from a network of hiking trails. Among the highlights is Cape Gorota, a beautiful cape in the northern part of the island. Motochi, an area in the south-west of the island, is characterized by its scenic, sheer coastline and rocks which are said to resemble a cat's head. There is a small village here with ryokan (traditional Japanese inns), which make a fascinating place to stay. Momoiwa (Peach Rock), a roundish hill, is nearby. The flowers here are stunning and the lovely views of Mount Rishiri can be enjoyed from the observation deck.

A view of Rishiri Island from Rebun Island

Kume-Shima

POPULATION:
9,250 (2003 estimate)
WHEN TO GO:
Year-round (avoid the typhoon season of September to October). Come for the Kume Marathon in balmy, beautiful October to November.
HOW TO GET THERE:
By air, via Naha (Okinawa) from Tokyo, Osaka or Taiwan, to Kume; by hydrofoil (April to October), from Naha, to Madomari Port, Kume; by ferry, from Naha, to Kanegusuku Port, Kume.
HIGHLIGHTS:
Windsurfing, jet skiing and all forms of water sports on Hatenohama and Eef beaches.
The turtles in the vast research tanks of the Kume Island Sea Museum and the fireflies glowing magically at the Firefly Centre.
The 250 year-old Uezu Family Residence, a designated National Important Cultural Asset – the superbly preserved manor house complex of a Ryukyuan noble family.
The booming taiko drums accompanying the children of Kumejima performing the Eisa (Ryukyuan traditional drum dance) in costume, either at Nakazato village or in the square in front of Umigame (Sea Turtle Hall). Any of the festivals or celebrations where you can see the Hatagashira – the traditional Ryukyuan sport of balancing huge cabers or flagpoles weighted at the top with heavy and elaborate decorations.

Kume-Shima is just 102 km (63 mi) southwest of Okinawa's capital, Naha, and for mainland Japanese it is the ultimate domestic destination. It has beautiful beaches and excellent dive sites. Its green interior presents shifting landscapes of fields, exuberant flowers, and hillside slopes of elegant Fukugi trees with the sea always sparkling in the background.

In the Maju district, a particular and extensive group of 200 year-old Fukugi is especially esteemed – along with a 250 year-old Ryukyu pine that looks like a paradoxical giant bonsai, and is a designated National Treasure. With a diameter of 4.3 m (15 ft), 6 m (20 ft) high, and covering 250 sq m (800 sq ft), this magnificent pine is celebrated in Ryukyuan poetry as one of the sacred natural beings – like the yonic lava tube called 'miifugaa' at Kume's north tip, or the offshore phallic lava column called 'garasaa-yama' in the south – revered by its animistic culture. Beneath the meticulous service culture of its resorts, Kume is an outstanding exemplar of a tradition rooted in its history as part of a once independent Ryukyu kingdom.

Kume's triumph is to have incorporated its fundamental beliefs into its tourist economy. Visitors love the textiles called Tsumugi, made by a process kept alive since the 15th century and considered an 'Intangible Cultural Property'. They adore the island's version of Awamori liquor, made from local spring water, Thai rice and black malt yeast. Like certain places, these are associated with ancestors, and regarded with reverence. The respect extends to Kume's magnificent indigenous fireflies and superb marine ecology.

Lack of respect causes real resentment: the US has used the nearby islet of Torishima, a traditionally brilliant fishing ground, for fifty years of regular bombing practice, carelessly pounding it to gravel in a culture that holds care for natural things as the highest human responsibility.

Miyako

Roughly 300 km (180 mi) southwest of Okinawa, a low plateau sits above the translucent, turquoise sea. This is Miyako, centrepiece of a small archipelago of the same name, and of the coral reefs, raised from the seabed thousands of years ago. Miyako's fame in Japan's main islands is based on its gorgeous white sand beaches, its golf courses and its reef dive sites. Two long bridges unite Miyako with its seven satellite islands, making their coral reefs and wildlife easily accessible. The islanders are justly proud of their status as a mainstream tourist destination.

Most visitors remain oblivious to Miyako's indigenous culture, a variant developed from the ancient Ryukyu kingdom centred in Okinawa. Over 15,000 islanders speak Miyako, a Ryukyuan language – and four of its satellites have their own distinct dialect, even though they are so close.

There are 15 surviving Gusuku sites scattered round Miyako, shrines sacred to a history and way of life veiled to beach holidaymakers. During the year, each district conducts its own sacred rite. Shimajiri district's Pantu rite consists of three local men daubed in grass and mud, and carrying sticks and a grotesque face-mask. They represent gods, and chase people to smear them with mud. Being caught and muddied-up guarantees a year of protection by the deities. The Karimata district has its Uyagan rite, a form of harvest festival. In the sugarcane fields not yet claimed for new tourist facilities, these rites are the public face of Miyako's cultural soul, and like the island itself, they have a rare and profound beauty.

POPULATION:
55, 914 (2006)
WHEN TO GO:
Year-round
HOW TO GET THERE:
By air, from Naha (Okinawa), Haneda or Kansai, to Miyako.
HIGHLIGHTS:
Diving the Tori-ike reef off Shimoji Island.
Exploring the 2 km (1.3 mi) long and 140-200 m (450-620 ft) wide Higashi-hennazaki, the extreme eastern cape of Miyako, with a lighthouse at the end. Its 360° panorama as the sun rises guarantees a place in Japan's top 100 beauty spots.
The replica of German fairytale Marksburg Castle at the Ueno German Culture Village – an improbable theme park built in 1993, commemorating the 1873 rescue of German sailors from a shipwreck, a story told since 1937 in Japan's schoolbooks.

Rock formations on Jodogahama Beach

Shikoku

POPULATION:
4,500,000 (2006)
WHEN TO GO:
Come for Oshiro Matsui, the late March/April cherry blossom festival of the 300 Sakura trees in Matsuyama Castle Park; or the dazzling fall foliage displays at Kankakei in Kagawa, or Iyakei in Tokushima, from October to mid-December. The Awa Odori Festival in Tokushima is in August.
HOW TO GET THERE:
By air, via Tokyo or Osaka, to the Prefectural capitals of Takamatsu (N), Matsuyama (W), Kochi (S) and Tokushima (E); by train/bus/car, via the three new bridges from Honshu; or – much the most fun – by ferry from Osaka's Nanko Port, to Matsuyama. The overnight ferries are miniature ocean liners, with panelled cabins and baths to match.
HIGHLIGHTS:
The turrets and fortifications of Matsuyama Castle (1627), including the extraordinary 10 m (32 ft) stone gates, all different, and with individual histories of national significance, eight of which are individually designated 'Japanese National Treasures'.
Watching a nocturnal performance of Noh theatre by the flickering light of bonfires, medieval-style, in the restored Matsuyama Castle Ninomaru Historical Garden.
The opulent merchant's mansion of Kami-Haga House, and traditional wax and candle-making at Uchiko, a beautifully preserved 19th century small town in Ehime.
Bathing at Japan's oldest hot spring, Dogo Onsen, near Matsuyama – even the no-frills 'Kami-no-Yu' ('Bath of the Gods') gets you the huge, traditional wooden Japanese buildings and marble trimmings.
YOU SHOULD KNOW:
Kobo Daishi is the posthumous title awarded to the scholar monk Kukai, the 9th century polymath who created the Kana syllabary, brought the tantric teachings of esoteric Buddhism from China, and developed them into the Japanese Shingon sect.

Cherry trees growing on the mountainside on Shikoku.

The smallest of Japan's four main islands, Shikoku has always been a backwater cut off from direct access to Honshu or Kyushu by the Inland Sea. Now, even after new bridges were supposed to integrate it culturally and economically with mainstream Japan, Shikoku remains isolated, and the loveliest and most bucolic region of the whole country. It helps that most of its population lives in the big cities along its north coast. The mountainous ridges running east-west concentrate both Shikoku's industry and its intensive agriculture: the wide, alluvial northeast produces two crops of rice and wheat each year, and is rich with citrus fruits, persimmons, peaches and grapes. A road map of the north also demonstrates the density of its express and freeway network, and the graphic distinction from the sparsely populated, deeply rural south. The south is the traditional Japan of fabulous mountain scenery, samurai castles, craft workshops, farming villages where oxen pull creaky wagons, and small terraces of vegetables or orange trees cut into the dense woods.

In Shikoku, ancient Japan is no ghost: each year 100,000 people complete the '88 Temple Pilgrimage', a rite originating around 1570-90 that requires followers of the 9th century Buddhist priest Kobo Daishi to visit his 88 special shrines over a 1,450 km (906 mi) route. In Uwajima in Shikoku's southwest corner, bullfighting is described as 'bovine sumo', because trainers, instead of killing the bulls, incite two immense and pampered creatures to push and barge each other out of a ring. Nearby, at Taga Jinja, a medieval Shinto shrine to fertility has developed into a full-blown, three-floor museum of sex and erotica – with no discernible loss of sanctity. Quirky, charming, and absolutely lovely, Shikoku keeps reminding you of the ancient soul behind Japan's façade of white-hot technological modernity.

Okinawa

Their English name means the chain of islands stretching from Kyushu to Taiwan, dividing the East China Sea from the Pacific Ocean, but in Japan, 'Ryukyu Islands' signifies only the southern half – Okinawa Prefecture. Okinawa is the largest island, still and always the capital of what was once an independent kingdom paying tribute to China from 1372 until a 1609 invasion by 2,500 Japanese samurai, and eventual (1879) annexation by the Japanese Meiji. Japan enforced its language, culture and identity on the islanders, but today, and especially in Okinawa, the indigenous Ryokyu culture (with at least seven distinct languages) is resurgent. Okinawans' desire for cultural separatism is in direct proportion to their poor treatment by Japan and the US since World War II, and is reinforced by their obvious geographical isolation, and their ecological and ethnic affinity to South East Asia.

Enduring evidence of Ryukyu tradition is in the breathtaking medieval castles and related buildings called Gusuku sites, which include hundreds of sacred groves called Utaki. The combination of ancestor-worship and animism underpins Okinawan culture: the castles are themselves sacred, and services are held within them. The best are UNESCO World Heritage Sites, cited for their modern relevance, not as historic ruins.

Although Okinawa's tourist credentials are first-class – beautiful beaches, subtropical forests full of wildlife and waterfalls, throbbing resort complexes, coral reefs and marine parks – what really catches your eye is the way of life in the canefields, orchards and vegetable gardens. Rural Okinawa is alive with myth and legend – you'll hear it in music and dance, and the hundreds of local country festivals. For visitors, the island feels like a lost world, fortuitously recovered from what, in more urban areas, looks like wholesale Americanization.

POPULATION:
1.3 million (2004 estimate)
WHEN TO GO:
Year-round
HOW TO GET THERE:
By air, from the Japanese main islands, Taiwan or Hong Kong, to Naha; then by train, bus or car around the island.
HIGHLIGHTS:
The World War II Peace Memorial at Mabuni, the Cornerstone of Peace, inscribed with the names of those who died in the battle for Okinawa in 1945, regardless of nationality.
Modern Ryukyu glassware – traditional Meiji-era skills developed a new style from melting down and re-using soft drink bottles discarded by US troops.
Hiking the dense forest trails between Kunigami and Higashi village areas in the north – from coastal mangroves up to rocky waterfalls, to the chorus of a parliament of birds.
Shuri Castle, overlooking Naha one of the biggest Gusuku, and the only one to have been part of Ryukyu royal history from its medieval inception to its end in 1879.
Shikina-En Gardens, near Naha – a former residence of Ryukyu kings. Rebuilt in 1800 for the coronation of King Sho On.
Sefa Utaki, in Chinen village on the southern Pacific coast – huge rocks and trees shelter ceremonial altars in this most sacred Ryukyu site. The highest-ranking priestesses, the Kikoe Ogimi, were consecrated here, and it attracts many Agari Umai pilgrims.

Sea-bleaching traditional fabrics

OCEANIA

Pelsaert Island, one of the Houtman Abrolhos Islands

Houtman Abrolhos Islands

POPULATION:
Uninhabited, apart from temporary commercial fishermen.

WHEN TO GO:
Very changeable weather, and often windy. The best months for boating in particular are from February to June, and September to October. But still best to avoid the cyclone season from November to April – when most of the annual rain also falls.

HOW TO GET THERE:
Day trips by boat (with fishing and snorkelling) or scenic flights out of Geraldton on the mainland.

HIGHLIGHTS:
The Long Island Dive Trail – in the Wallabi Group of islands. A self guided tour in an area of outstanding marine life.
Diving on the wrecks (eg *Batavia*, 1629) in the Wallabi Group.
Wooded, Morley and Leo islands – blue lagoons and sandy beaches.

YOU SHOULD KNOW:
The islands are named after the Dutch Commander Frederick de Houtman who came across them in June 1619. 'Abrolhos' is thought to derive from the Portuguese expression *Abre os olhos* – 'Keep your eyes open' – certainly sound advice on these reefs.

It might seem careless to forget a chain of 122 coral islands about 60 km (37 mi) off the coast of Geraldton, Western Australia -- but forgotten it is. This is the world's most southerly coral island formation, stretching across 100 km (62 mi) of ocean and bathed by the warm Leeuwin current where tropical and temperate waters meet. You can't stay on the archipelago itself, but to skim over in a seaplane or fish and dive among the coral reefs is magic.

The real beauty of these wild islands lies below the surface, where unique corals abound and colourful fish dart in and out of cover. The islands are also home to sea lion colonies and over 90 species of sea birds – not to mention golden orb spiders, carpet pythons, small Tammar wallabies and marine green turtles. The obvious beauty of the reefs masks a slightly darker side to their nature: they have sunk many a ship in their time. The Dutch East India Company's vessels, *Batavia* and *Zeewijk*, are probably the best known of the Abrolhos wrecks.

The 'Abrolhos', as they are know locally, guard their treasures jealously – the islands are highly protected and any industry is carefully monitored. In the past, the abundant bird droppings or 'guano' fuelled a fertilizer industry; now the waters around the Abrolhos are an important lobster-breeding site. During the lobster fishing season from March to June, licensed fishermen and their families take up camp on 22 designated islands. You may not be able to stay yourself, but to have the privilege of setting foot on these untouched islands is quite simply enough.

Barrow Island

Barrow Island is a life raft for Australia's rarest creatures. In many ways, it is a living record of how parts of mainland Australia might have looked prior to European occupation. Many animals here are now extinct elsewhere on the continent. This arid, antipodean 'Galapagos' lies in the Indian Ocean off the coast of northern West Australia – 56 km (36 mi) from the mainland and just 25 km long (15.5 mi). Not only is it rich in wildlife but also in that 'liquid gold' – oil.

Most of the human residents are male – a reflection of the island's somewhat schizophrenic nature. In 1954, geologists working for West Australian Petroleum realised the island's rich potential for oil fields. Today there are over 400 production wells here, but alongside this has recently come a greater understanding and empathy with the wild inhabitants. Amazingly, wells and wildlife seems to rub along pretty well – with no species having been lost in the 36 years of oil production. But battles still rage over its future.

Inland from white dunes and reefs, the limestone uplands are littered with tussocks of spinifex, a spiny leafed grass. Here live the somewhat bizarre nocturnal burrowing bettongs or 'rat kangaroos'. Holing up in underground burrows by day, these sociable animals forage at night, grunting and squealing as they feast on their favourite food, figs. Since European settlement, numbers elsewhere have dropped dramatically but here about 5,000 burrowing bettongs thrive – as long as no cats and dogs arrive.

At first this may not seem like an easy place to be, but it is a last refuge for Australia's weirdest and most wonderful wildlife, and for that it's a must-see.

POPULATION:
50 to 100 (2005 estimate)
WHEN TO GO:
November to February when the weather is fair. Avoid the cyclone season.
HOW TO GET THERE:
Flights to Barrow airport from the mainland.
HIGHLIGHTS:
Green turtles nesting and laying eggs along the West Coast – November to February.
The grand perentie – the world's second largest lizard, beaten only by the Komodo dragon.
YOU SHOULD KNOW:
Barrow is the largest of the Montebello Islands, which were the site of three British nuclear bomb tests in 1952 and 1956.

A green turtle returning to the sea at sunrise.

Montague Island

POPULATION:
Uninhabited
WHEN TO GO:
All year round for diving (but February to June is the best time). Whale watching from October to November.
HOW TO GET THERE:
Official boat tours out of Narooma.
HIGHLIGHTS:
Swallowing succulent mud oysters.
Swimming with playful fur seals.
Southern right and humpback whales migrating past.
Diving – one of the island's best-kept secrets.
YOU SHOULD KNOW:
The island has a major weed problem. Kikuyu was introduced in the early 19th century to help feed animals kept by the lighthouse keepers and their families, and it got out of control. It is now being cleared as it can prevent penguins and shearwaters from burrowing or moving.

Just 9 km (6 mi) off Narooma on the south coast of New South Wales lies Montague Island, a sanctuary for little penguins and seals, and a delightful retreat for divers, fishermen and eco-tourists alike.

Barunguba or Montague Island as it is now know was once fertile Aboriginal hunting ground – sea-bird eggs and meat were there for the taking. But the task wasn't easy – legend has it that an estimated 150 Aboriginal people were drowned in the early 1800s when their bark canoes where swamped in a squall.

Surrounded by rich but sometimes tricky waters, construction of Montague's lighthouse, designed by James Barnet, commenced in 1878. This striking 21 m (69 ft) landmark was hewn from the island's own granite. Barnet was responsible for at least 15 major lightstations along the coast of New South Wales. The lighthouse keepers and their families are long gone – it was automated in 1986. But since its completion in 1881, visitors have landed here to climb the lighthouse and take in the wildlife.

The island and surrounding waters are teeming with life – migrating whales and dolphins, little penguins and fur seals, manta rays and sunfish. Fortunately for the penguins, the island has no foxes or feral cats, and breeding boxes have increased their number to around 12,000. After feeding at sea, these delightful creatures waddle ashore at dusk and can be watched from a platform near the island's jetty.
Recently, lucky eco-tourists have been able to stay overnight in the heritage-listed lighthouse keeper's cottage, now restored in true Edwardian style. These visitors get the rare chance to stay on the island in return for a little work – maybe penguin monitoring, weed clearing or doing bird and whale counts. It seems to turn work into pleasure.

The granite lighthouse on Montague Island

Norfolk Island

A tiny jewel set in the azure seas of the South Pacific, Norfolk Island is just 8 km (5 mi) long, and 1,600 km (994 mi) northeast of Sydney. It is the biggest of a cluster of three islands on the Norfolk Ridge, fringed by coral reefs and crowned by pristine rainforest and some of the world's tallest tree ferns.

On 10 October 1774, James Cook first landed on this diminutive island and named it in honour of the then Duchess of Norfolk. Convicts started to arrive 14 years later and over time it gained quite a reputation, becoming known as 'hell in the Pacific'. Then in 1856, descendants of the Bounty mutineers with their Tahitian wives and children sailed for five weeks from Pitcairn Island to settle on Norfolk Island. These new settlers brought with them a distinct culture and language, and many held mutineers' names such as Adams, Buffett, Christian and McCoy. From that day, Norfolk Island began its steady climb out of hell and into heaven.

Once sustained by agriculture and fishing, visitors now keep the island alive. But traditional culture remains deep-rooted – with dancing, singing and a unique cuisine. Banana dumplings, fried fish and Hihi pie, concocted with periwinkles, can be sampled at one of the fine restaurants scattered across the island.

The blue waters around Norfolk Island are teeming with fish, and there are countless fishing charters and scuba-diving trips out to the reef to explore this kaleidoscope underwater world. In the sheltered waters of Emily Bay, you can also indulge in some lazy swimming and snorkelling, and endless relaxation.

Norfolk Island is favoured by well-heeled Australians and New Zealanders, and a few millionaires have migrated to this tax-free haven. There are over 70 low-tax shops and many eager customers. Yet the island seems to balance the old and the new perfectly – honouring its Pitcairn people, its rich environment and its visitors.

Norfolk pine trees flank the shoreline.

POPULATION:
1,800 (2007)

WHEN TO GO:
Idyllic in December-January, with temperatures ranging from 12°C (54° F) at night to 19-21°C (66-70° F) in the day.

HOW TO GET THERE:
Regular flights from Sydney, Brisbane, Newcastle and Auckland – with an average 2 hours flying time.

HIGHLIGHTS:
Bounty Day – 8 June. When the islanders re-enact the landing of their ancestors on the island.
Kingston – built by convicts of the second penal colony, with many historic buildings.
Bushwalks through the National Park – to see some of the 40 plants unique to the island.
Lazing under the Norfolk Island Pines – up to 57 m (187 ft) tall.
A hot-stone massage with heated basalt stones from the nearby beach.

YOU SHOULD KNOW:
English is the main language here, but the islanders still talk to each other in 'Norfolk' – a mix of 18th century English and Polynesian. *Wataweih yorlye?* means 'How are you?'

The main beach seen from Point Lookout.

North Stradbroke Island

POPULATION:
3,200 (2005) – but greater during the holiday season.
WHEN TO GO:
June to October for humpback whale watching, and to avoid the summer crowds.
HOW TO GET THERE:
Thirty min vehicle ferry or water taxi from Cleveland (just 30 km (19 mi) south of Brisbane). There's also a fast catamaran service.
HIGHLIGHTS:
North Gorge Headlands walk – spectacular, surf-crashing walk around the Point Lookout cliffs.
A cooling swim in Blue Lake, Blue Lake National Park.
Tours of Amenity Point and the lakes in glass-bottomed canoes.
Sandboarding, scuba diving, surfing and sea kayaking.
YOU SHOULD KNOW:
Stradbroke Island's most famous local was Oodgeroo Noonuccal, formerly known as Kath Walker, the Aboriginal poet and native-rights campaigner. She was one of the prime movers who lead the 1997 agreement between the local government council and the aboriginal people of the area claiming rights over the island and parts of Moreton Bay.

Affectionately known as 'Straddie' by the locals, North Stradbroke Island is the textbook beach get-away. Just 30 km (19 mi) southeast of Brisbane and the Gold Coast, it languishes at the southern end of Moreton Bay. At 30 km (19 mi) long, it is one of the world's largest sand islands, boasting pristine beaches, rugged coastline and inland freshwater lakes.

It lost its native name of Minijerribah in 1827, when one Captain H. J. Rous, or Viscount Dunwich, commander of the HMS *Rainbow*, named the island after his father the Earl of Stradbroke, the main town after his own title and Rainbow Beach after his ship.

A cluster of three picturesque villages – Dunwich, Amity Point and Point Lookout – act as convivial bases for many visitors. Dunwich was once a penal colony and quarantine station, and, as is often the case, its cemetery is a telling record of the island's past. At Point Lookout, the aptly named Whale Rock is the perfect spot from which to scan the vast oceans in search of migrating humpback whales, dolphins and turtles.

In the 1960s, sand mining operations began to impact on the fragile island environment, but by the 1990s environmental issues came to the fore and half of the island became a national park. Mining is still very active on the island, but mainly away in the restricted southern end.

Point Lookout on the eastern surf side of the island is a natural draw. Spreading across Straddie's single rocky headland it overlooks a string of white beaches. The western side enjoys the calmer waters of the bay and is safer for families. The island is famous for its fishing – with the annual 'Straddie Classic' every August being one of Australia's richest and best-known fishing competitions.

Rottnest Island

POPULATION:
128 (2006)
WHEN TO GO:
November to February.
HOW TO GET THERE:
By air or sea from Perth or Fremantle.
HIGHLIGHTS:
The cycle trail – explore all 24 km (15 mi) of coastline by bicycle. You will need at least 2½ hours for a leisurely trip.
Quokkas – these cute marsupials are almost tame and will come cadging when you are having a picnic.
The Quokka Arms – this hotel was constructed between 1859 and 1864 as the Governor's summer residence. More recently, it is open to the public as a hotel and is a popular drinking spot.
Snorkelling above the reefs – there are marked trails with underwater plaques to point out what to look for.
YOU SHOULD KNOW:
The island is very busy during school holidays so check dates before you go.

Sitting on the edge of the Australian continental shelf near Perth in western Australia, Rottnest Island is just 11 km (6 mi) long and 4.5 km (2.7 mi) at its widest point. An iconic holiday destination for Perth residents, with 70 per cent of visitors coming for a day out, the entire island is run as a nature reserve and the surrounding waters as a marine park.

Known to local Aboriginal people as Wadjemup, the island is believed to be a place of spirits and is of significance to the Aboriginal communities. Artefacts have been found at a number of sites on Rottnest Island which are at least 6,500 years old, and possibly older, so there were indigenous people living here before sea levels rose and the island was separated from the mainland.

The first Europeans to discover the island were Dutch navigators who were searching for a shorter route from the Cape of Good Hope to Batavia in the 17th century. At that time the island was uninhabited. Samuel Volkerson was the first European to actually land on the island in 1658. William de Vlamingh visited in 1696 and named the island Rottnest after the abundance of quokkas (small marsupials) he saw, mistaking them for rats. Other Europeans soon followed, believing the island had potential for salt harvesting, farming and fishing. From 1839 for almost a century the island housed a penal colony for Aboriginal men and boys. When the colony closed, the leisure potential of the island was realized and tourism took off.

The island is best explored by bicycle as private cars are not allowed. The 24-km (15-mi) route around the coast runs through some of the most beautiful scenery, passing small, sandy beaches in secluded coves. The island has a total of 63 beaches and 20 bays, some of the finest in the world, and the turquoise water makes swimming here a must.

There are lovely reefs here, with twenty species of colourful corals and 360 species of fish, which can be explored by snorkelling, diving or a trip in a glass-bottomed boat. There are also a number of shipwrecks close to the shore, making diving here a popular pastime. Look out for humpback whales, green and loggerhead turtles, rays and bottlenose dolphins.

The secluded Mary Cove

Fraser Island

POPULATION:
1,378 (1996)
WHEN TO GO:
Anytime, but the whale watching months are rightly busier (August to October) so book ahead.
HOW TO GET THERE:
Flights from Brisbane to Harvey Bay, then boat to the island.
Day trip – fast ferry from Urangan Marina to Kingfisher Bay resort.
Or barge from Urangan Harbour for more serious exploration by vehicle.
HIGHLIGHTS:
Lake Wabby – the deepest lake on the island.
The coloured cliffs at the Cathedrals.
A walk to the top of Indian Head – with sightings out to sea of dolphins, whales and sharks.
The Champagne Pools – a cluster of safe swimming pools just above the surf line.
Whale watching – 1,500 humpback whales visit Harvey Bay in August, September and October en route to Antarctic waters.
YOU SHOULD KNOW:
The island got its European name from James and Eliza Fraser (the captain of the *Stirling Castle*, and his wife) who were shipwrecked on the northwest coast in 1836. He died here, and she would have too but for the help of the Aborigines.

Ranked alongside Uluru and the Great Barrier Reef, Fraser Island is a World Heritage Site and much vaunted as one of Australia's great natural treasures. From the Queensland coast, it appears cloaked in lush, deep green forest. But for all its rainforests and lakes, Fraser Island is in fact the largest sand island in the world – 120 km (75 mi) by 15 km (9 mi) – with supposedly more sand than the Sahara Desert, and with dunes up to 224 m (735 ft) high. There is nowhere like it on earth.

The Buchulla tribe, who called the island K'gari, or 'Paradise', lived in harmony with their environment for thousands of years. Tragically, what they spent so many years creating the Europeans soon dismantled. Settlers woke up to the value of the timber and vast tracts of rainforest were cleared. Happily, in 1991, the island became part of the Great Sandy National Park and its future was secured.

The east coast forms the main highway, and other quieter tracks criss-cross the interior and pierce the island's wooded heart. Towering kauri pines and cycads encircle the blue and even 'tea'-tinted lakes. Lake turtles are a joy to encounter, and will sometimes pester you for bread. The west coast is given over to mangrove swamps and, with its more treacherous soft sand, is pretty inaccessible.

The authentic Fraser experience can only come with walking – and a three-day hike, with camping overnight, reveals the hidden depths of this paradise island.

Fraser Island is one of the few remaining strongholds for a pure race of wild dingoes. Sadly, in recent years these dingoes have gained something of a reputation, but some of the blame for their aggression seems to point back to tourism. Visitors are just asked never to feed them and admire them from afar – to be 'Dingo Smart'.

Dunes and lush forest on Fraser Island

The rocky beaches of Kangaroo Island

Kangaroo Island

Kangaroo in both name and nature, this large island just 13 km (8 mi) off the South Australian mainland has remained relatively untouched for thousands of years; and as such is an unblemished microcosm of the vast red continent. Towering cliffs protect the northern shores, giving way to more exposed sandy beaches in the south. Bushwalking is pretty compulsory, and trails meander across the national and conservation parks that cover a third of the island.

Wild koalas hug the trees and kangaroos hop down the streets. Isolated from the ravages of European diseases and introduced species that afflicted their near neighbours, the native animals and plants have flourished – echidnas, platypuses, possums and penguins are all on the wildlife fanatic's list.

In 1800, Captain Matthew Flinders was commissioned by the British Government to chart the southern coastline of Terra Australis in HMS *Investigator*. He first sighted this island in March 1802, came ashore and named it Kangaroo Island, after dining well on wild kangaroo meat. Just weeks later he spotted a French ship on the horizon, under the command of Nicholas Baudin. Despite their two countries being at war, the two men were civil, exchanging ideas and even vital supplies. Baudin went on to map the south and west coastlines, leaving many French names in his wake: Ravine des Casoars, D'Estress Bay and Cape de Couedic – now home to a colony of New Zealand fur seals.

Experienced divers may discover one of the 50 or so wrecks that litter this rocky coastline. Following the earliest recorded shipwreck in 1847, the first lighthouse in South Australia was built at Cape Willoughby, and stands to this day – 27 metres (89 ft) high and a healthy climb to the top. Ferries landing at Penneshaw on the eastern tip make it a hotspot for tourists, but it is easy enough to get away into the wilds and delight in this well-preserved refuge.

POPULATION:
4,500 (2003)

WHEN TO GO:
June through to August is fabulous. The countryside is lush and the wildlife active during the day: kangaroos are popping out of the pouch, koalas, Southern right whales are steaming by on migration, and the male echidnas are out looking for mates. September to November sees Kangaroo Island in full bloom, and eucalyptus oil in full production.

HOW TO GET THERE:
By regular ferries (45 mins) from Cape Jervis to Penneshaw. By air – from Adelaide (30 mins).

HIGHLIGHTS:
Flinders Chase National Park – incredible rock formations including Remarkable Rocks and Admiral's Arch.
Little penguins on parade around Kingscote and Penneshaw – as they head back from the water to their seaside burrows for the night.
Surfing or swimming at Vivonne Bay – Australia's top beach for clear, clean waters and privacy.
Emu Ridge Eucalyptus Distillery is the only commercial distillery of its type in South Australia, still employing 600 islanders.

YOU SHOULD KNOW:
Here you can taste honey from the only known pure strain of Ligurian bee in the world. Twelve hives were imported from Liguria, Italy in the 1880s and in splendid island isolation they have remained pure – untouched by other breeds of bees, and producing true nectar of the gods.

Melville and Bathurst

POPULATION:
2,500 (2007)
WHEN TO GO:
Tours available from May to October (the wet season is October to March).
HOW TO GET THERE:
Chartered planes/tours out of Darwin.
HIGHLIGHTS:
Early Catholic mission buildings.
Morning tea with the Tiwi women.
The Pukamani burial sites.
YOU SHOULD KNOW:
Football is a Tiwi passion. It was introduced in 1941 by the missionary John Pye. The Tiwi grand final (mainly barefoot) in April is a significant local event, and football here has the highest local participation rate of anywhere in Australia (35 per cent).

Just 80 km (50 mi) due north of Darwin, Melville and its intimate smaller neighbour Bathurst make up the Tiwi Islands, home of the Tiwi Aboriginal people. Most of these people now live on Bathurst having abandoned their hunter-gatherer lifestyle, but some return to their traditional lands on Melville for just a few weeks each year.

For thousands of years they had hardly any contact with their mainland neighbours, and are rightly proud of their unique land and culture. Today, these determined people have created their own success story; leading their own tours on the islands, and turning their talents to beautiful and highly valued art – crafting and selling bark painting, textiles and pottery.

The Tiwi people's presence on the islands is most clearly marked by their Pukumani wooden burial poles, erected around graves and carved and painted with symbolic figures. This decorative patterning extends to body painting for ceremonies, and has been practised for thousands of years. The traditional form of mark making was derived from the creation story, and the Tiwi people's positioning of line and dot is very distinctive.

Clear waters, empty beaches and lush forest are the trademarks of these big, flat islands. Eucalyptus forest gives way to bush, and the waters offshore are favoured by sharks and freshwater crocodiles cruising out from the mainland.

You need a permit to visit the islands – and it is almost essential to book a tour, which employs the Tiwi islanders and takes in the local craft workshops. Food gathering in the bush or offshore with the local people, and staying overnight in a bush camp, draws you even deeper into their ancient and forgotten culture.

Flinders Island

This remarkable 'mountain' in the sea is the main island of the Furneaux chain – 50 or so dots across the Bass Strait, stretching from Tasmania to Australia. These islands are all that remains of the land bridge that once fused Tasmania to the mainland.

In the late 1800s, George Bass and Matthew Flinders circumnavigated Tasmania and left their names indelibly on the map. Flinders was also the destination for the last surviving Tasmanian Aborigines. They were literally herded here under the supervision of Reverend George Augustus Robinson to 'save' them from extinction by civilizing them and converting them to Christianity. Isolated, hungry

and plagued by disease, they gradually died out, and a tiny chapel and cemetery at Wybalenna is all that remains.

On Flinders, rugged granite peaks give way to white crescent beaches and turquoise waters. Much of the land is now a natural reserve and Strezelecki National Park is a wonderful place, adored by hikers. From Settlement Point, you can gaze out over the vast mutton bird colony – where hundreds of thousands of birds scream in to their nests at dusk during the breeding season, from October to March.

On foot is the classic way to take in this island – six days from top to toe – or following one of the many shorter bushwalking trails. And to soothe those weary limbs, nothing compares with soaking in the tepid waters on one of the many fine beaches, interspersed with some gentle fishing off the rocks.

Trousers Point

POPULATION:
897 (2005)
WHEN TO GO:
Pleasant throughout the year, but January is the warmest with temperatures from 13-22° C (60-71° F), with cooling sea breezes.
HOW TO GET THERE:
Daily flights from Tasmania, also some flights from Victoria.
HIGHLIGHTS:
Trousers Point – an idyllic cove with swimming, camping and picnicking.
Settlement Point – for a short coastal walk with swimming, rock hopping and views.
Climbing to the top of Mount Strezelecki.
YOU SHOULD KNOW:
One of the more unusual pastimes here is fossicking for 'diamonds' – small fragments of topaz – on the beach and in the creek at Killiecrankie Bay.

Royal penguins out for a stroll on Macquarie Island

POPULATION:
Uninhabited (except 20-40 members of the Australian Antarctic Division who are based here every year).

WHEN TO GO:
In the breeding season – over the summer months and early autumn. Even then the weather can be challenging – cold with continuous drizzle.

HOW TO GET THERE:
Very limited access by permit only – approaching by sea, but there are no harbours or landing facilities. Most visitors some on cruise ships, spending up to two days on the island and tourist boats.

HIGHLIGHTS:
Getting there.
Sandy Bay king penguin colony – walkways and observation platforms.
Invigorating dips in the icy seas!

YOU SHOULD KNOW:
On steep hillsides grows the Macquarie Island cabbage. Brittle with big leaves, this cabbage actually tastes more like tough celery. It's a good source of vitamin C, and 100 years ago the sealers practically lived on it.

Macquarie Island

'Macca' rests at the ends of the earth. This remote wilderness is tucked away in the southeast corner of the Pacific, halfway between Australia and Antarctica. A tiny fragment of land, it is of huge significance on a world scale, yet was only discovered by accident by Frederick Hasselborough in 1810 while he was looking around for new sealing grounds.

Under Tasmania's wing, the only human inhabitants on this extraordinary wildlife sanctuary are from the Australian Antarctic Division, based on the north of the island. Over the centuries, scientists have been endlessly drawn to this unsung wonder of the natural world. On the animal front, the visitors are visually and audibly overwhelming. Each spring, around 3.5 million seabirds, mostly penguins, and 80,000 elephant seals pull themselves up on to the rocky shoreline to breed. There are penguins galore – rockhoppers, kings, royals and gentooes; and on occasion the fabulous sooty and wandering albatrosses. Rabbits are a less welcome sight and are literally eating away at this World Heritage Site. Their days may well be numbered.

You have to work extremely hard to get to this island, but the rewards for true lovers of wildlife and wilderness are unparalleled. It's a cold, inhospitable place at the best of times, but you don't come here for the weather.

Lord Howe Island

Unpolluted and untouched, Lord Howe Island is the ultimate eco-destination. Back in Victorian times, stories came to England of this 'gem of the sea', and to this day over two-thirds of the land is given over to a park reserve and only 400 people can visit at any one time. Often the animals outnumber the people.

There's only one road, and everyone tends to get around by bicycle, boat or on foot. Just 11 km (7 mi) long, this boomerang-shaped beauty is topped by the rainforest-clad Mount Gower and Mount Lidgbird and dips down into the cool Tasman Sea. Born of a volcanic eruption some seven million years ago, it has the southernmost coral reef in the world – safe haven for 500 species of fish and 90 species of corals.

Lord Howe Island was discovered in 1788 by Lieutenant Henry Lidgbird Ball of HMS *Supply*, while on his way from Botany Bay to Norfolk Island with convicts on board. Many government ships, whaling and trading vessels stopped here but a permanent settlement wasn't established until 1834, at an area now known as Old Settlement.

Nowadays, the locals are laidback and often barefoot, and set the tone for any visit. On the more popular northern end of the island, there are endless walks and lookouts, and ideal places for a picnic along Old Settlement Beach. Bushwalking apart, there are fabulous swimming, snorkelling and diving spots. This insanely beautiful island never appears crowded – and if it is, it's with exotic flora and fauna not human life.

POPULATION:
300 (2007)

WHEN TO GO:
Cheapest to get there out of season but it can be wetter and windier and some places may be closed. From September to April huge numbers of exotic seabirds nest here.

HOW TO GET THERE:
By air from Sydney or Brisbane.

HIGHLIGHTS:
Sooty terns on the accessible summit of Mount Eliza (from August to March).
Mist forests of Mount Gower in the south – strenuous guided walk of about 8 hours.
Ned's Beach – a daily fish feeding frenzy attracting reef and sharks.
Ball's Pyramid – dive trips around the world's tallest stack, rising from the sea 23 km (14 mi) to the southeast.

YOU SHOULD KNOW:
Some rare mushrooms on the island glow in the dark. These glowing mushrooms appear after heavy rain in the palm forests. If picked they glow for a number of days. The glow is so bright that you can read by it in the dark.

The twin peaks of Mounts Lidgbird and Gower

The Whitsunday Islands

POPULATION:
14,103 (2001)
WHEN TO GO:
Any time of year.
HOW TO GET THERE:
Fly to Hamilton Island direct, or to Proserpine on the mainland. Take a ferry from Shutehaven or Airlie Beach on the mainland.
HIGHLIGHTS:
Scenic flights over the Great Barrier Reef – these can most easily be arranged on Hamilton Island.
Whitehaven Beach – located on Whitsunday Island, this 7-km (4.3 mi) beach has brilliant white sand, so bring your sunglasses.
Aboriginal cave paintings – accessible by boat, the paintings can be found at Nara Inlet on Hook Island.
Migrating whales – if you visit the islands in July-September, look out for migrating whales as they make their way through the warm waters past the islands.
Hamilton Island Race Week – this yachting festival takes place in August each year. More than 150 yachts come from across Australia and New Zealand to compete in a week of races. On Whitehaven Day, the yachts descend on Whitehaven Beach and enjoy an enormous beach party.
YOU SHOULD KNOW:
The islands can get busy in the peak season.

A group of 74 islands lying off the coast of Queensland, Australia, between Townsville and Mackay, the Whitsunday Islands are part of the Great Barrier Reef and one of Australia's most popular destinations attracting over half a million visitors each year. These forested mountainous islands are surrounded by spectacular coral reefs, warm crystal-clear aquamarine waters and white sandy beaches. They were first discovered by Captain Cook in the 1770s on his fraught voyage to try to find an exit from the reef system without destroying his ship. He named the islands Whitsunday because he thought it was Whit Sunday on the day he discovered them, though it turned out he was wrong. The name, however, stuck.

Most of the islands are designated as national park, although some are privately owned. Apart from the bigger more developed islands, the majority are uninhabited, unspoiled wildernesses. There are small resorts on some of the islands, and camp sites on others if you really want to get away from it all.

Hamilton Island is the most developed and many visitors use it as a base from which to access the Great Barrier Reef. There are many other activities on offer from Hamilton, including sea kayaking, twilight sailing, game fishing, scenic flights over the Great Barrier Reef, diving, cuddling a koala, bushwalking and waterskiing. Despite its development, the island is still largely untouched and has some lovely beaches, coves and inlets.

Hook Island, the second largest of the islands, is another popular destination for tourists. It is best known for its colourful coral gardens, a great place for snorkelling and diving.

Whitsunday Island is the largest of the group and is best known among boating-types for Hill Inlet, the secure anchorage of Cid Harbour, the sheltered waterway of Gulnare Inlet, and the famous Whitehaven Beach, with its 7 km (4.3 mi) of pure white silica sand. This stunning beach attracts lots of day-trippers from the mainland ports of Airlie Beach and Shute Harbour.

The stunning Whitehaven Beach

There is a bewildering variety of organized tours on offers, with sailing boat, catamaran and cruise trips to the islands and reefs, many to sites where visitors can snorkel in the reefs and watch the fish. Several companies also run trips in glass-bottomed boats or semi-submersibles. The islands are not only worth visiting for the marine life, however. Many have walking trails up to their peaks through lovely rainforest full of birdsong, and there are so many beaches you are bound to find one to yourself.

The rugged, volcanic coastline of Christmas Island

Christmas Island

David Attenborough once famously sat on the beach here, in the pitch dark, as millions of red land crabs scuttled over his legs and marched determinedly down to the sea. Christmas Island is a scientist's heaven, and for the rest of us a retreat from reality. In Australia's remote Indian Ocean Territories, it lies 360 km (224 mi) south of Jakarta and 2,300 km (1,429 mi) northwest of Perth. Its people are a blend of Chinese, Malay and European-Australian, and so is its food, language, religion and customs.

It took millions of years for the island to emerge from the depths, and it remains of immense scientific importance. For centuries, Christmas Island's isolation and rugged coasts were a natural barrier to settlement. On 25 December 1643, Captain William Mynors of the British East India Company's *Royal Mary* had sighted the island and given it its name. And yet no humans resided here until the late nineteenth century; leaving many unique animal species to evolve without human interference.

Sixty percent of the island is now protected, and harbours wildlife found nowhere else in the world. The famous red land crabs are dotted across the forest floor; pneumatic robber crabs scale the coconut trees and frigatebirds, noddies and boobies nest on the cliffs and in the forests. The coastline is rugged, but notched with tiny sheltered bays and sand and coral beaches seemingly purpose built for a swim.

POPULATION:
1,600 (2007)

WHEN TO GO:
Dry season – April to November. November/December for the mammoth red land crab march.

HOW TO GET THERE:
Flights form Perth (via the Cocos Islands); and from Singapore and Jakarta.

HIGHLIGHTS:
Diving with whale sharks – October to April.
Cave dives.
Flying Fish Cove – swimming and snorkelling.
Walks through the rainforest.
Hugh's Waterfall.
The Blowholes – a series of rock formations that hiss and spurt water when it is forced through from the ocean swell.

YOU SHOULD KNOW:
This remote island unexpectedly hit the headlines in August 2001, when the Norwegian container ship *Tampa* with its cargo of rescued asylum seekers from Afghanistan was refused permission to land.

Hobart harbour

Tasmania

A world apart in every sense, Tasmania is Australia's only island state, and the very isolation that once made it an ideal location for penal settlements now helps preserve its natural riches. Tasmania would seem to have it all – from history and wilderness to friendly people and great food and wines.

Tasmania certainly seems to move at a much slower pace than the mainland – affording visitors the time and space to relax. Over 360 km (224 mi) long and 306 km (190 mi) wide, it's big enough to allow you to head for the hills on the back roads and escape everyday life. Along the way are magnificent peaks, old colonial settlements and empty beaches. It also purports to have some of the cleanest air in the world.

The first European to sight Tasmania was the Dutch navigator Abel Tasman in 1642, and from then on many explorers came this way, including James Cook and William Bligh. But the arrival of these men was bad news for the Tasmanian Aborigines. They lost their traditional hunting grounds and sometimes their lives, and were resettled to Flinders Island to be 'civilized'. Many Aboriginal sites are sacred, but on the cliffs around Woolnorth can be seen some of their unique art.

Corners of Tasmania are often likened to the green pastures of England but here there are also vast wildernesses: the west is wild and untamed, inland are glacial mountains and roaring rivers. For the less adventurous, there is the cosmopolitan capital Hobart – spread out over seven hills and with a waterfront location to match Sydney's. In the heart of the countryside lies sleepy old Richmond – with some of Australia's finest and most pristine colonial architecture it's now a Mecca for artists and artisans.

Tasmania appears to have been slightly overlooked. Yet this discreet island, roughly the size of Ireland, is both gentle and wild, charming and challenging.

POPULATION:
484,700 (2005)

WHEN TO GO:
October to March – when it's pleasantly warm and mild.

HOW TO GET THERE:
Flights from Melbourne and other mainland capitals. High speed ferries from Sydney and Melbourne.

HIGHLIGHTS:
The capital Hobart with its Salamanca market place.
Walking the rugged Overland Track through Cradale Mountain-Lake St Clair National Park.
Hiking through Freycinet National Park to Wineglass Bay.
White-water rafting on the wild Franklin River.

YOU SHOULD KNOW:
The tale of the Tasmania tiger – a striped carnivore that once roamed Tasmania – has two endings: one is that it was hunted to extinction by European settlers, while the other maintains that this large thylacine still leads a secretive life way out in Tasmania's great wilderness.

Torres Straits Islands

Dividing Australia from Papua New Guinea, the Torres Strait is one of the last frontiers on earth, and is sprinkled with stepping-stone islands. Of these islands, 17 are inhabited and Thursday Island is seen as the 'capital'. This tiny speck of an island, just visible from the Australian mainland, was once called the 'Sink of the Pacific', reflecting the sheer variety of people who have passed through since its pearling heydays – Aboriginal, Malay, Chinese, Japanese, Melanesian and Anglo. In this now lies its charm.

In the 19th century, Europeans quickly discovered the Strait's rich pearl beds and Thursday Island was once a thriving centre for pearl diving. For decades this was the only job on the island and many Japanese pearl divers tragically lost their lives here, and are buried in the local cemetery. Most died of compression sickness.

Many foreigners have influenced the islands' history. In the late 1800s the London Missionary Society landed on Darnley Island – and the advent of Christianity stabilized the community, but also led to the demise of traditional life. South Sea Island teachers also came, and brought with them a new dance culture and crops, and intermarried with the locals.

Access to the smaller more remote islands is limited, but a few are little gems. Badu is fringed by mangrove swamps and is the centre of the Straits burgeoning crayfish industry; and Saibai, just 16 km (10 mi) from the New Guinea mainland is the only place in Australia from which you can see another country. In many ways, Thursday Island is the easiest and most interesting island to visit, with its laid-back attitude and multicultural mix. Here the hotel clock has no hands – paying homage to the leisurely pace of life.

POPULATION:
8,089 (2001)
WHEN TO GO:
Avoid the monsoon season.
HOW TO GET THERE:
Ferry from mainland to Thursday Island. Access to other islands limited and more expensive.
Flights from Cairns to Thursday Island via Horn Island – a few minutes by water taxi from Thursday Island.
Small airline operators service other islands
HIGHLIGHTS:
Thursday Island:
Coming of Light festivities on 1 July.
All Souls Quetta Memorial Church – built in 1893 in memory of the shipwreck of the *Quetta*, with 133 lives lost.
Aplin Road Cemetery – tiled islander tombs, and the Japanese area filled with hundreds of pearl divers graves.
Thursday's colonial-style Customs House.
Pearling Museum on nearby Horn Island.
YOU SHOULD KNOW:
In any one season in the annual (July) Island of Origin rugby league matches up to 25 players may be hospitalized, and there is sadly an occasional death.

Waier Island, part of the Murray Island group in the Torres Straits

The rich variety of fish found in the waters surrounding Mayor Island make this a popular dive location.

POPULATION:
3 (2001)
WHEN TO GO:
October to May.
HOW TO GET THERE:
By boat from Whangamata or Tauranga.
HIGHLIGHTS:
The island offers great opportunities for off-shore activities, including big game fishing, diving and snorkelling, to appreciate the rich marine life here, including swordfish, marlin and mako sharks.
The hiking trails on the island allow good views of the crater, with its lakes and hot springs.
YOU SHOULD KNOW:
Strict quarantine measures are in place to protect the wildlife around the island, so you must contact the caretaker before landing here.

Mayor Island

Located off the Bay of Plenty coast of New Zealand's North Island, Mayor Island is the top of a dormant shield volcano, rising 355 m (1,164 ft) above the waves and believed to have formed about 7,000 years ago. Known as Tuhua by the indigenous Maori, the island was named Mayor Island by Captain Cook, who first sighted it three days before Lord Mayor's Day in 1769. The sides of the volcano rise fairly steeply from the sea, and the majority of its interior is a vast crater. Hot springs abound, and there are two small crater lakes on the island, Green Lake and Black Lake, which were formed by eruptions 36,000 and 6,000 years ago.

The island is best known for its lava flows and domes, containing deposits of obsidian, a black volcanic glass created by the rapid cooling of silica-rich lava. The obsidian, *tuhua* in Maori, was prized by the Maori for making cutting and scraping tools and pieces from the island have been found throughout New Zealand and the Kermadec Islands.

The waters around the island are renowned for game fishing, with marlin, mako sharks and swordfish being plentiful here. The island and the waters close to its shores are protected as a small marine reserve, but diving, snorkelling, sailing and swimming are all encouraged here. The old game-fishing centre on Sou'East Bay is on a beautiful beach and the clear waters and rich variety of fish here make it the most popular destination for divers.

There are several hiking tracks on the island, so visitors can explore the native bush and see the birdlife. Because it is protected, the easiest way to get here is with a registered tour operator.

Stewart Island

In Maori legend, if North Island was once the great fish and South Island the canoe, then Stewart Island was its anchor. Due south of Invercargill, the Maori name for the third largest island in New Zealand is Rakiura or Glowing Skies. Gazing at a crimson sun setting over the horizon or the Aurora Australis (Southern Lights) sweeping over inky skies, this is the end of that quest for paradise.

This laidback and unspoilt wilderness reverberates with the sound of birdsong. Parakeets, tui, kaka, bellbirds and robins flutter overhead and sing their hearts out. Eighty-five percent of the island is protected, and it is unadulterated heaven for walkers and birders. Just offshore are albatrosses, blue penguins and petrels. Added to that, the coast is punctuated by endless sandy coves for a swim in the somewhat bracing waters.

Searching for New Zealand's national bird, the kiwi, is at its easiest here. The birds are large and pretty common around the beaches, even during the day. They are so short-sighted and slow they may even bump into bathers.

The only real settlement on the island is Oban. This lazy little fishing village nestles in Halfmoon Bay and has enough shops and cafés to keep the relaxed traveller content. Despite its 7,000 km (4,350 mi) coastline, Stewart Island only has 20 km (12 mi) of roads. Shrug off the cares of the world and relax Stewart-style.

POPULATION:
420 (2006)

WHEN TO GO:
The weather can swing dramatically in any given day, but December and January are warmest with temperatures averaging 16.5° C (62 °F).

HOW TO GET THERE:
Flights from Invercargill.

HIGHLIGHTS:
Walking the 29 km (18 mi) Rakiura Track (a circuit out of Oban) with camping and huts along the way.
Eating crayfish as fresh as it gets.
Swim at isolated Mason Bay – the water may be cold but kiwis abound.
Ulva Island – tiny island just offshore and heaving with wildlife, and plenty of trails.
Paterson Inlet for kayaking and walking.

YOU SHOULD KNOW:
Bring a torch if you are staying in Oban – there are no streetlights at night.

The Aurora Australis over Stewart Island

Mokoia Island

POPULATION:
Uninhabited
WHEN TO GO:
Best to avoid the really busy summer months of December and January, when it is one of the sunniest places on North Island and the driest.
HOW TO GET THERE:
Flights from Auckland to Rotorua. Cruises and high-speed boats from the Rotorua lakefront jetty.
HIGHLIGHTS:
Maori cultural performances. Hinemoa's Pool (Walkimihia). Nature treks – spot the tui, weka and brown kiwi.
Food trails and tastings – hunt down and taste indigenous New Zealand herbs and learn about their historical, medicinal and culinary uses.

A sacred island in a lake, Mokoia is a green lava dome rising 180 m (590 ft) above the still waters of Lake Roturua in the heart of North Island. Stepping ashore, its deeply spiritual nature seems to reverberate through the air. This natural sanctuary for wildlife belongs to the Te Arawa people and was once know as Te Motu Tapu a Tinirau – the Sacred Island of Tinirau. Fertile and isolated for hundreds of years, it holds a unique *kumera* (sweet potato) plantation, which meant it was once hotly contested by warring tribes. It was once also a thriving village for Maori and missionaries, but is now stands quiet and alone.

Steeped in tradition, it is said that Mokoia was home to Tutanekai, a young warrior. It was to Mokoia that Hinemoa, the daughter of a famous chief, defying her family, swam some 2.5 km (1.5 mi) from the shores of Lake Rotorua at night guided only by the sound of her true love's flute. So deep and rich is this story that the two main streets in Rotorua are named after this lovestruck couple.

The shores of Mokoia hold geothermal springs and Roturua is New Zealand's most dynamic thermal area – with geysers, hot springs and bubbling mud pools. The area is also the epicentre of Maori culture, with one-third of its residents being Maori. 'Sulphur City' as it is known is a much-favoured spot for tourists and backpackers; so, to find more spiritual solace, cruise out to the hidden island of Mokoia.

A view of Mokoia Island across Lake Rotorua

Large colonies of fur seals can be found in the Chatham Islands.

Chatham Islands

Head due south of Christchurch, way out into the South Pacific, and you'll stumble upon the ten Chatham Islands. As befits this remote, brooding location, there are rugged coastlines, towering cliffs and endless, empty beaches. Its Moriori name of Rekohu or 'Misty Sun' respects a peaceful past with people of Polynesian extraction. Sadly the last full-blooded Moriori, Tommy Solomon, died over 70 years ago. But slowly the descendants of these people are gaining recognition for their rights and values.

The Chathams are the first inhabited land in the world to greet the dawn – on 1 January 2000 the dawn was greeted here at 4.00 am (NZST) with major international celebrations linking all nations of the world.

Only Chatham Island and Pitt Island are inhabited, and the best way to get around the islands is to ask these locals. Around the shores live many rare birds – from black robins and magenta petrels to mollyhawks; and inland ancient Moriori tree and rock carvings survive. At Blind Man's Creek 40 million-year-old sharks' teeth can be found – but visitors are asked to leave them where they find them, for obvious reasons!

This is an unworldly place, offering enormous peace and solitude. There are no public roads, no flashy resorts and limited accommodation; and the fiercely independent yet welcoming locals take good care of their guests. From the moment you arrive you are placed under the wing of an island family.

POPULATION:
770 (2006)

WHEN TO GO:
Best to visit from September to March, with temperatures of 15-24° C (59-75° F) – but these are also the busiest times.
All visitors must have confirmed accommodation before arriving. In summer the hotel and lodge are often filled by tours so book as far ahead as possible.

HOW TO GET THERE:
Direct flights from Wellington, Christchurch and Auckland.

HIGHLIGHTS:
Early Moriori settlement sites and middens.
Memorial to Tommy Solomon, the last full-blooded Moriori.
Crayfishing off the beach, and wonderful seafood to savour.
Fishing and diving tours.
Fur seal colony near Kaingaroa, Chatham Island.

YOU SHOULD KNOW:
The international date line lies to the east of the Chathams, even though the islands lie east of 180° longitude. Consequently, the Chatham Islands observe their own time, 45 minutes ahead of New Zealand time.

Sub-Antarctic Islands

With a past lost in sealing and shipwrecks, New Zealand's Sub-Antarctic Islands (Snares, Bounty, Campbell, Antipodes and Aucklands) have finally found their true vocation as wondrous, wild nature reserves and biodiversity 'hot spots'. Home to half the world's seabirds, they also offer fabulous breeding grounds for the 'giants' of the natural world – elephant seals, crested penguins and wandering albatrosses.

Many of the islands are rightly out of bounds, but some can be landed on with a permit. Landing on Campbell Island is a treat – to make acquaintance with over 7,500 pairs of southern royal albatrosses and the rare Campbell Island teal. One out-of-bounds group is the magical Antipodes Islands that got their name from their position at latitude 180° – exactly opposite 0° at Greenwich, England. Bobbing offshore you may catch a glimpse of the endemic Antipodes Island parakeet or the huge albatrosses nesting in the short grass. On the Bounty Islands there are literally thousands of penguins and mollyhawks –– definitely no room for humans.

The Auckland Islands were plagued by shipwrecks in the 1800s, and settlement here failed miserably when the introduced cattle had to be destroyed. So now the land is given over to wildlife. On the wondrously named Disappointment Island there are over 60,000 white-capped mollyhawks and more. But the plant life of these islands should not be forgotten. Sir Joseph Hooker, botanist aboard Sir James Clark Ross's 1840 Antarctic expedition wrote of 'a flora display second to none outside the tropics'. He was to become the curator of Kew Gardens.

The Sub-Antartics are not for the faint-hearted. Arrive armed with a sense of adventure and a love of the wilder side of life and you will leave all the wiser.

POPULATION:
Uninhabited
WHEN TO GO:
November to January
HOW TO GET THERE:
Most easily on ecotourism boat trips out of Manpouri.
HIGHLIGHTS:
Birds… a day ashore on Enderby (Auckland Islands) – to see flightless teal, snipe and yellow-eyed penguins.
Auckland Island – southern royal albatrosses among the flowering mega herbs.
Early morning on Snares Island with six million sooty shearwaters.
YOU SHOULD KNOW:
If you are very lucky you might just hitch a lift to the islands on board a scientific boat expedition as a 'casual explorer'. But there is often a long waiting list.

Surf surging through the kelp on Snares Island.

The Bay of Islands

Close to the northern tip of New Zealand, 60 km (40 mi) north-west of Whangarei, is one of the most popular fishing, sailing and diving destinations in the country. The clear blue waters of the Bay of Islands boast a rich variety of marine life, and are dotted with 144 small islands which together make a picture-postcard scene. The warm equatorial waters give the bay a mild climate which is pleasant all year round.

The Bay of Islands was the first part of New Zealand to be settled by Europeans. British explorer Captain Cook gave the bay its modern name when he stopped here in 1769 on his round-the-world voyage. He put down his anchor at Motoroahia (Roberton Island) where he met the local Maori tribes and began trading on (largely) friendly terms. This is also the place where 500 Maori chiefs and representatives of Queen Victoria signed the Waitangi Treaty in 1840. The treaty made New Zealand a British colony, but gave Maoris the rights of British citizens and the right to own their own lands and other property. The treaty has caused much controversy since it was signed, partly because there were differences between the Maori and British translations. You can find out more at the Waitangi Treaty Grounds, a half-hour stroll along the beach from Paihia.

The best way to enjoy the islands and their abundant wildlife is by boat, whether it is a kayak, yacht or cruiser. Dolphin and whale sightings are very common here. It is even possible to swim with dolphins on a licensed tour.

Jacques Cousteau described the diving around Poor Knights Islands as among the very best in the world, with an abundance of marine wildlife including manta rays and killer whales. There are more than a hundred dive sites in the bay, with coral reefs, rocky coastlines and ship wrecks to explore, including the wreck of the Greenpeace ship, *Rainbow Warrior*, sunk here by the French secret services in 1985. The bay is also famous for its fishing, with good populations of marlin, kingfish and snapper.

POPULATION:
149,600 (2006)
WHEN TO GO:
Any time of year.
HOW TO GET THERE:
By road or rail from Auckland to Russell or by air to Kerikiri then by road.
HIGHLIGHTS:
Swimming with the dolphins.
Whale-watching boat trips.
Watching penguins and gannets.
YOU SHOULD KNOW:
There are strict rules about how closely boats can approach whales and dolphins.

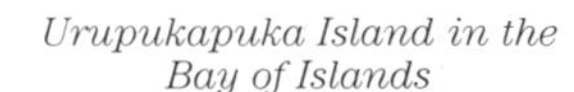

Urupukapuka Island in the Bay of Islands

Espiritu Santo Island

POPULATION:
31,000 (2007 estimate)
WHEN TO GO:
The temperate climate doesn't vary much, though November to February is the hottest, most humid time.
HOW TO GET THERE:
By light aircraft from Port Vila or direct Air Vanuatu flights from Australia (Sydney).
HIGHLIGHTS:
Informative tours for those who want to explore the island's delights with the help of knowledgeable guides.
Luganville market – for a wealth of colourful island produce (and characters).
For divers only – Million Dollar Point, where US forces dumped everything from aircraft to military vehicles into the sea after World War II; the wrecks of the SS *President Coolidge* and USS *Tucker*, both victims of 'friendly fire' (US-laid mines).
Big Bay National Park in the north of the island, a beautifully preserved and completely unspoiled area.
Guided trekking – magical jungle exploration in a small party with an experienced local leader.
YOU SHOULD KNOW:
Take what you need – only the most basic of necessities can be bought on the island.

With an area of 3,950 sq km (1,525 sq mi), this is the largest island in the Republic of Vanuatu, formerly known as the New Hebrides. Vanuatu consists of 83 islands in Melanesia, until recently an isolated part of the western Pacific visited only by the most intrepid of travellers. Now times are changing, but happily for those who like their tropical and sub-tropical islands unspoiled, not that fast.

Espiritu Santo (from the Spanish 'Holy Spirit') is often referred to simply as Santo. The main town and provincial capital is Luganville, the second largest settlement in Vanuatu. The name reflects the fact that the islands were once governed jointly by the British and French, with the latter rather more influential. However, it was the Americans who had bases on Espiritu Santo in World War II, and there are plenty of decaying reminders of their stay. The town has an excellent harbour that is an important centre of the trade in commodities like copra (dried coconut meat) and cacao. It has modernized to the extent that broadband internet access is available, and there are now plenty of buses and taxis to help visitors get around locally.

From Luganville, there are roads to the north and west, but they don't stray far from the coast, leaving the bulk of the island remote and inaccessible. It has a rocky spine, with Mount Tabwemasana rising to around 1,900 m (6,200 ft) – the highest point in Vanuatu. Cruise ships often visit Luganville, and the island is a popular destination with divers who like to get away from the underwater crowd to explore freshwater caves and extensive coral reefs. There are excellent beaches, like the aptly named Champagne Beach (sparkling water and pink sand). The number of annual visitors is still small, but that is changing – get there ahead of the crowd!

Champagne Beach

Tanna Island

In parts of this island, it seems that time has stood still for a thousand years – many villagers still wear traditional costume (which is pretty skimpy), follow the customs of their ancestors and shun all the trappings of modern life. Tanna is a small but interesting island in Vanuatu. Captain James Cook was the first European to arrive, in 1774, attracted by a glowing volcano in the night. Cook was followed by traders and missionaries, but the latter had little success in weaning the islanders off their old beliefs, and in the 19th century some were sadly cannibalized. Even today, outsiders are only welcome in rural villages if travelling with a local guide.

That notwithstanding, Tanna is trying to encourage tourism to supplement the traditional farming and fishing activities. There are a limited number of low-key resorts and bungalow accommodation on the west and east coasts, with wild trekking a major activity in the south around the island's highest mountain, Tukosmera, and nearby Mount Melen. There are one or two inland lodges behind Mount Yasur, on the northwest coast, said to be the world's most accessible active volcano. It is near Sulphur Bay and one-day volcano tours are the most common tourist activity, but the island merits a longer stay.

Tanna has the beautiful white beaches and tropical vegetation of many Pacific islands, but retains an atmosphere that will delight the traveller who dislikes wholesale modern development. There are still places in the world that still allow adventurous travellers to feel that they've discovered the idyllic back of beyond, but are not too difficult to reach. This is one of them.

POPULATION:
20,000 (2007 estimate)

WHEN TO GO:
The climate is at its best between March and October.

HOW TO GET THERE:
By Air Vanuatu from Port Vila on the island of Efate to White Grass airport on Tanna's east coast. On from there by public transport (usually a pickup truck).

HIGHLIGHTS:
Old-fashioned Port Resolution, founded by Captain Cook and named after his ship, HMS *Resolution*.
Friday evening meetings of the John Frums cargo cult, that still believes that gods in the USA are responsible for the miraculous appearance of modern goodies such as radios and fridges (visitors genuinely welcome).

YOU SHOULD KNOW:
There is a cargo cult on Tanna that worships...Prince Philip, Queen Elizabeth II's husband.

Mount Yasur, the world's most accessible active volcano

Lake Te Nggano, home to a rich variety of bird life

POPULATION:
1,500 (2007 estimate)
WHEN TO GO:
Beware of cyclones – the best chance of avoiding an inside-out golf umbrella is between May and October.
HOW TO GET THERE:
Solomon Airlines has five weekly flights to Rennell from Afutara Airport.
HIGHLIGHTS:
A visit to the ancient burial places, caves and temples of the legendary Hiti people.
The abundant and varied bird life on Lake Te Nggano.
Attending a *hetaki* bout – it's the island's traditional form of wrestling.
Visiting one of the villages that specializes in traditional wood carving of extraordinary quality.
YOU SHOULD KNOW:
Eight US Navy Catalina flying boats were scuttled in Lake Te Nggano at the end of World War II, after both Japanese and American forces had been based there.

Rennell Island

How about a trip to the world's largest raised coral atoll? That'll be Rennell Island, traditionally known as Mu Nggava, the southern-most of the Solomon Islands in the western Pacific. It is 80 km (50 mi) long and 40 km (25 mi) wide with an area of 630 sq km (245 sq mi), sparsely populated and largely covered with tropical forest. The island is surrounded by high cliffs, has no beaches and boasts the Pacific Ocean's largest freshwater lake – brackish Lake Te Nggano. There are no rivers or streams, so islanders rely on wells and rainwater tanks.

The inhabitants – who live in closely-knit clans – operate a subsistence economy involving horticulture, fishing, hunting and gathering, with coconuts, yams, taro and bananas being important staples. The profession of *mataisau* (carpenter and expert wood carver) is highly respected.

This is not a casual holiday destination for conventional tourists. Facilities are primitive and those wishing to see this remote place are advised to join an organized group. There are various specialized tours like birdwatching, scuba diving (by boat) and World War II battlefield tours (there was a naval battle off the island in 1943), whilst some basic guest-houses do cater for the bold solo artist – find them near Tingoa airfield or around the lake.

East Rennell (paradoxically the southern third of the island) is a UNESCO World Heritage Site, listed for its importance as a stepping-stone in the migration and evolution of species in the western Pacific. It is not protected by national legislation and – as with many of the Solomon Islands – logging is an ever-present threat.

Guadalcanal Island

In 1942 and 1943, Guadalcanal Island in the southern Solomons was the scene of the first major Allied assault on the Japanese Empire. The intense campaign raged for six months and involved three major land battles, five naval battles and daily air combat, as the Japanese strove to recapture their strategically vital airfield on Guadalcanal. The Allied victory marked a turning point in the Pacific theatre, with defence moving to successful offence. However, violence didn't altogether cease after World War II. There was a civil war at the end of the 20th century when the local people rose against immigrants from neighbouring Malaita, a conflict not resolved until 2003.

The island is large – at 5,330 sq km (2,050 sq mi) and it contains the national capital of the Solomon Islands, Honiara. This is on the north coast, home to the majority of the population and much of which is fringed by sandy beaches and steeply sloping raised coral reefs. The mountainous interior is mainly jungle, and the south coast is subject to such heavy rainfall that it is known as 'The Weather Coast'. There is a road along the north coast, but those hardy enough to head south must go by boat or helicopter.

This is not a well-developed tourist destination, but a great many visitors do arrive. They are drawn mainly by the wealth of World War II relics on land and sea – the latter contributing to the attraction of Guadalcanal as a top dive location. Other activities include sailing, sea kayaking and inland canoeing, cave exploration, bird and wildlife watching, cycling and hiking. There is a variety of accommodation available, from luxury hotels to budget lodges, and there are cars to be hired. Positively cosmopolitan by Solomon Islands' standards!

POPULATION:
73,000 (2007)
WHEN TO GO:
Avoid the (very) wet season (November to May).
HOW TO GET THERE:
Fly in to Honiara International Airport – formerly Henderson Field, which that World War II battle was all about.
HIGHLIGHTS:
The National Museum in Honiara, containing historical artefacts and traditional handicrafts.
Guided tours of World War II battle sites, and a visit to the Vilu War Museum.
Spectacular Mataniko Falls, which pour over the mouth of a cave with resident bats and swallows.
The giant clam farm west of Honiara – yes, they really are huge.
Local handicrafts (and war souvenirs!) on sale at Betikama High School, outside Honiara.
YOU SHOULD KNOW:
Guadalcanal is infested with mosquitoes and malaria is endemic.

The World War II memorial on Guadalcanal

New Caledonia

POPULATION:
240,000 (2007 estimate)
WHEN TO GO:
The best time for island activities and good weather is mid-May to November. December to March is hotter, wetter and hurricane-prone.
HOW TO GET THERE:
Fly to Nouméa from Paris, New Zealand, Australia, Japan, USA and via various other Pacific islands, notably Nada in Fiji.
HIGHLIGHTS:
A national symbol – the extraordinary flightless kagu, an endangered greyish-white bird with red legs and bill endemic to the island.
A day trip to the picture-postcard-perfect L'Ile-des-Pins off the southern tip of the island, by air or high-speed catamaran.
The stunning modern Jean-Marie Tjibaou Cultural Centre in Nouméa, designed by Renzo Piano.
Hienghène on the east coast – a place of extraordinary natural beauty where mountains plunge dramatically into the sea.
YOU SHOULD KNOW:
The New Caledonia Barrier Reef surrounding Grand Terre is the world's second longest, after Australia's Great Barrier Reef.

This is a French overseas territory, like other islands in various exotic locations around the globe. New Caledonia lies on the Tropic of Capricorn in Melanesia, and the main island (Grand Terre) is bundled up with the Loyalty Islands, 100 km (60 mi) to the west. It is 350 km (217 mi) long and 70 km (44 mi) across at the widest point. The island's shores are lapped by the Coral Sea and South Pacific Ocean. New Caledonia is a mountainous island, rising massively to Mount Panié at 1,630 m (5,340 ft). Seasonal rainfall on the higher, eastern side is double that of the west coast, which lies in a 'rain shadow' cast by the central spine of mountains. The east coast is lush and tropical, the west coast a more temperate zone.

Unlike many Pacific islands of relatively recent volcanic origin, New Caledonia is a fragment of the long-lost Gondwana continent that once also included New Zealand and Australia. The island had therefore preserved a fascinating biological heritage for tens of millions of years, though in a parable for our times this has been badly degraded in less than a century by extensive open-cast nickel mining and logging. The surrounding sea, however, is well protected, with the world's largest lagoon complex containing a stunning variety of marine life.

New Caledonia has a great deal to offer the visitor, and this tropical island is a popular destination, with an endless variety of landscapes and everything from beautiful white sand beaches lapped by emerald-green sea to cool mountain retreats – even fine French restaurants and lively night life in the rather glamorous capital, Nouméa.

The Gossanah tribal team playing cricket, a popular sport among the women of the indigenous Melanesian Kanak community.

Viti Levu Island

Fiji is renowned for its colourful coral and the clear waters around Vitu Levu are perfect for snorkelling.

Welcome to Fiji's largest island, at a chunky 145 km (90 mi) by 105 km (65 mi). Viti Levu is divided in half geographically and climatically by a rugged north-south mountain range peaking at Mount Victoria, also known as Tomanivi. To the east – heavy rainfall and a strong dairy industry. To the west – drier climate and sugar cane production. Other industries include gold mining, light manufacturing and – of rapidly increasing importance – tourism. The island is a major hub of air and sea communications in the southwest Pacific.

The Republic of Fiji's vibrant capital city, Suva, is here, along with some three-quarters of the nation's population. There is a good route around the island's perimeter, connecting Suva with the coastal towns of Sigatoka, Rakiraki, Nausori, Nadi, Lautoka and Ba. Most visitors arrive at Nadi International Airport on the dusty west coast, which serves as a good starting point for those who take the island driving tour. This involves a leisurely two- or three-day circumnavigation on the island's only paved roads – Queen's Road along the southern coast from Suva to Lautoka, and King's Road along the north shore from Lautoka back to Suva.

It is an excellent way to see the island, stopping frequently to explore intriguing tracks into the interior or down to the sea, and chatting with the famously friendly locals. King's Road is in poorer shape, is longer and not much travelled by tourists, passing through country that is less developed than the south. For those who prefer a classic Pacific beach holiday, there are numerous attractive resorts, both on the mainland and offshore islands.

Best of all, it doesn't have to stop there – Viti Levu is the gateway to the Fiji Archipelago's thousands of islands, at least 100 of which are inhabited and are waiting for visitors with open arms!

POPULATION:
435,000 (2007 estimate)

WHEN TO GO:
The temperature is pretty even (and hot) all year round, with the driest months being April, May and June, followed closely by October.

HOW TO GET THERE:
By air from almost anywhere – long or short haul, or a mixture of both.

HIGHLIGHTS:
The Sigatora Valley, Sand Dunes and the excellent beach at the mouth of the Sigatora River.
Kula Eco Park in the southern Coral Coast area, an excellent facility dedicated to the preservation of Fiji's flora and fauna.
Seeing it all in 25 minutes, by taking the helicopter tour offered by Island Hoppers out of Nadi.

YOU SHOULD KNOW:
The Garden of the Sleeping Giant at Lautoka is an impressive tropical garden rich in orchids that once belonged to Perry Mason – TV star Raymond Burr.

The village of Savusavu

Vanua Levu Island

POPULATION:
130,000 (2007 estimate)
WHEN TO GO:
Any time, though some prefer to miss high summer (January and February) which – although only a few degrees above average – seems hotter because of high humidity.
HOW TO GET THERE:
By helicopter or light aircraft from Viti Levu, to either Labasa or Savusavu. Also by local ferry from Viti Levu.
HIGHLIGHTS:
Treat yourself to a local speciality – a souvenir black pearl raised from local waters or a piece of jewellery containing the black beauties.
Saturday night at a classic South Seas haunt – the Planters Club in Savusavu, which is as good as Vanua Levu's nightlife gets. Guests welcome.
The Waisali Rainforest Reserve, complete with cooling waterfall.
Spectacular windsurfing in the fabulous setting of Savusavu Bay.
YOU SHOULD KNOW:
In 1789, the infamous Captain William Bligh called here on his way to Timor, after being cast adrift by the mutinous crew of HMS *Bounty*.

Formerly Sandalwood Island, this wedge-shaped island is Fiji's second largest, measuring 180 km (110 mi) in length and up to 50 km (31 mi) across. Cape Udu at its northeastern tip is the northernmost point in Fiji. A long peninsula sticks out from the southeastern portion of Vanua Levu, and the island is divided horizontally by a craggy mountain range capped by the twin peaks of Nasorolevu and Dikeva. The south of the island is the wetter half, with the dryer north supporting major sugarcane plantations.

In the north, three rivers form the delta where the island's largest town, Labasa, is located. This is the workaday centre of the sugar industry. In the south, the main settlement is Savusavu, beloved by the relatively small number of tourists who get to the island for its diving, kayaking and a stunning bay that is home to an active yachting community. There is an ill-maintained basic road system with few paved roads.

Although Savusavu is the place most visitors head for, it has rustic storefronts and many ramshackle buildings. Efforts are being made to spruce the town up, to encourage more tourists and cater for wealthy incomers who are buying ocean-front plots for serious money and building holiday homes. As a pointer to future development, a large new marina has been constructed and the process of 'tourist gentrification' will doubtless continue apace.

But for now, Vanua Levu has plenty of original character, and offers an ideal opportunity to study local culture and traditions before they are overwhelmed by tourism. That said, there are plenty of fine resorts in superb settings around the island for those who prefer to pursue the perfect suntan (though sadly there are few beaches to lie on).

Beqa Island

This tiny island extends to just 36 sq km (14 sq mi) and is some 10 km (6 mi) south of Navua off Viti Levu, Fiji's main island. There are nine coastal villages on Beqa, with some agriculture and fishing, but tourism is the main economic activity. The island rises steeply to a volcanic point. The villagers live in extended clans and trade fish and produce for essentials at mainland markets in Navua and Suva. There are several resorts on the island, including Beqa Lagoon, Lalati, Kula Bay and the exclusive Royal Davui on its own islet. More are planned, which may slightly dilute the get-away-from-it-all rationale of this exquisite place. As yet there are no roads and all transport is by boat.

The Shark Reef Marine Reserve on the fringes of Beqa Lagoon has been created to study the resident shark population and thus contribute to the long-term worldwide conservation of sharks. Up to eight species are to be found in the reserve at any one time, and those with the necessary diving skills and nerves of steel can get to meet them, with the help of experienced professional guides. Wreck diving is also popular and there are amazing reefs to explore.

Indeed, Beqa Lagoon is the island's crowning glory, with a fringing reef around the island extending into a barrier reef that together are nearly 70 km (43 mi) long, with the latter enclosing a deep lagoon with an area of just under 400 sq km (155 sq mi). The reefs are made up of colourful corals that have been developing for centuries.

POPULATION:
2,100 (2007 estimate)
WHEN TO GO:
All year round – the island is generally hot and humid, often with tropical storms, especially between December and April.
HOW TO GET THERE:
By boat from mainland Viti Levu.
HIGHLIGHTS:
Try and see the local tradition of sacred firewalking in action, especially in the villages of Rukua and Daku-I-Beqa.
Climbing to the virgin rain forest and finding one of the island's many cooling waterfalls.
World-famous dive sites like Side Streets, Golden Arches and Caesar's Rocks.
YOU SHOULD KNOW:
The correct pronunciation of Beqa is not 'becca' but 'mbenga'.

Sacred firewalking is a local tradition on Beqa.

An aerial view of the fabulous beaches of the Mamanuca

POPULATION:
2,100 (2007 estimate)
WHEN TO GO:
All year round – the weather is sunny, the seas calm and the breezes cooling.
HOW TO GET THERE:
By air to Nadi International Airport. Onward transfer by light aircraft, helicopter or boat to the island of your choice.
HIGHLIGHTS:
A trip around the islands in an old-fashioned South Sea schooner.
A self-drive/sail boat trip on a craft hired from the Musket Cove marina.
Game fishing or scuba diving along the renowned Malolo Reef.
YOU SHOULD KNOW:
Despite the large number of tourists in the Mamanucas, the island of Modriki was chosen as the setting for the miles-from-anywhere Tom Hanks film *Castaway*.

Mamanuca Islands

This archipelago is scattered off Nadi Bay on Viti Levu's west coast. There are about 20 islands, but be careful which one you choose – some are completely covered at high tide. The Mamanuca Islands are a serious visitor attraction, offering tiny coral islets to explore and numerous beach resorts to suit every pocket, plus all the watersports and diving activities for which Fiji is famous. Most resorts offer complementary kayaks, hobby cats and reef snorkelling trips.

These are not the most beautiful islands you will ever see, but the beaches are fabulous and the water is inviting. The resort islands are Malolo, Beachcomber, Mana, Malolo Lailai, Monu, Monuriki, Navini, Tavarua, Tavua, Tokoriki and (especially for Robert Louis Stevenson fans) Treasure Island. The inner Mamanucas consist of small, flat coral isles. The middle islands are the largest and offer gentle hills with paths to summits that offer stunning views over the archipelago, and the opportunity to find less crowded beaches. The outer islands are more rugged, with isolated bays and interesting volcanic rock formations. They have traditional fishing villages and – at 90 minutes from the mainland by fast catamaran – those outer islands are the destination of choice for people trying to get far from the madding crowd.

You will pay a premium to holiday on the Mamanuca Islands, but at many resorts you will share your island with more than enough people. However, as soon as you've settled comfortably into your space on the beach lots of day-trippers may suddenly invade from the mainland – a budget treat for them and a pain for you. And if it's traditional Fijian culture you're looking for, you won't find it here.

Yasawa Islands

Fiji's Yasawa Islands extend majestically to the north of the Mamanucas, and are much less commercially orientated than their southern cousins. The Yasawas form a thin broken line, consisting of 16 larger islands and dozens of smaller ones, stretching for 80 km (50 mi) from a point just off Kautoka on the northwestern coast of Viti Levu. Their scenic appeal is tremendous, with impressive panoramas and stunning beach vistas, whilst unchanging fishing villages provide an opportunity to observe the traditional way of life. These sun-drenched volcanic islands have fabulous beaches and clear lagoons, basic rest houses for backpackers, exclusive resorts for the well-heeled and plenty in between. It all adds up to the South Pacific at its most typical, so it's no accident that both versions of *The Blue Lagoon* were shot on location here.

Though the islands have been a popular cruise destination from the 1950s, land-based tourism was forbidden by the Fiji government until 1987. Since then, the popularity of the islands has been growing as they moved from back-packer heaven ('find a fishing boat to take you') towards mainstream tourism (from 2002, following the introduction of a catamaran service). New development is inevitable, but the wonderful island scenery has not been compromised thus far and there is more than enough coastline to go around. Resorts tend to be fairly isolated, most island villages are without electricity or running water and there is little public infrastructure. Indeed, the absence of sufficient fresh water to support a resort is a bar to development on some islands.

Many of the resorts are owned and operated by friendly islanders, retaining a rustic charm that combines with majestic scenery to ensure that visitors to the Yasawas feel they have indeed discovered the 'real' South Pacific.

POPULATION:
6,000 (2007 estimate)
WHEN TO GO:
There is no preferred special season – hot and dry conditions predominate, with cool nights.
HOW TO GET THERE:
From Lautoka by fast catamaran (2-4 hours) or seaplane (20 minutes). Arrange it all upon arrival at Nadi International Airport.
HIGHLIGHTS:
Sunrise (or sunset, for late risers) viewed from the top of Wayalailai Island.
A Sunday church service in one of the island villages for beautifully harmonious singing.
Overnight cruises to the Yasawas – visiting traditional villages, empty beaches and anchoring in remote lagoons. Lasting three to seven nights.
For those looking to treat themselves – the real Blue Lagoon, at the hugely expensive Turtle Island Resort on the privately owned island of Nanuya Levu, as patronized by the stars.
YOU SHOULD KNOW:
For those who want to explore the islands at leisure, a Yasawa Travel Pass gives unlimited return transfers on the fast catamaran *Yasawa Flyer*.

A beautiful beach on Matacawa Levu Island

Lau Islands

POPULATION:
15,000 (2007 estimate)
WHEN TO GO:
Unless you like singing in the rain, make it the cooler, drier months from April to October.
HOW TO GET THERE:
Stand by for a true flashback in modern tourist terms – the only way is to catch one of the cargo boats that sporadically serve the Lau Islands from Suva, then island-hop by fishing boat.
HIGHLIGHTS:
Wonderful wood-carvings and striking masi painting (on cloth made from the paper of the mulberry tree) produced by the locals.
Some of Fiji's most pristine dive sites – best to bring your own boat (and live on it).
The caves – Qara Bulu on Lakeba (once a prison) and the large sea cave on Vanau Balavu (used by people over a thousand years ago).
YOU SHOULD KNOW:
Anyone for cricket? Unlike the rest of Fiji (rugby mad, soccer crazy), the Lau islanders prefer cricket, and supply almost all the national team's players.

The relatively accessible Yasawa Islands may seem like the real thing, but to discover the true South Pacific of yesteryear it is necessary to mount an expedition to the Lau Islands. This cluster of one hundred or more islands and islets makes up Fiji's remote Eastern Archipelago. Around 30 are inhabited – by villagers who remain entirely traditional. To the south are low coral isles and to the north high volcanic islands, making for a wonderful variety of scenery. They are notable for producing a disproportionate number of people who have become prominent in the country's business and political life, including prime ministers and a president.

This is the place where Melanesian Fiji comes closest to Polynesian Tonga, acting as a mixing point for the two cultures. Tongan influence is apparent in names, language, food and buildings – Lauan houses tend to be rounded in Tongan fashion rather than square in Fijian style. The island of Lakeba in the south is a traditional meeting place, and one of the few islands where the intrepid traveller will find guest-houses.

Another is Kaimbu, a private resort island. Accommodation may also be found on Vanua Balavu, the archipelago's second-largest island and biggest in the northern group. It has an extensive reef system, steep undercut cliffs, hot springs and the Yanuyanu Island Resort built to advance tourist development in this hitherto 'undiscovered' archipelago (though a permit to visit must be obtained from the Ministry of Foreign Affairs in Suvu!). There is also an airfield and a small copra port on the island.

For those of adventurous bent who don't rely on advanced booking, the Lau Islands can deliver the trip of a lifetime. Catch it while you can – it's only a matter of time before the modern world arrives.

Taveuni Island

Fiji's third-largest island is shaped like a fat cigar. Taveuni lies just to the east of Vanua Levu, extending to around 42 km (26 mi) by 10 km (6 mi). It is the top of a shield volcano, dotted with volcanic cones that include Des Vœux Peak and Uluigalau, the country's second-highest peak at 1,195 m (3,920 ft). The island is divided by a volcanic spine, with verdant forests spilling down the sides. As with many Fijian islands the western end, sheltered by mountains from the trade winds, is drier than the rain-soaked eastern end.

Tourism is not yet a massive contributor to the local economy, which relies on copra production and speciality crops like tropical fruits, vanilla and kava. But there are a number of small resorts and guest-houses on the island, with more planned. Visitor numbers are set to rise dramatically, but for the moment Taveuni remains pleasantly uncrowded.

That's rather surprising as Taveuni has some great attractions. The climate is hot and humid, though not unbearably so, and the place retains much of its original natural character, having been subject to less land clearance than many Fijian islands. Indeed, it is known as 'The Garden Island' after the profusion of flowers and tropical plants found here. Some of the most famous dive sites in Fiji are around Taveuni, including Rainbow Reef and the extraordinary Great White Wall, a luminescent tunnel surrounded by glowing coral. The island has Fiji's most famous waterfall, Bouma Falls in the delightful Bouma National Heritage Park. There is also the spectacular Lake Tagimacuia in a volcanic crater at a height of 800 m (2,625 ft), where the eponymous red-and-white tagimacuia flower grows.

If unspoiled tropical islands are your idea of bliss, they truly don't come much better than this.

POPULATION:
9,500 (2007 estimate)

WHEN TO GO:
Any time, but take an umbrella – this is one of the wettest places in Fiji, with up to 2,600 mm (102 in) of rain each year. The driest months are April to October.

HOW TO GET THERE:
Fly in from Suvu or Nadi to Taveuni Airport in the northern part of the island.

HIGHLIGHTS:
Two sanctuaries designed to protect the island's flora and fauna – Taveuni Forest Preserve in the centre of the island and Ravilevu Nature Preserve on the east coast.
Birdlife – the mongoose was never introduced here so many birds that are no longer found on the other islands thrive (as does the magpie, introduced to destroy coconut pests).
The Vunivasa Tour – a visit to the archaeological site of a fortified Fijian village, followed by a waterfall visit that culminates in a toe-curling 'flight' in an airborne chair.
Wairiki Mission, a fine example of British colonial Romanesque architecture, overlooking the sea where Taveuni warriors once repulsed Tongan invaders.

YOU SHOULD KNOW:
The international dateline (180th Meridian) passes right through the island, so you can literally have one foot in today and one foot in yesterday – but it has been notionally 'moved' so the island can pretend to operate on the same day.

Sunset on Taveuni Island

Girls in a ceremonial dance on Rotuma Island

POPULATION:
2,800 (2007 estimate)
WHEN TO GO:
The rainy season is best avoided, so make it April to October. Even then the humidity may come as a shock, though cool sea breezes can dilute the impact.
HOW TO GET THERE:
Fly in to the airstrip on the north shore on Air Fiji's weekly flight from Suva.
HIGHLIGHTS:
The remarkable islet of Haf'lius (Split Island), with a fissure down the centre that's large enough to take a boat through.
Mount Suelhof – at 256 m (840 ft) it's a splendid vantage point for those willing to undertake the necessary hike.
A variety of old churches that serve as a reminder of the island's colonial past (in which Christian missionaries loomed large, and largely succeeded in converting the islanders).
The many traditional ceremonies, including the installation of chiefs (there are lots of those), religious occasions, weddings and funerals.
YOU SHOULD KNOW:
The first European sighting of Rotuma was by Captain Edward Edwards of HMS *Pandora*, who landed here in 1791 looking for Fletcher Christian and the mutinous crew of the *Bounty* (bad luck, wrong island).

Rotuma Island

Roughly 470 km (290 mi) north of Fiji, this small group – Rotuma Island plus four offshore islets – is a Fijian dependency and home to the unique race known as Rotumans. Actually, Rotuma isn't the home it once was – economic hardship has caused roughly four-fifths of the indigenous population (of under 15,000 in total) to migrate to the main Fijian islands. Rotumans more closely resemble Polynesians (physically and culturally) than Fiji's Melanesians, and those who remain live in coastal villages. Dependency status allows the island more political autonomy than other parts of Fiji, with the Ahau-based Council of Rotuma making key local decisions in conjunction with a government office.

It is possible to visit this isolated island, though the Rotumans voted against opening the place up to tourism as recently as 1985. Even now, the door is barely ajar, with visits strictly rationed by Rotuman elders who are determined that their island paradise will not be spoiled by the intrusive demands of mass tourism. The people are gracious, but expect visitors to respect their customs and be modest in behaviour and dress.

There are no hotels or resorts on Rotuma, though simple accommodation can be arranged. The determined voyager will find a rugged volcanic island with many small cones that is covered in lush vegetation, measuring 13 km (8 mi) by 4 km (2.5 mi). It has a large reef, spectacular coral, abundant sea life (including dolphins and turtles) and some of the most beautiful and untouched beaches in all Fiji. Give it a serious go – the rewards will more than repay the effort, and you'll be one of the tiny minority who've ever been privileged to visit this very special island.

Matareva Point on Upolu Island

Upolu

The most heavily populated of Samoa's islands is Upolu, a massive shield volcano that is 75 km (47 mi) long. The Samoans believe their islands were the cradle of Polynesian civilization, and Upolu is certainly the sort of place that would arrive from central casting if the director called for an unspoiled Pacific Island where real people live real lives. The interior is rugged, tropical and lush, with rushing rivers and spectacular waterfalls. The exquisite palm-fringed beaches with protective reefs are often totally secluded and mostly deserted. There are no big tourist hotels or over-developed resorts and the focus of the islanders is on extended family, tradition and culture. It is a point of honour that *fa'a Samoa* (the Samoan way) should continue to flourish. As a result, the whole atmosphere is wonderfully relaxed.

Samoa's capital Apia is here – a town of old colonial buildings, a harbour that screams 'South Seas schooner', giant pulu trees and shabby charm. This is the only place on Upolu where there are shops, markets, hotels, restaurants, banks and international communications. Maketi Fou is the vibrant main market, a centre of town life that offers an amazing range of fresh produce and seems to be busy 24/6 (the Samoans are very religious and everything closes on Sunday). There is a flea market in the market building on Beach Road that sells clothing, food and handicrafts.

Outside Apia, visitors should look for the traditional thatched huts, here called *fales*, which are scattered along the coast – usually owned and operated by locals to generate a little collective income for the village. This is an inexpensive way to see the island, and Samoa is actually one of the most affordable destinations in the Pacific.

POPULATION:
113,000 (2007 estimate)

WHEN TO GO:
No special season – Samoa is hot and humid all year round, though cooling trade winds blow from May to October.

HOW TO GET THERE:
Fly in to Faleolo International Airport on the western end of the island.

HIGHLIGHTS:
Vailma, the Robert Louis Stevenson Museum – former home of the *Treasure Island* author who died there in 1894 and is buried with his wife on the summit of Mount Vaea, overlooking Apia.
The Independence celebrations during the first week in June, culminating in the fautasi race when great longboat canoes with dozens of crewmen battle for supremacy.
Uafato Conservation Reserve – natural tropical forest with thriving bird life.
Togitogiga waterfall – several small falls running into the perfect plunge pool.

YOU SHOULD KNOW:
Land in Samoa is family-owned, so don't be offended if you find a wonderfully secluded beach, only for a local to appear and request a small payment for the privilege of using it.

Afu Aau Waterfall is set in virgin rainforest on Savaii.

POPULATION:
45,000 (2007 estimate)
WHEN TO GO:
Any time of year – even in the rainy season (November to April) there are plenty of sunny days. There are occasional hurricanes between December and March.
HOW TO GET THERE:
A local flight from Apia on Upolu, or by ferry (fast or slow) from Mulifanua in western Upolu.
HIGHLIGHTS:
Falealupo Rainforest Preserve, offering canopy walkways.
The Alofaaga Blowholes, near the village of Taga.
Lava landscape at Sale'aula.
Strolling round the picturesque little town of Asau, before trying to spot the bay's numerous turtles.
Pulemelei Mound, Polynesia's largest archaeological site – the grand pyramid is 60 m (200 ft) long and 15 m (50 ft) high.
YOU SHOULD KNOW:
Samoa's proximity to the international dateline means it is the last place on earth to see the sun set. Watch it from Falealupo on Savaii, one of the world's most westerly villages.

Savaii

This is the larger of Samoa's two main islands, but Savaii has fewer people than Upolu and is even less well developed. This is another volcanic shield island, and remains active (last eruption – 1911, lasting for four years). The island has a gently sloping profile, rising to a height of 1,860 m (6,100 ft) at Mount Silisili, and the evidence of lava flow is everywhere, often giving the landscape a dramatic quality. This really is the South Sea island that tourism forgot, with hardly any visitor-orientated development. But there is some basic accommodation, and an occasional low-key resort to be found by the determined traveller, whose reward will be some spectacular scenery and a close encounter with laid-back living, Polynesian style.

Salelologa on the island's southeastern corner has the airport, wharf and a colourful market. Otherwise it's pretty much a workaday place with little to attract the visitor. It's another matter south of town, where the Tafua Peninsula has a huge accessible crater and wonderful views of the wild coastline, which can be followed by a trip to the peninsula's lovely Aganoa Beach. Actually 'accessible' is a significant word in a Savaii context. There are irregular buses and a few expensive taxis, so the best plan is to hire a car and explore at leisure. Even then, the road system leaves a lot to be desired, but a circumnavigation of Savaii on the coast road will deliver some wonderful surprises – unspoiled traditional villages, huge churches, amazing lava formations, beautiful beaches and shimmering lagoons.

Tutuila

American Samoa is an unincorporated territory of the USA in the South Pacific, and Tutuila is its largest island with most of the population. The island is 30 km (18 mi) long and 10 km (6 mi) across at the widest point. The mountainous backbone culminates in Mount Matafao at 653 m (2,142 ft).

Tutuila is notable for the large natural Pago Pago harbour upon which is located the village of Pago Pago and the tuna canneries which are the island's principal economic activity. Pago Pago International Airport, on the other hand, is further down the coast between Tafuna and Fagatogo. Mount Alava overlooks the harbour from the north and a hike to the summit is rewarded with panoramic views of rugged coastline and virgin forest. There are few beaches and much of the north coast is inaccessible.

Fagatogo, Tutuila's capital and commercial centre, is also on Pago Pago Harbour, as is Utulei where government bureaucracy is concentrated. Most American Samoans (who are US nationals but not US citizens) live in villages along the south coast, serviced by regular buses from Fagatogo market. This is undoubtedly a South Pacific island, but American influence is pronounced and there are some messy corners. Tourism is not a major activity, though there are a number of motels, hotels and guesthouses around the harbour and west of Tafuna. Visitors come mainly for the wild scenery.

The National Park of American Samoa is on Tutuila and two neighbouring islands – Ofu and Ta'u. It includes coral reefs and some of the best coastal rainforest in the Pacific, with snorkelling, scuba diving and hiking permitted. There are many archaeological sites on the island, which is one of several (including nearby Ta'u) that lay claim to the title 'cradle of Polynesian civilization'.

POPULATION:
56,000 (2000)

WHEN TO GO:
To be different, try the rainy season between November and April, to see Tutuila's rainforest at its very best (the mornings are usually sunny, but beware mosquitoes!).

HOW TO GET THERE:
Fly to Apia on Western Samoa and from there to Tutuila by Polynesian Airlines or Samoa Air.

HIGHLIGHTS:
Leone village in the west, where large churches bear witness to zealous missionary activity during the 19th century.
A trip to Aunu'u Island National Landmark off the southeast corner of Tutuila, to see the unusual Red Lake.
The scenic south coast road from the airport via Cape Taputapu to the end of the line, Fagamalo village.
Picturesque Alega Beach, with its famous Tisa's Barefoot Bar.

YOU SHOULD KNOW:
Most beaches are village owned and both scanty dress and Sunday swimming are banned.

A church in the village of Afono

Manu'a Islands

POPULATION:
1,400 (2000)
WHEN TO GO:
Warm and wet (November to April) or warm and dry (May to October).
HOW TO GET THERE:
Via an internal flight from Pago Pago International Airport.
HIGHLIGHTS:
South Ofu Beach, for one of the most stunning panoramas of beach, sea and mountains in the entire Pacific Ocean.
An adventurous trek to the huge Judds Crater, a six-hour hike from Ta'u village.
Some of the world's tallest sea cliffs on the south coast of Ta'u.
YOU SHOULD KNOW:
Visitors are advised to bring their own necessities (including food), as supplies are not generally on sale in the Manu'a Islands.

Apart from the 'mainland' of Tutuila, American Samoa extends to Rose Atoll, Swains Island and the Manu'a Islands. The latter group consists of adjacent high volcanic islands – Ta'u, Ofu and Olosega – located 110 km (70 mi) east of Tutuila.

Ta'u is the largest of the three, and the most easterly volcanic island in Samoa. It has American Samoa's high point in Lata Mountain, rising to 966 m (3,170 ft), the group's main airport at Fiti'uta and a boat harbour at Faleasao. A road connects the small villages on the northern shore. The south of the island and its reefs are part of the National Park of American Samoa, which includes the sacred site of Saua – another contender for 'birthplace of the Polynesian people'. Unusually, the park is not owned by the US government, but leased from the islanders. There is no tourist infrastructure, though accommodation can be found in the sleepy villages.

Nearfby Ofu and Olosega are tropical Siamese twins. They are saw-tooth volcanic remains separated only by the narrow strait of Asaga, and effectively joined by a coral reef. Until recently, it was possible to wade from one island to the other at low tide, but now there is a bridge. Ofu Island has a small airport and boat harbour, together with one village, also Ofu, and a visitor lodge. The National Park extends to this most beautiful of islands, protecting a pristine southern coastline and rainforest. The park is being extended to Olosega, where the small population lives in Olosega village, after a second village (Sili) was destroyed by a hurricane.

There are many places that claim to offer serious travellers the opportunity to discover the 'real' South Pacific, untainted by commercialism – but these islands aren't kidding.

The stunning panorama of South Ofu Beach

Tongatapu

Spectacular blow-holes near the village of Houma

Captain Cook named Tonga 'The Friendly Islands' after arriving during a feast and finding natives who appeared welcoming. In fact, it is said that the chiefs wanted to kill him but couldn't agree on a plan. Tongatapu is Tonga's main island, and the location of the former British protectorate's capital, Nuku'alofa. The second city of Mu'a is also here, along with most of the commercial activity and the grandiose official residence of the king.

Nuku'alofa is full of Victorian buildings, churches, old graveyards, bustling markets (don't miss excellent local arts and crafts upstairs at Talamahu Market) and a classic Pacific waterfront. Most of the island's hotels are here, too, though this is very much a shabby working town that doesn't give excessive thought to pleasing tourists – a comment that might justifiably be applied to the island as a whole.

Indeed, most visitors make Tongatapu a stepping stone to the offshore coral islands of Fafa, Atata and Pangaimotu, which offer excellent beach holidays. Along with a number of other islands in the main lagoon off Nuku'alofa, they are very like the ever-popular Manamuca Islands in Fiji, but without the same tourist pressure.

But for all that Tongatapu itself is no resort island, it will reward the curious traveller with its interesting combination of history and natural beauty. Though much of this largely flat island is covered in plantations, the eastern end is relatively undeveloped, with deserted sandy beaches, coves and caves. There is also a wealth of monuments testifying to the island's long history and cultural traditions. The south coast is wild, with dramatic coastal scenery and high cliffs punctuated with sandy coves, well worth the effort needed to get there in a hire car that will have seen much better days.

POPULATION:
71,000 (2007 estimate)

WHEN TO GO:
Any time – the tropical climate is even all year round and Tongatapu is milder than Fiji or Samoa, with less rainfall.

HOW TO GET THERE:
Various international carriers serve the airport at Fu'amotu.

HIGHLIGHTS:
Tongan culture at its best (dancing and food, among other things!) – find it all at the Tongan National Centre just south of Nuku'alofa.
The ancient langi pyramids (royal burial tombs) near Mu'a, once the ancient capital of Tonga.
A flying fox preserve in the western district of Kolovai for close-up contact with the world's largest bats (there are plenty, as only the king is allowed to hunt them).
The 13th century stone trilithon, which is known as Ha'amonga 'a Maui, in the north of the island,.
Spectacular blow-holes near the village of Houma.

YOU SHOULD KNOW:
There have been recent pro-democracy riots in Nuku'alofa (accompanied by arson and several deaths) as younger Tongans protested at the country's rule by a feudal absolute monarchy.

Niue

POPULATION:
1,700 (2007 estimate)
WHEN TO GO:
To dodge the sometimes intense rainy season, avoid the summer months (November to April).
HOW TO GET THERE:
There's one flight a week from New Zealand.
HIGHLIGHTS:
Whale watching, or swimming with them – it's a proud boast that the whales often outnumber the tourists!
Game fishing in deep water right off the island.
The Huvalu Forest Conservation Area near Hakupu village, with a wonderful variety of flora and fauna.
Matapu Chasm – a swimming and snorkelling pool enclosed by cliffs, protected from sea currents.
Caves – lots of them, ripe for exploration, including Talava Arches, Palaha Cave and Liku Sea Track and Cave.
YOU SHOULD KNOW:
Perhaps sadly, as a result of sustained migration there are many more Niue Islanders living in New Zealand than on their native island.

Coral reef surrounding Niue Island

One of the world's largest coral islands is shaped rather like a human head, complete with pointed nose and chin. That still doesn't make it all that big – Niue has an area of only 270 sq km (105 sq mi). This tropical island is located in the South Pacific, within a triangle formed by the Cook Islands, Samoa and Tonga, and is nicknamed the 'Rock of Polynesia' or (by islanders) simply 'The Rock', because it is ringed by cliffs surrounding a central plateau. The coast is honeycombed with limestone caves. Niue is surrounded by a coral reef, which is only broken in one place – on the west coast near the capital, Alofi.

Niue was named 'Savage Island' by Captain Cook in 1774, when legend has it that the inhabitants not only refused to allow him to land, but also appeared to have blood-stained teeth (actually caused by eating red bananas). They remained resistant to the outside world until an islander who had been trained as a missionary introduced Christianity in the mid-19th century. Britain was the colonial power, but Niue is now a self-governing protectorate of New Zealand.

The economy has only recently started developing (slowly) from virtual subsistence level and dependence on New Zealand aid, with a newly liberated private sector and activities like mineral exploration, fishing and tourism earmarked for growth. With regard to the latter, there is very little accommodation on this friendly island, so a visit is almost like being welcomed into the family. Niue is a place where rainforest and an amazing shoreline go hand in hand, and it really is true to say that the visitor can experience unspoiled Polynesia, just the way it used to be. And that's without a white-sand beach to be seen!

Tuvalu Islands

This Polynesian island nation was formerly the Ellis Islands, part of the British Gilbert and Ellis Islands protectorate, and consists of three reef islands and six atolls. With a total land mass of just 26 sq km (10 sq mi) Tuvalu is one of the smallest independent countries in the world – and that tiny area is spread in a ragged line across some 1,500 km (930 mi) of the Central Pacific. Its nearest neighbours are Kiribati (formerly the Gilbert Islands), Samoa and Fiji.

The islands are Nanumanga, Niulakita and Niutao. The atolls are Funafuti (the capital and only relatively easy destination), Nanumea, Nui, Nukufetau, Nukulaelae and Vasafua. The atolls all have associated islets. Tuvalu has no natural resources and very little gainful economic activity, being kept afloat by international aid. Actually, keeping afloat may be a problem, as Tuvalu's highest point is just 5 m (16 ft) above sea level, so global warming could have catastrophic consequences.

Because of their remote location and scattered character, tourism has yet to become a significant part of life in Tuvalu. A serious shortage of drinking water means that there is not much likelihood of that changing, though the islands have all the attributes necessary to provide the typical South Seas vacation – coral reefs, white beaches, palm-fringed lagoons and friendly people. The upside is that determined visitors who do manage to reach Tuvalu find a few delightful guest-houses and lodges in an unspoiled corner of the Pacific that is ideal for R&R (that's rest and relaxation rather than rest and recreation). And the distinctive Polynesian culture is upheld by the island people, who maintain traditional social organization, arts and crafts, architecture, music and dance. And they mostly speak English.

POPULATION:
12,000 (2007 estimate)

WHEN TO GO:
Whenever – the pleasant tropical climate is consistent all year round. Rainfall is unpredictable, but is generally more prevalent between November and April.

HOW TO GET THERE:
Air Fiji flies in from Suvu to Funafuti twice a week, and the supply ships *Nivaga II* and *Manu Folau* make the same trip (rather more slowly) four times a year.

HIGHLIGHTS:
Funafuti Conservation area on the western side of the atoll, including lagoon, reef, channel, ocean and island habitats, rich in flora, fauna and marine life.
An old World War II American airbase on Nanumea, complete with the remains of abandoned aircraft, and there's also a wrecked landing craft on the reef.
Traditional dancing – performed on special occasions and to celebrate Christian holidays.

YOU SHOULD KNOW:
Tuvalu recently became the 189th member state of the United Nations.

An aerial view of Funafuti

Pitcairn Island

POPULATION:
50 (2007 estimate)
WHEN TO GO:
Whenever you can get there – weather-wise the climate is hot and humid, with occasional typhoons in summer (November to March).
HOW TO GET THERE:
Cruise ships (including dedicated Pitcairn cruises) visit, as do private yachts and occasional cargo ships. A licence is required to stay on Pitcairn for any length of time.
HIGHLIGHTS:
HMS *Bounty*'s anchor, on display in the town square.
Down Rope, a cliff with Polynesian petroglyphs, showing that the mutineers weren't the first inhabitants of this isolated place.
A quick return visit to the modern world – take a laptop and enjoy free wireless internet access via satellite.
The grave of John Adams – the only marked grave of a mutineer.
YOU SHOULD KNOW:
Actually, the determined Captain Edwards nearly did find Fletcher Christian and his men – in 1791 he got as close as Ducie Island (which he named), just 540 km (335 mi) east of Pitcairn.

It's no wonder that HMS *Pandora* under Captain Edward Edwards didn't find all the Bounty mutineers – despite catching most of them on Tahiti. In 1789 the rest, under ringleader Fletcher Christian, had hidden on one of the remotest islands in the Pacific, Pitcairn, and literally burnt their boat (the remains may still be seen in Bounty Bay). It ended badly; with mutineers and six Tahitian men they took with them killing each other. In 1808 when the American ship *Topaz* visited, only one mutineer (Alexander Smith, alias John Adams) was still alive.

This British Overseas Territory is officially the Pitcairn, Henderson, Ducie and Oeno Islands. The last three are uninhabited coral atolls scattered round the South Pacific some distance from Pitcairn – Henderson Island having the distinction of being a UNESCO World Heritage Site because of its bird life (including four species found only on Henderson).

Pitcairn is a volcanic peak jutting out of the ocean to a height of 337 m (1,100 ft) and is tiny – just 5 sq km (2 sq mi). It is a green, steep-sided island with cliffs that fall into the sea. Bounty Bay (in reality no more than a cove) is the only landing place, and then only for longboats that fetch visitors from boats anchored off shore. It is connected by the newly paved Hill of Difficulty to Adamstown, the settlement, where the few islanders live largely self-sufficient lives.

Every year, Bounty Day (23 January) is celebrated with a community feast and the ceremonial burning of a model *Bounty*. There's no getting away from it – Pitcairn and memories of the infamous mutiny will be inextricably linked for ever and a day. And if you do manage to visit this extraordinary place, you will have the travel experience of a lifetime to remember.

Commemorative plaque for HMS Bounty

Aitutaki is the archetypal desert island.

Aitutaki

North of Rarotonga, the beautiful island of Aitutaki is the second most populous of the Cook Islands, a group of 15 lovely islands in the South Pacific. This coral atoll boasts low rolling hills, banana plantations and coconut groves. This is an archetypal desert island and a wonderful place to unwind, with palm-fringed white sandy beaches, magnificent clear sea and a relaxed pace of life. Aitutaki has a main island and a string of small islets (including Mangere, Akaiami, and Tekopua), all surrounded by a barrier reef, thus creating the spectacular turquoise lagoon that makes it such a perfect place for swimming, snorkelling and scuba diving. Although it is the second most visited of the Cook Islands, Aitutaki is still unspoiled.

Polynesians probably first settled here around AD 900. The first European contact was with Captain Bligh and the crew of HMS *Bounty* who arrived on the island in 1789, just before the infamous mutiny. Hire a bicycle, scooter or car to explore this stunning island, taking a relaxed tour of the beaches and plantations. The highest peak, Maunga Pu, offers great views over the whole island.

A 20-minute boat ride will take you to Akaiami, one of the smaller islets at the far end of the lagoon. This remote and tranquil islet is surrounded by pristine turquoise lagoon and coral reef. The one inhabitant here owns the island and runs a small lodge.

One-Foot Island is probably the biggest tourist attraction and another must-see. Along with the blue lagoons and flawless white beach, there is a post office, one of the most remote in the world.

Several operators offer tours of the lagoon by boat, and if you haven't seen enough marine life, visit the Ministry of Marine Resources to learn about the sea life in the lagoon, and see baby sea turtles and giant clams. The lagoon also offers great scuba diving and fishing, both game fishing and fly fishing.

POPULATION:
2,194 (2006)

WHEN TO GO:
April to November

HOW TO GET THERE:
Fly from Auckland via Rarotonga

HIGHLIGHTS:
The church in Arutanga – the oldest church in the islands, this was built by two teachers from the London Missionary Society in the 1820s. Aitutaki was the first of the Cook Islands to accept Christianity.
A lagoon cruise to the islets of Akaiami and Tapuatae (One-Foot Island) – explore the perfect white sand beaches and spot marine life on the way.
Flyfishing for the fighting bonefish.
Ika mata – a local dish of marinated raw tuna with coconut sauce.
Aitutaki's dancers, who are famous throughout the Cook Islands – attend an 'Island Night' to see a dancing show and experience the local cuisine.

YOU SHOULD KNOW:
If you hire a car, you will need to buy a local driving licence from the police station at Arutanga

Aroa Beach

Rarotonga

The island's name means 'down south' and as the largest and most populated of the Cook Islands, it is the jumping off point for exploring the rest of the Cook Islands. At just 671 sq km (259 sq mi), Rarotonga is one of the most beautiful of the Cook Islands, and often referred to as the 'Jewel of the Pacific' and it's easy to see why.

Long palm fringed beaches and coral-filled seas make this island paradise an idyllic haven for travellers. Along the coastline, the lagoon is an ideal place for snorkeling and getting close to the wildlife in the water. The climate is equable and rarely ventures outside the margins of 18 °C to 29 °C (64 °F to 84 °F) . The interior is a volcanic mountainous region which is virtually uninhabited. The summit is called Te Rua Manga (The Needle), aptly named for its jagged peaks. It has dense jungle and a cloud forest beginning at 400 m (1,300 ft) above sea level, abundant in rare indigenous species of plants. The Cook Islands Natural Heritage Project was set up to educate people about the need for conservation and actively promotes eco-tourism.

In 1997 Japanese archaeologists found an undiscovered sacred site on Motu Tapu, an islet in the lagoon at Ngatangiia. This dated human life on Rarotonga to about 5,000 years ago. Statues of Tangaroa, the god of fertility, are still dotted around the island. The Polynesian dancing here is considered to be some of the best in Polynesia, and was described by a nineteenth century missionary as, 'positively obscene'.

Land tends to belong to families and is rarely sold and derelict houses pepper the island as without ownership of the land as well, they are un-saleable. There is much nineteenth century architecture to be seen, leftover from when the missionaries arrived on the island and one of note, is the Cook Island Christian Church. There are many of these scattered over the Cook Islands and this one has an interesting graveyard and pretty exterior.

POPULATION:
18,000 (2006)
WHEN TO GO:
The weeklong Te Maeva Nui Festival takes place annually at the end of July, and is worth a visit for this vibrant expression of Polynesian culture.
DON'T MISS:
The spectacular diving.
YOU SHOULD KNOW:
In areas of the lagoon marked by boundary poles, taking any fish, coral or shells is strictly prohibited.

Manihiki

Populated since 1500 AD and 'discovered' in 1832 by the American ship *Good Hope*, Captain Patrickson originally named Manihiki, Humphrey Island. This flat island paradise rises only a few metres above sea level and sits on top of an underwater mountain which stands 4,000 m (13,000 ft) above the ocean floor. This triangular coral atoll is 1054 km (655 mi) north-northwest of Rarotonga, which is its centre for administration.

The inhabitants of Manihiki had a close relationship with their sister island, Rakahanga. The inhabitants of both islands travelled between the two on wooden boats and canoes in search of food. This often resulted in death due to the distance between each island and the fact that it was impossible to see either at the mid-way point. The missionaries that arrived in the nineteenth century discouraged this practice, and their arrival heralded the end of native gods on the island. By 1852 Christianity was accepted and is still the religion of the islanders. An oral heritage survives though, and this makes the island rich in Polynesian culture.

The island is made up of a string of coconut palm covered islets and is shaped around the rim of a lagoon, 4km (2.5 mi) across. The lagoon is home to the black pearl, and most of the islanders are involved in farming the black-lip pearl oyster; the Cook Islands' most important export. A survey carried out for the Ministry of Marine Resources in 2000 recorded 111 pearl farms covering 7 km sq (4 mi sq).

POPULATION:
1,000 (2004)
WHEN TO GO:
The hurricane season is from November to April so it's best to avoid this period.
DON'T MISS:
A multitude of different types of coral and fish makes for spectacular diving in the region.
YOU SHOULD KNOW:
You will need to get a diving permit from the village of Tauhunu.

Islanders roast coconut crabs on a bed of hot stones.

Bora Bora

POPULATION:
7,250 (2002)
WHEN TO GO:
There isn't a bad time to go, but the high season is July to October.
HOW TO GET THERE:
By Air Tahiti to Motu Mute airport on the reef, which also accepts some direct international flights.
HIGHLIGHTS:
An excursion into the hills by 4 wheel drive vehicle to see the interior – don't miss the impressive World War II guns.
For daring sub-aquatic types, an expedition to feed sharks and manta rays in the lagoon.
Nightly sunset sailing trips that let you experience spectacular Pacific sunsets from the water.
Black pearl jewellery hand-crafted by locals.
YOU SHOULD KNOW:
There was an American supply base here in World War II, and many US personnel liked the place so much they stayed behind – until some were forcibly removed by the military following complaints from their families back home.

Welcome to French Polynesia, and one of the Pacific's most desirable destinations – or even, as the island's website proclaims with typical Gallic understatement, 'the most beautiful island in the world'. Even if that's going a bit far, this is certainly a romantic faraway place that attracts lots of people, and to be sure everyone gets the point there's plenty of the grass-skirt dancing that has become a Polynesian trademark.

Bora Bora is in the Leeward Islands, 230 km (140 mi) northwest of Tahiti, and now depends on visitors for its economic wellbeing. The only other commercial activities are fishing and harvesting coconuts, so the advent of tourism has given the island a huge fillip. The locals speak French and Tahitian, but most have a good grasp of English. The island is surrounded by a barrier reef that encloses the bluest of lagoons, and the land rises from white beaches through lush jungle-covered slopes to the dual peaks of an extinct volcano – Mounts Pahia and Otemanu. The main settlement of Vaitape is on the west coast, opposite the entrance to the lagoon.

The Hotel Bora Bora pioneered the use of palm-thatched tourist accommodation built out over the water on stilts, and this is now a standard feature of most resorts. Despite a deliberately rustic appearance, these are spacious, luxurious and priced accordingly. There are a number of high-end resorts on palm-fringed *motu* (islets) around the lagoon, and cheaper lodgings on shore.

There is one bus that shuttles back and forth around half the island, but exploring is best done by bicycle or on foot. The lagoon offers the usual activities – scuba diving, snorkeling, windsurfing, kitesurfing, water skiing and jetskiing – but in truth the key words on beautiful Bora Bora are 'relax' and 'enjoy'.

The brilliant blue lagoon of Bora Bora

Tahiti

This is the largest of the Windward Islands in French Polynesia, some 45 km (28 mi) long with an area of 1,050 sq km (405 sq mi). Tahiti's inhabitants are French citizens but enjoy considerable autonomy. The island consists of two oval portions, one large (Tahiti Nui) and one small (Tahiti Iti), connected by an isthmus. The capital, Papeete, is on heavily populated Tahiti Nui, which has quite good infrastructure, with *Le Truk* public buses offering an excellent and affordable way of getting around. But Tahiti Iti is less well developed, with its remote southeastern half accessible only by boat or on jungle-booted feet. Much of the island is covered in lush rainforest and the heavy scent of tropical flowers is everywhere. The national flower is the Tiare, a gardenia that forms the basis of traditional lei necklaces.

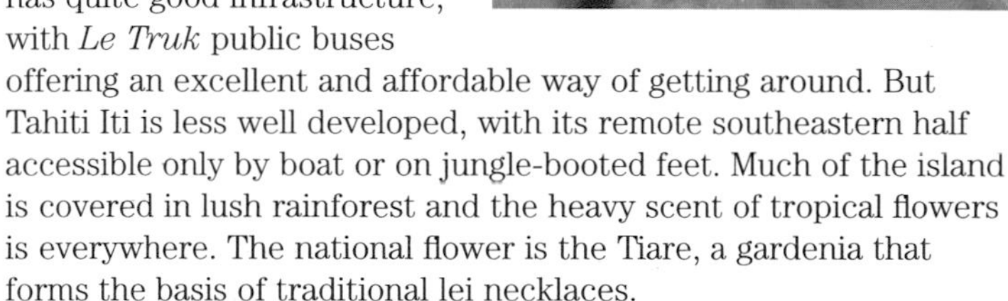

Although many visitors stop only long enough to catch onward flights to the popular islands of Bora Bora and Moorea, Tahiti itself has a lot to offer. The very name is enough to conjure up thoughts of an earthly paradise with a delightful climate, where palm-fringed beaches are lapped by aquamarine sea and handsome islanders extend the warmest of welcomes. It's all true!

Start at Papeete, a fascinating metropolis with a colourful morning market and bustling waterfront. But Tahiti is really an outdoor destination. It offers a wide choice of places to stay, from high-end beachfront resorts to hotels, motels, backpacker hostels and campsites. For those who want more from a holiday than sun, sea and sand, Tahiti offers endless possibilities – diving, snorkelling, wind surfing, sailing, game fishing, reef watching in glass-bottomed boats, horse riding, trekking, 4x4 expeditions into the interior... whatever takes your fancy, this magical 'Island of Love' will surely oblige.

A Tahitian dance festival in Papeete

POPULATION:
170,000 (2002)

WHEN TO GO:
It's warm all year round, but very wet, humid and stormy between November and April. If that doesn't appeal, be prepared to pay premium prices from May to October.

HOW TO GET THERE:
Fly in to Faa'a Airport, served by several international carriers.

HIGHLIGHTS:
Papeete's two-week Heiva Festival in July, celebrating the rather odd combination of Polynesian culture and Bastille Day (book your trip early if you want to be there).
For those with time and money to spare – a cruise to the distant Marquesas Islands on the passenger-carrying freighter *Aranui*.
The three Faarumai waterfalls – one of them is among the highest in French Polynesia.
Tahiti's longest bridge, crossing its longest river, at the end of its largest valley, by one if its largest rural villages – all called Papenoo.

YOU SHOULD KNOW:
The great but penniless Post-Impressionist French painter Paul Gauguin relocated to Tahiti in the 1890s and painted many Polynesian subjects. There is a small Gauguin museum on the island.

The lagoon at sunset

Moorea

POPULATION:
15,000 (2002)
WHEN TO GO:
If you're looking to set the date, May to October is ideal honeymoon weather (unless you prefer the other months when frequent heavy rain may keep you indoors).
HOW TO GET THERE:
By ferry or short air hop from Papeete.
HIGHLIGHTS:
A half-day photographic tour in an open-top or air-conditioned Jeep through tropical valleys and up to a panoramic viewpoint in the mountains.
Opunohu Agricultural College's three round-trip nature trails – to sample Moorea's abundant flora (walkable alone or with a guide).
A dolphin and whale-watching expedition outside the reef.
Viewing the reef and colourful lagoon life, without getting wet, from a half-submerged glass-bottomed boat.
YOU SHOULD KNOW:
Charles Darwin was inspired to formulate his theory of coral atoll formation after studying Moorea from atop a mountain in Tahiti.

This is definitely a case of high society – Moorea is a soaring island formed by volcanic action in French Polynesia's Society Islands (so named by Captain Cook). The island is 19 km (12 mi) to the east of Tahiti, and shaped like an inverted triangle with two deep bays nibbled out of the north coast. It isn't huge at 135 sq km (52 sq mi), but large enough to absorb the many tourists in reasonable comfort. There are three main settlements – Teavaro, Papetoai and Afareaitu, plus numerous resorts including those with the inevitable stilt houses extending into the lagoon.

This is the destination of choice for thousands of honeymooners each year, so be prepared to mingle with lots of love-struck fellow travellers. It's not hard to understand the romantic appeal. From the first glimpse of Moorea, rising steeply out of the ocean to eight impressive mountain ridges, it is apparent that this is a beautiful place with stunning scenery. Upon closer inspection, that initial impression is confirmed. The island is clad in lush vegetation, surrounded by a barrier reef sheltering a fabulous lagoon and is everything that a perfect tropical island should be. Indeed, there is a hilltop lookout between majestic Mount Tohivea and shark-toothed Mount Rotui, where the view down to the twin inlets of Cooks Bay and Opunohu Bay takes the breath away – it's so good that local tradition insists it was once reserved for the gods alone.

Of course Moorea offers all the usual holiday distractions for those who want to take advantage of them – watersports, sailing, fishing, tours on land and sea, adventure activities, hiking, biking, shopping and nightlife. But in truth, many visitors would honestly say that simply being here is enough.

Maupiti

Way out west in French Polynesia's Leeward Islands you come to the volcanic high island of Maupiti, a green postage stamp in the vast ocean with a surface area of just 11 sq km (4 sq mi), surrounded by long motu (islets) that enclose an immense shallow lagoon with just one access point for boats. Traditionally, Maupiti has strong cultural links with Bora Bora, 40 km (25 mi) to the east, and is sometimes described as 'Bora Bora's beautiful little cousin'.

If you really want a get-away-from-it-all holiday, this is the place for you. There are no resorts and no organized tours – just a few simple guest-houses and rooms to rent in family homes. Remember to take cash, because there's no way of getting any unless the bank is open (which is an infrequent occurrence). The pace of life here is slow and peaceful, ensuring that the only viable options are to relax, relax, relax.

It takes but two hours to stroll around the island, enjoying dramatic scenery (Mount Hotu Paraoa plunges straight into the sea at the island's southern tip) and wonderful sandy beaches (notably Tereia Beach at the western point). The main settlements of Farauru and Vaiea are on the eastern side. A three-hour hike takes you to the top of the central peak of Mount Teurafaatui, and the reward is a sensational panorama over the lagoon to Bora Bora and (on a clear day) Raiatea and Tahaa.

Maupiti is a genuine South Sea island paradise.

POPULATION:
1,200 (2002)

WHEN TO GO:
Any time – this is a magical island for all seasons, even more spectacular in the summer rainy season (December to April) when clouds and sudden storms enhance the drama.

HOW TO GET THERE:
By twice-weekly boat from Bora Bora (the *Maupiti Express*) or thrice weekly by air from Tahiti via Raiatea or Bora Bora.

HIGHLIGHTS:
The tiny islet of Motu Paeao on the north side of Maupiti, where archaeologists found graves and artefacts from the earliest period of Polynesian civilization.
Snorkelling around Onoiau Pass – the only boat access to the island.
Interesting petroglyphs carved into rock at the northern end of the island.

YOU SHOULD KNOW:
After tourism, Maupiti's chief economic activity is growing *noni* (Indian or beach mulberry), but don't be tempted to scrump one – an alternative name is 'vomit fruit'.

An aerial view of the volcanic island of Maupiti

Rangiroa

POPULATION:
3,400 (2007)
WHEN TO GO:
June to October.
HOW TO GET THERE:
Fly from Tahiti or Bora Bora.
HIGHLIGHTS:
The bird sanctuary on Motu Paio.
Take a lagoon cruise in a glass-bottomed boat to see the wonderful corals, sea fans and multitudinous fish species.
The Pink Sands – at the far south-west of the atoll, the sands are a lovely shade of pink, a beautiful contrast to the turquoise lagoon and blue sky.
The Island of the Reef – here raised coral formations create a dazzling tidepool environment.
Shooting the pass of Tiputa – here hundreds of fish, sharks and moray eels swim around you, swept along by the strong currents. You may even spot a rare black and white dolphin.
YOU SHOULD KNOW:
The numerous reef sharks in the lagoon will come up to investigate but they are nosy rather than aggressive.

Rangiroa is a stunning archipelago of 78 low islands spread over several hundred kilometres of the eastern Pacific around 200 km north of Tahiti. This is the second largest atoll in the world, the coral-encrusted rim of an ancient submerged volcano encircling an enormous shallow inland sea with more than 240 islets or *motu*. The *motu* are separated by at least 100 shallow channels and three passes, two of which are big enough for ships to enter the lagoon.

The lagoon waters are sparklingly clear, and vary in colour from jade-green to purple, a real surprise for first-time visitors. The marine life here is truly astonishing, with over 400 varieties of rainbow-hued fish glinting in the iridescent waters among the brightly coloured hard and soft corals, and the gently waving sea fans. The lagoon is understandably famous for its unsurpassed snorkelling and scuba diving, while outside the reefs there are amazing numbers of eagle rays, sharks, barracuda and tuna along the walls of the drop-offs.

The main villages in the archipelago are Avatoru and Tiputa, which offer the visitor a unique look at the South Pacific lifestyle, with their coral churches, craft centres, restaurants and tiny shops. Tiputa is situated at the eastern end. Its picturesque houses are ringed with bleached coral and flowering hedges, and nearby is the bird sanctuary on Motu Paio, well worth a visit.

There were more settlements on Rangiroa during the 14th and 15th centuries, and the remains of these can still be seen today, including cultivation pits and coral temples. To protect themselves from the aggressive Parata warriors from the atoll of Anaa, the Rangiroa inhabitants took refuge on the southwest side of the atoll. The village they created there was destroyed by a natural disaster, probably a tsunami, in 1560 and the entire population disappeared.

The Blue Lagoon at Taeo'o, an hour's boat ride from the village of Avatoru, is a natural pool of aquamarine water on the edge of the reef, and probably one of the most idyllic places in the world. This is like a gigantic natural aquarium with wonderful colourful corals and numerous reef sharks. The surrounding *motu* are home to rare birds, including the Vini ultramarine parakeet.

The blue lagoon and one of the many motu

The Marquesa Islands

Further from a continental landmass than any other islands on earth, the Marquesas lie in the Pacific Ocean about 1,400 km (870 mi) north-east of Tahiti. Due to their remoteness, these lush and rugged islands are almost entirely unspoiled. The wild, steep cliffs and valleys lead up to high central ridges, and sharp volcanic pinnacles pierce the skyline. This uncompromising landscape is, however, softened by the wonderful rampant vegetation, including colourful bougainvillea, orchids, lilies, ginger and jasmine. The wildlife is extraordinarily rich and varied, with 80 per cent of birds, half the native plants and insects, and many of the numerous marine species unique to the Marquesas.

The administrative capital of the southern group, Hiva Oa is perhaps the best known of the Marquesas. Paul Gauguin spent the last years of his life here and some of his paintings are on display in the museum. There are many archaeological sites on Hiva Oa, including characterful and fascinating rock carvings and tombs. Separated from Hiva Oa by a narrow channel only a few kilometres wide, Tahuata is the smallest inhabited island of the Marquesas. The first Europeans disembarked on the white sand here in 1595, but still today there are few visitors to this paradise.

The most populated island of the Marquesas, Ua Pou is said to be both young and old as its rocks and geographical features were formed in two different volcanic periods. The largest settlement is Hakahau, the centre of which is its Catholic church built from wood and stone.

At the far south of the island group, Fatu Iva is the most isolated and possibly the most beautiful island. There are around 500 inhabitants living in the valleys here, and they rely on small cargo ships to bring provisions. This makes it a relaxing place to explore, miles from the modern world. The inhabitants specialize in the making of tapa, a beaten bark cloth used for drawing on.

Ua Huka, in the northern Marquesas, is less fertile than its neighbouring islands and the vast tracts of scrubby land are grazed by wild goats and horses. The island's inhabitants live mainly on the south coast, in the villages of Vaipaee, Hane and Hokatu, each of which boasts a handicrafts centre. Also worth a visit are the arboretum and two interesting museums on the island.

Wherever in the Marquesas you choose to visit, you will discover an island paradise rich in both wildlife and cultural treasures.

Hiva Hoa Island

POPULATION:
8,632 (2007)

WHEN TO GO:
April to May, or September to October.

HOW TO GET THERE:
Fly from Papeete or Rangiroa to Nuku Hiva, or take a cruise ship or freighter from Papeete, calling at all six of the inhabited Marquesas.

HIGHLIGHTS:
Surfing – the size and quality of the ocean waves make these islands a hot spot for surfing. Relax on the beautiful deserted white sand beaches to get your breath back. The archeological remains – Oipona, on the island of Hiva Oa, is one of the most impressive sites presided over by a 7-foot stone tiki (statue) called Takaii, two large paepae (stone platforms), eighteen stone sculptures and two carved boulders. Another important site is the Taaoa Valley.

YOU SHOULD KNOW:
The islands are busiest in July and August, so book accommodation in advance for these months.

A church service on Tubuai

POPULATION:
6,700 (2002)
WHEN TO GO:
Any time – the islands enjoy a cooler climate than Tahiti, but the warmest season (November to February) is also the wettest.
HOW TO GET THERE:
There are three flights a week from Tahiti to Rurutu, Tubuai and Raivavae. Or spend a couple of days on the ocean – the supply ship *Tuhaa Pae II* sails three times a month from Tahiti (but only visits distant Rapa every six weeks).
HIGHLIGHTS:
The aamoraa ofai ceremony on Rurutu each January and July, when youngsters from different villages prove themselves by lifting heavy stones – followed by exuberant dancing and feasting.
Old hilltop fortresses (*pas*) and religious gathering places (*maraes*) on Rapa Island.
Close-up whale watching from the cliffs of Rurutu between July and November.
Elaborate hats, mats and bags woven by islanders from pandanus and coconut leaves. Also traditional wood and stone carvings.
YOU SHOULD KNOW:
Canoes in the Austral Islands are the only ones in Polynesia with outriggers on the right-hand side.

Austral Islands

At the southern extremity of French Polynesia's far-flung island collective, spread across some 1,280 km (800 mi) of ocean and straddling the Tropic of Capricorn, lie the Austral Islands. There are two distinct volcanic archipelagos. The Tubuai Islands consist of Iles Maria, Rimatara, Rurutu, Tubuai and Raivavae. The Bass Islands are Rapa and Marotiri, plus various uninhabited islets. Their combined land area is a mere 300 sq km (115 sq mi).

The remote Australs are largely self-sufficient and definitely not the place for those who like creature comforts. There are no resorts, and only four islands (Rurutu, Tubuai, Raivavae and Rapa) offer accommodation in small guest-houses and family pensions. These rather bare volcanic high islands are not even the prettiest in the South Pacific, though in truth some (notably Tubuai and Raivavae) have reefs and lagoons that are the equal of any in Polynesia. But those seeking a classic resort holiday must look elsewhere, because the Australs offer something completely different.

It's almost like stepping into a time machine and travelling backwards into the Polynesia discovered by Europeans centuries ago. The inhabitants live simply in villages where the houses and churches are often constructed in coral limestone. They catch fish, grow coffee, arrowroot, tobacco and coconuts, unworried by the cares of the modern world. Very religious, they have preserved the old rituals, celebrations, dance and polyphonic singing, giving the Australs an authenticity and traditional quality of life that can hardly fail to impress the adventurous traveller, who will be warmly welcomed to share (and respect) it. That's the reason for coming, and there couldn't be a better one.

Maui

Maui is the second largest of the islands in the Hawaiian Island chain, standing at 1,883 sq km (727 sq mi), and is also known as 'The Valley Isle'. Formed by six volcanoes, the islands of Maui, Lanai, Kahoolawe and Molokai were originally known as Maui Nui and were one landmass, which has since been separated by rising sea levels.

The shallow waters created by these sunken valleys provide excellent shelter to breeding humpback whales that can often been seen from the shore with their calves. The warm shallow waters are also host to huge numbers of fish and expanses of coral, making this a snorkelers' paradise.

The historic whaling village of Lahainha, on the west of the island, is a must-see. Steeped in history, the town was the home of King Kamehameha I, and later made the capital in 1790. It was also home to missionaries from 1824 who brought with them their religion and education for the masses but also measles and small pox. Today it is a bustling tourist town with a multitude of shops selling souvenirs and sea cruises. Ride the Lahainha Kaanapali Railroad, often referred to as Sugar Cane Train the only train in the whole of Hawaii, between Lahainha and Kaanapali for a different view of the island.

Haleakala National Park, famous for its endangered silversword plant, protects 122 sq km (47 sq mi) of land from the peaks of Haleakala, down to sea level along the Kipahulu coast. You'll need to purchase a pass on arrival at the park, but it is well worth it. For a swim, head down to the southeast part of the island to visit the Ohe'o Gulch, or Seven Sacred Pools. This stunning series of waterfalls and plunge pools progresses for four miles down to sea level and is often busy by the afternoon, so get there early.

POPULATION:
118,000 (2002)
WHEN TO GO:
Arrive between December and April and witness the majestic humpback whales breeding season.
DON'T MISS:
An authentic evening at a *luau* with traditional dancing and food.
YOU SHOULD KNOW:
Maui was voted 'the best island in the world' by independent travel magazine, *Condé Nast Traveller*.

Lava, palm trees and waterfalls blend in perfect harmony at the Seven Sacred Pools of Haleakala National Park

Kauai

POPULATION:
58,303 (2000)
WHEN TO GO:
January, or September to November.
HOW TO GET THERE:
Fly from Honolulu, California or Arizona.
HIGHLIGHTS:
The beaches around Poipu, near the southern tip of the island, are perfect for snorkelling and diving.
The Huleia National Wildlife Refuge – for native wild birds and animals.
Wailua Falls – this 60 m (173 ft) waterfall has three spouts of water. In ancient times, Hawaiian men would jump from the top of the falls to prove their manhood.
The Na Pali coast – the scenery is spectacular here and the best way to explore is by hiring a 4 wheel drive. Alternatively, book a helicopter ride over the coast for a view from above.
The Kauai Museum – located in the old part of Lihue, it features the history, geography and culture of the island.
YOU SHOULD KNOW:
Large parts of *Jurrassic Park*, *Fantasy Island*, *Raiders of the Lost Ark*, the original *King Kong* and *6 Days and 7 Nights* were filmed here.

Kauai is the northernmost of Hawaii's major islands which make up a volcanic archipelago in the Central Pacific. Known as 'the Garden Island', it is covered by tropical lush greenery due to its abundant rainfall. Because it is the oldest of the islands, formed more than six million years ago, it has been changed the most by erosion which has created some spectacular natural wonders such as Waimea Canyon and the Na Pali Coast. The island is less developed and more laid back than some of the other Hawaiian islands. This makes it popular with visitors and Hawaiians alike. It is also home to more white sandy beaches than any other major island in Hawaii..

The north and east coasts of Kauai are on the windward side of the island, where the winds blow onto the shore and deposit the most rain. These are the most lush and tropical sides of the island. By contrast, the south and west sides are sunnier and drier.

West Kauai is littered with spectacular natural wonders. Waimea Canyon, which has been likened to the Grand Canyon, is the main draw. At over 16 km (10 mi) long and an awe-inspiring 1,098 m (3,600 ft) deep, it is enormous. Carved over hundreds of thousands of years by runoff from Mount Waialeale, the canyon shows millions of years of geological history. The colours of its rocks rival that of its Arizona counterpart, except that Waimea Canyon also has touches of green. Also on the western side of the island is Kalalau Valley. Don't miss the views into the valley at sunset when the walls reflect beautiful shades of pink, orange, red and grey.

On the sunny south side of the island is the National Tropical Botanical Garden, home to a wide collection of colourful tropical plants. Nearby is Spouting Horn, named after the howling geyser effect created when water rushes into a series of natural lava tubes.

In the north is Hanalei Bay, a spectacular crescent of sandy beach at the foot of a sheer cliff. The town has good restaurants and shops, making this a great place for chilling out on the beach. Further west, the Na Pali coast is known for its lush valleys, enormous jagged cliffs towering above the ocean, lava tubes and caves, and its unspoilt, pristine beaches. The Na Pali coast State Park was formed to protect the Kalalau Valley, where overgrown gorges drop dramatically into the sea 1,219 m (4,000 ft) below. The park is a wonderful place for hiking or kayaking, and a helicopter ride over the awe-inspiring scenery is a truly memorable experience.

A beach on the spectacular Na Pali coast

Kiritimati Island

Feel like a trip to London and Paris? You'll find both on Kiritimati in mid-Pacific, also known as Christmas Island (Captain Cook arrived on 24 December 1777, in 'naming' mood). The world's largest coral atoll extends to a substantial 640 sq km (247 sq mi) and makes up 70 per cent of the land area in the scattered island republic of Kiribati. Its villages are London, Tabwakea, Banana, Poland and Paris (now sadly in ruins). And no, you don't have to take a Geiger counter – the radiation from Britain's 1950s H-bomb tests on Maiden Island, 320 km (200 mi) south of Kiritimati, has long dissipated on the four winds.

Many place names on Kiritimati date from the tenure of Emmanuel Rougier, a French priest who leased the island between the two World Wars, planting nearly a million coconut trees as his contribution to the islanders' future. London is the main village and has a modern port facility handling exports like coconuts, copra, seaweed and tropical saltwater aquarium fish. There is little tourism, because the island is a long way from anywhere and – despite some good beaches and a splendid lagoon – doesn't have much to offer that's worth going that far for, other than sport fishing and the opportunity to observe millions of nesting seabirds.

There is a hotel, but most of the Micronesian inhabitants live without electricity, running water or sanitation. This is one of the most primitive places on earth, but the people are very friendly and live a traditional community life, sheltered by thatched huts skilfully constructed from coconut palms and pandanus trees, subsisting on coconut products and the fruits of the sea.

The world's largest coral atoll

POPULATION:
5,000 (2005)

WHEN TO GO:
Any time, as there is no rainy season (indeed little rain at all). Avoid El Niño periods if you're a bird watcher – the birds vanish.

HOW TO GET THERE:
The weekly Aloha Airline flight from Honolulu to Cassidy International Airport (a three-and-a-half hour flight). Cruise ships visit frequently.

HIGHLIGHTS:
A lung-bursting climb to see the panoramic view from the island's highest point, La colline de Joe (Joe's Hill), at a dizzying 12m (40 ft) above sea level.
Fly fishing in the lagoon for that most prized of quarry species – bonefish.
Colourful cultural presentations to visitors from cruise ships on the main wharf at London – or uninhibited singing and dancing that takes place with the slimmest excuse.
The renowned Cook Islet Bird Sanctuary at the entrance to the enclosed lagoon.

YOU SHOULD KNOW:
This is the first inhabited place on earth to see in each New Year.

One of Tarawa's beautiful islets

Tarawa Island

This Micronesian atoll in the central Pacific used to be the capital of the British Gilbert and Ellis Islands, now fulfilling the same role for the Republic of Kiribati, an island nation of 33 atolls spread over 3,500,000 sq km (1,350,000 sq km) of otherwise empty sea. Kiribati extends north and south of the Equator, also east and west of the International Date Line.

Tarawa consists of a reef shaped like a rough triangle enclosing a lagoon, the eastern side of which is submerged and the remainder is made up of 24 thin islets, not all of which are connected. The largest is South Tarawa, extending along most of the lagoon's south side. Tarawa supports many more people than the basic way of life generally practised by the Kiribatis should allow, even though some have been relocated to other islands to ease the pressure. The majority are concentrated on South Tarawa, which only has an area of 16 sq km (6 sq mi). Despite an influx of foreign aid, this has led to problems of overcrowding, unemployment and poor health.

However, that does mean that many of Tarawa's other islets are uncrowded (some are unihabited) and these typical tropical treasures may be explored by boat. However, whilst accommodation is available (from a luxury hotel down to basic guest-houses), this is not a tourist destination. That doesn't mean it isn't interesting, if only because it demonstrates what real life can be like for tens of thousand of Pacific islanders where the magic wand of tourism has yet to wave.

One of the bloodiest battles in World War II's Pacific Theatre took place on Tarawa in 1943, when US marines landed and were met by 4,500 well-prepared Japanese defenders, who fought almost to the last man.

POPULATION:
29,500 (2007 estimate)
WHEN TO GO:
To avoid the heaviest rains, visiting in May to October is recommended.
HOW TO GET THERE:
Fly Air Nauru from Australia to Bonriki International Airport on South Tarawa.
HIGHLIGHTS:
Numerous World War II relics dating from the Japanese occupation.
Canoe racing in the lagoon off South Tarawata.
Ambo Islet, with its beautiful beach and the famous Ambo Lagoon Club.
The good diving and snorkelling in the lagoon and all around the eastern islets.
YOU SHOULD KNOW:
Visitors to Kiribati require a visa.

Chuuk Islands

This island group is a quarter of the Federated States of Micronesia, and the FSM's most populous state. It consists of more than 40 islands, some 15 of which are inside the main lagoon. There are five sets of outer islands – the Upper and Lower Mortlocks to the south, the Western Islands, the Hall Islands and Nomwin Atoll to the north. The outer islands need be of little concern to the visitor, as they can be reached only with great difficulty and have no tourist facilities.

The lagoon islands are another matter. Chuuk (sometimes called Truk) Lagoon has a diameter of 80 km (50 mi), and is up to 90 m (300 ft) deep. Reef diving alone would be rewarding, but the lagoon's true surprise is the 'Graveyard of the Pacific' – hundreds of wrecks including submarines, warships, freighters and planes that have lain undisturbed on the seabed since a fierce battle between the Japanese Imperial Fleet and American carrier planes in 1944. Over time, these have become an amazing underwater museum, where wrecks have become breathtaking coral gardens that provide a happy hunting ground for hundreds of exotic marine fish and animals. The phrase 'divers' heaven' is frequently used, and fully justified.

Life on the lagoon islands hasn't changed much for centuries. Weno is the main island, and has the airport, whilst other significant islands are Tonoas, Fefen, Uman and Udot. Through a combination of circumstances – extreme distance from anywhere and tourism centred on diving, whose participants are more interested in action than luxury accommodation – the islands have remained remarkably unspoiled, with islanders living peacefully on the fruits of nature and their own husbandry. The result, for those willing to make the not inconsiderable effort needed to get there, is enchanting.

POPULATION:
53,000 (2004)

WHEN TO GO:
The best time to visit is January to March, when there is generally little rainfall.

HOW TO GET THERE:
Fly from Hawaii on the island-hopper, or go via Guam.

HIGHLIGHTS:
Warrior masks and busts carved by islanders, who also make a selection of beautifully woven traditional goods.

Sapuk Lighthouse, built by the Japanese in the 1930s, with a superb view of the strategic northeast reef passage. Also marvel at the huge World War II guns nearby.

An incomparable panorama of the Chuuk Islands from Tonachau Mountain atop Weno, legendary home of the god Souwoniras and his divine son.

Tonata guns and caves, as a fine example of the many fortifications dating from World War II when Chuuk was a major Japanese base.

Nemwes and Fouman Rocks on Udot Island, symbolic sites that recall ancient rivalries between Chuuk and the Yap Islands.

YOU SHOULD KNOW:
The local courtship ritual involves unique tokens known as 'Chuukese Love Sticks' (don't ask).

The waters around Chuuk are often described as a diver's heaven.

Pohnpei

POPULATION:
35,000 (2007 estimate)
WHEN TO GO:
The (very) rainy season (July to October) is best avoided – otherwise the warm, tropical climate doesn't vary much.
HOW TO GET THERE:
By air, at considerable expense, flying Continental Micronesia from Guam. Or island-hop from Hawaii.
HIGHLIGHTS:
Nan Madol on Temwen Island, off Pohnpei's eastern shore, sometimes called the "Venice of the Pacific" – a network of canals and artificial islands covered in imposing stone ruins that date back to the 12th and 13th centuries.
The impressive Liduduhniap Twin Waterfalls on the Nanpil River, near Kolonia.
Kolonia's Spanish Wall, built in 1899 as part of Fort Alphonso XII, and the nearby Catholic Mission Bell Tower, all that remains of a church demolished by the Japanese in World War II.
A glass (one should be enough) of numbing sakau, a local drink made from pepper root used in traditional ceremonies and now sold in most bars.
YOU SHOULD KNOW:
Waterproof clothing is de rigueur – Pohnpei is one of the wettest places on earth with annual rainfall of 1,000 cm (400 in).

Micronesia's Federated States of Micronesia (FSM) consists of some 600 small islands spread across nearly 2,900,000 sq km (1,100,000 sq mi) of the Western Pacific just above the Equator. For all that, the FSM can only muster around 700 sq km (270 sq mi) of terra firma. The four states are Pohnpei, Chuuk, Kosrae and Yap. Each consists of one or more main high volcanic islands, with all but Kosrae including numerous outlying atolls.

Pohnpei is the FSM's largest island, with a circumference of 130 km (80 mi). It hosts a mixed population – as home to the national government, it has attracted employees from other states to join a hotch-potch of different Pacific islanders, Japanese, Americans, Australians and Europeans who have settled over the years. In addition to Pohnpei itself, whose reef encloses 25 islets and has eight atolls, the state consists of another 137 widely scattered atolls. Kolonia on the north coast is the island's commercial centre and capital.

Most of Pohnpei's shoreline is covered in mangrove swamps, but artificial beaches have been created on the mainland and reef atolls have excellent natural beaches. The island is rich in unspoiled coral reefs that delight divers and snorkelers, whilst a reef aperture known as Palikir Pass has acquired a well-deserved reputation as a surfing hotspot. Rugged mountain terrain and luxuriant rain forest cover the interior of the island, rising to the high point of Mount Nahnu Laud 788 m (2,585 ft). There are some fine nature trails and trekking opportunities, with numerous rushing streams, waterfalls and cooling plunge pools to enjoy along the way.

This is an island where tourists are welcomed by friendly people, that retains much original character simply because it has not yet become a well-known international resort destination. Enjoy!

The ruins of Nan Madol

Kosrae

This is said to be Micronesia's most remote destination and, unlike the other three Federated States of Micronesia, Kosrae has no outlying atolls. It is a high volcanic island extending to some 110 sq km (42 sq mi) in area with steep contours and dense vegetation that have prevented development. The island is sometimes called 'the sleeping lady' because it appears to have the female form when viewed from the sea. It is surrounded by coral reefs that are carefully protected against damage. More than 170 species of hard coral have been identified, plus ten soft corals, and the reefs and lagoons are home to over 250 different types of fish and marine animal. The Utwe-Walung Marine Park preserves untouched forest and mangrove ecosystems.

The island government is the main employer, and though the inhabitants continue to rely on traditional farming and fishing for subsistence, imported goods now meet their wider needs. They used to live in family groups surrounding a communal cookhouse, but this practice is in decline. For all that the 21st century has crept in, the islanders still delight in traditional singing, chanting, weaving, woodcarving, canoe building and house construction. They are extremely devout and welcome visitors warmly.

There are a few small resorts, but you won't be sharing the beauties of Kosrae with many others – this is the island that mass tourism has yet to discover. The visitors who do make it are inevitably captivated, and some do no more than unwind from the hectic pace of the modern world – sunbathing, snorkelling, meeting islanders and eating wholesome food. Others dive on the reefs and wrecks, or trek into the lush interior and discover the island's rich archaeological heritage. Whatever their preference, not one is disappointed by this wondrous tropical island.

Mangrove swamps and hanging tree ferns on Kosrae

POPULATION:
7,700 (2007 estimate)

WHEN TO GO:
December to April is the best time, July to October the wettest.

HOW TO GET THERE:
It's best to travel via Guam from whence (if you want to 'do' all four of the FSM's states) a 'Visit Micronesia' pass is available. Or go the other way on Continental's island-hopper flights from Hawaii.

HIGHLIGHTS:
The extended hike to the top of majestic Mount Finkol.
The remains of two 19th century whalers, *Henrietta* and *Waverly* – the former was burned in Okat Harbour as reprisal after crew members molested local women.
Exploring atmospheric mangrove swamps by canoe.
Spotting bottleneck dolphins and the occasional whale.

YOU SHOULD KNOW:
The last buccaneer, the American William 'Bully' Haynes, was shipwrecked here in 1874 – and is said to have buried his treasure here – it has never been found...

Babeldaob Island

POPULATION:
4,500 (2007 estimate)
WHEN TO GO:
At any time, though the monsoon season (June to October) does see intense rainfall almost every day.
HOW TO GET THERE:
Various international carriers fly in to Koror-Babeldaob Airport, often via Guam.
HIGHLIGHTS:
Paluan storyboards – traditional wood carvings depicting local myths and legends.
The bai (men's meeting house) in Airai, said to be the world's oldest.
Lake Ngardok near Melekeok, the largest natural freshwater lake in Micronesia – and home to crocodiles.
The many mysterious stone monoliths around Ngarchelong Province, in the north of the island.
The scenic Taki Falls at Ngardmau on the west coast.
YOU SHOULD KNOW:
Palauans have traditionally operated a matrilineal society where titles, land and property pass through the female line to eldest daughters.

This is the largest island in the Micronesian Republic of Palau, one of the world's youngest and smallest nations (independent only since 1994). Unlike many far-flung Pacific nations, Paulau's islands are well grouped, some 800 km (500 mi) east of the Philippines. Palau is mostly flat, but Babeldaob (also known as Babelthuap) is mountainous and contains the country's highest point, Mount Ngerchelchuus 242 m (794 ft) tall. It also has over two-thirds of the country's land mass and the main airport is there.

For many years, Babeldaob played second fiddle to its immediate neighbour, the urbanized Koror Island. But the recent construction of a bridge connecting the two (replacing one that collapsed) and a new highway that rings Babeldaob has altered the relationship. The new capital, Melekeok, is on Babeldaob and the island has been opened up for rapid economic exploitation and the promotion of tourism. This major infrastructure project has been controversial, as it will degrade the ecology of an environmental treasure – the Ngermeskang River (Micronesia's largest), its estuary and Ngaremeduu Bay. The designation of a large conservation area may not be enough to limit damage, but therein lies the dilemma of many small, poverty-stricken Pacific nations – an unspoiled environment and poverty, or development and improved living standards?

The decision has been made here, for better or worse, with an influx of middle-class professionals from Koror who are building commuter homes, and farmers who are clearing forest and mangrove swamps to plant cash crops. Despite existing tourist facilities, it's still possible to see the islanders living as they always have, by gathering food and fishing, and experience an island that still has extraordinary natural beauty. But hurry – it won't be long before Babeldaob changes almost beyond recognition.

Many mysterious stone monoliths can be found in the north of the island.

Ngercheu Island

Palau is a nation that really does live up to the description 'tropical paradise'. This archipelago consists of 343 islands where major ocean currents of the Pacific and Philippines Sea meet and mingle, creating a wonderful maze of small islands, incredible underwater features and a colourful variety of marine life. This has ensured that Palau, whilst no over-developed Pacific tourist trap, has become one of the world's top destinations for diving and snorkelling.

The famous Rock Islands are a collection of rounded, foliage-covered islets that seem to float above the water, an illusion caused by the fact that they have been undercut by the sea's action over millennia. They are occupied by birds, bats, monkeys and saltwater crocodiles. Ngercheu is right in the middle of the 'Rocks', some 25 km (15 mi) south of Palau's most populous island, Koror. It is a tiny uninhabited island that was developed as the Carp Island Resort, and Ngercheu is now often referred to as Carp Island. It offers panoramic views of the Rock Islands, white sandy beaches and proximity to world-famous dive sites to lure visitors, who stay in the simple accommodation or visit for the day from Koror's more developed tourist facilities. The 'resort' consists of a large central building ringed by thatched cottages and bungalows, and is mainly occupied by those who come not for a luxury beach holiday, but for tempting diving opportunities.

These include named wonders like Manta Ray Point, New Drop-Off, Big Drop-Off, Peleliu Wall (the deepest reef structure in Palau), Blue Hole and Blue Corner – a wonderland of multi-coloured coral, teeming tropical fish, turtles and reef sharks. But divers do require a permit and must be certified.

POPULATION:
Uninhabited
WHEN TO GO:
Any time – the weather matters not to divers. Even the rainy season from June to October generally sees a mixture of sunshine and showers.
HOW TO GET THERE:
By boat from Koror.
HIGHLIGHTS:
For divers – the Ngemelis Wall, considered by many to be the world's finest dive site.
A fascinating variety of bird life.
Spectacular sunrises and sunsets over the Rock Islands.
YOU SHOULD KNOW:
The local saltwater crocodiles are not as large or fearsome as their Australian brethren, with only one attack on a human ever reported.

The fantastic formations of the Rock Islands

COUNTRIES

ISLANDS

4Corners Images/Pavan Aldo/SIME 462; /Cossa Bruno/SIME 454; /Johanna Huber/SIME 254; /Fantuz Olimpio/SIME 250.
Alamy 64, 242, 226; /Peter Adams Photography 245; /Bryan & Cherry Alexander Photography 8 inset 2, 129; /AM Corporation 382 inset 1, 385; /Arco images 212; /Jon Arnold Images 7 centre top, 383 inset 1,165, 418, 424; /Atmotu Images 513; /B Mete Uz 327; /Bill Bachman 2 left, 478; /David Ball 181; /Banana Pancake 6 centre top, 76, 434; /David Beatty/Robert Harding Picture Library 294; /Pat Behnke 130 inset 2, 262; /Debra Behr 515; /Rieger Bertrand/Hemis 421; /Philip Bigg 377; /Bildarchiv Monheim GmbH; /Stephen Bond 534; /Mark Boulton 171; /Charles Bowman 194; /Box Archive, The 260; /Richard Broadwell 256; /CalatheaPhoto 240; /Thomas Cockrem 6 centre bottom, 477 inset 1, 512; /Gary Cook 111, 334, 356; /Bill Coster 368; /Gary Crabble 58; /Chris A. Crumley 535; /CuboImages srl 248, 253; /DAJ 466; /Cameron Davidson 48; /Danita Delimont 65, 216, 216; /Digital Archive Japan 465; /Reinhard Dirscherl 92, 456; /Chad Ehlers 3 right, 134; /Keith Erksine 370; /Robert Estall Photo Agency 342, 345; /Mark Eveleigh 330, 448; /f1 online 252; /Michele Falzone 120, 366; /FAN travelstock 312; /Neil Farrin 369; /David Fleetham 536; /Andrew Fox 50; /Chris Fredisson 143; /Danielle Gali/Jon Arnold Images 423; /Bertrand Gardel 360 inset 1; /Alain Le Garsmeur 12; /geogphotos 158; /Eddie Gerald 361 inset 2, 378; /David Gowans 11; /Greenshoots Communications 341; /Rainer Grosskopf 38; /David W. Hamilton 537; /Terry Harris/Just Greece Photo Library 291; 298, 309; /Philippe Hays 130 inset 3, 172; /Gavin Hellier/Jon Arnold Images 302; /Hemis 130 inset 1, 230, 232, 235, 292, 360 inset 2, 363, 371; /HJB 355; /Per-Andre Hoffman/LOOK Die Bildagentur der Fotografen GmbH 5 bottom, 426; /Andrew Holt 168, 347, 443; /Cindy Miller Hopkins/Danita Delimont 315; /Peter Horree 195, 383 inset 2, 438; /imagebroker 242; /Images&Stories 7 top, 326, 331, 407; /Images of Africa Photobank 334 inset 1, 349; /IML Image Group 293, 295, 299, 305, 316; /Interfoto Pressebildagentur 365; /Eric James 268; /Martin Jenkinson 324; /Norma Joseph 380; /Don Johnston 13; /Andrea Jones 163; /Huw Jones 269; /JTB Photo Communications, Inc. 468, 472; /Michael Juno 267; /Jupiterimages/Agence Images 233; /Christian Kapteyn 482; /Karsten 449; /Hideo Kurihara 300; /Kuttig - Travel 397; /Richard Laird 51; /J. C. Leacock 8 inset 3, 55; /Yadid Levy 352, 352; /Mark Lewis 61; /Suzanne Long 479; /Melvyn Longhurst 322; /LOOK Die Bildagentur der Fotografen GmbH 192, 199, 255; /Craig Lovell/Eagle Visions Photography 531; /David Lyons 160, 182; /Rebecca Marsden 402; /J. Marshall 353; /J. Marshall - Tribaleye Images 432; /Ian Masterton 218; /Neil McAllister 433; /Josh McCulloch 22; /Niall McDiarmid 155; /Chris McLennan 398, 477 inset 2, 490; /mediacolor's 228, 308, 372, 506; /Bernd Mellmann 208; /Bodo Muller/TopicMedia 281; /Nagelestock.com 131 inset 2, 178, 244, 331; /National Trust Photolibrary 161; /Nature Picture Library 376; /Peter Nicholson 113; /Julian Nieman 372; /Mirjana Nociar 274; /Nordic photos 138, 144; /M. Tomothy O'Keefe 28; /D. J. Paco 314; /Jiri PaleniCek/Profimedia International s.r.o. 430; /Doug Pearson/Jon Arnold Images 499; /Douglas Peebles Photography 533; /Photolibrary Wales 176, 445; /Pictor International/ImageState 384; /Pictures Colour Library 313; /B. Fabio Pili 116; /Nicholas Pitt 6 centre, 403, 415; /Pixonnet.com 132; /RF Company 207, 211; /RHK UW Productions 431; /Rolf Richardson 492; /Bill Rubie 427; /David Sanger Photography 135, 538; /Kevin Schafer 518; /Scottish Viewpoint 187; /Leonid Serebrennikov 439; /Mikael Svensson 136; /David South 412; /Rhys Stacker 417; /David Stares 247;
/Frances Stephane/Hemis 343; /Stock Connection Distribution 117; /Egmont Strigi 272; /Karen Su/China Span 362; /Jack Sullivan 334 inset 3, 344; /Ozil Thierry 128; /Richard Thompson 483; /Tom Till 25; /Travelib India 361 inset 1, 381; /Kirk Treakle 442; /Ian Trower 435; /Bob Turner 86; /Mikael Utterstrom 141; /John Warburton-Lee 340; /WaterFrame 93, 452; /Ron Watts 19; /Alois Weber/f1 online 288; /Westend61 360, 375; /Kim Westerskov 494; /Henry Westheim 43; /Michele Westmorland/Danita Delimont 455; /Chris Wilson 469; /Jan Wlodarczyck 318; /Robert Wojtowicz 53; /Worldwide Picture Library 338; /Ariadne Van Zandbergan 334 inset 2, 351; /Marek Zuk 282; /Zute Lightfoot 355.
Ardea/Kurt Amsler 112.
Art Directors and Trip/Colin Conway 457; /Robin Smith 460.
Axiom/Chris Caldicott 75; /Chris Coe 21; /Ian Cumming 9 inset 1, 67, 80; /Jim Holmes 470; /Ellen Roney 69; /M. Winch 522.
Bluegreen Pictures/Roberto Rinaldi 480.
Britain on View 175.
Camera Press/Thomas Ernsting 358; /Riehle 422.
Corbis 71; /Peter Adams 257, 264; /James L. Amos 26; /Arctic-Images 147, 148; /Jon Arnold/JAI 382, 463; /Yann Arthus-Bertrand 484; /Atlantide Phototravel 91; /Tom Bean 20, 30; /Remi Benali 476 inset 1, 504; /Niall Benvie 185, 186; /Walter Bibikow 84, 296, 297, 317; /Kristi J. Black 95; /Jonathan Blair 270; /Tibor Bognar 73; /Jean du Boisberranger/Hemis 508; /Christophe Boisvieux 139; /Gareth Brown 382 inset 3, 400; /Christiana Carvalho/Frank Lane Picture Agency 218; /Dian Cook & Len Jenshel 81; /Ashley Cooper 173, 519; /Guido Cozzi/Atlantide Phototravel 258; /Fridmar Damm 79; /James Davis/Eye Ubiquitous 310; /Design Pics 156, 159; /Julio Donoso 121; /Abbie Enock/Travel Ink 162; /EP travelstock 289; /Macduff Everton 9 inset 2, 36, 88, 140, 177; /Michele Falzone 123, 335 inset 2, 337; /Michele Falzone/JAI 6 bottom, 419; /Neil Farrin/JAI 514; /Kevin Fleming 49; /Franz-Marc Frei 517; /Patrick Frilet/Hemis 307, 529; /Bertrand Gardel 372; /Bertrand Gardel/Hemis 74, 236; /Robert Garvey 491; /Raymond Gehman 17; /Philippe Giraud/Goodlook 275, 279, 285; /Scott Gog 301; /Larry Dale Gordon/zefa 63; /Jean Guichard 130, 189; /Franck Guiziou/Hemis 311, 399; /Darrell Gulin 525; /Richard Hamilton 29; /Richard Hamilton Smith 102; /Blaine Harrington 27; /Lindsay Hebberd 437; /Gavin Hellier/JAI 180; /Jon Hicks 278; /Hobermann 42; /Jeremy Horner 261, 271, 280; /Jason Hosking/zefa 464; /Dave G. Houser 39; /George H.H. Huey 40; /Peter Hulme/Ecoscene 190; /Irish Image Collection, The 157; /Gavriel Jecan 395; /Ann Johansson 204; /Mark A. Johnson 367; /Ray Juno 249; /Wolfgang Kaehler 115, 286, 364, 476 inset 3, 488, 503; /Catherine Karnow 82; /Karen Kasmauski 475; /Layne Kennedy 70; /Richard Klune 174; /Wilfried Krecichwost/zefa 7 bottom, 146; /Bob Krist 5 top, 52, 124, 167, 539; /Frans Lanting 429, 498, 532; /Danny Lehman 8, 85, 103, 104; /Barry Lewis 145; /Massimo Listri 142; /Ludovic Maisant 2, 89; /William Manning 266; /Olivier Martel 222; /Medio Images 320; /Manfred Mehlig/zefa 206; /Wolfgang Meier/ zefa 198; /Angela Merker/dpa 501; /Momatiuk-Eastcott 33, 127; /Kevin M. Morris 410; /Amos Nachoum 68; /Richard T. Nowitz 24; /Owaki/Kulla 54; /Douglas Peebles 5 centre bottom, 59, 476, 520, 524; /Sergio Pitamitz 90, 122, 528; /Sergio Pitamitz/zefa 263; /Jose Fuste Raga 87; /Jose Fuste Raga/zefa 394; /Steve Raymer 225; /Phillippe Renault 66; /Bertrand Rieger/Hemis 166; /Joel W. Rogers 277; /Ellen Rooney/Robert Harding World Imagery 321; /Guenter Rossenbach/zefa 197, 205; /Hans Georg Roth 243, 283; /Andy Rouse 125, 126; /Galen Rowell 10; /Bob Sacha 5 centre top, 56, 72; /Kevin Schafer 8 inset 1, 60, 105, 192; /Michael St. Maur Sheil 131 inset 1, 150, 152, 154; /Marco Simoni/Robert Harding World Images 303; /Hugh Sitton/zefa 304; /Skyscan 169; /Jon Sparks 188; /George Steinmetz 458; /Svenja-Foto/zefa 137, 210; /Craig Tuttle 521; /Upperhall/Robert Harding World Imagery 348; /Sandro Vannini 251; /Volkmar Brockhaus/zefa 7 centre bottom, 325; /Onne van der Wal 500; /Patrick Ward 184; /Michele Westmorland 507, 511; /Stuart Westmorland 32; /Nik Wheeler 77, 83, 100, 276, 335 inset 1, 339; /Peter M. Wilson 306, 414; /Lawson Wood 179; /Adam Woolfitt 200; /Michael S. Yamashita 214; /Bo Zaunders 46; /David Jay Zimmerman 44.
Divevietnam.com/Caroline Istas 416.
DK Images/Stuart Isett 405.
Drummond Island Tourist Board 35.
FLPA/Christiana Carvalho 451; /Terry Whittaker 404; /Konrad Wothe/Minden Pictures 440.
Focus/Toomas Tuul 214.
Getty Images 62; /Peter Adams 290; /AFP 450; /Altrendo Travel 481; /Nina Buesing 94; /Robert Caputo 330; /Robert Caputo/Aurora 476 inset 2, 530; /Jason Childs 444; /Rene Frederick 505; /David A. Harvey 41; /Peter Hendrie 516; /Fred Hirschmann 34; /Philip Kramer 509; /Isao Kuroda/Sebun Photo 474; /Thorsten Milse 485; /Louise Murray 510; /Jean-Pierre Pieuchot 527; /Nobuaki Sumida 473; /Pete Turner 6 top, 47; /Norbert Wu 97; /Katsuhiro Yamanashi 471.
Imagestate/Jean-Erick Pasquier 31.
Lonely Planet Images/Grant Dixon 487; /Krzysztof Dydynski 110; /Michael Gebicki 459; /Peter Hendrie 502; /Peter Solness 224; /Oliver Strewe 3 centre, 493; /Tony Wheeler 453.
Polly Manguel 18.
National Geographic Image Collection/William Albert Allard 523.
Nature's Pic Images/Rob Suisted 496.
Panos/Andrew Testa 382 inset 2, 406.
Photolibrary/Robin Bush/Oxford Scientific Films 497.
Photoshot 96; /B & C Alexander/NHPA 441; /Gerald Cubitt/NHPA 436; /Martin Harvey 99; /Mauritius/World Pictures 203; /Stuart Pearce/World Pictures 389; /Martin Puddy/World Pictures 388; /Kevin Schafer/NHPA 489; /World Pictures 16, 108, 109, 114, 118, 119, 386.
Reuters/Steve Crisp 336.
Robert Harding Picture Library/Louise Murray 78.
Ted Rhodes 15.
Shutterstock/Bruce Amos 401; /Alexey Biryukov 265; /Castka 239; /Thierry Dagnelie 234; /Chean Mun Fei 390; /Imagemaker 387; /Olga Kolos 221; /Jason Maehl 396; /Holger Mette 447; /Salazkin Vladimir Mikhailovich 223; /Dimitrije Paunovic 323; /Jean Schweitzer 241; /Morozova Tatyana 446; /Lawrence Wee 392.
Still Pictures/Reinhard Dirscherl/WaterFrame.de 101; /Le Gal/ Andia 237; /Rainer Heubeck/Dasa Fotoarchive 107; /Juan Pablo Moreiras/FFI 98; /Ed Reschke 106; /Sandford/ Andia.fr 231
Travel Michigan/Raymond J. Malace 37.
Travel-images.com/R. Grove 14.
Visitdenmark.com 196.
Stephen Voss 495.

Organizational Behavior

edition
13

Organizational Behavior

Stephen P. Robbins
San Diego State University

Timothy A. Judge
University of Florida

Pearson Education International

Acquisitions Editor: Jennifer Collins
Editorial Director: Sally Yagan
Editor in Chief: David Parker
Director of Marketing: Patrice Jones
Marketing Manager: Nikki Jones
Marketing Assistant: Ian Gold
Director of Development: Steve Deitmer
Development Editor: Elisa Adams
Product Development Manager: Ashley Santora
Editorial Assistant: Elizabeth Davis
Permissions Project Manager: Charles Morris
Senior Managing Editor: Judy Leale
Senior Operations Specialist: Arnold Vila
Art Director: Patricia Smythe
Interior Design: Karen Quigley
Cover Design: Ray Cruz
Director, Image Resource Center: Melinda Patelli
Manager, Rights and Permissions: Zina Arabia
Manager, Visual Research: Beth Brenzel
Image Permission Coordinator: Cynthia Vincenti
Composition/Project Management: GGS Book Services
Printer/Binder: Quebecor World/Versailles
Typeface: NewBaskerville-Roman, 10.5/12

Credits and acknowledgments borrowed from other sources and reproduced, with permission, in this textbook appear on appropriate page within text (photo credits on page 682).

Pearson Education Ltd., London
Pearson Education Singapore, Pte. Ltd
Pearson Education, Canada, Inc.
Pearson Education–Japan
Pearson Education Australia PTY, Limited
Pearson Education North Asia, Ltd., Hong Kong
Pearson Educación de Mexico, S.A. de C.V.
Pearson Education Malaysia, Pte. Ltd.
Pearson Education Upper Saddle River, New Jersey

10 9 8 7 6 5 4 3 2 1
ISBN 13: 978-0-13-207964-8
ISBN 10: 0-13-207964-X

BRIEF CONTENTS

CONTENTS

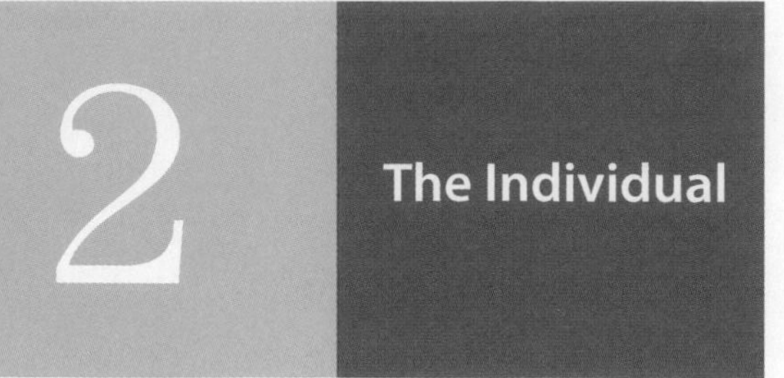

Chapter 2 Foundations of Individual Behavior 76

Chapter 3 Attitudes and Job Satisfaction 106

Chapter 6 Motivation Concepts 206

S
A
L

Chapter 12 Basic Approaches to Leadership 416

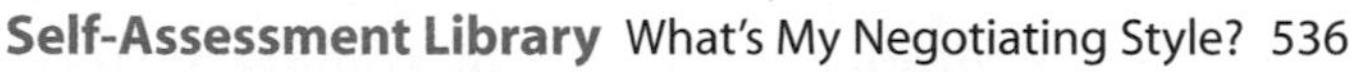

4 The Organization System

Chapter 16 Foundations of Organization Structure 550

Stephen P. Robbins

Education

Ph.D. University of Arizona

Professional Experience

Academic Positions: Professor, San Diego State University, Southern Illinois University at Edwardsville, University of Baltimore, Concordia University in Montreal, and University of Nebraska at Omaha.

Research: Research interests have focused on conflict, power, and politics in organizations, behavioral decision making, and the development of effective interpersonal skills.

Books Published: World's best-selling author of textbooks in both management and organizational behavior. His books are used at more than a thousand U.S. colleges and universities, have been translated into 16 languages, and have adapted editions for Canada, Australia, South Africa, and India. These include

- *Essentials of Organizational Behavior*, 8th ed. (Prentice Hall, 2005)
- *Management*, 8th ed. with Mary Coulter (Prentice Hall, 2005)
- *Human Resource Management*, 8th ed., with David DeCenzo (Wiley, 2005)
- *Prentice Hall's Self-Assessment Library 3.0* (Prentice Hall, 2005)
- *Fundamentals of Management*, 5th ed., with David DeCenzo (Prentice Hall, 2006)
- *Supervision Today!*, 4th ed., with David DeCenzo (Prentice Hall, 2004)
- *Training in Interpersonal Skills*, 3rd ed., with Phillip Hunsaker (Prentice Hall, 2003)
- *Managing Today!*, 2nd ed. (Prentice Hall, 2000)
- *Organization Theory*, 3rd ed. (Prentice Hall, 1990)
- *The Truth About Managing People . . . And Nothing But the Truth* (Financial Times/Prentice Hall, 2002)
- *Decide and Conquer: Make Winning Decisions and Take Control of Your Life* (Financial Times/Prentice Hall, 2004).

Other Interests

In his "other life," Dr. Robbins actively participates in masters' track competition. Since turning 50 in 1993, he's won 14 national championships, 11 world titles, and set numerous U.S. and world age-group records at 60, 100, 200, and 400 meters. In 2005, Dr. Robbins was elected into the USA Masters' Track & Field Hall of Fame.

Timothy A. Judge

Education

Ph.D. University of Illinois at Urbana-Champaign

Professional Experience

Academic Positions: Matherly-McKethan Eminent Scholar in Management, Warrington College of Business Administration, University of Florida; Stanley M. Howe Professor in Leadership, Henry B. Tippie College of Business, University of Iowa; Associate Professor (with tenure), Department of Human Resource Studies, School of Industrial and Labor Relations, Cornell University; Lecturer, Charles University, Czech Republic, and Comenius University, Slovakia; Instructor, Industrial/Organizational Psychology, Department of Psychology, University of Illinois at Urbana-Champaign.

Research: Dr. Judge's primary research interests are in (1) personality, moods, and emotions, (2) job attitudes, (3) leadership and influence behaviors, and (4) careers (person-organization fit, career success). Dr. Judge published more than 100 articles in these and other major topics in journals such as *Journal of Organizational Behavior, Personnel Psychology, Academy of Management Journal, Journal of Applied Psychology, European Journal of Personality, and European Journal of Work and Organizational Psychology.*

Fellowship: Dr. Judge is a fellow of the American Psychological Association, the Academy of Management, the Society for Industrial and Organizational Psychology, and the American Psychological Society.

Awards: In 1995, Dr. Judge received the Ernest J. McCormick Award for Distinguished Early Career Contributions from the Society for Industrial and Organizational Psychology, and in 2001, he received the Larry L. Cummings Award for mid-career contributions from the Organizational Behavior Division of the Academy of Management. In 2007, he received the Professional Practice Award from the Institute of Industrial and Labor Relations, University of Illinois.

Books Published: H. G. Heneman III, and T. A. Judge, *Staffing Organizations*, 5th ed. (Madison, WI: Mendota House/Irwin, 2006).

Other Interests

Although he cannot keep up (literally!) with Steve's accomplishments on the track, Dr. Judge enjoys golf, cooking and baking, literature (he's a particular fan of Thomas Hardy, and is a member of the Thomas Hardy Society), and keeping up with his three children, who range in age from 19 to 5.

PREFACE

Welcome to the thirteenth edition of *Organizational Behavior!* Long considered the standard for all organizational behavior textbooks, this edition continues its tradition of making current, relevant research come alive for students. While maintaining its hallmark features—clear writing style, cutting-edge content, and compelling pedagogy—the thirteenth edition has been updated to reflect the most recent research within the field of organizational behavior.

Key Changes to the Thirteenth Edition

New Global Emphasis. In addition to the International OB highlights, a Global Implications section—which discusses the global implications of each chapter's material—has been added to each chapter.

Updated and Expanded S.A.L. S.A.L. (Self-Assessment Library), the top-selling self-assessment product on the market, has been improved and updated. An additional 25 tests have been added to S.A.L. Moreover, the S.A.L. assessments have been integrated into each chapter, including a S.A.L. assessment at the beginning of each chapter, which allows a seamless self-assessment of a key concept in each chapter.

New Learning Objectives. Each chapter has new learning objectives to allow students to quickly grasp the core concepts in each chapter. In addition to being highlighted at the beginning of each chapter, these learning objectives are keyed to the presentation of the material in the text, and then are highlighted again in the chapter *Questions for Review.*

Experiential Exercises. An experiential, hands-on, in-class exercise is included in each chapter, along with material in the Instructor's Manual that will make for unique and entertaining exercises to highlight a key chapter concept.

Streamlined Length. The text has been streamlined—it is shorter than the last edition of Robbins/Judge, done so by eliminating older material that is less on the cutting edge.

Updated Material. In nearly every chapter, the *Opening Vignette, OB in the News,* and *Myth or Science?* sections are new. In addition, many of the *Case Incident, Ethical Dilemma,* and *Point/Counterpoint* sections are new to this edition.

Chapter-by-Chapter Changes

- New material on evidence-based management (Chapter 1).
- New section on creating a positive work environment and discussion of positive organizational scholarship (Chapter 1).
- New material on general mental ability (Chapter 2).
- New material on sexual orientation and gender identity in the workplace (Chapter 2).
- Revised treatment of cognitive dissonance (Chapter 3).

- Updated sections on personality determinants and how the Big Five predict behavior at work (Chapter 4).
- Updated and revised material on stereotyping and profiling (Chapter 5).
- Enhanced integration of material on the rational model of decision making, bounded rationality, and intuition (Chapter 5).
- Revised treatment of McClelland's Theory of Needs (Chapter 6).
- Streamlined treatment of implementing goal-setting theory and Management by Objectives (Chapter 6).
- Updated treatment of variable-pay programs (Chapter 7).
- New section on gender and emotions (Chapter 8).
- Revised treatment of group norms (Chapter 9).
- New material on virtual teams (Chapter 10).
- New material on personality and team performance (Chapter 10).
- Updated material on diversity effects on team performance (Chapter 10).
- New material on team reflexivity and team mental models (Chapter 10).
- Revised treatment of downward communication (Chapter 11).
- Revised and updated coverage of electronic communication, including new sections on networking software and Internet logs (blogs) (Chapter 11).
- New material on gender differences in communication (Chapter 11).
- Updated material on authentic and ethical leadership (Chapter 13).
- New section on how trust can be regained (Chapter 13).
- New section on political skill (Chapter 14).
- Updated treatment of sexual harassment (Chapter 14).
- Revised recommendations for effective use of distributive bargaining tactics (Chapter 15).
- Revised treatment of individual differences in negotiation, including new coverage of gender differences in negotiation (Chapter 15).
- Revised and updated treatment of the virtual organization (Chapter 16).
- New section on creating a positive organizational culture (Chapter 17).
- Updated material on forces for change in OB (Chapter 19).
- New section on implementing organizational changes fairly (Chapter 19).
- Additional material on challenge and hindrance stressors (Chapter 19).

Instructor's Resource Center

At www.prenhall.com/irc, instructors can access a variety of print, digital, and presentation resources available with this text in downloadable format. Registration is simple and gives you immediate access to new titles and new editions. As a registered faculty member, you can download resource files and receive immediate access and instructions for installing course management content on your campus server.

If you need assistance, our dedicated technical support team is ready to help with the media supplements that accompany this text. Visit www.247.prenhall.com for answers to frequently asked questions and toll-free user support phone numbers.

The following supplements are available to adopting instructors (for detailed descriptions, please visit www.prenhall.com/irc):

- **Instructor's Resource Center (IRC) on CD-ROM**—ISBN: 0-13-602669-9
- **Printed Instructor's Manual**—ISBN: 0-13-602670-2
- **Printed Test Item File**—ISBN: 0-13-602683-4
- **TestGen Test Generating Software**—Available at the IRC online
- **PowerPoint Slides**— Available at the IRC online and on CD-ROM
- **Custom Videos on DVD**—ISBN: 0-13-602675-3

AACSB Learning Standards Tags in Test Item File

What Is the AACSB?

AACSB is a not-for-profit corporation of educational institutions, corporations, and other organizations devoted to the promotion and improvement of higher education in business administration and accounting. A collegiate institution offering degrees in business administration or accounting may volunteer for AACSB accreditation review. The AACSB makes initial accreditation decisions and conducts periodic reviews to promote continuous quality improvement in management education. Pearson Education is a proud member of the AACSB and is pleased to provide advice to help you apply AACSB Learning Standards.

What Are AACSB Learning Standards?

One of the criteria for AACSB accreditation is the quality of the curricula. Although no specific courses are required, the AACSB expects a curriculum to include learning experiences in such areas as:

- Communication
- Ethical Reasoning
- Analytic Skills
- Use of Information Technology
- Multicultural and Diversity
- Reflective Thinking

These six categories are AACSB Learning Standards. Questions that test skills relevant to these standards are tagged with the appropriate standard. For example, a question testing the moral questions associated with externalities would receive the Ethical Reasoning tag.

How Can I Use These Tags?

Tagged questions help you measure whether students are grasping the course content that aligns with AACSB guidelines noted above. In addition, the tagged questions may help to identify potential applications of these skills. This in turn may suggest enrichment activities or other educational experiences to help students achieve these goals.

OneKey Online Courses: Convenience, Simplicity, and Success

OneKey offers complete teaching and learning online resources all in one place. OneKey is all that instructors need to plan and administer courses, and OneKey is all that students need for anytime, anywhere access to online course material. Conveniently organized by textbook chapter, these resources save time and help students reinforce and apply what they have learned. OneKey is available in three course management platforms: Blackboard, CourseCompass, and WebCT.

Vango Notes

Study on the go with VangoNotes (www.VangoNotes.com), detailed chapter reviews in downloadable MP3 format. Now wherever you are and whatever you're doing, you can study on the go by listening to the following for each chapter of your textbook:

- Big Ideas: Your "need to know" for each chapter
- Practice Test: Gut check for the Big Ideas—tells you if you need to keep studying
- Key Terms: Audio "flashcards"—help you review key concepts and terms
- Rapid Review: Quick-drill session—use it right before your test

VangoNotes are **flexible**: Download all the material (or only the chapters you need) directly to your player. And *VangoNotes* are **efficient**: Use them in your car, at the gym, walking to class, wherever you go. So get yours today, and get studying.

OneKey Online Course Management Materials

OneKey offers complete teaching and learning online resources all in one place. OneKey is all that instructors need to plan and administer courses, and OneKey is all that students need for anytime, anywhere access to online course material. Conveniently organized by textbook chapter, these resources save time and help students reinforce and apply what they have learned. OneKey is available in three course management platforms: Blackboard, CourseCompass, and WebCT.

What's Key for Students?

- **Learning Modules** — Every section of all 19 chapters is supported by section-level pretest, content summary for review, learning application exercise, and post-test. Learning modules are a great way to study for exams and are not connected to the instructor grade book, offering unlimited practice.
- **Prentice Hall's Self-Assessment Library (S.A.L.)**
- **Research Navigator™** is the easiest way for students to start a research assignment or research paper. Complete with extensive help on the research process and four exclusive databases of credible and reliable source material—including the EBSCO Academic Journal and Abstract Database, *New York Times* Search by Subject Archive, "Best of the Web" Link Library, and *Financial Times* Article Archive and Company Financials—Research Navigator helps students quickly and efficiently make the most of their research time.

What's Key for Instructors?

Instructor Resource Center — Faculty can access all instructor resources in one place.

Companion Website

This Web site serves as a student study and review site. Accessible at www.prenhall.com/robbins, this site includes chapter quizzes and student PowerPoints.

Updated and Expanded Self-Assessments

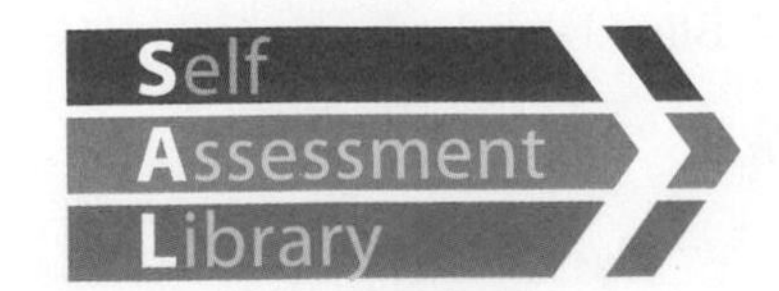

Prentice Hall's Self-Assessment Library (S.A.L.)

A hallmark of the Robbins series, S.A.L. is a unique learning tool that allows you to assess your knowledge, beliefs, feelings, and actions in regard to a wide range of personal skills, abilities, and interests. Self-Assessments have been integrated into each chapter, including a self-assessment at the beginning of each chapter.

S.A.L. helps students better understand their interpersonal and behavioral skills as they relate to the theoretical concepts presented in each chapter.

Highlights

- **68 research-based self-assessments** — Our entire collection of 68 instruments are from sources such as *Journal of Social Behavior and Personality, Harvard Business Review, Organizational Behavior: Experiences and Cases, Journal of Experimental Education, Journal of Applied Measurement,* and more.
- **Work–life and career focused** — All self-assessments are focused to help individuals better manage their work lives or careers. Organized in four parts, these instruments offer you one source from which to learn more about yourself.
- **Choice of Formats** — The Prentice Hall Self-Assessment Library is available in either CD-ROM or online format. It is integrated into the Robbins authored OneKey materials for use within the course-management context for his textbooks.
- **Save Feature** — Students can take the self-assessments an unlimited number of times, and save and print their scores for class discussion.
- **Scoring Key** — The key to the self-assessments has been edited by Steve Robbins to allow students to quickly make sense of the results of their score.
- **Instructor's Manual** — An *Instructor's Manual* guides instructors in interpreting self-assessments and helps facilitate better classroom discussion.

For the Thirteenth Edition, an access code for the online version of S.A.L is included with every new copy of the text. Additionally, faculty can select to Value Pack SAL in CD-ROM format or within your OneKey course management course offered in WebCT, Blackboard, or CourseCompass. SAL is also available for stand alone purchase.

Prentice Hall's Self-Assessment Library (S.A.L.) Table of Contents

I. WHAT ABOUT ME?

A. **Personality Insights**
1. What's My Basic Personality?
2. What's My Jungian 16-Type Personality?
3. Am I a Type-A?
4. How Well Do I Handle Ambiguity?
5. How Creative Am I?

B. **Values and Attitude Insights**
1. What Do I Value?
2. How Involved Am I In My Job?
3. How Satisfied Am I with My Job?
4. What Are My Attitudes Toward Workplace Diversity?

C. **Motivation Insights**
1. What Motivates Me?
2. What Are My Dominant Needs?
3. What Rewards Do I Value Most?
4. What's My View on the Nature of People?
5. What Are My Course Performance Goals?
6. How Confident Am I in My Abilities to Succeed?
7. What's My Attitude Toward Achievement?
8. How Sensitive Am I to Equity Differences?
9. What's My Job's Motivating Potential?
10. Do I Want an Enriched Job?

D. **Decision-Making Insights**
1. What's My Decision-Making Style?
2. Am I a Procrastinator?
3. How Do My Ethics Rate?

E. **Other**
1. What's My Emotional Intelligence Score?
2. What Time of Day Am I Most Productive?
3. How Good Am I at Personal Planning?
4. Am I Likely to Become an Entrepreneur?

II. WORKING WITH OTHERS

A. **Communication Skills**
1. What's My Face-to-Face Communication Style?
2. How Good Are My Listening Skills?

B. **Leadership and Team Skills**
1. What's My Leadership Style?
2. How Charismatic Am I?
3. Do I Trust Others?
4. Do Others See Me as Trusting?
5. How Good Am I at Disciplining Others?
6. How Good Am I at Building and Leading a Team?

C. **Power and Conflict Skills**
1. How Power-Oriented Am I?
2. What's My Preferred Type of Power?
3. How Good Am I at Playing Politics?
4. How Well Do I Manage Impressions?
5. What's My Preferred Conflict-Handling Style?
6. What's My Negotiating Style?

III. LIFE IN ORGANIZATIONS

A. **Organization Structure**
1. What Type of Organization Structure Do I Prefer?
2. How Willing Am I to Delegate?
3. How Good Am I at Giving Performance Feedback?

B. ***Careers***
1. What's the Right Organizational Culture for Me?
2. How Committed Am I to My Organization?
3. Am I Experiencing Work/Family Conflict?
4. How Motivated Am I to Manage?
5. Am I Well-Suited for a Career as a Global Manager?

C. **Change and Stress**
1. How Well Do I Respond to Turbulent Change?
2. How Stressful Is My Life?
3. Am I Burned Out?

IV. NEW ASSESSMENTS

A. **Personality Insights**
1. Am I a Narcissist?
2. Am I a Deliberate Decision Maker?
3. How Confident Am I in My Abilities to Succeed?
4. How Spiritual Am I?

B. **Motivation Insights**
1. Am I Engaged?

C. **Values and Attitude Insights**
1. What's My Attitude Toward Older People?
2. What Are My Gender Role Perceptions?

D. **Mood and Emotion Insights**
   1. How Are You Feeling Right Now?
   2. What's My Affect Intensity?

E. **Leadership and Team Skills**
   1. Do I Have a Negative Attitude Toward Working in Groups?
   2. What Is My Team Efficacy?
   3. Am I a Gossip?
   4. Am I an Ethical Leader?
   5. What Is My LPC Score?

F. **Organization Structure**
   1. Is My Workplace Political?
   2. Do I Like Bureaucracy?

G. **Other**
   1. How Much Do I Know about Organizational Behavior?
   2. How Much Do I Know about HRM?

ACKNOWLEDGMENTS

Getting this book into your hands was a team effort. It took faculty reviewers and a talented group of designers and production specialists, editorial personnel, and marketing and sales staff. Sincere appreciation goes to Bob Stretch, Southwestern College, for his skillful and dedicated work on the Instructor's Manual; Cara Cantarella, Acumen Enterprises, Inc., for her tireless work on perfecting the Test Item File; Kate Demarest, Carroll Community College, for her work on the imaginative Online Content; Nick Kaufman Productions for its professional work on the Videos; Brent Scott, Michigan State University, for his dedicated work on the updating of the Self-Assessment Library; and finally Donald Truxillo, Portland State University for his work on the VangoNotes.

More than 100 instructors reviewed parts or all of *Organizational Behavior, Thirteenth Edition.* Their comments, compliments, and suggestions have significantly improved the final product. The authors would like to extend their sincerest thank you to the following instructors:

David Abramis, California State University
Chris Adalikwu, Concordia College
Basil Adams, Notre Dame de Namur University
Vicky Aitken, St Louis Community College
Lois Antonen, CSUS
Lucy Arendt, University of Wisconsin, Green Bay
Mihran Aroian, University of Texas Austin
Christopher Barlow, DePaul University
Jacqui Bergman, Appalachian State University
Anne Berthelot, University of Texas at El Paso
David Bess, Shidler College of Business
Bruce Bikle, California State University Sacramento
Michael Bochenek, Elmhurst College
Alicia Boisnier, State University of New York
William H. Bommer, Cleveland State University
Bryan Bonner, University of Utah
Jessica Bradley, Clemson University
Dr. Jerry Bream, Empire State College/Niagara Frontier Center
Jeff Bruns, Bacone College
Pamela Buckle, Adelphi University
Patricia Buhler, Goldey-Beacom College
Edith Busija, University of Richmond
Michael Cafferky, Southern Adventist University
Scott Campbell, Francis Marion University
Elena Capella, University of San Francisco
Don Capener, Monmouth University
Dan Caprar, University of Iowa
Carol Carnevale, SUNY Empire State College
Donald W. Caudill, Bluefield College
Anthony Chelte, Midwestern State University
David Connelly, Western Illinois State University
Jeffrey Conte, San Diego State University
Jane Crabtree, Benedictine University
Suzanne Crampton, Grand Valley State University
Douglas Crawford, Wilson College
Michael Cruz, San Jose State University
Robert Cyr, Northwestern University
Nancy Da Silva, San Jose State University
Joseph Daly, Appalachian State University
Denise Daniels, Seattle Pacific University
Marie Dasborough, Oklahoma State University
Christine Day, Eastern Michigan University
Emmeline de Pillis, University of Hawaii Hilo
Roger Dean, Washington & Lee University
Robert DelCampo, University of New Mexico
Kristen Detienne, Brigham Young University
Cynthia Doil, Southern Illinois University
Jennifer Dose, Messiah College
David Duby, Liberty University
Ken Dunegan, Cleveland State University

Michael Dutch, Greensboro College
Lenny Favara, Central Christian College
Claudia Ferrante, U.S. Air Force Academy
Andy Fitorre, Nyack College
Kathleen Fleming, Averett University
Erin Fluegge University of Florida
Lucy Franks, Bellevue University
Diane Galbraith, Slippery Rock University
Janice Gates, Western Illinois University
James Gelatt, University of Maryland University College
Matthew Giblin, Southern Illinois University
Cindi Gilliland, The University of Arizona
David Glew, University of North Carolina at Wilmington
Leonard Glick, Northeastern University
Reginald Goodfellow, California State University
Richard Grover, University of Southern Maine
John Guarino, Averett University
Linda Hackleman, Concordia University Austin
Deniz Hackner, Tidewater Community College
Jonathon Halbesleben, University of Missouri-Columbia
Dan Hallock, University of North Alabama
Nell Hartley, Robert Morris University
Erin Hayes, George Washington University
Douglas Heeter, Ferris State University
David Henderson, University of Illinois at Chicago
Scott Henley, Oklahoma City University
Susan Herman, University of Alaska Fairbanks
James Hess, Ivy Tech Community College
Kim Hinrichs, Minnesota State University Mankato
Kathie Holland, University of Central Florida
Brooks Holtom, Georgetown University
Lisa Houts, California State University Fullerton
Paul Hudec, Milwaukee School of Engineering
Charlice Hurst, University of Florida
Warren Imada, Leeward Community College
Christine Jackson, Purdue University
Marsha Jackson, Bowie State University
Alan Jackson, Peru State College
Kathryn Jacobson, Arizona State University
Paul Jacques, Western Carolina University
Elizabeth Jamison, Radford University
Michael Johnson, University of Washington
David Jones, South University
Rusty Juban, Southeastern Illinois University
Carole L. Jurkiewicz, Louisiana State University
John Kammeyer-Mueller, University of Florida
Edward Kass, Saint Joseph's University
James Katzenstein, California State University
John Keiser, SUNY College at Brockport
Mark Kendrick, Methodist University
Mary Kern, Baruch College
Hal Kingsley, Erie Community College
Jeffrey Kobles, California State University San Marcos
Frederick Lane, Baruch College
Rebecca Lau, Virginia Polytechnic Institute and State University
Julia Levashina, Indiana State University Kokomo
Don Lifton, Ithaca College
Ginamarie Ligon, Villanova University
Beth Livingston, University of Florida
Barbara Low, Dominican University
Doyle Lucas, Anderson University
Alexandra Luong, University of Minnesota
Rick Maclin, Missouri Baptist University
Peter Madsen, Brigham Young University
J. David Martin, Midwestern State University
John Mattoon, State University of New York
Brenda McAleer, University of Maine at Augusta
Christina McCale, Regis Colllege
Don McCormick, California State University Northridge
Bonnie McNeely, Murray State University
Steven Meisel, La Salle University
Catherine Michael, St. Edwards University
Sandy Miles, Murray State University
Leann Mischel, Susquehanna University
Atul Mitra, University of Northern Iowa
Paula Morrow, Iowa State University
Mark Mortensen, Massachusetts Institute of Technology
Judy Nixon, University of Tennessee at Chattanooga
Jeffrey Nystrom, University of Colorado at Denver
Heather Odle-Dusseau, Clemson University
Miguel Olivas-Lujan, Lujan Clarion University
Laura Finnerty Paul, Skidmore College
Anette Pendergrass, Arkansas State University at Mountain Home
Jeff Peterson, University of Washington
Nanette Philibert, Missouri Southern State University
Larry Phillips, Indiana University Southbend
Eric Popkoff, Brooklyn College
Aarti Ramaswami, Indiana University Bloomington

Amy Randel, San Diego State University
Anne Reilly, Loyola University Chicago
Chris Roberts, University of Massachusetts Amherst
Sherry Robinson, Pennsylvania State University Hazleton
Andrea Roofe, Florida International University
Manjula Salimath, University of North Texas
Mary Saunders, Georgia Gwinnett College
Elizabeth Scott, Elizabeth City University
Mark Seabright, Western Oregon University
Joseph Seltzer, LaSalle University
John Shaw, Mississippi State University
John Sherlock, Western Carolina University
Heather Shields, Texas Tech University
Stuart Sidle, University of New Haven
Bret Simmons, University of Nevada Reno
Lynda St. Clair, Bryant University
John B. Stark, California State University, Bakersfield
Merwyn Strate, Purdue University
Karen Thompson, Sonoma State University
Linda Tibbetts, Antioch University McGregor
Ed Tomlinson, John Carroll University
Bob Trodella, Webster University
Albert Turner, Webster University
William Walker, University of Houston
Ian Walsh, Boston College
Charles F. Warren, Salem State College
Christa Washington, Saint Augustine
Jim Westerman, Appalachian State University
William J. White, Northwestern University
David Whitlock, Southwest Baptist University
Dan Wiljanen, Grand Valley State University
Dean Williamson, Brewton-Parker College
Hilda Williamson, Hampton University
Alice Wilson, Cedar Crest College
Craig Wishart, Fayetteville State University
Laura Wolfe, Louisiana State University
Melody Wollan, Eastern Illinois University
Evan Wood, Taylor University Fort Wayne
Chun-Sheng Yu, University of Houston-Victoria

Over the last editions this text has grown stronger with the contribution and feedback of the following instructors:

Janet Adams, Kennesaw State University
Cheryl Adkins, Longwood College
David Albritton, Northern Arizona University
Bradley Alge, Purdue University
Anke Arnaud, University of Central Florida
Gary Ballinger, Purdue University
Deborah Balser, University of Missouri at St. Louis
Joy Benson, University of Wisconsin at Green Bay
Lehman Benson III, University of Arizona
Richard Blackburn, University of North Carolina–Chapel Hill
Weldon Blake, Bethune-Cookman College
Bryan Bonner, University of Utah
Peggy Brewer, Eastern Kentucky University
Jim Breaugh, University of Missouri
Deborah Brown, North Carolina State University
Reginald Bruce, University of Louisville
Allen Bures, Radford University
Holly Buttner, University of North Carolina at Greensboro
David Carmichael, Oklahoma City University
Suzanne Chan, Tulane University
Bongsoon Cho, State University of New York–Buffalo
Savannah Clay, Central Piedmont Community College
Evelyn Dadzie, Clark Atlanta University
Emmeline de Pillis, University of Hawaii
Doug Dierking, University of Texas at Austin
Ceasar Douglas, Florida State University
Ken Dunegan, Cleveland State University
Kathleen Edwards, University of Texas at Austin
Berrin Erdogan, Portland State University
Ellen Fagenson Eland, George Mason University
Jann Freed, Central College
Carolyn Gardner, Radford University
Edward Fox, Wilkes University
Alison Fragale, University of North Carolina at Chapel Hill
Dean Frear, Wilkes University
Crissie Frye, Eastern Michigan University
Janice Gates, Western Illinois University
David Glew, University of North Carolina at Wilmington
Ellen Kaye Gehrke, Alliant International University
Joe Gerard, University of Wisconsin at Milwaukee
Donald Gibson, Fairfield University

Mary Giovannini, Truman State University
Jeffrey Goldstein, Adelphi University
Jodi Goodman, University of Connecticut
Claude Graeff, Illinois State University
W. Lee Grubb III, East Carolina University
Rebecca Guidice, University of Nevada at Las Vegas
Andra Gumbus, Sacred Heart University
Dan Hallock, University of North Alabama
Edward Hampton, University of Central Florida
Vernard Harrington, Radford University
Nell Hartley, Robert Morris University
Barbara Hassell, Indiana University, Kelley School of Business
Tom Head, Roosevelt University
Ted Herbert, Rollins College
Ronald Hester, Marymount University
Patricia Hewlin, Georgetown University
Chad Higgins, University of Washington
Kathie Holland, University of Central Florida
Elaine Hollensbe, University of Cincinnati
Kristin Holmberg-Wright, University of Wisconsin at Parkside
Abigail Hubbard, University of Houston
Stephen Humphrey, Florida State University
Gazi Islam, Tulane University
Elizabeth Jamison, Radford University
Stephen Jenner, California State University, Dominguez Hills
John Jermier, University of South Florida
Jack Johnson, Consumnes River College
Ray Jones, University of Pittsburgh
Anthony Jost, University of Delaware
Louis Jourdan, Clayton College
Marsha Katz, Governors State College
Robert Key, University of Phoenix
Sigrid Khorram, University of Texas at El Paso
Jack Kondrasuk, University of Portland
Leslie A. Korb, University of Nebraska at Kearney
Glen Kreiner, University of Cincinnati
James Kroeger, Cleveland State University
David Leuser, Plymouth State College
Benyamin Lichtenstein, University of Massachusetts at Boston
Robert Liden, University of Illinois at Chicago
Kathy Lund Dean, Idaho State University
Timothy A. Matherly, Florida State University
Lou Marino, University of Alabama
Paul Maxwell, Saint Thomas University
James McElroy, Iowa State University
Melony Mead, University of Phoenix
Nancy Meyer-Emerick, Cleveland State University
Janice Miller, University of Wisconsin at Milwaukee
Linda Morable, Richland College
Lori Muse, Western Michigan University
Padmakumar Nair, University of Texas at Dallas
Alison O'Brien, George Mason University
Kelly Ottman, University of Wisconsin at Milwaukee
Peg Padgett, Butler University
Jennifer Palthe, Western Michigan University
Dennis Passovoy, University of Texas at Austin
Karen Paul, Florida International University
Bryan Pesta, Cleveland State University
William Pinchuk, Rutgers University at Camden
Paul Preston, University of Montevallo
Scott Quatro, Grand Canyon University
Jere Ramsey, Cal Poly at San Luis Obispo
Clint Relyea, Arkansas State University
David Ritchey, University of Texas at Dallas
Christopher Ann Robinson-Easley, Governors State University
Tracey Rockett Hanft, University of Texas at Dallas
Joe Rode, Miami University
Bob Roller, LeTourneau University
Philip Roth, Clemson University
Craig Russell, University of Oklahoma at Norman
Andy Schaffer, North Georgia College and State University
Holly Schroth, University of California at Berkeley
Ted Shore, California State University at Long Beach
Daniel Sherman, University of Alabama, Huntsville
Stuart Sidle, DePaul University
Randy Sleeth, Virginia Commonwealth University
William Smith, Emporia State University
Kenneth Solano, Northeastern University
Shane Spiller, Morehead State University
John Stark, California State University at Bakersfield
Joo-Seng Tan, Cornell University
Tom Tudor, University of Arkansas at Little Rock
William D. Tudor, Ohio State University
Daniel Turban, University of Missouri
Jim Turner, Morehead State University
Leslie Tworoger, Nova Southeastern University
M.A. Viets, University of Vermont

Roger Volkema, American University
Barry Wisdom, Southeast Missouri State University
Jun Zhao, Governors State University
Lori Ziegler, University of Texas at Dallas
Gail Zwart, Riverside Community College

We owe a debt of gratitude to all those at Prentice Hall who have supported this text over the last 30 years and who have worked so hard on the development of this latest edition. On the development and editorial side, we want to thank Development Editor, Elisa Adams; Director of Development, Steve Deitmer; Editorial Assistant, Elizabeth Davis; Editor, Jennifer Collins; Editor in Chief, David Parker; and Editorial Director, Sally Yagan. On the design and production side, Senior Managing Editor Judy Leale did an outstanding job. Last but not least, we would like to thank Marketing Manager, Nikki Jones, and Director of Marketing, Patrice Jones and their sales staff who have been selling this book over its many editions. Thank you for the attention you've given this book.

What Is Organizational Behavior?

The stellar universe is not so difficult of comprehension as the real actions of other people.

—Writer Marcel Proust

LEARNING OBJECTIVES

After studying this chapter, you should be able to:

1 Demonstrate the importance of interpersonal skills in the workplace.

2 Describe the manager's functions, roles, and skills.

3 Define *organizational behavior (OB)*.

4 Show the value to OB of systematic study.

5 Identify the major behavioral science disciplines that contribute to OB.

6 Demonstrate why there are few absolutes in OB.

7 Identify the challenges and opportunities managers have in applying OB concepts.

8 Compare the three levels of analysis in this book's OB model.

Managers make a lot of mistakes. Some come from inexperience. Others reflect lack of knowledge. And some are just dumb.

But few mistakes could be considered as stupid as what managers of home security company Alarm One, Inc., did.

As part of a "team building" exercise, employees were paddled with rival companies' yard signs as part of a contest that pitted sales teams against one another. The winners threw pies at the losers, fed them baby food, made them wear diapers, and, yes, spanked them. Sometimes coworkers made comments such as, "bend over baby," and "you've been a bad girl."

Is That Any Way to Treat an Employee?

Outside the "team building" contests, Alarm One also routinely spanked employees who were late for work.

One of the employees who was spanked—Janet Orlando (see photo above)—was so humiliated that she quit shortly after the episode and later decided to sue Alarm One.

During the trial against Alarm One, in his closing arguments, Orlando's attorney said, "No reasonable middle-aged woman would want to be put up there before a group of young men, turned around to show her buttocks, get spanked and called abusive names, and told it was to increase sales and motivate employees."

It's not surprising that a U.S. jury of six men and six women ruled in favor of Orlando, awarding her more than she'd asked for: $500,000 in compensatory damages and $1.2 million in punitive damages.

Why did Alarm One do this in the first place? The California, company defended the spankings by saying they were part of a voluntary program to build camaraderie and were not discriminatory because they were given to both male and female workers.

After the trial, Orlando and Alarm One agreed to a payment of $1.4 million, in lieu of Alarm One's appealing. As of now, though, the company has not paid Orlando a dime, forcing her to sue all over again. "These guys have lied since day one," says Orlando.[1] ■

You might think incidents like the one at Alarm One illustrate that managing people is all about common sense. After all, you don't need a textbook to tell you not to spank employees. However, as we'll see, not all aspects of management are common sense. Mistakes like spanking employees are visible and obvious mistakes, but managers commonly make other mistakes due to their lack of knowledge. This is where organizational behavior comes into play.

To see how far common sense gets you, try the following from the Self-Assessment Library.

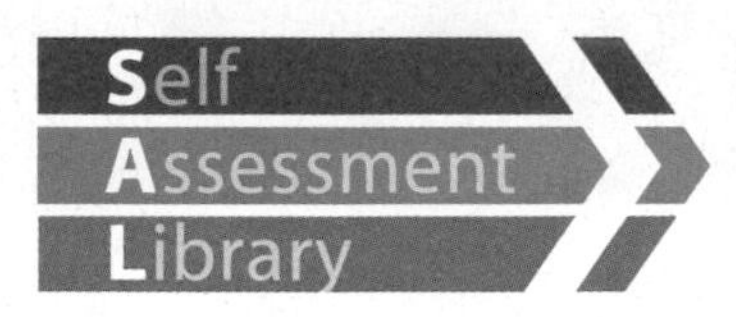

HOW MUCH DO I KNOW ABOUT ORGANIZATIONAL BEHAVIOR?

In the Self-Assessment Library (available on CD and online), take assessment IV.G.1 (How Much Do I Know About OB?) and answer the following questions:

1. *How did you score? Are you surprised by your score?*
2. *How much of effective management do you think is common sense? Did your score on the test change your answer to this question?*

The Importance of Interpersonal Skills

1 Demonstrate the importance of interpersonal skills in the workplace.

Although practicing managers have long understood the importance of interpersonal skills to managerial effectiveness, business schools have been slower to get the message. Until the late 1980s, business school curricula emphasized the technical aspects of management, specifically focusing on economics, accounting, finance, and quantitative techniques. Course work in human behavior and people skills received minimal attention relative to the technical aspects of management. Over the past 2 decades, however, business faculty have come to realize the importance that an understanding of human behavior plays in determining a manager's effectiveness, and required courses on people skills have been added to many curricula. As the director of leadership at Massachusetts Institute of Technology's Sloan

Succeeding in management today requires good people skills. Communication and leadership skills distinguish managers such as Jeffrey Immelt who rise to the top of their profession. Immelt, CEO of General Electric, joined the company in corporate marketing in 1982 and spent 20 years in sales, marketing, and product development leadership positions before moving into GE's top management job. Outgoing and adept at building relationships, Immelt travels the world, meeting with customers, employees, suppliers, and stockholders. In this photo, Immelt interacts with schoolchildren in a reading program funded by GE.

School of Management recently put it, "M.B.A. students may get by on their technical and quantitative skills the first couple of years out of school. But soon, leadership and communication skills come to the fore in distinguishing the managers whose careers really take off."[2]

Recognition of the importance of developing managers' interpersonal skills is closely tied to the need for organizations to get and keep high-performing employees. Regardless of labor market conditions, outstanding employees are always in short supply.[3] Companies with reputations as good places to work have a big advantage. A study of the U.S. workforce, for example, found that wages and fringe benefits are not the main reasons people like their jobs or stay with an employer. Far more important is the quality of the employee's job and the supportiveness of the work environment.[4] So having managers with good interpersonal skills is likely to make the workplace more pleasant, which, in turn, makes it easier to hire and keep qualified people. In addition, creating a pleasant workplace appears to make good economic sense. For instance, companies with reputations as good places to work (such as the companies that are included among the "Best Companies to Work for in America") have been found to generate superior financial performance.[5]

We have come to understand that technical skills are necessary, but they are not enough to succeed in management. In today's increasingly competitive and demanding workplace, managers can't succeed on their technical skills alone. They also have to have good people skills. This book has been written to help both managers and potential managers develop those people skills.

What Managers Do

2 *Describe the manager's functions, roles, and skills.*

Let's begin by briefly defining the terms *manager* and *organization*—the place where managers work. Then let's look at the manager's job; specifically, what do managers do?

Managers get things done through other people. They make decisions, allocate resources, and direct the activities of others to attain goals. Managers do their work in an **organization**, which is a consciously coordinated social unit, composed of two or more people, that functions on a relatively continuous basis to achieve a common goal or set of goals. On the basis of this definition, manufacturing and service firms are organizations, and so are schools, hospitals, churches, military units, retail stores, police departments, and local, state, and government agencies. The people who oversee the activities of others and who are responsible for attaining goals in these organizations are managers (although they're sometimes called *administrators*, especially in not-for-profit organizations).

Management Functions

In the early part of the twentieth century, a French industrialist by the name of Henri Fayol wrote that all managers perform five management functions: planning, organizing, commanding, coordinating, and controlling.[6] Today, we have condensed these to four: planning, organizing, leading, and controlling.

Because organizations exist to achieve goals, someone has to define those goals and the means for achieving them; management is that someone. The **planning** function encompasses defining an organization's goals, establishing an overall strategy for achieving those goals, and developing a comprehensive set of plans to integrate and coordinate activities. Evidence indicates that this function is the one that increases the most as managers move from lower-level to midlevel management.[7]

Managers are also responsible for designing an organization's structure. We call this function **organizing**. It includes determining what tasks are to be done, who is to do them, how the tasks are to be grouped, who reports to whom, and where decisions are to be made.

Every organization contains people, and it is management's job to direct and coordinate those people. This is the **leading** function. When managers motivate employees, direct the activities of others, select the most effective communication channels, or resolve conflicts among members, they're engaging in leading.

The final function managers perform is **controlling**. To ensure that things are going as they should, management must monitor the organization's performance. Actual performance is then compared with the previously set goals. If there are any significant deviations, it is management's job to get the organization back on track. This monitoring, comparing, and potential correcting is what is meant by the controlling function.

So, using the functional approach, the answer to the question "What do managers do?" is that they plan, organize, lead, and control.

Management Roles

In the late 1960s, Henry Mintzberg, a graduate student at Massachusetts Institute of Technology, undertook a careful study of five executives to determine what those managers did on their jobs. On the basis of his observations, Mintzberg concluded that managers perform 10 different, highly interrelated roles—or sets of behaviors—attributable to their jobs.[8] As shown in Exhibit 1-1, these 10 roles can be grouped as being primarily (1) interpersonal, (2) informational, and (3) decisional.

Interpersonal Roles All managers are required to perform duties that are ceremonial and symbolic in nature. For instance, when the president of a college hands out diplomas at commencement or a factory supervisor gives a group of students a tour of the plant, he or she is acting in a *figurehead* role. All

Exhibit 1-1 Mintzberg's Managerial Roles

Role	Description
Interpersonal	
Figurehead	Symbolic head; required to perform a number of routine duties of a legal or social nature
Leader	Responsible for the motivation and direction of employees
Liaison	Maintains a network of outside contacts who provide favors and information
Informational	
Monitor	Receives a wide variety of information; serves as nerve center of internal and external information of the organization
Disseminator	Transmits information received from outsiders or from other employees to members of the organization
Spokesperson	Transmits information to outsiders on organization's plans, policies, actions, and results; serves as expert on organization's industry
Decisional	
Entrepreneur	Searches organization and its environment for opportunities and initiates projects to bring about change
Disturbance handler	Responsible for corrective action when organization faces important, unexpected disturbances
Resource allocator	Makes or approves significant organizational decisions
Negotiator	Responsible for representing the organization at major negotiations

Source: Adapted from *The Nature of Managerial Work* by H. Mintzberg. Copyright © 1973 by H. Mintzberg. Reprinted by permission of Pearson Education.

managers also have a *leadership* role. This role includes hiring, training, motivating, and disciplining employees. The third role within the interpersonal grouping is the *liaison* role. Mintzberg described this activity as contacting outsiders who provide the manager with information. These may be individuals or groups inside or outside the organization. The sales manager who obtains information from the quality-control manager in his or her own company has an internal liaison relationship. When that sales manager has contacts with other sales executives through a marketing trade association, he or she has an outside liaison relationship.

Informational Roles All managers, to some degree, collect information from outside organizations and institutions. Typically, they obtain it by reading magazines and talking with other people to learn of changes in the public's tastes, what competitors may be planning, and the like. Mintzberg called this the

managers *Individuals who achieve goals through other people.*

organization *A consciously coordinated social unit, composed of two or more people, that functions on a relatively continuous basis to achieve a common goal or set of goals.*

planning *A process that includes defining goals, establishing strategy, and developing plans to coordinate activities.*

organizing *Determining what tasks are to be done, who is to do them, how the tasks are to be grouped, who reports to whom, and where decisions are to be made.*

leading *A function that includes motivating employees, directing others, selecting the most effective communication channels, and resolving conflicts.*

controlling *Monitoring activities to ensure that they are being accomplished as planned and correcting any significant deviations.*

monitor role. Managers also act as a conduit to transmit information to organizational members. This is the *disseminator* role. In addition, managers perform a *spokesperson* role when they represent the organization to outsiders.

Decisional Roles Mintzberg identified four roles that revolve around making choices. In the *entrepreneur* role, managers initiate and oversee new projects that will improve their organization's performance. As *disturbance handlers*, managers take corrective action in response to unforeseen problems. As *resource allocators*, managers are responsible for allocating human, physical, and monetary resources. Finally, managers perform a *negotiator* role, in which they discuss issues and bargain with other units to gain advantages for their own unit.

Management Skills

Still another way of considering what managers do is to look at the skills or competencies they need to achieve their goals. Robert Katz has identified three essential management skills: technical, human, and conceptual.[9]

Technical Skills **Technical skills** encompass the ability to apply specialized knowledge or expertise. When you think of the skills of professionals such as civil engineers or oral surgeons, you typically focus on their technical skills. Through extensive formal education, they have learned the special knowledge and practices of their field. Of course, professionals don't have a monopoly on technical skills, and not all technical skills have to be learned in schools or other formal training programs. All jobs require some specialized expertise, and many people develop their technical skills on the job.

Human Skills The ability to work with, understand, and motivate other people, both individually and in groups, defines **human skills**. Many people are technically proficient but interpersonally incompetent. They might be poor listeners, unable to understand the needs of others, or have difficulty managing conflicts. Because managers get things done through other people, they must have good human skills to communicate, motivate, and delegate.

Conceptual Skills Managers must have the mental ability to analyze and diagnose complex situations. These tasks require **conceptual skills**. Decision making, for instance, requires managers to identify problems, develop alternative solutions to correct those problems, evaluate those alternative solutions, and select the best one. Managers can be technically and interpersonally competent yet still fail because of an inability to rationally process and interpret information.

Effective Versus Successful Managerial Activities

Fred Luthans and his associates looked at the issue of what managers do from a somewhat different perspective.[10] They asked the question "Do managers who move up the quickest in an organization do the same activities and with the same emphasis as managers who do the best job?" You would tend to think that the managers who are the most effective in their jobs would also be the ones who are promoted the fastest. But that's not what appears to happen.

Luthans and his associates studied more than 450 managers. What they found was that these managers all engaged in four managerial activities:

1. **Traditional management.** Decision making, planning, and controlling
2. **Communication.** Exchanging routine information and processing paperwork

Exhibit 1-2 Allocation of Activities by Time

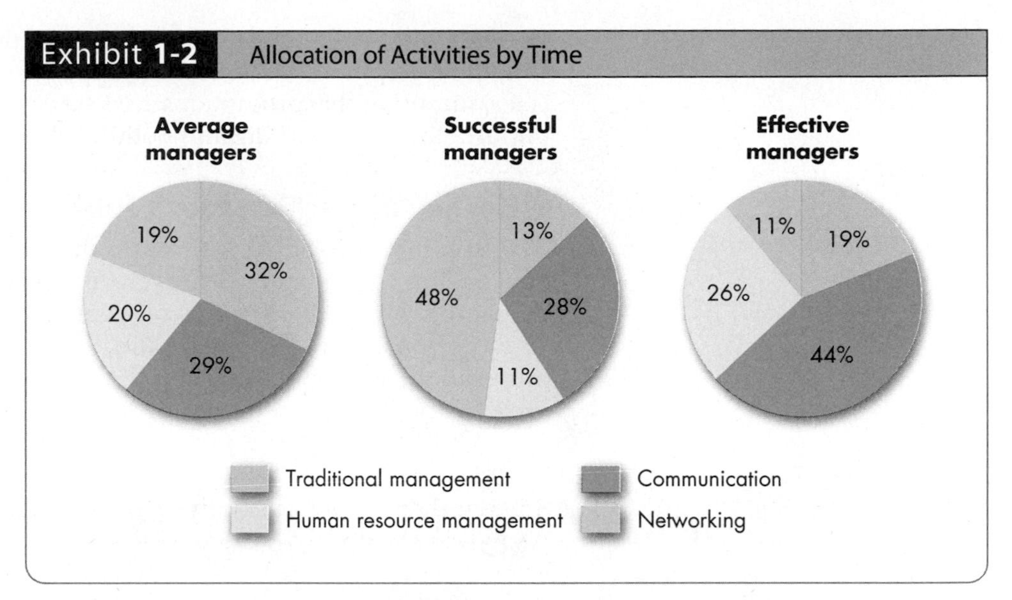

Source: Based on F. Luthans, R. M. Hodgetts, and S. A. Rosenkrantz, *Real Managers* (Cambridge, MA: Ballinger, 1988).

3. **Human resource management.** Motivating, disciplining, managing conflict, staffing, and training
4. **Networking.** Socializing, politicking, and interacting with outsiders

The "average" manager in the study spent 32 percent of his or her time in traditional management activities, 29 percent communicating, 20 percent in human resource management activities, and 19 percent networking. However, the amount of time and effort that different managers spent on those four activities varied a great deal. Specifically, as shown in Exhibit 1-2, managers who were *successful* (defined in terms of the speed of promotion within their organization) had a very different emphasis than managers who were *effective* (defined in terms of the quantity and quality of their performance and the satisfaction and commitment of their employees). Among successful managers, networking made the largest relative contribution to success, and human resource management activities made the least relative contribution. Among effective managers, communication made the largest relative contribution and networking the least. More recent studies, conducted in a variety of countries (Australia, Israel, Italy, Japan, and the United States), further confirm the link between networking and success within an organization.[11] For example, one study found that Australian managers who actively networked received more promotions and enjoyed other rewards associated with career success. And the connection between communication and effective managers is also clear. A study of 410 U.S. managers indicates that managers who seek information from colleagues and employees—even if it's negative—and who explain their decisions are the most effective.[12]

This research adds important insights to our knowledge of what managers do. On average, managers spend approximately 20 to 30 percent of their time on each of the four activities: traditional management, communication, human resource management, and networking. However, successful managers don't

technical skills *The ability to apply specialized knowledge or expertise.*

human skills *The ability to work with, understand, and motivate other people, both individually and in groups.*

conceptual skills *The mental ability to analyze and diagnose complex situations.*

give the same emphasis to each of those activities as do effective managers. In fact, their emphases are almost the opposite. This finding challenges the historical assumption that promotions are based on performance, and it illustrates the importance of networking and political skills in getting ahead in organizations.

A Review of the Manager's Job

One common thread runs through the functions, roles, skills, activities, and approaches to management: Each recognizes the paramount importance of managing people. Regardless of whether it is called "the leading function," "interpersonal roles," "human skills," or "human resource management, communication, and networking activities," it's clear that managers need to develop their people skills if they're going to be effective and successful.

Enter Organizational Behavior

We've made the case for the importance of people skills. But neither this book nor the discipline on which it is based is called "people skills." The term that is widely used to describe the discipline is *organizational behavior.*

3 *Define* organizational behavior (OB).

Organizational behavior (often abbreviated OB) is a field of study that investigates the impact that individuals, groups, and structure have on behavior within organizations, for the purpose of applying such knowledge toward improving an organization's effectiveness. That's a mouthful, so let's break it down.

Organizational behavior is a field of study, meaning that it is a distinct area of expertise with a common body of knowledge. What does it study? It studies three determinants of behavior in organizations: individuals, groups, and structure. In addition, OB applies the knowledge gained about individuals, groups, and the effect of structure on behavior in order to make organizations work more effectively.

Microsoft understands how organizational behavior affects an organization's performance. The company maintains good employee relationships by providing a great work environment, generous benefits, and challenging jobs. The two-story wall painting shown here is one of 4,500 pieces of contemporary art displayed at Microsoft's corporate campus for employees' enjoyment. Other benefits, such as valet parking, dry-cleaning and laundry service, free grocery delivery, and take-home meals, help employees focus on their work. At Microsoft, employee loyalty and productivity are high, contribuing to the company's growth to $44 billion in revenues since its founding in 1975.

To sum up our definition, OB is concerned with the study of what people do in an organization and how their behavior affects the organization's performance. And because OB is concerned specifically with employment-related situations, you should not be surprised to find that it emphasizes behavior as related to concerns such as jobs, work, absenteeism, employment turnover, productivity, human performance, and management.

There is increasing agreement as to the components or topics that constitute the subject area of OB. Although there is still considerable debate as to the relative importance of each, there appears to be general agreement that OB includes the core topics of motivation, leader behavior and power, interpersonal communication, group structure and processes, learning, attitude development and perception, change processes, conflict, work design, and work stress.[13]

Complementing Intuition with Systematic Study

Each of us is a student of behavior. Since our earliest years, we've watched the actions of others and have attempted to interpret what we see. Whether or not you've explicitly thought about it before, you've been "reading" people almost all your life. You watch what others do and try to explain to yourself why they have engaged in their behavior. In addition, you've attempted to predict what they might do under different sets of conditions. Unfortunately, your casual or commonsense approach to reading others can often lead to erroneous predictions. However, you can improve your predictive ability by supplementing your intuitive opinions with a more systematic approach.

4 *Show the value to OB of systematic study.*

The systematic approach used in this book will uncover important facts and relationships and will provide a base from which more accurate predictions of behavior can be made. Underlying this systematic approach is the belief that behavior is not random. Rather, there are certain fundamental consistencies underlying the behavior of all individuals that can be identified and then modified to reflect individual differences.

These fundamental consistencies are very important. Why? Because they allow predictability. Behavior is generally predictable, and the *systematic study* of behavior is a means to making reasonably accurate predictions. When we use the phrase **systematic study**, we mean looking at relationships, attempting to attribute causes and effects, and basing our conclusions on scientific evidence—that is, on data gathered under controlled conditions and measured and interpreted in a reasonably rigorous manner. (See Appendix A for a basic review of research methods used in studies of organizational behavior.)

An approach that complements systematic study is evidence-based management. **Evidence-based management (EBM)** involves basing managerial decisions

organizational behavior (OB) *A field of study that investigates the impact that individuals, groups, and structure have on behavior within organizations, for the purpose of applying such knowledge toward improving an organization's effectiveness.*

systematic study *Looking at relationships, attempting to attribute causes and effects, and drawing conclusions based on scientific evidence.*

evidence-based management (EBM) *Basing managerial decisions on the best available scientific evidence.*

MYTH OR SCIENCE? "Preconceived Notions Versus Substantive Evidence"

Assume that you signed up to take an introductory college course in finance. On the first day of class, your instructor asks you to take out a piece of paper and answer the following question: "What is the net present value at a discount rate of 12 percent per year of an investment made by spending $1,000,000 this year on a portfolio of stocks, with an initial dividend next year of $100,000 and an expected rate of dividend growth thereafter of 4 percent per year?" It's unlikely you'd be able to answer that question without some instruction in finance.

Now, change the scenario. You're in an introductory course in organizational behavior. On the first day of class, your instructor asks you to write the answer to the following question: "What's the most effective way to motivate employees at work?" At first you might feel a bit of reluctance, but once you began writing, you'd likely have no problem coming up with suggestions on motivation.

That's one of the main challenges of teaching, or taking, a course in OB. You enter an OB course with a lot of *preconceived notions* that you accept as *facts*. You think you already know a lot about human behavior.[14] That's not typically true in finance, accounting, or even marketing. So, in contrast to many other disciplines, OB not only introduces you to a comprehensive set of concepts and theories; it has to deal with a lot of commonly accepted "facts" about human behavior and organizations that you've acquired over the years. Some examples might include: "You can't teach an old dog new tricks," "leaders are born, not made," and "two heads are better than one." But these "facts" aren't necessarily true. So one of the objectives of a course in organizational behavior is to *replace* popularly held notions, often accepted without question, with science-based conclusions.

As you'll see in this book, the field of OB is built on decades of research. This research provides a body of substantive evidence that is able to replace preconceived notions. Throughout this book, we've included boxes titled "Myth or Science?" They call your attention to some of the most popular of these notions or myths about organizational behavior. We use the boxes to show how OB research has disproved them or, in some cases, shown them to be true. Hopefully, you'll find these boxes interesting. But more importantly, they'll help remind you that the study of human behavior at work is a science and that you need to be vigilant about "seat-of-the-pants" explanations of work-related behaviors. ■

on the best available scientific evidence. We'd want doctors to make decisions about patient care based on the latest available evidence, and EBM argues that we want managers to do the same. That means managers must become more scientific in how they think about management problems. For example, a manager might pose a managerial question, search for the best available evidence, and apply the relevant information to the question or case at hand. You might think it's difficult to argue against this (what manager would argue that decisions shouldn't be based on evidence?), but the vast majority of management decisions are still made "on the fly," with little or systematic study of available evidence.[15]

Systematic study and EBM add to **intuition**, or those "gut feelings" about "why I do what I do" and "what makes others tick." Of course, a systematic approach does not mean that the things you have come to believe in an unsystematic way are necessarily incorrect. As Jack Welch, the former CEO of General Electric, noted, "The trick, of course, is to know when to go with your gut." If we make all decisions with intuition or gut instinct, we're likely making decisions with incomplete information—sort of like making an investment decision with only half the data.

The limits of relying on intuition are made worse by the fact that we tend to overestimate the accuracy of what we think we know. A recent survey revealed that 86 percent of managers thought their organization was treating their employees well. However, only 55 percent of the employees thought they were well treated.

We find a similar problem in chasing the business and popular media for management wisdom. The business press tends to be dominated by fads. As one writer put it, "Every few years, new companies succeed, and they are scrutinized for the underlying truths they might reveal. But often there is no underlying truth; the companies just happened to be in the right place at the right time."[16] Although we try to avoid it, we might also fall into this trap. It's not that the business press stories are all wrong; it's that without a systematic approach, it's hard to separate the wheat from the chaff.

Some of the conclusions we make in this text, based on reasonably substantive research findings, will only support what you always knew was true. But you'll also be exposed to research evidence that runs counter to what you may have thought was common sense. One of the objectives of this text is to encourage you to enhance your intuitive views of behavior with a systematic analysis, in the belief that such analysis will improve your accuracy in explaining and predicting behavior.

We're not advising that you throw your intuition, or all the business press, out the window. Nor are we arguing that research is always right. Researchers make mistakes, too. What we are advising is to use evidence as much as possible to inform your intuition and experience. That is the promise of OB.

Disciplines That Contribute to the OB Field

Organizational behavior is an applied behavioral science that is built on contributions from a number of behavioral disciplines. The predominant areas are psychology and social psychology, sociology, and anthropology. As you shall learn, psychology's contributions have been mainly at the individual or micro level of analysis, while the other disciplines have contributed to our understanding of macro concepts such as group processes and organization. Exhibit 1-3 is an overview of the major contributions to the study of organizational behavior.

5 *Identify the major behavioral science disciplines that contribute to OB.*

Psychology

Psychology is the science that seeks to measure, explain, and sometimes change the behavior of humans and other animals. Psychologists concern themselves with studying and attempting to understand individual behavior. Those who have contributed and continue to add to the knowledge of OB are learning theorists, personality theorists, counseling psychologists, and, most important, industrial and organizational psychologists.

Early industrial/organizational psychologists concerned themselves with the problems of fatigue, boredom, and other factors relevant to working

intuition *A gut feeling not necessarily supported by research.*

psychology *The science that seeks to measure, explain, and sometimes change the behavior of humans and other animals.*

Exhibit 1-3 Toward an OB Discipline

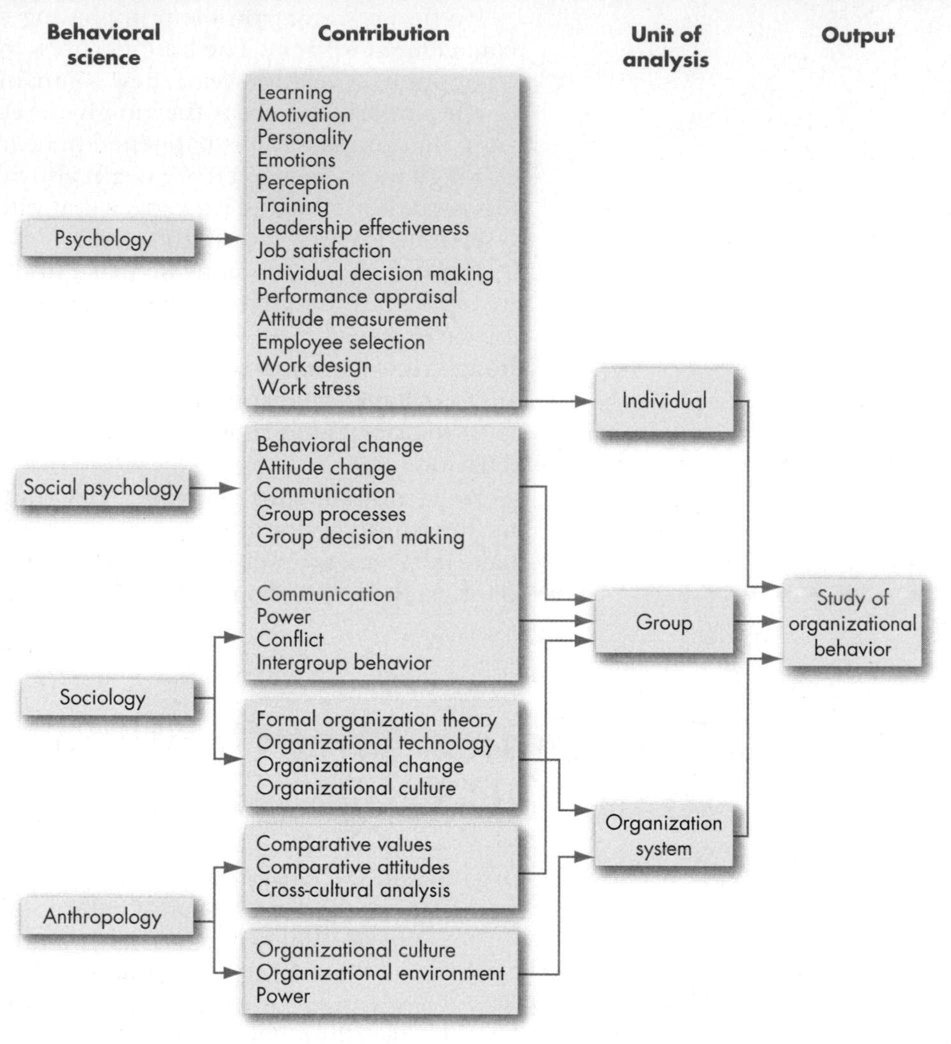

Behavioral science | Contribution | Unit of analysis | Output

Psychology
Learning
Motivation
Personality
Emotions
Perception
Training
Leadership effectiveness
Job satisfaction
Individual decision making
Performance appraisal
Attitude measurement
Employee selection
Work design
Work stress
Individual

Social psychology
Behavioral change
Attitude change
Communication
Group processes
Group decision making

Sociology
Communication
Power
Conflict
Intergroup behavior
Group

Formal organization theory
Organizational technology
Organizational change
Organizational culture

Anthropology
Comparative values
Comparative attitudes
Cross-cultural analysis

Organizational culture
Organizational environment
Power
Organization system

Study of organizational behavior

conditions that could impede efficient work performance. More recently, their contributions have been expanded to include learning, perception, personality, emotions, training, leadership effectiveness, needs and motivational forces, job satisfaction, decision-making processes, performance appraisals, attitude measurement, employee-selection techniques, work design, and job stress.

Social Psychology

Social psychology blends concepts from both psychology and sociology, though it is generally considered a branch of psychology. It focuses on peoples' influence on one another. One major area receiving considerable investigation from social psychologists has been *change*—how to implement it and how to reduce barriers to its acceptance. In addition, we find social psychologists making significant contributions in the areas of measuring, understanding, and changing attitudes; communication patterns; and building trust. Finally, social psychologists have made important contributions to our study of group behavior, power, and conflict.

OB *In the News*

Other Disciplines Make Use of OB Concepts

It may surprise you to learn that, increasingly, other business disciplines are employing OB concepts.

Of the business disciplines, marketing has the closest overlap with OB. One of the primary areas of marketing is consumer research, and trying to predict consumer behavior is not that different from trying to predict employee behavior. Both require an understanding of the dynamics and underlying causes of human behavior, and there's a lot of correspondence between the disciplines.

What's perhaps more surprising is the degree to which the so-called hard disciplines are making use of soft OB concepts. Behavioral finance, behavioral accounting, and behavioral economics (also called *economic psychology*) all have grown in importance and interest in the past several years.

On reflection, this shouldn't be so surprising. Your common sense will tell you that humans are not perfectly rational creatures, and in many cases, our actions don't conform to a rational model of behavior. Although some elements of irrationality are incorporated into economic thought, increasingly, finance, accounting, and economics researchers find it useful to draw from OB concepts.

For example, investors have a tendency to place more weight on private information (information that only they, or a limited group of people, know) than on public information, even when there is reason to believe that the public information is more accurate. To understand this phenomenon, finance researchers use OB concepts. In addition, behavioral accounting research might study how feedback influences auditors' behavior, or the functional and dysfunctional implications of earnings warnings on investor behavior.

The point is that while you take separate courses in various business disciplines, the lines between them are increasingly being blurred as researchers draw from common disciplines to explain behavior. We think that's a good thing because it more accurately matches the way managers actually work, think, and behave.

Source: Based on W. Chuang and B. Lee, "An Empirical Evaluation of the Overconfidence Hypothesis," *Journal of Banking and Finance*, September 2006, pp. 2489–2515; and A. R. Drake, J. Wong, and S. B. Salter, "Empowerment, Motivation, and Performance: Examining the Impact of Feedback and Incentives on Nonmanagement Employees," *Behavioral Research in Accounting* 19 (2007), pp. 71–89.

Sociology

While psychology focuses on the individual, **sociology** studies people in relation to their social environment or culture. Sociologists have contributed to OB through their study of group behavior in organizations, particularly formal and complex organizations. Perhaps most importantly, sociology has contributed to research on organizational culture, formal organization theory and structure, organizational technology, communications, power, and conflict.

Anthropology

Anthropology is the study of societies to learn about human beings and their activities. For instance, anthropologists' work on cultures and environments has helped us understand differences in fundamental values, attitudes, and behavior between people in different countries and within different organizations. Much of our current understanding of organizational culture, organizational environments, and differences between national cultures is a result of the work of anthropologists or those using their methods.

social psychology *An area of psychology that blends concepts from psychology and sociology and that focuses on the influence of people on one another.*

sociology *The study of people in relation to their social environment or culture.*

anthropology *The study of societies to learn about human beings and their activities.*

There Are Few Absolutes in OB

6 *Demonstrate why there are few absolutes in OB.*

There are few, if any, simple and universal principles that explain organizational behavior. There are laws in the physical sciences—chemistry, astronomy, physics—that are consistent and apply in a wide range of situations. They allow scientists to generalize about the pull of gravity or to be confident about sending astronauts into space to repair satellites. But as a noted behavioral researcher aptly concluded, "God gave all the easy problems to the physicists." Human beings are complex. Because we are not alike, our ability to make simple, accurate, and sweeping generalizations is limited. Two people often act very differently in the same situation, and the same person's behavior changes in different situations. For instance, not everyone is motivated by money, and you may behave differently at church on Sunday than you did at a party the night before.

That doesn't mean, of course, that we can't offer reasonably accurate explanations of human behavior or make valid predictions. However, it does mean that OB concepts must reflect situational, or contingency, conditions. We can say that *x* leads to *y*, but only under conditions specified in *z*—the **contingency variables**. The science of OB was developed by applying general concepts to a particular situation, person, or group. For example, OB scholars would avoid stating that everyone likes complex and challenging work (the general concept). Why? Because not everyone wants a challenging job. Some people prefer the routine over the varied or the simple over the complex. In other words, a job that is appealing to one person may not be to another, so the appeal of the job is contingent on the person who holds it.

As you proceed through this book, you'll encounter a wealth of research-based theories about how people behave in organizations. But don't expect to find a lot of straightforward cause-and-effect relationships. There aren't many! Organizational behavior theories mirror the subject matter with which they deal. People are complex and complicated, and so too must be the theories developed to explain their actions.

Challenges and Opportunities for OB

7 *Identify the challenges and opportunities managers have in applying OB concepts.*

Understanding organizational behavior has never been more important for managers than it is today. A quick look at a few of the dramatic changes now taking place in organizations supports this claim. For instance, the typical employee in many developed countries is getting older; more and more women and people of color are in the workplace; corporate downsizing and the heavy use of temporary workers are severing the bonds of loyalty that historically tied many employees to their employers; and global competition is requiring employees to become more flexible and to learn to cope with rapid change. The war on terror has brought to the forefront the challenges of working with and managing people during uncertain times.

In short, there are a lot of challenges and opportunities today for managers to use OB concepts. In this section, we review some of the most critical issues confronting managers for which OB offers solutions—or at least some meaningful insights toward solutions.

Responding to Globalization

Organizations are no longer constrained by national borders. Burger King is owned by a British firm, and McDonald's sells hamburgers in Moscow. ExxonMobil, a so-called American company, receives almost 75 percent of its revenues from sales

Pizza Hut is responding to globalization by expanding its restaurants and delivery services worldwide. Pizza Hut introduced pizza to Chinese consumers in 1990. Today, Pizza Hut management targets mainland China as the number-one market for new restaurant development because of the country's enormous growth potential. In this photo, Pizza Hut passes out free samples in Nanjing to promote its delivery service. Managers expect delivery to become increasingly important as economic activity continues to expand, placing increased time demands on Chinese families.

outside the United States. New employees at the Finland-based phone maker Nokia are increasingly being recruited from India, China, and other developing countries—with non-Finns now outnumbering Finns at Nokia's renowned research center in Helsinki. And all major automobile manufacturers now build cars outside their borders; for instance, Honda builds cars in the United States, Ford in Brazil, Volkswagen in Mexico, and both Mercedes and BMW in South Africa.

These examples illustrate that the world has become a global village. In the process, the manager's job is changing.

Increased Foreign Assignments If you're a manager, you are increasingly likely to find yourself in a foreign assignment—transferred to your employer's operating division or subsidiary in another country. Once there, you'll have to manage a workforce that is likely to be very different in needs, aspirations, and attitudes from those you are used to back home.

Working with People from Different Cultures Even in your own country, you're going to find yourself working with bosses, peers, and other employees who were born and raised in different cultures. What motivates you may not motivate them. Or your style of communication may be straightforward and open, but they may find this approach uncomfortable and threatening. To work effectively with people from different cultures, you need to understand how their culture, geography, and religion have shaped them and how to adapt your management style to their differences.

Coping with Anticapitalism Backlash Capitalism's focus on efficiency, growth, and profits may be generally accepted in Australia, Hong Kong, and the United States, but these capitalistic values aren't nearly as popular in places like

contingency variables *Situational factors: variables that moderate the relationship between two or more other variables.*

France, the Middle East, and the Scandinavian countries. For instance, because Finland's egalitarian values have created a "soak the rich" mentality among politicians, traffic fines are based on the offender's income rather than the severity of the offense.[17] So when one of Finland's richest men (he is heir to a sausage fortune), who was making close to $9 million a year, was ticketed for doing 80 kilometers per hour through a 40-kilometer zone in central Helsinki, the Finnish court hit him with a fine of $217,000!

Managers at global companies such as Volkswagen, McDonald's, Hitachi, and Coca-Cola have come to realize that economic values are not universally transferable. Management practices need to be modified to reflect the values of the different countries in which an organization operates.

Overseeing Movement of Jobs to Countries with Low-Cost Labor It's increasingly difficult for managers in advanced nations, where minimum wages are typically $6 or more an hour, to compete against firms who rely on workers from China and other developing nations where labor is available for 30 cents an hour. It's not by chance that a good portion of Americans wear clothes made in China, work on computers whose microchips came from Taiwan, and watch movies that were filmed in Canada. In a global economy, jobs tend to flow to places where lower costs provide business firms with a comparative advantage. Such practices, however, are often strongly criticized by labor groups, politicians, local community leaders, and others who see this exporting of jobs as undermining the job markets in developed countries. Managers must deal with the difficult task of balancing the interests of their organization with their responsibilities to the communities in which they operate.

Managing People During the War on Terror If you read the paper or watch the evening news, chances are you will find that the war on terror is one of the top stories. But when you think about the war, do you think about the workplace? Probably not. So you might be surprised to learn that the war on terror has had a profound effect on the business world. In fact, surveys suggest that fear of terrorism is the number-one reason business travelers have cut back on their trips. But travel isn't the only concern. Increasingly, organizations need to find ways to deal with employee fears about security precautions (in most cities, you can't get into an office building without passing through several layers of airport-like security) and assignments abroad (how would you feel about an assignment in a country with substantial sentiments against people from your country?).[18] An understanding of OB topics such as emotions, motivation, communication, and leadership can help managers to deal more effectively with their employees' fears about terrorism.

Managing Workforce Diversity

One of the most important and broad-based challenges currently facing organizations is adapting to people who are different. The term we use for describing this challenge is *workforce diversity.* Whereas globalization focuses on differences between people *from* different countries, workforce diversity addresses differences among people *within* given countries.

Workforce diversity means that organizations are becoming a more heterogeneous mix of people in terms of gender, age, race, ethnicity, and sexual orientation. A diverse workforce, for instance, includes women, people of color, the physically disabled, senior citizens, and gays and lesbians (see Exhibit 1-4, which shows how the U.S. workforce, for example, is becoming more diverse). Managing this diversity has become a global concern. For instance, managers in Canada and Australia are finding it necessary to adjust to large influxes of Asian workers. The "new" South Africa is increasingly

Exhibit 1-4 Major U.S. Workforce Diversity Categories

Gender

Nearly half of the U.S. workforce is now women, and women are a growing percentage of the workforce in most other countries throughout the world. Organizations need to ensure that hiring and employment policies create equal access and opportunities to individuals, regardless of gender.

Race

The percentage of Hispanics, blacks, and Asians in the U.S. workforce continues to increase. Organizations need to ensure that policies provide equal access and opportunities, regardless of race.

National Origin

A growing percentage of U.S. workers are immigrants or come from homes where English is not the primary language spoken. Because employers in the United States have the right to demand that English be spoken at the workplace on job-related activities, communication problems can occur when employees' English-language skills are weak.

Age

The U.S. workforce is aging, and recent polls indicate that an increasing percentage of employees expect to work past the traditional retirement age of 65. Organizations cannot discriminate on the basis of age and need to make accommodations to the needs of older workers.

Disability

Organizations need to ensure that jobs and workplaces are accessible to the mentally and physically challenged, as well as to the health challenged.

Domestic Partners

An increasing number of gay and lesbian employees, as well as employees with live-in partners of the opposite sex, are demanding the same rights and benefits for their partners that organizations have provided for traditional married couples.

Religion

Organizations need to be sensitive to the customs, rituals, and holidays, as well as the appearance and attire, of individuals of non-Christian faiths such as Judaism, Islam, Hinduism, Buddhism, and Sikhism, and ensure that these individuals suffer no adverse impact as a result of their appearance or practices.

characterized by blacks holding important technical and managerial jobs. Women, long confined to low-paying temporary jobs in Japan, are moving into managerial positions. And the European Union cooperative trade arrangement, which opened up borders throughout much of Western Europe, has increased workforce diversity in organizations that operate in countries such as Germany, Portugal, Italy, and France.

Embracing Diversity We used to take a melting-pot approach to differences in organizations, assuming that people who were different would somehow automatically want to assimilate. But we now recognize that employees don't set aside their cultural values, lifestyle preferences, and differences when they come to work. The challenge for organizations, therefore, is to make themselves more accommodating to diverse groups of people by addressing their different lifestyles, family needs, and work styles. The melting-pot assumption is being replaced by one that recognizes and values differences.[19]

workforce diversity *The concept that organizations are becoming more heterogeneous in terms of gender, age, race, ethnicity, sexual orientation, and inclusion of other diverse groups.*

Haven't organizations always included members of diverse groups? Yes, but they were a small percentage of the workforce and were, for the most part, ignored by large organizations. Moreover, it was assumed that these minorities would seek to blend in and assimilate. For instance, the bulk of the pre-1980s U.S. workforce were male Caucasians working full time to support their nonemployed wives and school-aged children. Now such employees are the true minority![20]

Changing U.S. Demographics The most significant change in the U.S. labor force during the last half of the twentieth century was the rapid increase in the number of female workers.[21] In 1950, for instance, only 29.6 percent of the workforce was women. By 2003, it was 46.7 percent. So today's workforce is rapidly approaching gender balance. In addition, with women now significantly outnumbering men on U.S. college campuses, we can expect an increasing number of technical, professional, and managerial jobs to be filled by the expanding pool of qualified female applicants.

In the same way that women dramatically changed the workplace in the latter part of the twentieth century, the first half of the twenty-first century will be notable for changes in racial and ethnic composition and an aging baby boom generation. By 2050, Hispanics will grow from today's 11 percent of the workforce to 24 percent, blacks will increase from 12 percent to 14 percent, and Asians will increase from 5 percent to 11 percent. Meanwhile, the labor force will be aging in the near term. The 55-and-older age group, which currently makes up 13 percent of the labor force, will increase to 20 percent by 2014.

Implications Workforce diversity has important implications for management practice. Managers have to shift their philosophy from treating everyone alike to recognizing differences and responding to those differences in ways that ensure employee retention and greater productivity while, at the same time, not discriminating. This shift includes, for instance, providing diversity training and revamping benefits programs to accommodate the different needs of different employees. Diversity, if positively managed, can increase creativity and innovation in organizations as well as improve decision making by providing different perspectives on

With more than 370,000 employees in 200 countries, United Parcel Service embraces the value of diversity. Since 1968, UPS senior managers participate in a 4-week community internship program that deepens their responsiveness to the needs of a diverse workforce and customer base while helping with charitable causes in the community. In this photo, UPS managers from Germany and California help a bicycle shop owner reorganize his business.

problems.[22] When diversity is not managed properly, there is a potential for higher turnover, more difficult communication, and more interpersonal conflicts.

Improving Quality and Productivity

In the 1990s, organizations around the world added capacity in response to increased demand. Companies built new facilities, expanded services, and added staff. The result? Today, almost every industry suffers from excess supply. The retail world suffers from too many malls and shopping centers. Automobile factories can build more cars than consumers can afford. The telecom industry is drowning in debt from building capacity that might take 50 years to absorb, and most cities and towns now have far more restaurants than their communities can support.

Excess capacity translates into increased competition. And increased competition is forcing managers to reduce costs and, at the same time, improve their organizations' productivity and the quality of the products and services they offer. Management guru Tom Peters says, "Almost all quality improvement comes via simplification of design, manufacturing, layout, processes, and procedures." To achieve these ends, managers are implementing programs such asquality management and process reengineering—programs that require extensive employee involvement.

Today's managers understand that the success of any effort at improving quality and productivity must include their employees. These employees will not only be a major force in carrying out changes but increasingly will actively participate in planning those changes. OB offers important insights into helping managers work through these changes.

Improving Customer Service

American Express recently turned Joan Weinbel's worst nightmare into a nonevent. It was 10:00 P.M. Joan was home in New Jersey, packing for a week-long trip, when she suddenly realized she had left her AmEx Gold Card at a restaurant in New York City earlier in the evening. The restaurant was 30 miles away. She had a flight to catch at 7:30 the next morning, and she wanted her card for the trip. She called American Express. The phone was quickly answered by a courteous and helpful AmEx customer service representative. He told Ms. Weinbel not to worry. He asked her a few questions and told her "help was on the way." To say Joan was flabbergasted would be an understatement when her doorbell rang at 11:45 P.M.—less than 2 hours after she had called AmEx. At her door was a courier with a new card. How the company was able to produce the card and get it to her so quickly still puzzles Joan. But she said the experience made her a customer for life.

Today, the majority of employees in developed countries work in service jobs. For instance, 80 percent of the U.S. labor force is employed in service industries. In Australia, 73 percent work in service industries. In the United Kingdom, Germany, and Japan, the percentages are 69, 68, and 65, respectively. Examples of these service jobs include technical support representatives, fast-food counter workers, sales clerks, waiters or waitresses, nurses, automobile repair technicians, consultants, credit representatives, financial planners, and flight attendants. The common characteristic of these jobs is that they require substantial interaction with an organization's customers. And because an organization can't exist without customers—whether that organization is Toyota, Gucci, Merrill Lynch, a law firm, a museum, a school, or a government agency—management needs to ensure that employees do what it takes to please customers.[23] For example, at Patagonia—a retail outfitter for climbers, mountain bikers, skiers and boarders, and other outdoor fanatics—managers are held directly responsible for

It's an annual tradition for Michael Dell to work the phone lines, helping customers in Dell, Inc.'s consumer department. Dell models the customer-responsive culture he created in founding Dell Computer Corporation in 1984 with the idea of building relationships directly with customers. He attributes his company's climb to market leadership as the world's top computer systems company to a persistent focus on the customer. Dell employees deliver superior customer service by communicating directly with customers via the Internet or by phone.

customer service. In fact, customer service is the store manager's most important general responsibility: "Instill in your employees the meaning and importance of customer service as outlined in the retail philosophy, 'our store is a place where the word "no" does not exist'; Empower staff to "use their best judgment" in all customer service matters."[24] OB can help managers at Patagonia achieve this goal and, more generally, can contribute to improving an organization's performance by showing managers how employee attitudes and behavior are associated with customer satisfaction.

Many an organization has failed because its employees failed to please customers. Management needs to create a customer-responsive culture. OB can provide considerable guidance in helping managers create such cultures—cultures in which employees are friendly and courteous, accessible, knowledgeable, prompt in responding to customer needs, and willing to do what's necessary to please the customer.[25]

Improving People Skills

We opened this chapter by demonstrating how important people skills are to managerial effectiveness. We said that "this book has been written to help both managers and potential managers develop those people skills."

As you proceed through the chapters, we'll present relevant concepts and theories that can help you explain and predict the behavior of people at work. In addition, you'll gain insights into specific people skills that you can use on the job. For instance, you'll learn ways to design motivating jobs, techniques for improving your listening skills, and how to create more effective teams.

Stimulating Innovation and Change

Whatever happened to Encyclopedia Brittanica, Woolworth, Smith Corona, TWA, Bethlehem Steel, and Worldcom? All these giants went bust. Why have other giants, such as Sears, Boeing, and Lucent Technologies implemented huge cost-cutting programs and eliminated thousands of jobs? To avoid going broke.

Today's successful organizations must foster innovation and master the art of change, or they'll become candidates for extinction. Victory will go to the organizations that maintain their flexibility, continually improve their quality, and beat their competition to the marketplace with a constant stream of innovative products and services. Domino's single-handedly brought on the demise of thousands of small pizza parlors whose managers thought they could continue doing what they had been doing for years. Amazon.com is putting a lot of independent bookstores out of business as it proves you can successfully sell books from an Internet Web site. After years of lackluster performance, Boeing realized it needed to change its business model. The result was its 787 "Dreamliner" and becoming again the world's largest airplane manufacturer.

An organization's employees can be the impetus for innovation and change, or they can be a major stumbling block. The challenge for managers is to stimulate their employees' creativity and tolerance for change. The field of OB provides a wealth of ideas and techniques to aid in realizing these goals.

Coping with "Temporariness"

With change comes temporariness. Globalization, expanded capacity, and advances in technology have combined in recent years to make it imperative that organizations be fast and flexible if they are to survive. The result is that most managers and employees today work in a climate best characterized as "temporary."

Evidence of temporariness is everywhere in organizations. Jobs are continually being redesigned; tasks are increasingly being done by flexible teams rather than individuals; companies are relying more on temporary workers; jobs are being subcontracted out to other firms; and pensions are being redesigned to move with people as they change jobs.

Workers need to continually update their knowledge and skills to perform new job requirements. For example, production employees at companies such as Caterpillar, Volvo Group, and Alcoa now need to know how to operate computerized production equipment. That was not part of their job descriptions 20 years ago. Work groups are also increasingly in a state of flux. In the past, employees were assigned to a specific work group, and that assignment was relatively permanent. There was a considerable amount of security in working with the same people day in and day out. That predictability has been replaced by temporary work groups, teams that include members from different departments and whose members change all the time, and the increased use of employee rotation to fill constantly changing work assignments. Finally, organizations themselves are in a state of flux. They continually reorganize their various divisions, sell off poor-performing businesses, downsize operations, subcontract noncritical services and operations to other organizations, and replace permanent employees with temporary workers.

Today's managers and employees must learn to cope with temporariness. They have to learn to live with flexibility, spontaneity, and unpredictability. The study of OB can provide important insights into helping you better understand a work world of continual change, how to overcome resistance to change, and how best to create an organizational culture that thrives on change.

Working in Networked Organizations

Computerization, the Internet, and the ability to link computers within organizations and between organizations have created a different workplace for many employees—a networked organization. These technology changes allow people to communicate and work together even though they may be thousands of miles apart. They also allow people to become independent contractors, who can telecommute via computer to workplaces around the globe and change employers as the demand for their services changes. Software programmers, graphic designers, systems analysts, technical writers, photo researchers, book editors, and medical transcribers are just a few examples of people who can work from home or other non-office locations.

The manager's job is different in a networked organization, especially when it comes to managing people. For instance, motivating and leading people and making collaborative decisions "online" requires different techniques than are needed in dealing with individuals who are physically present in a single location.

As more and more employees do their jobs linked to others through networks, managers need to develop new skills. OB can provide valuable insights to help with honing those skills.

Helping Employees Balance Work–Life Conflicts

The typical employee in the 1960s or 1970s showed up at the workplace Monday through Friday and did his or her job in 8- or 9-hour chunks of time. The workplace and hours were clearly specified. That's no longer true for a large segment of today's workforce. Employees are increasingly complaining that the line between work and nonwork time has become blurred, creating personal conflicts and stress.[26] At the same time, however, today's workplace presents opportunities for workers to create and structure their work roles.

A number of forces have contributed to blurring the lines between employees' work life and personal life. First, the creation of global organizations means their world never sleeps. At any time and on any day, for instance, thousands of Toyota Motor Corporation employees are working somewhere. The need to consult with colleagues or customers 8 or 10 time zones away means that many employees of global firms are "on call" 24 hours a day. Second, communication technology allows employees to do their work at home, in their cars, or on the beach in Tahiti. This lets many people in technical and professional jobs do their work any time and from any place. Third, organizations are asking employees to put in longer hours. For instance, over a recent 10-year period, the average American workweek increased from 43 to 47 hours; and the number of people working 50 or more hours a week jumped from 24 percent to 37

Merrill Lynch is committed to helping its employees achieve a work–life balance. The company provides adoption assistance to employees such as Keli Tuschman, shown here with her adopted daughter from China. Other employee-support systems include day-care facilities, paid time-off child-care leave for birth and adoption, a "school's out" program that provides child care during school holidays, and working-parent networks. Creating a family-friendly workplace helps Merrill Lynch attract and retain a motivated workforce.

Source: Jessica Kourkounis/ The New York Times

percent. Finally, fewer families have only a single breadwinner. Today's married employee is typically part of a dual-career couple. This makes it increasingly difficult for married employees to find the time to fulfill commitments to home, spouse, children, parents, and friends.

Employees are increasingly recognizing that work is infringing on their personal lives, and they're not happy about it. For example, recent studies suggest that employees want jobs that give them flexibility in their work schedules so they can better manage work–life conflicts.[27] In fact, evidence indicates that balancing work and life demands now surpasses job security as an employee priority.[28] In addition, the next generation of employees is likely to show similar concerns.[29] A majority of college and university students say that attaining a balance between personal life and work is a primary career goal. They want "a life" as well as a job. Organizations that don't help their people achieve work–life balance will find it increasingly difficult to attract and retain the most capable and motivated employees.

As you'll see in later chapters, the field of OB offers a number of suggestions to guide managers in designing workplaces and jobs that can help employees deal with work–life conflicts.

Creating a Positive Work Environment

Although competitive pressures on most organizations are stronger than ever, we've noticed an interesting turn in both OB research and management practice, at least in some organizations. Instead of responding to competitive pressures by "turning up the heat," some organizations are trying to realize a competitive advantage by fostering a positive work environment. For example, Jeff Immelt and Jim McNerney, both disciplines of Jack Welch (the former CEO of GE), have tried to maintain high performance expectations (a characteristic of GE's culture) while also fostering a positive work environment in their organizations (GE and Boeing). "In this time of turmoil and cynicism about business, you need to be passionate, positive leaders," Mr. Immelt recently told his top managers.

At the same time, a real growth area in OB research has been **positive organizational scholarship** (also called *positive organizational behavior*), which concerns how organizations develop human strengths, foster vitality and resilience, and unlock potential. Researchers in this area argue that too much of OB research and management practice has been targeted toward identifying what's wrong with organizations and their employees. In response, these researchers try to study what's *good* about organizations.[30]

For example, positive organizational scholars have studied a concept called "reflected best-self"—asking employees to think about situations in which they were at their "personal best" in order to understand how to exploit their strengths. These researchers argue that we all have things at which we are unusually good, yet too often we focus on addressing our limitations and too rarely think about how to exploit our strengths.[31]

Although positive organizational scholarship does not deny the presence (or even the value) of the negative (such as critical feedback), it does challenge researchers to look at OB through a new lens. It also challenges organizations to think about how to exploit their employees' strengths rather than dwell on their limitations.

positive organizational scholarship *An area of OB research that concerns how organizations develop human strength, foster vitality and resilience, and unlock potential.*

Improving Ethical Behavior

In an organizational world characterized by cutbacks, expectations of increasing worker productivity, and tough competition in the marketplace, it's not altogether surprising that many employees feel pressured to cut corners, break rules, and engage in other forms of questionable practices.

Members of organizations are increasingly finding themselves facing **ethical dilemmas**, situations in which they are required to define right and wrong conduct. For example, should they "blow the whistle" if they uncover illegal activities taking place in their company? Should they follow orders with which they don't personally agree? Do they give an inflated performance evaluation to an employee whom they like, knowing that such an evaluation could save that employee's job? Do they allow themselves to "play politics" in the organization if it will help their career advancement?

What constitutes good ethical behavior has never been clearly defined, and, in recent years, the line differentiating right from wrong has become even more blurred. Employees see people all around them engaging in unethical practices—elected officials are indicted for padding their expense accounts or taking bribes; corporate executives inflate company profits so they can cash in lucrative stock options; and university administrators "look the other way" when winning coaches encourage scholarship athletes to take easy courses in place of those needed for graduation in order to stay eligible. When caught, these people give excuses such as "everyone does it" or "you have to seize every advantage nowadays." Is it any wonder that employees are expressing decreased confidence and trust in management and that they're increasingly uncertain about what constitutes appropriate ethical behavior in their organizations?[32]

Managers and their organizations are responding to this problem from a number of directions.[33] They're writing and distributing codes of ethics to guide employees through ethical dilemmas. They're offering seminars, workshops, and other training programs to try to improve ethical behaviors. They're providing in-house advisors who can be contacted, in many cases anonymously, for assistance in dealing with ethical issues, and they're creating protection mechanisms for employees who reveal internal unethical practices.

Today's manager needs to create an ethically healthy climate for his or her employees, where they can do their work productively and confront a minimal degree of ambiguity regarding what constitutes right and wrong behaviors. In upcoming chapters, we'll discuss the kinds of actions managers can take to create an ethically healthy climate and help employees sort through ethically ambiguous situations. We'll also present ethical-dilemma exercises at the end of each chapter that will allow you to think through ethical issues and assess how you would handle them.

Coming Attractions: Developing an OB Model

We conclude this chapter by presenting a general model that defines the field of OB, stakes out its parameters, and identifies its primary dependent and independent variables. The end result will be a "coming attraction" of the topics in the remainder of this book.

8 *Compare the three levels of analysis in this book's OB model.*

An Overview

A **model** is an abstraction of reality, a simplified representation of some real-world phenomenon. A mannequin in a retail store is a model. So, too, is the

Exhibit 1-5

Basic OB Model, Stage I

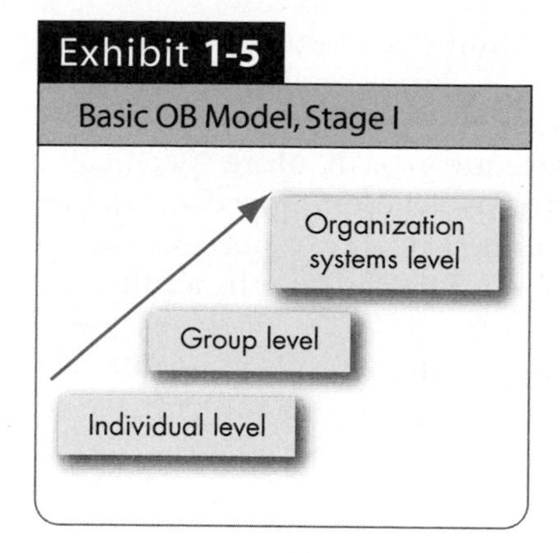

accountant's formula Assets + Liabilities = Owners' Equity. Exhibit 1-5 presents the skeleton on which we will construct our OB model. It proposes that there are three levels of analysis in OB and that, as we move from the individual level to the organization systems level, we add systematically to our understanding of behavior in organizations. The three basic levels are analogous to building blocks; each level is constructed on the previous level. Group concepts grow out of the foundation laid in the individual section; we overlay structural constraints on the individual and group in order to arrive at organizational behavior.

The Dependent Variables

A **dependent variable** is the key factor that you want to explain or predict and that is affected by some other factor. What are the primary dependent variables in OB? Scholars have historically tended to emphasize productivity, absenteeism, turnover, and job satisfaction. More recently, two more variables—deviant workplace behavior and organizational citizenship behavior—have been added to this list. We'll briefly discuss each of these variables to ensure that you understand what they mean and why they have achieved their level of distinction.

Productivity An organization is productive if it achieves its goals and does so by transferring inputs to outputs at the lowest cost. As such, **productivity** implies a concern for both **effectiveness** and **efficiency**.

A hospital, for example, is *effective* when it successfully meets the needs of its clientele. It is *efficient* when it can do so at a low cost. If a hospital manages to achieve higher output from its present staff by reducing the average number of days a patient is confined to a bed or by increasing the number of staff–patient contacts per day, we say that the hospital has gained productive efficiency. A business firm is effective when it attains its sales or market share goals, but its productivity also depends on achieving those goals efficiently. Popular measures of organizational efficiency include return on investment, profit per dollar of sales, and output per hour of labor.

We can also look at productivity from the perspective of the individual employee. Take the cases of Phillipe and Al, who are both long-distance truckers. If Phillipe is supposed to haul his fully loaded rig from Vancouver to Toronto in 75 hours or less, he is effective if he makes the 3,000-mile trip within that time period. But measures of productivity must take into account the costs incurred in reaching the goal. That's where efficiency comes in. Let's assume that, with identical rigs and loads, Phillipe made the Vancouver to Toronto run in 68 hours and averaged 7 miles per gallon. Al, however, made the trip in 68 hours also but averaged 9 miles per gallon. Both Phillipe and Al were effective—they accomplished their goal—but Al was more efficient than Phillipe because his rig consumed less gas and, therefore, he achieved his goal at a lower cost.

Organizations in service industries need to include attention to customer needs and requirements in assessing their effectiveness. Why? Because in these types of businesses, there is a clear chain of cause and effect running from employee attitudes and behavior to customer attitudes and behavior to an

ethical dilemmas *Situations in which individuals are required to define right and wrong conduct.*

model *An abstraction of reality. A simplified representation of some real-world phenomenon.*

dependent variable *A response that is affected by an independent variable.*

productivity *A performance measure that includes effectiveness and efficiency.*

effectiveness *Achievement of goals.*

efficiency *The ratio of effective output to the input required to achieve it.*

organization's productivity. Sears, in fact, has carefully documented this chain.[34] The company's management found that a 5 percent improvement in employee attitudes leads to a 1.3 percent increase in customer satisfaction, which in turn translates into a 0.5 percent improvement in revenue growth. More specifically, Sears found that by training employees to improve the employee–customer interaction, it was able to improve customer satisfaction by 4 percent over a 12-month period, which generated an estimated $200 million in additional revenues.

In summary, one of OB's major concerns is productivity. We want to know what factors will influence the effectiveness and efficiency of individuals, of groups, and of the overall organization.

Absenteeism **Absenteeism** is defined as the failure to report to work. Absenteeism is a huge cost and disruption to employers. For instance, a recent survey found that the average direct cost to U.K. employers of unscheduled absences is $694 per year per employee—and this doesn't include lost productivity or the additional costs for overtime pay or hiring temporary employees to cover for absent workers.[35] Comparable costs in the United States are also high—approximately $789 per year per employee.[36] In Sweden, an average of 10 percent of the country's workforce is on sick leave at any given time.[37]

It's obviously difficult for an organization to operate smoothly and to attain its objectives if employees fail to report to their jobs. The work flow is disrupted, and often important decisions must be delayed. In organizations that rely heavily on assembly-line production, absenteeism can be considerably more than a disruption; it can result in a drastic reduction in the quality of output, and, in some cases, it can bring about a complete shutdown of the production facility. Levels of absenteeism beyond the normal range in any organization have a direct impact on that organization's effectiveness and efficiency.

Are *all* absences bad? Probably not. Although most absences have a negative impact on the organization, we can conceive of situations in which the organization may benefit by an employee's voluntarily choosing not to come to

Employees of Worthington Industries take part in a lunchtime kickboxing class at the company's fitness center. The class is part of Worthington's employee health and wellness initiative that helps reduce absenteeism and increase productivity. Worthington also operates an on-site medical center staffed with doctors and nurses. The center helps reduce the time employees spend on doctors' visits and minimizes absenteeism through preventive screenings and wellness programs.

work. For instance, in jobs in which an employee needs to be alert—consider surgeons and airline pilots, for example—it may be better for the organization if an ill or fatigued employee does *not* report to work. The cost of an accident in such jobs could be disastrous. But these examples are clearly atypical. For the most part, we can assume that organizations benefit when employee absenteeism is low.

Turnover **Turnover** is the voluntary and involuntary permanent withdrawal from an organization. A high turnover rate results in increased recruiting, selection, and training costs. What are those costs? They're higher than you might think. For instance, the cost for a typical information technology company in the United States to replace a programmer or systems analyst has been estimated at $34,100; and the cost for a retail store to replace a lost sales clerk has been calculated as $10,445.[38] In addition, a high rate of turnover can disrupt the efficient running of an organization when knowledgeable and experienced personnel leave and replacements must be found and prepared to assume positions of responsibility.

All organizations, of course, have some turnover. The U.S. national turnover rate, for example, averages about 3 percent per month, which is about a 36 percent turnover per year. This average, of course, varies a lot by occupation (for example, the monthly turnover rate for government jobs is less than 1 percent versus 5 to 7 percent in the construction industry).[39] If the "right" people are leaving the organization—the marginal and submarginal employees—turnover can actually be positive. It can create an opportunity to replace an underperforming individual with someone who has higher skills or motivation, open up increased opportunities for promotions, and add new and fresh ideas to the organization.[40] In today's changing world of work, reasonable levels of employee-initiated turnover facilitate organizational flexibility and employee independence, and they can lessen the need for management-initiated layoffs.

But turnover often involves the loss of people the organization doesn't want to lose. For instance, one study covering 900 employees who had resigned from their jobs found that 92 percent earned performance ratings of "satisfactory" or better from their superiors.[41] So when turnover is excessive, or when it involves valuable performers, it can be a disruptive factor that hinders the organization's effectiveness.

Deviant Workplace Behavior Given the cost of absenteeism and turnover to employers, more and more OB researchers are studying these behaviors as indicators or markers of deviant behavior. Deviance can range from someone playing his music too loudly to violence. Managers need to understand this wide range of behaviors to address any form of employee dissatisfaction. If managers don't understand *why* an employee is acting up, the problem will never be solved.

We can define **deviant workplace behavior** (also called *antisocial behavior* or *workplace incivility*) as voluntary behavior that violates significant organizational norms and, in doing so, threatens the well-being of the organization or its members. What are organizational norms in this context? They can be company policies that prohibit certain behaviors such as stealing. They also can be

absenteeism *The failure to report to work.*

turnover *Voluntary and involuntary permanent withdrawal from an organization.*

deviant workplace behavior *Voluntary behavior that violates significant organizational norms and, in so doing, threatens the well-being of the organization or its members.*

International OB

Transfer Pricing and International Corporate Deviance

Workplace deviance isn't limited to the harmful behaviors of employees within one location. There are cases of corporate deviance that extend across country borders. Consider transfer pricing, which is the price that one part of a company charges another part of the same company for a product or service. What happens with transfer pricing if various parts of a company are located in different countries, which is becoming increasingly common as more and more companies extend their operations across the globe to become multinational businesses?

Tax rates on company profits differ—sometimes greatly—from country to country. Transfer pricing, when used to shift income from high-tax countries to low-tax countries, can be a deviant corporate policy if it is abused. One way to increase overall profit—that is, the combined profit of the multinational's headquarters and its subsidiaries—is to take profits in the country with the lower taxes.

Take the case of a multinational firm whose headquarters sold toothbrushes to a subsidiary for $5,000—each. The subsidiary, with the higher tax of the two, claimed a loss (after all, it paid $5,000 per toothbrush). The multinational firm, with the lower tax of the two, took the profit and paid the tax on it. Because the two firms were part of the same organization, they combined the results of the transaction, and the company made a staggering profit.

Transfer pricing, according to a survey by the international auditing firm Ernst & Young, has become a heated issue among multinational companies. Why? The U.S. Multistate Tax Commission estimated that states were losing almost one-third of their corporate tax income because of tax-sheltering practices by multinational companies—transfer pricing among them. The U.S. Internal Revenue Service is keeping a watchful eye on international transactions.

Source: Based on "Case of the U.S. $5000 Toothbrush," *Finance Week*, April 27, 2005, pp. 45–46.

unspoken rules that are widely shared, such as not playing loud music in one's workspace. Consider, for example, an employee who plays the rock band Metallica's "St. Anger" at work with the speakers amped up. Yes, he may be showing up at work, but he may not be getting his work done, and he could also be irritating coworkers or customers (unless they are Talli fans themselves). But deviant workplace behaviors can be much more serious than an employee playing loud music. For example, an employee may insult a colleague, steal, gossip excessively, or engage in sabotage, all of which can wreak havoc on an organization.

Managers want to understand the source of workplace deviance in order to avoid a chaotic work environment, and workplace deviance can also have a considerable financial impact. Although the annual costs are hard to quantify, estimates are that deviant behavior costs employers dearly, from $4.2 billion for violence to $7.1 billion for corporate security against cyberattacks to $200 billion for theft.[42]

Deviant workplace behavior is an important concept because it's a response to dissatisfaction, and employees express this dissatisfaction in many ways. Controlling one behavior may be ineffective unless one gets to the root cause. The sophisticated manager will deal with root causes of problems that may result in deviance rather than solve one surface problem (excessive absence) only to see another one crop up (increased theft or sabotage).

Organizational Citizenship Behavior **Organizational citizenship behavior (OCB)** is discretionary behavior that is not part of an employee's formal job requirements but that nevertheless promotes the effective functioning of the organization.[43]

Successful organizations need employees who will do more than their usual job duties—who will provide performance that is *beyond* expectations. In today's dynamic workplace, where tasks are increasingly done in teams and where flexibility is critical, organizations need employees who will engage in "good citizenship" behaviors such as helping others on their team, volunteering for extra work, avoiding unnecessary conflicts, respecting the spirit as well as the letter of rules and regulations, and gracefully tolerating occasional work-related impositions and nuisances.

Organizations want and need employees who will do those things that aren't in any job description. And the evidence indicates that organizations that have such employees outperform those that don't.[44] As a result, OB is concerned with OCB as a dependent variable.

Job Satisfaction The final dependent variable we will look at is **job satisfaction**, which we define as a positive feeling about one's job resulting from an evaluation of its characteristics. Unlike the previous five variables, job satisfaction represents an attitude rather than a behavior. Why, then, has it become a primary dependent variable? For two reasons: its demonstrated relationship to performance factors and the value preferences held by many OB researchers.

The belief that satisfied employees are more productive than dissatisfied employees has been a basic tenet among managers for years, though only now has research begun to support this theory after decades of questions about the satisfaction–performance relationship.[45] Recently, a study of more than 2,500 business units found that units scoring in the top 25 percent on the employee opinion survey were, on average, 4.6 percent *above* their sales budget for the year, while those scoring in the bottom 25 percent were 0.8 percent *below* budget. In real numbers, this was a difference of $104 million in sales per year between the two groups.[46]

Moreover, it can be argued that advanced societies should be concerned not only with the quantity of life—that is, concerns such as higher productivity and material acquisitions—but also with its quality. Researchers with strong humanistic values argue that satisfaction is a legitimate objective of an organization. Not only is satisfaction negatively related to absenteeism and turnover, but, they argue, organizations have a responsibility to provide employees with jobs that are challenging and intrinsically rewarding. Therefore, although job satisfaction represents an attitude rather than a behavior, OB researchers typically consider it an important dependent variable.

The Independent Variables

What are the major determinants of productivity, absenteeism, turnover, deviant workplace behavior, OCB, and job satisfaction? Our answer to that question brings us to the independent variables. An **independent variable** is the presumed cause of some change in a dependent variable.

Consistent with our belief that organizational behavior can best be understood when viewed essentially as a set of increasingly complex building blocks, the base, or first level, of our model lies in understanding individual behavior.

Individual-Level Variables It has been said that "managers, unlike parents, must work with used, not new, human beings—human beings whom others

organizational citizenship behavior (OCB) *Discretionary behavior that is not part of an employee's formal job requirements but that nevertheless promotes the effective functioning of the organization.*

job satisfaction *A positive feeling about one's job resulting from an evaluation of its characteristics.*

independent variable *The presumed cause of some change in a dependent variable.*

have gotten to first."[47] When individuals enter an organization, they are a bit like used cars. Each is different. Some are "low mileage"—they have been treated carefully and have had only limited exposure to the realities of the elements. Others are "well worn," having been driven over some rough roads. This metaphor indicates that people enter organizations with certain intact characteristics that will influence their behavior at work. The most obvious of these are personal or biographical characteristics such as age, gender, and marital status; personality characteristics; an inherent emotional framework; values and attitudes; and basic ability levels. These characteristics are essentially in place when an individual enters the workforce, and, for the most part, there is little management can do to alter them. Yet they have a very real impact on employee behavior. Therefore, each of these factors—biographical characteristics, ability, values, attitudes, personality, and emotions—will be discussed as independent variables in Chapters 2 through 4 and 8.

There are four other individual-level variables that have been shown to affect employee behavior: perception, individual decision making, learning, and motivation. Those topics will be introduced and discussed in Chapters 2, 5, 6, and 7.

Group-Level Variables The behavior of people in groups is more than the sum total of all the individuals acting in their own way. The complexity of our model is increased when we acknowledge that people's behavior when they are in groups is different from their behavior when they are alone. Therefore, the next step in the development of an understanding of OB is the study of group behavior.

Chapter 9 lays the foundation for an understanding of the dynamics of group behavior. That chapter discusses how individuals in groups are influenced by the patterns of behavior they are expected to exhibit, what the group considers to be acceptable standards of behavior, and the degree to which group members are attracted to each other. Chapter 10 translates our understanding of groups to the design of effective work teams. Chapters 11 through 15 demonstrate how communication patterns, leadership, power and politics, and levels of conflict affect group behavior.

Organization System-Level Variables Organizational behavior reaches its highest level of sophistication when we add formal structure to our previous knowledge of individual and group behavior. Just as groups are more than the sum of their individual members, so are organizations more than the sum of their member groups. The design of the formal organization; the organization's internal culture; and the organization's human resource policies and practices (that is, selection processes, training and development programs, performance evaluation methods) all have an impact on the dependent variables. These are discussed in detail in Chapters 16 through 18.

Toward a Contingency OB Model

Our final model is shown in Exhibit 1-6. It shows the six key dependent variables and a large number of independent variables, organized by level of analysis, that research indicates have varying effects on the former. As complicated as this model is, it still doesn't do justice to the complexity of the OB subject matter. However, it should help explain why the chapters in this book are arranged as they are and help you to explain and predict the behavior of people at work.

For the most part, our model does not explicitly identify the vast number of contingency variables because of the tremendous complexity that would be

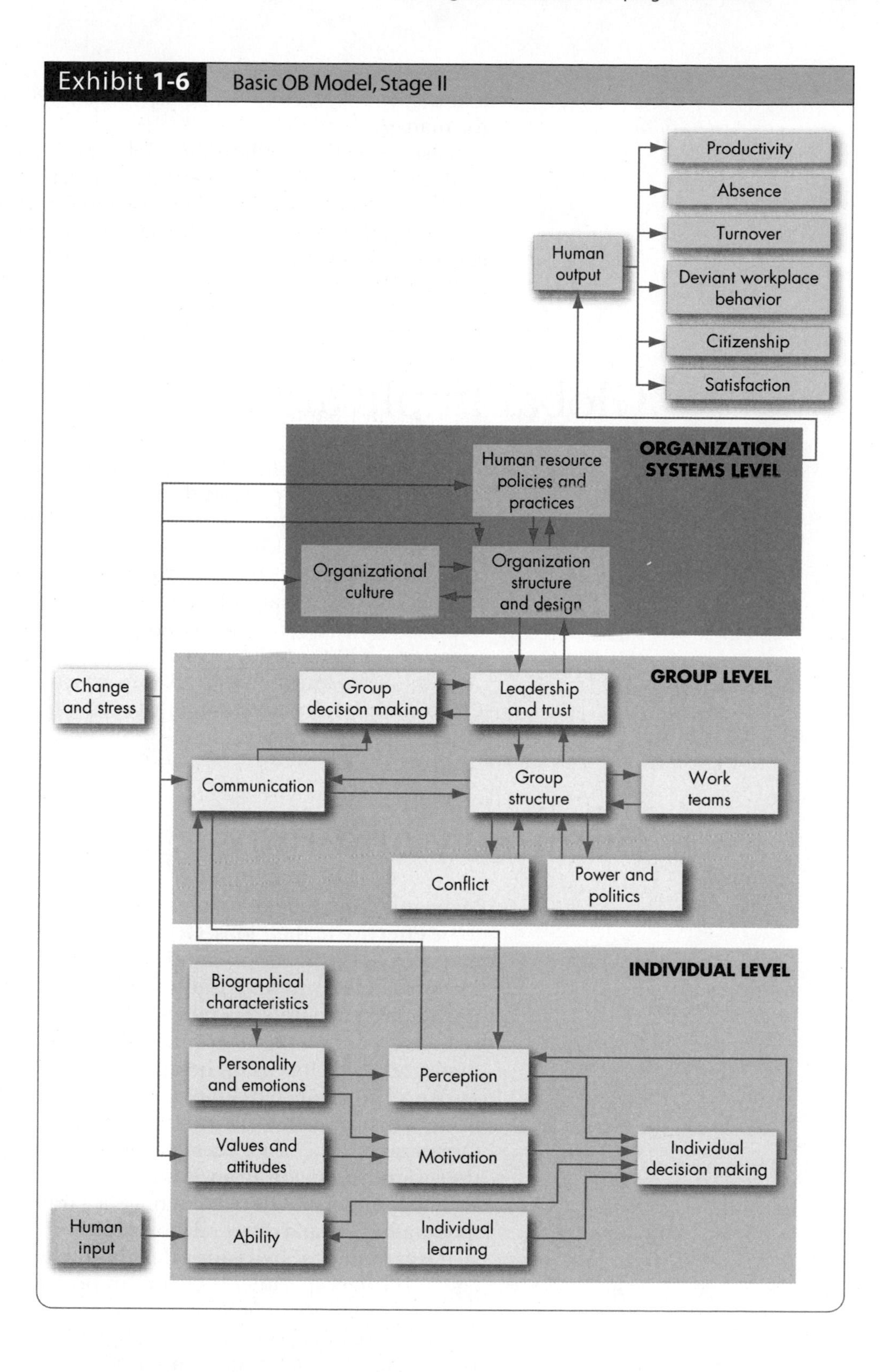

involved in such a diagram. Rather, throughout this book we will introduce important contingency variables that will improve the explanatory linkage between the independent and dependent variables in our OB model.

Note that we have included the concepts of change and stress in Exhibit 1-6, acknowledging the dynamics of behavior and the fact that work stress is an individual, group, and organizational issue. Specifically, in Chapter 19, we will discuss the change process, ways to manage organizational change, key change issues currently facing managers, consequences of work stress, and techniques for managing stress.

Also note that Exhibit 1-6 includes linkages between the three levels of analysis. For instance, organizational structure is linked to leadership. This link is meant to convey that authority and leadership are related; management exerts its influence on group behavior through leadership. Similarly, communication is the means by which individuals transmit information; thus, it is the link between individual and group behavior.

Global Implications

We've already discussed how globalization presents challenges and opportunities for OB. We want to draw your attention to this spot in the chapter, though, because in every subsequent chapter, we will have a section at this spot—titled "Global Implications"—that discusses how some of the things we know about OB are affected by cultural differences within and between countries. Most OB research has been conducted in Western cultures (especially the United States). That's changing, however, and compared to even a few years ago, we're now in a much better position to answer the question "How does what we know about OB vary based on culture?" You'll find that some OB principles don't vary much across cultures, but others vary a great deal from culture to culture.

Summary and Implications for Managers

Managers need to develop their interpersonal, or people, skills if they are going to be effective in their jobs. Organizational behavior (OB) is a field of study that investigates the impact that individuals, groups, and structure have on behavior within an organization, and it applies that knowledge to make organizations work more effectively. Specifically, OB focuses on how to improve productivity; reduce absenteeism, turnover, and deviant workplace behavior; and increase organizational citizenship behavior and job satisfaction.

We all hold generalizations about the behavior of people. Some of our generalizations may provide valid insights into human behavior, but many are erroneous. Organizational behavior uses systematic study to improve predictions of behavior that would be made from intuition alone. But because people are different, we need to look at OB in a contingency framework, using situational variables to moderate cause-and-effect relationships.

Organizational behavior offers both challenges and opportunities for managers. It offers specific insights to improve a manager's people skills. It recognizes differences and helps managers to see the value of workforce diversity and practices that may need to be changed when managing in different countries. It can improve quality and employee productivity by showing managers how to empower their people, design and implement change programs, improve customer service, and help employees balance work–life conflicts. It provides suggestions for helping managers meet chronic labor shortages. It can help managers to cope in a world of temporariness and to learn ways to stimulate innovation. Finally, OB can offer managers guidance in creating an ethically healthy work climate.

Point / Counterpoint

IN SEARCH OF THE QUICK FIX

Point

Walk into your nearest major bookstore. You'll undoubtedly find a large section of books devoted to management and managing human behavior. A close look at the titles will reveal that there is certainly no shortage of popular books on topics related to organizational behavior. To illustrate the point, consider the following popular books that are currently available on the topic of leadership:

- *Catch! A Fishmonger's Guide to Greatness* (Berrett-Koehler, 2003)
- *If Harry Potter Ran General Electric: Leadership Wisdom from the World of Wizards* (Currency/Doubleday, 2006)
- *Bhagavad Gita on Effective Leadership* (iUniverse, 2006)
- *Power Plays: Shakespeare's Lessons on Leadership and Management* (Simon & Schuster, 2000)
- *The Leadership Teachings of Geronimo* (Sterling House, 2002)
- *Leadership the Eleanor Roosevelt Way* (Prentice Hall, 2002)
- *Beyond Basketball: Coach K's Keywords for Success* (Warner Business Books, 2006)
- *Leadership Wisdom from the Monk Who Sold His Ferrari* (Hay House, 2003)
- *Tony Soprano on Management: Leadership Lessons Inspired by America's Favorite Mobster* (Berkley, 2004)

Organizations are always looking for leaders; and managers and manager-wannabes are continually looking for ways to hone their leadership skills. Publishers respond to this demand by offering hundreds of titles that promise insights into the subject of leadership. Books like these can provide people with the secrets to leadership that others know about.

Counterpoint

Beware of the quick fix! We all want to find quick and simple solutions to our complex problems. But here's the bad news: For problems related to organizational behavior, quick and simple solutions are often wrong because they fail to consider the diversity among organizations, situations, and individuals. As Einstein said, "everything should be made as simple as possible, but not simpler."

When it comes to trying to understand people at work, there is no shortage of simplistic ideas and books and consultants to promote them. And these books aren't just about leadership. Consider three recent bestsellers. *Who Moved My Cheese?* is a metaphor about two mice that is meant to convey the benefits of accepting change. *Fish!* tells how a fish market in Seattle made its jobs more motivating. And *Whale Done!* proposes that managers can learn a lot about motivating people from techniques used by whale trainers at Sea World in San Diego. Are the "insights" from these books generalizable to people working in hundreds of different countries, in a thousand different organizations, and doing a million different jobs? It's very unlikely.

Popular books on organizational behavior often have cute titles and are fun to read. But they can be dangerous. They make the job of managing people seem much simpler than it really is. They are also often based on the author's opinions rather than substantive research.

Organizational behavior is a complex subject. Few, if any, simple statements about human behavior are generalizable to all people in all situations. Should you really try to apply leadership insights you got from a book about Geronimo or Tony Soprano to managing software engineers in the twenty-first century?

Questions for Review

1 What is the importance of interpersonal skills?

2 What do managers do in terms of functions, roles, and skills?

3 What is organizational behavior (OB)?

4 Why is it important to complement intuition with systematic study?

5 What are the major behavioral science disciplines that contribute to OB?

6 Why are there few absolutes in OB?

7 What are the challenges and opportunities for managers in using OB concepts?

8 What are the three levels of analysis in this book's OB model?

Experiential Exercise

WORKFORCE DIVERSITY

Purpose

To learn about the different needs of a diverse workforce.

Time Required

Approximately 40 minutes.

Participants and Roles

Divide the class into six groups of approximately equal size. Assign each group one of the following roles:

Nancy is 28 years old. She is a divorced mother of three children, ages 3, 5, and 7. She is the department head. She earns $40,000 per year on her job and receives another $3,600 per year in child support from her ex-husband.

Ethel is a 72-year-old widow. She works 25 hours per week to supplement her $8,000 annual pension. Including her hourly wage of $8.50, she earns $19,000 per year.

John is a 34-year-old black male born in Trinidad who is now a U.S. resident. He is married and the father of two small children. John attends college at night and is within a year of earning his bachelor's degree. His salary is $27,000 per year. His wife is an attorney and earns approximately $50,000 per year.

Lu is a 26-year-old physically impaired male Asian American. He is single and has a master's degree in education. Lu is paralyzed and confined to a wheelchair as a result of an auto accident. He earns $32,000 per year.

Maria is a single, 22-year-old Hispanic woman. Born and raised in Mexico, she came to the United States only 3 months ago. Maria's English needs considerable improvement. She earns $20,000 per year.

Mike is a 16-year-old white male high school sophomore who works 15 hours per week after school and during vacations. He earns $7.20 per hour, or approximately $5,600 per year.

The members of each group are to assume the character consistent with their assigned role.

Background

The six participants work for a company that has recently installed a flexible benefits program. Instead of the traditional "one benefit package fits all," the company is allocating an additional 25 percent of each employee's annual pay to be used for discretionary benefits. Those benefits and their annual cost are as follows:

- Supplementary health care for employee:
  Plan A (no deductible and pays 90 percent) = $3,000
  Plan B ($200 deductible and pays 80 percent) = $2,000
  Plan C ($1,000 deductible and pays 70 percent) = $500
- Supplementary health care for dependents (same deductibles and percentages as above):
  Plan A = $2,000
  Plan B = $1,500
  Plan C = $500
- Supplementary dental plan = $500
- Life insurance:
  Plan A ($25,000 coverage) = $500
  Plan B ($50,000 coverage) = $1,000
  Plan C ($100,000 coverage) = $2,000
  Plan D ($250,000 coverage) = $3,000
- Mental health plan = $500
- Prepaid legal assistance = $300
- Vacation = 2 percent of annual pay for each week, up to 6 weeks a year
- Pension at retirement equal to approximately 50 percent of final annual earnings = $1,500
- Four-day workweek during the 3 summer months (available only to full-time employees) = 4 percent of annual pay

- Day-care services (after company contribution) = $2,000 for all of an employee's children, regardless of number
- Company-provided transportation to and from work = $750
- College tuition reimbursement = $1,000
- Language class tuition reimbursement = $500

The Task

1. Each group has 15 minutes to develop a flexible benefits package that consumes 25 percent (and no more!) of their character's pay.
2. After completing step 1, each group appoints a spokesperson who describes to the entire class the benefits package the group has arrived at for their character.
3. The entire class then discusses the results. How did the needs, concerns, and problems of each participant influence the group's decision? What do the results suggest for trying to motivate a diverse workforce?

Source: Special thanks to Professor Penny Wright (San Diego State University) for her suggestions during the development of this exercise.

Ethical Dilemma

LYING IN BUSINESS

Do you think it's ever okay to lie? If you were negotiating for the release of hostages, most people would probably agree that if lying would lead to the hostages' safety, it's okay. What about in business, where the stakes are rarely life or death? Business executives such as Martha Stewart have gone to jail for lying (submitting a false statement to federal investigators). Is misrepresentation or omitting factors okay as long as there is no outright lie?

Consider the negotiation process. A good negotiator never shows all his cards, right? And so omitting certain information is just part of the process. Well, it may surprise you to learn that the law will hold you liable for omitting information if partial disclosure is misleading or if one side has superior information not accessible to the other.

In one case (*Jordan v. Duff and Phelps*), a company (Duff and Phelps) withheld information from an employee—Jordan—about the impending sale of the company. The problem: Jordan was leaving the organization and therefore sold his shares in the company. Ten days later, when the sale of the company became public, those shares became worth much more. Jordan sued his former employer on the grounds that it should have disclosed this information to him. Duff and Phelps countered that it had never lied to Jordan. The Court of Appeals argued that in such situations, one party cannot take "opportunistic advantage" of the other. In the eyes of the law, sometimes omitting relevant facts can be as bad as lying.

Questions

1. In a business context, is it ever okay to lie? If yes, what are those situations? Why is it okay to lie in these situations?
2. A recent survey revealed that 24 percent of managers said they have fired someone for lying. Do you think it's fair to fire an employee who lies, no matter what the nature of the lie? Explain.
3. In business, is withholding information for your own advantage the same as lying? Why or why not?
4. In a business context, if someone has something to gain by lying, what percentage of people, do you think, would lie?

Source: Based on "Lying at Work Could Get You Fired," *UPI*, March 5, 2006; "Brain Scans Detect More Activity in Those Who Lie," Reuters, November 29, 2004; www.msnbc.msn.com/id/6609019; and P. Ekman and E. L. Rosenberg, *What the Fact Reveals: Basic and Applied Studies of Spontaneous Expression Using the Facial Action Coding System (CAPS)*, 2nd ed. (New York: Oxford University Press, 2004).

Case Incident 1

"DATA WILL SET YOU FREE"

Ford CEO Alan Mulally is known for starting meetings by saying "Data will set you free" and for trying to change Ford's culture to one that is based on increased accountability, more information sharing, and hard metrics. "You can't manage a secret," he is also fond of saying. Although it's not clear whether Mulally's approach will work at Ford, which is known for its self-contained fiefdoms where little information is shared, some companies have found that managing people according to hard metrics has paid off. Consider Freescale Semiconductor, a computer chip manufacturer based in Austin, Texas.

Freescale has discovered that in order to have the right people at the right time to do the right job, it needs an extensive and elaborate set of metrics to manage its 24,000 employees in 30 countries. Of particular concern to Freescale is retention. "There's no greater cost than human capital, especially in the technology industry," says Jignasha Patel, Freescale's director of global talent sourcing and inclusion. "When you've got a tenured employee that decides to walk out the door, it's not just one person leaving, it's that person's knowledge and network and skills."

To manage talent and prevent turnover, Freescale holds line managers accountable for recruiting, hiring, and retaining employees. To do that, managers need to project their talent needs into the future and reconcile those with projected availabilities. Patel provides line managers with census data that help them make their projections, but at the end of the day, the responsibility is theirs. "What we have done is taken all of our inclusion data, all our metrics, and we've moved the accountability over to the business unit," Patel says.

Patel also provides Freescale managers with benchmark data so they can compare their effectiveness with that of other units. The benchmark data include the number of people hired, turnovers, and promotions—and breakdowns by demographic categories. "There's [a return on investment] for everything we do," says Patel.

Questions

1. Why do you think Freescale focuses on metrics? Why don't more organizations follow its approach?
2. As a manager, would you want to be accountable for the acquisition and retention of employees you supervise? Why or why not?
3. In general, what do you think are the advantages and limitations of such metrics?
4. Freescale focused on metrics for the acquisition and retention of employees. Do you think metrics can be applied to other areas of management, such as employee attitudes, employee performance, or skill development? How might those metrics be measured and managed?

Source: Based on R. R. Hastings, "Metrics Drive Winning Culture," *SHRM Online*, April 9, 2007, www.shrm.org.

Case Incident 2

WORKPLACE VIOLENCE

On Wednesday, January 26, 2005, 54-year-old Myles Meyers walked into DaimlerChrysler's Toledo, Ohio, assembly plant holding a double-barrel shotgun under his coat. Myers, a Jeep repairman, approached Yiesha Martin, a 27-year-old stock supervisor, and stated his intentions. He was there to murder three supervisors: Mike Toney, 45, Roy Thacker, 50, and Carrie Woggerman, 24. Afterward, he said, he would turn the gun on himself. "I was shaking and I started to cry," said Martin. Meyers told her not to cry and to page Toney. Although he was usually eating lunch at his desk around this time, Toney was busy dealing with a problem on the production line. On Martin's second attempt, Toney responded.

Thacker, however, was the first of Meyer's intended victims to approach the former employee. When Thacker asked Meyers why he was at the office, "[Meyers] turned from the partition and just shot him," Martin recalled. "I just saw the shells go. He reloaded in front of me." Martin ran, grabbing a radio in the process. As she ran away, calling into her radio for help, she heard another gunshot. Mike Toney had just arrived and was now the second victim. Carrie Woggerman was able to flee after the first shot, but Paul Medlen, 41, while attempting to come to the aid of Toney, was shot in the chest by Meyers just before Meyers turned the gun on himself, taking his own life. Of the three employees shot by Meyers, two survived. Unfortunately, Thacker died from his wounds.

Regrettably, the shooting at the Toledo assembly plant was not an isolated incident. Just 2 years earlier, Doug Williams, an employee at Lockheed Martin, left in the middle of an ethics meeting, went to his car, and came back with several guns. He then shot six coworkers to death and wounded eight others before committing suicide. Every year, nearly half of U.S. workers report having faced aggression from coworkers, customers, or supervisors. And according to the Occupational Safety and Health Administration (OSHA), roughly 20,000 assaults and 792 homicides occurred at workplaces throughout the United States in 2005. Such violence prompted the Centers for Disease Control and Prevention to label workplace violence a "national epidemic."

In addition to the obvious devastation workplace violence causes victims and their families, businesses often experience serious repercussions, including legal action.

Lockheed Martin is still embroiled in a legal battle over whether the company should assume part of the responsibility for the shooting that took place at its plant. And Paul Medlen has filed suit against DaimlerChrysler and the plant's security firm, Wackenhut Corp., alleging that both failed to provide adequate security. Given the tremendous damage that companies and employees face following violent episodes, why aren't businesses doing more to curtail workplace violence? According to a recent study by the American Society of Safety Engineers, only 1 percent of U.S. businesses have formal antiviolence policies.

Advice on how to reduce workplace violence abounds. According to former FBI agent Doug Kane, people who behave violently often announce or hint at their intentions before the violence occurs. Managers, then, need to be aware of at-risk employees who may commit violent acts and should encourage employees to report any threatening or suspicious behavior. Some employees of the DaimlerChrysler plant are even suggesting that metal detectors be installed to prevent future violence. Whatever measures are taken, it is clear that workplace violence is an issue that needs to be addressed for employees to feel safe at work.

Questions

1. How liable should companies be for violent acts committed during work by their own employees?
2. Can companies completely prevent workplace violence? If not, what steps can they take to reduce it?
3. Why do you think only 1 percent of companies have formal antiviolence policies?
4. Some companies are considering installing metal detectors to prevent workplace violence. Do you think these measures infringe too much on individual privacy? In other words, can a company take prevention too far?
5. What factors might lead to violent acts in the workplace? Are these acts committed by only a few "sick" individuals, or are many individuals capable of committing acts given certain circumstances?

Source: Based on "Half of U.S. Workers Face On-the-Job Violence," *Forbes*, January 26, 2006, www.Forbes.com; A. K. Fisher, "How to Prevent Violence at Work," *Fortune*, February 21, 2005, pp. 42; and C. Hall, "Witness Recounts Moments of Horror and Heartbreak," *The Toledo Blade*, January 29, 2005, http://toledoblade.com/apps/pbcs.dll/article?AID=/20050129/NEWS03/501290378.

Endnotes

1. "Spanked Employee Seeks $1.2 Million," *CNN.com Law Center*, April 27, 2006, p. 1; and "Clovis Woman Who Sued Successfully over Spanking Is Suing Again," *Fresno Bee*, December 14, 2006, www.SFGate.com.
2. Cited in R. Alsop, "Playing Well with Others," *Wall Street Journal*, September 9, 2002.
3. See, for instance, C. Penttila, "Hiring Hardships," *Entrepreneur*, October 2002, pp. 34–35.
4. *The 2002 National Study of the Changing Workforce* (New York: Families and Work Institute, 2002).
5. I. S. Fulmer, B. Gerhart, and K. S. Scott, "Are the 100 Best Better? An Empirical Investigation of the Relationship Between Being a 'Great Place to Work' and Firm Performance," *Personnel Psychology*, Winter 2003, pp. 965–993.
6. H. Fayol, *Industrial and General Administration* (Paris: Dunod, 1916).
7. A. I. Kraut, P. R. Pedigo, D. D. McKenna, and M. D. Dunnette, "The Role of the Manager: What's Really Important in Different Management Jobs," *Academy of Management Executive* 19, no. 4 (2005), pp. 122–129.
8. H. Mintzberg, *The Nature of Managerial Work* (Upper Saddle River, NJ: Prentice Hall, 1973).
9. R. L. Katz, "Skills of an Effective Administrator," *Harvard Business Review*, September–October 1974, pp. 90–102.
10. F. Luthans, "Successful vs. Effective Real Managers," *Academy of Management Executive*, May 1988, pp. 127–132; and F. Luthans, R. M. Hodgetts, and S. A. Rosenkrantz, *Real Managers* (Cambridge, MA: Ballinger, 1988). See also F. Shipper and J Davy, "A Model and Investigation of Managerial Skills, Employees' Attitudes, and Managerial Performance," *Leadership Quarterly* 13 (2002), pp. 95–120.
11. P. H. Langford, "Importance of Relationship Management for the Career Success of Australian Managers," *Australian Journal of Psychology*, December 2000, pp. 163–169; and A. M. Konrad, R. Kashlak, I. Yoshioka, R. Waryszak, and N. Toren, "What Do Managers Like to Do? A Five-Country Study," *Group & Organization Management*, December 2001, pp. 401–433.
12. A. S. Tsui, S. J. Ashford, L. St. Clair, and K. R. Xin, "Dealing with Discrepant Expectations: Response Strategies and Managerial Effectiveness," *Academy of Management Journal*, December 1995, pp. 1515–1543.
13. See, for instance, C. Heath and S. B. Sitkin, "Big-B Versus Big-O: What Is *Organizational* about Organizational Behavior?" *Journal of Organizational Behavior*, February 2001, pp. 43–58. For a review of what one eminent researcher believes *should* be included in organizational behavior, based on survey data, see J. B. Miner, "The Rated Importance, Scientific Validity, and Practical Usefulness of Organizational Behavior Theories: A Quantitative Review," *Academy of Management Learning & Education*, September 2003, pp. 250–268.

14. See L. A. Burke and J. E. Moore, "A Perennial Dilemma in OB Education: Engaging the Traditional Student," *Academy of Management Learning & Education*, March 2003, pp. 37–52.
15. D. M. Rousseau and S. McCarthy, "Educating Managers from an Evidence-Based Perspective," *Academy of Management Learning & Education* 6, no. 1 (2007), pp. 84–101.
16. J. Surowiecki, "The Fatal-Flaw Myth," *The New Yorker*, July 31, 2006, p. 25.
17. "In Finland, Fine for Speeding Sets Record," *International Herald Tribune*, February 11, 2004, p. 2.
18. Chris Woodyard, "War, Terrorism Scare Off Business Travelers," *USA Today*, March 25, 2003.
19. O. C. Richard, "Racial Diversity, Business Strategy, and Firm Performance: A Resource-Based View," *Academy of Management Journal*, April 2000, pp. 164–177.
20. "Bye-Bye, Ozzie and Harriet," *American Demographics*, December 2000, p. 59.
21. This section is based on M. Toosi, "A Century of Change: The U.S. Labor Force, 1950–2050," *Monthly Labor Review*, May 2002, pp. 15–27; and *CBO's Projections of the Labor Force* (Washington, DC: Congressional Budget Office, September 2004).
22. See M. E. A. Jayne and R. L. Dipboye, "Leveraging Diversity to Improve Business Performance: Research Findings and Recommendations for Organizations," *Human Resource Management*, Winter 2004, pp. 409–424; S. E. Jackson and A. Joshi, "Research on Domestic and International Diversity in Organizations: A Merger That Works?" in N. Anderson et al (eds.), *Handbook of Industrial, Work & Organizational Psychology*, vol. 2 (Thousand Oaks, CA: Sage, 2001), pp. 206–231; and L. Smith, "The Business Case for Diversity," *Fortune*, October 13, 2003, pp. S8–S12.
23. See, for instance, S. D. Pugh, J. Dietz, J. W. Wiley, and S. M. Brooks, "Driving Service Effectiveness Through Employee-Customer Linkages," *Academy of Management Executive*, November 2002, pp. 73–84; and H. Liao and A. Chuang, "A Multilevel Investigation of Factors Influencing Employee Service Performance and Customer Outcomes," *Academy of Management Journal*, February 2004, pp. 41–58.
24. See www.patagonia.com/jobs/retail_asst_mgr.shtml; and "Patagonia Sets the Pace for Green Business," *Grist Magazine*, October 22, 2004, www.grist.org.
25. See, for instance, M. Workman and W. Bommer, "Redesigning Computer Call Center Work: A Longitudinal Field Experiment," *Journal of Organizational Behavior*, May 2004, pp. 317–337.
26. See, for instance, V. S. Major, K. J. Klein, and M. G. Ehrhart, "Work Time, Work Interference with Family, and Psychological Distress," *Journal of Applied Psychology*, June 2002, pp. 427–436; D. Brady, "Rethinking the Rat Race," *BusinessWeek*, August 26, 2002, pp. 142–143; J. M. Brett and L. K. Stroh, "Working 61 Plus Hours a Week: Why Do Managers Do It?" *Journal of Applied Psychology*, February 2003, pp. 67–78.
27. See, for instance, *The 2002 National Study of the Changing Workforce* (New York: Families and Work Institute, 2002).
28. Cited in S. Armour, "Workers Put Family First Despite Slow Economy, Jobless Fears."
29. S. Shellenbarger, "What Job Candidates Really Want to Know: Will I Have a Life?" *Wall Street Journal*, November 17, 1999, p. B1; and "U.S. Employers Polish Image to Woo a Demanding New Generation," *Manpower Argus*, February 2000, p. 2.
30. F. Luthans and C. M. Youssef, "Emerging Positive Organizational Behavior," *Journal of Management*, June 2007, pp. 321–349; and J. E. Dutton and S. Sonenshein, "Positive Organizational Scholarship," in C. Cooper and J. Barling (eds.), *Encyclopedia of Positive Psychology* (Thousand Oaks, CA: Sage, 2007).
31. L. M. Roberts, G. Spreitzer, J. Dutton, R. Quinn, E. Heaphy, and B. Barker, "How to Play to Your Strengths," *Harvard Business Review*, January 2005, pp. 1–6; and L. M. Roberts, J. E. Dutton, G. M. Spreitzer, E. D. Heaphy, and R. E. Quinn, "Composing the Reflected Best-Self Portrait: Becoming Extraordinary in Work Organizations," *Academy of Management Review* 30, no. 4 (2005), pp. 712–736.
32. J. Merritt, "For MBAs, Soul-Searching 101," *BusinessWeek*, September 16, 2002, pp. 64–66; and S. Greenhouse, "The Mood at Work: Anger and Anxiety," *New York Times*, October 29, 2002, p. E1.
33. See, for instance, G. R. Weaver, L. K. Trevino, and P. L. Cochran, "Corporate Ethics Practices in the Mid-1990's: An Empirical Study of the Fortune 1000," *Journal of Business Ethics*, February 1999, pp. 283–294; and C. De Mesa Graziano, "Promoting Ethical Conduct: A Review of Corporate Practices," *Strategic Investor Relations*, Fall 2002, pp. 29–35.
34. A. J. Rucci, S. P. Kirn, and R. T. Quinn, "The Employee–Customer–Profit Chain at Sears," *Harvard Business Review*, January–February 1998, pp. 83–97.
35. J. Britt, "Workplace No-Shows' Cost to Employers Rise Again," *HRMagazine*, December 2002, pp. 26–29.
36. "Absence-Minded Workers Cost Business Dearly," *Works Management*, June 2001, pp. 10–14.
37. W. Hoge, "Sweden's Cradle-to-Grave Welfare Starts to Get Ill," *International Herald Tribune*, September 25, 2002, p. 8.
38. "Employee Turnover Costs in the U.S.," *Manpower Argus*, January 2001, p. 5.
39. See http://data.bls.gov (May 11, 2005).
40. See, for example, M. C. Sturman and C. O. Trevor, "The Implications of Linking the Dynamic Performance and Turnover Literatures," *Journal of Applied Psychology*, August 2001, pp. 684–696.
41. Cited in "You Often Lose the Ones You Love," *IndustryWeek*, November 21, 1988, p. 5.
42. R. J. Bennett and S. L. Robinson, "Development of a Measure of Workplace Deviance," *Journal of Applied Psychology* 85, no. 3 (2000), pp. 349–360; A. M. O'Leary-Kelly, M. K. Duffy, and R. W. Griffin, "Construct Confusion in the Study of Antisocial Work Behavior," *Research in Personnel and Human Resources Management* 18 (2000), pp. 275–303; and C. Porath, C. Pearson, and D. L. Shapiro, "Turning the Other Cheek or an Eye for an Eye: Targets' Responses to Incivility," paper interactively presented at the annual meeting of the National Academy of Management, August 1999.
43. D. W. Organ, *Organizational Citizenship Behavior: The Good Soldier Syndrome* (Lexington, MA: Lexington Books, 1988), p. 4; and J. A. LePine, A. Erez, and D. E. Johnson, "The Nature and Dimensionality of Organizational Citizenship Behavior: A Critical Review and Meta-Analysis," *Journal of Applied Psychology*, February 2002, pp. 52–65.

44. P. M. Podsakoff, S. B. MacKenzie, J. B. Paine, and D. G. Bachrach, "Organizational Citizenship Behaviors: A Critical Review of the Theoretical and Empirical Literature and Suggestions for Future Research," *Journal of Management* 26, no. 3 (2000), pp. 543–548; and M. C. Bolino and W. H. Turnley, "Going the Extra Mile: Cultivating and Managing Employee Citizenship Behavior," *Academy of Management Executive*, August 2003, pp. 60–73.

45. T. A. Judge, C. J. Thoresen, J. E. Bono, and G. R. Patton, "The Job Satisfaction–Job Performance Relationship: A Qualitative and Quantitative Review," *Psychological Bulletin* 127 (2001), pp. 376–407.

46. M. Buckingham and C. Coffman, *First, Break All the Rules: What the World's Greatest Managers Do Differently* (New York: Simon & Schuster, 1999).

47. H. J. Leavitt, *Managerial Psychology*, rev. ed. (Chicago: University of Chicago Press, 1964), p. 3.

Foundations of Individual Behavior

I think that God in creating Man somewhat overestimated his ability.

—Writer Oscar Wilde

LEARNING OBJECTIVES

After studying this chapter, you should be able to:

1 Contrast the two types of ability.

2 Define *intellectual ability* and demonstrate its relevance to OB.

3 Identify the key biographical characteristics and describe how they are relevant to OB.

4 Define *learning* and outline the principles of the three major theories of learning.

5 Define *shaping* and show how it can be used in OB.

6 Show how culture affects our understanding of intellectual abilities, biographical characteristics, and learning.

Meet Alexandra Hai, the first woman to operate a gondola in Venice.

For more than a millennium, gondolas have been navigating the canals of Italy's most fabled city. And for more than a millennium, they've been operated by men. Until 2007, when Hai won her right to operate one. But it didn't come without a fight. Hai, a 40-year-old of German and Algerian descent, had to go to court. The court ruled in her favor but restricted her operations to transporting the guests of a local hotel.

Paddling Against the Tide

Source: Dave Yoder/The New York Times

Whenever Hai is out, people stop, gawk, take pictures, and shout ("Brava, Gondoliera! Brava!" shouted one resident from his balcony). Not all the reactions are so positive, though.

Roberto Luppi, president of the Venice gondoliers' association, said that Hai has been proven incapable of operating a gondola, having failed four tests. He says the court's decision to allow her to operate is a publicity stunt. He defends the threats she's received from some male gondoliers, arguing, "After a person accuses gondoliers of being racists and sexists, what does she expect?" he said. "That they are supposed to give her kisses?"

Compared to Scandinavian countries, for example, Italy differentiates markedly between gender roles (though, of course, there is a lot of individual variation within Italy, as within most countries). In Venice, the first women was allowed to wait on tables in St. Mark's Square only 8 years ago. That waitress, Ljubica Gunj, still waits on tables at the Aurora Café. However, next door, the Firoian Café allows women to wait on tables only indoors.

Even though Hai continues to operate her gondola, locals still dispute her right to be on the water. Hai maintains that she failed the tests because they were rigged against her. Luppi and many other Venetians see it differently. "She needs to look in the mirror and accept that she cannot drive," he said. To most of the gondoliers, the job is fit only for a man since it requires strength and the ability to navigate currents and paddle in reverse, and even for aesthetic reasons (relating to the traditional garb of the gondoliers). Says one gondolier, "Let's leave just one tradition intact. Being a gondolier is a tradition, and it is very difficult work."

For her part, Hai argues that her job has been doubly difficult because she's had to fight for her job. "There is nothing worse than to do something like this," she said. "I would have preferred to do something more useful in life, like helping save the rain forests."[1] ■

Gender is but one characteristic that people bring with them when they join an organization. In this chapter, we look at how individual differences in the form of ability (which includes intelligence) and biographical characteristics (such as age) affect employee performance and satisfaction. Then we show how people learn behaviors and what management can do to shape those behaviors.

But before we move on to the next section, check out the following Self-Assessment Library, where you can assess your views on one of the characteristics we'll discuss in this chapter—age.

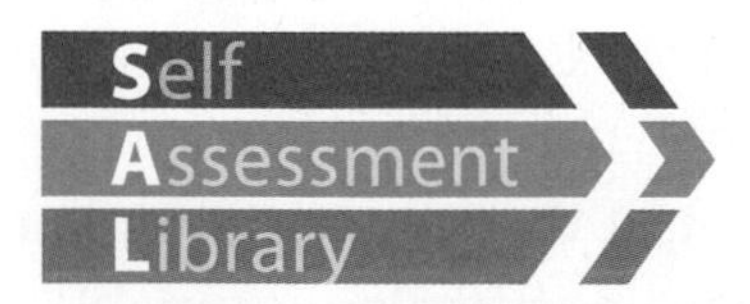

WHAT'S MY ATTITUDE TOWARD OLDER PEOPLE?

In the Self-Assessment Library (available on CD or online), take assessment IV.C.1 (What's My Attitude Toward Older People?) and answer the following questions:

1. *Are you surprised by your results?*
2. *How do your results compare to those of others?*

Ability

1 Contrast the two types of ability.

Contrary to what we were taught in grade school, we weren't all created equal. Most people are to the left or to the right of the median on some normally distributed ability curve. For example, regardless of how motivated you are, it's unlikely that you can act as well as Scarlett Johansson, play basketball as well as LeBron James, write as well as J. K. Rowling, or play the guitar as well as Pat Matheny. Of course, just because we aren't all equal in abilities does not imply that some individuals are inherently inferior to others. Everyone has strengths and weaknesses in terms of ability that make him or her relatively superior or inferior to others in performing certain tasks or activities. From management's standpoint, the issue is not whether people differ in terms of their abilities. They clearly do. The issue is knowing *how* people differ in abilities and using that knowledge to increase the likelihood that an employee will perform his or her job well.

What does *ability* mean? As we will use the term, **ability** refers to an individual's capacity to perform the various tasks in a job. It is a current assessment of what one can do. An individual's overall abilities are essentially made up of two sets of factors: intellectual and physical.

Intellectual Abilities

2 *Define* intellectual ability *and demonstrate its relevance to OB.*

Intellectual abilities are abilities needed to perform mental activities—for thinking, reasoning, and problem solving. People in most societies place a high value on intelligence, and for good reason. Compared to others, smart people generally earn more money and attain higher levels of education. Smart people are also more likely to emerge as leaders of groups. Intelligence quotient (IQ) tests, for example, are designed to ascertain a person's general intellectual abilities. So, too, are popular college admission tests, such as the SAT and ACT and graduate admission tests in business (GMAT), law (LSAT), and medicine (MCAT). Testing firms don't make the argument that their tests assess intelligence, but experts know that they do.[2] The seven most frequently cited dimensions making up intellectual abilities are number aptitude, verbal comprehension, perceptual speed, inductive reasoning, deductive reasoning, spatial visualization, and memory.[3] Exhibit 2-1 describes these dimensions.

Exhibit 2-1 Dimensions of Intellectual Ability

Dimension	Description	Job Example
Number aptitude	Ability to do speedy and accurate arithmetic	Accountant: Computing the sales tax on a set of items
Verbal comprehension	Ability to understand what is read or heard and the relationship of words to each other	Plant manager: Following corporate policies on hiring
Perceptual speed	Ability to identify visual similarities and differences quickly and accurately	Fire investigator: Identifying clues to support a charge of arson
Inductive reasoning	Ability to identify a logical sequence in a problem and then solve the problem	Market researcher: Forecasting demand for a product in the next time period
Deductive reasoning	Ability to use logic and assess the implications of an argument	Supervisor: Choosing between two different suggestions offered by employees
Spatial visualization	Ability to imagine how an object would look if its position in space were changed	Interior decorator: Redecorating an office
Memory	Ability to retain and recall past experiences	Salesperson: Remembering the names of customers

ability *An individual's capacity to perform the various tasks in a job.*

intellectual abilities *The capacity to do mental activities—thinking, reasoning, and problem solving.*

Intelligence dimensions are positively related, so that high scores on one dimension tend to be positively correlated with high scores on another. If you score high on verbal comprehension, for example, you're more likely to score high on spatial visualization. The correlations aren't perfect, meaning that people do have specific abilities. However, the correlations are high enough that for some time, researchers have recognized a general factor of intelligence, called **general mental ability (GMA)**. GMA doesn't deny that there are specific abilities, but it suggests that it makes sense to talk about overall, or general, intelligence.

Jobs differ in the demands they place on incumbents to use their intellectual abilities. The more complex a job is in terms of information-processing demands, the more general intelligence and verbal abilities will be necessary to perform the job successfully.[4] Of course, a high IQ is not a requirement for all jobs. For jobs in which employee behavior is highly routine and there are few or no opportunities to exercise discretion, a high IQ is not as important to performing well. However, that does not mean that people with high IQs cannot have an impact on jobs that are traditionally less complex.

It might surprise you that the most widely used intelligence test in hiring decisions takes only 12 minutes. It's called the Wonderlic Personnel Test. There are different forms of the test, and each form has 50 questions. Here are a few examples of questions from the Wonderlic:

- When rope is selling at $.10 a foot, how many feet can you buy for $.60?
- Assume the first two statements are true. Is the final one:
  1. true, 2. false, 3. not certain?
     a. The boy plays baseball.
     b. All baseball players wear hats.
     c. The boy wears a hat.

The Wonderlic tests both speed (almost nobody has time to answer every question) and power (questions get harder as you go along), so the average

International OB

The Benefits of Cultural Intelligence

Have you ever noticed that some individuals seem to have a knack for relating well to people from different cultures? Some researchers have labeled this skill *cultural intelligence*, which is an outsider's natural ability to interpret an individual's unfamiliar gestures and behaviors in the same way that others from the individual's culture would. Cultural intelligence is important because when conducting business with people from different cultures, misunderstandings can often occur, and, as a result, cooperation and productivity may suffer.

Consider the following example. An American manager was meeting with his fellow design team engineers, two of whom were German. As ideas floated around the table, his German colleagues quickly rejected them. The American thought the feedback was harsh and concluded that his German colleagues were rude. However, they were merely critiquing the ideas, not the individual—a distinction that the American was unable to make, perhaps due to a lack of cultural intelligence. As a result, the American became wary of contributing potentially good ideas. Had the American been more culturally intelligent, he likely would have recognized the true motives behind his colleagues' remarks and thus may have been able to use those remarks to improve his ideas.

It is unclear whether the notion of cultural intelligence is separate from other forms of intelligence, such as emotional intelligence, and even whether cultural intelligence is different from cognitive ability. However, it is clear that the ability to interact well with individuals from different cultures is a key asset in today's global business environment.

Source: Based on C. Earley and E. Mosakowski, "Cultural Intelligence," *Harvard Business Review*, October 2004, pp. 139–146.

score is pretty low—about 21/50. And because the Wonderlic is able to provide valid information at a cheap price ($2–$6/applicant), more and more companies are using the test in hiring decisions. For example, the Factory Card & Party Outlet, which has 182 stores in the United States, uses the Wonderlic. So do Subway, restaurants and the National Football League, as you'll see in Chapter 18 Most companies that use the Wonderlic don't use it in place of other hiring tools such as application forms or interviews. Rather, they add the Wonderlic as another source of information—in this case, because of the test's ability to provide valid data on applicants' intelligence levels.

Interestingly, while intelligence is a big help in performing a job well, it doesn't make people happier or more satisfied with their jobs. The correlation between intelligence and job satisfaction is about zero. Why? Research suggests that although intelligent people perform better and tend to have more interesting jobs, they are also more critical in evaluating their job conditions. Thus, smart people have it better, but they also expect more.[5]

Physical Abilities

Though the changing nature of work suggests that intellectual abilities are becoming increasingly important for many jobs, **physical abilities** have been and will remain important for successfully doing certain jobs. Research on the requirements needed in hundreds of jobs has identified nine basic abilities involved in the performance of physical tasks.[6] These are described in Exhibit 2-2. Individuals differ in the extent to which they have each of these abilities. Not surprisingly, there is also little

3 *Identify the key biographical characteristics and describe how they are relevant to OB.*

Exhibit 2-2 Nine Basic Physical Abilities

Strength Factors	
1. Dynamic strength	Ability to exert muscular force repeatedly or continuously over time
2. Trunk strength	Ability to exert muscular strength using the trunk (particularly abdominal) muscles
3. Static strength	Ability to exert force against external objects
4. Explosive strength	Ability to expend a maximum of energy in one or a series of explosive acts
Flexibility Factors	
5. Extent flexibility	Ability to move the trunk and back muscles as far as possible
6. Dynamic flexibility	Ability to make rapid, repeated flexing movements
Other Factors	
7. Body coordination	Ability to coordinate the simultaneous actions of different parts of the body
8. Balance	Ability to maintain equilibrium despite forces pulling off balance
9. Stamina	Ability to continue maximum effort requiring prolonged effort over time

general mental ability (GMA) *An overall factor of intelligence, as suggested by the positive correlations among specific intellectual ability dimensions.*

physical abilities *The capacity to do tasks that demand stamina, dexterity, strength, and similar characteristics.*

relationship among them: A high score on one is no assurance of a high score on others. High employee performance is likely to be achieved when management has ascertained the extent to which a job requires each of the nine abilities and then ensures that employees in that job have those abilities.

Biographical Characteristics

As discussed in Chapter 1, this textbook is essentially concerned with finding and analyzing the variables that have an impact on employee productivity, absence, turnover, deviance, citizenship, and satisfaction. The list of those variables—as shown in Exhibit 1-6—is long and contains some complicated concepts. Many of the concepts—motivation, say, or power and politics or organizational culture—are hard to assess. It might be valuable, then, to begin by looking at factors that are easily definable and readily available—data that can be obtained, for the most part, simply from information available in an employee's personnel file. What factors would these be? Obvious characteristics would be an employee's age, gender, race, and length of service with an organization. Fortunately, a sizable amount of research has specifically analyzed many of these **biographical characteristics**.

Age

The relationship between age and job performance is likely to be an issue of increasing importance during the next decade for at least three reasons. First, there is a widespread belief that job performance declines with increasing age. Regardless of whether this is true, a lot of people believe it and act on it. Second, as noted in Chapter 1, the workforce is aging. The third reason is U.S. legislation that, for all intents and purposes, outlaws mandatory retirement. Most U.S. workers today no longer have to retire at age 70.

What is the perception of older workers? Evidence indicates that employers hold mixed feelings.[7] They see a number of positive qualities that older workers

Home Depot values the work ethic of older employees such as assistant manager Ellen Van Valen shown here, who is in her late 60s. Home Depot is one of a growing number of firms that are recruiting older workers because, compared with younger workers, they have lower turnover rates and training costs and, in many cases, better work performance. Van Valen believes that age has little to do with the desire to work but says that "older folks seem to catch on a lot quicker."

Source: Douglas Healey/ The New York Times

bring to their jobs, such as experience, judgment, a strong work ethic, and commitment to quality. But older workers are also perceived as lacking flexibility and as being resistant to new technology. And in a time when organizations are actively seeking individuals who are adaptable and open to change, the negatives associated with age clearly hinder the initial hiring of older workers and increase the likelihood that they will be let go during cutbacks. Now let's take a look at the evidence. What effect does age actually have on turnover, absenteeism, productivity, and satisfaction?

The older you get, the less likely you are to quit your job. That conclusion is based on studies of the age–turnover relationship.[8] Of course, this shouldn't be too surprising. As workers get older, they have fewer alternative job opportunities. In addition, older workers are less likely to resign than are younger workers because their long tenure tends to provide them with higher wage rates, longer paid vacations, and more attractive pension benefits.

It's tempting to assume that age is also inversely related to absenteeism. After all, if older workers are less likely to quit, won't they also demonstrate higher stability by coming to work more regularly? Not necessarily. Most studies do show an inverse relationship, but close examination finds that the age–absence relationship is partially a function of whether the absence is avoidable or unavoidable.[9] In general, older employees have lower rates of avoidable absence than do younger employees. However, they have higher rates of unavoidable absence, probably due to the poorer health associated with aging and the longer recovery period that older workers need when injured.

How does age affect productivity? There is a widespread belief that productivity declines with age. It is often assumed that an individual's skills—particularly speed, agility, strength, and coordination—decay over time and that prolonged job boredom and lack of intellectual stimulation contribute to reduced productivity. The evidence, however, contradicts that belief and those assumptions. For instance, during a 3-year period, a large hardware chain staffed one of its stores solely with employees over 50 and compared its results with those of five stores with younger employees. The store staffed by the over-50 employees was significantly more productive (measured in terms of sales generated against labor costs) than two of the other stores and held its own with the other three.[10] Other reviews of the research find that age and job performance are unrelated.[11] Moreover, this finding seems to be true for almost all types of jobs, professional and nonprofessional. The natural conclusion is that the demands of most jobs, even those with heavy manual labor requirements, are not extreme enough for any declines in physical skills attributable to age to have an impact on productivity; or, if there is some decay due to age, it is offset by gains due to experience.[12]

Our final concern is the relationship between age and job satisfaction. On this issue, the evidence is mixed. Most studies indicate a positive association between age and satisfaction, at least up to age 60.[13] Other studies, however, have found a U-shaped relationship.[14] Several explanations could clear up these results, the most plausible being that these studies are intermixing professional and nonprofessional employees. When the two types are separated, satisfaction tends to continually increase among professionals as they age, whereas it falls among nonprofessionals during middle age and then rises again in the later years.

biographical characteristics *Personal characteristics—such as age, gender, race, and length of tenure—that are objective and easily obtained from personnel records.*

Gender

Few issues initiate more debates, misconceptions, and unsupported opinions than whether women perform as well on jobs as men do. In this section, we review the research on that issue.

The evidence suggests that the best place to begin is with the recognition that there are few, if any, important differences between men and women that will affect their job performance. There are, for instance, no consistent male–female differences in problem-solving ability, analytical skills, competitive drive, motivation, sociability, or learning ability.[15] Psychological studies have found that women are more willing to conform to authority and that men are more aggressive and more likely than women to have expectations of success, but those differences are minor. Given the significant changes that have taken place in the past 40 years in terms of increasing female participation rates in the workforce and rethinking what constitutes male and female roles, you should operate on the assumption that there is no significant difference in job productivity between men and women.[16]

One issue that does seem to differ between genders, especially when the employee has preschool-age children, is preference for work schedules.[17] Working mothers are more likely to prefer part-time work, flexible work schedules, and telecommuting in order to accommodate their family responsibilities.

But what about absence and turnover rates? Are women less stable employees than men? First, on the question of turnover, the evidence indicates no significant differences.[18] Women's quit rates are similar to those for men. The research on absence, however, consistently indicates that women have higher rates of absenteeism than men do.[19] The most logical explanation for this finding is that the research was conducted in North America, and North American culture has historically placed home and family responsibilities on the woman. When a child is ill or someone needs to stay home to wait for a plumber, it has been the woman who has traditionally taken time off from work. However, this research is undoubtedly time bound.[20] The historical role of the woman in caring for children and as secondary breadwinner has definitely changed in the past generation, and a large proportion of men nowadays are as interested in day care and the problems associated with child care in general as are women.

JPMorgan Chase, a global banking and financial services firm, believes that women perform as well on jobs as men do. Almost 60 percent of the firm's employees are women, and 50 percent of its managers and professionals are women. The many working moms at JPMorgan appreciate flexible work schedules such as job sharing, compressed workweeks, flextime, and telecommuting. JPMorgan also provides on-site, back-up child-care centers for employees whose usual child-care arrangements fall through. Shown here are stockbrokers and traders at the company's headquarters.

Race

Race is a controversial issue. It can be so contentious that it's tempting to avoid the topic. A complete picture of individual differences in OB, however, would be incomplete without a discussion of race.

What is race? Before we can discuss how race matters in OB, first we have to reach some consensus about what race is, and that's not easily done. Some scholars argue that it's not productive to discuss race for policy reasons (it's a divisive issue), for biological reasons (a large percentage of us are a mixture of races), or for genetic and anthropological reasons (many anthropologists and evolutionary scientists reject the concept of distinct racial categories).

Most people in the United States identify themselves according to a racial group. In contrast, in some countries, such as Brazil, people are less likely to define themselves according to distinct racial categories. The U.S. Department of Education classifies individuals according to five racial categories: African American, Native American (American Indian/Alaskan Native), Asian/Pacific Islander, Hispanic, and white. We'll define race as the biological heritage people use to identify themselves. This definition allows each individual to define his or her race. Golfer Tiger Woods, for example, refuses to place himself into a single racial category, emphasizing his multiethnic roots.

Race has been studied quite a bit in OB, particularly as it relates to employment outcomes such as personnel selection decisions, performance evaluations, pay, and workplace discrimination. Doing justice to all of this research isn't possible here, so let's summarize a few points.

First, in employment settings, there is a tendency for individuals to favor colleagues of their own race in performance evaluations, promotion decisions, and pay raises.[21] Second, there are substantial racial differences in attitudes toward affirmative action, with African Americans approving of such programs to a greater degree than whites.[22] Third, African Americans generally fare worse than whites in employment decisions. For example, African Americans receive lower ratings in employment interviews, are paid less, and are promoted less frequently.[23]

The major dilemma faced by employers who use mental ability tests for selection, promotion, training, and similar personnel decisions is concern that they may have a negative impact on racial and ethnic groups.[24] For instance, some minority groups score, on average, as much as 1 standard deviation lower than whites on verbal, numeric, and spatial ability tests, meaning that only 10 percent of minority group members score above the average for whites. However, after reviewing the evidence, researchers have concluded that "despite group differences in mean test performance, there is little convincing evidence that well-constructed tests are more predictive of educational, training, or occupational performance for members of the majority group than for members of minority groups."[25] The issue of racial differences in cognitive ability tests continues to be hotly debated.[26]

Other Biographical Characteristics: Tenure, Religion, Sexual Orientation, and Gender Identity

The last set of biographical characteristic we'll look are tenure, religion, and sexual orientation.

Tenure With the exception of gender and racial differences, few issues are more subject to misconceptions and speculations than the impact of seniority on job performance.

Extensive reviews have been conducted of the seniority–productivity relationship.[27] If we define *seniority* as time on a particular job, we can say that the

OB In the News

Are You More Biased Than You Think?

One late Wednesday afternoon, a 34-year-old white woman sat down in her Washington, DC, office to take a test. She prided herself on being a civil rights advocate, and her office décor gave ample testament to her liberal causes.

The woman accessed a test on a Web site run by a research team at Harvard University. The test was relatively simple; it asked her to distinguish between a series of black and white faces. When she saw a black face, she was to press a key on the left, and when she saw a white face, she was to press a key on the right. Next, she was asked to distinguish between a series of positive and negative words. Words such as "wonderful" required pressing the "i" key, words such as "terrible" required pressing the "e" key. The test remained simple when two categories were combined: The person pressed "e" if she saw either a white face or a positive word, and she pressed "i" if she saw either a black face or a negative word.

Then the groupings were reversed. The woman's index fingers hovered over her keyboard. The test now required her to group black faces with positive words and white faces with negative words. She leaned forward intently. She made no mistakes, but it took her longer to correctly sort the words and images.

Her result appeared on the screen, and the activist became very silent. The test found she had a bias for whites over blacks.

"It surprises me I have any preferences at all," she said. "By the work I do, by my education, my background. I'm progressive, and I think I have no bias. Being a minority myself, I don't feel I should or would have biases."

As it turns out, evidence is starting to accumulate—there are more than 60 studies so far—showing that most people have these sorts of implicit biases. They're implicit because we don't consciously realize they're there. But there they are. We may have implicit biases against minorities or women, or people of a certain religion or sexual orientation. Some people do not have an implicit bias in one area (say, toward race), but do in another area (say, toward Republicans).

Are these biases set in stone? Are they changed by experience? That's not yet clear. Some of the researchers argue that such biases are so primitive that simple training exercises or experiences are unlikely to change them. Like race or gender, they may be part of who we are. "Mind bugs operate without us being conscious of them," says one of the Harvard researchers. "They are not special things that happen in our heart because we are evil."

Source: Based on S. Vedantam, "See No Bias," *Washington Post*, January 23, 2005, p. W12; and A. S. Baron and M. R. Banaji, "The Development of Implicit Attitudes: Evidence of Race Evaluations from Ages 6 and 10 and Adulthood," *Psychological Science*, January 2006, pp. 53–58.

most recent evidence demonstrates a positive relationship between seniority and job productivity. So tenure, expressed as work experience, appears to be a good predictor of employee productivity.

The research relating tenure to absence is quite straightforward. Studies consistently demonstrate seniority to be negatively related to absenteeism.[28] In fact, in terms of both frequency of absence and total days lost at work, tenure is the single most important explanatory variable.[29]

Tenure is also a potent variable in explaining turnover. The longer a person is in a job, the less likely he or she is to quit.[30] Moreover, consistent with research which suggests that past behavior is the best predictor of future behavior,[31] evidence indicates that tenure on an employee's previous job is a powerful predictor of that employee's future turnover.[32]

The evidence indicates that tenure and job satisfaction are positively related.[33] In fact, when age and tenure are treated separately, tenure appears to be a more consistent and stable predictor of job satisfaction than is chronological age.

Religion Religion is a touchy subject. Not only do religious and nonreligious people question each other's belief systems, often people of different religious faiths conflict. As demonstrated by the war in Iraq and the past conflict in Northern Ireland, there are often violent differences among sects of the same religion. U.S. federal law prohibits employers from discriminating against employees based on their religion, with very few exceptions. However, that doesn't mean religion is a non-issue in OB.

Perhaps the greatest religious issue in the United States today revolves around Islam. There are nearly 2 million Muslims in the United States, and across the world, Islam is one of the most popular religions. For the most part, U.S. Muslims have attitudes similar to those of other U.S. citizens (though the differences tend to be greater for younger U.S. Muslims). Still, there are both perceived and real differences. Nearly 4 of 10 U.S. adults admit that they harbor negative feelings or prejudices toward U.S. Muslims. Fifty-two percent believe that U.S. Muslims are not respectful of women.

Some in the United States take these general biases a step further. Motaz Elshafi, a 28-year-old software engineer for Cisco Systems who was born and raised in New Jersey, received an e-mail from a coworker addressed, "Dear Terrorist." Although such acts are relatively isolated, they do occur.

There are limits to which workplaces can be adapted to fit the views of some Muslims. For example, it may be difficult for certain employers to accommodate some Muslims' practice of praying five times a day or wearing a beard or head scarf.

But we need to be careful of laying down blanket judgments of all Muslims; they're no more accurate than judgments of all Christians or all the people in any other group. As one Islamic scholar has noted, "There is no such thing as a single American Muslim community, much as there is no single Christian community. Muslims vary hugely by ethnicity, faith, tradition, education, income, and degree of religious observance."[34]

Sexual Orientation and Gender Identity Employers differ a lot in how they treat sexual orientation. Federal law does not prohibit discrimination against employees based on sexual orientation, though many states and municipalities do have anti-discrimination policies. Many employers ignore it (practicing some version of the "don't ask, don't tell" military policy), some do not hire gays, but an increasing number of employers are implementing policies and practices protecting the rights of gays in the workplace. Take defense contractor Raytheon, builder of Tomahawk cruise missiles and other defense systems. Raytheon offers domestic partner benefits, supports a wide array of gay rights groups, and wants to be an employer of choice for gays. Why has Raytheon done this? Because it believes these policies give it an advantage in the ever-competitive market of hiring engineers and scientists.

Raytheon is not alone. More than half of the Fortune 500 companies offer domestic partner benefits for gay couples. This includes companies such as American Express, IBM, Intel, Morgan Stanley, Motorola, and Wal-Mart. That doesn't mean, though, that all employers are on board. Some companies are against domestic partner benefits or nondiscrimination clauses for gay employees. Among those companies are Alltel, ADM, ExxonMobil, H. J. Heinz, Nissan, Nestle, and Rubbermaid.[35]

As for gender identity, companies are increasingly putting in place policies to govern how their organization treats employees who change genders (often called *transgender employees*). In 2001, only eight companies in the Fortune 500 had policies on gender identity. By 2006, that number had swelled to 124. IBM is one of them. Brad Salavich, a diversity manager for IBM, says, "We believe that having strong transgender and gender identification policies is a natural extension of IBM's corporate culture." Dealing with transgender employees requires some special considerations, such as bathrooms, names, and so on.[36]

Learning

4 *Define* learning *and outline the principles of the three major theories of learning.*

All complex behavior is learned. If we want to explain and predict behavior, we need to understand how people learn. In this section, we define *learning*, present three popular learning theories, and describe how managers can facilitate employee learning.

A Definition of *Learning*

What is **learning**? A psychologist's definition is considerably broader than the layperson's view that "it's what we did when we went to school." In actuality, each of us is continuously "going to school." Learning occurs all the time. Therefore, a generally accepted definition of *learning* is "any relatively permanent change in behavior that occurs as a result of experience."[37] Ironically, we can say that changes in behavior indicate that learning has taken place and that learning is a change in behavior.

The previous definition suggests that we can see changes taking place, but we can't see the learning itself. The concept is theoretical and, hence, not directly observable:

> You have seen people in the process of learning, you have seen people who behave in a particular way as a result of learning and some of you (in fact, I guess the majority of you) have "learned" at some time in your life. In other words, we infer that learning has taken place if an individual behaves, reacts, responds as a result of experience in a manner different from the way he formerly behaved.[38]

Our definition has several components that deserve clarification. First, learning involves change. Change may be good or bad from an organizational point of view. People can learn unfavorable behaviors—to hold prejudices or to shirk their responsibilities, for example—as well as favorable behaviors. Second,

The U.S. military uses cultural sensitivity training to provide soldiers with an experience that will lead to positive and permanent changes in their behavior. Soldiers learn how to communicate with village leaders in Afghanistan by practicing with role players who are Afghan citizens living in the United States. They learn in a realistic setting by sitting on the floor in a room decorated to resemble the home of an Afghan village leader. Instructors evaluate the training sessions to determine whether changes in behavior take place as a result of the learning process.

the change must become ingrained. Immediate changes may be only reflexive or a result of fatigue (or a sudden burst of energy) and thus may not represent learning. Third, some form of experience is necessary for learning. Experience may be acquired directly through observation or practice, or it may be acquired indirectly, as through reading. The crucial test still remains: Does this experience result in a relatively permanent change in behavior? If the answer is "yes," we can say that learning has taken place.

Theories of Learning

How do we learn? Three theories have been offered to explain the process by which we acquire patterns of behavior. These are classical conditioning, operant conditioning, and social learning.

Classical Conditioning **Classical conditioning** grew out of experiments to teach dogs to salivate in response to the ringing of a bell, conducted in the early 1900s by Russian physiologist Ivan Pavlov.[39] A simple surgical procedure allowed Pavlov to measure accurately the amount of saliva secreted by a dog. When Pavlov presented the dog with a piece of meat, the dog exhibited a noticeable increase in salivation. When Pavlov withheld the presentation of meat and merely rang a bell, the dog did not salivate. Then Pavlov proceeded to link the meat and the ringing of the bell. After repeatedly hearing the bell before getting the food, the dog began to salivate as soon as the bell rang. After a while, the dog would salivate merely at the sound of the bell, even if no food was offered. In effect, the dog had learned to respond—that is, to salivate—to the bell. Let's review this experiment to introduce the key concepts in classical conditioning.

In Pavlov's experiment, the meat was an *unconditioned stimulus*; it invariably caused the dog to react in a specific way. The reaction that took place whenever the unconditioned stimulus occurred was called the *unconditioned response* (or the noticeable increase in salivation, in this case). The bell was an artificial stimulus, or what we call the *conditioned stimulus*. Although it was originally neutral, after the bell was paired with the meat (an unconditioned stimulus), it eventually produced a response when presented alone. The last key concept is the *conditioned response*. This describes the behavior of the dog; it salivated in reaction to the bell alone.

Using these concepts, we can summarize classical conditioning. Essentially, learning a conditioned response involves building up an association between a conditioned stimulus and an unconditioned stimulus. When the stimuli, one compelling and the other one neutral, are paired, the neutral one becomes a conditioned stimulus and, hence, takes on the properties of the unconditioned stimulus.

Classical conditioning can be used to explain why Christmas carols often bring back pleasant memories of childhood; the songs are associated with the festive holiday spirit and evoke fond memories and feelings of euphoria. In an organizational setting, we can also see classical conditioning operating. For example, at one manufacturing plant, every time the top executives from the head office were scheduled to make a visit, the plant management would clean up the administrative offices and wash the windows. This went on for years.

learning *A relatively permanent change in behavior that occurs as a result of experience.*

classical conditioning *A type of conditioning in which an individual responds to some stimulus that would not ordinarily produce such a response.*

Eventually, employees would turn on their best behavior and look prim and proper whenever the windows were cleaned—even in those occasional instances when the cleaning was not paired with a visit from the top brass. People had learned to associate the cleaning of the windows with a visit from the head office.

Classical conditioning is passive. Something happens, and we react in a specific way. It is elicited in response to a specific, identifiable event. As such, it can explain simple reflexive behaviors. But most behavior—particularly the complex behavior of individuals in organizations—is emitted rather than elicited. That is, it's voluntary rather than reflexive. For example, employees *choose* to arrive at work on time, ask their boss for help with problems, or "goof off" when no one is watching. The learning of those behaviors is better understood by looking at operant conditioning.

Operant Conditioning **Operant conditioning** argues that behavior is a function of its consequences. People learn to behave to get something they want or to avoid something they don't want. Operant behavior means voluntary or learned behavior in contrast to reflexive or unlearned behavior. The tendency to repeat such behavior is influenced by the reinforcement or lack of reinforcement brought about by the consequences of the behavior. Therefore, reinforcement strengthens a behavior and increases the likelihood that it will be repeated.

What Pavlov did for classical conditioning, the Harvard psychologist B. F. Skinner did for operant conditioning.[40] Skinner argued that creating pleasing consequences to follow specific forms of behavior would increase the frequency of that behavior. He demonstrated that people will most likely engage in desired behaviors if they are positively reinforced for doing so; that rewards are most effective if they immediately follow the desired response; and that behavior that is not rewarded, or is punished, is less likely to be repeated. For example, we know a professor who places a mark by a student's name each time the student makes a contribution to class discussions. Operant conditioning would argue that this practice is motivating because it conditions a student to expect a reward (earning class credit) each time she demonstrates a specific behavior (speaking up in class). The concept of operant conditioning was part of Skinner's broader concept of **behaviorism**, which argues that behavior follows stimuli in a relatively unthinking manner. In Skinner's form of radical behaviorism, concepts such as feelings, thoughts, and other states of mind are rejected as causes of behavior. In short, people learn to associate stimulus and response, but their conscious awareness of this association is irrelevant.[41]

You see apparent illustrations of operant conditioning everywhere. For example, any situation in which it is either explicitly stated or implicitly suggested that reinforcements are contingent on some action on your part involves the use of operant learning. Your instructor says that if you want a high grade in the course, you must supply correct answers on the test. A commissioned salesperson wanting to earn a sizable income finds that doing so is contingent on generating high sales in her territory. Of course, the linkage can also work to teach the individual to engage in behaviors that work against the best interests of the organization. Assume that your boss tells you that if you will work overtime during the next 3-week busy season you'll be compensated for it at your next performance appraisal. However, when performance-appraisal time comes, you find that you are given no positive reinforcement for your overtime work. The next time your boss asks you to work overtime, what will you do? You'll probably decline! Your behavior can be explained by operant conditioning: If a behavior fails to be positively reinforced, the probability that the behavior will be repeated declines.

Toyota Motor Corporation applies social learning theory in teaching employees skills they need to meet the company's high standards of quality and efficiency. At its new Global Production Center training facility in Toyota City, Japan, employees from factories around the world learn production techniques through observation and direct experience. Trainees first watch computerized "visual manuals" to learn basic skills. Then, under the tutelage of an experienced production master, they practice the skills. In this photo, a trainer (left) models a spray-painting technique while a trainee practices the skill.

Social Learning Individuals can learn by observing what happens to other people and just by being told about something as well as through direct experiences. For example, much of what we have learned comes from watching models—parents, teachers, peers, motion picture and television performers, bosses, and so forth. This view that we can learn through both observation and direct experience is called **social-learning theory**.[42]

Although social-learning theory is an extension of operant conditioning—that is, it assumes that behavior is a function of consequences—it also acknowledges the existence of observational learning and the importance of perception in learning. People respond to how they perceive and define consequences, not to the objective consequences themselves.

The influence of models is central to the social-learning viewpoint. Four processes have been found to determine the influence that a model will have on an individual:

1. **Attentional processes.** People learn from a model only when they recognize and pay attention to its critical features. We tend to be most influenced by models that are attractive, repeatedly available, important to us, or similar to us in our estimation.
2. **Retention processes.** A model's influence depends on how well the individual remembers the model's action after the model is no longer readily available.
3. **Motor reproduction processes.** After a person has seen a new behavior by observing the model, the watching must be converted to doing. This process then demonstrates that the individual can perform the modeled activities.

operant conditioning *A type of conditioning in which desired voluntary behavior leads to a reward or prevents a punishment.*

behaviorism *A theory that argues that behavior follows stimuli in a relatively unthinking manner.*

social-learning theory *The view that people can learn through observation and direct experience.*

4. **Reinforcement processes.** Individuals are motivated to exhibit the modeled behavior if positive incentives or rewards are provided. Behaviors that are positively reinforced are given more attention, learned better, and performed more often.

Shaping: A Managerial Tool

5 *Define* shaping *and show how it can be used in OB.*

Because learning takes place on the job as well as prior to it, managers are concerned with how they can teach employees to behave in ways that most benefit the organization. When we attempt to mold individuals by guiding their learning in graduated steps, we are **shaping behavior**.

Consider a situation in which an employee's behavior is significantly different from that sought by management. If management rewarded the individual only when he showed desirable responses, there might be very little reinforcement taking place. In such a case, shaping offers a logical approach toward achieving the desired behavior.

We *shape* behavior by systematically reinforcing each successive step that moves the individual closer to the desired response. If an employee who has chronically been a half-hour late for work comes in only 20 minutes late, we can reinforce that improvement. Reinforcement would increase as responses more closely approximated the desired behavior.

Methods of Shaping Behavior There are four ways to shape behavior: through positive reinforcement, negative reinforcement, punishment, and extinction.

Following a response with something pleasant is called *positive reinforcement*. This would describe, for instance, a boss who praises an employee for a job well done. Following a response by the termination or withdrawal of something unpleasant is called *negative reinforcement*. If your college instructor asks a question and you don't know the answer, looking through your lecture notes is likely

MYTH OR SCIENCE? *"You Can't Teach an Old Dog New Tricks!"*

This statement is false. It reflects the widely held stereotype that older workers have difficulty adapting to new methods and techniques. Studies consistently demonstrate that older employees are perceived as being relatively inflexible, resistant to change, and less willing and able to be trained than their younger counterparts.[43] But these perceptions are mostly wrong.

Evidence does indicate that older workers (typically defined as people aged 50 and over) are less confident of their learning abilities (perhaps due to acceptance of societal stereotypes). Moreover, older workers do seem to be somewhat less efficient in acquiring complex or demanding skills, and, on average, they are not as fast in terms of reaction time or in solving problems. That is, they may take longer to train. However, once trained, research indicates that older workers actually learn more than their younger counterparts, and they are better at transferring what they have learned to the job.[44] And age actually improves some intellectual abilities, such as verbal ability, and older brains are packed with more so-called expert knowledge—meaning they tend to have better outlines for how to solve problems.[45]

The ability to acquire the skills, knowledge, or behavior necessary to perform a job at a given level—that is, trainability—has been the subject of much research. And the evidence indicates that there are differences between people in their trainability. A number of individual-difference factors (such as low ability and reduced motivation) have been found to impede learning and training outcomes. However, age has not been found to influence these outcomes. In fact, older employees actually benefit more from training. Still, the stereotypes persist.[46] ■

to preclude your being called on. This is a negative reinforcement because you have learned that looking busily through your notes prevents the instructor from calling on you. *Punishment* is causing an unpleasant condition in an attempt to eliminate an undesirable behavior. Giving an employee a 2-day suspension from work without pay for showing up drunk is an example of punishment. Eliminating any reinforcement that is maintaining a behavior is called *extinction*. When the behavior is not reinforced, it tends to be gradually extinguished. College instructors who wish to discourage students from asking questions in class can eliminate this behavior in their students by ignoring those who raise their hands to ask questions. Hand raising will become extinct when it is invariably met with an absence of reinforcement.

Both positive and negative reinforcement result in learning. They strengthen a response and increase the probability of repetition. In the preceding illustrations, praise strengthens and increases the behavior of doing a good job because praise is desired. The behavior of "looking busy" is similarly strengthened and increased by its terminating the undesirable consequence of being called on by the teacher. However, both punishment and extinction weaken behavior and tend to decrease its subsequent frequency. In shaping behavior, a critical issue is the timing of reinforcements. This is an issue we'll consider now.

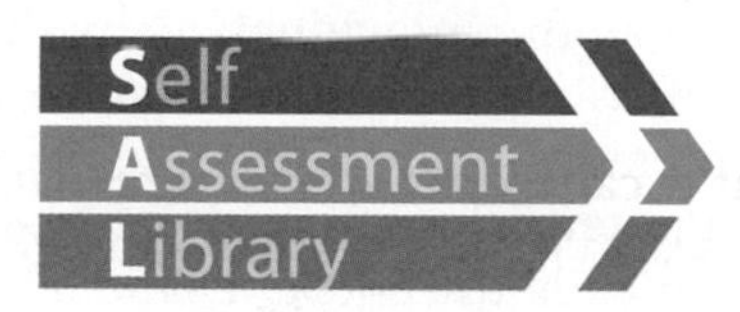

HOW GOOD AM I AT DISCIPLINING OTHERS?

In the Self-Assessment Library (available on CD or online), take assessment II.B.5 (How Good Am I at Disciplining Others?).

Schedules of Reinforcement The two major types of reinforcement schedules are *continuous* and *intermittent*. A **continuous reinforcement** schedule reinforces the desired behavior each and every time it is demonstrated. Take, for example, the case of someone who historically has had trouble arriving at work on time. Every time he is not tardy, his manager might compliment him on his desirable behavior. With **intermittent reinforcement**, on the other hand, not every instance of the desirable behavior is reinforced, but reinforcement is given often enough to make the behavior worth repeating. This latter schedule can be compared to the workings of a slot machine, which people will continue to play even when they know it is adjusted to give a considerable return to the casino. The intermittent payoffs occur just often enough to reinforce the behavior of slipping in coins and pulling the handle. Evidence indicates that the intermittent, or varied, form of reinforcement tends to promote more resistance to extinction than does the continuous form.[47]

An intermittent reinforcement can be of a ratio or interval type. *Ratio schedules* depend on how many responses the subject makes. The individual is reinforced after giving a certain number of specific types of behavior. *Interval schedules* depend on how much time has passed since the previous reinforcement. With interval schedules, the individual is reinforced on the first appropriate

shaping behavior *Systematically reinforcing each successive step that moves an individual closer to the desired response.*

continuous reinforcement *Reinforcing a desired behavior each time it is demonstrated.*

intermittent reinforcement *Reinforcing a desired behavior often enough to make the behavior worth repeating but not every time it is demonstrated.*

behavior after a particular time has elapsed. A reinforcement can also be classified as fixed or variable.

When rewards are spaced at uniform time intervals, the reinforcement schedule is a **fixed-interval schedule**. The critical variable is time, which is held constant. This is the predominant schedule for most salaried workers in North America. When you get your paycheck on a weekly, semimonthly, monthly, or other predetermined time basis, you're rewarded on a fixed-interval reinforcement schedule.

If rewards are distributed in time so that reinforcements are unpredictable, the schedule is a **variable-interval schedule**. When an instructor advises her class that pop quizzes will be given during the term (the exact number of which is unknown to the students) and the quizzes will account for 20 percent of the term grade, she is using a variable-interval schedule. Similarly, a series of randomly timed unannounced visits to a company office by the corporate audit staff is an example of a variable-interval schedule.

In a **fixed-ratio schedule**, after a fixed or constant number of responses are given, a reward is initiated. For example, a piece-rate incentive plan is a fixed-ratio schedule; the employee receives a reward based on the number of work pieces generated. If the piece rate for a zipper installer in a dressmaking factory is $5 per dozen, the reinforcement (money in this case) is fixed to the number of zippers sewn into garments. After every dozen is sewn in, the installer has earned another $5.

When the reward varies relative to the behavior of the individual, he or she is said to be reinforced on a **variable-ratio schedule**. Salespeople on commission are examples of individuals on such a reinforcement schedule. On some occasions, they may make a sale after only 2 calls on a potential customer. On other occasions, they might need to make 20 or more calls to secure a sale. The reward, then, is variable in relation to the number of successful calls the salesperson makes. Exhibit 2-3 summarizes the schedules of reinforcement.

Reinforcement Schedules and Behavior Continuous reinforcement schedules can lead to early satiation, and under this schedule, behavior tends to weaken rapidly when reinforcers are withheld. However, continuous reinforcers are appropriate for newly emitted, unstable, or low-frequency responses. In contrast, intermittent reinforcers preclude early satiation because they don't follow every response. They are appropriate for stable or high-frequency responses.

In general, variable schedules tend to lead to higher performance than fixed schedules (see Exhibit 2-4). For example, as noted previously, most

Exhibit 2-3 Schedules of Reinforcement

Reinforcement Schedule	Nature of Reinforcement	Effect on Behavior	Example
Continuous	Reward given after each desired behavior	Fast learning of new behavior but rapid extinction	Compliments
Fixed-interval	Reward given at fixed time intervals	Average and irregular performance with rapid extinction	Weekly paychecks
Variable-interval	Reward given at variable time intervals	Moderately high and stable performance with slow extinction	Pop quizzes
Fixed ratio	Reward given at fixed amounts of output	High and stable performance attained quickly but also with rapid extinction	Piece-rate pay
Variable-ratio	Reward given at variable amounts of output	Very high performance with slow extinction	Commissioned sales

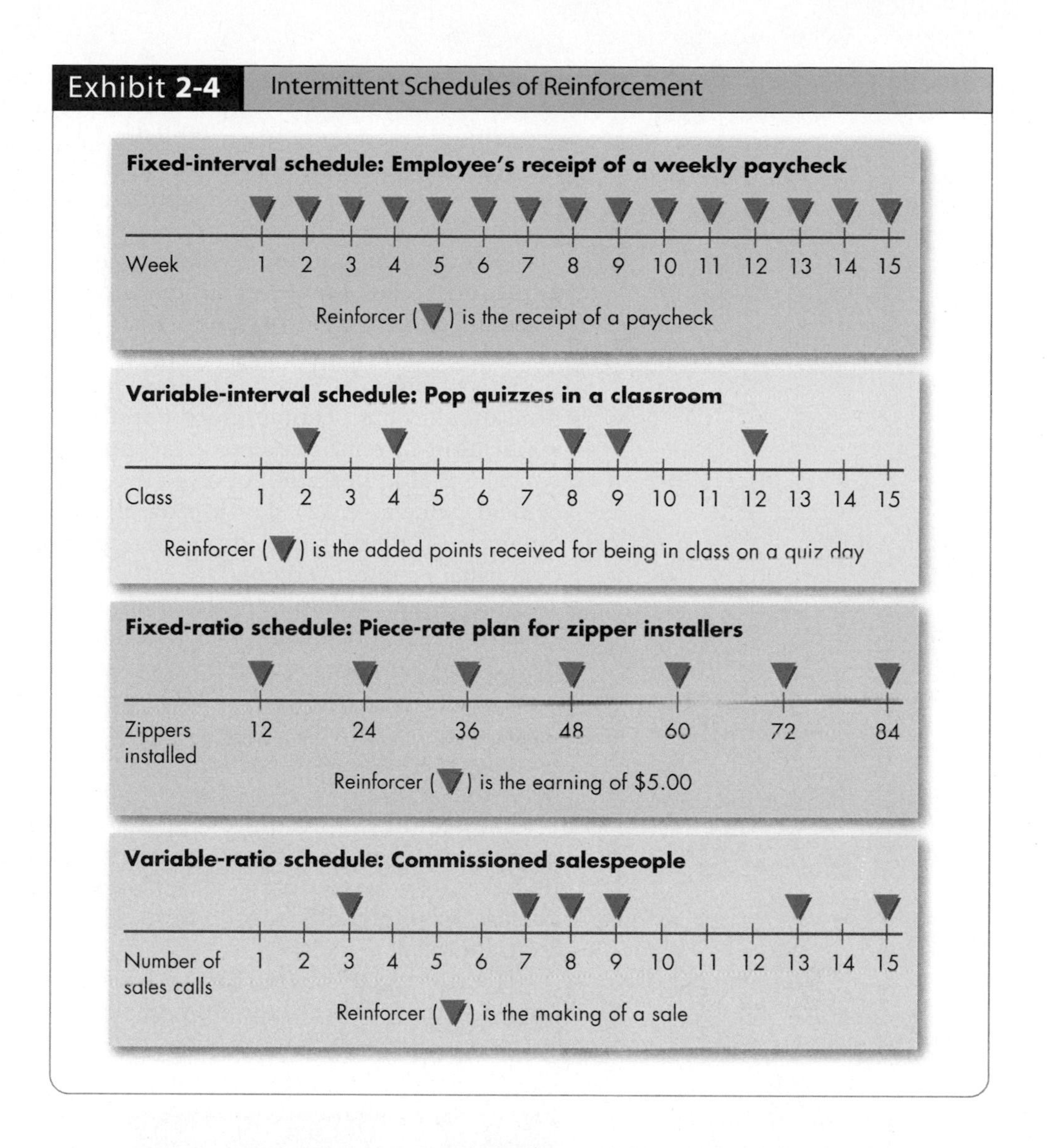

employees in organizations are paid on fixed-interval schedules. But such a schedule does not clearly link performance and rewards. The reward is given for time spent on the job rather than for a specific response (performance). In contrast, variable-interval schedules generate high rates of response and more stable and consistent behavior because of the high correlation between performance and reward and because of the uncertainty involved—the employee tends to be more alert because there is a surprise factor.

Behavior Modification A now-classic study took place a number of years ago with freight packers at Emery Air Freight (now part of FedEx).[48] Emery's management wanted packers to use freight containers for shipments whenever possible because of specific economic savings. When packers were asked about the percentage of shipments contained, the standard reply was

fixed-interval schedule *Spacing rewards at uniform time intervals.*

variable-interval schedule *Distributing rewards in time so that reinforcements are unpredictable.*

fixed-ratio schedule *Initiating rewards after a fixed or constant number of responses.*

variable-ratio schedule *Varying the reward relative to the behavior of the individual.*

90 percent. An analysis by Emery found, however, that the actual container utilization rate was only 45 percent. In order to encourage employees to use containers, management established a program of feedback and positive reinforcements. Each packer was instructed to keep a checklist of daily packings, both containerized and noncontainerized. At the end of each day, the packer computed the container utilization rate. Almost unbelievably, container utilization jumped to more than 90 percent on the first day of the program and held at that level. Emery reported that this simple program of feedback and positive reinforcements saved the company $2 million over a 3-year period.

This program at Emery Air Freight illustrates the use of behavior modification, or what has become more popularly called **OB Mod.**[49] It represents the application of reinforcement concepts to individuals in the work setting. The typical OB Mod program follows a five-step problem-solving model: (1) identify critical behaviors; (2) develop baseline data; (3) identify behavioral consequences; (4) develop and implement an intervention strategy; and (5) evaluate performance improvement.[50]

Everything an employee does on the job is not equally important in terms of performance outcomes. The first step in OB Mod, therefore, is to identify the critical behaviors that make a significant impact on the employee's job performance. These are those 5 to 10 percent of behaviors that may account for up to 70 or 80 percent of each employee's performance. Freight packers using containers whenever possible at Emery Air Freight is an example of a critical behavior.

The second step requires the manager to develop some baseline performance data. This is obtained by determining the number of times the identified behavior is occurring under present conditions. In the Emery freight-packing example, this was the revelation that 45 percent of all shipments were containerized.

The third step is to perform a functional analysis to identify the behavioral contingencies or consequences of performance. This tells the manager the

Convenience-store retailer 7-Eleven, Inc., uses OB Mod to strengthen desirable performance behaviors. Using employee performance software, 7-Eleven measures the efforts of 2,400 store managers and 30,000 employees at company-owned stores in Canada and the United States. The company ties employee compensation to performance outcomes based on 7-Eleven's five fundamental strategic initiatives—product assortment, value, quality, service, and cleanliness—as well as for meeting goals set for new products. The system identifies top performers and rewards them with incentive bonuses.

antecedent cues that emit the behavior and the consequences that are currently maintaining it. At Emery Air Freight, social norms and the greater difficulty in packing containers were the antecedent cues. This encouraged the practice of packing items separately. Moreover, the consequences for continuing the behavior, prior to the OB Mod intervention, were social acceptance and escaping more demanding work.

Once the functional analysis is complete, the manager is ready to develop and implement an intervention strategy to strengthen desirable performance behaviors and weaken undesirable behaviors. The appropriate strategy will entail changing some elements of the performance–reward linkage—structure, processes, technology, groups, or the task—with the goal of making high-level performance more rewarding. In the Emery example, the work technology was altered to require the keeping of a checklist. The checklist plus the computation, at the end of the day, of a container-utilization rate acted to reinforce the desirable behavior of using containers.

The final step in OB Mod is to evaluate performance improvement. In the Emery intervention, the immediate improvement in the container-utilization rate demonstrated that behavioral change took place. That it rose to 90 percent and held at that level further indicates that learning took place. That is, the employees underwent a relatively permanent change in behavior.

A number of organizations have used OB Mod to improve employee productivity; to reduce errors, absenteeism, tardiness, and accident rates; and to improve friendliness toward customers.[51] For instance, a clothing manufacturer saved $60,000 in 1 year due to fewer absences. A packing firm improved productivity 16 percent, cut errors by 40 percent, and reduced accidents by more than 43 percent—resulting in savings of over $1 million. A bank successfully used OB Mod to increase the friendliness of its tellers, which led to a demonstrable improvement in customer satisfaction.

Problems with OB Mod and Reinforcement Theory Although the effectiveness of reinforcements in the form of rewards and punishments has a lot of support in the literature, that doesn't necessarily mean that Skinner was right or that OB Mod is the best way to reward people. What if the power of reinforcements isn't due to operant conditioning or behaviorism? One problem with behaviorism is, as research shows, that thoughts and feelings immediately follow environmental stimuli, even those explicitly meant to shape behavior. This is contrary to the assumptions of behaviorism and OB Mod, which assume that people's innermost thoughts and feelings in response to the environment are irrelevant.

Think about praise from a supervisor. For example, assume your course instructor compliments you for asking a good question. A behaviorist would argue that this shapes your behavior because you find the stimulus (the compliment) pleasant and therefore respond by attempting to ask other questions that will generate the same reward. However, imagine, for example, that you had to weigh the pleasant feelings produced by your professor's praise against the snickers of jealous classmates who whispered "brown noser." Your choice of what to do would likely be dictated by weighing the value of these stimuli, which may be a rather complex mental process involving thinking and feeling.

OB Mod *The application of reinforcement concepts to individuals in the work setting.*

Also, is it really shaping if the compliment was given without an intention of molding behavior? Isn't it perhaps overly restrictive to view all stimuli as motivated to obtain a particular response? Is the only reason we tell someone we love them because we wish to obtain a reward or to mold their behavior?

Because of these problems, among others, operant conditioning and behaviorism have been superseded by other approaches that emphasize cognitive processes.[52] There is no denying, though, the contribution of these theories to our understanding of human behavior.

Global Implications

As you will see, there may be no global or cross-cultural research on some of the topics we discuss in a chapter, and this chapter is no exception. We therefore confine our comments here to areas where there has been the most cross-cultural research: (1) How does research on intellectual abilities generalize across cultures? (2) Do biographical characteristics such as gender and age operate similarly across cultures? and (3) Do the principles of learning work in different cultures?

6 Show how culture affects our understanding of intellectual abilities, biographical characteristics, and learning.

Intellectual Abilities

Evidence strongly supports the ideas that the structures and measures of intellectual abilities generalize across cultures. Thus, someone in Venezuela or Sudan does not have a different set of mental abilities than a Japanese or Czech worker. Moreover, data from across many cultures support the finding that specific mental abilities indicate a higher-order factor we call general mental ability (GMA). There is some evidence that IQ scores vary to some degree across cultures, but those differences are much smaller when we consider educational and economic differences.[53]

Biographical Characteristics

Obviously, some biographical characteristics vary across cultures. Some cultures are more racially homogenous than others, and the average age of citizens varies across countries (for example, in Italy and Japan, a far greater percentage of the population is over 65 than in India or China). That doesn't mean, however, that the relationships we've described between age and performance, or between gender and turnover, are different across cultures. Frankly, we don't have much good scientific evidence on whether, for example, gender or age affects absenteeism similarly across cultures. One survey of U.S. managers in eight countries revealed some surprising differences. Compared with British managers, female managers in the Philippines believed that their country was more supportive of women's advancement into leadership positions.[54] While such survey results are interesting, they don't substitute for systematic study. Thus, we really don't know the degree to which gender (or other biographical factors) varies in importance in predicting OB outcomes in different countries.

OB researchers don't always answer the questions we want them to answer. AACSB International, the largest accreditation association for business schools, frequently faults business schools for not producing research that's relevant to managers. Though we think OB research has a lot to offer, it's not perfect either, and this is a case in point.

Learning

There is little research on how theories of learning generalize to organizations and employees in different cultures. This is due in part to the fact that much of the research on learning theories is fairly old, conducted before there was a lot of cross-cultural research. For example, two major recent reviews of cross-cultural research in OB did not mention learning theories, reinforcement theory, or behavioral modification. That doesn't mean these theories are necessarily culturally bound; it means we really don't yet know one way or the other.

Summary and Implications for Managers

This chapter looked at three individual variables—ability, biographical characteristics, and learning. Let's now try to summarize what we found and consider their importance for a manager who is trying to understand organizational behavior.

Ability Ability directly influences an employee's level of performance. Given management's desire to get high-performing employees, what can be done?

First, an effective selection process will improve the fit. A job analysis will provide information about jobs currently being done and the abilities that individuals need to perform the jobs adequately. Applicants can then be tested, interviewed, and evaluated on the degree to which they possess the necessary abilities.

Second, promotion and transfer decisions affecting individuals already in the organization's employ should reflect the abilities of candidates. As with new employees, care should be taken to assess critical abilities that incumbents will need in the job and to match those requirements with the organization's human resources.

Third, the fit can be improved by fine-tuning the job to better match an incumbent's abilities. Often, modifications can be made in the job that, while not having a significant impact on the job's basic activities, better adapt it to the specific talents of a given employee. Examples would be changing some of the equipment used or reorganizing tasks within a group of employees.

Biographical Characteristics Biographical characteristics are readily observable to managers. However, just because they're observable doesn't mean they should be explicitly used in management decisions. We also need to be aware of implicit biases we or other managers may have.

Learning Any observable change in behavior is *prima facie* evidence that learning has taken place. Positive reinforcement is a powerful tool for modifying behavior. By identifying and rewarding performance-enhancing behaviors, management increases the likelihood that those behaviors will be repeated. Our knowledge about learning further suggests that reinforcement is a more effective tool than punishment. Although punishment eliminates undesired behavior more quickly than negative reinforcement does, punished behavior tends to be only temporarily suppressed rather than permanently changed. And punishment may produce unpleasant side effects, such as lower morale and higher absenteeism or turnover. In addition, the recipients of punishment tend to become resentful of the punisher. Managers, therefore, are advised to use reinforcement rather than punishment.

Point Counterpoint

ALL HUMAN BEHAVIOR IS LEARNED[55]

Point

Human beings are essentially blank slates that are shaped by their environment. B. F. Skinner, in fact, summarized his belief in the power of the environment to shape behavior when he said, "Give me a child at birth and I can make him into anything you want."

Following are some of the societal mechanisms that exist because of this belief in the power of learned behavior:

Role of parenting. We place a great deal of importance on the role of mothers and fathers in the raising of children. We believe, for instance, that children raised without fathers will be hindered by their lack of a male role model. And parents who have continual run-ins with the law risk having government authorities take their children from them. The latter action is typically taken because society believes that irresponsible parents don't provide the proper learning environment for their children.

Importance of education. Most advanced societies invest heavily in the education of their young. They typically provide 10 or more years of free education. And in countries such as the United States, going on to college after finishing high school has become the norm rather than the exception. This investment in education is undertaken because it is seen as a way for young people to learn knowledge and skills.

Job training. For individuals who don't go on to college, most will pursue job-training programs to develop specific work-related skills. They'll take courses to become proficient as auto mechanics, medical assistants, and the like. Similarly, people who seek to become skilled trades workers will pursue apprenticeships as carpenters, electricians, or pipe fitters. In addition, business firms invest billions of dollars each year in training and education to keep current employees' skills up-to-date.

Manipulation of rewards. Organizations design complex compensation programs to reward employees fairly for their work performance. But these programs are also designed with the intention to motivate employees. They are designed to encourage employees to engage in behaviors that management desires and to extinguish behaviors that management wants to discourage. Salary levels, for instance, typically reward employee loyalty, encourage the learning of new skills, and motivate individuals to assume greater responsibilities in the organization.

These mechanisms all exist and flourish because organizations and society believe that people can learn and change their behavior.

Counterpoint

Although people can learn and can be influenced by their environment, far too little attention has been paid to the role that evolution has played in shaping human behavior. Evolutionary psychology tells us that human beings are basically hardwired at birth. We arrive on Earth with ingrained traits, honed and adapted over millions of years, that shape and limit our behavior.

All living creatures are "designed" by specific combinations of genes. As a result of natural selection, genes that produce faulty design features are eliminated. Characteristics that help a species survive tend to endure and get passed on to future generations. Many of the characteristics that helped early *Homo sapiens* survive live on today and influence the way we behave. Here are a few examples:

Emotions. Stone Age people, at the mercy of wild predators and natural disasters, learned to trust their instincts. Those with the best instincts survived. Today, emotions remain the first screen to all information we receive. We know we are supposed to act rationally, but our emotions can never be fully suppressed.

Risk avoidance. Ancient hunter-gatherers who survived were not big risk takers. They were cautious. Today, when we're comfortable with the status quo, we typically see any change as risky and, thus, tend to resist it.

Stereotyping. To prosper in a clan society, Early humans had to quickly "size up" whom they could trust or not trust. Those who could do this quickly were more likely to survive. Today, like our ancestors, we naturally stereotype people based on very small pieces of evidence, mainly their looks and a few readily apparent behaviors.

Male competitiveness. Males in early human societies frequently had to engage in games or battles in which there were clear winners and losers. Winners attained high status, were viewed as more attractive mates, and were more likely to reproduce. The ingrained male desire to do public battle and display virility and competence persists today.

Evolutionary psychology challenges the notion that people are free to change their behavior if trained or motivated. It doesn't say that we can't engage in learning or exercise free will. What it does say is that nature predisposes us to act and interact in particular ways in particular circumstances. As a result, we find that people in organizational settings often behave in ways that don't appear to be beneficial to themselves or their employers.

Questions for Review

1 What are the two types of ability?

2 What is intellectual or cognitive ability, and how is it relevant to OB?

3 What are the key biographical characteristics, and why are they relevant to OB?

4 What is learning, and what are the major theories of learning?

5 What is shaping, and how can it be used as a management tool?

6 How does culture affect our understanding of intellectual abilities, biographical characteristics, and learning?

Experiential Exercise

POSITIVE REINFORCEMENT VERSUS PUNISHMENT

Exercise Overview (Steps 1–4)

This 10-step exercise takes approximately 20 minutes.

1. Two volunteers are selected to receive reinforcement or punishment from the class while performing a particular task. The volunteers leave the room.
2. The instructor identifies an object for the student volunteers to locate when they return to the room. (The object should be unobstructed but clearly visible to the class. Examples that have worked well include a small triangular piece of paper that was left behind when a notice was torn off a classroom bulletin board, a smudge on the chalkboard, and a chip in the plaster of a classroom wall.)
3. The instructor specifies the actions that will be in effect when the volunteers return to the room. For punishment, students should hiss or boo when the first volunteer is moving away from the object. For positive reinforcement, they should cheer and applaud when the second volunteer is getting closer to the object.
4. The instructor should assign a student to keep a record of the time it takes each of the volunteers to locate the object.

Volunteer 1 (Steps 5 and 6)

5. Volunteer 1 is brought back into the room and is told, "Your task is to locate and touch a particular object in the room, and the class has agreed to help you. You cannot use words or ask questions. Begin."
6. Volunteer 1 continues to look for the object until it is found, while the class engages in the punishing behavior.

Volunteer 2 (Steps 7 and 8)

7. Volunteer 2 is brought back into the room and is told, "Your task is to locate and touch a particular object in the room, and the class has agreed to help you. You cannot use words or ask questions. Begin."
8. Volunteer 2 continues to look for the object until it is found, while the class assists by giving positive reinforcement.

Class Review (Steps 9 and 10)

9. The timekeeper will present the results of how long it took each volunteer to find the object.
10. The class will discuss: What was the difference in behavior of the two volunteers? What are the implications of this exercise to shaping behavior in organizations?

Source: Adapted from an exercise developed by Larry Michaelson of the University of Oklahoma. Used with permission.

Ethical Dilemma

YOU MUST HAVE SEX

Recently, The University of Florida changed its policy to provide health benefits for cohabitating partners. The change in policy sparked some controversy. For example, Larry Cretul, a member of Congress whose district includes the university, introduced a bill to make it illegal to use taxpayer dollars to fund a domestic-partner benefit program. In explaining his bill, Cretul said, "I just happen to be one who supports the idea that marriage should continue to be held in the elevated position."

Another part of the policy sparked as much controversy—the requirement that the cohabitating partners sign an agreement indicating that they're having sex. The policy stipulates that enrollees "must have been in non-platonic relationship for the preceding 12 months." As part of qualifying for the benefits, employees must sign an agreement indicating that they have engaged in sexual activity with their partner.

One employee of the university said she was offended by the policy and wondered how the university was going to enforce it.

In response, the university's director of human resources, Kyle Cavanaugh, said that the "non-platonic" clause was increasingly common in domestic-partner benefit plans, to rule out qualification for people who happen to be living together but aren't in a romantic relationship. Cavanaugh promises that responses to the question are confidential, but some still wonder. "That's a personal question," said one employee.[56]

Questions

1. What do you think about same-sex domestic partner benefits? To what extent are your views affected by your religious or political views?
2. What do you think about the policy that requires employees to stipulate that they have sexual activity with their domestic partner? If you think it's a bad policy, what (if anything) would you propose in its place?

Case Incident 1

THE FLYNN EFFECT

Given that a substantial amount of intellectual ability (up to 80 percent) is inherited, it might surprise you to learn that intelligence test scores are rising. In fact, scores have risen so dramatically that today's great-grandparents seem mentally deficient by comparison.

First, let's review the evidence for rising test scores. Then, we'll review explanations for the results.

On an IQ scale where 100 is the average, scores have been rising about 3 points per decade, meaning that if your grandparent scored 100, the average score for your generation would be around 115. That's a pretty big difference—about a standard deviation—meaning that someone who's from your grandparent's generation whose score was at the 84th percentile would only be average (50th) percentile by today's norms.

James Flynn is a New Zealand researcher credited with first documenting the rising scores. He first reported the results in 1984, when he found that almost everyone who took a well-validated IQ test in the 1970s did better than those who took it in the 1940s.

The results appear to hold up across cultures. Test scores are rising not only in the United States but in most other countries in which the effect has been tested, too.

What explains the Flynn Effect? Researchers are not entirely sure, but some of the explanations offered are:

1. **Education.** Students today are better educated than their ancestors, and education leads to higher test scores.
2. **Smaller families.** In 1900, the average couple had four children; today the number is less than two. We know firstborns tend to have higher IQs than other children, probably because they receive more attention than their later-born siblings.
3. **Test-taking savvy.** Today's children have been tested so often that they are test savvy: They know how to take tests and how to do well on them.
4. **Genes.** Although smart couples tend to have fewer, not more, children, it's possible that due to better education, tracking, and testing, those who do have the right genes are better able to exploit those advantages. Some genetics researchers also have argued that if two people of different intelligence mate, because the gene of the more intelligent mate is stronger, it wins out, meaning the child's IQ will be closer to the IQ of the smarter parent.

Questions

1. Do you believe people are really getting smarter? Why or why not?
2. Which of the factors explaining the Flynn Effect do you buy?
3. Are there any societal advantages or disadvantages to the Flynn Effect?

Source: F. Greve, "Rise in Average IQ Scores Makes Kids Today Exceptional by Earlier Standards," *Jewish World Review*, February 14, 2006, pp. 1–3; and M. A. Mingroni, "Resolving the IQ Paradox: Heterosis as a Cause of the Flynn Effect and Other Trends," *Psychological Review*, July 2007, pp. 806–829.

Case Incident 2

PROFESSIONAL SPORTS: REWARDING AND PUNISHING THE SAME BEHAVIOR?

Baseball Commissioner Bud Selig has felt the heat for some time, and it's not the kind a 90-mile-per-hour fastball brings. When allegations of steroid use among some of Major League Baseball's biggest stars first surfaced, Selig argued that the league's policy on steroids was "as good as any in professional sports." The policy? Random drug testing, with a 10-day suspension for first-time offenders. Congress and the general public were not satisfied. So, Selig announced a tougher "three strikes and you're out" policy: A 50-game suspension for a first offense, a 100-game suspension for a second, and a permanent ban from baseball for a third. Players may incur fines as well. Other professional leagues have followed suit. The PGA Tour even announced its own drug-testing policy, which began in the 2008 season.

But here's the problem: The same system that punishes those who take performance-enhancing drugs may also reinforce such behavior. And the current repercussions for players may not serve as a strong deterrent. A fine of $10,000 or a 10-day suspension may be a relatively minor setback compared to the millions that can be earned for becoming an all-star power hitter.

Take Rafael Palmeiro as an example. He tested positive for steroids. Though Palmeiro insists he took them inadvertently, the type found in his system (stanozolol) is not the kind found in dietary supplements. His punishment? Palmeiro received a 10-day suspension and forfeited $167,000 of his $3 million salary, and a banner celebrating his 3,000th hit was removed from Camden Yards.

Now consider all-time home-run king Barry Bonds. Bonds has set records, and made millions, by hitting lots of home runs. Although there are widespread and detailed reports that he has taken performance-enhancing drugs (particularly between 1998 and 2003, when federal agents raided the company that was allegedly supplying him), the allegations have never been enough to get him banned from baseball. His fame and fortune continue. And the rewards of hitting home runs are not limited to the players. Revenues from increased game attendance and sports merchandise, as well as a team's rising popularity and success, are incentives for players to perform at high levels and for owners to reward them.

In the NFL, the situation is not much different. For example, Oakland Raiders safety Jarrod Cooper tested positive for steroids before the 2007–2008 season. His penalty? Suspension from the preseason games and the first four regular-season games. Although a four-game suspension can mean a large loss of income (the average NFL salary tops $1 million), such punishment still may not prevent steroid use because the money that can be made from endorsements and winning games can far exceed players' salaries.

It appears that professional sports may be trying to have their cake and eat it, too. As we have seen, behavior that may lead individuals and teams to fame and fortune may also be behavior that demands punishment.

Questions

1. What type of reinforcement schedule does random drug testing represent? Is this type of schedule typically effective or ineffective?
2. What are some examples of behaviors in typical organizations that supervisors reward but that may actually be detrimental to others or to the organization as a whole? As a manager, what might you do to try to avoid this quandary?
3. If you were the commissioner of baseball, what steps would you take to try to reduce the use of steroids in baseball? Is punishment likely to be the most effective deterrent? Why or why not?
4. Is it ever okay to allow potentially unethical behaviors, which on the surface may benefit organizations, to persist? Why or why not?

Source: "Bonds Exposed," *Sports Illustrated*, March 7, 2006; M. Lewis, "Absolutely, Power Corrupts," *New York Times Magazine*, April 24, 2005, p. 46; and "Former K-State Wildcat Jarrod Cooper Violates NFL Steroids Policy," *Kansas City Star*, July 20, 2007.

Endnotes

1. Based on P. Kiefer, "On the Canals, a Woman Paddles Against the Tide," *New York Times*, May 14, 2007, pp. A1, A4.
2. L. S. Gottfredson, "The Challenge and Promise of Cognitive Career Assessment," *Journal of Career Assessment* 11, no. 2 (2003), pp. 115–135.
3. M. D. Dunnette, "Aptitudes, Abilities, and Skills," in M. D. Dunnette (ed.), *Handbook of Industrial and Organizational Psychology* (Chicago: Rand McNally, 1976), pp. 478–483.
4. J. F. Salgado, N. Anderson, S. Moscoso, C. Bertua, F. de Fruyt, and J. P. Rolland, "A Meta-analytic Study of General Mental Ability Validity for Different Occupations in the European Community," *Journal of Applied Psychology*, December 2003, pp. 1068–1081; and F. L. Schmidt and

J. E. Hunter, "Select on Intelligence," in E. A. Locke (ed.), *Handbook of Principles of Organizational Behavior* (Malden, MA: Blackwell, 2004).

5. Y. Ganzach, "Intelligence and Job Satisfaction," *Academy of Management Journal* 41, no. 5 (1998), pp. 526–539; and Y. Ganzach, "Intelligence, Education, and Facets of Job Satisfaction," *Work and Occupations* 30, no. 1 (2003), pp. 97–122.
6. E. A. Fleishman, "Evaluating Physical Abilities Required by Jobs," *Personnel Administrator*, June 1979, pp. 82–92.
7. K. Greene, "Older Workers Can Get a Raw Deal—Some Employers Admit to Promoting, Challenging Their Workers Less," *Wall Street Journal*, April 10, 2003, p. D2; and K. A. Wrenn and T. J. Maurer, "Beliefs About Older Workers' Learning and Development Behavior in Relation to Beliefs About Malleability of Skills, Age-Related Decline, and Control," *Journal of Applied Social Psychology* 34, no. 2 (2004), pp. 223–242.
8. D. R. Davies, G. Matthews, and C. S. K. Wong, "Ageing and Work," in C. L. Cooper and I. T. Robertson (eds.), *International Review of Industrial and Organizational Psychology*, vol. 6 (Chichester, UK: Wiley, 1991), pp. 183–187.
9. R. D. Hackett, "Age, Tenure, and Employee Absenteeism," *Human Relations*, July 1990, pp. 601–619.
10. Cited in K. Labich, "The New Unemployed," *Fortune*, March 8, 1993, p. 43.
11. See G. M. McEvoy and W. F. Cascio, "Cumulative Evidence of the Relationship Between Employee Age and Job Performance," *Journal of Applied Psychology*, February 1989, pp. 11–17; and F. L. Schmidt and J. E. Hunter, "The Validity and Utility of Selection Methods in Personnel Psychology: Practical and Theoretical Implications of 85 Years of Research Findings," *Psychological Bulletin* 124 (1998), pp. 262–274.
12. See, for instance, F. J. Landy, et al., *Alternatives to Chronological Age in Determining Standards of Suitability for Public Safety Jobs* (University Park, PA: Center for Applied Behavioral Sciences, Pennsylvania State University, 1992).
13. R. Lee and E. R. Wilbur, "Age, Education, Job Tenure, Salary, Job Characteristics, and Job Satisfaction: A Multivariate Analysis," *Human Relations*, August 1985, pp. 781–791.
14. K. M. Kacmar and G. R. Ferris, "Theoretical and Methodological Considerations in the Age–Job Satisfaction Relationship," *Journal of Applied Psychology*, April 1989, pp. 201–207; and W. A. Hochwarter, G. R. Ferris, P. L. Perrewe, L. A. Witt, and C. Kiewitz, "A Note on the Nonlinearity of the Age–Job Satisfaction Relationship," *Journal of Applied Social Psychology*, June 2001, pp. 1223–1237.
15. See E. M. Weiss, G. Kemmler, E. A. Deisenhammer, W. W. Fleischhacker, and M. Delazer, "Sex Differences in Cognitive Functions," *Personality and Individual Differences*, September 2003, pp. 863–875; and A. F. Jorm, K. J. Anstey, H. Christensen, and B. Rodgers, "Gender Differences in Cognitive Abilities: The Mediating Role of Health State and Health Habits," *Intelligence*, January 2004, pp. 7–23.
16. See M. M. Black and E. W. Holden, "The Impact of Gender on Productivity and Satisfaction Among Medical School Psychologists," *Journal of Clinical Psychology in Medical Settings*, March 1998, pp. 117–131.
17. S. Shellenbarger, "More Job Seekers Put Family Needs First," *Wall Street Journal*, November 15, 1991, p. B1.
18. R. W. Griffeth, P. W. Hom, and S. Gaertner, "A Meta-analysis of Antecedents and Correlates of Employee Turnover: Update, Moderator Tests, and Research Implications for the Next Millennium," *Journal of Management* 26, no. 3 (2000), pp. 463–488.
19. See, for instance, K. D. Scott and E. L. McClellan, "Gender Differences in Absenteeism," *Public Personnel Management*, Summer 1990, pp. 229–253; and A. VandenHeuvel and M. Wooden, "Do Explanations of Absenteeism Differ for Men and Women?" *Human Relations*, November 1995, pp. 1309–1329.
20. See, for instance, M. Tait, M. Y. Padgett, and T. T. Baldwin, "Job and Life Satisfaction: A Reevaluation of the Strength of the Relationship and Gender Effects as a Function of the Date of the Study," *Journal of Applied Psychology*, June 1989, pp. 502–507; and M. B. Grover, "Daddy Stress," *Forbes*, September 6, 1999, pp. 202–208.
21. J. M. Sacco, C. R. Scheu, A. M. Ryan, and N. Schmitt, "An Investigation of Race and Sex Similarity Effects in Interviews: A Multilevel Approach to Relational Demography," *Journal of Applied Psychology* 88, no. 5 (2003), pp. 852–865; and G. N. Powell and D. A. Butterfield, "Exploring the Influence of Decision Makers' Race and Gender on Actual Promotions to Top Management," *Personnel Psychology* 55, no. 2 (2002), pp. 397–428.
22. D. A. Kravitz and S. L. Klineberg, "Reactions to Two Versions of Affirmative Action Among Whites, Blacks, and Hispanics," *Journal of Applied Psychology* 85, no. 4 (2000), pp. 597–611.
23. J. M. Sacco, C. R. Scheu, A. M. Ryan, and N. Schmitt, "An Investigation of Race and Sex Similarity Effects in Interviews: A Multilevel Approach to Relational Demography," *Journal of Applied Psychology* 88, no. 5 (2003), pp. 852–865.
24. P. Bobko, P. L. Roth, and D. Potosky, "Derivation and Implications of a Meta-Analytic Matrix Incorporating Cognitive Ability, Alternative Predictors, and Job Performance," *Personnel Psychology*, Autumn 1999, pp. 561–589.
25. M. J. Ree, T. R. Carretta, and J. R. Steindl, "Cognitive Ability," in N. Anderson, D. S. Ones, H. K. Sinangil, and C. Viswesvaran (eds.). *Handbook of Industrial, Work, and Organizational Psychology*, vol. 1 (London: Sage Publications, 2001), pp. 219–232.
26. See J. P. Rushton and A. R. Jenson, "Thirty Years of Research on Race Differences in Cognitive Ability," *Psychology, Public Policy, and the Law* 11, no. 2 (2005), pp. 235–295; and R. E. Nisbett, "Heredity, Environment, and Race Differences in IQ: A Commentary on Rushton and Jensen (2005)," *Psychology, Public Policy, and the Law* 11, no. 2 (2005), pp. 302–310.
27. M. A. Quinones, J. K. Ford, and M. S. Teachout, "The Relationship Between Work Experience and Job Performance: A Conceptual and Meta-analytic Review," *Personnel Psychology*, Winter 1995, pp. 887–910.
28. I. R. Gellatly, "Individual and Group Determinants of Employee Absenteeism: Test of a Causal Model," *Journal of Organizational Behavior*, September 1995, pp. 469–485.
29. P. O. Popp and J. A. Belohlav, "Absenteeism in a Low Status Work Environment," *Academy of Management Journal*, September 1982, p. 681.
30. Griffeth, Hom, and Gaertner, "A Meta-analysis of Antecedents," pp. 463–488.

31. R. D. Gatewood and H. S. Field, *Human Resource Selection* (Chicago: Dryden Press, 1987).

32. J. A. Breaugh and D. L. Dossett, "The Effectiveness of Biodata for Predicting Turnover," paper presented at the National Academy of Management Conference, New Orleans, August 1987.

33. W. van Breukelen, R. van der Vlist, and H. Steensma, "Voluntary Employee Turnover: Combining Variables from the 'Traditional' Turnover Literature with the Theory of Planned Behavior," *Journal of Organizational Behavior* 25, no. 7 (2004), pp. 893–914.

34. M. Elias, "USA's Muslims Under a Cloud," *USA Today*, August 10, 2006, pp. 1D, 2D; and R. R. Hastings, "Muslims Seek Acknowledgement of Mainstream Americans," *HRWeek*, May 11, 2007, p. 1.

35. *HRC Corporate Equality Index*, 2006, www.hrc.org/cei; and R. R. Hastings, "Necessity Breeds Inclusion: Reconsidering 'Don't Ask, Don't Tell'," *HRWeek*, January 2007, pp. 1–2.

36. B. Leonard, "Transgender Issues Test Diversity Limits," *HRMagazine*, June 2007, pp. 32–34.

37. See H. M. Weiss, "Learning Theory and Industrial and Organizational Psychology," in M. D. Dunnette and L. M. Hough (eds.), *Handbook of Industrial & Organizational Psychology*, 2nd ed., vol. 1 (Palo Alto, CA: Consulting Psychologists Press, 1990), pp. 172–173.

38. W. McGehee, "Are We Using What We Know About Training? Learning Theory and Training," *Personnel Psychology*, Spring 1958, p. 2.

39. I. P. Pavlov, *The Work of the Digestive Glands*, trans. W. H. Thompson (London: Charles Griffin, 1902). See also the special issue of *American Psychologist*, September 1997, pp. 933–972, commemorating Pavlov's work.

40. B. F. Skinner, *Contingencies of Reinforcement* (East Norwalk, CT: Appleton-Century-Crofts, 1971).

41. J. A. Mills, *Control: A History of Behavioral Psychology* (New York: New York University Press, 2000).

42. A. Bandura, *Social Learning Theory* (Upper Saddle River, NJ: Prentice Hall, 1977).

43. T. Maurer, K. Wrenn, and E. Weiss, "Toward Understanding and Managing Stereotypical Beliefs About Older Workers' Ability and Desire for Learning and Development," *Research in Personnel and Human Resources Management* 22 (2003), pp. 253–285.

44. J. A. Colquitt, J. A. LePine, and R. A. Noe, "Toward an Integrative Theory of Training Motivation: A Meta-Analytic Path Analysis of 20 Years of Research," *Journal of Applied Psychology* 85, no. 5 (2000), pp. 678–707.

45. S. Begley, "The Upside of Aging," *New York Times*, February 16, 2007, pp. W1, W4.

46. Wrenn and Maurer, "Beliefs About Older Workers' Learning and Development Behavior," pp. 223–242.

47. A. D. Stajkovic and F. Luthans, "A Meta-analysis of the Effects of Organizational Behavior Modification on Task Performance, 1975–95," *Academy of Management Journal*, October 1997, pp. 1122–1149.

48. "At Emery Air Freight: Positive Reinforcement Boosts Performance," *Organizational Dynamics*, Winter 1973, pp. 41–50.

49. F. Luthans and R. Kreitner, *Organizational Behavior Modification and Beyond: An Operant and Social Learning Approach* (Glenview, IL: Scott, Foresman, 1985); Stajkovic and Luthans, "A Meta-Analysis of the Effects of Organizational Behavior Modification on Task Performance, 1975–95," pp. 1122–1149; and A. D. Stajkovic and F. Luthans, "Behavioral Management and Task Performance in Organizations: Conceptual Background, Meta-Analysis, and Test of Alternative Models," *Personnel Psychology*, Spring 2003, pp. 155–192.

50. Stajkovic and Luthans, "A Meta-analysis of the Effects of Organizational Behavior Modification on Task Performance, 1975–95," p. 1123.

51. See F. Luthans and A. D. Stajkovic, "Reinforce for Performance: The Need to Go Beyond Pay and Even Rewards," *Academy of Management Executive*, May 1999, pp. 49–57; and A. D. Stajkovic and F. Luthans, "Differential Effects of Incentive Motivators on Work Performance," *Academy of Management Journal* 44, no. 3 (2001), pp. 580–590.

52. E. A. Locke, "Beyond Determinism and Materialism, or Isn't It Time We Took Consciousness Seriously?" *Journal of Behavior Therapy & Experimental Psychiatry* 26, no. 3 (1995), pp. 265–273.

53. N. Barber, "Educational and Ecological Correlates of IQ: A Cross-National Investigation," *Intelligence* (May–Jun 2005), pp. 273–284.

54. S. Falk, "The Anatomy of the Glass Ceiling," *Accenture*, 2006, www.accenture.com.

55. Points in this argument are based on N. Nicholson, "How Hardwired Is Human Behavior?" *Harvard Business Review*, July–August 1998, pp. 135–147; and B. D. Pierce and R. White, "The Evolution of Social Structure: Why Biology Matters," *Academy of Management Review*, October 1999, pp. 843–853.

56. J. Stripling, "UF Requirement for Partner Benefits: You Must Have Sex," *Gainesville (Florida) Sun*, January 20, 2006, pp. 1A, 7A.

Attitudes and Job Satisfaction

Attitude isn't everything, but it's close.

—*New York Times* headline, August 6, 2006

LEARNING OBJECTIVES

After studying this chapter, you should be able to:

1. Contrast the three components of an attitude.
2. Summarize the relationship between attitudes and behavior.
3. Compare and contrast the major job attitudes.
4. Define *job satisfaction* and show how it can be measured.
5. Summarize the main causes of job satisfaction.
6. Identify four employee responses to dissatisfaction.
7. Show whether job satisfaction is a relevant concept in countries other than the United States.

It seems that Google will spare no expense to keep its workers happy. Unlimited amounts of chef-prepared food all day. A huge gym with state-of-the-art equipment, including a climbing wall, a volleyball court, and two lap pools. A masseuse is there, too. On-site car washes, oil changes, haircuts, and dry cleaning. And free doctor checkups and free dental work, again on site. Child care next door and a backup child-care service in case the employee is running late.

Google: Is This a Great Place to Work or What?

Free transportation is the latest benefit. Silicon Valley, the location of Google's main operations, is home to some of the worst traffic in the United States. A recent survey of Silicon Valley residents indicated that traffic is their number-one concern—for the 10th straight year! So Google now provides its employees with free high-tech shuttle buses equipped with comfortable leather seats, bicycle racks, and wireless Internet access, powered by biodiesel engines. About one-quarter of Google's employees take advantage of the service. Riders can even sign up to receive alerts on their PCs and cellphones about changes in schedules or delays. The morning service starts at 5:05 A.M., and the evening run goes until 10:05 P.M.. During peak hours, pickups are as frequent as every 15 minutes. "We are basically running a small municipal transit agency," says Marty Lev, the Google director who oversees the program. Bent Hagemark, a software engineer, loves Google's shuttle so much he said, "If they cut the shuttle, it would be a disaster."

Although its free shuttle and other benefits programs have attracted the most attention, Google offers a host of other benefits, less flashy but no less valued, including:

- Automatic life insurance at two times annual salary
- For employees with 6 or more years of seniority, 25 vacation days per year
- For new parents, parental leave at 75 percent pay for 6 weeks and reimbursement for up to $500 for take-out meals during the first 4 weeks at home with the new baby
- Tuition reimbursement of $8,000 per calendar year
- A $2,000 bonus for referral of employees who are hired and stay at least 60 days
- A gift-matching program for employee contributions up to $3,000 per year to nonprofit organizations
- Reimbursement up to $5,000 to use toward adoption expenses

A recent survey suggested that of all the factors that might increase job satisfaction, employees believe benefits are the most important. Google seems to get that.[1] ■

Like Google, many organizations are very concerned with the attitudes of their employees. In this chapter, we look at attitudes, their link to behavior, and how employees' satisfaction or dissatisfaction with their jobs affects the workplace.

What are your attitudes toward your job? Use the following Self-Assessment Library to determine your level of satisfaction with your current or past jobs.

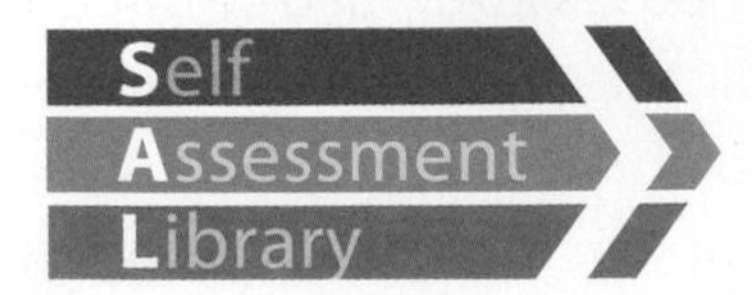

HOW SATISFIED AM I WITH MY JOB?

In the Self-Assessment Library (available on CD or online), take assessment I.B.3 (How Satisfied Am I with My Job?) and then answer the following questions. If you currently do not have a job, answer the questions for your most recent job.

1. *How does your job satisfaction compare to that of others in your class who have taken the assessment?*
2. *Why do you think your satisfaction is higher or lower than average?*

Attitudes

Attitudes are evaluative statements—either favorable or unfavorable—about objects, people, or events. They reflect how we feel about something. When I say "I like my job," I am expressing my attitude about work.

1 *Contrast the three components of an attitude.*

Attitudes are complex. If you ask people about their attitude toward religion, Paris Hilton, or the organization they work for, you may get a simple response, but the reasons underlying the response are probably complex. In order to fully understand attitudes, we need to consider their fundamental properties or components.

What Are the Main Components of Attitudes?

Typically, researchers have assumed that attitudes have three components: cognition, affect, and behavior.[2] Let's look at each.

The statement "my pay is low" is a description. It is the **cognitive component** of an attitude—the aspect of an attitude that is a description of or belief in the way things are. It sets the stage for the more critical part of an attitude—its **affective component**. Affect is the emotional or feeling segment of an attitude and is reflected in the statement "I am angry over how little I'm paid." Finally, and we'll discuss this issue at considerable length later in this section, affect can lead to behavioral outcomes. The **behavioral component** of an attitude refers to an intention to behave in a certain way toward someone or something (to continue the example, "I'm going to look for another job that pays better").

Viewing attitudes as being made up of three components—cognition, affect, and behavior—is helpful in understanding their complexity and the potential relationship between attitudes and behavior. Keep in mind that these components are closely related, and cognition and affect in particular are inseparable in many ways. For example, imagine you concluded that someone had just treated you unfairly. Aren't you likely to have feelings about that, occurring virtually instantaneously with the thought? Thus, cognition and affect are intertwined.

Exhibit 3-1 illustrates how the three components of an attitude are related. In this example, an employee didn't get a promotion he thought he deserved; a coworker got it instead. The employee's attitude toward his supervisor is illustrated as follows: the employee thought he deserved the promotion (cognition), the employee strongly dislikes his supervisor (affect), and the employee is looking for another job (behavior). As we previously noted, although we often think that cognition causes affect, which then causes behavior, in reality these components are often difficult to separate.

2 *Summarize the relationship between attitudes and behavior.*

In organizations, attitudes are important for their behavioral component. If workers believe, for example, that supervisors, auditors, bosses, and time-and-motion engineers are all in conspiracy to make employees work harder for the same or less money, it makes sense to try to understand how these attitudes formed, their relationship to actual job behavior, and how they might be changed.

attitudes *Evaluative statements or judgments concerning objects, people, or events.*

cognitive component *The opinion or belief segment of an attitude.*

affective component *The emotional or feeling segment of an attitude.*

behavioral component *An intention to behave in a certain way toward someone or something.*

Exhibit 3-1 The Components of an Attitude

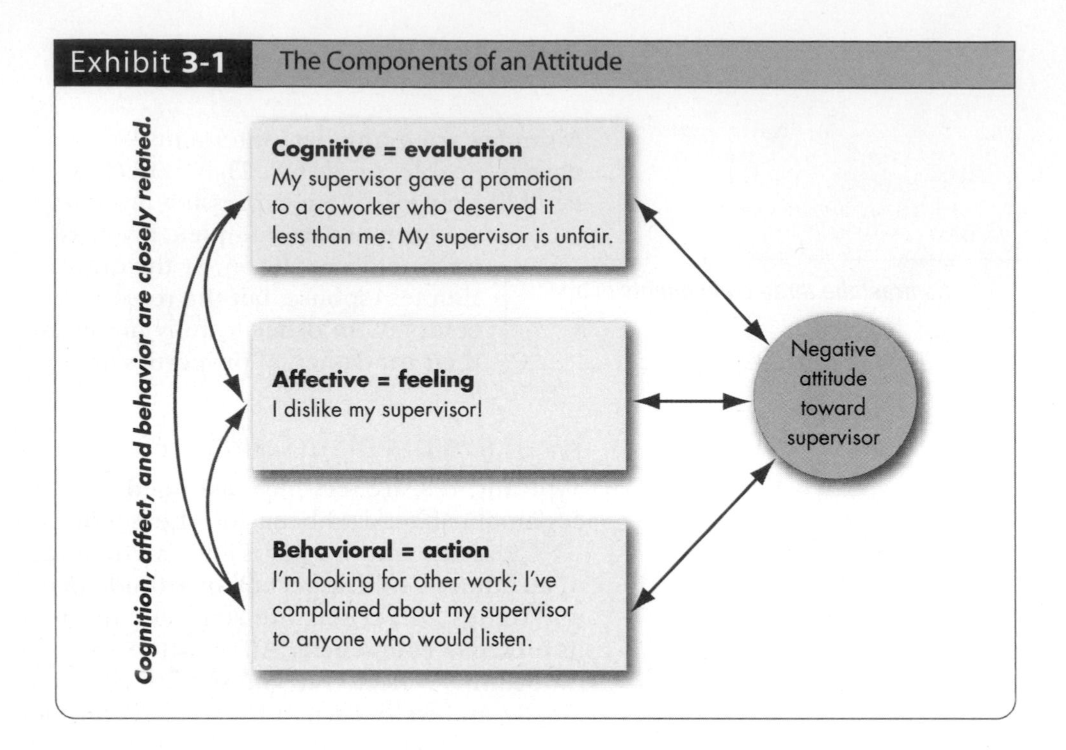

Does Behavior Always Follow from Attitudes?

Early research on attitudes assumed that they were causally related to behavior; that is, the attitudes people hold determine what they do. Common sense, too, suggests a relationship. Isn't it logical that people watch television programs they like, or that employees try to avoid assignments they find distasteful?

However, in the late 1960s, this assumed effect of attitudes on behavior was challenged by a review of the research.[3] One researcher—Leon Festinger—argued that attitudes *follow* behavior. Did you ever notice how people change what they say so it doesn't contradict what they do? Perhaps a U.S. friend of yours has consistently argued that the quality of American cars isn't up to that of imports and that he'd never own anything but a Japanese or German car. But his dad gives him a late-model Ford Mustang, and suddenly U.S. cars aren't so bad. Festinger argued that these cases of attitude following behavior illustrate the effects of **cognitive dissonance.**[4] *Cognitive dissonance* refers to any incompatibility an individual might perceive between two or more attitudes or between behavior and attitudes. Festinger argued that any form of inconsistency is uncomfortable and that individuals will attempt to reduce the dissonance and, hence, the discomfort. They will seek a stable state, in which there is a minimum of dissonance.

Research has generally concluded that people seek consistency among their attitudes and between their attitudes and their behavior.[5] They do this by altering either the attitudes or the behavior or by developing a rationalization for the discrepancy. Tobacco executives provide an example.[6] How, you might wonder, do these people cope with the ongoing barrage of data linking cigarette smoking and negative health outcomes? They can deny that any clear causation between smoking and cancer, for instance, has been established. They can brainwash themselves by continually articulating the benefits of tobacco. They can acknowledge the negative consequences of smoking but rationalize that people are going to smoke and that tobacco companies merely promote freedom of choice. They can accept the research evidence and begin actively working to make less dangerous cigarettes or at least reduce their

Marriott Corporation strives for consistency between attitudes and behavior through its motto "Spirit to Serve." CEO Bill Marriott (left in photo) models the behavior of service by visiting hotel employees throughout the year. "I want our associates to know that there really is a guy named Marriott who cares about them," he says. Marriott honors employees with job excellence awards for behavior that exemplifies the attitude of service.

availability to more vulnerable groups, such as teenagers. Or they can quit their job because the dissonance is too great.

No individual, of course, can completely avoid dissonance. You know that cheating on your income tax is wrong, but you "fudge" the numbers a bit every year and hope you're not audited. Or you tell your children to floss their teeth every day, but *you* don't. So how do people cope? Festinger would propose that the desire to reduce dissonance depends on the *importance* of the elements creating it and the degree of *influence* the individual believes he has over the elements; individuals will be more motivated to reduce dissonance when the attitudes or behavior are important or when they believe that the dissonance is due to something they can control. A third factor is the *rewards* of dissonance; high rewards accompanying high dissonance tend to reduce the tension inherent in the dissonance.

These moderating factors suggest that just individuals who experience dissonance will not necessarily move directly toward reducing it. If the issues underlying the dissonance are of minimal importance, if individuals perceive the dissonance is externally imposed and substantially uncontrollable, or if rewards are significant enough to offset it, an individual will not be under great tension to reduce the dissonance.

While Festinger questioned the attitudes–behavior relationship by arguing that, in many cases, attitudes follow behavior, other researchers asked whether there was any relationship at all. More recent research shows that attitudes predict future behavior and confirmed Festinger's original belief that certain "moderating variables" can strengthen the link.[7]

Moderating Variables The most powerful moderators of the attitudes–behavior relationship are the *importance* of the attitude, its *correspondence to behavior,*

cognitive dissonance *Any incompatibility between two or more attitudes or between behavior and attitudes.*

"Giving back to the communities in which we live and work" is an important value of Deloitte & Touche USA. The company gives its employees a direct experience with this attitude through its annual Impact Day, a one-day example of the company's year-round commitment to volunteer service. On this day, employees are allowed to leave their regular work to participate in a community service project. In this photo, the firm's CEO, Barry Salzberg (center), talks with an employee volunteer at a send-off party for a Make-A-Wish recipient.

its *accessibility*, whether there exist *social pressures*, and whether a person has *direct experience* with the attitude.[8]

Important attitudes reflect fundamental values, self-interest, or identification with individuals or groups that a person values. Attitudes that individuals consider important tend to show a strong relationship to behavior.

The more closely the attitude and the behavior are matched or correspond, the stronger the relationship. Specific attitudes tend to predict specific behaviors, whereas general attitudes tend to best predict general behaviors. For instance, asking someone specifically about her intention to stay with an organization for the next 6 months is likely to better predict turnover for that person than if you asked her how satisfied she was with her job overall. On the other hand, overall job satisfaction would better predict a general behavior such as whether the individual was engaged in her work or motivated to contribute to her organization.[9]

Attitudes we remember easily are more likely to predict our behavior. Interestingly, you're more likely to remember attitudes you frequently express. So the more you talk about your attitude on a subject, the more you're likely to remember it, and the more likely it is to shape your behavior.

Discrepancies between attitudes and behavior are more likely to occur when social pressures to behave in certain ways hold exceptional power. This situation tends to characterize behavior in organizations. It may explain why an employee who holds strong anti-union attitudes attends pro-union organizing meetings or why tobacco executives, who are not smokers themselves and who tend to believe the research linking smoking and cancer, don't actively discourage others from smoking in their offices.

Finally, the attitude–behavior relationship is likely to be much stronger if an attitude refers to something with which the individual has direct personal experience. Asking college students with no significant work experience how they would respond to working for an authoritarian supervisor is far less likely to predict actual behavior than asking that same question of employees who have actually worked for such an individual.

What Are the Major Job Attitudes?

3 *Compare and contrast the major job attitudes.*

A person can have thousands of attitudes, but OB focuses our attention on a very limited number of work-related attitudes. These tap positive or negative evaluations that employees hold about aspects of their work environment. Most of the research in OB has looked at three attitudes: job satisfaction, job involvement, and organizational commitment.[10] A few other attitudes attracting attention from researchers include perceived organizational support and employee engagement; we'll also briefly discuss these.

Job Satisfaction The term **job satisfaction** describes a positive feeling about a job, resulting from an evaluation of its characteristics. A person with a high level of job satisfaction holds positive feelings about his or her job, while a dissatisfied person holds negative feelings. When people speak of employee attitudes, they usually mean job satisfaction. In fact, the two are frequently used interchangeably. Because of the high importance OB researchers have given to job satisfaction, we'll review this attitude in detail later in this chapter.

Job Involvement Related to job satisfaction is **job involvement.**[11] Job involvement measures the degree to which people identify psychologically with their job and consider their perceived performance level important to self-worth.[12] Employees with a high level of job involvement strongly identify with and really care about the kind of work they do. Another closely related concept is **psychological empowerment**, which is employees' beliefs in the degree to which they influence their work environment, their competence, the meaningfulness of their job, and the perceived autonomy in their work.[13] For example, one study of nursing managers in Singapore found that good leaders empower their employees by involving them in decisions, making them feel their work is important, and giving them discretion to "do their own thing."[14]

High levels of both job involvement and psychological empowerment are positively related to organizational citizenship and job performance.[15] In addition, high job involvement has been found to be related to a reduced number of absences and lower resignation rates.[16]

Organizational Commitment The third job attitude we'll discuss is **organizational commitment**, a state in which an employee identifies with a particular organization and its goals and wishes to maintain membership in the organization.[17] So, high job involvement means identifying with your specific job, while high organizational commitment means identifying with your employing organization.

There are three separate dimensions to organizational commitment:[18]

1. **Affective commitment.** An **affective commitment** is an emotional attachment to the organization and a belief in its values. For example, a Petco

job satisfaction *A positive feeling about one's job resulting from an evaluation of its characteristics.*

job involvement *The degree to which a person identifies with a job, actively participates in it, and considers performance important to self-worth.*

psychological empowerment *Employees' belief in the degree to which they affect their work environment, their competence, the meaningfulness of their job, and their perceived autonomy in their work.*

organizational commitment *The degree to which an employee identifies with a particular organization and its goals and wishes to maintain membership in the organization.*

affective commitment *An emotional attachment to an organization and a belief in its values.*

employee may be affectively committed to the company because of its involvement with animals.

2. **Continuance commitment.** A **continuance commitment** is the perceived economic value of remaining with an organization compared to leaving it. An employee may be committed to an employer because she is paid well and feels it would hurt her family to quit.
3. **Normative commitment.** A **normative commitment** is an obligation to remain with the organization for moral or ethical reasons. For example, an employee who is spearheading a new initiative may remain with an employer because he feels he would "leave the employer in the lurch" if he left.

A positive relationship appears to exist between organizational commitment and job productivity, but it is a modest one.[19] A review of 27 studies suggested that the relationship between commitment and performance is strongest for new employees, and it is considerably weaker for more experienced employees.[20] And, as with job involvement, the research evidence demonstrates negative relationships between organizational commitment and both absenteeism and turnover.[21] In general, affective commitment seems more strongly related to organizational outcomes such as performance and turnover than the other two commitment dimensions. One study found that affective commitment was a significant predictor of various outcomes (perception of task characteristics, career satisfaction, intent to leave) in 72 percent of the cases, compared with only 36 percent for normative commitment and 7 percent for continuance commitment.[22] The weak results for continuance commitment make sense in that it really isn't a strong commitment at all. Rather than an allegiance (affective commitment) or an obligation (normative commitment) to an employer, a continuance commitment describes an employee who is "tethered" to an employer simply because there isn't anything better available.

International OB

Chinese Employees and Organizational Commitment

Are employees from different cultures committed to their organizations in similar ways? A 2003 study explored this question and compared the organizational commitment of Chinese employees to that of Canadian and South Korean workers. Although results revealed that the three types of commitment—normative, continuance, and affective—are present in all three cultures, they differ in importance.

Normative commitment, an obligation to remain with an organization for moral or ethical reasons, was higher in the Chinese sample of employees than in the Canadian and South Korean samples. Affective commitment, an emotional attachment to the organization and a belief in its values, was also stronger in China than in Canada and South Korea. Chinese culture may explain why. The Chinese emphasize loyalty to one's group, and in this case, one's "group" may be the employer, so employees may feel a certain loyalty from the start and become more emotionally attached as their time with the organization grows. To the extent that the Chinese view their organization as part of their group and become emotionally attached to that group, they will be more committed to their organization. Perhaps as a result of this emphasis on loyalty, the normative commitment of Chinese employees strongly predicted intentions to maintain employment with an organization.

Continuance commitment, the perceived economic value of remaining with an organization compared with leaving it, was lower in the Chinese sample than in the Canadian and South Korean samples. One reason is that Chinese workers value loyalty toward the group more than individual concerns.

So, although all three countries experience normative, continuance, and affective commitment, the degree to which each is important differs across countries.

Source: Based on Y. Cheng and M. S. Stockdale, "The Validity of the Three-Component Model of Organizational Commitment in a Chinese Context," *Journal of Vocational Behavior*, June 2003, pp. 465–489.

There is reason to believe that the concept of commitment may be less important to employers and employees today than it once was. The unwritten loyalty contract that existed 30 years ago between employees and employers has been seriously damaged, and the notion of employees staying with a single organization for most of their career has become increasingly irrelevant. Given that, "measures of employee–firm attachment, such as commitment, are problematic for new employment relations."[23] This suggests that *organizational commitment* is probably less important as a work-related attitude than it once was. In its place, we might expect something akin to *occupational commitment* to become a more relevant variable because it better reflects today's fluid workforce.[24]

Perceived Organizational Support **Perceived organizational support (POS)** is the degree to which employees believe the organization values their contribution and cares about their well-being (for example, an employee believes his organization would accommodate him if he had a child-care problem or would forgive an honest mistake on his part). Research shows that people perceive their organization as supportive when rewards are deemed fair, when employees have a voice in decisions, and when their supervisors are seen as supportive.[25] Although less research has linked POS to OB outcomes than is the case with other job attitudes, some findings suggest that employees with strong POS perceptions are more likely to have higher levels of organizational citizenship behaviors and job performance.[26]

Employee Engagement A new concept is **employee engagement**, an individual's involvement with, satisfaction with, and enthusiasm for, the work she does. For example, we might ask employees about the availability of resources and the opportunities to learn new skills, whether they feel their work is important and meaningful, and whether their interactions with coworkers and supervisors are rewarding.[27] Highly engaged employees have a passion for their work and feel a deep connection to their company; disengaged employees have essentially "checked out"—putting time but not energy or attention into their work. A recent study of nearly 8,000 business units in 36 companies found that, compared with other companies, those whose employees had high-average levels of engagement had higher levels of customer satisfaction, were more productive, had higher profits, and had lower levels of turnover and accidents.[28] The beer-maker Molson Coors found that engaged employees were five times less likely to have safety incidents, and when one did occur, it was much less serious, and less costly, for the engaged employee than for a disengaged one ($63 per incident versus $392). Engagement becomes a real concern for most organizations because surveys indicate that few employees—between 17 percent and 29 percent—are highly engaged by their work. The farm-equipment manufacturer Caterpillar set out to increase employee engagement and concluded that its initiative resulted in an 80 percent drop in grievances and a 34 percent increase in highly satisfied customers.[29]

Because of some of these promising findings, employee engagement has attracted quite a following in many business organizations and management consulting firms. However, the concept is relatively new, so we have a lot to learn about how engagement relates to other concepts, such as job satisfaction, organizational

continuance commitment *The perceived economic value of remaining with an organization compared with leaving it.*

normative commitment *An obligation to remain with an organization for moral or ethical reasons.*

perceived organizational support (POS) *The degree to which employees believe an organization values their contribution and cares about their well-being.*

employee engagement *An individual's involvement with, satisfaction with, and enthusiasm for the work he or she does.*

Employee engagement at Good People Company, Ltd., in Seoul, South Korea, includes a monthly "Pyjamas Day" during which all employees work in the clothing the company designs. Good People managers then hold meetings with employees to solicit their feedback and inspirations about company products, making employees feel that their contributions are important and meaningful.

commitment, job involvement, or intrinsic motivation to do one's job well. Engagement may be broad enough that it captures the intersection of these variables. In other words, it may be what these attitudes have in common.

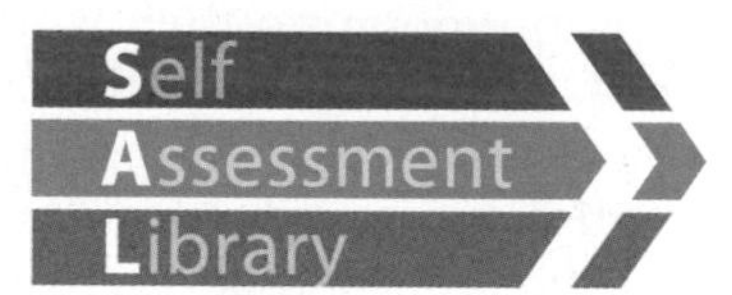

AM I ENGAGED?

In the Self-Assessment Library (available on CD or online), take assessment IV.B.1 (Am I Engaged?). (Note: If you do not currently have a job, answer the questions for your most recent job.)

Are These Job Attitudes Really All That Distinct? You might wonder whether these job attitudes are really distinct. After all, if people feel deeply involved in their job (high job involvement), isn't it probable that they like it (high job satisfaction)? Similarly, won't people who think their organization is supportive (high perceived organizational support) also feel committed to it (strong organizational commitment)? Evidence suggests that these attitudes are highly related, perhaps to a troubling degree. For example, the correlation between perceived organizational support and affective commitment is very strong.[30] The problem is that a strong correlation means the variables may be redundant (so, for example, if you know someone's affective commitment, you basically know her perceived organizational support).

But why is this redundancy so troubling? Why have two steering wheels on a car when you need only one? Why have two concepts—going by different labels—when you need only one? Redundancy is inefficient and confusing. Although we OB researchers like proposing new attitudes, often we haven't been good at showing how they compare and contrast with each other. There is some measure of distinctiveness among these attitudes, but they overlap greatly. The overlap may exist for various reasons, including the employee's personality. Some people are

OB *In the News*

Why Is Job Satisfaction Falling?

There is increasing evidence that job satisfaction levels in the United States are dropping. The Conference Board, which surveys large numbers of workers every year, reports the following percentages of individuals reporting that they are at least moderately satisfied with their jobs:

1987	61%
1995	59%
2000	51%
2005	52%
2006	47%

What are the strongest areas of dissatisfaction? Only one in five employees is satisfied with his company's promotions and bonus plans. Surprisingly, satisfaction has dropped the most among those making the highest incomes (although they still have somewhat higher satisfaction than those with relatively low earnings).

Even though U.S. workers remain relatively satisfied with their jobs, especially compared to employees in other countries, this doesn't explain why job satisfaction levels are dropping. One reason may be that in their drive to increase productivity, many companies continue to downsize, leaving the remaining workers overburdened. Downsizing also lowers the morale of layoff survivors. Why? Not only are the survivors saddled with the duties of their coworkers, but they often miss their coworkers and also wonder whether they'll be next. A recent survey suggested that only one in four employees believes her organization is loyal to her. It shouldn't be a surprise that job attitudes fall as a result.

Source: Based on K. Gurchiek, "Show Workers Their Value, Study Says," *HR Magazine*, October 2006, p. 40; "U.S. Job Satisfaction Declines," *USA Today*, April 9, 2007, p. 1B; S. Moore, L. Grunberg, and E. Greenberg, "The Effects of Similar and Dissimilar Layoff Experiences on Work and Well-Being Outcomes," *Journal of Occupational Health Psychology*, July 2004, pp. 247–257.

predisposed to be positive or negative about almost everything. If someone tells you she loves her company, it may not mean a lot if she is positive about everything else in her life. Or the overlap may mean that some organizations are just all-around better places to work than others. This may mean that if you as a manager know someone's level of job satisfaction you know most of what you need to know about how the person sees the organization.

Additional activities designed to change attitudes include arranging for people to do volunteer work in community or social service centers to meet individuals and groups from diverse backgrounds and using exercises that let participants feel what it's like to be different. For example, when people participate in the exercise *Blue Eyes–Brown Eyes*, in which people are segregated and stereotyped according to their eye color, participants see what it's like to be judged by something over which they have no control. Evidence suggests that this exercise reduces participants' negative attitudes toward individuals who are different from them.[31]

Job Satisfaction

4 *Define* job satisfaction *and show how it can be measured.*

We have already discussed job satisfaction briefly. Now let's dissect the concept more carefully. How do we measure job satisfaction? How satisfied are employees in their jobs? What causes an employee to have a high level of job satisfaction? How do dissatisfied and satisfied employees affect an organization?

Measuring Job Satisfaction

We've defined job satisfaction as a positive feeling about a job resulting from an evaluation of its characteristics. This definition is clearly a very broad one.[32] Yet breadth is inherent in the concept. Remember, a person's job is more than just the obvious activities of shuffling papers, writing programming code, waiting on customers, or driving a truck. Jobs require interacting with coworkers and bosses, following organizational rules and policies, meeting performance standards, living with working conditions that are often less than ideal, and the like.[33] This means that an employee's assessment of how satisfied he is with the job is a complex summation of a number of discrete job elements. How, then, do we measure the concept?

The two most widely used approaches are a single global rating and a summation score made up of a number of job facets. The single global rating method is nothing more than a response to one question, such as "All things considered, how satisfied are you with your job?" Respondents circle a number between 1 and 5 that corresponds to answers from "highly satisfied" to "highly dissatisfied." The other approach—a summation of job facets—is more sophisticated. It identifies key elements in a job and asks for the employee's feelings about each. Typical elements here are the nature of the work, supervision, present pay, promotion opportunities, and relations with coworkers.[34] Respondents rate them on a standardized scale, and researchers add the ratings to create an overall job satisfaction score.

Is one of these approaches superior to the other? Intuitively, summing up responses to a number of job factors seems likely to achieve a more accurate evaluation of job satisfaction. The research, however, doesn't support the intuition.[35] This is one of those rare instances in which simplicity seems to work as well as complexity, and comparisons of the two methods indicate that one is essentially as valid as the other. The best explanation for this outcome is that the concept of job satisfaction is inherently so broad that the single question captures its essence. Another explanation may be that some important facets are left out of the summation of job facets. Both methods are helpful. For example, the single global rating method isn't very time-consuming, which frees managers to address other workplace issues and problems. And the summation of job facets helps managers zero in on where problems exist, making it easier to deal with unhappy employees and solve problems faster and more accurately.

How Satisfied Are People in Their Jobs?

Are most people satisfied with their jobs? The answer seems to be a qualified "yes" in most developed countries. Independent studies conducted among U.S. workers over the past 30 years, for example, generally indicate that more workers are satisfied with their jobs than are dissatisfied.[36] However, two caveats need to be mentioned. First, as we noted earlier, job satisfaction levels in the United States appear to be dropping.

Second, research shows that satisfaction levels vary a lot, depending on which facet of job satisfaction you're talking about. As shown in Exhibit 3-2, people are, on average, satisfied with their jobs overall, with the work itself, and with their supervisors and coworkers. However, they tend to be less satisfied with their pay and with promotion opportunities. It's not really clear why people dislike their pay and promotion possibilities more than other aspects of their jobs.[37]

What Causes Job Satisfaction?

5 *Summarize the main causes of job satisfaction.*

Think about the best job you've ever had. What made it so? Chances are you probably liked the work you did. In fact, of the major job-satisfaction facets (work itself, pay, advancement opportunities, supervision, coworkers), enjoying the work is almost always the one most strongly correlated with high levels of overall job satisfaction. Interesting jobs that provide training, variety, independence, and control satisfy most employees.[38] In other words, most people prefer work that is challenging and stimulating over work that is predictable and routine.

Exhibit 3-2 Average Job Satisfaction Levels by Facet

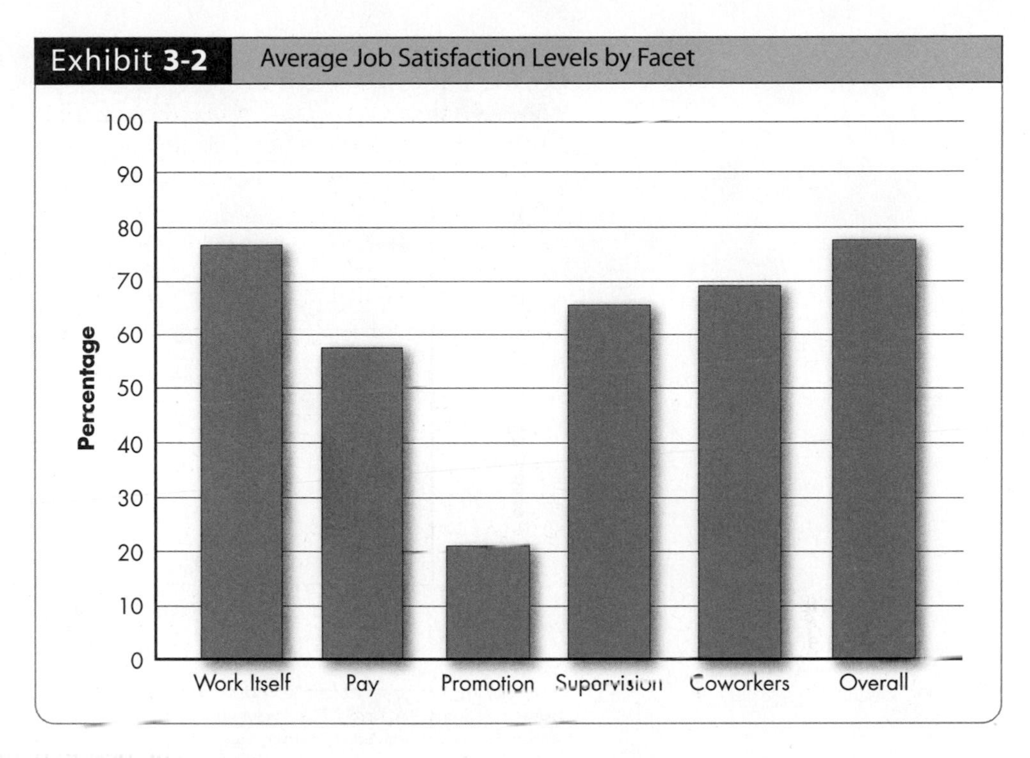

You've probably noticed that pay comes up often when people discuss job satisfaction. There is an interesting relationship between salary and job satisfaction. For people who are poor (for example, living below the poverty line) or who live in poor countries, pay does correlate with job satisfaction and with overall happiness. But, once an individual reaches a level of comfortable living (in the United States, that occurs at about $40,000 a year, depending on the region and family size), the relationship virtually disappears. In other words, people who earn $80,000 are, on average, no happier with their jobs than those who earn close to $40,000. Take a look at Exhibit 3-3. It shows the relationship between the average pay for a job and the average level of job satisfaction. As you can see, there isn't much of a relationship there. Jobs that are compensated handsomely have average job satisfaction levels no higher than those that are paid much less. To further illustrate this point, one researcher even found no significant difference when he compared the overall well-being of the richest people on the Forbes 400 list with that of Maasai herdsmen in East Africa.[39] As we saw in the Google example at the beginning of the chapter, good benefits do appear to satisfy employees, but high pay levels much less so.

Money does motivate people, as we will discover in Chapter 6. But what motivates us is not necessarily the same as what makes us happy. A recent poll by the University of California, Los Angeles and the American Council on Education found that entering college freshmen rated becoming "very well off financially" first on a list of 19 goals, ahead of choices such as helping others, raising a family, or becoming proficient in an academic pursuit. Maybe your goal isn't to be happy. But if it is, money's probably not going to do much to get you there.[40]

Job satisfaction is not just about job conditions. Personality also plays a role. People who are less positive about themselves are less likely to like their jobs. Research has shown that people who have positive **core self-evaluations**—who

core self-evaluations *Bottom-line conclusions individuals have about their capabilities, competence, and worth as a person.*

Exhibit 3-3 Relationship Between Average Pay in a Job and Job Satisfaction of Employees in That Job

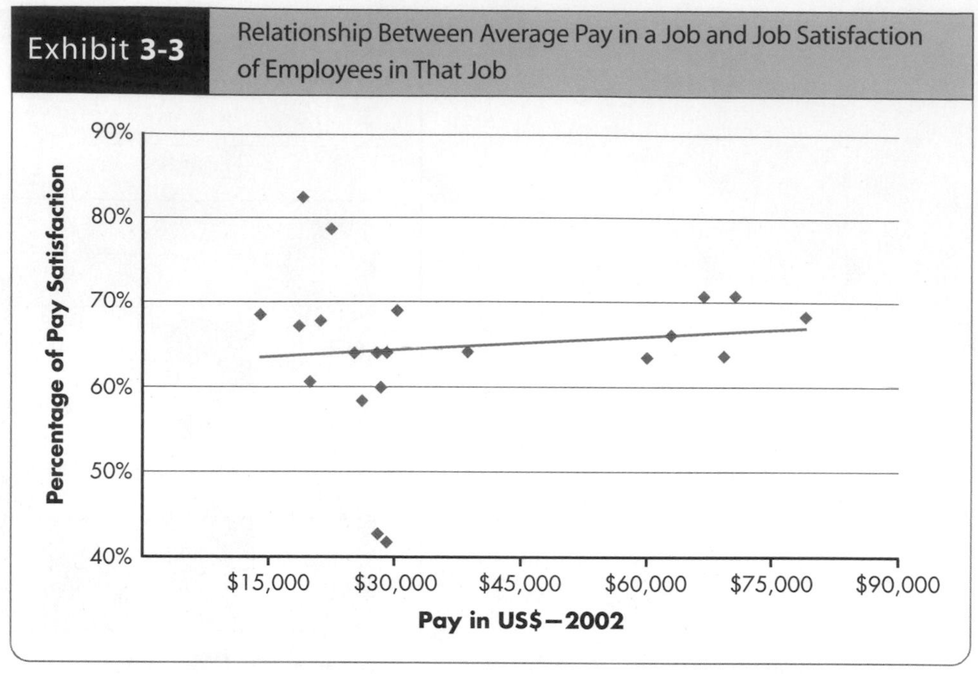

Source: T. A. Judge, R. F. Piccolo, N. P. Podsakoff, J. C. Shaw, and B. L. Rich, "Can Happiness Be "Earned"?: The Relationship Between Pay and Job Satisfaction," working paper, University of Florida, 2005.

believe in their inner worth and basic competence—are more satisfied with their jobs than those with negative core self-evaluations. Not only do they see their work as more fulfilling and challenging, they are more likely to gravitate toward challenging jobs in the first place. Those with negative core self-evaluations set less ambitious goals and are more likely to give up when confronting difficulties. Thus, they're more likely to be stuck in boring, repetitive jobs than those with positive core self-evaluations.[41]

MYTH OR SCIENCE? *"Happy Workers Are Productive Workers"*

This statement is generally true. The idea that "happy workers are productive workers" was developed in the 1930s and 1940s, largely as a result of findings drawn by researchers conducting the Hawthorne studies at the U.S. firm Western Electric. Based on those conclusions, managers worked to make their employees happier by focusing on working conditions and the work environment. Then, in the 1980s, an influential review of the research suggested that the relationship between job satisfaction and job performance was not particularly high. The authors of that review even went so far as to label the relationship as "illusory."[42]

More recently, a review of more than 300 studies corrected some errors in that earlier review. It estimated that the correlation between job satisfaction and job performance is moderately strong. This conclusion also appears to be generalizable across international contexts. The correlation is higher for complex jobs that provide employees with more discretion to act on their attitudes.[43]

The reverse causality might be true: Productive workers are likely to be happy workers, or productivity might lead to satisfaction.[44] In other words, if you do a good job, you intrinsically feel good about it. In addition, your higher productivity should increase your recognition, your pay level, and your likelihood of promotion. Cumulatively, these rewards, in turn, increase your level of satisfaction with the job.

Both arguments are probably right: Satisfaction can lead to high levels of performance for some people, while for others, high performance is satisfying. ■

Exhibit 3-4 Responses to Job Dissatisfaction

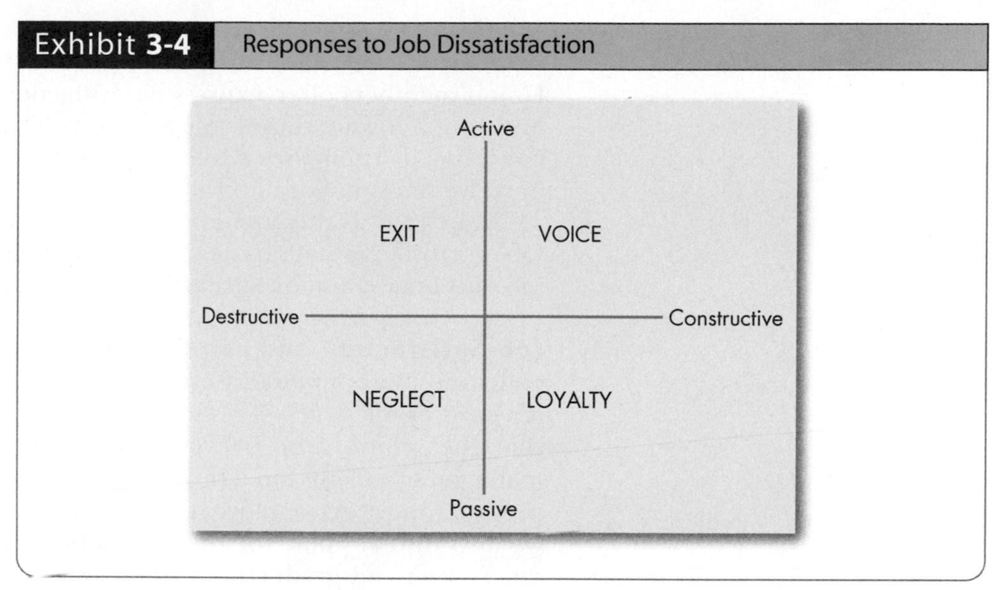

Source: Reprinted with permission from *Journal of Applied Social Psychology* 15, no. 1, p. 83. © V. H. Winston & Sons, Inc., 360 South Beach Boulevard, Palm Beach, FL 33480. All rights reserved.

The Impact of Satisfied and Dissatisfied Employees on the Workplace

6 Identify four employee responses to dissatisfaction.

There are consequences when employees like their jobs and when they dislike their jobs. One theoretical model—the exit–voice–loyalty–neglect framework—is helpful in understanding the consequences of dissatisfaction. Exhibit 3-4 illustrates the framework's four responses, which differ from one another along two dimensions: constructive/destructive and active/passive. The responses are defined as follows:[45]

- *Exit.* The **exit** response involves directing behavior toward leaving the organization, including looking for a new position as well as resigning.
- *Voice.* The **voice** response involves actively and constructively attempting to improve conditions, including suggesting improvements, discussing problems with superiors, and undertaking some forms of union activity.
- *Loyalty.* The **loyalty** response involves passively but optimistically waiting for conditions to improve, including speaking up for the organization in the face of external criticism and trusting the organization and its management to "do the right thing."
- *Neglect.* The **neglect** response involves passively allowing conditions to worsen, including chronic absenteeism or lateness, reduced effort, and increased error rate.

Exit and neglect behaviors encompass our performance variables—productivity, absenteeism, and turnover. But this model expands employee response to include voice and loyalty—constructive behaviors that allow individuals to tolerate unpleasant situations or to revive satisfactory working conditions.

exit *Dissatisfaction expressed through behavior directed toward leaving the organization.*

voice *Dissatisfaction expressed through active and constructive attempts to improve conditions.*

loyalty *Dissatisfaction expressed by passively waiting for conditions to improve.*

neglect *Dissatisfaction expressed through allowing conditions to worsen.*

It helps us to understand situations, such as those sometimes found among unionized workers, for whom low job satisfaction is coupled with low turnover.[46] Union members often express dissatisfaction through the grievance procedure or through formal contract negotiations. These voice mechanisms allow them to continue in their jobs while convincing themselves that they are acting to improve the situation.

As helpful as this framework is in presenting the possible consequences of job dissatisfaction, it's quite general. We now discuss more specific outcomes of job satisfaction and dissatisfaction in the workplace.

Job Satisfaction and Job Performance As the "Myth or Science?" box concludes, happy workers are more likely to be productive workers, although it's hard to tell which way the causality runs. Some researchers used to believe that the relationship between job satisfaction and job performance was a management myth. But a review of 300 studies suggested that the correlation is pretty strong.[47] As we move from the individual level to that of the organization, we also find support for the satisfaction–performance relationship.[48] When satisfaction and productivity data are gathered for the organization as a whole, we find that organizations with more satisfied employees tend to be more effective than organizations with fewer satisfied employees.

Job Satisfaction and OCB It seems logical to assume that job satisfaction should be a major determinant of an employee's organizational citizenship behavior (OCB).[49] Satisfied employees would seem more likely to talk positively about the organization, help others, and go beyond the normal expectations in their job. Moreover, satisfied employees might be more prone to go beyond the call of duty because they want to reciprocate their positive experiences. Consistent with this thinking, evidence suggests that job satisfaction is moderately correlated with OCBs, such that people who are more satisfied with their jobs are more likely to engage in OCBs.[50] More recent evidence suggests that satisfaction influences OCB through perceptions of fairness.

A major focus of Nissan Motor Company's Diversity Development Office in Japan is helping female employees develop their careers. Nissan provides women such as the assembly-line workers shown here with one-on-one counseling services of career advisors and training programs to develop applicable skills. Women can also visit Nissan's corporate intranet to read interviews with "role models," women who have made substantial contributions to the company. Nissan believes that hiring more women and supporting their careers will contribute to the company's competitive edge.

Why do those satisfied with their jobs contribute more OCBs? Research indicates that fairness perceptions explain the relationship, at least in part.[51] What does this mean? Basically, job satisfaction comes down to conceptions of fair outcomes, treatment, and procedures.[52] If you don't feel that your supervisor, the organization's procedures, or pay policies are fair, your job satisfaction is likely to suffer significantly. However, when you perceive organizational processes and outcomes to be fair, trust develops. And when you trust your employer, you're more willing to voluntarily engage in behaviors that go beyond your formal job requirements.

Job Satisfaction and Customer Satisfaction As we noted in Chapter 1, employees in service jobs often interact with customers. Since the management of service organizations should be concerned with pleasing those customers, it is reasonable to ask: Is employee satisfaction related to positive customer outcomes? For frontline employees who have regular contact with customers, the answer is "yes."

The evidence indicates that satisfied employees increase customer satisfaction and loyalty.[53] Why? In service organizations, customer retention and defection are highly dependent on how frontline employees deal with customers. Satisfied employees are more likely to be friendly, upbeat, and responsive—which customers appreciate. And because satisfied employees are less prone to turnover, customers are more likely to encounter familiar faces and receive experienced service. These qualities build customer satisfaction and loyalty. The relationship also seems to apply in reverse: Dissatisfied customers can increase an employee's job dissatisfaction. Employees who have regular contact with customers report that rude, thoughtless, or unreasonably demanding customers adversely affect the employees' job satisfaction.[54]

A number of companies are acting on this evidence. Service-oriented businesses such as FedEx, Singapore Airlines, Four Seasons Hotels, American Express, and Virgin Atlantic obsess about pleasing their customers. Toward that end, they also focus on building employee satisfaction—recognizing that

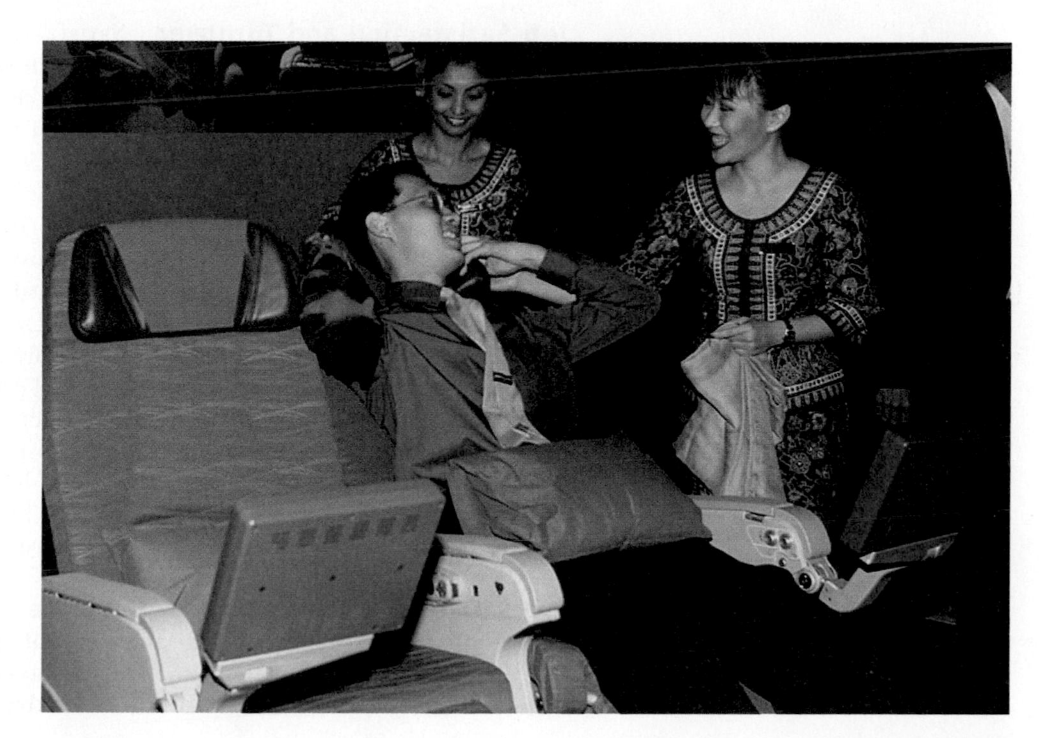

Service organizations know that whether customers are satisfied and loyal depends on how frontline employees deal with customers. Singapore Airlines has earned a reputation among world travelers for outstanding customer service. The airline's "putting people first" philosophy applies to both its employees and customers. In recruiting flight attendants, the airline selects people who are warm, hospitable, and happy to serve others. Through extensive training, Singapore molds recruits into attendants focused on complete customer satisfaction.

employee satisfaction will go a long way toward contributing to their goal of having happy customers. These firms seek to hire upbeat and friendly employees, they train employees in the importance of customer service, they reward customer service, they provide positive employee work climates, and they regularly track employee satisfaction through attitude surveys.

Job Satisfaction and Absenteeism We find a consistent negative relationship between satisfaction and absenteeism, but the correlation is moderate to weak.[55] While it certainly makes sense that dissatisfied employees are more likely to miss work, other factors have an impact on the relationship and reduce the correlation coefficient. For example, organizations that provide liberal sick leave benefits are encouraging all their employees—including those who are highly satisfied—to take days off. Assuming that you have a reasonable number of varied interests, you can find work satisfying and yet still want to take off to enjoy a 3-day weekend or tan yourself on a warm summer day if those days come free with no penalties.

An excellent illustration of how satisfaction directly leads to attendance, when there is minimal impact from other factors, is a study done at Sears, Roebuck.[56] Sears had a policy of not permitting employees to be absent from work for avoidable reasons without penalty. The occurrence of a freak April 2 snowstorm in Chicago created the opportunity to compare employee attendance at the Chicago office with attendance in New York, where the weather was quite nice. (Satisfaction data were available on employees at both locations.) The storm crippled Chicago's transportation system, and individuals knew they could miss work this day with no penalty. If satisfaction leads to attendance when there are no outside factors, the more satisfied employees should have come to work in Chicago, while dissatisfied employees should have stayed home. The study found that on this particular April 2, absenteeism rates in New York were just as high for satisfied groups of workers as for dissatisfied groups. But in Chicago, the workers with high satisfaction scores did indeed have much higher attendance than did those with lower satisfaction levels, exactly what we would have expected if satisfaction is negatively correlated with absenteeism.

Job Satisfaction and Turnover Satisfaction is also negatively related to turnover, but the correlation is stronger than what we found for absenteeism.[57] Yet, again, other factors, such as labor-market conditions, expectations about alternative job opportunities, and length of tenure with the organization, are important constraints on an employee's decision to leave her current job.[58]

Evidence indicates that an important moderator of the satisfaction–turnover relationship is the employee's level of performance.[59] Specifically, level of satisfaction is less important in predicting turnover for superior performers. Why? The organization typically makes considerable efforts to keep these people. They get pay raises, praise, recognition, increased promotional opportunities, and so forth. Just the opposite tends to apply to poor performers. The organization makes few attempts to retain them. There may even be subtle pressures to encourage them to quit. We would expect, therefore, that job satisfaction is more important in influencing poor performers to stay than in influencing superior performers to stay. Regardless of level of satisfaction, the latter are more likely to remain with the organization because the receipt of recognition, praise, and other rewards gives them more reasons to do so.

Job Satisfaction and Workplace Deviance Job dissatisfaction predicts a lot of specific behaviors, including unionization attempts, substance abuse, stealing at work, undue socializing, and tardiness. Researchers argue that these behaviors are indicators of a broader syndrome that we would term *deviant* *behavior in the workplace* (or *employee withdrawal*).[60] The key is that if employees don't like their work environment, they'll respond somehow. It is not always easy to forecast exactly *how* they'll respond. One worker's response might be to quit. Another might take work time to surf the Internet, take work supplies home for personal use, and so on. In short, evidence indicates that workers who don't like their jobs "get even" in various ways—and because employees can be quite creative in the ways they do that, controlling one behavior, such as having an absence control policy, leaves the root cause untouched. If employers want to control the undesirable consequences of job dissatisfaction, they should attack the source of the problem—the dissatisfaction—rather than try to control the different responses.

Managers Often "Don't Get It" Given the evidence we've just reviewed, it should come as no surprise that job satisfaction can affect the bottom line. One study by a management consulting firm separated large organizations into high morale (where more than 70 percent of employees expressed overall job satisfaction) and medium or low morale (lower than 70 percent). The stock prices of companies in the high morale group grew 19.4 percent, compared with 10 percent for the medium or low morale group. Despite these results, many managers are unconcerned about job satisfaction of their employees. Still others overestimate the degree to which their employees are satisfied with their jobs, so they don't think there's a problem when there is. One study of 262 large employers found that 86 percent of senior managers believed their organization treated its employees well, but only 55 percent of the employees agreed. Another study found 55 percent of managers thought morale was good in their organization, compared to only 38 percent of employees.[61] Managers first need to care about job satisfaction, and then they need to measure it rather than just assume that everything is going well.

Global Implications

Is Job Satisfaction a U.S. Concept?

7 *Show whether job satisfaction is a relevant concept in countries other than the United States.*

Most of the research on job satisfaction has been conducted in the United States. So, we might ask: Is job satisfaction a U.S. concept? The evidence strongly suggests that this is *not* the case; people in other cultures can and do form judgments of job satisfaction. Moreover, it appears that similar factors cause, and result from, job satisfaction across cultures. For example, we noted earlier that pay is positively, but relatively weakly, related to job satisfaction. This relationship appears to hold in other industrialized nations as well as in the United States.

Are Employees in Western Cultures More Satisfied with Their Jobs?

Although job satisfaction appears to be a relevant concept across cultures, that doesn't mean there are no cultural differences in job satisfaction. Evidence suggests that employees in Western cultures have higher levels of job satisfaction than those in Eastern cultures.[62] Exhibit 3-5 provides the results of a global study of the job satisfaction levels of workers in 15 countries. (This study included 23 countries, but for presentation purposes, we report the results for only the largest.) As the exhibit shows, the highest levels of job satisfaction appear to be in the United States and western Europe.

Exhibit 3-5 Average Levels of Job Satisfaction by Country

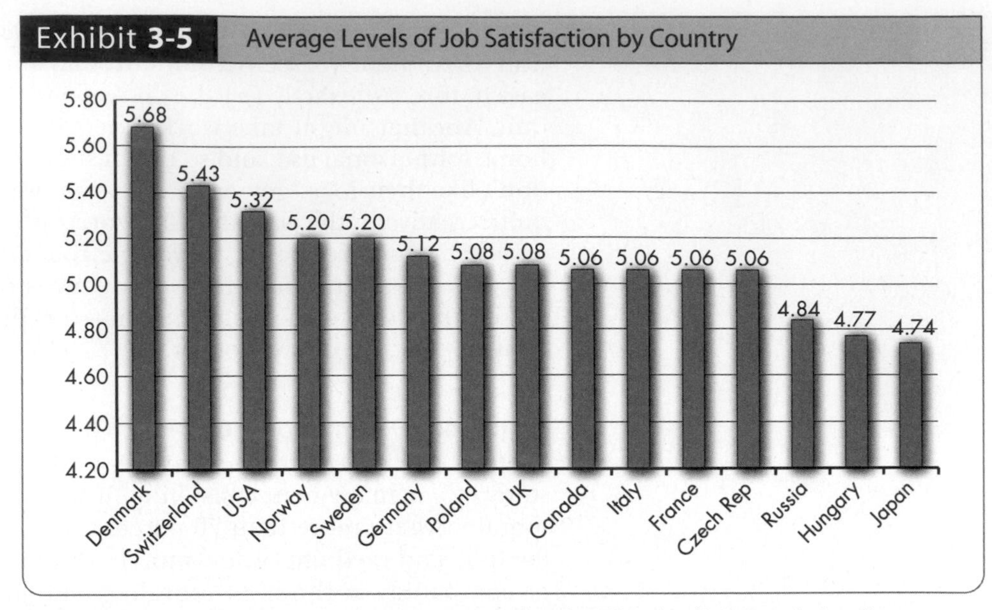

Source: M. Benz and B. S. Frey, "The Value of Autonomy: Evidence from the Self-Employed in 23 Countries," working paper 173, Institute for Empirical Research in Economics, University of Zurich, November 2003 (http://ssrn.com/abstract=475140).

Note: Scores represent average job-satisfaction levels in each country as rated on a 1 = very dissatisfied to 10 = very satisfied scale.

Is the reason that employees in Western cultures have better jobs? Or are individuals in Western cultures simply more positive (and less self-critical)? Although both factors are probably at play, evidence suggests that individuals in Eastern cultures value negative emotions more than do individuals in Western cultures, whereas those in Western cultures tend to emphasize positive emotions and individual happiness.[63] That may be why employees in Western cultures are more likely to have higher levels of satisfaction.

Summary and Implications for Managers

Managers should be interested in their employees' attitudes because attitudes give warnings of potential problems and because they influence behavior. Satisfied and committed employees, for instance, have lower rates of turnover, absenteeism, and withdrawal behaviors. They also perform better on the job. Given that managers want to keep resignations and absences down—especially among their most productive employees—they'll want to do things that generate positive job attitudes. As one review put it, "A sound measurement of overall job attitude is one of the most useful pieces of information an organization can have about its employees."[64]

The most important thing managers can do to raise employee satisfaction is focus on the intrinsic parts of the job, such as making the work challenging and interesting. Although paying employees poorly will likely not attract high-quality employees to the organization, or keep high performers, managers should realize that high pay alone is unlikely to create a satisfying work environment. Creating a satisfied workforce is hardly a guarantee of successful organizational performance, but evidence strongly suggests that whatever managers can do to improve employee attitudes will likely result in heightened organizational effectiveness.

Point

Counterpoint

MANAGERS CAN CREATE SATISFIED EMPLOYEES

A review of the evidence has identified four factors conducive to high levels of employee job satisfaction: mentally challenging work, equitable rewards, supportive working conditions, and supportive colleagues.[65] Management is able to control each of these factors:

Mentally challenging work. Generally, people prefer jobs that give them opportunities to use their skills and abilities and offer a variety of tasks, freedom, and feedback on how well they're doing. These characteristics make work mentally challenging.

Equitable rewards. Employees want pay systems that they perceive as just, unambiguous, and in line with their expectations. When pay is seen as fair—based on job demands, individual skill level, and community pay standards—satisfaction is likely to result.

Supportive working conditions. Employees want their work environment both to be safe and personally comfortable and to facilitate their doing a good job. In addition, most prefer working relatively close to home, in clean and relatively modern facilities, with adequate tools and equipment.

Supportive colleagues. People get more out of work than merely money and other tangible achievements. For most employees, work also fulfills the need for social interaction. Not surprisingly, therefore, having friendly and supportive coworkers leads to increased job satisfaction. The boss's behavior is also a major determinant of satisfaction. Studies find that employee satisfaction is increased when the immediate supervisor is understanding and friendly, offers praise for good performance, listens to employees' opinions, and shows a personal interest in employees.

The notion that managers and organizations can control the level of employee job satisfaction is inherently attractive. It fits nicely with the view that managers directly influence organizational processes and outcomes. Unfortunately, a growing body of evidence challenges the notion that managers control the factors that influence employee job satisfaction. The most recent findings indicate that it is largely genetically determined.[66]

Whether a person is happy or not is essentially determined by gene structure. Approximately 50 to 80 percent of people's differences in happiness, or subjective well-being, has been found to be attributable to their genes. Identical twins, for example, tend to have very similar careers, report similar levels of job satisfaction, and change jobs at similar rates.

Analysis of satisfaction data for a selected sample of individuals over a 50-year period found that individual results were stable over time, even when the subjects changed employers and occupations. This and other research suggests that an individual's disposition toward life—positive or negative—is established by genetic makeup, holds over time, and carries over into a disposition toward work.

Given these findings, there is probably little most managers can do to influence employee satisfaction. Despite the fact that managers and organizations go to extensive lengths to try to improve employee job satisfaction by manipulating job characteristics, working conditions, and rewards, people will inevitably return to their own "set point." A bonus may temporarily increase the satisfaction level of a negatively disposed worker, but it is unlikely to sustain it. Sooner or later, a dissatisfied worker will find new areas of fault with the job.

The only place managers will have any significant influence is in the selection process. If managers want satisfied workers, they need to screen out negative people who derive little satisfaction from their jobs, irrespective of work conditions.

Questions for Review

1. What are the main components of attitudes? Are these components related or unrelated?

2. Does behavior always follow from attitudes? Why or why not? Discuss the factors that affect whether behavior follows from attitudes.

3. What are the major job attitudes? In what ways are these attitudes alike? What is unique about each?

4. How do we measure job satisfaction?

5. What causes job satisfaction? For most people, is pay or the work itself more important?

6. What outcomes does job satisfaction influence? What implications does this have for management?

7. Is job satisfaction a uniquely U.S. concept? Does job satisfaction appear to vary by country?

Experiential Exercise

WHAT FACTORS ARE MOST IMPORTANT TO YOUR JOB SATISFACTION?

Most of us probably want a job we think will satisfy us. But because no job is perfect, we often have to trade off job attributes. One job may pay well but provide limited opportunities for advancement or skill development. Another may offer work we enjoy but have poor benefits. The following is a list of 21 job factors or attributes:

- Autonomy and independence
- Benefits
- Career advancement opportunities
- Career development opportunities
- Compensation/pay
- Communication between employees and management
- Contribution of work to organization's business goals
- Feeling safe in the work environment
- Flexibility to balance life and work issues
- Job security
- Job-specific training
- Management recognition of employee job performance
- Meaningfulness of job
- Networking
- Opportunities to use skills/abilities
- Organization's commitment to professional development
- Overall corporate culture
- Relationship with coworkers
- Relationship with immediate supervisor
- The work itself
- The variety of work

On a sheet of paper, rank-order these job factors from top to bottom so that number 1 is the job factor you think is most important to your job satisfaction, number 2 is the second most important factor to your job satisfaction, and so on.

Now gather in teams of three or four people and try the following:

1. Appoint a spokesperson who will take notes and report the answers to the following questions, on behalf of your group, back to the class.
2. Averaging across all members in your group, generate a list of the top five job factors.
3. Did most people in your group seem to value the same job factors? Why or why not?
4. Your instructor will provide you with the results of a study of a random sample of 600 employees conducted by the Society for Human Resource Management (SHRM). How do your group's rankings compare with the SHRM results?
5. The chapter says that pay doesn't correlate all that well with job satisfaction, but in the SHRM survey, people say it is relatively important. Can your group suggest a reason for the apparent discrepancy?
6. Now examine your own list again. Does your list agree with the group list? Does your list agree with the SHRM study?

Ethical Dilemma

ARE U.S. WORKERS OVERWORKED?

Europeans pride themselves on their quality of life, and rightly so. In a recent worldwide analysis of quality of life, the United States ranked 13th. The 12 nations that finished ahead of the United States were all from Europe. Factors considered in the analysis included material well-being, health, political stability, divorce rates, job security, political freedom, and gender equality.

Many Europeans would credit their high quality of life to their nations' free health care, generous unemployment benefits, and greater emphasis on leisure as opposed to work. Consider that most European nations mandate restricted workweek hours and a month or more of vacation time, but U.S. workers have among the fewest vacation days and longest average workweek in the world. Juliet Schor, a Harvard economist who has written on the subject, argues that the United States "is the world's standout workaholic nation" and that U.S. workers are trapped in a "squirrel cage" of overwork. Some argue that mandated leisure time would force companies to compete within their industry by raising productivity and product quality rather than by requiring workers to put in more hours.

Many European nations also place limits on the hours employers can require employees to work. France, Germany, and other nations limit the workweek to 35 hours. Recently, after much debate, the French parliament voted to do away with the rule that set 35 hours as the maximum workweek. The justification was that more flexible rules would allow French companies to compete more effectively so that, if business required it, they could pay employees for longer hours. Opponents of the new rule argue that it puts the decision about how much to work in the individual's hands and that it will inevitably detract from quality of life and give employers power to exploit workers. A French union leader said, "They say it's the worker who will choose how much to work, but they're lying because it's always the employer who decides."

Questions

1. Why do you think quality of life is lower in the United States than in many European nations? Do you think it would improve if the U.S. government required a minimum number of vacation days or limited workweek hours?
2. Do you think the French parliament was right to eliminate the 35-hour workweek limit? Do you think the quality of French life will suffer? Why or why not?
3. Do you think employers have an obligation to consider the quality of life of their employees? Could such an obligation mean protecting employees from being overworked?
4. Do you think it makes a difference in the research results that the unemployment rate in Europe is roughly double that of the United States and that Europe's gross domestic product (GDP) is about half that of the United States?

Sources: Juliet Schor, *The Overworked American: The Unexpected Decline of Leisure* (New York: Basic Books, 1992); C. S. Smith, "Effort to Extend Workweek Advances in France," *New York Times*, February 10, 2005, p. A9; "The Economist Intelligence Unit's Quality-of-Life Index," *The Economist*, 2005, www.economist.com/media/pdf/QUALITY_OF_LIFE.pdf; E. Olsen, "The Vacation Deficit," *Budget Travel*, October 29, 2004, www.msnbc.msn.com/id/6345416/.

Case Incident 1

ALBERTSONS WORKS ON EMPLOYEE ATTITUDES

Albertsons is a huge grocery and drug company. It has more than 2,400 supermarkets, and its Osco and Savon brands make it the fifth-largest drugstore company in the United States. In a typical year, shoppers make 1.4 billion trips through its stores.

Albertsons competes in tough businesses. Wal-Mart, in particular, has been eating away at its market share. With revenues flat and profits falling, the company hired Larry Johnston to turn the business around.

Johnston came to Albertsons from General Electric. And it was while he was at GE that Johnston met a training specialist named Ed Foreman. Foreman endeared himself to Johnston when the latter hired Foreman to help him with a serious problem. At the time, Johnston had been sent to Paris to fix the European division of GE Medical Systems, which made CT scanners. Over the previous decade, four executives had been brought in to turn the division around and try to make it profitable. All had failed. Johnston responded to the challenge by initiating some important changes: He made a number of acquisitions, he closed down inefficient plants, and he moved factories to eastern European countries to take advantage of lower labor costs. Then he brought in Ed Foreman to charge up the troops. "After we got Ed in," says Johnston, "people began to live their lives differently. They came to work with a spring in their step." In 3 years, the division was bringing in annual profits of $100 million. Johnston gives a large part of the credit for this turnaround to Foreman.

What is Foreman's secret? He provides motivation and attitude training. Here's an example of Foreman's primary program, called the Successful Life Course. It lasts 3 days and begins each morning at 6 A.M. The first day begins with a chapter from an inspirational handout, followed by 12 minutes of yoga-like stretching. Then participants march up a hill, chanting, "I know I can, I know I can." This is followed by breakfast and then a variety of lectures on attitude, diet, and exercise. But the primary focus of the program is on attitude. Says Foreman, "It's your attitude, not your aptitude, that determines your altitude." Other parts of the program include group hugs, team activities, and mind-control relaxation exercises.

Johnston believes strongly in Foreman's program. "Positive attitude is the single biggest thing that can change a business," says Johnston. He sees Foreman's program as being a critical bridge linking employees with customers: "We're in the business of the maintenance and acquisition of customers." And with so many shoppers going through his stores, Johnston says this "provides a lot of opportunities for customer service. We've got to energize the associates." To prove he's willing to put his money where his mouth is, Johnston has committed $10 million to this training. By year-end 2004, 10,000 managers had taken the course. They, in turn, are training all 190,000 Albertsons associates, with the help of tapes and books.

Foreman says his program works. He cites success at companies such as Allstate, Milliken & Co., and Abbott Labs. "The goal is to improve mental, physical, and emotional well-being," he says. "We as individuals determine the success of our own lives. Positive thoughts create positive actions."

Questions

1. Explain how Foreman's 3-day course could positively influence the profitability of Albertsons.
2. Johnston says, "Positive attitude is the single biggest thing that can change a business." How valid and generalizable do you think this statement is?
3. If you were Johnston, what would you do to evaluate the effectiveness of your $10 million investment in Foreman's training program?
4. If you were an Albertsons employee, how would you feel about going through Foreman's course? Explain your position.

Source: Based on M. Burke, "The Guru in the Vegetable Bin," *Forbes*, March 3, 2003, pp. 56–58.

Case Incident 2

LONG HOURS, HUNDREDS OF E-MAILS, AND NO SLEEP: DOES THIS SOUND LIKE A SATISFYING JOB?

Although the 40-hour workweek is now the exception rather than the norm, some individuals are taking things to the extreme:

- John Bishop, 31, is an investment banker who works for Citigroup's global energy team in New York. A recent workday for Bishop consisted of heading to the office for a conference call at 6:00 P.M. He left the office at 1:30 A.M. and had to be on a plane that same morning for a 9:00 A.M. presentation in Houston. Following the presentation, Bishop returned to New York the same day, and by 7:00 P.M., he was back in his office to work an additional 3 hours. Says Bishop, "I might be a little skewed to the workaholic, but realistically, expecting 90 to 100 hours a week is not at all unusual."
- Irene Tse, 34, heads the government bond-trading division at Goldman Sachs. For 10 years, she has seen the stock market go from all-time highs to recession levels. Such fluctuations can mean millions of dollars in either profits or losses. "There are days when you can make a lot, and other days where you lose so much you're just stunned by what you've done," says Tse. She also states that she hasn't slept completely through the night in years and frequently wakes up several times during the night to check the global market status. Her average workweek? Eighty hours. "I've done this for 10 years, and I can count on the fingers of one hand the number of days in my career when I didn't want to come to work. Every day I wake up and I can't wait to get here."

- Tony Kurtz, 33, is a managing director at Capital Alliance Partners, and he raises funds for real estate investments. However, these are not your average properties. He often travels to exotic locations such as Costa Rica and Hawaii to woo prospective clients. He travels more than 300,000 miles per year, often sleeping on planes and dealing with jet lag. Kurz is not the only one he knows with such a hectic work schedule. His girlfriend, Avery Baker, logs around 400,000 miles a year, working as the senior vice president of marketing for Tommy Hilfiger. "It's not easy to maintain a relationship like this," says Kurz. But do Kurz and Baker like their jobs? You bet.
- David Clark, 35, is the vice president of global marketing for MTV. His job often consists of traveling around the globe to promote the channel as well as to keep up with the global music scene. If he is not traveling (Clark typically logs 200,000 miles a year), a typical day consists of waking at 6:30 A.M. and immediately responding to numerous messages that have accumulated over the course of the night. He then goes to his office, where throughout the day he responds to another 500 or so messages from clients around the world. If he's lucky, he gets to spend an hour a day with his son, but then it's back to work until he finally goes to bed around midnight. Says Clark, "there are plenty of people who would love to have this job. They're knocking on the door all the time. So that's motivating."

Many individuals would balk at the prospect of a 60-hour or more workweek with constant traveling and little time for anything else. However, some individuals are exhilarated by such professions. According to the Bureau of Labor Statistics, in 2004, about 17 percent of managers worked more than 60 hours per week. But the demands of such jobs are clearly not for everyone. Many quit, with turnover levels at 55 percent for consultants and 30 percent for investment bankers, according to Vault.com. However, it is clear that such jobs, which are time-consuming and often stressful, can be satisfying to some individuals.

Questions

1. Do you think only certain individuals are attracted to these types of jobs, or is it the characteristics of the jobs themselves that are satisfying?
2. What characteristics of these jobs might contribute to increased levels of job satisfaction?
3. Given that the four individuals we just read about tend to be satisfied with their jobs, how might this satisfaction relate to their job performance, citizenship behavior, and turnover?
4. Recall David Clark's statement that "there are plenty of people who would love to have this job. They're knocking on the door all the time." How might Clark's perceptions that he has a job many others desire contribute to his job satisfaction?

Source: Based on L. Tischler, "Extreme Jobs (And the People Who Love Them)," *Fast Company,* April 2005, pp. 55–60, www.glo-jobs.com/article.php?article_no=87.

Endnotes

1. M. Helft, "Google's Buses Help Its Workers Beat the Rush," *New York Times,* March 10, 2007, pp. A1, B9; E. Esen, *SHRM Job Satisfaction Series: 2005 Job Satisfaction* (Alexandria, VA: Society for Human Resource Management, 2005); and "Benefits," *Google.com,* www.google.com/support/jobs/bin/static.py?page=benefits.html&benefits=us.
2. S. J. Breckler, "Empirical Validation of Affect, Behavior, and Cognition as Distinct Components of Attitude," *Journal of Personality and Social Psychology,* May 1984, pp. 1191–1205; and S. L. Crites, Jr., L. R. Fabrigar, and R. E. Petty, "Measuring the Affective and Cognitive Properties of Attitudes: Conceptual and Methodological Issues," *Personality and Social Psychology Bulletin,* December 1994, pp. 619–634.
3. A. W. Wicker, "Attitude Versus Action: The Relationship of Verbal and Overt Behavioral Responses to Attitude Objects," *Journal of Social Issues,* Autumn 1969, pp. 41–78.
4. L. Festinger, *A Theory of Cognitive Dissonance* (Stanford, CA: Stanford University Press, 1957).
5. See, for instance, I. R. Newby-Clark, I. McGregor, and M. P. Zanna, "Thinking and Caring About Cognitive Consistency: When and for Whom Does Attitudinal Ambivalence Feel Uncomfortable?" *Journal of Personality & Social Psychology,* February 2002, pp. 157–166; and D. J. Schleicher, J. D. Watt, and G. J. Greguras, "Reexamining the Job Satisfaction-Performance Relationship: The Complexity of Attitudes," *Journal of Applied Psychology* 89, no. 1 (2004), pp. 165–177.
6. See, for instance, J. Nocera, "If It's Good for Philip Morris, Can It also Be Good for Public Health?" *New York Times,* June 18, 2006.
7. See L. R. Glasman and D. Albarracín, "Forming Attitudes That Predict Future Behavior: A Meta-analysis of the Attitude–Behavior Relation," *Psychological Bulletin,* September 2006, pp. 778–822; I. Ajzen, "The Directive Influence of Attitudes on Behavior," in M. Gollwitzer and J. A. Bargh (eds.), *The Psychology of Action: Linking Cognition and Motivation to Behavior* (New York: Guilford, 1996), pp. 385–403; and I. Ajzen, "Nature and Operation of Attitudes," in S. T. Fiske, D. L. Schacter, and C. Zahn-Waxler (eds.), *Annual Review of Psychology,* vol. 52 (Palo Alto, CA: Annual Reviews, Inc., 2001), pp. 27–58.

8. Ibid.
9. D. A. Harrison, D. A. Newman, and P. L. Roth, "How Important Are Job Attitudes? Meta-analytic Comparisons of Integrative Behavioral Outcomes and Time Sequences," *Academy of Management Journal* 49, no. 2 (2006), pp. 305–325.
10. P. P. Brooke, Jr., D. W. Russell, and J. L. Price, "Discriminant Validation of Measures of Job Satisfaction, Job Involvement, and Organizational Commitment," *Journal of Applied Psychology*, May 1988, pp. 139–145; and R. T. Keller, "Job Involvement and Organizational Commitment as Longitudinal Predictors of Job Performance: A Study of Scientists and Engineers," *Journal of Applied Psychology*, August 1997, pp. 539–545.
11. See, for example, S. Rabinowitz and D. T. Hall, "Organizational Research in Job Involvement," *Psychological Bulletin*, March 1977, pp. 265–288; G. J. Blau, "A Multiple Study Investigation of the Dimensionality of Job Involvement," *Journal of Vocational Behavior*, August 1985, pp. 19–36; C. L. Reeve and C. S. Smith, "Refining Lodahl and Kejner's Job Involvement Scale with a Convergent Evidence Approach: Applying Multiple Methods to Multiple Samples," *Organizational Research Methods*, April 2000, pp. 91–111; and J. M. Diefendorff, D. J. Brown, and A. M. Kamin, "Examining the Roles of Job Involvement and Work Centrality in Predicting Organizational Citizenship Behaviors and Job Performance," *Journal of Organizational Behavior*, February 2002, pp. 93–108.
12. Based on G. J. Blau and K. R. Boal, "Conceptualizing How Job Involvement and Organizational Commitment Affect Turnover and Absenteeism," *Academy of Management Review*, April 1987, p. 290.
13. K. W. Thomas and B. A. Velthouse, "Cognitive Elements of Empowerment: An 'Interpretive' Model of Intrinsic Task Motivation," *Academy of Management Review* 15, no. 4 (1990), pp. 666–681; G. M. Spreitzer, "Psychological Empowerment in the Workplace: Dimensions, Measurement, and Validation," *Academy of Management Journal* 38, no. 5 (1995), pp. 1442–1465; G. Chen and R. J. Klimoski, "The Impact of Expectations on Newcomer Performance in Teams as Mediated by Work Characteristics, Social Exchanges, and Empowerment," *Academy of Management Journal* 46, no. 5 (2003), pp. 591–607; A. Ergeneli, G. Saglam, and S. Metin, "Psychological Empowerment and Its Relationship to Trust in Immediate Managers," *Journal of Business Research*, January 2007, pp. 41–49; and S. E. Seibert, S. R. Silver, and W. A. Randolph, "Taking Empowerment to the Next Level: A Multiple-Level Model of Empowerment, Performance, and Satisfaction," *Academy of Management Journal* 47, no. 3 (2004), pp. 332–349.
14. B. J. Avolio, W. Zhu, W. Koh, and P. Bhatia, "Transformational Leadership and Organizational Commitment: Mediating Role of Psychological Empowerment and Moderating Role of Structural Distance," *Journal of Organizational Behavior* 25, no. 8, 2004, pp. 951–968.
15. J. M. Diefendorff, D. J. Brown, A. M. Kamin, and R. G. Lord, "Examining the Roles of Job Involvement and Work Centrality in Predicting Organizational Citizenship Behaviors and Job Performance," *Journal of Organizational Behavior*, February 2002, pp. 93–108.
16. G. J. Blau, "Job Involvement and Organizational Commitment as Interactive Predictors of Tardiness and Absenteeism," *Journal of Management*, Winter 1986, pp. 577–584; K. Boal and R. Cidambi, "Attitudinal Correlates of Turnover and Absenteeism: A Meta Analysis," paper presented at the meeting of the American Psychological Association, Toronto, Canada, 1984; and M. R. Barrick, M. K. Mount, and J. P. Strauss, "Antecedents of Involuntary Turnover Due to a Reduction in Force," *Personnel Psychology* 47, no. 3 (1994), pp. 515–535.
17. Blau and Boal, "Conceptualizing," p. 290.
18. J. P. Meyer, N. J. Allen, and C. A. Smith, "Commitment to Organizations and Occupations: Extension and Test of a Three-Component Conceptualization," *Journal of Applied Psychology* 78, no. 4 (1993), pp. 538–551.
19. M. Riketta, "Attitudinal Organizational Commitment and Job Performance: A Meta-analysis," *Journal of Organizational Behavior*, March 2002, pp. 257–266.
20. T. A. Wright and D. G. Bonett, "The Moderating Effects of Employee Tenure on the Relation Between Organizational Commitment and Job Performance: A Meta-analysis," *Journal of Applied Psychology*, December 2002, pp. 1183–1190.
21. See, for instance, W. Hom, R. Katerberg, and C. L. Hulin, "Comparative Examination of Three Approaches to the Prediction of Turnover," *Journal of Applied Psychology*, June 1979, pp. 280–290; H. Angle and J. Perry, "Organizational Commitment: Individual and Organizational Influence," *Work and Occupations*, May 1983, pp. 123–146; J. L. Pierce and R. B. Dunham, "Organizational Commitment: Pre-Employment Propensity and Initial Work Experiences," *Journal of Management*, Spring 1987, pp. 163–178; and T. Simons and Q. Roberson, "Why Managers Should Care About Fairness: The Effects of Aggregate Justice Perceptions on Organizational Outcomes," *Journal of Applied Psychology* 88, no. 3 (2003), pp. 432–443.
22. R. B. Dunham, J. A. Grube, and M. B. Castañeda, "Organizational Commitment: The Utility of an Integrative Definition," *Journal of Applied Psychology* 79, no. 3 (1994), pp. 370–380.
23. D. M. Rousseau, "Organizational Behavior in the New Organizational Era," in J. T. Spence, J. M. Darley, and D. J. Foss (eds.), *Annual Review of Psychology*, vol. 48 (Palo Alto, CA: Annual Reviews, 1997), p. 523.
24. Ibid.; K. Lee, J. J. Carswell, and N. J. Allen, "A Meta-analytic Review of Occupational Commitment: Relations with Person- and Work-Related Variables," *Journal of Applied Psychology*, October 2000, pp. 799–811; G. Blau, "On Assessing the Construct Validity of Two Multidimensional Constructs: Occupational Commitment and Occupational Entrenchment," *Human Resource Management Review*, Fall 2001, pp. 279–298; and E. Snape and T. Redman, "An Evaluation of a Three-Component Model of Occupational Commitment: Dimensionality and Consequences Among United Kingdom Human Resource Management Specialists," *Journal of Applied Psychology* 88, no. 1 (2003), pp. 152–159.
25. L. Rhoades, R. Eisenberger, and S. Armeli, "Affective Commitment to the Organization: The Contribution of Perceived Organizational Support," *Journal of Applied Psychology* 86, no. 5 (2001), pp. 825–836.
26. Z. X. Chen, S. Aryee, and C. Lee, "Test of a Mediation Model of Perceived Organizational Support," *Journal of Vocational Behavior*, June 2005, pp. 457–470; and J. A. M. Coyle-Shapiro

and N. Conway, "Exchange Relationships: Examining Psychological Contracts and Perceived Organizational Support," *Journal of Applied Psychology*, July 2005, pp. 774–781.

27. D. R. May, R. L. Gilson, and L. M. Harter, "The Psychological Conditions of Meaningfulness, Safety and Availability and the Engagement of the Human Spirit at Work," *Journal of Occupational and Organizational Psychology* 77, no. 1 (2004), pp. 11–37.

28. J. K. Harter, F. L. Schmidt, and T. L. Hayes, "Business-Unit-Level Relationship Between Employee Satisfaction, Employee Engagement, and Business Outcomes: A Meta-analysis," *Journal of Applied Psychology* 87, no. 2 (2002), pp. 268–279.

29. N. R. Lockwood, *Leveraging Employee Engagement for Competitive Advantage* (Alexandria, VA: Society for Human Resource Management, 2007); and R. J. Vance, *Employee Engagement and Commitment* (Alexandria, VA: Society for Human Resource Management, 2006).

30. L. Rhoades and R. Eisenberger, "Perceived Organizational Support: A Review of the Literature," *Journal of Applied Psychology* 87, no. 4 (2002), pp. 698–714; and R. L. Payne and D. Morrison, "The Differential Effects of Negative Affectivity on Measures of Well-Being Versus Job Satisfaction and Organizational Commitment," *Anxiety, Stress & Coping: An International Journal* 15, no. 3 (2002), pp. 231–244.

31. T. L. Stewart, J. R. LaDuke, C. Bracht, B. A. M. Sweet, and K. E. Gamarel, "Do the 'Eyes' Have It? A Program Evaluation of Jane Elliott's 'Blue-Eyes/Brown-Eyes' Diversity Training Exercise," *Journal of Applied Social Psychology* 33, no. 9 (2003), pp. 1898–1921.

32. For problems with the concept of job satisfaction, see R. Hodson, "Workplace Behaviors," *Work and Occupations*, August 1991, pp. 271–290; and H. M. Weiss and R. Cropanzano, "Affective Events Theory: A Theoretical Discussion of the Structure, Causes and Consequences of Affective Experiences at Work," in B. M. Staw and L. L. Cummings (eds.), *Research in Organizational Behavior*, vol. 18 (Greenwich, CT: JAI Press, 1996), pp. 1–3.

33. The Wyatt Company's 1989 national WorkAmerica study identified 12 dimensions of satisfaction: work organization, working conditions, communications, job performance and performance review, coworkers, supervision, company management, pay, benefits, career development and training, job content and satisfaction, and company image and change.

34. See E. Spector, *Job Satisfaction: Application, Assessment, Causes, and Consequences* (Thousand Oaks, CA: Sage, 1997), p. 3.

35. J. Wanous, A. E. Reichers, and M. J. Hudy, "Overall Job Satisfaction: How Good Are Single-Item Measures?" *Journal of Applied Psychology*, April 1997, pp. 247–252.

36. A. F. Chelte, J. Wright, and C. Tausky, "Did Job Satisfaction Really Drop During the 1970s?" *Monthly Labor Review*, November 1982, pp. 33–36; "Job Satisfaction High in America, Says Conference Board Study," *Monthly Labor Review*, February 1985, p. 52; E. Graham, "Work May Be a Rat Race, but It's Not a Daily Grind," *Wall Street Journal*, September 19, 1997, p. R1; and K. Bowman, "Attitudes About Work, Chores, and Leisure in America," *AEI Opinion Studies*, August 25, 2003.

37. W. K. Balzer, J. A. Kihm, P. C. Smith, J. L. Irwin, P. D. Bachiochi, C. Robie, E. F. Sinar, and L. F. Parra, *Users' Manual for the Job Descriptive Index (JDI; 1997 Revision) and the Job In General Scales* (Bowling Green, OH: Bowling Green State University, 1997).

38. J. Barling, E. K. Kelloway, and R. D. Iverson, "High-Quality Work, Job Satisfaction, and Occupational Injuries," *Journal of Applied Psychology* 88, no. 2 (2003), pp. 276–283; F. W. Bond and D. Bunce, "The Role of Acceptance and Job Control in Mental Health, Job Satisfaction, and Work Performance," *Journal of Applied Psychology* 88, no. 6 (2003), pp. 1057–1067.

39. E. Diener, E. Sandvik, L. Seidlitz, and M. Diener, "The Relationship Between Income and Subjective Well-Being: Relative or Absolute?" *Social Indicators Research* 28 (1993), pp. 195–223.

40. E. Diener and M. E. P. Seligman, "Beyond Money: Toward an Economy of Well-Being," *Psychological Science in the Public Interest* 5, no. 1 (2004), pp. 1–31; and A. Grant, "Money= Happiness? That's Rich: Here's the Science Behind the Axiom," *The (South Mississippi) Sun Herald*, January 8, 2005.

41. T. A. Judge and C. Hurst, "The Benefits and Possible Costs of Positive Core Self-Evaluations: A Review and Agenda for Future Research," in D. Nelson & C. L. Cooper (eds.), *Positive Organizational Behavior* (London, UK: Sage Publications, 2007), pp. 159–174.

42. M. T. Iaffaldano and M. Muchinsky, "Job Satisfaction and Job Performance: A Meta-analysis," *Psychological Bulletin*, March 1985, pp. 251–273.

43. T. A. Judge, C. J. Thoresen, J. E. Bono, and G. K. Patton, "The Job Satisfaction–Job Performance Relationship: A Qualitative and Quantitative Review," *Psychological Bulletin*, May 2001, pp. 376–407; T. Judge, S. Parker, A. E. Colbert, D. Heller, and R. Ilies, "Job Satisfaction: A Cross-Cultural Review," in N. Anderson, D. S. Ones, H. K. Sinangil, and C. Viswesvaran (eds.), *Handbook of Industrial, Work, & Organizational Psychology*, vol. 2 (Thousand Oaks, CA: Sage, 2001), p. 41.

44. C. N. Greene, "The Satisfaction–Performance Controversy," *Business Horizons*, February 1972, pp. 31–41; E. E. Lawler III, *Motivation in Organizations* (Monterey, CA: Brooks/Cole, 1973); and M. M. Petty, G. W. McGee, and J. W. Cavender, "A Meta-analysis of the Relationship Between Individual Job Satisfaction and Individual Performance," *Academy of Management Review*, October 1984, pp. 712–721.

45. See D. Farrell, "Exit, Voice, Loyalty, and Neglect as Responses to Job Dissatisfaction: A Multidimensional Scaling Study," *Academy of Management Journal*, December 1983, pp. 596–606; C. E. Rusbult, D. Farrell, G. Rogers, and A. G. Mainous III, "Impact of Exchange Variables on Exit, Voice, Loyalty, and Neglect: An Integrative Model of Responses to Declining Job Satisfaction," *Academy of Management Journal*, September 1988, pp. 599–627; M. J. Withey and W. H. Cooper, "Predicting Exit, Voice, Loyalty, and Neglect," *Administrative Science Quarterly*, December 1989, pp. 521–539; J. Zhou and J. M. George, "When Job Dissatisfaction Leads to Creativity: Encouraging the Expression of Voice," *Academy of Management Journal*, August 2001, pp. 682–696; J. B. Olson-Buchanan and W. R. Boswell, "The Role of Employee Loyalty and Formality in Voicing Discontent," *Journal of Applied Psychology*, December 2002, pp. 1167–1174; and A. Davis-Blake, J. P. Broschak, and E. George, "Happy Together? How Using Nonstandard Workers Affects Exit, Voice, and Loyalty Among Standard

Employees," *Academy of Management Journal* 46, no. 4 (2003), pp. 475–485.

46. R. B. Freeman, "Job Satisfaction as an Economic Variable," *American Economic Review*, January 1978, pp. 135–141.

47. T. A. Judge, C. J. Thoresen, J. E. Bono, and G. K. Patton, "The Job Satisfaction–Job Performance Relationship: A Qualitative and Quantitative Review," *Psychological Bulletin*, May 2001, pp. 376–407.

48. C. Ostroff, "The Relationship Between Satisfaction, Attitudes, and Performance: An Organizational Level Analysis," *Journal of Applied Psychology*, December 1992, pp. 963–974; A. M. Ryan, M. J. Schmit, and R. Johnson, "Attitudes and Effectiveness: Examining Relations at an Organizational Level," *Personnel Psychology*, Winter 1996, pp. 853–882; and J. K. Harter, F. L. Schmidt, and T. L. Hayes, "Business-Unit Level Relationship Between Employee Satisfaction, Employee Engagement, and Business Outcomes: A Meta-analysis," *Journal of Applied Psychology*, April 2002, pp. 268–279.

49. See T. S. Bateman and D. W. Organ, "Job Satisfaction and the Good Soldier: The Relationship Between Affect and Employee 'Citizenship'," *Academy of Management Journal*, December 1983, pp. 587–595; P. Podsakoff, S. B. MacKenzie, J. B. Paine, and D. G. Bachrach, "Organizational Citizenship Behaviors: A Critical Review of the Theoretical and Empirical Literature and Suggestions for Future Research," *Journal of Management* 26, no. 3 (2000), pp. 513–563.

50. B. J. Hoffman, C. A. Blair, J. P. Maeriac, and D. J. Woehr, "Expanding the Criterion Domain? A Quantitative Review of the OCB Literature," *Journal of Applied Psychology* 92, no. 2 (2007), pp. 555–566; D. W. Organ and K. Ryan, "A Meta-analytic Review of Attitudinal and Dispositional Predictors of Organizational Citizenship Behavior," *Personnel Psychology*, Winter 1995, pp. 775–802; and J. A. LePine, A. Erez, and D. E. Johnson, "The Nature and Dimensionality of Organizational Citizenship Behavior: A Critical Review and Meta-analysis," *Journal of Applied Psychology*, February 2002, pp. 52–65.

51. J. Fahr, P. M. Podsakoff, and D. W. Organ, "Accounting for Organizational Citizenship Behavior: Leader Fairness and Task Scope Versus Satisfaction," *Journal of Management*, December 1990, pp. 705–722; R. H. Moorman, "Relationship Between Organization Justice and Organizational Citizenship Behaviors: Do Fairness Perceptions Influence Employee Citizenship?" *Journal of Applied Psychology*, December 1991, pp. 845–855; and M. A. Konovsky and D. W. Organ, "Dispositional and Contextual Determinants of Organizational Citizenship Behavior," *Journal of Organizational Behavior*, May 1996, pp. 253–266.

52. D. W. Organ, "Personality and Organizational Citizenship Behavior," *Journal of Management*, Summer 1994, p. 466.

53. See, for instance, B. Schneider and D. E. Bowen, "Employee and Customer Perceptions of Service in Banks: Replication and Extension," *Journal of Applied Psychology*, August 1985, pp. 423–433; D. J. Koys, "The Effects of Employee Satisfaction, Organizational Citizenship Behavior, and Turnover on Organizational Effectiveness: A Unit-Level, Longitudinal Study," *Personnel Psychology*, Spring 2001, pp. 101–114; and J. Griffith, "Do Satisfied Employees Satisfy Customers? Support-Services Staff Morale and Satisfaction Among Public School Administrators, Students, and Parents," *Journal of Applied Social Psychology*, August 2001, pp. 1627–1658.

54. M. J. Bitner, B. H. Booms, and L. A. Mohr, "Critical Service Encounters: The Employee's Viewpoint," *Journal of Marketing*, October 1994, pp. 95–106.

55. E. A. Locke, "The Nature and Causes of Job Satisfaction," in M. D. Dunnette (ed.), *Handbook of Industrial and Organizational Psychology* (Chicago: Rand McNally, 1976), p. 1331; R. D. Hackett and R. M. Guion, "A Reevaluation of the Absenteeism–Job Satisfaction Relationship," *Organizational Behavior and Human Decision Processes*, June 1985, pp. 340–381; K. D. Scott and G. S. Taylor, "An Examination of Conflicting Findings on the Relationship between Job Satisfaction and Absenteeism: A Meta-analysis," *Academy of Management Journal*, September 1985, pp. 599–612; R. Steel and J. R. Rentsch, "Influence of Cumulation Strategies on the Long-Range Prediction of Absenteeism," *Academy of Management Journal*, December 1995, pp. 1616–1634; and G. Johns, "The Psychology of Lateness, Absenteeism, and Turnover," p. 237.

56. F. J. Smith, "Work Attitudes as Predictors of Attendance on a Specific Day," *Journal of Applied Psychology*, February 1977, pp. 16–19.

57. W. Hom and R. W. Griffeth, *Employee Turnover* (Cincinnati, OH: South-Western Publishing, 1995); R. W. Griffeth, P. W. Hom, and S. Gaertner, "A Meta-analysis of Antecedents and Correlates of Employee Turnover: Update, Moderator Tests, and Research Implications for the Next Millennium," *Journal of Management* 26, no. 3 (2000), p. 479; G. Johns, "The Psychology of Lateness, Absenteeism, and Turnover," p. 237.

58. See, for example, C. L. Hulin, M. Roznowski, and D. Hachiya, "Alternative Opportunities and Withdrawal Decisions: Empirical and Theoretical Discrepancies and an Integration," *Psychological Bulletin*, July 1985, pp. 233–250; and J. M. Carsten and P. E. Spector, "Unemployment, Job Satisfaction, and Employee Turnover: A Meta-analytic Test of the Muchinsky Model," *Journal of Applied Psychology*, August 1987, pp. 374–381.

59. D. G. Spencer and R. M. Steers, "Performance as a Moderator of the Job Satisfaction–Turnover Relationship," *Journal of Applied Psychology*, August 1981, pp. 511–514.

60. K. A. Hanisch, C. L. Hulin, and M. Roznowski, "The Importance of Individuals' Repertoires of Behaviors: The Scientific Appropriateness of Studying Multiple Behaviors and General Attitudes," *Journal of Organizational Behavior* 19, no. 5 (1998), pp. 463–480.

61. K. Holland, "Inside the Minds of Your Employees," *New York Times* (January 28, 2007), p. B1; "Study Sees Link Between Morale and Stock Price," *Workforce Management* (February 27, 2006), p. 15; and "The Workplace as a Solar System," *New York Times* (October 28, 2006), p. B5.

62. M. J. Gelfand, M. Erez, and Z. Aycan, "Cross-Cultural Organizational Behavior," *Annual Review of Psychology* 58 (2007), pp. 479–514; A. S. Tsui, S. S. Nifadkar, and A. Y. Ou, "Cross-National, Cross-Cultural Organizational Behavior Research: Advances, Gaps, and Recommendations," *Journal of Management*, June 2007, pp. 426–478.

63. M. Benz and B. S. Frey, "The Value of Autonomy: Evidence from the Self-Employed in 23 Countries," working paper 173, Institute for Empirical Research in Economics, University of Zurich, November 2003 (http://ssrn.com/

abstract=475140); and P. Warr, *Work, Happiness, and Unhappiness* (Mahwah, NJ: Laurence Erlbaum, 2007).

64. Harrison, Newman, and Roth, "How Important Are Job Attitudes?" pp. 320–321.

65. Judge, et al., "Job Satisfaction: A Cross-Cultural Review"; T. A. Judge and A. H. Church, "Job Satisfaction: Research and Practice," in C. L. Cooper and E. A. Locke (eds.), *Industrial and Organizational Psychology: Linking Theory with Practice* (Oxford, UK: Blackwell, 2000), pp. 166–198; L. Saari and T. A. Judge, "Employee Attitudes and Job Satisfaction," *Human Resource Management* 43, no. 4 (2004), pp. 395–407.

66. See, for instance, R. D. Arvey, B. McCall, T. J. Bouchard, Jr., and P. Taubman, "Genetic Influences on Job Satisfaction and Work Values," *Personality and Individual Differences*, July 1994, pp. 21–33; D. Lykken and A. Tellegen, "Happiness Is a Stochastic Phenomenon," *Psychological Science*, May 1996, pp. 186–189; and D. Lykken and M. Csikszentmihalyi, "Happiness—Stuck with What You've Got?" *Psychologist*, September 2001, pp. 470–472; and "Double Take," *UNH Magazine*, Spring 2000, www.unhmagazine.unh.edu/sp00/twinssp00.html.

Personality and Values

I am driven by fear of failure.
It is a strong motivator for me.
—Dennis Manning, CEO of
Guardian Life Insurance Co.

LEARNING OBJECTIVES

After studying this chapter, you should be able to:

1 Define *personality*, describe how it is measured, and explain the factors that determine an individual's personality.

2 Describe the Myers-Briggs Type Indicator personality framework and assess its strengths and weaknesses.

3 Identify the key traits in the Big Five personality model.

4 Demonstrate how the Big Five traits predict behavior at work.

5 Identify other personality traits relevant to OB.

6 Define *values*, demonstrate the importance of values, and contrast terminal and instrumental values.

7 Compare generational differences in values and identify the dominant values in today's workforce.

8 Identify Hofstede's five value dimensions of national culture.

John Ruskin wrote that the first test of a truly great man is his humility. Don't tell that to Stephen Schwarzman, chief executive of the Blackstone Group. Schwarzman says his mission in life is to "inflict pain" and "kill off" his rivals. "I want war," he told the *Wall Street Journal*," not a series of skirmishes." And win in business he has. In 20 years, he has made Blackstone one of the most profitable—and most feared—investment groups on Wall Street, with assets approaching $100 billion.

The Seven-Billion-Dollar Man

Source: Fred R. Conrad/The New York Times

Recently, Blackstone went public, and Schwarzman profited to the tune of $7.75 billion. His successes as an investment banker are so legendary that, in 2007, *Fortune* dubbed him the "King of Wall Street." David Rubenstein, co-founder of rival buyout firm Carlyle Group, told Schwarzman, "I wish you would retire so you wouldn't compete with us on deals."

Not only is the 5′6″ Schwarzman combative, he likes the attention his success has produced. When he turned 60, his birthday party was anything but modest. The affair was enhanced by the performance of famous entertainers such as the comedian Martin Short and singers Rod Stewart and Patti LaBelle. Who staged this event? Why, Schwarzman himself. When Blackstone executives prepared a video tribute to him to be played at the event, Schwarzman intervened to squelch any roasting or other jokes played at his expense.

As you might imagine, Schwarzman is not the easiest guy to work for. When he was sunning himself at his 11,000-square-foot estate in Palm Beach, Florida, he complained that an employee wasn't wearing the proper black shoes with his uniform. On another occasion, he reportedly fired a Blackstone executive for the sound his nose made when he breathed.

The image of an enormously successful, demanding, and, yes, glamorous business leader does not daunt Schwarzman. "You wouldn't have a party for 500 people or buy trophy properties in Palm Beach if you didn't relish the notoriety," says one longtime Wall Street executive.

No matter what you think of what a Harvard roommate of Schwarzman calls his desire "to be above the crowd," there is no denying that Schwarzman has been a huge success. You may even be interested in working for him. If you do, just be careful how you breathe.[1] ■

Our personalities shape our behaviors. So if we want to better understand the behavior of someone in an organization, it helps if we know something about his or her personality. In the first half of this chapter, we review the research on personality and its relationship to behavior. In the latter half, we look at how values shape many of our work-related behaviors.

One of the personality traits we'll discuss is narcissism. Like many other CEOs and celebrities, Stephen Schwarzman might be described as relatively narcissistic. Check out the Self-Assessment Library to see how you score on narcissism (remember: be honest!).

AM I A NARCISSIST?

In the Self-Assessment Library (available on CD or online), take assessment IV.A.1 (Am I a Narcissist?) and answer the following questions.

1. *How did you score? Did your scores surprise you? Why or why not?*
2. *On which facet of narcissism was your highest score? your lowest?*
3. *Do you think this measure is accurate? Why or why not?*

Personality

1 Define personality, describe how it is measured, and explain the factors that determine an individual's personality.

Why are some people quiet and passive, while others are loud and aggressive? Are certain personality types better adapted than others for certain job types? Before we can answer these questions, we need to address a more basic one: What is personality?

What Is Personality?

When we talk of personality, we don't mean that a person has charm, a positive attitude toward life, a smiling face, or a place as a finalist for "Happiest and Friendliest" in this year's Miss Universe contest. When psychologists talk of personality, they mean a dynamic concept describing the growth and development of a person's whole psychological system. Rather than looking at parts of the person, personality looks at some aggregate whole that is greater than the sum of the parts.

Defining *Personality* The definition of *personality* we most frequently use was produced by Gordon Allport nearly 70 years ago. He said personality is "the dynamic organization within the individual of those psychophysical systems that determine his unique adjustments to his environment."[2] For our purposes, you should think of **personality** as the sum total of ways in which an individual reacts to and interacts with others. We most often describe it in terms of the measurable traits a person exhibits.

Measuring Personality The most important reason managers need to know how to measure personality is that research has shown that personality tests are useful in hiring decisions. Scores on personality tests help managers forecast who is the best bet for a job.[3] And some managers want to know how people score on personality tests to better understand and more effectively manage the people who work for them. Far and away the most common means of measuring personality is through self-report surveys, with which individuals evaluate themselves by rating themselves on a series of factors such as "I worry a lot about the future." Though self-report measures work well when well constructed, one weakness of these measures is that the respondent might lie or practice impression management—that is, the person could "fake good" on the test to create a good impression. This is especially a concern when the survey is the basis for employment. Another problem is accuracy. In other words, a perfectly good candidate could have just been in a bad mood when the survey was taken.

Observer-ratings surveys provide an independent assessment of personality. Instead of self-reporting, a coworker or another observer does the rating (sometimes with the subject's knowledge and sometimes not). Even though the results of self-report surveys and observer-ratings surveys are strongly correlated, research suggests that observer-ratings surveys are a better predictor of success on the job.[4] However, each can tell us something unique about an individual's behavior in the workplace.

Personality Determinants An early debate in personality research centered on whether an individual's personality was the result of heredity or of environment. Was the personality predetermined at birth, or was it the result of the individual's interaction with his or her surroundings? Clearly, there's no simple black-and-white answer. Personality appears to be a result of both hereditary and environmental factors. However, it might surprise you that research in personality development has tended to better support the importance of heredity over the environment.

Heredity refers to factors determined at conception. Physical stature, facial attractiveness, gender, temperament, muscle composition and reflexes, energy

personality *The sum total of ways in which an individual reacts to and interacts with others.*

heredity *Factors determined at conception, one's biological, physiological, and inherent psychological makeup.*

International OB

A Global Personality

Determining which employees will succeed on overseas business assignments is often difficult for an organization's managers because the same qualities that predict success in one culture may not in another. However, researchers are naming personality traits that can help managers zero in on which employees would be suited for foreign assignments.

You might think that of the Big Five traits, openness to experience would be most important to effectiveness in international assignments. Open people are more likely to be culturally flexible—to "go with the flow" when things are different in another country. Although research is not fully consistent on the issue, most does suggest that managers who score high on openness perform better than others in international assignments.

James Eyring, Dell Computer's director of learning and development for Asia, agrees that personality is important for success in overseas assignments. "I've seen people fail the openness test—they worked exactly as they would in the U.S. They just weren't open to understanding how things work in a different culture," says Eyring.

What does the research mean for organizations? When it comes to choosing employees for global assignments, personality can make a difference.

Source: Based on M. A. Shaffer, D. A. Harrison, and H. Gregersen, "You Can Take It with You: Individual Differences and Expatriate Effectiveness," *Journal of Applied Psychology*, January 2006, pp. 109–125; and E. Silverman, "The Global Test," *Human Resource Executive Online*, June 16, 2006, www.hreonline.com/HRE/story.jsp?storyId=5669803.

their favor. Proactives are more likely than others to seek out job and organizational information, develop contacts in high places, engage in career planning, and demonstrate persistence in the face of career obstacles.

Having discussed personality traits—the enduring characteristics that describe a person's behavior—we now turn to values. Although personality and values are related, they're not the same. Values are often very specific and describe belief systems rather than behavioral tendencies. Some beliefs or values don't say much about a person's personality, and we don't always act in ways that are consistent with our values.

Values

Is capital punishment right or wrong? If a person likes power, is that good or bad? The answers to these questions are value laden. Some might argue, for example, that capital punishment is right because it is an appropriate retribution for crimes such as murder and treason. Others might argue, just as strongly, that no government has the right to take anyone's life.

6 *Define values, demonstrate the importance of values, and contrast terminal and instrumental values.*

Values represent basic convictions that "a specific mode of conduct or end-state of existence is personally or socially preferable to an opposite or converse mode of conduct or end-state of existence."[53] They contain a judgmental element in that they carry an individual's ideas as to what is right, good, or desirable. Values have both content and intensity attributes. The content attribute says that a mode of conduct or an end-state of existence is *important.* The intensity attribute specifies *how important* it is. When we rank an individual's values in terms of their intensity, we obtain that person's **value system**. All of us have a hierarchy of values that forms our value system. This system is identified by the relative importance we assign to values such as freedom, pleasure, self-respect, honesty, obedience, and equality.

Are values fluid and flexible? Generally speaking, no. They tend to be relatively stable and enduring.[54] A significant portion of the values we hold is established in our early years—from parents, teachers, friends, and others. As children, we are told that certain behaviors or outcomes are *always* desirable or *always* undesirable, with few gray areas. You were told, for example, that you should be honest and responsible. You were never taught to be just a little bit honest or a little bit responsible. It is this absolute, or "black-or-white," learning of values that more or less ensures their stability and endurance. The process of questioning our values, of course, may result in a change. More often, our questioning merely acts to reinforce the values we hold.

The Importance of Values

Values are important to the study of organizational behavior because they lay the foundation for our understanding of people's attitudes and motivation and because they influence our perceptions. Individuals enter an organization with preconceived notions of what "ought" and "ought not" to be. Of course, these notions are not value free. On the contrary, they contain interpretations of right and wrong. Furthermore, they imply that certain behaviors or outcomes are preferred over others. As a result, values cloud objectivity and rationality.

Values generally influence attitudes and behavior.[55] Suppose you enter an organization with the view that allocating pay on the basis of performance is right, while allocating pay on the basis of seniority is wrong. How are you going to react if you find that the organization you've just joined rewards seniority and not performance? You're likely to be disappointed—and this can lead to job dissatisfaction and a decision not to exert a high level of effort because "it's probably not going to lead to more money anyway." Would your attitudes and behavior be different if your values aligned with the organization's pay policies? Most likely.

Terminal Versus Instrumental Values

Can we classify values? Yes. In this section, we review two approaches to developing value typologies.

Rokeach Value Survey Milton Rokeach created the Rokeach Value Survey (RVS).[56] It consists of two sets of values, each containing 18 individual value items. One set, called **terminal values**, refers to desirable end-states. These are the goals a person would like to achieve during his or her lifetime. The other set, called **instrumental values**, refers to preferable modes of behavior, or means of achieving the terminal values. Exhibit 4-3 gives common examples for each of these sets.

values *Basic convictions that a specific mode of conduct or end-state of existence is personally or socially preferable to an opposite or converse mode of conduct or end-state of existence.*

value system *A hierarchy based on a ranking of an individual's values in terms of their intensity.*

terminal values *Desirable end-states of existence; the goals a person would like to achieve during his or her lifetime.*

instrumental values *Preferable modes of behavior or means of achieving one's terminal values.*

Exhibit 4-3 Terminal and Instrumental Values in the Rokeach Value Survey

Terminal Values	Instrumental Values
A comfortable life (a prosperous life)	Ambitious (hardworking, aspiring)
An exciting life (a stimulating, active life)	Broad-minded (open-minded)
A sense of accomplishment (lasting contribution)	Capable (competent, efficient)
A world at peace (free of war and conflict)	Cheerful (lighthearted, joyful)
A world of beauty (beauty of nature and the arts)	Clean (neat, tidy)
Equality (brotherhood, equal opportunity for all)	Courageous (standing up for your beliefs)
Family security (taking care of loved ones)	Forgiving (willing to pardon others)
Freedom (independence, free choice)	Helpful (working for the welfare of others)
Happiness (contentedness)	Honest (sincere, truthful)
Inner harmony (freedom from inner conflict)	Imaginative (daring, creative)
Mature love (sexual and spiritual intimacy)	Independent (self-reliant, self-sufficient)
National security (protection from attack)	Intellectual (intelligent, reflective)
Pleasure (an enjoyable, leisurely life)	Logical (consistent, rational)
Salvation (saved, eternal life)	Loving (affectionate, tender)
Self-respect (self-esteem)	Obedient (dutiful, respectful)
Social recognition (respect, admiration)	Polite (courteous, well-mannered)
True friendship (close companionship)	Responsible (dependable, reliable)
Wisdom (a mature understanding of life)	Self-controlled (restrained, self-disciplined)

Source: Reprinted with the permission of The Free Press, a Division of Simon & Schuster Adult Publishing Group, from The Nature of Human Values by Milton Rokeach.

Several studies confirm that RVS values vary among groups.[57] People in the same occupations or categories (for example, corporate managers, union members, parents, students) tend to hold similar values. For instance, one study compared corporate executives, members of the steelworkers' union, and members of a community activist group. Although there was a good deal of overlap among the three groups,[58] there were also some very significant differences (see Exhibit 4-4). The activists had value preferences that were quite different from those of the other two groups. They ranked "equality" as their most important terminal value; executives and union members ranked this value 12 and 13, respectively. Activists ranked "helpful" as their second-highest instrumental value. The other two groups both ranked it 14. These differences are important, because executives, union members, and activists all have a vested interest in what corporations do. These differences make things difficult for groups that have to negotiate with each other and can create serious conflicts when they contend with each other over an organization's economic and social policies.[59]

Exhibit 4-4 Mean Value Ranking of Executives, Union Members, and Activists (Top Five Only)

EXECUTIVES		UNION MEMBERS		ACTIVISTS	
Terminal	Instrumental	Terminal	Instrumental	Terminal	Instrumental
1. Self-respect	1. Honest	1. Family security	1. Responsible	1. Equality	1. Honest
2. Family security	2. Responsible	2. Freedom	2. Honest	2. A world of peace	2. Helpful
3. Freedom	3. Capable	3. Happiness	3. Courageous	3. Family security	3. Courageous
4. A sense of accomplishment	4. Ambitious	4. Self-respect	4. Independent	4. Self-respect	4. Responsible
5. Happiness	5. Independent	5. Mature love	5. Capable	5. Freedom	5. Capable

Source: Based on W. C. Frederick and J. Weber, "The Values of Corporate Managers and Their Critics: An Empirical Description and Normative Implications," in W. C. Frederick and L. E. Preston (eds.), *Business Ethics: Research Issues and Empirical Studies* (Greenwich, CT: JAI Press, 1990), pp. 123–144.

7 *Compare generational differences in values and identify the dominant values in today's workforce.*

Generational Values

Contemporary Work Cohorts Researchers have integrated several recent analyses of work values into four groups that attempt to capture the unique values of different cohorts or generations in the U.S. workforce.[60] Exhibit 4-5 proposes that employees can be segmented by the era in which they entered the workforce. Because most people start work between the ages of 18 and 23, the eras also correlate closely with the chronological age of employees.

Before going any further, let's look at some limitations of this analysis. First, we make no assumption that the framework would apply universally across all cultures. Second, while there is a steady stream of press coverage, there is very little rigorous research on generational values, so we have to rely on an intuitive framework. Finally, these are imprecise categories. There is no law that someone born in 1985 can't have similar values to someone born in 1955. You may see your values better reflected in other generations than in your own. Despite these limitations, values do change over generations,[61] and we can gain some useful insights from analyzing values this way.

Workers who grew up influenced by the Great Depression, World War II, and the Berlin blockade entered the workforce through the 1950s and early 1960s, believing in hard work, the status quo, and authority figures. We call them *Veterans* (some use the label *Traditionalists*). Once hired, Veterans tended to be loyal to their employer and respectful of authority, hardworking, and practical. These are the people former NBC anchor Tom Brokaw wrote about in his book *The Greatest Generation.* In terms of terminal values on the RVS, these employees are likely to place the greatest importance on a comfortable life and family security.

Boomers (*Baby Boomers*) are a large cohort born after World War II when veterans returned to their families and times were good. Boomers entered the workforce from the mid-1960s through the mid-1980s. This cohort was influenced heavily by the civil rights movement, the women's movement, the Beatles, the Vietnam War, and baby boom competition. They brought with them a large measure of the "hippie ethic" and distrust of authority. But they place a great deal of emphasis on achievement and material success. They work hard and want to enjoy the fruits of their labors. They're pragmatists who believe that ends can justify means. Boomers see the organizations that employ them merely as vehicles for their careers. Terminal

Exhibit 4-5 Dominant Work Values in Today's Workforce

Cohort	Entered the Workforce	Approximate Current Age	Dominant Work Values
Veterans	1950s or early 1960s	65+	Hardworking, conservative, conforming; loyalty to the organization
Boomers	1965–1985	Mid-40s to mid-60s	Success, achievement, ambition, dislike of authority; loyalty to career
Xers	1985–2000	Late 20s to early 40s	Work/life balance, team-oriented, dislike of rules; loyalty to relationships
Nexters	2000 to present	Under 30	Confident, financial success, self-reliant but team-oriented; loyalty to both self and relationships

Companies such as Patagonia, Inc., a marketer of outdoor clothing and equipment, understand the dominant work values of young people in the workforce who value work/life balance and relationships. Patagonia was one of the first U.S. firms to offer employees flexible working hours, maternity and paternity leave, and on-site day care. Through an internship program, employees can leave their jobs for up to 2 months to work full time for the environmental group of their choice while Patagonia continues to pay their salaries and benefits.

values such as a sense of accomplishment and social recognition rank high with them.

The lives of *Xers* (*Generation Xers*) have been shaped by globalization, two-career parents, MTV, AIDS, and computers. They value flexibility, life options, and the achievement of job satisfaction. Family and relationships are very important to this cohort. Unlike Veterans, Xers are skeptical, particularly of authority. They also enjoy team-oriented work. Money is important as an indicator of career performance, but Xers are willing to trade off salary increases, titles, security, and promotions for increased leisure time and expanded lifestyle options. In search of balance in their lives, Xers are less willing to make personal sacrifices for the sake of their employer than previous generations were. On the RVS, they rate high on true friendship, happiness, and pleasure.

The most recent entrants to the workforce, the *Nexters* (also called *Netters*, *Millennials*, *Generation Yers*, and *Generation Nexters*) grew up during prosperous times. They have high expectations and seek meaning in their work. Nexters have life goals more oriented toward becoming rich (81 percent) and famous (51 percent) than do Generation Xers (62 percent and 29 percent, respectively). Nexters are at ease with diversity and are the first generation to take technology for granted. They've lived much of their lives with ATMs, DVDs, cellphones, laptops, and the Internet. More than other generations, they tend to be questioning, socially conscious, and entrepreneurial. At the same time, some have described Nexters as needy. One employer said, "This is the most high-maintenance workforce in the history of the world. The good news is they're also going to be the most high-performing."[62]

An understanding that individuals' values differ but tend to reflect the societal values of the period in which they grew up can be a valuable aid in explaining and predicting behavior. Employees in their late 60s, for instance, are more likely to accept authority than their coworkers who are 10 or 15 years younger. And workers in their 30s are more likely than their parents to balk at having to work weekends and more prone to leave a job in mid-career to pursue another that provides more leisure time.

OB In the News

Are U.S. Values Different?

People in the United States are used to being criticized. After all, it was more than a century ago when the Irish playwright George Barnard Shaw wrote, "Americans adore me and will go on adoring me until I say something nice about them."

But as a result of the Iraq War and the fact that the United States is the world's lone remaining superpower, its citizens are taking unprecedented criticism abroad. One critic sneered, "The American pursuit of wealth, size, and abundance—as material surrogates for happiness—is aesthetically unpleasing and ecologically catastrophic." And many Europeans think that U.S. adults are obsessed with work. Some have even argued that the United States and Europe are becoming increasingly polarized.

Overall, the United States is wealthier than Europe and has higher productivity. But what's wrong with that? Well, some stats are not very positive. For example, compared to Europe, the United States is much more violent; it has 685 prisons for every 100,000 people, compared to 87 in the European Union. The United States has also increasingly seemed to reward power with money. For example, in 1980, the average CEO in the United States earned 40 times the annual income of the average manufacturing employee. Today, that ratio is 475:1! By comparison, the ratios are 24:1 in the U.K., 15:1 in France, and 13:1 in Sweden. Finally, the United States contains 5 percent of the world's population, but it is responsible for 25 percent of the world's greenhouse gas output—which is, many scientists argue, responsible for global warming.

Values may account for some of these differences. For example, in a study of people in 14 countries, those in the United States were more likely than others to see natural resources as elements at their disposal. And compared to Europeans, U.S. adults are more likely to believe that war is often necessary, that it is right to kill to defend property, and that physical punishment of children is necessary.

Do you think U.S. values are an underlying factor behind some of these social phenomena? Or is this academic U.S. bashing?

Source: Based on: T. Judt, "Europe vs. America," *New York Review of Books*, February 20, 2005, www.nybooks.com/articles/17726; P. W. Schultz and L. Zelezny, "Values as Predictors of Environmental Attitudes: Evidence for Consistency Across 14 Countries," *Journal of Environmental Psychology*, September 1999, pp. 255–265; and A. McAlister, P. Sandström, P. Puska, A. Veijo, R. Chereches, and L. Heidmets, "Attitudes Towards War, Killing, and Punishment of Children Among Young People in Estonia, Finland, Romania, the Russian Federation, and the USA," *Bulletin of the World Health Organization* 79, no. 5 (2001), pp. 382–387.

Linking an Individual's Personality and Values to the Workplace

Thirty years ago, organizations were concerned only with personality because their primary focus was to match individuals to specific jobs. That concern still exists. But, in recent years, that interest has expanded to include how well the individual's personality *and* values match the *organization*. Why? Because managers today are less interested in an applicant's ability to perform a *specific* job than with the *flexibility* to meet changing situations and commitment to the organization.

We'll now discuss person–job fit and person–organization fit in more detail.

Person–Job Fit

The effort to match job requirements with personality characteristics is best articulated in John Holland's **personality–job fit theory**.[63] Holland presents six

personality–job fit theory *A theory that identifies six personality types and proposes that the fit between personality type and occupational environment determines satisfaction and turnover.*

Exhibit 4-6 Holland's Typology of Personality and Congruent Occupations

Type	Personality Characteristics	Congruent Occupations
Realistic: Prefers physical activities that require skill, strength, and coordination	Shy, genuine, persistent, stable, conforming, practical	Mechanic, drill press operator, assembly-line worker, farmer
Investigative: Prefers activities that involve thinking, organizing, and understanding	Analytical, original, curious, independent	Biologist, economist, mathematician, news reporter
Social: Prefers activities that involve helping and developing others	Sociable, friendly, cooperative, understanding	Social worker, teacher, counselor, clinical psychologist
Conventional: Prefers rule-regulated, orderly, and unambiguous activities	Conforming, efficient, practical, unimaginative, inflexible	Accountant, corporate manager, bank teller, file clerk
Enterprising: Prefers verbal activities in which there are opportunities to influence others and attain power	Self-confident, ambitious, energetic, domineering	Lawyer, real estate agent, public relations specialist, small business manager
Artistic: Prefers ambiguous and unsystematic activities that allow creative expression	Imaginative, disorderly, idealistic, emotional, impractical	Painter, musician, writer, interior decorator

personality types and proposes that satisfaction and the propensity to leave a position depend on the degree to which individuals successfully match their personalities to a job. Each one of the six personality types has a congruent occupation. Exhibit 4-6 describes the six types and their personality characteristics and gives examples of congruent occupations.

Holland developed the Vocational Preference Inventory questionnaire, which contains 160 occupational titles. Respondents indicate which of these occupations they like or dislike, and their answers form personality profiles. Research strongly supports the resulting hexagonal diagram shown in Exhibit 4-7.[64] The closer two fields or orientations are in the hexagon, the more compatible they are. Adjacent categories are quite similar, whereas diagonally opposite ones are highly dissimilar.

What does all this mean? The theory argues that satisfaction is highest and turnover is lowest when personality and occupation are in agreement. Social individuals should be in social jobs, conventional people in conventional jobs, and so forth. A realistic person in a realistic job is in a more congruent situation

Exhibit 4-7 Relationships Among Occupational Personality Types

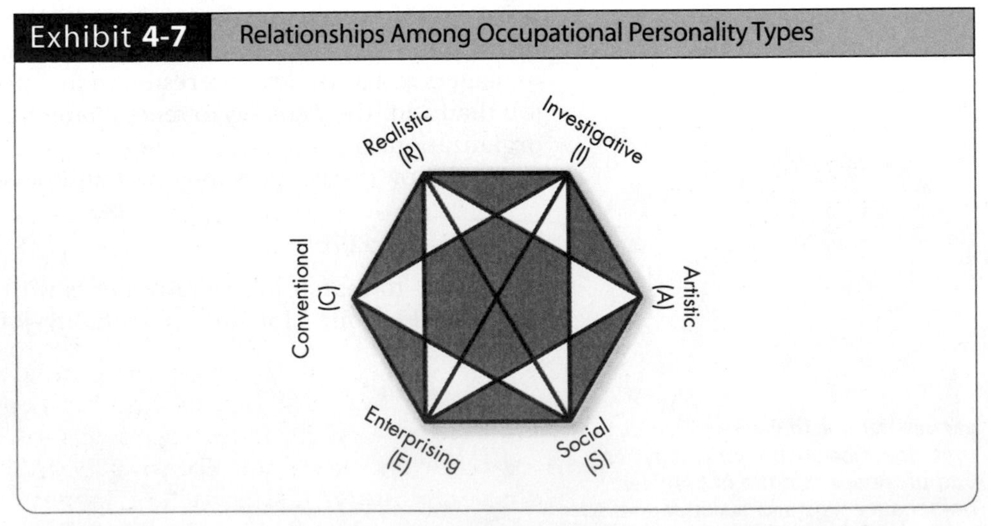

Source: Reprinted by special permission of the publisher, Psychological Assessment Resources, Inc., from Making Vocational Choices, copyright 1973, 1985, 1992 by Psychological Assessment Resources, Inc. All rights reserved.

than a realistic person in an investigative job. A realistic person in a social job is in the most incongruent situation possible. The key points of this model are that (1) there do appear to be intrinsic differences in personality among individuals, (2) there are different types of jobs, and (3) people in jobs congruent with their personality should be more satisfied and less likely to voluntarily resign than people in incongruent jobs.

Person–Organization Fit

We've noted that researchers in recent years have looked at matching people to *organizations* as well as to jobs. If an organization faces a dynamic and changing environment and requires employees who are able to readily change tasks and move easily between teams, it's more important that employees' personalities fit with the overall organization's culture than with the characteristics of any specific job.

The person–organization fit essentially argues that people are attracted to and selected by organizations that match their values, and they leave organizations that are not compatible with their personalities.[65] Using the Big Five terminology, for instance, we could expect that people high on extraversion fit well with aggressive and team-oriented cultures, that people high on agreeableness match up better with a supportive organizational climate than one that focuses on aggressiveness, and that people high on openness to experience fit better into organizations that emphasize innovation rather than standardization.[66] Following these guidelines at the time of hiring should lead to selecting new employees who fit better with the organization's culture, which should, in turn, result in higher employee satisfaction and reduced turnover. Research on person–organization fit has also looked at people's values and whether they match the organization's culture. The fit of employees' values with the culture of their organization predicts job satisfaction, commitment to the organization, and low turnover.[67]

Global Implications

Personality

Do personality frameworks, such as the Big Five model, transfer across cultures? Are dimensions such as the Type A personality relevant in all cultures? Let's try to answer these questions.

8 *Identify Hofstede's five value dimensions of national culture.*

The five personality factors identified in the Big Five model appear in almost all cross-cultural studies.[68] These studies have included a wide variety of diverse cultures—such as China, Israel, Germany, Japan, Spain, Nigeria, Norway, Pakistan, and the United States. Differences tend to be in the emphasis on dimensions and whether countries are predominantly individualistic or collectivistic. For example, Chinese managers use the category of conscientiousness more often and the category of agreeableness less often than do U.S. managers. And the Big Five appear to predict a bit better in individualistic than in collectivist cultures.[69] But there is a surprisingly high amount of agreement, especially among individuals from developed countries. As a case in point, a comprehensive review of studies covering people from the 15-nation European Community found that conscientiousness was a valid predictor of performance across jobs and occupational groups.[70] This is exactly what U.S. studies have found.

Values

Because values differ across cultures, an understanding of these differences should be helpful in explaining and predicting behavior of employees from different countries.

Hofstede's Framework for Assessing Cultures One of the most widely referenced approaches for analyzing variations among cultures was done in the late 1970s by Geert Hofstede.[71] He surveyed more than 116,000 IBM employees in 40 countries about their work-related values and found that managers and employees vary on five value dimensions of national culture:

- *Power distance.* **Power distance** describes the degree to which people in a country accept that power in institutions and organizations is distributed unequally. A high rating on power distance means that large inequalities of power and wealth exist and are tolerated in the culture, as in a class or caste system that discourages upward mobility of its citizens. A low power distance rating characterizes societies that stress equality and opportunity.
- *Individualism versus collectivism.* **Individualism** is the degree to which people prefer to act as individuals rather than as members of groups and believe in individual rights above all else. **Collectivism** emphasizes a tight social framework in which people expect others in groups of which they are a part to look after them and protect them.
- *Masculinity versus femininity.* Hofstede's construct of **masculinity** is the degree to which the culture favors traditional masculine roles such as achievement, power, and control, as opposed to viewing men and women as equals. A high masculinity rating indicates the culture has separate roles for men and women, with men dominating the society. A high **femininity** rating means the culture sees little differentiation between male and female roles and treats women as the equals of men in all respects.
- *Uncertainty avoidance.* The degree to which people in a country prefer structured over unstructured situations defines their uncertainty avoidance. In cultures that score high on uncertainty avoidance, people have an increased level of anxiety about uncertainty and ambiguity and use laws and controls to reduce uncertainty. Cultures low on **uncertainty avoidance** are more accepting of ambiguity and are less rule oriented, take more risks, and more readily accept change.
- *Long-term versus short-term orientation.* This is the newest addition to Hofstede's typology. It focuses on the degree of a society's long-term devotion to traditional values. People in a culture with **long-term orientation** look to the future and value thrift, persistence, and tradition. In a **short-term orientation**, people value the here and now; they accept change more readily and don't see commitments as impediments to change.

How do different countries score on Hofstede's dimensions? Exhibit 4-8 shows the ratings for the countries for which data are available. For example, power distance is higher in Malaysia than in any other country. The United States is very individualistic. In fact, it's the most individualistic nation of all (closely followed by Australia and Great Britain). The United States also tends to be short term in orientation and is low in power distance (people in the United States tend not to accept built-in class differences between people). The United States is also relatively low on uncertainty avoidance, meaning that most adults are relatively tolerant of uncertainty and ambiguity. The United States scores relatively high on masculinity, meaning that most people emphasize traditional gender roles (at least relative to countries such as Denmark, Finland, Norway, and Sweden).

You'll notice regional differences. Western and Northern nations such as Canada and the Netherlands tend to be more individualistic. Compared with other countries, poorer countries such as Mexico and the Philippines tend to be higher on power distance. South American nations tend to be higher than other countries on uncertainty avoidance, and Asian countries tend to have a long-term orientation.

Hofstede's culture dimensions have been enormously influential on OB researchers and managers. Nevertheless, his research has been criticized. First, although the data have since been updated, the original work is more than 30 years old and was based on a single company (IBM). A lot has happened on the world scene since then. Some of the most obvious changes include the fall of the Soviet Union, the transformation of central and eastern Europe, the end of apartheid in South Africa, the spread of Islam throughout the world today, and the rise of China as a global power. Second, few researchers have read the details of Hofstede's methodology closely and are therefore unaware of the many decisions and judgment calls he had to make (for example, reducing the number of cultural values to just five). Some results are unexpected. For example, Japan, which is often considered a highly collectivist nation, is considered only average on collectivism under Hofstede's dimensions.[72] Despite these concerns, Hofstede has been one of the most widely cited social scientists ever, and his framework has left a lasting mark on OB.

The GLOBE Framework for Assessing Cultures Begun in 1993, the Global Leadership and Organizational Behavior Effectiveness (GLOBE) research program is an ongoing cross-cultural investigation of leadership and national culture. Using data from 825 organizations in 62 countries, the GLOBE team identified nine dimensions on which national cultures differ.[73] Some of these—such as power distance, individualism/collectivism, uncertainty avoidance, gender differentiation (similar to masculinity versus femininity), and future orientation (similar to long-term versus short-term orientation)—resemble the Hofstede dimensions. The main difference in the GLOBE framework is that it added dimensions, such as humane orientation (the degree to which a society rewards individuals for being altruistic, generous, and kind to others) and performance orientation (the degree to which a society encourages and rewards group members for performance improvement and excellence).

Which framework is better? That's hard to say, and each has its adherents. We give more emphasis to Hofstede's dimensions here because they have stood the test of time and the GLOBE study confirmed them. However, researchers continue to debate the differences between these frameworks, and future studies may, in time, favor the more nuanced perspective of the GLOBE study.[74]

power distance *A national culture attribute that describes the extent to which a society accepts that power in institutions and organizations is distributed unequally.*

individualism *A national culture attribute that describes the degree to which people prefer to act as individuals rather than as members of groups.*

collectivism *A national culture attribute that describes a tight social framework in which people expect others in groups of which they are a part to look after them and protect them.*

masculinity *A national culture attribute that describes the extent to which the culture favors traditional masculine work roles of achievement, power, and control. Societal values are characterized by assertiveness and materialism.*

femininity *A national culture attribute that has little differentiation between male and female roles, where women are treated as the equals of men in all aspects of the society.*

uncertainty avoidance *A national culture attribute that describes the extent to which a society feels threatened by uncertain and ambiguous situations and tries to avoid them.*

long-term orientation *A national culture attribute that emphasizes the future, thrift, and persistence.*

short-term orientation *A national culture attribute that emphasizes the past and present, respect for tradition, and fulfillment of social obligations.*

Exhibit 4-8 Hofstede's Cultural Values by Nation

	Power Distance		Individualism Versus Collectivism		Masculinity Versus Femininity		Uncertainty Avoidance		Long-Versus Short-Term Orientation	
Country	**Index**	**Rank**	**Index**	**Rank**	**Index**	**Rank**	**Index**	**Rank**	**Index**	**Rank**
Argentina	49	35–36	46	22–23	56	20–21	86	10–15		
Australia	36	41	90	2	61	16	51	37	31	22–24
Austria	11	53	55	18	79	2	70	24–25	31	22–24
Belgium	65	20	75	8	54	22	94	5–6	38	18
Brazil	69	14	38	26–27	49	27	76	21–22	65	6
Canada	39	39	80	4–5	52	24	48	41–42	23	30
Chile	63	24–25	23	38	28	46	86	10–15		
Colombia	67	17	13	49	64	11–12	80	20		
Costa Rica	35	42–44	15	46	21	48–49	86	10–15		
Denmark	18	51	74	9	16	50	23	51	46	10
Ecuador	78	8–9	8	52	63	13–14	67	28		
El Salvador	66	18–19	19	42	40	40	94	5–6		
Finland	33	46	63	17	26	47	59	31–32	41	14
France	68	15–16	71	10–11	43	35–36	86	10–15	39	17
Germany	35	42–44	67	15	66	9–10	65	29	31	22–24
Great Britain	35	42–44	89	3	66	9–10	35	47–48	25	28–29
Greece	60	27–28	35	30	57	18–19	112	1		
Guatemala	95	2–3	6	53	37	43	101	3		
Hong Kong	68	15–16	25	37	57	18–19	29	49–50	96	2
India	77	10–11	48	21	56	20–21	40	45	61	7
Indonesia	78	8–9	14	47–48	46	30–31	48	41–42		
Iran	58	29–30	41	24	43	35–36	59	31–32		
Ireland	28	49	70	12	68	7–8	35	47–48	43	13
Israel	13	52	54	19	47	29	81	19		
Italy	50	34	76	7	70	4–5	75	23	34	19
Jamaica	45	37	39	25	68	7–8	13	52		
Japan	54	33	46	22–23	95	1	92	7	80	4
Korea (South)	60	27–28	18	43	39	41	85	16–17	75	5
Malaysia	104	1	26	36	50	25–26	36	46		
Mexico	81	5–6	30	32	69	6	82	18		
The Netherlands	38	40	80	4–5	14	51	53	35	44	11–12
New Zealand	22	50	79	6	58	17	49	39–40	30	25–26
Norway	31	47–48	69	13	8	52	50	38	44	11–12
Pakistan	55	32	14	47–48	50	25–26	70	24–25	0	34
Panama	95	2–3	11	51	44	34	86	10–15		
Peru	64	21–23	16	45	42	37–38	87	9		
Philippines	94	4	32	31	64	11–12	44	44	19	31–32
Portugal	63	24–25	27	33–35	31	45	104	2	30	25–26
Singapore	74	13	20	39–41	48	28	8	53	48	9
South Africa	49	35–36	65	16	63	13–14	49	39–40		
Spain	57	31	51	20	42	37–38	86	10–15	19	31–32
Sweden	31	47–48	71	10–11	5	53	29	49–50	33	20
Switzerland	34	45	68	14	70	4–5	58	33	40	15–16
Taiwan	58	29–30	17	44	45	32–33	69	26	87	3
Thailand	64	21–23	20	39–41	34	44	64	30	56	8
Turkey	66	18–19	37	28	45	32–33	85	16–17		
United States	40	38	91	1	62	15	46	43	29	27
Uruguay	61	26	36	29	38	42	100	4		
Venezuela	81	5–6	12	50	73	3	76	21–22		
Yugoslavia	76	12	27	33–35	21	48–49	88	8		
Regions:										
Arab countries	80	7	38	26–27	53	23	68	27		
East Africa	64	21–23	27	33–35	41	39	52	36	25	28–29
West Africa	77	10–11	20	39–41	46	30–31	54	34	16	33

Scores range from 0 = extremely low on dimension to 100 = extremely high.

Note: 1 = highest rank. LTO ranks: 1 = China; 15-16 = Bangladesh; 21 = Poland; 34 = lowest.

Summary and Implications for Managers

Personality What value, if any, does the Big Five model provide to managers? From the early 1900s through the mid-1980s, researchers sought to find a link between personality and job performance. "The outcome of those 80-plus years of research was that personality and job performance were not meaningfully related across traits or situations."[75] However, the past 20 years have been more promising, largely due to the findings surrounding the Big Five. Screening candidates for jobs who score high on conscientiousness—as well as the other Big Five traits, depending on the criteria an organization finds most important—should pay dividends. Each of the Big Five traits has numerous implications for important OB criteria. Of course, managers still need to take situational factors into consideration.[76] Factors such as job demands, the degree of required interaction with others, and the organization's culture are examples of situational variables that moderate the personality–job performance relationship. You need to evaluate the job, the work group, and the organization to determine the optimal personality fit. Other traits, such as core self-evaluation or narcissism, may be relevant in certain situations, too.

Although the MBTI has been widely criticized, it may have a place in organizations. In training and development, it can help employees to better understand themselves, and it can help team members to better understand each other. And it can open up communication in work groups and possibly reduce conflicts.

Values Why is it important to know an individual's values? Values often underlie and explain attitudes, behaviors, and perceptions. So knowledge of an individual's value system can provide insight into what "makes the person tick."

Employees' performance and satisfaction are likely to be higher if their values fit well with the organization. For instance, the person who places great importance on imagination, independence, and freedom is likely to be poorly matched with an organization that seeks conformity from its employees. Managers are more likely to appreciate, evaluate positively, and allocate rewards to employees who "fit in," and employees are more likely to be satisfied if they perceive that they do fit in. This argues for management to strive during the selection of new employees to find job candidates who have not only the ability, experience, and motivation to perform but also a value system that is compatible with the organization's.

Point

Counterpoint

TRAITS ARE POWERFUL PREDICTORS OF BEHAVIOR[77]

The essence of trait approaches in OB is that employees possess stable personality characteristics that significantly influence their attitudes toward, and behavioral reactions to, organizational settings. People with particular traits tend to be relatively consistent in their attitudes and behavior over time and across situations.

Of course, trait theorists recognize that all traits are not equally powerful. They tend to put them into one of three categories. *Cardinal traits* are those so strong and generalized that they influence every act a person performs. *Primary traits* are generally consistent influences on behavior, but they may not show up in all situations. Finally, *secondary traits* are attributes that do not form a vital part of the personality but come into play only in particular situations. For the most part, trait theories have focused on the power of primary traits to predict employee behavior.

Trait theorists do a fairly good job of meeting the average person's face-validity test. Think of friends, relatives, and acquaintances you have known for a number of years. Do they have traits that have remained essentially stable over time? Most of us would answer that question in the affirmative. If Cousin Anne was shy and nervous when we last saw her 10 years ago, we would be surprised to find her outgoing and relaxed now.

Managers seem to have a strong belief in the power of traits to predict behavior. If managers believed that situations determined behavior, they would hire people almost at random and structure the situation properly. But the employee selection process in most organizations places a great deal of emphasis on how applicants perform in interviews and on tests. Assume that you're an interviewer and ask yourself "What am I looking for in job candidates?" If you answered with terms such as *conscientious, hard-working, persistent, confident,* and *dependable*, you're a trait theorist.

Few people would dispute that some stable individual attributes affect reactions to the workplace. But trait theorists go beyond that and argue that individual behavior consistencies are widespread and account for much of the differences in behavior among people.

Two problems with using traits to explain a large proportion of behavior in organizations are that the evidence isn't all that impressive, and individuals are highly adaptive so that personality traits change in response to organizational situations.

First, though personality does influence workplace attitudes and behaviors, the effects aren't all that strong; traits explain a minority of the variance in attitudes and behavior. Why is this so? The effects of traits are likely to be strongest in relatively weak situations and weakest in relatively strong situations. Organizational settings tend to be strong situations because they have rules and other formal regulations that define acceptable behavior and punish deviant behavior; and they have informal norms that dictate appropriate behaviors. These formal and informal constraints minimize the effects of personality traits.

By arguing that employees possess stable traits that lead to cross-situational consistencies in behaviors, trait theorists imply that individuals don't really adapt to different situations. But a growing body of evidence suggests that an individual's traits are changed by the organizations the individual participates in. If the individual's personality changes as a result of exposure to organizational settings, in what sense can that individual be said to have traits that persistently and consistently affect his or her reactions to those very settings? Moreover, people typically belong to multiple organizations that often include very different kinds of members. And they adapt to those different situations, too. Instead of being prisoners of a rigid and stable personality framework, as trait theorists propose, people regularly adjust their behavior to reflect the requirements of various situations.

Questions for Review

1 What is personality? How do we typically measure it? What factors determine personality?

2 What is the Myers-Briggs Type Indicator (MBTI), and what does it measure?

3 What are the Big Five personality traits?

4 How do the Big Five traits predict work behavior?

5 Besides the Big Five, what other personality traits are relevant to OB?

6 What are values, why are they important, and what is the difference between terminal and instrumental values?

7 Do values differ across generations? How so?

8 Do values differ across cultures? How so?

Experiential Exercise

WHAT ORGANIZATIONAL CULTURE DO YOU PREFER?

The Organizational Culture Profile (OCP) can help assess whether an individual's values match the organization's.[78] The OCP helps individuals sort their characteristics in terms of importance, which indicates what a person values.

1. Working on your own, complete the OCP below.
2. Your instructor may ask you the following questions individually or as group of three or four students (with a spokesperson appointed to speak to the class for each group):
   a. What were your most preferred and least preferred values? Do you think your most preferred and least preferred values are similar to those of other class or group members?
   b. Do you think there are generational differences in the most preferred and least preferred values?
   c. Research has shown that individuals tend to be happier, and perform better, when their OCP values match those of their employer. How important do you think a "values match" is when you're deciding where you want to work?

Ethical Dilemma

HIRING BASED ON BODY ART

Leonardo's Pizza in Gainesville, Florida, regularly employs heavily tattooed workers. Tina Taladge and Meghan Dean, for example, are covered from their shoulders to their ankles in colorful tattoos. So many of the employees at Leonardo's sport tattoos that body art could almost be a qualification for the job. Many employers, however, are not that open to tattoos. Consider Russell Parrish, 29, who lives near Orlando, Florida, and has dozens of tattoos on his arms, hands, torso, and neck. In searching for a job, Parrish walked into 100 businesses, and in 60 cases, he was refused an application. "I want a career," Parrish says, "I want same the shot as everybody else."

Parrish isn't alone. Many employers, including Walt Disney World, GEICO, SeaWorld, the U.S. Postal Service, and Wal-Mart, have policies against visible tattoos. A survey of employers revealed that 58 percent indicated that they would be less likely to hire someone with visible tattoos or body piercings. "Perception is everything when it comes to getting a job," says Elaine Stover, associate director of career services at Arizona State University. "Some employers and clients could perceive body art negatively."

However, other employers—such as Bank of America, Allstate, and IBM—allow tattoos. Bank of America goes so far as to have a policy against using tattoos as a factor in hiring decisions.

Policies toward tattoos vary because, legally, employers can do as they wish. As long as the rule is applied equally to everyone (it would not be permissible to allow tattoos on men but not on women, for example), policies against tattoos are perfectly legal. Though not hiring people with tattoos is discrimination, "it's legal discrimination," said Gary Wilson, a Florida employment lawyer.

Thirty-six percent of those aged 18 to 25, and 40 percent of those aged 26 to 40, have at least one tattoo, whereas only 15 percent of those over 40 do, according to a fall 2006 survey by the Pew Research Center. One study in *American Demographics* suggested that 57 percent of senior citizens viewed visible tattoos as "freakish."

Clint Womack, like most other people with multiple tattoos, realizes there's a line that is dangerous to cross. While the 33-year-old hospital worker's arms, legs, and much of his torso are covered with tattoos, his hands, neck, and face are clear. "Tattoos are a choice you make," he says, "and you have to live with your choices."

Questions

1. Why do some employers ban tattoos while others don't mind them?
2. Is it fair for employers to reject applicants who have tattoos? Is it fair to require employees, if hired, to conceal their tattoos?
3. Should it be illegal to allow tattoos to be a factor at all in the hiring process?

Sources: R. R. Hastings, "Survey: The Demographics of Tattoos and Piercings," *HRWeek*, February 2007, www.shrm.org; and H. Wessel, "Taboo of Tattoos in the Workplace," *Orlando (Florida) Sentinel*, May 28, 2007, www.tmcnet.com/usubmit/2007/05/28/2666555.htm.

Case Incident 1

THE RISE OF THE NICE CEO?

If asked to describe the traits of an effective CEO, most people would probably use adjectives such as *driven*, *competitive*, and *tough*. While it's clear that some hard-nosed CEOs, like Blackstone chief executive Stephen Schwarzman (see the chapter opener), are successful, recently some authors have suggested that being "nice" is really important in today's workplace, even in the CEO suite. In a recent book titled *The No A–hole Rule: Building a Civilized Workplace and Surviving One That Isn't*, Stanford management professor Robert Sutton argues that getting along well with others is important to the successful functioning of organizations.

Many companies, such as Google, have developed policies to weed out those who habitually behave in an uncivil manner. Lars Dalgaard, CEO of SuccessFactors, a business software company, identifies himself as a recovering Fortune 500 "a--hole." Now, Dalgaard has implemented a strict "no a--hole" rule in his company. Job interviews are lengthy and feature probing questions designed to uncover any browbeating tendencies. Last year, Dalgaard took candidates vying for a chief financial officer vacancy to lunch at a local restaurant to see how they treated the wait staff. Some got a free lunch but nothing more. When managers and employees are hired, they get a welcome letter from Dalgaard that spells out 15 corporate values, the last of which is "I will not be an a--hole."

Although it's not clear whether they've read Sutton's book, some CEOs of Fortune 500 companies do seem to project the image of a "kinder, gentler CEO." Let's consider three examples, all of whom were protégés of Jack Welch when he was CEO of General Electric (GE) and were candidates to be his successor: Bob Nardelli, James McNerney, and Jeff Immelt.

Bob Nardelli, former CEO, Home Depot

When Bob Nardelli wasn't chosen to be CEO of GE, he demanded to know why. Didn't he have the best numbers? His bitterness was palpable, say GE insiders. When Nardelli became CEO of Home Depot, in his first few months on the job, he became notorious for his imperious manner and explosive temper. At one meeting, he yelled, "You guys don't know how to run a f---ing business." When Nardelli was fired as CEO in 2006, it was due to a combination of factors, including Home Depot's lackluster stock price, but his abrasive personality played no small part. *BusinessWeek* wrote: "With the stock price recently stuck at just over 40, roughly the same as when Nardelli arrived 6 years ago, he could no longer rely on other sterile metrics to assuage the quivering anger his arrogance provoked within every one of his key constituencies: employees, customers, and shareholders."

James McNerney, CEO, Boeing

These are heady days at Boeing, which commands record levels of new orders and dominates its European rival Airbus as never before. Most CEOs would take credit for this success. Not James McNerney, who gives the credit to Boeing's engineers and employees. "I view myself as a value-added facilitator here more than as someone who's crashing through the waves on the bridge of a frigate," he says. A former GE colleague compared Nardelli and McNerney, saying, "Jim's problems have been as tough, or tougher, than the ones that Bob had to face. But he has tried to solve them in a much more pleasant way. The guy is loved over there at Boeing."

Jeff Immelt, CEO, General Electric

Although Jeff Immelt is the first to point out that the nickname "Neutron Jack" for his predecessor Jack Welch was misleading, and that the differences between him and Welch are not as dramatic as some claim, Immelt is noted for his calm demeanor and trusting approach. In speaking of his approach, he said, "I want to believe the best in terms of what people can do. And if you want to make a growth culture, you've got to have a way to nurture people and not make them fight so goddamn hard to get any idea through the door."

Questions

1. Do you think Sutton is wrong and that the contrasting fortunes, and personalities, of Nardelli, McNerney, and Immelt are coincidental? Why or why not?
2. Do you think the importance of being "nice" varies by industry or type of job? How so?
3. How comfortable would you be working in a culture like that of SuccessFactors, where a certain level of "niceness" is part of the job description?
4. Do you think being "nice" is the same as the Big Five trait of agreeableness? If so, do you think companies should screen out those who score low on agreeableness?
5. Earlier we discussed the fact that entrepreneurs score significantly lower than managers on agreeableness. How would you reconcile this finding with Sutton's point?

Sources: D. Brady, "Being Mean Is So Last Millennium," *BusinessWeek*, January 15, 2007, p. 61; G. Colvin, "How One CEO Learned to Fly," *Fortune*, October 16, 2006; B. Grow, "Out at Home Depot," *BusinessWeek*, January 9, 2007; J. Guynn, "Crusade Against the Jerk at Work," *San Francisco (California) Chronicle*, February 24, 2007; and "The Fast Company Interview: Jeff Immelt," *Fast Company*, July 2005, p. 60.

Case Incident 2

A DIAMOND PERSONALITY

Ask Oscar Rodriguez about the dot-com burst, and he may grin at you as if to say, "What burst?" Rodriguez, a 38-year-old entrepreneur, owns an Internet business that sells loose diamonds to various buyers. Business is booming. In 2004, Rodriguez had sales of $2.06 million—a 140 percent increase from 2003. Rodriguez's database of almost 60,000 available diamonds is one of the largest in the industry and is valued, according to him, at over $350 million. Needless to say, he's optimistic about his business venture.

The future wasn't always so bright. In 1985, Rodriguez moved from his native Puerto Rico to Gainesville, Florida, with little ability to speak English. There, he attended community college and worked at a local mall to support himself. After graduation, his roommate's girlfriend suggested that he work at a local jeweler. "I thought she was crazy. I didn't know anything about jewelry," says Rodriguez, but he took her advice. Though he worked hard and received his Diamonds and Diamonds Grading certification from the Gemological Institute of America, he wasn't satisfied with his progress. "I quickly realized that working there, I was just going to get a salary with a raise here and there. I would never become anything. That drove me to explore other business ventures. I also came to really know diamonds—their pricing and their quality."

In 1997, tired of working for someone else, Rodriguez decided to open his own jewelry store. However, business didn't boom. "Some of my customers were telling me they could find diamonds for less on the Internet. It blew my mind." Rodriguez recognized an opportunity and began contacting well-known diamond dealers to see whether they would be interested in selling their gems online. Rodriguez recalls one conversation with a prominent dealer who told him, "You cannot sell diamonds on the Internet. You will not survive." Discouraged, Rodriguez says he then made a mistake. "I stopped working on it. If you have a dream, you have to keep working harder at it."

A year later, Rodriguez did work harder at his dream and found a dealer who agreed to provide him with some diamonds. Says Rodriguez, "Once I had one, I could approach others. Business started to build. The first three months I sold $200,000 worth of diamonds right off the bat. And that was just me. I started to add employees and eventually closed the jewelry store and got out of retail." Although Rodriquez does have some diamonds in inventory, he primarily acts as a connection point between buyers and suppliers, giving his customers an extraordinary selection from which to choose.

Rodriguez is now a savvy entrepreneur, and his company, Abazias.com, went public in October 2003.

Why is Rodriguez successful? Just ask two people who have known him over the years. Gary Schneider, a realtor who helped build Rodriguez's building, says, "Oscar is a very ambitious young man. I am not surprised at all how successful he is. He is an entrepreneur in the truest sense of the word." One of Rodriguez's former real-estate instructors, Howard Freeman, concurs. "I am not surprised at all at his success," says Freeman. "Oscar has always been an extremely motivated individual with a lot of resources. He has a wonderful personality and pays close attention to detail. He also has an ability to stick to things. You could tell from the beginning that he was going to persevere, and I am proud of him."

Rodriguez is keeping his success in perspective, but he also realizes his business's potential: "I take a very small salary, and our overhead is $250,000 a year. I am not in debt, and the business is breaking even. I care about the company. I want to keep everything even until we take off, and then it may be another ball game."

Questions

1. What factors do you think have contributed to Rodriguez's success? Was he merely "in the right place at the right time," or are there characteristics about him that contribute to his success?
2. How do you believe Rodriguez would score on the Big Five dimensions of personality (extraversion, agreeableness, conscientiousness, emotional stability, openness to experience)? Which ones would he score high on? Which ones might he score low on?
3. Do you believe that Rodriguez is high or low on core self-evaluation? On what information did you base your decision?
4. What information about Rodriguez suggests that he has a proactive personality?

Source: Based on M. Blombert, "Cultivating a Career," *The Gainesville (Florida) Sun*, May 9, 2005, p. D1.

Endnotes

1. N. D. Schwartz, "Wall Street's Man of the Moment," *Fortune*, February 21, 2007, http://money.cnn.com/magazines/fortune/fortune_archive/2007/03/05/8401261; and H. Sender and M. Langley, "How Blackstone's Chief Became $7 Billion Man," *Wall Street Journal*, June 13, 2007, pp. A1, A13.
2. G. W. Allport, *Personality: A Psychological Interpretation* (New York: Holt, Rinehart & Winston, 1937), p. 48. For a brief critique of current views on the meaning of personality, see R. T. Hogan and B. W. Roberts, "Introduction: Personality and Industrial and Organizational Psychology," in B. W. Roberts and R. Hogan (eds.), *Personality Psychology in the Workplace* (Washington, DC: American Psychological Association, 2001), pp. 11–12.
3. K. I. van der Zee, J. N. Zaal, and J. Piekstra, "Validation of the Multicultural Personality Questionnaire in the Context of Personnel Selection," *European Journal of Personality* 17 (2003), pp. S77–S100.
4. T. A. Judge, C. A. Higgins, C. J. Thoresen, and M. R. Barrick, "The Big Five Personality Traits, General Mental Ability, and Career Success Across the Life Span," *Personnel Psychology* 52, no. 3 (1999), pp. 621–652.
5. See, for instance, M. B. Stein, K. L. Jang, and W. J. Livesley, "Heritability of Social Anxiety-Related Concerns and Personality Characteristics: A Twin Study," *Journal of Nervous and Mental Disease*, April 2002, pp. 219–224; and S. Pinker, *The Blank Slate: The Modern Denial of Human Nature* (New York: Viking, 2002).
6. See R. D. Arvey and T. J. Bouchard, Jr., "Genetics, Twins, and Organizational Behavior," in B. M. Staw and L. L. Cummings (eds.), *Research in Organizational Behavior*, vol. 16 (Greenwich, CT: JAI Press, 1994), pp. 65–66; W. Wright, *Born That Way: Genes, Behavior, Personality* (New York: Knopf, 1998); and T. J. Bouchard, Jr., and J. C. Loehlin, "Genes, Evolution, and Personality," *Behavior Genetics*, May 2001, pp. 243–273.
7. S. Srivastava, O. P. John, and S. D. Gosling, "Development of Personality in Early and Middle Adulthood: Set Like Plaster or Persistent Change?" *Journal of Personality and Social Psychology*, May 2003, pp. 1041–1053.
8. See A. H. Buss, "Personality as Traits," *American Psychologist*, November 1989, pp. 1378–1388; R. R. McCrae, "Trait Psychology and the Revival of Personality and Culture Studies," *American Behavioral Scientist*, September 2000, pp. 10–31; and L. R. James and M. D. Mazerolle, *Personality in Work Organizations* (Thousand Oaks, CA: Sage, 2002).
9. See, for instance, G. W. Allport and H. S. Odbert, "Trait Names, A Psycholexical Study," *Psychological Monographs*, no. 47 (1936); and R. B. Cattell, "Personality Pinned Down," *Psychology Today*, July 1973, pp. 40–46.
10. R. B. Kennedy and D. A. Kennedy, "Using the Myers-Briggs Type Indicator in Career Counseling," *Journal of Employment Counseling*, March 2004, pp. 38–44.
11. G. N. Landrum, *Profiles of Genius* (New York: Prometheus, 1993).
12. See, for instance, D. J. Pittenger, "Cautionary Comments Regarding the Myers-Briggs Type Indicator," *Consulting Psychology Journal: Practice and Research*, Summer 2005, pp. 210–221; L. Bess and R. J. Harvey, "Bimodal Score Distributions and the Myers-Briggs Type Indicator: Fact or Artifact?" *Journal of Personality Assessment*, February 2002, pp. 176–186; R. M. Capraro and M. M. Capraro, "Myers-Briggs Type Indicator Score Reliability Across Studies: A Meta-analytic Reliability Generalization Study," *Educational & Psychological Measurement*, August 2002, pp. 590–602; and R. C. Arnau, B. A. Green, D. H. Rosen, D. H. Gleaves, and J. G. Melancon, "Are Jungian Preferences Really Categorical? An Empirical Investigation Using Taxometric Analysis," *Personality & Individual Differences*, January 2003, pp. 233–251.
13. See, for example, J. M. Digman, "Personality Structure: Emergence of the Five-Factor Model," in M. R. Rosenzweig and L. W. Porter (eds.), *Annual Review of Psychology*, vol. 41 (Palo Alto, CA: Annual Reviews, 1990), pp. 417–440; R. R. McCrae, "Special Issue: The Five-Factor Model: Issues and Applications," *Journal of Personality*, June 1992; D. B. Smith, P. J. Hanges, and M. W. Dickson, "Personnel Selection and the Five-Factor Model: Reexamining the Effects of Applicant's Frame of Reference," *Journal of Applied Psychology*, April 2001, pp. 304–315; and M. R. Barrick and M. K. Mount, "Yes, Personality Matters: Moving on to More Important Matters," *Human Performance* 18, no. 4 (2005), pp. 359–372.

14. See, for instance, M. R. Barrick and M. K. Mount, "The Big Five Personality Dimensions and Job Performance: A Meta-analysis," *Personnel Psychology*, Spring 1991, pp. 1–26; G. M. Hurtz and J. J. Donovan, "Personality and Job Performance: The Big Five Revisited," *Journal of Applied Psychology*, December 2000, pp. 869–879; J. Hogan and B. Holland, "Using Theory to Evaluate Personality and Job-Performance Relations: A Socioanalytic Perspective," *Journal of Applied Psychology*, February 2003, pp. 100–112; and M. R. Barrick and M. K. Mount, "Select on Conscientiousness and Emotional Stability," in E. A. Locke (ed.), *Handbook of Principles of Organizational Behavior* (Malden, MA: Blackwell, 2004), pp. 15–28.
15. M. K. Mount, M. R. Barrick, and J. P. Strauss, "Validity of Observer Ratings of the Big Five Personality Factors," *Journal of Applied Psychology*, April 1994, p. 272. Additionally confirmed by G. M. Hurtz and J. J. Donovan, "Personality and Job Performance: The Big Five Revisited"; and M. R. Barrick, M. K. Mount, and T. A. Judge, "The FFM Personality Dimensions and Job Performance: Meta-analysis of Meta-analyses," *International Journal of Selection and Assessment* 9 (2001), pp. 9–30.
16. F. L. Schmidt and J. E. Hunter, "The Validity and Utility of Selection Methods in Personnel Psychology: Practical and Theoretical Implications of 85 Years of Research Findings," *Psychological Bulletin*, September 1998, p. 272.
17. M. Tamir and M. D. Robinson, "Knowing Good from Bad: The Paradox of Neuroticism, Negative Affect, and Evaluative Processing," *Journal of Personality & Social Psychology* 87, no. 6 (2004), pp. 913–925.
18. R. J. Foti and M. A. Hauenstein, "Pattern and Variable Approaches in Leadership Emergence and Effectiveness," *Journal of Applied Psychology*, March 2007, pp. 347–355.
19. L. I. Spirling and R. Persaud, "Extraversion as a Risk Factor," *Journal of the American Academy of Child & Adolescent Psychiatry* 42, no. 2 (2003), p. 130.
20. J. A. LePine, J. A. Colquitt, and A. Erez, "Adaptability to Changing Task Contexts: Effects of General Cognitive Ability, Conscientiousness, and Openness to Experience," *Personnel Psychology* 53 (2000), pp. 563–595.
21. B. Laursen, L. Pulkkinen, and R. Adams, "The Antecedents and Correlates of Agreeableness in Adulthood," *Developmental Psychology* 38, no. 4 (2002), pp. 591–603.
22. B. Barry and R. A. Friedman, "Bargainer Characteristics in Distributive and Integrative Negotiation," *Journal of Personality and Social Psychology*, February 1998, pp. 345–359.
23. T. Bogg and B. W. Roberts, "Conscientiousness and Health-Related Behaviors: A Meta-Analysis of the Leading Behavioral Contributors to Mortality," *Psychological Bulletin* 130, no. 6 (2004), pp. 887–919.
24. S. Lee and H. J. Klein, "Relationships Between Conscientiousness, Self-Efficacy, Self-Deception, and Learning over Time," *Journal of Applied Psychology* 87, no. 6 (2002), pp. 1175–1182; G. J. Feist, "A Meta-analysis of Personality in Scientific and Artistic Creativity," *Personality and Social Psychology Review* 2, no. 4 (1998), pp. 290–309.
25. T. A. Judge and J. E. Bono, "A Rose by Any Other Name . . . Are Self-Esteem, Generalized Self-Efficacy, Neuroticism, and Locus of Control Indicators of a Common Construct?" in B. W. Roberts and R. Hogan (eds.), *Personality Psychology in the Workplace* (Washington, DC: American Psychological Association), pp. 93–118.
26. A. Erez and T. A. Judge, "Relationship of Core Self-Evaluations to Goal Setting, Motivation, and Performance," *Journal of Applied Psychology* 86, no. 6 (2001), pp. 1270–1279.
27. U. Malmendier and G. Tate, "CEO Overconfidence and Corporate Investment," *Journal of Finance* 60, no. 6 (December 2005), pp. 2661–2700.
28. R. Sandomir, "Star Struck," *New York Times*, January 12, 2007, pp. C10, C14.
29. R. G. Vleeming, "Machiavellianism: A Preliminary Review," *Psychological Reports*, February 1979, pp. 295–310.
30. R. Christie and F. L. Geis, *Studies in Machiavellianism* (New York: Academic Press, 1970), p. 312; and N. V. Ramanaiah, A. Byravan, and F. R. J. Detwiler, "Revised Neo Personality Inventory Profiles of Machiavellian and Non-Machiavellian People," *Psychological Reports*, October 1994, pp. 937–938.
31. Christie and Geis, *Studies in Machiavellianism*.
32. "Linda Wachner, 61," *Fortune*, April 16, 2007, p. 106.
33. M. Maccoby, "Narcissistic Leaders: The Incredible Pros, the Inevitable Cons," *The Harvard Business Review*, January–February 2000, pp. 69–77, www.maccoby.com/Articles/NarLeaders.shtml.
34. W. K. Campbell and C. A. Foster, "Narcissism and Commitment in Romantic Relationships: An Investment Model Analysis," *Personality and Social Psychology Bulletin* 28, no. 4 (2002), pp. 484–495.
35. T. A. Judge, J. A. LePine, and B. L. Rich, "The Narcissistic Personality: Relationship with Inflated Self-Ratings of Leadership and with Task and Contextual Performance," *Journal of Applied Psychology* 91, no. 4 (2006), pp. 762–776.
36. See M. Snyder, *Public Appearances/Private Realities: The Psychology of Self-Monitoring* (New York: W. H. Freeman, 1987); and S. W. Gangestad and M. Snyder, "Self-Monitoring: Appraisal and Reappraisal," *Psychological Bulletin*, July 2000, pp. 530–555.
37. Snyder, *Public Appearances/Private Realities*.
38. D. V. Day, D. J. Shleicher, A. L. Unckless, and N. J. Hiller, "Self-Monitoring Personality at Work: A Meta-analytic Investigation of Construct Validity," *Journal of Applied Psychology*, April 2002, pp. 390–401.
39. M. Kilduff and D. V. Day, "Do Chameleons Get Ahead? The Effects of Self-Monitoring on Managerial Careers," *Academy of Management Journal*, August 1994, pp. 1047–1060; and A. Mehra, M. Kilduff, and D. J. Brass, "The Social Networks of High and Low Self-Monitors: Implications for Workplace Performance," *Administrative Science Quarterly*, March 2001, pp. 121–146.
40. R. N. Taylor and M. D. Dunnette, "Influence of Dogmatism, Risk-Taking Propensity, and Intelligence on Decision-Making Strategies for a Sample of Industrial Managers," *Journal of Applied Psychology*, August 1974, pp. 420–423.
41. I. L. Janis and L. Mann, *Decision Making: A Psychological Analysis of Conflict, Choice, and Commitment* (New York: The Free Press, 1977); W. H. Stewart, Jr., and L. Roth, "Risk Propensity Differences Between Entrepreneurs and Managers: A Meta-analytic Review," *Journal of Applied*

Psychology, February 2001, pp. 145–153; J. B. Miner and N. S. Raju, "Risk Propensity Differences Between Managers and Entrepreneurs and Between Low- and High-Growth Entrepreneurs: A Reply in a More Conservative Vein," *Journal of Applied Psychology* 89, no. 1 (2004), pp. 3–13; and W. H. Stewart, Jr., and P. L. Roth, "Data Quality Affects Meta-analytic Conclusions: A Response to Miner and Raju (2004) Concerning Entrepreneurial Risk Propensity," *Journal of Applied Psychology* 89, no. 1 (2004), pp. 14–21.

42. N. Kogan and M. A. Wallach, "Group Risk Taking as a Function of Members' Anxiety and Defensiveness," *Journal of Personality*, March 1967, pp. 50–63.

43. M. Friedman and R. H. Rosenman, *Type A Behavior and Your Heart* (New York: Alfred A. Knopf, 1974), p. 84.

44. Ibid., pp. 84–85.

45. R. E. White, S. Thornhill, and E. Hampson, "Entrepreneurs and Evolutionary Biology: The Relationship Between Testosterone and New Venture Creation," *Organizational Behavior and Human Decision Processes* 100 (2006), pp. 21–34; and H. Zhao and S. E. Seibert, "The Big Five Personality Dimensions and Entrepreneurial State: A Meta-analytical Review," *Journal of Applied Psychology* 91, no. 2 (2006), pp. 259–271.

46. K. W. Cook, C. A. Vance, and E. Spector, "The Relation of Candidate Personality with Selection-Interview Outcomes," *Journal of Applied Social Psychology* 30 (2000), pp. 867–885.

47. J. M. Crant, "Proactive Behavior in Organizations," *Journal of Management* 26, no. 3 (2000), p. 436.

48. S. E. Seibert, M. L. Kraimer, and J. M. Crant, "What Do Proactive People Do? A Longitudinal Model Linking Proactive Personality and Career Success," *Personnel Psychology*, Winter 2001, p. 850.

49. T. S. Bateman and J. M. Crant, "The Proactive Component of Organizational Behavior: A Measure and Correlates," *Journal of Organizational Behavior*, March 1993, pp. 103–118; and J. M. Crant and T. S. Bateman, "Charismatic Leadership Viewed from Above: The Impact of Proactive Personality," *Journal of Organizational Behavior*, February 2000, pp. 63–75.

50. Crant, "Proactive Behavior in Organizations," p. 436.

51. See, for instance, R. C. Becherer and J. G. Maurer, "The Proactive Personality Disposition and Entrepreneurial Behavior Among Small Company Presidents," *Journal of Small Business Management*, January 1999, pp. 28–36.

52. S. E. Seibert, J. M. Crant, and M. L. Kraimer, "Proactive Personality and Career Success," *Journal of Applied Psychology*, June 1999, pp. 416–427; Seibert, Kraimer, and Crant, "What Do Proactive People Do?" p. 850; and J. D. Kammeyer-Mueller, and C. R. Wanberg, "Unwrapping the Organizational Entry Process: Disentangling Multiple Antecedents and Their Pathways to Adjustment," *Journal of Applied Psychology* 88, no. 5 (2003), pp. 779–794.

53. M. Rokeach, *The Nature of Human Values* (New York: The Free Press, 1973), p. 5.

54. M. Rokeach and S. J. Ball-Rokeach, "Stability and Change in American Value Priorities, 1968–1981," *American Psychologist* 44, no. 5 (1989), pp. 775–784; and B. M. Meglino and E. C. Ravlin, "Individual Values in Organizations: Concepts, Controversies, and Research," *Journal of Management* 24, no. 3 (1998), p. 355.

55. See, for instance, Meglino and Ravlin, "Individual Values in Organizations," pp. 351–389.

56. Rokeach, *The Nature of Human Values*, p. 6.

57. J. M. Munson and B. Z. Posner, "The Factorial Validity of a Modified Rokeach Value Survey for Four Diverse Samples," *Educational and Psychological Measurement*, Winter 1980, pp. 1073–1079; and W. C. Frederick and J. Weber, "The Values of Corporate Managers and Their Critics: An Empirical Description and Normative Implications," in W. C. Frederick and L. E. Preston (eds.), *Business Ethics: Research Issues and Empirical Studies* (Greenwich, CT: JAI Press, 1990), pp. 123–144.

58. Frederick and Weber, "The Values of Corporate Managers and Their Critics," pp. 123–144.

59. Ibid., p. 132.

60. See, for example, J. Levitz, "Pitching 401(k)s to Generation Y Is a Tough Sell," *Wall Street Journal*, September 27, 2006, pp. B1, B2; P. Paul, "Global Generation Gap," *American Demographics*, March 2002, pp. 18–19; and N. Watson, "Generation Wrecked," *Fortune*, October 14, 2002, pp. 183–190.

61. K. W. Smola and C. D. Sutton, "Generational Differences: Revisiting Generational Work Values for the New Millennium," *Journal of Organizational Behavior* 23 (2002), pp. 363–382; and K. Mellahi and C. Guermat, "Does Age Matter? An Empirical Examination of the Effect of Age on Managerial Values and Practices in India," *Journal of World Business* 39, no. 2 (2004), pp. 199–215.

62. N. A. Hira, "You Raised Them, Now Manage Them," *Fortune*, May 28, 2007, pp. 38–46; R. R. Hastings, "Surveys Shed Light on Generation Y Career Goals," *SHRM Online*, March 2007, www. shrm. org; and S. Jayson, "The 'Millennials' Come of Age," *USA Today*, June 29, 2006, pp. 1D, 2D.

63. J. L. Holland, *Making Vocational Choices: A Theory of Vocational Personalities and Work Environments* (Odessa, FL: Psychological Assessment Resources, 1997).

64. See, for example, J. L. Holland and G. D. Gottfredson, "Studies of the Hexagonal Model: An Evaluation (or, The Perils of Stalking the Perfect Hexagon)," *Journal of Vocational Behavior*, April 1992, pp. 158–170; T. J. Tracey and J. Rounds, "Evaluating Holland's and Gati's Vocational-Interest Models: A Structural Meta-Analysis," *Psychological Bulletin*, March 1993, pp. 229–246; J. L. Holland, "Exploring Careers with a Typology: What We Have Learned and Some New Directions," *American Psychologist*, April 1996, pp. 397–406; and S. X. Day and J. Rounds, "Universality of Vocational Interest Structure Among Racial and Ethnic Minorities," *American Psychologist*, July 1998, pp. 728–736.

65. See B. Schneider, "The People Make the Place," *Personnel Psychology*, Autumn 1987, pp. 437–453; B. Schneider, H. W. Goldstein, and D. B. Smith, "The ASA Framework: An Update," *Personnel Psychology*, Winter 1995, pp. 747–773; A. L. Kristof, "Person–Organization Fit: An Integrative Review of Its Conceptualizations, Measurement, and Implications," *Personnel Psychology*, Spring 1996, pp. 1–49; B. Schneider, D. B. Smith, S. Taylor, and J. Fleenor, "Personality and Organizations: A Test of the Homogeneity of Personality Hypothesis," *Journal of Applied Psychology*, June 1998, pp. 462–470; W. Arthur, Jr., S. T. Bell, A. J. Villado, and D. Doverspike, "The Use of Person-Organization Fit in Employment Decision-Making: An Assessment of Its

Criterion-Related Validity," *Journal of Applied Psychology* 91, no. 4 (2006), pp. 786–801; and J. R. Edwards, D. M. Cable, I. O. Williamson, L. S. Lambert, and A. J. Shipp, "The Phenomenology of Fit: Linking the Person and Environment to the Subjective Experience of Person–Environment Fit," *Journal of Applied Psychology* 91, no. 4 (2006), pp. 802–827.

66. Based on T. A. Judge and D. M. Cable, "Applicant Personality, Organizational Culture, and Organization Attraction," *Personnel Psychology*, Summer 1997, pp. 359–394.

67. M. L. Verquer, T. A. Beehr, and S. E. Wagner, "A Meta-analysis of Relations Between Person–Organization Fit and Work Attitudes," *Journal of Vocational Behavior* 63, no. 3 (2003), pp. 473–489.

68. See, for instance, J. E. Williams, J. L. Saiz, D. L. Formy-Duval, M. L. Munick, E. E. Fogle, A. Adom, A. Haque, F. Neto, and J. Yu, "Cross-Cultural Variation in the Importance of Psychological Characteristics: A Seven-Country Study," *International Journal of Psychology*, October 1995, pp. 529–550; R. R. McCrae and P. T. Costa, Jr., "Personality Trait Structure as a Human Universal," *American Psychologist*, May 1997, pp. 509–516; R. R. McCrae, "Trait Psychology and the Revival of Personality-and-Culture Studies," *American Behavioral Scientist*, September 2000, pp. 10–31; S. V. Paunonen, M. Zeidner, H. A. Engvik, P. Oosterveld, and R. Maliphant, "The Nonverbal Assessment of Personality in Five Cultures," *Journal of Cross-Cultural Psychology*, March 2000, pp. 220–239; H. C. Triandis and E. M. Suh, "Cultural Influences on Personality," in S. T. Fiske, D. L. Schacter, and C. Zahn-Waxler (eds.), *Annual Review of Psychology*, vol. 53 (Palo Alto, CA: Annual Reviews, 2002), pp. 133–160; R. R. McCrae and J. Allik, *The Five-Factor Model of Personality Across Cultures* (New York: Kluwer Academic/Plenum, 2002); and R. R. McCrae, P. T. Costa, Jr., T. A. Martin, V. E. Oryol, A. A. Rukavishnikov, I. G. Senin, M. Hrebickova, and T. Urbanek, "Consensual Validation of Personality Traits Across Cultures," *Journal of Research in Personality* 38, no. 2 (2004), pp. 179–201.

69. A. T. Church and M. S. Katigbak, "Trait Psychology in the Philippines," *American Behavioral Scientist*, September 2000, pp. 73–94.

70. J. F. Salgado, "The Five Factor Model of Personality and Job Performance in the European Community," *Journal of Applied Psychology*, February 1997, pp. 30–43.

71. G. Hofstede, *Culture's Consequences: International Differences in Work-Related Values* (Beverly Hills, CA: Sage, 1980); G. Hofstede, *Cultures and Organizations: Software of the Mind* (London: McGraw-Hill, 1991); G. Hofstede, "Cultural Constraints in Management Theories," *Academy of Management Executive* 7, no. 1 (1993), pp. 81–94; G. Hofstede and M. F. Peterson, "National Values and Organizational Practices," in N. M. Ashkanasy, C. M. Wilderom, and M. F. Peterson (eds.), *Handbook of Organizational Culture and Climate* (Thousand Oaks, CA: Sage, 2000), pp. 401–416; and G. Hofstede, *Culture's Consequences: Comparing Values, Behaviors, Institutions, and Organizations Across Nations*, 2nd ed. (Thousand Oaks, CA: Sage, 2001). For criticism of this research, see B. McSweeney, "Hofstede's Model of National Cultural Differences and Their Consequences: A Triumph of Faith—A Failure of Analysis," *Human Relations* 55, no. 1 (2002), pp. 89–118.

72. M. H. Bond, "Reclaiming the Individual from Hofstede's Ecological Analysis—A 20-Year Odyssey: Comment on Oyserman et al. (2002). *Psychological Bulletin* 128, no. 1 (2002), pp. 73–77; G. Hofstede, "The Pitfalls of Cross-National Survey Research: A Reply to the Article by Spector et al. on the Psychometric Properties of the Hofstede Values Survey Module 1994," *Applied Psychology: An International Review* 51, no. 1 (2002), pp. 170–178; and T. Fang, "A Critique of Hofstede's Fifth National Culture Dimension," *International Journal of Cross-Cultural Management* 3, no. 3 (2003), pp. 347–368.

73. M. Javidan and R. J. House, "Cultural Acumen for the Global Manager: Lessons from Project GLOBE," *Organizational Dynamics* 29, no. 4 (2001), pp. 289–305; and R. J. House, P. J. Hanges, M. Javidan, and P. W. Dorfman (eds.), *Leadership, Culture, and Organizations: The GLOBE Study of 62 Societies* (Thousand Oaks, CA: Sage, 2004).

74. P. C. Early, "Leading Cultural Research in the Future: A Matter of Paradigms and Taste," *Journal of International Business Studies*, September 2006, pp. 922–931; G. Hofstede, "What Did GLOBE Really Measure? Researchers' Minds Versus Respondents' Minds," *Journal of International Business Studies*, September 2006, pp. 882–896; and M. Javidan, R. J. House, P. W. Dorfman, P. J. Hanges, and M. S. de Luque, "Conceptualizing and Measuring Cultures and Their Consequences: A Comparative Review of GLOBE's and Hofstede's Approaches," *Journal of International Business Studies*, September 2006, pp. 897–914.

75. L. A. Witt, "The Interactive Effects of Extraversion and Conscientiousness on Performance," *Journal of Management* 28, no. 6 (2002), p. 836.

76. R. P. Tett and D. D. Burnett, "A Personality Trait–Based Interactionist Model of Job Performance," *Journal of Applied Psychology*, June 2003, pp. 500–517.

77. R. Hogan, "In Defense of Personality Measurement: New Wine for Old Whiners," *Human Performance* 18, no. 4 (2005), pp. 331–341; and N. Schmitt, "Beyond the Big Five: Increases in Understanding and Practical Utility," *Human Performance* 17, no. 3 (2004), pp. 347–357.

78. B. Adkins and D. Caldwell, "Firm or Subgroup Culture: Where Does Fitting in Matter Most?" *Journal of Organizational Behavior* 25, no. 8 (2004), pp. 969–978; H. D. Cooper-Thomas, A. van Vianen, and N. Anderson, "Changes in Person–Organization Fit: The Impact of Socialization Tactics on Perceived and Actual P–O Fit," *European Journal of Work & Organizational Psychology* 13, no. 1 (2004), pp. 52–78; and C. A. O'Reilly, J. Chatman, and D. F. Caldwell, "People and Organizational Culture: A Profile Comparison Approach to Assessing Person–Organization Fit," *Academy of Management Journal* 34, no. 3 (1991), pp. 487–516.

Perception and Individual Decision Making

Indecision may or may not be my problem.
—Musician Jimmy Buffett

LEARNING OBJECTIVES

After studying this chapter, you should be able to:

1. Define *perception* and explain the factors that influence it.
2. Explain attribution theory and list the three determinants of attribution.
3. Identify the shortcuts individuals use in making judgments about others.
4. Explain the link between perception and decision making.
5. Apply the rational model of decision making and contrast it with bounded rationality and intuition.
6. List and explain the common decision biases or errors.
7. Explain how individual differences and organizational constraints affect decision making.
8. Contrast the three ethical decision criteria.
9. Define *creativity* and discuss the three-component model of creativity.

Muslim Americans: Perception and Reality

A rental car company employee was told she couldn't wear a head scarf during Ramadan and then was fired for complaining. Hotel employees were cursed at and nicknamed "Osama" and "Taliban."

Among the many ramifications of the September 11, 2001, terrorist attacks are heightened negative perceptions of Muslims and Arabs, including those living and working in the United States. More than 6 years after the attacks, 4 of 10 U.S. adults admitted they still harbored

Source: Joyce Dopkeen/The New York Times

negative feelings or prejudices against Muslims living in the United States, according to a *USA Today*/Gallup poll. A poll of Muslim Americans revealed that 53 percent perceived that life has been more difficult for them since the 9/11 terrorist attacks.

There are 2.35 million Muslims in the United States. *BusinessWeek* concluded, "as a group, they offer a model of assimilation and material success." Although estimates differ, one study suggested that Muslim Americans (59 percent) are twice as likely as the general U.S. population (28 percent) to have a college degree. The median family income of Muslim Americans exceeds the national average of $55,800. In a 2007 poll, 71 percent of American Muslims agreed with the statement "most people who want to get ahead can make it if they work hard," compared to 64 percent of the general U.S. population. Forty percent of U.S. Muslims attend mosque weekly, compared to 45 percent of U.S. Christians who say they attend church weekly. Overall, U.S. Muslims are much more like typical U.S. citizens than Muslims in other Western democracies, such as France, Spain, or the United Kingdom, where the typical Muslim is more likely to be less educated and have a lower income.

There are, however, areas of divergence and concern. Roughly one in four U.S. Muslims under 30 said they believed suicide bombings to defend their religion are acceptable, at least in some circumstances. (Only 9 percent of U.S. Muslims over 30 believed that suicide bombings were ever justified.) And accommodation of Islamic practices is not always easy for U.S. employers. For example, a devout Muslim corrections officer sued the state of New York when he was ordered to remove his kufi, or skullcap; the state eventually settled the suit. A group of female Muslim employees won their challenge against the uniform policy of the in-flight catering company LSG Sky Chefs, which required pants and sports shirts. USAir kept a Muslim flight attendant from working after she chose to wear a hijab (a Muslim head scarf), and Dunkin' Donuts fired a Muslim employee after she refused to remove her hijab. Recently, Aicha Baha sued Walt Disney World, alleging that she was fired because she wouldn't remove her hijab at work.

For the average U.S. citizen, reconciling the two perceptions of Muslim Americans—that most are much like the typical U.S. citizen, while a few clearly are not—often proves difficult. Moreover, for employers, establishing dress codes, attendance policies, and other workplace standards is often difficult. UPS, for example, has a policy that its drivers be clean shaven, but it makes an exception for religious accommodation.

But there are positive signs. The Equal Employment Opportunity Commission (EEOC) witnessed a significant spike in discrimination claims by Muslim Americans in the year after the 9/11 attacks. Since that time, discrimination claims have "slowed considerably and declined in frequency," according to EEOC spokesman David Ginsburg. Moreover, negative attitudes and distrust are less evident in the workplace. But according to a recent survey by the Society for Human Resource Management, 75 percent of U.S. HR professionals thought negative attitudes toward Muslim employees have stayed the same since 9/11, while 16 percent thought they've increased, and 9 percent thought they've decreased.

It's not easy to be an American Muslim. Born and raised in Philadelphia, and now living in Kansas, Mahnaz Shabbir is president of Shabbir Advisors, an integrated strategic management consulting company. Shabbir says, "For most of my life, my identification as a first generation American Muslim has been a struggle."[1] ■

The chapter-opening story considers perceptions, in this case of Muslim Americans. In the following Self-Assessment Library, consider your perceptions of appropriate gender roles.

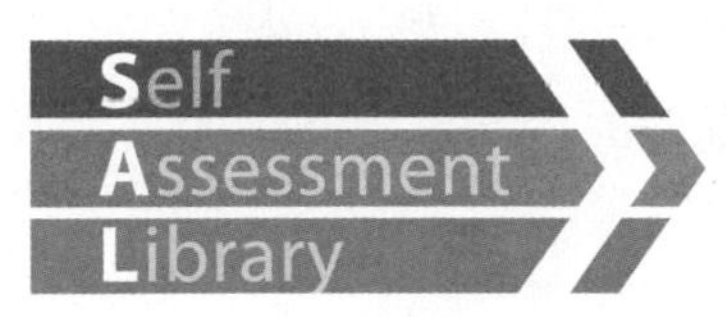

WHAT ARE MY GENDER ROLE PERCEPTIONS?

In the Self-Assessment Library (available on CD or online), take assessment IV.C.2 (What Are My Gender Role Perceptions?) and answer the following questions.

1. *Did you score as high as you thought you would?*
2. *Do you think a problem with measures like this is that people aren't honest in responding?*
3. *If others, such as friends, classmates, and family members, rated you, would they rate you differently? Why or why not?*
4. *Research has shown that people's gender role perceptions are becoming less traditional over time. Why do you suppose this is so?*

What Is Perception?

1 *Define* perception *and explain the factors that influence it.*

Perception is a process by which individuals organize and interpret their sensory impressions in order to give meaning to their environment. However, what we perceive can be substantially different from objective reality. For example, all employees in a firm may view it as a great place to work—favorable working conditions, interesting job assignments, good pay, excellent benefits, understanding and responsible management—but, as most of us know, it's very unusual to find such agreement.

Why is perception important in the study of OB? Simply because people's behavior is based on their perception of what reality is, not on reality itself. *The world as it is perceived is the world that is behaviorally important.*

Factors That Influence Perception

How do we explain the fact that individuals may look at the same thing yet perceive it differently? A number of factors operate to shape and sometimes distort perception. These factors can reside in the *perceiver*, in the object, or *target*, being perceived; or in the context of the *situation* in which the perception is made (see Exhibit 5-1).

perception *A process by which individuals organize and interpret their sensory impressions in order to give meaning to their environment.*

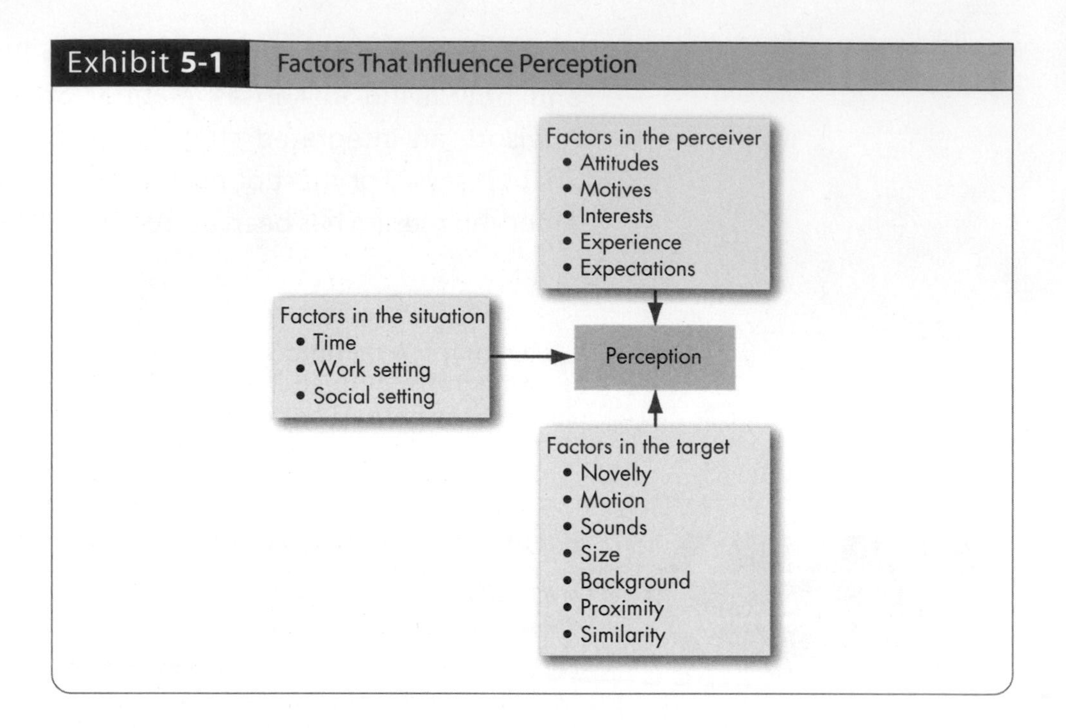

When an individual looks at a target and attempts to interpret what he or she sees, that interpretation is heavily influenced by the personal characteristics of the individual perceiver. Personal characteristics that affect perception include a person's attitudes, personality, motives, interests, past experiences, and expectations. For instance, if you expect police officers to be authoritative, young people to be lazy, or individuals holding public office to be unscrupulous, you may perceive them as such, regardless of their actual traits.

Characteristics of the target we observe can affect what we perceive. Loud people are more likely to be noticed in a group than quiet ones. So, too, are extremely attractive or unattractive individuals. Because we don't look at targets in isolation, the relationship of a target to its background also influences perception, as does our tendency to group close things and similar things together. For instance, women, people of color, or members of any other group that has clearly distinguishable characteristics are often perceived as alike in other, unrelated ways as well.

The context in which we see objects or events is also important. The time at which we see an object or event can influence attention, as can location, light, heat, or any number of situational factors. For example, at a nightclub on Saturday night, you may not notice a young guest "dressed to the nines." Yet that same person so attired for your Monday morning management class would certainly catch your attention (and that of the rest of the class). Neither the perceiver nor the target changed between Saturday night and Monday morning, but the situation is different.

Person Perception: Making Judgments About Others

2 *Explain attribution theory and list the three determinants of attribution.*

Now we turn to the most relevant application of perception concepts to OB. This is the issue of *person perception*, or the perceptions people form about each other.

Attribution Theory

Nonliving objects such as desks, machines, and buildings are subject to the laws of nature, but they have no beliefs, motives, or intentions. People do. That's why when we observe people, we attempt to develop explanations of why they behave in certain ways. Our perception and judgment of a person's actions, therefore, will be significantly influenced by the assumptions we make about that person's internal state.

Attribution theory tries to explain the ways in which we judge people differently, depending on the meaning we attribute to a given behavior.[2] It suggests that when we observe an individual's behavior, we attempt to determine whether it was internally or externally caused. That determination, however, depends largely on three factors: (1) distinctiveness, (2) consensus, and (3) consistency. First, let's clarify the differences between internal and external causation and then we'll elaborate on each of the three determining factors.

Internally caused behaviors are those we believe to be under the personal control of the individual. *Externally* caused behavior is what we imagine the situation forced the individual to do. For example, if one of your employees is late for work, you might attribute his lateness to his partying into the wee hours of the morning and then oversleeping. This is an internal attribution. But if you attribute his arriving late to an automobile accident that tied up traffic, then you are making an external attribution.

Now let's discuss each of the three determining factors. *Distinctiveness* refers to whether an individual displays different behaviors in different situations. Is the employee who arrives late today also the one coworkers say regularly "blows off" commitments? What we want to know is whether this behavior is unusual. If it is, we are likely to give it an external attribution. If it's not unusual, we will probably judge the behavior to be internal.

If everyone who faces a similar situation responds in the same way, we can say the behavior shows *consensus*. The behavior of our tardy employee meets this criterion if all employees who took the same route to work were also late. From an attribution perspective, if consensus is high, you would probably give an external attribution to the employee's tardiness, whereas if other employees who took the same route made it to work on time, you would attribute his lateness to an internal cause.

Finally, an observer looks for *consistency* in a person's actions. Does the person respond the same way over time? Coming in 10 minutes late for work is not perceived in the same way for an employee for whom it is an unusual case (she hasn't been late for several months) as it is for an employee for whom it is part of a routine pattern (she is late two or three times a week). The more consistent the behavior, the more we are inclined to attribute it to internal causes.

Exhibit 5-2 summarizes the key elements in attribution theory. It tells us, for instance, that if an employee, Maria Romano, generally performs at about the same level on other related tasks as she does on her current task (low distinctiveness), if other employees frequently perform differently—better or worse—than Kim does on that current task (low consensus), and if Kim's performance

attribution theory *An attempt to determine whether an individual's behavior is internally or externally caused.*

Exhibit 5-2 Attribution Theory

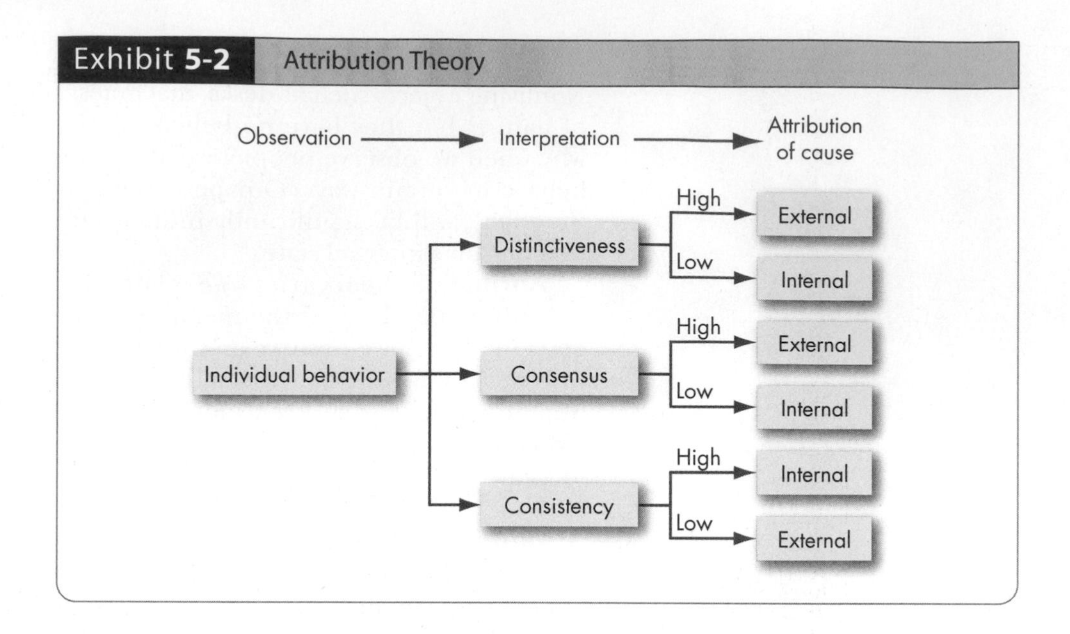

on this current task is consistent over time (high consistency), you or anyone else judging Maria's work will be likely to hold her primarily responsible for her task performance (internal attribution).

One of the most interesting findings from attribution theory is that errors or biases distort attributions. For instance, substantial evidence suggests that when we make judgments about the behavior of other people, we tend to underestimate the influence of external factors and overestimate the influence of internal or personal factors.[3] This **fundamental attribution error** can explain why a sales manager is prone to attribute the poor performance of her sales agents to laziness rather than to the innovative product line introduced by a competitor. Individuals and organizations also tend to attribute their own successes to internal factors such as ability or effort, while putting the blame for failure on external factors such as bad luck or unproductive coworkers. This is the **self-serving bias.**[4] For example, when former (and now deceased) Enron CEO Ken Lay was tried for fraud after the company collapsed amid a financial scandal, he blamed former Chief Financial Officer Andrew Fastow, saying, "I think the primary reason for Enron's collapse was Andy Fastow and his little group of people and what they did."

Frequently Used Shortcuts in Judging Others

We use a number of shortcuts when we judge others. These techniques are frequently valuable: They allow us to make accurate perceptions rapidly and provide valid data for making predictions. However, they are not foolproof. They can and do get us into trouble. Understanding these shortcuts can help you recognize when they can result in significant distortions.

3 *Identify the shortcuts individuals use in making judgments about others.*

Selective Perception Any characteristic that makes a person, an object, or an event stand out will increase the probability that we will perceive it. Why? Because it is impossible for us to assimilate everything we see; we can take in only certain stimuli. This tendency explains why you're more likely to notice cars like your own or why a boss may reprimand some people and not others who are doing the same thing. Because we can't observe everything going on about us, we engage in **selective perception.** A classic example shows how vested interests can significantly influence which problems we see.

Dearborn and Simon performed a perceptual study in which 23 business executives read a comprehensive case describing the organization and activities of a steel company.[5] Six were in sales, 5 in production, 4 in accounting, and 8 in miscellaneous functions. Each manager was asked to write down the most important problem he found in the case. Eighty-three percent of the sales executives rated sales important; only 29 percent of the others did so. The researchers concluded that participants perceived as important the aspects of a situation specifically related to their own unit's activities and goals. A group's perception of organizational activities is selectively altered to align with the vested interests they represent.

Because we cannot assimilate all that we observe, we take in bits and pieces. But we don't choose them randomly; rather, we select them according to our interests, background, experience, and attitudes. Selective perception allows us to "speed-read" others, but not without the risk of drawing an inaccurate picture. Because we see what we want to see, we can draw unwarranted conclusions from an ambiguous situation.

Halo Effect When we draw a general impression about an individual on the basis of a single characteristic, such as intelligence, sociability, or appearance, a **halo effect** is operating.[6] Consider former Hewlett Packard CEO Carly Fiorina. Early in her tenure, she was lauded as articulate, decisive, charismatic, savvy, and visionary. At the time of her appointment, *BusinessWeek* said, "She has it all." After Fiorina was fired, though, she was described as unproven, egotistical, inflexible, and uncompromising. *BusinessWeek* faulted her for her unwillingness to delegate and her inability to execute.[7] So, when Fiorina was deemed effective, everything about her was good. But when she was fired for supposed ineffectiveness, the same people who lauded her before now saw few if any redeeming features. That's both sides of the halo (halo or horns, you might say).

The reality of the halo effect was confirmed in a classic study in which subjects were given a list of traits such as intelligent, skillful, practical, industrious, determined, and warm and asked to evaluate the person to whom those traits applied.[8] Subjects judged the person to be wise, humorous, popular, and imaginative. When the same list was modified to include "cold" instead of "warm," a completely different picture emerged. Clearly, the subjects were allowing a single trait to influence their overall impression of the person they were judging.

Contrast Effects An old adage among entertainers says, "Never follow an act that has kids or animals in it." Why? Audiences love children and animals so much that you'll look bad in comparison. This example demonstrates how **contrast effects** can distort perceptions. We don't evaluate a person in isolation. Our reaction to a person is influenced by other persons we have recently encountered.

In a series of job interviews, for instance, interviewers can make distortions in any given candidate's evaluation as a result of his place in the interview

fundamental attribution error *The tendency to underestimate the influence of external factors and overestimate the influence of internal factors when making judgments about the behavior of others.*

self-serving bias *The tendency for individuals to attribute their own successes to internal factors and put the blame for failures on external factors.*

selective perception *The tendency to selectively interpret what one sees on the basis of one's interests, background, experience, and attitudes.*

halo effect *The tendency to draw a general impression about an individual on the basis of a single characteristic.*

contrast effects *Evaluation of a person's characteristics that is affected by comparisons with other people recently encountered who rank higher or lower on the same characteristics.*

International OB

Can Negative Perceptions Dampen International Business Relations?

Japan and China would seem to be natural economic partners, given that they're geographically so close to each other. However, Japanese companies currently lag behind both Europe and the United States in terms of trade with China. Although the Japanese auto industry has had enormous success in other countries, including the United States, the top-selling foreign cars in China are produced by GM (a U.S. company) and Volkswagen (a German company). Also, Japan's booming electronics industry currently captures only 5 percent of the Chinese market.

But who or what is to blame for the dismal business relationship between Japan and China? The perceptions of the public—in both countries—may be the answer. For example, many Chinese citizens are still angered about a report that employees of a Japanese construction company hired Chinese prostitutes for a corporate party. And many Japanese citizens believe that Chinese immigrants are to blame for many of the violent crimes taking place in Japan. In addition to these recent events, historically, relations between the two countries have been strained. Beijing is still upset about Japan's military invasion of China in the 1930s and 1940s, for which Japan refuses to make amends.

These negative perceptions may be difficult to reverse if perceptual errors such as fundamental attribution error and the halo effect are operating. That is, both countries blame each other for their behaviors (internal attribution), and both countries tend to view each other's actions as negative (negative halo effect). Because of these errors, future behaviors, even if they are ambiguous, may be perceived negatively by the other country.

Source: Based on C. Chandler, "Business Is Hot, Relations Are Not," *Fortune (Europe)*, April 19, 2004, pp. 20–21; and "China Urges Japan to Do More to Improve Ties," The Associated Press, March 14, 2005.

schedule. A candidate is likely to receive a more favorable evaluation if preceded by mediocre applicants and a less favorable evaluation if preceded by strong applicants.

Stereotyping When we judge someone on the basis of our perception of the group to which he or she belongs, we are using the shortcut called

Jin, an Asian American rapper, performs at the Garden of Eden in Hollywood, hoping for a hit song in an industry that lacks Asian American pop stars. But Asian American artists and scholars argue that racial stereotyping inaccurately generalizes Asian Americans as studious geeks and that someone who looks Asian must be a foreigner. This stereotyping doesn't fit the "cool" image and born-in-the-U.S.A. authenticity required for musicians like Jin who aspire to become American pop stars.

Source: Misha Erwitt/ The New York Times

stereotyping.[9] We saw the problems stereotyping can create at the opening of this chapter: All Muslims are not terrorists!

We rely on generalizations every day because they help us make decisions quickly. They are a means of simplifying a complex world. It's less difficult to deal with an unmanageable number of stimuli if we use heuristics or stereotypes. The problem occurs, of course, when we generalize inaccurately or too much. In organizations, we frequently hear comments that represent stereotypes based on gender, age, race, religion, ethnicity, and even weight:[10] "Women won't relocate for a promotion," "men aren't interested in child care," "older workers can't learn new skills," "Asian immigrants are hardworking and conscientious," "overweight people lack discipline." Stereotypes can be so deeply ingrained and powerful that they influence life-and-death decisions. One study showed that, controlling for a wide array of factors (such as aggravating or mitigating circumstances), the degree to which black defendants in murder trails looked stereotypically black essentially doubled their odds of receiving a death sentence if convicted.[11]

One specific manifestation of stereotypes is **profiling**—a form of stereotyping in which a group of individuals is singled out, typically on the basis of race or ethnicity, for intensive inquiry, scrutiny, or investigation. Since 9/11, ethnic profiling has become the subject of much debate.[12] On one side, proponents argue that profiling people of Arab descent is necessary in order to prevent terrorism. After all, a good percentage of the large-scale terrorist attacks that have taken place over the past 30 years have been perpetrated by Muslim terrorists.[13] On the other side, critics argue that profiling is demeaning, discriminatory, and an ineffective way to find potential terrorists and that Muslim Americans are as law abiding as other citizens. The debate is important and implies the need to balance the rights of individuals against the greater good of society. Organizations need to sensitize employees and managers to the damage that profiling can create. Many are expanding their diversity training programs, which we discuss in Chapter 18, to particularly address ethnic stereotyping and profiling.

One of the problems of stereotypes is that they *are* widespread and often useful generalizations, despite the fact that they may not contain a shred of truth when applied to a particular person or situation. So we constantly have to check ourselves to make sure we're not unfairly or inaccurately applying a stereotype in our evaluations and decisions. Stereotypes are an example of the warning, "The more useful, the more danger from misuse."

Specific Applications of Shortcuts in Organizations

People in organizations are always judging each other. Managers must appraise their employees' performances. We evaluate how much effort our coworkers are putting into their jobs. When a new person joins a work team, the other members immediately "size her up." In many cases, our judgments have important consequences for the organization. Let's briefly look at a few of the most obvious applications.

stereotyping *Judging someone on the basis of one's perception of the group to which that person belongs.*

profiling *A form of stereotyping in which a group of individuals is singled out—typically on the basis of race or ethnicity—for intensive inquiry, scrutiny, or investigation.*

Employment Interview A major input into who is hired and who is rejected in an organization is the employment interview. It's fair to say that few people are hired without an interview. But evidence indicates that interviewers make perceptual judgments that are often inaccurate.[14] They generally draw early impressions that very quickly become entrenched. Research shows that we form impressions of others within a tenth of a second, based on our first glance at them.[15] If these first impressions are negative, they tend to be more heavily weighted in the interview than if that same information came out later.[16] Most interviewers' decisions change very little after the first 4 or 5 minutes of an interview. As a result, information elicited early in the interview carries greater weight than does information elicited later, and a "good applicant" is probably characterized more by the absence of unfavorable characteristics than by the presence of favorable characteristics.

Performance Expectations People attempt to validate their perceptions of reality, even when those perceptions are faulty.[17] This characteristic is particularly relevant when we consider performance expectations on the job. The terms **self-fulfilling prophecy** and *Pygmalion effect* have evolved to characterize the fact that an individual's behavior is determined by other people's expectations. In other words, if a manager expects big things from her people, they're not likely to let her down. Similarly, if a manager expects people to perform minimally, they'll tend to behave so as to meet those low expectations. The expectations become reality. The self-fulfilling prophecy has been found to affect the performance of students in school, soldiers in combat, and even accountants.[18]

Performance Evaluation We'll discuss performance evaluations more fully in Chapter 18, but note for now that they are very much dependent on the perceptual process.[19] An employee's future is closely tied to the appraisal—promotions, pay raises, and continuation of employment are among the most obvious outcomes. Although the appraisal can be objective (for example, a salesperson is appraised on how many dollars of sales he generates in his territory), many jobs are evaluated in subjective terms. Subjective evaluations of performance, though often necessary, are problematic because all the errors we've discussed thus far—selective perception, contrast effects, halo effects, and so on—affect them. Ironically, sometimes performance ratings say as much about the evaluator as they do about the employee!

The Link Between Perception and Individual Decision Making

4 *Explain the link between perception and decision making.*

Individuals in organizations make **decisions**. That is, they make choices from among two or more alternatives. Top managers, for instance, determine their organization's goals, what products or services to offer, how best to finance operations, or where to locate a new manufacturing plant. Middle- and lower-level managers determine production schedules, select new employees, and decide how pay raises are to be allocated. Of course, making decisions is not the sole province of managers. Nonmanagerial employees also make decisions that affect their jobs and the organizations for which they work. They decide whether to come to work on

John Thompson, the CEO of the software company Symantec, made a decision in reaction to the problem of an explosion of Internet viruses. Thompson said, "About every 15 to 18 months, there's a new form of attack that makes old technologies less effective." So he decided to acquire 13 companies that specialize in products such as personal firewalls, intrusion detection, and early warning systems that protect everything from corporate intranets to consumer e-mail inboxes.

any given day, how much effort to put forth at work, and whether to comply with a request made by the boss. In recent years, organizations have been empowering their nonmanagerial employees with job-related decision-making authority that was historically reserved for managers alone. Individual decision making, therefore, is an important part of organizational behavior. But how individuals in organizations make decisions and the quality of their final choices are largely influenced by their perceptions.

Decision making occurs as a reaction to a **problem**.[20] That is, a discrepancy exists between the current state of affairs and some desired state, requiring us to consider alternative courses of action. For example, if your car breaks down and you rely on it to get to work, you have a problem that requires a decision on your part. Unfortunately, most problems don't come neatly packaged and labeled "problem." One person's *problem* is another person's *satisfactory state of affairs*. One manager may view her division's 2 percent decline in quarterly sales to be a serious problem requiring immediate action on her part. In contrast, her counterpart in another division of the same company, who also had a 2 percent sales decrease, might consider that percentage quite acceptable. So the awareness that a problem exists and whether a decision needs to be made is a perceptual issue.

Moreover, every decision requires us to interpret and evaluate information. We typically receive data from multiple sources and need to screen, process, and interpret it. Which data, for instance, are relevant to the decision and which are not? The perceptions of the decision maker will answer that question. We also need to develop alternatives and evaluate the strengths and weaknesses of each. Again, because alternatives don't come with their strengths and weaknesses clearly marked, an individual decision maker's perceptual process will have a large bearing on the final outcome. Finally, throughout the entire decision-making process, perceptual distortions often surface that can bias analysis and conclusions.

Decision Making in Organizations

5 *Apply the rational model of decision making and contrast it with bounded rationality and intuition.*

Business schools generally train students to follow rational decision-making models. While these models have considerable merit, they don't always describe how people actually make decisions. This is where OB enters the picture: If we are to improve how we make decisions in organizations, we need to understand the decision-making errors that people commit (in addition to the perception errors just discussed). In the sections that follow, we describe these errors, and we begin with a brief overview of the rational decision-making model.

The Rational Model, Bounded Rationality, and Intuition

Rational Decision Making We often think the best decision maker is **rational** and makes consistent, value-maximizing choices within specified constraints.[21]

self-fulfilling prophecy *A situation in which a person inaccurately perceives a second person, and the resulting expectations cause the second person to behave in ways consistent with the original perception.*

decisions *Choices made from among two or more alternatives.*

problem *A discrepancy between the current state of affairs and some desired state.*

rational *Characterized by making consistent, value-maximizing choices within specified constraints.*

Exhibit 5-3 Steps in the Rational Decision-Making Model

1. Define the problem.
2. Identify the decision criteria.
3. Allocate weights to the criteria.
4. Develop the alternatives.
5. Evaluate the alternatives.
6. Select the best alternative.

These decisions follow a six-step **rational decision-making model**.[22] The six steps are listed in Exhibit 5-3.

The rational decision-making model relies on a number of assumptions, including that the decision maker has complete information, is able to identify all the relevant options in an unbiased manner, and chooses the option with the highest utility.[23] As you might imagine, most decisions in the real world don't follow the rational model. For instance, people are usually content to find an acceptable or reasonable solution to a problem rather than an optimal one. Choices tend to be limited to the neighborhood of the problem symptom and of the current alternative. As one expert in decision making put it, "Most significant decisions are made by judgment, rather than by a defined prescriptive model."[24] What's more, people are remarkably unaware of making suboptimal decisions.[25]

Bounded Rationality Most people respond to a complex problem by reducing it to a level at which they can readily understand it. The limited information-processing capability of human beings makes it impossible to assimilate and understand all the information necessary to optimize.[26] So people *satisfice*, that is, they seek solutions that are satisfactory and sufficient.

Operating within the confines of bounded rationality, Rose Marie Bravo revitalized the British retailer Burberry Group PLC when she became CEO. Bravo's decisions during her 10 years as CEO transformed a dormant brand into a profitable luxury label. Based on her retail experience at Saks in the United States, Bravo decided to capitalize on Burberry's quality heritage and trademark plaid design as the solution to the company's stagnant growth. She repositioned Burberry as a global luxury brand by running a celebrity ad campaign to redefine the brand's image as hip for the younger generation and by using the plaid design on new lines of swimwear and children's clothing. Bravo stepped down in July 2005 when her contract expired.

When you considered which college to attend, did you look at every viable alternative? Did you carefully identify all the criteria that were important in your decision? Did you evaluate each alternative against the criteria in order to find the optimal college? The answers are probably "no." Well, don't feel bad. Few people made their college choice this way. Instead of optimizing, you probably satisficed.

Because the human mind cannot formulate and solve complex problems with full rationality, we operate within the confines of **bounded rationality**. We construct simplified models that extract the essential features from problems without capturing all their complexity.[27] We can then behave rationally within the limits of the simple model.

How does bounded rationality work for the typical individual? Once we've identified a problem, we begin to search for criteria and alternatives. But the list of criteria is likely to be far from exhaustive. We identify a limited list of the most conspicuous choices, both easy to find and highly visible, that usually represent familiar criteria and tried-and-true solutions. Next, we begin reviewing them, but our review will not be comprehensive. Instead, we focus on alternatives that differ only in a relatively small degree from the choice currently in effect. Following familiar and well-worn paths, we review alternatives only until we identify one that is "good enough"—that meets an acceptable level of performance. That ends our search. So the solution represents a satisficing choice—the first *acceptable* one we encounter—rather than an optimal one.

Intuition Perhaps the least rational way of making decisions is to rely on intuition. **Intuitive decision making** is a nonconscious process created from distilled experience.[28] Its defining qualities are that it occurs outside conscious thought; it relies on holistic associations, or links between disparate pieces of information; it's fast; and it's affectively charged, meaning that it usually engages the emotions.[29]

Intuition is not rational, but that doesn't necessarily make it wrong. And intuition doesn't necessarily operate in opposition to rational analysis; rather, the two can complement each other. And intuition can be a powerful force in decision making. Research on chess playing provides an excellent illustration of how intuition works.[30]

Novice chess players and grand masters were shown an actual, but unfamiliar, chess game with about 25 pieces on the board. After 5 or 10 seconds, the pieces were removed, and each subject was asked to reconstruct the pieces by position. On average, the grand master could put 23 or 24 pieces in their correct squares, while the novice was able to replace only 6. Then the exercise was changed. This time, the pieces were placed randomly on the board. Again, the novice got only about 6 correct, but so did the grand master! The second exercise demonstrated that the grand master didn't have any better memory than the novice. What the grand master *did* have was the ability, based on the experience of having played thousands of chess games, to recognize patterns and clusters of pieces that occur on chessboards in the course of games. Studies also show

rational decision-making model *A decision-making model that describes how individuals should behave in order to maximize some outcome.*

bounded rationality *A process of making decisions by constructing simplified models that extract the essential features from problems without capturing all their complexity.*

intuitive decision making *An unconscious process created out of distilled experience.*

that chess professionals can play 50 or more games simultaneously, making decisions in seconds, and exhibit only a moderately lower level of skill than when playing 1 game under tournament conditions, where decisions take half an hour or longer. The expert's experience allows him or her to recognize the pattern in a situation and draw on previously learned information associated with that pattern to arrive at a decision choice quickly. The result is that the intuitive decision maker can decide rapidly based on what appears to be very limited information.

For most of the twentieth century, experts believed that decision makers' use of intuition was irrational or ineffective. That's no longer the case.[31] There is growing recognition that rational analysis has been overemphasized and that, in certain instances, relying on intuition can improve decision making.[32] But while intuition can be invaluable in making good decisions, we can't rely on it too much. Because it is so unquantifiable, it's hard to know when our hunches are right or wrong. The key is not to either abandon or rely solely on intuition but to supplement it with evidence and good judgment.

Common Biases and Errors in Decision Making

6 *List and explain the common decision biases or errors.*

Decision makers engage in bounded rationality, but an accumulating body of research tells us that decision makers also allow systematic biases and errors to creep into their judgments.[33] These come from attempts to shortcut the decision process. To minimize effort and avoid difficult trade-offs, people tend to rely too heavily on experience, impulses, gut feelings, and convenient rules of thumb. In many instances, these shortcuts are helpful. However, they can lead to severe distortions of rationality. Following are the most common biases in decision making.

Overconfidence Bias It's been said that "no problem in judgment and decision making is more prevalent and more potentially catastrophic than overconfidence."[34] When we're given factual questions and asked to judge the probability that our answers are correct, we tend to be far too optimistic. For instance, studies have found that, when people say they're 65 to 70 percent confident that they're right, they are actually correct only about 50 percent of the time.[35] And when they say they're 100 percent sure, they tend to be 70 to 85 percent correct.[36] Here's another interesting example. In one random-sample national poll, 90 percent of U.S. adults said they expected to go to heaven. But in another random-sample national poll, only 86 percent thought Mother Theresa was in heaven. Talk about an overconfidence bias!

From an organizational standpoint, one of the most interesting findings related to overconfidence is that those individuals whose intellectual and interpersonal abilities are *weakest* are most likely to overestimate their performance and ability.[37] So as managers and employees become more knowledgeable about an issue, they become less likely to display overconfidence.[38] And overconfidence is most likely to surface when organizational members are considering issues or problems that are outside their area of expertise.[39]

Anchoring Bias The **anchoring bias** is a tendency to fixate on initial information and fail to adequately adjust for subsequent information.[40] The anchoring bias occurs because our mind appears to give a disproportionate amount of emphasis to the first information it receives.[41] Anchors are widely used by people in professions where persuasion skills are important—such as advertising, management, politics, real estate, and law. For instance, in a mock jury trial, the plaintiff's attorney asked one set of jurors to make an award in the range of $15 million to $50 million. The plaintiff's attorney asked another set of jurors for an award in the range of $50 million to $150 million. Consistent with the anchoring bias, the median awards were $15 million and $50 million, respectively.[42]

Consider the role of anchoring in negotiations. Any time a negotiation takes place, so does anchoring. As soon as someone states a number, your ability to ignore that number has been compromised. For instance, when a prospective employer asks how much you were making in your prior job, your answer typically anchors the employer's offer. You may want to keep this in mind when you negotiate your salary, but remember to set the anchor only as high as you realistically can.

Confirmation Bias The rational decision-making process assumes that we objectively gather information. But we don't. We *selectively* gather it. The **confirmation bias** represents a specific case of selective perception. We seek out information that reaffirms our past choices, and we discount information that contradicts them.[43] We also tend to accept at face value information that confirms our preconceived views, while we are critical and skeptical of information that challenges these views. Therefore, the information we gather is typically biased toward supporting views we already hold. This confirmation bias influences where we go to collect evidence because we tend to seek out sources most likely to tell us what we want to hear. It also leads us to give too much weight to supporting information and too little to contradictory information.

Availability Bias Many more people fear flying than fear driving in a car. But if flying on a commercial airline were as dangerous as driving, the equivalent of two 747s filled to capacity would have to crash every week, killing all aboard, to match the risk of being killed in a car accident. Yet the media gives much more attention to air accidents, so we tend to overstate the risk of flying and understate the risk of driving.

This illustrates the **availability bias**, which is the tendency for people to base their judgments on information that is readily available to them.[44] Events that evoke emotions, that are particularly vivid, or that have occurred more recently tend to be more available in our memory. As a result, we tend to overestimate the chances of unlikely events such as an airplane crash. The availability bias can also explain why managers, when doing annual performance appraisals, tend to give more weight to recent employee behaviors than to behaviors of 6 or 9 months ago.

Escalation of Commitment Another distortion that creeps into decisions in practice is a tendency to escalate commitment when making a series of decisions.[45] **Escalation of commitment** refers to staying with a decision even when

anchoring bias *A tendency to fixate on initial information, from which one then fails to adequately adjust for subsequent information.*

confirmation bias *The tendency to seek out information that reaffirms past choices and to discount information that contradicts past judgments.*

availability bias *The tendency for people to base their judgments on information that is readily available to them.*

escalation of commitment *An increased commitment to a previous decision in spite of negative information.*

MYTH OR SCIENCE? *"No One Thinks They're Biased"*

This statement is mostly true. Few of us are truly objective. Consider the telecommunications firm Verizon and its CEO, Ivan G. Seidenberg. Even though Verizon's earnings dropped by more than 5 percent and its stock price fell by more than 25 percent, Seidenberg received a nearly 50 percent increase in compensation. The consulting firm that Verizon used to set Seidenberg's pay said it adhered to "strict policies in place to ensure the independence and objectivity of our consultants."

Or take the case of Lawrence M. Small, former head of the Smithsonian Institution based in Washington, D.C. Small was appointed for his money-raising prowess, but external funding for the Smithsonian actually fell during his tenure. His pay, however, rose dramatically—to $915,698 in 2007. Small's deputy, Sheila P. Burke, also earned a handsome salary, accumulated more than $10 million in outside income from 2000 to 2007, and was absent for 400 business days. When confronted with these points, Burke replied, "There is every indication that I am in fact an extraordinary individual with a very strong work ethic."

These may be extreme examples. But they point to an alarming human tendency that may characterize all of us: Not only do we think we're objective when we evaluate ourselves or others, we don't recognize our biases and lack of objectivity. As one author noted, "Much of what happens in the brain is not evident in the brain itself, and thus people are better at playing these sorts of tricks on themselves than at catching themselves in the act."

A study of doctors, who are often lavished with gifts from pharmaceutical sales representatives, showed this tendency all too well. When asked about whether gifts might influence their prescribing practices, 84 percent thought that their colleagues were influenced by gifts, but only 16 percent thought that they were similarly influenced.[46] It may well be that we think others are *less* truthful or objective than they really are and that we think we are *more* truthful or objective than we really are. The lesson? We should recognize the self-serving biases that contaminate our evaluations of others—and of ourselves. ■

there is clear evidence that it's wrong. For example, consider a friend who has been dating his girlfriend for several years. Although he admits to you that things aren't going too well in the relationship, he says he is still going to marry her. His justification: "I have a lot invested in the relationship!"

It has been well documented that individuals escalate commitment to a failing course of action when they view themselves as responsible for the failure.[47] That is, they "throw good money after bad" to demonstrate that their initial decision wasn't wrong and to avoid having to admit that they made a mistake.[48] Escalation of commitment has obvious implications for managerial decisions. Many an organization has suffered large losses because a manager was determined to prove his original decision was right by continuing to commit resources to what was a lost cause from the beginning.

Randomness Error Human beings have a lot of difficulty dealing with chance. Most of us like to believe we have some control over our world and our destiny. Although we undoubtedly can control a good part of our future through rational decision making, the truth is that the world will always contain random events. Our tendency to believe we can predict the outcome of random events is the **randomness error**.

Decision making becomes impaired when we try to create meaning out of random events. One of the most serious impairments occurs when we turn imaginary patterns into superstitions.[49] These can be completely contrived ("I never make important decisions on Fridays) or evolve from a certain pattern of behavior that has been reinforced previously (golfer Tiger Woods often wears a red shirt during the final round of a golf tournament because he won many junior golf tournaments while wearing red shirts). Although many of us engage in some superstitious behavior, it can be debilitating when it affects daily judgments or biases major decisions. At the extreme, some decision makers become controlled by their superstitions—making it nearly impossible for them to change routines or objectively process new information.

Winner's Curse The **winner's curse** argues that the winning participants in a competitive auction typically pay too much for the item. Some buyers will underestimate the value of an item, and others will overestimate it, and the highest bidder (the winner) will be the one who overestimated the most. Therefore, unless the bidders dramatically undervalue, there is a good chance that the "winner" will pay too much.

Logic predicts that the winner's curse gets stronger as the number of bidders increases. The more bidders there are, the more likely that some of them have greatly overestimated the good's value. So, beware of auctions with an unexpectedly large number of bidders.

Hindsight Bias The **hindsight bias** is the tendency to believe falsely, after the outcome of an event is actually known, that we'd have accurately predicted that outcome.[50] When something happens and we have accurate feedback on the outcome, we seem to be pretty good at concluding that the outcome was relatively obvious. Do you think the 9/11 terrorist attacks should have been prevented? We'll never know, but we have to realize that things always seem much clearer when we know all the facts (or the connections among the facts). As Malcolm Gladwell, author of *Blink* and *The Tipping Point*, writes, "What is clear in hindsight is rarely clear before the fact. It's an obvious point, but one that nonetheless bears repeating, particularly when we're in the midst of assigning blame for the surprise attack of September 11th."[51]

The hindsight bias reduces our ability to learn from the past. It permits us to think that we're better at making predictions than we really are and can result in our being more confident about the accuracy of future decisions than we have a right to be. If, for instance, your actual predictive accuracy is only 40 percent, but you think it's 90 percent, you're likely to become falsely overconfident and less vigilant in questioning your predictive skills.

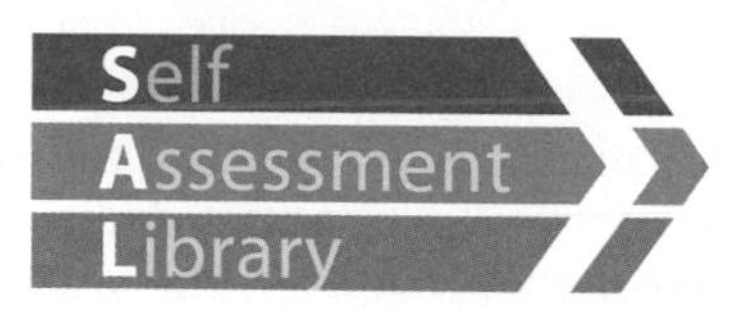

AM I A DELIBERATE DECISION MAKER?

In the Self-Assessment Library (available on CD or online), take assessment IV.A.2 (Am I a Deliberate Decision Maker?). Would it be better to be a more deliberate decision maker? Why or why not?

Influences on Decision Making: Individual Differences and Organizational Constraints

7 *Explain how individual differences and organizational constraints affect decision making.*

Having examined the rational decision-making model, bounded rationality, and some of the most salient biases and errors in decision making, we turn here to a discussion of factors that influence how people make decisions and the degree to which they are susceptible

randomness error *The tendency of individuals to believe that they can predict the outcome of random events.*

winner's curse *A decision-making dictum which argues that the winning participants in an auction typically pay too much for the winning item.*

hindsight bias *The tendency to believe falsely, after an outcome of an event is actually known, that one would have accurately predicted that outcome.*

OB In the News

Google and the Winner's Curse

One way the winner's curse is revealed is in initial public offering (IPO) pricing schemes. IPOs occur when a company decides to "go public"—offer itself for sale to investors. In such a case, potential investors need to estimate what the market value of a company's stock will be, lest they pay too much for the company's stock. Here's how the winner's curse operated, so some thought, with the pricing of Google.

Google auctioned off a portion of its stock, with the shares sold to those who paid the most per share. Google explicitly warned potential investors of the winner's curse in its U.S. Securities Exchange Commision registration statement (the company wrote: "The auction process for our public offering may result in a phenomenon known as the 'winner's curse,' and, as a result, investors may experience significant losses"). Despite this warning, the winning investors paid more than 10 times the estimated pre-IPO value for Google shares, often as much as $200/share. Yet, even 2 years after Google's IPO, its stock price was well above $200 and was trading for more than $600 in June 2007.

Clearly, the Google IPO turned out not to be the winner's curse many thought. So, how can we know when we have the winner's curse and avoid it?

There is no surefire way to avoid the winner's curse without knowing the future value of a good, and of course that's impossible. But bidders can reduce the odds of the winner's curse by doing their homework so they can forecast future value as accurately as possible and by bid shading, or placing a bid below what they believe the good is worth. This may make it less likely the bidder will win the auction, but it will protect her from overpaying when she does win. Savvy bidders know they don't want to win if it means they'll pay more than a good is worth.

Sources: Based on J. D. Miller, "Google's 'Winner's Curse,'" May 4, 2004; G. Deltas and R. Engelbrecht-Wiggans, "Naive Bidding," *Management Science*, March 2005, pp. 328–338; G. P. Zachary, "Google's Dirty Little Secrets: Investors May Suffer from Winner's Curse," August 8, 2004, p. E3; and D. Marasco, "The Winner's Curse—Oil Field Economics and Baseball," http://economics.about.com/cs/baseballeconomics/a/winners_curse.htm.

to errors and biases. We discuss individual differences and organizational constraints.

Individual Differences

Decision making in practice is characterized by bounded rationality, common biases and errors, and the use of intuition. In addition, individual differences create deviations from the rational model. In this section, we look at two differences: personality and gender.

Personality There hasn't been much research on personality and decision making. One possible reason is that most researchers who conduct decision-making research aren't trained to investigate personality. However, the studies that have been conducted suggest that personality does influence decision making. Research has considered conscientiousness and self-esteem (both of which we discussed in Chapter 4). Let's look at each in the context of decision making.

Some research has shown that specific facets of conscientiousness—rather than the broad trait itself—affect escalation of commitment (see p. 151).[52] Interestingly, one study revealed that two facets of conscientiousness—achievement striving and dutifulness—actually had opposite effects on escalation of commitment. For example, achievement-striving people were more likely to escalate their commitment, whereas dutiful people were less likely. Why might this be the case? Generally, achievement-oriented people hate to fail, so they escalate their commitment, hoping to forestall failure. Dutiful people, however, are more inclined to do what they see as best for the organization. Second, achievement-striving individuals appear to be more susceptible to the hindsight bias, perhaps because they have a greater need to justify the appropriateness of their actions.[53] Unfortunately, we don't have evidence on whether dutiful people are immune to the hindsight bias.

Finally, people with high self-esteem appear to be especially susceptible to the self-serving bias. Why? Because they are strongly motivated to maintain their self-esteem, so they use the self-serving bias to preserve it. That is, they blame others for their failures while taking credit for successes.[54]

Gender Recent research on rumination offers insights into gender differences in decision making.[55] Overall, the evidence indicates that women analyze decisions more than men do.

Rumination refers to reflecting at length. In terms of decision making, it means overthinking problems. Women, in general, are more likely than men to engage in rumination. Twenty years of study find that women spend much more time than men analyzing the past, present, and future. They're more likely to overanalyze problems before making a decision and to rehash a decision once it has been made. On the positive side, this is likely to lead to more careful consideration of problems and choices. However, it can make problems harder to solve, increase regret over past decisions, and increase depression. On this last point, women are nearly twice as likely as men to develop depression.[56]

Why women ruminate more than men is not clear. Several theories have been suggested. One view is that parents encourage and reinforce the expression of sadness and anxiety more in girls than in boys. Another theory is that women, more than men, base their self-esteem and well-being on what others think of them. A third theory is that women are more empathetic and more affected by events in others' lives, so they have more to ruminate about.

Gender differences surface early. By age 11, for instance, girls are ruminating more than boys. But this gender difference seems to lessen with age. Differences are largest during young adulthood and smallest after age 65, when both men and women ruminate the least.[57]

Organizational Constraints

Organizations can constrain decision makers, creating deviations from the rational model. For instance, managers shape their decisions to reflect the organization's performance evaluation and reward system, to comply with the organization's formal regulations, and to meet organizationally imposed time constraints. Previous organizational decisions also act as precedents to constrain current decisions.

Performance Evaluation Managers are strongly influenced in their decision making by the criteria on which they are evaluated. If a division manager believes the manufacturing plants under his responsibility are operating best when he hears nothing negative, we shouldn't be surprised to find his plant managers spending a good part of their time ensuring that negative information doesn't reach him.

Reward Systems The organization's reward system influences decision makers by suggesting to them what choices are preferable in terms of personal payoff. For example, if the organization rewards risk aversion, managers are more likely to make conservative decisions. From the 1930s through the mid-1980s, General Motors consistently gave out promotions and bonuses to managers who kept a low profile and avoided controversy. The result was that GM managers became very adept at dodging tough issues and passing controversial decisions on to committees.

Formal Regulations David Gonzalez, a shift manager at a Taco Bell restaurant in San Antonio, Texas, describes constraints he faces on his job: "I've got rules and regulations covering almost every decision I make—from how to

At McDonald's restaurants throughout the world, formal regulations shape employee decisions by standardizing the behavior of restaurant crew members. McDonald's requires that employees follow rules and regulations for food preparation and service to meet the company's standards of food quality and safety and reliable and friendly service. For example, McDonald's requires 72 safety protocols to be conducted every day in each restaurant as part of a daily monitoring routine for restaurant managers.

make a burrito to how often I need to clean the restrooms. My job doesn't come with much freedom of choice." David's situation is not unique. All but the smallest of organizations create rules and policies to program decisions, which are intended to get individuals to act in the intended manner. And of course, in so doing, they limit the decision maker's choices.

System-Imposed Time Constraints Organizations impose deadlines on decisions. For instance, a report on new-product development may have to be ready for the executive committee to review by the first of the month. Almost all important decisions come with explicit deadlines. These conditions create time pressures on decision makers and often make it difficult, if not impossible, to gather all the information they might like to have before making a final choice.

Historical Precedents Decisions aren't made in a vacuum. They have a context. In fact, individual decisions are accurately characterized as points in a stream of decisions. Decisions made in the past are ghosts that continually haunt current choices—that is, commitments that have already been made constrain current options. It's common knowledge that the largest determinant of the size of any given year's budget is last year's budget.[58] Choices made today, therefore, are largely a result of choices made over the years.

What About Ethics in Decision Making?

8 *Contrast the three ethical decision criteria.*

Ethical considerations should be an important criterion in organizational decision making. This is certainly more true today than at any time in the recent past, given the increasing scrutiny business is under to behave in an ethical and socially responsible way. In this section, we present three different ways to frame decisions ethically.

Three Ethical Decision Criteria

An individual can use three different criteria in making ethical choices.[59] The first is the *utilitarian* criterion, in which decisions are made solely on the basis of their outcomes or consequences. The goal of **utilitarianism** is to provide the greatest good for the greatest number. This view tends to dominate business decision making. It is consistent with goals such as efficiency, productivity, and high profits. By maximizing profits, for instance, a business executive can argue that he is securing the greatest good for the greatest number—as he hands out dismissal notices to 15 percent of his employees.

Another ethical criterion is to focus on *rights*. This calls on individuals to make decisions consistent with fundamental liberties and privileges, as set forth in documents such as the U.S. Bill of Rights. An emphasis on rights in decision making means respecting and protecting the basic rights of individuals, such as the right to privacy, to free speech, and to due process. For instance, this criterion protects **whistle-blowers** when they reveal unethical practices by their organization to the press or government agencies, on the grounds of their right to free speech.

A third criterion is to focus on *justice*. This requires individuals to impose and enforce rules fairly and impartially so that there is an equitable distribution of benefits and costs. Union members typically favor this view. It justifies paying people the same wage for a given job, regardless of performance differences, and using seniority as the primary determination in making layoff decisions.

Each of these criteria has advantages and liabilities. A focus on utilitarianism promotes efficiency and productivity, but it can result in ignoring the rights of some individuals, particularly those with minority representation in the organization. The use of rights as a criterion protects individuals from injury and is consistent with freedom and privacy, but it can create an overly legalistic work environment that hinders productivity and efficiency. A focus on justice protects the interests of the underrepresented and less powerful, but it can encourage a sense of entitlement that reduces risk taking, innovation, and productivity.

Decision makers, particularly in for-profit organizations, tend to feel safe and comfortable when they use utilitarianism. A lot of questionable actions can be justified when framed as being in the best interests of "the organization" and stockholders. But many critics of business decision makers argue that this perspective needs to change.[60] Increased concern in society about individual rights and social justice suggests the need for managers to develop ethical standards based on nonutilitarian criteria. This presents a solid challenge to today's managers because making decisions using criteria such as individual rights and social justice involves far more ambiguities than using utilitarian criteria such as effects on efficiency and profits. This helps to explain why managers are increasingly criticized for their actions. Raising prices, selling products with questionable effects on consumer health, closing down inefficient plants, laying off large numbers of employees, moving production overseas to cut costs, and similar decisions can be justified in utilitarian terms. But that may no longer be the single criterion by which good decisions should be judged.

utilitarianism *A system in which decisions are made to provide the greatest good for the greatest number.*

whistle-blowers *Individuals who report unethical practices by their employer to outsiders.*

Unleashing the creative potential of employees is paramount to the continued success of videogame maker Electronic Arts in developing innovative entertainment software. Designed to stimulate employees' creativity, EA's work environment is casual and fun, and employees are given the freedom to manage their own work time. To recharge their creativity, they can take a break from their projects and relax at a serenity pool, work out in a state-of-the-art fitness center, play pool or table tennis in a games room, or play basketball, soccer, or beach volleyball in an outdoor recreation area.

Improving Creativity in Decision Making

Although following the steps of the rational decision-making model will often improve decisions, a rational decision maker also needs **creativity**, that is, the ability to produce novel and useful ideas.[61] These are ideas that are different from what's been done before but that are appropriate to the problem or opportunity presented.

9 *Define* creativity *and discuss the three-component model of creativity.*

Why is creativity important to decision making? It allows the decision maker to more fully appraise and understand the problem, including seeing problems others can't see. Such thinking is becoming more important. Experts estimate that the United States alone will add 10 million "creative class" jobs—in science, technology, entertainment, design, and entrepreneurship—over the next decade. And both companies and business schools are trying to increase the creative potential of their employees and graduates.[62] The beauty-products manufacturer L'Oréal puts its managers through creative exercises such as cooking or making music, and the University of Chicago's business school has added a requirement for MBA students to make short movies about their experiences.

Creative Potential Most people have creative potential they can use when confronted with a decision-making problem. But to unleash that potential, they have to get out of the psychological ruts many of us fall into and learn how to think about a problem in divergent ways.

People differ in their inherent creativity, and exceptional creativity is scarce. We all know of creative geniuses in science (Albert Einstein), art (Pablo Picasso), and business (Steve Jobs). But what about the typical individual? People who score high on openness to experience (see Chapter 4), for example, are more likely than others to be creative. Intelligent people also are more likely than others to be creative.[63] Other traits associated with creative people include independence, self-confidence, risk taking, an internal locus of control, tolerance for ambiguity, a low need for structure, and perseverance in the face of frustration.[64]

A study of the lifetime creativity of 461 men and women found that fewer than 1 percent were exceptionally creative.[65] But 10 percent were highly creative and about 60 percent were somewhat creative. This suggests that most of us have creative potential; we just need to learn to unleash it.

Three-Component Model of Creativity Given that most people have the capacity to be at least somewhat creative, what can individuals and organizations do to stimulate employee creativity? The best answer to this question lies in the **three-component model of creativity**.[66] Based on an extensive body of research, this model proposes that individual creativity essentially requires expertise, creative thinking skills, and intrinsic task motivation (see Exhibit 5-4). Studies confirm that the higher the level of each of these three components, the higher the creativity.

Expertise is the foundation for all creative work. The film writer, producer, and director Quentin Tarantino spent his youth working in a video rental store, where he built up an encyclopedic knowledge of movies. The potential for creativity is enhanced when individuals have abilities, knowledge, proficiencies, and similar expertise in their field of endeavor. For example, you wouldn't expect someone with a minimal knowledge of programming to be very creative as a software engineer.

The second component is *creative-thinking skills.* This encompasses personality characteristics associated with creativity, the ability to use analogies, and the talent to see the familiar in a different light.

Research suggests that we are more creative when we're in good moods, so if we need to be creative, we should do things that make us happy, such as listening to music we enjoy, eating foods we like, watching funny movies, or socializing with others.[67]

Evidence also suggests that being around others who are creative can actually make us more inspired, especially if we're creatively "stuck."[68] One study found that "weak ties" to creative people—knowing creative people but not all that closely—facilitates creativity because the people are there as a resource if

Exhibit 5-4 The Three Components of Creativity

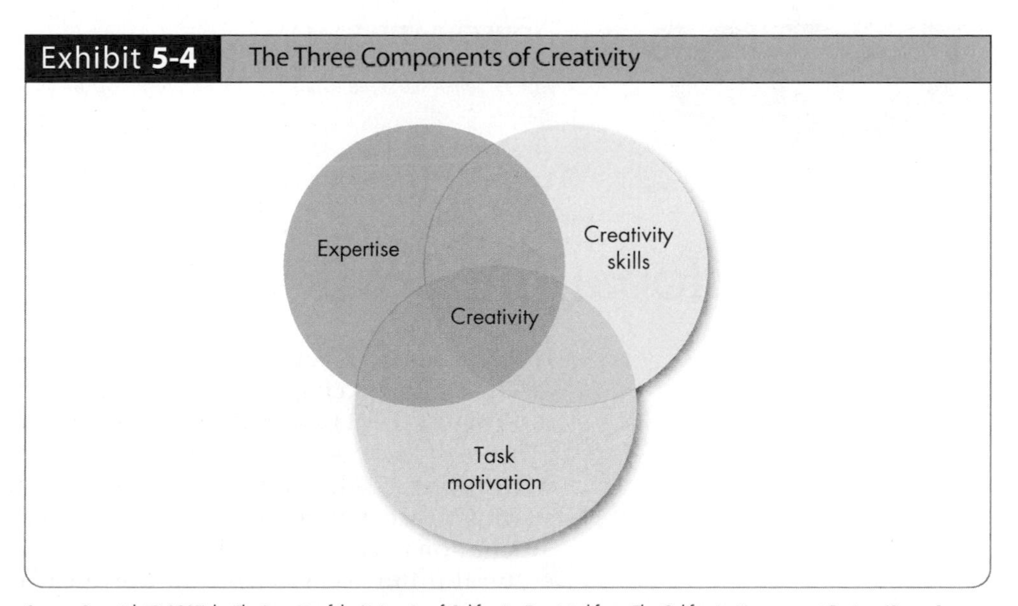

Source: Copyright © 1997, by The Regents of the University of California. Reprinted from *The California Management Review* 40, no. 1. By permission of The Regents.

creativity *The ability to produce novel and useful ideas.*

three-component model of creativity *The proposition that individual creativity requires expertise, creative thinking skills, and intrinsic task motivation.*

we need them, but they are not so close as to stunt our own independent thinking.[69]

The effective use of analogies allows decision makers to apply an idea from one context to another. One of the most famous examples in which analogy resulted in a creative breakthrough was Alexander Graham Bell's observation that it might be possible to apply the way the ear operates to his "talking box." He noticed that the bones in the ear are operated by a delicate, thin membrane. He wondered why, then, a thicker and stronger piece of membrane shouldn't be able to move a piece of steel. From that analogy, the telephone was conceived.

Some people have developed their creative skills because they are able to see problems in a new way. They're able to make the strange familiar and the familiar strange.[70] For instance, most of us think of hens laying eggs. But how many of us have considered that a hen is only an egg's way of making another egg?

The final component in the three-component model of creativity is *intrinsic task motivation.* This is the desire to work on something because it's interesting, involving, exciting, satisfying, or personally challenging. This motivational component is what turns creativity *potential* into *actual* creative ideas. It determines the extent to which individuals fully engage their expertise and creative skills. Creative people often love their work, to the point of seeming obsession. Our work environment can have a significant effect on intrinsic motivation. Stimulants that foster creativity include a culture that encourages the flow of ideas; fair and constructive judgment of ideas; rewards and recognition for creative work; sufficient financial, material, and information resources; freedom to decide what work is to be done and how to do it; a supervisor who communicates effectively, shows confidence in others, and supports the work group; and work group members who support and trust each other.[71]

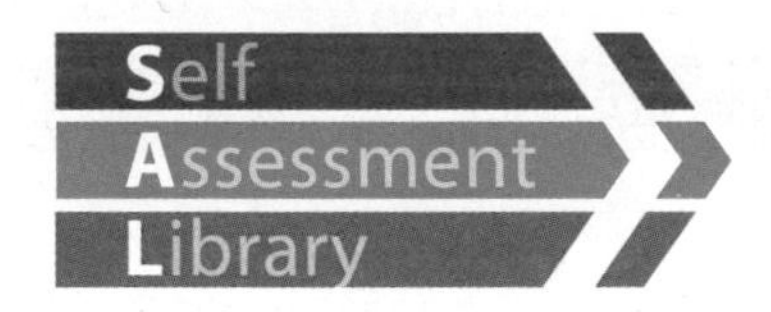

HOW CREATIVE AM I?

In the Self-Assessment Library (available on CD or online), take assessment I.A.5 (How Creative Am I?).

Global Implications

In considering whether there are global differences in the concepts we've discussed in this chapter, let's consider the three areas that have attracted the most research: (1) attributions, (2) decision making, and (3) ethics.

Attributions Although research on cultural differences in perception is just starting to accumulate, there has been some research on cultural differences in attributions. The evidence is mixed, but most of it suggests that there *are* cultural differences across cultures in the attributions people make.[72] For instance, a study of Korean managers found that, contrary to the self-serving bias, they tended to accept responsibility for group failure "because I was not a capable leader" instead of attributing failure to group members.[73] Attribution theory was developed largely based on experiments with U.S. and western European workers. But the Korean study suggests caution in making attribution theory predictions in non-Western societies, especially in countries with strong collectivist traditions.

Decision Making The rational model makes no acknowledgment of cultural differences, nor does the bulk of OB research literature on decision making. A 2007 review of cross-cultural OB research covered 25 areas, but cultural influence on decision making was not among them. Another 2007 review identified 15 topics, but the result was the same: no research on culture and decision making.[74] It seems that most OB research assumes that culture doesn't matter to decision making.

But Indonesians, for instance, don't necessarily make decisions the same way Australians do. Therefore, we need to recognize that the cultural background of a decision maker can have a significant influence on the selection of problems, the depth of analysis, the importance placed on logic and rationality, and whether organizational decisions should be made autocratically by an individual manager or collectively in groups.[75]

Cultures differ, for example, in terms of time orientation, the importance of rationality, their belief in the ability of people to solve problems, and their preference for collective decision making. Differences in time orientation help us understand why managers in Egypt make decisions at a much slower and more deliberate pace than their U.S. counterparts. While rationality is valued in North America, that's not true elsewhere in the world. A North American manager might make an important decision intuitively but know it's important to appear to proceed in a rational fashion because rationality is highly valued in the West. In countries such as Iran, where rationality is not as paramount as other factors, efforts to appear rational are not necessary.

Some cultures emphasize solving problems, while others focus on accepting situations as they are. The United Kingdom falls in the first category; Thailand and Indonesia are examples of the second. Because problem-solving managers believe they can and should change situations to their benefit, U.K. managers might identify a problem long before their Thai or Indonesian counterparts would choose to recognize it as such. Decision making by Japanese managers is much more group oriented than in the United Kingdom. The Japanese value conformity and cooperation. So before Japanese CEOs make an important decision, they collect a large amount of information, which they use in consensus-forming group decisions.

In short, we have reason to believe there are important cultural differences in decision making. Unfortunately, though, there is not yet much research to substantiate these beliefs. OB is a research-based discipline, but research does not always respond quickly to important practical concerns.

Ethics What is seen as an ethical decision in China may not be seen as such in Canada. The reason is that there are no global ethical standards.[76] Contrasts between Asia and the West provide an illustration.[77] Because bribery is commonplace in countries such as China, a Canadian working in China might face a dilemma: Should I pay a bribe to secure business if it is an accepted part of that country's culture? A manager of a large U.S. company operating in China caught an employee stealing. Following company policy, she fired him and turned him over to the local authorities. Later, she was horrified to learn that the employee had been summarily executed.[78]

Although ethical standards may seem ambiguous in the West, criteria defining right and wrong are actually much clearer in the West than in Asia. Few issues are black and white there; most are gray. The need for global organizations to establish ethical principles for decision makers in countries such as India and China and to modify them to reflect cultural norms may be critical if high standards are to be upheld and if consistent practices are to be achieved.

Summary and Implications for Managers

Perception Individuals base their behavior not on the way their external environment actually is but rather on what they see or believe it to be. Whether a manager successfully plans and organizes the work of employees and actually helps them to structure their work more efficiently and effectively is far less important than how employees perceive the manager's efforts. Similarly, employees judge issues such as fair pay for work performed, the validity of performance appraisals, and the adequacy of working conditions in very individual ways; we cannot be assured that they will interpret conditions about their jobs in a favorable light. Therefore, to influence productivity, it's necessary to assess how workers perceive their jobs.

Absenteeism, turnover, and job satisfaction are also reactions to an individual's perceptions. Dissatisfaction with working conditions and the belief that an organization lacks promotion opportunities are judgments based on attempts to create meaning out of the job. The employee's conclusion that a job is good or bad is an interpretation. Managers must spend time understanding how each individual interprets reality and, when there is a significant difference between what someone sees and what exists, try to eliminate the distortions.

Individual Decision Making Individuals think and reason before they act. This is why an understanding of how people make decisions can be helpful for explaining and predicting their behavior.

In some decision situations, people follow the rational decision-making model. But few important decisions are simple or unambiguous enough for the rational model's assumptions to apply. So we find individuals looking for solutions that satisfice rather than optimize, injecting biases and prejudices into the decision process, and relying on intuition.

Given the evidence we've described on how decisions are actually made in organizations, what can managers do to improve their decision making? We offer four suggestions.

First, analyze the situation. Adjust your decision-making approach to the national culture you're operating in and to the criteria your organization evaluates and rewards. For instance, if you're in a country that doesn't value rationality, don't feel compelled to follow the rational decision-making model or even to try to make your decisions appear rational. Similarly, organizations differ in terms of the importance they place on risk, the use of groups, and the like. Adjust your decision approach to ensure that it's compatible with the organization's culture.

Second, be aware of biases. Then try to minimize their impact. Exhibit 5-5 offers some suggestions.

Third, combine rational analysis with intuition. These are not conflicting approaches to decision making. By using both, you can actually improve your decision-making effectiveness. As you gain managerial experience, you should feel increasingly confident in imposing your intuitive processes on top of your rational analysis.

Finally, try to enhance your creativity. Actively look for novel solutions to problems, attempt to see problems in new ways, and use analogies. In addition, try to remove work and organizational barriers that might impede your creativity.

Exhibit 5-5 Reducing Biases and Errors

Focus on Goals. Without goals, you can't be rational, you don't know what information you need, you don't know which information is relevant and which is irrelevant, you'll find it difficult to choose between alternatives, and you're far more likely to experience regret over the choices you make. Clear goals make decision making easier and help you eliminate options that are inconsistent with your interests.

Look for Information That Disconfirms Your Beliefs. One of the most effective means for counteracting overconfidence and the confirmation and hindsight biases is to actively look for information that contradicts your beliefs and assumptions. When we overtly consider various ways we could be wrong, we challenge our tendencies to think we're smarter than we actually are.

Don't Try to Create Meaning out of Random Events. The educated mind has been trained to look for cause-and-effect relationships. When something happens, we ask why. And when we can't find reasons, we often invent them. You have to accept that there are events in life that are outside your control. Ask yourself if patterns can be meaningfully explained or whether they are merely coincidence. Don't attempt to create meaning out of coincidence.

Increase Your Options. No matter how many options you've identified, your final choice can be no better than the best of the option set you've selected. This argues for increasing your decision alternatives and for using creativity in developing a wide range of diverse choices. The more alternatives you can generate, and the more diverse those alternatives, the greater your chance of finding an outstanding one.

Source: S. P. Robbins, *Decide & Conquer: Making Winning Decisions and Taking Control of Your Life* (Upper Saddle River, NJ: Financial Times/Prentice Hall, 2004), pp. 164–168.

Point Counterpoint

WHEN IN DOUBT, DO!

Life is full of decisions and choices. The real question is not "To be, or not to be" but rather "To do, or not to do?" For example, should I confront my professor about my midterm grade? Should I buy a new car? Should I accept a new job? Should I choose this major? Very often, we are unsure of our decision. In such cases, it is almost always better to choose action over inaction. In life, people more often regret inaction than action. Take the following simple example:

Act	State	
	RAIN	***SHINE***
Carry umbrella	Dry (except your feet!)	Inconvenience
Don't carry umbrella	Miserable drenching	Unqualified bliss

Say you carry an umbrella and it doesn't rain, or you don't carry an umbrella and it does rain. In which situation are you worse off? Would you rather experience the mild inconvenience of the extra weight of the umbrella or get drenched? Chances are you'll regret inaction more than action. Research shows that after we make a decision, we regret inaction more than action. Although we often regret actions in their immediate aftermath, over time, regrets over actions decline markedly, whereas regrets over missed opportunities increase. For example, you finally decide to take a trip to Europe. You have an amazing time, but a few weeks after you get back, your credit card bill arrives—and it isn't pretty. Unfortunately, you have to work overtime and miss a few dinners out with friends to pay off the bills. A few months down the road, however, you decide to reminisce by looking through your photos from the trip, and you can't imagine not having gone. So, when in doubt, just do!

It's just silly to think that when in doubt, you should always act. People will undoubtedly make mistakes following such simple advice. For example, you're out of work, but you still decide to purchase your dream car—a BMW, fully loaded. Not the smartest idea. So why is the motto "just do it" dangerous? Because there are two types of regrets: hot regret, in which an individual kicks herself for having caused something bad, and wistful regret, in which she fantasizes about how else things might have turned out. The danger is that actions are more likely to lead to anguish or hot regret, and inaction is more likely to lead to wistful regret. So the bottom line is that we can't apply simple rules such as "just do it" to important decisions.[79]

Questions for Review

1 What is perception, and what factors influence our perception?

2 What is attribution theory? What are the three determinants of attribution? What are its implications for explaining organizational behavior?

3 What shortcuts do people frequently use in making judgments about others?

4 What is the link between perception and decision making? How does one affect the other?

5 What is the rational model of decision making? How is it different from bounded rationality and intuition?

6 What are some of the common decision biases or errors that people make?

7 What are the influences of individual differences, organizational constraints, and culture on decision making?

8 Are unethical decisions more a function of an individual decision maker or the decision maker's work environment? Explain.

9 What is creativity, and what is the three-component model of creativity?

Experiential Exercise

BIASES IN DECISION MAKING

Step 1

Answer each of the following problems.

1. *Fortune* magazine ranked the following 10 corporations as being among the 500 largest United States–based firms according to sales volume for 2005:

   Group A: Apple Computer, Hershey Foods, Hilton Hotels, Mattel, Levi Strauss

   Group B: American International Group, Cardinal Health, Conagra Foods, Ingram Micro, Valero Energy

   Which group would you say (A or B) had the larger total sales volume? By what percentage (10 percent, 50 percent, 100 percent)?
2. The best student in your introductory MBA class this past semester writes poetry and is rather shy and small in stature. What was the student's undergraduate major: Chinese studies or psychology?
3. Which of the following causes more deaths in the United States each year?
   a. Stomach cancer
   b. Motor vehicle accidents
4. Which would you choose?
   a. A sure gain of $240
   b. A 25 percent chance of winning $1,000 and a 75 percent chance of winning nothing
5. Which would you choose?
   a. A sure loss of $750
   b. A 75 percent chance of losing $1,000 and a 25 percent chance of losing nothing
6. Which would you choose?
   a. A sure loss of $3,000
   b. An 80 percent chance of losing $4,000 and a 20 percent chance of losing nothing

Step 2

Break into groups of three to five students. Compare your answers. Explain why you chose the answers you did.

Step 3

Your instructor will give you the correct answers to each problem. Now discuss the accuracy of your decisions; the biases evident in the decisions you reached; and how you might improve your decision making to make it more accurate.

Source: These problems are based on examples provided in M. H. Bazerman, *Judgment in Managerial Decision Making,* 3rd ed. (New York: Wiley, 1994).

Ethical Dilemma

FIVE ETHICAL DECISIONS: WHAT WOULD YOU DO?

How would you respond to each of the following situations?

1. Assume that you're a middle manager in a company with about 1,000 employees. You're negotiating a contract with a very large potential customer whose representative has hinted that you could almost certainly be assured of getting his business if you gave him and his wife an all-expenses-paid cruise to the Caribbean. You know the representative's employer wouldn't approve of such a "payoff," but you have the discretion to authorize such an expenditure. What would you do?
2. You have an autographed CD by Sean Combs (signed "PuffD"). You have put the CD up for sale on eBay. So far, the highest bid is $74.50. A friend has offered you $100 for the CD, commenting that he could get $150 for the CD on eBay in a year. You know this is highly unlikely. Should you sell your friend the CD for what he offered ($100)? Do you have an obligation to tell your friend you have listed your CD on eBay?
3. Your company's policy on reimbursement for meals while traveling on business is that you will be repaid for your out-of-pocket costs, not to exceed $80 per day. You don't need receipts for these expenses—the company will take your word. When traveling, you tend to eat at fast-food places and rarely spend in excess of $20 a day. Most of your colleagues put in reimbursement requests in the range of $55 to $60 per day, regardless of what their actual expenses are. How much would you request for your meal reimbursements?
4. You work for a company that manufactures, markets, and distributes various products, including nutritional supplements, to health food and nutrition stores. One of the company's best-selling products is an herbal supplement called Rosalife. The company advertises that Rosalife "achieves all the gains of estrogen hormone replacement therapy without any of the side effects." One day, a research assistant stops by your office with some troubling information. She tells you that while researching another product, she came across a recent study that suggests Rosalife does not offer the benefits the company claims it does. You show this study to your supervisor, who says, "We're not responsible for validating non-FDA-controlled products, and nobody's hurt anyway." Indeed, you know this is not the case. What is your ethical responsibility?
5. Assume that you're the manager at a gaming company, and you're responsible for hiring a group to outsource the production of a highly anticipated new game. Because your company is a giant in the industry, numerous companies are trying to get the bid. One of them offers you some kickbacks if you give that firm the bid, but ultimately, it is up to your bosses to decide on the company. You don't mention the incentive, but you push upper management to give the bid to the company that offered you the kickback. Is withholding the truth as bad as lying? Why or why not?

Case Incident 1

NATURAL DISASTERS AND THE DECISIONS THAT FOLLOW

Jeff Rommel's introduction to Florida could be described as trial by hurricane. Rommel took over Florida operations in 2004 for Nationwide Insurance. Over a 2-month period in 2004, Florida experienced its worst hurricane season in history—four major hurricanes (Charley, Frances, Ivan, and Jeanne) slammed the state, causing an estimated $40 billion in damage. In the hurricanes' wake, Nationwide received more than 119,000 claims, collectively worth $850 million.

Although dealing with those claims was difficult, even more difficult was Rommel's later decision to cancel approximately 40,000 homeowners' policies. Nationwide received a huge amount of media attention as a result, almost all negative. In reflecting on the decision, Rommel said, "Pulling out was a sound business decision. Was it good for the individual customer? No, I can't say it was. But the rationale was sound."

Hurricanes aren't the only weapons in nature's arsenal, and the insurance industry is hardly the only industry affected by nature. Consider the airline industry. American Airlines has 80,000 employees, 4 of whom make decisions to cancel flights. One of them is Danny Burgin. When weather systems approach, Burgin needs to consider a host of factors in deciding which flights to cancel and how to reroute affected passengers. He argues that of two major weather factors, winter snowstorms and summer thunderstorms, snowstorms are easier to handle because they are more predictable.

Don't tell that to JetBlue, however. On February 14, 2007, JetBlue was unprepared for a snowstorm that hit the East Coast. Due to the lack of planning, JetBlue held hundreds of passengers on its planes at JFK, in some cases for as long as 10 hours (with bathrooms closed!). To the stranded travelers, JetBlue's tepid offer of a refund was just

Psychology, vol. 47 (Palo Alto, CA: Annual R
237–271.
10. See, for example, G. N. Powell, "The
Business Students' Stereotypes of Japanese
Stereotypes of American Managers," *Group
Management*, March 1992, pp. 44–56; W.
Chan, E. Snape, and T. Redman, "Age
Discriminatory Attitudes Towards Old
East–West Comparison," *Human Relation*
629–661; C. Ostroff and L. E. Atwater, "
Work with Matter? Effects of Referent Gr
Age Composition on Managers' Compens
Applied Psychology, August 2003, pp. 725
Heilman, A. S. Wallen, D. Fuchs, and
"Penalties for Success: Reactions to Wome
Male Gender-Typed Tasks," *Journal of Appli*
2004, pp. 416–427.
11. J. L. Eberhardt, P. G. Davies, V. J. Purdic-V
Johnson, "Looking Deathworthy: Perceive
of Black Defendants Predicts Capital-Sente
Psychological Science 17, no. 5 (2006), pp. 38
12. See, for example, J. Wilgoren, "Struggling
and American," *New York Times*, Novemb
J. Q. Wilson and H. R. Higgins, "Profiles i
Street Journal, January 10, 2002, p. A12; a
"Profiling," *America*, March 18, 2002, pp. 1
13. See the List of Terrorist Incidents Infor
http://www.localcolorart.com/search
List_of_terrorist_incidents/.
14. H. G. Heneman III and T. A. Judge, *Staf*
(Middleton, WI: Mendota House, 2006).
15. J. Willis and A. Todorov, "First Impressions
Mind After a 100ms Exposure to a Face," *P*
July 2006, pp. 592–598.
16. See, for example, E. C. Webster, *Decisi
Employment Interview* (Montreal: McGill Un
Relations Center, 1964).
17. See, for example, D. Eden, *Pygmalion*
(Lexington, MA: Lexington Books, 1
"Leadership and Expectations: Pygmalion
Self-Fulfilling Prophecies," *Leadership Quarter*
271–305; D. B. McNatt, "Ancient Pygmalion
rary Management: A Meta-analysis of the
Applied Psychology, April 2000, pp. 314–32
and D. Eden, "Remedial Self-Fulfilling Pr
Experiments to Prevent Golem Effects Amo
Women," *Journal of Applied Psychology*, June
and D. Eden, "Self-Fulfilling Prophecies in
J. Greenberg (ed.), *Organizational Behavi
Science*, 2nd ed. (Mahwah, NJ: Lawrence Er
91–122.
18. D. Eden and A. B. Shani, "Pygmalion Go
Expectancy, Leadership, and Trainee Perf
of Applied Psychology, April 1982, pp. 19
McNatt and T. A. Judge, "Boundary C
Galatea Effect: A Field Experiment a
Replication," *Academy of Management Jour*
pp. 550–565.
19. See, for example, R. D. Bretz, Jr., G. T. Milko
"The Current State of Performance Appra

as outrageous. For an airline that prided itself on customer service and had regularly been rated as the top U.S. airline in customer satisfaction, it was a public relations disaster. Linda Hirneise, an analyst at J.D. Power, said, "It did not appear JetBlue had a plan." In defending the airline, JetBlue's founder and CEO, David Neeleman, said, "Is our good will gone? No, it isn't. We fly 30 million people a year. Ten thousand were affected by this." In responding to another interviewer, he said, "You're overdoing it. Delta screwed people for two days, and we did it for three and a half, okay? So go ask Delta what they did about it. Why don't you grill them?" Eventually, though, Neeleman himself was affected by it, and he stepped down.

Questions

1. Insurance companies in the state of Florida earned record profits in 2006, suggesting that Nationwide's decision to cancel policies in light of the calm hurricane seasons (in Florida) in 2005–2007 may have cost the company potential revenue and customer goodwill. Do you think Rommel's quote about making a "sound business decision" reveals any perceptual or decision-making biases? Why or why not?
2. Review the section on common biases and errors in decision making. For companies such as Nationwide, American Airlines, and JetBlue that must respond to natural events, which of these biases and errors are relevant and why?
3. In each of the three cases discussed here, which organizational constraints were factors in the decisions that were made?
4. How do you think people like Rommel, Burgin, and Neeleman factor ethics into their decisions? Do you think the welfare of policy owners and passengers enter into their decisions?

Sources: M. Blomberg, "Insuring the Nation," *Gainesville (Florida) Sun*, February 27, 2006, pp. 1D, 8D; M. Trottman, "Choices in Stormy Weather," *Wall Street Journal*, February 14, 2006, pp. B1, B2; C. Salter, "Lessons from the Tarmac," *Fast Company*, May 2007, pp. 31–32; and D. Q. Wilber, "Tale of Marooned Passengers Galvanizes Airline Opponents," *Washington Post*, February 16, 2007, p. D1.

Case Incident 2

WHISTLE-BLOWERS: SAINTS OR SINNERS?

Corporate whistle-blowers, individuals who report company wrongdoings, are often lauded for their courage and integrity. For example, Jeffrey Wigand is well known (especially after the docudrama starring Russell Crowe) for exposing the Big Tobacco scandal. Similarly, Sherron Watkins is credited for bringing the Enron scandal to light. Given that whistle-blowers face unemployment, and, often, ridicule from their company, many people do not come forward to report illegal activity. To encourage whistle-blowers, a whistle-blower law adopted in 1986 pays informants as much as 30 percent of legal fines reaped during lawsuits. With settlements often exceeding $100 million, whistle-blowers can sometimes see huge payoffs. Some experts are concerned that these payoffs are creating a culture in which employees quickly report wrongdoings instead of trying to rectify the situation internally.

For example, Douglas Durand was a former vice president of sales at TAP Pharmaceutical Products. In 1995, he began to suspect that TAP was conspiring with doctors to defraud Medicare. Pharmaceutical companies routinely provide doctors with free samples of the latest drugs; however, Durand believed that TAP was working with doctors to bill Medicare for the free drugs, a practice that is against federal law. Later that same year, Durand became more worried when he discovered that TAP had decided to pay a 2 percent fee to individual doctors to cover "administrative costs"—a kickback in Durand's opinion. Durand then began preparing to blow the whistle on TAP and its affiliates. "I wanted to do the right thing," he says. After being referred to attorney Elizabeth Ainslie by one of his colleagues, Durand started keeping notes and collecting company documents, while his lawyer attempted to get the federal government involved.

In February 1996, Durand received a $35,000 bonus from TAP and then quit the company. Three months later, he and Ainslie filed suits against TAP. For the next 5 years, Durand and Ainslie built their case against TAP. At one point, Durand even obtained some of his former coworkers' home phone numbers and called them while the FBI listened in. During one call to a former TAP colleague, Durand lied, saying that he had been subpoenaed, in an attempt to get his former colleague to incriminate himself. All in all, more than 500 boxes of documents were collected, containing evidence against TAP. Although TAP fought the lawsuit, it finally settled in April 2001. Durand's take was a cool $126 million.

On the day TAP settled, prosecutors filed criminal fraud charges against the company. One of those prosecutors, Michael Sullivan, said the charges were filed to send "a very strong signal to the pharmaceutical industry." However, as the trial progressed, holes in Durand's story began to appear. The kickbacks that Durand claimed TAP

paid to doctors never occurred, the compa
charge Medicare, and a conference that D
TAP used to bribe doctors into using its dr
paid for by the doctors themselves. Finally,
federal jury in Boston cleared TAP of the c
before the company had incurred over $1
fees. Durand is now retired and lives wit
daughter in Florida.

Supporters of whistle-blowing, such as S
Grassley (R-Iowa), say that having inform
company wrongdoings is the best way to
activity. "There can never be enough bur
courage fraudulent use of taxpayers' mo
ing colleagues might squeal can be a
states. However, others disagree. Accor
Stetler, defense attorney for TAP, "It's ab
of extortion." Whatever position you take
that whistle-blowing is a strong means to c
wrongdoing. However, when this right is a
blowers can become as unethical as the c
they are blowing the whistle on.

Source: Based on N. Weinberg, "The Dark Side c

Endnotes

1. P. Babcock, "Discriminatory Backlash Lir 11," *SHRM Online*, September 5, 2006, hrnews_published; "Muslim Americans: M Mostly Mainstream," Pew Research Cente http://pewresearch.org/assets/pdf/muslir and "They're Muslims, and Yankees, To January 15, 2007, www.businessweek.com/n
2. H. H. Kelley, "Attribution in Social Interac et al. (eds.), *Attribution: Perceiving the C* (Morristown, NJ: General Learning Press, 1
3. See L. Ross, "The Intuitive Psychologist comings," in L. Berkowitz (ed.), *Advance Social Psychology*, vol. 10 (Orlando, FL: 1977), pp. 174–220; and A. G. Miller and Effect of an Informational Option on t Attribution Error," *Personality and Social P* June 1989, pp. 194–204.
4. See, for instance, G. Johns, "A Multi-Leve Serving Behavior in and by Organizations and B. M. Staw (eds.), *Research in Organi* vol. 21 (Stamford, CT: JAI Press, 1999), pp and D. Dunning, "Feeling 'Holier Than Serving Assessments Produced by Errors Prediction?" *Journal of Personality and* December 2000, pp. 861–875; and M. G S. Schulz-Hardt, U. Napiersky, and D. Fr Fault—But Only I Can Change It': Cou Prefactual Thoughts of Managers," *Jo Psychology*, April 2004, pp. 279–292.

Motivation Concepts

Luke: "I don't believe it."

Yoda: "That is why you fail."

—from the film *The Empire Strikes Back*

LEARNING OBJECTIVES

After studying this chapter, you should be able to:

1. Describe the three key elements of motivation.
2. Identify four early theories of motivation and evaluate their applicability today.
3. Apply the predictions of cognitive evaluation theory to intrinsic and extrinsic rewards.
4. Compare and contrast goal-setting theory and management by objectives.
5. Contrast reinforcement theory and goal-setting theory.
6. Demonstrate how organizational justice is a refinement of equity theory.
7. Apply the key tenets of expectancy theory to motivating employees.
8. Compare contemporary theories of motivation.
9. Explain to what degree motivation theories are culture bound.

In 1982, Chris Gardner was homeless, raising a 20-month-old son in San Francisco and peddling medical devices few wanted to buy. Unable to afford both housing and child care, Gardner boarded himself and his son where he could—in cheap hotels in Oakland, in a church shelter when they couldn't afford that, and even in the bathroom at the Bay Area Rapid Transit office when the shelter was full. A happy ending was nowhere in sight.

Chris Gardner's Pursuit of Happyness

A turning point in Gardner's life came in a parking lot, when he met a man driving a red Ferrari. "He was looking for a parking space. I said, 'You can have mine, but I gotta ask you two questions.' The two questions were: What do you do? And how do you do that? Turns out this guy was a stockbroker and he was making $80,000 a month." From that moment, Gardner resolved that he'd be a stockbroker, too. A while later, he looked up the offices of Dean Witter, then one of the largest investment banking firms (it later merged with Morgan Stanley). Gardner was able to line up an interview for a spot in the firm's internship program.

The night before his interview, Gardner was taken to jail for a backlog of parking tickets he couldn't afford to pay. So he went to his interview unshaven, disheveled, in yesterday's clothes. He explained his situation, and Dean Witter took a chance on him. The firm advised him it was only a trial program and that only a few of the most promising prospects would be hired to full-time positions. Gardner remembered advice his mother had given him: "You can only depend on yourself. The cavalry ain't coming."

At Dean Witter, Gardner made 200 calls a day. "Every time I picked up the phone," he said, "I knew I was getting closer to digging myself out of the hole." Gardner made it at Dean Witter, spent 1983–1987 at Bear Stearns & Co., where he became a top earner, and 5 years later, opened his own brokerage firm in Chicago. Named Gardner Rich, it's still thriving today. Now 14 people work at the firm's offices, a few blocks from the Sears Tower in Chicago. Not that Gardner is coasting. Sitting in his Chicago office, dressed in Bermuda shorts, sandals, and two watches (which he always wears to make sure he's never late), Gardner says he's a bit tired of talking about himself and how far he's come.

No wonder. He's given scores of interviews and has been featured on many major TV talk shows. His life story was made into a best-selling book and a Columbia Pictures film, which he helped produce and which starred Will Smith. When he's not working at his investment bank, Gardner is a motivational speaker and helps various charities in Chicago and San Francisco. For example, with the Cara Program, which assists the homeless and at-risk populations in Chicago with comprehensive job training and placement, Gardner speaks at counseling sessions and assists with permanent job placement. A table in his office is piled high with letters from people inspired by his story. On occasion, he'll call one of the letter writers. He says: "I find myself saying over and over: 'Baby steps count.'"[1] ■

What motivates people like Chris Gardner to excel? Is there anything organizations can do to encourage that sort of motivation in their employees? Before we answer that question, try a self-assessment of your confidence in your ability to succeed.

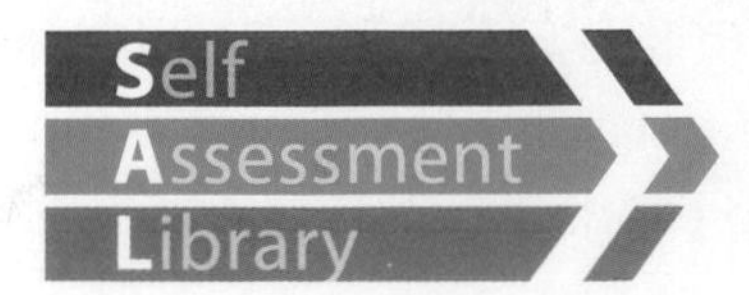

HOW CONFIDENT AM I IN MY ABILITIES TO SUCCEED?

In the Self-Assessment Library (available on CD or online), take assessment IV.A.3 (How Confident Am I in My Abilities to Succeed?) and answer the following questions.

1. *How did you score relative to other class members? Does that surprise you?*
2. *Do you think self-confidence is critical to success? Can a person be too confident?*

Motivation is one of the most frequently researched topics in OB.[2] One reason for its popularity is revealed in a recent Gallup poll, which found that a majority of U.S. employees—55 percent—have no enthusiasm for their work.[3] Moreover, another study suggested that, by workers' own reports, they waste roughly 2 hours per day, not counting lunch and scheduled breaks (the biggest time-wasters were Internet surfing and talking with coworkers).[4] Clearly, motivation seems to be an issue. The good news is that all this research provides us with considerable insights into how to improve motivation.

In this chapter, we'll review the basics of motivation, assess a number of motivation theories, and provide an integrative model that shows how the best of these theories fit together.

Defining *Motivation*

What is motivation? It's the result of the interaction between an individual and a situation. Certainly, some individuals, such as Chris Gardner, seem to be driven to succeed. But the same student who finds it difficult to read a textbook for more than 20 minutes may devour a Harry Potter book in a day. For this student, the difference in motivation is driven by the situation. So as we analyze the concept of motivation, keep in mind that the level of motivation varies both between individuals and within individuals at different times.

1 *Describe the three key three elements of motivation.*

We define **motivation** as the processes that account for an individual's intensity, direction, and persistence of effort toward attaining a goal.[5] While general motivation is concerned with effort toward *any* goal, we'll narrow the focus to *organizational* goals in order to reflect our singular interest in work-related behavior.

The three key elements in our definition are intensity, direction, and persistence. *Intensity* is concerned with how hard a person tries. This is the element most of us focus on when we talk about motivation. However, high intensity is unlikely to lead to favorable job-performance outcomes unless the effort is channeled in a *direction* that benefits the organization. Therefore, we have to consider the quality of effort as well as its intensity. Effort that is directed toward, and consistent with, the organization's goals is the kind of effort that we should be seeking. Finally, motivation has a *persistence* dimension. This is a measure of how long a person can maintain effort. Motivated individuals stay with a task long enough to achieve their goal.

Early Theories of Motivation

2 *Identify four early theories of motivation and evaluate their applicability today.*

The 1950s were a fruitful period in the development of motivation concepts. Four specific theories were formulated during this period, which although heavily attacked and now questionable in terms of validity, are probably still the best-known explanations for employee motivation. As you'll see later in this chapter, we have

motivation *The processes that account for an individual's intensity, direction, and persistence of effort toward attaining a goal.*

since developed more valid explanations of motivation, but you should know these early theories for at least two reasons: (1) They represent a foundation from which contemporary theories have grown, and (2) practicing managers still regularly use these theories and their terminology in explaining employee motivation.

Hierarchy of Needs Theory

It's probably safe to say that the most well-known theory of motivation is Abraham Maslow's **hierarchy of needs**.[6] Maslow hypothesized that within every human being, there exists a hierarchy of five needs:

1. **Physiological.** Includes hunger, thirst, shelter, sex, and other bodily needs
2. **Safety.** Security and protection from physical and emotional harm
3. **Social.** Affection, belongingness, acceptance, and friendship
4. **Esteem.** Internal factors such as self-respect, autonomy, and achievement, and external factors such as status, recognition, and attention
5. **Self-actualization.** Drive to become what one is capable of becoming; includes growth, achieving one's potential, and self-fulfillment

As each of these needs becomes substantially satisfied, the next need becomes dominant. In terms of Exhibit 6-1, the individual moves up the steps of the hierarchy. From the standpoint of motivation, the theory would say that, although no need is ever fully gratified, a substantially satisfied need no longer motivates. So if you want to motivate someone, according to Maslow, you need to understand what level of the hierarchy that person is currently on and focus on satisfying the needs at or above that level.

Maslow separated the five needs into higher and lower orders. Physiological and safety needs were described as **lower-order needs** and social, esteem, and **self-actualization** as **higher-order needs**. The differentiation between the two orders was made on the premise that higher-order needs are satisfied internally (within the person), whereas lower-order needs are predominantly satisfied externally (by things such as pay, union contracts, and tenure).

Maslow's needs theory has received wide recognition, particularly among practicing managers. This can be attributed to the theory's intuitive logic and ease of understanding. Unfortunately, however, research does not validate the theory. Maslow provided no empirical substantiation, and several studies that sought to validate the theory found no support for it.[7]

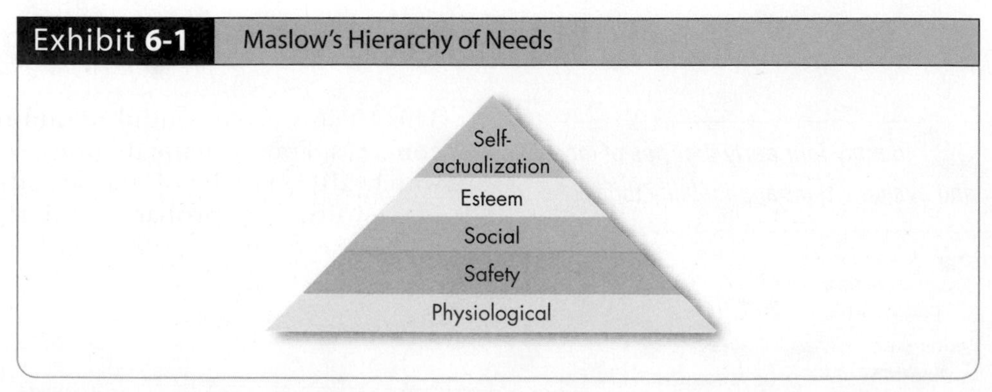

Source: A. H. Maslow, *Motivation and Personality*, 3rd ed., R. D. Frager and J. Fadiman (eds.). © 1997. Adapted by permission of Pearson Education, Inc., Upper Saddle River, New Jersey.

Clayton Alderfer attempted to rework Maslow's need hierarchy to align it more closely with empirical research. His revised need hierarchy is labeled **ERG theory**.[8] Alderfer argued that there are three groups of core needs—*existence* (similar to Maslow's physiological and safety needs), *relatedness* (similar to Maslow's social and status needs), and *growth* (similar to Maslow's esteem needs and self-actualization). Unlike Maslow, Alderfer didn't assume that these needs existed in a rigid hierarchy. An individual could be focusing on all three need categories simultaneously. Despite these differences, empirical research hasn't been any more supportive of ERG theory than of the need hierarchy.[9]

Old theories, especially ones that are intuitively logical, apparently die hard. Although the need hierarchy theory and its terminology have remained popular with practicing managers, there is little evidence that need structures are organized along the dimensions proposed by Maslow or Alderfer, that unsatisfied needs motivate, or that a satisfied need activates movement to a new need level.[10]

Theory X and Theory Y

Douglas McGregor proposed two distinct views of human beings: one basically negative, labeled **Theory X**, and the other basically positive, labeled **Theory Y**.[11] After viewing the way in which managers dealt with employees, McGregor concluded that managers' views of the nature of human beings are based on a certain grouping of assumptions and that managers tend to mold their behavior toward employees according to these assumptions.

Under Theory X, managers believe that employees inherently dislike work and must therefore be directed or even coerced into performing it. In contrast to these negative views about the nature of human beings, under Theory Y, managers assume that employees can view work as being as natural as rest or play, and therefore the average person can learn to accept, and even seek, responsibility.

To understand Theory X and Theory Y more fully, think in terms of Maslow's hierarchy. Theory Y assumes that higher-order needs dominate individuals. McGregor himself held to the belief that Theory Y assumptions were more valid than Theory X. Therefore, he proposed such ideas as participative decision making, responsible and challenging jobs, and good group relations as approaches that would maximize an employee's job motivation.

Unfortunately, there is no evidence to confirm that either set of assumptions is valid or that accepting Theory Y assumptions and altering one's actions accordingly will lead to more motivated workers. OB theories need to have empirical support before we can accept them. Such empirical support is lacking for Theory X and Theory Y as it is for the hierarchy of needs theories.

hierarchy of needs theory *A hierarchy of five needs—physiological, safety, social, esteem, and self-actualization—in which, as each need is substantially satisfied, the next need becomes dominant.*

lower-order needs *Needs that are satisfied externally, such as physiological and safety needs.*

self-actualization *The drive to become what a person is capable of becoming.*

higher-order needs *Needs that are satisfied internally, such as social, esteem, and self-actualization needs.*

ERG theory *A theory that posits three groups of core needs: existence, relatedness, and growth.*

Theory X *The assumption that employees dislike work, are lazy, dislike responsibility, and must be coerced to perform.*

Theory Y *The assumption that employees like work, are creative, seek responsibility, and can exercise self-direction.*

MYTH OR SCIENCE? "Women Are More Motivated to Get Along, and Men Are More Motivated to Get Ahead"

This statement is generally true. Compared with women, men are relatively more motivated to excel at tasks and jobs. Compared with men, women are more motivated to maintain relationships.

Before proceeding any further, though, it is important to note that these gender differences do not mean that every man is more motivated by his career than every woman. There are differences, but think of it like gender and longevity. Women, on average, live longer than men, but in a significant percentage of couples (roughly 45 percent), a husband will outlive his wife. So, there are differences, but you need to resist the human tendency to turn a group difference into a universal generalization or stereotype.

Research indicates that men are more likely to be described by what are called "agentic traits," such as *active, decisive*, and *competitive*. Women are more likely to be described by what are termed "communal" traits, such as *caring, emotional*, and *considerate*. This evidence, however, might reflect gender stereotypes. We might hold stereotypes of the traits of men and women, but that doesn't necessarily prove that men and women are motivated by different things.

Other evidence, though, suggests that this is not just a gender stereotype. A study of 1,398 working Germans revealed that men were more motivated by agentic strivings and women more by communal strivings, and these gender differences did not change over the 17-month course of the study. As a result of these differences, men had higher levels of "objective" career success (income, occupational status) than women. Women, however, were more involved in their families than were men.

We don't know whether these differences are ingrained or socialized. If they are socialized, though, evidence suggests that it begins early. A study of the stories that children aged 4 through 9 told about their lives revealed that girls were more likely to emphasize communion (friendships, helping others, affectionate contact) than were boys.[12] ■

Two-Factor Theory

Psychologist Frederick Herzberg proposed the **two-factor theory**—also called *motivation-hygiene theory*.[13] Believing that an individual's relation to work is basic and that one's attitude toward work can very well determine success or failure, Herzberg investigated the question "What do people want from their jobs?" He asked people to describe, in detail, situations in which they felt exceptionally *good* or *bad* about their jobs. The responses were then tabulated and categorized.

From the categorized responses, Herzberg concluded that the replies people gave when they felt good about their jobs were significantly different from the replies given when they felt bad. As shown in Exhibit 6-2, certain characteristics tend to be consistently related to job satisfaction and others to job dissatisfaction. Intrinsic factors such as advancement, recognition, responsibility, and achievement seem to be related to job satisfaction. Respondents who felt good about their work tended to attribute these factors to themselves. On the other hand, dissatisfied respondents tended to cite extrinsic factors, such as supervision, pay, company policies, and working conditions.

The data suggest, said Herzberg, that the opposite of satisfaction is not dissatisfaction, as was traditionally believed. Removing dissatisfying characteristics from a job does not necessarily make the job satisfying. As illustrated in Exhibit 6-3, Herzberg proposed that his findings indicated the existence of a dual continuum: The opposite of "satisfaction" is "no satisfaction," and the opposite of "dissatisfaction" is "no dissatisfaction."

According to Herzberg, the factors that lead to job satisfaction are separate and distinct from those that lead to job dissatisfaction. Therefore, managers who seek to eliminate factors that can create job dissatisfaction may bring about

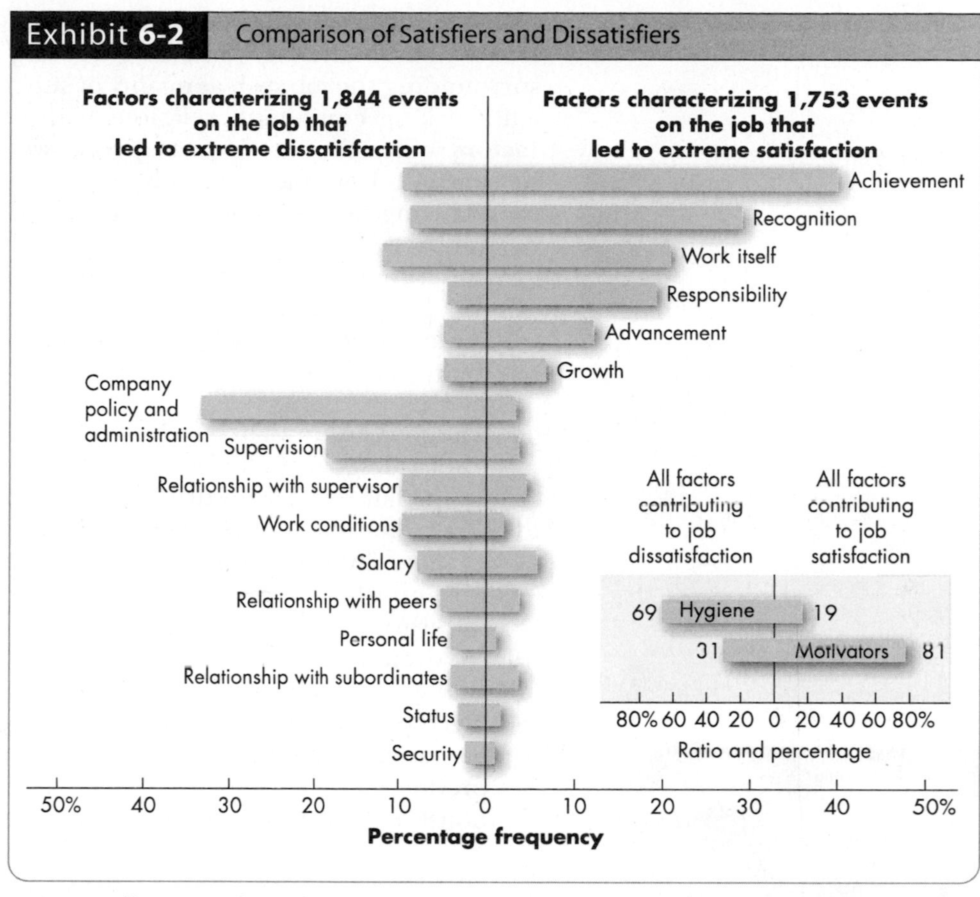

Source: Reprinted by permission of *Harvard Business Review*. "Comparison of Satisfiers and Dissatisfiers." An exhibit from *One More Time: How Do You Motivate Employees?* by Frederick Herzberg, January 2003.

Exhibit 6-3 Contrasting Views of Satisfaction and Dissatisfaction

Traditional view

Satisfaction — Dissatisfaction

Herzberg's view

Motivators

Satisfaction — No satisfaction

Hygiene factors

No dissatisfaction — Dissatisfaction

two-factor theory *A theory that relates intrinsic factors to job satisfaction and associates extrinsic factors with dissatisfaction. Also called* motivation-hygiene *theory.*

peace but not necessarily motivation. They will be placating their workforce rather than motivating workers. As a result, Herzberg characterized conditions surrounding the job such as quality of supervision, pay, company policies, physical working conditions, relations with others, and job security as **hygiene factors**. When they're adequate, people will not be dissatisfied; neither will they be satisfied. If we want to motivate people on their jobs, Herzberg suggested emphasizing factors associated with the work itself or with outcomes directly derived from it, such as promotional opportunities, opportunities for personal growth, recognition, responsibility, and achievement. These are the characteristics that people find intrinsically rewarding.

The two-factor theory has not been well supported in the literature, and it has many detractors.[14] The criticisms of the theory include the following:

1. The procedure that Herzberg used is limited by its methodology. When things are going well, people tend to take credit themselves. Contrarily, they blame failure on the extrinsic environment.
2. The reliability of Herzberg's methodology is questioned. Raters have to make interpretations, so they may contaminate the findings by interpreting one response in one manner while treating a similar response differently.
3. No overall measure of satisfaction was utilized. A person may dislike part of a job yet still think the job is acceptable overall.
4. Herzberg assumed a relationship between satisfaction and productivity, but the research methodology he used looked only at satisfaction and not at productivity. To make such research relevant, one must assume a strong relationship between satisfaction and productivity.

Anne Sweeney is a high achiever. Since joining The Walt Disney Company in 1996, Sweeney has led the transition of the struggling Disney Channel from a premium cable service to a basic network, quintupling the channel's subscriber base. As co-chair of Disney's Media Networks, Sweeney is trying to achieve a turnaround for Disney's ABC Family channel. In addition, when Sweeney became president of ABC Television in 2004, she accepted the challenging goal of lifting the network from its last-place position.

Regardless of the criticisms, Herzberg's theory has been widely read, and few managers are unfamiliar with its recommendations.

It's important to realize that even though we may intuitively *like* a theory, that does not mean that we should accept it. Many managers find need theories intuitively appealing, but remember that at one time the world seemed intuitively flat. Sometimes science backs up intuition, and sometimes it doesn't. In the case of the two-factor theory—as with the need hierarchy and Theory X/Theory Y—it doesn't.

McClelland's Theory of Needs

You have one beanbag, and there are five targets set up in front of you. Each one is progressively farther away and, hence, more difficult to hit. Target A is a cinch. It sits almost within arm's reach. If you hit it, you get $2. Target B is a bit farther out, but about 80 percent of the people who try can hit it. It pays $4. Target C pays $8, and about half the people who try can hit it. Very few people can hit Target D, but the payoff is $16 for those who do. Finally, Target E pays $32, but it's almost impossible to achieve. Which target would you try for? If you selected C, you're likely to be a high achiever. Why? Read on.

McClelland's theory of needs was developed by David McClelland and his associates.[15] The theory focuses on three needs, defined as follows:

- **Need for achievement (nAch)** is the drive to excel, to achieve in relation to a set of standards, to strive to succeed.
- **Need for power (nPow)** is the need to make others behave in a way in which they would not have behaved otherwise.
- **Need for affiliation (nAff)** is the desire for friendly and close interpersonal relationships.

Of the three needs, McClelland and subsequent researchers focused most of their attention on nAch. High achievers perform best when they perceive their probability of success as 0.5—that is, when they estimate that they have a 50–50 chance of success. They dislike gambling with high odds because they get no achievement satisfaction from success that comes by pure chance. Similarly, they dislike low odds (high probability of success) because then there is no challenge to their skills. They like to set goals that require stretching themselves a little.

Relying on an extensive amount of research, we can make some reasonably well-supported predictions of the relationship between achievement need and job performance. Although less research has been done on power and affiliation needs, there are consistent findings there, too. First, when jobs have a high degree of personal responsibility and feedback and an intermediate degree of risk, high achievers are strongly motivated. High achievers, for example, are successful in entrepreneurial activities such as running their own businesses and managing self-contained units within large organizations.[16] Second, a high need to achieve does not necessarily make someone a good manager, especially in large organizations. People with a high achievement need are interested in how well they do personally and not in influencing others to do well. High-nAch salespeople do not necessarily make good sales managers, and the good general manager in a large organization does not typically have a high need to achieve.[17] Third, the needs for affiliation and power tend to be closely related to managerial success. The best managers are high in their need for power and low in their need for affiliation.[18] In fact, a high power motive may be a requirement for managerial effectiveness.[19]

As you might have gathered, of the early theories of motivation, McClelland's has had the best research support. Unfortunately, it has less practical effect than the others. Because McClelland argued that the three needs are subconscious—meaning that we may be high on these needs but not know it—measuring them is not easy. In the most common approach, a trained expert presents pictures to individuals, asks them to tell a story about each, and then scores their responses in terms of the three needs. However, because measuring the needs is time-consuming and expensive, few organizations have been willing to invest time and resources in measuring McClelland's concept.

Contemporary Theories of Motivation

The previously described theories are well known but, unfortunately, have either not held up well under close examination or fallen out of favor. However, there are a number of contemporary theories, and they have one thing in common: Each has a reasonable degree of valid supporting documentation.

hygiene factors *Factors—such as company policy and administration, supervision, and salary—that, when adequate in a job, placate workers. When these factors are adequate, people will not be dissatisfied.*

McClelland's theory of needs *A theory which states that achievement, power, and affiliation are three important needs that help explain motivation.*

need for achievement (nAch) *The drive to excel, to achieve in relationship to a set of standards, and to strive to succeed.*

need for power (nPow) *The need to make others behave in a way in which they would not have behaved otherwise.*

need for affiliation (nAff) *The desire for friendly and close interpersonal relationships.*

Of course, this doesn't mean that the theories we are about to introduce are unquestionably right. We call them "contemporary theories" not because they were all developed recently but because they represent the current state of thinking in explaining employee motivation.

Cognitive Evaluation Theory

"It's strange," said Kenda. "I started working as a volunteer. I put in 15 hours a week helping people adopt pets. And I loved coming to work. Then, 3 months ago, they hired me full-time at $11 an hour. I'm doing the same work I did before. But I'm not finding it near as much fun."

3 Apply the predictions of cognitive evaluation theory to intrinsic and extrinsic rewards.

There's an explanation for Kenda's reaction. It's called **cognitive evaluation theory**, which proposes that the introduction of extrinsic rewards, such as pay, for work effort that was previously intrinsically rewarding due to the pleasure associated with the content of the work itself tends to decrease overall motivation.[20] Cognitive evaluation theory has been extensively researched, and a large number of studies have supported it.[21] As we'll show, the major implications of this theory relate to work rewards.

Historically, motivation theorists generally assumed that intrinsic rewards such as interesting work were independent of extrinsic rewards such as high pay. But cognitive evaluation theory suggests otherwise. It argues that when extrinsic rewards are used by organizations as payoffs for superior performance, the intrinsic rewards, which are derived from individuals doing what they like, are reduced. In other words, when extrinsic rewards are given to someone for performing an interesting task, it causes intrinsic interest in the task itself to decline.

Why would such an outcome occur? The popular explanation is that an individual experiences a loss of control over her own behavior so that the previous

OB In the News

Paying Employees Not to Work

There is no better illustration of the woes of the Detroit, Michigan automakers than the fact that each of "Big Three" has been forced to pay employees for work they *don't* do. This pay has taken two major forms.

First, Ford and General Motors have offered employees cash payments to leave their jobs. The employees are unionized, and their labor agreements guarantee full employment, so the companies must offer buyout deals that workers will accept. Because, in the words of a labor relations specialist, employees "almost see their job as a property right," the cash payments have been substantial—often in the six-figures range. Ford and GM also pay workers to go to college, paying half their salary and up to $15,000 per year in tuition, as long as they quit when they're done.

A second, more controversial, policy is the "Jobs Bank" in which Ford and GM have paid more than 15,000 employees full salary and benefits to produce nothing. Although some of these employees are paid to perform some company-approved activity, such as volunteer work, many report to what is called "the rubber room"—a windowless old storage shed—where their job is to, literally, do nothing. The Jobs Bank is estimated to cost Ford and GM between $1.4 and $2 billion each year. Why does it exist? It was negotiated as part of the automakers' agreement to full employment policies in the 1980s.

As expensive as the Jobs Bank has proven to be for the automakers, it is not exactly motivating for some employees. Jerry Mellon said time in the rubber room "makes you want to bang your head against the wall." Others, though, love it. Tom Adams said, "The Jobs Bank has been wonderful for me. It's doing what it is supposed to do, which is make it so I won't be a burden on society."

In 2007 GM and Ford entered into new contracts with the UAW. Despite some restrictions, the jobs banks lives on.

Sources: M. Maynard and J. W. Peters, "Getting Auto Workers to Leave a Golden Job," *New York Times*, March 22, 2006, pp. C1, C8; and J. McCracken, "Detroit's Symbol of Dysfunction: Paying Employees Not to Work," *Wall Street Journal*, March 1, 2006, pp. A1, A12.

intrinsic motivation diminishes. Furthermore, the elimination of extrinsic rewards can produce a shift—from an external to an internal explanation—in an individual's perception of causation of why she works on a task. If you're reading a novel a week because your English literature instructor requires you to, you can attribute your reading behavior to an external source. However, after the course is over, if you find yourself continuing to read a novel a week, your natural inclination is to say, "I must enjoy reading novels because I'm still reading one a week."

If the cognitive evaluation theory is valid, it should have major implications for managerial practices. It has been a truism among compensation specialists for years that if pay or other extrinsic rewards are to be effective motivators, they should be made contingent on an individual's performance. But cognitive evaluation theorists would argue that this will only tend to decrease the internal satisfaction that the individual receives from doing the job. In fact, if cognitive evaluation theory is correct, it would make sense to make an individual's pay *noncontingent* on performance in order to avoid decreasing intrinsic motivation.

We noted earlier that the cognitive evaluation theory has been supported in a number of studies. Yet it has also been met with attacks, specifically on the

Exhibit 6-4

Source: From the *Wall Street Journal*, February 8, 1995. Reprinted with permission of Cartoon Features Syndicate.

cognitive evaluation theory *A theory that states that allocating extrinsic rewards for behavior that had been previously intrinsically rewarding tends to decrease the overall level of motivation.*

methodology used in these studies[22] and in the interpretation of the findings.[23] But where does this theory stand today? Can we say that when organizations use extrinsic motivators such as pay and promotions and verbal rewards to stimulate workers' performance, they do so at the expense of reducing intrinsic interest and motivation in the work being done? The answer is not a simple "yes" or a simple "no."

Extrinsic rewards that are verbal (for example, receiving praise from a supervisor or coworker) or tangible (for example, money) can actually have different effects on individuals' intrinsic motivation. That is, verbal rewards increase intrinsic motivation, whereas tangible rewards undermine it. When people are told they will receive a tangible reward, they come to count on it and focus more on the reward than on the task.[24] Verbal rewards, however, seem to keep people focused on the task and encourage them to do it better.

A recent outgrowth of the cognitive evaluation theory is **self-concordance**, which considers the degree to which peoples' reasons for pursuing goals are consistent with their interests and core values. For example, if individuals pursue goals because of an intrinsic interest, they are more likely to attain their goals and are happy even if they do not attain them. Why? Because the process of striving toward them is fun. In contrast, people who pursue goals for extrinsic reasons (money, status, or other benefits) are less likely to attain their goals and are less happy even when they do achieve them. Why? Because the goals are less meaningful to them.[25] OB research suggests that people who pursue work goals for intrinsic reasons are more satisfied with their jobs, feel like they fit into their organizations better, and may perform better.[26]

How Managers Evaluate Their Employees Depends on Culture

A recent study found interesting differences in managers' perceptions of employee motivation. The study examined managers from three distinct cultural regions: Asia, Latin America, and North America. The results of the study revealed that North American managers perceive their employees as being motivated more by extrinsic factors (for example, pay) than intrinsic factors (for example, doing meaningful work). Asian managers perceive their employees as being motivated by both extrinsic and intrinsic factors, while Latin American managers perceive their employees as being motivated by intrinsic factors.

Even more interesting, these differences affected evaluations of employee performance. As expected, Asian managers focused on both types of motivation when evaluating their employees' performance, and Latin American managers focused on intrinsic motivation. Oddly, North American managers, though believing that employees are motivated primarily by extrinsic factors, actually focused more on *intrinsic* factors when evaluating employee performance. Why the paradox? One explanation is that North Americans value uniqueness, so any deviation from the norm—such as being perceived as being unusually high in intrinsic motivation—is rewarded.

Latin American managers' focus on intrinsic motivation when evaluating employees may be related to a cultural norm termed *simpatía*, a tradition that compels employees to display their internal feelings. Consequently, Latin American managers are more sensitized to these displays and can more easily notice their employees' intrinsic motivation.

So, from an employee perspective, the cultural background of your manager can play an important role in how you are evaluated.

Source: Based on S. E. DeVoe and S. S. Iyengar, "Managers' Theories of Subordinates: A Cross-Cultural Examination of Manager Perceptions of Motivation and Appraisal of Performance," *Organizational Behavior and Human Decision Processes,* January 2004, pp. 47–61.

What does all of this mean? It means choose your job carefully. Make sure you're choosing to do something for reasons other than extrinsic rewards. For organizations, managers need to provide intrinsic rewards in addition to extrinsic incentives. In other words, managers need to make the work interesting, provide recognition, and support employee growth and development. Employees who feel that what they do is within their control and a result of free choice are likely to be more motivated by their work and committed to their employers.[27]

Goal-Setting Theory

4 Compare and contrast goal-setting theory and management by objectives.

Gene Broadwater, the coach of a cross-country running team, gave his squad these last words before they approached the starting line for the league championship race: "Each one of you is physically ready. Now, get out there and do your best. No one can ever ask more of you than that."

You've heard the sentiment a number of times yourself: "Just do your best. That's all anyone can ask for." But what does "do your best" mean? Do we ever know if we've achieved that vague goal? Would the cross-country runners have recorded faster times if Coach Broadwater had given each a specific goal to shoot for? Might you have done better in math class if your parents had said, "You should strive for 85 percent or higher on all your work in math" rather than telling you to "do your best"? The research on **goal-setting theory** addresses these issues, and the findings, as you'll see, are impressive in terms of the effect that goal specificity, challenge, and feedback have on performance.

In the late 1960s, Edwin Locke proposed that intentions to work toward a goal are a major source of work motivation.[28] That is, goals tell an employee what needs to be done and how much effort will need to be expended.[29] The evidence strongly supports the value of goals. More to the point, we can say that specific goals increase performance; that difficult goals, when accepted, result in higher performance than do easy goals; and that feedback leads to higher performance than does nonfeedback.[30]

Specific goals produce a higher level of output than does the generalized goal of "do your best." Why? The specificity of the goal itself seems to act as an internal stimulus. For instance, when a trucker commits to making 12 round-trip hauls between Toronto and Montreal, each week, this intention gives him a specific objective to try to attain. We can say that, all things being equal, the trucker with a specific goal will outperform a counterpart operating with no goals or the generalized goal of "do your best."

If factors such as acceptance of the goals are held constant, we can also state that the more difficult the goal, the higher the level of performance. Of course, it's logical to assume that easier goals are more likely to be accepted. But once a hard task is accepted, the employee can be expected to exert a high level of effort to try to achieve it.

But why are people motivated by difficult goals?[31] First, difficult goals direct our attention to the task at hand and away from irrelevant distractions. Challenging goals get our attention and thus tend to help us focus. Second, difficult goals energize us because we have to work harder to attain them. For

self-concordance *The degree to which a person's reasons for pursuing a goal is consistent with the person's interests and core values.*

goal-setting theory *A theory that says that specific and difficult goals, with feedback, lead to higher performance.*

example, think of your study habits. Do you study as hard for an easy exam as you do for a difficult one? Probably not. Third, when goals are difficult, people persist in trying to attain them. Finally, difficult goals lead us to discover strategies that help us perform the job or task more effectively. If we have to struggle for a way to solve a difficult problem, we often think of a better way to go about it.

People do better when they get feedback on how well they are progressing toward their goals because feedback helps to identify discrepancies between what they have done and what they want to do; that is, feedback acts to guide behavior. But all feedback is not equally potent. Self-generated feedback—for which employees are able to monitor their own progress—has been shown to be a more powerful motivator than externally generated feedback.[32]

If employees have the opportunity to participate in the setting of their own goals, will they try harder? The evidence is mixed regarding the superiority of participative over assigned goals.[33] In some cases, participatively set goals elicited superior performance, while in other cases, individuals performed best when assigned goals by their boss. But a major advantage of participation may be in increasing acceptance of the goal itself as a desirable one toward which to work.[34] As we'll note shortly, commitment is important. If participation isn't used, then the individual assigning the goal needs to clearly explain the purpose and importance of the goal.[35]

Are there any contingencies in goal-setting theory, or can we take it as a universal truth that difficult and specific goals will *always* lead to higher performance? In addition to feedback, three other factors have been found to influence the goals–performance relationship: goal commitment, task characteristics, and national culture.

Goal-setting theory presupposes that an individual is committed to the goal; that is, an individual is determined not to lower or abandon the goal. Behaviorally, this means that an individual (1) believes he or she can achieve the goal and (2) wants to achieve it.[36] Goal commitment is most likely to occur when goals are made public, when the individual has an internal locus of control (see Chapter 4), and when the goals are self-set rather than assigned.[37] Research indicates that goal-setting theory doesn't work equally well on all tasks. The evidence suggests that goals seem to have a more substantial effect on performance when tasks are simple rather than complex, well learned rather than novel, and independent rather than interdependent.[38] On interdependent tasks, group goals are preferable.

Finally, goal-setting theory is culture bound. It's well adapted to countries such as Canada and the United States because its key components align reasonably well with North American cultures. It assumes that employees will be reasonably independent (that is, not too high a score on power distance), that managers and employees will seek challenging goals (that is, low in uncertainty avoidance), and that performance is considered important by both (that is, high in achievement). So we can't expect goal setting to necessarily lead to higher employee performance in countries such as Portugal or Chile, where the opposite conditions exist.

Our overall conclusion is that intentions—as articulated in terms of difficult and specific goals—are a potent motivating force. The motivating power of goal-setting theory has been demonstrated on more than 100 tasks involving more than 40,000 participants in many different kinds of industries—from lumber, to insurance, to automobiles. Basically, setting specific, challenging goals for employees is the best thing managers can do to improve performance.

Hasso Plattner, co-founder of the German software firm SAP, motivates employees by setting stretch goals. Plattner set a shockingly optimistic goal of 15 percent annual growth for SAP's software license revenues. Employees responded by achieving an even higher growth rate of 18 percent. Plattner set another stretch goal by announcing a bonus plan that would pay $381 million to hundreds of managers and key employees if they could double the company's market capitalization, from a starting point of $57 billion, by the end of 2010. For Plattner, setting stretch goals is a way to inject entrepreneurial energy into the 35-year-old company.

Self Assessment Library

WHAT ARE MY COURSE PERFORMANCE GOALS?

In the Self-Assessment Library (available on CD or online), take assessment I.C.5 (What Are My Course Performance Goals?).

Implementing Goal-Setting Goal-setting theory has an impressive base of research support. But as a manager, how do you make it operational? That's often left up to the individual manager or leader. Some managers explicitly set aggressive performance targets—what General Electric called "stretch goals." For example, some CEOs, such as Procter & Gamble's A. G. Laffey and SAP's Hasso Plattner, are known for the demanding performance goals they set. The problem with leaving it up to the individual manager is that, in many cases, managers don't set goals. A recent survey revealed that when asked whether their job had clearly defined goals, only a minority of employees agreed.[39]

A more systematic way to utilize goal setting is with a management by objectives program. **Management by objectives (MBO)** emphasizes participatively set goals that are tangible, verifiable, and measurable. As depicted in Exhibit 6-5, the organization's overall objectives are translated into specific objectives for each succeeding level (that is, divisional, departmental, individual) in the organization. But because lower-unit managers jointly participate in setting their own goals,

management by objectives (MBO) *A program that encompasses specific goals, participatively set, for an explicit time period, with feedback on goal progress.*

Exhibit 6-5 Cascading of Objectives

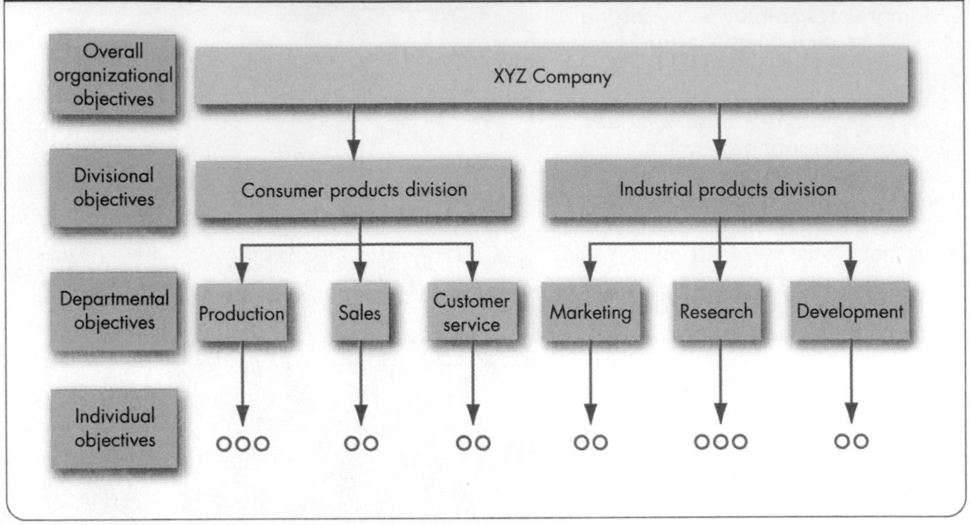

Overall organizational objectives: XYZ Company

Divisional objectives: Consumer products division; Industrial products division

Departmental objectives: Production; Sales; Customer service; Marketing; Research; Development

Individual objectives: OOO; OO; OO; OO; OOO; OO

MBO works from the "bottom up" as well as from the "top down." The result is a hierarchy that links objectives at one level to those at the next level. And for the individual employee, MBO provides specific personal performance objectives.

Four ingredients are common to MBO programs: goal specificity, participation in decision making (including participation in the setting of goals or objectives), an explicit time period, and performance feedback.[40] Many of the elements in MBO programs match propositions of goal-setting theory. For example, having an explicit time period to accomplish objectives matches goal-setting theory's emphasis on goal specificity. Similarly, we noted earlier that feedback about goal progress is a critical element of goal-setting theory. The only area of possible disagreement between MBO and goal-setting theory relates to the issue of participation: MBO strongly advocates it, whereas goal-setting theory demonstrates that managers assigning goals is usually just as effective.

You'll find MBO programs in many business, health care, educational, government, and nonprofit organizations.[41] MBO's popularity should not be construed to mean that it always works. There are a number of documented cases in which MBO has been implemented but failed to meet management's expectations.[42] When MBO doesn't work, the culprits tend to be factors such as unrealistic expectations regarding results, lack of commitment by top management, and an inability or unwillingness of management to allocate rewards based on goal accomplishment. Failures can also arise out of cultural incompatibilities. For instance, Fujitsu recently scrapped its MBO-type program because management found it didn't fit well with the Japanese culture's emphasis on minimizing risk and emphasizing long-term goals.

Self-Efficacy Theory

Self-efficacy (also known as *social cognitive theory* or *social learning theory*) refers to an individual's belief that he or she is capable of performing a task.[43] The higher your self-efficacy, the more confidence you have in your ability to succeed in a task. So, in difficult situations, people with low self-efficacy are more likely to lessen their effort or give up altogether, while those with high self-efficacy will try harder to master the challenge.[44] In addition, individuals high in self-efficacy seem to respond to negative feedback with increased effort and motivation, while those low in self-efficacy are likely to

5 *Contrast reinforcement theory and goal-setting theory.*

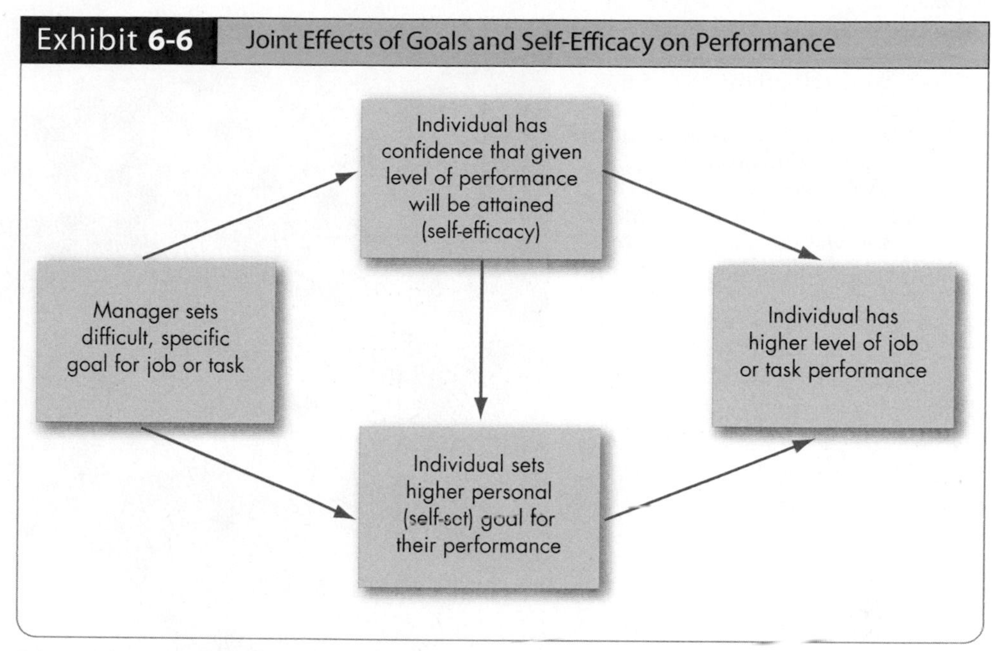

Source: Based on E. A. Locke and G. P. Latham, "Building a Practically Useful Theory of Goal Setting and Task Motivation: A 35-Year Odyssey," *American Psychologist*, September 2002, pp. 705–717.

lessen their effort when given negative feedback.[45] How can managers help their employees achieve high levels of self-efficacy? By bringing together goal-setting theory and self-efficacy theory.

Goal-setting theory and self-efficacy theory don't compete with one another; rather, they complement each other. As Exhibit 6-6 shows, when a manager sets difficult goals for employees, this leads employees to have a higher level of self-efficacy and also leads them to set higher goals for their own performance. Why is this the case? Research has shown that setting difficult goals for people communicates confidence. For example, imagine that your boss sets a high goal for you, and you learn it is higher than the goals she has set for your coworkers. How would you interpret this? As long as you didn't feel you were being picked on, you would probably think, "Well, I guess my boss thinks I'm capable of performing better than others." This then sets into motion a psychological process in which you're more confident in yourself (higher self-efficacy) and you set higher personal goals, causing you to perform better both in the workplace and outside it.

The researcher who developed self-efficacy theory, Albert Bandura, argues that there are four ways self-efficacy can be increased:[46]

1. Enactive mastery
2. Vicarious modeling
3. Verbal persuasion
4. Arousal

According to Bandura, the most important source of increasing self-efficacy is what he calls *enactive mastery*—that is, gaining relevant experience with the task

self-efficacy *An individual's belief that he or she is capable of performing a task.*

The U.S. Coast Guard illustrates the importance of enactive mastery in increasing self-efficacy. Since the September 11 terrorist attacks, the duties of the Coast Guard have expanded in protecting U.S. ports, ships, and waterways. The Coast Guard men and women shown here participate in a tactical law enforcement training program by playing out a hostage scenario. Practicing and building their skills in boarding ships helps the Coast Guard personnel increase their confidence to succeed at their task.

or job. If you've been able to do the job successfully in the past, then you're more confident you'll be able to do it in the future.

The second source is *vicarious modeling*—or becoming more confident because you see someone else doing the task. For example, if your friend loses weight, then it increases your confidence that you can lose weight, too. Vicarious modeling is most effective when you see yourself as similar to the person you are observing. Watching Tiger Woods play a difficult golf shot might not increase your confidence in being able to play the shot yourself, but if you watch a golfer with a handicap similar to yours, it's persuasive.

The third source is *verbal persuasion*, which is becoming more confident because someone convinces you that you have the skills necessary to be successful. Motivational speakers use this tactic a lot.

Finally, Bandura argues that *arousal* increases self-efficacy. Arousal leads to an energized state, which drives a person to complete a task. The person gets "psyched up" and performs better. But when arousal is not relevant, then arousal hurts performance. In other words, if the task is something that requires a steady, lower-key perspective (say, carefully editing a manuscript), arousal may in fact hurt performance.

What are the OB implications of self-efficacy theory? Well, it's a matter of applying Bandura's sources of self-efficacy to the work setting. Training programs often make use of enactive mastery by having people practice and build their skills. In fact, one of the reasons training works is because it increases self-efficacy.[47]

The best way for a manager to use verbal persuasion is through the *Pygmalion effect* or the *Galatea effect*. As discussed in Chapter 5, the Pygmalion effect is a form of a self-fulfilling prophecy in which believing something to be true can make it true. In the Pygmalion effect, self-efficacy is increased by communicating to an individual's teacher or supervisor that the person is of high ability. For example, studies were done in which teachers were told their students had very high IQ scores (when in fact they had a range of IQs—some high, some low, and some in between). Consistent with a Pygmalion effect, the teachers spent more time with the students they *thought* were smart, gave them more challenging assignments, and expected more of them—all of which led to higher student self-efficacy and better student grades.[48] This also has been used in the workplace.[49] The Galatea effect occurs when high performance expectations are communicated directly to an employee. For example, sailors who were told, in a convincing manner, that they would not get seasick in fact were much less likely to get seasick.[50]

Note that intelligence and personality are absent from Bandura's list. A lot of research shows that intelligence and personality (especially conscientiousness and emotional stability) can increase self-efficacy.[51] Those individual traits are so strongly related to self-efficacy (people who are intelligent, conscientiousness, and emotionally stable are much more likely to have high self-efficacy than those who score low on these characteristics) that some researchers would argue that self-efficacy does not exist.[52] What this means is that self-efficacy may simply be a by-product in a smart person with a confident personality, and the term *self-efficacy* is superfluous and unnecessary. Although Bandura strongly disagrees with this conclusion, more research on the issue is needed.

Reinforcement Theory

A counterpoint to goal-setting theory is **reinforcement theory**. The former is a cognitive approach, proposing that an individual's purposes direct his action. Reinforcement theory takes a behavioristic approach, arguing that reinforcement conditions behavior. The two theories are clearly at odds philosophically. Reinforcement theorists see behavior as being environmentally caused. You need not be concerned, they would argue, with internal cognitive events; what controls behavior is reinforcers—any consequences that, when immediately following responses, increase the probability that the behavior will be repeated.

6 *Demonstrate how organizational justice is a refinement of equity theory.*

Reinforcement theory ignores the inner state of the individual and concentrates solely on what happens to a person when he or she takes some action. Because it does not concern itself with what initiates behavior, it is not, strictly speaking, a theory of motivation. But it does provide a powerful means of analysis of what controls behavior, and for this reason it is typically considered in discussions of motivation.[53]

We discussed the reinforcement process in detail in Chapter 2. Although it's clear that so-called reinforcers such as pay can motivate people, it's just as clear that for people the process is much more complicated than stimulus–response. In its pure form, reinforcement theory ignores feelings, attitudes, expectations, and other cognitive variables that are known to affect behavior. In fact, some researchers look at the same experiments that reinforcement theorists use to support their position and interpret the findings in a cognitive framework.[54]

Reinforcement is undoubtedly an important influence on behavior, but few scholars are prepared to argue that it is the only influence. The behaviors you engage in at work and the amount of effort you allocate to each task are affected by the consequences that follow from your behavior. For instance, if you're consistently reprimanded for outproducing your colleagues, you'll likely reduce your productivity. But your lower productivity may also be explained in terms of goals, inequity, or expectancies.

reinforcement theory *A theory that says that behavior is a function of its consequences.*

In perceiving inequity in pay, American Airlines flight attendants used an *other–inside* referent comparison when comparing their pay to that of the airline's managers. Flight attendants marched in protest after the company earned a profit of $230 million and decided to give 874 executives more than $200 million in bonuses. But almost 80,000 other employees received no bonuses and continued to receive reduced pay and benefits per an agreement the flight attendants had made 3 years earlier to keep the company from declaring bankruptcy.

Equity Theory

8 *Apply the key tenets of expectancy theory to motivating employees.*

Jane Pearson graduated last year from the Oxford Brookes University Business School with a degree in accounting. After interviews with a number of organizations on campus, she accepted a position with a top public accounting firm and was assigned to the firm's London office. Jane was very pleased with the offer she received: challenging work with a prestigious firm, an excellent opportunity to gain valuable experience, and the highest salary any accounting major at her university was offered last year—£2,396 per month. But Jane was the top student in her class; she was articulate and mature, and she fully expected to receive a commensurate salary.

Twelve months have passed since Jane joined her employer. The work has proved to be as challenging and satisfying as she had hoped. Her employer is extremely pleased with her performance; in fact, Jane recently received a £100-per-month raise. However, Jane's motivational level has dropped dramatically in the past few weeks. Why? Her employer has just hired a fresh college graduate, who lacks the 1-year experience Jane has gained, for £2,422 per month—£25 more than Jane now makes! Jane is irate. She is even talking about looking for another job.

Jane's situation illustrates the role that equity plays in motivation. Employees make comparisons of their job inputs (for example, effort, experience, education, competence) and outcomes (for example, salary levels, raises, recognition) relative to those of others. We perceive what we get from a job situation (outcomes) in relation to what we put into it (inputs), and then we compare our outcome–input ratio with the outcome–input ratios of relevant others. This is shown in Exhibit 6-7. If we perceive our ratio to be equal to that of the relevant others with whom we compare ourselves, a state of equity is said to exist; we perceive our situation as fair and that justice prevails. When we see the ratio as unequal, we experience equity tension. When we see ourselves as underrewarded, the tension creates anger; when we see ourselves as overrewarded, the tension creates guilt. J. Stacy Adams has proposed that this negative state of tension provides the motivation to do something to correct it.[55]

Exhibit 6-7 Equity Theory

Ratio Comparisons*	Perception
$\frac{O}{I_A} < \frac{O}{I_B}$	Inequity due to being underrewarded
$\frac{O}{I_A} = \frac{O}{I_B}$	Equity
$\frac{O}{I_A} > \frac{O}{I_B}$	Inequity due to being overrewarded

*Where $\frac{O}{I_A}$ represents the employee; and $\frac{O}{I_B}$ represents relevant others

The referent that an employee selects adds to the complexity of **equity theory**.[56] There are four referent comparisons that an employee can use:

1. *Self–inside.* An employee's experiences in a different position inside the employee's current organization
2. *Self–outside.* An employee's experiences in a situation or position outside the employee's current organization
3. *Other–inside.* Another individual or group of individuals inside the employee's organization
4. *Other–outside.* Another individual or group of individuals outside the employee's organization

Employees might compare themselves to friends, neighbors, coworkers, or colleagues in other organizations or compare their present job with past jobs they themselves have had. Which referent an employee chooses will be influenced by the information the employee holds about referents as well as by the attractiveness of the referent. This has led to focusing on four moderating variables: gender, length of tenure, level in the organization, and amount of education or professionalism.[57]

Research shows that both men and women prefer same-sex comparisons. The research also demonstrates that women are typically paid less than men in comparable jobs and have lower pay expectations than men for the same work.[58] So a woman who uses another woman as a referent tends to calculate a lower comparative standard. This leads us to conclude that employees in jobs that are not sex segregated will make more cross-sex comparisons than those in jobs that are either male or female dominated. This also suggests that if women are tolerant of lower pay, it may be due to the comparative standard they use. Of course, employers' stereotypes about women (for example, the belief that women are less committed to the organization or that "women's work" is less valuable) also may contribute to the pay gap.[59]

Employees with short tenure in their current organizations tend to have little information about others inside the organization, so they rely on their own personal experiences. However, employees with long tenure rely more heavily on coworkers for comparison. Upper-level employees, those in the professional

equity theory *A theory that says that individuals compare their job inputs and outcomes with those of others and then respond to eliminate any inequities.*

ranks, and those with higher amounts of education tend to have better information about people in other organizations. Therefore, these types of employees will make more other–outside comparisons.

Based on equity theory, when employees perceive inequity, they can be predicted to make one of six choices:[60]

1. Change their inputs (for example, exert less effort)
2. Change their outcomes (for example, individuals paid on a piece-rate basis can increase their pay by producing a higher quantity of units of lower quality)
3. Distort perceptions of self (for example, "I used to think I worked at a moderate pace, but now I realize that I work a lot harder than everyone else.")
4. Distort perceptions of others (for example, "Geert's job isn't as desirable as I previously thought it was.")
5. Choose a different referent (for example, "I may not make as much as my brother-in-law, but I'm doing a lot better than my Dad did when he was my age.")
6. Leave the field (for example, quit the job)

The theory establishes the following propositions relating to inequitable pay:

A. *Given payment by time, overrewarded employees will produce more than will equitably paid employees.* Hourly and salaried employees will generate high quantity or quality of production in order to increase the input side of the ratio and bring about equity.

B. *Given payment by quantity of production, overrewarded employees will produce fewer, but higher-quality, units than will equitably paid employees.* Individuals paid on a piece-rate basis will increase their effort to achieve equity, which can result in greater quality or quantity. However, increases in quantity will only increase inequity because every unit produced results in further overpayment. Therefore, effort is directed toward increasing quality rather than increasing quantity.

C. *Given payment by time, underrewarded employees will produce less or poorer quality of output.* Effort will be decreased, which will bring about lower productivity or poorer-quality output than equitably paid subjects.

D. *Given payment by quantity of production, underrewarded employees will produce a large number of low-quality units in comparison with equitably paid employees.* Employees on piece-rate pay plans can bring about equity because trading off quality of output for quantity will result in an increase in rewards, with little or no increase in contributions.

Some of these propositions have been supported, but others haven't.[61] First, inequities created by overpayment do not seem to have a very significant impact on behavior in most work situations. Apparently, people have a great deal more tolerance of overpayment inequities than of underpayment inequities or are better able to rationalize them. It's pretty damaging to a theory when one-half of the equation (how people respond to overreward) falls apart. Second, not all people are equity sensitive.[62] For example, there is a small part of the working population who actually prefer that their outcome–input ratios be less than the referent comparison's. Predictions from equity theory are not likely to be very accurate with these "benevolent types."

It's also important to note that while most research on equity theory has focused on pay, employees seem to look for equity in the distribution of other organizational rewards. For instance, it has been shown that the use of high-status job titles as well as large and lavishly furnished offices may function as outcomes for some employees in their equity equation.[63]

Finally, recent research has been directed at expanding what is meant by *equity*, or *fairness*.[64] Historically, equity theory focused on **distributive justice**, which is the employee's perceived fairness of the *amount and allocation* of rewards among individuals. But increasingly equity is thought of from the standpoint of **organizational justice**, which we define as an overall perception of what is fair in the workplace. Employees perceive their organizations as just when they believe the outcomes they have received and the way in which the outcomes were received are fair. One key element of organizational justice is an individual's *perception* of justice. In other words, under organizational justice, fairness or equity can be subjective, and it resides in the perception of the person. What one person may see as unfair another may see as perfectly appropriate. In general, people have an egocentric, or self-serving, bias. They see allocations or procedure favoring themselves as fair.[65] For example, in a recent poll, 61 percent of respondents said that they are personally paying their fair share of taxes, but an almost equal number (54 percent) of those polled felt the system as a whole is unfair, saying that some people skirt the system.[66] Fairness often resides in the eye of the beholder, and we tend to be fairly self-serving about what we see as fair.

Beyond its focus on perceptions of fairness, the other key element of organizational justice is the view that justice is multidimensional. Organizational justice argues that distributive justice is important. For example, how much we get paid relative to what we think we should be paid (distributive justice) is obviously important. But, according to justice researchers, *how* we get paid is just as important. Exhibit 6-8 shows a model of organizational justice.

Beyond distributive justice, the key addition under organizational justice was **procedural justice**—which is the perceived fairness of the *process* used to determine the distribution of rewards. Two key elements of procedural justice are process control and explanations. *Process control* is the opportunity to present one's point of view about desired outcomes to decision makers. *Explanations* are clear reasons for the outcome that management gives to a person. Thus, for employees to see a process as fair, they need to feel that they have some control over the outcome and feel that they were given an adequate explanation about why the outcome occurred. Also, for procedural fairness, it's important that a manager is *consistent* (across people and over time), is *unbiased*, makes decisions based on *accurate information*, and is *open to appeals*.[67]

Research shows that the effects of procedural justice become more important when distributive justice is lacking. This makes sense. If we don't get what we want, we tend to focus on *why*. For example, if your supervisor gives a cushy office to a coworker instead of to you, you're much more focused on your supervisor's treatment of you than if you had gotten the office. Explanations are beneficial when they take the form of post hoc excuses (for example, admitting that the act is unfavorable but denying sole responsibility for it) rather than justifications (for example, accepting full responsibility but denying that the outcome is unfavorable or inappropriate).[68] In the office example, an excuse would be "I know this is bad. I wanted to give you

distributive justice *Perceived fairness of the amount and allocation of rewards among individuals.*

organizational justice *An overall perception of what is fair in the workplace, composed of distributive, procedural, and interactional justice.*

procedural justice *The perceived fairness of the process used to determine the distribution of rewards.*

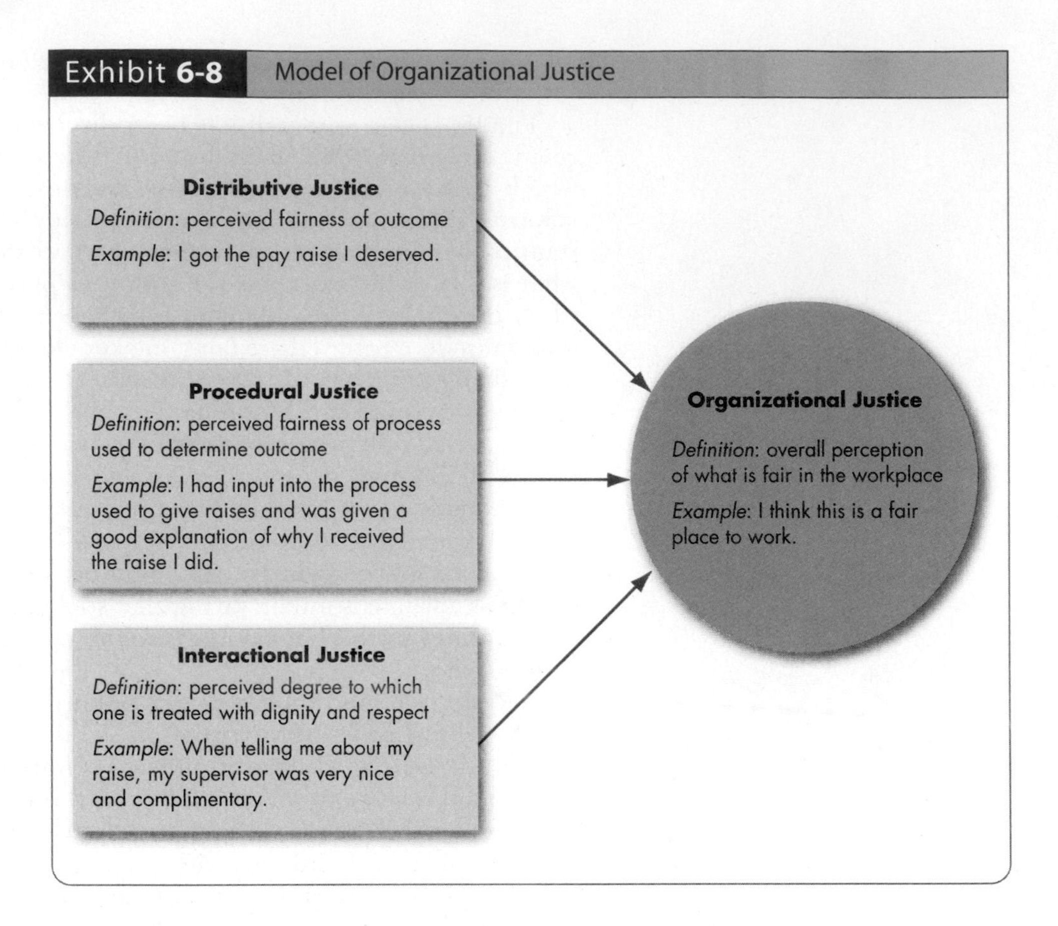

the office, but it was not my decision" and a justification would be "Yes, I decided to give the office to Sam, but having the corner office is not that big of a deal."

A recent addition to research on organizational justice is **interactional justice**, which is an individual's perception of the degree to which she is treated with dignity, concern, and respect. When people are treated in an unjust manner (at least in their own eyes), they respond by retaliating (for example, bad-mouthing a supervisor).[69] Because interactional justice or injustice is intimately tied to the conveyer of the information (usually one's supervisor), whereas procedural injustice often results from impersonal policies, we would expect perceptions of injustice to be more closely related to one's supervisor. Generally, that's what the evidence suggests.[70]

Of these three forms of justice, distributive justice is most strongly related to satisfaction with outcomes (for example, satisfaction with pay) and organizational commitment. Procedural justice relates most strongly to job satisfaction, employee trust, withdrawal from the organization, job performance, and citizenship behaviors. There is less evidence on interactional justice.[71]

Managers can take several steps to foster employees' perceptions of fairness. First, they should realize that employees are especially sensitive to unfairness in procedures when bad news has to be communicated (that is, when distributive justice is low). Thus, when managers have bad news to communicate, it's especially important to openly share information about how allocation decisions are made, follow consistent and unbiased procedures, and engage in similar practices to increase the perception of procedural justice. Second, when addressing perceived injustices, managers need to focus their actions on the source of the problem. For example, in one weekend in June 2007, Northwest Airlines was forced to cancel 352 flights because many pilots and flight attendants called in sick to protest their pay. The pilot's union instructed the pilots: "Fly safe. Fly the contract. Don't fly sick. Don't fly fatigued. Don't fly hungry." In a situation like this, Northwest should realize that the remedy needs to be tangible rather than apologies or changes in procedures.[72]

Expectancy Theory

8 *Compare contemporary theories of motivation.*

Currently, one of the most widely accepted explanations of motivation is Victor Vroom's **expectancy theory**.[73] Although it has its critics, most of the evidence supports the theory.[74]

Expectancy theory argues that the strength of a tendency to act in a certain way depends on the strength of an expectation that the act will be followed by a given outcome and on the attractiveness of that outcome to the individual. In more practical terms, expectancy theory says that employees will be motivated to exert a high level of effort when they believe that effort will lead to a good performance appraisal; that a good appraisal will lead to organizational rewards such as bonuses, salary increases, or promotions; and that the rewards will satisfy the employees' personal goals. The theory, therefore, focuses on three relationships (see Exhibit 6-9):

1. *Effort–performance relationship.* The probability perceived by the individual that exerting a given amount of effort will lead to performance.
2. *Performance–reward relationship.* The degree to which the individual believes that performing at a particular level will lead to the attainment of a desired outcome.
3. *Rewards–personal goals relationship.* The degree to which organizational rewards satisfy an individual's personal goals or needs and the attractiveness of those potential rewards for the individual.[75]

Exhibit 6-9 Expectancy Theory

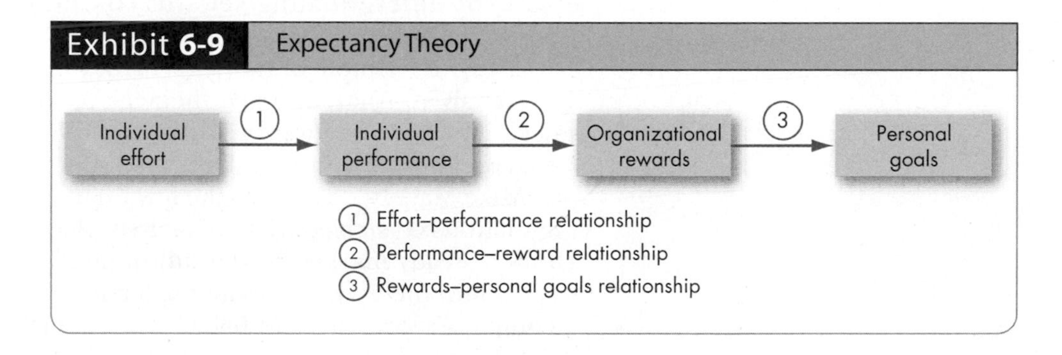

interactional justice *The perceived degree to which an individual is treated with dignity, concern, and respect.*

expectancy theory *A theory that says that the strength of a tendency to act in a certain way depends on the strength of an expectation that the act will be followed by a given outcome and on the attractiveness of that outcome to the individual.*

Expectancy theory helps explain why a lot of workers aren't motivated on their jobs and do only the minimum necessary to get by. This is evident when we look at the theory's three relationships in a little more detail. We present them as questions employees need to answer in the affirmative if their motivation is to be maximized.

First, *if I give a maximum effort, will it be recognized in my performance appraisal*? For a lot of employees, the answer is "no." Why? Their skill level may be deficient, which means that no matter how hard they try, they're not likely to be high performers. The organization's performance appraisal system may be designed to assess nonperformance factors such as loyalty, initiative, or courage, which means more effort won't necessarily result in a higher evaluation. Another possibility is that employees, rightly or wrongly, perceive that the boss doesn't like them. As a result, they expect to get a poor appraisal, regardless of level of effort. These examples suggest that one possible source of low employee motivation is the belief by employees that, no matter how hard they work, the likelihood of getting a good performance appraisal is low.

Second, *if I get a good performance appraisal, will it lead to organizational rewards*? Many employees see the performance–reward relationship in their job as weak. The reason is that organizations reward a lot of things besides just performance. For example, when pay is allocated to employees based on factors such as seniority, being cooperative, or "kissing up" to the boss, employees are likely to see the performance–reward relationship as being weak and demotivating.

Finally, *if I'm rewarded, are the rewards ones that I find personally attractive*? The employee works hard in the hope of getting a promotion but gets a pay raise instead. Or the employee wants a more interesting and challenging job but receives only a few words of praise. Or the employee puts in extra effort to be relocated to the company's Paris office but instead is transferred to Singapore. These examples illustrate the importance of the rewards being tailored to individual employee needs. Unfortunately, many managers are limited in the rewards they can distribute, which makes it difficult to individualize rewards. Moreover, some managers incorrectly assume that all employees want the same thing, thus overlooking the motivational effects of differentiating rewards. In either case, employee motivation is submaximized.

As a vivid example of how expectancy theory can work, consider the case of stock analysts. Analysts make their living by trying to forecast the future of a stock's price; the accuracy of their buy, sell, or hold recommendations is what keeps them in work or gets them fired. But it's not quite that simple. For example, Mike Mayo, 42, is one of the few financial analysts willing to put sell recommendations on stocks. Why do analysts place so few sell ratings on stocks? After all, in a steady market, by definition, as many stocks are falling as are rising. Expectancy theory provides an explanation: Analysts who place a sell rating on a company's stock have to balance the benefits they receive by being accurate against the risks they run by drawing the company's ire. What are these risks? They include public rebuke, professional blackballing, and exclusion from information. As Mayo said, "There is no recourse for analysts." When analysts place a buy rating on a stock, they face no such trade-off because, obviously, companies love that they are recommending that investors buy their stock. So, the incentive structure suggests that the expected outcome of buy ratings is higher than the expected outcome of sell ratings, and that's why buy ratings vastly outnumber sell ratings.[76]

Does expectancy theory work? Attempts to validate the theory have been complicated by methodological, criterion, and measurement problems. As a result, many published studies that purport to support or negate the theory must be viewed with caution. Importantly, most studies have failed to replicate the methodology as it was originally proposed. For example, the theory proposes to explain different levels of effort from the same person under different circumstances, but almost all replication studies have looked at different people. Correcting for this flaw has greatly improved support for the validity of expectancy theory.[77] Some critics suggest that the theory has only limited use, arguing that it tends to be more valid for predicting in situations in which effort–performance and performance–reward linkages are clearly perceived by the individual.[78] Because few individuals perceive a high correlation between performance and rewards in their jobs, the theory tends to be idealistic. If organizations actually rewarded individuals for performance rather than according to criteria such as seniority, effort, skill level, and job difficulty, then the theory's validity might be considerably greater. However, rather than invalidating expectancy theory, this criticism can be used in support of the theory because it explains why a significant segment of the workforce exerts low levels of effort in carrying out job responsibilities.

Integrating Contemporary Theories of Motivation

9 *Explain to what degree motivation theories are culture bound.*

We've looked at a lot of motivation theories in this chapter. The fact that a number of these theories have been supported only complicates the matter. It would be simpler if, after presenting half a dozen theories, only one was found valid. But the theories we presented are not all in competition with one another. Because one is valid doesn't automatically make the others invalid. In fact, many of the theories presented in this chapter are complementary. The challenge is now to tie these theories together to help you understand their interrelationships.[79]

Exhibit 6-10 presents a model that integrates much of what we know about motivation. Its basic foundation is the expectancy model shown in Exhibit 6-9. Let's work through Exhibit 6-10. (We will look at job design closely in Chapter 7.)

We begin by explicitly recognizing that opportunities can either aid or hinder individual effort. The individual effort box also has another arrow leading into it. This arrow flows out of the person's goals. Consistent with goal-setting theory, this goals–effort loop is meant to remind us that goals direct behavior.

Expectancy theory predicts that employees will exert a high level of effort if they perceive that there is a strong relationship between effort and performance, performance and rewards, and rewards and satisfaction of personal goals. Each of these relationships, in turn, is influenced by certain factors. For effort to lead to good performance, the individual must have the requisite ability to perform, and the performance appraisal system that measures the individual's performance must be perceived as being fair and objective. The performance–reward relationship will be strong if the individual perceives that it is performance (rather than seniority, personal favorites, or other criteria) that is rewarded. If cognitive evaluation theory were fully valid in the actual

Exhibit 6-10 Integrating Contemporary Theories of Motivation

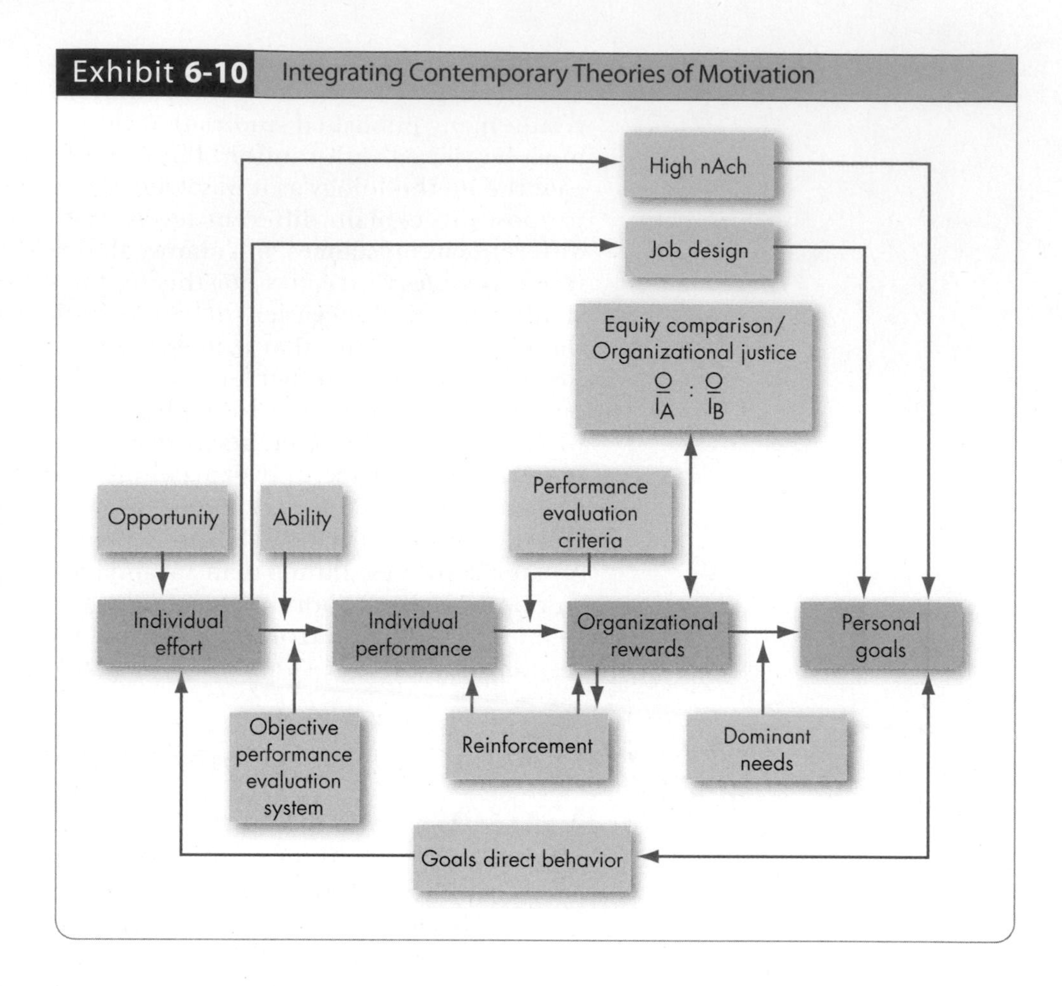

workplace, we would predict here that basing rewards on performance should decrease the individual's intrinsic motivation. The final link in expectancy theory is the rewards–goals relationship. Motivation would be high to the degree that the rewards an individual received for high performance satisfied the dominant needs consistent with individual goals.

A closer look at Exhibit 6-10 also reveals that the model considers achievement motivation, job design, reinforcement, and equity theories/organizational justice. A high achiever is not motivated by an organization's assessment of performance or organizational rewards, hence the jump from effort to personal goals for those with a high nAch. Remember, high achievers are internally driven as long as the jobs they are doing provide them with personal responsibility, feedback, and moderate risks. They are not concerned with the effort–performance, performance–rewards, or rewards–goal linkages.

Reinforcement theory enters the model by recognizing that the organization's rewards reinforce the individual's performance. If management has designed a reward system that is seen by employees as "paying off" for good performance, the rewards will reinforce and encourage continued good performance. Rewards also play the key part in organizational justice research. Individuals will judge the favorability of their outcomes (for example, their pay) relative to what others receive but also with respect to how they are treated: When people are disappointed in their rewards, they are likely to be sensitive to the perceived fairness of the procedures used and the consideration given to them by their supervisor.

Global Implications

In our discussion of goal-setting theory, we said that care needs to be taken in applying this theory because it assumes cultural characteristics that are not universal. This is true for many of the theories presented in this chapter because most current motivation theories were developed in the United States by and about U.S. adults.[80] For instance, both goal-setting and expectancy theories emphasize goal accomplishment as well as rational and individual thought—characteristics consistent with U.S. culture. Let's take a look at several motivation theories and consider their cross-cultural transferability.

Maslow's needs hierarchy argues that people start at the physiological level and then move progressively up the hierarchy in this order: physiological, safety, social, esteem, and self-actualization. This hierarchy, if it has any application at all, aligns with U.S. culture. In countries such as Japan, Greece, and Mexico, where uncertainty-avoidance characteristics are strong, security needs would be on top of the need hierarchy. Countries that score high on nurturing characteristics—such as Denmark, Sweden, Norway, the Netherlands, and Finland—would have social needs on top.[81] We would predict, for instance, that group work will motivate employees more when the country's culture scores high on the nurturing criterion.

Another motivation concept that clearly has a U.S. bias is the achievement need. The view that a high achievement need acts as an internal motivator presupposes two cultural characteristics—a willingness to accept a moderate degree of risk (which excludes countries with strong uncertainty avoidance characteristics) and a concern with performance (which applies almost singularly to countries with strong achievement characteristics). This combination is found in Anglo-American countries such as the United States, Canada, and Great Britain.[82] However, these characteristics are relatively absent in countries such as Chile and Portugal.

U.S. firms expanding their operations in China are learning that motivation concepts that succeed in the United States don't always apply to Chinese employees. For example, compensation for salespeople in China is based on seniority, not on performance. And most Chinese firms do not offer any nonmonetary motivation such as employee recognition programs. For the Chinese salesperson shown here assisting a customer interested in GM's Cadillac CTS, motivation may come from satisfying her economic and achievement needs.

Equity theory has gained a relatively strong following in the United States. That's not surprising because U.S.-style reward systems are based on the assumption that workers are highly sensitive to equity in reward allocations. And in the United States equity is meant to closely tie pay to performance. However, evidence suggests that in collectivist cultures, especially in the former socialist countries of central and eastern Europe, employees expect rewards to reflect their individual needs as well as their performance.[83] Moreover, consistent with a legacy of communism and centrally planned economies, employees exhibited an entitlement attitude—that is, they expected outcomes to be *greater* than their inputs.[84] These findings suggest that U.S.-style pay practices may need modification, especially in Russia and former communist countries, in order to be perceived as fair by employees.

But don't assume there are *no* cross-cultural consistencies. For instance, the desire for interesting work seems important to almost all workers, regardless of their national culture. In a study of seven countries, employees in Belgium, Britain, Israel, and the United States ranked "interesting work" number one among 11 work goals. And workers in Japan, the Netherlands, and Germany ranked this factor either second or third.[85] Similarly, in a study comparing job-preference outcomes among graduate students in the United States, Canada, Australia, and Singapore, growth, achievement, and responsibility were rated the top three and had identical rankings.[86] Both of these studies suggest some universality to the importance of intrinsic factors in the two-factor theory.

Summary and Implications for Managers

The theories we've discussed in this chapter address different outcome variables. Some, for instance, are directed at explaining turnover, while others emphasize productivity. The theories also differ in their predictive strength. In this section, we (1) review the most established motivation theories to determine their relevance in explaining the dependent variables, and (2) assess the predictive power of each.[87]

Need Theories We introduced four theories that focused on needs: Maslow's hierarchy, ERG, McClelland's needs, and the two-factor theory. None of these theories has found widespread support, although the strongest of them is probably McClelland's theory, particularly regarding the relationship between achievement and productivity. In general, need theories (Maslow and ERG) are not very valid explanations of motivation.

Goal-Setting Theory There is little dispute that clear and difficult goals lead to higher levels of employee productivity. This evidence leads us to conclude that goal-setting theory provides one of the most powerful explanations of this dependent variable. The theory, however, does not address absenteeism, turnover, or satisfaction.

Reinforcement Theory This theory has an impressive record for predicting factors such as quality and quantity of work, persistence of effort, absenteeism, tardiness, and accident rates. It does not offer much insight into employee satisfaction or the decision to quit.

Equity Theory/Organizational Justice Equity theory deals with productivity, satisfaction, absence, and turnover variables. However, its strongest legacy probably is that it provided the spark for research on organizational justice, which has more support in the literature.

Expectancy Theory Our final theory, expectancy theory, focuses on performance variables. It has proved to offer a relatively powerful explanation of employee productivity, absenteeism, and turnover. But expectancy theory assumes that employees have few constraints on their decision discretion. It makes many of the same assumptions that the rational model makes about individual decision making (see Chapter 5), and this limits its applicability. Expectancy theory has some validity because for many behaviors people consider expected outcomes. However, the rational model goes only so far in explaining behavior.

Point Counterpoint

FAILURE MOTIVATES!

It's sad but true that many of the best lessons we learn in life are from our failures. Often when we're riding on the wings of success, we coast—until we crash to earth.

Take the example of Dan Doctoroff. Doctoroff is a successful New York investment banker who spent 5 years obsessed with bringing the 2012 Olympics to New York. In his efforts, he used $4 million of his own money, traveled half a million miles, worked 100-hour weeks, and staked his reputation on achieving a goal many thought was foolhardy.

What happened? New York wasn't selected, and all Doctoroff's efforts were in vain. His immediate reaction? He felt "emotionally paralyzed." But Doctoroff is not sorry he made the effort. He said he learned a lot about himself in trying to woo Olympic decision makers in 78 countries. Colleagues had once described him as brash and arrogant. As a result of his efforts, Doctoroff said, he learned to listen more and talk less. He also said that losing made him realize how supportive his wife and three teenage children could be.

Not only does failure bring perspective to people such as Doctoroff, it often provides important feedback on how to improve. The important thing is to learn from the failure and to persist. As Doctoroff says, "The only way to ensure you'll lose is not to try."

One of the reasons successful people fail so often is that they set their own bars so high. Harvard's Rosabeth Moss Kanter, who has spent her career studying executives, says, "Many successful people set the bar so high that they don't achieve the distant goal. But they do achieve things that wouldn't have been possible without that bigger goal."[88]

Do people learn from failure? We've seen that one of the decision-making errors people make is escalation of commitment: They persist in a failed venture just because they think persistence is a virtue or because their ego is involved, even when logic suggests they should move on. One research study found that managers often illogically persist in launching new products, even when the evidence becomes clear that the product is going nowhere. As the authors note, "It sometimes takes more courage to kill a product that's going nowhere than to sustain it." So, the thought of learning from failure is a nice ideal, but most people are too defensive to do that.

Moreover, there is ample evidence that when people fail they often rationalize their failures to preserve their self-esteem and thus don't learn at all. Although the example of Dan Doctoroff is interesting, it's not clear he's done anything but rationalize his failure. It's human nature. Research shows that when we fail, we often engage in external attributions—blaming the failure on bad luck or powerful others—or we devalue what we failed to get ("It wasn't that important to me anyway," we may tell ourselves). These rationalizations may not be correct, but that's not the point. We engage in them not to be right but to preserve our often fragile self-esteem. We need to believe in ourselves to motivate ourselves, and because failing undermines that self-belief, we have to do what we can to recover our self-confidence.[89]

In sum, although it is a nice story that failure is actually good, as one songwriter wrote, "the world is not a song." Failure hurts, and to either protect ourselves or recover from the pain, we often do *not* learn from failure—we rationalize it away.

Questions for Review

1 Define *motivation*. What are the key elements of motivation?

2 What are the early theories of motivation? How well have they been supported by research?

3 What is cognitive evaluation theory? What does it assume about the effects of intrinsic and extrinsic rewards on behavior?

4 What are the major predictions of goal-setting theory? Have these predictions been supported by research?

5 What is reinforcement theory? How is it related to goal-setting theory? Has research supported reinforcement theory?

6 What is equity theory? Why has it been supplanted by organizational justice?

7 What are the key tenets of expectancy theory? What has research had to say about this theory?

8 How do the contemporary theories of work motivation complement one another?

9 Do you think motivation theories are often culture bound? Why or why not?

Experiential Exercise

GOAL-SETTING TASK

Purpose

This exercise will help you learn how to write tangible, verifiable, measurable, and relevant goals that might evolve from an MBO program.

Time

Approximately 20 to 30 minutes.

Instructions

1. Break into groups of three to five.
2. Spend a few minutes discussing your class instructor's job. What does he or she do? What defines good performance? What behaviors lead to good performance?
3. Each group is to develop a list of five goals that, although not established participatively with your instructor, you believe might be developed in an MBO program at your college. Try to select goals that seem most critical to the effective performance of your instructor's job.
4. Each group will select a leader who will share the group's goals with the entire class. For each group's goals, class discussion should focus on the goals' (a) specificity, (b) ease of measurement, (c) importance, and (d) motivational properties.

Ethical Dilemma

IS GOAL-SETTING MANIPULATION?

Managers are interested in the subject of motivation because they're concerned with learning how to get the most effort from their employees. Is this ethical? For example, when managers set hard, specific goals for employees, aren't they manipulating them?

Manipulate is defined as "(1) to handle, manage, or use, especially with skill, in some process of treatment or performance; (2) to manage or influence by artful skill; (3) to adapt or change to suit one's purpose or advantage." Aren't these definitions compatible with the notion of managers skillfully seeking to influence employee productivity for the benefit of the manager and the organization?

Do managers have the right to seek control over their employees? Does anyone, for that matter, have the right to control others? Does control imply manipulation? And if so, is there anything wrong with managers manipulating employees through goal setting or other motivational techniques?

Case Incident 1

DO U.S. WORKERS "LIVE TO WORK"?

Many people around the world believe that U.S. adults live only to work. Do we really work that much harder than people in other countries? To answer this question, we turn to data collected by OECD, an organization that does research on economic development issues. The following figures represent the average hours worked per week (total number of hours an average employee works per year, divided by 52), averaged over the more recent 5 years available, for countries that are members of the OECD:

1. South Korea	46.7
2. Greece	39.9
3. Hungary	38.6
4. Czech Republic	38.2
5. Poland	38.1
6. Mexico	36.0
7. Italy	35.2
8. Iceland	34.9
9. New Zealand	34.9
10. Japan	34.5
11. Canada	33.6
12. Slovak Republic	33.5
13. Australia	33.4
14. Finland	33.2
15. United States	33.0
16. Spain	32.7
17. Portugal	32.5
18. United Kingdom	32.4
19. Ireland	31.8
20. Switzerland	31.7
21. Austria	31.6
22. Luxembourg	30.5
23. Sweden	30.4
24. Denmark	29.8
25. France	29.8
26. Belgium	29.6
27. Germany	27.8
28. Netherlands	26.1
29. Norway	26.0

Questions

1. Do these results surprise you? Why or why not?
2. Why do you think U.S. employees have a reputation for "living to work"?
3. Do these results prove that Koreans, for example, are more motivated to work than their U.S. counterparts? Why or why not?
4. A research study has suggested that changes in hours worked over time are due, in part, to changes in tax rates. "If taxes and [government expenditures] are high, that may lead to less work," said one of the researchers. Supporting this theory, since 2001, workers in the United States have increased their hours worked while tax rates have dropped. What theory or theories of motivation might support such a change?

Sources: L. Ohanian, A. Raffo, and R. Rogerson, *Long-Term Changes in Labor Supply and Taxes: Evidence from OECD Countries, 1956–2004*, NBER working paper 12786, December 2006; and J. J. Smith, "Taxes Likely Causing Some Countries' Workers to Labor Fewer Hours," *SHRM Online*, May 2007, www.shrm.org.

Case Incident 2

BULLYING BOSSES

"It got to where I was twitching, literally, on the way into work," states Carrie Clark, a 52-year-old retired teacher and administrator. After enduring 10 months of repeated insults and mistreatment from her supervisor, she finally quit her job. "I had to take care of my health."

Although many individuals recall bullies from their elementary school days, some are realizing that bullies can exist in the workplace as well. And these bullies do not just pick on the weakest in the group; rather, any subordinate in their path may fall prey to their torment, according to Dr. Gary Namie, director of the Workplace Bullying and Trauma Institute. Dr. Namie further says workplace bullies are not limited to men—women are at least as likely to be bullies. However, gender discrepancies are found in victims of bullying, as women are more likely to be targets.

What motivates a boss to be a bully? Dr. Harvey Hornstein, a retired professor from Teachers College at Columbia University, suggests that supervisors may use bullying as a means to subdue a subordinate who poses a threat to the supervisor's status. In addition, supervisors may bully individuals to vent frustrations. Many times, however, the sheer desire to wield power may be the primary reason for bullying.

What is the impact of bullying on employee motivation and behavior? Surprisingly, even though victims of workplace bullies may feel less motivated to go to work every day, it does not appear that they discontinue performing their required job duties. However, it does appear that victims of bullies are less motivated to perform extra-role or citizenship behaviors. Helping others, speaking positively about the organization, and going beyond the call of duty are behaviors that are reduced as a result of bullying. According to Dr. Bennett Tepper of the University of North Carolina, fear may be the reason that many workers continue to perform their job duties. And not all individuals reduce their citizenship behaviors. Some continue to engage in extra-role behaviors to make themselves look better than their colleagues.

What should you do if your boss is bullying you? Don't necessarily expect help from coworkers. As Emelise Aleandri, an actress and a producer from New York who left her job after being bullied, stated, "Some people were afraid to do anything. But others didn't mind what was happening at all, because they wanted my job." Moreover, according to Dr. Michelle Duffy of the University of Kentucky, coworkers often blame victims of bullying in order to resolve their guilt. "They do this by wondering whether maybe the person deserved the treatment, that he or she has been annoying, or lazy, they did something to earn it," states Dr. Duffy. One example of an employee who observed this phenomenon firsthand is Sherry Hamby, who was frequently verbally abused by her boss and then eventually fired. She stated, "This was a man who insulted me, who insulted my family, who would lay into me while everyone else in the office just sat there and let it happen. The people in my office eventually started blaming me."

What can a bullied employee do? Dr. Hornstein suggests that employees try to ignore the insults and respond only to the substance of the bully's gripe. "Stick with the substance, not the process, and often it won't escalate," he states. Of course, that is easier said than done.

Questions

1. Of the three types of organizational justice, which one does workplace bullying most closely resemble?
2. What aspects of motivation might workplace bullying reduce? For example, are there likely to be effects on an employee's self-efficacy? If so, what might those effects be?
3. If you were a victim of workplace bullying, what steps would you take to try to reduce its occurrence? What strategies would be most effective? What strategies might be ineffective? What would you do if one of your colleagues were a victim of an abusive supervisor?
4. What factors do you believe contribute to workplace bullying? Are bullies a product of the situation, or do they have flawed personalities? What situations and what personality factors might contribute to the presence of bullies?

Source: Based on C. Benedict, "The Bullying Boss," *New York Times*, June 22, 2004, p. F1.

Endnotes

1. J. L. Yang, "'Happyness' for Sale," *Fortune*, September 18, 2006, pp. 56–58.
2. C. A. O'Reilly III, "Organizational Behavior: Where We've Been, Where We're Going," in M. R. Rosenzweig and L. W. Porter (eds.), *Annual Review of Psychology*, vol. 42 (Palo Alto, CA: Annual Reviews, 1991), p. 431. See also M. L. Ambrose and C. T. Kulik, "Old Friends, New Faces: Motivation Research in the 1990s," *Journal of Management* 25, no. 3 (1999), pp. 231–292.
3. Cited in D. Jones, "Firms Spend Billions to Fire Up Workers—With Little Luck," *USA Today*, May 10, 2001, p. 1A.
4. "Wasted Time at Work Costs Employers Billions," *IPMA-HR Bulletin*, August 11, 2006, pp. 1–7.
5. See, for instance, T. R. Mitchell, "Matching Motivational Strategies with Organizational Contexts," in L. L. Cummings and B. M. Staw (eds.), *Research in Organizational Behavior*, vol. 19 (Greenwich, CT: JAI Press, 1997), pp. 60–62.
6. A. Maslow, *Motivation and Personality* (New York: Harper & Row, 1954).
7. See, for example, E. E. Lawler III and J. L. Suttle, "A Causal Correlation Test of the Need Hierarchy Concept," *Organizational Behavior and Human Performance*, April 1972, pp. 265–287; D. T. Hall and K. E. Nougaim, "An Examination of Maslow's Need Hierarchy in an Organizational Setting," *Organizational Behavior and Human Performance*, February 1968, pp. 12–35; A. K. Korman, J. H. Greenhaus, and I. J. Badin, "Personnel Attitudes and Motivation," in M. R. Rosenzweig and L. W. Porter (eds.), *Annual Review of Psychology* (Palo Alto, CA: Annual Reviews, 1977), pp. 178–179; and J. Rauschenberger, N. Schmitt, and J. E. Hunter, "A Test of the Need Hierarchy Concept by a Markov Model of Change in Need Strength," *Administrative Science Quarterly*, December 1980, pp. 654–670.
8. C. P. Alderfer, "An Empirical Test of a New Theory of Human Needs," *Organizational Behavior and Human Performance*, May 1969, pp. 142–175.
9. C. P. Schneider and C. P. Alderfer, "Three Studies of Measures of Need Satisfaction in Organizations," *Administrative Science Quarterly*, December 1973, pp. 489–505; and I. Borg and M. Braun, "Work Values in East and West Germany: Different Weights, but Identical Structures," *Journal of Organizational Behavior* 17, special issue (1996), pp. 541–555.

10. M. A. Wahba and L. G. Bridwell, "Maslow Reconsidered: A Review of Research on the Need Hierarchy Theory," *Organizational Behavior and Human Performance*, April 1976, pp. 212–240.
11. D. McGregor, *The Human Side of Enterprise* (New York: McGraw-Hill, 1960). For an updated analysis of Theory X and Theory Y constructs, see R. J. Summers and S. F. Cronshaw, "A Study of McGregor's Theory X, Theory Y and the Influence of Theory X, Theory Y Assumptions on Causal Attributions for Instances of Worker Poor Performance," in S. L. McShane (ed.), Organizational Behavior, *ASAC 1988 Conference Proceedings*, vol. 9, Part 5. Halifax, Nova Scotia, 1988, pp. 115–123.
12. A. E. Abele, "The Dynamics of Masculine-Agentic and Feminine-Communal Traits: Findings from a Prospective Study," *Journal of Personality and Social Psychology*, October 2003, pp. 768–776; and R. Ely, G. Melzi, and L. Hadge, "Being Brave, Being Nice: Themes of Agency and Communion in Children's Narratives," *Journal of Personality*, April 1998, pp. 257–284.
13. F. Herzberg, B. Mausner, and B. Snyderman, *The Motivation to Work* (New York: Wiley, 1959).
14. R. J. House and L. A. Wigdor, "Herzberg's Dual-Factor Theory of Job Satisfaction and Motivations: A Review of the Evidence and Criticism," *Personnel Psychology*, Winter 1967, pp. 369–389; D. P. Schwab and L. L. Cummings, "Theories of Performance and Satisfaction: A Review," *Industrial Relations*, October 1970, pp. 403–430; and J. Phillipchuk and J. Whittaker, "An Inquiry into the Continuing Relevance of Herzberg's Motivation Theory," *Engineering Management Journal* 8 (1996), pp. 15–20.
15. D. C. McClelland, *The Achieving Society* (New York: Van Nostrand Reinhold, 1961); J. W. Atkinson and J. O. Raynor, *Motivation and Achievement* (Washington, DC: Winston, 1974); D. C. McClelland, *Power: The Inner Experience* (New York: Irvington, 1975); and M. J. Stahl, *Managerial and Technical Motivation: Assessing Needs for Achievement, Power, and Affiliation* (New York: Praeger, 1986).
16. D. C. McClelland and D. G. Winter, *Motivating Economic Achievement* (New York: The Free Press, 1969); and J. B. Miner, N. R. Smith, and J. S. Bracker, "Role of Entrepreneurial Task Motivation in the Growth of Technologically Innovative Firms: Interpretations from Follow-up Data," *Journal of Applied Psychology*, October 1994, pp. 627–630.
17. D. C. McClelland, *Power*; D. C. McClelland and D. H. Burnham, "Power Is the Great Motivator," *Harvard Business Review*, March–April 1976, pp. 100–110; and R. E. Boyatzis, "The Need for Close Relationships and the Manager's Job," in D. A. Kolb, I. M. Rubin, and J. M. McIntyre, *Organizational Psychology: Readings on Human Behavior in Organizations*, 4th ed. (Upper Saddle River, NJ: Prentice Hall, 1984), pp. 81–86.
18. D. G. Winter, "The Motivational Dimensions of Leadership: Power, Achievement, and Affiliation," in R. E. Riggio, S. E. Murphy, and F. J. Pirozzolo (eds.), *Multiple Intelligences and Leadership* (Mahwah, NJ: Lawrence Erlbaum, 2002), pp. 119–138.
19. J. B. Miner, *Studies in Management Education* (New York: Springer, 1965).
20. R. de Charms, *Personal Causation: The Internal Affective Determinants of Behavior* (New York: Academic Press, 1968).
21. E. L. Deci, *Intrinsic Motivation* (New York: Plenum, 1975); J. Cameron and W. D. Pierce, "Reinforcement, Reward, and Intrinsic Motivation: A Meta-analysis," *Review of Educational Research*, Fall 1994, pp. 363–423; S. Tang and V. C. Hall, "The Overjustification Effect: A Meta-analysis," *Applied Cognitive Psychology*, October 1995, pp. 365–404; E. L. Deci, R. Koestner, and R. M. Ryan, "A Meta-analytic Review of Experiments Examining the Effects of Extrinsic Rewards on Intrinsic Motivation," *Psychological Bulletin* 125, no. 6 (1999), pp. 627–668; R. M. Ryan and E. L. Deci, "Intrinsic and Extrinsic Motivations: Classic Definitions and New Directions," *Contemporary Educational Psychology*, January 2000, pp. 54–67; and N. Houlfort, R. Koestner, M. Joussemet, A. Nantel-Vivier, and N. Lekes, "The Impact of Performance-Contingent Rewards on Perceived Autonomy and Competence," *Motivation & Emotion* 26, no. 4 (2002), pp. 279–295.
22. W. E. Scott, "The Effects of Extrinsic Rewards on 'Intrinsic Motivation': A Critique," *Organizational Behavior and Human Performance*, February 1976, pp. 117–119; B. J. Calder and B. M. Staw, "Interaction of Intrinsic and Extrinsic Motivation: Some Methodological Notes," *Journal of Personality and Social Psychology*, January 1975, pp. 76–80; and K. B. Boal and L. L. Cummings, "Cognitive Evaluation Theory: An Experimental Test of Processes and Outcomes," *Organizational Behavior and Human Performance*, December 1981, pp. 289–310.
23. G. R. Salancik, "Interaction Effects of Performance and Money on Self-Perception of Intrinsic Motivation," *Organizational Behavior and Human Performance*, June 1975, pp. 339–351; and F. Luthans, M. Martinko, and T. Kess, "An Analysis of the Impact of Contingency Monetary Rewards on Intrinsic Motivation," *Proceedings of the Nineteenth Annual Midwest Academy of Management*, St. Louis, 1976, pp. 209–221.
24. Deci, Koestner, and Ryan, "A Meta-analytic Review of Experiments Examining the Effects of Extrinsic Rewards on Intrinsic Motivation," pp. 627–668.
25. K. M. Sheldon, A. J. Elliot, and R. M. Ryan, "Self-Concordance and Subjective Well-being in Four Cultures," *Journal of Cross-Cultural Psychology* 35, no. 2 (2004), pp. 209–223.
26. J. E. Bono and T. A. Judge, "Self-Concordance at Work: Toward Understanding the Motivational Effects of Transformational Leaders," *Academy of Management Journal* 46, no. 5 (2003), pp. 554–571.
27. J. P. Meyer, T. E. Becker, and C. Vandenberghe, "Employee Commitment and Motivation: A Conceptual Analysis and Integrative Model," *Journal of Applied Psychology* 89, no. 6 (2004), pp. 991–1007.
28. E. A. Locke, "Toward a Theory of Task Motivation and Incentives," *Organizational Behavior and Human Performance*, May 1968, pp. 157–189.
29. P. C. Earley, P. Wojnaroski, and W. Prest, "Task Planning and Energy Expended: Exploration of How Goals Influence Performance," *Journal of Applied Psychology*, February 1987, pp. 107–114.
30. See M. E. Tubbs "Goal Setting: A Meta-analytic Examination of the Empirical Evidence," *Journal of Applied Psychology*, August 1986, pp. 474–483; E. A. Locke and G. P. Latham, "Building a Practically Useful Theory of Goal Setting and Task Motivation," *American Psychologist*, September 2002, pp. 705–717; and E. A. Locke and G. P. Latham, "New

Directions in Goal-Setting Theory," *Current Directions in Psychological Science* 15, no. 5 (2006), pp. 265–268.

31. E. A. Locke and G. P. Latham, "Building a Practically Useful Theory of Goal Setting and Task Motivation: A 35-Year Odyssey," *American Psychologist* 57, no. 9 (2002), pp. 705–717.

32. J. M. Ivancevich and J. T. McMahon, "The Effects of Goal Setting, External Feedback, and Self-Generated Feedback on Outcome Variables: A Field Experiment," *Academy of Management Journal,* June 1982, pp. 359–372; and E. A. Locke, "Motivation through Conscious Goal Setting," *Applied and Preventive Psychology* 5 (1996), pp. 117–124.

33. See, for example, G. P. Latham, M. Erez, and E. A. Locke, "Resolving Scientific Disputes by the Joint Design of Crucial Experiments by the Antagonists: Application to the Erez-Latham Dispute Regarding Participation in Goal Setting," *Journal of Applied Psychology,* November 1988, pp. 753–772; T. D. Ludwig and E. S. Geller, "Assigned Versus Participative Goal Setting and Response Generalization: Managing Injury Control among Professional Pizza Deliverers," *Journal of Applied Psychology,* April 1997, pp. 253–261; and S. G. Harkins and M. D. Lowe, "The Effects of Self-Set Goals on Task Performance," *Journal of Applied Social Psychology,* January 2000, pp. 1–40.

34. M. Erez, P. C. Earley, and C. L. Hulin, "The Impact of Participation on Goal Acceptance and Performance: A Two-Step Model," *Academy of Management Journal,* March 1985, pp. 50–66.

35. E. A. Locke, "The Motivation to Work: What We Know," *Advances in Motivation and Achievement* 10 (1997), pp. 375–412; and Latham, Erez, and Locke, "Resolving Scientific Disputes by the Joint Design of Crucial Experiments by the Antagonists," pp. 753–772.

36. H. J. Klein, M. J. Wesson, J. R. Hollenbeck, P. M. Wright, and R. D. DeShon, "The Assessment of Goal Commitment: A Measurement Model Meta-analysis," *Organizational Behavior and Human Decision Processes* 85, no. 1 (2001), pp. 32–55.

37. J. R. Hollenbeck, C. R. Williams, and H. J. Klein, "An Empirical Examination of the Antecedents of Commitment to Difficult Goals," *Journal of Applied Psychology,* February 1989, pp. 18–23. See also J. C. Wofford, V. L. Goodwin, and S. Premack, "Meta-analysis of the Antecedents of Personal Goal Level and of the Antecedents and Consequences of Goal Commitment," *Journal of Management,* September 1992, pp. 595–615; M. E. Tubbs, "Commitment as a Moderator of the Goal-Performance Relation: A Case for Clearer Construct Definition," *Journal of Applied Psychology,* February 1993, pp. 86–97; and J. E. Bono and A. E. Colbert, "Understanding Responses to Multi-Source Feedback: The Role of Core Self-evaluations," *Personnel Psychology,* Spring 2005, pp. 171–203.

38. See R. E. Wood, A. J. Mento, and E. A. Locke, "Task Complexity as a Moderator of Goal Effects: A Meta-analysis," *Journal of Applied Psychology,* August 1987, pp. 416–425; R. Kanfer and P. L. Ackerman, "Motivation and Cognitive Abilities: An Integrative/Aptitude-Treatment Interaction Approach to Skill Acquisition," *Journal of Applied Psychology (monograph),* vol. 74, 1989, pp. 657–690; T. R. Mitchell and W. S. Silver, "Individual and Group Goals When Workers Are Interdependent: Effects on Task Strategies and Performance," *Journal of Applied Psychology,* April 1990, pp. 185–193; and A. M. O'Leary-Kelly, J. J. Martocchio, and D. D. Frink, "A Review of the Influence of Group Goals on Group Performance," *Academy of Management Journal,* October 1994, pp. 1285–1301.

39. "KEYGroup Survey Finds Nearly Half of All Employees Have No Set Performance Goals," *IPMA-HR Bulletin,* March 10, 2006, p. 1; S. Hamm, "SAP Dangles a Big, Fat Carrot," *BusinessWeek,* May 22, 2006, pp. 67–68; and "P&G CEO Wields High Expectations but No Whip," *USA Today,* February 19, 2007, p. 3B.

40. See, for instance, S. J. Carroll and H. L. Tosi, *Management by Objectives: Applications and Research* (New York: Macmillan, 1973); and R. Rodgers and J. E. Hunter, "Impact of Management by Objectives on Organizational Productivity," *Journal of Applied Psychology,* April 1991, pp. 322–336.

41. See, for instance, R. C. Ford, F. S. MacLaughlin, and J. Nixdorf, "Ten Questions About MBO," *California Management Review,* Winter 1980, p. 89; T. J. Collamore, "Making MBO Work in the Public Sector," *Bureaucrat,* Fall 1989, pp. 37–40; G. Dabbs, "Nonprofit Businesses in the 1990s: Models for Success," *Business Horizons,* September–October 1991, pp. 68–71; R. Rodgers and J. E. Hunter, "A Foundation of Good Management Practice in Government: Management by Objectives," *Public Administration Review,* January–February 1992, pp. 27–39; T. H. Poister and G. Streib, "MBO in Municipal Government: Variations on a Traditional Management Tool," *Public Administration Review,* January/February 1995, pp. 48–56; and C. Garvey, "Goalsharing Scores," *HRMagazine,* April 2000, pp. 99–106.

42. See, for instance, C. H. Ford, "MBO: An Idea Whose Time Has Gone?" *Business Horizons,* December 1979, p. 49; R. Rodgers and J. E. Hunter, "Impact of Management by Objectives on Organizational Productivity," *Journal of Applied Psychology,* April 1991, pp. 322–336; R. Rodgers, J. E. Hunter, and D. L. Rogers, "Influence of Top Management Commitment on Management Program Success," *Journal of Applied Psychology,* February 1993, pp. 151–155; and M. Tanikawa, "Fujitsu Decides to Backtrack on Performance-Based Pay," *New York Times,* March 22, 2001, p. W1.

43. A. Bandura, *Self-Efficacy: The Exercise of Control* (New York: Freeman, 1997).

44. A. D. Stajkovic and F. Luthans, "Self-Efficacy and Work-Related Performance: A Meta-analysis," *Psychological Bulletin,* September 1998, pp. 240–261; and A. Bandura, "Cultivate Self-Efficacy for Personal and Organizational Effectiveness," in E. Locke (ed.), *Handbook of Principles of Organizational Behavior* (Malden, MA: Blackwell, 2004), pp. 120–136.

45. A. Bandura and D. Cervone, "Differential Engagement in Self-Reactive Influences in Cognitively-Based Motivation," *Organizational Behavior and Human Decision Processes,* August 1986, pp. 92–113.

46. A. Bandura, *Self-Efficacy: The Exercise of Control* (New York: Freeman, 1997).

47. C. L. Holladay and M. A. Quiñones, "Practice Variability and Transfer of Training: The Role of Self-Efficacy Generality," *Journal of Applied Psychology* 88, no. 6 (2003), pp. 1094–1103.

48. R. C. Rist, "Student Social Class and Teacher Expectations: The Self-Fulfilling Prophecy in Ghetto Education," *Harvard Educational Review* 70, no. 3 (2000), pp. 266–301.

49. D. Eden, "Self-Fulfilling Prophecies in Organizations," in J. Greenberg (ed.), *Organizational Behavior: The State of the Science,* 2nd ed. (Mahwah, NJ: Erlbaum, 2003), pp. 91–122.

50. Ibid.

51. T. A. Judge, C. L. Jackson, J. C. Shaw, B. Scott, and B. L. Rich, "Self-Efficacy and Work-Related Performance: The Integral Role of Individual Differences," *Journal of Applied Psychology* 92, no. 1 (2007), pp. 107–127.

52. Ibid.

53. J. L. Komaki, T. Coombs, and S. Schepman, "Motivational Implications of Reinforcement Theory," in R. M. Steers, L. W. Porter, and G. Bigley (eds.), *Motivation and Work Behavior*, 6th ed. (New York: McGraw-Hill, 1996), pp. 87–107.

54. E. A. Locke, "Latham vs. Komaki: A Tale of Two Paradigms," *Journal of Applied Psychology*, February 1980, pp. 16–23.

55. J. S. Adams, "Inequity in Social Exchanges," in L. Berkowitz (ed.), *Advances in Experimental Social Psychology* (New York: Academic Press, 1965), pp. 267–300.

56. P. S. Goodman, "An Examination of Referents Used in the Evaluation of Pay," *Organizational Behavior and Human Performance*, October 1974, pp. 170–195; S. Ronen, "Equity Perception in Multiple Comparisons: A Field Study," *Human Relations*, April 1986, pp. 333–346; R. W. Scholl, E. A. Cooper, and J. F. McKenna, "Referent Selection in Determining Equity Perception: Differential Effects on Behavioral and Attitudinal Outcomes," *Personnel Psychology*, Spring 1987, pp. 113–127; and T. P. Summers and A. S. DeNisi, "In Search of Adams' Other: Reexamination of Referents Used in the Evaluation of Pay," *Human Relations*, June 1990, pp. 497–511.

57. C. T. Kulik and M. L. Ambrose, "Personal and Situational Determinants of Referent Choice," *Academy of Management Review*, April 1992, pp. 212–237.

58. C. Ostroff and L. E. Atwater, "Does Whom You Work with Matter? Effects of Referent Group Gender and Age Composition on Managers' Compensation," *Journal of Applied Psychology* 88, no. 4 (2003), pp. 725–740.

59. Ibid.

60. See, for example, E. Walster, G. W. Walster, and W. G. Scott, *Equity: Theory and Research* (Boston: Allyn & Bacon, 1978); and J. Greenberg, "Cognitive Reevaluation of Outcomes in Response to Underpayment Inequity," *Academy of Management Journal*, March 1989, pp. 174–184.

61. P. S. Goodman and A. Friedman, "An Examination of Adams' Theory of Inequity," *Administrative Science Quarterly*, September 1971, pp. 271–288; R. P. Vecchio, "An Individual-Differences Interpretation of the Conflicting Predictions Generated by Equity Theory and Expectancy Theory," *Journal of Applied Psychology*, August 1981, pp. 470–481; J. Greenberg, "Approaching Equity and Avoiding Inequity in Groups and Organizations," in J. Greenberg and R. L. Cohen (eds.), *Equity and Justice in Social Behavior* (New York: Academic Press, 1982), pp. 389–435; R. T. Mowday, "Equity Theory Predictions of Behavior in Organizations," in R. Steers, L. W. Porter, and G. Bigley (eds.), *Motivation and Work Behavior*, 6th ed. (New York: McGraw-Hill, 1996), pp. 111–131; S. Werner and N. P. Mero, "Fair or Foul? The Effects of External, Internal, and Employee Equity on Changes in Performance of Major League Baseball Players," *Human Relations*, October 1999, pp. 1291–1312; R. W. Griffeth and S. Gaertner, "A Role for Equity Theory in the Turnover Process: An Empirical Test," *Journal of Applied Social Psychology*, May 2001, pp. 1017–1037; and L. K. Scheer, N. Kumar, and J.-B. E. M. Steenkamp, "Reactions to Perceived Inequity in U.S. and Dutch Interorganizational Relationships," *Academy of Management* 46, no. 3 (2003), pp. 303–316.

62. See, for example, R. C. Huseman, J. D. Hatfield, and E. W. Miles, "A New Perspective on Equity Theory: The Equity Sensitivity Construct," *Academy of Management Journal*, April 1987, pp. 222–234; K. S. Sauley and A. G. Bedeian, "Equity Sensitivity: Construction of a Measure and Examination of Its Psychometric Properties," *Journal of Management* 26, no. 5 (2000), pp. 885–910; M. N. Bing and S. M. Burroughs, "The Predictive and Interactive Effects of Equity Sensitivity in Teamwork-Oriented Organizations," *Journal of Organizational Behavior*, May 2001, pp. 271–290; and J. A. Colquitt, "Does the Justice of One Interact with the Justice of Many? Reactions to Procedural Justice in Teams," *Journal of Applied Psychology* 89, no. 4 (2004), pp. 633–646.

63. J. Greenberg and S. Ornstein, "High Status Job Title as Compensation for Underpayment: A Test of Equity Theory," *Journal of Applied Psychology*, May 1983, pp. 285–297; and J. Greenberg, "Equity and Workplace Status: A Field Experiment," *Journal of Applied Psychology*, November 1988, pp. 606–613.

64. See, for instance, J. Greenberg, *The Quest for Justice on the Job* (Thousand Oaks, CA: Sage, 1996); R. Cropanzano and J. Greenberg, "Progress in Organizational Justice: Tunneling through the Maze," in C. L. Cooper and I. T. Robertson (eds.), *International Review of Industrial and Organizational Psychology*, vol. 12 (New York: Wiley, 1997); J. A. Colquitt, D. E. Conlon, M. J. Wesson, C. O. L. H. Porter, and K. Y. Ng, "Justice at the Millennium: A Meta-Analytic Review of the 25 Years of Organizational Justice Research," *Journal of Applied Psychology*, June 2001, pp. 425–445; T. Simons and Q. Roberson, "Why Managers Should Care About Fairness: The Effects of Aggregate Justice Perceptions on Organizational Outcomes," *Journal of Applied Psychology*, June 2003, pp. 432–443; and G. P. Latham and C. C. Pinder, "Work Motivation Theory and Research at the Dawn of the Twenty-First Century," *Annual Review of Psychology* 56 (2005), pp. 485–516.

65. K. Leung, K. Tong, and S. S. Ho, "Effects of Interactional Justice on Egocentric Bias in Resource Allocation Decisions," *Journal of Applied Psychology* 89, no. 3 (2004), pp. 405–415.

66. "Americans Feel They Pay Fair Share of Taxes, Says Poll," *NewsTarget.com*, May 2, 2005, www.newstarget.com/007297.html.

67. G. S. Leventhal, "What Should Be Done with Equity Theory? New Approaches to the Study of Fairness in Social Relationships," in K. Gergen, M. Greenberg, and R. Willis (eds.), *Social Exchange: Advances in Theory and Research* (New York: Plenum, 1980), pp. 27–55.

68. J. C. Shaw, E. Wild, and J. A. Colquitt, "To Justify or Excuse? A Meta-Analytic Review of the Effects of Explanations," *Journal of Applied Psychology* 88, no. 3 (2003), pp. 444–458.

69. D. P. Skarlicki and R. Folger, "Retaliation in the Workplace: The Roles of Distributive, Procedural, and Interactional Justice," *Journal of Applied Psychology* 82, no. 3 (1997), pp. 434–443.

70. R. Cropanzano, C. A. Prehar, and P. Y. Chen, "Using Social Exchange Theory to Distinguish Procedural from Interactional Justice," *Group & Organization Management* 27, no. 3 (2002), pp. 324–351; and S. G. Roch and L. R. Shanock, "Organizational Justice in an Exchange Framework: Clarifying

Organizational Justice Dimensions," *Journal of Management*, April 2006, pp. 299–322.

71. Colquitt, Conlon, Wesson, Porter, and Ng, "Justice at the Millennium," pp. 425–445.

72. J. Reb, B. M. Goldman, L. J. Kray, and R. Cropanzano, "Different Wrongs, Different Remedies? Reactions to Organizational Remedies After Procedural and Interactional Injustice," *Personnel Psychology* 59 (2006), pp. 31–64; and "Northwest Airlines Flight Cancellations Mount as Labor Woes Continue," *Aero-News.net*, June 26, 2007, www.aero-news.net.

73. V. H. Vroom, *Work and Motivation* (New York: Wiley, 1964).

74. For criticism, see H. G. Heneman III and D. P. Schwab, "Evaluation of Research on Expectancy Theory Prediction of Employee Performance," *Psychological Bulletin*, July 1972, pp. 1–9; T. R. Mitchell, "Expectancy Models of Job Satisfaction, Occupational Preference and Effort: A Theoretical, Methodological and Empirical Appraisal," *Psychological Bulletin*, November 1974, pp. 1053–1077; and W. Van Eerde and H. Thierry, "Vroom's Expectancy Models and Work-Related Criteria: A Meta-analysis," *Journal of Applied Psychology*, October 1996, pp. 575–586. For support, see L. W. Porter and E. E. Lawler III, *Managerial Attitudes and Performance* (Homewood, IL: Irwin, 1968); and J. J. Donovan, "Work Motivation," in N. Anderson et al (eds.), *Handbook of Industrial, Work & Organizational Psychology*, vol. 2 (Thousand Oaks, CA: Sage, 2001), pp. 56–59.

75. Vroom refers to these three variables as expectancy, instrumentality, and valence, respectively.

76. J. Nocera, "The Anguish of Being an Analyst," *New York Times*, March 4, 2006, pp. B1, B12.

77. P. M. Muchinsky, "A Comparison of Within- and Across-Subjects Analyses of the Expectancy-Valence Model for Predicting Effort," *Academy of Management Journal*, March 1977, pp. 154–158; and C. W. Kennedy, J. A. Fossum, and B. J. White, "An Empirical Comparison of Within-Subjects and Between-Subjects Expectancy Theory Models," *Organizational Behavior and Human Decision Process*, August 1983, pp. 124–143.

78. R. J. House, H. J. Shapiro, and M. A. Wahba, "Expectancy Theory as a Predictor of Work Behavior and Attitudes: A Re-evaluation of Empirical Evidence," *Decision Sciences*, January 1974, pp. 481–506.

79. For other examples of models that seek to integrate motivation theories, see H. J. Klein, "An Integrated Control Theory Model of Work Motivation," *Academy of Management Review*, April 1989, pp. 150–172; E. A. Locke, "The Motivation Sequence, the Motivation Hub, and the Motivation Core," *Organizational Behavior and Human Decision Processes*, December 1991, pp. 288–299; and T. R. Mitchell, "Matching Motivational Strategies with Organizational Contexts," pp. 60–62.

80. N. J. Adler, *International Dimensions of Organizational Behavior*, 4th ed. (Cincinnati, OH: South-Western Publishing, 2002), p. 174.

81. G. Hofstede, "Motivation, Leadership, and Organization: Do American Theories Apply Abroad?" *Organizational Dynamics*, Summer 1980, p. 55.

82. Ibid.

83. J. K. Giacobbe-Miller, D. J. Miller, and V. I. Victorov, "A Comparison of Russian and U.S. Pay Allocation Decisions, Distributive Justice Judgments, and Productivity Under Different Payment Conditions," *Personnel Psychology*, Spring 1998, pp. 137–163.

84. S. L. Mueller and L. D. Clarke, "Political Economic Context and Sensitivity to Equity: Differences Between the United States and the Transition Economies of Central and Eastern Europe," *Academy of Management Journal*, June 1998, pp. 319–329.

85. I. Harpaz, "The Importance of Work Goals: An International Perspective," *Journal of International Business Studies*, First Quarter 1990, pp. 75–93.

86. G. E. Popp, H. J. Davis, and T. T. Herbert, "An International Study of Intrinsic Motivation Composition," *Management International Review*, January 1986, pp. 28–35.

87. This section is based on F. J. Landy and W. S. Becker, "Motivation Theory Reconsidered," in L. L. Cummings and B. M. Staw (eds.), *Research in Organizational Behavior*, vol. 9 (Greenwich, CT: JAI Press, 1987), pp. 24–35.

88. J. Zaslow, "Losing Well: How a Successful Man Deal with a Rare and Public Failure," *Wall Street Journal*, March 2, 2006, p. D1.

89. E. Biyalogorsky, W. Boulding, and R. Staelin, "Stuck in the Past: Why Managers Persist with New Product Failures," *Journal of Marketing*, April 2006, pp. 108–121.

Motivation: From Concepts to Applications

Money is better than poverty,
if only for financial reasons.
—Filmmaker Woody Allen

LEARNING OBJECTIVES

After studying this chapter, you should be able to:

1 Describe the job characteristics model and evaluate the way it motivates by changing the work environment.

2 Compare and contrast the three main ways jobs can be redesigned.

3 Identify three alternative work arrangements and show how they might motivate employees.

4 Give examples of employee involvement measures and show how they can motivate employees.

5 Demonstrate how the different types of variable-pay programs can increase employee motivation.

6 Show how flexible benefits turn benefits into motivators.

7 Identify the motivational benefits of intrinsic rewards.

Free as a Bird at Best Buy

How would you like to work wherever you want, whenever you want? Although Best Buy, the big-box retailer based in Minnesota, does not run its headquarters with quite that degree of flexibility, it's close.

One afternoon last year, Chap Allen, who oversees online orders at the electronics retailer Best Buy, turned off his computer at 2 P.M. and told his staff, "See you tomorrow. I'm going to a matinee." Steve Hance has taken to going

Source: Tom Strattman/The New York Times

hunting on workdays, his 12-gauge shotgun in one hand, his Verizon LG cellphone in the other. Best Buy e-learning specialist Mark Wells has been spending some workdays following the Dave Matthews Band around the country. Single parent Kelly McDevitt, an online promotions manager, has started leaving work at 2:30 P.M. to pick up her daughter from school. Scott Jauman began spending one-third of his work schedule at his Northwoods cabin.

What is going on at Best Buy? Is this any way to run a business?

For most jobs, lack of flexibility is still the norm, and flexibility is often dictated by the nature of the business. For example, if you are a manager with Kohl's Department Stores, your schedule needs to conform to the hours the store is open. With changes in technology, though, more managerial jobs place no such restrictions on managers' time.

This is what caused Best Buy HR managers Jody Thompson and Cali Ressler to wonder whether there was a better way to do business. In 2003, two senior managers complained to them that their top performers were under an unsustainable level of stress. They also knew from survey data that employees gave Best Buy low marks for jobs with high demands and low control. They asked Best Buy's senior management to partake in an experiment—allow managers to set their own schedules and abolish meetings, as long as managers' performance evaluation was based on output.

There was some resistance. Senior VP John Thompson, a former GE executive, was highly skeptical. But even he was won over by the results of the experiment. Best Buy found that in the three divisions that implemented the program—dot-com, logistics, and sourcing—voluntary turnover dropped 90 percent, 52 percent, and 75 percent, respectively. Thompson and Ressler also estimate that productivity has increased 35 percent in these departments over the same time span. They argue that morale and engagement are higher than they have ever been in the company.

Best Buy is not alone. One survey of employers revealed that 85 percent expect a large increase in the number of "unleashed" workers at their companies. The changes at some of the biggest corporations have already been dramatic. IBM estimates that 40 percent of its workforce has no formal office. One-third of AT&T's managers also don't have any dedicated office space. Sun Microsystems allows its employees to work anywhere they want.

It's possible that such programs are a fad. However, as Ressler says, "The old way of managing and looking at work isn't going to work anymore."[1] ■

As the Best Buy experiment shows, companies vary a lot in the practical approach they take to motivating employees. Best Buy's approach assumes that employees do their best work when given a lot of autonomy in deciding how (and where and when) they go about doing it. The following self-assessment will provide some information on how motivating *your* job might be.

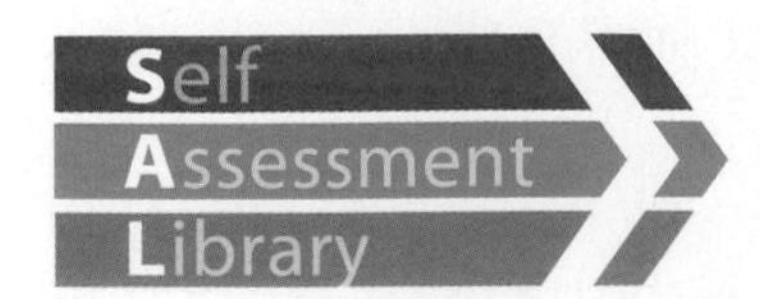

WHAT'S MY JOB'S MOTIVATING POTENTIAL?

In the Self-Assessment Library (available on CD or online), take assessment I.C.9 (What's My Job's Motivating Potential?) and answer the following questions. If you currently do not have a job, answer the questions for your most recent job.

1. *How did you score relative to your classmates?*
2. *Did your score surprise you? Why or why not?*
3. *How might your results affect your career path?*

In Chapter 6, we focused on motivation theories. In this chapter, we focus on applying motivation concepts. We link motivation theories to practices such as employee involvement and skill-based pay. Why? Because it's one thing to be able to know specific motivation theories; it's quite another to see how, as a manager, you can use them.

Motivating by Job Design: The Job Characteristics Model

Increasingly, research on motivation is focused on approaches that link motivational concepts to changes in the way work is structured.

1 *Describe the job characteristics model and evaluate the way it motivates by changing the work environment.*

Research in **job design** provides stronger evidence that the way the elements in a job are organized can act to increase or decrease effort. This research also offers detailed insights into what those elements are. We'll first review the job characteristics model and then discuss some ways jobs can be redesigned. Finally, we'll explore some alternative work arrangements.

The Job Characteristics Model

Developed by J. Richard Hackman and Greg Oldham, the **job characteristics model (JCM)** proposes that any job can be described in terms of five core job dimensions:[2]

1. **Skill variety.** **Skill variety** is the degree to which a job requires a variety of different activities so the worker can use a number of different skills and talent. For instance, an example of a job scoring high on skill variety would be the job of an owner-operator of a garage who does electrical repairs, rebuilds engines, does body work, and interacts with customers. A job scoring low on this dimension would be the job of a body shop worker who sprays paint 8 hours a day.
2. **Task identity.** **Task identity** is the degree to which a job requires completion of a whole and identifiable piece of work. An example of a job scoring high on identity would be the job of a cabinetmaker who designs a piece of furniture, selects the wood, builds the object, and finishes it to perfection. A job scoring low on this dimension would be the job of a worker in a furniture factory who operates a lathe solely to make table legs.
3. **Task significance.** **Task significance** is the degree to which a job has a substantial impact on the lives or work of other people. An example of a job scoring high on significance would be the job of a nurse handling the diverse needs of patients in a hospital intensive care unit. A job scoring low on this dimension would be the job of a janitor sweeping floors in a hospital.

job design *The way the elements in a job are organized.*

job characteristics model (JCM) *A model that proposes that any job can be described in terms of five core job dimensions: skill variety, task identity, task significance, autonomy, and feedback.*

skill variety *The degree to which a job requires a variety of different activities.*

task identity *The degree to which a job requires completion of a whole and identifiable piece of work.*

task significance *The degree to which a job has a substantial impact on the lives or work of other people.*

4. **Autonomy.** **Autonomy** is the degree to which a job provides substantial freedom, independence, and discretion to the individual in scheduling the work and in determining the procedures to be used in carrying it out. An example of a job scoring high on autonomy is the job of a salesperson who schedules his or her own work each day and decides on the most effective sales approach for each customer without supervision. A job scoring low on this dimension would be the job of a salesperson who is given a set of leads each day and is required to follow a standardized sales script with each potential customer.
5. **Feedback.** **Feedback** is the degree to which carrying out the work activities required by a job results in the individual obtaining direct and clear information about the effectiveness of his or her performance. An example of a job with high feedback is the job of a factory worker who assembles iPods and tests them to see if they operate properly. A job scoring low on feedback would be the job of a factory worker who, after assembling an iPod, is required to route it to a quality-control inspector who tests it for proper operation and makes needed adjustments.

Exhibit 7-1 presents the job characteristics model. Note how the first three dimensions—skill variety, task identity, and task significance—combine to create meaningful work. That is, if these three characteristics exist in a job, the model predicts that the incumbent will view the job as being important, valuable, and worthwhile. Note, too, that jobs with high autonomy give job incumbents a feeling of personal responsibility for the results and that, if a job provides feedback, employees will know how effectively they are performing. From a motivational standpoint, the JCM says that individuals obtain internal rewards when they learn (knowledge of results) that they personally (experienced responsibility) have performed well on a task that they care about (experienced meaningfulness).[3] The more these three psychological states are present, the greater will be employees' motivation, performance, and satisfaction and the lower their absenteeism and likelihood of leaving the organization.

Exhibit 7-1 The Job Characteristics Model

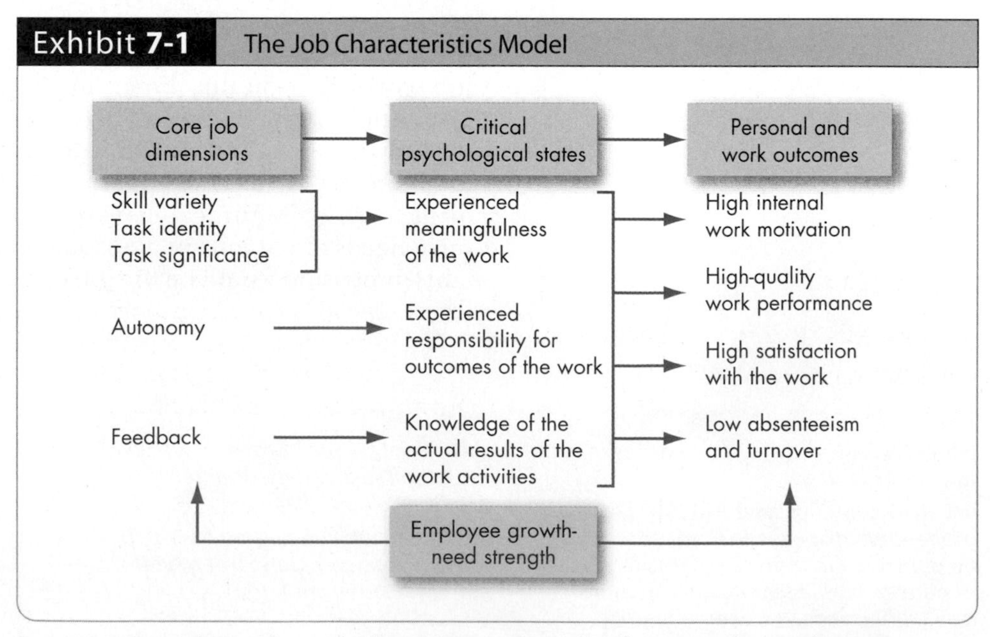

Source: J. R. Hackman and G. R. Oldham, *Work Redesign* © 1980; pp. 78–80. Adapted by permission of Pearson Education, Inc., Upper Saddle River, New Jersey.

As Exhibit 7-1 shows, the links between the job dimensions and the outcomes are moderated or adjusted by the strength of the individual's growth need—that is, by the employee's desire for self-esteem and self-actualization. This means that individuals with a high growth need are more likely to experience the psychological states when their jobs are enriched than are their counterparts with low growth need. Moreover, the individuals with a high growth need will respond more positively to the psychological states when they are present than will individuals with a low growth need.

The core dimensions can be combined into a single predictive index, called the **motivating potential score (MPS)**, which is calculated as follows:

$$\text{MPS} = \frac{\text{Skill variety} + \text{Task identity} + \text{Task significance}}{3} \times \text{Autonomy} \times \text{Feedback}$$

Jobs that are high on motivating potential must be high on at least one of the three factors that lead to experienced meaningfulness, and they must be high on both autonomy and feedback. If jobs score high on motivating potential, the model predicts that motivation, performance, and satisfaction will be positively affected and that the likelihood of absence and turnover will be reduced.

The JCM has been well researched. And most of the evidence supports the general framework of the theory—that is, there is a set of job characteristics, and these characteristics affect behavioral outcomes.[4] But it appears that the MPS model doesn't work—that is, we can better derive motivating potential by adding the characteristics rather than using the complex MPS formula.[5] Beyond employee growth-need strength, other variables, such as the employee's perception of his or her work load compared with that of others, may also moderate the link between the core job dimensions and personal and work outcomes.[6] Overall, though, it appears that jobs that have the intrinsic elements of variety, identity, significance, autonomy, and feedback are more satisfying and generate higher performance from people than jobs that lack these characteristics.

Take some time to think about your job. Do you have the opportunity to work on different tasks, or is your day pretty routine? Are you able to work independently, or do you constantly have a supervisor or coworker looking over your shoulder? What do you think your answers to these questions say about your job's motivating potential? Revisit your answers to the self-assessment at the beginning of this chapter and then calculate your MPS from the job characteristics model.

How Can Jobs Be Redesigned?

2 Compare and contrast the three main ways jobs can be redesigned.

"Every day was the same thing," Frank Greer said. "Stand on that assembly line. Wait for an instrument panel to be moved into place. Unlock the mechanism and drop the panel into the Jeep Liberty as it moved by on the line. Then I plugged in the harnessing wires. I repeated that for eight hours a day. I don't care that they were paying me $24 an hour. I was

autonomy *The degree to which a job provides substantial freedom and discretion to the individual in scheduling the work and in determining the procedures to be used in carrying it out.*

feedback *The degree to which carrying out the work activities required by a job results in the individual obtaining direct and clear information about the effectiveness of his or her performance.*

motivating potential score (MPS) *A predictive index that suggests the motivating potential in a job.*

Job rotation adds va
assembly task
automobile airbag
plant. Autoliv repla
line with U-shaped
that cons
workstations staffed
employees. Work
jobs every 24 minut
announces a job ro
rock music from
Steam through the
address system: "Na
hey,

Exhibit 7-3 Example of a Flextime Schedule

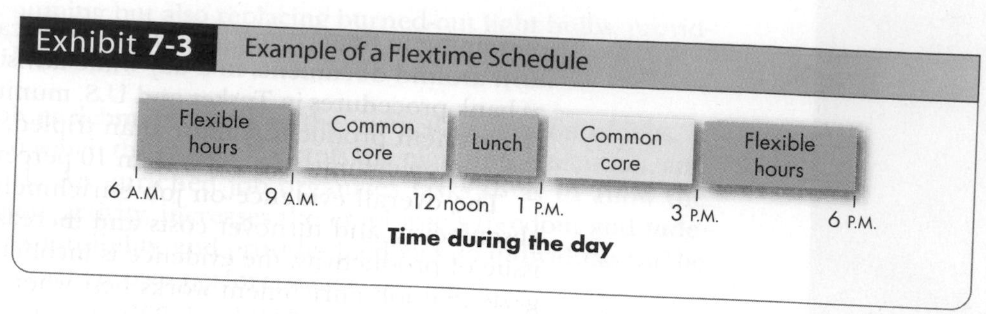

7 P.M. It's up to her how she schedules her 8-hour day within this 13-hour period. Because Susan is a morning person and also has a 7-year-old son who gets out of school at 3 P.M. every day, she opts to work from 6 A.M. to 3 P.M. "My work hours are perfect. I'm at the job when I'm mentally most alert, and I can be home to take care of my son after he gets out of school."

Susan Ross's work schedule at The Hartford is an example of **flextime**. The term is short for "flexible work time." It allows employees some discretion over when they arrive at work and when they leave. Employees have to work a specific number of hours a week, but they are free to vary the hours of work within certain limits. As shown in Exhibit 7-3, each day consists of a common core, usually 6 hours, with a flexibility band surrounding the core. For example, exclusive of a 1-hour lunch break, the core may be 9 A.M. to 3 P.M., with the office actually opening at 6 A.M. and closing at 6 P.M. All employees are required to be at their jobs during the common core period, but they are allowed to accumulate their other 2 hours before and/or after the core time. Some flextime programs allow extra hours to be accumulated and turned into a free day off each month.

Flextime has become an extremely popular scheduling option. In Germany, for instance, 29 percent of businesses have flextime for their employees.[18] The proportion of full-time U.S. employees on flextime more than doubled between the late 1980s and 2005. Approximately 43 percent of the U.S. full-time workforce now has flexibility in their daily arrival and departure times.[19]

The benefits claimed for flextime are numerous. They include reduced absenteeism, increased productivity, reduced overtime expenses, reduced hostility toward management, reduced traffic congestion around work sites, elimination of tardiness, and increased autonomy and responsibility for employees that may increase employee job satisfaction.[20] But beyond the claims, what's flextime's record?

Most of the performance evidence stacks up favorably. Flextime tends to reduce absenteeism and frequently improves worker productivity,[21] probably for several reasons. Employees can schedule their work hours to align with personal demands, thus reducing tardiness and absences, and employees can adjust their work activities to those hours in which they are individually most productive.

Flextime's major drawback is that it's not applicable to every job. It works well with clerical tasks for which an employee's interaction with people outside his or her department is limited. It is not a viable option for receptionists, sales personnel in retail stores, or similar jobs for which comprehensive service demands that people be at their workstations at predetermined times.

Job Sharing A recent work scheduling innovation is **job sharing**. It allows two or more individuals to split a traditional 40-hour-a-week job. So, for example, one person might perform the job from 8 A.M. to noon, while another performs the same job from 1 P.M. to 5 P.M.; or the two could work full, but alternate, days. As a case in point, Sue Manix and Charlotte Schutzman share the title of vice president of employee communications in the Philadelphia office of Verizon.[22] Schutzman works Monday and Tuesday, Manix works Thursday and Friday, and they alternate Wednesdays. The two women have job-shared for 10 years, acquiring promotions, numerous bonuses, and a 20-person staff along the way. With each having children at home, this arrangement allows them the flexibility to better balance their work and family responsibilities.

Approximately 31 percent of large organizations now offer their employees job sharing.[23] However, despite its availability, it doesn't seem to be widely adopted by employees. This is probably because of the difficulty of finding compatible partners to share a job and the negative perceptions historically held of individuals not completely committed to their job and employer.

Job sharing allows an organization to draw on the talents of more than one individual in a given job. A bank manager who oversees two job sharers describes it as an opportunity to get two heads but "pay for one."[24] It also opens up the opportunity to acquire skilled workers—for instance, women with young children and retirees—who might not be available on a full-time basis.[25] Many Japanese firms are increasingly considering job sharing—but for a very different reason.[26] Because Japanese executives are extremely reluctant to fire people, job sharing is seen as a potentially humanitarian means for avoiding layoffs due to overstaffing.

From the employee's perspective, job sharing increases flexibility. As such, it can increase motivation and satisfaction for those to whom a 40-hour-a-week job is just not practical. But the major drawback from management's perspective is finding compatible pairs of employees who can successfully coordinate the intricacies of one job.[27]

Telecommuting It might be close to the ideal job for many people. No commuting, flexible hours, freedom to dress as you please, and few or no interruptions from colleagues. It's called **telecommuting**, and it refers to employees who do their work at home at least 2 days a week on a computer that is linked to their office.[28] (A closely related term—*the virtual office*—is increasingly being used to describe employees who work out of their home on a relatively permanent basis.)

Recent estimates indicate that between 9 million and 24 million people telecommute in the United States, depending on exactly how the term is defined.[29] This translates to about 10 percent or more of the workforce. Well-known organizations that actively encourage telecommuting include AT&T, IBM, Merrill Lynch, American Express, Hewlett-Packard, and a number of U.S. government agencies.[30] The concept is also catching on elsewhere in the world. In Finland, Sweden, Britain, and Germany, telecommuters represent 17, 15, 8, and 6 percent of their workforces, respectively.[31]

What kinds of jobs lend themselves to telecommuting? Three categories have been identified as most appropriate: routine information-handling tasks, mobile activities, and professional and other knowledge-related tasks.[32] Writers, attorneys, analysts, and employees who spend the majority of their time on computers or the telephone are natural candidates for telecommuting. For instance, telemarketers, customer-service representatives, reservation agents, and product-support specialists spend most of their time on the phone.

job sharing *An arrangement that allows two or more individuals to split a traditional 40-hour-a-week job.*

telecommuting *Working from home at least two days a week on a computer that is linked to the employee's office.*

flextime *Flexible work hours.*

Telecommuting is appropriate for the knowledge-based work of employees at KPMG, a global network of professional firms that provides audit, tax, and advisory services. Kelvin Brown, a senior manager in KPMG's research and development tax concession section, works on his laptop at his beef cattle farm near Harden, Australia, a 4-hour drive away from the company's office in Sydney. For Brown, working from home increases his productivity and allows him more time to spend with his family.

As telecommuters, they can access information on their computers at home as easily as in the company's office.

There are numerous stories of telecommuting's success.[33] For instance, 3,500 Merrill Lynch employees telecommute. And after the program was in place just a year, management reported an increase in productivity of between 15 and 20 percent among their telecommuters, 3.5 fewer sick days a year, and a 6 percent decrease in turnover. Putnam Investments, located in Boston, has found telecommuting to be an attractive recruitment tool. The company was having difficulty attracting new hires. But after introducing telecommuting, the number of its applicants grew 20-fold. And Putnam's management calculates that the 12 percent of its employees who telecommute have substantially higher productivity than in-office staff and about one-tenth the attrition rate.

The potential pluses of telecommuting for management include a larger labor pool from which to select, higher productivity, less turnover, improved morale, and reduced office-space costs. The major downside for management is less direct supervision of employees. In addition, in today's team-focused workplace, telecommuting may make it more difficult for management to coordinate teamwork.[34] From the employee's standpoint, telecommuting offers a considerable increase in flexibility. But not without costs. For employees with a high social need, telecommuting can increase feelings of isolation and reduce job satisfaction. And all telecommuters potentially suffer from the "out of sight, out of mind" effect. Employees who aren't at their desks, who miss meetings, and who don't share in day-to-day informal workplace interactions may be at a disadvantage when it comes to raises and promotions. It can be easy for bosses to overlook or undervalue the contribution of employees whom they don't see regularly.

Ability and Opportunity

Robin and Anwar both graduated from college a couple years ago, with degrees in elementary education. They both took jobs as first-grade teachers but in different school districts. Robin immediately confronted a number of obstacles on the job: a large class (42 students), a small and dingy classroom, and inadequate supplies. Anwar's situation couldn't have been more different. He had only 15 students in his class, plus a teaching aide for 15 hours each week, a modern and well-lighted room, a well-stocked supply cabinet, an iMac computer for every student, and a highly supportive principal. Not surprisingly, at the end of their first school year, Anwar had been considerably more effective as a teacher than had Robin.

The preceding episode illustrates an obvious but often overlooked fact. Success on a job is facilitated or hindered by the existence or absence of support resources.

A popular, although arguably simplistic, way of thinking about employee performance is as a function (f) of the interaction of ability (A) and motivation (M); that is, Performance = $f(A \times M)$. If either ability or motivation is inadequate, performance will be negatively affected. This helps to explain, for instance, a hard-working athlete or student with modest abilities who consistently outperforms a more gifted, but lazy, rival. So, as noted in Chapter 2, an individual's intelligence and skills (subsumed under the label *ability*) must be considered in addition to motivation if we are to accurately explain and predict employee performance. But a piece of the puzzle is still missing. We need to add **opportunity to perform** (O) to our equation: Performance = $f(A \times M \times O)$.[35] Even though an individual may be willing and able, there may be obstacles that constrain performance.

When you attempt to assess why an employee is not performing to the level at which you believe he or she is capable of performing, take a look at the work environment to see if it's supportive. Does the employee have adequate tools, equipment, materials, and supplies? Does the employee have favorable working conditions, helpful coworkers, supportive work rules and procedures, sufficient information to make job-related decisions, adequate time to do a good job, and the like? If not, performance will suffer.

Employee Involvement

4 *Give examples of employee involvement measures and show how they can motivate employees.*

What specifically do we mean by **employee involvement**? We define it as a participative process that uses the input of employees to increase their commitment to the organization's success. The underlying logic is that if we involve workers in the decisions that affect them and increase their autonomy and control over their work lives, employees will become more motivated, more committed to the organization, more productive, and more satisfied with their jobs.[36]

Examples of Employee Involvement Programs

Let's look at the three major forms of employee involvement—participative management, representative participation, and quality circles—in more detail.

Participative Management The distinct characteristic common to all **participative management** programs is the use of joint decision making. That is,

opportunity to perform *Absence of obstacles that constrain the employee. High levels of performance are partially a function of the opportunity to perform.*

employee involvement *A participative process that uses the input of employees and is intended to increase employee commitment to an organization's success.*

participative management *A process in which subordinates share a significant degree of decision-making power with their immediate superiors.*

subordinates actually share a significant degree of decision-making power with their immediate superiors. Participative management has, at times, been promoted as a panacea for poor morale and low productivity. But for it to work, the issues in which employees get involved must be relevant to their interests so they'll be motivated, employees must have the competence and knowledge to make a useful contribution, and there must be trust and confidence between all parties involved.[37]

Dozens of studies have been conducted on the participation–performance relationship. The findings, however, are mixed.[38] A careful review of the research seems to show that participation typically has only a modest influence on variables such as employee productivity, motivation, and job satisfaction. Of course, this doesn't mean that the use of participative management can't be beneficial under the right conditions. What it says, however, is that the use of participation is not a sure means for improving employee performance.

Representative Participation Almost every country in western Europe has some type of legislation that requires companies to practice **representative participation**. That is, rather than participating directly in decisions, workers are represented by a small group of employees who actually participate. Representative participation has been called "the most widely legislated form of employee involvement around the world."[39] The goal of representative participation is to redistribute power within an organization, putting labor on a more equal footing with the interests of management and stockholders.

Wegmans grocery stores involve their employees in making decisions that affect their work and please their customers. For example, Wegmans bakery employee Maria Benjamin, shown here, persuaded the company president to sell her chocolate meatball cookies that were made using a recipe passed down from Benjamins's Italian ancestors. Wegmans encourages employees to make on-the-spot decisions without consulting their immediate supervisors. That could include an employee's decision to cook customers' Thanksgiving turkeys because the ones they bought were too big for their home ovens.

The two most common forms representative participation takes are works councils and board representatives.[40] Works councils are groups of nominated or elected employees who must be consulted when management makes decisions involving personnel. Board representatives are employees who sit on a company's board of directors and represent the interests of the firm's employees.

The overall influence of representative participation on working employees seems to be minimal.[41] For instance, the evidence suggests that works councils are dominated by management and have little impact on employees or the organization. And although this form of employee involvement might increase the motivation and satisfaction of the individuals who are doing the representing, there is little evidence that this trickles down to the operating employees whom they represent. Overall, "the greatest value of representative participation is symbolic. If one is interested in changing employee attitudes or in improving organizational performance, representative participation would be a poor choice."[42]

Quality Circles Initially developed in Japan, **quality circles** became popular in Europe, and North America during the 1980s.[43] Companies such as Toyota, Hewlett-Packard, General Electric, Xerox, Procter & Gamble, IBM, Motorola, and American Airlines used quality circles. A quality circle is defined as a work group of 8 to 10 employees and supervisors who have a shared area of responsibility and who meet regularly—typically once a week, on company time and on company premises—to discuss their quality problems, investigate causes of the problems, recommend solutions, and take corrective actions.

A review of the evidence on quality circles indicates that they tend to show little or no effect on employee satisfaction, and although many studies report positive results from quality circles on productivity, these results are by no means guaranteed.[44] The failure of many quality circle programs to produce measurable benefits has also led to a large number of them being discontinued. One of the reasons for their failure is that managers deal with employee involvement in only a limited way. "At most, these programs operate for one hour per week, with the remaining 39 hours unchanged. Why should changes in 2.5 percent of a person's job have a major impact?"[45] Basically, quality circles were an easy way for management to get on the employee involvement bandwagon without really involving employees.

Linking Employee Involvement Programs and Motivation Theories

Employee involvement draws on a number of the motivation theories discussed in Chapter 6. For instance, Theory Y is consistent with participative management, and Theory X aligns with the more traditional autocratic style of managing people. In terms of two-factor theory, employee involvement programs could provide employees with intrinsic motivation by increasing opportunities for growth, responsibility, and involvement in the work itself. Similarly, the opportunity to make and implement decisions—and then seeing them work out—can help satisfy an employee's needs for responsibility, achievement, recognition, growth, and enhanced self-esteem. So employee involvement is compatible with ERG theory and efforts to stimulate the achievement need. And extensive employee involvement programs clearly have the potential to increase employee intrinsic motivation in work tasks.

Using Rewards to Motivate Employees

5 *Demonstrate how the different types of variable-pay programs can increase employee motivation.*

As we saw in Chapter 3, pay is not a primary factor driving job satisfaction. However, it does motivate people, and companies often underestimate the importance of pay in keeping top talent. A 2006 study found that whereas only 45 percent of employers thought that pay was a key factor in losing top talent, 71 percent of top performers indicated that it was a top reason.[46]

Given that pay is so important, we need to understand what to pay employees and how to pay them. To do that, management must make some strategic decisions. Will the organization lead, match, or lag the market in pay? How will individual contributions be recognized? In this section, we consider four major strategic rewards decisions that need to be made: (1) what to pay employees (which is decided by establishing a pay structure); (2) how to pay individual employees (which is decided through

representative participation *A system in which workers participate in organizational decision making through a small group of representative employees.*

quality circle *A work group of employees who meet regularly to discuss their quality problems, investigate causes, recommend solutions, and take corrective actions.*

variable pay plans and skill-based pay plans); (3) what benefits to offer, especially whether to offer employees choice in benefits (flexible benefits); and (4) how to construct employee recognition programs.

What to Pay: Establishing a Pay Structure

There are many ways to pay employees. The process of initially setting pay levels can be rather complex and entails balancing *internal equity*—the worth of the job to the organization (usually established through a technical process called job evaluation)—and *external equity*—the external competitiveness of an organization's pay relative to pay elsewhere in its industry (usually established through pay surveys). Obviously, the best pay system pays the job what it is worth (internal equity) while also paying competitively relative to the labor market.

Some organizations prefer to be pay leaders by paying above the market, while some may lag the market because they can't afford to pay market rates, or they are willing to bear the costs of paying below market (namely, higher turnover as people are lured to better-paying jobs). Wal-Mart, for example, pays less than its competitors and often outsources jobs overseas. Chinese workers in Shenzhen earn $120 a month (that's $1,440 per year) to make stereos for Wal-Mart. Of the 6,000 factories that are worldwide suppliers to Wal-Mart, 80 percent are located in China. In fact, one-eighth of all Chinese exports to the United States go to Wal-Mart.[47]

Pay more, and you may get better-qualified, more highly motivated employees who will stay with the organization longer. But pay is often the highest single operating cost for an organization, which means that paying too much can make the organization's products or services too expensive. It's a strategic decision an organization must make, with clear trade-offs.

How to Pay: Rewarding Individual Employees Through Variable-Pay Programs

"Why should I put any extra effort into this job?" asked Anne Garcia, a fourth-grade elementary schoolteacher in Denver, Colorado. "I can excel or I can do the bare minimum. It makes no difference. I get paid the same. Why do anything above the minimum to get by?"

Comments similar to Anne's have been voiced by schoolteachers for decades because pay increases were tied to seniority. Recently, however, a number of schools have begun revamping their compensation systems to motivate people like Anne to strive for excellence in their jobs. For instance, some U.S. states have introduced programs that tie teacher pay to the performance of the students in their classrooms.[48] In California, some teachers are now eligible for performance bonuses as high as $25,000 per year.[49]

A number of organizations—business firms as well as school districts and other government agencies—are moving away from paying people based solely on credentials or length of service and toward using variable-pay programs. Piece-rate plans, merit-based pay, bonuses, profit-sharing, gainsharing, and employee stock ownership plans are all forms of **variable-pay programs**. Instead of paying a person only for time on the job or seniority, a variable-pay program bases a portion of an employee's pay on some individual and/or organizational measure of performance. Earnings therefore fluctuate up and down with the measure of performance.[50] Variable-pay plans have long been used to compensate salespeople and executives. Recently they have begun to be applied to other employees. IBM, Wal-Mart, Pizza Hut, Cigna Corp., and John Deere are

Science teacher John Roper-Batker at Seward Montessori School in Minneapolis, Minnesota, supports the variable-pay initiative being adopted by many school districts in Minnesota. The new pay plan motivates teachers by basing their pay on their performance in raising student achievement rather than on seniority or degrees. The move toward rewarding teachers with bonuses for their individual performance follows the widespread adoption of variable-pay plans in many businesses and government agencies.

Source: Ben Garvin/ The New York Times

just a few examples of companies using variable pay with rank-and-file employees.[51] Today, more than 70 percent of U.S. companies have some form of variable-pay plan, up from only about 5 percent in 1970.[52] Unfortunately, recent survey data indicate that most employees still don't see a strong connection between pay and performance. Only 29 percent say that when they do a good job, their performance is rewarded.[53]

It is precisely the fluctuation in variable pay that has made these programs attractive to management. It turns part of an organization's fixed labor costs into a variable cost, thus reducing expenses when performance declines. So when economies around the world encountered a recession in 2001, companies with variable pay were able to reduce their labor costs much faster than companies that had maintained non-performance-based compensation systems.[54] In addition, when pay is tied to performance, the employee's earnings recognize contribution rather than being a form of entitlement. Low performers find, over time, that their pay stagnates, while high performers enjoy pay increases commensurate with their contributions.

Let's examine the different types of variable-pay programs in more detail.

Piece-Rate Pay Piece-rate wages have been popular for more than a century as a means of compensating production workers. In **piece-rate pay plans**, workers are paid a fixed sum for each unit of production completed. When an employee gets no base salary and is paid only for what he or she produces, this is a pure piece-rate plan. People who work in ballparks selling peanuts and soda are frequently paid this way. If they sell only 40 bags of peanuts, their take

variable-pay program *A pay plan that bases a portion of an employee's pay on some individual and/or organizational measure of performance.*

piece-rate pay plan *A pay plan in which workers are paid a fixed sum for each unit of production completed.*

is only $40. The harder they work and the more peanuts they sell, the more they earn. The limitation of these plans is that they're not feasible for many jobs. For example, Alabama college football coach Nick Saban earns $4 million per year. That salary is paid regardless of how many games he wins. Would it be better to pay Saban, for example, $400,000 for each win? It seems unlikely he would accept such a deal, and it may cause unanticipated consequences as well (such as cheating). So, although incentives are motivating and relevant for some jobs, it is unrealistic to think they can constitute the only piece of some employees' pay.

Merit-Based Pay Merit-based pay plans pay for individual performance. However, unlike piece-rate plans, which pay based on objective output, **merit-based pay plans** are based on performance appraisal ratings. A main advantage of merit pay plans is that they allow employers to differentiate pay based on performance so that those people thought to be high performers are given bigger raises. The plans can be motivating because, if they are designed correctly, individuals perceive a strong relationship between their performance and the rewards they receive. The evidence supports the importance of this linkage.[55]

Most large organizations have merit pay plans, especially for salaried employees. IBM's merit pay plan, for example, provides increases to employees' base salary based on their annual performance evaluation. Since the 1990s, when the economy stumbled badly, an increasing number of Japanese companies have abandoned seniority-based pay in favor of merit-based pay. Koichi Yanashita, of Takeda Chemical Industries, commented, "The merit-based salary system is an important means to achieve goals set by the company's top management, not just a way to change wages."[56]

In an effort to motivate and retain top performers, more companies are increasing the differential between top and bottom performers. The consulting firm Hewitt Associates found that, in 2006, employers gave their best performers roughly 10 percent raises, compared to 3.6 percent for average performers and 1.3 percent for below-average performers. They've also found that these differences have increased over time. Martyn Fisher of Imperial Chemical in the United Kingdom said that his company has widened the merit pay gap between top and average performers because, "as much as we would regret our average performers leaving, we'd regret more an above-target performer leaving."[57]

Despite the intuitive appeal of pay for performance, merit pay plans have several limitations. One of them is that, typically, such plans are based on an annual performance appraisal. Thus, the merit pay is as valid or invalid as the performance ratings on which it is based. Another limitation of merit pay is that sometimes the pay raise pool fluctuates based on economic conditions or other factors that have little to do with an individual employee's performance. One year, a colleague at a top university who performed very well in teaching and research was given a pay raise of $300. Why? Because the pay raise pool was very small. Yet that is hardly pay-for-performance. Finally, unions typically resist merit pay plans. Because the largest teachers' unions have generally resisted it, relatively few teachers are covered by merit pay. Instead, seniority-based pay, where all employees get the same raises, predominates.

Bonuses For many jobs, annual bonuses are a significant component of the total compensation. Among Fortune 100 CEOs, the bonus (with a mean of $1.01 million) generally exceeds the base salary (with a mean of $863,000). Increasingly, bonus plans are casting a larger net within organizations to include lower-ranking employees. Many companies now routinely reward production employees with bonuses in the thousands of dollars when company profits improve. The steel company Nucor, for example, guarantees its employees only about $10/hour, but its bonuses can be substantial; the average Nucor worker made roughly $91,000 last year. One advantage of bonuses over merit pay is that **bonuses** reward employees for recent performance rather than historical performance. The incentive effects of performance should be higher because, rather than paying people for performance that may have occurred years ago (and was rolled into their base pay), bonuses reward only recent performance. The downside of bonuses is that employees may view them as pay—after all, any worker would choose a $5,000 raise rolled into her base pay over a one-time payment of $5,000. KeySpan Corp., a 9,700-employee utility company in New York, tried to manage this trade-off by combining yearly bonuses with a smaller merit-pay raise. Elaine Weinstein, KeySpan's senior vice president of HR, credits the plan with changing the culture from "entitlement to meritocracy."[58]

Skill-Based Pay **Skill-based pay** is an alternative to job-based pay. Rather than having an individual's job title define his or her pay category, skill-based pay (also called *competency-based* or *knowledge-based pay*) sets pay levels on the basis of how many skills employees have or how many jobs they can do.[59] For instance, employees at American Steel & Wire can boost their annual salaries by up to $12,480 by acquiring as many as 10 new skills. The food-products manufacturer Frito-Lay Corporation ties its compensation for frontline operations managers to developing their skills in leadership, workforce development, and functional excellence. For employers, the lure of skill-based pay plans is that they increase the flexibility of the workforce: Filling staffing needs is easier when employee skills are interchangeable. Skill-based pay also facilitates communication across the organization because people gain a better understanding of each others' jobs.

What about the downside of skill-based pay? People can "top out"—that is, they can learn all the skills the program calls for them to learn. This can frustrate employees after they've become challenged by an environment of learning, growth, and continual pay raises. There is also a problem created by paying people for acquiring skills for which there may be no immediate need. This happened at IDS Financial Services.[60] The company found itself paying people more money even though there was little immediate use for their new skills. IDS eventually dropped its skill-based pay plan and replaced it with one that equally balances individual contribution and gains in work-team productivity. Finally, skill-based plans don't address the level of performance. They deal only with whether someone can perform the skill.

Profit-Sharing Plans **Profit-sharing plans** are organizationwide programs that distribute compensation based on some established formula designed around a company's profitability. These can be direct cash outlays or, particularly

merit-based pay plan *A pay plan based on performance appraisal ratings.*

bonus *A pay plan that rewards employees for recent performance rather than historical performance.*

skill-based pay *A pay plan that sets pay levels on the basis of how many skills employees have or how many jobs they can do.*

profit-sharing plan *An organizationwide program that distributes compensation based on some established formula designed around a company's profitability.*

Continental Airlines President Jeff Smisek (center) celebrates with employees after distributing $111 million in profit-sharing checks to the company's 44,000 employees who helped return the airline to profitability. In addition, employees received stock options valued at about $250 million.

in the case of top managers, allocations of stock options. When you read about executives like Reuben Mark, the CEO at Colgate-Palmolive, earning $148 million in a year, almost all this comes from cashing in stock options previously granted based on company profit performance. Not all profit-sharing plans, though, need be so grand in scale. Jacob Luke, 13, started his own lawn-mowing business after getting a mower from his uncle. Jacob employs his brother, Isaiah, and friend, Marcel Monroe, and pays them each 25 percent of the profits he makes on each yard.

Gainsharing A variable-pay program that has gotten a great deal of attention in recent years is **gainsharing**.[61] This is a formula-based group incentive plan. Improvements in group productivity from one period to another determine the total amount of money that is to be allocated. Gainsharing's popularity seems to be narrowly focused among large manufacturing companies such as Champion Spark Plug and Mead Paper. For instance, approximately 45 percent of Fortune 1000 firms have implemented gainsharing plans.[62] Gainsharing is different from profit-sharing in that rewards are tied to productivity gains rather than on profits. Employees in a gainsharing plan can receive incentive awards even when the organization isn't profitable.

Employee Stock Ownership Plans **Employee stock ownership plans (ESOPs)** are company-established benefit plans in which employees acquire stock, often at below-market prices, as part of their benefits. Companies as varied as Publix Supermarkets and W.L. Gore & Associates are now over 50 percent employee owned.[63] But most of the 10,000 or so ESOPs in the United States, for example, are in small, privately held companies.[64]

The research on ESOPs indicates that they increase employee satisfaction.[65] But their impact on performance is less clear. ESOPs have the potential to increase employee job satisfaction and work motivation. But for this potential to be realized, employees need to psychologically experience ownership.[66] That is, in addition to merely having a financial stake in the company, employees

OB In the News

Motivating with Performance Reviews

The past few years have witnessed some pretty dramatic changes in the ways employers are reviewing employees' performance. Traditionally, almost all employees participated in a yearly performance review, where performance was thoroughly reviewed in a sit-down with their immediate supervisor, a written letter or form was completed, and the employee was given an annual raise.

Although a lot of companies still do it this way, increasingly employers are turning to more frequent and less formal performance reviews. The appliance company Whirlpool Coporation has switched from an annual performance review to a quarterly review. Jeffrey Davidoff, a marketing manager at Whirlpool, reviews each of his eight immediate subordinates for 45 minutes each quarter. When asked about the new program, Davidoff commented, "I'm noticing much better results. I am pleasantly surprised at how many day-to-day behaviors have changed."

In today's business environment, short-term results matter, and performance varies too much on a day-to-day basis to leave it to an annual review. For these reasons, many other employers besides Whirlpool are conducting more frequent performance reviews. National Cooperative Bank in Washington, DC, now conducts more frequent reviews, as does forest products company Weyerhauser.

Whirlpool's Davidoff has found that the more frequent appraisal process has changed his behavior, too. Rather than doing the marketing work himself, he now focuses more on coaching and developing his employees to take on some of his responsibilities. "This is how work gets done," he says. "If you believe in your people, the time with them is literally the best way to spend your time."

Source: Based on E. White, "For Relevance, Firms Revamp Worker Reviews," *Wall Street Journal*, July 17, 2006, pp. B1, B5.

need to be kept regularly informed of the status of the business and also have the opportunity to exercise influence over it. The evidence consistently indicates that it takes ownership and a participative style of management to achieve significant improvements in an organization's performance.[67]

Evaluation of Variable Pay Do variable-pay programs increase motivation and productivity? The answer is a qualified "yes." For example, studies generally support the idea that organizations with profit-sharing plans have higher levels of profitability than those without them.[68] Similarly, gainsharing has been found to improve productivity in a majority of cases and often has a positive impact on employee attitudes.[69] Another study found that whereas piece-rate pay-for-performance plans stimulated higher levels of productivity, this positive affect was not observed for risk-averse employees. Thus, in general, what economist Ed Lazear has said seems generally right: "Workers respond to prices just as economic theory predicts. Claims by sociologists and others that monetizing incentives may actually reduce output are unambiguously refuted by the data." But that doesn't mean everyone responds positively to variable-pay plans.[70]

Flexible Benefits: Developing a Benefits Package

6 Show how flexible benefits turn benefits into motivators.

Hans Drickhamer, Evans and Allison Murphy both work for Citigroup, but they have very different needs in terms of employee benefits. Hans is married and has three young children and a wife who is at home full time. Allison, too, is married, but her husband has a high-paying job with the

gainsharing *A formula-based group incentive plan.*

employee stock ownership plan (ESOP) *A company-established benefits plan in which employees acquire stock, often at below-market prices, as part of their benefits.*

Software developer Oracle Corporation in Redwood City, California, provides employees with basic benefits and then enables them to choose coverage levels and additional benefits that meet their individual needs and those of their dependents. Flexible benefits are consistent with the expectancy theory thesis that links rewards to individual employees' goals. The OracleFlex plan gives employees flex credits they can use to purchase benefits so they can control the amount they spend for each benefit option. Employees with remaining credits may direct them toward taxable income or to their 401(k) savings plan, health care reimbursement, or dependent care reimbursement accounts.

federal government, and they have no children. Hans is concerned about having a good medical plan and enough life insurance to support his family in case it's needed. In contrast, Allison's husband already has her medical needs covered on his plan, and life insurance is a low priority for both Allison and her husband. Allison is more interested in extra vacation time and long-term financial benefits such as a tax-deferred savings plan.

A standardized benefits package for all employees at Citigroup would be unlikely to satisfactorily meet the needs of both Hans and Allison. Citigroup could, however, cover both sets of needs if it offered flexible benefits.

Flexible benefits allow each employee to put together a benefits package individually tailored to his or her own needs and situation. It replaces the traditional "one-benefit-plan-fits-all" programs that dominated organizations for more than 50 years.[71] Consistent with expectancy theory's thesis that organizational rewards should be linked to each individual employee's goals, flexible benefits individualize rewards by allowing each employee to choose the compensation package that best satisfies his or her current needs. The average organization provides fringe benefits worth approximately 40 percent of an employee's salary. Traditional benefits programs were designed for the typical employee of the 1950s—a male with a wife and two children at home. Less than 10 percent of employees now fit this stereotype. About 25 percent of today's employees are single, and one-third are part of two-income families with no children. Traditional programs don't meet their diverse needs, but flexible benefits do. They can be uniquely tailored to accommodate differences in employee needs based on age, marital status, spouses' benefit status, number and age of dependents, and the like.

The three most popular types of benefits plans are modular plans, core-plus options, and flexible spending accounts.[72] *Modular plans* are predesigned packages of benefits, with each module put together to meet the needs of a specific group of employees. So a module designed for single employees with no dependents might include only essential benefits. Another, designed for single parents, might have additional life insurance, disability insurance, and expanded health coverage. *Core-plus plans* consist of a core of essential benefits and a menu-like selection of other benefit options from which employees can select and add to the core. Typically, each employee is given "benefit credits," which allow the "purchase" of additional benefits that uniquely meet his or her needs. *Flexible spending plans* allow employees to set aside up to the dollar amount offered in the plan to pay for particular services. It's a convenient way, for example, for employees to pay for health care and dental premiums. Flexible spending accounts can increase employee take-home pay because employees don't have to pay taxes on the dollars they spend out of these accounts.

Intrinsic Rewards: Employee Recognition Programs

Laura Schendell makes only $8.50 per hour working at her fast-food job in Vancouver, British Columbia, and the job isn't very challenging or interesting. Yet Laura talks enthusiastically about her job, her boss, and the company that employs her. "What I like is the fact that Guy [her supervisor] appreciates the effort I make. He compliments me regularly in front of the other people on my shift, and I've been chosen Employee of the Month twice in the past six months. Did you see my picture on that plaque on the wall?"

7 *Identify the motivational benefits of intrinsic rewards.*

Organizations are increasingly recognizing what Laura Schendell knows: Important work rewards can be both intrinsic and extrinsic. Rewards are intrinsic in the form of employee recognition programs and extrinsic in the form of compensation systems. In this section,

Exhibit 7-4

Source: From the *Wall Street Journal*, October 21, 1997. Reprinted by permission of Cartoon Features Syndicate.

we deal with ways in which managers can reward and motivate employee performance.

Employee recognition programs range from a spontaneous and private "thank you" up to widely publicized formal programs in which specific types of behavior are encouraged and the procedures for attaining recognition are clearly identified. Some research has suggested that whereas financial incentives may be more motivating in the short term, in the long run, nonfinancial incentives are more motivating.[73]

Nichols Foods Ltd., a British bottler of soft drinks and syrups, has a comprehensive recognition program.[74] The central hallway in its production area is lined with "bragging boards," where the accomplishments of various individuals and teams are regularly updated. Monthly awards are presented to people who have been nominated by peers for extraordinary effort on the job. And monthly award winners are eligible for further recognition at an annual off-site meeting for all employees. In contrast, most managers use a far more informal approach. Julia Stewart, president of Applebee's restaurants, frequently leaves sealed notes on the chairs of employees after everyone has gone home.[75] These notes explain how critical Stewart thinks the person's work is or how much she appreciates the completion of a recent project. Stewart also relies heavily on voice mail messages left after office hours to tell employees how appreciative she is for a job well done.

A few years ago, 1,500 employees were surveyed in a variety of work settings to find out what they considered to be the most powerful workplace motivator. Their response? Recognition, recognition, and more recognition.[76] As illustrated in Exhibit 7-5, Phoenix Inn, a U.S. chain of small hotels, encourages employees to smile by letting customers identify this desirable behavior and

flexible benefits *A benefits plan that allows each employee to put together a benefits package individually tailored to his or her own needs and situation.*

Exhibit 7-5

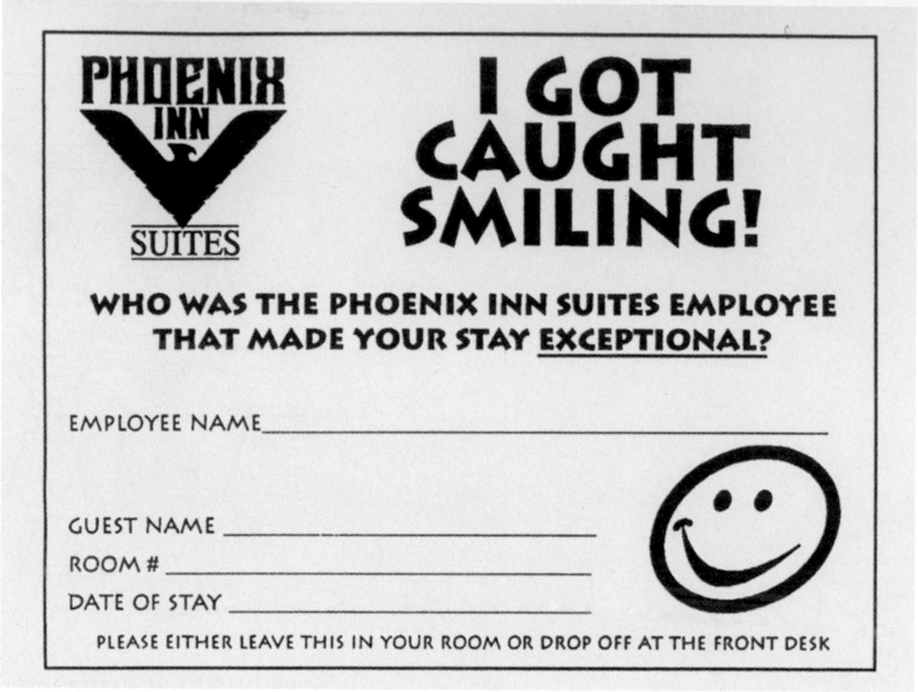

PHOENIX INN SUITES

I GOT CAUGHT SMILING!

WHO WAS THE PHOENIX INN SUITES EMPLOYEE THAT MADE YOUR STAY EXCEPTIONAL?

EMPLOYEE NAME________________

GUEST NAME ________________

ROOM # ________________

DATE OF STAY ________________

PLEASE EITHER LEAVE THIS IN YOUR ROOM OR DROP OFF AT THE FRONT DESK

then recognizing employees who are identified smiling most often by giving them rewards and publicity.

An obvious advantage of recognition programs is that they are inexpensive (praise, of course, is free!).[77] It shouldn't be surprising, therefore, to find that employee recognition programs have grown in popularity. A 2002 survey of 391 companies found that 84 percent had some program to recognize worker achievements and that 4 in 10 said they were doing more to foster employee recognition than they had been just a year earlier.[78]

Despite the increased popularity of employee recognition programs, critics argue that these programs are highly susceptible to political manipulation by management.[79] When applied to jobs where performance factors are relatively objective, such as sales, recognition programs are likely to be perceived by employees as fair. However, in most jobs, the criteria for good performance aren't self-evident, which allows managers to manipulate the system and recognize their favorite employees. Abuse of such a system can undermine the value of recognition programs and lead to demoralizing employees.

Global Implications

Do the motivational approaches discussed in this chapter vary by culture? Because we've discussed some very different approaches in this chapter, let's break down our analysis by approach. Not every approach has been studied by cross-cultural researchers, so we don't discuss every motivational approach. However, we consider cross-cultural differences in the following approaches: (1) job characteristics and job enrichment, (2) telecommuting, (3) variable pay, (4) flexible benefits, and (5) employee involvement.

International OB

Cultural Differences in Job Characteristics and Job Satisfaction

How do various factors of one's job contribute to satisfaction in different cultures? A recent study attempted to answer this question in a survey of about 50 countries. The authors of the study distinguished between intrinsic job characteristics (for example, having a job that allows one to use one's skills, frequently receiving recognition from one's supervisor) and extrinsic job characteristics (for example, receiving pay that is competitive within a given industry, working in an environment that has comfortable physical conditions) and assessed differences between the two in predicting employee job satisfaction.

The study found that, across all countries, extrinsic job characteristics were consistently and positively related to satisfaction with one's job. However, countries differed in the extent to which intrinsic job characteristics predicted job satisfaction. Wealthier countries, countries with stronger social security, countries that stress individualism rather than collectivism, and countries with a smaller power distance (those that value a more equal distribution of power in organizations and institutions) showed a stronger relationship between the presence of intrinsic job characteristics and job satisfaction.

What explains these findings? One explanation is that in countries with greater wealth and social security, concerns over survival are taken for granted, and thus employees have the freedom to place greater importance on intrinsic aspects of the job. Another explanation is that cultural norms that emphasize the individual and have less power asymmetry socialize individuals to focus on the intrinsic aspects of their job. In other words, such norms tell individuals that it is okay to want jobs that are intrinsically rewarding.

Source: Based on X. Huang and E. Van De Vliert, "Where Intrinsic Job Satisfaction Fails to Work: National Moderators of Intrinsic Motivation," *Journal of Organizational Behavior* 24, no. 2 (2003), pp. 159–179.

Job Characteristics and Job Enrichment Although a few studies have tested the job characteristics model in different cultures, the results aren't very consistent. One study suggested that when employees are "other-oriented" (that is, concerned with the welfare of others at work), the relationship between intrinsic job characteristics and job satisfaction was weaker. As the authors note, because the job characteristics model is relatively individualistic (considering the relationship between the employee and his or her work), this suggests that job enrichment strategies may not have the same effects in more collectivistic cultures that they do in individualistic cultures.[80] However, another study suggested that the degree to which jobs had intrinsic job characteristics predicted job satisfaction and job involvement equally well for Japanese, Hungarian, and U.S. employees.[81]

Telecommuting Does the degree to which employees telecommute vary by nation? Does it effectiveness depend on culture? First, one study suggests that telecommuting is more common in the United States than in all the European Union (EU) nations except the Netherlands. In the study, 24.6 percent of U.S. employees engaged in telecommuting, compared to only 13.0 percent of EU employees. Of the EU countries, the Netherlands had the highest rate of telecommuting (26.4 percent); the lowest rates were in Spain (4.9 percent) and Portugal (3.4 percent). Thus, telecommuting appears to be more common in the United States than in Europe. What about the rest of the world? Unfortunately, there are very little data comparing telecommuting rates in other parts of the world. Similarly, we don't really know whether telecommuting works better in the United States than in other countries. However, the same study that compared telework rates between the United States and the EU determined that employees in Europe appeared to have the same level of interest in telework: Regardless of country, interest is higher among employees than among employers.[82]

Variable Pay You'd probably think that individual pay systems (such as merit pay or pay-for-performance) would work better in individualistic cultures like the United States than in collectivistic cultures like China or Venezuela. Similarly, you'd probably hypothesize that group-based rewards such as gainsharing or profit-sharing would work better in collectivistic cultures than in individualistic cultures. Unfortunately, there isn't much research on the issue. One recent study did suggest, though, that beliefs about the fairness of a group incentive plan were more predictive of pay satisfaction for employees in the United States than for employees in Hong Kong. One interpretation of these findings is that U.S. employees are more critical in appraising a group pay plan, and therefore it's more critical that the plan be communicated clearly and administered fairly.[83]

Flexible Benefits Today, almost all major corporations in the United States offer flexible benefits. And they're becoming the norm in other countries, too. For instance, a recent survey of 136 Canadian organizations found that 93 percent have adopted or will adopt flexible benefits in the near term.[84] And a similar survey of 307 firms in the United Kingdom found that while only 16 percent have flexible benefits programs in place, another 60 percent are either in the process of implementing them or are seriously considering it.[85]

Employee Involvement Employee involvement programs differ among countries.[86] For instance, a study comparing the acceptance of employee involvement programs in four countries, including the United States and India, confirmed the importance of modifying practices to reflect national culture.[87] Specifically, while U.S. employees readily accepted these programs, managers in India who tried to empower their employees through employee involvement programs were rated low by those employees. Employee satisfaction also decreased. These reactions are consistent with India's high power–distance culture, which accepts and expects differences in authority.

Summary and Implications for Managers

We've presented a number of motivation theories and applications in Chapter 6 and in this chapter. Although it's always dangerous to synthesize a large number of complex ideas into a few simple guidelines, the following suggestions summarize the essence of what we know about motivating employees in organizations.

Recognize Individual Differences Managers should be sensitive to individual differences. For example, employees from Asian cultures prefer not to be singled out as special because it makes them uncomfortable.

Employees have different needs. Don't treat them all alike. Moreover, spend the time necessary to understand what's important to each employee. This allows you to individualize goals, level of involvement, and rewards to align with individual needs. Also, design jobs to align with individual needs and therefore maximize the motivation potential in jobs.

Use Goals and Feedback Employees should have firm, specific goals, and they should get feedback on how well they are faring in pursuit of those goals.

Allow Employees to Participate in Decisions That Affect Them Employees can contribute to a number of decisions that affect them: setting work goals, choosing their own benefits packages, solving productivity and quality problems, and the like. This can increase employee productivity, commitment to work goals, motivation, and job satisfaction.

Link Rewards to Performance Rewards should be contingent on performance. Importantly, employees must perceive a clear linkage between performance and rewards. Regardless of how closely rewards are actually correlated to performance criteria, if individuals perceive this relationship to be low, the results will be low performance, a decrease in job satisfaction, and an increase in turnover and absenteeism.

Check the System for Equity Employees should perceive rewards as equating with the inputs they bring to the job. At a simplistic level, this should mean that experience, skills, abilities, effort, and other obvious inputs should explain differences in performance and, hence, pay, job assignments, and other obvious rewards.

Point / Counterpoint

PRAISE MOTIVATES

Some of the most memorable, and meaningful, words we've ever heard have probably been words of praise. Genuine compliments mean a lot to people—and can go a long way toward inspiring the best performance. Numerous research studies show that students who receive praise from their teachers are more motivated, and often this motivation lasts well after the praise is given. Too often we assume that simple words of praise mean little, but most of us yearn for genuine praise from people who are in a position to evaluate us.

Companies are starting to learn this lesson. Walt Disney, Lands' End, and Hallmark have worked on how to use praise as a work reward to motivate employees. The 1,000-employee Scooter Store even has a "celebrations assistant" whose job is to celebrate employee successes. The Container Store estimates that 1 of its 4,000 employees receives praise every 20 seconds. Bank of America also believes in the power of praise. It "encourage[s] managers to start every meeting with informal recognition," says Bank of American VP Kevin Cronin.

Praise even seems to be important to long-term relationships. The Gottman Institute, a relationship research and training firm in Seattle, says its research suggests that the happiest marriages are those in which couples make five times as many positive statements to and about each other as negative ones. Of course, praise is not everything, but it is a very important and often underutilized motivator. And best of all, it's free.

Praise is highly overrated. Sure, in theory, it's nice to receive compliments, but in practice, praise has some real pitfalls.

First, a lot of praise is not genuine. Falsely praising people breeds narcissism. Jean Twenge, a researcher who studies narcissism, has said that scores on narcissism have risen steadily since 1982. As she notes, lavishing praise may be the culprit. Told we're wonderful time after time, we start to believe it, even when we aren't.

Second, praise is paradoxical in that the more it's given, the less meaningful it is. If we go around telling everyone they're special, soon it means nothing to those who do achieve something terrific. In the animated film *The Incredibles*, a superhero's mom tells her son, "Everyone's special!" His reply, "Which is another way of saying no one is."

Third, some of the most motivating people are those who are difficult to please. Think of Jack Welch, former CEO of GE, or A. G. Lafley, current CEO of Procter & Gamble. They are known for being difficult to please, which means most people will work harder to meet their expectations. Conversely, what happens when you dish out kudos for an employee who just shows up? What you've done is send a message that simply showing up is enough. Praise may seem like it's free, but when it's "dumbing down" performance expectations—so that employees think mediocrity is okay—the price may be huge.

Often what people really need is a gentle kick in the pants. As Steve Smolinsky of the Wharton School at the University of Pennsylvania says, "You have to tell students, 'It's not as good as you can do. . . . You can do better.' "

As one management consultant says, "People want to know how they're doing. Don't sugarcoat it. Just give them the damn data."[88]

Questions for Review

1 What is the job characteristics model? How does it motivate employees?

2 What are the three major ways that jobs can be redesigned? In your view, in what situations would one of the methods be favored over the others?

3 What are the three alternative work arrangements of flextime, job sharing, and telecommuting? What are the advantages and disadvantages of each?

4 What are employee involvement programs? How might they increase employee motivation?

5 What is variable pay? What are the variable-pay programs that are used to motivate employees? What are their advantages and disadvantages?

6 How can flexible benefits motivate employees?

7 What are the motivational benefits of intrinsic rewards?

Experiential Exercise

ASSESSING EMPLOYEE MOTIVATION AND SATISFACTION USING THE JOB CHARACTERISTICS MODEL

Purpose

This exercise will help you examine outcomes of the job characteristics model for different professions.

Time

Approximately 30 to 45 minutes.

Background

Data were collected on 6,930 employees in 56 different organizations in the United States, using the Job Diagnostic Survey. The following table contains data on the five core job dimensions of the job characteristics model for several professions. Also included are growth-needs strength, internal motivation, and pay satisfaction for each profession. The values are averages based on a 7-point scale.

Instructions

1. Break into groups of three to five.
2. Calculate the MPS score for each of the professions and compare them. Discuss whether you think these scores accurately reflect your perceptions of the motivating potential of these professions.
3. Graph the relationship between each profession's core job dimensions and its corresponding value for internal motivation and for pay satisfaction, using the core job dimensions as independent variables. What conclusions can you draw about motivation and satisfaction of employees in these professions?

Job Characteristics Averages for Six Professions

	Profession					
Variable	***Professional/ Technical***	***Managerial***	***Sales***	***Service***	***Clerical***	***Machine Trades***
Skill variety	5.4	5.6	4.8	5.0	4.0	5.1
Task identity	5.1	4.7	4.4	4.7	4.7	4.9
Task significance	5.6	5.8	5.5	5.7	5.3	5.6
Autonomy	5.4	5.4	4.8	5.0	4.5	4.9
Feedback	5.1	5.2	5.4	5.1	4.6	4.9
Growth-needs strength	5.6	5.3	5.7	5.4	5.0	4.8
Internal motivation	5.8	5.8	5.7	5.7	5.4	5.6
Pay satisfaction	4.4	4.6	4.2	4.1	4.0	4.2

Source: J. R. Hackman and G. R. Oldham, *Work Redesign* (Reading, MA: Addison-Wesley, 1980).

Ethical Dilemma

ARE U.S. EXECUTIVES PAID TOO MUCH?

There is no question that executive pay is growing. From 1999 to 2003, the pay of the top five executives from the 1,500 largest companies in the United States amounted to $122 billion, compared with $68 billion from 1993 to 1997. In comparison, from 2001 to 2003, top executive compensation amounted to 9.8 percent of the companies' net income, and the figure was 5 percent from 1993 to 1995. Perks, bonuses, and stock options are often particularly controversial. Ford's CEO Alan Mulally pulled in $28.2 million in 2006, including a bonus of $18.5 million, and free corporate jet travel for his wife, Nicki (which cost Ford $172,974 for the first quarter of 2006). Verizon's CEO Ivan Seidenberg received stock options worth $27 million in 2005, despite the fact that the company's stock dropped 25 percent that year. One of the members of Verizon's board of directors argued that the options were granted to make up for the fact that Seidenberg had been underpaid in the past.

The value of stock options is boosted when companies grant executive stock options when prices are low. You've probably heard of backdating, a practice in which executives are given the right to purchase their company's stock at some prior price, generally when the price of the stock was low. For example, when the stock market tanked after the 9/11 terrorist attacks, many companies granted executives stock options (Home Depot issued $19.2 million worth of options to its top five executives on September 17, and Merrill Lynch gave $14.4 million to its CEO on September 27) even though September is usually a month in which stock options are rarely issued. Some companies, such as Apple, went even further and backdated stock options so that a stock could be purchased at some retroactive lower price.

Even though bonuses, perks, and stock options have caused the ratio of executive pay to employee pay to grow dramatically over the past 25 years, some say this represents a classic economic response with a situation in which the demand is great for high-quality top executive talent and the supply is low. Ira Kay, a compensation consultant, says: "It's not fair to compare [executives] with hourly workers. Their market is the global market for executives." However, executive pay is considerably higher in the United States than in most other countries. U.S. CEOs are paid more than twice as much as Canadian CEOs, nearly three times as much as British CEOs, and four times as much as German CEOs. This difference is even greater when compared with what average workers make. U.S. CEOs make 531 times the pay of their average hourly employees. In contrast, British CEOs make 25 times as much as their workers, Canadians 21 times as much, and Germans 11 times as much.

Critics of executive pay practices in the United States argue that CEOs choose board members whom they can count on to support ever-increasing pay (including lucrative bonus and stock-option plans) for top management. If board members fail to "play along," they risk losing their positions, their fees, and the prestige and power inherent in board membership. Mutual funds own a significant percentage of the stock of publicly traded companies. So you would think they would reign in excessive pay to executives. Mutual fund companies, however, vote in favor of management pay plans 76 percent of the time, while they vote for shareholder proposals only 28 percent of the time. Don Phillips of the research firm Morningstar, commented, "Most asset managers are reluctant to pick fights with management because these big corporations are the ones who can write big checks to money-management firms for business."

Is high compensation of U.S. executives a problem? If so, does the blame for the problem lie with CEOs or with the shareholders and boards that knowingly allow the practice? Are U.S. CEOs greedy? Are they acting unethically? What do you think?

Sources: J. S. Lublin, "For CEO Spouses, Corporate Jets Are the Perfect Perk," *Wall Street Journal*, June 30, 2007, p. A1, A8; J. Levitz, "Do Mutual Funds Back CEO Pay? *Wall Street Journal*, March 28, 2006, pp. C1, C4; and J. Eisinger, "Lavish Pay Puts a Bit on Profits," *Wall Street Journal*, November 11, 2006, pp. C1, C7.

Case Incident 1

REDUCING TRAVEL COSTS AT APPLEBEE'S

Applebee's International is a large restaurant chain—with roughly 2,000 restaurants in the United States and 16 other countries—headquartered in the Kansas City area. Applebee's has been growing over time, opening roughly 100 new restaurants per year. As it has grown, the chain has found that its travel expenses have grown as well. Although much of the roughly $6 million Applebee's was spending on travel was money well spent, the firm was interested in finding ways to contain the costs. Andrew Face, Applebee's senior manager of human resources, was asked by his boss, the senior vice president of HR, to redesign Applebee's travel system. Face's job was to eliminate non-essential travel costs at the same time that he increased corporate travel benefits.

Face's first idea was to outsource—to look to an off-site call center, through which he would be able to negotiate group discounts for travel costs. But Face's boss thought outsourcing to a vendor wouldn't offer the type of support Applebee's needed for its employee travelers. For example, managers' plans would often change, and they needed flexibility in the travel system to accommodate that.

Face eventually decided on QualityAgent, a Web-based system that offered employee support. Because Applebee's was concerned about weaning users off the old system (using travel agents), participation was voluntary. But Face got an e-mail every time an employee used QualityAgent to make an airline reservation that didn't fall within the Applebee's travel policy, so he could send an e-mail before the employee purchased the ticket to remind the person of the policy. He also got weekly reports on travel usage to control costs and usage patterns better.

Although these elements alone saved Applebee's money, Face wasn't finished. He decided to provide incentives for using the system. To employees who followed travel policy and took six or more trips per year, Face promised a pair of domestic airline tickets if the company saved $100,000 in costs that first year. Eventually he got usage up to 55 percent to 60 percent of employee travel.

Questions

1. Consider the variable-pay programs discussed in this chapter. Of which type of program is Applebee's program an example? Explain.
2. If you were asked to revise the Applebee's program to include more individual incentives, how might you do that?
3. How would you react to such a program? Explain your reactions.
4. Why do you think more companies do not use these sorts of incentives?

Source: L. Thornburg, "Applebee's International Cuts Travel Costs," *SHRM Online*, February 9, 2007, www.shrm.org.

Case Incident 2

THANKS FOR NOTHING

Although it may seem fairly obvious that receiving praise and recognition from one's company is a motivating experience, sadly, many companies are failing miserably when it comes to saying thanks to their employees. According to Curt Coffman, global practice leader at Gallup, 71 percent of U.S. workers are "disengaged," essentially meaning that they couldn't care less about their organization. Coffman states, "We're operating at one-quarter of the capacity in terms of managing human capital. It's alarming." Employee recognition programs, which became more popular as the U.S. economy shifted from industrial to knowledge based, can be an effective way to motivate employees and make them feel valued. In many cases, however, recognition programs are doing "more harm than good," according to Coffman.

Take Ko, a 50-year-old former employee of a dot-com in California. Her company proudly instituted a rewards program designed to motivate employees. What were the rewards for a job well done? Employees would receive a badge that read "U Done Good" and, each year, would receive a T-shirt as a means of annual recognition. Once an employee received 10 "U Done Good" badges, he or she could trade them in for something bigger and better—a paperweight. Ko states that she would have preferred a raise. "It was patronizing. There wasn't any deep thought involved in any of this." To make matters worse, she says, the badges were handed out arbitrarily and were not tied to performance. And what about those T-shirts? Ko states that the company instilled a strict dress code, so employees couldn't even wear the shirts if they wanted to. Needless to say, the employee recognition program seemed like an empty gesture rather than a motivator.

Even programs that provide employees with more expensive rewards can backfire, especially if the rewards are given insincerely. Eric Lange, an employee of a trucking company, recalls a time when one of the company's vice presidents achieved a major financial goal for the company. The vice president, who worked in an office next to Lange, received a Cadillac Seville as his company car and a new Rolex wristwatch that cost the company $10,000. Both were lavish gifts, but the way they were distributed left a sour taste in the vice president's mouth. He entered his office to find the Rolex in a cheap cardboard box sitting on his desk, along with a brief letter explaining that he would be receiving a 1099 tax form in order to pay taxes on the watch. Lange states of the vice president, "He came into my office, which was right next door, and said, 'Can you believe this?'" A mere 2 months later, the vice president pawned the watch. Lange explains, "It had absolutely no meaning for him."

Such experiences resonate with employees who may find more value in a sincere pat on the back than in gifts from management that either are meaningless or aren't conveyed with respect or sincerity. However, sincere pats on the back may be hard to come by. Gallup's poll found that 61 percent of employees stated that they haven't received a sincere "thank you" from management in the past year. Findings such as these are troubling, as verbal rewards are not only inexpensive for companies to hand out but also quick and easy to distribute. Of course, verbal rewards do need to be paired sometimes with tangible benefits that employees value—after all, money talks. In addition, when praising employees for a job well done, managers need to ensure that the praise is given in conjunction with the specific accomplishment. In this way, employees may not only feel valued by their organization but will also know what actions to take to be rewarded in the future.

Questions

1. If praising employees for doing a good job seems to be a fairly easy and obvious motivational tool, why do you think companies and managers don't often do it?
2. As a manager, what steps would you take to motivate your employees after observing them perform well?
3. Are there any downsides to giving employees too much verbal praise? What might these downsides be and how could you alleviate them as a manager?
4. As a manager, how would you ensure that recognition given to employees is distributed fairly and justly?

Source: Based on J. Sandberg, "Been Here 25 Years and All I Got Was This Lousy T-Shirt," *Wall Street Journal*, January 28, 2004, p. B1.

Endnotes

1. M. Conlin, "Smashing the Clock," *BusinessWeek*, December 11, 2006, pp. 60–68.
2. J. R. Hackman and G. R. Oldham, "Motivation Through the Design of Work: Test of a Theory," *Organizational Behavior and Human Performance*, August 1976, pp. 250–279; and J. R. Hackman and G. R. Oldham, *Work Redesign* (Reading, MA: Addison-Wesley, 1980).
3. J. R. Hackman, "Work Design," in J. R. Hackman and J. L. Suttle (eds.), *Improving Life at Work* (Santa Monica, CA: Goodyear, 1977), p. 129.
4. See "Job Characteristics Theory of Work Redesign," in J. B. Miner, *Theories of Organizational Behavior* (Hinsdale, IL: Dryden Press, 1980), pp. 231–266; B. T. Loher, R. A. Noe, N. L. Moeller, and M. P. Fitzgerald, "A Meta-analysis of the Relation of Job Characteristics to Job Satisfaction," *Journal of Applied Psychology*, May 1985, pp. 280–289; W. H. Glick, G. D. Jenkins, Jr., and N. Gupta, "Method Versus Substance: How Strong Are Underlying Relationships Between Job haracteristics and Attitudinal Outcomes?" *Academy of Management Journal*, September 1986, pp. 441–464; Y. Fried and G. R. Ferris, "The Validity of the Job Characteristics Model: A Review and Meta-analysis," *Personnel Psychology*, Summer 1987, pp. 287–322; S. J. Zaccaro and E. F. Stone, Incremental Validity of an Empirically Based Measure of Job haracteristics," *Journal of Applied Psychology*, May 1988, pp. 245–252; J. R. Rentsch and R. P. Steel, "Testing the Durability of Job Characteristics as Predictors of Absenteeism over a Six-Year Period," *Personnel Psychology*, Spring 1998, pp. 165–190; S. J. Behson, E. R. Eddy, and S. J. Lorenzet, "The Importance of the Critical Psychological States in the Job Characteristics Model: A Meta-analytic and Structural Equations Modeling Examination," *Current Research in Social Psychology*, May 2000, pp. 170–189; and T. A. Judge, "Promote Job atisfaction Through Mental Challenge," in E. A. Locke (ed.), *Handbook of Principles of Organizational Behavior*, pp. 75–89.
5. T. A. Judge, S. K. Parker, A. E. Colbert, D. Heller, and R. Ilies, "Job Satisfaction: A Cross-Cultural Review," in N. Anderson, D. S. Ones (eds.), *Handbook of Industrial, Work and* Organizational Psychology, vol. 2 (Thousand Oaks, CA: Sage Publications, 2002), pp. 25–52.
6. C. A. O'Reilly and D. F. Caldwell, "Informational Influence as a Determinant of Perceived Task Characteristics and Job Satisfaction," *Journal of Applied Psychology*, April 1979, pp. 157–165; R. V. Montagno, "The Effects of Comparison [to] Others and Prior Experience on Responses to Task Design," *Academy of Management Journal*, June 1985, pp. 491–498; and P. C. Bottger and I. K.-H. Chew, "The Job Characteristics Model and Growth Satisfaction: Main Effects of Assimilation of Work Experience and Context Satisfaction," *Human Relations*, June 1986, pp. 575–594.
7. C. Ansberry, "In the New Workplace, Jobs Morph to Suit Rapid Pace of Change," *Wall Street Journal*, March 22, 2002, p. A1.
8. Hackman, "Work Design," pp. 115–120.
9. J. P. Wanous, "Individual Differences and Reactions to Job Characteristics," *Journal of Applied Psychology*, October 1974, pp. 616–622; and H. P. Sims and A. D. Szilagyi, "Job Characteristic Relationships: Individual and Structural Moderators," *Organizational Behavior and Human Performance*, June 1976, pp. 211–230.
10. M. Fein, "The Real Needs and Goals of Blue-Collar Workers," *The Conference Board Record*, February 1972, pp. 26–33.
11. J. Ortega, "Job Rotation as a Learning Mechanism," *Management Science*, October 2001, pp. 1361–1370.
12. See, for instance, data on job enlargement described in M. A. Campion and C. L. McClelland, "Follow-up and Extension of the Interdisciplinary Costs and Benefits of Enlarged Jobs," *Journal of Applied Psychology*, June 1993, pp. 339–351.
13. Hackman and Oldham, *Work Redesign*.
14. A. M. Grant, E. M. Campbell, G. Chen, K. Cottone, D. Lapedis, and K. Lee, "Impact and the Art of Motivation Maintenance: The Effects of Contact with Beneficiaries on Persistence Behavior," *Organizational Behavior and Human Decision Processes* 103 (2007), pp. 53–67.
15. Cited in *U.S. News & World Report*, May 31, 1993, p. 63.
16. See, for example, Hackman and Oldham, *Work Redesign*; Miner, *Theories of Organizational Behavior*, pp. 231–266;

R. W. Griffin, "Effects of Work Redesign on Employee Perceptions, Attitudes, and Behaviors: A Long-Term Investigation," *Academy of Management Journal* 34, no. 2 (1991), pp. 425–435; and J. L. Cotton, *Employee Involvement* (Newbury Park, CA: Sage, 1993), pp. 141–172.

17. F. P. Morgeson, M. D. Johnson, M. A. Campion, G. J. Medsker, and T. V. Mumford, "Understanding Reactions to Job Redesign: A Quasi-Experimental Investigation of the Moderating Effects of Organizational Contact on Perceptions of Performance Behavior," *Personnel Psychology* 39 (2006), pp. 333–363.

18. From the National Study of the Changing Workforce, cited in S. Shellenbarger, "Number of Women Managers Rise," *Wall Street Journal*, September 30, 2003, p. D2.

19. Cited in "Flextime Gains in Popularity in Germany," *Manpower Argus*, September 2000, p. 4.

20. D. R. Dalton and D. J. Mesch, "The Impact of Flexible Scheduling on Employee Attendance and Turnover," *Administrative Science Quarterly*, June 1990, pp. 370–387; K. S. Kush and L. K. Stroh, "Flextime: Myth or Reality," *Business Horizons*, September–October 1994, p. 53; and L. Golden, "Flexible Work Schedules: What Are We Trading Off to Get Them?" *Monthly Labor Review*, March 2001, pp. 50–55.

21. See, for example, D. A. Ralston and M. F. Flanagan, "The Effect of Flextime on Absenteeism and Turnover for Male and Female Employees," *Journal of Vocational Behavior*, April 1985, pp. 206–217; D. A. Ralston, W. P. Anthony, and D. J. Gustafson, "Employees May Love Flextime, but What Does It Do to the Organization's Productivity?" *Journal of Applied Psychology*, May 1985, pp. 272–279; J. B. McGuire and J. R. Liro, "Flexible Work Schedules, Work Attitudes, and Perceptions of Productivity," *Public Personnel Management*, Spring 1986, pp. 65–73; P. Bernstein, "The Ultimate in Flextime: From Sweden, by Way of Volvo," *Personnel*, June 1988, pp. 70–74; Dalton and Mesch, "The Impact of Flexible Scheduling on Employee Attendance and Turnover," pp. 370–387; and B. B. Baltes, T. E. Briggs, J. W. Huff, J. A. Wright, and G. A. Neuman, "Flexible and Compressed Workweek Schedules: A Meta-analysis of Their Effects on Work-Related Criteria," *Journal of Applied Psychology* 84, no. 4 (1999), pp. 496–513.

22. Cited in S. Caminiti, "Fair Shares," *Working Woman*, November 1999, pp. 52–54.

23. Ibid., p. 54.

24. S. Shellenbarger, "Two People, One Job: It Can Really Work," *Wall Street Journal*, December 7, 1994, p. B1.

25. "Job-Sharing: Widely Offered, Little Used," *Training*, November 1994, p. 12.

26. C. Dawson, "Japan: Work-Sharing Will Prolong the Pain," *BusinessWeek*, December 24, 2001, p. 46.

27. Shellenbarger, "Two People, One Job," p. B1.

28. See, for example, T. H. Davenport and K. Pearlson, "Two Cheers for the Virtual Office," *Sloan Management Review*, Summer 1998, pp. 61–65; E. J. Hill, B. C. Miller, S. P. Weiner, and J. Colihan, "Influences of the Virtual Office on Aspects of Work and Work/Life Balance," *Personnel Psychology*, Autumn 1998, pp. 667–683; K. E. Pearlson and C. S. Saunders, "There's No Place Like Home: Managing Telecommuting Paradoxes," *Academy of Management Executive*, May 2001, pp. 117–128; S. J. Wells, "Making Telecommuting Work," *HRMagazine*, October 2001, pp. 34–45; and E. J. Hill, M. Ferris, and V. Martinson, "Does It Matter Where You Work? A Comparison of How Three Work Venues (Traditional Office, Virtual Office, and Home Office) Influence Aspects of Work and Personal/Family Life," *Journal of Vocational Behavior* 63, no. 2 (2003), pp. 220–241.

29. N. B. Kurland and D. E. Bailey, "Telework: The Advantages and Challenges of Working Here, There, Anywhere, and Anytime," *Organizational Dynamics*, Autumn 1999, pp. 53–68; and Wells, "Making Telecommuting Work," p. 34.

30. See, for instance, J. D. Glater, "Telecommuting's Big Experiment," *New York Times*, May 9, 2001, p. C1; and S. Shellenbarger, "Telework Is on the Rise, but It Isn't Just Done from Home Anymore, " *Wall Street Journal*, January 23, 2001, p. B1.

31. U. Huws, "Wired in the Country," *People Management*, November 1999, pp. 46–47.

32. Cited in R. W. Judy and C. D'Amico, *Workforce 2020* (Indianapolis: Hudson Institute, 1997), p. 58.

33. Cited in Wells, "Making Telecommuting Work," pp. 34–45.

34. J. M. Stanton and J. L. Barnes-Farrell, "Effects of Electronic Performance Monitoring on Personal Control, Task Satisfaction, and Task Performance," *Journal of Applied Psychology*, December 1996, pp. 738–745; B. Pappas, "They Spy," *Forbes*, February 8, 1999, p. 47; S. Armour, "More Bosses Keep Tabs on Telecommuters," *USA Today*, July 24, 2001, p. 1B; and D. Buss, "Spies Like Us," *Training*, December 2001, pp. 44–48.

35. L. H. Peters, E. J. O'Connor, and C. J. Rudolf, "The Behavioral and Affective Consequences of Performance-Relevant Situational Variables," *Organizational Behavior and Human Performance*, February 1980, pp. 79–96; M. Blumberg and C. D. Pringle, "The Missing Opportunity in Organizational Research: Some Implications for a Theory of Work Performance," *Academy of Management Review*, October 1982, pp. 560–569; D. A. Waldman and W. D. Spangler, "Putting Together the Pieces: A Closer Look at the Determinants of Job Performance," *Human Performance* 2 (1989), pp. 29–59; and J. Hall, "Americans Know How to Be Productive if Managers Will Let Them," *Organizational Dynamics*, Winter 1994, pp. 33–46.

36. See, for example, the increasing body of literature on empowerment, such as W. A. Randolph, "Re-Thinking Empowerment: Why Is It So Hard to Achieve?" *Organizational Dynamics*, 29, no. 2 (2000), pp. 94–107; K. Blanchard, J. P. Carlos, and W. A. Randolph, *Empowerment Takes More Than a Minute*, 2nd ed. (San Francisco: Berrett-Koehler, 2001); D. P. Ashmos, D. Duchon, R. R. McDaniel, Jr., and J. W. Huonker, "What a Mess! Participation as a Simple Managerial Rule to 'Complexify' Organizations," *Journal of Management Studies*, March 2002, pp. 189–206; and S. E. Seibert, S. R. Silver, and W. A. Randolph, "Taking Empowerment to the Next Level: A Multiple-Level Model of Empowerment, Performance, and Satisfaction" *Academy of Management Journal* 47, no. 3 (2004), pp. 332–349.

37. F. Heller, E. Pusic, G. Strauss, and B. Wilpert, *Organizational Participation: Myth and Reality* (Oxford, UK: Oxford University Press, 1998).

38. See, for instance, K. L. Miller and P. R. Monge, "Participation, Satisfaction, and Productivity: A Meta-analytic Review," *Academy of Management Journal*, December 1986, pp. 727–753; J. A. Wagner III and R. Z. Gooding, "Shared Influence and Organizational Behavior: A Meta-analysis of Situational Variables Expected to Moderate Participation–Outcome Relationships," *Academy of Management Journal*, September 1987, pp. 524–541; J. A. Wagner III, "Participation's Effects on Performance and Satisfaction: A Reconsideration of Research Evidence," *Academy of Management Review*, April 1994, pp. 312–330; C. Doucouliagos, "Worker Participation and Productivity in Labor-Managed and Participatory Capitalist Firms: A Meta-Analysis," *Industrial and Labor Relations Review*, October 1995, pp. 58–77; J. A. Wagner III, C. R. Leana, E. A. Locke, and D. M. Schweiger, "Cognitive and Motivational Frameworks in U.S. Research on Participation: A Meta-analysis of Primary Effects," *Journal of Organizational Behavior* 18 (1997), pp. 49–65; J. S. Black and H. B. Gregersen, "Participative Decision-Making: An Integration of Multiple Dimensions," *Human Relations*, July 1997, pp. 859–878; E. A. Locke, M. Alavi, and J. A. Wagner III, "Participation in Decision Making: An Information Exchange Perspective," in G. R. Ferris (ed.), *Research in Personnel and Human Resource Management*, vol. 15 (Greenwich, CT: JAI Press, 1997), pp. 293–331; and J. A. Wagner III and J. A. LePine, "Effects of Participation on Performance and Satisfaction: Additional Meta-analytic Evidence," *Psychological Reports*, June 1999, pp. 719–725.
39. Cotton, *Employee Involvement*, p. 114.
40. See, for example, M. Gilman and P. Marginson, "Negotiating European Works Council: Contours of Constrained Choice," *Industrial Relations Journal*, March 2002, pp. 36–51; J. T. Addison and C. R. Belfield, "What Do We Know About the New European Works Council? Some Preliminary Evidence from Britain," *Scottish Journal of Political Economy*, September 2002, pp. 418–444; and B. Keller, "The European Company Statute: Employee Involvement—And Beyond," *Industrial Relations Journal*, December 2002, pp. 424–445.
41. Cotton, *Employee Involvement*, pp. 129–130, 139–140.
42. Ibid., p. 140.
43. See, for example, G. W. Meyer and R. G. Stott, "Quality Circles: Panacea or Pandora's Box?" *Organizational Dynamics*, Spring 1985, pp. 34–50; E. E. Lawler III, and S. A. Mohrman, "Quality Circles: After the Honeymoon," *Organizational Dynamics*, Spring 1987, pp. 42–54; T. R. Miller, "The Quality Circle Phenomenon: A Review and Appraisal," *SAM Advanced Management Journal*, Winter 1989, pp. 4–7; K. Buch and R. Spangler, "The Effects of Quality Circles on Performance and Promotions," *Human Relations*, June 1990, pp. 573–582; P. R. Liverpool, "Employee Participation in Decision-Making: An Analysis of the Perceptions of Members and Nonmembers of Quality Circles," *Journal of Business and Psychology*, Summer 1990, pp. 411–422, E. E. Adams, Jr., "Quality Circle Performance," *Journal of Management*, March 1991, pp. 25–39; and L. I. Glassop, "The Organizational Benefits of Teams," *Human Relations* 55, no. 2 (2002), pp. 225–249.
44. T. L. Tang and E. A. Butler, "Attributions of Quality Circles' Problem-Solving Failure: Differences Among Management, Supporting Staff, and Quality Circle Members," *Public Personnel Management*, Summer 1997, pp. 203–225; G. Hammersley and A. Pinnington, "Quality Circles Reach End of the Line at Land Rover," *Human Resource Management International Digest*, May/June 1999, pp. 4–5; and D. Nagar and M. Takore, "Effectiveness of Quality Circles in a Large Public Sector," *Psychological Studies*, January–July 2001, pp. 63–68.
45. Cotton, *Employee Involvement*, p. 87.
46. E. White, "Opportunity Knocks, and It Pays a Lot Better," *Wall Street Journal*, November 13, 2006, p. B3.
47. P. S. Goodman and P. P. Pan, "Chinese Workers Pay for Wal-Mart's Low Prices," *The Washington Post*, February 8, 2004; p. A1.
48. See T. Henry, "States to Tie Teacher Pay to Results," *USA Today*, September 30, 1999, p. 1A.
49. D. Kollars, "Some Educators Win $25,000 Bonus as Test Scores Rise," *Sacramento (California) Bee*, January 8, 2001, p. 1.
50. Based on J. R. Schuster and P. K. Zingheim, "The New Variable Pay: Key Design Issues," *Compensation & Benefits Review*, March–April 1993, p. 28; K. S. Abosch, "Variable Pay: Do We Have the Basics in Place?" *Compensation & Benefits Review*, July–August 1998, pp. 12–22; and K. M. Kuhn and M. D. Yockey, "Variable Pay as a Risky Choice: Determinants of the Relative Attractiveness of Incentive Plans," *Organizational Behavior and Human Decision Processes*, March 2003, pp. 323–341.
51. W. Zellner, "Trickle-Down Is Trickling Down at Work," *BusinessWeek*, March 18, 1996, p. 34; and "Linking Pay to Performance Is Becoming a Norm in the Workplace," *Wall Street Journal*, April 6, 1999, p. A1.
52. L. Wiener, "Paycheck Plus," *U.S. News & World Report*, February 24/March 3, 2003, p. 58.
53. Cited in "Pay Programs: Few Employees See the Pay-for-Performance Connection," *Compensation & Benefits Report*, June 2003, p. 1.
54. B. Wysocki, Jr., "Chilling Reality Awaits Even the Employed," *Wall Street Journal*, November 5, 2001, p. A1.
55. M. Fein, "Work Measurement and Wage Incentives," *Industrial Engineering*, September 1973, pp. 49–51. For updated reviews of the effect of pay on performance, see G. D. Jenkins, Jr., N. Gupta, A. Mitra, and J. D. Shaw, "Are Financial Incentives Related to Performance? A Meta-analytic Review of Empirical Research," *Journal of Applied Psychology*, October 1998, pp. 777–787; and S. L. Rynes, B. Gerhart, and L. Parks, "Personnel Psychology: Performance Evaluation and Pay for Performance," *Annual Review of Psychology* 56, no. 1 (2005), pp. 571–600.
56. E. Arita, "Teething Troubles Aside, Merit-Based Pay Catching On," *Japan Times*, April 23, 2004, http://search.japantimes.co.jp/cgi-bin/nb20040423a3.html.
57. E. White, "The Best vs. the Rest," *Wall Street Journal*, January 30, 2006, pp. B1, B3.
58. E. White, "Employers Increasingly Favor Bonuses to Raises," *Wall Street Journal*, August 28, 2006, p. B3; and J. S. Lublin, "Boards Tie CEO Pay More Tightly to Performance," *Wall Street Journal*, February 21, 2006, pp. A1, A14.
59. G. E. Ledford, Jr., "Paying for the Skills, Knowledge, and Competencies of Knowledge Workers," *Compensation & Benefits Review*, July–August 1995, pp. 55–62; B. Murray and B. Gerhart, "An Empirical Analysis of a Skill-Based Pay Program and Plant Performance Outcomes," *Academy of Management Journal*, February 1998, pp. 68–78; J. R. Thompson and C. W. LeHew, "Skill-Based Pay as an Organizational Innovation," *Review of Public Personnel Administration*, Winter 2000, pp. 20–40; and J. D. Shaw, N. Gupta, A. Mitra, and

G. E. Ledford, Jr., "Success and Survival of Skill-Based Pay Plans," *Journal of Management*, February 2005, pp. 28–49.

60. "Tensions of a New Pay Plan," *New York Times*, May 17, 1992, p. F5.
61. See, for instance, D.-O. Kim, "Determinants of the Survival of Gainsharing Programs," *Industrial & Labor Relations Review*, October 1999, pp. 21–42; "Why Gainsharing Works Even Better Today Than in the Past," *HR Focus*, April 2000, pp. 3–5; L. R. Gomez-Mejia, T. M. Welbourne, and R. M. Wiseman, "The Role of Risk Sharing and Risk Taking Under Gainsharing," *Academy of Management Review*, July 2000, pp. 492–507; W. Atkinson, "Incentive Pay Programs That Work in Textile," *Textile World*, February 2001, pp. 55–57; M. Reynolds, "A Cost-Reduction Strategy That May Be Back," *Healthcare Financial Management*, January 2002, pp. 58–64; and M. R. Dixon, L. J. Hayes, and J. Stack, "Changing Conceptions of Employee Compensation," *Journal of Organizational Behavior Management* 23, no. 2–3 (2003), pp. 95–116.
62. Employment Policy Foundation, *U.S. Wage and Productivity Growth Attainable Through Gainsharing*, May 10, 2000.
63. "The Employee Ownership 100," *National Center for Employee Ownership*, July 2003, www.nceo. org.
64. Cited in K. Frieswick, "ESOPs: Split Personality," *CFO*, July 7, 2003, p. 1.
65. A. A. Buchko, "The Effects of Employee Ownership on Employee Attitudes: A Test of Three Theoretical Perspectives," *Work and Occupations* 19, no. 1 (1992), 59–78.
66. J. L. Pierce and C. A. Furo, "Employee Ownership: Implications for Management," *Organizational Dynamics* 18 no. 3 (1990), pp. 32–43.
67. See data in D. Stamps, "A Piece of the Action," *Training*, March 1996, p. 66.
68. C. G. Hanson and W. D. Bell, *Profit Sharing and Profitability: How Profit Sharing Promotes Business Success* (London: Kogan Page, 1987); M. Magnan and S. St-Onge, "Profit-Sharing and Firm Performance: A Comparative and Longitudinal Analysis," paper presented at the 58th annual meeting of the Academy of Management, San Diego, August 1998; and D. D'Art and T. Turner, "Profit Sharing, Firm Performance, and Union Influence in Selected European Countries," *Personnel Review* 33, no. 3 (2004), pp. 335–350.
69. T. M. Welbourne and L. R. Gomez-Mejia, "Gainsharing: A Critical Review and a Future Research Agenda," *Journal of Management* 21, no. 3 (1995), pp. 559–609.
70. C. B. Cadsby, F. Song, and F. Tapon, "Sorting and Incentive Effects of Pay for Performance: An Experimental Investigation," *Academy of Management Journal* 50, no. 2 (2007), pp. 387–405.
71. See, for instance, M. W. Barringer and G. T. Milkovich, "A Theoretical Exploration of the Adoption and Design of Flexible Benefit Plans: A Case of Human Resource Innovation," *Academy of Management Review*, April 1998, pp. 305–324; D. Brown, "Everybody Loves Flex," *Canadian HRReporter*, November 18, 2002, p. 1; J. Taggart, "Putting Flex Benefits Through Their Paces," *Canadian HR Reporter*, December 2, 2002, p. G3; and N. D. Cole and D. H. Flint, "Perceptions of Distributive and Procedural Justice in Employee Benefits: Flexible Versus Traditional Benefit Plans," *Journal of Managerial Psychology* 19, no. 1 (2004), pp. 19–40.
72. D. A. DeCenzo and S. P. Robbins, *Human Resource Management*, 7th ed. (New York: Wiley, 2002), pp. 346–348.
73. S. E. Markham, K. D. Scott, and G. H. McKee, "Recognizing Good Attendance: A Longitudinal, Quasi-Experimental Field Study," *Personnel Psychology*, Autumn 2002, p. 641; and S. J. Peterson and F. Luthans, "The Impact of Financial and Nonfinancial Incentives on Business Unit Outcomes over Time," *Journal of Applied Psychology* 91, no. 1 (2006), pp. 156–165.
74. D. Drickhamer, "Best Plant Winners: Nichols Foods Ltd.," *IndustryWeek*, October 1, 2001, pp. 17–19.
75. M. Littman, "Best Bosses Tell All," *Working Woman*, October 2000, p. 54.
76. Cited in S. Caudron, "The Top 20 Ways to Motivate Employees," *IndustryWeek*, April 3, 1995, pp. 15–16. See also B. Nelson, "Try Praise," *INC.*, September 1996, p. 115.
77. A. D. Stajkovic and F. Luthans, "Differential Effects of Incentive Motivators on Work Performance," *Academy of Management Journal*, June 2001, p. 587. See also F. Luthans and A. D. Stajkovic, "Provide Recognition for Performance Improvement," in E. A. Locke (ed.), *Handbook of Principles of Organizational Behavior* (Malden, MA: Blackwell, 2004), pp. 166–180.
78. Cited in K. J. Dunham, "Amid Shrinking Workplace Morale, Employers Turn to Recognition," *Wall Street Journal*, November 19, 2002, p. B8.
79. Ibid.
80. B. M. Meglino and A. M. Korsgaard, "The Role of Other Orientation in Reactions to Job Characteristics," *Journal of Management*, February 2007, pp. 57–83.
81. M. F. Peterson and S. A. Ruiz-Quintanilla, "Cultural Socialization as a Source of Intrinsic Work Motivation," *Group & Organization Management*, June 2003, pp. 188–216.
82. P. Peters and L. den Dulk, "Cross Cultural Differences in Managers' Support for Home-Based Telework: A Theoretical Elaboration," *International Journal of Cross Cultural Management*, December 2003, pp. 329–346.
83. S. C. L. Fong and M. A. Shaffer, "The Dimensionality and Determinants of Pay Satisfaction: A Cross-Cultural Investigation of a Group Incentive Plan," *International Journal of Human Resource Management*, June 2003, pp. 559–580.
84. Brown, "Everybody Loves Flex.," p. 1.
85. E. Unsworth, "U.K. Employers Find Flex Benefits Helpful: Survey," *Business Insurance*, May 21, 2001, pp. 19–20.
86. See, for instance, A. Sagie and Z. Aycan, "A Cross-Cultural Analysis of Participative Decision-Making in Organizations," *Human Relations*, April 2003, pp. 453–473; and J. Brockner, "Unpacking Country Effects: On the Need to Operationalize the Psychological Determinants of Cross-National Differences," in R. M. Kramer and B. M. Staw (eds.), *Research in Organizational Behavior*, vol. 25 (Oxford, UK: Elsevier, 2003), pp. 336–340.
87. C. Robert, T. M. Probst, J. J. Martocchio, R. Drasgow, and J. J. Lawler, "Empowerment and Continuous Improvement in the United States, Mexico, Poland, and India: Predicting Fit on the Basis of the Dimensions of Power Distance and Individualism," *Journal of Applied Psychology*, October 2000, pp. 643–658.
88. "The Most Praised Generation Goes to Work," *Gainesville (Florida) Sun*, April 29, 2007, pp. 5G, 6G; and J. Zaslow, "In Praise of Less Praise," *Wall Street Journal*, May 3, 2007, p. D1.

Emotions and Moods

Time cools, time clarifies; no mood can be maintained quite unaltered through the course of hours.

—Writer Mark Twain

LEARNING OBJECTIVES

After studying this chapter, you should be able to:

1 Differentiate emotions from moods and list the basic emotions and moods.

2 Discuss whether emotions are rational and what functions they serve.

3 Identify the sources of emotions and moods.

4 Show the impact emotional labor has on employees.

5 Describe affective events theory and identify its applications.

6 Contrast the evidence for and against the existence of emotional intelligence.

7 Apply concepts about emotions and moods to specific OB issues.

8 Contrast the experience, interpretation, and expression of emotions across cultures.

Can revenge be a motivator? Absolutely. Consider what Terry Garnett says: "I do hold grudges. Am I motivated by that? Absolutely."

In the 1990s, Garnett was a senior vice president at the software company Oracle, reporting to Oracle CEO Larry Ellison. The two traveled around the world together, rubbed elbows with media and movie moguls, and became friends. The families even vacationed together in Japan. Ellison, an ardent admirer of all things Japanese, invited Garnett to join

Sweet Revenge

him in the famed Philosopher's Walk to the Ginkakuji Temple in Kyoto.

A few weeks after returning from their trip to Japan, Ellison called Garnett into his office and summarily fired him. Feeling numb and lacking a clear explanation for his dismissal, Garnett walked the 30 feet from Ellison's office to his own, packed up his things, and left. "I tried to keep composed," he said. Privately, though, he was seething, telling himself, "There will be a day of reckoning."

Channeling his anger, Garnett started competing directly with Ellison and Oracle by investing in promising start-up projects. A recent example is Ingres, a low-cost software provider that Garnett hopes will compete directly with Oracle's bread-and-butter offering: its high-price database business (together, Oracle and IBM claim 70 percent of the global database business). Garnett has hired away numerous Oracle employees, forming a small army of engineers and managers to help him take the battle to the enemy. In 2004, Garnett and David Helfrich founded Garnett & Helfrich Capital, a $350 million private equity fund for midsized technology spinouts. Rather than focusing on start-ups or buyouts of well-established companies, Garnett & Helfrich focuses on existing technology businesses or product lines that have struggled.

In reflecting on his successes, Garnett says, "The simplest way to create a culture is to pick an enemy. We have an enemy. It's Oracle."[1] ■

As the example of Terry Garnett shows, emotions can spur us to action. Before we delve further into emotions and moods, get an assessment of your mood state right now. Take the following self-assessment to find out what sort of mood you're in.

HOW ARE YOU FEELING RIGHT NOW?

In the Self-Assessment Library (available on CD or online), take assessment IV.D.1 (How Are You Feeling Right Now?) and answer the following questions.

1. *What was higher—your positive mood score or negative mood score? How do these scores compare with those of your classmates?*
2. *Did your score surprise you? Why or why not?*
3. *What sorts of things influence your positive moods? your negative moods?*

Given the obvious role that emotions play in our work and everyday lives, it might surprise you to learn that, until recently, the field of OB has given the topic of emotions little or no attention.[2] How could this be? We can offer two possible explanations.

The first is the *myth of rationality*.[3] From the late nineteenth century and the rise of scientific management until very recently, the protocol of the work world was to keep a damper on emotions. A well-run organization didn't allow employees to express frustration, fear, anger, love, hate, joy, grief, and similar feelings. The prevailing thought was that such emotions were the antithesis of rationality. Even though researchers and managers knew that emotions were an inseparable part of everyday life, they tried to create organizations that were emotion free. That, of course, wasn't possible.

The second explanation is that many believed that emotions of any kind are disruptive.[4] When researchers considered emotions, they looked at strong negative emotions—especially anger—that interfered with an employee's ability to work effectively. They rarely viewed emotions as constructive or contributing to enhanced performance.

Certainly some emotions, particularly when exhibited at the wrong time, can hinder employee performance. But this doesn't change the fact that employees bring their emotional sides with them to work every day and that no study of OB would be comprehensive without considering the role of emotions in workplace behavior.

What Are Emotions and Moods?

1 Differentiate emotions from moods and list the basic emotions and moods.

Although we don't want to belabor definitions, before we can proceed with our analysis, we need to clarify three terms that are closely intertwined: *affect, emotions,* and *moods.*

Affect is a generic term that covers a broad range of feelings that people experience. It's an umbrella concept that encompasses both emotions and moods.[5] **Emotions** are intense feelings that are directed at someone or something.[6] **Moods** are feelings that tend to be less intense than emotions and that often (though not always) lack a contextual stimulus.[7]

Most experts believe that emotions are more fleeting than moods.[8] For example, if someone is rude to you, you'll feel angry. That intense feeling of anger probably comes and goes fairly quickly, maybe even in a matter of seconds. When you're in a bad mood, though, you can feel bad for several hours.

Emotions are reactions to a person (for example, seeing a friend at work may make you feel glad) or event (for example, dealing with a rude client may make you feel angry). You show your emotions when you're "happy about something, angry at someone, afraid of something."[9] Moods, in contrast, aren't usually directed at a person or an event. But emotions can turn into moods when you lose focus on the event or object that started the feeling. And, by the same token, good or bad moods can make you more emotional in response to an event. So when a colleague criticizes how you spoke to a client, you might become angry at him. That is, you show emotion (anger) toward a specific object (your colleague). But as the specific emotion dissipates, you might just feel generally dispirited. You can't attribute this feeling to any single event; you're just not your normal self. You might then overreact to other events. This affect state describes a mood. Exhibit 8-1 shows the relationships among affect, emotions, and mood.

Exhibit 8-1 Affect, Emotions, and Moods

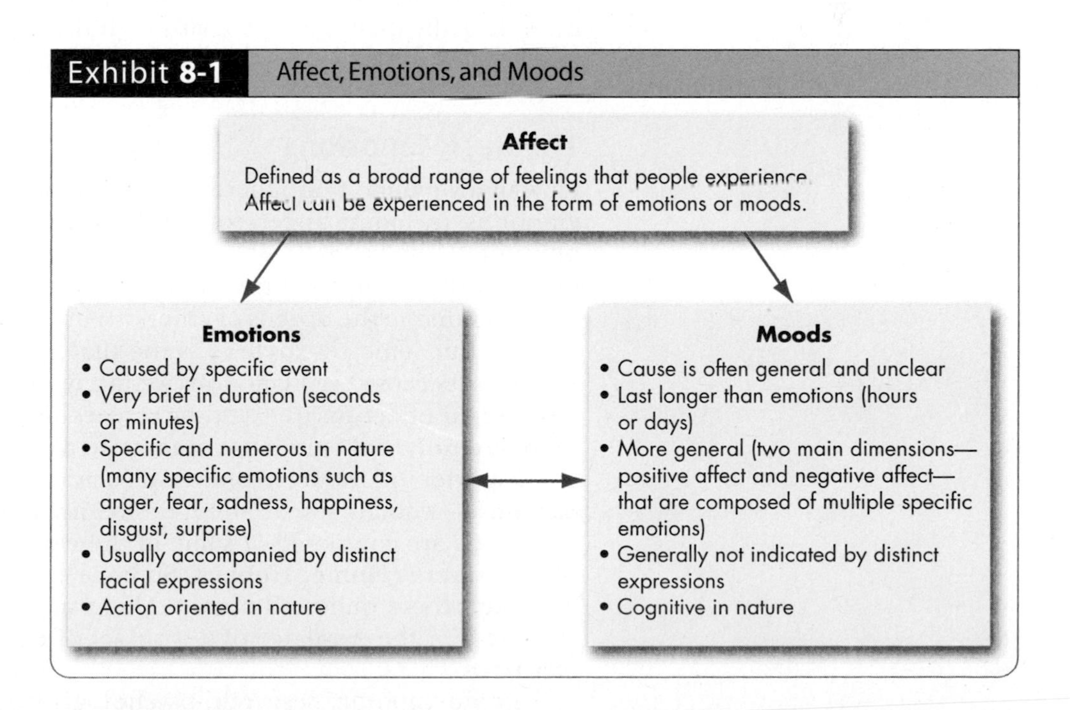

affect *A broad range of feelings that people experience.*

emotions *Intense feelings that are directed at someone or something.*

moods *Feelings that tend to be less intense than emotions and that lack a contextual stimulus.*

First, as the exhibit shows, affect is a broad term that encompasses emotions and moods. Second, there are differences between emotions and moods. Some of these differences—that emotions are more likely to be caused by a specific event, and emotions are more fleeting than moods—we just discussed. Other differences are subtler. For example, unlike moods, emotions tend to be more clearly revealed with facial expressions (for example, anger, disgust). Also, some researchers speculate that emotions may be more action-oriented—they may lead us to some immediate action—while moods may be more cognitive, meaning they may cause us to think or brood for a while.[10]

Finally, the exhibit shows that emotions and moods can mutually influence each other. For example, an emotion, if it's strong and deep enough, can turn into a mood: Getting your dream job may generate the emotion of joy, but it also can put you in a good mood for several days. Similarly, if you're in a good or bad mood, it might make you experience a more intense positive or negative emotion than would otherwise be the case. For example, if you're in a bad mood, you might "blow up" in response to a coworker's comment when normally it would have just generated a mild reaction. Because emotions and moods can mutually influence each other, there will be many points throughout the chapter where emotions and moods will be closely connected.

Although affect, emotions, and moods are separable in theory, in practice the distinction isn't always crystal clear. In fact, in some areas, researchers have studied mostly moods, and in other areas, mainly emotions. So, when we review the OB topics on emotions and moods, you may see more information on emotions in one area and moods in another. This is simply the state of the research.

Also, the terminology can be confusing. For example, the two main mood dimensions are positive affect and negative affect, yet we have defined affect more broadly than mood. So, although the topic can be fairly dense in places, hang in there. The material is interesting—and applicable to OB.

The Basic Emotions

How many emotions are there? In what ways do they vary? There are dozens of emotions, including anger, contempt, enthusiasm, envy, fear, frustration, disappointment, embarrassment, disgust, happiness, hate, hope, jealousy, joy, love, pride, surprise, and sadness. There have been numerous research efforts to limit and define the dozens of emotions into a fundamental or basic set of emotions.[11] But some researchers argue that it makes no sense to think of basic emotions because even emotions we rarely experience, such as shock, can have a powerful effect on us.[12] Other researchers, even philosophers, argue that there are universal emotions common to all of us. René Descartes, often called the founder of modern philosophy, identified six "simple and primitive passions"—wonder, love, hatred, desire, joy, and sadness—and argued that "all the others are composed of some of these six or are species of them."[13] Other philosophers (Hume, Hobbes, Spinoza) identified categories of emotions. Although these philosophers were helpful, the burden to provide conclusive evidence for the existence of a basic set of emotions still rests with contemporary researchers.

In contemporary research, psychologists have tried to identify basic emotions by studying facial expressions.[14] One problem with this approach is that some emotions are too complex to be easily represented on our faces. Take love, for example. Many think of love as the most universal of all emotions,[15] yet it's not easy to express a loving emotion with one's face only. Also, cultures have norms that govern emotional expression, so how we *experience* an emotion isn't always the same as how we *show* it. And many companies today offer anger-management programs to teach people to contain or even hide their inner feelings.[16]

It's unlikely that psychologists or philosophers will ever completely agree on a set of basic emotions, or even whether it makes sense to think of basic emotions. Still, enough researchers have agreed on six essentially universal emotions—anger, fear, sadness, happiness, disgust, and surprise—with most other emotions subsumed under one of these six categories.[17] Some researchers even plot these six emotions along a continuum: happiness—surprise—fear—sadness—anger—disgust.[18] The closer any two emotions are to each other on this continuum, the more likely it is that people will confuse them. For instance, we sometimes mistake happiness for surprise, but rarely do we confuse happiness and disgust. In addition, as we'll see later on, cultural factors can also influence interpretations.

The Basic Moods: Positive and Negative Affect

One way to classify emotions is by whether they are positive or negative.[19] Positive emotions—such as joy and gratitude—express a favorable evaluation or feeling. Negative emotions—such as anger or guilt—express the opposite. Keep in mind that emotions can't be neutral. Being neutral is being nonemotional.[20]

When we group emotions into positive and negative categories, they become mood states because we are now looking at them more generally instead of isolating one particular emotion. In Exhibit 8-2, excited is a specific emotion that is a pure marker of high positive affect, while boredom is a pure marker of low positive affect. Similarly, nervous is a pure marker of high negative affect, while relaxed is a pure marker of low negative affect. Finally, some emotions—such as contentment (a mixture of high positive affect and low negative affect) and sadness (a mixture of low positive affect and high negative affect)—are in between. You'll notice that this model does not include all emotions. There are two reasons. First, we can fit other emotions such as enthusiasm or depression into the model, but we're short on space. Second, some emotions, such as surprise, don't fit well because they're not as clearly positive or negative.

Exhibit 8-2 The Structure of Mood

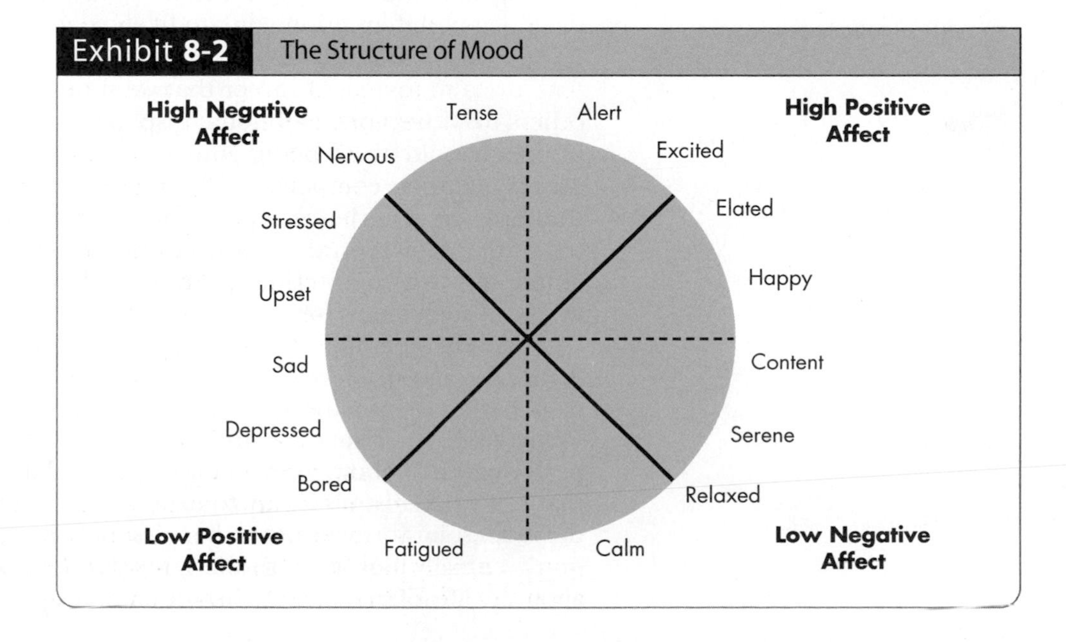

So, we can think of **positive affect** as a mood dimension consisting of positive emotions such as excitement, self-assurance, and cheerfulness at the high end and boredom, sluggishness, and tiredness at the low end. **Negative affect** is a mood dimension consisting of nervousness, stress, and anxiety at the high end and relaxation, tranquility, and poise at the low end. (Note that positive and negative affect *are* moods. We're using these labels, rather than *positive mood* and *negative mood* because that's how researchers label them.)

Positive affect and negative affect play out at work (and beyond work, of course) in that they color our perceptions, and these perceptions can become their own reality. For example, one flight attendant posted an anonymous blog on the Web that said: "I work in a pressurized aluminum tube and the environment outside my 'office' cannot sustain human life. That being said, the human life inside is not worth sustaining sometimes . . . in fact, the passengers can be jerks, and idiots. I am often treated with no respect, nobody listens to me . . . until I threaten to kick them off the plane."[21] Clearly, if a flight attendant is in a bad mood, it's going to influence his perceptions of passengers, which will, in turn, influence his behavior.

Importantly, negative emotions are likely to translate into negative moods. People think about events that created strong negative emotions five times as long as they do about events that created strong positive ones.[22] So, we should expect people to recall negative experiences more readily than positive ones. Perhaps one of the reasons is that, for most of us, they're also more unusual. Indeed, research shows that there is a **positivity offset**, meaning that at zero input (when nothing in particular is going on), most individuals experience a mildly positive mood.[23] So, for most people, positive moods are somewhat more common than negative moods. The positivity offset also appears to operate at work. For example, one study of customer-service representatives in a British call center (probably a job where it's pretty difficult to feel positive) revealed that people reported experiencing positive moods 58 percent of the time.[24]

The Function of Emotions

2 *Discuss whether emotions are rational and what functions they serve.*

Do Emotions Make Us Irrational? How often have you heard someone say, "Oh, you're just being emotional"? You might have been offended. The famous astronomer Carl Sagan once wrote, "Where we have strong emotions, we're liable to fool ourselves." These observations suggest that rationality and emotion are in conflict with one another and that if you exhibit emotion you are likely to act irrationally. One team of authors argues that displaying emotions such as sadness, to the point of crying, is so toxic to a career that we should leave the room rather than allow others to witness our emotional display.[25] The author Lois Frankel advises that women should avoid being emotional at work because it will undermine how others rate their competence.[26] These perspectives suggest that the demonstration or even experience of emotions is likely to make us seem weak, brittle, or irrational. However, the research disagrees and is increasingly showing that emotions are actually critical to rational thinking.[27] In fact, there has been evidence of such a link for a long time.

Take the example of Phineas Gage, a railroad worker in Vermont. One September day in 1848, while Gage was setting an explosive charge at work, a 3′7″ iron bar flew into his lower-left jaw and out through the top of his skull. Remarkably, Gage survived his injury. He was still able to read and speak, and he performed well above average on cognitive ability tests. However, it became clear that Gage had lost his ability to experience emotion. He was emotionless at even the saddest misfortunes or the happiest occasions. Gage's inability to express emotion eventually took away his ability to reason. He started making irrational choices about his life, often behaving erratically and against his self-interests. Despite being

By studying brain injuries, such as the one experienced by Phineas Gage, whose skull is shown here, researchers discovered an important link between emotions and rational thinking. They found that losing the ability to emote led to the loss of the ability to reason. From this discovery, researchers learned that our emotions provide us with valuable information that helps our thinking process.

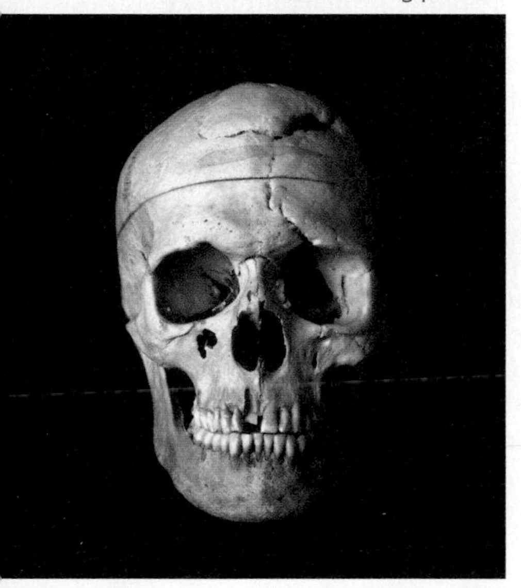

an intelligent man whose intellectual abilities were unharmed by the accident, Gage drifted from job to job, eventually taking up with a circus. In commenting on Gage's condition, one expert noted, "Reason may not be as pure as most of us think it is or wish it were . . . emotions and feelings may not be intruders in the bastion of reason at all: they may be enmeshed in its networks, for worse *and* for better."[28]

The examples of Phineas Gage and many other brain injury studies show us that emotions are critical to rational thinking. We must have the ability to experience emotions to be rational. Why? Because our emotions provide important information about how we understand the world around us. Although we might think of a computer as intellectually superior, a human so void of emotion would be unable to function. Think about a manager making a decision to fire an employee. Would you really want the manager to make the decision without regarding either his or the employee's emotions? The key to good decision making is to employ both thinking *and* feeling in one's decisions.

What Functions Do Emotions Serve? Why do we have emotions? What role do they serve? We just discussed one function—that we need them to think rationally. Charles Darwin, however, took a broader approach. In *The Expression of the Emotions in Man and Animals*, Darwin argued that emotions developed over time to help humans solve problems. Emotions are useful, he said, because they motivate people to engage in actions that are important for survival—actions such as foraging for food, seeking shelter, choosing mates, guarding against predators, and predicting others' behaviors. For example, disgust (an emotion) motivates us to avoid dangerous or harmful things (such as rotten foods). Excitement (also an emotion) motivates us to take on situations in which we require energy and initiative (for example, tackling a new career).

Drawing from Darwin are researchers who focus on **evolutionary psychology**. This field of study says we must experience emotions—whether they are positive or negative—because they serve a purpose.[29] For example, you would probably consider jealousy to be a negative emotion. Evolutionary psychologists would argue that it exists in people because it has a useful purpose. Mates may feel jealousy to increase the chance that their genes, rather than a rival's genes, are passed on to the next generation.[30] Although we tend to think of anger as being "bad," it actually can help us protect our rights when we feel they're being violated. For example, a person showing anger when she's double-crossed by a colleague is serving a warning for others not to repeat the same behavior. Consider another example. Rena Weeks was a secretary at a prominent law firm. Her boss wouldn't stop touching and grabbing her. His treatment of her made her angry. So she did more than quit—she sued, and won a multimillion-dollar case.[31] It's not that anger is always good. But as with all other emotions, it exists because it serves a useful purpose. Positive emotions also serve a purpose. For example, a service employee who feels empathy for a customer may provide better customer service than an seemingly unfeeling employee.

But some researchers are not firm believers of evolutionary psychology. Why? Think about fear (an emotion). It's just as easy to think of the harmful effects of

positive affect *A mood dimension that consists of specific positive emotions such as excitement, self-assurance, and cheerfulness at the high end and boredom, sluggishness, and tiredness at the low end.*

negative affect *A mood dimension that consists of emotions such as nervousness, stress, and anxiety at the high end and relaxation, tranquility, and poise at the low end.*

positivity offset *The tendency of most individuals to experience a mildly positive mood at zero input (when nothing in particular is going on).*

evolutionary psychology *An area of inquiry which argues that we must experience the emotions we do because they serve a purpose.*

fear as it is the beneficial effects. For example, running in fear from a predator increases the likelihood of survival. But what benefit does freezing in fear serve? Evolutionary psychology provides an interesting perspective on the functions of emotions, but it's difficult to know whether this perspective is valid all the time.[32]

Sources of Emotions and Moods

3 Identify the sources of emotions and moods.

Have you ever said, "I got up on the wrong side of the bed today"? Have you ever snapped at a coworker or family member for no particular reason? If you have, it probably makes you wonder where emotions and moods come from. Here we discuss some of the primary influences on moods and emotions.

Personality Moods and emotions have a trait component—most people have built-in tendencies to experience certain moods and emotions more frequently than others do. Moreover, people naturally differ in how intensely they experience the same emotions. Contrast Texas Technical University basketball coach Bobby Knight to Microsoft CEO Bill Gates. One is easily moved to anger, while the other is relatively distant and unemotional. Knight and Gates probably differ in **affect intensity**, or how strongly they experience their emotions.[33] Affectively intense people experience both positive and negative emotions more deeply—when they're sad, they're really sad, and when they're happy, they're really happy.

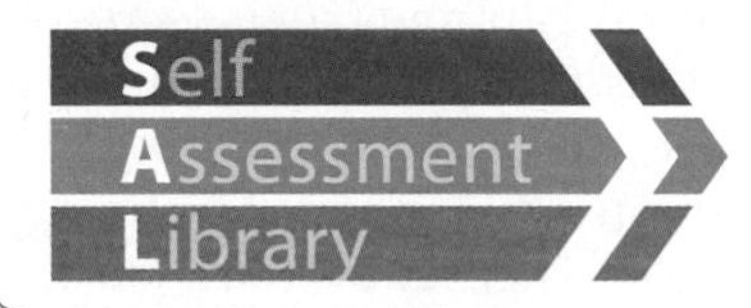

WHAT'S MY AFFECT INTENSITY?

In the Self-Assessment Library (available on CD or online), take assessment IV.D.2 (What's My Affect Intensity?).

Day of the Week and Time of the Day Are people in their best moods on the weekends? Well, sort of. As Exhibit 8-3 shows, people tend to be in their worst moods (highest negative affect and lowest positive affect) early in the week and in their best moods (highest positive affect and lowest negative affect) late in the week.[34]

What about time of the day? (See Exhibit 8-4.) We often think that people differ, depending on whether they are "morning" or "evening" people. However, the vast majority of us follow the same pattern. Regardless of what time people go to bed at night or get up in the morning, levels of positive affect tend to peak around the halfway point between waking and sleeping. Negative affect, however, shows little fluctuation throughout the day.[35] This basic pattern seems to hold whether people describe themselves as morning people or evening people.[36]

What does this mean for organizational behavior? Monday morning is probably not the best time to ask someone for a favor or convey bad news. Our workplace interactions will probably be more positive from midmorning onward and also later in the week.

Weather When do you think you would be in a better mood—when it's 70 degrees and sunny or when it's a gloomy, cold, rainy day? Many people believe their mood is tied to the weather. However, evidence suggests that weather has little effect on mood. One expert concluded, "Contrary to the prevailing cultural view, these data indicate that people do not report a better mood on bright and sunny days (or, conversely, a worse mood on dark and rainy days)."[37] *Illusory correlation* explains why people tend to *think* that nice weather improves their mood. **Illusory correlation** occurs when people associate two events but in reality there is no connection.

Exhibit 8-3 Our Moods Are Affected by the Day of the Week

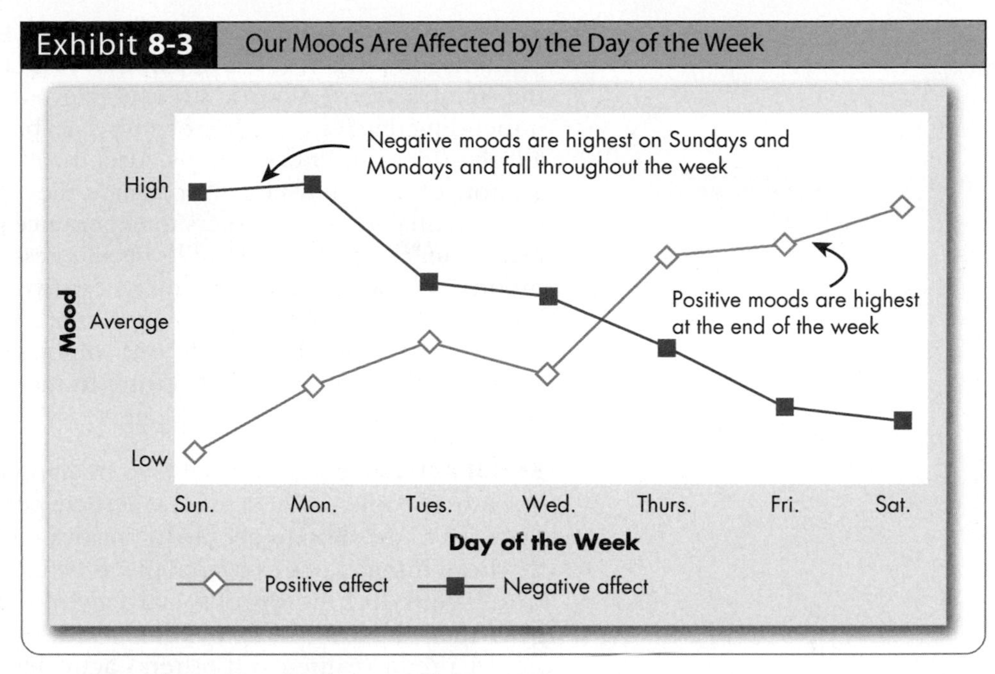

Source: D. Watson, *Mood and Temperament* (New York: Guilford Press, 2000).

Exhibit 8-4 Our Moods Are Affected by the Time of the Day

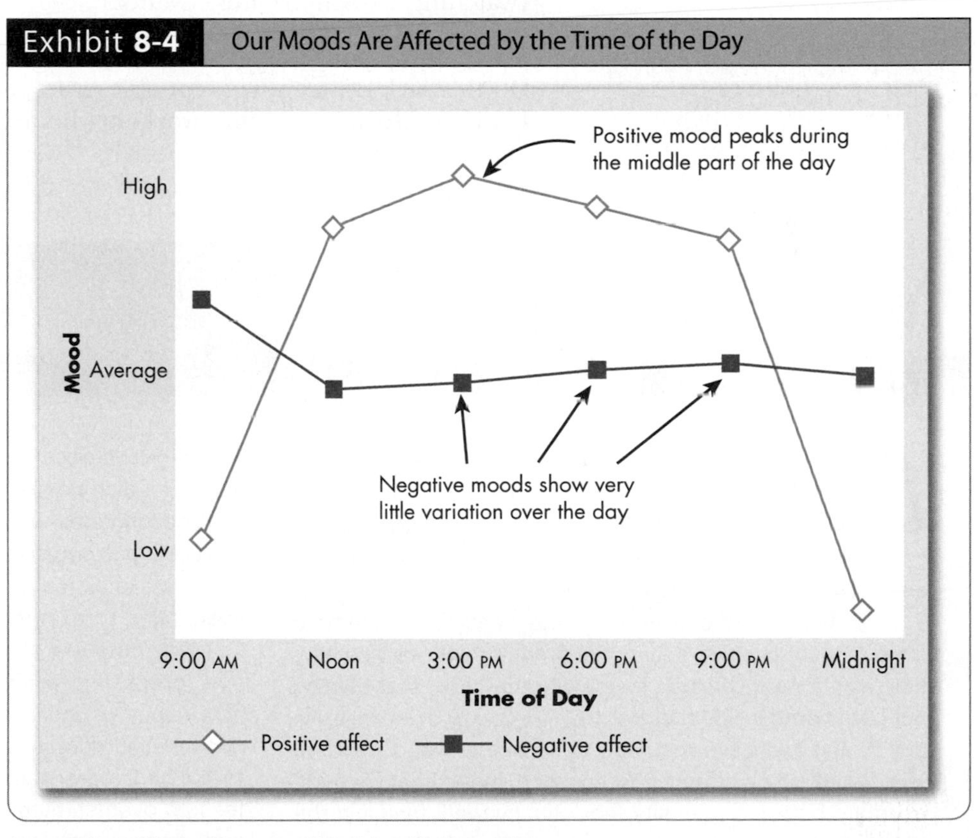

Source: D. Watson, *Mood and Temperament* (New York: Guilford Press, 2000).

affect intensity *Individual differences in the strength with which individuals experience their emotions.*

illusory correlation
The tendency of people to associate two events when in reality there is no connection.

Stress As you might imagine, stress affects emotions and moods. For example, students have higher levels of fear before an exam, but their fear dissipates once the exam is over.[38] At work, stressful daily events (for example, a nasty e-mail, an impending deadline, the loss of a big sale, being reprimanded by your boss) negatively affect employees' moods. Also, the effects of stress build over time. As the authors of one study note, "a constant diet of even low-level stressful events has the potential to cause workers to experience gradually increasing levels of strain over time."[39] Such mounting levels of stress and strain at work can worsen our moods, and we experience more negative emotions. Consider the following entry from a worker's blog: "i'm in a bit of a blah mood today . . . physically, i feel funky, though and the weather out combined with the amount of personal and work i need to get done are getting to me." Although sometimes we thrive on stress, for most of us, like this blogger, stress takes a toll on our mood.[40]

Social Activities Do you tend to be happiest when you are out with friends? For most people, social activities increase positive mood and have little effect on negative mood. But do people in positive moods seek out social interactions, or do social interactions cause people to be in good moods? It seems that both are true.[41] And does the *type* of social activity matter? Indeed it does. Research suggests that physical (skiing or hiking with friends), informal (going to a party), or epicurean (eating with others) activities are more strongly associated with increases in positive mood than formal (attending a meeting) or sedentary (watching TV with friends) events.[42]

Sleep U.S. adults report that they sleep less than they did a generation ago.[43] Do this lack of sleep make people grumpier? Sleep quality does affect mood. Undergraduates and adult workers who are sleep deprived report greater feelings of fatigue, anger, and hostility.[44] One of the reasons less sleep, or poor sleep quality, puts people in a bad mood is that it impairs decision making and

MYTH OR SCIENCE? *"People Can't Accurately Forecast Their Own Emotions"*

This statement is essentially true. People tend to do a pretty bad job of predicting how they're going to feel when something happens. The research on this topic—called *affective forecasting*—shows that our poor job of affective forecasting takes two forms.

First, we tend to overestimate the pleasure we'll receive from a future positive event. We tend to think we'll be happier with a new car than is actually the case, that owning our own home will feel better than it actually does once we buy it, and even that marriage will make us happier than it will. Research on affective forecasting shows that we overestimate both the intensity (how happy we'll feel) and the duration (how long we'll feel happy) of future positive events. For example, when Joakim Noah was contemplating being a first-round basketball draft pick, a reporter asked him what he'd most look forward to. Noah said he couldn't wait to have "the best bathroom in the NBA." Noah was a first-round pick (by the Chicago Bulls), so chances are he got his world-class bathroom in Chicago, but chances also are that it didn't make him as happy as he thought it would.

A second area where we are not very good at affective forecasting is negative events. Just as positive events tend not to make us feel as good as we think they will, negative events don't make us feel as bad as we think they will.

Many different studies have supported our poor affective forecasting abilities: College students overestimate how happy or unhappy they'll be after being assigned to a good or bad dormitory, people overestimate how unhappy they'll be 2 months after a break-up, untenured college professors overestimate how happy they will be with tenure, and women overestimate the emotional impact of unwanted results for a pregnancy test.[45]

So, there is good news and bad news in this story: It's true that the highs aren't as high as we think, but it's also true that the lows aren't as low as we fear. Odds are, the future isn't as bright as you hope, but neither is it as bleak as you fear. ■

Sweat therapy enhances the mood of Mark Saunders, senior marketing manager at GlaxoSmithKline, a pharmaceutical firm. Saunders regularly works out with the help of a trainer at the company's fitness center. Saunders says exercise makes him more energetic and sharp and boosts his creativity and productivity. "Especially in winter, this keeps my engine going," he says. Like many other companies that provide fitness centers for employees, GlaxoSmithKline believes that exercise increases positive moods, resulting in happier, healthier, and more productive employees.

makes it difficult to control emotions.[46] A recent study suggests that poor sleep the previous night also impairs peoples' job satisfaction the next day, mostly because people feel fatigued, irritable, and less alert.[47]

Exercise You often hear that people should exercise to improve their mood. But does "sweat therapy" really work? It appears so. Research consistently shows that exercise enhances peoples' positive mood.[48] It appears that the therapeutic effects of exercise are strongest for those who are depressed. Although the effects of exercise on moods are consistent, they are not terribly strong. So, exercise may help put you in a better mood, but don't expect miracles.

Age Do you think that young people experience more extreme, positive emotions (so-called "youthful exuberance") than older people do? If you answered "yes," you were wrong. One study of people aged 18 to 94 years revealed that negative emotions seem to occur less as people get older. Periods of highly positive moods lasted longer for older individuals, and bad moods faded for them more quickly than for younger people.[49] The study implies that emotional experience tends to improve with age, so that as we get older, we experience fewer negative emotions.

Gender The common belief is that women are more emotional than men. Is there any truth to this? The evidence does confirm that women are more emotionally expressive than are men;[50] they experience emotions more intensely, they tend to "hold onto" emotions longer than men, and they display more frequent expressions of both positive and negative emotions, except anger.[51] Although there may be innate differences between the genders, research suggests that emotional differences also are due to the different ways men and women have been socialized.[52] Men are taught to be tough and brave. Showing emotion is inconsistent with this image. Women, in contrast, are socialized to be nurturing. For instance, women are expected to express more positive emotions on the job (shown by smiling) than men, and they do.[53]

Emotional Recognition: Universal or Culture Specific?

Early researchers studying how we understand emotions based on others' expressions believed that all individuals, regardless of their culture, could recognize the same emotion. So, for example, a frown would be recognized as indicating the emotion sadness, no matter where one was from. However, more recent research suggests that this universal approach to the study of emotions is incorrect because there are subtle differences in the degree to which we can tell what emotions people from different cultures are feeling, based on their facial expressions.

One study examined how quickly and accurately we can read the facial expressions of people of different cultural backgrounds. Although individuals were at first faster at recognizing the emotional expression of others from their own culture, when living in a different culture, the speed and accuracy at which they recognized others' emotions increased as they became more familiar with the culture. For example, as Chinese residing in the United States adapted to their surroundings, they were able to recognize the emotions of people native to the United States more quickly. In fact, foreigners are sometimes better at recognizing emotions among the citizens in their non-native country than are those citizens themselves.

Interestingly, these effects begin to occur relatively quickly. For example, Chinese students living in the United States for an average of 2.4 years were better at recognizing the facial expressions of U.S. citizens than they were at reading the facial expressions of Chinese citizens. Why is this the case? According to the authors of the study, it could be that because they are limited in speaking the language, they rely more on nonverbal communication. What is the upshot for OB? When conducting business in a foreign country, the ability to correctly recognize others' emotions can facilitate interactions and lead to less miscommunication. Otherwise, a slight smile that is intended to communicate disinterest may be mistaken for happiness.

Source: Based on H. A. Elfenbein and N. Ambady, "When Familiarity Breeds Accuracy: Cultural Exposure and Facial Emotion Recognition," *Journal of Personality and Social Psychology*, August 2003, pp. 276–290.

Emotional Labor

If you've ever had a job working in retail sales or waiting on tables in a restaurant, you know the importance of projecting a friendly demeanor and smiling. Even though there were days when you didn't feel cheerful, you knew management expected you to be upbeat when dealing with customers. So you faked it, and in so doing, you expressed emotional labor.

4 *Show the impact emotional labor has on employees.*

Every employee expends physical and mental labor when they put their bodies and cognitive capabilities, respectively, into their job. But jobs also require **emotional labor**. Emotional labor is an employee's expression of organizationally desired emotions during interpersonal transactions at work.[54]

The concept of emotional labor emerged from studies of service jobs. Airlines expect their flight attendants, for instance, to be cheerful; we expect funeral directors to be sad; and we expect doctors to be emotionally neutral. But really, emotional labor is relevant to almost every job. Your managers expect you, for example, to be courteous, not hostile, in interactions with coworkers. The true challenge arises when employees have to project one emotion while simultaneously feeling another.[55] This disparity is **emotional dissonance**, and it can take a heavy toll on employees. Bottled-up feelings of frustration, anger, and resentment can eventually lead to emotional exhaustion and burnout.[56] It's from the increasing importance of emotional labor as a key component of effective job performance that an understanding of emotion has gained heightened relevance within the field of OB.

When Apple's iPhone first went on sale at an Apple Store in San Francisco, employees enthusiastically greeted the first customers. Giving customers a warm reception with smiling faces and applause is an example of displayed emotions, those an organization requires employees to show and considers appropriate in a given job.

Emotional labor creates dilemmas for employees. There are people with whom you have to work that you just plain don't like. Maybe you consider their personality abrasive. Maybe you know they've said negative things about you behind your back. Regardless, your job requires you to interact with these people on a regular basis. So you're forced to feign friendliness.

It can help you, on the job especially, if you separate emotions into *felt* or *displayed emotions*.[57] **Felt emotions** are an individual's actual emotions. In contrast, **displayed emotions** are those that the organization requires workers to show and considers appropriate in a given job. They're not innate; they're learned. "The ritual look of delight on the face of the first runner-up as the new Miss America is announced is a product of the display rule that losers should mask their sadness with an expression of joy for the winner."[58] Similarly, most of us know that we're expected to act sad at funerals, regardless of whether we consider the person's death to be a loss, and to pretend to be happy at weddings, even if we don't feel like celebrating.[59]

Effective managers have learned to be serious when giving an employee a negative performance evaluation and to hide their anger when they've been passed over for promotion. And a salesperson who hasn't learned to smile and appear friendly, regardless of his true feelings at the moment, isn't typically going to last long on most sales jobs. How we *experience* an emotion isn't always the same as how we *show* it.[60]

Yet another point is that displaying fake emotions requires us to suppress the emotions we really feel (not showing anger toward a customer, for example). In other words, the individual has to "act" to keep her job. **Surface acting** is hiding

emotional labor *A situation in which an employee expresses organizationally desired emotions during interpersonal transactions at work.*

emotional dissonance *Inconsistencies between the emotions people feel and the emotions they project.*

felt emotions *An individual's actual emotions.*

displayed emotions *Emotions that are organizationally required and considered appropriate in a given job.*

surface acting *Hiding one's inner feelings and forgoing emotional expressions in response to display rules.*

Exhibit 8-5 Relationship of Pay to Cognitive and Emotional Demands of Jobs

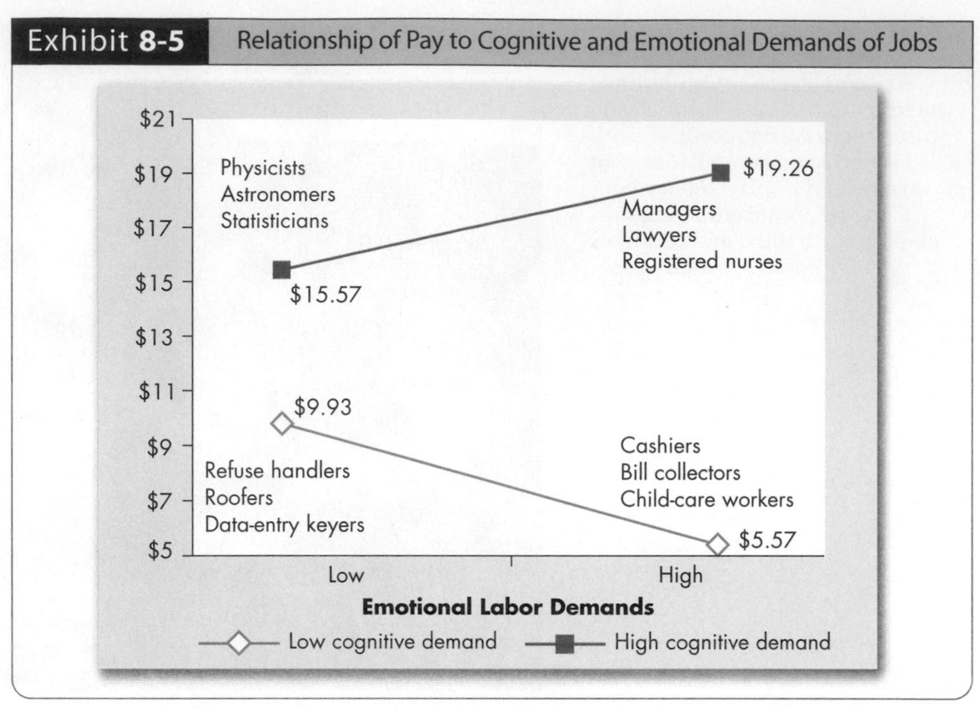

Source: Based on: T. M. Glomb, J. D. Kammeyer-Mueller, and M. Rotundo, "Emotional Labor Demands and Compensating Wage Differentials," *Journal of Applied Psychology* 89, no. 4 (August 2004), pp. 700–714.

one's inner feelings and forgoing emotional expressions in response to display rules. For example, when a worker smiles at a customer even when he doesn't feel like it, he is surface acting. **Deep acting** is trying to modify one's true inner feelings based on display rules. A health care provider trying to genuinely feel more empathy for her patients is deep acting.[61] Surface acting deals with one's *displayed* emotions, and deep acting deals with one's *felt* emotions. Research shows that surface acting is more stressful to employees than deep acting because it entails feigning one's true emotions.[62]

Interestingly, as important as managing emotions is to many jobs, it seems that the market does not necessarily reward emotional labor. A recent study found that emotional demands matter in setting compensation levels, but only when jobs are already cognitively demanding—such as jobs in law and nursing. But, for instance, child-care workers and waiters—holders of jobs with high emotional demands but relatively low cognitive demands—receive little compensation for the emotional demands of their work.[63] Exhibit 8-5 shows the relationship between cognitive and emotional demands and pay. The model doesn't seem to depict a fair state of affairs. After all, why should emotional demands be rewarded in only cognitively complex jobs? One explanation may be that it's hard to find qualified people who are willing and able to work in such jobs.

Affective Events Theory

5 *Describe affective events theory and identify its applications.*

As we have seen, emotions and moods are an important part of our lives, especially our work lives. But how do our emotions and moods influence our job performance and satisfaction? A model called **affective events theory (AET)** has increased our understanding of the links.[64] AET demonstrates that employees react emotionally to things that happen to them at work and that this reaction influences their job performance and satisfaction.

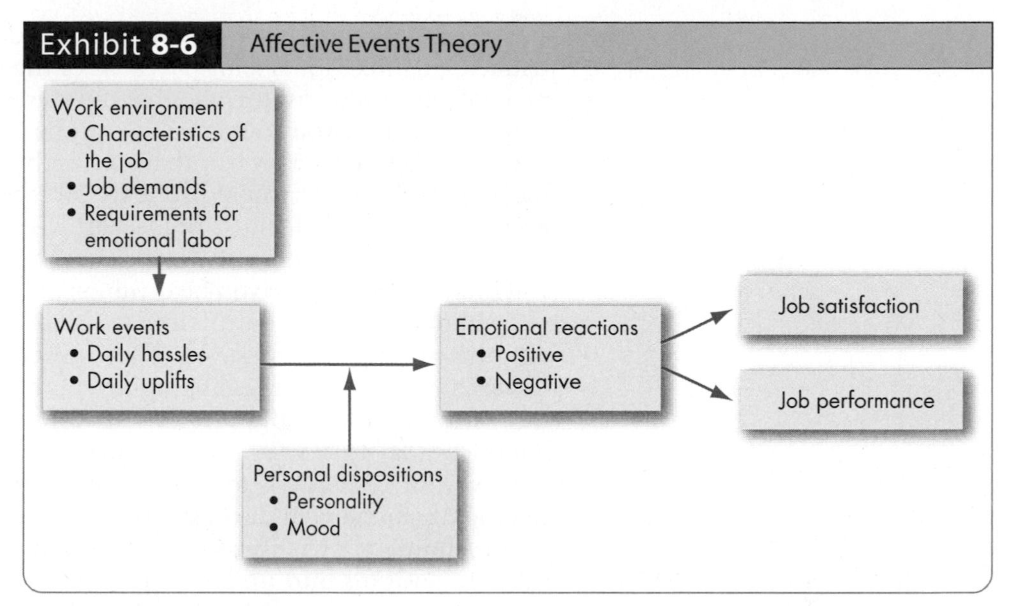

Source: Based on N. M. Ashkanasy and C. S. Daus, "Emotion in the Workplace: The New Challenge for Managers," *Academy of Management Executive*, February 2002, p. 77.

Exhibit 8-6 summarizes AET. The theory begins by recognizing that emotions are a response to an event in the work environment. The work environment includes everything surrounding the job—the variety of tasks and degree of autonomy, job demands, and requirements for expressing emotional labor. This environment creates work events that can be hassles, uplifting events, or both. Examples of hassles are colleagues who refuse to carry their share of work, conflicting directions from different managers, and excessive time pressures. Examples of uplifting events include meeting a goal, getting support from a colleague, and receiving recognition for an accomplishment.[65]

These work events trigger positive or negative emotional reactions. But employees' personalities and moods predispose them to respond with greater or lesser intensity to the event. For instance, people who score low on emotional stability are more likely to react strongly to negative events. And their mood introduces the reality that their general affect cycle creates fluctuations. So a person's emotional response to a given event can change, depending on mood. Finally, emotions influence a number of performance and satisfaction variables, such as organizational citizenship behavior, organizational commitment, level of effort, intentions to quit, and workplace deviance.

In addition, tests of the theory suggest that (1) an emotional episode is actually a series of emotional experiences precipitated by a single event. It contains elements of both emotions and mood cycles. (2) Current emotions influence job satisfaction at any given time, along with the history of emotions surrounding the event. (3) Because moods and emotions fluctuate over time, their effect on performance also fluctuates. (4) Emotion-driven behaviors are typically short in duration and of high variability. (5) Because emotions, even positive ones, tend to be incompatible with behaviors required to do a job, they typically have a negative influence on job performance.[66]

deep acting *Trying to modify one's true inner feelings based on display rules.*

affective events theory (AET) *A model that suggests that workplace events cause emotional reactions on the part of employees, which then influence workplace attitudes and behaviors.*

An example might help better explain AET.[67] Say that you work as an aeronautical engineer for Boeing. Because of the downturn in the demand for commercial jets, you've just learned that the company is considering laying off 10,000 employees. This layoff could include you. This event is likely to make you feel negative emotions, especially fear that you might lose your job and primary source of income. And because you're prone to worry a lot and obsess about problems, this event increases your feelings of insecurity. The layoff also puts into place a series of smaller events that create an episode: You talk with your boss, and he assures you that your job is safe; you hear rumors that your department is high on the list to be eliminated; and you run into a former colleague who was laid off 6 months ago and still hasn't found work. These events, in turn, create emotional ups and downs. One day, you're feeling upbeat and that you'll survive the cuts. The next day, you might be depressed and anxious. These emotional swings take your attention away from your work and lower your job performance and satisfaction. Finally, your response is magnified because this is the fourth-largest layoff that Boeing has initiated in the past 3 years.

In summary, AET offers two important messages.[68] First, emotions provide valuable insights into understanding employee behavior. The model demonstrates how workplace hassles and uplifting events influence employee performance and satisfaction. Second, employees and managers shouldn't ignore emotions and the events that cause them, even when they appear to be minor, because they accumulate.

Emotional Intelligence

(a) Def

6 *Contrast the evidence for and against the existence of emotional intelligence.*

Diane Marshall is an office manager. Her awareness of her own and others' emotions is almost nil. She's moody and unable to generate much enthusiasm or interest in her employees. She doesn't understand why employees get upset with her. She often overreacts to problems and chooses the most ineffectual responses to emotional situations.[69] Diane Marshall has low emotional intelligence. **Emotional intelligence (EI)** is a person's ability to (1) be self-aware (to recognize her own emotions when she experiences them), (2) detect emotions in others, and (3) manage emotional cues and information. People who know their own emotions and are good at reading emotion cues—for instance, knowing why they're angry and how to express themselves without violating norms—are most likely to be effective.[70]

Several studies suggest that EI plays an important role in job performance. One study looked at the characteristics of engineers at Lucent Technologies who were rated as stars by their peers. The researchers concluded that stars were better at relating to others. That is, it was EI, not IQ, that characterized high performers. Another illuminating study looked at the successes and failures of 11 American presidents—from Franklin Roosevelt to Bill Clinton. They were evaluated on six qualities—communication, organization, political skill, vision, cognitive style, and emotional intelligence. It was found that the key quality that differentiated the successful (such as Roosevelt, Kennedy, and Reagan) from the unsuccessful (such as Johnson, Carter, and Nixon) was emotional intelligence.[71]

EI has been a controversial concept in OB. It has supporters and detractors. In the following sections, we review the arguments for and against the viability of EI in OB.

The Case for EI

Adv

The arguments in favor of EI include its intuitive appeal, the fact that EI predicts criteria that matter, and the idea that EI is biologically based.

Meg Whitman, the former CEO of eBay, is a leader with high emotional intelligence. After eBay founder Pierre Omidyar selected Whitman to transform his start-up into a global enterprise, she emerged as a star performer in a job that demands interacting socially with employees, customers, and political leaders throughout the world. Whitman is described as self-confident yet humble, trustworthy, culturally sensitive, and expert at building teams and leading change. Shown here, Whitman welcomed Gloria Arroyo, president of the Philippine Islands where eBay has an auction site, to eBay headquarters.

Intuitive Appeal There's a lot of intuitive appeal to the EI concept. Almost everyone would agree that it is good to possess street smarts and social intelligence. People who can detect emotions in others, control their own emotions, and handle social interactions well will have a powerful leg up in the business world, so the thinking goes. As just one example, partners in a multinational consulting firm who scored above the median on an EI measure delivered $1.2 million more in business than did the other partners.[72]

EI Predicts Criteria That Matter More and more evidence is suggesting that a high level of EI means a person will perform well on the job. One study found that EI predicted the performance of employees in a cigarette factory in China.[73] Another study found that being able to recognize emotions in others' facial expressions and to emotionally "eavesdrop" (that is, pick up subtle signals about peoples' emotions) predicted peer ratings of how valuable those people were to their organization.[74] Finally, a review of 59 studies indicated that, overall, EI correlated moderately with job performance.[75]

EI Is Biologically Based One study has shown that people with damage to the part of the brain that governs emotional processing (lesions in an area of the prefrontal cortex) score significantly lower than others on EI tests. Even though these brain-damaged people scored no lower on standard measures of intelligence than people without the same brain damage, they were still impaired in normal decision making. Specifically, when people were playing a card game in which there is a reward (money) for picking certain types of cards and a punishment (a loss of money) for picking other types of cards, the

emotional intelligence (EI)
The ability to detect and to manage emotional cues and information.

participants with no brain damage learned to succeed in the game, while the performance of the brain-damaged group worsened over time. This study suggests that EI is neurologically based in a way that's unrelated to standard measures of intelligence and that people who suffer neurological damage score lower on EI and make poorer decisions than people who are healthier in this regard.[76]

The Case Against EI

For all its supporters, EI has just as many critics. Its critics say that EI is vague and impossible to measure, and they question its validity.

EI Is Too Vague a Concept To many researchers, it's not clear what EI is. Is it a form of intelligence? Most of us wouldn't think that being self-aware or self-motivated or having empathy is a matter of intellect. So, is EI a misnomer? Moreover, many times different researchers focus on different skills, making it difficult to get a definition of EI. One researcher may study self-discipline. Another may study empathy. Another may look at self-awareness. As one reviewer noted, "The concept of EI has now become so broad and the components so variegated that . . . it is no longer even an intelligible concept."[77]

EI Can't Be Measured Many critics have raised questions about measuring EI. Because EI is a form of intelligence, for instance, there must be right and wrong answers about it on tests, they argue. Some tests do have right and wrong answers, although the validity of some of the questions on these measures is questionable. For example, one measure asks you to associate particular feelings with specific colors, as if purple always makes us feel cool and not warm. Other measures are self-reported, meaning there is no right or wrong answer. For example, an EI test question might ask you to respond to the statement, "I'm good at 'reading' other people." In general, the measures of EI are diverse, and researchers have not subjected them to as much rigorous study as they have measures of personality and general intelligence.[78]

The Validity of EI Is Suspect Some critics argue that because EI is so closely related to intelligence and personality, once you control for these factors, EI has nothing unique to offer. There is some foundation to this argument. EI appears to be highly correlated with measures of personality, especially emotional stability.[79] But there hasn't been enough research on whether EI adds insight beyond measures of personality and general intelligence in predicting job performance. Still, among consulting firms and in the popular press, EI is wildly popular. For example, one company's promotional materials for an EI measure claimed, "EI accounts for more than 85 percent of star performance in top leaders."[80] To say the least, it's difficult to validate this statement with the research literature.

Weighing the arguments for and against EI, it's still too early to tell whether the concept is useful. It *is* clear, though, that the concept is here to stay.

WHAT'S MY EMOTIONAL INTELLIGENCE SCORE?

In the Self-Assessment Library (available on CD or online), take assessment I.E.1 (What's My Emotional Intelligence Score?).

OB Applications of Emotions and Moods

7 *Apply concepts about emotions and moods to specific OB issues.*

In this section, we assess how an understanding of emotions and moods can improve our ability to explain and predict the selection process in organizations, decision making, creativity, motivation, leadership, interpersonal conflict, negotiation, customer service, job attitudes, and deviant workplace behaviors. We also look at how managers can influence our moods.

Selection

One implication from the evidence to date on EI is that employers should consider it a factor in hiring employees, especially in jobs that demand a high degree of social interaction. In fact, more and more employers are starting to use EI measures to hire people. A study of U.S. Air Force recruiters showed that top-performing recruiters exhibited high levels of EI. Using these findings, the Air Force revamped its selection criteria. A follow-up investigation found that future hires who had high EI scores were 2.6 times more successful than those who didn't. At the beauty-products company L'Oreal, salespersons selected on EI scores outsold those hired using the company's old selection procedure. On an annual basis, salespeople selected on the basis of emotional competence sold \$91,370 more than other salespeople did, for a net revenue increase of \$2,558,360.[81]

Decision Making

As you saw in Chapter 5, traditional approaches to the study of decision making in organizations have emphasized rationality. More and more OB researchers, though, are finding that moods and emotions have important effects on decision making.

Positive moods and emotions seem to help decision making. People in good moods or those experiencing positive emotions are more likely than others to use heuristics, or rules of thumb,[82] to help make good decisions quickly.

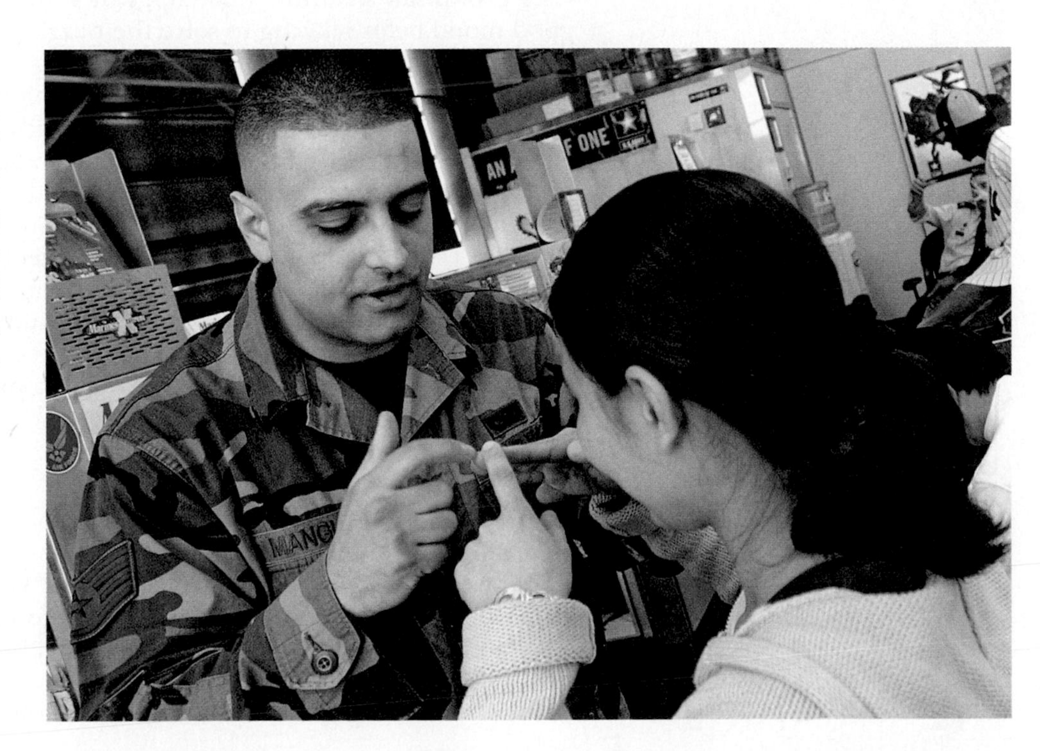

The U.S. Air Force uses emotional intelligence as a selection criterion for recruiters, whose jobs demand a high degree of social interaction. By hiring recruiters with high EI scores, the Air Force has reduced turnover rates among new recruiters and decreased hiring and training costs. The recruiter shown here interacts with a new enlistee by teaching her the proper way to salute before she reports to boot camp.

Positive emotions also enhance problem-solving skills so that positive people find better solutions to problems.[83]

OB researchers continue to debate the role of negative emotions and moods in decision making. Although one often-cited study suggested that depressed people reach more accurate judgments,[84] more recent evidence has suggested that people who are depressed make poorer decisions. Why? Because depressed people are slower at processing information and tend to weigh all possible options rather than the most likely ones.[85] Although it would seem that weighing all possible options is a good thing, the problem is that depressed people search for the perfect solution when rarely is any solution perfect.

Creativity

People who are in good moods tend to be more creative than people in bad moods.[86] They produce more ideas, others think their ideas are original, and they tend to identify more creative options to problems.[87] It seems that people who are experiencing positive moods or emotions are more flexible and open in their thinking, which may explain why they're more creative.[88] Supervisors should actively try to keep employees happy because doing so creates more good moods (employees like their leaders to encourage them and provide positive feedback on a job well done), which in turn leads people to be more creative.[89]

Some researchers, however, do not believe that a positive mood makes people more creative. They argue that when people are in positive moods, they may relax ("If I'm in a good mood, things must be going okay, and I must not need to think of new ideas") and not engage in the critical thinking necessary for some forms of creativity.[90] However, this view is controversial.[91] Until there are more studies on the subject, we can safely conclude that for many tasks, positive moods increase our creativity.

Motivation

Two studies have highlighted the importance of moods and emotions on motivation. The first study had two groups of people solve a number of word puzzles. One group saw a funny video clip, which was intended to put the group in a good mood before having to solve the puzzles. The other group was not shown the clip and just started working on solving the word puzzles right away. The results? The positive-mood group reported higher expectations of being able to solve the puzzles, worked harder at them, and solved more puzzles as a result.[92]

The second study found that giving people feedback—whether real or fake—about their performance influenced their mood, which then influenced their motivation.[93] So a cycle can exist in which positive moods cause people to be more creative, which leads to positive feedback from those observing their work. This positive feedback then further reinforces their positive mood, which may then make them perform even better, and so on.

Both of these studies highlight the effects of mood and emotions on motivation and suggest that organizations that promote positive moods at work are likely to have more motivated workers.

Leadership

Effective leaders rely on emotional appeals to help convey their messages.[94] In fact, the expression of emotions in speeches is often the critical element that makes us accept or reject a leader's message. "When leaders feel excited, enthusiastic, and active, they may be more likely to energize their subordinates and convey a sense of efficacy, competence, optimism, and enjoyment."[95] Politicians, as a case in point, have learned to show enthusiasm when talking about their chances of winning an election, even when polls suggest otherwise.

Known as an enthusiastic cheerleader for Microsoft, CEO Steve Ballmer travels the world, delivering impassioned speeches to inspire employees and business partners. Through his emotionally charged speeches, Ballmer presents a road map for employees and partners of Microsoft's competitive focus and company vision. "I want everyone to share my passion for our products and services," he says. "I want people to understand the amazing positive way our software can make leisure time more enjoyable and work and businesses more successful."

Corporate executives know that emotional content is critical if employees are to buy into their vision of their company's future and accept change. When higher-ups offer new visions, especially when the visions contain distant or vague goals, it is often difficult for employees to accept those visions and the changes they'll bring. By arousing emotions and linking them to an appealing vision, leaders increase the likelihood that managers and employees alike will accept change.[96]

Negotiation

Negotiation is an emotional process; however, we often say a skilled negotiator has a "poker face." The founder of Britain's Poker Channel, Crispin Nieboer, stated, "It is a game of bluff and there is fantastic human emotion and tension, seeing who can bluff the longest."[97] Several studies have shown that a negotiator who feigns anger has an advantage over the opponent. Why? Because when a negotiator shows anger, the opponent concludes that the negotiator has conceded all that she can, so the opponent gives in.[98]

Displaying a negative emotion (such as anger) can be effective, but feeling bad about your performance appears to impair future negotiations. Individuals who do poorly in a negotiation experience negative emotions, develop negative perceptions of their counterpart, and are less willing to share information or be cooperative in future negotiations.[99] Interestingly, then, while moods and emotions have benefits at work, in negotiation, unless we're putting up a false front (feigning anger), it seems that emotions may impair negotiator performance. In fact, a 2005 study found that people who suffered damage to the emotional centers of their brains (damage to the same part of the brain as Phineas Gage) may be the *best* negotiators because they're not likely to overcorrect when faced with negative outcomes.[100]

Customer Service

A worker's emotional state influences customer service, which influences levels of repeat business and levels of customer satisfaction.[101] Providing quality customer service makes demands on employees because it often puts them in a state of emotional dissonance. Over time, this state can lead to job burnout, declines in job performance, and lower job satisfaction.[102]

In addition, employees' emotions may transfer to the customer. Studies indicate a matching effect between employee and customer emotions, an effect that is called **emotional contagion**—the "catching" of emotions from others.[103] How does emotional contagion work? The primary explanation is that when someone experiences positive emotions and laughs and smiles at you, you begin to copy that person's behavior. So when employees express positive emotions, customers tend to respond positively. Emotional contagion is important because when customers catch the positive moods or emotions of employees they shop longer. But what about negative emotions and moods? Are they contagious, too? Absolutely. When an employee feels unfairly treated by a customer, for example, it's harder for him to display the positive emotions his organization expects of him.[104]

Job Attitudes

Ever hear the advice "Never take your work home with you," meaning that people should forget about their work once they go home? As it turns out, that's easier said than done. Several studies have shown that people who had a good day at work tend to be in a better mood at home that evening. And people who had a bad day tend to be in a bad mood once they're at home.[105] Evidence also suggests that people who have a stressful day at work have trouble relaxing after they get off work.[106]

Even though people do emotionally take their work home with them, by the next day, the effect is usually gone.[107] So, although it may be difficult or even unnatural to "never take your work home with you," it doesn't appear that, for most people, a negative mood resulting from a bad day at work carries over to the next day.

Deviant Workplace Behaviors

Negative emotions can lead to a number of deviant workplace behaviors.

Anyone who has spent much time in an organization realizes that people often behave in ways that violate established norms and that threaten the organization, its members, or both. As we saw in Chapter 1, these actions are called *workplace deviant behaviors*.[108] Many of these deviant behaviors can be traced to negative emotions.

For instance, envy is an emotion that occurs when you resent someone for having something that you don't have but that you strongly desire—such as a better work assignment, larger office, or higher salary.[109] It can lead to malicious deviant behaviors. An envious employee, for example, could then act hostilely by backstabbing another employee, negatively distorting others' successes, and positively distorting his own accomplishments.[110] Evidence suggests that people who feel negative emotions, particularly those who feel angry or hostile, are more likely than people who don't feel negative emotions to engage in deviant behavior at work.[111]

How Managers Can Influence Moods

In general, you can improve peoples' moods by showing them a funny video clip, giving them a small bag of candy, or even having them taste a pleasant beverage.[112] But what can companies do to improve their employees' moods? Managers can use humor and give their employees small tokens of appreciation for work well done. Also, research indicates that when leaders are in good moods, group members are more positive, and as a result, the members cooperate more.[113]

Finally, selecting positive team members can have a contagion effect as positive moods transmit from team member to team member. One study of professional cricket teams (cricket is a sport played in countries such as Great Britain and India that's a little like baseball) found that players' happy moods affected the moods of their team members and also positively influenced their performance.[114] It makes sense, then, for managers to select team members who are predisposed to experience positive moods.

Crying at Work Gains Acceptance

As we have noted, many employers discourage the expression of emotions at work, especially when those emotions are negative. Recently, though, there are signs that situation is starting to change.

One day, only 4 months into her first job, Hannah Seligson, now 24, was called into the big boss's office and told that her immediate supervisor was not happy with her work. She bawled on the spot. "I was just floored," she said. "I had been working so hard."

Kathryn Brady, 34, is a finance manager for a large corporation in Atlanta. Occasionally she has had bosses who have driven her to tears. Brady argues that when she has cried, it has been out of frustration, not weakness. "The misinterpretation that I'm whiny or weak is just not fair," she says.

To many, however, these emotional displays are signs of weakness. On the reality show *The Apprentice*, Martha Stewart warned one of the contestants not to cry. "Cry, and you're out of here," she said. "Women in business don't cry, my dear."

Although that "old school" wisdom still holds true in many places, it is changing in others. George Merkle, CEO of a San Antonio credit company, does not mind if his employees cry. If someone cries, he says, "No apology needed. I know it's upsetting, and we can work our way through it."

Surveys indicate that women are more likely to cry at work than men, but that may be changing, too. When 6'3" 253-pound football tight end Vernon Davis cried after being selected in the first round of the NFL draft, nobody accused him of being a wimp.

Sources: P. Kitchen, "Experts: Crying at Work on the Rise," *Newsday*, June 10, 2007; and S. Shellenbarger, "Read This and Weep," *Wall Street Journal*, April 26, 2007, p. D1.

Global Issues

8 *Contrast the experience, interpretation, and expression of emotions across cultures.*

Does the degree to which people *experience* emotions vary across cultures? Do peoples' *interpretations* of emotions vary across cultures? Finally, do the norms for the *expression* of emotions differ across cultures? Let's tackle each of these questions.

Does the Degree to Which People Experience Emotions Vary Across Cultures? Yes. In China, for example, people report experiencing fewer positive and negative emotions than people in other cultures, and the emotions they experience are less intense than what other cultures report. Compared with Mainland Chinese, Taiwanese are more like U.S. workers in their experience of emotions: On average, Taiwanese report more positive and fewer negative emotions than their Chinese counterparts.[115] In general, people in most cultures appear to experience certain positive and negative emotions, but the frequency of their experience and their intensity varies to some degree.[116]

Do Peoples' Interpretations of Emotions Vary Across Cultures? In general, people from all over the world interpret negative and positive emotions the same way. We all view negative emotions, such as hate, terror, and rage, as dangerous and destructive. And we all desire positive emotions, such as joy, love, and happiness. However, some cultures value certain emotions more than others. For example, U.S. culture values enthusiasm, while the Chinese consider negative emotions to be more useful and constructive than do people in the United States. In general, pride is seen as a positive emotion in Western, individualistic cultures such as the United States, but Eastern cultures such as China and Japan tend to view pride as undesirable.[117]

emotional contagion *The process by which peoples' emotions are caused by the emotions of others.*

Do the Norms for the Expression of Emotions Differ Across Cultures? Absolutely. For example, Muslims see smiling as a sign of sexual attraction, so women have learned not to smile at men.[118] And research has shown that in collectivist countries people are more likely to believe the emotional displays of another have something to do with their own relationship with the person expressing the emotion, while people in individualistic cultures don't think that another's emotional expressions are directed at them. Evidence indicates that in the United States there's a bias against expressing emotions, especially intense negative emotions. French retail clerks, in contrast, are infamous for being surly toward customers. (A report from the French government itself confirmed this.) There are also reports that serious German shoppers have been turned off by Wal-Mart's friendly greeters and helpful personnel.[119]

In general, and not surprisingly, it's easier for people to accurately recognize emotions within their own culture than in other cultures. For example, a Chinese businessperson is more likely to accurately label the emotions underlying the facial expressions of a fellow Chinese colleague than those of a U.S. colleague.[120]

Interestingly, some cultures lack words for emotional terms such as *anxiety, depression*, and *guilt*. Tahitians, as a case in point, don't have a word directly equivalent to *sadness*. When Tahitians are sad, their peers attribute their state to a physical illness.[121] Our discussion illustrates the need to consider the fact that cultural factors influence what managers think is emotionally appropriate.[122] What's acceptable in one culture may seem extremely unusual or even dysfunctional in another. Managers need to know the emotional norms in each culture they do business in or with so they don't send unintended signals or misread the reactions of others. For example, a U.S. manager in Japan should know that while U.S. culture tends to view smiling positively, the Japanese attribute frequent smiling to a lack of intelligence.[123]

Summary and Implications for Managers

Emotions and moods are similar in that both are affective in nature. But they're also different—moods are more general and less contextual than emotions. And events do matter. The time of day and day of the week, stressful events, social activities, and sleep patterns are some of the factors that influence emotions and moods.

Emotions and moods have proven themselves to be relevant for virtually every OB topic we study. Increasingly, organizations are selecting employees they believe have high levels of emotional intelligence. Emotions, especially positive moods, appear to facilitate effective decision-making and creativity. Although the research is relatively recent, research suggests that mood is linked to motivation, especially through feedback, and that leaders rely on emotions to increase their effectiveness. The display of emotions is important to negotiation and customer service, and the experience of emotions is closely linked to job attitudes and behaviors that follow from attitudes, such as deviant behavior in the workplace.

Can managers control their colleagues' and employees' emotions and moods? Certainly there are limits, practical and ethical. Emotions and moods are a natural part of an individual's makeup. Where managers err is in ignoring their coworkers' and employees' emotions and assessing others' behavior as if it were completely rational. As one consultant aptly put it, "You can't divorce emotions from the workplace because you can't divorce emotions from people."[124] Managers who understand the role of emotions and moods will significantly improve their ability to explain and predict their coworkers' and employees' behavior.

Point

Counterpoint

THE COSTS AND BENEFITS OF ORGANIZATIONAL DISPLAY RULES

Organizations today realize that good customer service means good business. After all, who wants to end a shopping trip at the grocery store with a surly checker? Research clearly shows that organizations that provide good customer service have higher profits than those with poor customer service.[125] An integral part of customer-service training is to set forth display rules to teach employees to interact with customers in a friendly, helpful, professional way—and evidence indicates that such rules work: Having display rules increases the odds that employees will display the emotions expected of them.[126]

As one Starbucks manager says, "What makes Starbucks different is our passion for what we do. We're trying to provide a great experience for people, with a great product. That's what we all care about."[127] Starbucks may have good coffee, but a big part of the company's growth has been the customer experience. For instance, the cashiers are friendly and will get to know you by name if you are a repeat customer.

Asking employees to act friendly is good for them, too. Research shows that employees of organizations that require them to display positive emotions actually feel better as a result.[128] And, if someone feels that being asked to smile is bad for him, he doesn't belong in the service industry in the first place.

Organizations have no business trying to regulate the emotions of their employees. Companies should not be "the thought police" and force employees to feel and act in ways that serve only organizational needs. Service employees should be professional and courteous, yes, but many companies expect them to take abuse and refrain from defending themselves. That's wrong. As the philosopher Jean Paul Sartre wrote, we have a responsibility to be authentic—true to ourselves—and within reasonable limits organizations have no right to ask us to be otherwise.

Service industries have no business teaching their employees to be smiling punching bags. Most customers might even prefer that employees be themselves. Employees shouldn't be openly nasty or hostile, of course, but who appreciates a fake smile? Think about trying on an outfit in a store and the clerk automatically says it looks "absolutely wonderful" when you know it doesn't and you sense the clerk is lying. Most customers would rather talk with a "real" person than someone enslaved to an organization's display rules. Furthermore, if an employee doesn't feel like slapping on an artificial smile, then it's only going to create dissonance between her and her employer.[129]

Finally, research shows that forcing display rules on employees takes a heavy emotional toll.[130] It's unnatural to expect someone to smile all the time or to passively take abuse from customers, clients, or fellow employees. Organizations can improve their employees' psychological health by encouraging them to be themselves, within reasonable limits.

Questions for Review

1 What are the similarities and differences between emotions and moods? What are the basic emotions and the basic mood dimensions?

2 Are emotions and moods rational? What functions do emotions and moods serve?

3 What are the primary sources of emotions and moods?

4 What is emotional labor, and why is it important to understanding OB?

5 What is affective events theory? Why is it important to understanding emotions?

6 What is emotional intelligence, and what are the arguments for and against its importance?

7 What effect do emotions and moods have on different OB issues? As a manager, what steps would you take to improve your employees' moods?

8 Does the degree to which people *experience* emotions vary across cultures? Do peoples' *interpretations* of emotions vary across cultures, and do different norms across cultures govern the expression of emotions?

Experiential Exercise

WHO CAN CATCH A LIAR?

In this chapter, we discussed how people determine emotions from facial expressions. There has been research on whether people can tell whether someone is lying based on facial expression. Let's see who is good at catching liars.

Split up into teams and follow these instructions.

1. Randomly choose someone to be the team organizer. Have this person write down on a piece of paper "T" for truth and "L" for lie. If there are, say, six people in the group (other than the organizer), then three people will get a slip with a "T" and three a slip with an "L." It's important that all team members keep what's on their paper a secret.
2. Each team member who holds a T slip needs to come up with a true statement, and each team member who holds an L slip needs to come up with a false statement. Try not to make the statement so outrageous that no one would believe it (for example, "I have flown to the moon").
3. The organizer will have each member make his or her statement. Group members should then examine the person making the statement closely to try to determine whether he or she is telling the truth or lying. Once each person has made his or her statement, the organizer will ask for a vote and record the tallies.
4. Each person should now indicate whether the statement was the truth or a lie.
5. How good was your group at catching the liars? Were some people good liars? What did you look for to determine if someone was lying?

Ethical Dilemma

ARE WORKPLACE ROMANCES UNETHICAL?

A large percentage of married individuals first met in the workplace. A 2006 survey revealed that 40 percent of all employees have been in an office romance. Another survey of singles showed that most employees would be open to such a romance. Given the amount of time people spend at work, this isn't terribly surprising. Yet office romances pose sensitive ethical issues for organizations and employees. What rights and responsibilities do organizations have to regulate the romantic lives of their employees?

Take the example of Julie Roehm, senior VP of marketing at Wal-Mart, who began dating Sean Womack, VP of communications architecture. When Wal-Mart learned of the relationship, it fired both Roehm and Womack, arguing that the undisclosed relationship violated its policy against workplace romances. After her firing, Roehm sued Wal-Mart, claiming that the company breached her contract and damaged her reputation. Wal-Mart then countersued, alleging that Roehm showed favoritism on Womack's behalf. Eventually, Roehm dropped her lawsuit in exchange for Wal-Mart dropping its countersuit.

The Wal-Mart, Julie Roehm, and Sean Womack saga shows that while workplace romances are personal matters, it's hard to keep them out of the political complexities of organizational life.

Questions

1. Nearly three-quarters of organizations have no policies governing workplace romances. Do you think organizations should have such policies in place?
2. Do you agree with Wal-Mart's policy against workplace romantic relationships? Why or why not?
3. Do you think it is ever appropriate for a supervisor to date an employee under his or her supervision? Why or why not?
4. Some companies, such as Nike and Southwest Airlines, openly try to recruit couples. Do you think this is a good idea? How would you feel working in a department with a "couple"?

Sources: J. Geenwald, "Employers Are the Losers in the Dating Game," *Workforce Week*, June 3, 2007, pp. 1–2; and "My Year at Wal-Mart," *BusinessWeek*, February 12, 2007.

Case Incident 1

THE UPSIDE OF ANGER?

A researcher doing a case study on emotions in organizations interviewed Laura, a 22-year-old customer-service representative in Australia. The following is a summary of the interview (with some paraphrasing of the interviewer questions):

Interviewer: How would you describe your workplace?

Laura: *Very cold, unproductive, [a] very, umm, cold environment, atmosphere.*

Interviewer: What kinds of emotions are prevalent in your organization?

Laura: *Anger, hatred towards other people, other staff members.*

Interviewer: So it seems that managers keep employees in line using fear tactics?

Laura: *Yeah. [The General Manager's] favorite saying is, "Nobody's indispensable." So, it's like, "I can't do that because I'll get sacked!"*

Interviewer: How do you survive in this situation?

Laura: *You have to cater your emotions to the sort of situation, the specific situation . . . because it's just such a hostile environment, this is sort of the only way you can survive.*

Interviewer: Are there emotions you have to hide?

Laura: *Managers don't like you to show your emotions. . . . They don't like to show that there is anything wrong or anything emotional in the working environment.*

Interviewer: Why do you go along?

Laura: *I feel I have to put on an act because . . . to show your true emotions, especially towards my managers [Laura names two of her senior managers], it would be hatred sometimes. So, you just can't afford to do that because it's your job and you need the money.*

Interviewer: Do you ever rebel against this system?

Laura: *You sort of put on a happy face just so you can annoy [the managers]. I find that they don't like people being happy, so you just annoy them by being happy. So, yeah. It just makes you laugh. You just "put it on" just because you know it annoys [management]. It's pretty vindictive and manipulative but you just need to do that.*

Interviewer: Do you ever find that this gets to you?

Laura: *I did care in the beginning and I think it just got me into more trouble. So now I just tell myself, "I don't care." If you tell yourself something for long enough, eventually you believe it. Yeah, so now I just go "Oh well."*

Interviewer: Do you intend to keep working here?

Laura: *It's a means to an end now. So every time I go [to work] and every week I just go, "Well, one week down, one week less until I go away." But if I knew that I didn't have this goal, I don't know if I could handle it, or if I would even be there now.*

Interviewer: Is there an upside to working here?

Laura: *I'm so much better at telling people off now than I ever used to be. I can put people in place in about three sentences. Like, instead of, before I would walk away from it. But now I just stand there and fight. . . . I don't know if that's a good thing or a bad thing.*

Questions

1. Do you think Laura is justified in her responses to her organization's culture? Why or why not?
2. Do you think Laura's strategic use and display of emotions serve to protect her?

3. Assuming that Laura's description is accurate, how would *you* react to the organization's culture?
4. Research shows that acts of coworkers (37 percent) and management (22 percent) cause more negative emotions for employees than do acts of customers (7 percent).[131] What can Laura's company do to change its emotional climate?

Source: J. Perrone and M. H. Vickers, "Emotions as Strategic Game in a Hostile Workplace: An Exemplar Case," *Employee Responsibilities and Rights Journal* 16, no. 3 (2004), pp. 167–178.

Case Incident 2

ABUSIVE CUSTOMERS CAUSE EMOTIONS TO RUN HIGH

Telephone customer-service representatives have a tough time these days. With automated telephone systems that create a labyrinth for customers, result in long hold times, and make it difficult for them to speak to an actual human being, a customer's frustration often settles in before the representative has had time to say "hello." Says Donna Earl, an owner of a customer-service consulting firm in San Francisco, "By the time you get to the person you need to talk to, you're mad."

Erin Calabrese knows all too well just how mad customers can get. A customer-service representative at a financial services company, she still vividly recalls one of her worst experiences—with a customer named Jane. Jane called Calabrese over some charges on her credit card and began "ranting and raving." "Your #%#% company, who do you think you are?" yelled Jane. Though Calabrese tried to console the irate customer by offering a refund, Jane only called Calabrese an "idiot." The heated conversation continued for almost 10 minutes before Calabrese, shaking, handed the phone to her supervisor and left her desk.

Sometimes customers can be downright racist. One customer-service representative finally quit her job at a New Jersey company because she constantly heard racial remarks from customers after, she contends, they heard her Spanish accent. "By the time you leave, your head is spinning with all the complaints," she said.

Unfortunately, these employees have little choice but to take the abuse. Many companies require customer-service employees to display positive emotions at all times to maintain satisfied customers. But the result could be an emotional nightmare that doesn't necessarily end once the calls stop. Calabrese stated that she would frequently take her negative emotions home. The day after she received the abusive call from Jane, Calabrese went home and started a fight with her roommate. It was "an all-out battle," recalls Calabrese, "I just blew up." The former customer-service representative who worked in New Jersey also recalls the effects of the abusive calls on her family. "My children would say, 'Mom, stop talking about your work. You're home.' My husband would say the same thing," she said.

Emma Parsons, who quit her job as a customer-service representative for the travel industry, was frustrated by the inability to do anything about abusive customers and the mood they'd put her in. "Sometimes you'd finish a call and you'd want to smash somebody's face. I had no escape, no way of releasing." She said that if she did retaliate toward an abusive customer, her boss would punish her.

Some companies train their representatives to defuse a customer's anger and to avoid taking abuse personally, but the effort isn't enough. Liz Aherarn of Radclyffe Group, a consulting firm in Lincoln Park, New Jersey, says customer-service employees who work the phones are absent more frequently, are more prone to illness, and are more likely to make stress-related disability claims than other employees. Thus, it is apparent that in the world of customer service, particularly when interactions take place over the phone, emotions can run high, and the effects can be damaging. Although the adage "the customer comes first" has been heard by many, companies should empower employees to decide when it is appropriate to put the customer second. Otherwise, employees are forced to deal with abusive customers, the effects of which can be detrimental to both the individual and the company.

Questions

1. From an emotional labor perspective, how does dealing with an abusive customer lead to stress and burnout?
2. If you were a recruiter for a customer-service call center, what personality types would you prefer to hire and why? In other words, what individual differences are likely to affect whether an employee can handle customer abuse on a day-to-day basis?
3. Emotional intelligence is one's ability to detect and manage emotional cues and information. How might emotional intelligence play a role in responding to

abusive customers? What facets of emotional intelligence might employees who are able to handle abusive customers possess?

4. What steps should companies take to ensure that their employees are not victims of customer abuse? Should companies allow a certain degree of abuse if that abuse results in satisfied customers and perhaps greater profit? What are the ethical implications of this?

Source: Based on S. Shellenbarger, "Domino Effect: The Unintended Results of Telling Off Customer-Service Staff," *Wall Street Journal*, February 5, 2004, p. D.1.

Endnotes

1. Based on J. McGregor, "Sweet Revenge," *BusinessWeek*, January 22, 2007, pp. 64–70.
2. See, for instance, C. D. Fisher and N. M. Ashkanasy, "The Emerging Role of Emotions in Work Life: An Introduction," *Journal of Organizational Behavior*, Special Issue 2000, pp. 123–129; N. M. Ashkanasy, C. E. J. Hartel, and W. J. Zerbe (eds.), *Emotions in the Workplace: Research, Theory, and Practice* (Westport, CT: Quorum Books, 2000); N. M. Ashkanasy and C. S. Daus, "Emotion in the Workplace: The New Challenge for Managers," *Academy of Management Executive*, February 2002, pp. 76–86; and N. M. Ashkanasy, C. E. J. Hartel, and C. S. Daus, "Diversity and Emotion: The New Frontiers in Organizational Behavior Research," *Journal of Management* 28, no. 3 (2002), pp. 307–338.
3. See, for example, L. L. Putnam and D. K. Mumby, "Organizations, Emotion and the Myth of Rationality," in S. Fineman (ed.), *Emotion in Organizations* (Thousand Oaks, CA: Sage, 1993), pp. 36–57; and J. Martin, K. Knopoff, and C. Beckman, "An Alternative to Bureaucratic Impersonality and Emotional Labor: Bounded Emotionality at the Body Shop," *Administrative Science Quarterly*, June 1998, pp. 429–469.
4. B. E. Ashforth and R. H. Humphrey, "Emotion in the Workplace: A Reappraisal," *Human Relations*, February 1995, pp. 97–125.
5. S. G. Barsade and D. E. Gibson, "Why Does Affect Matter in Organizations?" *Academy of Management Perspectives*, February 2007, pp. 36–59.
6. See N. H. Frijda, "Moods, Emotion Episodes and Emotions," in M. Lewis and J. M. Haviland (eds.), *Handbook of Emotions* (New York: Guilford Press, 1993), pp. 381–403.
7. H. M. Weiss and R. Cropanzano, "Affective Events Theory: A Theoretical Discussion of the Structure, Causes and Consequences of Affective Experiences at Work," in B. M. Staw and L. L. Cummings (eds.), *Research in Organizational Behavior*, vol. 18 (Greenwich, CT: JAI Press, 1996), pp. 17–19.
8. See P. Ekman and R. J. Davidson (eds.), *The Nature of Emotions: Fundamental Questions* (Oxford, UK: Oxford University Press, 1994).
9. Frijda, "Moods, Emotion Episodes and Emotions," p. 381.
10. See Ekman and Davidson (eds.), *The Nature of Emotions*.
11. See, for example, P. Ekman, "An Argument for Basic Emotions," *Cognition and Emotion*, May/July 1992, pp. 169–200; C. E. Izard, "Basic Emotions, Relations Among Emotions, and Emotion–Cognition Relations," *Psychological Bulletin*, November 1992, pp. 561–565; and J. L. Tracy and R. W. Robins, "Emerging Insights into the Nature and Function of Pride," *Current Directions in Psychological Science* 16, no. 3 (2007), pp. 147–150.
12. R. C. Solomon, "Back to Basics: On the Very Idea of 'Basic Emotions,'" *Journal for the Theory of Social Behaviour* 32, no. 2 (June 2002), pp. 115–144.
13. R. Descartes, *The Passions of the Soul* (Indianapolis: Hackett, 1989).
14. P. Ekman, *Emotions Revealed: Recognizing Faces and Feelings to Improve Communication and Emotional Life* (New York: Times Books/Henry Holt and Co., 2003).
15. P. R. Shaver, H. J. Morgan, and S. J. Wu, "Is Love a 'Basic' emotion?" *Personal Relationships* 3, no. 1 (March 1996), pp. 81–96.
16. Solomon, "Back to Basics."
17. Weiss and Cropanzano, "Affective Events Theory," pp. 20–22.
18. Cited in R. D. Woodworth, *Experimental Psychology* (New York: Holt, 1938).
19. D. Watson, L. A. Clark, and A. Tellegen, "Development and Validation of Brief Measures of Positive and Negative Affect: The PANAS Scales," *Journal of Personality and Social Psychology*, 1988, pp. 1063–1070.
20. A. Ben-Ze'ev, *The Subtlety of Emotions* (Cambridge, MA: MIT Press, 2000), p. 94.
21. "Flight Attendant War Stories . . . Stewardess," *AboutMyJob.com*, www.aboutmyjob.com/main.php3?action=displayarticle&artid=2111.
22. Cited in Ibid., p. 99.
23. J. T. Cacioppo and W. L. Gardner, "Emotion," in *Annual Review of Psychology*, vol. 50 (Palo Alto, CA: Annual Reviews, 1999), pp. 191–214.
24. D. Holman, "Call Centres," in D. Holman, T. D. Wall, C. Clegg, P. Sparrow, and A. Howard (eds.), *The Essentials of the New Work Place: A Guide to the Human Impact of Modern Working Practices* (Chichester, UK: Wiley, 2005), pp. 111–132.
25. L. M. Poverny and S. Picascia, "There Is No Crying in Business," *Womensmedia.com*, www.womensmedia.com/new/Crying-at-Work.shtml.
26. L. P. Frankel, *Nice Girls Don't Get the Corner Office* (New York: Warner Book, 2004).
27. A. R. Damasio, *Descartes' Error: Emotion, Reason, and the Human Brain* (New York: Quill, 1994).
28. Ibid.
29. L. Cosmides and J. Tooby, "Evolutionary Psychology and the Emotions," in M. Lewis and J. M. Haviland-Jones (eds.), *Handbook of Emotions*, 2nd ed. (New York: Guilford Press, 2000), pp. 91–115.
30. D. M. Buss, "Cognitive Biases and Emotional Wisdom in the Evolution of Conflict Between the Sexes," *Current Directions in Psychological Science* 10, no. 6 (December 2001), pp. 219–223.

31. K. Hundley, "An Unspoken Problem: Two-Thirds of Female Lawyers Say They Have Experienced or Seen Harassment at Work. But Few Want to Talk About It," *St. Petersburg (Florida) Times*, April 25, 2004, www.sptimes.com/2005/04/24/Business/An_unspoken_problem.shtml.
32. K. N. Laland and G. R. Brown, *Sense and Nonsense: Evolutionary Perspectives on Human Behaviour* (Oxford, UK: Oxford University Press, 2002).
33. R. J. Larsen and E. Diener, "Affect Intensity as an Individual Difference Characteristic: A Review," *Journal of Research in Personality* 21 (1987), pp. 1–39.
34. D. Watson, *Mood and Temperament* (New York: Guilford Press, 2000).
35. Ibid.
36. Ibid.
37. Ibid., p. 100.
38. Ibid., p. 73.
39. J. A. Fuller, J. M. Stanton, G. G. Fisher, C. Spitzmüller, S. S. Russell, and P. C. Smith, "A Lengthy Look at the Daily Grind: Time Series Analysis of Events, Mood, Stress, and Satisfaction," *Journal of Applied Psychology* 88, no. 6 (December 2003), pp. 1019–1033.
40. See "Monday Blahs," May 16, 2005, www.ashidome.com/blogger/housearrest.asp?c=809&m=5&y=2005.
41. A. M. Isen, "Positive Affect as a Source of Human Strength," in L. G. Aspinwall and U. Staudinger (eds.), *The Psychology of Human Strengths* (Washington, DC: American Psychological Association, 2003), pp. 179–195.
42. Watson, *Mood and Temperament* (2000).
43. *Sleep in America Poll* (Washington, DC: National Sleep Foundation, 2005).
44. M. Lavidor, A. Weller, and H. Babkoff, "How Sleep Is Related to Fatigue," *British Journal of Health Psychology* 8 (2003), pp. 95–105; and J. J. Pilcher and E. Ott, "The Relationships Between Sleep and Measures of Health and Well-Being in College Students: A Repeated Measures Approach," *Behavioral Medicine* 23 (1998), pp. 170–178.
45. T. D. Wilson and D. T. Gilbert, "Affective Forecasting: Knowing What to Want," *Current Directions in Psychological Science*, June 2005, pp. 131–134.
46. E. K. Miller and J. D. Cohen, "An Integrative Theory of Prefrontal Cortex Function," *Annual Review of Neuroscience* 24 (2001), pp. 167–202.
47. B. A. Scott and T. A. Judge, "Tired and Cranky? The Effects of Sleep Quality on Employee Emotions and Job Satisfaction," working paper, Department of Management, University of Florida, 2005.
48. P. R. Giacobbi, H. A. Hausenblas, and N. Frye, "A Naturalistic Assessment of the Relationship Between Personality, Daily Life Events, Leisure-Time Exercise, and Mood," *Psychology of Sport & Exercise* 6, no. 1 (January 2005), pp. 67–81.
49. L. L. Carstensen, M. Pasupathi, M. Ulrich, and J. R. Nesselroade, "Emotional Experience in Everyday Life Across the Adult Life Span," *Journal of Personality and Social Psychology* 79, no. 4 (2000), pp. 644–655.
50. K. Deaux, "Sex Differences," in M. R. Rosenzweig and L. W. Porter (eds.), *Annual Review of Psychology*, vol. 26 (Palo Alto, CA: Annual Reviews, 1985), pp. 48–82; M. LaFrance and M. Banaji, "Toward a Reconsideration of the Gender–Emotion Relationship," in M. Clark (ed.), *Review of Personality and Social Psychology*, vol. 14 (Newbury Park, CA: Sage, 1992), pp. 178–197; and A. M. Kring and A. H. Gordon, "Sex Differences in Emotion: Expression, Experience, and Physiology," *Journal of Personality and Social Psychology*, March 1998, pp. 686–703.
51. L. R. Brody and J. A. Hall, "Gender and Emotion," in M. Lewis and J. M. Haviland (eds.), *Handbook of Emotions* (New York: Guilford Press, 1993), pp. 447–460; M. G. Gard and A. M. Kring, "Sex Differences in the Time Course of Emotion," *Emotion* 7, no. 2 (2007), pp. 429–437; and M. Grossman and W. Wood, "Sex Differences in Intensity of Emotional Experience: A Social Role Interpretation," *Journal of Personality and Social Psychology*, November 1992, pp. 1010–1022.
52. N. James, "Emotional Labour: Skill and Work in the Social Regulations of Feelings," *Sociological Review*, February 1989, pp. 15–42; A. Hochschild, *The Second Shift* (New York: Viking, 1989); and F. M. Deutsch, "Status, Sex, and Smiling: The Effect of Role on Smiling in Men and Women," *Personality and Social Psychology Bulletin*, September 1990, pp. 531–540.
53. A. Rafaeli, "When Clerks Meet Customers: A Test of Variables Related to Emotional Expression on the Job," *Journal of Applied Psychology*, June 1989, pp. 385–393; and LaFrance and Banaji, "Toward a Reconsideration of the Gender–Emotion Relationship."
54. See J. A. Morris and D. C. Feldman, "Managing Emotions in the Workplace," *Journal of Managerial Issues* 9, no. 3 (1997), pp. 257–274; S. Mann, *Hiding What We Feel, Faking What We Don't: Understanding the Role of Your Emotions at Work* (New York: HarperCollins, 1999); and S. M. Kruml and D. Geddes, "Catching Fire Without Burning Out: Is There an Ideal Way to Perform Emotion Labor?" in N. M. Ashkansay, C. E. J. Hartel, and W. J. Zerbe, *Emotions in the Workplace* (New York: Quorum Books, 2000), pp. 177–188.
55. P. Ekman, W. V. Friesen, and M. O'sullivan, "Smiles When Lying," in P. Ekman and E. L. Rosenberg (eds.), *What the Face Reveals: Basic and Applied Studies of Spontaneous Expression Using the Facial Action Coding System (FACS)* (London: Oxford University Press, 1997), pp. 201–216.
56. A. Grandey, "Emotion Regulation in the Workplace: A New Way to Conceptualize Emotional Labor," *Journal of Occupational Health Psychology* 5, no. 1 (2000), pp. 95–110; and R. Cropanzano, D. E. Rupp, and Z. S. Byrne, "The Relationship of Emotional Exhaustion to Work Attitudes, Job Performance, and Organizational Citizenship Behavior," *Journal of Applied Psychology*, February 2003, pp. 160–169.
57. A. R. Hochschild, "Emotion Work, Feeling Rules, and Social Structure," *American Journal of Sociology*, November 1979, pp. 551–575; W.-C. Tsai, "Determinants and Consequences of Employee Displayed Positive Emotions," *Journal of Management* 27, no. 4 (2001), pp. 497–512; M. W. Kramer and J. A. Hess, "Communication Rules for the Display of Emotions in Organizational Settings," *Management Communication Quarterly*, August 2002, pp. 66–80; and J. M. Diefendorff and E. M. Richard, "Antecedents and Consequences of Emotional Display Rule Perceptions," *Journal of Applied Psychology*, April 2003, pp. 284–294.
58. B. M. DePaulo, "Nonverbal Behavior and Self-Presentation," *Psychological Bulletin*, March 1992, pp. 203–243.
59. C. S. Hunt, "Although I Might Be Laughing Loud and Hearty, Deep Inside I'm Blue: Individual Perceptions Regarding Feeling and Displaying Emotions at Work," paper

presented at the Academy of Management Conference, Cincinnati, August 1996, p. 3.

60. Solomon, "Back to Basics."

61. C. M. Brotheridge and R. T. Lee, "Development and Validation of the Emotional Labour Scale," *Journal of Occupational & Organizational Psychology* 76, no. 3 (September 2003), pp. 365–379.

62. A. A. Grandey, "When 'the Show Must Go On': Surface Acting and Deep Acting as Determinants of Emotional Exhaustion and Peer-Rated Service Delivery," *Academy of Management Journal*, February 2003, pp. 86–96; and A. A. Grandey, D. N. Dickter, and H. Sin, "The Customer Is Not Always Right: Customer Aggression and Emotion Regulation of Service Employees," *Journal of Organizational Behavior* 25, no. 3 (May 2004), pp. 397–418.

63. T. M. Glomb, J. D. Kammeyer-Mueller, and M. Rotundo, "Emotional Labor Demands and Compensating Wage Differentials," *Journal of Applied Psychology* 89, no. 4 (August 2004), pp. 700–714.

64. H. M. Weiss and R. Cropanzano, "An Affective Events Approach to Job Satisfaction," *Research in Organizational Behavior* 18 (1996), pp. 1–74.

65. J. Basch and C. D. Fisher, "Affective Events–Emotions Matrix: A Classification of Work Events and Associated Emotions," in N. M. Ashkanasy, C. E. J. Hartel, and W. J. Zerbe, (eds.), *Emotions in the Workplace* (Westport, CT: Quorum Books, 2000), pp. 36–48.

66. See, for example, H. M. Weiss and R. Cropanzano, "Affective Events Theory"; and C. D. Fisher, "Antecedents and Consequences of Real-Time Affective Reactions at Work," *Motivation and Emotion*, March 2002, pp. 3–30.

67. Based on H. M. Weiss and R. Cropanzano, "Affective Events Theory," p. 42.

68. N. M. Ashkanasy, C. E. J. Hartel, and C. S. Daus, "Diversity and Emotion: The New Frontiers in Organizational Behavior Research," *Journal of Management* 28, no. 3 (2002), p. 324.

69. Based on D. R. Caruso, J. D. Mayer, and P. Salovey, "Emotional Intelligence and Emotional Leadership," in R. E. Riggio, S. E. Murphy, and F. J. Pirozzolo (eds.), *Multiple Intelligences and Leadership* (Mahwah, NJ: Lawrence Erlbaum, 2002), p. 70.

70. This section is based on Daniel Goleman, *Emotional Intelligence* (New York: Bantam, 1995); P. Salovey and D. Grewal, "The Science of Emotional Intelligence," *Current Directions in Psychological Science* 14, no. 6 (2005), pp. 281–285; M. Davies, L. Stankov, and R. D. Roberts, "Emotional Intelligence: In Search of an Elusive Construct," *Journal of Personality and Social Psychology*, October 1998, pp. 989–1015; D. Geddes and R. R. Callister, "Crossing the Line(s): A Dual Threshold Model of Anger in Organizations," *Academy of Management Review* 32, no. 3 (2007), pp. 721–746; and J. Ciarrochi, J. P. Forgas, and J. D. Mayer (eds.), *Emotional Intelligence in Everyday Life* (Philadelphia: Psychology Press, 2001).

71. F. I. Greenstein, *The Presidential Difference: Leadership Style from FDR to Clinton* (Princeton, NJ: Princeton University Press, 2001).

72. C. Cherniss, "The Business Case for Emotional Intelligence," *Consortium for Research on Emotional Intelligence in Organizations*, 1999, www.eiconsortium.org/research/business_case_for_ei.pdf.

73. K. S. Law, C. Wong, and L. J. Song, "The Construct and Criterion Validity of Emotional Intelligence and Its Potential Utility for Management Studies," *Journal of Applied Psychology* 89, no. 3 (2004), pp. 483–496.

74. H. A. Elfenbein and N. Ambady, "Predicting Workplace Outcomes from the Ability to Eavesdrop on Feelings," *Journal of Applied Psychology* 87, no. 5 (October 2002), pp. 963–971.

75. D. L. Van Rooy and C. Viswesvaran, "Emotional Intelligence: A Meta-analytic Investigation of Predictive Validity and Nomological Net," *Journal of Vocational Behavior* 65, no. 1 (August 2004), pp. 71–95.

76. R. Bar-On, D. Tranel, N. L. Denburg, and A. Bechara, "Exploring the Neurological Substrate of Emotional and Social Intelligence," *Brain* 126, no. 8 (August 2003), pp. 1790–1800.

77. E. A. Locke, "Why Emotional Intelligence Is an Invalid Concept," *Journal of Organizational Behavior* 26, no. 4 (June 2005), pp. 425–431.

78. J. M. Conte, "A Review and Critique of Emotional Intelligence Measures," *Journal of Organizational Behavior* 26, no. 4 (June 2005), pp. 433–440; and M. Davies, L. Stankov, and R. D. Roberts, "Emotional Intelligence: In Search of an Elusive Construct," *Journal of Personality and Social Psychology* 75, no. 4 (1998), pp. 989–1015.

79. T. Decker, "Is Emotional Intelligence a Viable Concept?" *Academy of Management Review* 28, no. 2 (April 2003), pp. 433–440; and Davies, Stankov, and Roberts, "Emotional Intelligence: In Search of an Elusive Construct."

80. F. J. Landy, "Some Historical and Scientific Issues Related to Research on Emotional Intelligence," *Journal of Organizational Behavior* 26, no. 4 (June 2005), pp. 411–424.

81. L. M. J. Spencer, D. C. McClelland, and S. Kelner, *Competency Assessment Methods: History and State of the Art* (Boston: Hay/McBer, 1997).

82. J. Park and M. R. Banaji, "Mood and Heuristics: The Influence of Happy and Sad States on Sensitivity and Bias in Stereotyping," *Journal of Personality and Social Psychology* 78, no. 6 (2000), pp. 1005–1023.

83. See A. M. Isen, "Positive Affect and Decision Making," in M. Lewis and J. M. Haviland-Jones (eds.), *Handbook of Emotions*, 2nd ed. (New York: Guilford, 2000), pp. 261–277.

84. L. B. Alloy and L. Y. Abramson, "Judgement of Contingency in Depressed and Nondepressed Students: Sadder but Wiser?" *Journal of Experimental Psychology: General* 108 (1979), pp. 441–485.

85. N. Ambady and H. M. Gray, "On Being Sad and Mistaken: Mood Effects on the Accuracy of Thin-Slice Judgments," *Journal of Personality and Social Psychology* 83, no. 4 (2002), pp. 947–961.

86. A. M. Isen, "On the Relationship Between Affect and Creative Problem Solving," in S. W. Russ (ed.), *Affect, Creative Experience and Psychological Adjustment* (Philadelphia, PA: Brunner/Mazel, 1999), pp. 3–17; and S. Lyubomirsky, L. King, and E. Diener, "The Benefits of Frequent Positive Affect: Does Happiness Lead to Success?" *Psychological Bulletin* 131, no. 6 (2005), pp. 803–855.

87. M. J. Grawitch, D. C. Munz, and E. K. Elliott, "Promoting Creativity in Temporary Problem-Solving Groups: The Effects of Positive Mood and Autonomy in Problem

Definition on Idea-Generating Performance," *Group Dynamics* 7, no. 3 (September 2003), pp. 200–213.

88. S. Lyubomirsky, L. King, and E. Diener, "The Benefits of Frequent Positive Affect: Does Happiness Lead to Success?" *Psychological Bulletin* 131, no. 6 (2005), pp. 803–855.

89. N. Madjar, G. R. Oldham, and M. G. Pratt, "There's No Place Like Home? The Contributions of Work and Nonwork Creativity Support to Employees' Creative Performance," *Academy of Management Journal* 45, no. 4 (2002), pp. 757–767.

90. J. M. George and J. Zhou, "Understanding When Bad Moods Foster Creativity and Good Ones Don't: The Role of Context and Clarity of Feelings," *Journal of Applied Psychology* 87, no. 4 (August 2002), pp. 687–697; and J. P. Forgas and J. M. George, "Affective Influences on Judgments and Behavior in Organizations: An Information Processing Perspective," *Organizational Behavior and Human Decision Processes* 86, no. 1 (2001), pp. 3–34.

91. L. L. Martin, "Mood as Input: A Configural View of Mood Effects," in L. L. Martin and G. L. Clore (eds.), *Theories of Mood and Cognition: A User's Guidebook* (Mahwah, NJ: Lawrence Erlbaum, 2001), pp. 135–157.

92. A. Erez and A. M. Isen, "The Influence of Positive Affect on the Components of Expectancy Motivation," *Journal of Applied Psychology* 87, no. 6 (2002), pp. 1055–1067.

93. R. Ilies and T. A. Judge, "Goal Regulation Across Time: The Effect of Feedback and Affect," *Journal of Applied Psychology* 90, no. 3 (May 2005), pp. 453–467.

94. K. M. Lewis, "When Leaders Display Emotion: How Followers Respond to Negative Emotional Expression of Male and Female Leaders," *Journal of Organizational Behavior*, March 2000, pp. 221–234; and J. M. George, "Emotions and Leadership: The Role of Emotional Intelligence," *Human Relations*, August 2000, pp. 1027–1055.

95. George, "Trait and State Affect," p. 162.

96. Ashforth and Humphrey, "Emotion in the Workplace," p. 116.

97. N. Reynolds, "Whiz-Kids Gamble on TV Channel for Poker," *telegraph.co.uk*, April 16, 2005, www.telegraph.co.uk.

98. G. A. Van Kleef, C. K. W. De Dreu, and A. S. R. Manstead, "The Interpersonal Effects of Emotions in Negotiations: A Motivated Information Processing Approach," *Journal of Personality and Social Psychology* 87, no. 4 (2004), pp. 510–528; and G. A. Van Kleef, C. K. W. De Dreu, and A. S. R. Manstead, "The Interpersonal Effects of Anger and Happiness in Negotiations," *Journal of Personality and Social Psychology* 86, no. 1 (2004), pp. 57–76.

99. K. M. O'Connor and J. A. Arnold, "Distributive Spirals: Negotiation Impasses and the Moderating Role of Disputant Self-Efficacy," *Organizational Behavior and Human Decision Processes* 84, no. 1 (2001), pp. 148–176.

100. B. Shiv, G. Loewenstein, A. Bechara, H. Damasio, and A. R. Damasio, "Investment Behavior and the Negative Side of Emotion," *Psychological Science* 16, no. 6 (2005), pp. 435–439.

101. W.-C. Tsai and Y.-M. Huang, "Mechanisms Linking Employee Affective Delivery and Customer Behavioral Intentions," *Journal of Applied Psychology*, October 2002, pp. 1001–1008.

102. Grandey, "When 'the Show Must Go On.'"

103. See P. B. Barker and A. A. Grandey, "Service with a Smile and Encounter Satisfaction: Emotional Contagion and Appraisal Mechanisms," *Academy of Management Journal* 49, no. 6 (2006), pp. 1229–1238; and S. D. Pugh, "Service with a Smile: Emotional Contagion in the Service Encounter," *Academy of Management Journal*, October 2001, pp. 1018–1027.

104. D. E. Rupp and S. Spencer, "When Customers Lash Out: The Effects of Customer Interactional Injustice on Emotional Labor and the Mediating Role of Emotions, *Journal of Applied Psychology* 91, no. 4 (2006), pp. 971–978; and Tsai and Huang, "Mechanisms Linking Employee Affective Delivery and Customer Behavioral Intentions."

105. R. Ilies and T. A. Judge, "Understanding the Dynamic Relationships Among Personality, Mood, and Job Satisfaction: A Field Experience Sampling Study," *Organizational Behavior and Human Decision Processes* 89 (2002), pp. 1119–1139.

106. R. Rau, "Job Strain or Healthy Work: A Question of Task Design," *Journal of Occupational Health Psychology* 9, no. 4 (October 2004), pp. 322–338; and R. Rau and A. Triemer, "Overtime in Relation to Blood Pressure and Mood During Work, Leisure, and Night Time," *Social Indicators Research* 67, no. 1–2 (June 2004), pp. 51–73.

107. T. A. Judge and R. Ilies, "Affect and Job Satisfaction: A Study of Their Relationship at Work and at Home," *Journal of Applied Psychology* 89 (2004), pp. 661–673.

108. See R. J. Bennett and S. L. Robinson, "Development of a Measure of Workplace Deviance," *Journal of Applied Psychology*, June 2000, pp. 349–360. See also P. R. Sackett and C. J. DeVore, "Counterproductive Behaviors at Work," in N. Anderson, D. S. Ones, H. K. Sinangil, and C. Viswesvaran (eds.), *Handbook of Industrial, Work & Organizational Psychology*, vol. 1 (Thousand Oaks, CA: Sage, 2001), pp. 145–164.

109. A. G. Bedeian, "Workplace Envy," *Organizational Dynamics*, Spring 1995, p. 50; and Ben-Ze'ev, *The Subtlety of Emotions*, pp. 281–326.

110. Bedeian, "Workplace Envy," p. 54.

111. K. Lee and N. J. Allen, "Organizational Citizenship Behavior and Workplace Deviance: The Role of Affect and Cognition," *Journal of Applied Psychology* 87, no. 1 (2002), pp. 131–142; and T. A. Judge, B. A. Scott, and R. Ilies, "Hostility, Job Attitudes, and Workplace Deviance: Test of a Multilevel Model," *Journal of Applied Psychology* 91, no. 1 (2006) 126–138.

112. A. M. Isen, A. A. Labroo, and P. Durlach, "An Influence of Product and Brand Name on Positive Affect: Implicit and Explicit Measures," *Motivation & Emotion* 28, no. 1 (March 2004), pp. 43–63.

113. T. Sy, S. Côté, and R. Saavedra, "The Contagious Leader: Impact of the Leader's Mood on the Mood of Group Members, Group Affective Tone, and Group Processes," *Journal of Applied Psychology* 90, no. 2 (2005), pp. 295–305.

114. P. Totterdell, "Catching Moods and Hitting Runs: Mood Linkage and Subjective Performance in Professional Sports Teams," *Journal of Applied Psychology* 85, no. 6 (2000), pp. 848–859.

115. M. Eid and E. Diener, "Norms for Experiencing Emotions in Different Cultures: Inter- and International Differences," *Journal of Personality & Social Psychology* 81, no. 5 (2001), pp. 869–885.

116. S. Oishi, E. Diener, and C. Napa Scollon, "Cross-Situational Consistency of Affective Experiences Across Cultures," *Journal of Personality & Social Psychology* 86, no. 3 (2004), pp. 460–472.

117. Eid and Diener, "Norms for Experiencing Emotions in Different Cultures."
118. Ibid.
119. Ashforth and Humphrey, "Emotion in the Workplace," p. 104; B. Plasait, "Accueil des Touristes Dans les Grands Centres de Transit Paris," *Rapport du Bernard Plasait*, October 4, 2004, www.tourisme.gouv.fr/fr/navd/presse/dossiers/att00005767/dp_plasait.pdf; B. Mesquita, "Emotions in Collectivist and Individualist Contexts," *Journal of Personality and Social Psychology* 80, no. 1 (2001), pp. 68–74; and D. Rubin, "Grumpy German Shoppers Distrust the Wal-Mart Style," *Seattle Times*, December 30, 2001, p. A15.
120. H. A. Elfenbein and N. Ambady, "When Familiarity Breeds Accuracy: Cultural Exposure and Facial Emotional Recognition," *Journal of Personality and Social Psychology* 85, no. 2 (2003), pp. 276–290.
121. R. I. Levy, *Tahitians: Mind and Experience in the Society Islands* (Chicago: University of Chicago Press, 1973).
122. B. Mesquita and N. H. Frijda, "Cultural Variations in Emotions: A Review," *Psychological Bulletin*, September 1992, pp. 179–204; and B. Mesquita, "Emotions in Collectivist and Individualist Contexts," *Journal of Personality and Social Psychology*, January 2001, pp. 68–74.
123. D. Matsumoto, "Cross-Cultural Psychology in the 21st Century," http://teachpsych.lemoyne.edu/teachpsych/faces/script/Ch05.htm.
124. S. Nelton, "Emotions in the Workplace," *Nation's Business*, February 1996, p. 25.
125. H. Liao and A. Chuang, "A Multilevel Investigation of Factors Influencing Employee Service Performance and Customer Outcomes," *Academy of Management Journal* 47, no. 1 (2004), pp. 41–58.
126. D. J. Beal, J. P. Trougakos, H. M. Weiss, and S. G. Green, "Episodic Processes in Emotional Labor: Perceptions of Affective Delivery and Regulation Strategies," *Journal of Applied Psychology* 91, no. 5 (2006), pp. 1057–1065.
127. *Starbucks.com*, May 16, 2005, www.starbucks.com.
128. D. Zapf and M. Holz, "On the Positive and Negative Effects of Emotion Work in Organizations," *European Journal of Work and Organizational Psychology* 15, no. 1 (2006), pp. 1–28.
129. D. Zapf, "Emotion Work and Psychological Well-Being: A Review of the Literature and Some Conceptual Considerations," *Human Resource Management Review* 12, no. 2 (2002), pp. 237–268.
130. J. E. Bono and M. A. Vey, "Toward Understanding Emotional Management at Work: A Quantitative Review of Emotional Labor Research," in C. E. Härtel and W. J. Zerbe (eds.), *Emotions in Organizational Behavior* (Mahwah, NJ: Lawrence Erlbaum, 2005), pp. 213–233.
131. Kruml and Geddes, "Catching Fire Without Burning Out."

Foundations of Group Behavior

Madness is the exception in individuals but the rule in groups.
—Philosopher Friedrich Nietzsche

LEARNING OBJECTIVES

After studying this chapter, you should be able to:

1 Define *group* and differentiate between different types of groups.

2 Identify the five stages of group development.

3 Show how role requirements change in different situations.

4 Demonstrate how norms and status exert influence on an individual's behavior.

5 Show how group size affects group performance.

6 Contrast the benefits and disadvantages of cohesive groups.

7 Contrast the strengths and weaknesses of group decision making.

8 Compare the effectiveness of interacting, brainstorming, nominal, and electronic meeting groups.

9 Evaluate evidence for cultural differences in group status and social loafing as well as the effects of diversity in groups.

You know the drill. Gather a small group of people together. Appoint someone to write the ideas on an easel with paper (or type them on a laptop). It's called brainstorming, and it's been around for a long time.

Some brainstorming sessions founder because group members are afraid of saying something stupid. Joe Polidoro, a manager who has worked at several banks, says of brainstorming sessions, "We sit there looking embarrassed like we're all new to a nudist colony."

Brainstorming: A Lousy Idea for Ideas?

Others struggle with the scheduled nature of such sessions. Some feel as if they're put in a room and told, "Okay, be creative now." "I'm more mercurial than that," says Kate Lee, a former manager at GE.

Others think the whole idea of brainstorming is fatally flawed, that such sessions rarely produce the creative ideas they are meant to produce. Martha McGuire, senior VP of a bank, argued that the majority of recommendations resulting from brainstorming sessions are obvious. "You end up with a more pedestrian solution than you would have had, had you not held the session," she says.

Some argue that the real purpose of brainstorming sessions is not to produce the best idea. Rather, it's to get buy-in for decisions that have already been made. Christopher Holland, a policy analyst for the Australian government, said, "These things are usually designed to give people the idea that they have input into decisions when the decisions have already been decided."

One researcher argues that the problems of brainstorming demonstrate the problems of groups. "If you leave groups to their own devices," he says, "they're going to do a very miserable job."[1] ■

From what you just read, you might think groups are hopeless, but that's not the case. Groups have their place—and their pitfalls. Before we launch into a discussion of these issues, first examine your own attitude toward working in groups. Take the following self-assessment and answer the accompanying questions.

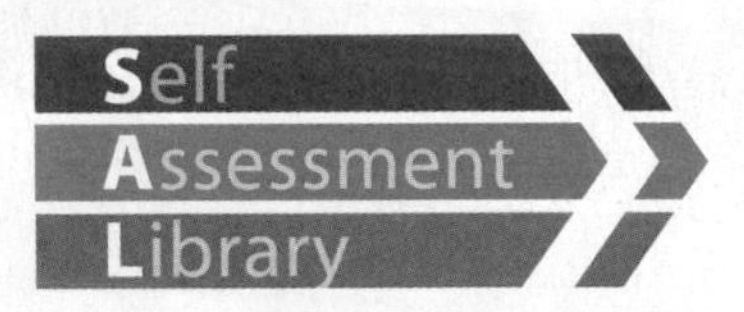

DO I HAVE A NEGATIVE ATTITUDE TOWARD WORKING IN GROUPS?

In the Self-Assessment Library (available on CD or online), take assessment IV.E.1 (Do I Have a Negative Attitude Toward Working in Groups?) and answer the following questions.

1. *Are you surprised by your results? If yes, why? If not, why not?*
2. *Do you think it is important to always have a positive attitude toward working in groups? Why or why not?*

The objectives of this chapter and Chapter 10 are to introduce you to basic group concepts, provide you with a foundation for understanding how groups work, and show you how to create effective teams. Let's begin by defining *group* and explaining why people join groups.

Defining and Classifying Groups

1 Define group and differentiate between different types of groups.

A **group** is defined as two or more individuals, interacting and interdependent, who have come together to achieve particular objectives. Groups can be either formal or informal. By **formal groups**, we mean those defined by the organization's structure, with designated work assignments establishing tasks. In formal groups, the behaviors that team members should engage in are stipulated by and directed toward organizational goals. The six members making up an airline flight crew are an example of a formal group. In contrast, **informal groups** are alliances that are neither formally structured nor organizationally determined. These groups are natural formations in the work environment that appear in response to the need for social contact. Three employees from different departments who regularly eat lunch or have coffee together are an example of an informal group. These types of interactions among individuals, even though informal, deeply affect their behavior and performance.

It's possible to further subclassify groups as command, task, interest, or friendship groups.[2] Command and task groups are dictated by formal organization, whereas interest and friendship groups are informal alliances.

A **command group** is determined by the organization chart. It is composed of the individuals who report directly to a given manager. An elementary school principal and her 18 teachers form a command group, as do a director of postal audits and his five inspectors.

Task groups, also organizationally determined, represent individuals working together to complete a job task. However, a task group's boundaries are not limited to its immediate hierarchical superior. It can cross command relationships. For instance, if a college student is accused of a campus crime, dealing with the problem might require communication and coordination among the dean of academic affairs, the dean of students, the registrar, the director of security, and the student's advisor. Such a formation would constitute a task group. It should be noted that all command groups are also task groups, but because task groups can cut across the organization, the reverse need not be true.

People who may or may not be aligned into common command or task groups may affiliate to attain a specific objective with which each is concerned. This is an **interest group**. Employees who band together to have their vacation schedules altered, to support a peer who has been fired, or to seek improved working conditions represent the formation of a united body to further their common interest.

Groups often develop because the individual members have one or more common characteristics. We call these formations **friendship groups**. Social alliances, which frequently extend outside the work situation, can be based on similar age or ethnic heritage, support for Notre Dame football, interest in the same alternative rock band, or the holding of similar political views, to name just a few such characteristics.

There is no single reason why individuals join groups. Because most people belong to a number of groups, it's obvious that different groups provide different benefits to their members. Exhibit 9-1 summarizes the most popular reasons people have for joining groups.

Exhibit 9-1 Why Do People Join Groups?

Security. By joining a group, individuals can reduce the insecurity of "standing alone." People feel stronger, have fewer self-doubts, and are more resistant to threats when they are part of a group.

Status. Inclusion in a group that is viewed as important by others provides recognition and status for its members.

Self-esteem. Groups can provide people with feelings of self-worth. That is, in addition to conveying status to those outside the group, membership can also give increased feelings of worth to the group members themselves.

Affiliation. Groups can fulfill social needs. People enjoy the regular interaction that comes with group membership. For many people, these on-the-job interactions are their primary source for fulfilling their needs for affiliation.

Power. What cannot be achieved individually often becomes possible through group action. There is power in numbers.

Goal achievement. There are times when it takes more than one person to accomplish a particular task—there is a need to pool talents, knowledge, or power in order to complete a job. In such instances, management will rely on the use of a formal group.

group *Two or more individuals, interacting and interdependent, who have come together to achieve particular objectives.*

formal group *A designated work group defined by an organization's structure.*

informal group *A group that is neither formally structured nor organizationally determined; such a group appears in response to the need for social contact.*

command group *A group composed of the individuals who report directly to a given manager.*

task group *People working together to complete a job task.*

interest group *People working together to attain a specific objective with which each is concerned.*

friendship group *People brought together because they share one or more common characteristics.*

Stages of Group Development

2 *Identify the five stages of group development.*

Groups generally pass through a standardized sequence in their evolution. We call this sequence the five-stage model of group development. Although research indicates that not all groups follow this pattern,[3] it is a useful framework for understanding group development. In this section, we describe the five-stage general model and an alternative model for temporary groups with deadlines.

The Five-Stage Model

As shown in Exhibit 9-2, the **five-stage group-development model** characterizes groups as proceeding through five distinct stages: forming, storming, norming, performing, and adjourning.[4]

The first stage, **forming**, is characterized by a great deal of uncertainty about the group's purpose, structure, and leadership. Members "test the waters" to determine what types of behaviors are acceptable. This stage is complete when members have begun to think of themselves as part of a group.

The **storming stage** is one of intragroup conflict. Members accept the existence of the group, but there is resistance to the constraints that the group imposes on individuality. Furthermore, there is conflict over who will control the group. When this stage is complete, there will be a relatively clear hierarchy of leadership within the group.

The third stage is one in which close relationships develop and the group demonstrates cohesiveness. There is now a strong sense of group identity and camaraderie. This **norming stage** is complete when the group structure solidifies and the group has assimilated a common set of expectations of what defines correct member behavior.

The fourth stage is **performing**. The structure at this point is fully functional and accepted. Group energy has moved from getting to know and understand each other to performing the task at hand.

For permanent work groups, performing is the last stage in the group development. However, for temporary committees, teams, task forces, and similar groups that have a limited task to perform, there is an **adjourning stage**. In this stage, the group prepares for its disbandment. High task performance is no longer the group's top priority. Instead, attention is directed toward wrapping up activities. Responses of group members vary in this stage. Some are upbeat, basking in the group's accomplishments. Others may be depressed over the loss of camaraderie and friendships gained during the work group's life.

Many interpreters of the five-stage model have assumed that a group becomes more effective as it progresses through the first four stages. Although this assumption may be generally true, what makes a group effective is more complex than this model acknowledges.[5] Under some conditions, high levels of conflict may be conducive to high group performance. So we might expect to find situations in

Exhibit 9-2 Stages of Group Development

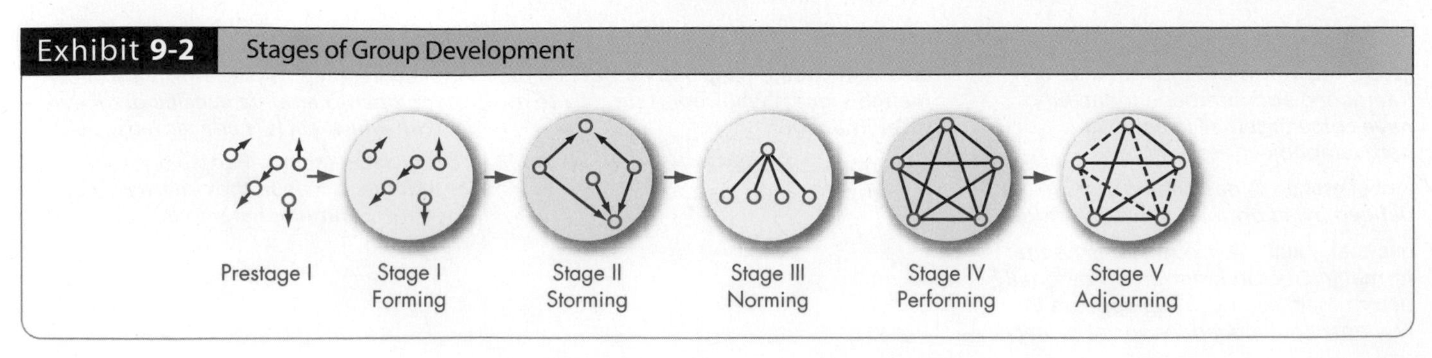

Having passed through the forming, storming, and norming phases of group development, this group of women at a Delphi Delco Electronics factory in Mexico now function as a permanent work group in the performing stage. Their structure is functional and accepted, and each day they begin their work with a small shift meeting before performing their tasks.

which groups in Stage II outperform those in Stage III or IV. Similarly, groups do not always proceed clearly from one stage to the next. Sometimes, in fact, several stages go on simultaneously, as when groups are storming and performing at the same time. Groups even occasionally regress to previous stages. Therefore, even the strongest proponents of this model do not assume that all groups follow its five-stage process precisely or that Stage IV is always the most preferable.

Another problem with the five-stage model, in terms of understanding work-related behavior, is that it ignores organizational context.[6] For instance, a study of a cockpit crew in an airliner found that within 10 minutes three strangers assigned to fly together for the first time had become a high-performing group. What allowed for this speedy group development was the strong organizational context surrounding the tasks of the cockpit crew. This context provided the rules, task definitions, information, and resources needed for the group to perform. They didn't need to develop plans, assign roles, determine and allocate resources, resolve conflicts, and set norms the way the five-stage model predicts.

An Alternative Model for Temporary Groups with Deadlines

Temporary groups with deadlines don't seem to follow the usual five-stage model. Studies indicate that they have their own unique sequencing of actions (or inaction): (1) Their first meeting sets the group's direction; (2) this first phase of group activity is one of inertia; (3) a transition takes place at the end of this first phase, which occurs exactly when the group has used up half its allotted time; (4) a transition initiates major changes; (5) a second phase of inertia

five-stage group-development model *The five distinct stages groups go through: forming, storming, norming, performing, and adjourning.*

forming stage *The first stage in group development, characterized by much uncertainty.*

storming stage *The second stage in group development, characterized by intragroup conflict.*

norming stage *The third stage in group development, characterized by close relationships and cohesiveness.*

performing stage *The fourth stage in group development, during which the group is fully functional.*

adjourning stage *The final stage in group development for temporary groups, characterized by concern with wrapping up activities rather than task performance.*

Exhibit 9-3 The Punctuated-Equilibrium Model

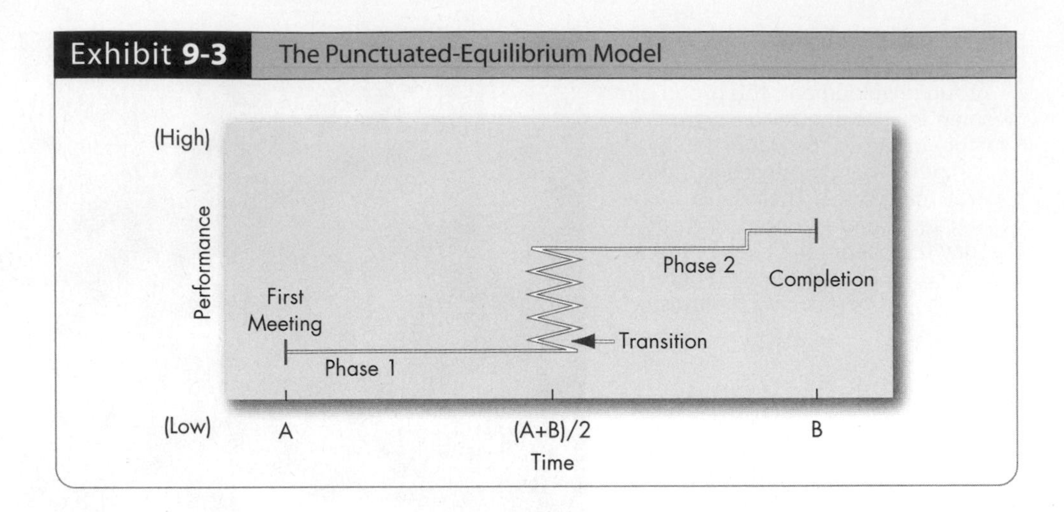

follows the transition; and (6) the group's last meeting is characterized by markedly accelerated activity.[7] This pattern, called the **punctuated-equilibrium model**, is shown in Exhibit 9-3.

The first meeting sets the group's direction. A framework of behavioral patterns and assumptions through which the group will approach its project emerges in this first meeting. These lasting patterns can appear as early as the first few seconds of the group's existence. Once set, the group's direction becomes "written in stone" and is unlikely to be reexamined throughout the first half of the group's life. This is a period of inertia—that is, the group tends to stand still or become locked into a fixed course of action. Even if it gains new insights that challenge initial patterns and assumptions, the group is incapable of acting on these new insights in Phase 1.

One of the most interesting discoveries made in studies of groups[8] was that each group experienced its transition at the same point in its calendar—precisely halfway between its first meeting and its official deadline—despite the fact that some groups spent as little as an hour on their project while others spent 6 months. It was as if the groups universally experienced a midlife crisis at this point. The midpoint appears to work like an alarm clock, heightening members' awareness that their time is limited and that they need to "get moving." This transition ends Phase 1 and is characterized by a concentrated burst of changes, dropping of old patterns, and adoption of new perspectives. The transition sets a revised direction for Phase 2. Phase 2 is a new equilibrium or period of inertia. In this phase, the group executes plans created during the transition period.

The group's last meeting is characterized by a final burst of activity to finish its work. In summary, the punctuated-equilibrium model characterizes groups as exhibiting long periods of inertia interspersed with brief revolutionary changes triggered primarily by their members' awareness of time and deadlines. Keep in mind, however, that this model doesn't apply to all groups. It's essentially limited to temporary task groups who are working under a time-constrained completion deadline.[9]

Group Properties: Roles, Norms, Status, Size, and Cohesiveness

Work groups are not unorganized mobs. Work groups have properties that shape the behavior of members and make it possible to explain and predict a large portion of individual behavior within the group as well as the perfor-

Trumpeter Wynton Marsalis plays a number of diverse roles. As artistic director of the Jazz at Lincoln Center Orchestra, Marsalis serves on the senior management team in leading the world's largest not-for-profit arts organization dedicated to jazz. He is also a composer, performer, music teacher, fundraiser, and goodwill ambassador as a United Nations Messenger of Peace. Each of these positions imposes different role requirements on Marsalis. This photo shows Marsalis joining Chef Emeril Lagasse at a free educational event for schoolchildren in New Orleans that explored two aspects of the city's culture: jazz and food.

mance of the group itself. Some of these properties are roles, norms, status, group size, and the degree of group cohesiveness.

Group Property 1: Roles

3 *Show how role requirements change in different situations.*

Writer and dramatist William Shakespeare said, "All the world's a stage, and all the men and women merely players." Using the same metaphor, all group members are actors, each playing a **role**. By this term, we mean a set of expected behavior patterns attributed to someone occupying a given position in a social unit. The understanding of role behavior would be dramatically simplified if each of us chose one role and "played it out" regularly and consistently. Unfortunately, we are required to play a number of diverse roles, both on and off our jobs. As we'll see, one of the tasks in understanding behavior is grasping the role that a person is currently playing.

For example, Bill Patterson is a plant manager with EMM Industries, a large electrical equipment manufacturer in Phoenix, Arizona. He has a number of roles that he fulfills on that job—for instance, EMM employee, member of middle management, electrical engineer, and primary company spokesperson in the community. Off the job, Bill Patterson finds him in still more roles: husband, father, Catholic, Rotarian, tennis player, member of the Thunderbird Country Club, and president of his homeowners' association. Many of these roles are compatible; some create conflicts. For instance, how does his religious involvement influence his managerial decisions regarding layoffs, expense account padding, and provision of accurate information to government agencies? A recent offer of promotion requires Bill to relocate, yet his family very much wants to stay in Phoenix. Can the role demands of his job be reconciled with the demands of his husband and father roles?

punctuated-equilibrium model *A set of phases that temporary groups go through that involves transitions between inertia and activity.*

role *A set of expected behavior patterns attributed to someone occupying a given position in a social unit.*

The issue should be clear: Like Bill Patterson, we are all required to play a number of roles, and our behavior varies with the role we are playing. Bill's behavior when he attends church on Sunday morning is different from his behavior on the golf course later that same day. So different groups impose different role requirements on individuals.

Role Identity Certain attitudes and actual behaviors are consistent with a role, and they create the **role identity**. People have the ability to shift roles rapidly when they recognize that a situation and its demands clearly require major changes. For instance, when union stewards were promoted to supervisory positions, it was found that their attitudes changed from pro-union to pro-management within a few months of their promotion. When these promotions had to be rescinded later because of economic difficulties in the firm, it was found that the demoted supervisors had once again adopted their pro-union attitudes.[10]

Role Perception Our view of how we're supposed to act in a given situation is a **role perception**. Based on an interpretation of how we believe we are supposed to behave, we engage in certain types of behavior. Where do we get these perceptions? We get them from stimuli all around us—friends, books, television. For example, we may form an impression of the work of doctors from watching television shows about doctors. Of course, the primary reason apprenticeship programs exist in many trades and professions is to allow beginners to watch an "expert" so they can learn to act as they are supposed to.

Role Expectations **Role expectations** are defined as the way others believe you should act in a given situation. How you behave is determined to a large extent by the role defined in the context in which you are acting. For instance, the role of a U.S. federal judge is viewed as having propriety and dignity, while a football coach is seen as aggressive, dynamic, and inspiring to his players.

In the workplace, it can be helpful to look at the topic of role expectations through the perspective of the **psychological contract**—an unwritten agreement that exists between employees and their employer. This psychological contract sets out mutual expectations—what management expects from workers and vice versa.[11] In effect, this contract defines the behavioral expectations that go with every role. For instance, management is expected to treat employees justly, provide acceptable working conditions, clearly communicate what is a fair day's work, and give feedback on how well an employee is doing. Employees are expected to respond by demonstrating a good attitude, following directions, and showing loyalty to the organization.

What happens when role expectations as implied in the psychological contract are not met? If management is derelict in keeping up its part of the bargain, we can expect negative repercussions on employee performance and satisfaction. When employees fail to live up to expectations, the result is usually some form of disciplinary action up to and including firing.

Role Conflict When an individual is confronted by divergent role expectations, the result is **role conflict**. It exists when an individual finds that compliance with one role requirement may make it difficult to comply with another.[12] At the extreme, it would include situations in which two or more role expectations are mutually contradictory.

Our previous discussion of the many roles Bill Patterson had to deal with included several role conflicts—for instance, Bill's attempt to reconcile the expectations placed on him as a husband and father with those placed on him as an executive with EMM Industries. The former, as you will remember, emphasizes stability and concern for the desire of his wife and children to remain in Phoenix. EMM, on the other hand, expects its employees to be responsive to the needs and requirements of the company. Although it might be in Bill's financial and career interests to accept a relocation, the conflict comes down to choosing between family and career role expectations.

An Experiment: Zimbardo's Prison Experiment One of the most illuminating role experiments was done a number of years ago by Stanford University psychologist Philip Zimbardo and his associates.[13] They created a "prison" in the basement of the Stanford psychology building, hired at $15 a day two dozen emotionally stable, physically healthy, law-abiding students who scored "normal average" on extensive personality tests, randomly assigned them the role of either "guard" or "prisoner," and established some basic rules.

To get the experiment off to a "realistic" start, Zimbardo got the cooperation of the local police department. The police went, unannounced, to each future prisoners' home, arrested and handcuffed them, put them in a squad car in front of friends and neighbors, and took them to police headquarters, where they were booked and fingerprinted. From there, they were taken to the Stanford prison.

At the start of the planned 2-week experiment, there were no measurable differences between the individuals assigned to be guards and those chosen to be prisoners. In addition, the guards received no special training in how to be prison guards. They were told only to "maintain law and order" in the prison and not to take any nonsense from the prisoners. Physical violence was forbidden. To simulate further the realities of prison life, the prisoners were allowed visits from relatives and friends. And although the mock guards worked 8-hour shifts, the mock prisoners were kept in their cells around the clock and were allowed out only for meals, exercise, toilet privileges, head-count lineups, and work details.

It took the "prisoners" little time to accept the authority positions of the guards or the mock guards to adjust to their new authority roles. After the guards crushed a rebellion attempt on the second day, the prisoners became increasingly passive. Whatever the guards "dished out," the prisoners took. The prisoners actually began to believe and act as if they were, as the guards constantly reminded them, inferior and powerless. And every guard, at some time during the simulation, engaged in abusive, authoritative behavior. For example, one guard said, "I was surprised at myself. . . . I made them call each other names and clean the toilets out with their bare hands. I practically considered the prisoners cattle, and I kept thinking: 'I have to watch out for them in case they try something.'" Another guard added, "I was tired of seeing the prisoners in their rags and smelling the strong odors of their bodies that filled the cells. I watched them tear at each other on orders given by us. They didn't see it as an experiment. It was real and they were fighting to keep their identity. But we were always there to show them who was boss." Surprisingly, during the entire experiment—even after days of abuse—not one prisoner said, "Stop this. I'm a student like you. This is just an experiment!"

The simulation actually proved *too successful* in demonstrating how quickly individuals learn new roles. The researchers had to stop it after only 6 days

role identity *Certain attitudes and behaviors consistent with a role.*

role perception *An individual's view of how he or she is supposed to act in a given situation.*

role expectations *How others believe a person should act in a given situation.*

psychological contract *An unwritten agreement that sets out what management expects from an employee and vice versa.*

role conflict *A situation in which an individual is confronted by divergent role expectations.*

because of the participants' pathological reactions. And remember, these were individuals chosen precisely for their normalcy and emotional stability.

What can we conclude from this prison simulation? The participants in this experiment had, like the rest of us, learned stereotyped conceptions of guard and prisoner roles from the mass media and their own personal experiences in power and powerlessness relationships gained at home (parent–child), in school (teacher–student), and in other situations. This, then, allowed them easily and rapidly to assume roles that were very different from their inherent personalities. In this case, we saw that people with no prior personality pathology or training in their roles could execute extreme forms of behavior consistent with the roles they were playing.

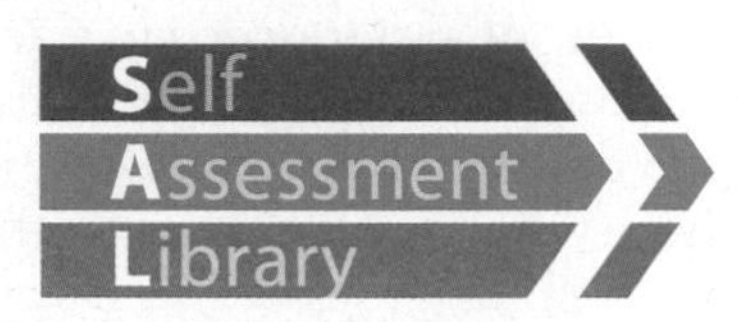

DO I TRUST OTHERS?

In the Self-Assessment Library (available on CD or online), take assessment II.B.3 (Do I Trust Others?). You can also check out assessment II.B.4 (Do Others See Me as Trusting?).

Group Properties 2 and 3: Norms and Status

Did you ever notice that golfers don't speak while their partners are putting on the green or that employees don't criticize their bosses in public? Why? The answer is norms.

4 *Demonstrate how norms and status exert influence on an individual's behavior.*

All groups have established **norms**—that is, acceptable standards of behavior that are shared by the group's members. Norms tell members what they ought and ought not to do under certain circumstances. From an individual's standpoint, they tell what is expected of you in certain situations. When agreed to and accepted by the group, norms act as a means of influencing the behavior of group members with a minimum of external controls. Different groups, communities, and societies have different norms, but they all have them.[14]

Norms can cover virtually any aspect of group behavior.[15] Probably the most common group norm is a *performance norm.* Work groups typically provide their members with explicit cues to how hard they should work, how to get the job done, what their level of output should be, what level of tardiness is appropriate, and the like. These norms are extremely powerful in affecting an individual employee's performance—they are capable of significantly modifying a performance prediction that was based solely on the employee's ability and level of personal motivation. Although arguably the most important, performance norms aren't the only kind. Other types include *appearance norms* (for example, dress codes, unspoken rules about when to look busy), *social arrangement norms* (for example, with whom group members eat lunch, whether to form friendships on and off the job), and *resource allocation norms* (for example, assignment of difficult jobs, distribution of resources like pay or equipment).

The Hawthorne Studies Behavioral scientists generally agree that full-scale appreciation of the importance norms play in influencing worker behavior did not occur until the early 1930s. This enlightenment grew out of a series of studies undertaken at Western Electric Company's Hawthorne Works in Chicago between 1924 and 1932.[16] Originally initiated by Western Electric officials and later overseen by Harvard University professor Elton Mayo, the Hawthorne studies concluded that a worker's behavior and sentiments were closely related, that group influences were significant in affecting individual

From the Hawthorne studies, observers gained valuable insights into how individual behavior is influenced by group norms. The group of workers determined the level of fair output and established norms for individual work rates that conformed to the output. To enforce the group norms, workers used sarcasm, ridicule, and even physical force to influence individual behaviors that were not acceptable to the group.

behavior, that group standards were highly effective in establishing individual worker output, and that money was less a factor in determining worker output than were group standards, sentiments, and security. Let us briefly discuss the Hawthorne investigations and demonstrate the importance of these findings in explaining group behavior.

The Hawthorne researchers began by examining the relationship between the physical environment and productivity. Illumination and other working conditions were selected to represent this physical environment. The researchers' initial findings contradicted their anticipated results.

They began with illumination experiments with various groups of workers. The researchers manipulated the intensity of illumination upward and downward, while at the same time noting changes in group output. Results varied, but one thing was clear: In no case was the increase or decrease in output in proportion to the increase or decrease in illumination. So the researchers introduced a control group: An experimental group was presented with varying intensity of illumination, while the controlled unit worked under a constant illumination intensity. Again, the results were bewildering to the Hawthorne researchers. As the light level was increased in the experimental unit, output rose for both the control group and the experimental group. But to the surprise of the researchers, as the light level was dropped in the experimental group, productivity continued to increase in both groups. In fact, a productivity decrease was observed in the experimental group only when the light intensity had been reduced to that of moonlight. The Hawthorne researchers concluded that illumination intensity was only a minor influence among the many influences that affected an employee's productivity, but they could not explain the behavior they had witnessed.

As a follow-up to the illumination experiments, the researchers began a second set of experiments in the relay assembly test room at Western Electric.

norms *Acceptable standards of behavior within a group that are shared by the group's members.*

A small group of women was isolated from the main work group so that their behavior could be more carefully observed. They went about their job of assembling small telephone relays in a room laid out similarly to their normal department. The only significant difference was the placement in the room of a research assistant who acted as an observer—keeping records of output, rejects, working conditions, and a daily log sheet describing everything that happened. Observations covering a multiyear period found that this small group's output increased steadily. The number of personal absences and those due to sickness was approximately one-third of those recorded by women in the regular production department. What became evident was that this group's performance was significantly influenced by its status of being a "special" group. The women in the test room thought that being in the experimental group was fun, that they were in sort of an elite group, and that management was concerned with their interest by engaging in such experimentation. In essence, workers in both the illumination and assembly-test-room experiments were reacting to the increased attention they were receiving.

A third study, in the bank wiring observation room, was introduced to ascertain the effect of a sophisticated wage incentive plan. The assumption was that individual workers would maximize their productivity when they saw that it was directly related to economic rewards. The most important finding to come out of this study was that employees did not individually maximize their outputs. Rather, their output became controlled by a group norm that determined what was a proper day's work. Output was not only being restricted, but individual workers were giving erroneous reports. The total for a week would check with the total week's output, but the daily reports showed a steady level of output, regardless of actual daily production. What was going on?

Interviews determined that the group was operating well below its capability and was leveling output in order to protect itself. Members were afraid that if they significantly increased their output, the unit incentive rate would be cut, the expected daily output would be increased, layoffs might occur, or slower workers would be reprimanded. So the group established its idea of a fair output—neither too much nor too little. They helped each other out to ensure that their reports were nearly level.

The norms the group established included a number of "don'ts." *Don't* be a rate-buster, turning out too much work. *Don't* be a chiseler, turning out too little work. *Don't* be a squealer on any of your peers. How did the group enforce these norms? Their methods were neither gentle nor subtle. They included sarcasm, name-calling, ridicule, and even physical punches to the upper arm of any member who violated the group's norms. Members would also ostracize individuals whose behavior was against the group's interest.

The Hawthorne studies made an important contribution to our understanding of group behavior—particularly the significant place that norms have in determining individual work behavior.

Conformity As a member of a group, you desire acceptance by the group. Because of your desire for acceptance, you are susceptible to conforming to the group's norms. There is considerable evidence that groups can place strong pressures on individual members to change their attitudes and behaviors to conform to the group's standard.[17]

Do individuals conform to the pressures of all the groups to which they belong? Obviously not, because people belong to many groups, and their norms vary. In some cases, they may even have contradictory norms. So what do people do? They conform to the important groups to which they belong or hope to belong. The important groups have been called **reference groups**, and they're characterized as ones in which a person is aware of other members,

Exhibit 9-4 Examples of Cards Used in Asch's Study

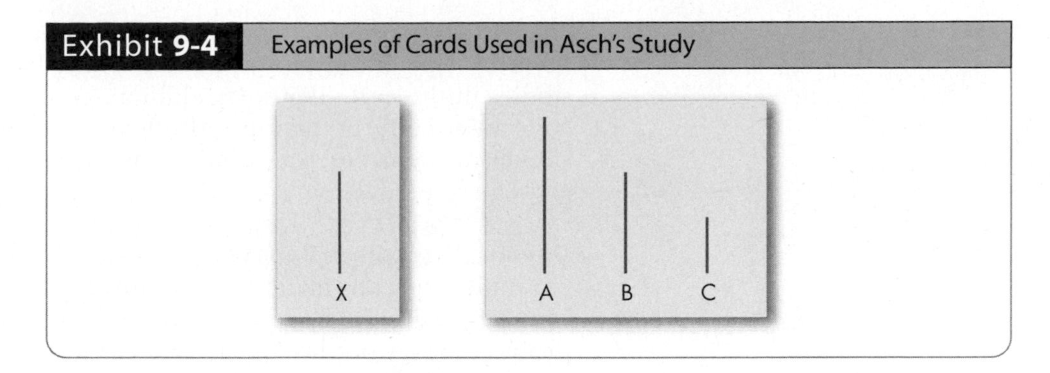

defines himself or herself as a member or would like to be a member, and feels that the group members are significant to him or her.[18] The implication, then, is that all groups do not impose equal conformity pressures on their members.

The impact that group pressures for **conformity** can have on an individual member's judgment and attitudes was demonstrated in the now-classic studies by Solomon Asch.[19] Asch made up groups of seven or eight people, who sat around a table and were asked to compare two cards held by the experimenter. One card had one line, and the other had three lines of varying length. As shown in Exhibit 9-4, one of the lines on the three-line card was identical to the line on the one-line card. Also as shown in Exhibit 9-4, the difference in line length was quite obvious; in fact, under ordinary conditions, subjects made fewer than 1 percent errors. The object was to announce aloud which of the three lines matched the single line. But what happens if the members in the group begin to give incorrect answers? Will the pressures to conform result in an unsuspecting subject (USS) altering an answer to align with the others? That was what Asch wanted to know. So he arranged the group so that only the USS was unaware that the experiment was "fixed." The seating was prearranged: The USS was placed so as to be one of the last to announce a decision.

The experiment began with several sets of matching exercises. All the subjects gave the right answers. On the third set, however, the first subject gave an obviously wrong answer—for example, saying "C" in Exhibit 9-4. The next subject gave the same wrong answer, and so did the others until it got to the unknowing subject. He knew "B" was the same as "X," yet everyone else had said "C." The decision confronting the USS was this: Do you publicly state a perception that differs from the preannounced position of the others in your group? Or do you give an answer that you strongly believe is incorrect in order to have your response agree with that of the other group members?

The results obtained by Asch demonstrated that over many experiments and many trials 75 percent of the subjects gave at least one answer that conformed—that is, that they knew was wrong but that was consistent with the replies of other group members—and the average for conformers was 37 percent. What meaning can we draw from these results? They suggest that there are group norms that press us toward conformity. That is, we desire to be one of the group and avoid being visibly different.

The preceding conclusions are based on research that was conducted 50 years ago. Has time altered their validity? And should we consider these findings generalizable across cultures? The evidence indicates that there have been

reference groups *Important groups to which individuals belong or hope to belong and with whose norms individuals are likely to conform.*

conformity *The adjustment of one's behavior to align with the norms of the group.*

changes in the level of conformity over time; and Asch's findings are culture bound.[20] Specifically, levels of conformity have steadily declined since Asch's studies in the early 1950s. In addition, conformity to social norms is higher in collectivist cultures than in individualistic cultures. Nevertheless, even in individualistic countries, you should consider conformity to norms to still be a powerful force in groups.

Deviant Workplace Behavior Ted Vowinkel is frustrated by a coworker who constantly spreads malicious and unsubstantiated rumors about him. Debra Hundley is tired of a member of her work team who, when confronted with a problem, takes out his frustration by yelling and screaming at her and other work team members. And Rhonda Lieberman recently quit her job as a dental hygienist after being constantly sexually harassed by her employer.

What do these three episodes have in common? They represent employees being exposed to acts of *deviant workplace behavior*.[21] **Deviant workplace behavior** (also called *antisocial behavior* or *workplace incivility*) is voluntary behavior that violates significant organizational norms and, in doing so, threatens the well-being of the organization or its members. Exhibit 9-5 provides a typology of deviant workplace behaviors, with examples of each.

Few organizations will admit to creating or condoning conditions that encourage and maintain deviant norms. Yet they exist. Employees report, for example, an increase in rudeness and disregard toward others by bosses and coworkers in recent years. And nearly half of employees who have suffered this incivility report that it has led them to think about changing jobs, with 12 percent actually quitting because of it.[22]

As with norms in general, individual employees' antisocial actions are shaped by the group context within which they work. Evidence demonstrates that the antisocial behavior exhibited by a work group is a significant predictor of an individual's antisocial behavior at work.[23] In other words, deviant workplace behavior is likely to flourish where it's supported by group norms. What this means for managers is that when deviant workplace norms surface, employee cooperation, commitment, and motivation are likely to suffer. This, in turn, can lead to reduced employee productivity and job satisfaction and increased turnover.

In addition, just being part of a group can increase an individual's deviant behavior. In other words, someone who ordinarily wouldn't engage in deviant

Exhibit 9-5 Typology of Deviant Workplace Behavior

Category	Examples
Production	Leaving early Intentionally working slowly Wasting resources
Property	Sabotage Lying about hours worked Stealing from the organization
Political	Showing favoritism Gossiping and spreading rumors Blaming coworkers
Personal aggression	Sexual harassment Verbal abuse Stealing from coworkers

Source: Adapted from S. L. Robinson and R. J. Bennett, "A Typology of Deviant Workplace Behaviors: A Multidimensional Scaling Study," *Academy of Management Journal*, April 1995, p. 565.

Exhibit 9-6 Groups and Deviant Behavior

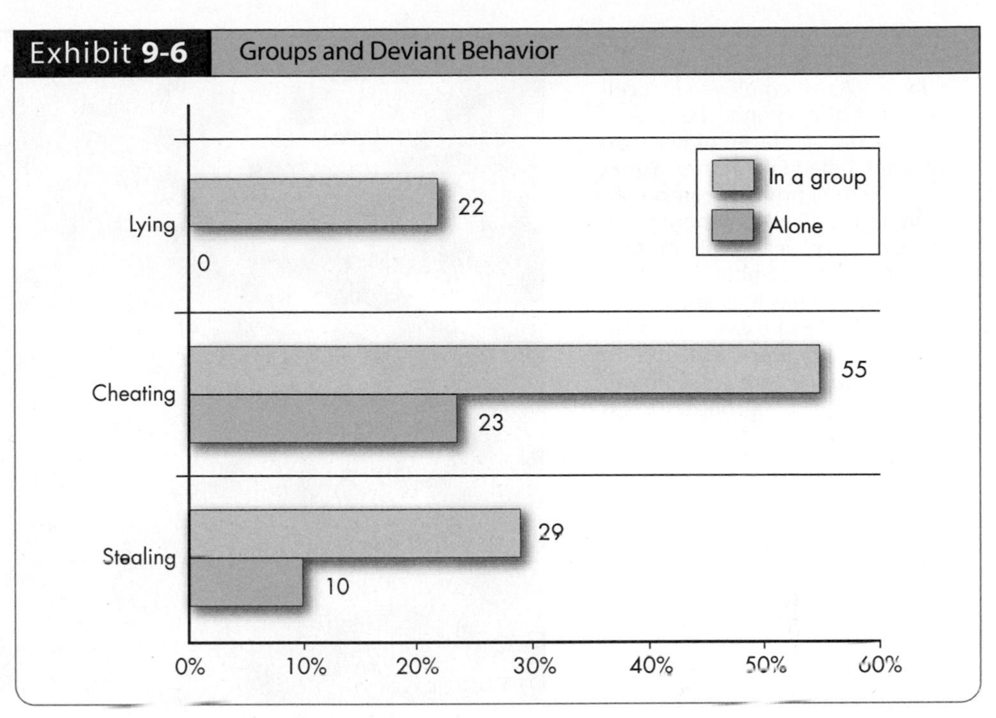

Source: A. Erez, H. Elms, and E. Fong, "Lying, Cheating, Stealing: Groups and the Ring of Gyges," paper presented at the Academy of Management Annual Meeting, Honolulu, HI, August 8, 2005.

behavior might be more likely to do so when working in a group. In fact, a recent study suggests that, compared with individuals working alone, those working in a group were more likely to lie, cheat, and steal. As shown in Exhibit 9-6, in this study, no individual working alone lied, but 22 percent of those working in groups did. Moreover, individuals working in groups also were more likely to cheat (55 percent of individuals working in a group cheated on a task versus 23 percent of individuals working alone) and steal (29 percent of individuals working in a group stole compared to only 10 percent working alone).[24] Groups provide a shield of anonymity so that someone who ordinarily might be afraid of getting caught for stealing can rely on the fact that other group members had the same opportunity or reason to steal. This creates a false sense of confidence that may result in more aggressive behavior. Thus, deviant behavior depends on the accepted norms of the group—or even whether an individual is part of a group.[25]

Status

Status—that is, a socially defined position or rank given to groups or group members by others—permeates every society. Even the smallest group will develop roles, rights, and rituals to differentiate its members. Status is an important factor in understanding human behavior because it is a significant motivator and has major behavioral consequences when individuals perceive a disparity between what they believe their status to be and what others perceive it to be.

deviant workplace behavior *Voluntary behavior that violates significant organizational norms and, in so doing, threatens the well-being of the organization or its members. Also called* antisocial behavior *or* workplace incivility.

status *A socially defined position or rank given to groups or group members by others.*

Otsuka Yuriko has high status at the Canon manufacturing plant in Ami, Japan. As an employee in a cell-manufacturing unit, she wears a badge on the sleeve of her work uniform labeled Eiji Meister. Yuriko earned the badge by completing an apprenticeship program and becoming proficient in all the tasks required to assemble a machine. Because she has mastered all the tasks, Yuriko can train other employees in her work unit, and her contributions are critical to her group's success.

What Determines Status? According to **status characteristics theory**, status tends to be derived from one of three sources:[26]

1. **The power a person wields over others.** Because they likely control the group's resources, people who control the outcomes of a group through their power tend to be perceived as high status.
2. **A person's ability to contribute to a group's goals.** People whose contributions are critical to the group's success tend to have high status.
3. **An individual's personal characteristics.** Someone whose personal characteristics are positively valued by the group (for example, good looks, intelligence, money, or a friendly personality) typically has higher status than someone who has fewer valued attributes.

Status and Norms Status has been shown to have some interesting effects on the power of norms and pressures to conform. For instance, high-status members of groups are often given more freedom to deviate from norms than are other group members.[27] High-status people are also better able to resist conformity pressures than their lower-status peers. An individual who is highly valued by a group but who doesn't much need or care about the social rewards the group provides is particularly able to pay minimal attention to conformity norms.[28]

The previous findings explain why many star athletes, celebrities, top-performing salespeople, and outstanding academics seem oblivious to appearance or social norms that constrain their peers. As high-status individuals, they're given a wider range of discretion. But this is true only as long as the high-status person's activities aren't severely detrimental to group goal achievement.[29]

Status and Group Interaction Interaction among members of groups is influenced by status. We find, for instance, that high-status people tend to be more assertive.[30] They speak out more often, criticize more, state more commands, and interrupt others more often. But status differences actually inhibit diversity of ideas and creativity in groups because lower-status members tend to be less active participants in group discussions. In situations in which lower-status members possess expertise and insights that could aid the group, their expertise and insights are not likely to be fully utilized, thus reducing the group's overall performance.

Status Inequity It is important for group members to believe that the status hierarchy is equitable. Perceived inequity creates disequilibrium, which results in various types of corrective behavior.[31]

The concept of equity presented in Chapter 6 applies to status. People expect rewards to be proportionate to costs incurred. If Dana and Liam are the two finalists for the head nurse position in a hospital, and it is clear that Dana has more seniority and better preparation for assuming the promotion, Liam will view the selection of Dana to be equitable. However, if Liam is chosen because she is the daughter-in-law of the hospital director, Dana will believe an injustice has been committed.

Groups generally agree within themselves on status criteria and, hence, there is usually high concurrence in group rankings of individuals. However, individuals can find themselves in a conflict situation when they move between groups whose status criteria are different or when they join groups whose members have heterogeneous backgrounds. For instance, business executives may use personal income or the growth rate of their companies as determinants of status. Government bureaucrats may use the size of their budgets. Blue-collar workers may use years of seniority. In groups made up of heterogeneous individuals or when heterogeneous groups are forced to be interdependent, status differences may initiate conflict as the group attempts to reconcile and align the differing hierarchies. As we'll see in Chapter 10, this can be a particular problem when management creates teams made up of employees from across varied functions within the organization.

Group Property 4: Size

Does the size of a group affect the group's overall behavior? The answer to this question is a definite "yes," but the effect is contingent on what dependent variables you look at.[32] The evidence indicates, for instance, that smaller groups are faster at completing tasks than are larger ones and that individuals perform better in smaller groups than in larger ones.[33] However, for groups engaged in problem solving, large groups consistently get better marks than their smaller counterparts.[34] Translating these results into specific numbers is a bit more hazardous, but we can offer some parameters. Large groups—those with a dozen or more members—are good for gaining diverse input. So if the goal of the group is fact-finding, larger groups should be more effective. On the other hand, smaller groups are better at doing something productive with that input. Groups of approximately seven members tend to be more effective for taking action.

5 *Show how group size affects group performance.*

One of the most important findings related to the size of a group has been labeled **social loafing**. Social loafing is the tendency for individuals to expend less effort when working collectively than when working individually.[35] It directly challenges the logic that the productivity of the group as a whole should at least equal the sum of the productivity of the individuals in that group.

status characteristics theory *A theory that states that differences in status characteristics create status hierarchies within groups.*

social loafing *The tendency for individuals to expend less effort when working collectively than when working individually.*

Studies indicate that these employees in Miles, China, collecting harvest grapes for the production of red wine, perform better in a group than when working alone. In collectivist societies such as China, employees show less propensity to engage in social loafing. Unlike individualistic cultures such as the United States, where people are dominated by self-interest, the Chinese are motivated by in-group goals.

A common stereotype about groups is that the sense of team spirit spurs individual effort and enhances the group's overall productivity. But that stereotype may be wrong. In the late 1920s, a German psychologist named Max Ringelmann compared the results of individual and group performance on a rope-pulling task.[36] He expected that the group's effort would be equal to the sum of the efforts of individuals within the group. That is, three people pulling together should exert three times as much pull on the rope as one person, and eight people should exert eight times as much pull. Ringelmann's results, however, didn't confirm his expectations. One person pulling on a rope alone exerted an average of 63 kilograms of force. In groups of three, the per-person force dropped to 53 kilograms. And in groups of eight, it fell to only 31 kilograms per person.

Replications of Ringelmann's research with similar tasks have generally supported his findings.[37] Group performance increases with group size, but the addition of new members to the group has diminishing returns on productivity. So more may be better in the sense that the total productivity of a group of four is greater than that of three people, but the individual productivity of each group member declines.

What causes this social loafing effect? It may be due to a belief that others in the group are not carrying their fair share. If you see others as lazy or inept, you can reestablish equity by reducing your effort. Another explanation is the dispersion of responsibility. Because the results of the group cannot be attributed to any single person, the relationship between an individual's input and the group's output is clouded. In such situations, individuals may be tempted to become "free riders" and coast on the group's efforts. In other words, there will be a reduction in efficiency when individuals think that their contribution cannot be measured.

The implications for OB of this effect on work groups are significant. When managers use collective work situations to enhance morale and teamwork, they must also provide means by which they can identify individual efforts. If this isn't done, management must weigh the potential losses in productivity from using groups against any possible gains in worker satisfaction.[38]

There are several ways to prevent social loafing : (1) Set group goals so that the group has a common purpose to strive toward; (2) increase intergroup competition, which again focuses the group on the shared outcome; (3) engage in peer evaluation so that each person's contribution to the group is evaluated by each group member; and (4) if possible, distribute group rewards, in part, based on each member's unique contributions.[39] Although none of these actions is a "magic bullet" that will prevent social loafing in all cases, they should help minimize its effect.

Group Property 5: Cohesiveness

6 Contrast the benefits and disadvantages of cohesive groups.

Groups differ in their **cohesiveness**—that is, the degree to which members are attracted to each other and are motivated to stay in the group.[40] For instance, some work groups are cohesive because the members have spent a great deal of time together, or the group's small size facilitates high interaction, or the group has experienced external threats that have brought members close together. Cohesiveness is important because it has been found to be related to group productivity.[41]

Studies consistently show that the relationship between cohesiveness and productivity depends on the performance-related norms established by the group.[42] If performance-related norms are high (for example, high output, quality work, cooperation with individuals outside the group), a cohesive group will be more productive than will a less cohesive group. But if cohesiveness is high and performance norms are low, productivity will be low. If cohesiveness is low and performance norms are high, productivity increases, but it increases less than in the high-cohesiveness/high-norms situation. When cohesiveness and performance-related norms are both low, productivity tends to fall into the low-to-moderate range. These conclusions are summarized in Exhibit 9-7.

What can you do to encourage group cohesiveness? You might try one or more of the following suggestions: (1) Make the group smaller, (2) encourage agreement with group goals, (3) increase the time members spend together, (4) increase the status of the group and the perceived difficulty of attaining membership in the group, (5) stimulate competition with other groups, (6) give rewards to the group rather than to individual members, and (7) physically isolate the group.[43]

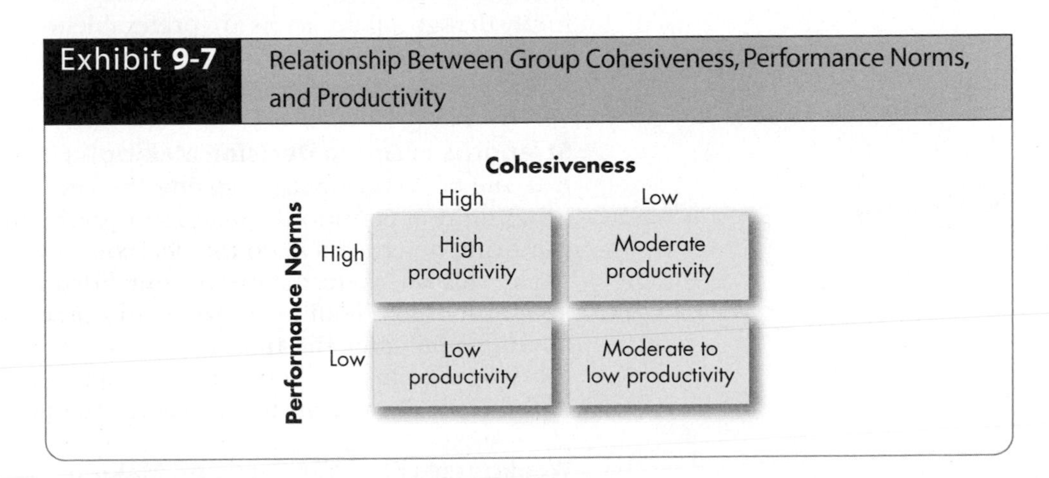

cohesiveness *The degree to which group members are attracted to each other and are motivated to stay in the group.*

Group Cohesiveness Across Cultures

Arecent study attempted to determine whether motivating work groups by giving them more complex tasks and greater autonomy resulted in increased group cohesiveness. Researchers studied bank teams in the United States, an individualist culture, and in Hong Kong, a collectivist culture. Both teams were composed of individuals from each respective country. The results showed that, regardless of what culture the teams were from, giving teams difficult tasks and more freedom to accomplish those tasks created a more tight-knit group. Consequently, team performance was enhanced.

However, the teams differed in the extent to which increases in task complexity and autonomy resulted in greater group cohesiveness. Teams in individualist cultures responded more strongly than did teams in collectivist cultures, became more united and committed, and, as a result, received higher performance ratings from their supervisors than teams from collectivist cultures.

Why do these cultural differences exist? One explanation is that collectivist teams already have a strong predisposition to work together as a group, so there's less need for increased teamwork. What's the lesson? Managers in individualist cultures may need to work harder to increase team cohesiveness. One way to do this is to give teams more challenging assignments and provide them with more independence.

Source: Based on D. Man and S. S. K. Lam, "The Effects of Job Complexity and Autonomy on Cohesiveness in Collectivist and Individualistic Work Groups: A Cross-Cultural Analysis," *Journal of Organizational Behavior*, December 2003, pp. 979–1001.

Group Decision Making

7 *Contrast the strengths and weaknesses of group decision making.*

The belief—characterized by juries—that two heads are better than one has long been accepted as a basic component of North American and many other countries' legal systems. This belief has expanded to the point that, today, many decisions in organizations are made by groups, teams, or committees.[44] In this section, we discuss group decision making.

Groups Versus the Individual

Decision-making groups may be widely used in organizations, but does that imply that group decisions are preferable to those made by an individual alone? The answer to this question depends on a number of factors. Let's begin by looking at the strengths and weaknesses of group decision making.[45]

Strengths of Group Decision Making Groups generate *more complete information and knowledge.* By aggregating the resources of several individuals, groups bring more input into the decision process. In addition to more input, groups can bring heterogeneity to the decision process. They offer *increased diversity of views.* This opens up the opportunity for more approaches and alternatives to be considered. Finally, groups lead to increased *acceptance of a solution.* Many decisions fail after the final choice is made because people don't accept the solution. Group members who participated in making a decision are likely to enthusiastically support the decision and encourage others to accept it.

Weaknesses of Group Decision Making In spite of the pluses noted, group decisions have their drawbacks. They're time-consuming because groups typically take more time to reach a solution than would be the case if an individual were making the decision. There are *conformity pressures in groups.* The desire by group members to be accepted and considered an asset to the group can result in squashing any overt disagreement. Group discussion can be *dominated by one* *or a few members.* If this dominant coalition is composed of low- and medium-ability members, the group's overall effectiveness will suffer. Finally, group decisions suffer from *ambiguous responsibility.* In an individual decision, it's clear who is accountable for the final outcome. In a group decision, the responsibility of any single member is watered down.

Effectiveness and Efficiency Whether groups are more effective than individuals depends on the criteria you use to define effectiveness. In terms of *accuracy*, group decisions are generally more accurate than the decisions of the average individual in a group, but they are less accurate than the judgments of the most accurate group member.[46] If decision effectiveness is defined in terms of *speed*, individuals are superior. If *creativity* is important, groups tend to be more effective than individuals. And if effectiveness means the degree of *acceptance* the final solution achieves, the nod again goes to the group.[47]

But effectiveness cannot be considered without also assessing efficiency. In terms of efficiency, groups almost always stack up as a poor second to the individual decision maker. With few exceptions, group decision making consumes more work hours than if an individual were to tackle the same problem alone. The exceptions tend to be the instances in which, to achieve comparable quantities of diverse input, the single decision maker must spend a great deal of time reviewing files and talking to people. Because groups can include members from diverse areas, the time spent searching for information can be reduced. However, as we noted, these advantages in efficiency tend to be the exception. Groups are generally less efficient than individuals. In deciding whether to use groups, then, consideration should be given to assessing whether increases in effectiveness are more than enough to offset the reductions in efficiency.

Summary In summary, groups offer an excellent vehicle for performing many of the steps in the decision-making process. They are a source of both breadth and depth of input for information gathering. If the group is composed of individuals with diverse backgrounds, the alternatives generated should be more extensive and the analysis more critical. When the final solution is agreed on, there are more people in a group decision to support and implement it. These pluses, however, can be more than offset by the time

MYTH OR SCIENCE? *"Are Two Heads Better Than One?"*

Two heads are not necessarily always better than one. In fact, the evidence generally confirms the superiority of individuals over groups when brainstorming. The best individual in a group also makes better decisions than groups as a whole, though groups do tend to do better than the average group member.[48]

Research also indicates that groups are superior only when they meet certain criteria.[49] These criteria include:

1. **The group must have diversity among members.** To get benefits from "two heads," the heads must differ in relevant skills and abilities.
2. **The group members must be able to communicate their ideas freely and openly.** This requires an absence of hostility and intimidation.
3. **The task being undertaken must be complex.** Relative to individuals, groups do better on complex rather than simple tasks. ■

consumed by group decisions, the internal conflicts they create, and the pressures they generate toward conformity. Therefore, in some cases, individuals can be expected to make better decisions than groups.

Groupthink and Groupshift

Two byproducts of group decision making have received a considerable amount of attention from researchers in OB. As we'll show, these two phenomena have the potential to affect a group's ability to appraise alternatives objectively and to arrive at quality decision solutions.

The first phenomenon, called **groupthink**, is related to norms. It describes situations in which group pressures for conformity deter the group from critically appraising unusual, minority, or unpopular views. Groupthink is a disease that attacks many groups and can dramatically hinder their performance. The second phenomenon we shall discuss is called **groupshift**. It indicates that, in discussing a given set of alternatives and arriving at a solution, group members tend to exaggerate the initial positions they hold. In some situations, caution dominates, and there is a conservative shift. More often, however, the evidence indicates that groups tend toward a risky shift. Let's look at each of these phenomena in more detail.

Groupthink Have you ever felt like speaking up in a meeting, a classroom, or an informal group but decided against it? One reason may have been shyness. On the other hand, you may have been a victim of groupthink, a phenomenon that occurs when group members become so enamored of seeking concurrence that the norm for consensus overrides the realistic appraisal of alternative courses of action and the full expression of deviant, minority, or unpopular views. It describes a deterioration in an individual's mental efficiency, reality testing, and moral judgment as a result of group pressures.[50]

We have all seen the symptoms of the groupthink phenomenon:

1. Group members rationalize any resistance to the assumptions they have made. No matter how strongly the evidence may contradict their basic assumptions, members behave so as to reinforce those assumptions continually.
2. Members apply direct pressures on those who momentarily express doubts about any of the group's shared views or who question the validity of arguments supporting the alternative favored by the majority.
3. Members who have doubts or hold differing points of view seek to avoid deviating from what appears to be group consensus by keeping silent about misgivings and even minimizing to themselves the importance of their doubts.
4. There appears to be an illusion of unanimity. If someone doesn't speak, it's assumed that he or she is in full accord. In other words, abstention becomes viewed as a "yes" vote.[51]

In studies of historic American foreign policy decisions, these symptoms were found to prevail when government policy-making groups failed—unpreparedness at the battle of Pearl Harbor in 1941, the U.S. invasion of North Korea in the 1950s, the Bay of Pigs fiasco and the escalation of the Vietnam War in the 1960s.[52] More recently, the U.S. *Challenger* and *Columbia* space shuttle disasters and the failure of the main mirror on the *Hubble* telescope have been linked to decision processes at the U.S. National Aeronautics and Space Administration NASA in which groupthink symptoms were evident.[53] And groupthink was found to be a primary factor leading to setbacks at both British Airways and retailer Marks & Spencer as they tried to implement globalization strategies.[54]

Groupthink appears to be closely aligned with the conclusions Asch drew in his experiments with a lone dissenter. Individuals who hold a position that is different from that of the dominant majority are under pressure to suppress,

OB In the News

Groupthink for an Enron Jury?

Although most of us view the U.S. energy company Enron as the very symbol of corporate corruption, not every Enron employee behaved unethically. Twenty former Enron employees—most notably Ken Lay, Jeff Skilling, and Andrew Fastow—were either convicted of or pleaded guilty to fraudulent behavior. The conviction of another Enron executive you've probably never heard of—former broadband finance chief Kevin Howard—provides a fascinating, and disturbing, glimpse into how juries use group pressure to reach decisions.

Howard's first trial ended in a hung jury. In the second trial, he was found guilty of conspiracy, fraud, and falsifying records. However, shortly after his conviction, two jurors and two alternate jurors said they were pressured by other jurors to reach a unanimous decision even though they believed Howard was innocent. Juror Ann Marie Campbell said, in a sworn statement, "There was just so much pressure to change my vote that I felt like we had to compromise and give in to the majority because I felt like there was no other choice." Campbell said at one point a male juror tried to "grab her by the shoulders" to convince her, and another "banged his first on the table during deliberations." Another jury member said, "There was an atmosphere of 'let's fry them.' "

On appeal, a judge threw out Howard's conviction, based, in part, on the earlier judge's instruction to the convicting jury which pressured them to reach a unanimous decision. The Kevin Howard case shows how strong groupthink pressures can be and the degree to which individuals can be pressured to give in to the majority.

Source: K. Hays, "Judge Dismisses Enron Convictions," *Houston (Texas) Chronicle*, February 1, 2007.

withhold, or modify their true feelings and beliefs. As members of a group, we find it more pleasant to be in agreement—to be a positive part of the group—than to be a disruptive force, even if disruption is necessary to improve the effectiveness of the group's decisions.

Does groupthink attack all groups? No. It seems to occur most often when there is a clear group identity, when members hold a positive image of their group that they want to protect, and when the group perceives a collective threat to this positive image.[55] So groupthink is not a dissenter-suppression mechanism as much as it's a means for a group to protect its positive image. For NASA, its problems stem from its attempt to confirm its identity as "the elite organization that could do no wrong."[56]

What can managers do to minimize groupthink?[57] First, they can monitor group size. People grow more intimidated and hesitant as group size increases, and, although there is no magic number that will eliminate groupthink, individuals are likely to feel less personal responsibility when groups get larger than about 10. Managers should also encourage group leaders to play an impartial role. Leaders should actively seek input from all members and avoid expressing their own opinions, especially in the early stages of deliberation. In addition, managers should appoint one group member to play the role of devil's advocate; this member's role is to overtly challenge the majority position and offer divergent perspectives. Still another suggestion is to use exercises that stimulate active discussion of diverse alternatives without threatening the group and intensifying identity protection. One such exercise is to have group members talk about dangers or risks involved in a decision and delaying discussion of any

groupthink *A phenomenon in which the norm for consensus overrides the realistic appraisal of alternative courses of action.*

groupshift *A change in decision risk between a group's decision and an individual decision that a member within the group would make; the shift can be toward either conservatism or greater risk.*

potential gains. Requiring members to first focus on the negatives of a decision alternative makes the group less likely to stifle dissenting views and more likely to gain an objective evaluation.

Groupshift In comparing group decisions with the individual decisions of members within the group, evidence suggests that there are differences.[58] In some cases, group decisions are more conservative than individual decisions. More often, the shift is toward greater risk.[59]

What appears to happen in groups is that the discussion leads to a significant shift in the positions of members toward a more extreme position in the direction in which they were already leaning before the discussion. So conservative types become more cautious, and more aggressive types take on more risk. The group discussion tends to exaggerate the initial position of the group.

Groupshift can be viewed as actually a special case of groupthink. The decision of the group reflects the dominant decision-making norm that develops during the group's discussion. Whether the shift in the group's decision is toward greater caution or more risk depends on the dominant prediscussion norm.

The greater occurrence of the shift toward risk has generated several explanations for the phenomenon.[60] It's been argued, for instance, that discussion creates familiarization among the members. As they become more comfortable with each other, they also become more bold and daring. Another argument is that most societies in developed nations value risk, that they admire individuals who are willing to take risks, and that group discussion motivates members to show that they are at least as willing as their peers to take risks. The most plausible explanation of the shift toward risk, however, seems to be that the group diffuses responsibility. Group decisions free any single member from accountability for the group's final choice. Greater risk can be taken because even if the decision fails no one member can be held wholly responsible.

So how should you use the findings on groupshift? You should recognize that group decisions exaggerate the initial position of the individual members, that the shift has been shown more often to be toward greater risk, and that whether a group will shift toward greater risk or caution is a function of the members' prediscussion inclinations.

Having discussed group decision making and its pros and cons, we now turn to the techniques by which groups make decisions. These techniques reduce some of the dysfunctional aspects of group decision making.

Group Decision-Making Techniques

The most common form of group decision making takes place in **interacting groups**. In these groups, members meet face-to-face and rely on both verbal and nonverbal interaction to communicate with each other. But as our discussion of groupthink demonstrated, interacting groups often censor themselves and pressure individual members toward conformity of opinion. Brainstorming, the nominal group technique, and electronic meetings have been proposed as ways to reduce many of the problems inherent in the traditional interacting group.

8 *Compare the effectiveness of interacting, brainstorming, nominal, and electronic meeting groups.*

Brainstorming is meant to overcome pressures for conformity in an interacting group that retard the development of creative alternatives.[61] It does this by utilizing an idea-generation process that specifically encourages any and all alternatives while withholding any criticism of those alternatives.

In a typical brainstorming session, a half-dozen to a dozen people sit around a table. The group leader states the problem in a clear manner so that it is understood by all participants. Members then "freewheel" as many alternatives as they can in a given length of time. No criticism is allowed, and all the

Exhibit 9-8

Source: S. Adams, *Build a Better Life by Stealing Office Supplies* (Kansas City, MO: Andrews & McMeal, 1991), p. 31. Dilbert reprinted with permission of United Features Syndicate, Inc.

alternatives are recorded for later discussion and analysis. One idea stimulates others, and judgments of even the most bizarre suggestions are withheld until later to encourage group members to "think the unusual."

Brainstorming may indeed generate ideas—but not in a very efficient manner. Research consistently shows that individuals working alone generate more ideas than a group in a brainstorming session. Why? One of the primary reasons is because of "production blocking." In other words, when people are generating ideas in a group, there are many people talking at once, which blocks the thought process and eventually impedes the sharing of ideas.[62] The following two techniques go further than brainstorming by offering methods that help groups arrive at a preferred solution.[63]

The **nominal group technique** restricts discussion or interpersonal communication during the decision-making process, hence the term *nominal.* Group members are all physically present, as in a traditional committee meeting, but members operate independently. Specifically, a problem is presented and then the group takes the following steps:

1. Members meet as a group, but before any discussion takes place, each member independently writes down ideas on the problem.
2. After this silent period, each member presents one idea to the group. Each member takes a turn, presenting a single idea, until all ideas have been

interacting groups *Typical groups in which members interact with each other face-to-face.*

brainstorming *An idea-generation process that specifically encourages any and all alternatives while withholding any criticism of those alternatives.*

nominal group technique *A group decision-making method in which individual members meet face-to-face to pool their judgments in a systematic but independent fashion.*

presented and recorded. No discussion takes place until all ideas have been recorded.
3. The group discusses the ideas for clarity and evaluates them.
4. Each group member silently and independently rank-orders the ideas. The idea with the highest aggregate ranking determines the final decision.

The chief advantage of the nominal group technique is that it permits a group to meet formally but does not restrict independent thinking, as does an interacting group. Research generally shows that nominal groups outperform brainstorming groups.[64]

The most recent approach to group decision making blends the nominal group technique with sophisticated computer technology.[65] It's called a computer-assisted group, or an **electronic meeting**. Once the required technology is in place, the concept is simple. Up to 50 people sit around a horseshoe-shaped table, empty except for a series of computer terminals. Issues are presented to participants, who type their responses into their computers. Individual comments, as well as aggregate votes, are displayed on a projection screen. The proposed advantages of electronic meetings are anonymity, honesty, and speed. Participants can anonymously type any message they want, and it flashes on the screen for all to see at the push of a participant's keyboard key. This technique also allows people to be brutally honest without penalty. And it's supposedly fast because chitchat is eliminated, discussions don't digress, and many participants can "talk" at once without stepping on one another's toes. The early evidence, however, indicates that electronic meetings don't achieve most of their proposed benefits. Evaluations of numerous studies found that electronic meetings actually led to *decreased* group effectiveness, required *more* time to complete tasks, and resulted in *reduced* member satisfaction compared with face-to-face groups.[66] Nevertheless, current enthusiasm for computer-mediated communications suggests that this technology is here to stay and is likely to increase in popularity in the future.

Each of these four group decision techniques has its own set of strengths and weaknesses. The choice of one technique over another depends on what criteria you want to emphasize and the cost–benefit trade-off. For instance, as Exhibit 9-9 indicates, an interacting group is good for achieving commitment to a solution, brainstorming develops group cohesiveness, the nominal group technique is an inexpensive means for generating a large number of ideas, and electronic meetings minimize social pressures and conflicts.

Exhibit 9-9 Evaluating Group Effectiveness

	Type of Group			
Effectiveness Criteria	**Interacting**	**Brainstorming**	**Nominal**	**Electronic**
Number and quality of ideas	Low	Moderate	High	High
Social pressure	High	Low	Moderate	Low
Money costs	Low	Low	Low	High
Speed	Moderate	Moderate	Moderate	Moderate
Task orientation	Low	High	High	High
Potential for interpersonal conflict	High	Low	Moderate	Low
Commitment to solution	High	Not applicable	Moderate	Moderate
Development of group cohesiveness	High	High	Moderate	Low

Global Implications

9 *Evaluate evidence for cultural differences in group status and social loafing, as well as the effects of diversity in groups.*

As in most other areas of OB, most of the research on groups has been conducted in North America, but that situation is changing quickly. There are three areas of groups research where cross-cultural issues are particularly important.

Status and Culture Do cultural differences affect status? The answer is a resounding "yes."[67]

The importance of status does vary between cultures. The French, for example, are highly status conscious. Countries also differ on the criteria that create status. For instance, status for Latin Americans and Asians tends to be derived from family position and formal roles held in organizations. In contrast, although status is still important in countries such as the United States and Australia, it is often bestowed more for accomplishments than on the basis of titles and family trees.[68]

The message here is to make sure you understand who and what holds status when interacting with people from a culture different from your own. A U.S. manager who doesn't understand that physical office size is not a measure of a Japanese executive's position or who fails to grasp the importance the British place on family genealogy and social class is likely to unintentionally offend his overseas counterparts and, in so doing, lessen his interpersonal effectiveness.

Social Loafing Social loafing appears to have a Western bias. It's consistent with individualistic cultures, such as the United States and Canada, that are dominated by self-interest. It is *not* consistent with collective societies, in which individuals are motivated by in-group goals. For instance, in studies comparing employees from the United States with employees from the People's Republic of China and Israel (both collectivist societies), the Chinese and Israelis showed no propensity to engage in social loafing. In fact, the Chinese and Israelis actually performed better in a group than when working alone.

Group Diversity More and more research is being done on how diversity influences group performance. Some of this research looks at cultural diversity, and some of it considers diversity on other characteristics (such as race or gender). Collectively, the research points to both benefits and costs from group diversity.

In terms of costs, diversity appears to lead to increased group conflict, especially in the early stages of a group's tenure. This conflict often results in lower group morale and group members dropping out. One study of groups that were either culturally diverse (composed of people from different countries) or homogeneous (composed of people from the same country) found that, on a wilderness survival exercise (not unlike the Experiential Exercise in this chapter), the diverse and homogenous groups performed equally well, but the diverse groups were less satisfied with their groups, were less cohesive, and had more conflict.[69]

In terms of the benefits to diversity, more evidence is accumulating that, over time, culturally and demographically diverse groups may perform better, if they can get over their initial conflicts. Why might this be the case?

electronic meeting *A meeting in which members interact on computers, allowing for anonymity of comments and aggregation of votes.*

Research shows that surface-level diversity—observable characteristics such as national origin, race, and gender—actually cues people to possible differences in deep-level diversity—underlying attitudes, values, and opinions. One researcher argues, "The mere presence of diversity you can see, such as a person's race or gender, actually cues a team that there's likely to be differences of opinion." Although those differences of opinion can lead to conflict, they also provide an opportunity to solve problems in unique ways.

One study of jury behavior, for example, found that diverse juries were more likely to deliberate longer, share more information, and make fewer factual errors when discussing evidence. Interestingly, two studies of MBA student groups found that surface-level diversity led to greater openness even when there was no deep-level diversity. In such cases, the surface-level diversity of a group may subconsciously cue team members to be more open-minded in their views.[70]

In sum, the impact of cultural diversity on groups is a mixed bag. It is difficult to be in a diverse group in the short term. However, if the group members can weather their differences, over time, diversity may help them be more open-minded and creative, thus allowing them to do better in the long run. However, we should realize that even when there are positive effects of diversity on group performance, they are unlikely to be especially strong. As one review stated, "the business case (in terms of demonstrable financial results) for diversity remains hard to support based on the extant research."[71]

Summary and Implications for Managers

Performance A number of group properties show a relationship with performance. Among the most prominent are role perception, norms, status differences, size of the group, and cohesiveness.

There is a positive relationship between role perception and an employee's performance evaluation.[72] The degree of congruence that exists between an employee and the boss in the perception of the employee's job influences the degree to which the boss will judge that employee as an effective performer. To the extent that the employee's role perception fulfills the boss's role expectations, the employee will receive a higher performance evaluation.

Norms control group member behavior by establishing standards of right and wrong. The norms of a given group can help to explain the behaviors of its members for managers. When norms support high output, managers can expect individual performance to be markedly higher than when group norms aim to restrict output. Similarly, norms that support antisocial behavior increase the likelihood that individuals will engage in deviant workplace activities.

Status inequities create frustration and can adversely influence productivity and the willingness to remain with an organization. Among individuals who are equity sensitive, incongruence is likely to lead to reduced motivation and an increased search for ways to bring about fairness (for example, taking another job). In addition, because lower-status people tend to participate less in group discussions, groups characterized by high status differences among members are likely to inhibit input from the lower-status members and to underperform their potential.

The impact of size on a group's performance depends on the type of task in which the group is engaged. Larger groups are more effective at fact-finding activities. Smaller groups are more effective at action-taking tasks. Our knowledge of social loafing suggests that, if management uses larger groups, efforts should be made to provide measures of individual performance within the group.

Cohesiveness can play an important function in influencing a group's level of productivity. Whether it does depends on the group's performance-related norms.

Satisfaction As with the role perception–performance relationship, high congruence between a boss and an employee as to the perception of the employee's job shows a significant association with high employee satisfaction.[73] Similarly, role conflict is associated with job-induced tension and job dissatisfaction.[74]

Most people prefer to communicate with others at their own status level or a higher one rather than with those below them.[75] As a result, we should expect satisfaction to be greater among employees whose job minimizes interaction with individuals who are lower in status than themselves.

The group size–satisfaction relationship is what one would intuitively expect: Larger groups are associated with lower satisfaction.[76] As size increases, opportunities for participation and social interaction decrease, as does the ability of members to identify with the group's accomplishments. At the same time, having more members also prompts dissension, conflict, and the formation of subgroups, which all act to make the group a less pleasant entity of which to be a part.

Point Counterpoint

ALL JOBS SHOULD BE DESIGNED AROUND GROUPS

Groups, not individuals, are the ideal building blocks for an organization. There are several reasons for designing all jobs around groups.

First, in general, groups make better decisions than the average individual acting alone.

Second, with the growth in technology, society is becoming more intertwined. Look at the growth of social networking sites such as MySpace, Facebook, and YouTube. People are connected anyway, so why not design work in the same way?

Third, small groups are good for people. They can satisfy social needs and provide support for employees in times of stress and crisis. Evidence indicates that social support—both when they provide it and when they receive it—makes people happier and even allows them to live longer.

Fourth, groups are very effective tools for implementation for decisions. Groups gain commitment from their members so that group decisions are likely to be willingly and more successfully carried out.

Fifth, groups can control and discipline individual members in ways that are often extremely difficult through impersonal quasi-legal disciplinary systems. Group norms are powerful control devices.

Sixth, groups are a means by which large organizations can fend off many of the negative effects of increased size. Groups help prevent communication lines from growing too long, the hierarchy from growing too steep, and individuals from getting lost in the crowd.

The rapid growth of team-based organizations in recent years suggests that we may well be on our way toward a day when almost all jobs are designed around groups.

Capitalistic countries such as the United States, Canada, Australia, and the United Kingdom value the individual. Designing jobs around groups is inconsistent with the economic values of these countries. Moreover, as capitalism and entrepreneurship have spread throughout eastern Europe, Asia, and other more collective societies, we should expect to see *less* emphasis on groups and *more* on the individual in workplaces throughout the world. Let's look at the United States to see how cultural and economic values shape employee attitudes toward groups.

The United States was built on the ethic of the individual. Its culture strongly values individual achievement and encourages competition. Even in team sports, people want to identify individuals for recognition. U.S. adults enjoy being part of a group in which they can maintain a strong individual identity. They don't enjoy sublimating their identity to that of the group. When they are assigned to groups, all sorts of bad things happen, including conflict, groupthink, social loafing, and deviant behavior.

The U.S. worker likes a clear link between individual effort and a visible outcome. It's not by chance that the United States, as a nation, has a considerably larger proportion of high achievers than exists in most of the rest of the world. It breeds achievers, and achievers seek personal responsibility. They would be frustrated in job situations in which their contribution was commingled and homogenized with the contributions of others.

U.S. workers want to be hired, evaluated, and rewarded on their individual achievements. They are not likely to accept a group's decision on such issues as their job assignments and wage increases, nor are they comfortable in a system in which the sole basis for their promotion or termination is the performance of their group.

Though teams have grown in popularity as a device for employers to organize people and tasks, we should expect resistance to any effort to treat individuals solely as members of a group—especially among workers raised in capitalistic economies.

Questions for Review

1 Define *group*? What are the different types of groups?

2 What are the five stages of group development?

3 Do role requirements change in different situations? If so, how?

4 How do group norms and status influence an individual's behavior?

5 How does group size affect group performance?

6 What are the advantages and limitations of cohesive groups?

7 What are the strengths and weaknesses of group (versus individual) decision making?

8 How effective are interacting, brainstorming, nominal, and electronic meeting groups?

9 What is the evidence for the effect of culture on group status and social loafing? How does diversity affect groups and their effectiveness over time?

Experiential Exercise

WILDERNESS SURVIVAL

You are a member of a hiking party. After reaching base camp on the first day, you decide to take a quick sunset hike by yourself. After a few exhilarating miles, you decide to return to camp. On your way back, you realize that you are lost. You have shouted for help, to no avail. It is now dark. And getting cold.

Your Task

Without communicating with anyone else in your group, read the following scenarios and choose the best answer. Keep track of your answers on a sheet of paper. You have 10 minutes to answer the 10 questions.

1. The first thing you decide to do is to build a fire. However, you have no matches, so you use the bow-and-drill method. What is the bow-and-drill method?
   a. A dry, soft stick is rubbed between one's hands against a board of supple green wood.
   b. A soft green stick is rubbed between one's hands against a hardwood board.
   c. A straight stick of wood is quickly rubbed back-and-forth against a dead tree.
   d. Two sticks (one being the bow, the other the drill) are struck to create a spark.

2. It occurs to you that you can also use the fire as a distress signal. When signaling with fire, how do you form the international distress signal?
   a. 2 fires
   b. 4 fires in a square
   c. 4 fires in a cross
   d. 3 fires in a line

3. You are very thirsty. You go to a nearby stream and collect some water in the small metal cup you have in your backpack. How long should you boil the water?
   a. 15 minutes
   b. A few seconds
   c. 1 hour
   d. It depends on the altitude.

4. You are very hungry, so you decide to eat what appear to be edible berries. When performing the universal edibility test, what should you do?
   a. Do not eat for 2 hours before the test.
   b. If the plant stings your lip, confirm the sting by holding it under your tongue for 15 minutes.
   c. If nothing bad has happened 2 hours after digestion, eat half a cup of the plant and wait again.
   d. Separate the plant into its basic components and eat each component, one at a time.

5. Next, you decide to build a shelter for the evening. In selecting a site, what do you *not* have to consider?
   a. It must contain material to make the type of shelter you need.
   b. It must be free of insects, reptiles, and poisonous plants.
   c. It must be large enough and level enough for you to lie down comfortably.
   d. It must be on a hill so you can signal rescuers and keep an eye on your surroundings.

6. In the shelter that you built, you notice a spider. You heard from a fellow hiker that black widow spiders populate the area. How do you identify a black widow spider?
   a. Its head and abdomen are black; its thorax is red.
   b. It is attracted to light.
   c. It runs away from light.
   d. It is a dark spider with a red or orange marking on the female's abdomen.
7. After getting some sleep, you notice that the night sky has cleared, so you decide to try to find your way back to base camp. You believe you should travel north and can use the North Star for navigation. How do you locate the North Star?
   a. Hold your right hand up as far as you can and look between your index and middle fingers.
   b. Find Sirius and look 60 degrees above it and to the right.
   c. Look for the Big Dipper and follow the line created by its cup end.
   d. Follow the line of Orion's belt.
8. You come across a fast-moving stream. What is the best way to cross it?
   a. Find a spot downstream from a sandbar, where the water will be calmer.
   b. Build a bridge.
   c. Find a rocky area, as the water will be shallow and you will have hand- and footholds.
   d. Find a level stretch where it breaks into a few channels.
9. After walking for about an hour, you feel several spiders in your clothes. You don't feel any pain, but you know some spider bites are painless. Which of these spider bites is painless?
   a. Black widow
   b. Brown recluse
   c. Wolf spider
   d. Harvestman (daddy longlegs)
10. You decide to eat some insects. Which insects should you avoid?
    a. Adults that sting or bite
    b. Caterpillars and insects that have a pungent odor
    c. Hairy or brightly colored ones
    d. All the above

Group Task

Break into groups of five or six people. Now imagine that your whole group is lost. Answer each question as a group, employing a consensus approach to reach each decision. Once the group comes to an agreement, write the decision down on the same sheet of paper that you used for your individual answers. You will have approximately 20 minutes for the group task.

Scoring Your Answers

Your instructor will provide you with the correct answers, which are based on expert judgments in these situations. Once you have received the answers, calculate (A) your individual score; (B) your group's score; (C) the average individual score in the group; (D) the best individual score in the group. Write these down and consult with your group to ensure that these scores are accurate.

(A) Your individual score __________

(B) Your group's score __________

(C) Average individual score in group __________

(D) Best individual score in group __________

Discussion Questions

1. How did your group (B) perform relative to yourself (A)?
2. How did your group (B) perform relative to the average individual score in the group (C)?
3. How did your group (B) perform relative to the best individual score in the group (D)?
4. Compare your results with those of other groups. Did some groups do a better job of outperforming individuals than others?
5. What do these results tell you about the effectiveness of group decision making?
6. What can groups do to make group decision-making more effective?

Ethical Dilemma

DEALING WITH SHIRKERS

We've noted that one of the most common problems in groups is social loafing, which means group members contribute less than if they were working on their own. We might call such individuals "shirkers"—those who are contributing far less than other group members.

Most of us have experienced social loafing, or shirking, in groups. And we may even admit to times when we shirked ourselves. We discussed earlier in the chapter some ways of discouraging social loafing, such as limiting group size, holding individuals responsible for their contributions, and setting group goals. While these tactics may be effective, in our experience, many students simply work around shirkers. "We just did it ourselves—it was easier that way," says one group member.

Consider the following questions for dealing with shirking in groups:

1. If group members end up "working around" shirkers, do you think this information should be communicated to the instructor so that individual's contribution to the project is judged more fairly? If so, does the group have an ethical responsibility to communicate this to the shirking group member? If not, isn't the shirking group member unfairly reaping the rewards of a "free ride"?
2. Do you think confronting the shirking group member is justified? Does this depend on the skills of the shirker (whether he is capable of doing good-quality work)?
3. Social loafing has been found to be higher in Western, more individualist nations, than in other countries. Do you think this means we should tolerate shirking on the part of U.S. workers to a greater degree than if it occurred with someone from Asia?

Case Incident 1

"IF TWO HEADS ARE BETTER THAN ONE, ARE FOUR EVEN BETTER?"

Maggie Becker, 24, is a marketing manager for Kavu, a small chain of coffee shops in eastern Ohio. Recently, Maggie's wealthy uncle passed away and left to Maggie, his only niece, $100,000. Maggie considers her current salary to be adequate to meet her current living expenses, so she'd like to invest the money so that when she buys a house she'll have a nice nest egg on which to draw.

One of Maggie's neighbors, Brian, is a financial advisor. Brian told Maggie there was a virtually endless array of investment options. She asked him to present her with two of the best options, and this is what he came up with:

1. **A very low-risk AAA municipal bond fund.** With this option, based on the information Brian provided, Maggie estimates that after 5 years she stands virtually zero chance of losing money, with an expected gain of approximately $7,000.
2. **A moderate-risk mutual fund.** Based on the information Brian provided her, Maggie estimates that with this option she stands a 50 percent chance of making $40,000 but also a 50 percent chance of losing $20,000.

Maggie prides herself on being rational and objective in her thinking. However, she's unsure of what to do in this case. Brian refuses to help her, telling her that she's already limited herself by asking for only two options. While driving to her parents' house for the weekend, Maggie finds herself vacillating between the two options. Her older brother is also visiting the folks this weekend, so Maggie decides to gather her family around the table after dinner, lay out the two options, and go with their decision. "You know the old saying—two heads are better than one," she says to herself, "so four heads should be even better."

Questions

1. Has Maggie made a good decision about the way she is going to make the decision?
2. Which investment would you choose? Why?
3. Which investment do you think most people would choose?
4. Based on what you have learned about groupshift, which investment do you think Maggie's family will choose?

Case Incident 2

THE DANGERS OF GROUPTHINK

Sometimes, the desire to maintain group harmony overrides the importance of making sound decisions. When that occurs, team members are said to engage in groupthink. Here are some examples:

- A civilian worker at a large Air Force base recalls a time that groupthink overcame her team's decision-making ability. She was a member of a process improvement team that an Air Force general had formed to develop a better way to handle the base's mail, which included important letters from high-ranking military individuals. The team was composed mostly of civilians, and it took almost a month to come up with a plan. The problem: The plan was not a process improvement. Recalls the civilian worker, "I was horrified. What used to be 8 steps; now there were 19." The team had devised a new system that resulted in each piece of mail being read by several middle managers before reaching its intended recipient. The team's new plan slowed down the mail considerably, with an average delay of 2 weeks. Even though the team members all knew that the new system was worse than its predecessor, no one wanted to question the team's solidarity. The problems lasted for almost an entire year. It wasn't until the general who formed the team complained about the mail that the system was changed.

- During the dot-com boom of the late 1990s, Virginia Turezyn, managing director of Infinity Capital, states that she was a victim of groupthink. At first, Turezyn was skeptical about the stability of the boom. But after continually reading about start-ups turning into multimillion-dollar payoffs, she felt different. Turezyn decided to invest millions in several dot-coms, including I-drive, a company that provided electronic data storage. The problem was that I-drive was giving the storage away for free, and as a result, the company was losing money. Turezyn recalls one board meeting at I-drive where she spoke up to no avail. "We're spending way too much money," she screamed. The younger executives shook their heads and replied that if they charged for storage they would lose their customers. Says Turezyn, "I started to think, 'Maybe I'm just too old. Maybe I really don't get it.'" Unfortunately, Turezyn did get it. I-drive later filed for bankruptcy.
- Steve Blank, an entrepreneur, also fell victim to groupthink. Blank was a dot-com investor, and he participated on advisory boards of several Internet start-ups. During meetings for one such start-up, a Web photo finisher, Blank tried to persuade his fellow board members to change the business model to be more traditional. Recalls Blank, "I went to those meetings and started saying things like 'Maybe you should spend that $10 million you just raised on acquiring a customer base rather than building a brand.' The CEO told me, 'Steve, you just don't get it—all the rules have changed.'" The team didn't take Blank's advice, and Blank says that he lost hundreds of thousands of dollars on the deal.

According to Michael Useem, a professor at the University of Pennsylvania's Wharton College of Business, one of the main reasons that groupthink occurs is a lack of conflict. "A single devil's advocate or whistle-blower faces a really uphill struggle," he states. "But if you [the naysayer] have one ally that is enormously strengthening."

Questions

1. What are some factors that led to groupthink in the cases described here? What can teams do to attempt to prevent groupthink from occurring?
2. How might differences in status among group members contribute to groupthink? For example, how might lower-status members react to a group's decision? Are lower-status members more or less likely to be dissenters? Why might higher-status group members be more effective dissenters?
3. Microsoft CEO Steve Ballmer says that he encourages dissent. Can such norms guard against the occurrence of groupthink? As a manager, how would you try to cultivate norms that prevent groupthink?
4. How might group characteristics such as size and cohesiveness affect groupthink?

Source: Based on C. Hawn, "Fear and Posing," *Forbes,* March 25, 2002, pp. 22–25; and J. Sandberg, "Some Ideas Are So Bad That Only Team Efforts Can Account for Them," *Wall Street Journal,* September 29, 2004, p. B1.

Endnotes

1. J. Sandberg, "Brainstorming Works Best if People Scramble for Ideas on Their Own," *Wall Street Journal,* June 13, 2006, p. B1.
2. L. R. Sayles, "Work Group Behavior and the Larger Organization," in C. Arensburg, et al. (eds.), *Research in Industrial Relations* (New York: Harper & Row, 1957), pp. 131–145.
3. J. F. McGrew, J. G. Bilotta, and J. M. Deeney, "Software Team Formation and Decay: Extending the Standard Model for Small Groups," *Small Group Research* 30, no. 2, (1999), pp. 209–234.
4. B. W. Tuckman, "Developmental Sequences in Small Groups," *Psychological Bulletin,* June 1965, pp. 384–399; B. W. Tuckman and M. C. Jensen, "Stages of Small-Group Development Revisited," *Group and Organizational Studies,* December 1977, pp. 419–427; and M. F. Maples, "Group Development: Extending Tuckman's Theory," *Journal for Specialists in Group Work,* Fall 1988, pp. 17–23; and K. Vroman and J. Kovacich, "Computer-Mediated Interdisciplinary Teams: Theory and Reality," *Journal of Interprofessional Care* 16, no. 2 (2002), pp. 159–170.
5. J. F. George and L. M. Jessup, "Groups over Time: What Are We Really Studying?" *International Journal of Human-Computer Studies* 47, no. 3 (1997), pp. 497–511.
6. R. C. Ginnett, "The Airline Cockpit Crew," in J. R. Hackman (ed.), *Groups That Work (and Those That Don't)* (San Francisco: Jossey-Bass, 1990).
7. C. J. G. Gersick, "Time and Transition in Work Teams: Toward a New Model of Group Development," *Academy of Management Journal,* March 1988, pp. 9–41; C. J. G. Gersick, "Marking Time: Predictable Transitions in Task Groups," *Academy of Management Journal,* June 1989, pp. 274–309; M. J. Waller, J. M. Conte, C. B. Gibson, and M. A. Carpenter,

"The Effect of Individual Perceptions of Deadlines on Team Performance," *Academy of Management Review*, October 2001, pp. 586–600; and A. Chang, P. Bordia, and J. Duck, "Punctuated Equilibrium and Linear Progression: Toward a New Understanding of Group Development," *Academy of Management Journal*, February 2003, pp. 106–117; see also H. Arrow, M. S. Poole, K. B. Henry, S. Wheelan, and R. Moreland, "Time, Change, and Development: The Temporal Perspective on Groups," *Small Group Research*, February 2004, pp. 73–105.

8. Gersick, "Time and Transition in Work Teams;" and Gersick, "Marking Time."

9. A. Seers and S. Woodruff, "Temporal Pacing in Task Forces: Group Development or Deadline Pressure?" *Journal of Management* 23, no. 2 (1997), pp. 169–187.

10. S. Lieberman, "The Effects of Changes in Roles on the Attitudes of Role Occupants," *Human Relations*, November 1956, pp. 385–402.

11. See D. M. Rousseau, *Psychological Contracts in Organizations: Understanding Written and Unwritten Agreements* (Thousand Oaks, CA: Sage, 1995); E. W. Morrison and S. L. Robinson, "When Employees Feel Betrayed: A Model of How Psychological Contract Violation Develops," *Academy of Management Review*, April 1997, pp. 226–256; D. Rousseau and R. Schalk (eds.), *Psychological Contracts in Employment: Cross-Cultural Perspectives* (San Francisco: Jossey-Bass, 2000); L. Sels, M. Janssens, and I. Van den Brande, "Assessing the Nature of Psychological Contracts: A Validation of Six Dimensions," *Journal of Organizational Behavior*, June 2004, pp. 461–488; and C. Hui, C. Lee, and D. M. Rousseau, "Psychological Contract And Organizational Citizenship Behavior in China: Investigating Generalizability and Instrumentality," *Journal of Applied Psychology*, April 2004, pp. 311–321.

12. See M. F. Peterson et al., "Role Conflict, Ambiguity, and Overload: A 21-Nation Study," *Academy of Management Journal*, April 1995, pp. 429–452; and I. H. Settles, R. M. Sellers, and A. Damas, Jr., "One Role or Two? The Function of Psychological Separation in Role Conflict," *Journal of Applied Psychology*, June 2002, pp. 574–582.

13. P. G. Zimbardo, C. Haney, W. C. Banks, and D. Jaffe, "The Mind Is a Formidable Jailer: A Pirandellian Prison," *New York Times*, April 8, 1973, pp. 38–60; and C. Haney and P. G. Zimbardo, "Social Roles and Role-Playing: Observations from the Stanford Prison Study," *Behavioral and Social Science Teacher*, January 1973, pp. 25–45.

14. For a review of the research on group norms, see J. R. Hackman, "Group Influences on Individuals in Organizations," in M. D. Dunnette and L. M. Hough (eds.), *Handbook of Industrial & Organizational Psychology*, 2nd ed., vol. 3 (Palo Alto, CA: Consulting Psychologists Press, 1992), pp. 235–250. For a more recent discussion, see M. G. Ehrhart and S. E. Naumann, "Organizational Citizenship Behavior in Work Groups: A Group Norms Approach," *Journal of Applied Psychology*, December 2004, pp. 960–974.

15. Adapted from P. S. Goodman, E. Ravlin, and M. Schminke, "Understanding Groups in Organizations," in L. L. Cummings and B. M. Staw (eds.), *Research in Organizational Behavior*, vol. 9 (Greenwich, CT: JAI Press, 1987), p. 159.

16. E. Mayo, *The Human Problems of an Industrial Civilization* (New York: Macmillan, 1933); and F. J. Roethlisberger and W. J. Dickson, *Management and the Worker* (Cambridge, MA: Harvard University Press, 1939).

17. C. A. Kiesler and S. B. Kiesler, *Conformity* (Reading, MA: Addison-Wesley, 1969).

18. Ibid., p. 27.

19. S. E. Asch, "Effects of Group Pressure upon the Modification and Distortion of Judgments," in H. Guetzkow (ed.), *Groups, Leadership and Men* (Pittsburgh: Carnegie Press, 1951), pp. 177–190; and S. E. Asch, "Studies of Independence and Conformity: A Minority of One Against a Unanimous Majority," *Psychological Monographs: General and Applied* 70, no. 9 (1956), pp. 1–70.

20. R. Bond and P. B. Smith, "Culture and Conformity: A Meta-analysis of Studies Using Asch's (1952, 1956) Line Judgment Task," *Psychological Bulletin*, January 1996, pp. 111–137.

21. See S. L. Robinson and R. J. Bennett, "A Typology of Deviant Workplace Behaviors: A Multidimensional Scaling Study," *Academy of Management Journal*, April 1995, pp. 555–572; S. L. Robinson and A. M. O'Leary-Kelly, "Monkey See, Monkey Do: The Influence of Work Groups on the Antisocial Behavior of Employees," *Academy of Management Journal*, December 1998, pp. 658–672; and R. J. Bennett and S. L. Robinson, "The Past, Present, and Future of Workplace Deviance," in J. Greenberg (ed.), *Organizational Behavior: The State of the Science*, 2nd ed. (Mahwah, NJ: Erlbaum, 2003), pp. 237–271.

22. C. M. Pearson, L. M. Andersson, and C. L. Porath, "Assessing and Attacking Workplace Civility," *Organizational Dynamics* 29, no. 2 (2000), p. 130; see also C. Pearson, L. M. Andersson, and C. L. Porath, "Workplace Incivility," in S. Fox and P. E. Spector (eds.), *Counterproductive Work Behavior: Investigations of Actors and Targets* (Washington, DC American Psychological Association, 2005), pp. 177–200.

23. Robinson and O'Leary-Kelly, "Monkey See, Monkey Do."

24. A. Erez, H. Elms, and E. Fong, "Lying, Cheating, Stealing: It Happens More in Groups," paper presented at the European Business Ethics Network Annual Conference, Budapest, Hungary, August 30, 2003.

25. S. L. Robinson and M. S. Kraatz, "Constructing the Reality of Normative Behavior: The Use of Neutralization Strategies by Organizational Deviants," in R. W. Griffin and A. O'Leary-Kelly (eds.), *Dysfunctional Behavior in Organizations: Violent and Deviant Behavior* (Greenwich, CT: JAI Press, 1998), pp. 203–220.

26. See R. S. Feldman, *Social Psychology*, 3rd ed. (Upper Saddle River, NJ: Prentice Hall, 2001), pp. 464–465.

27. Cited in Hackman, "Group Influences on Individuals in Organizations," p. 236.

28. O. J. Harvey and C. Consalvi, "Status and Conformity to Pressures in Informal Groups," *Journal of Abnormal and Social Psychology*, Spring 1960, pp. 182–187.

29. J. A. Wiggins, F. Dill, and R. D. Schwartz, "On 'Status-Liability,'" *Sociometry*, April–May 1965, pp. 197–209.

30. See J. M. Levine and R. L. Moreland, "Progress in Small Group Research," in J. T. Spence, J. M. Darley, and D. J. Foss (eds.), *Annual Review of Psychology*, vol. 41 (Palo Alto, CA: Annual Reviews, 1990), pp. 585–634; S. D. Silver, B. P. Cohen, and J. H. Crutchfield, "Status Differentiation and Information Exchange in Face-to-Face and Computer-Mediated Idea Generation," *Social Psychology Quarterly*, 1994, pp. 108–123; and J. M. Twenge, "Changes in Women's Assertiveness in Response to Status and Roles: A Cross-Temporal Meta-analysis, 1931–1993," *Journal of Personality and Social Psychology*, July 2001, pp. 133–145.

31. J. Greenberg, "Equity and Workplace Status: A Field Experiment," *Journal of Applied Psychology*, November 1988, pp. 606–613.

32. E. J. Thomas and C. F. Fink, "Effects of Group Size," *Psychological Bulletin*, July 1963, pp. 371–384; A. P. Hare, *Handbook of Small Group Research* (New York: The Free Press, 1976); and M. E. Shaw, *Group Dynamics: The Psychology of Small Group Behavior*, 3rd ed. (New York: McGraw-Hill, 1981).

33. G. H. Seijts and G. P. Latham, "The Effects of Goal Setting and Group Size on Performance in a Social Dilemma," *Canadian Journal of Behavioural Science* 32, no. 2 (2000), pp. 104–116.

34. Shaw, *Group Dynamics: The Psychology of Small Group Behavior.*

35. See, for instance, D. R. Comer, "A Model of Social Loafing in Real Work Groups," *Human Relations*, June 1995, pp. 647–667; S. M. Murphy, S. J. Wayne, R. C. Liden, and B. Erdogan, "Understanding Social Loafing: The Role of Justice Perceptions and Exchange Relationships," *Human Relations*, January 2003, pp. 61–84; and R. C. Liden, S. J. Wayne, R. A. Jaworski, and N. Bennett, "Social Loafing: A Field Investigation," *Journal of Management*, April 2004, pp. 285–304.

36. W. Moede, "Die Richtlinien der Leistungs-Psychologie," *Industrielle Psychotechnik* 4 (1927), pp. 193–207. See also D. A. Kravitz and B. Martin, "Ringelmann Rediscovered: The Original Article," *Journal of Personality and Social Psychology*, May 1986, pp. 936–941.

37. See, for example, J. A. Shepperd, "Productivity Loss in Performance Groups: A Motivation Analysis," *Psychological Bulletin*, January 1993, pp. 67–81; and S. J. Karau and K. D. Williams, "Social Loafing: A Meta-analytic Review and Theoretical Integration," *Journal of Personality and Social Psychology*, October 1993, pp. 681–706.

38. S. G. Harkins and K. Szymanski, "Social Loafing and Group Evaluation," *Journal of Personality and Social Psychology*, December 1989, pp. 934–941.

39. A. Gunnthorsdottir and A. Rapoport, "Embedding Social Dilemmas in Intergroup Competition Reduces Free-Riding," *Organizational Behavior and Human Decision Processes* 101 (2006), pp. 184–199.

40. For some of the controversy surrounding the definition of cohesion, see J. Keyton and J. Springston, "Redefining Cohesiveness in Groups," *Small Group Research*, May 1990, pp. 234–254.

41. B. Mullen and C. Cooper, "The Relation Between Group Cohesiveness and Performance: An Integration," *Psychological Bulletin*, March 1994, pp. 210–227; P. M. Podsakoff, S. B. MacKenzie, and M. Ahearne, "Moderating Effects of Goal Acceptance on the Relationship Between Group Cohesiveness and Productivity," *Journal of Applied Psychology*, December 1997, pp. 974–983; and D. J. Beal, R. R. Cohen, M. J. Burke, and C. L. McLendon, "Cohesion and Performance in Groups: A Meta-analytic Clarification of Construct Relations," *Journal of Applied Psychology*, December 2003, pp. 989–1004.

42. Ibid.

43. Based on J. L. Gibson, J. M. Ivancevich, and J. H. Donnelly, Jr., *Organizations*, 8th ed. (Burr Ridge, IL: Irwin, 1994), p. 323.

44. N. Foote, E. Matson, L. Weiss, and E. Wenger, "Leveraging Group Knowledge for High-Performance Decision-Making," *Organizational Dynamics* 31, no. 2 (2002), pp. 280–295.

45. See N. R. F. Maier, "Assets and Liabilities in Group Problem Solving: The Need for an Integrative Function," *Psychological Review*, April 1967, pp. 239–249; G. W. Hill, "Group Versus Individual Performance: Are *N*+1 Heads Better Than One?" *Psychological Bulletin*, May 1982, pp. 517–539; A. E. Schwartz and J. Levin, "Better Group Decision Making," *Supervisory Management*, June 1990, p. 4; and R. F. Martell and M. R. Borg, "A Comparison of the Behavioral Rating Accuracy of Groups and Individuals," *Journal of Applied Psychology*, February 1993, pp. 43–50.

46. D. Gigone and R. Hastie, "Proper Analysis of the Accuracy of Group Judgments," *Psychological Bulletin*, January 1997, pp. 149–167; and B. L. Bonner, S. D. Sillito, and M. R. Baumann, "Collective Estimation: Accuracy, Expertise, and Extroversion as Sources of Intra-Group Influence," *Organizational Behavior and Human Decision Processes* 103 (2007), pp. 121–133.

47. See, for example, W. C. Swap and Associates, *Group Decision Making* (Newbury Park, CA: Sage, 1984).

48. D. D. Henningsen, M. G. Cruz, and M. L. Miller, "Role of Social Loafing in Predeliberation Decision Making," *Group Dynamics: Theory, Research, and Practice* 4, no. 2 (June 2000), pp. 168–175.

49. J. H. Davis, *Group Performance* (Reading, MA: Addison-Wesley, 1969); J. P. Wanous and M. A. Youtz, "Solution Diversity and the Quality of Group Decisions," *Academy of Management Journal*, March 1986, pp. 149–159; and R. Libby, K. T. Trotman, and I. Zimmer, "Member Variation, Recognition of Expertise, and Group Performance," *Journal of Applied Psychology*, February 1987, pp. 81–87.

50. I. L. Janis, *Groupthink* (Boston: Houghton Mifflin, 1982); W. Park, "A Review of Research on Groupthink," *Journal of Behavioral Decision Making*, July 1990, pp. 229–245; J. N. Choi and M. U. Kim, "The Organizational Application of Groupthink and Its Limits in Organizations," *Journal of Applied Psychology*, April 1999, pp. 297–306; and W. W. Park, "A Comprehensive Empirical Investigation of the Relationships Among Variables of the Groupthink Model," *Journal of Organizational Behavior*, December 2000, pp. 873–887.

51. Janis, *Groupthink.*

52. Ibid.

53. G. Moorhead, R. Ference, and C. P. Neck, "Group Decision Fiascos Continue: Space Shuttle Challenger and a Revised Groupthink Framework," *Human Relations*, May 1991, pp. 539–550; E. J. Chisson, *The Hubble Wars* (New York: HarperPerennial, 1994); and C. Covault, "*Columbia* Revelations Alarming E-Mails Speak for Themselves. But Administrator O'Keefe Is More Concerned About Board Findings on NASA Decision-Making," *Aviation Week & Space Technology*, March 3, 2003, p. 26.

54. J. Eaton, "Management Communication: The Threat of Groupthink," *Corporate Communication* 6, no. 4 (2001), pp. 183–192.

55. M. E. Turner and A. R. Pratkanis, "Mitigating Groupthink by Stimulating Constructive Conflict," in C. De Dreu and E. Van de Vliert (eds.), *Using Conflict in Organizations* (London: Sage, 1997), pp. 53–71.

56. Ibid., p. 68.

57. See N. R. F. Maier, *Principles of Human Relations* (New York: Wiley, 1952); I. L. Janis, *Groupthink: Psychological Studies of Policy Decisions and Fiascoes*, 2nd ed. (Boston: Houghton Mifflin, 1982); C. R. Leana, "A Partial Test of Janis' Groupthink Model: Effects of Group Cohesiveness and Leader Behavior on Defective Decision Making," *Journal of Management*, Spring 1985, pp. 5–17; and N. Richardson Ahlfinger and J. K. Esser, "Testing the Groupthink Model: Effects of Promotional Leadership and Conformity Predisposition," *Social Behavior & Personality* 29, no. 1 (2001), pp. 31–41.

58. See D. J. Isenberg, "Group Polarization: A Critical Review and Meta-Analysis," *Journal of Personality and Social Psychology*, December 1986, pp. 1141–1151; J. L. Hale and F. J. Boster, "Comparing Effect Coded Models of Choice Shifts," *Communication Research Reports*, April 1988, pp. 180–186; and P. W. Paese, M. Bieser, and M. E. Tubbs, "Framing Effects and Choice Shifts in Group Decision Making," *Organizational Behavior and Human Decision Processes*, October 1993, pp. 149–165.

59. See, for example, N. Kogan and M. A. Wallach, "Risk Taking as a Function of the Situation, the Person, and the Group," in *New Directions in Psychology*, vol. 3 (New York: Holt, Rinehart and Winston, 1967); and M. A. Wallach, N. Kogan, and D. J. Bem, "Group Influence on Individual Risk Taking," *Journal of Abnormal and Social Psychology* 65 (1962), pp. 75–86.

60. R. D. Clark III, "Group-Induced Shift Toward Risk: A Critical Appraisal," *Psychological Bulletin*, October 1971, pp. 251–270.

61. A. F. Osborn, *Applied Imagination: Principles and Procedures of Creative Thinking*, 3rd ed. (New York: Scribner, 1963). See also T. Rickards, "Brainstorming Revisited: A Question of Context," *International Journal of Management Reviews*, March 1999, pp. 91–110; and R. P. McGlynn, D. McGurk, V. S. Effland, N. L. Johll, and D. J. Harding, "Brainstorming and Task Performance in Groups Constrained by Evidence," *Organizational Behavior and Human Decision Processes*, January 2004, pp. 75–87.

62. N. L. Kerr and R. S. Tindale, "Group Performance and Decision-Making," *Annual Review of Psychology* 55 (2004), pp. 623–655.

63. See A. L. Delbecq, A. H. Van deVen, and D. H. Gustafson, *Group Techniques for Program Planning: A Guide to Nominal and Delphi Processes* (Glenview, IL: Scott, Foresman, 1975); and P. B. Paulus and H.-C. Yang, "Idea Generation in Groups: A Basis for Creativity in Organizations," *Organizational Behavior and Human Decision Processing*, May 2000, pp. 76–87.

64. C. Faure, "Beyond Brainstorming: Effects of Different Group Procedures on Selection of Ideas and Satisfaction with the Process," *Journal of Creative Behavior* 38 (2004), pp. 13–34.

65. See, for instance, A. B. Hollingshead and J. E. McGrath, "Computer-Assisted Groups: A Critical Review of the Empirical Research," in R. A. Guzzo and E. Salas (eds.), *Team Effectiveness and Decision Making in Organizations* (San Francisco: Jossey-Bass, 1995), pp. 46–78.

66. B. B. Baltes, M. W. Dickson, M. P. Sherman, C. C. Bauer, and J. LaGanke, "Computer-Mediated Communication and Group Decision Making: A Meta-Analysis," *Organizational Behavior and Human Decision Processes*, January 2002, pp. 156–179.

67. See G. Hofstede, *Cultures and Organizations: Software of the Mind* (New York, McGraw-Hill, 1991).

68. This section is based on P. R. Harris and R. T. Moran, *Managing Cultural Differences*, 5th ed. (Houston: Gulf Publishing, 1999).

69. D. S. Staples and L. Zhao, "The Effects of Cultural Diversity in Virtual Teams Versus Face-to-Face Teams," *Group Decision and Negotiation*, July 2006, pp. 389–406.

70. K. W. Phillips and D. L. Loyd, "When Surface and Deep-Level Diversity Collide: The Effects on Dissenting Group Members," *Organizational Behavior and Human Decision Processes* 99 (2006), pp. 143–160; and S. R. Sommers, "On Racial Diversity and Group Decision Making: Identifying Multiple Effects of Racial Composition on Jury Deliberations," *Journal of Personality and Social Psychology*, April 2006, pp. 597–612.

71. E. Mannix and M. A. Neale, "What Differences Make a Difference? The Promise and Reality of Diverse Teams in Organizations," *Psychological Science in the Public Interest*, October 2005, pp. 31–55.

72. T. P. Verney, "Role Perception Congruence, Performance, and Satisfaction," in D. J. Vredenburgh and R. S. Schuler (eds.), *Effective Management: Research and Application*, Proceedings of the 20th Annual Eastern Academy of Management, Pittsburgh, PA, May 1983, pp. 24–27.

73. Ibid.

74. A. G. Bedeian and A. A. Armenakis, "A Path-Analytic Study of the Consequences of Role Conflict and Ambiguity," *Academy of Management Journal*, June 1981, pp. 417–424; and P. L. Perrewe, K. L. Zellars, G. R. Ferris, A. M. Rossi, C. J. Kacmar, and D. A. Ralston, "Neutralizing Job Stressors: Political Skill as an Antidote to the Dysfunctional Consequences of Role Conflict," *Academy of Management Journal*, February 2004, pp. 141–152.

75. Shaw, *Group Dynamics*.

76. B. Mullen, C. Symons, L. Hu, and E. Salas, "Group Size, Leadership Behavior, and Subordinate Satisfaction," *Journal of General Psychology*, April 1989, pp. 155–170.

Understanding Work Teams

We're going to turn this team around 360 degrees.

—professional basketball player Jason Kidd

LEARNING OBJECTIVES

After studying this chapter, you should be able to:

1 Analyze the growing popularity of using teams in organizations.

2 Contrast groups and teams.

3 Compare and contrast four types of teams.

4 Identify the characteristics of effective teams.

5 Show how organizations can create team players.

6 Decide when to use individuals instead of teams.

7 Show how the understanding of teams differs in a global context.

In the competitive search for top talent, it is not unusual for top employees to be hired away from successful companies. Google, for example, has seen a lot of companies hire away its people.

A new wrinkle in the talent wars is hiring away an entire team. Take Mark Metz, the CEO of Optimus Solutions, a computer systems and services company. When Metz founded Optimus, he brought on board 7 of his former colleagues to help start the company. Even though he was sued for hiring them

Poaching the Whole Team

away, he wasn't deterred. In 2001, he recruited another team of 10. In 2005, he topped that, hiring away a manager's entire 30-person team. Experience matters in the IT area, and Metz believes he was able to gain valuable experience quickly without having to develop it over time. "You get the dynamics of a functioning team without having to create that yourself," he said.

Although some have accused Metz of raiding, executive recruiters see such "lift-outs" as a growing trend. Although the practice has been around in industries such as financial services and law, it's becoming increasingly common in other sectors, such as IT, management consulting, medical services, and accounting.

"We've even seen it happen between recruiters, which is its own irony," says one expert.

One factor explaining the rise in lift-outs, as Metz recognized, is speed. When organizations need to enter a competitive market as soon as possible, they don't have time to spend months hiring and then training team members. Hiring an entire team may be the quickest way to enter a new market or launch a product or service.

Another factor is private equity buyouts. Private equity firms seek to turn around a company quickly so that, in most cases, they can resell it for a profit (like "flipping" in real estate). Time is money, and poaching whole teams can reduce the time necessary to return the company to profitability.

Hiring away whole teams does have disadvantages. One is legality: Most companies have noncompete clauses in place, and some lift-outs run the risk of drawing a lawsuit from the company whose team was poached. Another challenge is that the team may act like a team and use its cohesion against the new employer. Metz found that after he recruited one of his teams to Optimus, the team started to negotiate en masse for better benefits. "You think you're just hiring many people," Metz said, "But they turn into mini acquisitions."[1] ■

Teams are increasingly becoming the primary means for organizing work in contemporary business firms. In fact, this trend is so widespread that companies such as Optimus are hiring whole teams. What do you think of your skills in leading and building a team? Take the following self-assessment to find out.

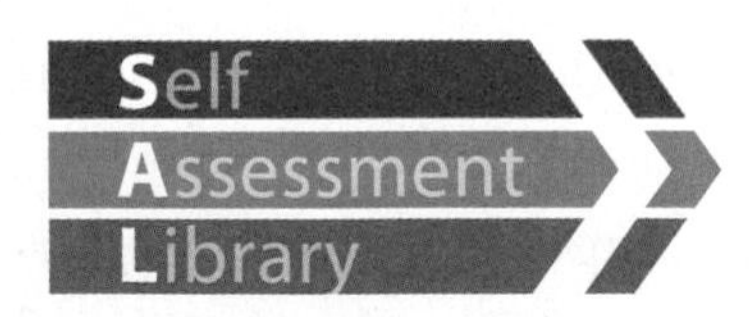

HOW GOOD AM I AT BUILDING AND LEADING A TEAM?

In the Self-Assessment Library (available on CD or online), take assessment II.B.6 (How Good Am I at Building and Leading a Team?) and answer the following questions.

1. *Did you score as high as you thought you would? Why or why not?*
2. *Do you think you can improve your score? If so, how? If not, why not?*
3. *Do you think there is such a thing as team players? If yes, what are their behaviors?*

Why Have Teams Become So Popular?

1 Analyze the growing popularity of using teams in organizations.

Decades ago, when companies such as W. L. Gore, Volvo, and General Foods introduced teams into their production processes, it made news because no one else was doing it. Today, it's just the opposite. It's the organization that *doesn't* use teams that has become newsworthy. Teams are everywhere.

How do we explain the current popularity of teams? As organizations have restructured themselves to compete more effectively and efficiently, they have turned to teams as a better way to use employee talents. Management has found that teams are more flexible and responsive to changing events than are traditional departments or other forms of permanent groupings. Teams have the capability to quickly assemble, deploy, refocus, and disband. But don't overlook the motivational properties of teams. Consistent with our discussion in Chapter 7 of the role of employee involvement as a motivator, teams facilitate employee participation in operating decisions. So another explanation for the popularity of teams is that they are an effective means for management to democratize their organizations and increase employee motivation.

The fact that organizations have turned to teams doesn't necessarily mean they're always effective. Decision makers, as humans, can be swayed by fads and herd mentality. Are teams truly effective? What conditions affect their potential? How do teams work together? These are some of the questions we'll answer in this chapter.

Differences Between Groups and Teams

2 *Contrast groups and teams.*

Groups and teams are not the same thing. In this section, we define and clarify the difference between work groups and work teams.[2]

In Chapter 9, we defined a *group* as two or more individuals, interacting and interdependent, who have come together to achieve particular objectives. A **work group** is a group that interacts primarily to share information and to make decisions to help each member perform within his or her area of responsibility.

Work groups have no need or opportunity to engage in collective work that requires joint effort. So their performance is merely the summation of each group member's individual contribution. There is no positive synergy that would create an overall level of performance that is greater than the sum of the inputs.

A **work team** generates positive synergy through coordinated effort. The individual efforts result in a level of performance that is greater than the sum of those individual inputs. Exhibit 10-1 highlights the differences between work groups and work teams.

These definitions help clarify why so many organizations have recently restructured work processes around teams. Management is looking for positive synergy that will allow the organizations to increase performance. The extensive use of teams creates the *potential* for an organization to generate greater outputs with no increase in inputs. Notice, however, that we said *potential*. There is nothing inherently magical in the creation of teams that ensures the achievement of positive synergy. Merely calling a *group* a *team* doesn't automatically increase its performance. As we show later in this chapter, effective teams have certain common characteristics. If management hopes to gain increases in organizational performance through the use of teams, it needs to ensure that its teams possess these characteristics.

work group *A group that interacts primarily to share information and to make decisions to help each group member perform within his or her area of responsibility.*

work team *A group whose individual efforts result in performance that is greater than the sum of the individual inputs.*

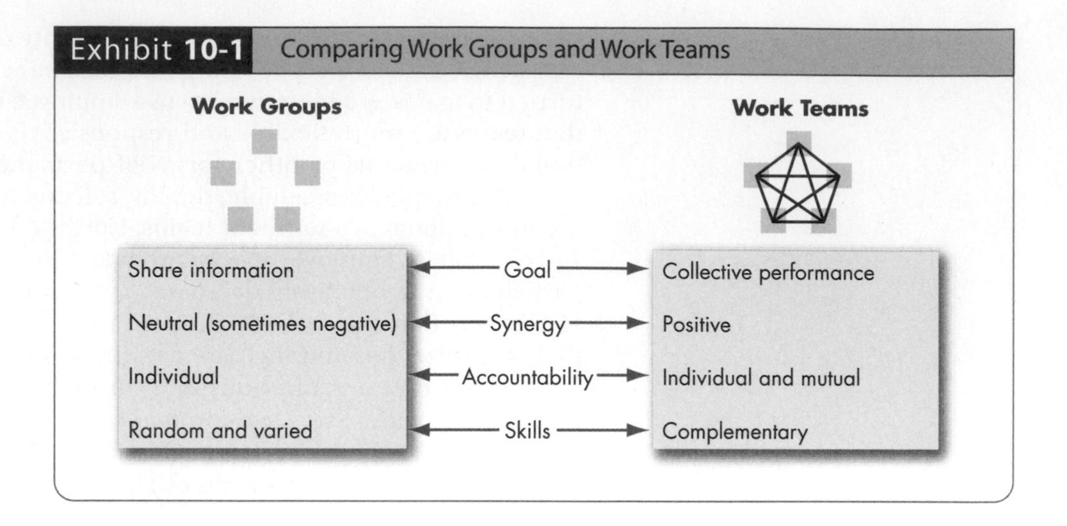

Types of Teams

3 *Compare and contrast four types of teams.*

Teams can do a variety of things. They can make products, provide services, negotiate deals, coordinate projects, offer advice, and make decisions.[3] In this section, we'll describe the four most common types of teams you're likely to find in an organization: *problem-solving teams, self-managed work teams, cross-functional teams,* and *virtual teams* (see Exhibit 10-2).

Problem-Solving Teams

Twenty years ago or so, teams were just beginning to grow in popularity, and most of those teams took similar form. They were typically composed of 5 to 12 hourly employees from the same department who met for a few hours each week to discuss ways of improving quality, efficiency, and the work environment.[4] We call these **problem-solving teams.**

In problem-solving teams, members share ideas or offer suggestions on how work processes and methods can be improved; they rarely have the authority to unilaterally implement any of their suggested actions. For instance, Merrill Lynch created a problem-solving team to specifically figure out ways to reduce the number of days it took to open up a new cash management account.[5] By suggesting cuts in the number of steps in the process from 46 to 36, the team was able to reduce the average number of days from 15 to 8.

Self-Managed Work Teams

Although problem-solving teams involve employees in decisions, they "only" make recommendations. Some organizations have gone further and created teams that can not only solve problems but implement solutions and take responsibility for outcomes.

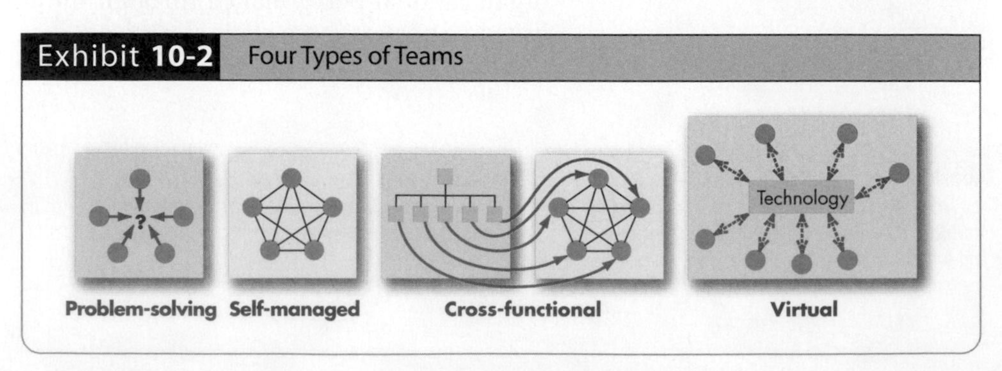

At the Louis Vuitton factory in Ducey, France, all employees work in problem-solving teams, with each team focusing on one product at a time. Team members are encouraged to suggest improvements in manufacturing work methods and processes as well as product quality. When a team was asked to make a test run on a prototype of a new handbag, team members discovered that decorative studs were causing the bag's zipper to bunch up. The team alerted managers, who had technicians move the studs away from the zipper, which solved the problem.

Self-managed work teams are groups of employees (typically 10 to 15 in number) who perform highly related or interdependent jobs and take on many of the responsibilities of their former supervisors.[6] Typically, these tasks are involved in planning and scheduling work, assigning tasks to members, making operating decisions, taking action on problems, and working with suppliers and customers. Fully self-managed work teams even select their own members and have the members evaluate each other's performance. As a result, supervisory positions take on decreased importance and may even be eliminated.

Business periodicals have been chock-full of articles describing successful applications of self-managed teams. But a word of caution needs to be offered: The overall research on the effectiveness of self-managed work teams has not been uniformly positive.[7] Moreover, although individuals on these teams do tend to report higher levels of job satisfaction compared to other individuals, they also sometimes have higher absenteeism and turnover rates. Inconsistency in findings suggests that the effectiveness of self-managed teams depends on the strength and make-up of team norms, the type of tasks the team undertakes, and the reward structure the team operates under—each of which can significantly influence how well the team performs.

Cross-Functional Teams

The Boeing Company created a team made up of employees from production, planning, quality, tooling, design engineering, and information systems to automate shims on the company's C-17 program. The team's suggestions

problem-solving teams *Groups of 5 to 12 employees from the same department who meet for a few hours each week to discuss ways of improving quality, efficiency, and the work environment.*

self-managed work teams *Groups of 10 to 15 people who take on responsibilities of their former supervisors.*

resulted in drastically reduced cycle time and cost as well as improved quality on the C-17 program.[8]

This Boeing example illustrates the use of **cross-functional teams**. These are teams made up of employees from about the same hierarchical level but from different work areas, who come together to accomplish a task.

Many organizations have used horizontal, boundary-spanning groups for decades. For example, IBM created a large task force in the 1960s—made up of employees from across departments in the company—to develop its highly successful System 360. But today cross-functional teams are so widely used that it is hard to imagine a major organizational initiative without one. For instance, all the major automobile manufacturers—including Toyota, Honda, Nissan, BMW, GM, Ford, and Chrysler—currently use this form of team to coordinate complex projects. And Harley-Davidson relies on specific cross-functional teams to manage each line of its motorcycles. These teams include Harley employees from design, manufacturing, and purchasing as well as representatives from key outside suppliers.[9]

Cross-functional teams are an effective means for allowing people from diverse areas within an organization (or even between organizations) to exchange information, develop new ideas and solve problems, and coordinate complex projects. Of course, cross-functional teams are no picnic to manage. Their early stages of development are often very time-consuming, as members learn to work with diversity and complexity. It takes time to build trust and teamwork, especially among people from different backgrounds with different experiences and perspectives.

Virtual Teams

The previously described types of teams do their work face-to-face. **Virtual teams** use computer technology to tie together physically dispersed members in order to achieve a common goal.[10] They allow people to collaborate online—using communication links such as wide-area networks, video conferencing, or e-mail—whether they're only a room away or continents apart. Virtual teams are so pervasive, and technology has advanced so far, that it's probably a bit of a misnomer to call these teams "virtual." Nearly all teams today do at least some of their work remotely.

Despite their ubiquity, virtual teams face special challenges. They may suffer because there is less social rapport and less direct interaction among members. They aren't able to duplicate the normal give-and-take of face-to-face discussion. Especially when members haven't personally met, virtual teams tend to be more task oriented and exchange less social–emotional information than face-to-face teams. Not surprisingly, virtual team members report less satisfaction with the group interaction process than do face-to-face teams. For virtual teams to be effective, management should ensure that (1) trust is established among team members (research has shown that one inflammatory remark in a team member e-mail can severely undermine team trust); (2) team progress is monitored closely (so the team doesn't lose sight of its goals and no team member "disappears"); and (3) the efforts and products of the virtual team are publicized throughout the organization (so the team does not become invisible).[11]

Creating Effective Teams

Many have tried to identify factors related to team effectiveness.[12] However, recent studies have organized what was once a "veritable laundry list of characteristics"[13] into a relatively focused model.[14] Exhibit 10-3 summarizes what we currently know

International OB

Global Virtual Teams

Years ago, before the vast working public ever dreamed of e-mail, instant messaging, or live video conferencing, work teams used to be in the same locations, with possibly one or two members a train or plane ride away. Today, however, the reach of corporations spans many countries, so the need for teams to work together across international lines has increased. To deal with this challenge, multinationals use global virtual teams to gain a competitive advantage.

Global virtual teams have advantages and disadvantages. On the positive side, because team members come from different countries with different knowledge and points of view, they may develop creative ideas and solutions to problems that work for multiple cultures. On the negative side, global virtual teams face more challenges than traditional teams that meet face-to-face. For one thing, miscommunication can lead to misunderstandings, which can create stress and conflict among team members. Also, members who do not accept individuals from different cultures may hesitate to share information openly, which can create problems of trust.

To create and implement effective global virtual teams, managers must carefully select employees whom they believe will thrive in such an environment. Employees must be comfortable with communicating electronically with others, and they must be open to different ideas. When dealing with team members in other countries, speaking multiple languages may also be necessary. Team members also must realize that the values they hold may be vastly different from their teammates' values. For instance, an individual from a country that values relationships and sensitivity, such as Sweden, might face a challenge when interacting with someone from Spain, which values assertiveness and competitiveness.

Although global virtual teams face many challenges, companies that implement them effectively can realize tremendous rewards through the diverse knowledge they gain.

Source: Based on N. Zakaria, A. Amelinckx, and D. Wilemon, "Working Together Apart? Building a Knowledge-Sharing Culture for Global Virtual Teams," *Creativity and Innovation Management*, March 2004, pp. 15–29.

4 *Identify the characteristics of effective teams.*

about what makes teams effective. As you'll see, it builds on many of the group concepts introduced in Chapter 9.

The following discussion is based on the model in Exhibit 10-3. Keep in mind two caveats before we proceed. First, teams differ in form and structure. Because the model we present attempts to generalize across all varieties of teams, you need to be careful not to rigidly apply the model's predictions to all teams.[15] You should use the model as a guide. Second, the model assumes that it's already been determined that teamwork is preferable to individual work. Creating "effective" teams in situations in which individuals can do the job better is equivalent to solving the wrong problem perfectly.

The key components of effective teams can be subsumed into four general categories. First are the resources and other *contextual* influences that make teams effective. The second relates to the team's *composition.* The third category is *work design.* Finally, *process* variables reflect those things that go on in the team that influences effectiveness. What does *team effectiveness* mean in this model? Typically, it has included objective measures of the team's productivity, managers' ratings of the team's performance, and aggregate measures of member satisfaction.

cross-functional teams *Employees from about the same hierarchical level, but from different work areas, who come together to accomplish a task.*

virtual teams *Teams that use computer technology to tie together physically dispersed members in order to achieve a common goal.*

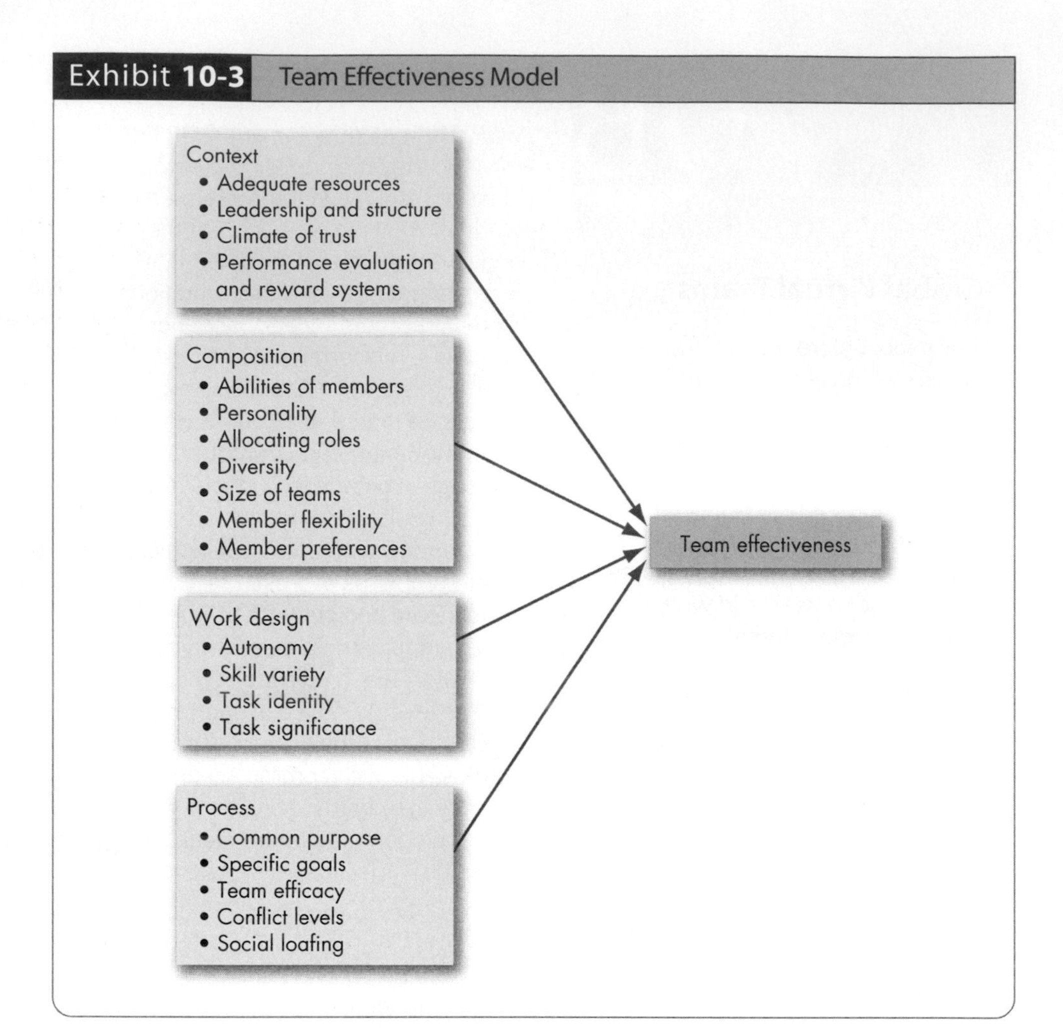

Context: What Factors Determine Whether Teams Are Successful

The four contextual factors that appear to be most significantly related to team performance are the presence of adequate resources, effective leadership, a climate of trust, and a performance evaluation and reward system that reflects team contributions.

Adequate Resources Teams are part of a larger organization system. As such, every work team relies on resources outside the group to sustain it. A scarcity of resources directly reduces the ability of a team to perform its job effectively. As one set of researchers concluded, after looking at 13 factors potentially related to group performance, "perhaps one of the most important characteristics of an effective work group is the support the group receives from the organization."[16] This support includes timely information, proper equipment, adequate staffing, encouragement, and administrative assistance. Teams must receive the necessary support from management and the larger organization if they are to succeed in achieving their goals.

Leadership and Structure Teams can't function if they can't agree on who is to do what and ensure that all members contribute equally in sharing the work load. Agreeing on the specifics of work and how they fit together to integrate individual skills requires team leadership and structure. This can be provided directly by management or by the team members themselves. Although you might think there is no role for leaders in self-managed teams, that couldn't be further from the truth. It is true that, in self-managed teams, team members absorb many of the duties typically assumed by managers. However, a manager's job becomes managing *outside* (rather than inside) the team.

Leadership is especially important in **multi-team systems**—where different teams need to coordinate their efforts to produce a desired outcome. In such systems, leaders need to empower teams by delegating responsibility to them, and they need to play the role of facilitator, making sure the teams are coordinating their efforts so that they work together rather than against one another.[17]

Climate of Trust Members of effective teams trust each other. And they also exhibit trust in their leaders.[18] Interpersonal trust among team members facilitates cooperation, reduces the need to monitor each others' behavior, and bonds members around the belief that others on the team won't take advantage of them. Team members, for instance, are more likely to take risks and expose vulnerabilities when they believe they can trust others on their team. Similarly, as discussed in Chapter 13, trust is the foundation of leadership. Trust in leadership is important in that it allows a team to be willing to accept and commit to its leader's goals and decisions.

Performance Evaluation and Reward Systems How do you get team members to be both individually and jointly accountable? The traditional, individually oriented evaluation and reward system must be modified to reflect team performance.[19] Individual performance evaluations and incentives may interfere with the development of high-performance teams. So in addition to evaluating and rewarding employees for their individual contributions, management should consider group-based appraisals, profit-sharing, gainsharing, small-group incentives, and other system modifications that reinforce team effort and commitment.

Surgical Teams Lack Teamwork

Surgery is almost always performed by a team, but in many cases, it's a team in name only. So says a new study of more than 2,100 surgeons, anesthesiologists, and nurses.

When the researchers surveyed these surgery team members, they asked them to "describe the quality of communication and collaboration you have experienced" with other members of the surgical unit. Perhaps not surprisingly, surgeons were given the lowest ratings for teamwork and nurses the highest ratings. "The study is somewhat humbling to me," said Martin Makary, the lead author on the study and a surgeon at the U.S. hospital Johns Hopkins. "There's a lot of pride in the surgical community. We need to balance out the captain-of-the-ship doctrine."

The researchers attribute many operating room errors, such as sponges left in patients and operations performed on the wrong part of the body, to poor teamwork. But improving the system is easier said than done. One recent study in Pennsylvania found that, over an 18-month period, there were 174 cases of surgeons operating on the wrong limb or body part. For its part, Johns Hopkins is modeling surgical team training after airline crew training. "Teamwork is an important component of patient safety," says Makary.

Sources: E. Nagourney, "Surgical Teams Found Lacking, in Teamwork," *New York Times*, May 9, 2006, p. D6; and "Nurses Give Surgeons Poor Grades on Teamwork in OR," *Forbes*, May 5, 2006.

multi-team systems *Systems in which different teams need to coordinate their efforts to produce a desired outcome.*

Team Composition

The team composition category includes variables that relate to how teams should be staffed. In this section, we address the ability and personality of team members, allocation of roles and diversity, size of the team, and members' preference for teamwork.

Abilities of Members Part of a team's performance depends on the knowledge, skills, and abilities of its individual members.[20] It's true that we occasionally read about an athletic team composed of mediocre players who, because of excellent coaching, determination, and precision teamwork, beats a far more talented group of players. But such cases make the news precisely because they represent an aberration. As the old saying goes, "The race doesn't always go to the swiftest nor the battle to the strongest, but that's the way to bet." A team's performance is not merely the summation of its individual members' abilities. However, these abilities set parameters for what members can do and how effectively they will perform on a team.

To perform effectively, a team requires three different types of skills. First, it needs people who have *technical expertise*. Second, it needs people who have the *problem-solving and decision-making skills* to be able to identify problems, generate alternatives, evaluate those alternatives, and make competent choices. Finally, teams need people who have good listening, feedback, conflict resolution, and other *interpersonal skills*.[21] No team can achieve its performance potential without developing all three types of skills. The right mix is crucial. Too much of one at the expense of others will result in lower team performance. But teams don't need to have all the complementary skills in place at their beginning. It's not uncommon for one or more members to take responsibility for learning the skills in which the group is deficient, thereby allowing the team to reach its full potential.

Research on the abilities of team members has revealed some interesting insights into team composition and performance. First, when the task entails considerable thought (for example, solving a complex problem such as reengineering an assembly line), high-ability teams (that is, teams composed of mostly

Senior product scientists Syed Abbas and Albert Post and technology team manager Laurie Coyle functioned as a high-ability team in developing Unilever's new Dove Nutrium bar soap. In solving the complex problems involved in product innovation, the intelligent members of Unilever's research and development teams have advanced science degrees, the ability to think creatively, and the interpersonal skills needed to perform effectively with other team members.
Source: Ruth Fremson/The New York Times

intelligent members) do better than lower-ability teams, especially when the work load is distributed evenly. (That way, team performance does not depend on the weakest link.) High-ability teams are also more adaptable to changing situations in that they can more effectively adapt prior knowledge to suit a set of new problems.

Second, although high-ability teams generally have an advantage over lower-ability teams, this is not always the case. For example, when tasks are simple (for example, tasks that individual team members might be able to solve on their own), high-ability teams do not perform as well, perhaps because, in such tasks, high-ability teams become bored and turn their attention to other activities that are more stimulating, whereas low-ability teams stay on task. High-ability teams should be "saved" for tackling the tough problems. So matching team ability to the task is important.

Finally, the ability of the team's leader also matters. Research shows that smart team leaders help less intelligent team members when they struggle with a task. But a less intelligent leader can neutralize the effect of a high ability team.[22]

Personality of Members We demonstrated in Chapter 4 that personality has a significant influence on individual employee behavior. This can also be extended to team behavior. Many of the dimensions identified in the Big Five personality model have been shown to be relevant to team effectiveness. A recent review of the literature suggested that three of the Big Five traits were especially important for team performance.[23] Specifically, teams that rate higher on mean levels of conscientiousness and openness to experience tend to perform better. Moreover, the minimum level of team member agreeableness also matters: Teams did worse when they had one or more highly disagreeable members. Perhaps one bad apple *can* spoil the whole bunch!

Research has also provided us with a good idea about why these personality traits are important to teams. Conscientious people are valuable in teams because they're good at backing up other team members, and they're also good at sensing when that support is truly needed. Open team members communicate better with one another and throw out more ideas, which leads teams composed of open people to be more creative and innovative.[24]

Even if an organization does a really good job of selecting individuals for team roles, most likely they'll find there aren't enough, say, conscientious people to go around. Suppose an organization needs to create 20 teams of 4 people each and has 40 highly conscientious people and 40 who score low on conscientiousness. Would the organization be better off (A) putting all the conscientious people together (forming 10 teams with the highly conscientious people and 10 teams of members low on conscientiousness) or (B) "seeding" each team with 2 people who scored high and 2 who scored low on conscientiousness?

Perhaps surprisingly, the evidence tends to suggest that option A is the best choice; performance across the teams will be higher if the organization forms 10 highly conscientious teams and 10 teams low in conscientiousness. "This may be because, in such teams, members who are highly conscientious not only must perform their own tasks but also must perform or re-do the tasks of low-conscientious members. It may also be because such diversity leads to feelings of contribution inequity."[25]

Allocation of Roles Teams have different needs, and people should be selected for a team to ensure that all the various roles are filled.

We can identify nine potential team roles (see Exhibit 10-4). Successful work teams have people to fill all these roles and have selected people to play these roles based on their skills and preferences.[26] (On many teams, individuals will play multiple roles.) Managers need to understand the individual strengths that

Exhibit 10-4 Key Roles of Teams

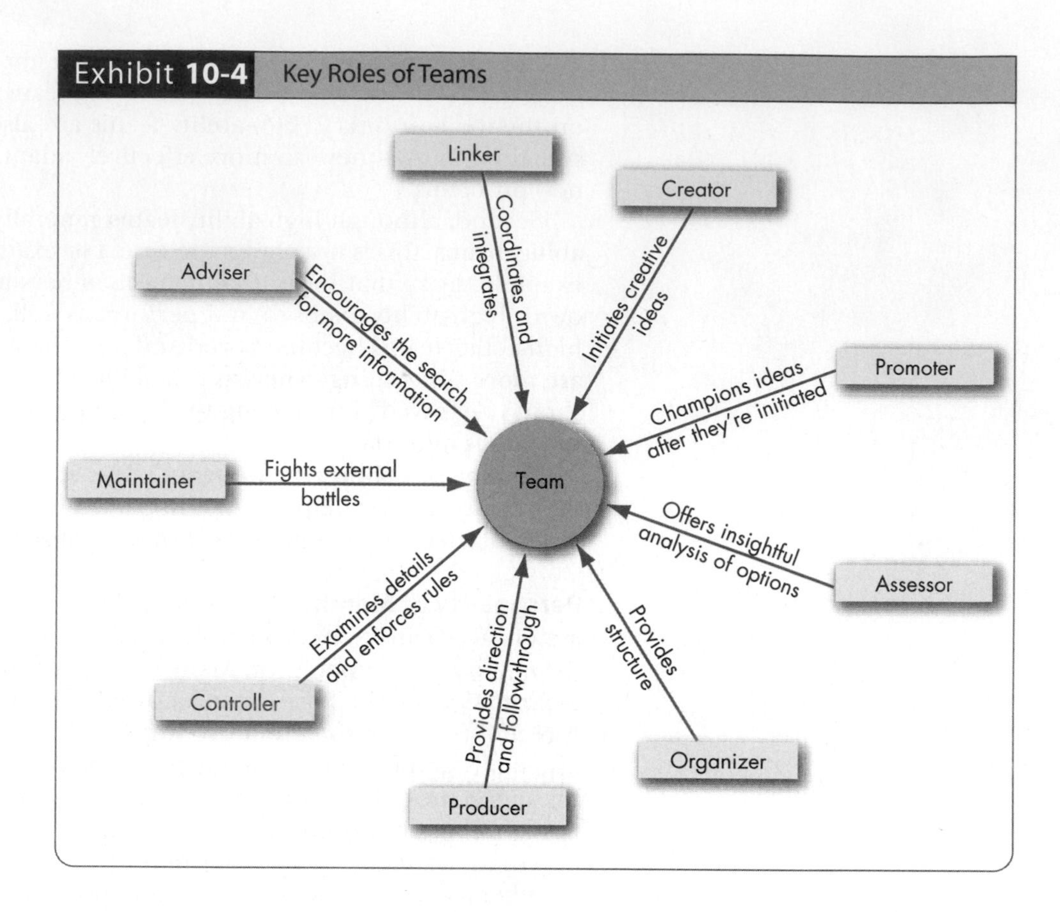

each person can bring to a team, select members with their strengths in mind, and allocate work assignments that fit with members' preferred styles. By matching individual preferences with team role demands, managers increase the likelihood that the team members will work well together.

Diversity of Members In Chapter 9, we discussed research on the effect of diversity on groups. How does *team* diversity affect *team* performance?

Many of us hold the optimistic view that diversity should be a good thing—diverse teams should benefit from differing perspectives and do better. Unfortunately, the evidence appears to favor the pessimists. One review concluded, "Studies on diversity in teams from the last 50 years have shown that surface-level social-category differences such as race/ethnicity, gender, and age tend to... have negative effects" on the performance of teams.[27] As in the literature on groups, there is some evidence that the disruptive effects of diversity decline over time, but unlike in the groups literature, there is less evidence that diverse teams perform better eventually.

One of the pervasive problems with teams is that while diversity may have real potential benefits, a team is deeply focused on commonly held information. But if diverse teams are to realize their creative potential, they need to focus not on their similarities but on their differences. There is some evidence, for example, that when team members believe others have more expertise, they will work to support those members, leading to higher levels of effectiveness.[28] The key is for diverse teams to communicate what they uniquely know and also what they don't know.

An offshoot of the diversity issue has received a great deal of attention from group and team researchers. This is the degree to which members of a work unit (group, team, or department) share a common demographic

Many team members share the common demographic of age at Yahoo!, where more than half of employees are age 34 or younger. Young team members of Yahoo!'s oneSearch team shown here, grew up during the information revolution, are well educated, and are results driven. The sharing of these attributes should result in better communication among team members, low turnover, and few power struggles.

Source: Jim Wilson/ The New York Times

attribute, such as age, sex, race, educational level, or length of service in the organization, and the impact of that attribute on turnover. We call this variable **organizational demography**. Organizational demography suggests that attributes such as age or the date that someone joins a specific work team or organization should help us to predict turnover. Essentially, the logic goes like this: Turnover will be greater among those with dissimilar experiences because communication is more difficult. Conflict and power struggles are more likely, and they are more severe when they occur. The increased conflict makes unit membership less attractive, so employees are more likely to quit. Similarly, the losers in a power struggle are more apt to leave voluntarily or to be forced out.[29]

Size of Teams The president of AOL Technologies says the secret to a great team is to "think small. Ideally, your team should have seven to nine people."[30] His advice is supported by evidence.[31] Generally speaking, the most effective teams have five to nine members. And experts suggest using the smallest number of people who can do the task. Unfortunately, there is a pervasive tendency for managers to err on the side of making teams too large. While a minimum of four or five may be necessary to develop diversity of views and skills, managers seem to seriously underestimate how coordination problems can exponentially increase as team members are added. When teams have excess members, cohesiveness and mutual accountability decline, social loafing increases, and more and more people do less talking relative to others. Moreover, large teams have trouble coordinating with one another, especially when under time pressure.

organizational demography *The degree to which members of a work unit share a common demographic attribute, such as age, sex, race, educational level, or length of service in an organization, and the impact of this attribute on turnover.*

MYTH OR SCIENCE? *"Old Teams Can't Learn New Tricks"*

This statement is true for some types of teams and false for others. Let's look at why.

To study this question, researchers at Michigan State University composed 80 four-person teams from undergraduate business students. The teams engaged in a networked computer simulation that was developed for the U.S. Department of Defense. In the simulation, teams played a command-and-control simulation in which each team member sat at a networked computer connected to his or her other team members' computers. The team's mission was to monitor a geographic area, keep unfriendly forces from moving in, and support friendly forces. Performance was measured by both speed (how quickly they identified targets and friendly forces) and accuracy (the number of friendly fire errors and missed opportunities).

Teams were rewarded either cooperatively (in which case team members shared rewards equally) or competitively (in which case team members were rewarded based on their individual contributions). After playing a few rounds, the reward structures were switched so that the cooperatively rewarded teams were switched to competitive rewards and the competitively rewarded teams were now cooperatively rewarded.

The researchers found that the initially cooperatively rewarded teams easily adapted to the competitive reward conditions and learned to excel. However, the formerly competitively rewarded teams could not adapt to cooperative rewards. As the authors note, their results may shed light on the intelligence failures of the U.S. Central Intelligence Agency and Federal Bureau of Investigation; when these formerly separate organizations were asked to cooperate, they found it very difficult to do so.

If the results of this study generalize to actual teams, it seems that teams that "cut their teeth" being cooperative can learn to be competitive, but competitive teams find it much harder to learn to cooperate.

Source: M. D. Johnson, S. E. Humphrey, D. R. Ilgen, D. Jundt, and C. J. Meyer, "Cutthroat Cooperation: Asymmetrical Adaptation to Changes in Team Reward Structures," *Academy of Management Journal* 49, vol. 1 (2006), pp. 103–119. ■

So in designing effective teams, managers should try to keep them at nine or fewer members. If a natural working unit is larger and you want a team effort, consider breaking the group into subteams.[32]

Member Preferences Not every employee is a team player. Given the option, many employees will select themselves *out* of team participation. When people who would prefer to work alone are required to team up, there is a direct threat to the team's morale and to individual member satisfaction.[33] This suggests that, when selecting team members, individual preferences should be considered as along with abilities, personalities, and skills. High-performing teams are likely to be composed of people who prefer working as part of a group.

Work Design

Effective teams need to work together and take collective responsibility for completing significant tasks. An effective team must be more than a "team in name only."[34] Based on terminology introduced in Chapter 7, the work-design category includes variables such as freedom and autonomy, the opportunity to use different skills and talents (skill variety), the ability to complete a whole and identifiable task or product (task identity), and work on a task or project that has a substantial impact on others (task significance). The evidence indicates that these characteristics enhance member motivation and increase team effectiveness.[35] These work-design characteristics motivate because they increase members' sense of responsibility and ownership of the work and because they make the work more interesting to perform.[36]

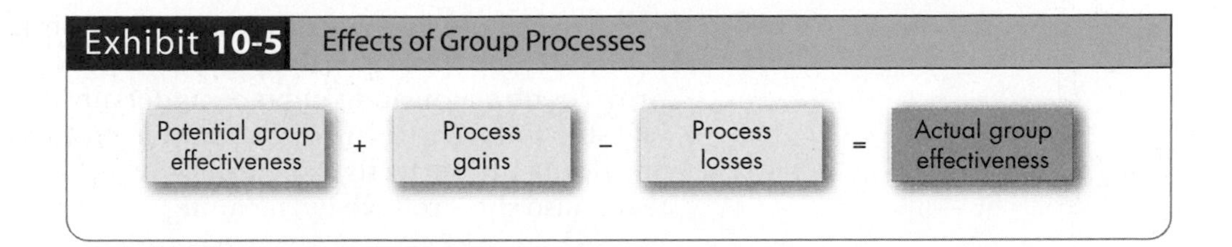

Team Processes

The final category related to team effectiveness is process variables. These include member commitment to a common purpose, establishment of specific team goals, team efficacy, a managed level of conflict, and minimization of social loafing.

Why are processes important to team effectiveness? One way to answer this question is to return to the topic of social loafing. We found that 1 + 1 + 1 doesn't necessarily add up to 3. In team tasks for which each member's contribution is not clearly visible, there is a tendency for individuals to decrease their effort. Social loafing, in other words, illustrates a process loss as a result of using teams. But team processes should produce positive results. That is, teams should create outputs greater than the sum of their inputs. The development of creative alternatives by a diverse group would be one such instance. Exhibit 10-5 illustrates how group processes can have an impact on a group's actual effectiveness.[37] Research teams are often used in research laboratories because they can draw on the diverse skills of various individuals to produce more meaningful research as a team than could be generated by all the researchers working independently. That is, they produce positive synergy. Their process gains exceed their process losses.

Common Plan and Purpose An effective team has a common plan and purpose that provides direction, momentum, and commitment for members.[38] This purpose is a vision, or master plan. It's broader than specific goals.

Members of successful teams put a tremendous amount of time and effort into discussing, shaping, and agreeing on a purpose that belongs to them both

Employee teams at the sports-apparel maker New Balance share the common purpose of continuously improving their work processes. In the company's stitching department, shown here, sharing the purpose of quality improvement motivated members of team CS-39 to develop a cross-training program so all members could learn and perform each other's job skills.

collectively and individually. This common purpose, when accepted by the team, becomes the equivalent of what celestial navigation is to a ship captain: It provides direction and guidance under any and all conditions. Like the proverbial ship following the wrong course, teams that don't have good planning skills are doomed; perfectly executing the wrong plan is a lost cause.[39] Effective teams also show **reflexivity**, meaning that they reflect on and adjust their master plan when necessary. A team has to have a good plan, but it also has to be willing and able to adapt when condition call for it.[40]

Specific Goals Successful teams translate their common purpose into specific, measurable, and realistic performance goals. Just as we demonstrated in Chapter 6 how goals lead individuals to higher performance, goals also energize teams. Specific goals facilitate clear communication. They also help teams maintain their focus on getting results.

Also, consistent with the research on individual goals, team goals should be challenging. Difficult goals have been found to raise team performance on those criteria for which they're set. So, for instance, goals for quantity tend to raise quantity, goals for speed tend to raise speed, goals for accuracy raise accuracy, and so on.[41]

Team Efficacy Effective teams have confidence in themselves. They believe they can succeed. We call this *team efficacy*.[42] Success breeds success. Teams that have been successful raise their beliefs about future success, which, in turn, motivates them to work harder. What, if anything, can management do to increase team efficacy? Two possible options are helping the team to achieve small successes and providing skill training. Small successes build team confidence. As a team develops an increasingly stronger performance record, it also increases the collective belief that future efforts will lead to success. In addition, managers should consider providing training to improve members' technical and interpersonal skills. The greater the abilities of team members, the greater the likelihood that the team will develop confidence and the capability to deliver on that confidence.

Mental Models Effective teams have accurate and common **mental models**—knowledge and beliefs (a "psychological map") about how the work gets done. If team members have the wrong mental models, which is particularly likely to happen with teams under acute stress, their performance suffers.[43] For example, in the Iraq war, many military leaders said they underestimated the power of the insurgency and the infighting among Iraqi religious sects. The similarity of team members' mental models matters, too. If team members have different ideas about how to do things, the teams will fight over how to do things rather than focus on what needs to be done.[44]

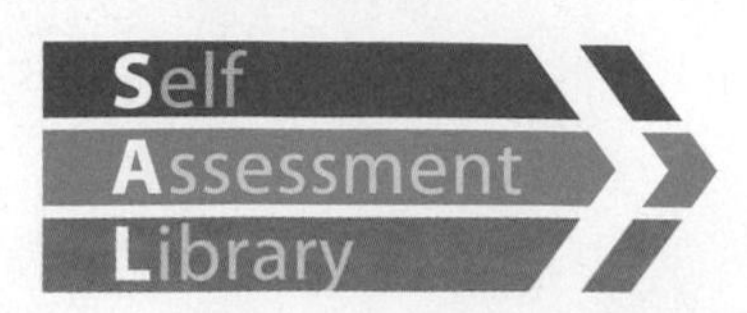

WHAT IS MY TEAM EFFICACY?

In the Self-Assessment Library (available on CD or online), take assessment IV.E.2 (What Is My Team Efficacy?).

Conflict Levels Conflict on a team isn't necessarily bad. As discussed in more depth in Chapter 15, teams that are completely void of conflict are likely to become apathetic and stagnant. So conflict can actually improve team effectiveness.[45] But not all types of conflict. Relationship conflicts—those based on interpersonal incompatibilities, tension, and animosity toward others—are almost always dysfunctional. However, on teams performing nonroutine activities, disagreements among members about task content (called *task conflicts*) is not detrimental. In fact, it is often beneficial because it reduces the likelihood of groupthink. Task conflicts stimulate discussion, promote critical assessment of problems and options, and can lead to better team decisions. So effective teams can be characterized as having an appropriate level of conflict.

Social Loafing We talked in Chapter 9 about the fact that individuals can hide inside a group. They can engage in social loafing and coast on the group's effort because their individual contributions can't be identified. Effective teams undermine this tendency by holding themselves accountable at both the individual and team levels. Successful teams make members individually and jointly accountable for the team's purpose, goals, and approach.[46] Therefore, members should be clear on what they are individually responsible for and what they are jointly responsible for.

Turning Individuals into Team Players

5 *Show how organizations can create team players.*

To this point, we've made a strong case for the value and growing popularity of teams. But many people are not inherently team players. There are also many organizations that have historically nurtured individual accomplishments. Finally, countries differ in terms of how they rate on individualism and collectivism. Teams fit well with countries that score high on collectivism. But what if an organization wants to introduce teams into a work population that is made up largely of individuals born and raised in an individualistic society? A veteran employee of a large company, who had done well working in an individualistic company in an individualist country, described the experience of joining a team: "I'm learning my lesson. I just had my first negative performance appraisal in 20 years."[47]

So what can organizations do to enhance team effectiveness—to turn individual contributors into team members? The following are the primary options managers have for trying to turn individuals into team players.

Selection: Hiring Team Players Some people already possess the interpersonal skills to be effective team players. When hiring team members, in addition to the technical skills required to fill the job, care should be taken to ensure that candidates can fulfill their team roles as well as technical requirements.[48]

Many job candidates don't have team skills. This is especially true for those socialized around individual contributions. When faced with such candidates, managers basically have three options. The candidates can undergo training to "make them into team players." If this isn't possible or doesn't work, the other two options are to transfer the individual to another unit within the organization that does not have teams (if this possibility exists) or not to hire the candidate. In established organizations that decide to redesign jobs around teams, it should be expected that some employees will resist being team players

reflexivity *A team characteristic of reflecting on and adjusting the master plan when necessary.*

mental models *Team members' knowledge and beliefs about how the work gets done by the team.*

The grocery-store chain Whole Foods Market uses a team structure throughout its entire organization, with each store averaging 10 self-managed teams. Team members participate in both the interview and selection processes. After new hires are trained during an orientation period, other team members vote on whether to add the candidate to their team, based on criteria such as positive job performance, adherence to policies and procedures, customer-service skills, and teamwork. The team voting process empowers team members to share in the building of a quality team.

and may be untrainable. Unfortunately, such people typically become casualties of the team approach.

Training: Creating Team Players A large proportion of people raised on the importance of individual accomplishments can be trained to become team players. Training specialists conduct exercises that allow employees to experience the satisfaction that teamwork can provide. They typically offer workshops to help employees improve their problem-solving, communication, negotiation, conflict-management, and coaching skills. Employees also learn the five-stage group development model described in Chapter 9. At the telecommunications firm Verizon, for example, trainers focus on how a team goes through various stages before it finally gels. And employees are reminded of the importance of patience—because teams take longer to make decisions than do employees acting alone.[49]

Emerson Electric's Specialty Motor Division in the state of Missouri, for instance, has achieved remarkable success in getting its 650-member workforce not only to accept but to welcome team training.[50] Outside consultants were brought in to give workers practical skills for working in teams. After less than a year, employees were enthusiastically accepting the value of teamwork.

Rewarding: Providing Incentives to Be a Good Team Player An organization's reward system needs to be reworked to encourage cooperative efforts rather than competitive ones.[51] For instance, Hallmark Cards, Inc., added to its basic individual-incentive system an annual bonus based on achievement of team goals. The insurance company Trigon Blue Cross/Blue Shield changed its system to reward an even split between individual goals and team-like behaviors.[52]

Promotions, pay raises, and other forms of recognition should be given to individuals who work effectively as collaborative team members. This doesn't mean individual contributions should be ignored; rather, they should be balanced with selfless contributions to the team. Examples of behaviors that should be rewarded include training new colleagues, sharing information with teammates, helping to resolve team conflicts, and mastering new skills that the team needs but in which it is deficient.

Finally, don't forget the intrinsic rewards that employees can receive from teamwork. Teams provide camaraderie. It's exciting and satisfying to be an integral part of a successful team. The opportunity to engage in personal development and to help teammates grow can be a very satisfying and rewarding experience for employees.

Beware! Teams Aren't Always the Answer

6 Decide when to use individuals instead of teams.

Teamwork takes more time and often more resources than individual work. For instance, teams have increased communication demands, conflicts to be managed, and meetings to be run. So the benefits of using teams have to exceed the costs. And that's not always the case.[53] In the excitement to enjoy the benefits of teams, some managers have introduced them into situations in which the work is better done by individuals. So before you rush to implement teams, you should carefully assess whether the work requires or will benefit from a collective effort.

How do you know if the work of your group would be better done in teams? It's been suggested that three tests be applied to see if a team fits the situation.[54] First, can the work be done better by more than one person? A good indicator is the complexity of the work and the need for different perspectives. Simple tasks that don't require diverse input are probably better left to individuals. Second, does the work create a common purpose or set of goals for the people in the group that is more than the aggregate of individual goals? For instance, many new-car dealer service departments have introduced teams that link customer-service personnel, mechanics, parts specialists, and sales representatives. Such teams can better manage collective responsibility for ensuring that customer needs are properly met. The final test to assess whether teams fit the situation is to determine whether the members of the group are interdependent. Using teams makes sense when there is interdependence between tasks—when the success of the whole depends on the success of each one *and* the success of each one depends on the success of the others. Soccer, for instance, is an obvious *team* sport. Success requires a great deal of coordination between interdependent players. Conversely, except possibly for relays, swim teams are not really teams. They're groups of individuals, performing individually, whose total performance is merely the aggregate summation of their individual performances.

Global Implications

7 Show how the understanding of teams differs in a global context.

Although research on global considerations in the use of teams is just beginning, three areas are particularly worth mentioning: the extent of teamwork, self-managed teams, and team cultural diversity.

Extent of Teamwork Although the use of work teams is pervasive in the United States, some evidence suggests that the extent of teamwork—the degree to which U.S. teams deeply affect the way work is done—is not as significant in the United States as in other countries. One study comparing U.S. workers to Canadian and Asian workers revealed that 51 percent of workers in Asia-Pacific and 48 percent of Canadian employees report high levels of teamwork. But only about one-third (32 percent) of U.S. employees say their organization has a high level of teamwork.[55] Thus, although teamwork is widely used in the United States, this evidence suggests that there still is a heavy role for individual contributions. Given that U.S. culture is highly individualistic, that may continue to be true for quite some time.

Self-Managed Teams Although self-managed teams have not proven to be the panacea many thought they would be, special care needs to be taken when introducing self-managed teams globally. For instance, evidence suggests that these types of teams have not fared well in Mexico, largely due to that culture's low tolerance of ambiguity and uncertainty and employees' strong respect for hierarchical authority.[56] Thus, in countries that are relatively high in power distance—meaning that roles of leaders and followers are clearly delineated—a team may need to be structured so that leadership roles are spelled out and power relationships are identified.

Team Cultural Diversity and Team Performance Earlier, we discussed research on team diversity in terms of factors such as race or gender. But what about diversity created by national differences? Like the earlier research, evidence indicates that these elements of diversity interfere with team processes, at least in the short term.[57] Cultural diversity does seem to be an asset for tasks that call for a variety of viewpoints. But culturally heterogeneous teams have more difficulty learning to work with each other and solving problems. The good news is that these difficulties seem to dissipate with time. Although newly formed culturally diverse teams underperform newly formed culturally homogeneous teams, the differences disappear after about 3 months.[58] The reason is that it takes culturally diverse teams a while to learn how to work through disagreements and different approaches to solving problems.

Summary and Implications for Managers

Few trends have influenced jobs as much as the massive movement to introduce teams into the workplace. The shift from working alone to working on teams requires employees to cooperate with others, share information, confront differences, and sublimate personal interests for the greater good of the team.

Effective teams have common characteristics. They have adequate resources, effective leadership, a climate of trust, and a performance evaluation and reward system that reflects team contributions. These teams have individuals with technical expertise as well as problem-solving, decision-making, and interpersonal skills and the right traits, especially conscientiousness and openness. Effective teams also tend to be small—with fewer than 10 people, preferably of diverse backgrounds. They have members who fill role demands and who prefer to be part of a group. And the work that members do provides freedom and autonomy, the opportunity to use different skills and talents, the ability to complete a whole and identifiable task or product, and work that has a substantial impact on others. Finally, effective teams have members who believe in the team's capabilities and are committed to a common plan and purpose, an accurate shared mental model of what is to be accomplished, specific team goals, a manageable level of conflict, and a minimal degree of social loafing.

Because individualistic organizations and societies attract and reward individual accomplishments, it is can be difficult to create team players in these environments. To make the conversion, management should try to select individuals who have the interpersonal skills to be effective team players, provide training to develop teamwork skills, and reward individuals for cooperative efforts.

Point / Counterpoint

SPORTS TEAMS ARE GOOD MODELS FOR WORKPLACE TEAMS

Point

Studies from football, soccer, basketball, hockey, and baseball have found a number of elements of successful sports teams that can be extrapolated to successful work teams.

Successful teams integrate cooperation and competition. Sports teams with the best win–loss record had coaches who promote a strong spirit of cooperation and a high level of healthy competition among their players.

Successful teams score early wins. Early successes build teammates' faith in themselves and their capacity as a team. Research on hockey teams of relatively equal ability found that 72 percent of the time, the team that was ahead at the end of the first period went on to win. So managers should provide teams with early tasks that are simple and provide "easy wins."

Successful teams avoid losing streaks. A couple failures can lead to a downward spiral if a team becomes demoralized. Managers need to instill confidence in team members that they can turn things around when they encounter setbacks.

Practice makes perfect. Successful sport teams execute on game day but learn from their mistakes in practice. Practice should be used to try new things and fail. A wise manager encourages work teams to experiment and learn.

Successful teams use half-time breaks. The best coaches in basketball and football use half-time during a game to reassess what is working and what isn't. Managers of work teams should similarly build in assessments at the approximate halfway point in a team project to evaluate what it can do to improve.

Winning teams have stable membership. Stability improves performance. Studies of professional basketball teams have found that when teammates have more time together they are more able to anticipate one another's moves, and they are clearer about one another's roles.

Successful teams debrief after failures and successes. The best sports teams study the game video. Similarly, work teams should routinely assess their successes and failures and should learn from them.

Sports metaphors are useful. For example, a recent *Harvard Business Review* issue had as the lead story "Playing to Win . . . Five Killer Strategies for Trouncing the Competition." The article argues that winners in business play hardball, which means they pick their shots, seek out competitive encounters, set the pace of innovation, and test the edges of the possible. Like sports teams, in business you have to play hardball, which means playing to win. That is what the sports model can teach us.

Counterpoint

There are flaws in using sports as a model for developing effective work teams. Here are just four caveats.

All sport teams aren't alike. In baseball, for instance, there is little interaction among teammates. Rarely are more than two or three players directly involved in a play. The performance of the team is largely the sum of the performance of its individual players. In contrast, basketball has much more interdependence among players. Geographic distribution is dense. Usually all players are involved in every play, team members have to be able to switch from offense to defense at a moment's notice, and there is continuous movement by all, not just the player who has the ball. The performance of the team is more than the sum of its individual players. So when using sports teams as a model for work teams, you have to make sure you're making the correct comparison. As one expert noted, "The problem with sports metaphors is that the meaning you extract from a sports metaphor is entirely dependent on the sport you pick."

Work teams are more varied and complex than sports teams. In an athletic league, the design of the task, the design of the team, and the team's context vary relatively little from team to team. But these variables can vary tremendously between work teams. As a result, coaching plays a much more significant part of a sports team's performance than in that of a work team. Performance of work teams is a function of getting the team's structural and design variables right. So, in contrast to sports, managers of work teams should focus more on getting the team set up for success than on coaching.

A lot of employees can't relate to sports metaphors. Not everyone on work teams is conversant in sports. Some people aren't as interested in sports as "sports hounds" and aren't as savvy about sports terminology. And team members from different cultures may not know the sports metaphors you're using. Most Americans, for instance, are unfamiliar with the rules and terminology of Australian Rules football.

Work team outcomes aren't easily defined in terms of wins and losses. Sports teams typically measure success in terms of wins and losses. Such measures of success are rarely as clear for work teams. When managers try to define success in wins and losses, it tends to infer that the workplace is ethically no more complex than the playing field, which is rarely true.

Source: See N. Katz, "Sports Teams as a Model for Workplace Teams: Lessons and Liabilities," *Academy of Management Executive*, August 2001, pp. 56–67; "Talent Inc.," *The New Yorker Online Only*, July 22, 2002, www.newyorker.com/online; and D. Batstone, "HBR Goes CG?," *Worthwhile.com*, April 14, 2004 www.worthwhilemag.com.

Questions for Review

1 How do you explain the growing popularity of teams in organizations?

2 What is the difference between a group and a team?

3 What are the four types of teams?

4 What conditions or context factors determine whether teams are effective?

5 How can organizations create team players?

6 When is work performed by individuals preferred over work performed by teams?

7 What are three ways in which our understanding of teams differs in a global context?

Experiential Exercise

FIXED VERSUS VARIABLE FLIGHT CREWS

Break into teams of five. Assume that you've been hired by AJet, a start-up airline based in St. Louis. Your team has been formed to consider the pros and cons of using variable flight crews and to arrive at a recommendation on whether to follow this industry practice at AJet.

Variable flight crews are crews formed when pilots, copilots, and flight attendants typically bid for schedules on specific planes (for instance, Boeing 737s, 757s, or 767s) based on seniority. Then they're given a monthly schedule made up of 1- to 4-day trips. So any given flight crew on a plane is rarely together for more than a few days at a time. A complicated system is required to complete the schedules. Because of this system, it's not unusual for a senior pilot at a large airline to fly with a different copilot on every trip during any given month. And a pilot and copilot who work together for 3 days in January may never work together again the rest of the year. (In contrast, a fixed flight crew consists of the same group of pilots and attendants who fly together for a period of time.)

In considering whether to use variable flight crews, your team is to answer the following questions:

1. What are the primary advantages of variable flight crews?
2. If you were to recommend some version of fixed flight crews, drawing from the material in this chapter, on what criteria would you assign AJet crews?

When your team has considered the advantages and disadvantages of variable flight crews and answered these questions, be prepared to present to the class your recommendations and justification.

Ethical Dilemma

PRESSURE TO BE A TEAM PLAYER

"Okay, I admit it. I'm not a team player. I work best when I work alone and am left alone," says Zachery Sanders.

Zach's employer, Broad's Furniture, an office furniture manufacturer, recently reorganized around teams. All production in the company's Michigan factory is now done in teams. And Zach's design department has been broken up into three design teams. To Zach's dismay, he was assigned to the modular-office design (MOD) team, which does work that Zach finds less interesting and challenging than other work he's done. What's worse, Zach believes that some low-performing individuals have been put in the team. Maddie Saunders, MOD's new team leader, seems to agree with Zach. She told him, "Zach, listen, I know you're not wild about the work MOD is doing, and it's true some weaker individual contributors have been assigned to the team. But that's why we formed the team. We really think that when we work together, the strengths of the team will be magnified and the weaknesses limited."

Although Zach respects Maggie, he's not convinced. "I've worked here for 4 years. I'm very good at what I do. And my performance reviews confirm that. I've been rated in the highest performance category every year I've been here. But now everything is changing. My evaluations and pay raises are going to depend on how well the team does. And, get this, 50 percent of my evaluation will depend on how well the team does—and this isn't a great team. I'm really frustrated and demoralized. They hired me for my design skills. They knew I wasn't a social type. Now they're forcing me to be a team player. This doesn't play to my strengths at all."

Is it unethical for Zach's employer to force him to be a team leader? Is his firm breaking an implied contract that it made with him at the time he was hired? Does this employer have any responsibility to provide Zach with an alternative that would allow him to continue to work independently? If you were Zach, how would you respond?

Case Incident 1

TEAMWORK: ONE COMPANY'S APPROACH TO HIGH PERFORMANCE

At ICU Medical Inc., teams haven't always been the answer. A maker of medical devices, the San Clemente, California, company was founded in 1984 by current chief executive officer Dr. George Lopez. At first, most of the major decisions were made by Lopez. Business was good—so good, in fact—that the company was ready for a public offering by the early 1990s. The company's products were in high demand, but dealing with that demand "was an overwhelming task for one entrepreneur CEO," states Lopez.

A solution to dealing with the increasing growth came to Lopez while watching his son play hockey. During a game, the opposing team had a star player who dominated his teammates and tried to make most of the plays himself. His son's team, however, worked together as a group and overwhelmed the star player. Lopez clearly saw that "the team was better than one player." He decided to reorganize his company to rely on teams that would not merely share in the decision-making process, but instead would have full autonomy to make their own decisions—setting their own meeting times, assigning their own tasks, and creating their own deadlines, and even deciding whether to form a team in the first place.

At that time, his company employed around 100 employees, but they weren't used to making decisions for themselves. Lopez put his new plan in place, telling his employees to form teams to come up with ideas to handle the increasing demand. At first, it didn't work as expected. Angered by the new team-based approach, the chief financial officer of the company quit. The new teams weren't faring well either. According to Lopez, "nothing was getting done, except people were spending a lot of time talking." Confident that teams were the answer, Lopez persisted and instructed teams to elect leaders. Team guidelines were put in place (e.g., "Challenge the issue, not the person"), and the company began using group rewards to motivate teamwork.

The new strategies paid off. Employees began to enjoy working together and making decisions for themselves, and ICU was able to easily handle the increasing demand. Since then, ICU has continued to prosper. Currently, the company employs close to 1,500 individuals. The company's stock price is six times higher than it was when the company first went public, and in 2006, revenue increased 28% to over $200 million. Each year, nearly 60 different teams, usually composed of five to seven members, finish projects. Those teams that are successful share in the $300,000 in team bonuses that the company allots annually.

Although teams at ICU have largely been beneficial, they are not without their problems. In particular, the team-based reward structure has sometimes created competitiveness and tension among employees. Colleen Wilder, who has worked on many teams at ICU over the years, recounts an incident where she refused to share a reward with coworkers who were not pulling their share. "You did nothing, and I propose you get nothing," she informed them. The team members evaluated what each person had contributed to the project and agreed that those who did not contribute should not receive a bonus. In addition, although Dr. Lopez's original vision was of teams that are completely autonomous, over the years the company has instituted more rules and policies, such as a 25-page handbook that tells teams how to operate. Although the goal of these rules is to help teams work together more smoothly, they take away some of the ability of teams to completely make their own decisions.

Despite these potential downsides, Dr. Lopez isn't about to change his reliance on teams. His reason is simple: "Top-down decisions are frequently wrong."

Questions

1. Using the terms from this chapter, how would you characterize the teams at ICU Medical Inc.? What are some advantages and disadvantages of giving teams a lot of autonomy to make decisions?
2. Four contextual factors (adequate resources, leadership and structure, climate of trust, and performance evaluation and reward systems) influence team performance. Which of these appear to be present in the above case? If present, are they supportive or unsupportive? How?
3. If you were to compose a team that will be given decision-making responsibility to solve complex problems, what types of members would you select in terms of abilities and personalities?
4. What are some processes losses that are likely to occur in teams such as those at ICU Medical Inc? How can these processes losses be avoided?

Source: Based on E. White, "How a Company Made Everyone a Team Player," *Wall Street Journal*, August 13, 2007, p. B.1

Case Incident 2

TEAM-BUILDING RETREATS

Team-building retreats are big business. Companies believe such retreats, where team members participate in activities ranging from mountain climbing, to trust-building exercises (where team members let themselves fall backwards into their colleagues' arms), to *Iron Chef*-inspired cooking contests (used by UBS, Hewlett-Packard, and Verizon) can foster effective teamwork. But why do organizations have teammates participate in activities that seem irrelevant to the organization's primary activities? Howard Atkins, chief financial officer at Wells Fargo, believes that corporate retreats aid team building, which in turn improves company performance. At a luxury hotel in Sonoma, California, Atkins—along with several other corporate executives—participated in an exercise in which he and his team had to build a bridge out of boxes and unstable wooden planks. To the delight of his colleagues, Atkins was able to make it across the bridge. The team succeeded. According to Atkins, "What I have been trying to do is get them to see the power of acting more like a team. It's really a terrific success."

Part of the success that Atkins is referring to is the double-digit gains in earnings by Wells Fargo—gains that he says are one of the effects of the corporate retreats. "Success more often than not is a function of execution, and execution is really about people, so we invest pretty heavily into our people." How heavy is the investment? Wells Fargo paid $50,000 for the retreat in Sonoma.

Given the level of expense, some companies are now discontinuing their team-building activities outside the organization. According to Susan Harper, a business psychologist, "team-building has definitely gone down. People are reluctant to spend money on what they think is not an absolute necessity." Atkins believes otherwise: "I know intuitively the payback here is huge. It's a very small investment to make for the payback we are going to get."

Hard drive maker Seagate takes it even further. Every year, Seagate flies roughly 200 managers to New Zealand to participate in "Eco Seagate," its annual team-building exercise. The tab? $9,000 per manager. Chief Financial Officer Charles Pope says it's one of the last things he's cut from Seagate's budget.

It's clear that companies that invest in team-building retreats think they're worth the investment. Sometimes, though, they have unintended consequences. In 2001, a dozen Burger King employees burned themselves while participating in a "fire walk"—a team-building exercise that requires teammates to walk barefoot across an 8-foot pit of burning-hot coals. The results were injured employees and some very negative publicity for Burger King. In 2006, an employee of security systems company Alarm One was award $1.7 million in damages in a lawsuit in which she claimed she had been spanked on the job as part of a camaraderie-building exercise. One observer of these retreats said, "Most of the time, people asking for these activities aren't interested in real teamwork building. What they really want is entertainment."

Some companies are taking team-building exercises in a different direction, having their employees engage in hands-on volunteer work. When the breweries Coors and Molson merged, they wanted to use a team-building exercise to acquaint the executive teams, but they didn't want to go the route of the typical golf outings or ropes course. So they helped Habitat for Humanity build a home. UPS has new managers participate in various community projects, such as distributing secondhand medical equipment in developing countries.

It is questionable whether team-building exercises such as mountain climbing, cooking contests, and fire walks result in improved company financial performance, and it may be better to think of such activities as morale boosters. According to Merianne Liteman, a professional corporate retreat organizer, "Where good retreats have a quantifiable effect is on retention, on morale, on productivity." Daryl Jesperson, CEO of RE/MAX International, says, "There is a productivity boost anytime you have one of these. People feel better about themselves, they feel better about the company, and as a result will do a better job."

Questions

1. Do you believe that team-building activities increase productivity? Why or why not? What other factors might be responsible for increases in profitability following a corporate retreat?
2. What are some other ways besides those described here to build effective teams and increase teamwork among company employees? How might these alternatives be better or worse than corporate retreats?
3. What should companies do about employees who lack athletic talent but are still pressured to participate in physical activities with their colleagues? How might poor performance by those with low athletic ability affect their status within the organization?
4. How might you increase teamwork when team members are not often in direct contact with one another? Can you think of any "electronic" team-building exercises?

Sources: Based on C. Dahle, "How to Avoid a Rout at the Company Retreat," *New York Times*, October 31, 2004, p. 10; S. Max, "Seagate's Morale-athon," *BusinessWeek*, April 3, 2006, pp. 110–112; M. C. White, "Doing Good on Company Time," *New York Times*, May 8, 2007, p. C6; and N. H. Woodward, "Making the Most of Team Building," *HRMagazine*, September 2006, pp. 73–76.

Endnotes

1. J. McGregor, "I Can't Believe They Took the Whole Team," *BusinessWeek*, December 18, 2006, pp. 120–122.
2. This section is based on J. R. Katzenbach and D. K. Smith, *The Wisdom of Teams* (Cambridge, MA: Harvard University Press, 1993), pp. 21, 45, 85; and D. C. Kinlaw, *Developing Superior Work Teams* (Lexington, MA: Lexington Books, 1991), pp. 3–21.
3. See, for instance, E. Sunstrom, K. DeMeuse, and D. Futrell, "Work Teams: Applications and Effectiveness," *American Psychologist*, February 1990, pp. 120–133.
4. J. H. Shonk, *Team-Based Organizations* (Homewood, IL: Business One Irwin, 1992); and M. A. Verespej, "When Workers Get New Roles," *IndustryWeek*, February 3, 1992, p. 11.
5. G. Bodinson and R. Bunch, "AQP's National Team Excellence Award: Its Purpose, Value and Process," *The Journal for Quality and Participation*, Spring 2003, pp. 37–42.
6. See, for example, S. G. Cohen, G. E. Ledford, Jr., and G. M. Spreitzer, "A Predictive Model of Self-Managing Work Team Effectiveness," *Human Relations*, May 1996, pp. 643–676; C. E. Nicholls, H. W. Lane, and M. Brehm Brechu, "Taking Self-Managed Teams to Mexico," *Academy of Management Executive*, August 1999, pp. 15–27; and A. Erez, J. A. LePine, and H. Elms, "Effects of Rotated Leadership and Peer Evaluation on the Functioning and Effectiveness of Self-Managed Teams: A Quasi-experiment," *Personnel Psychology*, Winter 2002, pp. 929–948.
7. See, for instance, J. L. Cordery, W. S. Mueller, and L. M. Smith, "Attitudinal and Behavioral Effects of Autonomous Group Working: A Longitudinal Field Study," *Academy of Management Journal*, June 1991, pp. 464–476; R. A. Cook and J. L. Goff, "Coming of Age with Self-Managed Teams: Dealing with a Problem Employee," *Journal of Business and Psychology*, Spring 2002, pp. 485–496; and C. W. Langfred, "Too Much of a Good Thing? Negative Effects of High Trust and Individual Autonomy in Self-Managing Teams," *Academy of Management Journal*, June 2004, pp. 385–399.
8. Bodinson and Bunch, "AQP's National Team Excellence Award."
9. M. Brunelli, "How Harley-Davidson Uses Cross-Functional Teams," *Purchasing Online*, November 4, 1999, www.purchasing.com/article/CA147865.html.
10. See, for example, J. Lipnack and J. Stamps, *Virtual Teams: People Working Across Boundaries and Technology*, 2nd ed. (New York: Wiley, 2000); C. B. Gibson and S. G. Cohen (eds.), *Virtual Teams That Work* (San Francisco: Jossey-Bass, 2003); and L. L. Martins, L. L. Gilson, and M. T. Maynard, "Virtual Teams: What Do We Know and Where Do We Go from Here?" *Journal of Management*, November 2004, pp. 805–835.
11. A. Malhotra, A. Majchrzak, and B. Rosen, "Leading Virtual Teams," *Academy of Management Perspectives*, February 2007, pp. 60–70; and J. M. Wilson, S. S. Straus, and B. McEvily, "All in Due Time: The Development of Trust in Computer-Mediated and Face-to-Face Teams," *Organizational Behavior and Human Decision Processes* 19 (2006), pp. 16–33.
12. See, for instance, J. R. Hackman, "The Design of Work Teams," in J. W. Lorsch (ed.), *Handbook of Organizational Behavior* (Upper Saddle River, NJ: Prentice Hall, 1987), pp. 315–342; and M. A. Campion, G. J. Medsker, and C. A. Higgs, "Relations Between Work Group Characteristics and Effectiveness: Implications for Designing Effective Work Groups," *Personnel Psychology*, Winter 1993, pp. 823–850.
13. D. E. Hyatt and T. M. Ruddy, "An Examination of the Relationship Between Work Group Characteristics and Performance: Once More into the Breech," *Personnel Psychology*, Autumn 1997, p. 555.
14. This model is based on M. A. Campion, E. M. Papper, and G. J. Medsker, "Relations Between Work Team Characteristics and Effectiveness: A Replication and Extension," *Personnel Psychology*, Summer 1996, pp. 429–452; D. E. Hyatt and T. M. Ruddy, "An Examination of the Relationship Between Work Group Characteristics and Performance," pp. 553–585; S. G. Cohen and D. E. Bailey, "What Makes Teams Work: Group Effectiveness Research from the Shop Floor to the Executive Suite," *Journal of Management* 23, no. 3 (1997), pp. 239–290; L. Thompson, *Making the Team* (Upper Saddle River, NJ: Prentice Hall, 2000), pp. 18–33; and J. R. Hackman, *Leading Teams: Setting the Stage for Great Performance* (Boston: Harvard Business School Press, 2002).
15. See M. Mattson, T. V. Mumford, and G. S. Sintay, "Taking Teams to Task: A Normative Model for Designing or Recalibrating Work Teams," paper presented at the National Academy of Management Conference, Chicago, August 1999; and G. L. Stewart and M. R. Barrick, "Team Structure and Performance: Assessing the Mediating Role of Intrateam Process and the Moderating Role of Task Type," *Academy of Management Journal*, April 2000, pp. 135–148.
16. Hyatt and Ruddy, "An Examination of the Relationship Between Work Group Characteristics and Performance," p. 577.
17. P. Balkundi and D. A. Harrison, "Ties, Leaders, and Time in Teams: Strong Inference About Network Structure's Effects on Team Viability and Performance," *Academy of Management Journal* 49, no. 1 (2006), pp. 49–68; G. Chen, B. L. Kirkman, R. Kanfer, D. Allen, and B. Rosen, "A Multilevel Study of Leadership, Empowerment, and Performance in Teams," *Journal of Applied Psychology* 92, no. 2 (2007), pp. 331–346; L. A. DeChurch and M. A. Marks, "Leadership in Multiteam Systems," *Journal of Applied Psychology* 91, no. 2 (2006), pp. 311–329; A. Srivastava, K. M. Bartol, and E. A. Locke, "Empowering Leadership in Management Teams: Effects on Knowledge Sharing, Efficacy, and Performance," *Academy of Management Journal* 49, no. 6 (2006), pp. 1239–1251; and J. E. Mathieu, K. K. Gilson, and T. M. Ruddy, "Empowerment and Team Effectiveness: An Empirical Test of an Integrated Model," *Journal of Applied Psychology* 91, no. 1 (2006), pp. 97–108.
18. K. T. Dirks, "Trust in Leadership and Team Performance: Evidence from NCAA Basketball," *Journal of Applied Psychology*, December 2000, pp. 1004–1012; and M. Williams, "In Whom We Trust: Group Membership as an Affective Context for Trust Development," *Academy of Management Review*, July 2001, pp. 377–396.
19. See S. T. Johnson, "Work Teams: What's Ahead in Work Design and Rewards Management," *Compensation & Benefits Review*, March–April 1993, pp. 35–41; and L. N. McClurg, "Team Rewards: How Far Have We Come?" *Human Resource Management*, Spring 2001, pp. 73–86.

20. R. R. Hirschfeld, M. H. Jordan, H. S. Feild, W. F. Giles, and A. A. Armenakis, "Becoming Team Players: Team Members' Mastery of Teamwork Knowledge as a Predictor of Team Task Proficiency and Observed Teamwork Effectiveness," *Journal of Applied Psychology* 91, no. 2 (2006), pp. 467–474.

21. For a more detailed breakdown of team skills, see M. J. Stevens and M. A. Campion, "The Knowledge, Skill, and Ability Requirements for Teamwork: Implications for Human Resource Management," *Journal of Management*, Summer 1994, pp. 503–530.

22. H. Moon, J. R. Hollenbeck, and S. E. Humphrey, "Asymmetric Adaptability: Dynamic Team Structures as One-Way Streets," *Academy of Management Journal* 47, no. 5 (October 2004), pp. 681–695; A. P. J. Ellis, J. R. Hollenbeck, and D. R. Ilgen, "Team Learning: Collectively Connecting the Dots," *Journal of Applied Psychology* 88, no. 5 (October 2003), pp. 821–835; C. L. Jackson and J. A. LePine, "Peer Responses to a Team's Weakest Link: A Test and Extension of LePine and Van Dyne's Model," *Journal of Applied Psychology* 88, no. 3 (June 2003), pp. 459–475; and J. A. LePine, "Team Adaptation and Postchange Performance: Effects of Team Composition in Terms of Members' Cognitive Ability and Personality," *Journal of Applied Psychology* 88, no. 1 (February 2003), pp. 27–39.

23. S. T. Bell, "Deep-Level Composition Variables as Predictors of Team Performance: A Meta-analysis," *Journal of Applied Psychology* 92, no. 3 (2007), pp. 595–615; and M. R. Barrick, G. L. Stewart, M. J. Neubert, and M. K. Mount, "Relating Member Ability and Personality to Work-Team Processes and Team Effectiveness," *Journal of Applied Psychology*, June 1998, pp. 377–391.

24. Ellis, Hollenbeck, and Ilgen, "Team Learning"; C. O. L. H. Porter, J. R. Hollenbeck, and D. R. Ilgen, "Backing Up Behaviors in Teams: The Role of Personality and Legitimacy of Need," *Journal of Applied Psychology* 88, no. 3 (June 2003), pp. 391–403; A. Colquitt, J. R. Hollenbeck, and D. R. Ilgen, "Computer-Assisted Communication and Team Decision-Making Performance: The Moderating Effect of Openness to Experience," *Journal of Applied Psychology* 87, no. 2 (April 2002), pp. 402–410; J. A. LePine, J. R. Hollenbeck, D. R. Ilgen, and J. Hedlund, "The Effects of Individual Differences on the Performance of Hierarchical Decision Making Teams: Much More Than G," *Journal of Applied Psychology* 82 (1997), pp. 803–811; Jackson and LePine, "Peer Responses to a Team's Weakest Link"; and LePine, "Team Adaptation and Postchange Performance."

25. Barrick, Stewart, Neubert, and Mount, "Relating Member Ability and Personality to Work-Team Processes and Team Effectiveness," p. 388; and S. E. Humphrey, J. R. Hollenbeck, C. J. Meyer, and D. R. Ilgen, "Trait Configurations in Self-Managed Teams: A Conceptual Examination of the Use of Seeding for Maximizing and Minimizing Trait Variance in Teams," *Journal of Applied Psychology* 92, no. 3 (2007), pp. 885–892.

26. C. Margerison and D. McCann, *Team Management: Practical New Approaches* (London: Mercury Books, 1990).

27. E. Mannix and M. A. Neale, "What Differences Make a Difference: The Promise and Reality of Diverse Teams in Organizations," *Psychological Science in the Public Interest*, October 2005, pp. 31–55.

28. G. S. Van Der Vegt, J. S. Bunderson, and A. Oosterhof, "Expertness Diversity and Interpersonal Helping in Teams: Why Those Who Need the Most Help End Up Getting the Least," *Academy of Management Journal* 49, no. 5 (2006), pp. 877–893.

29. K. Y. Williams and C. A. O'Reilly III, "Demography and Diversity in Organizations: A Review of 40 Years of Research," in B. M. Staw and L. L. Cummings (eds.), *Research in Organizational Behavior*, vol. 20, pp. 77–140; and A. Joshi, "The Influence of Organizational Demography on the External Networking Behavior of Teams," *Academy of Management Review*, July 2006, pp. 583–595.

30. J. Katzenbach, "What Makes Teams Work?" *Fast Company*, November 2000, p. 110.

31. The evidence in this section is described in Thompson, *Making the Team*, pp. 65–67. See also L. A. Curral, R. H. Forrester, and J. F. Dawson, "It's What You Do and the Way That You Do It: Team Task, Team Size, and Innovation-Related Group Processes," *European Journal of Work & Organizational Psychology* 10, no. 2 (June 2001), pp. 187–204; R. C. Liden, S. J. Wayne, and R. A. Jaworski, "Social Loafing: A Field Investigation," *Journal of Management* 30, no. 2 (2004), pp. 285–304; and J. A. Wagner, "Studies of Individualism–Collectivism: Effects on Cooperation in Groups," *Academy of Management Journal* 38, no. 1 (February 1995), pp. 152–172.

32. "Is Your Team Too Big? Too Small? What's the Right Number? *Knowledge@Wharton*, June 14, 2006, pp. 1–5.

33. Hyatt and Ruddy, "An Examination of the Relationship Between Work Group Characteristics and Performance"; J. D. Shaw, M. K. Duffy, and E. M. Stark, "Interdependence and Preference for Group Work: Main and Congruence Effects on the Satisfaction and Performance of Group Members," *Journal of Management* 26, no. 2 (2000), pp. 259–279; and S. A. Kiffin-Peterson and J. L. Cordery, "Trust, Individualism, and Job Characteristics of Employee Preference for Teamwork," *International Journal of Human Resource Management*, February 2003, pp. 93–116.

34. R. Wageman, "Critical Success Factors for Creating Superb Self-Managing Teams," *Organizational Dynamics*, Summer 1997, p. 55.

35. Campion, Papper, and Medsker, "Relations Between Work Team Characteristics and Effectiveness," p. 430; B. L. Kirkman and B. Rosen, "Powering Up Teams," *Organizational Dynamics*, Winter 2000, pp. 48–66; and D. C. Man and S. S. K. Lam, "The Effects of Job Complexity and Autonomy on Cohesiveness in Collectivist and Individualist Work Groups: A Cross-Cultural Analysis," *Journal of Organizational Behavior*, December 2003, pp. 979–1001.

36. Campion, Papper, and Medsker, "Relations Between Work Team Characteristics and Effectiveness," p. 430.

37. I. D. Steiner, *Group Processes and Productivity* (New York: Academic Press, 1972).

38. K. Hess, *Creating the High-Performance Team* (New York: Wiley, 1987); Katzenbach and Smith, *The Wisdom of Teams*, pp. 43–64; K. D. Scott and A. Townsend, "Teams: Why Some Succeed and Others Fail," *HRMagazine*, August 1994, pp. 62–67; and K. Blanchard, D. Carew, and E. Parisi-Carew, "How to Get Your Group to Perform Like a Team," *Training and Development*, September 1996, pp. 34–37.

39. J. E. Mathieu and W. Schulze, "The Influence of Team Knowledge and Formal Plans on Episodic Team Process—Performance Relationships," *Academy of Management Journal* 49, no. 3 (2006), pp. 605–619.
40. A. Gurtner, F. Tschan, N. K. Semmer, and C. Nagele, "Getting Groups to Develop Good Strategies: Effects of Reflexivity Interventions on Team Process, Team Performance, and Shared Mental Models," *Organizational Behavior and Human Decision Processes* 102 (2007), pp. 127–142; M. C. Schippers, D. N. Den Hartog, and P. L. Koopman, "Reflexivity in Teams: A Measure and Correlates," *Applied Psychology: An International Review* 56, no. 2 (2007), pp. 189–211; and C. S. Burke, K. C. Stagl, E. Salas, L. Pierce, and D. Kendall, "Understanding Team Adaptation: A Conceptual Analysis and Model," *Journal of Applied Psychology* 91, no. 6 (2006), pp. 1189–1207.
41. E. Weldon and L. R. Weingart, "Group Goals and Group Performance," *British Journal of Social Psychology*, Spring 1993, pp. 307–334. See also R. P. DeShon, S. W. J. Kozlowski, A. M. Schmidt, K. R. Milner, and D. Wiechmann, "A Multiple-Goal, Multilevel Model of Feedback Effects on the Regulation of Individual and Team Performance," *Journal of Applied Psychology*, December 2004, pp. 1035–1056.
42. K. Tasa, S. Taggar, and G. H. Seijts, "The Development of Collective Efficacy in Teams: A Multilevel and Longitudinal Perspective," *Journal of Applied Psychology* 92, no. 1 (2007), pp. 17–27; C. B. Gibson, "The Efficacy Advantage: Factors Related to the Formation of Group Efficacy," *Journal of Applied Social Psychology*, October 2003, pp. 2153–2086; and D. I. Jung and J. J. Sosik, "Group Potency and Collective Efficacy: Examining Their Predictive Validity, Level of Analysis, and Effects of Performance Feedback on Future Group Performance," *Group & Organization Management*, September 2003, pp. 366–391.
43. A. P. J. Ellis, "System Breakdown: The Role of Mental Models and Transactive Memory on the Relationships Between Acute Stress and Team Performance," *Academy of Management Journal* 49, no. 3 (2006), pp. 576–589.
44. S. W. J. Kozlowski and D. R. Ilgen, "Enhancing the Effectiveness of Work Groups and Teams," *Psychological Science in the Public Interest*, December 2006, pp. 77–124; and B. D. Edwards, E. A. Day, W. Arthur, Jr., and S. T. Bell, "Relationships Among Team Ability Composition, Team Mental Models, and Team Performance," *Journal of Applied Psychology* 91, no. 3 (2006), pp. 727–736.
45. K. A. Jehn, "A Qualitative Analysis of Conflict Types and Dimensions in Organizational Groups," *Administrative Science Quarterly*, September 1997, pp. 530–557. See also R. S. Peterson and K. J. Behfar, "The Dynamic Relationship Between Performance Feedback, Trust, and Conflict in Groups: A Longitudinal Study," *Organizational Behavior and Human Decision Processes*, September–November 2003, pp. 102–112.
46. K. H. Price, D. A. Harrison, and J. H. Gavin, "Withholding Inputs in Team Contexts: Member Composition, Interaction Processes, Evaluation Structure, and Social Loafing," *Journal of Applied Psychology* 91, no. 6 (2006), pp. 1375–1384.
47. See, for instance, B. L. Kirkman and D. L. Shapiro, "The Impact of Cultural Values on Employee Resistance to Teams: Toward a Model of Globalized Self-Managing Work Team Effectiveness," *Academy of Management Review*, July 1997, pp. 730–757; and B. L. Kirkman, C. B. Gibson, and D. L. Shapiro, "'Exporting' Teams: Enhancing the Implementation and Effectiveness of Work Teams in Global Affiliates," *Organizational Dynamics* 30, no. 1 (2001), pp. 12–29.
48. G. Hertel, U. Konradt, and K. Voss, "Competencies for Virtual Teamwork: Development and Validation of a Web-Based Selection Tool for Members of Distributed Teams," *European Journal of Work and Organizational Psychology* 15, no. 4 (2006), pp. 477–504.
49. T. D. Schellhardt, "To Be a Star Among Equals, Be a Team Player," *Wall Street Journal*, April 20, 1994, p. B1.
50. "Teaming Up for Success," *Training*, January 1994, p. s41.
51. J. S. DeMatteo, L. T. Eby, and E. Sundstrom, "Team-Based Rewards: Current Empirical Evidence and Directions for Future Research," in B. M. Staw and L. L. Cummings (eds.), *Research in Organizational Behavior*, vol. 20, pp. 141–183.
52. B. Geber, "The Bugaboo of Team Pay," *Training*, August 1995, pp. 27, 34.
53. C. E. Naquin and R. O. Tynan, "The Team Halo Effect: Why Teams Are Not Blamed for Their Failures," *Journal of Applied Psychology*, April 2003, pp. 332–340.
54. A. B. Drexler and R. Forrester, "Teamwork—Not Necessarily the Answer," *HRMagazine*, January 1998, pp. 55–58. See also R. Saavedra, P. C. Earley, and L. Van Dyne, "Complex Interdependence in Task-Performing Groups," *Journal of Applied Psychology*, February 1993, pp. 61–72; and K. A. Jehn, G. B. Northcraft, and M. A. Neale, "Why Differences Make a Difference: A Field Study of Diversity, Conflict, and Performance in Workgroups," *Administrative Science Quarterly*, December 1999, pp. 741–763.
55. "Watson Wyatt's Global Work Studies." *WatsonWyatt.com*, www.watsonwyatt.com/research/featured/workstudy.asp
56. Nicholls, Lane, and Brehm Brechu, "Taking Self-Managed Teams to Mexico."
57. W. E. Watson, K. Kumar, and L. K. Michaelsen, "Cultural Diversity's Impact on Interaction Process and Performance: Comparing Homogeneous and Diverse Task Groups," *Academy of Management Journal*, June 1993, pp. 590–602; P. C. Earley and E. Mosakowski, "Creating Hybrid Team Cultures: An Empirical Test of Transnational Team Functioning," *Academy of Management Journal*, February 2000, pp. 26–49; and S. Mohammed and L. C. Angell, "Surface- and Deep-Level Diversity in Workgroups: Examining the Moderating Effects of Team Orientation and Team Process on Relationship Conflict," *Journal of Organizational Behavior*, December 2004, pp. 1015–1039.
58. Watson, Kumar, and Michaelsen, "Cultural Diversity's Impact on Interaction Process and Performance: Comparing Homogeneous and Diverse Task Groups."

Communication

Constantly talking isn't necessarily communicating.

—Joel, a character in the 2004 film *Eternal Sunshine of the Spotless Mind*

11

LEARNING OBJECTIVES

After studying this chapter, you should be able to:

1. Identify the main functions of communication.
2. Describe the communication process and distinguish between formal and informal communication.
3. Contrast downward, upward, and lateral communication and provide examples of each.
4. Contrast oral, written, and nonverbal communication.
5. Contrast formal communication networks and the grapevine.
6. Analyze the advantages and challenges of electronic communication.
7. Show how channel richness underlies the choice of communication channel.
8. Identify common barriers to effective communication.
9. Show how to overcome the potential problems in cross-cultural communication.

Although gossip often seems benign, it can have some pretty serious consequences. Just ask four former employees of the town of Hooksett, New Hampshire (population 11,721), who were fired by the town council for gossiping about their boss. (Pictured below: from left, Sandra Piper, Joann Drewniak, Jessica Skorupski, and Michelle Bonsteel.)

The longtime employees—two administrative assistants and two department heads—were fired because one had referred to the town administrator in derogatory

Gossip at Work: The Hooksett Four

terms and because all four had discussed a rumor that he was having an affair with a female subordinate. One of the employees supposedly referred to the town administrator, David Jodoin, as "a little f__________." The fired employees (all of whom are female) also acknowledged feeling resentment toward the woman, who worked in a specially created position and was paid more than two of the employees, despite having less experience and seniority.

The four employees appealed their dismissal. The Hooksett council denied the appeal and issued a statement arguing "These employees do not represent the best interests of the town of Hooksett and the false rumors, gossip and derogatory statements have contributed to a negative working environment and malcontent among their fellow employees."

B. J. Branch, an attorney representing the four women, said his clients were "legitimately questioning the conduct of their supervisor, and whether the female subordinate was getting preferential treatment. It almost cheapens it to call it gossip. It might have been idle, not particularly thoughtful, talk. But there was no harm intended."

The fired employees—Michelle Bonsteel (code enforcement officer), Sandra Piper (tax assessor), and Jessica Skorupski and Joann Drewniak (both administrative assistants)—who have come to be known as the "Hooksett Four," also claimed they heard the rumor of the affair from a town resident, who questioned the late hours shared by the administrator and his female subordinate.

Some employers have policies against office gossip. Balliet's, U.S. department store, recently added a malicious-gossip paragraph to the store's personnel policies and procedures manual. It reads: "Malicious gossip by employees about other employees or customers is strictly forbidden, as is researching personal information about employees or customers on the Internet or other records. Violation of this policy may result in immediate termination of employment." The policy grew out of two incidents that occurred recently—one in which after-hours socializing led to things being said about people at work, and the other in which three employees went online to check out a situation about a coworker. "Both created enormous tension in the store," owner Bob Benham said. "Someone wouldn't talk to someone else, creating a mood customers could feel."

Since they were fired, the Hooksett Four have appeared on *Good Morning America*, and they are considering their legal options. A petition calling for their reinstatement was signed by 419 Hooksett residents and forwarded to the town council. "If we didn't fire them, we would have been sued for sexual harassment and malicious slander. We would have been liable for a lawsuit if we had done nothing," said George Longfellow, town council chair. "I'm definitely not going away, that's for sure," Drewniak said. "They wrongfully fired me, and I shouldn't be out of work."

Whatever the legal merits of the Hooksett Four's claim, it's clear that what may have seemed like benign gossip had pretty malignant consequences.[1] ■

The preceding examples illustrate the profound consequences of communication. In this chapter, we'll analyze the power of communication and ways in which it can be made more effective. One of the topics we'll discuss is gossip. Consider the following self-assessment and how you score on your attitudes toward gossip at work.

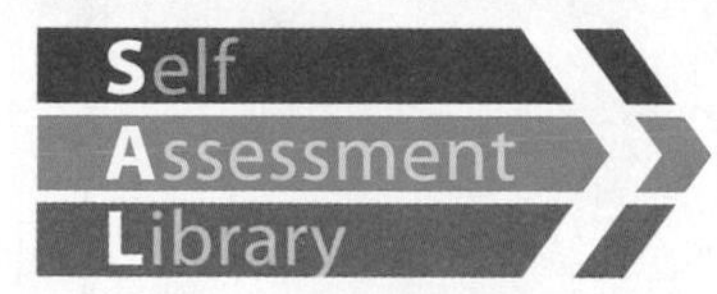

AM I A GOSSIP?

In the Self-Assessment Library (available on CD or online), take assessment IV.E.3 (Am I a Gossip?) and answer the following questions.

1. *How did you score relative to your classmates?*
2. *Do you think gossiping is morally wrong? Why or why not?*

Gossip is one communication issue. There are many others. Research indicates that poor communication is probably the most frequently cited source of interpersonal conflict.[2] Because individuals spend nearly 70 percent of their waking hours communicating—writing, reading, speaking, listening—it seems reasonable to conclude that one of the most inhibiting forces to successful group performance is a lack of effective communication. And good communication skills are very important to your career success. A 2007 study of recruiters found that they rated communication skills as *the* most important characteristic of an ideal job candidate.[3]

No individual, group, or organization can exist without communication: the transfer of meaning among its members. It is only through transmitting meaning from one person to another that information and ideas can be conveyed. Communication, however, is more than merely imparting meaning. It must also be understood. In a group in which one member speaks only German and the others do not know German, the individual speaking German will not be fully understood. Therefore, **communication** must include both the *transfer and the understanding of meaning.*

An idea, no matter how great, is useless until it is transmitted and understood by others. Perfect communication, if there were such a thing, would exist when a thought or an idea was transmitted so that the mental picture perceived by the receiver was exactly the same as that envisioned by the sender. Although elementary in theory, perfect communication is never achieved in practice, for reasons we shall expand on later in the chapter.

Before making too many generalizations concerning communication and problems in communicating effectively, we need to review briefly the functions that communication performs and describe the communication process.

Functions of Communication

Communication serves four major functions within a group or organization: control, motivation, emotional expression, and information.[4]

1 Identify the main functions of communication.

Communication acts to *control* member behavior in several ways. Organizations have authority hierarchies and formal guidelines that employees are required to follow. For instance, when employees are required to communicate any job-related grievance to their immediate boss, to follow their job description, or to comply with company policies, communication is performing a control function. But informal communication also controls behavior. When work groups tease or harass a member who produces too much (and makes the rest of the group look bad), they are informally communicating with, and controlling, the member's behavior.

communication *The transfer and understanding of meaning.*

Globalization has changed the way Toyota Motor Corporation provides employees with the information they need for decision making. In the past, Toyota transferred employee knowledge on the job from generation to generation through "tacit understanding," a common communication method used in the conformist and subdued Japanese culture. Today, however, as a global organization, Toyota transfers knowledge of its production methods to overseas employees by bringing them to its training center in Japan, shown here, to teach them production methods by using how-to manuals, practice drills, and lectures.

Communication fosters *motivation* by clarifying to employees what is to be done, how well they are doing, and what can be done to improve performance if it's subpar. We saw this operating in our review of goal-setting and reinforcement theories in Chapter 6. The formation of specific goals, feedback on progress toward the goals, and reinforcement of desired behavior all stimulate motivation and require communication.

For many employees, their work group is a primary source for social interaction. The communication that takes place within the group is a fundamental mechanism by which members show their frustrations and feelings of satisfaction. Communication, therefore, provides a release for the *emotional expression* of feelings and for fulfillment of social needs.

The final function that communication performs relates to its role in facilitating decision making. It provides the *information* that individuals and groups need to make decisions by transmitting the data to identify and evaluate alternative choices.

No one of these four functions should be seen as being more important than the others. For groups to perform effectively, they need to maintain some form of control over members, stimulate members to perform, provide a means for emotional expression, and make decision choices. You can assume that almost every communication interaction that takes place in a group or an organization performs one or more of these four functions.

The Communication Process

2 Describe the communication process and distinguish between formal and informal communication.

Before communication can take place, a purpose, expressed as a message to be conveyed, is needed. It passes between a sender and a receiver. The message is encoded (converted to a symbolic form) and passed by way of some medium (channel) to the receiver, who retranslates (decodes) the message initiated by the sender. The result is transfer of meaning from one person to another.[5]

Exhibit 11-1 The Communication Process

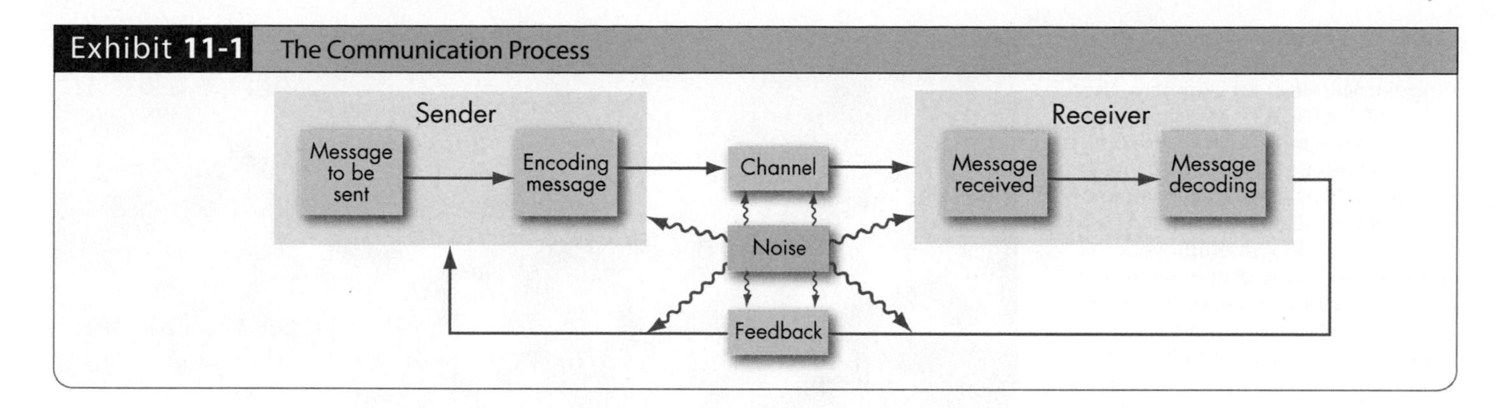

Exhibit 11-1 depicts this **communication process**. The key parts of this model are: (1) the sender, (2) encoding, (3) the message, (4) the channel, (5) decoding, (6) the receiver, (7) noise, and (8) feedback.

The *sender* initiates a message by encoding a thought. The *message* is the actual physical product from the sender's *encoding*. When we speak, the speech is the message. When we write, the writing is the message. When we gesture, the movements of our arms and the expressions on our faces are the message. The *channel* is the medium through which the message travels. It is selected by the sender, who must determine whether to use a formal or informal channel. **Formal channels** are established by the organization and transmit messages that are related to the professional activities of members. They traditionally follow the authority chain within the organization. Other forms of messages, such as personal or social, follow **informal channels** in the organization. These informal channels are spontaneous and emerge as a response to individual choices.[6] The *receiver* is the object to whom the message is directed. But before the message can be received, the symbols in it must be translated into a form that can be understood by the receiver. This step is the *decoding* of the message. *Noise* represents communication barriers that distort the clarity of the message. Examples of possible noise sources include perceptual problems, information overload, semantic difficulties, or cultural differences. The final link in the communication process is a feedback loop. *Feedback* is the check on how successful we have been in transferring our messages as originally intended. It determines whether understanding has been achieved.

Direction of Communication

3 *Contrast downward, upward, and lateral communication and provide examples of each.*

Communication can flow vertically or laterally. The vertical dimension can be further divided into downward and upward directions.[7]

Downward Communication

Communication that flows from one level of a group or organization to a lower level is downward communication. When we think of managers communicating with employees, the downward pattern is the one we are usually thinking of.

communication process *The steps between a source and a receiver that result in the transfer and understanding of meaning.*

formal channels *Communication channels established by an organization to transmit messages related to the professional activities of members.*

informal channels *Communication channels that are created spontaneously and that emerge as responses to individual choices.*

After the telecommunications firm AT&T acquired BellSouth and Cingular Wireless, Ed Whitacre, then CEO of AT&T, used downward communication to inform the former BellSouth and Cingular employees about the company's acquisition strategy. Whitacre held meetings to assure employees that he understood the changes resulting from the acquisition caused turmoil and confusion in the short term and asked them to continually provide excellent customer service during the transitional period. The face-to-face meetings gave employees the opportunity to ask questions.

Source: Erik S. Lesser/ The New York Times

It's used by group leaders and managers to assign goals, provide job instructions, inform employees of policies and procedures, point out problems that need attention, and offer feedback about performance. But downward communication doesn't have to be oral or face-to-face contact. When management sends letters to employees' homes to advise them of the organization's new sick leave policy, it's using downward communication. Another example of downward communication is an e-mail from a team leader to the members of her team, reminding them of an upcoming deadline.

When engaging in downward communication, managers must explain the reasons *why* a decision was made. One study found that employees were twice as likely to be committed to changes when the reasons behind them were fully explained. Although this may seem like common sense, many managers feel they are too busy to explain things, or that explanations will "open up a big can of worms." Evidence clearly indicates, though, that explanations increase employee commitment and support of decisions.[8]

Another problem in downward communication is its one-way nature; generally, managers inform employees but rarely solicit their advice or opinions. A 2006 study revealed that nearly two-thirds of employees say their boss rarely or never asks their advice. The author of the study noted, "Organizations are always striving for higher employee engagement, but evidence indicates they unnecessarily create fundamental mistakes. People need to be respected and listened to." Anne Mulcahy, CEO of Xerox, finds that listening takes work: "Listening is one of those things that is easy to talk about, difficult to do."[9]

The best communicators are those who explain the reasons behind their downward communications, but also solicit upward communication from the employees they supervise. That leads us to the next direction: upward communication.

Upward Communication

Upward communication flows to a higher level in the group or organization. It's used to provide feedback to higher-ups, inform them of progress toward goals, and relay current problems. Upward communication keeps managers aware of how employees feel about their jobs, coworkers, and the organization in general. Managers also rely on upward communication for ideas on how things can be improved.

Given that job responsibilities of most managers and supervisors have expanded, upward communication is increasingly difficult because managers are overwhelmed and easily distracted. To engage in effective upward communication, try to reduce distractions (meet in a conference room if you can, rather than your boss's office or cubicle), communicate in headlines not paragraphs (your job is to get your boss's attention, not to engage in a meandering discussion), support your headlines with actionable items (what you believe should happen), and prepare an agenda to make sure you use your boss's attention well.[10]

Lateral Communication

When communication takes place among members of the same work group, among members of work groups at the same level, among managers at the same level, or among any other horizontally equivalent personnel, we describe it as lateral communications.

Why would there be a need for horizontal communications if a group or an organization's vertical communications are effective? The answer is that horizontal communication is often necessary to save time and facilitate coordination. In some cases, such lateral relationships are formally sanctioned. More often, they are informally created to short-circuit the vertical hierarchy and expedite action. So lateral communications can, from management's viewpoint, be good or bad. Because strict adherence to the formal vertical structure for all communications can impede the efficient and accurate transfer of information, lateral communications can be beneficial. In such cases, they occur with the knowledge and support of superiors. But they can create dysfunctional conflicts when the formal vertical channels are breached, when members go above or around their superiors to get things done, or when bosses find out that actions have been taken or decisions have been made without their knowledge.

Interpersonal Communication

4 Contrast oral, written, and nonverbal communication.

How do group members transfer meaning between and among each other? There are three basic methods. People essentially rely on oral, written, and nonverbal communication.

Oral Communication

The chief means of conveying messages is oral communication. Speeches, formal one-on-one and group discussions, and the informal rumor mill, or grapevine, are popular forms of oral communication.

The advantages of oral communication are speed and feedback. A verbal message can be conveyed and a response received in a minimal amount of time. If the receiver is unsure of the message, rapid feedback allows for early detection by the sender and, hence, allows for early correction. As one professional put it, "Face-to-face communication on a consistent basis is still the best way to get information to and from employees."[11]

The major disadvantage of oral communication surfaces whenever a message has to be passed through a number of people. The more people a message must pass through, the greater the potential distortion. If you've ever played the game "telephone," you know the problem. Each person interprets the message in his or her own way. The message's content, when it reaches its destination, is often

MYTH OR SCIENCE? "People Are Good at Catching Liars at Work"

This statement is essentially false. The core purpose of communication in the workplace may be to convey business-related information. However, in the workplace, we also communicate in order to manage impressions others form of us. Some of this impression management is unintentional and harmless (for example, complimenting your boss on his clothing). However, sometimes people manage impressions through outright lies, such as making up an excuse for missing work or failing to make a deadline.

One of the reasons people lie—in the workplace and elsewhere—is that it works. Although most of us think we're good at detecting a lie, research shows that most people perform no better than chance at detecting whether someone is lying or telling the truth.

A recent review of 108 studies revealed that people detect lies at a rate, on average, only 4.2 percent better than chance. This study also found that people's confidence in their judgments of whether someone was lying bore almost no relationship to their actual accuracy; we think we're a lot better at catching people lying than we really are. What's even more discouraging is that so-called experts—police officers, parole officers, detectives, judges, and psychologists—perform no better than other people. As the authors of this review conclude, "People are not good detectors of deception regardless of their age, sex, confidence, and experience."

The point? Don't believe everything you hear and don't place too much weight on your ability to catch a liar based just on your intuition. When someone makes a claim that it's reasonable to doubt, ask her or him to back it up with evidence. ■

Source: M. G. Aamodt and H. Custer, "Who Can Best Catch a Liar? A Meta-analysis of Individual Differences in Detecting Deception," *The Forensic Examiner*, Spring 2006, pp. 6–11.

very different from that of the original. In an organization, where decisions and other communiqués are verbally passed up and down the authority hierarchy, there are considerable opportunities for messages to become distorted.

Written Communication

Written communications include memos, letters, fax transmissions, e-mail, instant messaging, organizational periodicals, notices placed on bulletin boards, or any other device that is transmitted via written words or symbols.

Why would a sender choose to use written communications? They're often tangible and verifiable. When they're printed, both the sender and receiver have a record of the communication; and the message can be stored for an indefinite period. If there are questions concerning the content of the message, it is physically available for later reference. This feature is particularly important for complex and lengthy communications. The marketing plan for a new product, for instance, is likely to contain a number of tasks spread out over several months. By putting it in writing, those who have to initiate the plan can readily refer to it over the life of the plan. A final benefit of all written communication comes from the process itself. People are usually more careful with the written word than with the oral word. They're forced to think more thoroughly about what they want to convey in a written message than in a spoken one. Thus, written communications are more likely to be well thought out, logical, and clear.

Of course, written messages have drawbacks. They're time-consuming. You could convey far more information to a college instructor in a 1-hour oral exam than in a 1-hour written exam. In fact, you could probably say the same thing in 10 to 15 minutes that it would take you an hour to write. So, although writing may be more precise, it also consumes a great deal of time. The other major disadvantage is feedback, or lack of it. Oral communication allows the receiver to respond rapidly to what he thinks he hears. Written communication, however, does not have a built-in feedback mechanism. The result is that the mailing of a memo is no assurance that it has been received, and, if received, there is no guarantee the recipient will interpret it as the sender intended. The latter point is also relevant in oral communiqués, except it's easy in such cases merely to ask the receiver to summarize what you've said. An accurate summary presents feedback evidence that the message has been received and understood.

Nonverbal Communication

Every time we verbally give a message to someone, we also impart a nonverbal message.[12] In some instances, the nonverbal component may stand alone. For example, in a singles bar, a glance, a stare, a smile, a frown, and a provocative body movement all convey meaning. Therefore, no discussion of communication would be complete without consideration of *nonverbal communication*—which includes body movements, the intonations or emphasis we give to words, facial expressions, and the physical distance between the sender and receiver.

It can be argued that every *body movement* has a meaning, and no movement is accidental. For example, through body language, we say, "Help me, I'm lonely"; "Take me, I'm available"; and "Leave me alone, I'm depressed." Rarely do we send our messages consciously. We act out our state of being with nonverbal body language. We lift one eyebrow for disbelief. We rub our noses for puzzlement. We clasp our arms to isolate ourselves or to protect ourselves. We shrug our shoulders for indifference, wink one eye for intimacy, tap our fingers for impatience, slap our forehead for forgetfulness.[13]

The two most important messages that body language conveys are (1) the extent to which an individual likes another and is interested in his or her views and (2) the relative perceived status between a sender and receiver.[14] For instance, we're more likely to position ourselves closer to people we like and touch them more often. Similarly, if you feel that you're of higher status than another, you're more likely to display body movements—such as crossed legs or a slouched seated position—that reflect a casual and relaxed manner.[15]

Body language adds to, and often complicates, verbal communication. A body position or movement does not by itself have a precise or universal meaning, but when it is linked with spoken language, it gives fuller meaning to a sender's message.

If you read the verbatim minutes of a meeting, you wouldn't grasp the impact of what was said in the same way you would if you had been there or if you saw the meeting on video. Why? There is no record of nonverbal communication. The emphasis given to words or phrases is missing. Exhibit 11-2

Exhibit 11-2 Intonations: It's the Way You Say It!

Change your tone and you change your meaning:

Placement of the emphasis	What it means
Why don't I take **you** to dinner tonight?	I was going to take someone else.
Why don't **I** take you to dinner tonight?	Instead of the guy you were going with.
Why **don't** I take you to dinner tonight?	I'm trying to find a reason why I **shouldn't** take you.
Why don't I take you to dinner tonight?	Do you have a problem with me?
Why don't I **take** you to dinner tonight?	Instead of going on your own.
Why don't I take you to **dinner** tonight?	Instead of lunch tomorrow.
Why don't I take you to dinner **tonight**?	Not tomorrow night.

Source: Based on M. Kiely, "When 'No' Means 'Yes,'" *Marketing*, October 1993, pp. 7–9. Reproduced in A. Huczynski and D. Buchanan, *Organizational Behavior*, 4th ed. (Essex, UK: Pearson Education, 2001), p. 194.

illustrates how *intonations* can change the meaning of a message. *Facial expressions* also convey meaning. A snarling face says something different from a smile. Facial expressions, along with intonations, can show arrogance, aggressiveness, fear, shyness, and other characteristics that would never be communicated if you read a transcript of what had been said.

The way individuals space themselves in terms of *physical distance* also has meaning. What is considered proper spacing is largely dependent on cultural norms. For example, what is considered a businesslike distance in some European countries would be viewed as intimate in many parts of North America. If someone stands closer to you than is considered appropriate, it may indicate aggressiveness or sexual interest; if farther away than usual, it may mean disinterest or displeasure with what is being said.

It's important for the receiver to be alert to these nonverbal aspects of communication. You should look for nonverbal cues as well as listen to the literal meaning of a sender's words. You should particularly be aware of contradictions between the messages. Your boss may say she is free to talk to you about a pressing budget problem, but you may see nonverbal signals suggesting that this is not the time to discuss the subject. Regardless of what is being said, an individual who frequently glances at her wristwatch is giving the message that she would prefer to terminate the conversation. We misinform others when we express one message verbally, such as trust, but nonverbally communicate a contradictory message that reads, "I don't have confidence in you."

Organizational Communication

5 *Contrast formal communication networks and the grapevine.*

In this section, we move from interpersonal communication to organizational communication. Our first focus will be to describe and distinguish formal networks and the grapevine. In the following section, we discuss technological innovations in communication.

Formal Small-Group Networks

Formal organizational networks can be very complicated. They can, for instance, include hundreds of people and a half-dozen or more hierarchical levels. To simplify our discussion, we've condensed these networks into three common small groups of five people each (see Exhibit 11-3). These three networks are the

Exhibit 11-3 Three Common Small-Group Networks

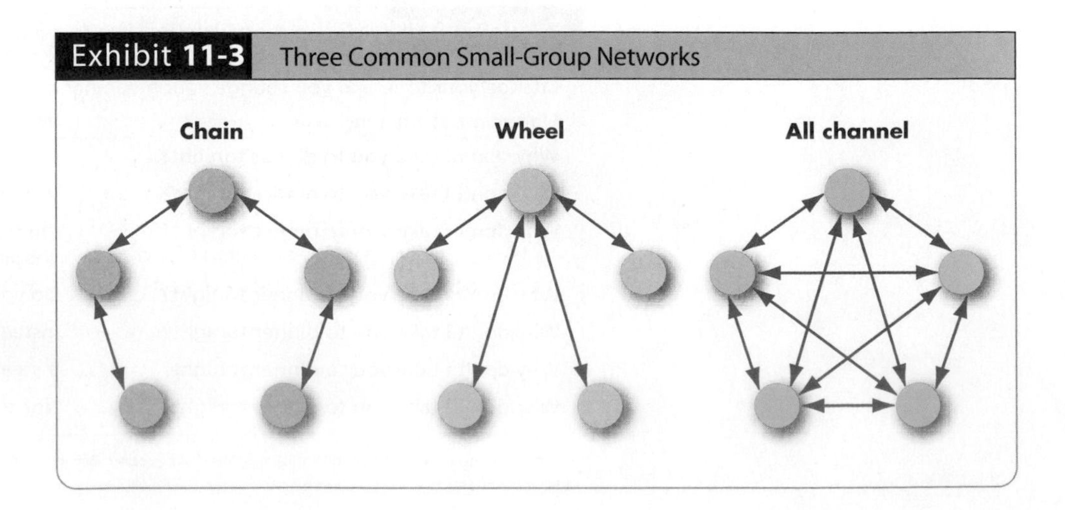

Exhibit 11-4 Small-Group Networks and Effective Criteria

Criteria	Networks Chain	Wheel	All Channel
Speed	Moderate	Fast	Fast
Accuracy	High	High	Moderate
Emergence of a leader	Moderate	High	None
Member satisfaction	Moderate	Low	High

chain, wheel, and all channel. Although these three networks have been extremely simplified, they allow us to describe the unique qualities of each.

The *chain* rigidly follows the formal chain of command. This network approximates the communication channels you might find in a rigid three-level organization. The *wheel* relies on a central figure to act as the conduit for all of the group's communication. It simulates the communication network you would find on a team with a strong leader. The *all-channel* network permits all group members to actively communicate with each other. The all-channel network is most often characterized in practice by self-managed teams, in which all group members are free to contribute and no one person takes on a leadership role.

As Exhibit 11-4 demonstrates, the effectiveness of each network depends on the dependent variable you're concerned about. For instance, the structure of the wheel facilitates the emergence of a leader, the all-channel network is best if you are concerned with having high member satisfaction, and the chain is best if accuracy is most important. Exhibit 11-4 leads us to the conclusion that no single network will be best for all occasions.

The Grapevine

The formal system is not the only communication network in a group or organization. There is also an informal one, called the **grapevine**.[16] Although the grapevine may be informal, it's still an important source of information. For instance, a survey found that 75 percent of employees hear about matters first through rumors on the grapevine.[17]

The grapevine has three main characteristics.[18] First, it is not controlled by management. Second, it is perceived by most employees as being more believable and reliable than formal communiqués issued by top management. Finally, it is largely used to serve the self-interests of the people within it.

One of the most famous studies of the grapevine investigated the communication pattern among 67 managerial personnel in a small manufacturing firm.[19] The basic approach used was to learn from each communication recipient how he or she first received a given piece of information and then trace it back to its source. It was found that, while the grapevine was an important source of information, only 10 percent of the executives acted as liaison individuals (that is, passed the information on to more than one other person). For example, when one executive decided to resign to enter the insurance business, 81 percent of the executives knew about it, but only 11 percent transmitted this information to others.

grapevine *An organization's informal communication network.*

Exhibit 11-5 Suggestions for Reducing the Negative Consequences of Rumors

1. Announce timetables for making important decisions.
2. Explain decisions and behaviors that may appear inconsistent or secretive.
3. Emphasize the downside, as well as the upside, of current decisions and future plans.
4. Openly discuss worst-case possibilities—it is almost never as anxiety provoking as the unspoken fantasy.

Source: Adapted from L. Hirschhorn, "Managing Rumors," in L. Hirschhorn (ed.), *Cutting Back* (San Francisco: Jossey-Bass, 1983), pp. 54–56. Used with permission.

Is the information that flows along the grapevine accurate? The evidence indicates that about 75 percent of what is carried is accurate.[20] But what conditions foster an active grapevine? What gets the rumor mill rolling?

It's frequently assumed that rumors start because they make titillating gossip. This is rarely the case. Rumors emerge as a response to situations that are *important* to us, when there is *ambiguity*, and under conditions that arouse *anxiety*.[21] The fact that work situations frequently contain these three elements explains why rumors flourish in organizations. The secrecy and competition that typically prevail in large organizations—around issues such as the appointment of new bosses, the relocation of offices, downsizing decisions, and the realignment of work assignments—create conditions that encourage and sustain rumors on the grapevine. A rumor will persist either until the wants and expectations creating the uncertainty underlying the rumor are fulfilled or until the anxiety is reduced.

What can we conclude from the preceding discussion? Certainly the grapevine is an important part of any group or organization communication network and is well worth understanding. It gives managers a feel for the morale of their organization, identifies issues that employees consider important, and helps tap into employee anxieties. The grapevine also serves employees' needs: Small talk serves to create a sense of closeness and friendship among those who share information, although research suggests that it often does so at the expense of those in the "out" group.[22]

Can management entirely eliminate rumors? No. What management should do, however, is minimize the negative consequences of rumors by limiting their range and impact. Exhibit 11-5 offers a few suggestions for minimizing those negative consequences.

Electronic Communications

6 Analyze the advantages and challenges of electronic communication.

An indispensable—and in 71 percent of cases, the primary—medium of communication in today's organizations is electronic. Electronic communications include e-mail, text messaging, networking software, Internet or Web logs (blogs), and video conferencing. Let's discuss each.

E-mail E-mail uses the Internet to transmit and receive computer-generated text and documents. Its growth has been spectacular, and its use is now so pervasive that it's hard to imagine life without it.

When Bill Gates goes to work, he has three screens synchronized, two of which are for e-mail (the other is Internet Explorer). As a communication tool, e-mail has a long list of benefits. E-mail messages can be quickly written, edited, and stored. They can be distributed to one person or thousands with a click of a mouse. They can be read, in their entirety, at the convenience of the recipient. And the cost of sending formal e-mail messages to employees is a fraction of the cost of printing, duplicating, and distributing a comparable letter or brochure.[23]

E-mail, of course, is not without drawbacks. The following are some of the most significant limitations of e-mail and what organizations should do to reduce or eliminate these problems:

- *Misinterpreting the message.* It's true that we often misinterpret verbal messages, but the potential for misinterpretation with e-mail is even greater. One research team found that we can accurately decode an e-mail's intent and tone only 50 percent of the time, yet most of us vastly overestimate our ability to send and interpret clear messages. If you're sending an important message, make sure you reread it for clarity. And if you're upset about the presumed tone of someone else's message, keep in mind that you may be misinterpreting it.[24]
- *Communicating negative messages.* When companies have negative information to communicate, managers need to think carefully. E-mail may not be the best way to communicate the message. When the electronics maker Radio Shack decided to lay off 400 employees, it drew down an avalanche of scorn inside and outside the company by doing it via e-mail. Employees need to be careful communicating negative messages via e-mail, too. Justen Deal, 22, wrote an e-mail critical of some strategic decisions made by his employer, pharmaceutical giant Kaiser Permanente. In the e-mail, he criticized the "misleadership" of Kaiser CEO George Halvorson and questioned the financing of several information technology projects. Within hours, Deal's computer was seized; he was later fired.[25]
- *Overuse of e-mail.* An estimated 6 trillion e-mails are sent every year, and someone has to answer all those messages! As people become established in their careers and their responsibilities expand, so do their inboxes. A survey of Canadian managers revealed that 58 percent spent 2 to 4 hours per day reading and responding to e-mails. Some people, such as venture capitalist Fred Wilson, have become so overwhelmed by e-mail that they've declared "e-mail bankruptcy." Recording artist Moby sent an e-mail to all those in his address book announcing that he was taking a break from e-mail for the rest of the year. Although you probably don't want to declare e-mail bankruptcy, or couldn't get away with it even if you did, you should use e-mail judiciously, especially when you're contacting people inside the organization who may already be wading through lots of e-mail messages every day.[26]
- *E-mail emotions.* We tend to think of e-mail as a sort of sterile, faceless form of communication. But that doesn't mean it's unemotional. As you no doubt know, e-mails are often highly emotional. One CEO said, "I've seen people not talk to each other, turf wars break out and people quit their jobs as a result of e-mails." E-mail tends to have a disinhibiting effect on people; senders write things they'd never be comfortable saying in person. Facial expressions tend to temper our emotional expressions, but in e-mail, there is no other face to look at, and so many of us fire away. An increasingly common way of communicating emotions in e-mail is with emoticons. For example, Yahoo!'s e-mail software allows the user to pick from 32 emoticons. Although emoticons used to be considered for personal use only, increasingly adults are using them in business e-mails. Still, some see them as too informal for business use.

  When others send flaming messages, remain calm and try not to respond in kind. Also, when writing new e-mails, try to temper your own tendencies to quickly fire off messages.[27]
- *Privacy concerns.* There are two privacy issues with e-mail. First, you need to be aware that your e-mails may be, and often are, monitored. Also, you can't always trust that the recipient of your e-mail will keep it confidential. For these reasons, you shouldn't write anything you wouldn't want made public. Before Wal-Mart fired marketing VP Julie Roehm, its managers examined

her e-mails for evidence of an inappropriate romantic relationship. Second, you need to exercise caution in forwarding e-mail from your company's e-mail account to a personal, or "public," (for example, Gmail, Yahoo!, MSN) e-mail account. These accounts often aren't as secure as corporate accounts, so when you forward a company e-mail to them, you may be violating your organization's policy or unintentionally disclosing confidential data. Many employers hire vendors that sift through e-mails, using software to catch not only the obvious ("insider trading") but the vague ("that thing we talked about") or guilt ridden ("regret"). Another survey revealed that nearly 40 percent of companies have employees whose only job is to read other employees' e-mail. You are being watched—so be careful what you e-mail![28]

Instant Messaging and Text Messaging Like e-mail, instant messaging (IM) and text messaging (TM) use electronic messages. Unlike e-mail, though, IM and TM are either in "real" time (IM) or use portable communication devices (TM). In just a few years, IM/TM has become pervasive. As you no doubt know from experience, IM is usually sent via desktop or laptop computer, whereas TM is transmitted via cellphones or handheld devices such as Blackberrys.

The growth of TM has been spectacular. In 2001, for instance, just 8 percent of U.S. employees were using it. Now that number is more than 50 percent.[29] Why? Because IM and TM represent fast and inexpensive means for managers to stay in touch with employees and for employees to stay in touch with each other. In an increasing number of cases, this isn't just a luxury, it's a business imperative. For example, Bill Green, CEO of the consulting firm Accenture, doesn't have a permanent office. Since he's on the road all the time, visiting Accenture's 100 locations scattered across the globe, TM is essential for him keep in touch. Although there aren't many other examples so dramatic, the great advantage of TM is that it is flexible; with it, you can be reached almost anywhere, anytime.[30]

Despite their advantages, IM and TM aren't going to replace e-mail. E-mail is still probably a better device for conveying long messages that need to be saved. IM is preferable for one- or two-line messages that would just clutter up an e-mail inbox. On the downside, some IM/TM users find the technology intrusive and distracting. Their continual presence can make it hard for employees to concentrate and stay focused. For example, a survey of managers revealed that in 86 percent of meetings, at least some participants checked TM. Finally, because instant messages can be intercepted easily, many organizations are concerned about the security of IM/TM.[31]

One other point: It's important to not let the informality of text messaging ("omg! r u serious? brb") spill over into business e-mails. Many prefer to keep business communication relatively formal. A survey of employers revealed that 58 percent rate grammar, spelling, and punctuation as "very important" in e-mail messages.[32] By making sure your professional communications are, well, professional, you'll show yourself to be mature and serious. That doesn't mean, of course, that you have to give up TM or IM; you just need to maintain the boundaries between how you communicate with your friends and how you communicate professionally.

Networking Software Nowhere has communication been transformed more than in the area of networking. You are doubtless familiar with and perhaps a user of social networking Web sites such as Facebook and MySpace.

Rather than being one huge site, Facebook, which has 30 million active users, is actually composed of separate networks based on schools, companies, or regions. It might surprise you to learn that individuals over 25 are the fastest-growing users of Facebook.

Facebook founder and CEO Mark Zuckerberg continues to transform communication. He announced a new platform strategy that allows third parties to develop services on the Facebook site, which allows communication opportunities for business entrepreneurs. For Zuckerberg, Facebook is more than a social networking site. He describes it as a communication tool that facilitates the flow of information between users and their friends, family members, and professional connections.

Source: Noah Berger/ The New York Times

More than 100 million users have created accounts at MySpace. This site averages more than 40 billion hits per month. MySpace profiles contain two "blurbs": "About Me" and "Who I'd Like to Meet" sections. Profiles can also contain "Interests" and "Details" sections, photos, blog entries, and other details. Compared to Facebook, MySpace is relatively more likely to be used for purely personal reasons, as illustrated by the "Friends Space" portion of a user's account.

Amid the growth of Facebook and MySpace, professional networking sites have entered the marketplace and expanded as well. LinkedIn, Ziggs, and ZoomInfo are all professional Web sites that allow users to set up lists of contacts and do everything from casually "pinging" them with updates to hosting chat rooms for all or some of the users' contacts. Some companies, such as IBM, have their own social networks (IBM's is called BluePages); IBM is selling the BluePages tool to companies and individual users. Microsoft is doing the same thing with its SharePoint tool.

To get the most out of social networks, while avoiding irritating your contacts, use them "for high-value items only"—not as an everyday or even every-week tool. Also, remember that a prospective employer might check your MySpace or Facebook entry. In fact, some entrepreneurs have developed software that mines such Web sites for companies (or individuals) that want to check up on a job applicant (or potential date). So keep in mind that what you post may be read by people other than your intended contacts.[33]

Web Logs (Blogs) Sun Microsystems CEO Jonathan Schwartz is a big fan of Web logs (**blogs**), Web sites about a single person or company that are usually updated daily. He encourages his employees to have them and has one himself (http://blogs.sun.com/jonathan). Schwartz's blog averages 400,000 hits per

blog (Web log) *A Web site where entries are written, generally displayed in reverse chronological order, about news, events, and personal diary entries.*

month, and Schwartz, like Apple's managers, allows Sun customers to post comments about the company's products on its Web site.

Obviously, Schwartz is not the only fan of blogs. Experts estimate that more than 10 million U.S. workers have blogs, and nearly 40 million people read blogs on a regular basis. Thousands of Microsoft employees have blogs. Google, GM, Nike, IBM, and many other large organizations also have corporate blogs.

So what's the downside? Although some companies have policies in place governing the content of blogs, many don't, and 39 percent of individual bloggers say they have posted comments that could be construed as harmful to their company's reputation. Many bloggers think their personal blogs are outside their employer's purview, but if someone else in a company happens to read a blog entry, there is nothing to keep him or her from sharing that information with others, and the employee could be dismissed as a result. Schwartz says that Sun would not fire an employee over any blog entry short of one that broke the law. "Our blogging policy is 'Be authentic. Period,'" he says. But most organizations are unlikely to be so forgiving of any blog entry that might cast a negative light on them.

When Andrew McDonald landed an internship with the cable channel Comedy Central, his first day at work, he started a blog. His supervisors asked him to change various things about the blog, essentially removing all specific references to his employer. Kelly Kreth was fired from her job as a marketing director for blogging about her coworkers. So was Jessa Werner, who later said, "I came to the realization that I probably shouldn't have been blogging about work."

One legal expert notes, "Employee bloggers mistakenly believe that First Amendment gives them the right to say whatever they want on their personal blogs. Wrong!" Also, beware of posting personal blog entries at work. More than three-quarters of employers actively monitor employees' Web site connections. In short, if you are going to have a personal blog, maintain a strict work–personal "firewall."[34]

Video Conferencing *Video conferencing* permits employees in an organization to have meetings with people at different locations. Live audio and video images of members allow them to see, hear, and talk with each other. Video conferencing technology, in effect, allows employees to conduct interactive meetings without the necessity of all being physically in the same location.

In the late 1990s, video conferencing was basically conducted from special rooms equipped with television cameras, located at company facilities. More recently, cameras and microphones are being attached to individual computers, allowing people to participate in video conferences without leaving their desks. As the cost of this technology drops, video conferencing is likely to be increasingly seen as an alternative to expensive and time-consuming travel.

Knowledge Management

Our final topic under organizational communication is **knowledge management (KM)**. This is a process of organizing and distributing an organization's collective wisdom so the right information gets to the right people at the right time. When done properly, KM provides an organization with both a competitive edge and improved organizational performance because it makes its employees smarter. It can also help control leaks of vital company information so that an organization's competitive advantage is preserved for as long as possible. Despite its importance, KM gets low marks from most business leaders. When consulting firm Bain & Co. asked 960 executives about the effectiveness of 25 management tools, KM ranked near the bottom of the list. One expert concluded, "Most organizations are still managing as if we were in the industrial era."[35]

More companies are beginning to use video conferencing as an alternative to expensive and time-consuming travel.

Effective KM begins by identifying what knowledge matters to the organization.[36] Management needs to review processes to identify those that provide the most value. Then it can develop computer networks and databases that can make that information readily available to the people who need it the most. But KM won't work unless the culture supports sharing of information.[37] As we'll show in Chapter 14, information that is important and scarce can be a potent source of power. And people who hold that power are often reluctant to share it with others. So KM requires an organizational culture that promotes, values, and rewards sharing knowledge. Finally, KM must provide the mechanisms and the motivation for employees to share knowledge that employees find useful on the job and enables them to achieve better performance.[38] *More* knowledge isn't necessarily *better* knowledge. Information overload needs to be avoided by designing the system to capture only pertinent information and then organizing it so it can be quickly accessed by the people whom it can help.

knowledge management (KM) *The process of organizing and distributing an organization's collective wisdom so the right information gets to the right people at the right time.*

With the average age of its aerospace engineers at 54, defense contractor Northrop Grumman has developed a knowledge-based system to transfer knowledge from older to younger employees. Northrop has created a culture of knowledge sharing by forming "communities of practice," groups from different divisions that meet in person and online to share information. Aerospace engineer Tamra Johnson, shown here, started a community of practice for new engineers so they could learn from retired project managers and older employees.

Finally, security is a huge concern with any KM system. A Merrill Lynch survey of 50 executives found that 52 percent rated leaks of company information as their number-one information security concern, topping viruses and hackers. In response, most companies actively monitor employee Internet use and e-mail records, and some even use video surveillance and record phone conversations. Necessary though they may be, such surveillance and monitoring practices may seem invasive to employees. An organization can buttress employee concerns by involving them in the creation of information-security policies and giving them some control over how their personal information is used.[39]

Choice of Communication Channel

7 *Show how channel richness underlies the choice of communication channel.*

Neal L. Patterson, CEO at medical software maker Cerner Corp., likes e-mail. Maybe too much so. Upset with his staff's work ethic, he recently sent a seething e-mail to his firm's 400 managers.[40] Here are some of that e-mail's highlights:

> Hell will freeze over before this CEO implements ANOTHER EMPLOYEE benefit in this Culture. . . . We are getting less than 40 hours of work from a large number of our Kansas City-based employees. The parking lot is sparsely used at 8 A.M.; likewise at 5 P.M. As managers—you either do not know what your EMPLOYEES are doing; or YOU do not CARE. . . . You have a problem and you will fix it or I will replace you. . . . What you are doing, as managers, with this company makes me SICK.

Patterson's e-mail additionally suggested that managers schedule meetings at 7 A.M., 6 P.M., and Saturday mornings; promised a staff reduction of 5 percent and institution of a time-clock system; and Patterson's intention to charge unapproved absences to employees' vacation time.

Within hours of this e-mail, copies of it had made its way onto a Yahoo! Web site. And within 3 days, Cerner's stock price had plummeted 22 percent.

Although one can argue whether such harsh criticism should be communicated at all, one thing is certainly clear: Patterson erred by selecting the wrong channel for his message. Such an emotional and sensitive message would likely have been better received in a face-to-face meeting.

Why do people choose one channel of communication over another—for instance, a phone call instead of a face-to-face talk? Is there any general insight we might be able to provide regarding choice of communication channel? The answer to the latter question is a qualified "yes." A model of media richness has been developed to explain channel selection among managers.[41]

Research has found that channels differ in their capacity to convey information. Some are rich in that they have the ability to (1) handle multiple cues simultaneously, (2) facilitate rapid feedback, and (3) be very personal. Others are lean in that they score low on these three factors. As Exhibit 11-6 illustrates, face-to-face conversation scores highest in terms of **channel richness** because it provides for the maximum amount of information to be transmitted during a communication episode. That is, it offers multiple information cues (words, postures, facial expressions, gestures, intonations), immediate feedback (both verbal and nonverbal), and the personal touch of "being there." Impersonal written media such as formal reports and bulletins rate lowest in richness.

The choice of one channel over another depends on whether the message is routine or nonroutine. The former types of messages tend to be straightforward and have a minimum of ambiguity. The latter are likely to be complicated and have the potential for misunderstanding. Managers can communicate routine messages efficiently through channels that are lower in richness. However, they can communicate nonroutine messages effectively only by selecting rich channels. Referring back to the Cerner Corp. example, it appears that Neal Patterson used a channel relatively low in richness (e-mail) to convey a

Exhibit 11-6 Information Richness of Communication Channels

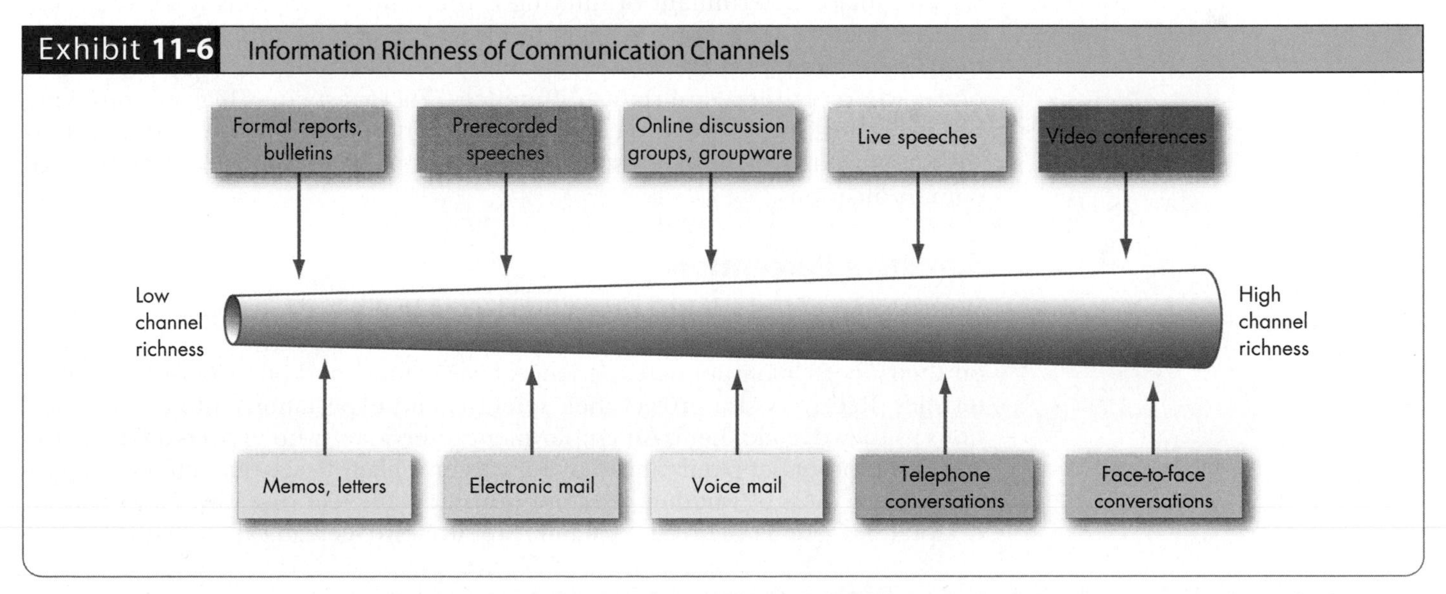

Source: Based on R. H. Lengel and R. L. Daft, "The Selection of Communication Media as an Executive Skill," *Academy of Management Executive*, August 1988, pp. 225–232; and R. L. Daft and R. H. Lengel, "Organizational Information Requirements, Media Richness, and Structural Design," *Managerial Science*, May 1996, pp. 554–572. Reproduced from R. L. Daft and R. A. Noe, *Organizational Behavior* (Fort Worth, TX: Harcourt, 2001), p. 311.

channel richness *The amount of information that can be transmitted during a communication episode.*

message that, because of its nonroutine nature and complexity, should have been conveyed using a rich communication medium.

Evidence indicates that high-performing managers tend to be more media sensitive than low-performing managers.[42] That is, they're better able to match appropriate media richness with the ambiguity involved in the communication.

The media richness model is consistent with organizational trends and practices of the past decade. It is not just coincidence that more and more senior managers have been using meetings to facilitate communication and regularly leaving the isolated sanctuary of their executive offices to manage by walking around. These executives are relying on richer channels of communication to transmit the more ambiguous messages they need to convey. The past decade has been characterized by organizations closing facilities, imposing large layoffs, restructuring, merging, consolidating, and introducing new products and services at an accelerated pace—all nonroutine messages high in ambiguity and requiring the use of channels that can convey a large amount of information. It is not surprising, therefore, to see the most effective managers expanding their use of rich channels.

Barriers to Effective Communication

8 *Identify common barriers to effective communication.*

A number of barriers can retard or distort effective communication. In this section, we highlight the most important of these barriers.

Filtering

Filtering refers to a sender's purposely manipulating information so it will be seen more favorably by the receiver. For example, when a manager tells his boss what he feels his boss wants to hear, he is filtering information.

The major determinant of filtering is the number of levels in an organization's structure. The more vertical levels in the organization's hierarchy, the more opportunities there are for filtering. But you can expect some filtering to occur wherever there are status differences. Factors such as fear of conveying bad news and the desire to please one's boss often lead employees to tell their superiors what they think those superiors want to hear, thus distorting upward communications.

Selective Perception

We have mentioned selective perception before in this book. It appears again here because the receivers in the communication process selectively see and hear based on their needs, motivations, experience, background, and other personal characteristics. Receivers also project their interests and expectations into communications as they decode them. An employment interviewer who expects a female job applicant to put her family ahead of her career is likely to see that in female applicants, regardless of whether the applicants actually feel that way. As we said in Chapter 5, we don't see reality; we interpret what we see and call it reality.

Information Overload

Individuals have a finite capacity for processing data. When the information we have to work with exceeds our processing capacity, the result is **information overload**. And with e-mails, IM, phone calls, faxes, meetings, and the need to keep current in one's field, the potential for today's managers and professionals to suffer from information overload is high.

What happens when individuals have more information than they can sort out and use? They tend to select, ignore, pass over, or forget information. Or

Call-center operators at Wipro Spectramind in New Delhi, India, speak English in serving their customers from the United States and the United Kingdom. But even though the operators and customers speak a common language, communication barriers exist because of differences in the countries' cultures and language accents. To overcome these barriers, the operators receive training in American and British pop culture so they can make small talk and are taught to speak with Western accents so they can be more easily understood by the calling clients.

they may put off further processing until the overload situation is over. In any case, the result is lost information and less effective communication.

Emotions

How the receiver feels at the time of receipt of a communication influences how he or she interprets it. The same message received when you're angry or distraught is often interpreted differently than it is when you're happy. Extreme emotions such as jubilation or depression are most likely to hinder effective communication. In such instances, we are most prone to disregard our rational and objective thinking processes and substitute emotional judgments.

Language

Even when we're communicating in the same language, words mean different things to different people. Age and context are two of the biggest factors that influence the language a person uses and the definitions he or she gives to words.

When Michael Schiller, a business consultant, was talking with his 15-year-old daughter about where she was going with her friends, he told her, "You need to recognize your ARAs and measure against them." Schiller said that in response, his daughter "looked at him like he was from outer space." (For the record, ARA stands for accountability, responsibility, and authority.) Those of you new to corporate lingo may find acronyms such as ARA, words such as "skeds" (schedules), or phrases such as "bake your noodle" (provide a service) to be bewildering, much in the same way that your parents may be mystified by the slang of your generation.[43]

The point is that although you and I probably speak a common language—English—our use of that language is far from uniform. If we knew how each of us modified the language, communication difficulties would be minimized.

filtering *A sender's manipulation of information so that it will be seen more favorably by the receiver.*

information overload *A condition in which information inflow exceeds an individual's processing capacity.*

The problem is that members in an organization usually don't know how those with whom they interact have modified the language. Senders tend to assume that the words and terms they use mean the same to the receiver as they do to them. This assumption is often incorrect.

Communication Apprehension

Another major barrier to effective communication is that some people—an estimated 5 to 20 percent of the population[44]—suffer from debilitating **communication apprehension**, or anxiety. Lots of people dread speaking in front of a group, but communication apprehension is a more serious problem because it affects a whole category of communication techniques. People who suffer from it experience undue tension and anxiety in oral communication, written communication, or both.[45] For example, oral apprehensives may find it extremely difficult to talk with others face-to-face or may become extremely anxious when they have to use the telephone. As a result, they may rely on memos or faxes to convey messages when a phone call would be not only faster but more appropriate.

Studies demonstrate that oral-communication apprehensives avoid situations that require them to engage in oral communication.[46] We should expect to find some self-selection in jobs so that such individuals don't take positions, such as teacher, for which oral communication is a dominant requirement.[47] But almost all jobs require some oral communication. And of greater concern is the evidence that high-oral-communication apprehensives distort the communication demands of their jobs in order to minimize the need for communication.[48] So we need to be aware that there is a set of people in organizations who severely limit their oral communication and rationalize this practice by telling themselves that more communication isn't necessary for them to do their job effectively.

Gender Differences

Gender differences are sometimes a barrier to effective communication. Deborah Tannen's research shows that men tend to use talk to emphasize status, whereas women tend to use it to create connections. These tendencies, of course, don't apply to *every* man and *every* woman. As Tannen puts it, her generalization means "a larger percentage of women or men *as a group* talk in a particular way, or individual women and men *are more likely* to talk one way or the other."[49] She has found that women speak and hear a language of connection and intimacy; men speak and hear a language of status, power, and independence. So, for many men, conversations are primarily a means to preserve independence and maintain status in a hierarchical social order. For many women, conversations are negotiations for closeness in which people try to seek and give confirmation and support.

For example, men frequently complain that women talk on and on about their problems. Women criticize men for not listening. What's happening is that when men hear a problem, they frequently assert their desire for independence and control by offering solutions. Many women, on the other hand, view telling a problem as a means to promote closeness. The women present the problem to gain support and connection, not to get advice. Mutual understanding is symmetrical. But giving advice is asymmetrical—it sets up the advice giver as more knowledgeable, more reasonable, and more in control. This contributes to distancing men and women in their efforts to communicate.

"Politically Correct" Communication

A final barrier to effective communication is politically correct communication, communication so concerned with being inoffensive that meaning and simplicity are lost or free expression is hampered. When Don Imus used inappropriate

language to describe the Rutgers women's basketball team, he lost his job. There is no doubt that what Imus said was wrong. But is one consequence of his downfall that people will become even more politically correct in what they say, at least in certain company?

There are plenty of words and phrases we can use that invoke neither racial slur nor politically correct language. But there are also situations in which our desire to avoid offense blocks communication (by keeping us from saying what's really on our mind) or alters our communication in such a way as to make it unclear. When does being respectful turn into being politically correct? Consider a few examples:[50]

- The *Los Angeles Times* allows its journalists to use the term *old age* but cautions that the onset of old age varies from "person to person," so a group of 75-year-olds aren't necessarily all old.
- CNN has fined its broadcasters for using the word *foreign* instead of *international.*
- Little People of America (LPA) association prefers the term *little people* to *dwarfs* or *midgets.*

Certain words can and do stereotype, intimidate, and insult individuals. In an increasingly diverse workforce, we must be sensitive to how words might offend others. But there's a downside to political correctness: It can complicate

communication apprehension
Undue tension and anxiety about oral communication, written communication, or both.

our vocabulary, making it more difficult for people to communicate. To illustrate, you probably know what these three terms mean: *garbage*, *quotas*, and *women*. But each of these words also has been found to offend one or more groups. They've been replaced with terms such as *postconsumer waste materials*, *educational equity*, and *people of gender*. The problem is that this latter group of terms is much less likely to convey a uniform message than the words they replaced. By removing certain words from our vocabulary, we make it harder to communicate accurately. When we further replace these words with new terms whose meanings are less well understood, we reduce the likelihood that our messages will be received as we intended them.

We must be sensitive to how our choice of words might offend others. But we also have to be careful not to sanitize our language to the point at which it clearly restricts clarity of communication. There is no simple solution to this dilemma. However, you should be aware of the trade-offs and the need to find a proper balance.

Global Implications

Effective communication is difficult under the best of conditions. Cross-cultural factors clearly create the potential for increased communication problems. This is illustrated in Exhibit 11-8. A gesture that is well understood and acceptable in one culture can be meaningless or lewd in another. Unfortunately, as business has become more global, companies' communication approaches have not kept pace. Only 18 percent of

9 *Show how to overcome the potential problems in cross-cultural communication.*

Exhibit 11-8 Hand Gestures Mean Different Things in Different Countries

The A-OK Sign

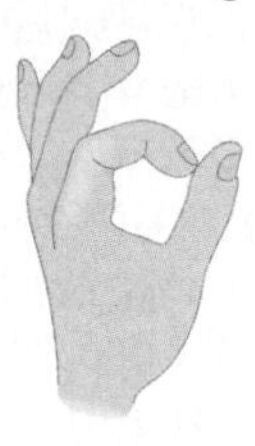

In the United States, this is just a friendly sign for "All right!" or "Good going." In Australia and Islamic countries, it is equivalent to what generations of high school students know as "flipping the bird."

The "Hook'em Horns" Sign

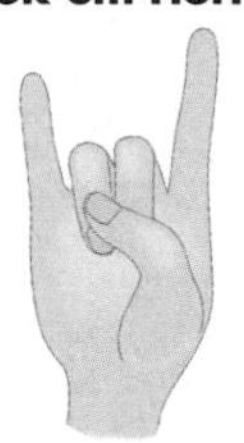

This sign encourages University of Texas athletes, and it's a good luck gesture in Brazil and Venezuela. In parts of Africa, it is a curse. In Italy, it is signaling to another that "your spouse is being unfaithful."

"V" for Victory Sign

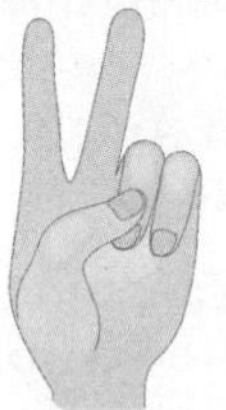

In many parts of the world, this means "victory" or "peace." In England, if the palm and fingers face inward, it means "Up yours!" especially if executed with an upward jerk of the fingers.

Finger-Beckoning Sign

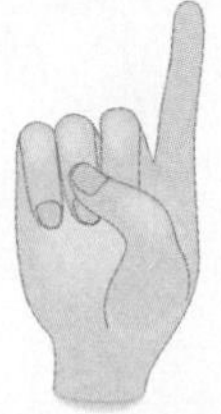

This sign means "come here" in the United States. In Malaysia, it is used only for calling animals. In Indonesia and Australia, it is used for beckoning "ladies of the night."

Source: "What's A-O-K in the U.S.A. Is Lewd and Worthless Beyond," *New York Times*, August 18, 1996, p. E7. From Roger E. Axtell, *GESTURES: The Do's and Taboos of Body Language Around the World*. Copyright © 1991. This material is used by permission of Wiley.

Lost in Translation?

In global commerce, language can be a barrier to conducting business effectively. Many U.S. companies have overseas parents, including AG, Bertelsmann, Diageo PLC, and Anglo-Dutch Unilever PLC. Similarly, U.S. companies have an overseas presence; for example, Ford has manufacturing plants in Belgium, Germany, Spain, Sweden, Turkey, and the United Kingdom. To make matters more complicated, as a result of mergers and acquisitions, companies are often owned by multiple overseas parents, creating an even greater strain on communication. Although English is the dominant language at many multinational companies, failing to speak a host country's language can make it tougher for managers to do their jobs well, especially if they are misinterpreted or if they misinterpret what others are saying. Such communication problems make it tougher to conduct business effectively and efficiently and may result in lost business opportunities.

To avoid communication problems, many companies require their managers to learn the local language. For example, German-based Siemens requires its managers to learn the language of their host country. Ernst Behrens, the head of Siemens's China operations, learned to speak Mandarin fluently. Robert Kimmett, a former Siemens board member, believes that learning a host country's language gives managers "a better grasp of what is going on inside a company . . . not just the facts and figures but also texture and nuance."

However, learning a foreign language can be difficult for managers. The challenge for North Americans is often deepened when the language is Asian, such as Japanese or Mandarin, because it is so different. To compensate, U.S. managers sometimes rely solely on body language and facial expressions to communicate. The problem? Cultural differences in these nonverbal forms of communication may result in serious misunderstandings. To avoid this pitfall, managers should to familiarize themselves with their host country's culture.

Source: Based on K. Kanhold, D. Bilefsky, M. Karnitschnig, and G. Parker, "Lost in Translation? Managers at Multinationals May Miss the Job's Nuances If They Speak Only English," *Wall Street Journal*, May 18, 2004, p. B.1.

companies have documented strategies for communicating with employees across cultures, and only 31 percent of companies require that corporate messages be customized for consumption in other cultures. P&G seems to be an exception; more than half of the company's employees don't speak English as their first language, so the company focuses on simple messages to make sure everyone knows what's important.[51]

Cultural Barriers One author has identified four specific problems related to language difficulties in cross-cultural communications.[52]

First, there are *barriers caused by semantics.* As we've noted previously, words mean different things to different people. This is particularly true for people from different national cultures. Some words, for instance, don't translate between cultures. Understanding the word *sisu* will help you in communicating with people from Finland, but this word is untranslatable into English. It means something akin to "guts" or "dogged persistence." Similarly, the new capitalists in Russia may have difficulty communicating with their British or Canadian counterparts because English terms such as *efficiency*, *free market*, and *regulation* are not directly translatable into Russian.

Second, there are *barriers caused by word connotations.* Words imply different things in different languages. Negotiations between Americans and Japanese executives, for instance, can be difficult because the Japanese word *hai* translates as "yes," but its connotation is "yes, I'm listening" rather than "yes, I agree."

Third are *barriers caused by tone differences.* In some cultures, language is formal, and in others, it's informal. In some cultures, the tone changes, depending on the context: People speak differently at home, in social situations, and at work. Using a personal, informal style in a situation in which a more formal style is expected can be embarrassing and off-putting.

Fourth, there are *barriers caused by differences among perceptions.* People who speak different languages actually view the world in different ways. Eskimos perceive snow

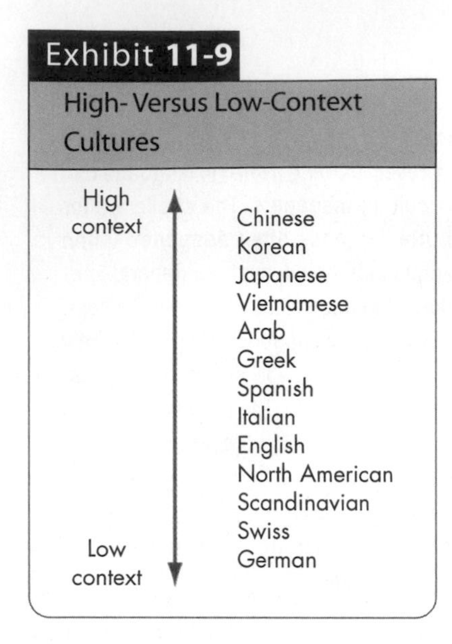

differently because they have many words for it. Thais perceive "no" differently than do Americans because the former have no such word in their vocabulary.

Cultural Context A better understanding of the cultural barriers just discussed and their implications for communicating across cultures can be achieved by considering the concepts of high- and low-context cultures.[53]

Cultures tend to differ in the importance to which context influences the meaning that individuals take from what is actually said or written in light of who the other person is. Countries such as China, Korea, Japan, and Vietnam are **high-context cultures**. They rely heavily on nonverbal and subtle situational cues in communicating with others. What is *not* said may be more significant than what *is* said. A person's official status, place in society, and reputation carry considerable weight in communications. In contrast, people from Europe and North America reflect their **low-context cultures**. They rely essentially on words to convey meaning. Body language and formal titles are secondary to spoken and written words (see Exhibit 11-9).

What do these contextual differences mean in terms of communication? Actually, quite a lot. Communication in high-context cultures implies considerably more trust by both parties. What may appear, to an outsider, as casual and insignificant conversation is important because it reflects the desire to build a relationship and create trust. Oral agreements imply strong commitments in high-context cultures. And who you are—your age, seniority, rank in the organization—is highly valued and heavily influences your credibility. But in low-context cultures, enforceable contracts tend to be in writing, precisely worded, and highly legalistic. Similarly, low-context cultures value directness. Managers are expected to be explicit and precise in conveying intended meaning. It's quite different in high-context cultures, in which managers tend to "make suggestions" rather than give orders.

A Cultural Guide When communicating with people from a different culture, what can you do to reduce misperceptions, misinterpretations, and misevaluations? You can begin by trying to assess the cultural context. You're likely to have fewer difficulties if people come from a similar cultural context to you. In addition, the following four rules can be helpful:[54]

1. *Assume differences until similarity is proven.* Most of us assume that others are more similar to us than they actually are. But people from different countries are often very different from us. You are therefore far less likely to make an error if you assume that others are different from you rather than assume similarity until difference is proven.
2. *Emphasize description rather than interpretation or evaluation.* Interpreting or evaluating what someone has said or done, in contrast to description, is based more on the observer's culture and background than on the observed situation. As a result, delay judgment until you've had sufficient time to observe and interpret the situation from the differing perspectives of all the cultures involved.
3. *Practice empathy.* Before sending a message, put yourself in the recipient's shoes. What are his or her values, experiences, and frames of reference? What do you know about his or her education, upbringing, and background that can give you added insight? Try to see the other person as he or she really is.
4. *Treat your interpretations as a working hypothesis.* Once you've developed an explanation for a new situation or think you empathize with someone from a foreign culture, treat your interpretation as a hypothesis that needs further testing rather than as a certainty. Carefully assess the feedback provided by recipients to see if it confirms your hypothesis. For important decisions or communiqués, you can also check with other foreign and home-country colleagues to make sure that your interpretations are on target.

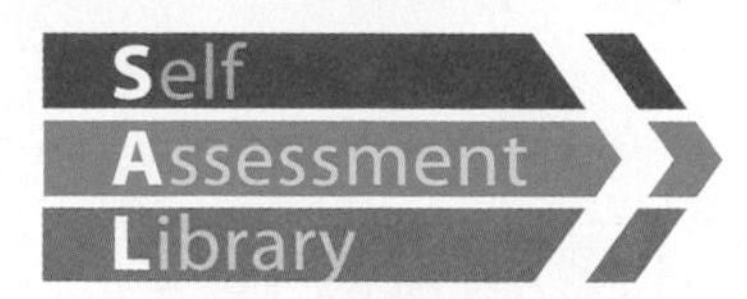

HOW GOOD ARE MY LISTENING SKILLS?

In the Self-Assessment Library (available on CD or online), take assessment II.A.2 (How Good Are My Listening Skills?).

Summary and Implications for Managers

A careful review of this chapter yields a common theme regarding the relationship between communication and employee satisfaction: The less the uncertainty, the greater the satisfaction. Distortions, ambiguities, and incongruities in communications all increase uncertainty and, hence, they have a negative impact on satisfaction.[55]

The less distortion that occurs in communication, the more that goals, feedback, and other management messages to employees will be received as they were intended.[56] This, in turn, should reduce ambiguities and clarify the group's task. Extensive use of vertical, lateral, and informal channels will increase communication flow, reduce uncertainty, and improve group performance and satisfaction. We should also expect incongruities between verbal and nonverbal communiqués to increase uncertainty and to reduce satisfaction.

Findings in the chapter further suggest that the goal of perfect communication is unattainable. Yet there is evidence that demonstrates a positive relationship between effective communication (which includes factors such as perceived trust, perceived accuracy, desire for interaction, top-management receptiveness, and upward information requirements) and worker productivity.[57] Choosing the correct channel, being an effective listener, and using feedback may, therefore, make for more effective communication. But the human factor generates distortions that can never be fully eliminated. The communication process represents an exchange of messages, but the outcome is meanings that may or may not approximate those that the sender intended. Whatever the sender's expectations, the decoded message in the mind of the receiver represents his or her reality. And it is this "reality" that will determine performance, along with the individual's level of motivation and degree of satisfaction.

Paying close attention to communication effectiveness is all the more important given the ways in which communication technology has transformed the workplace. Despite the great advantages of electronic communication formats, the pitfalls are numerous. Because we gather so much meaning from how a message is communicated (voice tone, facial expressions, body language), the potential for misunderstandings in electronic communication is great. E-mail, IM and TM, and networking software are vital aspects of organizational communication, but we need to use these tools wisely, or we'll not be as effective as managers as we might be.

Finally, there are a lot of barriers to effective communication, such as gender and culture. By keeping these barriers in mind, we can overcome them and increase our communication effectiveness.

high-context cultures *Cultures that rely heavily on nonverbal and subtle situational cues in communication.*

low-context cultures *Cultures that rely heavily on words to convey meaning in communication.*

Point Counterpoint

KEEP IT A SECRET

We're better off keeping more things to ourselves.[58] Workplace gossip is out of control, and very often, we can't trust people with secrets. Tell a friend never, ever to tell something to someone else, and you've aroused in them an irresistible desire to share the "juicy news" with others. A good rule of thumb is that if you're sure a confidante has told no one else, that probably means he or she has told only three other people. You might think this is a paranoid reaction, but research suggests that so-called confidantes rarely keep secrets, even when they swear they will.

Keeping our own secrets is normal, and most children learn to do it at any early age. People survive by protecting themselves, and when someone is keeping a secret, he usually has a good reason for doing so.

Even when we feel like confiding in someone else, it's prudent to keep confidential information to ourselves. Research shows that few of us are able to keep secrets and that if we fear certain negative consequences of telling our secrets (for example, our confidante will think less of us or will tell others), those fears not only don't keep us from blabbing, they are often justified.

Organizational secrets are all the more important to keep quiet. Organizations are rumor mills, and we can permanently damage our careers and the organizations for which we work by disclosing confidential information. Improper disclosure of organizational proprietary information is a huge cost and concern for organizations. Look at the HP debacle when board chair Patricia Dunn lost her job and two other board members resigned. The cause of this disaster? Board members telling reporters secrets they had no business telling.

The problem with keeping secrets is that they're expensive to maintain.

One social psychologist found that when people are instructed not to disclose certain information, it becomes more distracting and difficult for them to do so. In fact, the more people are instructed to keep something to themselves, the more they see the secret in everything they do. "We don't realize that in keeping it secret we've created an obsession in a jar," he says. So keeping things hidden takes a toll on our psyche—it (usually unnecessarily) adds to the mental burdens we carry with us.

Another psychologist has found that these costs are real. This researcher found that young people who experienced a traumatic experience often had more health problems later in life. As he researched the topic further, he found out why. Generally, these people conceal the event from others. He even did an experiment which showed that when people who have experienced traumatic events shared them, they later had fewer health problems than people who hadn't shared them. There isn't one identifiable reason why sharing these traumatic events seems to help people, but the result has been found repeatedly.

Thus, for mental and physical health reasons, we're better off not keeping secrets from others.

Questions for Review

1 What are the primary functions of the communication process in organizations?

2 What are the key parts of the communication process, and how do you distinguish formal and informal communication?

3 What are the differences among downward, upward, and lateral communication?

4 What are the unique challenges to oral, written, and nonverbal communication?

5 How are formal communication networks and the grapevine similar and different?

6 What are the main forms of electronic communication? What are their unique benefits and challenges?

7 Why is channel richness fundamental to the choice of communication channels?

8 What are some common barriers to effective communication?

9 What unique problems underlie cross-cultural communication?

Experiential Exercise

AN ABSENCE OF NONVERBAL COMMUNICATION

This exercise will help you to see the value of nonverbal communication to interpersonal relations.

1. The class is to split up into pairs (Party A and Party B).
2. Party A is to select a topic from the following list:
   a. Managing in the Middle East is significantly different from managing in North America.
   b. Employee turnover in an organization can be functional.
   c. Some conflict in an organization is good.
   d. Whistle-blowers do more harm than good for an organization.
   e. An employer has a responsibility to provide every employee with an interesting and challenging job.
   f. Everyone should register to vote.
   g. Organizations should require all employees to undergo regular drug tests.
   h. Individuals who have majored in business or economics make better employees than those who have majored in history or English.
   i. The place where you get your college degree is more important in determining your career success than what you learn while you're there.
   j. It's unethical for a manager to purposely distort communications to get a favorable outcome.
3. Party B is to choose a position on this topic (for example, arguing *against* the view that "some conflict in an organization is good"). Party A now must automatically take the opposite position.
4. The two parties have 10 minutes in which to debate their topic. The catch is that the individuals can only communicate verbally. They may *not* use gestures, facial movements, body movements, or any other nonverbal communication. It may help for each party to sit on their hands to remind them of their restrictions and to maintain an expressionless look.
5. After the debate is over, form groups of six to eight and spend 15 minutes discussing the following:
   a. How effective was communication during these debates?
   b. What barriers to communication existed?
   c. What purposes does nonverbal communication serve?
   d. Relate the lessons learned in this exercise to problems that might occur when communicating on the telephone or through e-mail.

Ethical Dilemma

DEFINING THE BOUNDARIES OF TECHNOLOGY

You work for a company that has no specific policies regarding non-work-related uses of computers and the Internet. It also has no electronic monitoring devices to determine what employees are doing on their computers. Are any of the following actions unethical? Explain your position on each.

a. Using the company's e-mail system for personal reasons during the workday
b. Playing computer games during the workday
c. Using your office computer for personal use (to check ESPN.com, shop online) during the workday
d. Looking for a mate on an Internet dating service Web site during the workday
e. Visiting "adult" Web sites on your office computer during the workday
f. Using your employer's portable communication device (Blackberry) for personal use
g. Conducting any of the above activities at work but before or after normal work hours
h. For telecommuters working from home, using a computer and Internet access line paid for by your employer to visit online shopping or dating-service sites during normal working hours

Case Incident 1

DIANNA ABDALA

To illustrate how precious e-mail is, consider the case of Dianna Abdala. In 2005, Abdala was a recent graduate of Suffolk University's law school, and she passed the bar exam. She then interviewed with and was offered a job at a law firm started by William Korman, a former state prosecutor.

The following is a summary of their e-mail communications:

-----Original Message-----
From: Dianna Abdala
Sent: Friday, February 03, 2006 9:23 p.m.
To: William A. Korman
Subject: Thank you

Dear Attorney Korman,

At this time, I am writing to inform you that I will not be accepting your offer. After careful consideration, I have come to the conclusion that the pay you are offering would neither fulfill me nor support the lifestyle I am living in light of the work I would be doing for you. I have decided instead to work for myself, and reap 100% of the benefits that I sew [sic].

Thank you for the interviews.

Dianna L. Abdala, Esq.

-----Original Message-----
From: William A. Korman
To: Dianna Abdala
Sent: Monday, February 06, 2006 12:15 p.m.
Subject: RE: Thank you

Dianna--

Given that you had two interviews, were offered and accepted the job (indeed, you had a definite start date), I am surprised that you chose an e-mail and a 9:30 p.m. voicemail message to convey this information to me. It smacks of immaturity and is quite unprofessional. Indeed, I did rely upon your acceptance by ordering stationary [sic] and business cards with your name, reformatting a computer and setting up both internal and external e-mails for you here at the office. While I do not quarrel with your reasoning, I am extremely disappointed in the way this played out. I sincerely wish you the best of luck in your future endeavors.

Will Korman

-----Original Message-----
From: Dianna Abdala
Sent: Monday, February 06, 2006 4:01 p.m.
To: William A. Korman
Subject: Re: Thank you

A real lawyer would have put the contract into writing and not exercised any such reliance until he did so.

Again, thank you.

-----Original Message-----
From: William A. Korman
To: Dianna Abdala
Sent: Monday, February 06, 2006 4:18 p.m.
Subject: RE: Thank you

Thank you for the refresher course on contracts. This is not a bar exam question. You need to realize that this is a very small legal community, especially the criminal defense bar. Do you really want to start pissing off more experienced lawyers at this early stage of your career?

-----Original Message-----
From: Dianna Abdala
To: William A. Korman
Sent: Monday, February 06, 2006 4:28 p.m.
Subject: Re: Thank you

bla bla bla

After this e-mail exchange, Korman forwarded the correspondence to several colleagues, and it quickly spread exponentially.

Questions

1. With whom do you side here—Abdala or Korman?
2. What mistakes do you think each party made?
3. Do you think this exchange will damage Abdala's career? Korman's firm?
4. What does this exchange tell you about the limitations of e-mail?

Sources: "Dianna Abdala," *Wikipedia* (http://en.wikipedia.org/wiki/Dianna_Abdala); and J. Sandberg, "Infamous Email Writers Aren't Always Killing Their Careers After All," *Wall Street Journal*, February 21, 2006, p. B1.

Case Incident 2

DO YOU NEED A SPEECH COACH?

Speech coaching is a growing business. In a way, this is surprising. As noted earlier, more and more communication is electronic, seemingly making the quality of one's speaking skills less important. Although electronic forms of communication clearly have grown exponentially, that doesn't mean that oral communication no longer matters, especially for some jobs.

Consider Michael Sipe, president of Private Equities, a small mergers and acquisitions firm in Silicon Valley. Sipe worked with a communications coach to give him the edge when pitching his company's services relative to competitors. "If a customer can't determine who is any better or different or worse, then they are left with a conversation about price," says Snipe. "And as a business owner, if you're only in a price conversation, that's a losing conversation. It is really important to paint a picture of why should do business with them in a very compelling way." Snipe felt a speech coach helped him do that.

To look at it another way, you can have all the expertise in the world, but if you can't effectively communicate that expertise, then you're not getting the most from your talents. R. W. Armstrong & Associates, an Indianapolis-based engineering project management company, has used speech coaches to refine its pitches. Although the investment wasn't small—the company estimates it paid $8,000 to $10,000 per day to train 25 employees—the firm believes it helped land several lucrative contracts.

Asset manager David Freeman agrees. "We may fly across the country to present for 45 minutes to a pension fund or consulting firm that can be worth $25 million, $50 million, or $100 million in the amount of money we are being given to manage," he says. "You want to increase the probability that you are going to be remembered."

So what do these coaches do? Some of their training is oriented around speech—how to communicate with excitement, how to use inflection effectively—and body language. One of the big areas is to teach people to use short sentences, to speak in sound bites, and to pause so listeners can absorb what's been said.

Questions

1. What do you think explains the growth of speech coaches in business?
2. Do you think hiring a speech coach is a good investment for managers to make?
3. Do you think you would benefit from the help of a speech coach? Why or why not?

Source: H. Chura, "Um, Uh, Like Call in the Speech Coach," *New York Times*, January 11, 2007, p. C7.

Endnotes

1. P. B. Erickson, "Drawing the Line Between Gossip, Watercooler Chat," *NewsOK.com* (June 15, 2007); and G. Cuyler, "'Hooksett 4' to Seek Judge's Aid in Getting Jobs Back," *Union Leader* (June 25, 2007).
2. See, for example, K. W. Thomas and W. H. Schmidt, "A Survey of Managerial Interests with Respect to Conflict," *Academy of Management Journal*, June 1976, p. 317.
3. "Employers Cite Communication Skills, Honesty/Integrity as Key for Job Candidates," *IPMA-HR Bulletin* (March 23, 2007), p. 1.

4. W. G. Scott and T. R. Mitchell, *Organization Theory: A Structural and Behavioral Analysis* (Homewood, IL: Irwin, 1976).
5. D. K. Berlo, *The Process of Communication* (New York: Holt, Rinehart & Winston, 1960), pp. 30–32.
6. J. Langan-Fox, "Communication in Organizations: Speed, Diversity, Networks, and Influence on Organizational Effectiveness, Human Health, and Relationships," in N. Anderson, D. S. Ones, H. K. Sinangil, and C. Viswesvaran (eds.), *Handbook of Industrial, Work and Organizational Psychology*, vol. 2 (Thousand Oaks, CA: Sage, 2001), p. 190.
7. R. L. Simpson, "Vertical and Horizontal Communication in Formal Organizations," *Administrative Science Quarterly*, September 1959, pp. 188–196; B. Harriman, "Up and Down the Communications Ladder," *Harvard Business Review*, September–October 1974, pp. 143–151; A. G. Walker and J. W. Smither, "A Five-Year Study of Upward Feedback: What Managers Do with Their Results Matter," *Personnel Psychology*, Summer 1999, pp. 393–424; and J. W. Smither and A. G. Walker, "Are the Characteristics of Narrative Comments Related to Improvement in Multirater Feedback Ratings Over Time?" *Journal of Applied Psychology* 89, no. 3 (June 2004), pp. 575–581.
8. P. Dvorak, "How Understanding the 'Why' of Decisions Matters," *Wall Street Journal* (March 19, 2007), p. B3.
9. K. Gurchiek, "Employers Show 'Top-Down Bias' on Employee Input," *HRWeek*, September 26, 2006, p. 1; and A. Pomeroy, "CEOs Emphasize Listening to Employees," *HRMagazine*, January 2007, p. 14.
10. E. Nichols, "Hyper-Speed Managers," *HRMagazine*, April 2007, pp. 107–110.
11. L. Dulye, "Get Out of Your Office," *HRMagazine*, July 2006, pp. 99–101.
12. L. S. Rashotte, "What Does That Smile Mean? The Meaning of Nonverbal Behaviors in Social Interaction," *Social Psychology Quarterly*, March 2002, pp. 92–102.
13. J. Fast, *Body Language* (Philadelphia: M. Evan, 1970), p. 7.
14. A. Mehrabian, *Nonverbal Communication* (Chicago: Aldine-Atherton, 1972).
15. N. M. Henley, "Body Politics Revisited: What Do We Know Today?" in P. J. Kalbfleisch and M. J. Cody (eds.), *Gender, Power, and Communication in Human Relationships* (Hillsdale, NJ: Erlbaum, 1995), pp. 27–61.
16. See, for example, N. B. Kurland and L. H. Pelled, "Passing the Word: Toward a Model of Gossip and Power in the Workplace," *Academy of Management Review*, April 2000, pp. 428–438; and N. Nicholson, "The New Word on Gossip," *Psychology Today*, June 2001, pp. 41–45.
17. Cited in "Heard It Through the Grapevine," *Forbes*, February 10, 1997, p. 22.
18. See, for instance, J. W. Newstrom, R. E. Monczka, and W. E. Reif, "Perceptions of the Grapevine: Its Value and Influence," *Journal of Business Communication*, Spring 1974, pp. 12–20; and S. J. Modic, "Grapevine Rated Most Believable," *IndustryWeek*, May 15, 1989, p. 14.
19. K. Davis, "Management Communication and the Grapevine," *Harvard Business Review*, September–October 1953, pp. 43–49.
20. K. Davis, cited in R. Rowan, "Where Did That Rumor Come From?" *Fortune*, August 13, 1979, p. 134.
21. R. L. Rosnow and G. A. Fine, *Rumor and Gossip: The Social Psychology of Hearsay* (New York: Elsevier, 1976).
22. J. K. Bosson, A. B. Johnson, K. Niederhoffer, and W. B. Swann, Jr., "Interpersonal Chemistry Through Negativity: Bonding by Sharing Negative Attitudes About Others," *Personal Relationships* 13 (2006), pp. 135–150.
23. B. Gates, "How I Work," *Fortune*, April 17, 2006, http://money.cnn.com/2006/03/30/news/newsmakers/gates_howiwork_fortune/.
24. D. Brady, "*!#?@ the E-mail. Can We Talk?" *BusinessWeek*, December 4, 2006, p. 109.
25. E. Binney, "Is E-mail the New Pink Slip?" *HR Magazine*, November 2006, pp. 32–33; and R. L. Rundle, "Critical Case: How an Email Rant Jolted a Big HMO," *Wall Street Journal*, April 24, 2007, pp. A1, A16.
26. "Some Email Recipients Say 'Enough Already'," *Gainesville (Florida) Sun*, June 3, 2007, p. 1G.
27. D. Goleman, "Flame First, Think Later: New Clues to E-mail Misbehavior," *New York Times*, February 20, 2007, p. D5; and E. Krell, "The Unintended Word," *HRMagazine*, August 2006, pp. 50–54.
28. R. Zeidner, "Keeping E-mail in Check," *HRMagazine*, June 2007, pp. 70–74; "E-mail May Be Hazardous to Your Career," *Fortune*, May 14, 2007, p. 24; "More Firms Fire Employees for E-mail Violations," *Gainesville (Florida) Sun*, June 6, 2006, p. B1.
29. Cited in C. Y. Chen, "The IM Invasion," *Fortune*, May 26, 2003, pp. 135–138.
30. C. Hymowitz, "Have Advice, Will Travel," *Wall Street Journal*, June 5, 2006, pp. B1, B3.
31. "Survey Finds Mixed Reviews on Checking E-mail During Meetings," *IPMA-HR Bulletin*, April 27, 2007, p. 1.
32. K. Gurchiek, "Shoddy Writing Can Trip Up Employees, Organizations," *SHRM Online*, April 27, 2006, pp. 1–2.
33. D. Lidsky, "It's Not Just Who You Know," *Fast Company*, May 2007, p. 56.
34. A. Bahney, "Interns? No Bloggers Need Apply," *New York Times*, May 25, 2006, pp. 1–2; "Bosses Battle Risk by Firing E-mail, IM & Blog Violators," *IPMA-HR Bulletin*, January 12, 2007, pp. 1–2; G. Krants, "Blogging with a Vendetta," *Workforce Week* 8, no. 25 (June 10, 2007), www.workforce.com/section/quick_takes/49486_3.html. D. Jones, "Sun CEO Sees Competitive Advantage in Blogging," *USA Today*, June 26, 2006, p. 7B; and B. Leonard, "Blogs Can Present New Challenges to Employers," *SHRM Online*, March 13, 2006, pp. 1–2.
35. P. R. Carlile, "Transferring, Translating, and Transforming: An Integrative Framework for Managing Knowledge Across Boundaries," *Organization Science* 15, no. 5 (September–October 2004), pp. 555–568; and S. Thurm, "Companies Struggle to Pass on Knowledge That Workers Acquire," *Wall Street Journal*, January 23, 2006, p. B1.
36. B. Fryer, "Get Smart," *INC*, September 15, 1999, p. 63.
37. E. Truch, "Managing Personal Knowledge: The Key to Tomorrow's Employability," *Journal of Change Management*, December 2001, pp. 102–105; and D. Mason and D. J. Pauleen, "Perceptions of Knowledge Management: A Qualitative Analysis," *Journal of Knowledge Management* 7, no. 4 (2003), pp. 38–48.
38. J. Gordon, "Intellectual Capital and You," *Training*, September 1999, p. 33.
39. "At Many Companies, Hunt for Leakers Expands Arsenal of Monitoring Tactics," *Wall Street Journal* September 11, 2006, pp. B1, B3; and B. J. Alge, G. A. Ballinger, S. Tangirala, and J. L.

Oakley, "Information Privacy in Organizations: Empowering Creative and Extrarole Performance," *Journal of Applied Psychology* 91, no. 1 (2006), pp. 221–232.

40. T. M. Burton and R. E. Silverman, "Lots of Empty Spaces in Cerner Parking Lot Get CEO Riled Up," *Wall Street Journal*, March 30, 2001, p. B3; and E. Wong, "A Stinging Office Memo Boomerangs," *New York Times*, April 5, 2001, p. C1.

41. See R. L. Daft and R. H. Lengel, "Information Richness: A New Approach to Managerial Behavior and Organization Design," in B. M. Staw and L. L. Cummings (eds.), *Research in Organizational Behavior*, vol. 6 (Greenwich, CT: JAI Press, 1984), pp. 191–233; R. L. Daft and R. H. Lengel, "Organizational Information Requirements, Media Richness, and Structural Design," *Managerial Science*, May 1986, pp. 554–572; R. E. Rice, "Task Analyzability, Use of New Media, and Effectiveness," *Organization Science*, November 1992, pp. 475–500; S. G. Straus and J. E. McGrath, "Does the Medium Matter? The Interaction of Task Type and Technology on Group Performance and Member Reaction," *Journal of Applied Psychology*, February 1994, pp. 87–97; L. K. Trevino, J. Webster, and E. W. Stein, "Making Connections: Complementary Influences on Communication Media Choices, Attitudes, and Use," *Organization Science*, March–April 2000, pp. 163–182; and N. Kock, "The Psychobiological Model: Towards a New Theory of Computer-Mediated Communication Based on Darwinian Evolution," *Organization Science* 15, no. 3 (May–June 2004), pp. 327–348.

42. R. L. Daft, R. H. Lengel, and L. K. Trevino, "Message Equivocality, Media Selection, and Manager Performance: Implications for Information Systems," *MIS Quarterly*, September 1987, pp. 355–368.

43. J. Sandberg, "The Jargon Jumble," *Wall Street Journal*, October 24, 2006, p. B1.

44. J. C. McCroskey, J. A. Daly, and G. Sorenson, "Personality Correlates of Communication Apprehension," *Human Communication Research*, Spring 1976, pp. 376–380.

45. See, for instance, B. H. Spitzberg and M. L. Hecht, "A Competent Model of Relational Competence," *Human Communication Research*, Summer 1984, pp. 575–599; and S. K. Opt and D. A. Loffredo, "Rethinking Communication Apprehension: A Myers-Briggs Perspective," *Journal of Psychology*, September 2000, pp. 556–570.

46. See, for example, L. Stafford and J. A. Daly, "Conversational Memory: The Effects of Instructional Set and Recall Mode on Memory for Natural Conversations," *Human Communication Research*, Spring 1984, pp. 379–402; and T. L. Rodebaugh, "I Might Look OK, But I'm Still Doubtful, Anxious, and Avoidant: The Mixed Effects of Enhanced Video Feedback on Social Anxiety Symptoms," *Behaviour Research & Therapy* 42, no. 12 (December 2004), pp. 1435–1451.

47. J. A. Daly and J. C. McCroskey, "Occupational Desirability and Choice as a Function of Communication Apprehension," *Journal of Counseling Psychology* 22, no. 4 (1975), pp. 309–313.

48. J. A. Daly and M. D. Miller, "The Empirical Development of an Instrument of Writing Apprehension," *Research in the Teaching of English*, Winter 1975, pp. 242–249.

49. D. Tannen, *Talking from 9 to 5: Men and Women at Work* (New York: Harper, 2001), p. 15.

50. Cited in J. Leo, "Falling for Sensitivity," *U.S. News & World Report*, December 13, 1993, p. 27.

51. R. E. Axtell, *Gestures: The Do's and Taboos of Body Language Around the World* (New York: Wiley, 1991); "Effective Communication: A Leading Indicator of Financial Performance," Watson Wyatt 2006, www.watsonwyatt.com; and A. Markels, "Turning the Tide at P&G," *U.S. News & World Report*, October 30, 2006, p. 69.

52. See M. Munter, "Cross-Cultural Communication for Managers," *Business Horizons*, May–June 1993, pp. 75–76.

53. See E. T. Hall, *Beyond Culture* (Garden City, NY: Anchor Press/Doubleday, 1976); E. T. Hall, "How Cultures Collide," *Psychology Today*, July 1976, pp. 67–74; E. T. Hall and M. R. Hall, *Understanding Cultural Differences* (Yarmouth, ME: Intercultural Press, 1990); R. E. Dulek, J. S. Fielden, and J. S. Hill, "International Communication: An Executive Primer," *Business Horizons*, January–February 1991, pp. 20–25; D. Kim, Y. Pan, and H. S. Park, "High- Versus Low-Context Culture: A Comparison of Chinese, Korean, and American Cultures," *Psychology and Marketing*, September 1998, pp. 507–521; M. J. Martinko and S. C. Douglas, "Culture and Expatriate Failure: An Attributional Explication," *International Journal of Organizational Analysis*, July 1999, pp. 265–293; and W. L. Adair, "Integrative Sequences and Negotiation Outcome in Same- and Mixed-Culture Negotiations," *International Journal of Conflict Management* 14, no. 3–4 (2003), pp. 1359–1392.

54. N. Adler, *International Dimensions of Organizational Behavior*, 4th ed. (Cincinnati, OH: South-Western Publishing, 2002), p. 94.

55. See, for example. R. S. Schuler, "A Role Perception Transactional Process Model for Organizational Communication-Outcome Relationships," *Organizational Behavior and Human Performance*, April 1979, pp. 268–291.

56. J. P. Walsh, S. J. Ashford, and T. E. Hill, "Feedback Obstruction: The Influence of the Information Environment on Employee Turnover Intentions," *Human Relations*, January 1985, pp. 23–46.

57. S. A. Hellweg and S. L. Phillips, "Communication and Productivity in Organizations: A State-of-the-Art Review," in *Proceedings of the 40th Annual Academy of Management Conference*, Detroit, 1980, pp. 188–192. See also B. A. Bechky, "Sharing Meaning Across Occupational Communities: The Transformation of Understanding on a Production Floor," *Organization Science* 14, no. 3 (May–June 2003), pp. 312–330.

58. Based on E. Jaffe, "The Science Behind Secrets," *APS Observer*, July 2006, pp. 20–22.

Basic Approaches to Leadership

I am more afraid of an army of 100 sheep led by a lion than an army of 100 lions led by a sheep.
—the French diplomat Talleyrand

LEARNING OBJECTIVES

After studying this chapter, you should be able to:

1 Define *leadership* and contrast leadership and management.

2 Summarize the conclusions of trait theories.

3 Identify the central tenets and main limitations of behavioral theories.

4 Assess contingency theories of leadership by their level of support.

5 Contrast the interactive theories path-goal and leader–member exchange.

6 Identify the situational variables in the leader-participation model.

7 Show how managers might need to adjust their leadership approaches in different countries.

The First Wrigley CEO Whose Name Isn't Wrigley

It probably doesn't surprise you to learn that Wrigley has been making chewing gum for more than a century. What may surprise you is that until 2006, the firm had always been run by Wrigleys. Bill Wrigley, Jr., great-grandson of Wrigley founder William Wrigley, Jr., is still executive chairman of the board and actively involved in the company. However, when Wrigley, who had been CEO since 1999, shifted roles from CEO to chairman and hired William Perez, both moves surprised industry insiders.

Perez, after all, had recently been unceremoniously dumped by Nike founder and Chairman Philip Knight. Knight claimed that Perez had failed to "wrap his arms around" Nike's culture and replaced him with a longtime Nike company veteran. Bob Nardelli (fired at Home Depot, now CEO of Chrysler) notwithstanding, fired CEOs are usually not prime candidates to become CEOs of other large companies, especially ones that had such a strong family lineage as Wrigley.

Adding to the surprise is that Perez hardly seems to fit the profile of a CEO. He is a self-described introvert who, some say, prefers numbers to people. As we'll learn in this chapter, extraversion tends to be a good predictor of leadership, especially of whether a leader will emerge. So how did Perez emerge as the first non-Wrigley to be CEO, and can an introvert really lead a Fortune 500 company?

As it turns out, Perez has been down this road before. Before joining Nike, he was CEO of S.C. Johnson, the large household products company. When Perez took over, S.C. Johnson was in the hands of Samuel C. Johnson who, like Bill Wrigley, Jr., was a fourth-generation CEO. Despite being an outsider, Perez worked so well with Johnson that staffers couldn't tell whether directives had come from Johnson or Perez.

Moreover, Wrigley's culture bears striking similarities to S.C. Johnson's. Though Wrigley is a publicly traded company and S.C. Johnson is private, both have low-key cultures and are reluctant to share many details with Wall Street investors or the business press. Since becoming CEO, Perez has worked as closely with Wrigley as he did with Johnson. The two exchange emails three or four times a day.

It's too soon to tell whether Perez will thrive as Wrigley's first outside CEO. However, it's clear that his personality and leadership style are a fit with the company's culture, even if his introverted nature doesn't fit the CEO prototype. Speaking of Perez, Wrigley said he is a "unique fit and brings in some tremendous skills."[1] ■

As Wrigley's hiring of William Perez shows, leadership is all about finding managers with "the right stuff"—the qualities to successfully lead work groups or organizations. But what is the right stuff? Personality traits, discussed in Chapter 4 and elsewhere in the text, are only some of the qualities we might associate with effective leadership. To assess yourself on another set of qualities that we'll discuss shortly, take the following self-assessment.

WHAT'S MY LEADERSHIP STYLE?

In the Self-Assessment Library (available on CD and online) take assessment II.B.1 (What's My Leadership Style?) and answer the following questions.

1. *How did you score on the two scales?*
2. *Do you think a leader can be both task oriented and people oriented? Do you think there are situations in which a leader has to make a choice between the two styles?*
3. *Do you think your leadership style will change over time? Why or why not?*

In this chapter, we'll look at the basic approaches to determining what makes an effective leader and what differentiates leaders from nonleaders. First, we'll present trait theories, which dominated the study of leadership up to the late 1940s. Then we'll discuss behavioral theories, which were popular until the late 1960s. Next, we'll introduce contingency theories and interactive theories. But before we review these approaches, let's first clarify what we mean by the term *leadership*.

What Is Leadership?

1 *Define* leadership *and contrast leadership and management.*

Leadership and *management* are two terms that are often confused. What's the difference between them?

John Kotter of the Harvard Business School argues that management is about coping with complexity.[2] Good management brings about order and consistency by drawing up formal plans, designing rigid organization structures, and monitoring results against the plans. Leadership, in contrast, is about coping with change. Leaders establish direction by developing a vision of the future; then they align people by communicating this vision and inspiring them to overcome hurdles.

Robert House of the Wharton School at the University of Pennsylvania basically concurs when he says that managers use the authority inherent in their designated formal rank to obtain compliance from organizational members.[3] Management consists of implementing the vision and strategy provided by leaders, coordinating and staffing the organization, and handling day-to-day problems.

Although Kotter and House provide separate definitions of the two terms, both researchers and practicing managers frequently make no such distinctions. So we need to present leadership in a way that can capture how it is used in theory and practice.

We define **leadership** as the ability to influence a group toward the achievement of a vision or set of goals. The source of this influence may be formal, such as that provided by the possession of managerial rank in an organization. Because management positions come with some degree of formally designated authority, a person may assume a leadership role simply because of the position

The personal qualities of Richard Branson, chairman of Virgin Group, make him a great leader. Branson is described as fun loving, sensitive to the needs of others, hard working, innovative, charismatic, enthusiastic, energetic, decisive, and risk taking. These traits helped the British entrepreneur build one of the most recognized and respected brands in the world.

leadership *The ability to influence a group toward the achievement of a vision or set of goals.*

he or she holds in the organization. But not all leaders are managers, nor, for that matter, are all managers leaders. Just because an organization provides its managers with certain formal rights is no assurance that they will be able to lead effectively. We find that nonsanctioned leadership—that is, the ability to influence that arises outside the formal structure of the organization—is often as important or more important than formal influence. In other words, leaders can emerge from within a group as well as by formal appointment to lead a group.

One last comment before we move on: Organizations need strong leadership *and* strong management for optimal effectiveness. In today's dynamic world, we need leaders to challenge the status quo, to create visions of the future, and to inspire organizational members to want to achieve the visions. We also need managers to formulate detailed plans, create efficient organizational structures, and oversee day-to-day operations.

Trait Theories

2 *Summarize the conclusions of trait theories.*

Throughout history, strong leaders—Buddha, Napoleon, Mao, Churchill, Roosevelt, Thatcher, Reagan—have all been described in terms of their traits. For example, when Margaret Thatcher was prime minister of Great Britain, she was regularly described as confident, iron willed, determined, and decisive.

Trait theories of leadership differentiate leaders from nonleaders by focusing on personal qualities and characteristics. Individuals such as Margaret Thatcher, South Africa's Nelson Mandela, Virgin Group CEO Richard Branson, Apple co-founder Steve Jobs, and American Express chairman Ken Chenault are recognized as leaders and described in terms such as *charismatic*, *enthusiastic*, and *courageous*. The search for personality, social, physical, or intellectual attributes that would describe leaders and differentiate them from nonleaders goes back to the earliest stages of leadership research.

Research efforts at isolating leadership traits resulted in a number of dead ends. For instance, a review in the late 1960s of 20 different studies identified nearly 80 leadership traits, but only 5 of these traits were common to 4 or more of the investigations.[4] By the 1990s, after numerous studies and analyses, about the best thing that could be said was that most "leaders are not like other people," but the particular traits that were isolated varied a great deal from review to review.[5] It was a pretty confusing state of affairs.

A breakthrough, of sorts, came when researchers began organizing traits around the Big Five personality framework (see Chapter 4).[6] It became clear that most of the dozens of traits emerging in various leadership reviews could be subsumed under one of the Big Five and that this approach resulted in consistent and strong support for traits as predictors of leadership. For instance, ambition and energy—two common traits of leaders—are part of extraversion. Rather than focus on these two specific traits, it is better to think of them in terms of the more general trait of extraversion.

A comprehensive review of the leadership literature, when organized around the Big Five, has found that extraversion is the most important trait of effective leaders.[7] But results show that extraversion is more strongly related to leader emergence than to leader effectiveness. This is not totally surprising since sociable and dominant people are more likely to assert themselves in group situations. While the assertive nature of extraverts is a positive, leaders need to make sure they're not too assertive—one study found that leaders who scored very high on assertiveness were less effective than those who were moderately high.[8]

Conscientiousness and openness to experience also showed strong and consistent relationships to leadership, though not quite as strong as extraversion. The traits of agreeableness and emotional stability weren't as strongly correlated with leadership. Overall, it does appear that the trait approach does have something to offer. Leaders who are extraverted (individuals who like being around people and are able to assert themselves), conscientious (individuals who are disciplined and keep commitments they make), and open (individuals who are creative and flexible) do seem to have an advantage when it comes to leadership, suggesting that good leaders do have key traits in common.

Recent studies are indicating that another trait that may indicate effective leadership is emotional intelligence (EI), which we discussed in Chapter 8. Advocates of EI argue that without it, a person can have outstanding training, a highly analytical mind, a compelling vision, and an endless supply of terrific ideas but still not make a great leader. This may be especially true as individuals move up in an organization.[9] But why is EI so critical to effective leadership? A core component of EI is empathy. Empathetic leaders can sense others' needs, listen to what followers say (and don't say), and are able to read the reactions of others. As one leader noted, "The caring part of empathy, especially for the people with whom you work, is what inspires people to stay with a leader when the going gets rough. The mere fact that someone cares is more often than not rewarded with loyalty."[10]

Despite these claims for its importance, the link between EI and leadership effectiveness is much less investigated than other traits. One reviewer noted, "Speculating about the practical utility of the EI construct might be premature.

OB In the News

Bad Bosses Abound

Although much is expected of leaders, what's surprising is how rarely they seem to meet the most basic definitions of effectiveness. A recent study of 700 workers by Florida State University revealed that many employees believe their supervisors don't give credit when it's due, gossip about them behind their backs, and don't keep their word. The situation is so bad that for many employees, the study's lead author says, "they don't leave their company, they leave their boss."

Among the other findings of the study:

- 39 percent said their supervisor failed to keep promises.
- 37 percent said their supervisor failed to give credit when due.
- 31 percent said their supervisor gave them the "silent treatment" in the past year.
- 27 percent said their supervisor made negative comments about them to other employees or managers.
- 24 percent said their supervisor invaded their privacy.
- 23 percent said their supervisor blames others to cover up mistakes or minimize embarrassment.

Why do companies promote such people into leadership positions? One reason may be the Peter Principle: When people are promoted into one job (say, as a supervisor or coach) based on how well they did another (say, salesperson or player), that assumes that the skills of one role are the same as the other. The only time such people stop being promoted is when they reach their level of incompetence. Judging from the results of this study, that level of leadership incompetence is reached all too often.

Another study of CEOs revealed that while, on average, the performance of companies led by narcissistic CEOs was not worse, it was significantly more variable. The authors of this study argue this is because narcissistic CEOs encourage excessive risk-taking, noting: "They changed the rules so as to encourage more extremism, more flamboyance, go-for-broke types."

Sources: D. Fost, "Survey Finds Many Workers Mistrust Bosses," *San Francisco Chronicle,* January 3, 2007,www.SFGate.com. T. Weiss, "The Narcissistic CEO," Forbes (Aug. 29, 2006); http://www.forbes.com/.

trait theories of leadership *Theories that consider personal qualities and characteristics that differentiate leaders from nonleaders.*

MYTH OR SCIENCE? *"Narcissists Make Better Leaders"*

This statement is false. Narcissism—the tendency to be self-absorbed, to be exploitive of others, and to have a grandiose self-regard—has sometimes been argued to be a necessary condition for effective leadership. If you don't admire yourself, the thinking goes, who else will? A recent research effort, however, suggests that narcissistic self-admiration is toxic to effective leadership.

The authors conducted two studies—one of lifeguards on the U.S. East Coast and another of MBA students in the U.S. Southeast. In these studies, the authors first used a standard measure of narcissism, containing items such as "I am more capable than other people," to assess participants' level of narcissism. Then they asked the participants to describe their leadership effectiveness and, independently and confidentially, they asked the participants' peers for their views of the participants' leadership effectiveness.

The authors found, for both lifeguards and MBA students, that those who scored high on narcissism thought they were better-than-average leaders. However, their peers not only disagreed, they rated them as *worse* than average. So narcissists tend to think they're very good leaders when, in the eyes of others, they are very bad leaders. It's ironic that narcissism may cause people to want to be leaders and to believe they can be good leaders when in fact they are the very people who should *not* be leaders.

This study arouses particular concern because we all may be becoming more narcissistic. Some researchers who have studied narcissism over time have found that narcissism levels in the population are rising. Poet Tony Hoagland argues that "American culture encourages self-involvement to a degree that makes it difficult for us to pay attention to anything but ourselves."[11] ■

Despite such warnings, EI is being viewed as a panacea for many organizational malaises with recent suggestions that EI is essential for leadership effectiveness."[12] But until more rigorous evidence accumulates, we can't be confident about the connection.

Based on the latest findings, we offer two conclusions. First, traits can predict leadership. Twenty years ago, the evidence suggested otherwise. But this was probably due to the lack of a valid framework for classifying and organizing traits. The Big Five seems to have rectified that. Second, traits do a better job at predicting the emergence of leaders and the appearance of leadership than in actually distinguishing between *effective* and *ineffective* leaders.[13] The fact that an individual exhibits the traits and others consider that person to be a leader does not necessarily mean that the leader is successful at getting his or her group to achieve its goals.

Behavioral Theories

> 3 *Identify the central tenets and main limitations of behavioral theories.*

The failures of early trait studies led researchers in the late 1940s through the 1960s to go in a different direction. They began looking at the behaviors exhibited by specific leaders. They wondered if there was something unique in the way that effective leaders behave. To use contemporary examples, Siebel Systems Chairman Tom Siebel and Oracle CEO Larry Ellison have been very successful in leading their companies through difficult times.[14] And they both rely on a common leadership style that is tough-talking, intense, and autocratic. Does this suggest that autocratic behavior is a preferred style for all leaders? In this section, we look at three different **behavioral theories of leadership** to answer that question. First, however, let's consider the practical implications of the behavioral approach.

If the behavioral approach to leadership were successful, it would have implications quite different from those of the trait approach. Trait research provides a basis for *selecting* the "right" persons to assume formal positions in groups and organizations requiring leadership. In contrast, if behavioral studies were to turn up critical behavioral determinants of leadership, we could *train* people to be leaders. The difference between trait and behavioral theories, in terms of application, lies in their underlying assumptions. Trait theories assume that leaders are born rather than made. However, if there were specific behaviors that identified leaders, then we could teach leadership; we could design programs that implanted these behavioral patterns in individuals who desired to be effective leaders. This was surely a more exciting avenue, for it meant that the supply of leaders could be expanded. If training worked, we could have an infinite supply of effective leaders.

Ohio State Studies

The most comprehensive and replicated of the behavioral theories resulted from research that began at Ohio State University in the late 1940s.[15] Researchers at Ohio State sought to identify independent dimensions of leader behavior. Beginning with over 1,000 dimensions, they eventually narrowed the list to two categories that substantially accounted for most of the leadership behavior described by employees. They called these two dimensions *initiating structure* and *consideration.*

Initiating structure refers to the extent to which a leader is likely to define and structure his or her role and those of employees in the search for goal attainment. It includes behavior that attempts to organize work, work relationships, and goals. A leader characterized as high in initiating structure could be described as someone who "assigns group members to particular tasks," "expects workers to maintain definite standards of performance," and "emphasizes the meeting of deadlines."

Consideration is described as the extent to which a person is likely to have job relationships that are characterized by mutual trust, respect for employees' ideas, and regard for their feelings. We could describe a leader high in consideration as one who helps employees with personal problems, is friendly and approachable, treats all employees as equals, and expresses appreciation and support. A recent survey of employees revealed that, when asked to indicate the factors that most motivated them at work, 66 percent mentioned appreciation. This speaks to the motivating potential of considerate leadership behavior.[16]

At one time, the results of the Ohio State studies were thought to be disappointing. One 1992 review concluded, "Overall, the research based on a two-factor conceptualization of leadership behavior has added little to our knowledge about effective leadership."[17] However, a more recent review suggests that this two-factor conceptualization was given a premature burial. A review of 160 studies found that both initiating structure and consideration were associated with effective leadership. Specifically, consideration was more strongly related to the individual. In other words, the followers of leaders who

behavioral theories of leadership *Theories proposing that specific behaviors differentiate leaders from nonleaders.*

initiating structure *The extent to which a leader is likely to define and structure his or her role and those of subordinates in the search for goal attainment.*

consideration *The extent to which a leader is likely to have job relationships characterized by mutual trust, respect for subordinates' ideas, and regard for their feelings.*

were high in consideration were more satisfied with their jobs and more motivated and also had more respect for their leader. Initiating structure, however, was more strongly related to higher levels of group and organization productivity and more positive performance evaluations.

University of Michigan Studies

Leadership studies undertaken at the University of Michigan's Survey Research Center at about the same time as those being done at Ohio State had similar research objectives: to locate behavioral characteristics of leaders that appeared to be related to measures of performance effectiveness.

The Michigan group also came up with two dimensions of leadership behavior that they labeled *employee oriented* and *production oriented*.[18] The **employee-oriented leaders** were described as emphasizing interpersonal relations; they took a personal interest in the needs of their employees and accepted individual differences among members. The **production-oriented leaders**, in contrast, tended to emphasize the technical or task aspects of the job; their main concern was in accomplishing their group's tasks, and the group members were a means to that end. These dimensions—employee oriented and production oriented—are closely related to the Ohio State dimensions. Employee-oriented leadership is similar to consideration, and production-oriented leadership is similar to initiating structure. In fact, most leadership researchers use the terms synonymously.[19]

Sally Jewell, CEO of Recreational Equipment, Inc., is an employee-oriented leader. During her tenure as CEO, Jewell has turned a struggling company into one with record sales. But she credits REI's success to the work of employees, stating that she doesn't believe in "hero CEOs." Jewell respects each employee's contribution to the company and includes in her leadership people who are very different from herself. Described as a leader high in consideration, she listens to employees' ideas and empowers them in performing their jobs.

The conclusions the Michigan researchers arrived at strongly favored the leaders who were employee oriented in their behavior. Employee-oriented leaders were associated with higher group productivity and greater job satisfaction. Production-oriented leaders tended to be associated with low group productivity and lower job satisfaction. Although the Michigan studies emphasized employee-oriented leadership (or consideration) over production-oriented leadership (or initiating structure), the Ohio State studies garnered more research attention and suggested that *both* consideration and initiating structure are important to effective leadership.

Drawing from the Ohio State and Michigan studies, Blake and Mouton proposed a **managerial grid** (sometimes called the *leadership grid*) based on the styles of "concern for people" and "concern for production," which essentially represent the Ohio State dimensions of consideration and initiating structure or the Michigan dimensions of employee oriented and production oriented.[20]

The grid, depicted in Exhibit 12-1, has 9 possible positions along each axis, creating 81 different positions in which the leader's style may fall. The grid does not show results produced; rather, it shows the dominating factors in a leader's thinking in regard to getting results. Based on the findings of Blake and Mouton, managers were found to perform best under a 9,9 style, as contrasted, for example, with a 9,1 (authority type) or 1,9 (laissez-faire type) style.[21] Unfortunately, the grid offers a better framework for conceptualizing leadership style than for presenting any tangible new information in clarifying the leadership quandary because it doesn't really convey any new information in addition to the Ohio State and the University of Michigan research.[22]

Summary of Trait Theories and Behavioral Theories

Judging from the evidence, the behavioral theories, like the trait theories, add to our understanding of leadership effectiveness. Leaders who have certain traits and who display consideration and structuring behaviors, do appear to be more effective. Perhaps trait theories and behavioral theories should be

Exhibit 12-1 The Managerial Grid

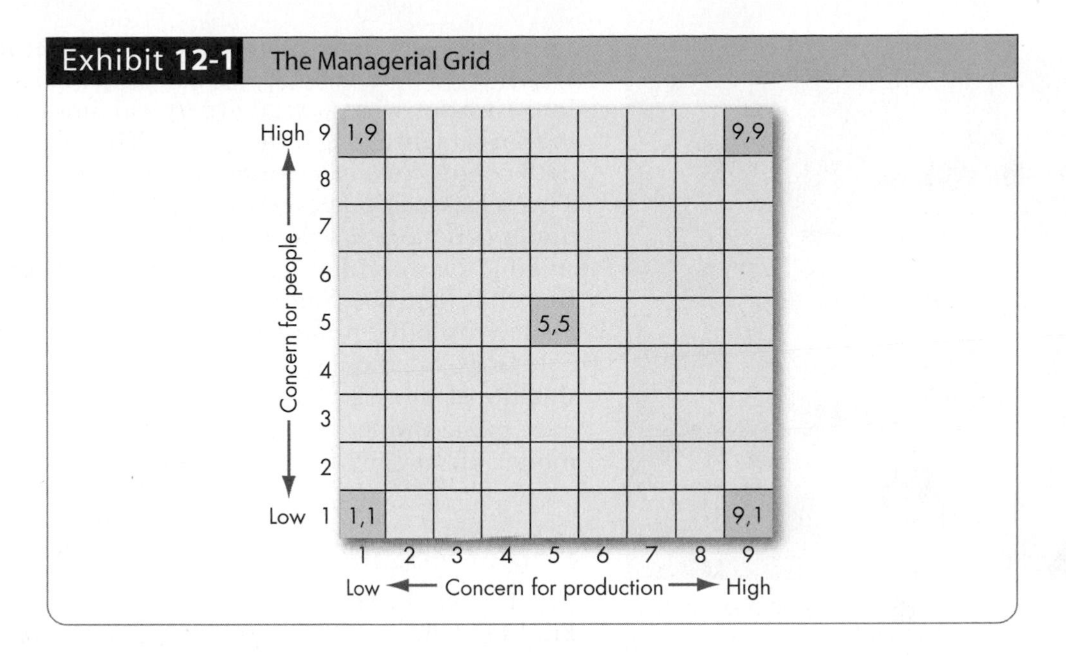

integrated. For example, you would think that conscientious leaders (conscientiousness is a trait) are more likely to be structuring (structuring is a behavior). And maybe extraverted leaders (extraversion is a trait) are more likely to be considerate (consideration is a behavior). Unfortunately, we can't be sure there is a connection. Future research is needed to integrate these approaches.

Trait theories and behavioral theories aren't the last word on leadership. Missing is consideration of the situational factors that influence success or failure. Some leaders may have the right traits or display the right behaviors and still fail. For example, former Hewlett-Packard CEO Carly Fiorina seemed to have "the right stuff" but still was ousted after HP failed to perform up to expectations. As important as trait theories and behavioral theories are in determining effective versus ineffective leaders, they do not guarantee a leader's success. The context matters, too.

Contingency Theories: Fiedler Model and Situational Leadership Theory

Some tough-minded leaders—such as former Home-Depot CEO Bob Nardelli or former Warnaco CEO Linda Wachner—seem to gain a lot of admirers when they take over struggling companies and help lead them out of the doldrums. However, these tough-minded leaders don't seem to "wear" well. Both Nardelli and Wachner were ousted after they had successfully transformed their companies, and Nardelli was later picked to lead another turnaround, this time at Chrysler.

4 *Assess contingency theories of leadership by their level of support.*

employee-oriented leader *A leader who emphasizes interpersonal relations, takes a personal interest in the needs of employees, and accepts individual differences among members.*

production-oriented leader *A leader who emphasizes technical or task aspects of the job.*

managerial grid *A nine-by-nine matrix outlining 81 different leadership styles.*

When Home Depot hired Robert Nardelli as CEO, the company believed he was "the right guy" to improve the company's performance. Under his leadership, Home Depot's profits, sales, and number of stores doubled. But shareholders criticized his leadership because he failed to improve the company's stock price relative to his huge pay package. After leaving Home Depot, Nardelli was hired as "the right guy" to revitalize Chrysler based on his turnaround expertise. Predicting the effectiveness of Nardelli's leadership as CEO of Home Depot and Chrysler illustrates the premise of contingency theories that leadership effectiveness is dependent on situational influences.

The rise and fall of Nardelli and Wachner illustrates that predicting leadership success is more complex than isolating a few traits or preferable behaviors. In their cases, what worked in very bad times and in very good times didn't seem to translate into long-term success. The failure by researchers in the mid-twentieth century to obtain consistent results led to a focus on situational influences. The relationship between leadership style and effectiveness suggested that under condition *a*, style *x* would be appropriate, whereas style *y* would be more suitable for condition *b*, and style *z* would be more suitable for condition *c*. But what were the conditions *a*, *b*, *c*, and so forth? It was one thing to say that leadership effectiveness was dependent on the situation and another to be able to isolate those situational conditions. Several approaches to isolating key situational variables have proven more successful than others and, as a result, have gained wider recognition. We shall consider three of these: the Fiedler model, Hersey and Blanchard's situational theory, and the path-goal theory.

Fiedler Model

The first comprehensive contingency model for leadership was developed by Fred Fiedler.[23] The **Fiedler contingency model** proposes that effective group performance depends on the proper match between the leader's style and the degree to which the situation gives control to the leader.

Identifying Leadership Style Fiedler believes a key factor in leadership success is the individual's basic leadership style. So he begins by trying to find out what that basic style is. Fiedler created the **least preferred coworker (LPC) questionnaire** for this purpose; it purports to measure whether a person is task- or relationship-oriented. The LPC questionnaire contains sets of 16 contrasting adjectives (such as pleasant–unpleasant, efficient–inefficient, open–guarded, supportive–hostile). It asks respondents to think of all the coworkers they have ever had and to describe the one person they *least enjoyed* working with by rating that person on a scale of 1 to 8 for each of the 16 sets of contrasting adjectives. Fiedler believes that based on the respondents' answers to this LPC questionnaire, he can determine their basic leadership style. If the least preferred coworker is described in relatively positive terms (a high LPC score), then the respondent is primarily interested in good personal relations with this coworker. That is, if you essentially describe the person you are least able to work with in favorable terms, Fiedler would label you *relationship oriented*. In contrast, if the least preferred coworker is seen in relatively unfavorable terms (a low LPC score), the respondent is primarily interested in productivity and thus would be labeled *task oriented*. About 16 percent of respondents score in the middle range.[24] Such individuals cannot be classified as either relationship oriented or task oriented and thus fall outside the theory's predictions. The rest of our discussion, therefore, relates to the 84 percent who score in either the high or low range of the LPC questionnaire.

Fiedler assumes that an individual's leadership style is fixed. As we'll show, this is important because it means that if a situation requires a task-oriented

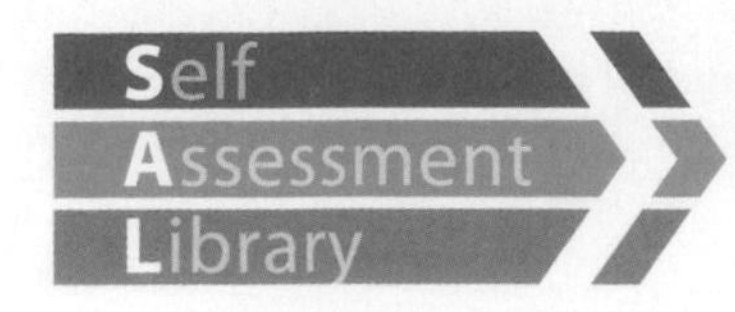

WHAT'S MY LPC SCORE?

In the Self-Assessment Library (available on CD and online) take assessment IV.E.5 (What's My LPC Score?).

leader and the person in that leadership position is relationship oriented, either the situation has to be modified or the leader has to be replaced in order to achieve optimal effectiveness.

Defining the Situation After an individual's basic leadership style has been assessed through the LPC questionnaire, it is necessary to match the leader with the situation. Fiedler has identified three contingency dimensions that, he argues, define the key situational factors that determine leadership effectiveness. These are leader–member relations, task structure, and position power. They are defined as follows:

1. **Leader–member relations** is the degree of confidence, trust, and respect members have in their leader.
2. **Task structure** is the degree to which the job assignments are procedurized (that is, structured or unstructured).
3. **Position power** is the degree of influence a leader has over power variables such as hiring, firing, discipline, promotions, and salary increases.

The next step in the Fiedler model is to evaluate the situation in terms of these three contingency variables. Leader–member relations are either good or poor, task structure is either high or low, and position power is either strong or weak.

Fiedler states that the better the leader–member relations, the more highly structured the job, and the stronger the position power, the more control the leader has. For example, a very favorable situation (in which the leader would have a great deal of control) might involve a payroll manager who is well respected and whose employees have confidence in her (good leader–member relations), for which the activities to be done—such as wage computation, check writing, and report filing—are specific and clear (high task structure), and the job provides considerable freedom for her to reward and punish her employees (strong position power). However, an unfavorable situation might be the disliked chairperson of a voluntary United Way fundraising team. In this job, the leader has very little control. Altogether, by mixing the three contingency dimensions, there are potentially eight different situations or categories in which leaders could find themselves (see Exhibit 12-2).

Matching Leaders and Situations With knowledge of an individual's LPC score and an assessment of the three contingency dimensions, the Fiedler model proposes matching them up to achieve maximum leadership effectiveness.[25] Based on his research, Fiedler concluded that task-oriented leaders tend to perform better in situations that were very

Fiedler contingency model *The theory that effective groups depend on a proper match between a leader's style of interacting with subordinates and the degree to which the situation gives control and influence to the leader.*

least preferred coworker (LPC) questionnaire *An instrument that purports to measure whether a person is task or relationship oriented.*

leader–member relations *The degree of confidence, trust, and respect subordinates have in their leader.*

task structure *The degree to which job assignments are procedurized.*

position power *Influence derived from one's formal structural position in the organization; includes power to hire, fire, discipline, promote, and give salary increases.*

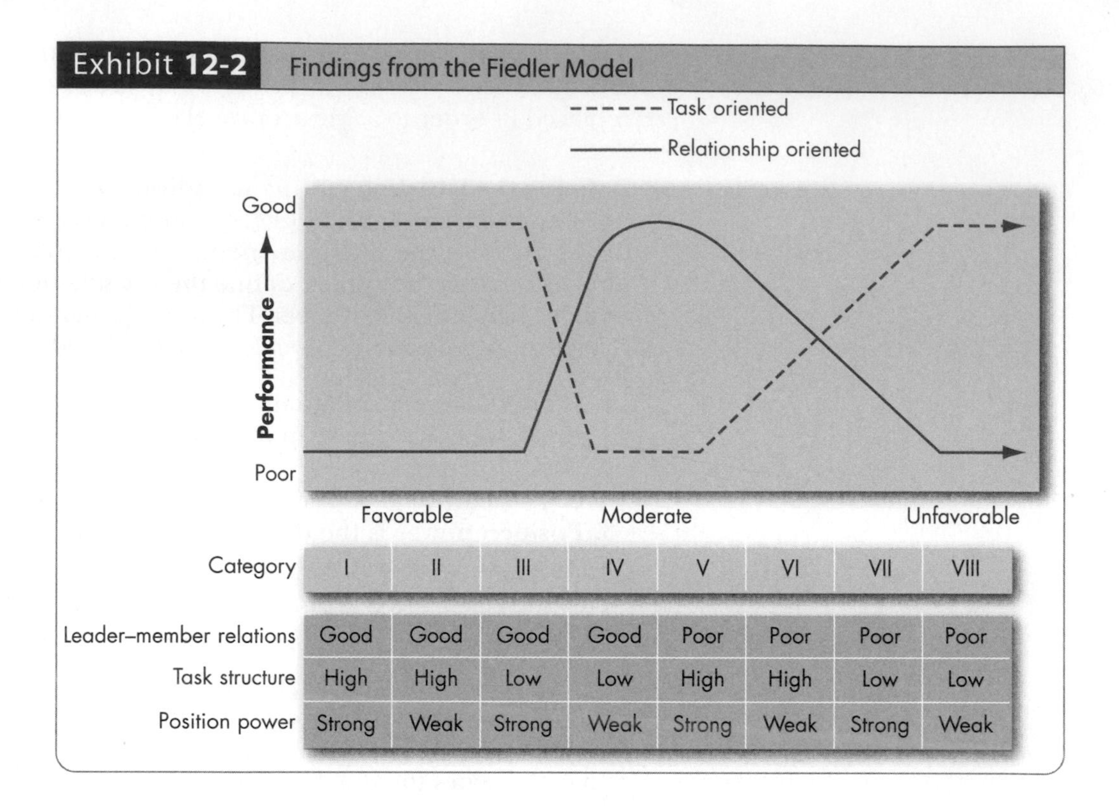

favorable to them and in situations that were very unfavorable (see Exhibit 12-2). So Fiedler would predict that when faced with a category I, II, III, VII, or VIII situation, task-oriented leaders perform better. Relationship-oriented leaders, however, perform better in moderately favorable situations—categories IV through VI. In recent years, Fiedler has condensed these eight situations down to three.[26] He now says that task-oriented leaders perform best in situations of high and low control, while relationship-oriented leaders perform best in moderate control situations.

How would you apply Fiedler's findings? You would seek to match leaders and situations. Individuals' LPC scores would determine the type of situation for which they were best suited. That "situation" would be defined by evaluating the three contingency factors of leader–member relations, task structure, and position power. But remember that Fiedler views an individual's leadership style as being fixed. Therefore, there are really only two ways in which to improve leader effectiveness.

First, you can change the leader to fit the situation—as in a baseball game, where a manager can put a right-handed pitcher or a left-handed pitcher into the game, depending on the situational characteristics of the hitter. So, for example, if a group situation rates as highly unfavorable but is currently led by a relationship-oriented manager, the group's performance could be improved by replacing that manager with one who is task oriented. The second alternative would be to change the situation to fit the leader. That could be done by restructuring tasks or increasing or decreasing the power that the leader has to control factors such as salary increases, promotions, and disciplinary actions.

Evaluation As a whole, reviews of the major studies that have tested the overall validity of the Fiedler model lead to a generally positive conclusion. That is, there is considerable evidence to support at least substantial parts of the model.[27] If predictions from the model use only three categories rather than the original eight, there is ample evidence to support Fiedler's conclusions.[28] But there are problems with the LPC questionnaire and the practical use of the model that need to be addressed. For instance, the logic underlying the LPC questionnaire is not well understood, and studies have shown that respondents' LPC scores are not stable.[29] Also, the contingency variables are complex and difficult for practitioners to assess. It's often difficult in practice to determine how good the leader–member relations are, how structured the task is, and how much position power the leader has.[30]

Cognitive Resource Theory More recently, Fiedler has reconceptualized his original theory.[31] In this refinement, called **cognitive resource theory**, he focuses on the role of stress as a form of situational unfavorableness and how a leader's intelligence and experience influence his or her reaction to stress.

The essence of the new theory is that stress is the enemy of rationality. It's difficult for leaders (or anyone else, for that matter) to think logically and analytically when they're under stress. Moreover, the importance of a leader's intelligence and experience to effectiveness differs under low- and high-stress situations. Fiedler and associates found that a leader's intellectual abilities correlate positively with performance under low stress but negatively under high stress. And, conversely, a leader's experience correlates negatively with performance under low stress but positively under high stress. So, it's the level of stress in the situation that determines whether an individual's intelligence or experience will contribute to leadership performance.

In spite of its newness, cognitive resource theory is developing a solid body of research support.[32] In fact, a study confirmed that when the stress level was low and the leader was directive (that is, when the leader was willing to tell people what to do), intelligence was important to a leader's effectiveness.[33] And in high-stress situations, intelligence was of little help because the leader was too cognitively taxed to put smarts to good use. Similarly, if a leader is nondirective, intelligence is of little help because the leader is afraid to put these smarts to use to tell people what to do. These results are exactly what cognitive resource theory predicts.

Hersey and Blanchard's Situational Theory

Paul Hersey and Ken Blanchard have developed a leadership model that has gained a strong following among management development specialists.[34] This model—called **situational leadership theory (SLT)**—has been incorporated into leadership training programs at more than 400 of the Fortune 500 companies; and more than 1 million managers per year from a wide variety of organizations are being taught its basic elements.[35]

Situational leadership is a contingency theory that focuses on the followers. Successful leadership is achieved by selecting the right leadership style, which Hersey and Blanchard argue is contingent on the level of the followers' readiness. Before we proceed, we should clarify two points: Why focus on the followers? And what do they mean by the term *readiness*?

The emphasis on the followers in leadership effectiveness reflects the reality that it is the followers who accept or reject the leader. Regardless of what the

cognitive resource theory *A theory of leadership that states that stress unfavorably affects a situation and that intelligence and experience can reduce the influence of stress on the leader.*

situational leadership theory (SLT) *A contingency theory that focuses on followers' readiness.*

These researchers at Cytos Biotechnology in Zurich, Switzerland, are developing anti-smoking and anti-obesity vaccines. The biologists and chemists at Cytos use their expertise in immunology and biotechnology in developing vaccines to treat the cause and progression of common chronic diseases that afflict millions of people worldwide. They have a high level of follower readiness. As highly educated, experienced, and responsible employees, they are able and willing to complete their tasks under leadership that gives them freedom to make and implement decisions. This leader–follower relationship is consistent with Hersey and Blanchard's situational leadership theory.

leader does, effectiveness depends on the actions of the followers. This is an important dimension that has been overlooked or underemphasized in most other leadership theories. The term *readiness*, as defined by Hersey and Blanchard, refers to the extent to which people have the ability and willingness to accomplish a specific task.

SLT essentially views the leader–follower relationship as analogous to that between a parent and a child. Just as a parent needs to relinquish control as a child becomes more mature and responsible, so too should leaders. Hersey and Blanchard identify four specific leader behaviors—from highly directive to highly laissez-faire. The most effective behavior depends on a follower's ability and motivation. SLT says that if followers are *unable* and *unwilling* to do a task, the leader needs to give clear and specific directions; if followers are *unable* and *willing*, the leader needs to display high task orientation to compensate for the followers' lack of ability and high relationship orientation to get the followers to "buy into" the leader's desires; if followers are *able* and *unwilling*, the leader needs to use a supportive and participative style; and if the employee is both *able* and *willing*, the leader doesn't need to do much.

SLT has an intuitive appeal. It acknowledges the importance of followers and builds on the logic that leaders can compensate for ability and motivational limitations in their followers. Yet research efforts to test and support the theory have generally been disappointing.[36] Why? Possible explanations include internal ambiguities and inconsistencies in the model itself as well as problems with research methodology in tests of the theory. So despite its intuitive appeal and wide popularity, any enthusiastic endorsement, at least at this time, has to be cautioned against.

Path-Goal Theory

Developed by Robert House, path-goal theory extracts elements from the Ohio State leadership research on initiating structure and consideration and the expectancy theory of motivation.[37]

The Theory The essence of **path-goal theory** is that it's the leader's job to provide followers with the information, support, or other resources necessary for them to achieve their goals. The term *path-goal* is derived from the belief that effective leaders clarify the path to help their followers get from where they are to the achievement of their work goals and to make the journey along the path easier by reducing roadblocks.

Leader Behaviors House identified four leadership behaviors. The *directive leader* lets followers know what is expected of them, schedules work to be done, and gives specific guidance as to how to accomplish tasks. The *supportive leader* is friendly and shows concern for the needs of followers. The *participative leader* consults with followers and uses their suggestions before making a decision. The *achievement-oriented leader* sets challenging goals and expects followers to perform at their highest level. In contrast to Fiedler, House assumes leaders are flexible and that the same leader can display any or all of these behaviors depending on the situation.

Path-Goal Variables and Predictions

As Exhibit 12-3 illustrates, path-goal theory proposes two classes of contingency variables that moderate the leadership behavior–outcome relationship: those in the environment that are outside the control of the employee (task structure, the formal authority system, and the work group) and those that are part of the personal characteristics of the employee (locus of control, experience, and perceived ability). Environmental factors determine the type of leader behavior required as a complement if follower outcomes are to be maximized, while personal characteristics of the employee determine how the environment and leader behavior are interpreted. So the theory proposes that leader behavior

Exhibit 12-3 Path-Goal Theory

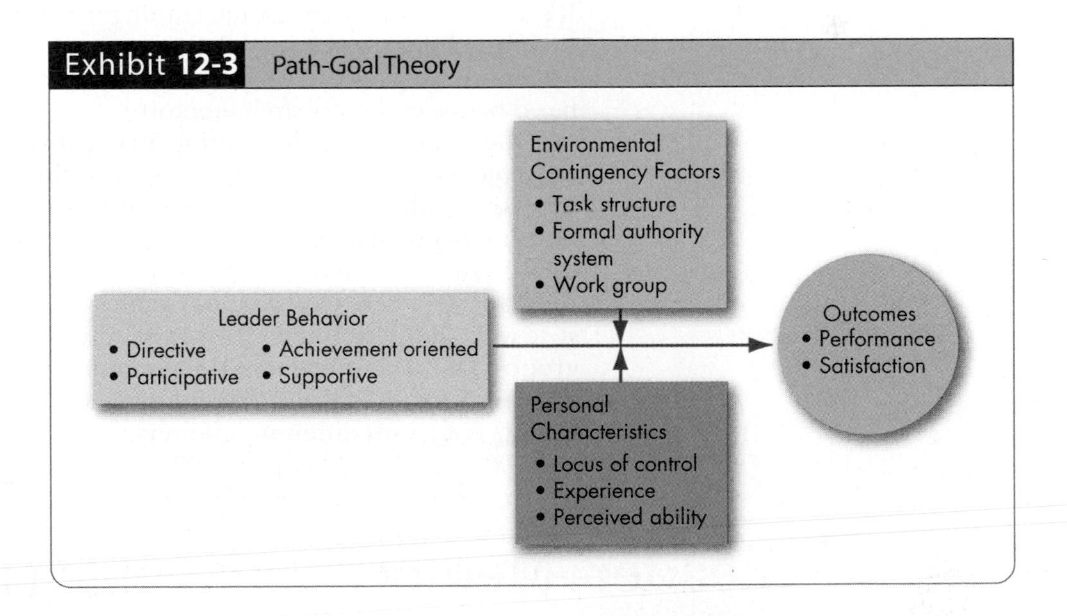

path-goal theory *A theory that states that it is the leader's job to assist followers in attaining their goals and to provide the necessary direction and/or support to ensure that their goals are compatible with the overall objectives of the group or organization.*

will be ineffective when it is redundant with sources of environmental structure or incongruent with employee characteristics. For example, the following are illustrations of predictions based on path-goal theory:

- Directive leadership leads to greater satisfaction when tasks are ambiguous or stressful than when they are highly structured and well laid out.
- Supportive leadership results in high employee performance and satisfaction when employees are performing structured tasks.
- Directive leadership is likely to be perceived as redundant among employees with high perceived ability or with considerable experience.
- Employees with an internal locus of control will be more satisfied with a participative style.
- Achievement-oriented leadership will increase employees' expectancies that effort will lead to high performance when tasks are ambiguously structured.

Evaluation Due to the complexity of the theory, testing path-goal theory has not proven to be easy. A review of the evidence suggests mixed support. As the authors of this review commented, "These results suggest that either effective leadership does not rest in the removal of roadblocks and pitfalls to employee path instrumentalities as path-goal theories propose or that the nature of these hindrances is not in accord with the proposition of the theories." Another review concluded that the lack of support was "shocking and disappointing."[38] These conclusions have been challenged by others who argue that adequate tests of the theory have yet to be conducted.[39] Thus, it is safe to say that the jury is still out regarding the validity of path-goal theory. Because it is so complex to test, that may remain the case for some time to come.

Summary of Contingency Theories

It's fair to say that none of the contingency theories have panned out as well as their developers had hoped. In particular, results for situational leadership theory and path-goal theory have been disappointing. Fiedler's LPC theory has fared better in the research literature.

One limitation of the contingency theories, and indeed of all the theories we've covered so far, is that they ignore the followers. Yet, as one leadership scholar noted, "leaders do not exist in a vacuum"; leadership is a symbiotic relationship between leaders and followers.[40] But the leadership theories we've covered to this point have largely assumed that leaders treat all their followers in the same manner. That is, they assume that leaders use a fairly homogeneous style with all the people in their work unit. But think about your experiences in groups. Did you notice that leaders often act very differently toward different people? Next we look at a theory that considers differences in the relationships leaders form with different followers.

Leader–Member Exchange (LMX) Theory

Think of a leader you know. Did this leader tend to have favorites who made up his or her "in-group"? If you answered "yes," you're acknowledging the foundation of leader–member exchange theory.[41] The **leader–member exchange (LMX) theory** argues that, because of time pressures, leaders establish a special relationship with a small group of their followers. These individuals make up the in-group—they are trusted, get a disproportionate amount of the leader's attention, and are more likely to

5 *Contrast the interactive theories path-goal and leader–member exchange.*

receive special privileges. Other followers fall into the out-group. They get less of the leader's time, get fewer of the preferred rewards that the leader controls, and have leader–follower relations based on formal authority interactions.

The theory proposes that early in the history of the interaction between a leader and a given follower, the leader implicitly categorizes the follower as an "in" or an "out," and that relationship is relatively stable over time. Leaders induce LMX by rewarding those employees with whom they want a closer linkage and punishing those with whom they do not.[42] But for the LMX relationship to remain intact, the leader and the follower must invest in the relationship.

Just precisely how the leader chooses who falls into each category is unclear, but there is evidence that leaders tend to choose in-group members because they have demographic, attitude, and personality characteristics that are similar to the leader's or a higher level of competence than out-group members[43] (see Exhibit 12-4). For example, leaders of the same gender tend to have closer (higher LMX) relationships than when leaders and followers are of different genders.[44] The key point to note here is that, even though it is the leader who is doing the choosing, it is the follower's characteristics that are driving the leader's categorizing decision.

Research to test LMX theory has been generally supportive. More specifically, the theory and research surrounding it provide substantive evidence that leaders do differentiate among followers; that these disparities are far from random; and that followers with in-group status will have higher performance ratings, engage in more helping or "citizenship" behaviors at work, and report greater satisfaction with their superior.[45] These positive findings for in-group members shouldn't be totally surprising, given our knowledge of self-fulfilling prophecy (see Chapter 5). Leaders invest their resources with those they expect to perform best. And "knowing" that in-group members are the most competent, leaders treat them as such and unwittingly fulfill their prophecy.[46]

Exhibit 12-4 Leader–Member Exchange Theory

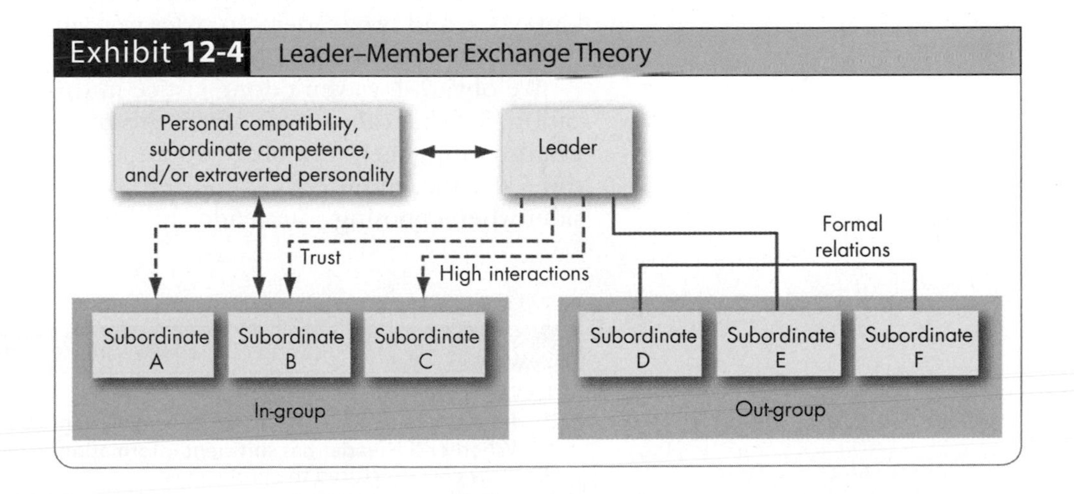

leader–member exchange (LMX) theory *A theory that supports leaders' creation of in-groups and out-groups; subordinates with in-group status will have higher performance ratings, less turnover, and greater job satisfaction.*

Decision Theory: Vroom and Yetton's Leader-Participation Model

6 *Identify the situational variables in the leader-participation model.*

The final theory we'll cover in this chapter argues that *the way* the leader makes decisions is as important as *what* she or he decides. Victor Vroom and Phillip Yetton developed a **leader-participation model** that relates leadership behavior and participation in decision making.[47] Recognizing that task structures have varying demands for routine and nonroutine activities, these researchers argued that leader behavior must adjust to reflect the task structure. Vroom and Yetton's model is normative—it provides a sequential set of rules that should be followed in determining the form and amount of participation in decision making, as determined by different types of situations. The model is a decision tree incorporating seven contingencies (whose relevance can be identified by making "yes" or "no" choices) and five alternative leadership styles. More recent work by Vroom and Arthur Jago has resulted in a revision of this model.[48] The revised model retains the same five alternative leadership styles—from the leader's making the decision completely alone to sharing the problem with the group and developing a consensus decision—but adds a set of problem types and expands the contingency variables to 12. The 12 contingency variables are listed in Exhibit 12-5.

Research testing both the original and revised leader-participation models has not been encouraging, although the revised model rates higher in effectiveness.[49] Criticism has tended to focus on variables that have been omitted and on the model's overall complexity.[50] Other contingency theories demonstrate that stress, intelligence, and experience are important situational variables. Yet the leader-participation model fails to include them. But more important, at least from a practical point of view, is the fact that the model is far too complicated for the typical manager to use on a regular basis. Although Vroom and Jago have developed a computer program to guide managers through all the decision branches in the revised model, it's not very realistic to expect practicing managers to consider 12 contingency variables, eight problem types, and five leadership styles in trying to select the appropriate decision process for a specific problem.

We obviously haven't done justice in this discussion to the model's sophistication. So what can you gain from this brief review? Additional insights into relevant contingency variables. Vroom and his associates have provided us with some specific, empirically supported contingency variables that you should consider when choosing your leadership style.

Exhibit 12-5 Contingency Variables in the Revised Leader-Participation Model

1. Importance of the decision
2. Importance of obtaining follower commitment to the decision
3. Whether the leader has sufficient information to make a good decision
4. How well structured the problem is
5. Whether an autocratic decision would receive follower commitment
6. Whether followers "buy into" the organization's goals
7. Whether there is likely to be conflict among followers over solution alternatives
8. Whether followers have the necessary information to make a good decision
9. Time constraints on the leader that may limit follower involvement
10. Whether costs to bring geographically dispersed members together is justified
11. Importance to the leader of minimizing the time it takes to make the decision
12. Importance of using participation as a tool for developing follower decision skills

Cultivating an International Perspective: A Necessity for Leaders

Accounting and consulting firm PricewaterhouseCoopers (PwC) is serious about expanding the worldview of its up-and-coming leaders. So the company started the Ulysses Program, which sends the company's potential leaders to foreign countries to gain knowledge and experience in cultural diversity.

For example, PwC sent one group of managers on an 8-week consulting assignment in the Namibian outback. Their job? To help village leaders deal with the growing AIDS crisis. Without PowerPoint presentations and e-mail, the managers quickly learned to communicate in a more traditional way—face-to-face. The managers were forced to rely less on quick technologies and more on forging connections by cultivating relationships with diverse clients. By experiencing diversity firsthand at what is perhaps its extreme, PwC hopes that its managers will be better equipped to handle issues in any culture in which they conduct business. The company says that the program gives its future leaders a broad, international perspective on business issues and makes it more likely that they will find creative, unconventional solutions to complex problems. In addition, participants can realize what they are able to accomplish when they do not have access to their usual resources. In essence, they are forced to become leaders.

The jury is still out on whether the program is effective at increasing the global leadership skills of those who participate. Nevertheless, participants of the Ulysses Program tout its benefits, and other companies have taken notice; Johnson & Johnson and Cisco Systems are just two of several companies that have adopted similar programs.

Source: Based on J. Hempel, and S. Porges, "It Takes a Village—And a Consultant," *BusinessWeek*, September 6, 2004, p. 76.

Global Implications

Most of the research on the leadership theories discussed in this chapter has been conducted in English-speaking countries. Thus, we know very little about how culture might influence their validity, particularly in Eastern cultures. However, a recent analysis of the Global Leadership and Organizational Behavior Effectiveness (GLOBE) research project (see Chapter 4 for more details on this study) has produced some useful, if preliminary, insights into cultural issues that leaders need to consider.[51]

7 Show how U.S. managers might need to adjust their leadership approaches in Brazil, France, Egypt, and China.

In this article, the authors sought to answer the practical question of how culture might affect a U.S. manager if he or she had been given two years to lead a project in four prototypical countries whose cultures diverged from that of the United States in different ways: Brazil, France, Egypt, and China. Let's consider each case in turn.

Brazil Based on the GLOBE study findings of the values of Brazilian employees, a U.S. manager leading a team in Brazil would need to be team oriented, participative, and humane. This would suggest that leaders who are high on consideration, who emphasize participative decision making, and who have

leader-participation model *A leadership theory that provides a set of rules to determine the form and amount of participative decision making in different situations.*

high LPC scores would be best suited to managing employees in this culture. As one Brazilian manager said in the study, "We do not prefer leaders who take self-governing decisions and act alone without engaging the group. That's part of who we are."

France Compared to U.S. employees, the French tend to have a more bureaucratic view of leaders and are less likely to expect them to be humane and considerate. Thus, a leader who is high on initiating structure, or relatively task oriented, will do best, and she can make decisions in a relatively autocratic manner. A manager who scores high on consideration (people-oriented) leadership may find that style backfiring in France.

Egypt Like those in Brazil, employees in Egypt are more likely to value team-oriented and participative leadership than U.S. employees. However, Egypt is also a relatively high-power-distance culture, meaning that status differences between leaders and followers are expected. How would a U.S. manager be participative and yet act in a manner that shows his or her high level of status? According to the authors, the leaders should ask employees for their opinions, try to minimize conflicts, but also not be afraid to take charge and make the final decision (after consulting team members).

China According to the GLOBE study, Chinese culture emphasizes being polite, considerate, and unselfish. But the culture also has a high performance orientation. These two factors suggest that both consideration and initiating structure may be important. Although Chinese culture is relatively participative compared to that of the United States, there are also status differences between leaders and employees. This suggests that, as in Egypt, a moderately participative style may work best.

Though we have little research to confirm the conclusions of this study, and of course there will always be variation across employees (not every Brazilian is more collective than every U.S. employee), the GLOBE study suggests that leaders need to take culture into account whenever they are managing employees from different cultures.

Summary and Implications for Managers

Leadership plays a central part in understanding group behavior, for it's the leader who usually provides the direction toward goal attainment. Therefore, a more accurate predictive capability should be valuable in improving group performance.

The early search for a set of universal leadership traits failed. However, recent efforts using the Big Five personality framework have generated much more encouraging results. Specifically, the traits of extraversion, conscientiousness, and openness to experience show strong and consistent relationships to leadership.

The behavioral approach's major contribution was narrowing leadership into task-oriented (initiating structure) and people-oriented (consideration) styles. As with the trait approach, results from the behavioral school were initially dismissed. But recent efforts have confirmed the importance of task- and people-oriented leadership styles.

A major shift in leadership research came when we recognized the need to develop contingency theories that included situational factors. At present, the evidence indicates that relevant situational variables include the task structure of the job; level of situational stress; level of group support; leader's intelligence and experience; and follower characteristics, such as personality, experience, ability, and motivation. Although contingency theories haven't lived up to their initial promise, the literature has provided basic support for Fiedler's LPC theory.

Finally, two other theories—leader–member exchange (LMX) theory and the leader-participation model—also contribute to our understanding of leadership. LMX theory has proved influential for its analysis of followers—whether they are included in the leader's "in-group" or were relegated to the "out group." Vroom's leader-participation model focuses on the leader's role as decision maker and considers *how* leaders make decisions (such as whether to involve followers in their decision making).

As a group, these traditional theories have enhanced our understanding of effective leadership. As we'll discover in the next chapter, however, more recent theories have shown even more promise in describing effective leadership.

Point Counterpoint

LEADERS ARE BORN, NOT MADE

In the United States, people are socialized to believe they can be whoever they want to be—and that includes being a leader. While that makes for a nice children's tale (think *The Little Engine That Could*—"I think I can, I think I can"), the world's affairs and people's lives are not always wrapped in pretty little packages, and this is one example. Being an effective leader has more to do with what you're born with than what you do with what you have.

That leaders are born, not made, isn't a new idea. The Victorian-era historian Thomas Carlyle wrote, "History is nothing but the biography of a few great men." Although today we should modify this to include women, his point still rings true: Great leaders are what make teams, companies, and even countries great. Can anyone disagree that people like Abraham Lincoln and Franklin Roosevelt were gifted political leaders? Or that Joan of Arc and George Patton were brilliant and courageous military leaders? Or that Henry Ford, Jack Welch, Steve Jobs, and Rupert Murdoch are gifted business leaders? As one reviewer of the literature put it, "Leaders are not like other people." These leaders are great leaders because they have the right stuff—stuff the rest of us don't have, or have in lesser quantities.

If you're not yet convinced, there is new evidence to support this position. A recent study of several hundred identical twins separated at birth found an amazing correlation in their ascendance into leadership roles. These twins were raised in totally different environments—some rich, some poor, some by educated parents, others by relatively uneducated parents, some in cities, others in small towns. But the researchers found that, despite their different environments, each pair of twins had striking similarities in terms of whether they became leaders.

Other research has found that shared environment—being raised in the same household, for example—has very little influence on leadership emergence. Despite what we might like to believe, the evidence is clear: A substantial part of leadership is a product of our genes. If we have the right stuff, we're destined to be effective leaders. If we have the wrong stuff, we're unlikely to excel in that role. Leadership cannot be for everyone, and we make a mistake in thinking that everyone is equally capable of being a good leader.[52]

Of course, personal qualities and characteristics matter to leadership, as they do to most other behaviors. But the real key is what you do with what you have.

First, if great leadership were merely the possession of a few key traits—say intelligence and personality—we could simply give people a test and select the most intelligent, extraverted, and conscientious people to be leaders. But that would be a disaster. It helps to have these traits, but leadership is much too complex to be reduced to a simple formula of traits. As smart as Steve Jobs is, there are smarter and more extraverted people out there—thousands of them. That isn't the essence of what makes him, or political or military leaders, great. It is a combination of factors—upbringing, early business experiences, learning from failure, and driving ambition.

Second, great leaders tell us that the key to their leadership success is not the characteristics they had at birth but what they learned along the way.

Take Warren Buffett, who is admired not only for his investing prowess but also as a leader and boss. Being a great leader, according to Buffett, is a matter of acquiring the right habits. "The chains of habit are too light to be noticed until they are too heavy to be broken," he says. Buffett argues that characteristics or habits such as intelligence, trustworthiness, and integrity are the most important to leadership—and at least the latter two can be developed. He says, "You need integrity, intelligence and energy to succeed. Integrity is totally a matter of choice—and it is habit-forming."

Finally, this focus on "great men and great women" is not very productive. Even if it were true that great leaders were born, it's a very impractical approach to leadership. People need to believe in something, and one of those things is that they can improve themselves. If we walked around thinking we were just some accumulation of genetic markers and our entire life was just a stage in which our genes played themselves out who would want to live that way? People like the optimistic story of *The Little Engine That Could* because we have a choice to think positively (we can become good leaders) or negatively (leaders are predetermined), and it's better to be positive.[53]

said of Obama, "I've
known anyone with
ent. He just seems to
across what are im
Although some have
sents an emphasis of
years of acrimonious
important as the *wha*
to the White House,
rise reflects people's

Sources: Based on J. H
Sensitive Side," *HRMa*
Pays . . . Or Does It?"
USA Today, January 23

Endnote

1. J. Weber and P. C
Other," *Business*
Carpenter, "Wri
Washington Post, C
2. J. P. Kotter, "Wh
Review, May–June
for Change: How L
The Free Press, 1
3. R. J. House and F
Leadership: Quo
(1997), p. 445.
4. J. G. Geier, "A Tr
Small Groups," *J*
pp. 316–323.
5. S. A. Kirkpatrick
Matter?" *Academ*
48–60; and S. J.
Monitoring and
Investigation of
Situations," *Jour*
308–315.
6. See T. A. Judge
"Personality and
the 15th Annual
and Organizatio
T. A. Judge, J.
"Personality and
Review," *Journal*
765–780.
7. Judge, Bono,
Leadership."
8. D. R. Ames and
Curvilinear R
Leadership," *Jou*
2 (2007), pp. 30
9. This section is
Leader?" *Harva*
1998, pp. 93–10
The Role of E

Questions for Review

1 Are leadership and management different from one another? If so, how?

2 What is the premise of trait theories? What traits are associated with leadership?

3 What are the central tenets and main limitations of behavioral theories?

4 What is Fiedler's contingency model? Has it been supported in research?

5 What are the main tenets of path-goal theory? What about leader–member exchange theory?

6 What are the predictions of the leader-participation model?

7 How specifically might an American leader need to adapt to the Brazilian, French, Egyptian, and Chinese cultures?

Experiential Exercise

WHAT IS A LEADER?

1. Working on your own, write down 12 adjectives that describe an effective business leader.
2. Break into groups of four or five people each. Appoint a note-taker and spokesperson. Compare your lists, making a new list of adjectives common across two or more persons' list. (Count synonyms—decisive and forceful, for example—as the same.)
3. Each spokesperson should present the group's list to the class.
4. Across the lists, are there many similarities? What does this tell you about the nature of leadership?

Ethical Dilemma

DO ENDS JUSTIFY THE MEANS?

The power that comes from being a leader can be used for evil as well as for good. When you assume the benefits of leadership, you also assume ethical burdens. But many highly successful leaders have relied on questionable tactics to achieve their ends. These include manipulation, verbal attacks, physical intimidation, lying, fear, and control. Consider a few examples:

- Jack Welch, former head of General Electric, provided the leadership that made GE the most valuable company in the United States. He also earned the label "Neutron Jack" by firing the lowest-performing 10 percent of the company's employees every year.
- Apple CEO Steve Jobs received backdated stock options: He was allowed to purchase shares of Apple at prices well below their market price at the time he was given the options. In fact, the options were backdated so that he could buy the shares at the lowest possible price. Former Apple CFO Fred Anderson argues that he warned Jobs about the accounting problems produced by backdating but says he (Anderson) is the one who took the fall.
- Cisco Systems CEO John Chambers commented that the tough times were "likely to be just a speed bump." Tell that to the 17,000 workers—nearly 20 percent of the company's workforce—he laid off. And yet Cisco has returned to profitability.

Questions

1. What is more important in judging a leader—his or her actions or the outcomes? Which *should* be more important?
2. How much of leadership success is due to luck or other factors beyond a leader's control?
3. Are employees, shareholders, and society too quick to excuse leaders who use questionable means if they are successful in achieving their goals?
4. Is it impossible for leaders to be both ethical *and* successful?

Some business model, you might think. Preach doom and gloom and be the worst critic of your own products. But that's how Chouinard's vision works. By portraying the future of mankind in its darkest terms, Patagonia builds the case for its way of doing business. If humans are on the verge of extinguishing themselves, then it becomes all the more important to buy from environmentally conscious companies. Patagonia's mission statement, featured prominently on its Web site, is *Build the best product, do no unnecessary harm, use business to inspire and implement solutions to the environmental crisis.*

Chouinard's pessimistic vision seems to be working. The company continues to grow, Chouinard regularly declines offers to buy the firm ("I don't want some Wall Street greaseball running my company," he says), and Patagonia receives 900 applications for every position it fills. Although Patagonia is not as large as some retailers, its use of environmentalism to its advantage has influenced other retailers—such as The Gap, Levi Strauss, and, most recently, Wal-Mart—to follow in its footsteps.

You would think all this would make Chouinard optimistic about the future. Not a chance. "I know everything's going to hell," he says.[1] ■

Although he's uncharacteristic of leaders in some ways, Yvon Chouinard embodies the qualities of an inspirational leader—that is, he has a vision, sticks with it, and inspires followers to transcend their own self-interests in pursuing it. One form of inspirational leadership is charismatic leadership. Take the following self-assessment to see how you score on charismatic leadership.

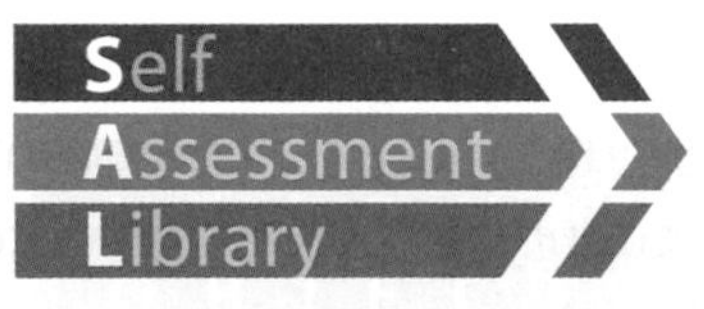

HOW CHARISMATIC AM I?

In the Self-Assessment Library (available on CD and online), take assessment II.B.2 (How Charismatic Am I?) and answer the following questions.

1. *How did you score compared to your classmates? Do you think your score is accurate?*
2. *Why do you think you scored as you did? Do you think the reason is in your genes? Are your parents charismatic? Or do you think your score has to do with your environment? Were there factors in your upbringing or early life experiences that affected your charisma?*
3. *Based on the material presented in the chapter, do you think you could become more charismatic? If yes, how might you go about it?*

Inspirational Approaches to Leadership

1 Show how framing influences leadership effectiveness.

Traditional approaches to leadership—those we considered in Chapter 12—ignore the importance of the leader as a communicator. **Framing** is a way of communicating to shape meaning. It's a way for leaders to influence how others see and understand events. It includes selecting and highlighting one or more aspects of a subject while excluding others.

Framing is especially important to an aspect of leadership ignored in the traditional theories: the ability of the leader to inspire others to act beyond their immediate self-interests.

In this section, we present two contemporary leadership theories with a common theme. They view leaders as individuals who inspire followers through their words, ideas, and behaviors. These theories are charismatic leadership and transformational leadership.

Charismatic Leadership

2 *Define* charismatic leadership *and show how it influences followers.*

John F. Kennedy, Martin Luther King, Jr., Nelson Mandela, Bill Clinton, Richard Branson (founder of the Virgin Group), Mary Kay Ash (founder of Mary Kay Cosmetics), and Steve Jobs (co-founder of Apple Computer) are individuals frequently cited as being charismatic leaders. So what do they have in common?

What Is Charismatic Leadership? Max Weber, a sociologist, was the first scholar to discuss charismatic leadership. More than a century ago, he defined *charisma* (from the Greek for "gift") as "a certain quality of an individual personality, by virtue of which he or she is set apart from ordinary people and treated as endowed with supernatural, superhuman, or at least specifically exceptional powers or qualities. These are not accessible to the ordinary person, but are regarded as of divine origin or as exemplary, and on the basis of them the individual concerned is treated as a leader."[2] Weber argued that charismatic leadership was one of several ideal types of authority.

The first researcher to consider charismatic leadership in terms of OB was Robert House. According to House's **charismatic leadership theory**, followers make attributions of heroic or extraordinary leadership abilities when they observe certain behaviors.[3] There have been a number of studies that have attempted to identify the characteristics of the charismatic leader. One of the best reviews of the literature has documented four—they have a vision, they are willing to take personal risks to achieve that vision, they are sensitive to follower needs, and they exhibit behaviors that are out of the ordinary.[4] These characteristics are described in Exhibit 13-1.

Exhibit 13-1 Key Characteristics of Charismatic Leaders

1. *Vision and articulation.* Has a vision—expressed as an idealized goal—that proposes a future better than the status quo; and is able to clarify the importance of the vision in terms that are understandable to others.
2. *Personal risk.* Willing to take on high personal risk, incur high costs, and engage in self-sacrifice to achieve the vision.
3. *Sensitivity to follower needs.* Perceptive of others' abilities and responsive to their needs and feelings.
4. *Unconventional behavior.* Engages in behaviors that are perceived as novel and counter to norms.

Source: Based on J. A. Conger and R. N. Kanungo, *Charismatic Leadership in Organizations* (Thousand Oaks, CA: Sage, 1998), p. 94.

framing *A way of using language to manage meaning.*

charismatic leadership theory *A leadership theory that states that followers make attributions of heroic or extraordinary leadership abilities when they observe certain behaviors.*

Are Charismatic Leaders Born or Made? Are charismatic leaders born with their qualities? Or can people actually learn how to be charismatic leaders? The answer to both questions is yes.

It is true that individuals are born with traits that make them charismatic. In fact, studies of identical twins have found that they score similarly on charismatic leadership measures, even if they were raised in different households and had never met. Research suggests that personality is also related to charismatic leadership. Charismatic leaders are likely to be extraverted, self-confident, and achievement oriented.[5] Consider Ted Turner, the co-founder of the cable channel CNN. When referring to himself, he has said, "A full moon blanks out all the stars around it" and "If I only had humility, I'd be perfect." Although not all charismatic leaders are as bold or colorful as Turner, most of them do have an alluring, interesting, and dynamic nature.

Although a small minority thinks that charisma is inherited and therefore cannot be learned, most experts believe that individuals also can be trained to exhibit charismatic behaviors and can thus enjoy the benefits that accompany being labeled "a charismatic leader."[6] After all, just because we inherit certain tendencies doesn't mean that we can't learn to change. One set of authors proposes that a person can learn to become charismatic by following a three-step process.[7] First, an individual needs to develop an aura of charisma by maintaining an optimistic view; using passion as a catalyst for generating enthusiasm; and communicating with the whole body, not just with words. Second, an individual draws others in by creating a bond that inspires others to follow. Third, the individual brings out the potential in followers by tapping into their emotions.

The three-step approach seems to work, as evidenced by researchers who have succeeded in actually scripting undergraduate business students to "play" charismatic.[8] The students were taught to articulate an overarching goal, communicate high performance expectations, exhibit confidence in the ability of followers to meet these expectations, and empathize with the needs of their followers; they learned to project a powerful, confident, and dynamic presence; and they practiced using a captivating and engaging voice tone. To further

The inspiring vision of Apple's charismatic co-founder and CEO Steve Jobs is to make state-of-the-art technology easy for people to use. Through this vision, Jobs inspires, motivates, and leads employees to develop products such as McIntosh computers, iPod music players, and iPhones. "The iPhone is like having your life in your pocket," says Jobs; Apple's entry into the mobile phone market includes an iPod, a camera, an alarm clock, and Internet communication capabilities with an easy-to-use touch-screen design.

capture the dynamics and energy of charisma, the leaders were trained to evoke charismatic nonverbal characteristics: They alternated between pacing and sitting on the edges of their desks, leaned toward the subjects, maintained direct eye contact, and had relaxed postures and animated facial expressions. These researchers found that the students could learn how to project charisma. Moreover, followers of these leaders had higher task performance, task adjustment, and adjustment to the leader and to the group than did followers who worked under groups led by noncharismatic leaders.

How Charismatic Leaders Influence Followers How do charismatic leaders actually influence followers? The evidence suggests a four-step process.[9] It begins by the leader articulating an appealing **vision**. A vision is a long-term strategy for how to attain a goal or goals. The vision provides a sense of continuity for followers by linking the present with a better future for the organization. For example, at Apple, Steve Jobs championed the iPod, noting, "It's as Apple as anything Apple has ever done." The creation of the iPod achieved Apple's goal of offering groundbreaking and easy-to-use-technology. Apple's strategy was to create a product that had a user-friendly interface where songs could be quickly uploaded and easily organized. It was the first major-market device to link data storage capabilities with music downloading.

A vision is incomplete unless it has an accompanying vision statement. A **vision statement** is a formal articulation of an organization's vision or mission. Charismatic leaders may use vision statements to "imprint" on followers an overarching goal and purpose. Once a vision and vision statement are established, the leader then communicates high performance expectations and expresses confidence that followers can attain them. This enhances follower self-esteem and self-confidence.

Next, the leader conveys, through words and actions, a new set of values and, by his or her behavior, sets an example for followers to imitate. One study of Israeli bank employees showed, for example, that charismatic leaders were more effective because their employees personally identified with the leaders. Finally, the charismatic leader engages in emotion-inducing and often unconventional behavior to demonstrate courage and convictions about the vision. There is an emotional contagion in charismatic leadership whereby followers "catch" the emotions their leader is conveying.[10] The next time you see Martin Luther King, Jr.'s "I Have a Dream" speech, focus on the reactions of the crowd, and it will bring to light how a charismatic leader can spread his emotion to his followers.

Because the vision is such a critical component of charismatic leadership, we should clarify exactly what we mean by the term, identify specific qualities of an effective vision, and offer some examples.[11]

A review of various definitions finds that a vision differs from other forms of direction setting in several ways: "A vision has clear and compelling imagery that offers an innovative way to improve, which recognizes and draws on traditions, and connects to actions that people can take to realize change. Vision taps people's emotions and energy. Properly articulated, a vision creates the enthusiasm that people have for sporting events and other leisure-time activities, bringing this energy and commitment to the workplace."[12]

The key properties of a vision seem to be inspirational possibilities that are value centered, realizable, with superior imagery and articulation.[13] Visions should be able to create possibilities that are inspirational and unique and that

vision *A long-term strategy for attaining a goal or goals.*

vision statement *A formal articulation of an organization's vision or mission.*

offer a new order that can produce organizational distinction. A vision is likely to fail if it doesn't offer a view of the future that is clearly and demonstrably better for the organization and its members. Desirable visions fit the times and circumstances and reflect the uniqueness of the organization. People in the organization must also believe that the vision is attainable. It should be perceived as challenging yet doable. Also, visions that have clear articulation and powerful imagery are more easily grasped and accepted.

What are some examples of visions? Rupert Murdoch had a vision of the future of the communication industry by combining entertainment and media. Through News Corporation, Murdoch has successfully integrated a broadcast network, TV stations, movie studio, publishing, and global satellite distribution. John Malone of Liberty Media calls News Corporation "the best run, most strategically positioned vertically integrated media company in the world."[14] The late Mary Kay Ash's vision of women as entrepreneurs selling products that improved their self-image gave impetus to her cosmetics company. And Michael Dell has created a vision of a business that allows Dell Computer to sell and deliver a finished PC directly to a customer in fewer than 8 days.

Does Effective Charismatic Leadership Depend on the Situation? There is an increasing body of research that shows impressive correlations between charismatic leadership and high performance and satisfaction among followers.[15] People working for charismatic leaders are motivated to exert extra work effort and, because they like and respect their leader, express greater satisfaction. It also appears that organizations with charismatic CEOs are more profitable. And charismatic college professors enjoy higher course evaluations.[16] However, there is a growing body of evidence indicating that charisma may not always be generalizable; that is, its effectiveness may depend on the situation. Charisma appears to be most successful when the follower's task has an ideological component or when the environment involves a high degree of stress and uncertainty.[17] This may explain why, when charismatic leaders surface, it's likely to be in politics, religion, wartime, or when a business firm is in its infancy or facing a life-threatening crisis. For example, in the 1930s, Franklin D.

Sony Corporation chose a charismatic leader to inspire the company to return to its innovative roots. As Sony's first CEO and chairman from outside Japan, Howard Stringer, from Wales, is reorganizing the company to lead the change in making the Sony brand more relevant to digital-age consumers. Stringer's strong sense of humor, optimism, boundless energy, and confidence are motivating employees worldwide, from engineers to executives. One top manager says, "Howard's personality and his character and the way he communicates have been good for the company." In this photo, the fun-loving Stringer jokes with Sony top executives about the color of their ties during a press conference announcing his new job as CEO.

Roosevelt offered a vision to get Americans out of the Great Depression. In the early 1970s, when Chrysler Corp. was on the brink of bankruptcy, it needed a charismatic leader with unconventional ideas like Lee Iacocca to reinvent the company. In 1997, when Apple Computer was floundering and lacking direction, the board persuaded charismatic co-founder Steve Jobs to return as interim CEO and to inspire the company to return to its innovative roots.

In addition to ideology and uncertainty, another situational factor limiting charisma appears to be level in the organization. Remember that the creation of a vision is a key component of charisma. But visions typically apply to entire organizations or major divisions. They tend to be created by top executives. Charisma therefore probably has more direct relevance to explaining the success and failures of chief executives than of lower-level managers. So even though an individual may have an inspiring personality, it's more difficult to utilize the person's charismatic leadership qualities in lower-level management jobs. Lower-level managers *can* create visions to lead their units. It's just harder to define such visions and align them with the larger goals of the organization as a whole.

Finally, charismatic leadership may affect some followers more than others. Research suggests, for example, that people are especially receptive to charismatic leadership when they sense a crisis, when they are under stress, or when they fear for their lives. More generally, some peoples' personalities are especially susceptible to charismatic leadership.[18] Consider self-esteem. If an individual lacks self-esteem and questions his self-worth, he is more likely to absorb a leader's direction rather than establish his own way of leading or thinking.

The Dark Side of Charismatic Leadership Charismatic business leaders like AIG's Hank Greenberg, GE's Jack Welch, Tyco's Dennis Kozlowski, Southwest Airlines's Herb Kelleher, Disney's Michael Eisner, and Hewlett Packard's Carly Fiorina became celebrities in their own right. Every company wanted a charismatic CEO. And to attract these people, boards of directors gave them unprecedented autonomy and resources. They had private jets at their beck and call, use of $30 million penthouses, interest-free loans to buy beach homes and artwork, security staffs provided by their companies, and similar benefits befitting royalty. One study showed that charismatic CEOs were able to use their charisma to leverage higher salaries even when their performance was mediocre.[19]

Unfortunately, charismatic leaders who are larger-than-life don't necessarily act in the best interests of their organizations.[20] Many of these leaders used their power to remake their companies in their own image. These leaders often completely blurred the boundary separating their personal interests from their organization's interests. The perils of this ego-driven charisma at its worst are leaders who allow their self-interest and personal goals to override the goals of the organization. Intolerant of criticism, they surround themselves with yes-people who are rewarded for pleasing the leader and create a climate where people are afraid to question or challenge the "king" or "queen" when they think he or she is making a mistake. The results at companies such as Enron, Tyco, Worldcom, and HealthSouth were leaders who recklessly used organizational resources for their personal benefit and executives who broke laws and crossed ethical lines to generate financial numbers that temporarily inflated stock prices and allowed leaders to cash in millions of dollars in stock options.

A study of 29 companies that went from good to great (based on the fact that their cumulative stock returns were all at least three times better than the general stock market over 15 years) found an *absence* of ego-driven charismatic leaders. Although the leaders of these firms were fiercely ambitious and driven, their ambition was directed toward their company rather than themselves. They generated extraordinary results but with little fanfare or hoopla. They took responsibility for mistakes and poor results and gave credit for successes to other people. They prided themselves on developing strong leaders inside the firm who could direct the company to greater heights after they were gone. These individuals have been called **level-5 leaders** because they have four basic leadership qualities—individual capability, team skills, managerial competence, and the ability to stimulate others to high performance—plus a fifth dimension: a paradoxical blend of personal humility and professional will. Level-5 leaders channel their ego needs away from themselves and into the goal of building a great company. So while level-5 leaders are highly effective, they tend to be people you've never heard of and who get little notoriety in the business press—people like Orin Smith at Starbucks, Kristine McDivitt of Patagonia, John Whitehead of Goldman Sachs, and Jack Brennan of Vanguard, the mutual fund company. This study is important because it confirms that leaders don't necessarily need to be charismatic to be effective, especially where charisma is enmeshed with an outsized ego.[21]

We don't mean to suggest that charismatic leadership isn't effective. Overall, its effectiveness is well supported. The point is that a charismatic leader isn't always the answer. Yes, an organization with a charismatic leader at the helm is more likely to be successful, but that success depends, to some extent, on the situation and on the leader's vision. Some charismatic leaders—Hitler, for example—are all too successful at convincing their followers to pursue a vision that can be disastrous.

Transformational Leadership

3 *Contrast transformational leadership and transactional leadership and discuss how transformational leadership works.*

A stream of research has focused on differentiating transformational leaders from transactional leaders.[22] Most of the leadership theories presented in Chapter 12—for instance, the Ohio State studies, Fiedler's model, and path-goal theory—have concerned **transactional leaders**. These kinds of leaders guide or motivate their followers in the direction of established goals by clarifying role and task requirements. **Transformational leaders** inspire followers to transcend their own self-interests for the good of the organization and are capable of having a profound and extraordinary effect on their followers. Andrea Jung at Avon, Richard Branson of the Virgin Group, and Jim McNerney of Boeing are all

A. G. Lafley is a transformational leader. Since joining Procter & Gamble as CEO in 2000, he has brought flexibility and creativity to a slow-growing company. He expanded core brands like Crest toothpaste to innovations such as teeth whiteners and toothbrushes. He shifted P&G's focus from in-house innovation by setting a goal that 50 percent of new products be developed with outside partners. With more than half of P&G's business outside the United States, Lafley recast his top management group to be 50 percent non-American. These changes have raised P&G's revenues, profits, and stock price. Shown here with Iams pet-food mascot Euka, Lafley helped move the brand from the No. 5 position in the United States to the No. 1 spot and doubled worldwide sales of Iams.

Exhibit 13-2 Characteristics of Transactional and Transformational Leaders

Transactional Leader

Contingent Reward: Contracts exchange of rewards for effort, promises rewards for good performance, recognizes accomplishments.

Management by Exception (active): Watches and searches for deviations from rules and standards, takes correct action.

Management by Exception (passive): Intervenes only if standards are not met.

Laissez-Faire: Abdicates responsibilities, avoids making decisions.

Transformational Leader

Idealized Influence: Provides vision and sense of mission, instills pride, gains respect and trust.

Inspirational Motivation: Communicates high expectations, uses symbols to focus efforts, expresses important purposes in simple ways.

Intellectual Stimulation: Promotes intelligence, rationality, and careful problem solving.

Individualized Consideration: Gives personal attention, treats each employee individually, coaches, advises.

Source: B. M. Bass, "From Transactional to Transformational Leadership: Learning to Share the Vision," *Organizational Dynamics*, Winter 1990, p. 22.

examples of transformational leaders. They pay attention to the concerns and developmental needs of individual followers; they change followers' awareness of issues by helping them to look at old problems in new ways; and they are able to excite, arouse, and inspire followers to put out extra effort to achieve group goals. Exhibit 13-2 briefly identifies and defines the characteristics that differentiate these two types of leaders.

Transactional and transformational leadership shouldn't be viewed as opposing approaches to getting things done.[23] Transformational and transactional leadership complement each other, but that doesn't mean they're equally important. Transformational leadership builds *on top of* transactional leadership and produces levels of follower effort and performance that go beyond what would occur with a transactional approach alone. But the reverse isn't true. So if you are a good transactional leader but do not have transformational qualities, you'll likely only be a mediocre leader. The best leaders are transactional *and* transformational.

Full Range of Leadership Model Exhibit 13-3 shows the full range of leadership model. Laissez-faire is the most passive and therefore the least effective of the leader behaviors. Leaders using this style are rarely viewed as effective. Management by exception—regardless of whether it is active or passive—is slightly better than laissez-faire, but it's still considered ineffective leadership. Leaders who practice management by exception leadership tend to be available only when there is a problem, which is often too late. Contingent reward leadership can be an effective style of leadership. However, leaders will not get their employees to go above and beyond the call of duty when practicing this style of leadership. Only with the four remaining leadership styles—which are all

level-5 leaders *Leaders who are fiercely ambitious and driven but whose ambition is directed toward their company rather than themselves.*

transactional leaders *Leaders who guide or motivate their followers in the direction of established goals by clarifying role and task requirements.*

transformational leaders *Leaders who inspire followers to transcend their own self-interests and who are capable of having a profound and extraordinary effect on followers.*

Exhibit 13-3 Full Range of Leadership Model

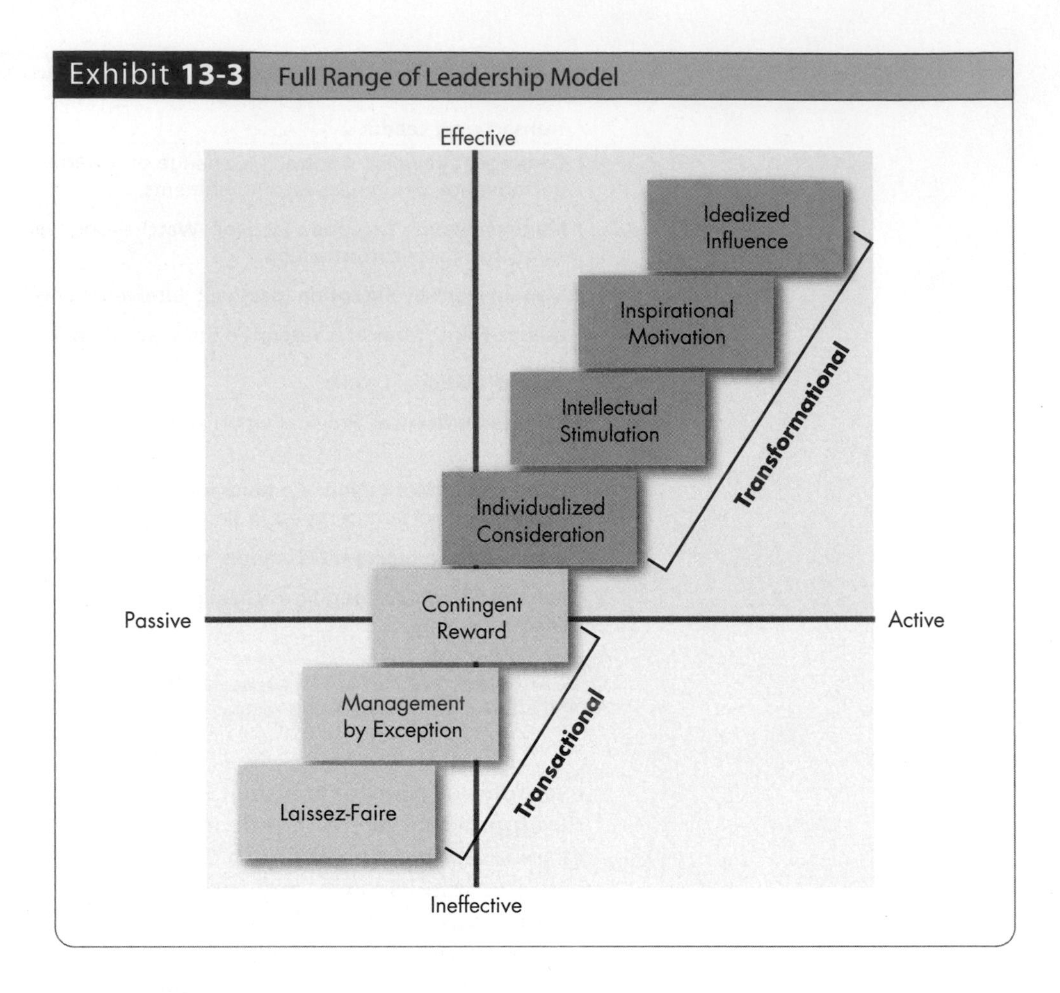

aspects of transformational leadership—are leaders able to motivate followers to perform above expectations and transcend their own self-interest for the sake of the organization. Individualized consideration, intellectual stimulation, inspirational motivation, and idealized influence all result in extra effort from workers, higher productivity, higher morale and satisfaction, higher organizational effectiveness, lower turnover, lower absenteeism, and greater organizational adaptability. Based on this model, leaders are generally most effective when they regularly use each of the four transformational behaviors.

How Transformational Leadership Works In the past few years, a great deal of research has been conducted to explain how transformational leadership works. Transformational leaders encourage their followers to be more innovative and creative.[24] For example, U.S. Army Colonel Leonard Wong found that, in the Iraq war, the Army was encouraging "reactive instead of proactive thought, compliance instead of creativity, and adherence instead of audacity." In response, Colonel Leonard Wong is working to empower junior officers to be creative and to take more risks.[25] Transformational leaders are more effective because they themselves are more creative, but they're also more effective because they encourage those who follow them to be creative, too.

Goals are another key mechanism that explains how transformational leadership works. Followers of transformational leaders are more likely to pursue ambitious goals, be familiar with and agree on the strategic goals of the organization, and believe that the goals they are pursuing are personally important.[26] VeriSign's CEO, Stratton Sclavos, says, "It comes down to charting a course—having the ability to articulate for your employees where you're headed and how you're going to get there. Even more important is choosing people to work with who have that same level of passion, commitment, fear, and competitiveness to drive toward those same goals."

Sclavos's remark about goals brings up vision. Just as research has shown that vision is important in explaining how charismatic leadership works, research has also shown that vision explains part of the effect of transformational leadership. Indeed, one study found that vision was even more important than a charismatic (effusive, dynamic, lively) communication style in explaining the success of entrepreneurial firms.[27] Finally, transformational leadership also engenders commitment on the part of followers and instills in them a greater sense of trust in the leader.[28]

Evaluation of Transformational Leadership The evidence supporting the superiority of transformational leadership over transactional leadership is impressive. Transformational leadership has been supported in disparate occupations (for example, school principals, marine commanders, ministers, presidents of MBA associations, military cadets, union shop stewards, school teachers, sales reps) and at various job levels. One recent study of R&D firms found, for example, that teams led by project leaders who scored high on transformational leadership produced better-quality products as judged 1 year later and were more profitable 5 years later.[29] A review of 87 studies testing transformational leadership found that it was related to the motivation and satisfaction of followers and to the higher performance and perceived effectiveness of leaders.[30]

Transformational leadership theory is not perfect. There are concerns about whether contingent reward leadership is strictly a characteristic of transactional leaders only. And contrary to the full range of leadership model, contingent reward leadership is sometimes more effective than transformational leadership.

In summary, the overall evidence indicates that transformational leadership is more strongly correlated than transactional leadership with lower turnover rates, higher productivity, lower employee stress and burnout, and higher employee satisfaction.[31] Like charisma, it appears that transformational leadership can be learned. One study of Canadian bank managers found that those managers who underwent transformational leadership training had bank branches that performed significantly better than branches with managers who did not undergo training. Other studies show similar results.[32]

Transformational Leadership Versus Charismatic Leadership There is some debate about whether transformational leadership and charismatic leadership are the same. The researcher most responsible for introducing charismatic leadership to OB, Robert House, considers them synonymous, calling the differences "modest" and "minor." However, the individual who first researched transformational leadership, Bernard Bass, considers charisma to be part of transformational leadership but argues that transformational leadership is broader than charisma, suggesting that charisma is, by itself, insufficient to "account for the transformational process."[33] Another researcher commented, "The purely charismatic [leader] may want followers to adopt the charismatic's world view and go no further; the transformational leader will attempt to instill in followers the ability to question not only established views but eventually those established by the leader."[34] Although many researchers believe that transformational leadership is broader than charismatic leadership, studies show that in reality a leader who scores high on transformational leadership is also likely to score high on charisma. Therefore, in practice, measures of charisma and transformational leadership may be roughly equivalent.

Authentic Leadership: Ethics and Trust Are the Foundation of Leadership

4 *Define* authentic leadership *and show why ethics and trust are vital to effective leadership.*

Although charismatic leadership theories and transformational leadership theories have added greatly to our understanding of effective leadership, they do not explicitly deal with the role of ethics and trust. Some scholars have argued that a consideration of ethics and trust is essential to complete the picture of effective leadership. Here we consider these two concepts under the rubric of authentic leadership.[35]

What Is Authentic Leadership?

Douglas R. Conant is not your typical CEO. His style is decidedly understated. When asked to reflect on the strong performance of Campbell Soup, he demurs, "We're hitting our stride a little bit more (than our peers)." He regularly admits mistakes and often says, "I can do better." Conant appears to be a good exemplar of authentic leadership.[36]

Authentic leaders know who they are, know what they believe in and value, and act on those values and beliefs openly and candidly. Their followers would consider them to be ethical people. The primary quality, therefore, produced by authentic leadership is trust. How does authentic leadership build trust? Authentic leaders share information, encourage open communication, and stick to their ideals. The result: People come to have faith in authentic leaders.

Because the concept is so recent, there hasn't been a lot of research on authentic leadership. However, we believe it's a promising way to think about ethics and trust in leadership because it focuses on the moral aspects of being a leader. Transformational or charismatic leaders can have a vision, and communicate it persuasively, but sometimes the vision is wrong (as in the case of Hitler), or the leader is more concerned with his own needs or pleasures, as in the case with the disgraced business leaders Dennis Kozlowski (ex-CEO of Tyco) and Jeff Skilling (ex-CEO of Enron).[37]

Campbell Soup CEO Douglas Conant exemplifies authentic leadership. In leading the company to becoming one of the best performers in the food industry, Conant motivates employees by giving them credit for innovation while deflecting praise of himself. During his 6 years as CEO, Conant has written 16,000 thank-you notes to employees, from the receptionist to the chief investment officer. Campbell's chairman says, "He's an extraordinary leader who behaves with the utmost integrity. People follow him and believe in him.

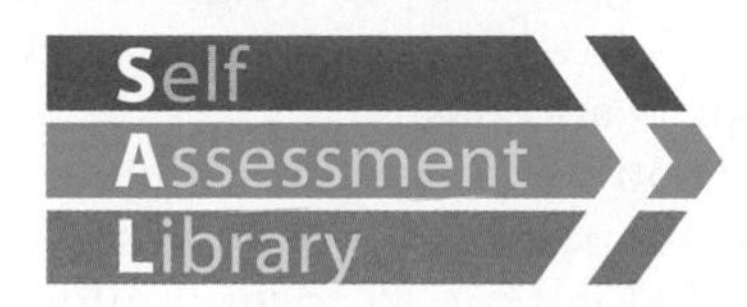

AM I AN ETHICAL LEADER?

In the Self-Assessment Library (available on CD and online), take assessment IV.E.4 (Am I an Ethical Leader?).

Ethics and Leadership

The topic of ethics and leadership has received surprisingly little attention. Only recently have ethicists and leadership researchers begun to consider the ethical implications in leadership.[38] Why now? One reason may be the growing general interest in ethics throughout the field of management. Another reason may be the discovery by probing biographers that many leaders—including Martin Luther King, Jr and John F. Kennedy—suffered from ethical shortcomings. Ethical lapses by business leaders are never absent from the headlines. Some companies, like Boeing, are even tying executive compensation to ethics. They've done so to reinforce the idea that "there's no compromise between doing things the right way and performance," in the words of Boeing's CEO Jim McNerney.[39]

Ethics touches on leadership at a number of junctures. Transformational leaders, for instance, have been described by one authority as fostering moral virtue when they try to change the attitudes and behaviors of followers.[40] Charisma, too, has an ethical component. Unethical leaders are more likely to use their charisma to enhance *power over* followers, directed toward self-serving ends. Ethical leaders are considered to use their charisma in a socially constructive way to serve others.[41] There is also the issue of abuse of power by leaders, for example, when they give themselves large salaries, bonuses, and stock options while, at the same time, they seek to cut costs by laying off long-time employees. Because top executives set the moral tone for an organization, they need to set high ethical standards, demonstrate those standards through their own behavior, and encourage and reward integrity in others.

Leadership effectiveness needs to address the *means* a leader uses in trying to achieve goals, as well as the content of those goals. Recently, scholars have tried to integrate ethical and charismatic leadership by advancing the idea of **socialized charismatic leadership**—leadership that conveys values that are other-centered versus self-centered by leaders who model ethical conduct.[42]

Leadership is not value free. Before we judge any leader to be effective, we should consider both the means used by the leader to achieve goals and the moral content of those goals.

Now let's examine the issue of trust and its role in shaping strong leaders.

What Is Trust?

Trust, or lack of trust, is an increasingly important leadership issue in today's organizations.[43] In this section, we define *trust* and provide you with some guidelines for helping build credibility and trust.

authentic leaders *Leaders who know who they are, know what they believe in and value, and act on those values and beliefs openly and candidly. Their followers would consider them to be ethical people.*

socialized charismatic leadership *A leadership concept that states that leaders convey values that are other-centered versus self-centered and who role model ethical conduct.*

Trust is a positive expectation that another will not—through words, actions, or decisions—act opportunistically.[44] The two most important elements of our definition are that it implies familiarity and risk.

The phrase *positive expectation* in our definition assumes knowledge and familiarity about the other party. Trust is a history-dependent process based on relevant but limited samples of experience.[45] It takes time to form, building incrementally and accumulating. Most of us find it hard, if not impossible, to trust someone immediately if we don't know anything about them. At the extreme, in the case of total ignorance, we can gamble, but we can't trust.[46] But as we get to know someone and the relationship matures, we gain confidence in our ability to form a positive expectation.

The term *opportunistic* refers to the inherent risk and vulnerability in any trusting relationship. Trust involves making oneself vulnerable as when, for example, we disclose intimate information or rely on another's promises.[47] By its very nature, trust provides the opportunity for disappointment or to be taken advantage of.[48] But trust is not taking risk per se; rather, it is a *willingness* to take risk.[49] So when I trust someone, I expect that they will not take advantage of me. This willingness to take risks is common to all trust situations.[50]

What are the key dimensions that underlie the concept of trust? Evidence has identified five: integrity, competence, consistency, loyalty, and openness[51] (see Exhibit 13-4).

Exhibit 13-4

Trust Dimensions

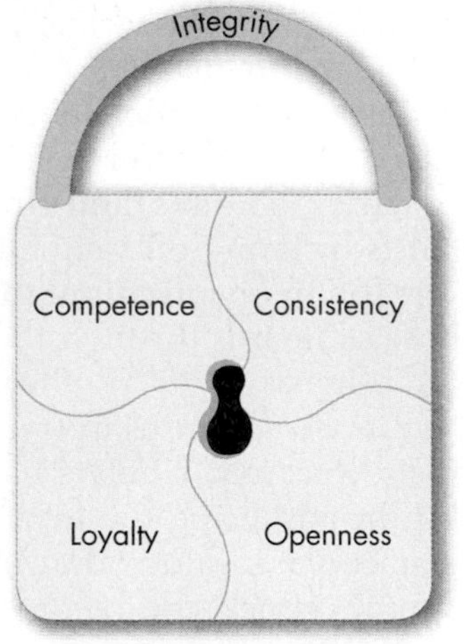

Integrity refers to honesty and truthfulness. Of the five dimensions, this one seems to be most critical when someone assesses another's trustworthiness.[52] For instance, when 570 white-collar employees were recently given a list of 28 attributes related to leadership, honesty was rated the most important by far.[53]

Competence encompasses an individual's technical and interpersonal knowledge and skills. Does the person know what he or she is talking about? You're unlikely to listen to or depend on someone whose abilities you don't respect. You need to believe that the person has the skills and abilities to carry out what he or she says they will do.

Consistency relates to an individual's reliability, predictability, and good judgment in handling situations. "Inconsistencies between words and action decrease trust."[54] This dimension is particularly relevant for managers. "Nothing is noticed more quickly. . . than a discrepancy between what executives preach and what they expect their associates to practice."[55]

Loyalty is the willingness to protect and save face for another person. Trust requires that you can depend on someone not to act opportunistically.

The final dimension of trust is *openness.* Can you rely on the person to give you the full truth?

Trust and Leadership

As we have shown in discussing ethical and authentic leadership, trust is a primary attribute associated with leadership; and when this trust is broken, it can have serious adverse effects on a group's performance.[56] As one author noted: "Part of the leader's task has been, and continues to be, working with people to find and solve problems, but whether leaders gain access to the knowledge and creative thinking they need to solve problems depends on how much people trust them. Trust and trust-worthiness modulate the leader's access to knowledge and cooperation."[57]

When followers trust a leader, they are willing to be vulnerable to the leader's actions—confident that their rights and interests will not be abused.[58] People are unlikely to look up to or follow someone whom they perceive as dishonest or who is likely to take advantage of them. Honesty, for instance, consistently ranks at the top of most people's list of characteristics they admire in their leaders. "Honesty is absolutely essential to leadership. If people are going to follow someone willingly, whether it be into battle or into the boardroom, they first want to assure themselves that the person is worthy of their trust."[59]

Three Types of Trust

5 *Identify the three types of trust.*

There are three types of trust in organizational relationships: *deterrence* based, *knowledge* based, and *identification* based.[60]

Deterrence-Based Trust The most fragile relationships are contained in **deterrence-based trust**. One violation or inconsistency can destroy the relationship. This form of trust is based on fear of reprisal if the trust is violated. Individuals who are in this type of relationship do what they do because they fear the consequences from not following through on their obligations.

Deterrence-based trust will work only to the degree that punishment is possible, consequences are clear, and the punishment is actually imposed if the trust is violated. To be sustained, the potential loss of future interaction with the other party must outweigh the profit potential that comes from violating expectations. Moreover, the potentially harmed party must be willing to introduce harm (for example, "I have no qualms about speaking badly of you if you betray my trust") to the person acting distrustingly.

Most new relationships begin on a base of deterrence. Take, as an illustration, a situation in which you're selling your car to a friend of a friend. You don't know the buyer. You might be motivated to refrain from telling this buyer all the problems with the car that you know about. Such behavior would increase your chances of selling the car and securing the highest price. But you don't withhold information. You openly share the car's flaws. Why? Probably because of fear of reprisal. If the buyer later thinks you deceived him, he is likely to share this with your mutual friend. If you knew that the buyer would never say anything to the mutual friend, you might be tempted to take advantage of the opportunity. If it's clear that the buyer would tell and that your mutual friend would think considerably less of you for taking advantage of this buyer-friend, your honesty could be explained in deterrence terms.

Another example of deterrence-based trust is a new manager–employee relationship. As an employee, you typically trust a new boss even though you have little experience on which to base that trust. The bond that creates this trust lies in the authority held by the boss and the punishment he or she can impose if you fail to fulfill your job-related obligations.

Knowledge-Based Trust Most organizational relationships are rooted in **knowledge-based trust**—that is, trust is based on the behavioral predictability that comes from a history of interaction. It exists when you have adequate information about someone to understand them well enough to be able to accurately predict his or her behavior.

Knowledge-based trust relies on information rather than deterrence. Knowledge of the other party and predictability of his or her behavior replaces the contracts, penalties, and legal arrangements more typical of deterrence-based trust. This knowledge develops over time, largely as a function of experience that builds confidence of trustworthiness and predictability. The better you know someone, the more accurately you can predict what he or she will do.

trust *A positive expectation that another will not act opportunistically.*

deterrence-based trust *Trust based on fear of reprisal if the trust is violated.*

knowledge-based trust *Trust based on behavioral predictability that comes from a history of interaction.*

Organizational relationships with Shelly Lazarus, CEO and chairman of Ogilvy & Mather Worldwide, are founded on knowledge-based trust. With the advertising agency for more than 30 years, Lazarus has earned a reputation for being honest, passionate about her work, intelligent, loyal, an excellent communicator, and respectful of employees' ideas. Lazarus believes her job as a leader is to be a role model for ethical behavior and to influence everyone at the agency to move productively in the same direction. Her vision is credited with the agency serving some of the world's most recognizable brands.

Predictability enhances trust—even if the other is predictably untrustworthy—because the ways that the other will violate the trust can be predicted! The more communication and regular interaction you have with someone else, the more this form of trust can be developed and depended on.

Interestingly, at the knowledge-based level, trust is not necessarily broken by inconsistent behavior. If you believe you can adequately explain or understand another's apparent violation, you can accept it, forgive the person, and move on in the relationship. However, the same inconsistency at the deterrence level is likely to irrevocably break the trust.

In an organizational context, most manager–employee relationships are knowledge based. Both parties have enough experience working with each other that they know what to expect. A long history of consistently open and honest interactions, for instance, is not likely to be permanently destroyed by a single violation.

Identification-Based Trust The highest level of trust is achieved when there is an emotional connection between the parties. It allows one party to act as an agent for the other and substitute for that person in interpersonal transactions. This is called **identification-based trust**. Trust exists because the parties understand each other's intentions and appreciate each other's wants and desires. This mutual understanding is developed to the point that each can effectively act for the other. Controls are minimal at this level. You don't need to monitor the other party because there exists unquestioned loyalty.

The best example of identification-based trust is a long-term, happily married couple. A husband comes to learn what's important to his wife and anticipates those actions. She, in turn, trusts that he will anticipate what's important to her without having to ask. Increased identification enables each to think like the other, feel like the other, and respond like the other.

You see identification-based trust occasionally in organizations among people who have worked together for long periods of time and have a depth of experience that allows them to know each other inside and out. This is also the type of trust that managers ideally seek in teams. Team members are comfortable with and trusting of each other that they can anticipate each other and act freely in each other's absence. In the current work world, it's probably accurate to say that most large corporations have broken the bonds of identification trust that were built with long-term employees. Broken promises have led to a breakdown in what was, at one time, a bond of unquestioned loyalty. It's likely to have been replaced with knowledge-based trust.

Basic Principles of Trust

Research allows us to offer some principles for better understanding the creation of both trust and mistrust.[61]

Mistrust Drives Out Trust People who are trusting demonstrate their trust by increasing their openness to others, disclosing relevant information, and expressing their true intentions. People who mistrust do not reciprocate. They conceal information and act opportunistically to take advantage of others. To defend against repeated exploitation, trusting people are driven to mistrust. A few mistrusting people can poison an entire organization.

Trust Begets Trust In the same way that mistrust drives out trust, exhibiting trust in others tends to encourage reciprocity. Effective leaders increase trust in small increments and allow others to respond in kind. By offering trust in only small increments, leaders limit penalty or loss that might occur if their trust is exploited.

Trust Can Be Regained Once it is violated, trust can be regained, but only in certain situations. When an individual's trust in another is broken because the other party failed to do what was expected of him, it can be restored when the individual observes a consistent pattern of trustworthy behaviors by the transgressor. However, when the same untrustworthy behavior occurs with deception, trust never fully recovers, even when the deceived is given apologies, promises, or a consistent pattern of trustworthy actions.[62]

Mistrusting Groups Self-destruct The corollary to the previous principle is that when group members mistrust each other, they repel and separate. They pursue their own interests rather than the group's. Members of mistrusting groups tend to be suspicious of each other, are constantly on guard against exploitation, and restrict communication with others in the group. These actions tend to undermine and eventually destroy the group.

Mistrust Generally Reduces Productivity Although we cannot say that trust necessarily *increases* productivity, though it usually does, mistrust almost always *reduces* productivity. Mistrust focuses attention on the differences in member interests, making it difficult for people to visualize common goals. People respond by concealing information and secretly pursuing their own interests. When employees encounter problems, they avoid calling on others, fearing that those others will take advantage of them. A climate of mistrust tends to stimulate dysfunctional forms of conflict and retard cooperation.

identification-based trust *Trust based on a mutual understanding of each other's intentions and appreciation of each other's wants and desires.*

Contemporary Leadership Roles

6 Demonstrate the importance of mentoring, self-leadership, and virtual leadership to our understanding of leadership.

Why are many effective leaders also active mentors? How can leaders develop self-leadership skills in their employees? And how does leadership work when face-to-face interaction is gone? In this section, we briefly address these three leadership role issues.

Mentoring

Many leaders create mentoring relationships. A **mentor** is a senior employee who sponsors and supports a less-experienced employee (a protégé). Successful mentors are good teachers. They can present ideas clearly, listen well, and empathize with the problems of their protégés. Mentoring relationships have been described in terms of two broad categories of functions—career functions and psychosocial functions:

Career Functions

- Lobbying to get the protégé challenging and visible assignments
- Coaching the protégé to help develop her skills and achieve work objectives
- Assisting the protégé by providing exposure to influential individuals within the organization
- Protecting the protégé from possible risks to her reputation
- Sponsoring the protégé by nominating her for potential advances or promotions
- Acting as a sounding board for ideas that the protégé might be hesitant to share with her direct supervisor

Psychosocial Functions

- Counseling the protégé about anxieties and uncertainty to help bolster her self-confidence
- Sharing personal experiences with the protégé
- Providing friendship and acceptance
- Acting as a role model[63]

Narayana Murtha (right in photo), one of the founders of Infosys Technologies in Bangalore, India, stepped down as CEO to serve the firm as chief mentor. In this role, Murtha shares his experiences, knowledge, and lessons learned while he built the company he started in 1981 and grew to 75,000 employees with sales of $3 billion. In mentoring Infosys's core management team, he wants to provide next-generation leadership for the firm. His goal is to build leadership qualities among Infosys employees by spending time at various corporate campuses and discussing issues that add value to the company. Murtha is shown here mentoring the new Infosys CEO, Nandan Nilekani.

Some organizations, such as Edward Jones, a financial services firm with 24,000 employees, have formal mentoring programs that officially assign mentors to new or high-potential employees. However, in contrast to Edward Jones's formal system, most organizations rely on informal mentoring—with senior managers personally selecting an employee and taking on that employee as a protégé. Informal mentoring is the most effective mentoring relationship outside the immediate boss–subordinate interface.[64] The boss–subordinate context has an inherent conflict of interest and tension, mostly attributable to managers' directly evaluating the performance of subordinates, limiting openness and meaningful communication.

Why would a leader want to be a mentor? There are personal benefits to the leader as well as benefits for the organization. The mentor–protégé relationship gives the mentor unfiltered access to the attitudes and feelings of lower-ranking employees, and protégés can be an excellent source of early warning signals that identify potential problems. Research suggests that mentor commitment to a program is key to its effectiveness, so if a program is to be successful, it's critical that mentors be on board and see the relationship as beneficial to themselves and the protégé. It's also important that the protégé feel that he has input into the relationship; if it's something he feels is foisted on him, he'll just go through the motions, too.[65]

Are all employees in an organization equally likely to participate in a mentoring relationship? Unfortunately, the answer is no.[66] Evidence indicates that minorities and women are less likely to be chosen as protégés than are white males and thus are less likely to accrue the benefits of mentorship. Mentors tend to select protégés who are similar to themselves in terms of criteria such as background, education, gender, race, ethnicity, and religion. "People naturally move to mentor and can more easily communicate with those with whom they most closely identify."[67] In the United States, for instance, upper-management positions in most organizations have been traditionally staffed by white males, so it is hard for minorities and women to be selected as protégés. In addition, in terms of cross-gender mentoring, senior male managers may select male protégés to minimize problems such as sexual attraction or gossip. Organizations have responded to this dilemma by increasing formal mentoring programs and providing training and coaching for potential mentors of special groups such as minorities and women.[68]

You might assume that mentoring is important, but the research has been fairly disappointing. Two large-scale reviews suggest that the benefits are primarily psychological rather than tangible. Based on these reviews, it appears that the objective outcomes of mentoring, in terms of career success (compensation, job performance), are very small. One of these reviews concluded, "Though mentoring may not be properly labeled an utterly useless concept to careers, neither can it be argued to be as important as the main effects of other influences on career success such as ability and personality."[69] It may *feel* nice to have a mentor, but it does not appear that having a mentor, or even having a good mentor who provides both support and advice, is important to one's career.

Some managers seem to recognize the limits of mentoring. When Scott Flanders became CEO of Freedom Communications, he told his managers to *limit* the time they spent mentoring their staffs. Tom Mattia, a manager at Coca-Cola who oversees 90 direct reports, finds that he has to practice "mentoring on the go."[70]

mentor *A senior employee who sponsors and supports a less-experienced employee, called a protégé.*

Self-Leadership

Is it possible for people to lead themselves? An increasing body of research suggests that many can.[71] Proponents of **self-leadership** propose that there are a set of processes through which individuals control their own behavior. And effective leaders (or what advocates like to call *superleaders*) help their followers to lead themselves. They do this by developing leadership capacity in others and nurturing followers so they no longer need to depend on formal leaders for direction and motivation.

The underlying assumptions behind self-leadership are that people are responsible, capable, and able to exercise initiative without the external constraints of bosses, rules, or regulations. Given the proper support, individuals can monitor and control their own behavior. The importance of self-leadership has increased with the expanded popularity of teams. Empowered, self-managed teams need individuals who are themselves self-directed. Management can't expect individuals who have spent their organizational lives under boss-centered leadership to suddenly adjust to self-managed teams. Therefore, training in self-leadership is an excellent means to help employees make the transition from dependence to autonomy.

To engage in effective self-leadership: (1) make your mental organizational chart horizontal rather than vertical (although vertical reporting relationships matter, often your most trusted colleagues and people of greatest possible impact are peers); (2) focus on influence and not control (do your job *with* your colleagues, not *for* them or *to* them); and (3) don't wait for the right time to make your mark; create your opportunities rather than wait for them.[73]

MYTH OR SCIENCE? *"Men Make Better Leaders Than Women"*

This statement is false. There is little evidence to support the belief that men make better leaders than women; indeed, though the differences are small, evidence suggests just the opposite.

From the dawn of the "great man" theory through the late 1980s, the common belief regarding gender and leadership effectiveness was that men made better leaders than women. This stereotype was predicated on the belief that men were inherently better skilled for leadership due to having a stronger task focus, lower emotionality, and a greater propensity to be directive.

The most recent assessment of the evidence concludes that women actually have a leadership advantage. Although the differences are fairly small, meaning that there is a great deal of overlap between males and females in their leadership styles, women do have, on average, a slight edge over men. A recent review of 45 companies found that female leaders were more transformational than male leaders. The authors concluded, "These data attest to the ability of women to perform very well in leadership roles in contemporary organizations."

It is true that men continue to dominate leadership positions. Only 2 percent of the CEOs of Fortune 500 companies are women. But being chosen as leader is not the same as performing well once selected. Research suggests that more individuals prefer male leaders. Given the evidence we've reviewed here, those preferences deserve serious reexamination.[72] ■

self-leadership *A set of processes through which individuals control their own behavior.*

Exhibit **13-5**

"So, does anyone in the group feel like responding to what Richard has just shared with us?"

Online Leadership

How do you lead people who are physically separated from you and with whom your interactions are basically reduced to written digital communications? This is a question that, to date, has received minimal attention from OB researchers.[74] Leadership research has been directed almost exclusively to face-to-face and verbal situations. But we can't ignore the reality that today's managers and their employees are increasingly being linked by networks rather than geographic proximity. Obvious examples include managers who regularly use e-mail to communicate with their staff, managers who oversee virtual projects or teams, and managers whose telecommuting employees are linked to the office by a computer and an Internet connection.

If leadership is important for inspiring and motivating dispersed employees, we need to offer some guidance as to how leadership might function in this context. Keep in mind, however, that there is limited research on this topic. So our intention here is not to provide definitive guidelines for leading online. Rather, it's to introduce you to an increasingly important issue and get you to think about how leadership changes when relationships are defined by network interactions.

In face-to-face communications, harsh *words* can be softened by nonverbal action. A smile and comforting gesture, for instance, can lessen the blow behind strong words like *disappointed*, *unsatisfactory*, *inadequate*, or *below expectations*. That nonverbal component doesn't exist with online interactions. The *structure* of words in a digital communication also has the power to motivate or demotivate the receiver. A manager who inadvertently sends a message in short phrases and in all caps may get a very different response than if she sent that same message in full sentences using mixed case.

We know that messages convey more than surface information. From a leadership standpoint, messages can convey trust or lack of trust, status, task directives, or emotional warmth. Concepts such as task structure, supportive behavior, and vision can be conveyed in written form as well as verbally. It may even be possible for leaders to convey charisma through the written word. But to effectively convey online leadership, managers must recognize that they have choices in the words and structure of their digital communications. They also need to develop the skills of "reading between the lines" in the messages they receive. In the same way that emotional intelligence taps an individual's ability to monitor and assess others' emotions, effective online leaders need to develop the skill of deciphering the emotional components of messages.

We propose that online leaders have to think carefully about what actions they want their digital messages to initiate. Networked communication is a powerful channel. When used properly, it can build and enhance an individual's leadership effectiveness. But when misused, it has the potential to undermine a great deal of what a leader has been able to achieve through his or her verbal actions.

In addition, online leaders confront unique challenges, the greatest of which appears to be developing and maintaining trust. Identification-based trust, for instance, is particularly difficult to achieve when there is a lack of intimacy and face-to-face interaction.[75] And online negotiations have also been found to be hindered because parties express lower levels of trust.[76] At this time, it's not clear whether it's even possible for employees to identify with or trust leaders with whom they only communicate electronically.[77]

This discussion leads us to the tentative conclusion that, for an increasing number of managers, good interpersonal skills may include the abilities to communicate support and leadership through written words on a computer screen and to read emotions in others' messages. In this "new world" of communications, writing skills are likely to become an extension of interpersonal skills.

Challenges to the Leadership Construct

7 *Identify when leadership may not be necessary.*

A noted management expert takes issue with the omnipotent role that academicians, practicing managers, and the general public have given to the concept of leadership. He says, "In the 1500s, people ascribed all events they didn't understand to God. Why did the crops fail? God. Why did someone die? God. Now our all-purpose explanation is leadership."[78] He notes that when a company succeeds, people need someone to give the credit to. And that's typically the firm's CEO. Similarly, when a company does poorly, people need someone to blame. CEOs also play this role. But much of an organization's success or failure is due to factors outside the influence of leadership. In many cases, success or failure is just a matter of being in the right or wrong place at a given time.

In this section, we present two perspectives that challenge the widely accepted belief in the importance of leadership. The first argument proposes that leadership is more about appearances than reality. You don't have to *be* an effective leader as long as you *look* like one. The second argument directly attacks the notion that some leadership *will always be effective,* regardless of the situation. This argument contends that in many situations, whatever actions leaders exhibit are irrelevant.

Leadership as an Attribution

We introduced attribution theory in Chapter 5. As you may remember, it deals with the ways in which people try to make sense out of cause-and-effect relationships. We said that when something happens, we want to attribute it to something else. The **attribution theory of leadership** says that leadership is merely an attribution that people make about other individuals.[79] The attribution theory has shown that people characterize leaders as having such traits as intelligence, outgoing personality, strong verbal skills, aggressiveness, understanding, and industriousness.[80] At the organizational level, the attribution framework accounts for the conditions under which people use leadership to explain organizational outcomes. Those conditions are extremes in organizational performance. When an organization has either extremely negative or extremely positive performance, people are prone to make leadership attributions to explain the performance.[81] As noted earlier, this tendency helps to account for the vulnerability of CEOs (and high-ranking state officials) when their organizations suffer a major financial setback, regardless of whether they had much to do with it, and it also accounts for why CEOs tend to be given credit for extremely positive financial results—again, regardless of how much or how little they contributed.

One longitudinal study of 128 major corporations provided important support for the attributional approach. Analyzing top management team members' perceptions of the charisma of their CEOs and their companies' objective performance, this study found that, whereas perceptions of CEO charisma did not lead to objective company performance, company performance did lead to perceptions of charisma.[82]

Following the attribution theory of leadership, we'd say that what's important in being characterized as an "effective leader" is projecting the *appearance* of being a leader rather than focusing on *actual accomplishments.* Leader-wannabes can attempt to shape the perception that they're smart, personable, verbally adept, aggressive, hardworking, and consistent in their style. By doing so, they increase the probability that their bosses, colleagues, and employees will *view* them as an effective leader.

International OB

Cultural Variation in Charismatic Attributions

Do people from different cultures make different attributions about their leaders' charisma? One recent study attempted to answer this question.

A team of researchers conducted a study in which individuals from the United States and Turkey read short stories about a hypothetical leader. Each story portrayed the leader's behaviors and the performance of the leader's company differently. In both cultures, individuals believed that the leader possessed more charisma when displaying behaviors such as promoting the company's vision and involving subordinates *and* when the leader's company performed well. However, the participants from the United States, who are more individualistic, focused on the leader's behaviors when attributing charisma. In contrast, the participants from Turkey, who are more collectivistic, focused on the company's performance when attributing charisma.

Why do these differences exist? The researchers speculated that people from individualistic cultures place more emphasis on the person than on the situation and so they attribute charisma when a leader displays certain traits. People from collectivistic cultures, in contrast, place more emphasis on the situation and assume that the leader is charismatic when the company performs well. So whether others see you as charismatic may, in part, depend on what culture you work in.

Source: Based on N. Ensari and S. E. Murphy, "Cross-Cultural Variations in Leadership Perceptions and Attribution of Charisma to the Leader," *Organizational Behavior and Human Decision Processes*, September 2003, pp. 52–66.

attribution theory of leadership *A leadership theory that says that leadership is merely an attribution that people make about other individuals.*

Substitutes for and Neutralizers of Leadership

Contrary to the arguments made throughout this chapter and Chapter 12, leadership may not always be important. A theory of leadership suggests that, in many situations, whatever actions leaders exhibit are irrelevant. Certain individual, job, and organizational variables can act as *substitutes* for leadership or *neutralize* the leader's influence on his or her followers.[83]

Neutralizers make it impossible for leader behavior to make any difference to follower outcomes. They negate the leader's influence. Substitutes, however, make a leader's influence not only impossible but also unnecessary. They act as a replacement for the leader's influence. For instance, characteristics of employees such as their experience, training, "professional" orientation, or indifference toward organizational rewards can substitute for, or neutralize the effect of, leadership. Experience and training can replace the need for a leader's support or ability to create structure and reduce task ambiguity. Jobs that are inherently unambiguous and routine or that are intrinsically satisfying may place fewer demands on the leadership variable. Organizational characteristics such as explicit, formalized goals, rigid rules and procedures, and cohesive work groups can also replace formal leadership (see Exhibit 13-6).

This recognition that leaders don't always have an impact on follower outcomes should not be that surprising. After all, we have introduced a number of variables in this text—attitudes, personality, ability, and group norms, to name but a few—that have been documented as having an effect on employee performance and satisfaction. Yet supporters of the leadership concept place an undue burden on this variable for explaining and predicting behavior. It's too simplistic to consider employees as guided to goal accomplishments solely by the actions of their leader. It's important, therefore, to recognize explicitly that leadership is merely another independent variable in our overall OB model. In some situations, it may contribute a lot to explaining employee productivity, absence, turnover, satisfaction, and citizenship behavior, but in other situations, it may contribute little toward that end.

OB In the News

Before and After

In case you're tempted to dismiss the attribution theory of leadership as another esoteric theory that lacks real-world relevance, consider the case of former Home Depot CEO Bob Nardelli (now head of Chrysler).

In March 2006, Nardelli was featured on *BusinessWeek's* cover. The article noted that Home Depot was "thriving" under Nardelli's "diamond-cut" leadership style. The article went on to argue that "Nardelli's feisty spirit is rekindling stellar financial performance."

Just 10 months later, in January 2007, Nardelli was back on *BusinessWeek's* cover. Confronted with a languishing stock price that had never performed up to the level of rival Lowe's, Home Depot's board asked Nardelli to restructure his pay package so that it was more closely tied to the company's stock price. When Nardelli refused, he was out.

What is striking, though, is how, in the same publication, things had changed so quickly after only a few months. In this article, Nardelli was described as "notoriously imperious," "arrogant," "autocratic," and "stubborn." The article explained his dismissal as evidence that "he could no longer rely on other sterile metrics to assuage the quivering anger his arrogance provoked within every one of his constituencies."

Are these two articles, by the same writer, really describing the same person? Sure they are. What changed was the results. Just as the attribution theory would predict, the same leader's behavior is attributed differently, depending on the results. In reflecting on the Nardelli saga, we might paraphrase the writer William Shakespeare and conclude, "There is no good or bad leader, but success makes it so."

Sources: B. Grow, "Renovating Home Depot," *BusinessWeek*, March 6, 2006, pp. 50–58; and B. Grow, "Out at Home Depot," *BusinessWeek*, January 15, 2007, pp. 56–62.

Exhibit 13-6 Substitutes for Neutralizers of Leadership

Defining Characteristics	Relationship-Oriented Leadership	Task-Oriented Leadership
Individual		
Experience/training	No effect on	Substitutes for
Professionalism	Substitutes for	Substitutes for
Indifference to rewards	Neutralizes	Neutralizes
Job		
Highly structured task	No effect on	Substitutes for
Provides its own feedback	No effect on	Substitutes for
Intrinsically satisfying	Substitutes for	No effect on
Organization		
Explicit formalized goals	No effect on	Substitutes for
Rigid rules and procedures	No effect on	Substitutes for
Cohesive work groups	Substitutes for	Substitutes for

Source: Based on S. Kerr and J. M. Jermier, "Substitutes for Leadership: Their Meaning and Measurement," *Organizational Behavior and Human Performance*, December 1978, p. 378.

The validity of substitutes and neutralizers is controversial. One of the problems is that the theory is very complicated: There are many possible substitutes for and neutralizers of many different types of leader behaviors across many different situations. Moreover, sometimes the difference between substitutes and neutralizers is fuzzy. For example, if I'm working on a task that's intrinsically enjoyable, the theory predicts that leadership will be less important because the task itself provides enough motivation. But does that mean that intrinsically enjoyable tasks neutralize leadership effects, or substitute for them, or both? Another problem that this review points out is that substitutes for leadership (such as employee characteristics, the nature of the task, and so forth) matter, but it does not appear that they substitute for or neutralize leadership.[84]

Finding and Creating Effective Leaders

8 Explain how to find and create effective leaders.

We have covered a lot of ground in these two chapters on leadership. But the ultimate goal of our review is to answer this question: How can organizations find or create effective leaders? Let's try to answer that question.

Selecting Leaders

The entire process that organizations go through to fill management positions is essentially an exercise in trying to identify individuals who will be effective leaders. Your search might begin by reviewing the specific requirements for the position to be filled. What knowledge, skills, and abilities are needed to do the job effectively? You should try to analyze the situation to find candidates who will make a proper match.

Testing is useful for identifying and selecting leaders. Personality tests can be used to look for traits associated with leadership—extraversion, conscientiousness, and openness to experience. Testing to find a leadership-candidate's score on self-monitoring also makes sense. High self-monitors are likely to outperform their low-scoring counterparts because the former are better at reading situations and adjusting their behavior accordingly. You can also assess candidates for emotional intelligence. Given the importance of social skills to

The French couturier Chanel developed an ascension plan for selecting a global CEO, a new position the firm created to manage the intense competition in the luxury-goods business. Selection criteria included a combination of business analytical skills and the ability to think creatively, a requirement for articulating the vision of Chanel's creative leaders. After interviewing 10 executives from the retailing, consumer-goods, and luxury-goods industries, Chanel selected Maureen Chiquet, an American who was president of The Gap's Banana Republic. Chiquet spent a year in Paris learning Chanel's culture and then served as president of Chanel's U.S. division before she became the firm's global CEO.

managerial effectiveness, candidates with a high EI should have an advantage, especially in situations requiring transformational leadership.[85]

Interviews also provide an opportunity to evaluate leadership candidates. For instance, we know that experience is a poor predictor of leader effectiveness, but situation-specific experience is relevant. You can use an interview to determine whether a candidate's prior experience fits with the situation you're trying to fill. Similarly, the interview is a reasonably good vehicle for identifying the degree to which a candidate has leadership traits such as extraversion, self-confidence, a vision, the verbal skills to frame issues, or a charismatic physical presence.

The most important event organizations need to plan for is leadership changes. Nothing lasts forever, so it's always simply a matter of *when* a leader exits, not whether. University of Florida athletic director Jeremy Foley always keeps a list of replacements. He has in place a successful football coach (Urban Meyer) and basketball coach (Billy Donovan). When Donovan surprised Foley in 2007 by announcing that he would coach an NBA team, the same day, Foley put his list in action and was about to offer the job to another candidate before Donovan had a change of heart and decided to stay. Unfortunately, some companies just aren't prepared. Frank Lanza is the 75-year-old chairman and CEO of L-3 Communications Holdings, and even though he recently underwent serious surgery, he's engaged in no planning for his successor. "I don't go for that," he said. That means when Lanza is no longer CEO, his replacement will have to be selected quickly and perhaps haphazardly.[86]

Training Leaders

Organizations, in aggregate, spend billions of dollars, yen, and euros on leadership training and development.[87] These efforts take many forms—from $50,000 executive leadership programs offered by universities such as Harvard to sailing experiences at the Outward Bound, a nonprofit organization that helps people achieve personal growth through adventure-based wilderness programs. Business schools, including some elite programs, are placing renewed emphasis on leadership development. Some companies, too, place a lot of emphasis on leadership development. For example, Goldman Sachs is well known for developing leaders, so much so that *BusinessWeek* called it the "Leadership Factory."[88]

Although much of the money spent on training may provide dubious benefits, our review suggests that there are some things managers can do to get the maximum effect from their leadership-training budgets.[89]

First, let's recognize the obvious. People are not equally trainable. Leadership training of any kind is likely to be more successful with individuals who are high self-monitors than with low self-monitors. Such individuals have the flexibility to change their behavior.

What kinds of things can individuals learn that might be related to higher leader effectiveness? It may be a bit optimistic to believe that we can teach "vision creation," but we can teach implementation skills. We can train people to develop "an understanding about content themes critical to effective visions."[90] We can also teach skills such as trust building and mentoring. And leaders can be taught situational-analysis skills. They can learn how to evaluate situations, how to modify situations to make them fit better with their style, and how to assess which leader behaviors might be most effective in given situations. A number of companies have recently turned to executive coaches to help senior managers improve their leadership skills.[91] For instance, the firms Charles Schwab, eBay, Pfizer, Unilever, and American Express have hired executive coaches to provide specific one-on-one training for their top executives to help them improve their interpersonal skills and to learn to act less autocratically.[92]

On an optimistic note, there is evidence suggesting that behavioral training through modeling exercises can increase an individual's ability to exhibit charismatic leadership qualities. The success of the researchers mentioned earlier (see "Are Charismatic Leaders Born or Made?" on page 413) in actually scripting undergraduate business students to "play" charismatic is a case in point.[93] Finally, there is accumulating research showing that leaders can be trained in transformational leadership skills. Once learned, these skills have bottom-line results, whether in the financial performance of Canadian banks or the training effectiveness of soldiers in the Israeli Defense Forces.[94]

Global Implications

9 *Assess whether charismatic and transformational leadership generalize across cultures.*

We noted in Chapter 12 that while there is little cross-cultural research on the traditional theories of leadership, there is reason to believe that certain types of leadership behaviors work better in some cultures than in others. What about the more contemporary leadership roles covered in this chapter? Is there cross-cultural research on charismatic/transformational leadership? Does it generalize across cultures? Yes and yes. There has been cross-cultural research on charismatic/transformational leadership, and it seems to suggest that the leadership style works in different cultures.

The GLOBE research program, which we introduced in Chapter 4, has gathered data on approximately 18,000 middle managers in 825 organizations, covering 62 countries. It's the most comprehensive cross-cultural study of leadership ever undertaken. So its findings should not be quickly dismissed. It's illuminating that one of the results coming from the GLOBE program is that there *are* some universal aspects to leadership. Specifically, a number of the elements making up transformational leadership appear to be associated with effective leadership, regardless of what country the leader is in.[95] This conclusion is very important because it flies in the face of the contingency view that leadership style needs to adapt to cultural differences.

What elements of transformational leadership appear universal? Vision, foresight, providing encouragement, trustworthiness, dynamism, positiveness, and proactiveness. The results led two members of the GLOBE team to conclude that "effective business leaders in any country are expected by their subordinates to provide a powerful and proactive vision to guide the company into the future, strong motivational skills to stimulate all employees to fulfill the vision, and excellent planning skills to assist in implementing the vision."[96]

What might explain the universal appeal of these transformational leader attributes? It's been suggested that pressures toward common technologies and management practices, as a result of global competition and multinational influences, may make some aspects of leadership universally accepted. If that's true, we may be able to select and train leaders in a universal style and thus significantly raise the quality of leadership worldwide.

None of this is meant to suggest that a certain cultural sensitivity or adaptation in styles might not be important when leading teams in different cultures. A vision is important in any culture, but how that vision is formed and communicated may still need to vary by culture. This is true even for companies that are known worldwide for their emphasis on vision. For example, a GE executive recalls the following of using his U.S. leadership style in Japan: "Nothing happened. I quickly realized that I had to adapt my approach, to act more as a consultant to my colleagues and to adopt a team-based motivational decision-making process rather than the more vocal style which tends to be common in the West. In Japan the silence of a leader means far more than a thousand words uttered by somebody else."[97]

Summary and Implications for Managers

Organizations are increasingly searching for managers who can exhibit transformational leadership qualities. They want leaders with vision and the charisma to carry out their vision. And although true leadership effectiveness may be a result of exhibiting the right behaviors at the right time, the evidence is quite strong that people have a relatively uniform perception of what a leader should look like. They attribute "leadership" to people who are smart, personable, verbally adept, and the like. To the degree that managers project these qualities, others are likely to deem them leaders. There is increasing evidence that the effectiveness of charismatic and transformational leadership crosses cultural boundaries.

Effective managers today must develop trusting relationships with those they seek to lead because, as organizations have become less stable and predictable, strong bonds of trust are likely to be replacing bureaucratic rules in defining expectations and relationships. Managers who aren't trusted aren't likely to be effective leaders.

For managers concerned with how to fill key positions in their organization with effective leaders, we have shown that tests and interviews help to identify people with leadership qualities. In addition to focusing on leadership selection, managers should also consider investing in leadership training. Many individuals with leadership potential can enhance their skills through formal courses, workshops, rotating job responsibilities, coaching, and mentoring.

Point Counterpoint

KEEP LEADERS ON A SHORT LEASH

A company's leaders need to be managed just like everyone else. Often they cause more harm than good. There is a long list of CEOs who practically drove their companies into the ground: Carly Fiorina (HP), Harry Stonecipher (Boeing), Raymond Gilmartin (Merck), Will McGuire (UnitedHealth), Franklin Raines (Fannie Mae), Henry McKinnell (Pfizer), Peter Dolan (Bristol-Myers Squibb), and the list could go on and on. Although the names always change, this sad fact never does: CEOs are often given the "run of the house" and are reined in only after the damage is done. So what happens? A new CEO is hired, and all too often, the same pattern repeats itself.

The key is not who the leader is but how he or she is managed. CEOs are given far too much influence and treated with kid gloves by their board of directors (who generally end up selecting, and rewarding, one another). They make nice while they're being interviewed, but once hired, most turn into autocrats, running their empires with little room for participation, dissent, and, heaven forbid, any limits on their power. When ex-Pfizer CEO Henry McKinnell was forced out, he complained about the "war against the corporation." Actually, the war was against his out-of-control pay package. After he was forced out, Hank Greenberg groused, "If I were starting over, I'd move to China or India." Poor Hank just didn't have enough room to run his empire with those darned stakeholders to answer to.

Yes, CEOs need to be hired carefully, but there are limits to how well we can see the "real" CEO. Much more important is having an autonomous board that will limit the CEO's powers and make him strongly accountable based on performance metrics.

Yes, some CEOs fail, but that's business. If everyone succeeded, why would you need a CEO in the first place? The key to leading companies is to choose wisely.

Select poorly, and you need to put systems in place to manage the leader. But this is a losing game. If you're stuck with a dog as CEO, you'll never be able to manage all aspects of her job. Blessed with a good one, and you won't need to worry about managing her performance—the CEO will do that job quite well on her own. Take the example of Boeing's CEO Jim McNerney. He is the first to point out the limits of his own power. "I'm just one of eleven with a point of view," he says. "I have to depend on my power to persuade."

To treat him as if he were some child to be rewarded and punished at every step is to eliminate any benefits of the job altogether. Boeing hired well, and though every CEO needs some metrics, mostly the board should stay out of his way and focus on the big picture—strategic planning, meeting long-term objectives, and so on. It is fine and good to pay CEOs based on performance, but the devil is often in the details. Link all of a CEO's pay to stock price, and what do you think will happen? Some good CEOs won't take the job because they realize they can't perfectly control stock price. Others will take the job only to cynically manipulate it to their short-term advantage. Either way, in the long run, the company loses.

Some companies have limited the leader's authority by slicing up the leader's job and micromanaged him or her at every turn. For example, when Citigroup's Chairman and CEO Charles Prince was forced out in late 2007, many argued in favor of separating the role of Chairman and CEO because the CEO couldn't and shouldn't be trusted to do the job. What company, and what leader, can excel under such a handicap?

There is nothing better than hiring the right CEO. There is nothing worse than hiring the wrong one.[98]

Questions for Review

1 How does framing influence leadership effectiveness?

2 What is charismatic leadership and how does it work?

3 What is transformational leadership? How is it different from transactional and charismatic leadership?

4 What is authentic leadership? Why do ethics and trust matter to leadership?

5 What are the three types of trust?

6 What are the importance of mentoring, self-leadership, and virtual leadership?

7 Are there situations in which leadership is not necessary?

8 How can organizations select and develop effective leaders?

9 Do charismatic and transformational leadership generalize across cultures?

Experiential Exercise

YOU BE THE JUDGE: WHICH VISION STATEMENT IS EFFECTIVE

There has been a lot of research about what makes an effective vision statement. A good vision statement is said to have the following qualities:

a. Identifies values and beliefs.
b. Is idealistic or utopian.
c. Represents broad and overarching (versus narrow and specific) goals.
d. Is inspiring.
e. Is future oriented.
f. Is bold and ambitious.
g. Reflects the uniqueness of the organization.
h. Is well articulated and easily understood.

Now that you know what makes a good vision statement, you can rate vision statements from actual companies.

1. Break into groups of four or five people each.
2. Each group member should rate each of the following vision statements—based on the eight qualities listed here—on a scale from 1 = very poor to 10 = excellent.
3. Compare your ratings. Did your group agree or disagree?
4. What do you think caused the agreement or disagreement?
5. How would you improve these vision statements?

Vision Statements

- *DuPont.* Our vision is to be the world's most dynamic science company, creating sustainable solutions essential to a better, safer and healthier life for people everywhere.
- *Nucor.* Nucor Corporation is made up of 11,900 teammates whose goal is to "Take Care of Our Customers." We are accomplishing this by being the safest, highest quality, lowest cost, most productive and most profitable steel and steel products company in the world. We are committed to doing this while being cultural and environmental stewards in our communities where we live and work. We are succeeding by working together.
- *Toshiba.* Toshiba delivers technology and products remarkable for their innovation and artistry—contributing to a safer, more comfortable, more productive life. We bring together the spirit of innovation with our passion and conviction to shape the future and help protect the global environment—our shared heritage. We foster close relationships, rooted in trust and respect, with our customers, business partners and communities around the world.
- *University of Northern Iowa.* The University of Northern Iowa offers a world-class university education, providing personalized experiences and creating a lifetime of opportunities. Hallmarks of UNI's success include: (1) An environment that places "Students First," (2) A commitment to Great Learning through Great Teaching, and (3) A broad range of services designed to enhance the lives and livelihoods of Iowans.
- *Nissan.* Call us zealous, even overzealous, but at Nissan we know that settling for just any solution is just that. Settling. And, not to mention, the fastest way to go from being an automotive company fueled by imagination to just another automotive company, period. That's why we think beyond the answer. And ask. Because only through this process of constant challenge can real change occur. One question at a time.

Source: The vision attributes are based on S. A. Kirkpatrick, E. A. Locke, and G. P. Latham, "Implementing the Vision: How Is It Done?" *Polish Psychological Bulletin* 27 (1996), pp. 93–106.

Ethical Dilemma

WHOLE FOODS'S RAHODEB

Whole Foods, a fast-growing chain of upscale grocery stores, has long been a Wall Street and business press favorite. It regularly appears high on *Fortune*'s list of *100 Best Companies to Work For* (it was 5th in 2007), and it has spawned its share of competitors, including Fresh Market, Trader Joe's, and Wild Oats.

Given that most industry analysts see a bright future for upscale, organic markets like Whole Foods, it's no surprise that the market has attracted its share of investor blogs. One of the prominent bloggers (filing hundreds of blog entries), "Rahodeb" has consistently extolled the virtues of Whole Foods's stock and derided Wild Oats. Rahodeb predicted that Wild Oats would eventually be forced into bankruptcy and that the stock price of Whole Foods would grow at an annual rate of 18 percent. Rahodeb's Yahoo! Finance blog entries were widely read because he seemed to have special insights into the industry and into Whole Foods in particular.

Would it surprise you to learn that in 2007, Rahodeb was exposed as Whole Foods co-founder and CEO John Mackey? ("Rahodeb" is an anagram of "Deborah," Mackey's wife.) What's more, while Rahodeb was talking down Wild Oats's stock, Whole Foods was in the process of acquiring Wild Oats, and talking down the company may have made the acquisition easier, and cheaper. Because the companies often have stores in the same cities, the Federal Trade Commission (FTC) is attempting to block the acquisition, and the FTC was responsible for "outing" Mackey.

It's not clear that Mackey's behavior was illegal. Mackey said, "I posted on Yahoo! under a pseudonym because I had fun doing it. Many people post on bulletin boards using pseudonyms. The views articulated by rahodeb sometimes represented what I believed and sometimes they didn't."

Do you think it is unethical for a company leader like Mackey to pose as an investor, talking up his or her company's stock price while talking down his competitor's? Would Mackey's behavior affect your willingness to work for or invest in Whole Foods?

Source: D. Kesmodel and J. R. Wilke, "Whole Foods Is Hot, Wild Oats a Dud—So Said 'Rahodeb,'" *Wall Street Journal*, July 12, 2007, pp. A1, A10; and G. Farrell and P. Davidson, "Whole Foods' CEO Was Busy Guy Online," *USA Today*, July 13, 2007, p. 4B.

Case Incident 1

THE MAKING OF A GREAT PRESIDENT

What does it take to be a great U.S. president? A survey of 78 history, political science, and law scholars rated the U.S. presidents from George Washington to Bill Clinton. Here are the presidents who were rated "great" and "near great."

Great
George Washington
Abraham Lincoln
Franklin D. Roosevelt (FDR)

Near Great
Thomas Jefferson
Theodore Roosevelt
Ronald Reagan
Harry Truman
Dwight Eisenhower
James Polk
Andrew Jackson

Among recent presidents, Presidents Nixon, Ford, and Carter were rated "Below Average," and Presidents G. H. W. Bush and Clinton were rated "Average."

What about George W. Bush? Given his relative unpopularity, you might think that he will go down in history as a failure. However, popularity is not a perfect indicator of whether a president's accomplishments stand the test of time. Harry Truman left office with an approval rating in the low 30s, whereas Bill Clinton left office with an approval rating in the mid-60s. Yet historians have judged Truman the more effective president.

Questions

1. Would you rate George W. Bush as a charismatic or transformational leader? What about Bill Clinton?
2. Do you think leaders in other contexts (for example, business, sports, religion) exhibit the same qualities as great or near-great U.S. presidents?
3. Do you think being in the right place at the right time could influence presidential greatness?

Source: "Presidential Leadership: The Rankings," *OpinionJournal.com*, September 12, 2005, www.opinionjournal.com/extra/?id=110007243.

Case Incident 2

GENERATION GAP: MENTORS AND PROTÉGÉS

As the baby boom generation nears retirement, many Boomers are mentoring their future work replacements—Generation Xers. Some Boomers have found the process difficult. William Slater, a 47-year-old computer engineer who participates in his company's formal mentoring program, has had negative experiences with three protégés. He recalls that one tried, unsuccessfully, to take his job, while another repeatedly spoke badly about him to his boss. "I have an ax to grind with Generation X. They're stabbing aging Baby Boomers in the back," says Slater.

It is not only Baby Boomers who have had bad experiences. Joel Bershok, a 24-year-old, was optimistic about the prospects of having a mentor. However, his mentor dissolved the relationship after only 3 weeks. Says Bershok: "He just wanted it for his resume." To Bershok, one of the major problems with a mentoring relationship is a lack of trust. With an uncertain economy and companies making frequent layoff announcements, Boomers are wary of teaching their younger counterparts too much for fear that those counterparts, who usually make less—and so cost the company less than Boomers—may replace them.

The fear may be justified. For example, Janet Wheeler, a 49-year-old broker, saw her job replaced by two younger workers after her company let her go. Wheeler thinks that other Boomers are beginning to notice the risks of mentoring and are responding by not teaching their protégés as much as they could. "You see young people being brought along just enough to get the job done, but not so much that they'll take your job," she states.

Given that some studies have demonstrated the beneficial effects of mentoring on employee outcomes such as performance, job satisfaction, and employee retention, many analysts are concerned that Baby Boomers are failing to see mentoring as a responsibility. According to a study by Menttium Corporation, a firm that aids companies in installing mentoring programs, almost 90 percent of formal mentoring relationships end prematurely. The primary reasons include poor matching of mentors to protégés and a lack of effort to keep the relationship going.

But some workers have strongly benefited from mentoring programs and are trying to maintain mentoring programs in their companies. Three years after joining Dell, Lynn Tyson, 41, helped start a formal mentoring program open to all of Dell's 42,000 employees. "I never had a formal mentor in my entire career. Most of the time I was shaking in my shoes," says Tyson. Her program has been successful so far—and she mentors 40 protégés. "I'm not trying to make this sound sappy, but I have the ability to make a difference in somebody's career, and that excites me every day." The benefits are especially apparent for women and minorities who, historically, have had greater difficulty than white males in climbing to top management positions. According to a study by Harvard University professor David A. Thomas, the most successful racial minorities at three different corporations had a strong network of mentors. In addition, research has shown that women also benefit from having positive mentoring experiences in that they have greater career success and career satisfaction.

With the right amount of effort, protégés, mentors, and the companies that sponsor such relationships can realize tremendous benefits. However, individuals in mentoring relationships may need to look past generational and other individual differences to achieve such benefits. Though Slater has had his share of bad mentoring experiences, he is still optimistic. "Mentoring is a time-honored concept. Those of us who've been mentored should mentor others. Otherwise, we've short-circuited the process and the future," he says.

Questions

1. What factors do you believe lead to successful mentoring programs? If you were designing a mentoring program, what might it look like?
2. In what ways might a protégé benefit from having a mentor? In what ways might a mentor benefit from having a protégé?
3. Of the three types of trust discussed in the chapter, which one may be the primary type in mentoring relationships and why?
4. What types of leaders, in terms of personality traits and behavioral tendencies, would most likely be good mentors? What types of leaders might be poor mentors?

Source: Based on J. Zaslow, "Moving On: Don't Trust Anyone Under 30: Boomers Struggle with Their New Role as Mentors," *Wall Street Journal*, June 5, 2003, p. D1; P. Garfinkel, "Putting a Formal Stamp on Mentoring," *New York Times*, January 18, 2004, p. 10; and J. E. Wallace, "The Benefits of Mentoring for Female Lawyers," *Journal of Vocational Behavior*, June 2001, pp. 366–391.

Endnotes

1. "Endless Summer," *Fortune*, April 2, 2007, pp. 63–70.
2. M. Weber, *The Theory of Social and Economic Organization*, A. M. Henderson and T. Parsons (trans.) (New York: The Free Press, 1947).
3. J. A. Conger and R. N. Kanungo, "Behavioral Dimensions of Charismatic Leadership," in J. A. Conger, R. N. Kanungo and Associates (eds.), *Charismatic Leadership* (San Francisco: Jossey-Bass, 1988), p. 79.
4. J. A. Conger and R. N. Kanungo, *Charismatic Leadership in Organizations* (Thousand Oaks, CA: Sage, 1998); and R. Awamleh and W. L. Gardner, "Perceptions of Leader Charisma and Effectiveness: The Effects of Vision Content, Delivery, and Organizational Performance," *Leadership Quarterly*, Fall 1999, pp. 345–373.
5. R. J. House and J. M. Howell, "Personality and Charismatic Leadership," *Leadership Quarterly* 3 (1992), pp. 81–108; D. N. Den Hartog and P. L., "Leadership in Organizations," in N. Anderson and D. S. Ones (eds.), *Handbook of Industrial, Work and Organizational Psychology*, vol. 2 (Thousand Oaks, CA: Sage, 2002), pp. 166–187.
6. See J. A. Conger and R. N. Kanungo, "Training Charismatic Leadership: A Risky and Critical Task," *Charismatic Leadership* (San Francisco: Jossey-Bass, 1988), pp. 309–323; A. J. Towler, "Effects of Charismatic Influence Training on Attitudes, Behavior, and Performance," *Personnel Psychology*, Summer 2003, pp. 363–381; and M. Frese, S. Beimel, and S. Schoenborn, "Action Training for Charismatic Leadership: Two Evaluations of Studies of a Commercial Training Module on Inspirational Communication of a Vision," *Personnel Psychology*, Autumn 2003, pp. 671–697.
7. R. J. Richardson and S. K. Thayer, *The Charisma Factor: How to Develop Your Natural Leadership Ability* (Upper Saddle River, NJ: Prentice Hall, 1993).
8. J. M. Howell and P. J. Frost, "A Laboratory Study of Charismatic Leadership," *Organizational Behavior and Human Decision Processes*, April 1989, pp. 243–269. See also Frese, Beimel, and Schoenborn, "Action Training for Charismatic Leadership."
9. B. Shamir, R. J. House, and M. B. Arthur, "The Motivational Effects of Charismatic Leadership: A Self-Concept Theory," *Organization Science*, November 1993, pp. 577–594.
10. B. Kark, R. Gan, and B. Shamir, "The Two Faces of Transformational Leadership: Empowerment and Dependency," *Journal of Applied Psychology*, April 2003, pp. 246–255; and P. D. Cherlunik, K. A. Donley, T. S. R. Wiewel, and S. R. Miller, "Charisma Is Contagious: The Effect of Leaders' Charisma on Observers' Affect," *Journal of Applied Social Psychology*, October 2001, pp. 2149–2159.
11. For reviews on the role of vision in leadership, see S. J. Zaccaro, "Visionary and Inspirational Models of Executive Leadership: Empirical Review and Evaluation," in S. J. Zaccaro (ed.), *The Nature of Executive Leadership: A Conceptual and Empirical Analysis of Success* (Washington, DC: American Psychological Assoc., 2001), pp. 259–278; and M. Hauser and R. J. House, "Lead Through Vision and Values," in E. A. Locke (ed.), *Handbook of Principles of Organizational Behavior* (Malden, MA: Blackwell, 2004), pp. 257–273.
12. P. C. Nutt and R. W. Backoff, "Crafting Vision," *Journal of Management Inquiry*, December 1997, p. 309.
13. Ibid., pp. 312–314.
14. J. L. Roberts, "A Mogul's Migraine," *Newsweek*, November 29, 2004, pp. 38–40.
15. D. A. Waldman, B. M. Bass, and F. J. Yammarino, "Adding to Contingent-Reward Behavior: The Augmenting Effect of Charismatic Leadership," *Group & Organization Studies*, December 1990, pp. 381–394; and S. A. Kirkpatrick and E. A. Locke, "Direct and Indirect Effects of Three Core Charismatic Leadership Components on Performance and Attitudes," *Journal of Applied Psychology*, February 1996, pp. 36–51.
16. A. H. B. de Hoogh, D. N. den Hartog, P. L. Koopman, H. Thierry, P. T. van den Berg, and J. G. van der Weide, "Charismatic Leadership, Environmental Dynamism, and Performance," *European Journal of Work & Organizational Psychology*, December 2004, pp. 447–471; S. Harvey, M. Martin, and D. Stout, "Instructor's Transformational Leadership: University Student Attitudes and Ratings," *Psychological Reports*, April 2003, pp. 395–402; and D. A. Waldman, M. Javidan, and P. Varella, "Charismatic Leadership at the Strategic Level: A New Application of Upper Echelons Theory," *Leadership Quarterly*, June 2004, pp. 355–380.
17. R. J. House, "A 1976 Theory of Charismatic Leadership," in J. G. Hunt and L. L. Larson (eds.), *Leadership: The Cutting Edge* (Carbondale, IL: Southern Illinois University Press, 1977), pp. 189–207; and Robert J. House and Ram N. Aditya, "The Social Scientific Study of Leadership," *Journal of Management* 23, no. 3 (1997), p. 441.
18. F. Cohen, S. Solomon, M. Maxfield, T. Pyszczynski, and J. Greenberg, "Fatal Attraction: The Effects of Mortality Salience on Evaluations of Charismatic, Task-Oriented, and Relationship-Oriented Leaders," *Psychological Science*, December 2004, pp. 846–851; and M. G. Ehrhart and K. J. Klein, "Predicting Followers' Preferences for Charismatic Leadership: The Influence of Follower Values and Personality," *Leadership Quarterly*, Summer 2001, pp. 153–179.
19. H. L. Tosi, V. Misangyi, A. Fanelli, D. A. Waldman, and F. J. Yammarino, "CEO Charisma, Compensation, and Firm Performance," *Leadership Quarterly*, June 2004, pp. 405–420.
20. See, for instance, R. Khurana, *Searching for a Corporate Savior: The Irrational Quest for Charismatic CEOs* (Princeton, NJ: Princeton University Press, 2002); and J. A. Raelin, "The Myth of Charismatic Leaders," *Training & Development*, March 2003, pp. 47–54.
21. J. Collins, "Level 5 Leadership: The Triumph of Humility and Fierce Resolve," *Harvard Business Review*, January 2001, pp. 67–76; J. Collins, "Good to Great," *Fast Company*, October 2001, pp. 90–104; J. Collins, "The Misguided Mix-up," *Executive Excellence*, December 2002, pp. 3–4; and Tosi et al., "CEO Charisma, Compensation, and Firm Performance."
22. See, for instance, B. M. Bass, B. J. Avolio, D. I. Jung, and Y. Berson, "Predicting Unit Performance by Assessing Transformational and Transactional Leadership," *Journal of Applied Psychology*, April 2003, pp. 207–218; and T. A. Judge, and R. F. Piccolo, "Transformational and Transactional Leadership: A Meta-analytic Test of Their Relative Validity," *Journal of Applied Psychology*, October 2004, pp. 755–768.

23. B. M. Bass, "Leadership: Good, Better, Best," *Organizational Dynamics*, Winter 1985, pp. 26–40; and J. Seltzer and B. M. Bass, "Transformational Leadership: Beyond Initiation and Consideration," *Journal of Management*, December 1990, pp. 693–703.

24. D. I. Jung, C. Chow, and A. Wu, "The Role of Transformational Leadership in Enhancing Organizational Innovation: Hypotheses and Some Preliminary Findings," *Leadership Quarterly*, August–October 2003, pp. 525–544; D. I. Jung, "Transformational and Transactional Leadership and Their Effects on Creativity in Groups," *Creativity Research Journal* 13, no. 2 (2001), pp. 185–195; and S. J. Shin and J. Zhou, "Transformational Leadership, Conservation, and Creativity: Evidence from Korea," *Academy of Management Journal*, December 2003, pp. 703–714.

25. D. Baum, "Battle Lessons: What the Generals Don't Know," *New Yorker*, January 17, 2005, pp. 42–48.

26. J. E. Bono and T. A. Judge, "Self-Concordance at Work: Toward Understanding the Motivational Effects of Transformational Leaders," *Academy of Management Journal*, October 2003, pp. 554–571; Y. Berson and B. J. Avolio, "Transformational Leadership and the Dissemination of Organizational Goals: A Case Study of a Telecommunication Firm," *Leadership Quarterly*, October 2004, pp. 625–646; and S. Shinn, "21st-Century Engineer," *BizEd*, January/February, 2005, pp. 18–23.

27. J. R. Baum, E. A. Locke, and S. A. Kirkpatrick, "A Longitudinal Study of the Relation of Vision and Vision Communication to Venture Growth in Entrepreneurial Firms," *Journal of Applied Psychology*, February 2000, pp. 43–54.

28. B. J. Avolio, W. Zhu, W. Koh, and P. Bhatia, "Transformational Leadership and Organizational Commitment: Mediating Role of Psychological Empowerment and Moderating Role of Structural Distance," *Journal of Organizational Behavior*, December 2004, pp. 951–968; and T. Dvir, Taly, N. Kass, and B. Shamir, "The Emotional Bond: Vision and Organizational Commitment Among High-Tech Employees," *Journal of Organizational Change Management* 17, no. 2 (2004), pp. 126–143.

29. R. T. Keller, "Transformational Leadership, Initiating Structure, and Substitutes for Leadership: A Longitudinal Study of Research and Development Project Team Performance," *Journal of Applied Psychology* 91, no. 1 (2006), pp. 202–210.

30. Judge and Piccolo, "Transformational and Transactional Leadership."

31. H. Hetland, G. M. Sandal, and T. B. Johnsen, "Burnout in the Information Technology Sector: Does Leadership matter?" *European Journal of Work and Organizational Psychology* 16, no. 1 (2007), pp. 58–75; and K. B. Lowe, K. G. Kroeck, and N. Sivasubramaniam, "Effectiveness Correlates of Transformational and Transactional Leadership: A Meta-Analytic Review of the MLQ Literature," *Leadership Quarterly*, Fall 1996, pp. 385–425.

32. See, for instance, J. Barling, T. Weber, and E. K. Kelloway, "Effects of Transformational Leadership Training on Attitudinal and Financial Outcomes: A Field Experiment," *Journal of Applied Psychology*, December 1996, pp. 827–832; and T. Dvir, D. Eden, and B. J. Avolio, "Impact of Transformational Leadership on Follower Development and Performance: A Field Experiment," *Academy of Management Journal*, August 2002, pp. 735–744.

33. R. J. House and P. M. Podsakoff, "Leadership Effectiveness: Past Perspectives and Future Directions for Research," in J. Greenberg (ed.), *Organizational Behavior: The State of the Science* (Hillsdale, NJ: Erlbaum, 1994), pp. 45–82; and B. M. Bass, *Leadership and Performance Beyond Expectations* (New York: The Free Press, 1985).

34. B. J. Avolio and B. M. Bass, "Transformational Leadership, Charisma and Beyond," working paper, School of management, State University of New York, Binghamton, 1985, p. 14.

35. See B. J. Avolio, W. L. Gardner, F. O. Walumbwa, F. Luthans, and D. R. May, "Unlocking the Mask: A Look at the Process by Which Authentic Impact Follower Attitudes and Behaviors," *Leadership Quarterly*, December 2004, pp. 801–823; W. L. Gardner and J. R. Schermerhorn, Jr., "Performance Gains Through Positive Organizational Behavior and Authentic Leadership," *Organizational Dynamics*, August 2004, pp. 270–281; and M. M. Novicevic, M. G. Harvey, M. R. Buckley, J. A. Brown-Radford, and R. Evans, "Authentic Leadership: A Historical Perspective," *Journal of Leadership and Organizational Behavior* 13, no. 1 (2006), pp. 64–76.

36. A. Carter, "Lighting a Fire Under Campbell," *BusinessWeek*, December 4, 2006, pp. 96–101.

37. R. Ilies, F. P. Morgeson, and J. D. Nahrgang, "Authentic Leadership and Eudaemonic Wellbeing: Understanding Leader-Follower Outcomes," *Leadership Quarterly* 16 (2005), pp. 373–394.

38. This section is based on E. P. Hollander, "Ethical Challenges in the Leader–Follower Relationship," *Business Ethics Quarterly*, January 1995, pp. 55–65; J. C. Rost, "Leadership: A Discussion About Ethics," *Business Ethics Quarterly*, January 1995, pp. 129–142; L. K. Treviño, M. Brown, and L. P. Hartman, "A Qualitative Investigation of Perceived Executive Ethical Leadership: Perceptions from Inside and Outside the Executive Suite," *Human Relations*, January 2003, pp. 5–37; and R. M. Fulmer, "The Challenge of Ethical Leadership," *Organizational Dynamics* 33, no. 3 (2004), pp. 307–317.

39. J. L. Lunsford, "Piloting Boeing's New Course," *Wall Street Journal*, June 13, 2006, pp. B1, B3.

40. J. M. Burns, *Leadership* (New York: Harper & Row, 1978).

41. J. M. Howell and B. J. Avolio, "The Ethics of Charismatic Leadership: Submission or Liberation?" *Academy of Management Executive*, May 1992, pp. 43–55.

42. M. E. Brown and L. K. Treviño, "Socialized Charismatic Leadership, Values Congruence, and Deviance in Work Groups," *Journal of Applied Psychology* 91, no. 4 (2006), pp. 954–962.

43. See, for example, K. T. Dirks and D. L. Ferrin, "Trust in Leadership: Meta-Analytic Findings and Implications for Research and Practice," *Journal of Applied Psychology*, August 2002, pp. 611–628; the special issue on trust in an organizational context, B. McEvily, V. Perrone, A. Zaheer, guest editors, *Organization Science*, January–February 2003; and R. Galford and A. S. Drapeau, *The Trusted Leader* (New York: The Free Press, 2003).

44. Based on S. D. Boon and J. G. Holmes, "The Dynamics of Interpersonal Trust: Resolving Uncertainty in the Face of

Risk," in R. A. Hinde and J. Groebel (eds.), *Cooperation and Prosocial Behavior* (Cambridge, UK: Cambridge University Press, 1991), p. 194; D. J. McAllister, "Affect- and Cognition-Based Trust as Foundations for Interpersonal Cooperation in Organizations," *Academy of Management Journal*, February 1995, p. 25; and D. M. Rousseau, S. B. Sitkin, R. S. Burt, and C. Camerer, "Not So Different After All: A Cross-Discipline View of Trust," *Academy of Management Review*, July 1998, pp. 393–404.

45. J. B. Rotter, "Interpersonal Trust, Trustworthiness, and Gullibility," *American Psychologist*, January 1980, pp. 1–7.
46. J. D. Lewis and A. Weigert, "Trust as a Social Reality," *Social Forces*, June 1985, p. 970.
47. J. K. Rempel, J. G. Holmes, and M. P. Zanna, "Trust in Close Relationships," *Journal of Personality and Social Psychology*, July 1985, p. 96.
48. M. Granovetter, "Economic Action and Social Structure: The Problem of Embeddedness," *American Journal of Sociology*, November 1985, p. 491.
49. R. C. Mayer, J. H. Davis, and F. D. Schoorman, "An Integrative Model of Organizational Trust," *Academy of Management Review*, July 1995, p. 712.
50. C. Johnson-George and W. Swap, "Measurement of Specific Interpersonal Trust: Construction and Validation of a Scale to Assess Trust in a Specific Other," *Journal of Personality and Social Psychology*, September 1982, p. 1306.
51. P. L. Schindler and C. C. Thomas, "The Structure of Interpersonal Trust in the Workplace," *Psychological Reports*, October 1993, pp. 563–573.
52. H. H. Tan and C. S. F. Tan, "Toward the Differentiation of Trust in Supervisor and Trust in Organization," *Genetic, Social, and General Psychology Monographs*, May 2000, pp. 241–260.
53. Cited in D. Jones, "Do You Trust Your CEO?" *USA Today*, February 12, 2003, p. 7B.
54. D. McGregor, *The Professional Manager* (New York: McGraw-Hill, 1967), p. 164.
55. B. Nanus, *The Leader's Edge: The Seven Keys to Leadership in a Turbulent World* (Chicago: Contemporary Books, 1989), p. 102.
56. See, for instance, Dirks and Ferrin, "Trust in Leadership"; D. I. Jung and B. J. Avolio, "Opening the Black Box: An Experimental Investigation of the Mediating Effects of Trust and Value Congruence on Transformational and Transactional Leadership," *Journal of Organizational Behavior*, December 2000, pp. 949–964; and A. Zacharatos, J. Barling, and R. D. Iverson, "High-Performance Work Systems and Occupational Safety," *Journal of Applied Psychology*, January 2005, pp. 77–93.
57. D. E. Zand, *The Leadership Triad: Knowledge, Trust, and Power* (New York: Oxford University Press, 1997), p. 89.
58. Based on L. T. Hosmer, "Trust: The Connecting Link Between Organizational Theory and Philosophical Ethics," *Academy of Management Review*, April 1995, p. 393; and R. C. Mayer, J. H. Davis, and F. D. Schoorman, "An Integrative Model of Organizational Trust," *Academy of Management Review*, July 1995, p. 712.
59. J. M. Kouzes and B. Z. Posner, *Credibility: How Leaders Gain and Lose It, and Why People Demand It* (San Francisco: Jossey-Bass, 1993), p. 14.
60. D. Shapiro, B. H. Sheppard, and L. Cheraskin, "Business on a Handshake," *Negotiation Journal*, October 1992, pp. 365–377; R. J. Lewicki, E. C. Tomlinson, and N. Gillespie, "Models of Interpersonal Trust Development: Theoretical Approaches, Empirical Evidence, and Future Directions," *Journal of Management*, December 2006, pp. 991–1022; and J. Child, "Trust—The Fundamental Bond in Global Collaboration," *Organizational Dynamics* 29, no. 4 (2001), pp. 274–288.
61. This section is based on Zand, *The Leadership Triad*, pp. 122–134; and A. M. Zak, J. A. Gold, R. M. Ryckman, and E. Lenney, "Assessments of Trust in Intimate Relationships and the Self-Perception Process," *Journal of Social Psychology*, April 1998, pp. 217–228.
62. M. E. Schweitzer, J. C. Hershey, and E. T. Bradlow, "Promises and Lies: Restoring Violated Trust," *Organizational Behavior and Human Decision Processes* 101 (2006), pp. 1–19.
63. See, for example, M. Murray, *Beyond the Myths and Magic of Mentoring: How to Facilitate an Effective Mentoring Process*, rev. ed. (New York: Wiley, 2001); K. E. Kram, "Phases of the Mentor Relationship," *Academy of Management Journal*, December 1983, pp. 608–625; R. A. Noe, "An Investigation of the Determinants of Successful Assigned Mentoring Relationships," *Personnel Psychology*, Fall 1988, pp. 559–580; and L. Eby, M. Butts, and A. Lockwood, "Protégés' Negative Mentoring Experiences: Construct Development and Nomological Validation," *Personnel Psychology*, Summer 2004, pp. 411–447.
64. J. A. Wilson and N. S. Elman, "Organizational Benefits of Mentoring," *Academy of Management Executive*, November 1990, p. 90; and J. Reingold, "Want to Grow as a Leader? Get a Mentor?" *Fast Company*, January 2001, pp. 58–60.
65. T. D. Allen, E. T. Eby, and E. Lentz, "The Relationship Between Formal Mentoring Program Characteristics and Perceived Program Effectiveness," *Personnel Psychology* 59 (2006), pp. 125–153; and T. D. Allen, L. T. Eby, and E. Lentz, "Mentorship Behaviors and Mentorship Quality Associated with Formal Mentoring Programs: Closing the Gap Between Research and Practice," *Journal of Applied Psychology* 91, no. 3 (2006), pp. 567–578.
66. See, for example, K. E. Kram and D. T. Hall, "Mentoring in a Context of Diversity and Turbulence," in E. E. Kossek and S. A. Lobel (eds.), *Managing Diversity* (Cambridge, MA: Blackwell, 1996), pp. 108–136; B. R. Ragins and J. L. Cotton, "Mentor Functions and Outcomes: A Comparison of Men and Women in Formal and Informal Mentoring Relationships," *Journal of Applied Psychology*, August 1999, pp. 529–550; and D. B. Turban, T. W. Dougherty, and F. K. Lee, "Gender, Race, and Perceived Similarity Effects in Developmental Relationships: The Moderating Role of Relationship Duration," *Journal of Vocational Behavior*, October 2002, pp. 240–262.
67. Wilson and Elman, "Organizational Benefits of Mentoring," p. 90.
68. See, for instance, K. Houston Philpot, "Leadership Development Partnerships at Dow Corning Corporation," *Journal of Organizational Excellence*, Winter 2002, pp. 13–27.
69. T. D. Allen, L. T. Eby, M. L. Poteet, Mark L., E. Lentz, and L. Lizzette, "Career Benefits Associated with Mentoring for Protégés: A Meta-Analysis," *Journal of Applied Psychology*,

February 2004, pp. 127–136; and J. D. Kammeyer-Mueller and T. A. Judge, "A Quantitative Review of the Mentoring Literature: Test of a Model," Working paper, University of Florida, 2005.

70. C. Hymowitz, "Today's Bosses Find Mentoring Isn't Worth the Time and Risks," *Wall Street Journal*, March 13, 2006, p. B1.

71. See C. C. Manz, "Self-Leadership: Toward an Expanded Theory of Self-Influence Processes in Organizations," *Academy of Management Review*, July 1986, pp. 585–600; C. C. Manz and H. P. Sims, Jr., *The New Superleadership: Leading Others to Lead Themselves* (San Francisco: Berrett-Koehler, 2001); C. L. Dolbier, M. Soderstrom, M. A. Steinhardt, "The Relationships Between Self-Leadership and Enhanced Psychological, Health, and Work Outcomes," *Journal of Psychology*, September 2001, pp. 469–485; and J. D. Houghton, T. W. Bonham, C. P. Neck, and K. Singh, "The Relationship Between Self-Leadership and Personality: A Comparison of Hierarchical Factor Structures," *Journal of Managerial Psychology* 19, no. 4 (2004), pp. 427–441.

72. A. H. Eagly, "Female Leadership Advantage and Disadvantage: Resolving the Contradictions," *Psychology of Women Quarterly*, March 2007, pp. 1–12; and A. H. Eagly, M. C. Johannesen-Schmidt, and M. L. van Engen, "Transformational, Transactional, and Laissez-Faire Leadership Styles: A Meta-analysis Comparing Women and Men," *Psychological Bulletin*, July 2003, pp. 569–591.

73. J. Kelly and S. Nadler, "Leading from Below," *Wall Street Journal*, March 3, 2007, pp. R4, R10.

74. L. A. Hambley, T. A. O'Neill, and T. J. B. Kline, "Virtual Team Leadership: The Effects of Leadership Style and Communication Medium on Team Interaction Styles and Outcomes," *Organizational Behavior and Human Decision Processes* 103 (2007), pp. 1–20; and B. J. Avolio and S. S. Kahai, "Adding the 'E' to E-Leadership: How it May Impact Your Leadership," *Organizational Dynamics* 31, no. 4 (2003), pp. 325–338.

75. S. J. Zaccaro and P. Bader, "E-Leadership and the Challenges of Leading E-Teams: Minimizing the Bad and Maximizing the Good," *Organizational Dynamics* 31, no. 4 (2003), pp. 381–385.

76. C. E. Naquin and G. D. Paulson, "Online Bargaining and Interpersonal Trust," *Journal of Applied Psychology*, February 2003, pp. 113–120.

77. B. Shamir, "Leadership in Boundaryless Organizations: Disposable or Indispensable?" *European Journal of Work and Organizational Psychology* 8, no. 1 (1999), pp. 49–71.

78. Comment by Jim Collins and cited in J. Useem, "Conquering Vertical Limits," *Fortune*, February 19, 2001, p. 94.

79. See, for instance, J. R. Meindl, "The Romance of Leadership as a Follower-Centric Theory: A Social Constructionist Approach," *Leadership Quarterly*, Fall 1995, pp. 329–341; and S. A. Haslam, M. J. Platow, J. C. Turner, K. J. Reynolds, C. McGarty, P. J. Oakes, S. Johnson, M. K. Ryan, and K. Veenstra, "Social Identity and the Romance of Leadership: The Importance of Being Seen to Be 'Doing It for Us,'" *Group Processes & Intergroup Relations*, July 2001, pp. 191–205.

80. R. G. Lord, C. L. DeVader, and G. M. Alliger, "A Meta-analysis of the Relation Between Personality Traits and Leadership Perceptions: An Application of Validity Generalization Procedures," *Journal of Applied Psychology*, August 1986, pp. 402–410.

81. J. R. Meindl, S. B. Ehrlich, and J. M. Dukerich, "The Romance of Leadership," *Administrative Science Quarterly*, March 1985, pp. 78–102.

82. B. R. Agle, N. J. Nagarajan, J. A. Sonnenfeld, and D. Srinivasan, "Does CEO Charisma Matter?" *Academy of Management Journal* 49, no. 1 (2006), pp. 161–174.

83. S. Kerr and J. M. Jermier, "Substitutes for Leadership: Their Meaning and Measurement," *Organizational Behavior and Human Performance*, December 1978, pp. 375–403; J. M. Jermier and S. Kerr, "Substitutes for Leadership: Their Meaning and Measurement—Contextual Recollections and Current Observations," *Leadership Quarterly* 8, no. 2 (1997), pp. 95–101; and E. de Vries Reinout, R. A. Roe, and T. C. B. Taillieu, "Need for Leadership as a Moderator of the Relationships Between Leadership and Individual Outcomes," *Leadership Quarterly*, April 2002, pp. 121–138.

84. S. D. Dionne, F. J. Yammarino, L. E. Atwater, and L. R. James, "Neutralizing Substitutes for Leadership Theory: Leadership Effects and Common-Source Bias," *Journal of Applied Psychology*, 87 (2002), pp. 454–464; and J. R. Villa, J. P. Howell, P. W. Dorfman, and D. L. Daniel, "Problems with Detecting Moderators in Leadership Research Using Moderated Multiple Regression," *Leadership Quarterly* 14 (2002), pp. 3–23.

85. B. M. Bass, "Cognitive, Social, and Emotional Intelligence of Transformational Leaders," in R. E. Riggio, S. E. Murphy, and F. J. Pirozzolo (eds.), *Multiple Intelligences and Leadership* (Mahwah, NJ: Erlbaum, 2002), pp. 113–114.

86. J. Karp, "Tough Question for L-3's CEO: Who's Next?" *Wall Street Journal*, May 8, 2006, pp. B1, B3.

87. See, for instance, P. Dvorak, "M.B.A. Programs Hone 'Soft Skills,'" *Wall Street Journal*, February 12, 2007, p. B3.

88. J. Weber, "The Leadership Factor," *BusinessWeek*, June 12, 2006, pp. 60–64.

89. See, for instance, Barling, Weber, and Kelloway, "Effects of Transformational Leadership Training on Attitudinal and Financial Outcomes"; and D. V. Day, "Leadership Development: A Review in Context," *Leadership Quarterly*, Winter 2000, pp. 581–613.

90. M. Sashkin, "The Visionary Leader," in J. A. Conger, R. N. Kanungo et al. (eds.), *Charismatic Leadership* (San Francisco: Jossey-Bass, 1988), p. 150.

91. D. V. Day, "Leadership Development: A Review in Context," *Leadership Quarterly*, Winter 2000, pp. 590–593.

92. M. Conlin, "CEO Coaches," *BusinessWeek*, November 11, 2002, pp. 98–104.

93. Howell and Frost, "A Laboratory Study of Charismatic Leadership."

94. Dvir, Eden, and Avolio, "Impact of Transformational Leadership on Follower Development and Performance"; B. J. Avolio and B. M. Bass, *Developing Potential Across a Full Range of Leadership: Cases on Transactional and Transformational Leadership* (Mahwah, NJ: Lawrence Erlbaum, 2002); A. J. Towler, "Effects of Charismatic Influence Training on Attitudes, Behavior, and Performance," *Personnel Psychology*, Summer 2003, pp. 363–381; and Barling, Weber, and Kelloway, "Effects of Transformational Leadership Training on Attitudinal and Financial Outcomes."

95. R. J. House, M. Javidan, P. Hanges, and P. Dorfman, "Understanding Cultures and Implicit Leadership Theories Across the Globe: An Introduction to Project GLOBE," *Journal of World Business,* Spring 2002, pp. 3–10.

96. D. E. Carl and M. Javidan, "Universality of Charismatic Leadership: A Multi-Nation Study," paper presented at the National Academy of Management Conference, Washington, DC, August 2001, p. 29.

97. N. Beccalli, "European Business Forum Asks: Do Companies Get the Leaders They Deserve?" *European Business Forum,* 2003, www.pwcglobal.com/extweb/pwcpublications.nsf/DocID/D1EC3380F589844585256D7300346A1B.

98. A. Murray, "After the Revolt, Creating a New CEO," *Wall Street Journal,* May 5, 2007, pp. A1, A18.

Power and Politics

Power is not revealed by striking hard or often, but by striking true.

—Novelist and Playwright Honoré de Balzac

LEARNING OBJECTIVES

After studying this chapter, you should be able to:

1 Define *power* and contrast leadership and power.

2 Contrast the five bases of power.

3 Identify nine power or influence tactics and their contingencies.

4 Show the connection between sexual harassment and the abuse of power.

5 Distinguish between legitimate and illegitimate political behavior.

6 Identify the causes and consequences of political behavior.

7 Apply impression management techniques.

8 Determine whether a political action is ethical.

9 Show the influence of culture on the uses and perceptions of politics.

You would think investment analysts are nothing if not objective. After all, if an analyst's buy, sell, or hold ratings are tainted by personal relationships, power plays, or office politics, the very credibility the analyst depends on is undermined. Analysts, though, are finding that they're coming under increasing pressure from companies whose stock they're evaluating, and by shareholders themselves.

"You Better Change It"

Consider Michael Krensavage, who has been an analyst for more than 11 years and is senior vice president of Equity Research for Raymond James & Associates. Although a veteran like Krensavage has seen his share of disappointed and angry managers, a recent phone message he received was particularly nasty. "Hey, ah, Mike," the caller said. "Let me tell you something right now. I am going to have an SEC investigation into your company for you downgrading the Bentley Pharmaceutical. You took a stock, your company is putting a short in and manipulating the stock down. I know about it; I'm going to get to the bottom of it. You better, you better upgrade that goddamn thing. Because let me tell you something right now my friend, you're going to go to jail. That stock had 90 percent better earnings this year than last year and then you hit it down. We know what you're doing, and I am going to get the [U.S. Securities and Exchange Commission] to investigate you and your company. You better believe it. You better change it."

What spawned this phone message was a report Krensavage had filed a few days earlier about Bentley, noting that the company's stock continued to underperform and urging investors to consider selling their Bentley shares.

Sometimes the threats come not from individual investors but from the companies themselves. When Krensavage downgraded his rating of AAIPharmia, a drug development company, the company bad-mouthed him at every opportunity. At one point, it launched an effort to get him fired, calling several of Krensavage's bosses. Although Krensavage wasn't fired, the situation reveals the political pressures many analysts face and succumb to.

"It's not easy putting a sell rating on a stock," Krensavage said. "You often face significant repercussions."[1] ■

Power and *politics* have been described as the last dirty words. It is easier for most of us to talk about sex or money than it is to talk about power or political behavior. People who have power deny it, people who want it try not to look like they're seeking it, and those who are good at getting it are secretive about how they do so.[2] To see whether you think your work environment is political, take the following self-assessment.

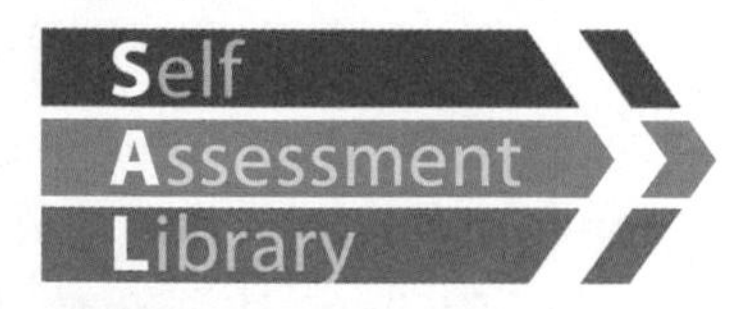

IS MY WORKPLACE POLITICAL?

In the Self-Assessment Library (available on CD and online), take assessment IV.F.1 (Is My Workplace Political?); if you don't currently have a job, answer for your most recent job. Then answer the following questions.

1. *How does your score relate to those of your classmates? Do you think your score is accurate? Why or why not?*
2. *Do you think a political workplace is a bad thing? If yes, why? If no, why not?*
3. *What factors cause your workplace to be political?*

A major theme of this chapter is that power and political behavior are natural processes in any group or organization. Given that, you need to know how power is acquired and exercised if you are to fully understand organizational behavior. Although you may have heard the phrase "power corrupts and absolute power corrupts absolutely," power is not always bad. As one author has noted, most medicines can kill if taken in the wrong amount, and thousands die each year in automobile accidents, but we don't abandon chemicals or cars because of the dangers associated with them. Rather, we consider danger an incentive to get training and information that will help us to use these forces productively.[3] The same applies to power. It's a reality of organizational life, and it's not going to go away. Moreover, by learning how power works in organizations, you'll be better able to use your knowledge to become a more effective manager.

A Definition of *Power*

1 *Define* power *and contrast leadership and* power.

Power refers to a capacity that *A* has to influence the behavior of *B* so that *B* acts in accordance with *A*'s wishes.[4] This definition implies a *potential* that need not be actualized to be effective, and a *dependency* relationship.

Power may exist but not be used. It is, therefore, a capacity or potential. Someone can have power but not impose it. Probably the most important aspect of power is that it is a function of **dependency**. The greater *B*'s dependence on *A*, the greater is *A*'s power in the relationship. Dependence, in turn, is based on alternatives that *B* perceives and the importance that *B* places on the alternative(s) that *A* controls. A person can have power over you only if he or she controls something you desire. If you want a college degree and have to pass a certain course to get it, and your current instructor is the only faculty member in the college who teaches that course, he or she has power over you. Your alternatives are highly limited, and you place a high degree of importance on obtaining a passing grade. Similarly, if you're attending college on funds totally provided by your parents, you probably recognize the power that they hold over you. You're dependent on them for financial support. But once you're out of school, have a job, and are making a good income, your parents' power is reduced significantly. Who among us, though, has not known or heard of a rich relative who is able to control a large number of family members merely through the implicit or explicit threat of "writing them out of the will"?

Contrasting Leadership and Power

A careful comparison of our description of power with our description of leadership in Chapters 12 and 13 reveals that the concepts are closely intertwined. Leaders use power as a means of attaining group goals. Leaders achieve goals, and power is a means of facilitating their achievement.

What differences are there between the two terms? One difference relates to goal compatibility. Power does not require goal compatibility, merely dependence. Leadership, on the other hand, requires some congruence between the goals of the leader and those being led. A second difference relates to the direction of influence. Leadership focuses on the downward influence on one's followers. It minimizes the importance of lateral and upward influence patterns. Power does not. Still another difference deals with research emphasis. Leadership research, for the most part, emphasizes style. It seeks answers to questions such as: How supportive should a leader be? How much decision making should be shared with followers? In contrast, the research on power has tended to encompass a broader area and to focus on tactics for gaining compliance. It has gone beyond the individual as the exerciser of power because power can be used by groups as well as by individuals to control other individuals or groups.

power *A capacity that A has to influence the behavior of B so that B acts in accordance with A's wishes.*

dependency *B's relationship to A when A possesses something that B requires.*

Bases of Power

2 *Contrast the five bases of power.*

Where does power come from? What is it that gives an individual or a group influence over others? We answer these questions by dividing the bases or sources of power into two general groupings—formal and personal—and then breaking each of these down into more specific categories.[5]

Formal Power

Formal power is based on an individual's position in an organization. Formal power can come from the ability to coerce or reward, or it can come from formal authority.

Coercive Power The **coercive power** base is dependent on fear. A person reacts to this power out of fear of the negative results that might occur if she failed to comply. It rests on the application, or the threat of application, of physical sanctions such as the infliction of pain, the generation of frustration through restriction of movement, or the controlling by force of basic physiological or safety needs.

At the organizational level, *A* has coercive power over *B* if *A* can dismiss, suspend, or demote *B*, assuming that *B* values his or her job. Similarly, if *A* can assign *B* work activities that *B* finds unpleasant or treat *B* in a manner that *B* finds embarrassing, *A* possesses coercive power over *B*. Coercive power can also come from withholding key information. People in an organization who have data or knowledge that others need can make those others dependent on them.

Dr. Julie Gerberding, director of the Centers for Disease Control and Prevention, has both legitimate power and expert power. As director of the CDC, she has formal authority to use the government agency's resources in protecting the health and safety of the U.S. population. Gerberding is able to wield power because of her expertise in infectious diseases gained through her education and work experience. She earned undergraduate degrees in biology and chemistry and an M.D. degree. Before becoming the CDC director, Gerberding was acting deputy director of the National Center for Infectious Diseases.

Reward Power The opposite of coercive power is **reward power**. People comply with the wishes or directives of another because doing so produces positive benefits; therefore, one who can distribute rewards that others view as valuable will have power over those others. These rewards can be either financial—such as controlling pay rates, raises, and bonuses; or nonfinancial—including recognition, promotions, interesting work assignments, friendly colleagues, and preferred work shifts or sales territories.[6]

Coercive power and reward power are actually counterparts of each other. If you can remove something of positive value from another or inflict something of negative value, you have coercive power over that person. If you can give someone something of positive value or remove something of negative value, you have reward power over that person.

Legitimate Power In formal groups and organizations, probably the most frequent access to one or more of the power bases is one's structural position. This is called **legitimate power**. It represents the formal authority to control and use organizational resources.

Positions of authority include coercive and reward powers. Legitimate power, however, is broader than the power to coerce and reward. Specifically, it includes acceptance by members in an organization of the authority of a position. When school principals, bank presidents, or army captains speak (assuming that their directives are viewed to be within the authority of their positions), teachers, tellers, and first lieutenants listen and usually comply.

Personal Power

You don't have to have a formal position in an organization to have power. Many of the most competent and productive chip designers at Intel, for instance, have power, but they aren't managers and have no formal power.

What they have is personal power—power that comes from an individual's unique characteristics. In this section, we look at two bases of personal power—expertise and the respect and admiration of others.

Expert Power **Expert power** is influence wielded as a result of expertise, special skill, or knowledge. Expertise has become one of the most powerful sources of influence as the world has become more technologically oriented. As jobs become more specialized, we become increasingly dependent on experts to achieve goals. It is generally acknowledged that physicians have expertise and hence expert power—most of us follow the advice that our doctors give us. But it's also important to recognize that computer specialists, tax accountants, economists, industrial psychologists, and other specialists are able to wield power as a result of their expertise.

Referent Power **Referent power** is based on identification with a person who has desirable resources or personal traits. If I like, respect, and admire you, you can exercise power over me because I want to please you.

Referent power develops out of admiration of another and a desire to be like that person. It helps explain, for instance, why celebrities are paid millions of dollars to endorse products in commercials. Marketing research shows that people such as the sports professionals David Beckham and Yao Ming have the power to influence your choice of athletic shoes and credit cards. With a little practice, you and I could probably deliver as smooth a sales pitch as these celebrities, but the buying public doesn't identify with you and me. One of the ways in which individuals acquire referent power is through charisma. Some people have referent power who, while not in formal leadership positions, nevertheless are able to exert influence over others because of their charismatic dynamism, likability, and emotional effects on us.

Which Bases of Power Are Most Effective?

Of the three bases of formal power (coercive, reward, legitimate) and two bases of personal power (expert, referent), which is most important to have? Interestingly, research suggests pretty clearly that the personal sources of power are most effective. Both expert and referent power are positively related to employees' satisfaction with supervision, their organizational commitment, and their performance, whereas reward and legitimate power seem to be unrelated to these outcomes. Moreover, one source of formal power—coercive power—actually can backfire in that it is negatively related to employee satisfaction and commitment.[7]

Consider Steve Stoute's company, Translation, which matches pop-star spokespersons with corporations that want to promote their brands. Stoute has paired prominent rock stars with firms such as McDonald's, and Reebok. Stoute's business seems to be all about referent power. As one record company executive commented when reflecting on Stoute's successes, "He's the right guy for guiding brands in using the record industry to reach youth culture in a credible way."[8] In other words, using pop stars to market products works

coercive power *A power base that is dependent on fear.*

reward power *Compliance achieved based on the ability to distribute rewards that others view as valuable.*

legitimate power *The power a person receives as a result of his or her position in the formal hierarchy of an organization.*

expert power *Influence based on special skills or knowledge.*

referent power *Influence based on possession by an individual of desirable resources or personal traits.*

Exhibit **14-1**

"I was just going to say 'Well, I don't make the rules.' But, of course, I do make the rules."

Source: Drawing by Leo Cullum in *The New Yorker*, copyright © 1986 *The New Yorker Magazine*. Reprinted by permission.

because of referent power: People buy products associated with cool figures because they wish to identify with these figures and emulate them.

Dependency: The Key to Power

Earlier in this chapter we said that probably the most important aspect of power is that it is a function of dependency. In this section, we show how having an understanding of dependency is central to furthering your understanding of power itself.

The General Dependency Postulate

Let's begin with a general postulate: *The greater* B*'s dependency on* A*, the greater the power* A *has over* B. When you possess anything that others require but that you alone control, you make them dependent on you, and, therefore, you gain power over them.[9] Dependency, then, is inversely proportional to the alternative sources of supply. If something is plentiful, possession of it will not increase your power. If everyone is intelligent, intelligence gives no special advantage. Similarly, among the superrich, money is no longer power. But, as the old saying goes, "In the land of the blind, the one-eyed man is king!" If you can create a monopoly by controlling information, prestige, or anything else that others crave, they become dependent on you. Conversely, the more that you can expand your options, the less power you place in the hands of others. This

Because Xerox Corporation has staked its future on development and innovation, Sophie Vandebroek is in a position of power at Xerox. As the company's chief technology officer, she leads the Xerox Innovation Group of 5,000 scientists and engineers at the company's global research centers. The group's mission is "to pioneer high-impact technologies that enable us to lead in our core markets and to create future markets for Xerox." Xerox depends on Vandebroek to make that mission a reality.

explains, for example, why most organizations develop multiple suppliers rather than give their business to only one. It also explains why so many of us aspire to financial independence. Financial independence reduces the power that others can have over us.

What Creates Dependency?

Dependency is increased when the resource you control is important, scarce, and nonsubstitutable.[10]

Importance If nobody wants what you have, it's not going to create dependency. To create dependency, the thing(s) you control must be perceived as being important. Organizations, for instance, actively seek to avoid uncertainty.[11] We should, therefore, expect that the individuals or groups who can absorb an organization's uncertainty will be perceived as controlling an important resource. For instance, a study of industrial organizations found that the marketing departments in these firms were consistently rated as the most powerful.[12] The researcher concluded that the most critical uncertainty facing these firms was selling their products. This might suggest that engineers, as a group, would be more powerful at the electronics manufacturer Matsushita than at the household-goods manufacturer Procter & Gamble. These inferences appear to be generally valid. An organization such as Matsushita, which is heavily technologically oriented, is highly dependent on its engineers to maintain its products' technical advantages and quality. And, at Matsushita, engineers are clearly a powerful group. At Procter & Gamble, marketing is the name of the game, and marketers are the most powerful occupational group.

Scarcity As noted previously, if something is plentiful, possession of it will not increase your power. A resource needs to be perceived as scarce to create dependency. This can help explain how low-ranking members in an organization who have important knowledge not available to high-ranking members gain power over the high-ranking members. Possession of a scarce resource—in this case, important knowledge—makes the high-ranking member dependent on the low-ranking member. This also helps to make sense out of behaviors of low-ranking members that otherwise might seem illogical, such as destroying the procedure manuals that describe how a job is done, refusing to train people in their jobs or even to show others exactly what they do, creating specialized language and terminology that inhibit others from understanding their jobs, or operating in secrecy so an activity will appear more complex and difficult than it really is. Ferruccio Lamborghini, the guy who created the exotic supercars that continue to carry his name, understood the importance of scarcity and used it to his advantage during World War II. Lamborghini was in Rhodes with the Italian army. His superiors were impressed with his mechanical skills, as he demonstrated an almost uncanny ability to repair tanks and cars that no one else could fix. After the war, he admitted that his ability was largely due to having been the first person on the island to receive the repair manuals, which he memorized and then destroyed so as to become indispensable.[13]

The scarcity–dependency relationship can further be seen in the power of occupational categories. Individuals in occupations in which the supply of personnel is low relative to demand can negotiate compensation and benefits packages that are far more attractive than can those in occupations for which there is an abundance of candidates. U.S. college administrators have no problem today finding English instructors. The market for network systems analysts, in contrast, is extremely tight, with the demand high and the supply limited. The result is that the bargaining power of computer-engineering faculty allows them to negotiate higher salaries, lighter teaching loads, and other benefits.

Nonsubstitutability The fewer viable substitutes for a resource, the more power the control over that resource provides. Higher education again provides an excellent example. At universities in which there are strong pressures for the faculty to publish, we can say that a department head's power over a faculty member is inversely related to that member's publication record. The more recognition the faculty member receives through publication, the more mobile he or she is; that is, because other universities want faculty who are highly published and visible, there is an increased demand for that person's services. Although the concept of tenure can act to alter this relationship by restricting the department head's alternatives, faculty members who have few or no publications have the least mobility and are subject to the greatest influence from their superiors.

Power Tactics

What **power tactics** do people use to translate power bases into specific action? That is, what options do individuals have for influencing their bosses, coworkers, or employees? And are some of these options more effective than others? In this section, we review popular tactical options and the conditions under which one may be more effective than another.

3 *Identify nine power or influence tactics and their contingencies.*

Research has identified nine distinct influence tactics:[14]

- *Legitimacy.* Relying on one's authority position or stressing that a request is in accordance with organizational policies or rules.
- *Rational persuasion.* Presenting logical arguments and factual evidence to demonstrate that a request is reasonable.

- *Inspirational appeals.* Developing emotional commitment by appealing to a target's values, needs, hopes, and aspirations.
- *Consultation.* Increasing the target's motivation and support by involving him or her in deciding how the plan or change will be accomplished.
- *Exchange.* Rewarding the target with benefits or favors in exchange for following a request.
- *Personal appeals.* Asking for compliance based on friendship or loyalty.
- *Ingratiation.* Using flattery, praise, or friendly behavior prior to making a request.
- *Pressure.* Using warnings, repeated demands, and threats.
- *Coalitions.* Enlisting the aid of other people to persuade the target or using the support of others as a reason for the target to agree.

Some tactics are more effective than others. Specifically, evidence indicates that rational persuasion, inspirational appeals, and consultation tend to be the most effective. On the other hand, pressure tends to frequently backfire and is typically the least effective of the nine tactics.[15] You can also increase your chance of success by using more than one type of tactic at the same time or sequentially, as long as your choices are compatible.[16] For instance, using both ingratiation and legitimacy can lessen the negative reactions that might come from the appearance of being "dictated to" by the boss.

To see how these tactics can work in practice, let's consider the most effective way of getting a raise. You can start with rational persuasion. That means doing your homework and carefully thinking through the best way to build your case: Figure out how your pay compares to that of peers, or land a competing job offer, or show objective results that testify to your performance. For example, Kitty Dunning, a vice president at the sales promotion agency Don Jagoda Associates, landed a 16 percent raise when she emailed her boss numbers showing she had increased sales.[17] You can also make good use of salary calculators such as Salary.com to compare your pay with comparable other.

But the effectiveness of some influence tactics depends on the direction of influence.[18] As shown in Exhibit 14-2, studies have found that rational persuasion is the only tactic that is effective across organizational levels. Inspirational appeals work best as a downward-influencing tactic with subordinates. When pressure works, it's generally only to achieve downward influence. And the use of personal appeals and coalitions are most effective with lateral influence attempts. In addition to the direction of influence, a number of other factors

Exhibit 14-2 Preferred Power Tactics by Influence Direction

Upward Influence	Downward Influence	Lateral Influence
Rational persuasion	Rational persuasion	Rational persuasion
	Inspirational appeals	Consultation
	Pressure	Ingratiation
	Consultation	Exchange
	Ingratiation	Legitimacy
	Exchange	Personal appeals
	Legitimacy	Coalitions

power tactics *Ways in which individuals translate power bases into specific actions.*

International OB

Influence Tactics in China

Researchers usually examine cross-cultural influences in business by comparing two very different cultures, such as those from Eastern and Western societies. However, it is also important to examine differences within a given culture because those differences can sometimes be greater than differences between cultures.

For example, although we might view all Chinese people as being alike due to their shared heritage and appearance, China is a big country, housing different cultures and traditions. A recent study examining Mainland Chinese, Taiwanese, and Hong Kong managers explored how the three cultural subgroups differ according to the influence tactics they prefer to use.

Though managers from all three places believe that rational persuasion and exchange are the most effective influence tactics, managers in Taiwan tend to use inspirational appeals and ingratiation more than managers from either Mainland China or Hong Kong. The study also found that managers from Hong Kong rate pressure as more effective in influencing others than do managers in Taiwan or Mainland China. Such differences have implications for business relationships. For example, Taiwanese or Mainland Chinese managers may be taken aback by the use of pressure tactics by a Hong Kong manager. Likewise, managers from Hong Kong may not be persuaded by managers from Taiwan, who tend to use ingratiating tactics. Such differences in influence tactics may make business dealings difficult. Companies should address these issues, perhaps making their managers aware of the differences within cultures.

Managers need to know what variations exist within their local cultures so they can be better prepared to deal with others. Managers who fail to realize these differences may miss out on opportunities to deal effectively with others.

Source: Based on P. P. Fu, T. K. Peng, J. C. Kennedy, and G. Yukl, "A Comparison of Chinese Managers in Hong Kong, Taiwan, and Mainland China," *Organizational Dynamics*, February 2004, pp. 32–46.

have been found to affect which tactics work best. These include the sequencing of tactics, a person's skill in using the tactic, and the culture of the organization.

You're more likely to be effective if you begin with "softer" tactics that rely on personal power such as personal and inspirational appeals, rational persuasion, and consultation. If these fail, you can move to "harder" tactics (which emphasize formal power and involve greater costs and risks), such as exchange, coalitions, and pressure.[19] Interestingly, it's been found that using a single soft tactic is more effective than using a single hard tactic and that combining two soft tactics or a soft tactic and rational persuasion is more effective than any single tactic or a combination of hard tactics.[20]

Recently, research has shown that people differ in their **political skill**, or the ability to influence others in such a way as to enhance their own objectives. Those who are politically skilled are more effective in their use of influence tactics, regardless of the tactics they're using. Political skill also appears to be more effective when the stakes are high—such as when the individual is accountable for important organizational outcomes. That's also why pro golfer Tiger Woods sticks to the majors and other big tournaments. Finally, the politically skilled are able to exert their influence without others detecting it, which is a key element in being effective (it's damaging to be labeled political).[21]

Finally, we know that cultures within organizations differ markedly—for example, some are warm, relaxed, and supportive; others are formal and conservative. The organizational culture in which a person works, therefore, will have a bearing on defining which tactics are considered appropriate. Some cultures encourage the use of participation and consultation, some encourage reason, and still others rely on pressure. So the organization itself will influence which subset of power tactics is viewed as acceptable for use.

Sexual Harassment: Unequal Power in the Workplace

4 *Show the connection between sexual harassment and the abuse of power.*

Sexual harassment is wrong. It can also be costly to employers. Just ask executives at the cigarette manufacturer Philip Morris, the consumer-products maker Dial, and UPS.[22] A U.S. jury awarded $2 million to a Philip Morris plant supervisor who suffered through more than a year of sexual harassment by men she supervised. Dial agreed to pay $10 million to resolve widespread sexual harassment practices at one of its soap factories. And a former UPS manager won an $80 million suit against UPS for fostering a hostile work environment when it failed to listen to her complaints of sexual harassment.

Not only are there legal dangers to sexual harassment, it obviously can have a negative impact on the work environment, too. Research shows that sexual harassment negatively affects job attitudes and leads those who feel harassed to withdraw from the organization. Moreover, in many cases, reporting sexual harassment doesn't improve the situation because the organization responds in a negative or unhelpful way. When organizational leaders make honest efforts to stop the harassment, the outcomes are much more positive.[23]

This employee was one of 90 workers who filed a sexual harassment lawsuit against Dial Corporation. The female employees alleged that male coworkers and supervisors at a Dial soap factory in Illinois fostered a "permissive culture" that condoned groping, sexual insults, and displays of pornography and that women who reported harassment faced retaliation or inaction by upper management. Although Dial denied wrongdoing, the company agreed to pay $10 million to settle the lawsuit, to revise its harassment policies and procedures, and to comply with federal compliance monitoring at its plant for 2½ years.

Sexual harassment is defined as any unwanted activity of a sexual nature that affects an individual's employment and creates a hostile work environment. The U.S. Supreme Court helped to clarify this definition by adding that the key test for determining if sexual harassment has occurred is whether comments or behavior in a work environment "would reasonably be perceived, and [are] perceived, as hostile or abusive."[24] But there continues to be disagreement as to what *specifically* constitutes sexual harassment. Organizations have generally made considerable progress in the past decade toward limiting overt forms of sexual harassment. This includes unwanted physical touching, recurring requests for dates when it is made clear the person isn't interested, and coercive threats that a person will lose the job if he or she refuses a sexual proposition. The problems today are likely to surface around more subtle forms of sexual harassment—unwanted looks or comments, off-color jokes, sexual artifacts like pin-ups posted in the workplace, or misinterpretations of where the line between being friendly ends and harassment begins.

A recent review concluded that 58 percent of women report having experienced potentially harassing behaviors and 24 percent report having experienced sexual harassment at work.[25] One problem with sexual harassment is that it is, to some degree, in the eye of the beholder. For example, women are more likely than men to see a given behavior or sets of behaviors as constituting sexual harassment. Men are less likely to see as harassment such behaviors as kissing someone, asking for a date, or making sex-stereotyped jokes. As the authors of this study note, "Although progress has been made at defining sexual harassment, it is still unclear as to whose perspective should be taken."[26] Thus, although some behaviors indisputably constitute harassment, men and women continue to differ to some degree on what constitutes harassment. For you, the best approach is to be careful—refrain from any behavior that may be taken as harassing, even if that was not your intent. Realize that what you see as an innocent joke or hug may be seen as harassment by the other party.

Most studies confirm that the concept of power is central to understanding sexual harassment.[27] This seems to be true whether the harassment comes from a

political skill *The ability to influence others in such a way as to enhance one's objectives.*

sexual harassment *Any unwanted activity of a sexual nature that affects an individual's employment and creates a hostile work environment.*

supervisor, a coworker, or an employee. And sexual harassment is more likely to occur when there are large power differentials. The supervisor–employee dyad best characterizes an unequal power relationship, where formal power gives the supervisor the capacity to reward and coerce. Because employees want favorable performance reviews, salary increases, and the like, it's clear that supervisors control resources that most employees consider important and scarce. Because of power inequities, sexual harassment by one's boss typically creates the greatest difficulty for those who are being harassed. If there are no witnesses, it is the victim's word against the harasser's. Are there others this boss has harassed, and, if so, will they come forward? Because of the supervisor's control over resources, many of those who are harassed are afraid of speaking out for fear of retaliation by the supervisor.

Although coworkers don't have legitimate power, they can have influence and use it to sexually harass peers. In fact, although coworkers appear to engage in somewhat less severe forms of harassment than do supervisors, coworkers are the most frequent perpetrators of sexual harassment in organizations. How do coworkers exercise power? Most often it's by providing or withholding information, cooperation, and support. For example, the effective performance of most jobs requires interaction and support from coworkers. This is especially true today because work is often assigned to teams. By threatening to withhold or delay providing information that's necessary for the successful achievement of your work goals, coworkers can exert power over you.

Although it doesn't get nearly as much attention as harassment by a supervisor, as seen in the lawsuit against Philip Morris, women in positions of power can be subjected to sexual harassment from males who occupy less powerful positions within the organization. This is usually achieved by the employee devaluing the woman through highlighting traditional gender stereotypes (such as helplessness, passivity, lack of career commitment) that reflect negatively on the woman in power. An employee may engage in such practices to attempt to gain some power over the higher-ranking female or to minimize power differentials. Increasingly, too, there are cases of women in positions of power harassing male employees.

The topic of sexual harassment is about power. It's about an individual controlling or threatening another individual. It's wrong. And whether perpetrated against women or men, it's illegal. But you can understand how sexual harassment surfaces in organizations if you analyze it in terms of power.

A recent review of the literature shows the damage caused by sexual harassment. As you would expect, individuals who are sexually harassed report more negative job attitudes (lower job satisfaction, diminished organizational commitment) as a result. This review also revealed that sexual harassment undermines the victims' mental and physical health. However, sexual harassment also negatively affects the group in which the victim works, lowering its level of productivity. The authors of this study conclude that sexual harassment "is significantly and substantively associated with a host of harms."[28]

We have seen how sexual harassment can wreak havoc on an organization, not to mention on the victims themselves. But it can be avoided. A manager's role in preventing sexual harassment is critical. Some ways managers can protect themselves and their employees from sexual harassment follow:

1. Make sure a policy is in place that defines what constitutes sexual harassment, that informs employees that they can be fired for sexually harassing another employee, and that establishes procedures for how complaints can be made.
2. Ensure employees that they will not encounter retaliation if they issue a complaint.
3. Investigate every complaint and include the legal and human resource departments.
4. Make sure that offenders are disciplined or terminated.

5. Set up in-house seminars to raise employee awa
ing sexual harassment.

The bottom line is that managers have a respor
ees from a hostile work environment, but they a
Managers may be unaware that one of their empl
But being unaware does not protect them or th
believe a manager could have known about the haras
and the company can be held liable.

Politics: Power in Action

5 *Distinguish between legitimate and illegitimate political behavior.*

When people get together in groups, power will be exerted. People want to carve out a niche from which to exert influence, to earn rewards, and to advance their careers.[29] When employees in organizations convert their power into action, we describe them as being engaged in politics. Those with good political skills have the ability to use their bases of power effectively.[30]

Definition of *Organizational Politics*

There has been no shortage of definitions of *organizational politics*. Essentially, however, they have focused on the use of power to affect decision making in an organization or on behaviors by members that are self-serving and organizationally nonsanctioned.[31] For our purposes, we shall define **political behavior** in organizations as activities that are not required as part of one's formal role in the organization but that influence, or attempt to influence, the distribution of advantages and disadvantages within the organization.[32] This definition encompasses key elements from what most people mean when they talk about organizational politics. Political behavior is outside one's specified job requirements. The behavior requires some attempt to use one's power bases. In addition, our definition encompasses efforts to influence the goals, criteria, or processes used for *decision making* when we state that politics is concerned with "the distribution of advantages and disadvantages within the organization." Our definition is broad enough to include varied political behaviors such as withholding key information from decision makers, joining a coalition, whistle-blowing, spreading rumors, leaking confidential information about organizational activities to the media, exchanging favors with others in the organization for mutual benefit, and lobbying on behalf of or against a particular individual or decision alternative.

A final comment relates to what has been referred to as the "legitimate–illegitimate" dimension in political behavior.[33] **Legitimate political behavior** refers to normal everyday politics—complaining to your supervisor, bypassing the chain of command, forming coalitions, obstructing organizational policies or decisions through inaction or excessive adherence to rules, and developing contacts outside the organization through one's professional activities. On the other hand, there are also **illegitimate political behaviors** that violate the

political behavior *Activities that are not required as part of a person's formal role in the organization but that influence, or attempt to influence, the distribution of advantages and disadvantages within the organization.*

legitimate political behavior *Normal everyday politics.*

illegitimate political behavior *Extreme political behavior that violates the implied rules of the game.*

In 2002, David Welch, chief financial officer of Bank of Floyd, blew the whistle on the bank's president, alleging that he had engaged in the unethical business practice of buying stocks before the announcement of a bank merger. As a result, Welch was fired. Since then, Welch has compiled piles of documents supporting his allegation. He was the first whistle-blower the U.S. government ordered to be reinstated to a job under the country's Sarbanes-Oxley Act, but the reinstatement order was overturned by a U.S. Labor Department judge. Welch continues his legal battle in an appeal to a circuit court.

implied rules of the game. Those who pursue such extreme activities are often described as individuals who "play hardball." Illegitimate activities include sabotage, whistle-blowing, and symbolic protests such as wearing unorthodox dress or protest buttons and groups of employees simultaneously calling in sick.

The vast majority of all organizational political actions are of the legitimate variety. The reasons are pragmatic: The extreme illegitimate forms of political behavior pose a very real risk of loss of organizational membership or extreme sanctions against those who use them and then fall short in having enough power to ensure that they work.

The Reality of Politics

Politics is a fact of life in organizations. People who ignore this fact of life do so at their own peril. But why, you may wonder, must politics exist? Isn't it possible for an organization to be politics free? It's *possible* but unlikely.

Organizations are made up of individuals and groups with different values, goals, and interests.[34] This sets up the potential for conflict over resources. Departmental budgets, space allocations, project responsibilities, and salary adjustments are just a few examples of the resources about whose allocation organizational members will disagree.

Resources in organizations are also limited, which often turns potential conflict into real conflict.[35] If resources were abundant, then all the various constituencies within the organization could satisfy their goals. But because they are limited, not everyone's interests can be provided for. Furthermore, whether true or not, gains by one individual or group are often *perceived* as being at the expense of others within the organization. These forces create competition among members for the organization's limited resources.

Maybe the most important factor leading to politics within organizations is the realization that most of the "facts" that are used to allocate the limited resources are open to interpretation. What, for instance, is *good* performance? What's an *adequate* improvement? What constitutes an *unsatisfactory* job? One person's view that an act is a "selfless effort to benefit the organization" is seen by another as a "blatant attempt to further one's interest."[36] The manager of any major league baseball team knows a .400 hitter is a high performer and a .125 hitter is a poor performer. You don't need to be a baseball genius to know you should play your .400 hitter and send the .125 hitter back to the minors. But what if you have to choose between players who hit .280 and .290? Then other factors—less objective ones—come into play: fielding expertise, attitude, potential, ability to perform in a clutch, loyalty to the team, and so on. More managerial decisions resemble choosing between a .280 and a .290 hitter than deciding between a .125 hitter and a .400 hitter. It is in this large and ambiguous middle ground of organizational life—where the facts *don't* speak for themselves—that politics flourish (see Exhibit 14-3).

Finally, because most decisions have to be made in a climate of ambiguity—where facts are rarely fully objective and thus are open to interpretation—people within organizations will use whatever influence they can to taint the facts to support their goals and interests. That, of course, creates the activities we call *politicking.*

Therefore, to answer the earlier question of whether it is possible for an organization to be politics free, we can say "yes," if all members of that organization hold the same goals and interests, if organizational resources are not scarce, and if performance outcomes are completely clear and objective. But that doesn't describe the organizational world that most of us live in.

Exhibit 14-3 Politics Is in the Eye of the Beholder

A behavior that one person labels as "organizational politics" is very likely to be characterized as an instance of "effective management" by another. The fact is not that effective management is necessarily political, although in some cases it might be. Rather, a person's reference point determines what he or she classifies as organizational politics. Take a look at the follwing labels used to describe the same phenomenon. These suggest that politics, like beauty, is in the eye of the beholder.

"Political" Label		"Effective Management" Label
1. Blaming others	vs.	Fixing responsibility
2. "Kissing up"	vs.	Developing working relationships
3. Apple polishing	vs.	Demonstrating loyalty
4. Passing the buck	vs.	Delegating authority
5. Covering your rear	vs.	Documenting decisions
6. Creating conflict	vs.	Encouraging change and innovation
7. Forming coalitions	vs.	Facilitating teamwork
8. Whistle-blowing	vs.	Improving efficiency
9. Scheming	vs.	Planning ahead
10. Overachieving	vs.	Competent and capable
11. Ambitious	vs.	Career minded
12. Opportunistic	vs.	Astute
13. Cunning	vs.	Practical minded
14. Arrogant	vs.	Confident
15. Perfectionist	vs.	Attentive to detail

Source: Based on T. C. Krell, M. E. Mendenhall, and J. Sendry, "Doing Research in the Conceptual Morass of Organizational Politics," paper presented at the Western Academy of Management Conference, Hollywood, CA, April 1987.

Causes and Consequences of Political Behavior

6 *Identify the causes and consequences of political behavior.*

Factors Contributing to Political Behavior

Not all groups or organizations are equally political. In some organizations, for instance, politicking is overt and rampant, while in others, politics plays a small role in influencing outcomes. Why is there this variation? Recent

MYTH OR SCIENCE?

"Power Breeds Contempt"

This statement appears to be true. When people have power bestowed on them, they appear to be inclined to ignore the perspectives and interests of those without power, so says a study completed by a team of U.S. researchers.[37]

In this study, researchers made one group of participants feel powerful by asking them to recall and write about a situation in which they had power over another person. Another group of participants was instructed to recall and write about an incident in which someone had power over them. When the groups were then asked to work together on a problem, participants in the powerful group were much more likely to ignore the perspectives of those in the less powerful group, were less able to accurately read their emotional expressions, and were less interested in understanding how other individuals see things. The authors of this study conclude that power leads to "the tendency to view other people only in terms of qualities that serve one's personal goals and interests, while failing to consider those features of others that define their humanity."

So, while power has perks, it also appears to have costs—especially in terms of seeing things from the perspective of those with less of it. ■

Exhibit 14-4 Factors That Influence Political Behavior

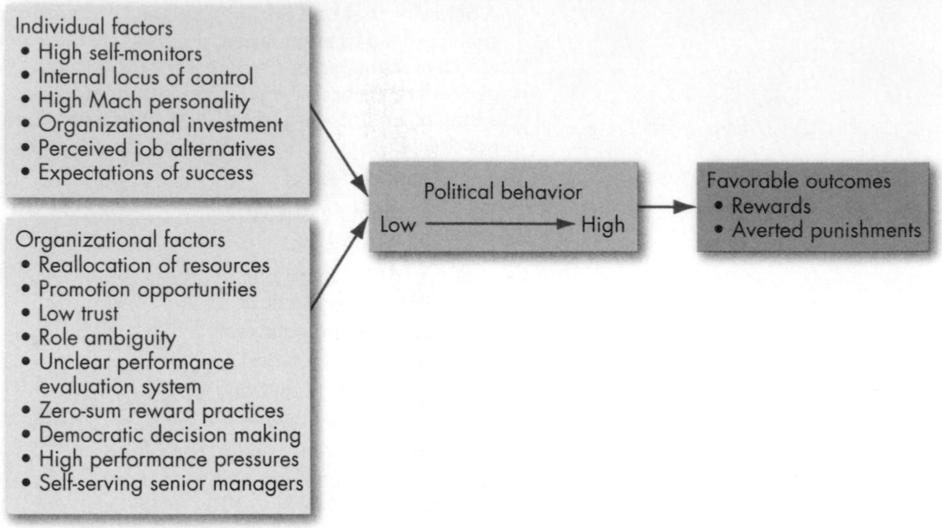

research and observation have identified a number of factors that appear to encourage political behavior. Some are individual characteristics, derived from the unique qualities of the people the organization employs; others are a result of the organization's culture or internal environment. Exhibit 14-4 illustrates how both individual and organizational factors can increase political behavior and provide favorable outcomes (increased rewards and averted punishments) for both individuals and groups in the organization.

Individual Factors At the individual level, researchers have identified certain personality traits, needs, and other factors that are likely to be related to political behavior. In terms of traits, we find that employees who are high self-monitors, possess an internal locus of control, and have a high need for power are more likely to engage in political behavior.[38] The high self-monitor is more sensitive to social cues, exhibits higher levels of social conformity, and is more likely to be skilled in political behavior than the low self-monitor. Individuals with an internal locus of control, because they believe they can control their environment, are more prone to take a proactive stance and attempt to manipulate situations in their favor. Not surprisingly, the Machiavellian personality—characterized by the will to manipulate and the desire for power—is comfortable using politics as a means to further his or her self-interest.

In addition, an individual's investment in the organization, perceived alternatives, and expectations of success will influence the degree to which he or she will pursue illegitimate means of political action.[39] The more a person has invested in the organization in terms of expectations of increased future benefits, the more that person has to lose if forced out and the less likely he or she is to use illegitimate means. The more alternative job opportunities an individual has—due to a favorable job market or the possession of scarce skills or knowledge, a prominent reputation, or influential contacts outside the organization—the more likely that individual is to risk illegitimate political actions. Finally, if an individual has a low expectation of success in using illegitimate means, it is unlikely that he or she will attempt to do so. High expectations of success in the use of illegitimate means are most likely to be the province of both experienced and powerful individuals with polished political skills and inexperienced and naive employees who misjudge their chances.

Politicking is more likely to surface when organizational resources are declining. From 2000 to 2006, Delta Airlines suffered losses of $14.5 billion and then filed for bankruptcy protection. To address the company's severe financial problems, the airline devised a $3 billion cost-cutting plan that included eliminating jobs and reducing pay for pilots and frontline employees. These actions stimulated conflict and increased politicking, such as the informational picketing shown here, as the pilots wanted to safeguard their pay.

Organizational Factors Political activity is probably more a function of an organization's characteristics than of individual difference variables. Why? Because many organizations have a large number of employees with the individual characteristics we listed, yet the extent of political behavior varies widely.

Although we acknowledge the role that individual differences can play in fostering politicking, the evidence more strongly supports the idea that certain situations and cultures promote politics. Specifically, when an organization's resources are declining, when the existing pattern of resources is changing, and when there is opportunity for promotions, politicking is more likely to surface.[40] In addition, cultures characterized by low trust, role ambiguity, unclear performance evaluation systems, zero-sum reward allocation practices, democratic decision making, high pressures for performance, and self-serving senior managers will create breeding grounds for politicking.[41]

When organizations downsize to improve efficiency, reductions in resources have to be made. Threatened with the loss of resources, people may engage in political actions to safeguard what they have. But any changes, especially those that imply significant reallocation of resources within the organization, are likely to stimulate conflict and increase politicking.

Promotion decisions have consistently been found to be one of the most political actions in organizations. The opportunity for promotions or advancement encourages people to compete for a limited resource and to try to positively influence the decision outcome.

The less trust there is within the organization, the higher the level of political behavior and the more likely that the political behavior will be of the illegitimate kind. So high trust should suppress the level of political behavior in general and inhibit illegitimate actions in particular.

Role ambiguity means that the prescribed behaviors of the employee are not clear. There are fewer limits, therefore, to the scope and functions of the employee's political actions. Because political activities are defined as those not required as part of one's formal role, the greater the role ambiguity, the more one can engage in political activity with little chance of it being visible.

The practice of performance evaluation is far from a perfect science. The more that organizations use subjective criteria in the appraisal, emphasize a single outcome measure, or allow significant time to pass between the time of an action and its appraisal, the greater the likelihood that an employee can get away with politicking. Subjective performance criteria create ambiguity. The use of a single outcome measure encourages individuals to do whatever is necessary to "look good" on that measure, but often at the expense of performing well on other important parts of the job that are not being appraised. The amount of time that elapses between an action and its appraisal is also a relevant factor. The longer the time, the more unlikely that the employee will be held accountable for his political behaviors.

The more that an organization's culture emphasizes the zero-sum or win/lose approach to reward allocations, the more employees will be motivated to engage in politicking. The zero-sum approach treats the reward "pie" as fixed so that any gain one person or group achieves has to come at the expense of another person or group. If I win, you must lose! If $15,000 in annual raises is to be distributed among five employees, then any employee who gets more than $3,000 takes money away from one or more of the others. Such a practice encourages making others look bad and increasing the visibility of what you do.

In the past 25 years, there has been a general move in North America and among most developed nations toward making organizations less autocratic. Managers in these organizations are being asked to behave more democratically. They're told that they should allow employees to advise them on decisions and that they should rely to a greater extent on group input into the decision process. Such moves toward democracy, however, are not necessarily embraced by all individual managers. Many managers sought their positions in order to have legitimate power so as to be able to make unilateral decisions. They fought hard and often paid high personal costs to achieve their influential positions. Sharing their power with others runs directly against their desires. The result is that managers, especially those who began their careers in the 1960s and 1970s, may use the required committees, conferences, and group meetings in a superficial way, as arenas for maneuvering and manipulating.

The more pressure that employees feel to perform well, the more likely they are to engage in politicking. When people are held strictly accountable for outcomes, this puts great pressure on them to "look good." If a person perceives that his or her entire career is riding on next quarter's sales figures or next month's plant productivity report, there is motivation to do whatever is necessary to make sure the numbers come out favorably.

Finally, when employees see the people on top engaging in political behavior, especially when they do so successfully and are rewarded for it, a climate is created that supports politicking. Politicking by top management, in a sense, gives permission to those lower in the organization to play politics by implying that such behavior is acceptable.

How Do People Respond to Organizational Politics?

Trish O'Donnell loves her job as a writer on a weekly television comedy series but hates the internal politics. "A couple of the writers here spend more time kissing up to the executive producer than doing any work. And our head writer clearly has his favorites. While they pay me a lot and I get to really use my creativity, I'm sick of having to be on alert for backstabbers and constantly having to self-promote my contributions. I'm tired of doing most of the work and getting little of the credit." Are Trish O'Donnell's comments typical of people who work in highly politicized workplaces? We all know of friends or relatives who

Exhibit 14-5 Employee Responses to Organizational Politics

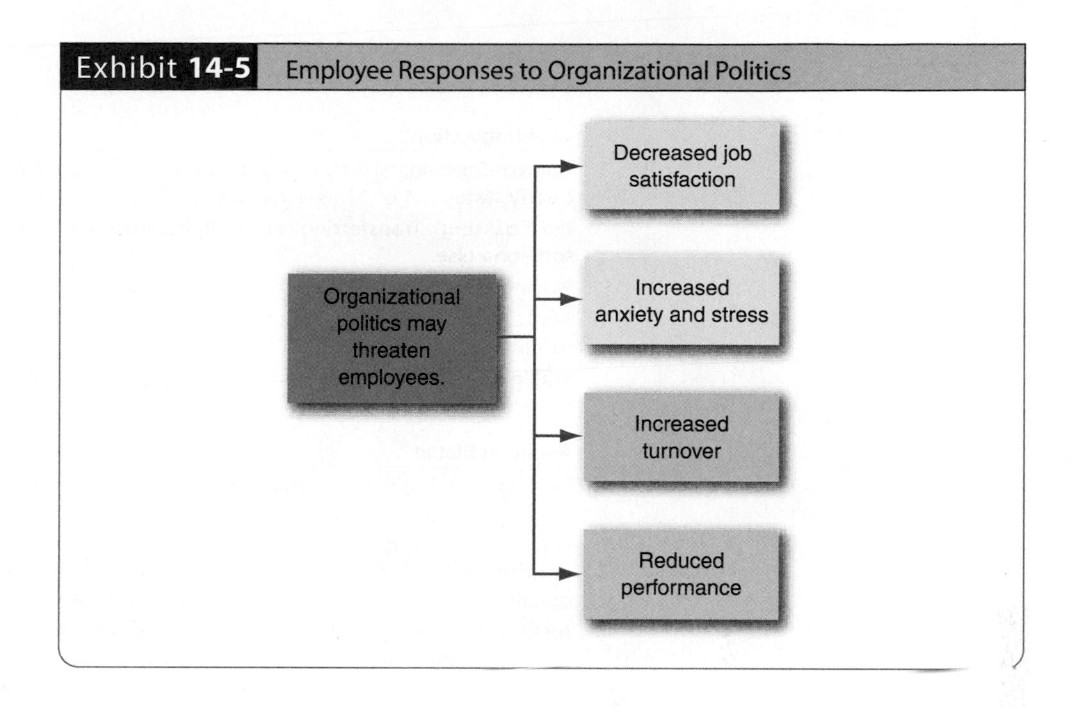

regularly complain about the politics at their job. But how do people in general react to organizational politics? Let's look at the evidence.

In our discussion earlier in this chapter of factors that contribute to political behavior, we focused on the favorable outcomes for individuals who successfully engage in politicking. But for most people—who have modest political skills or are unwilling to play the politics game—outcomes tend to be predominantly negative. Exhibit 14-5 summarizes the extensive research on the relationship between organizational politics and individual outcomes.[42] There is, for instance, very strong evidence indicating that perceptions of organizational politics are negatively related to job satisfaction.[43] The perception of politics also tends to increase job anxiety and stress. This seems to be due to the perception that, by not engaging in politics, a person may be losing ground to others who are active politickers; or, conversely, because of the additional pressures individuals feel because of having entered into and competing in the political arena.[44] Not surprisingly, when politicking becomes too much to handle, it can lead to employees quitting.[45] Finally, there is preliminary evidence suggesting that politics leads to self-reported declines in employee performance. This may occur because employees perceive political environments to be unfair, which demotivates them.[46]

In addition to these conclusions, several interesting qualifiers have been noted. First, the politics–performance relationship appears to be moderated by an individual's understanding of the "hows" and "whys" of organizational politics. "An individual who has a clear understanding of who is responsible for making decisions and why they were selected to be the decision makers would have a better understanding of how and why things happen the way they do than someone who does not understand the decision-making process in the organization."[47] When both politics and understanding are high, performance is likely to increase because the individual will see political actions as an opportunity. This is consistent with what you might expect among individuals with well-honed political skills. But when understanding is low, individuals are more likely to see politics as a threat, which would have a negative effect on job performance.[48] Second, when politics is seen as a threat and consistently responded to with defensiveness, negative outcomes are almost sure to surface eventually. When people perceive politics as a threat rather than as an opportunity, they

Exhibit 14-6 Defensive Behaviors

Avoiding Action

Overconforming. Strictly interpreting your responsibility by saying things like, "The rules clearly state . . . " or "This is the way we've always done it."

Buck passing. Transferring responsibility for the execution of a task or decision to someone else.

Playing dumb. Avoiding an unwanted task by falsely pleading ignorance or inability.

Stretching. Prolonging a task so that one person appears to be occupied—for example, turning a two-week task into a four-month job.

Stalling. Appearing to be more or less supportive publicly while doing little or nothing privately.

Avoiding Blame

Buffing. This is a nice way to refer to "covering your rear." It describes the practice of rigorously documenting activity to project an image of competence and thoroughness.

Playing safe. Evading situations that may reflect unfavorably. It includes taking on only projects with a high probability of success, having risky decisions approved by superiors, qualifying expressions of judgment, and taking neutral positions in conflicts.

Justifying. Developing explanations that lessen one's responsibility for a negative outcome and/or apologizing to demonstrate remorse.

Scapegoating. Placing the blame for a negative outcome on external factors that are not entirely blameworthy.

Misrepresenting. Manipulation of information by distortion, embellishment, deception, selective presentation, or obfuscation.

Avoiding Change

Prevention. Trying to prevent a threatening change from occurring.

Self-protection. Acting in ways to protect one's self-interest during change by guarding information or other resources.

often respond with **defensive behaviors**—reactive and protective behaviors to avoid action, blame, or change.[49] (Exhibit 14-6 provides some examples of these defensive behaviors.) And defensive behaviors are often associated with negative feelings toward the job and work environment.[50] In the short run, employees may find that defensiveness protects their self-interest. But in the long run, it wears them down. People who consistently rely on defensiveness find that, eventually, it is the only way they know how to behave. At that point, they lose the trust and support of their peers, bosses, employees, and clients.

Are our conclusions about responses to politics globally valid? Should we expect employees in Israel, for instance, to respond the same way to workplace politics that employees in the United States do? Almost all our conclusions on employee reactions to organizational politics are based on studies conducted in North America. The few studies that have included other countries suggest some minor modifications.[51] Israelis and Brits, for instance, seem to generally respond as do North Americans. That is, the perception of organizational politics among employees in these countries is related to decreased job satisfaction and increased turnover.[52] But in countries that are more politically unstable, such as Israel, employees seem to demonstrate greater tolerance of intense political processes in the workplace. This is likely to be because people in these countries are used to power struggles and have more experience in coping with them.[53] This suggests that people from politically turbulent countries in the Middle East or Latin America might be more accepting of organizational politics, and even more willing to use aggressive political tactics in the workplace, than people from countries such as Great Britain or Switzerland.

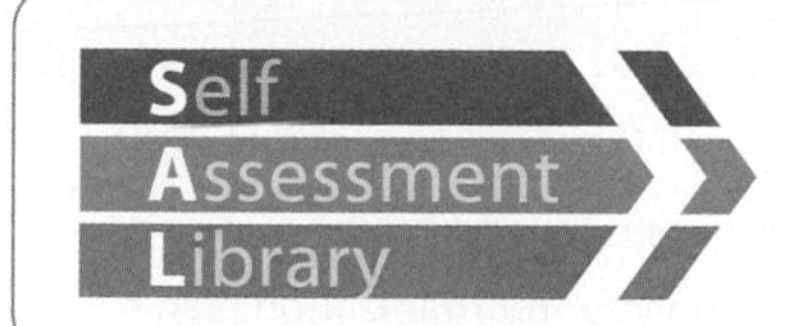

HOW GOOD AM I AT PLAYING POLITICS?

In the Self-Assessment Library (available on CD and online), take assessment II.C.3 (How Good Am I at Playing Politics?).

Impression Management

7 *Apply impression management techniques.*

We know that people have an ongoing interest in how others perceive and evaluate them. For example, North Americans spend billions of dollars on diets, health club memberships, cosmetics, and plastic surgery—all intended to make them more attractive to others.[54] Being perceived positively by others should have benefits for people in organizations. It might, for instance, help them initially to get the jobs they want in an organization and, once hired, to get favorable evaluations, superior salary increases, and more rapid promotions. In a political context, it might help sway the distribution of advantages in their favor. The process by which individuals attempt to control the impression others form of them is called **impression management (IM)**.[55] It's a subject that has gained the attention of OB researchers only recently.[56]

Is everyone concerned with IM? No! Who, then, might we predict to engage in IM? No surprise here. It's our old friend, the high self-monitor.[57] Low self-monitors tend to present images of themselves that are consistent with their personalities, regardless of the beneficial or detrimental effects for them. In contrast, high self-monitors are good at reading situations and molding their appearances and behavior to fit each situation. If you want to control the impression others form of you, what techniques can you use? Exhibit 14-7 summarizes some of the most popular IM techniques and provides an example of each.

Keep in mind that IM does not imply that the impressions people convey are necessarily false (although, of course, they sometimes are).[58] Excuses, for instance, may be offered with sincerity. Referring to the example used in Exhibit 14-7, you can *actually* believe that ads contribute little to sales in your region. But misrepresentation can have a high cost. If the image claimed is false, you may be discredited.[59] If you "cry wolf" once too often, no one is likely to believe you when the wolf really comes. So the impression manager must be cautious not to be perceived as insincere or manipulative.[60]

Are there *situations* in which individuals are more likely to misrepresent themselves or more likely to get away with it? Yes—situations that are characterized by high uncertainty or ambiguity provide relatively little information for challenging a fraudulent claim and reduce the risks associated with misrepresentation.[61]

Most of the studies undertaken to test the effectiveness of IM techniques have related it to two criteria: interview success and performance evaluations. Let's consider each of these.

The evidence indicates that most job applicants use IM techniques in interviews[62] and that, when IM behavior is used, it works.[63] In one study, for instance, interviewers felt that applicants for a position as a customer service representative who used IM techniques performed better in the interview, and they seemed somewhat more inclined to hire these people.[64] Moreover, when the researchers considered applicants' credentials, they concluded that it was the IM techniques alone that influenced the interviewers. That is, it didn't seem

defensive behaviors *Reactive and protective behaviors to avoid action, blame, or change.*

impression management (IM) *The process by which individuals attempt to control the impression others form of them.*

Exhibit 14-7 Impression Management (IM) Techniques

Conformity

Agreeing with someone else's opinion in order to gain his or her approval.

Example: A manager tells his boss, "You're absolutely right on your reorganization plan for the western regional office. I couldn't agree with you more."

Excuses

Explanations of a predicament-creating event aimed at minimizing the apparent severity of the predicament.

Example: Sales manager to boss, "We failed to get the ad in the paper on time, but no one responds to those ads anyway."

Apologies

Admitting responsibility for an undesirable event and simultaneously seeking to get a pardon for the action.

Example: Employee to boss, "I'm sorry I made a mistake on the report. Please forgive me."

Self-Promotion

Highlighting one's best qualities, downplaying one's deficits, and calling attention to one's achievements.

Example: A salesperson tells his boss: "Matt worked unsuccessfully for three years to try to get that account. I sewed it up in six weeks. I'm the best closer this company has."

Flattery

Complimenting others about their virtues in an effort to make oneself appear perceptive and likeable.

Example: New sales trainee to peer, "You handled that client's complaint so tactfully! I could never have handled that as well as you did."

Favors

Doing something nice for someone to gain that person's approval.

Example: Salesperson to prospective client, "I've got two tickets to the theater tonight that I can't use. Take them. Consider it a thank-you for taking the time to talk with me."

Association

Enhancing or protecting one's image by managing information about people and things with which one is associated.

Example: A job applicant says to an interviewer, "What a coincidence. Your boss and I were roommates in college."

Source: Based on B. R. Schlenker, *Impression Management* (Monterey, CA: Brooks/Cole, 1980); W. L. Gardner and M. J. Martinko, "Impression Management in Organizations," *Journal of Management*, June 1988, p. 332; and R. B. Cialdini, "Indirect Tactics of Image Management Beyond Basking," in R. A. Giacalone and P. Rosenfeld (eds.), *Impression Management in the Organization* (Hillsdale, NJ: Lawrence Erlbaum, 1989), pp. 45–71.

to matter if applicants were well or poorly qualified. If they used IM techniques, they did better in the interview.

Research indicates that some IM techniques work better than others in the interview. Researchers have compared applicants who used IM techniques that focused on promoting one's accomplishments (called *self-promotion*) to applicants who used techniques that focused on complimenting the interviewer and finding areas of agreement (referred to as *ingratiation*). In general, applicants appear to use self-promotion more than ingratiation.[65] What's more, self-promotion tactics may be more important to interviewing success. Applicants who work to create an appearance of competence by enhancing their accomplishments, taking credit for successes, and explaining away failures do better in interviews. These effects reach beyond the interview: Applicants who use more self-promotion tactics also seem to get more follow-up job-site visits, even after adjusting for grade-point average, gender, and job type. Ingratiation also works well in interviews, meaning

OB In the News

Excuses Are Everywhere

As we've noted, excuses are one means of managing impressions so as to avoid negative repercussions of our actions. However, judging from some recent evidence on absenteeism, excuses are also a chance for workers to engage their creative side.

A 2007 survey of nearly 7,000 employees and 3,000 hiring managers revealed some pretty creative excuses for being late for work or absent from work:

"Someone was following me and I drove all around town trying to lose them."

"My dog called the police, who wanted to question me about what really happened."

"My girlfriend got mad and destroyed all of my undergarments."

"A buffalo escaped from a game preserve and kept charging me every time I tried to leave my house."

"A skunk got into my house and sprayed all my uniforms."

"My mother-in-law poisoned me."

"My mother-in-law is in jail."

"I blew my nose so hard my back went out."

"My cow bit me."

"I'm too fat to get into my work pants."

Though you have to give the excuse makers high marks for originality, we seriously doubt supervisors bought these excuses. The making of excuses may be one of the few areas in which creativity is bad.

Sources: Based on K. Gurchiek, "'Sorry I'm Late; A Raccoon Stole My Shoe,'" *HRWeek*, May 29, 2007, www.shrm.org/hrnews_published/archives/CMS_021684.asp; and K. Gurchiek, "Runaway Horses, Charging Buffalo Kept Workers Home in '06," December 28, 2006, *HRWeek*, www.shrm.org/hrnews_published/archives/CMS_019743.asp.

that applicants who compliment the interviewer, agree with his or her opinions, and emphasize areas of fit do better than those who don't.[66]

In terms of performance ratings, the picture is quite different. Ingratiation is positively related to performance ratings, meaning that those who ingratiate with their supervisors get higher performance evaluations. However, self-promotion appears to backfire: Those who self-promote actually seem to receive *lower* performance evaluations.[67] Another study of 760 boards of directors found that individuals who ingratiate themselves to current board members (express agreement with the director, point out shared attitudes and opinions, compliment the director) increase their chances of landing on a board.[68]

What explains these results? If you think about them, they make sense. Ingratiating always works because everyone—both interviewers and supervisors—likes to be treated nicely. However, self-promotion may work only in interviews and backfire on the job because, whereas the interviewer has little idea whether you're blowing smoke about your accomplishments, the supervisor knows because it's his or her job to observe you. Thus, if you're going to self-promote, remember that what works in an interview will not always work once you're on the job.

The Ethics of Behaving Politically

8 Determine whether a political action is ethical.

We conclude our discussion of politics by providing some ethical guidelines for political behavior. Although there are no clear-cut ways to differentiate ethical from unethical politicking, there are some questions you should consider. For example, what is the utility of engaging in politicking? Sometimes we engage in political behaviors for little good reason. For example, major league baseball player Al Martin claimed he played football at a prominent U.S. college when in fact he never did. Because Martin was playing baseball, not football, there was little to be gained by his lie. Outright lies like this may be a rather extreme example of impression management, but many of us have distorted information to make a favorable impression. The point is that, before we do so, one thing to keep in mind is whether it's really worth the risk. Another question to ask is an ethical one: How does the utility of engaging in the political behavior balance out any harm (or potential harm) it will do to others? For example, complimenting a supervisor on his or her appearance to curry favor is probably much less harmful than grabbing credit for a project that is deserved by others.

Finally, does the political activity conform to standards of equity and justice? Sometimes it is hard to weigh the costs and benefits of a political action, but its ethicality is clear. The department head who inflates the performance evaluation of a favored employee and deflates the evaluation of a disfavored employee—and then uses these evaluations to justify giving the former a big raise and nothing to the latter—has treated the disfavored employee unfairly.

Unfortunately, the answers to these questions are often argued in ways to make unethical practices seem ethical. Powerful people, for example, can become very good at explaining self-serving behaviors in terms of the organization's best interests. Similarly, they can persuasively argue that unfair actions are really fair and just. Our point is that immoral people can justify almost any behavior. Those who are powerful, articulate, and persuasive are most vulnerable because they are likely to be able to get away with unethical practices successfully. When faced with an ethical dilemma regarding organizational politics, try to consider the preceding issues (is playing politics worth the risk, and will others be harmed in the process?). If you have a strong power base, recognize the ability of power to corrupt. Remember that it's a lot easier for the powerless than the powerful to act ethically, if for no other reason than they typically have very little political discretion to exploit.

Global Implications

9 Show the influence of culture on the uses and perceptions of politics.

Although culture might enter any of the topics we've covered to this point, three questions are particularly important: (1) Does culture influence politics perceptions? (2) Does culture affect the power of influence tactics people prefer to use? and (3) Does culture influence the effectiveness of different tactics?

Politics Perceptions

We noted earlier that when people see their work environment as political, negative consequences in their overall work attitudes and behaviors generally result. Most of the research on politics perceptions has been conducted in the United States. A recent study, however, suggested that politics perceptions have the same negative effects in Nigeria. When employees of two agencies in Nigeria viewed their work environments as political, they reported higher levels of job distress and were less likely to help their coworkers. Thus, although developing countries such as Nigeria are perhaps more ambiguous and more political environments in which to work, the negative consequences appear to be the same as in the United States.[69]

Preference for Power Tactics

Evidence indicates that people in different countries tend to prefer different power tactics.[70] For instance, a study comparing managers in the United States and China found that U.S. managers prefer rational appeal, whereas Chinese managers preferred coalition tactics.[71] These differences tend to be consistent with the values in these two countries. Reason is consistent with the U.S. preference for direct confrontation and the use of rational persuasion to influence others and resolve differences. Similarly, coalition tactics are consistent with the Chinese preference for using indirect approaches for difficult or controversial requests. Research also has shown that individuals in Western, individualistic cultures tend to engage in more self-enhancement (such as self-promotion) behaviors than individuals in Eastern, more collectivistic cultures.[72]

Effectiveness of Power Tactics

Unfortunately, while we know people in different cultures seem to have different preferences for the use of power or influence tactics, there is much less evidence as to whether these tactics work better in some cultures than in others. One study of managers in U.S. culture and three Chinese cultures (People's Republic of China, Hong Kong, Taiwan) found that U.S. managers evaluated "gentle persuasion" tactics such as consultation and inspirational appeal as more effective than did their Chinese counterparts.[73]

Summary and Implications for Managers

If you want to get things done in a group or an organization, it helps to have power. As a manager who wants to maximize your power, you will want to increase others' dependence on you. You can, for instance, increase your power in relation to your boss by developing knowledge or a skill that she needs and for which she perceives no ready substitute. But power is a two-way street. You will not be alone in attempting to build your power bases. Others, particularly employees and peers, will be seeking to make you dependent on them. The result is a continual battle. While you seek to maximize others' dependence on you, you will be seeking to minimize your dependence on others. And, of course, others you work with will be trying to do the same.

Few employees relish being powerless in their job and organization. It's been argued, for instance, that when people in organizations are difficult, argumentative, and temperamental, it may be because they are in positions of powerlessness positions in which the performance expectations placed on them exceed their resources and capabilities.[74]

There is evidence that people respond differently to the various power bases.[75] Expert and referent power are derived from an individual's personal qualities. In contrast, coercion, reward, and legitimate power are essentially organizationally derived. Because people are more likely to enthusiastically accept and commit to an individual whom they admire or whose knowledge they respect (rather than someone who relies on his or her position for influence), the effective use of expert and referent power should lead to higher employee motivation, performance, commitment, and satisfaction.[76] Competence especially appears to offer wide appeal, and its use as a power base results in high performance by group members. The message for managers seems to be "Develop and use your expert power base!"

The power of your boss may also play a role in determining your job satisfaction. "One of the reasons many of us like to work for and with people who are powerful is that they are generally more pleasant—not because it is their native disposition, but because the reputation and reality of being powerful permits them more discretion and more ability to delegate to others."[77]

An effective manager accepts the political nature of organizations. By assessing behavior in a political framework, you can better predict the actions of others and use that information to formulate political strategies that will gain advantages for you and your work unit.

Some people are significantly more "politically astute" than others, meaning that they are aware of the underlying politics and can manage impressions. Those who are good at playing politics can be expected to get higher performance evaluations and, hence, larger salary increases and more promotions than the politically naive or inept.[78] The politically astute are also likely to exhibit higher job satisfaction and be better able to neutralize job stressors.[79] For employees with poor political skills or who are unwilling to play the politics game, the perception of organizational politics is generally related to lower job satisfaction and self-reported performance, increased anxiety, and higher turnover.

Point / Counterpoint

MANAGING IMPRESSIONS IS UNETHICAL

Point

Managing impressions is wrong for both ethical and practical reasons.

First, managing impressions is just another name for lying. Don't we have a responsibility, both to ourselves and to others, to present ourselves as we really are? The Australian philosopher Tony Coady wrote, "Dishonesty has always been perceived in our culture, and in all cultures but the most bizarre, as a central human vice." Immanuel Kant's categorical imperative asks us to consider the following: If you want to know whether telling a lie on a particular occasion is justifiable, you must try to imagine what would happen if everyone were to lie. Surely you would agree that a world in which no one lies is preferable to one in which lying is common because in such a world we could never trust anyone. Thus, we should try to present the truth as best we can. Impression management goes against this virtue.

Practically speaking, impression management generally backfires in the long run. Remember Sir Walter Scott's quote, "Oh what a tangled web we weave, when first we practice to deceive!" Once we start to distort the facts, where do we stop? When George O'Leary was hired as Notre Dame's football coach, he said on his résumé that 30 years before, he had obtained a degree from Stony Brook University that he never earned. Obviously, this information was unimportant to his football accomplishments, and ironically, he had written it on his resume 20 years earlier when hired for a job at Syracuse University; he had simply never corrected the inaccuracy. But when the truth came out, O'Leary was finished.

At Indiana University's Kelley School of Business, the code of ethics instructs students to provide only truthful information on their résumés and obligates them to be honest in interviews.

People are most satisfied with their jobs when their values match the culture of the organizations. If either side misrepresents itself in the interview process, then odds are, people won't fit in the organizations they choose. What's the benefit in this?

This doesn't imply that a person shouldn't put his or her best foot forward. But that means exhibiting qualities that are good no matter the context—being friendly, being positive and self-confident, being qualified and competent, while still being honest.

Counterpoint

Oh, come on. Get off your high horse. *Everybody* fudges to some degree in the process of applying for a job. If you really told the interviewer what your greatest weakness or worst mistake was, you'd never get hired. What if you answered, "I find it hard to get up in the morning and get to work"?

These sorts of "white lies" are expected and act as a kind of social lubricant. If we really knew what people where thinking, we'd go crazy. Moreover, you can quote all the philosophy you want, but sometimes it's necessary to lie. You mean you wouldn't lie to save the life of your family? It's naïve to think we can live in a world without lying.

Sometimes a bit of deception is necessary to get a job. I know a gay applicant who was rejected from a job he really wanted because he told the interviewer he had written two articles for gay magazines. What if he had told the interviewer a little lie? Would harm really have been done? At least he'd have a job.

As another example, when an interviewer asks you what you earned on your previous job, that information will be used against you, to pay you a salary lower than you deserve. Is it wrong to boost your salary a bit? Or would it be better to disclose your actual salary and be taken advantage of?

The same goes for complimenting interviewers, agreeing with their opinions, and so forth. If an interviewer tells you, "We believe in community involvement," are you supposed to tell the interviewer you've never volunteered for anything?

Of course you can go too far. We're not advocating that people totally fabricate their backgrounds. What we are talking about here is a reasonable amount of enhancement. If we can help ourselves without doing any real harm, then impression management is not the same as lying and actually is something we should teach others.

Questions for Review

1 How would you define *power*? How is it different from leadership?

2 What are the five bases of power?

3 What are the nine power or influence tactics?

4 In what way is sexual harassment about the abuse of power?

5 What is political behavior and how would you distinguish between legitimate and illegitimate political behavior?

6 What are the causes and consequences of political behavior?

7 What is impression management and what are the techniques for managing impressions?

8 How can one determine whether a political action is ethical?

9 How does culture influence politics perceptions, preferences for different power or influence tactics, and the effectiveness of those tactics?

Experiential Exercise

UNDERSTANDING POWER DYNAMICS

Create Groups

Each student is to turn in a dollar bill (or similar value of currency) to the instructor, and students are then divided into three groups, based on criteria given by the instructor, assigned to their workplaces, and instructed to read the following rules and tasks. The money is divided into thirds, and two-thirds of it is given to the top group, one-third to the middle group, and none to the bottom group.

Conduct Exercise

Groups go to their assigned workplaces and have 30 minutes to complete their tasks.

Rules

Members of the top group are free to enter the space of either of the other groups and to communicate whatever they wish, whenever they wish. Members of the middle group may enter the space of the lower group when they wish but must request permission to enter the top group's space (which the top group can refuse). Members of the lower group may not disturb the top group in any way unless specifically invited by the top. The lower group does have the right to knock on the door of the middle group and request permission to communicate with them (which can also be refused).

The members of the top group have the authority to make any change in the rules that they wish, at any time, with or without notice.

Tasks

- *Top group.* To be responsible for the overall effectiveness and learning from the exercise and to decide how to use its money.
- *Middle group.* To assist the top group in providing for the overall welfare of the organization and to decide how to use its money.
- *Bottom group.* To identify its resources and to decide how best to provide for learning and the overall effectiveness of the organization.

Debriefing

Each of the three groups chooses two representatives to go to the front of the class and discuss the following:

1. Summarize what occurred within and among the three groups.
2. What are some of the differences between being in the top group and being in the bottom group?
3. What can we learn about power from this experience?
4. How accurate do you think this exercise is in reflecting the reality of resource allocation decisions in large organizations?

Source: Adapted from L. Bolman and T. E. Deal, *Exchange* 3, no. 4 (1979), pp. 38–42. Reprinted by permission of Sage Publications, Inc.

Ethical Dilemma

SWAPPING PERSONAL FAVORS?

Jack Grubman was a powerful man on Wall Street. As a star analyst of telecom companies for the Salomon Smith Barney unit of Citigroup, he made recommendations that carried a lot of weight with investors.

For years, Grubman had been negative on the stock of AT&T. But in November 1999, he changed his opinion. Based on e-mail evidence, it appears that Grubman's decision to upgrade AT&T wasn't based on the stock's fundamentals. There were other factors involved.

At the time, his boss at Citigroup, Sanford "Sandy" Weill, was in the midst of a power struggle with co-CEO John Reed to become the single head of the company. Meanwhile, Salomon was looking for additional business to increase its revenues. Getting investment banking business fees from AT&T would be a big plus. And Salomon's chances of getting that AT&T business would definitely be improved if Grubman would upgrade his opinion on the stock. Furthermore, Weill sought Grubman's upgrade to win favor with AT&T CEO Michael Armstrong, who sat on Citigroup's board. Weill wanted Armstrong's backing in his efforts to oust Reed.

Grubman had his own concerns. Though earning tens of millions a year in his job, as the son of a city worker in Philadelphia, he was a man of modest background. He wanted the best for his twin daughters, including entry to an exclusive New York City nursery school (the posh 92nd Street Y)—a school that a year earlier had reportedly turned down Madonna's daughter. Weill made a call to the school on Grubman's behalf and pledged a $1 million donation from Citigroup. At approximately the same time, Weill also asked Grubman to "take a fresh look" at his neutral rating on AT&T. Shortly after being asked to review his rating, Grubman raised it, and AT&T awarded Salomon an investment-banking job worth nearly $45 million. Shares of AT&T soared.

Did Sandy Weill do anything unethical? How about Jack Grubman? What do you think?

Source: Based on C. Gasparino, "Out of School," *Newsweek*, January 17, 2005, pp. 38–39.

Case Incident 1

DRESSING FOR SUCCESS

Jennifer Cohen thought she had a good grip on her company's dress code. She was wrong.

Cohen works for a marketing firm in Philadelphia. Before a meeting, an older colleague pulled 24-year-old Cohen aside and told her that she was dressing inappropriately by wearing Bermuda shorts, sleeveless tops, and Capri pants. Cohen was stunned by the rebuke. "Each generation seems to have a different idea of what is acceptable in the workplace," she said. "In this case, I was highly offended."

What offended Cohen even more was what came next: Cohen wasn't allowed to attend the meeting because her attire was deemed inappropriate.

Cohen's employer is not alone. Although many employers have "casual" days at work, the number of employers who are enforcing more formal dress codes has increased, according to a survey of employers by the Society for Human Resource Management. In 2001, 53 percent of employers allowed causal dress every day. Now that figure is 38 percent. Silicon Valley marketing firm McGrath/Power used to allow causal attire. Now, it enforces a more formal dress code. "The pendulum has swung," says CEO Jonathan Bloom, "We went through a too-causal period.... When we were very casual, the quality of the work wasn't as good."

Ironically, as more employers enforce more formal dress codes, other employers known for their formality are going the other way. IBM, which once had a dress code of business suits with white shirts, has thrown out dress codes altogether. IBM researcher Dan Gruhl typically goes to work at IBM's San Jose, California, office in flip-flops and shorts. "Having a relaxed environment encourages you to think more openly," he says. Although not going quite as far as IBM, other traditional employers, such as Ford, General Motors, and Procter & Gamble, have relaxed dress codes.

Still, for every IBM, there are more companies that have tightened the rules. Even the NBA has adopted an off-court dress code for its players. As for Cohen, she still bristles at the dress code. "When you're comfortable, you don't worry," she says. "You focus on your work."

Questions

1. Do you think Cohen had a right to be offended? Why or why not?

2. In explaining why she was offended, Cohen argued, "People my age are taught to express themselves, and saying something negative about someone's fashion is saying something negative about them." Do you agree with Cohen?
3. Does an employer have an unfettered right to set a company's dress code? Why or why not?
4. How far would you go to conform to an organization's dress code? If your boss dressed in a relatively formal manner, would you feel compelled to dress in a like manner to manage impressions?

Source: Based on S. Armour, "'Business Casual' Causes Confusion," *USA Today*, July 10, 2007, pp. 1B, 2B.

Case Incident 2

THE POLITICS OF BACKSTABBING

Scott Rosen believed that he was making progress as an assistant manager of a financial-services company—until he noticed that his colleague, another assistant manager, was attempting to push him aside. On repeated occasions, Rosen would observe his colleague speaking with their manager behind closed doors. During these conversations, Rosen's colleague would attempt to persuade the supervisor that Rosen was incompetent and mismanaging his job, a practice that Mr. Rosen found out after the fact. Rosen recounts one specific instance of his colleague's backstabbing efforts: When a subordinate asked Rosen a question to which Rosen did not know the answer, his colleague would say to their supervisor, "I can't believe he didn't know something like that." On other occasions, after instructing a subordinate to complete a specific task, Rosen's colleague would say, "I wouldn't make you do something like that." What was the end result of such illegitimate political tactics? Rosen was demoted, an action that led him to resign shortly after, while his colleague was promoted. "Whatever I did, I lost," recounts Rosen.

What leads individuals to behave this way? According to Judith Briles, a management consultant who has extensively studied the practice of backstabbing, a tight job market is often a contributing factor. Fred Nader, another management consultant, believes that backstabbing is the result of "some kind of character disorder."

One executive at a technology company in Seattle admits that blind ambition was responsible for the backstabbing he did. In 1999, he was assigned as an external sales representative, partnered with a colleague who worked internally at their client's office. The executive wanted the internal sales position for himself. To reach this goal, he systematically engaged in backstabbing to shatter his colleague's credibility. Each time he heard a complaint, however small, from the client, he would ask for it in an e-mail and then forward the information to his boss. He'd include a short message about his colleague, such as: "I'm powerless to deal with this. She's not being responsive and the customer is beating on me." In addition, he would fail to share important information with her before presentations with their boss, to convey the impression that she did not know what she was talking about. He even went so far as to schedule meetings with their boss on an electronic calendar but then altered her version so that she was late. Eventually, he convinced his boss that she was overworked. He was transferred to the client's office, while his colleague was moved back to the main office.

Incidents such as these may not be uncommon in the workplace. Given today's competitive work environment, employees may be using political games to move ahead. To guard against backstabbing, Bob McDonald, a management consultant, recommends telling supervisors and other key personnel that the backstabber is not a friend. He states that this may be effective because backstabbers often claim to be friends of their victims and then act as if they are hesitant about sharing negative information with others because of this professed friendship. In any event, it is clear that employees in organizations need to be aware of illegitimate political behavior. Companies may need to adopt formal policies to safeguard employees against such behavior; however, it may be the case that behaviors such as backstabbing and spreading negative rumors are difficult to detect. Thus, both employees and managers should try to verify information to avoid the negative repercussions that can come from backstabbing and other illegitimate behaviors.

Questions

1. What factors, in addition to those cited here, do you believe lead to illegitimate political behaviors such as backstabbing?
2. Imagine that a colleague is engaging in illegitimate political behavior toward you. What steps might you take to reduce or eliminate this behavior?

3. Do you believe that it is ever justifiable to engage in illegitimate political behaviors such as backstabbing? If so, what are some conditions that might justify such behavior?

4. In addition to the obvious negative effects of illegitimate political behavior on victims, such as those described in this case, what might be some negative effects on the perpetrators? on the organization as a whole?

Source: Based on J. Sandberg, "Sabotage 101: The Sinister Art of Backstabbing," *Wall Street Journal*, February 11, 2004, p. B1.

Endnotes

1. G. Morgenson, "Downgrade a Stock, Then Duck and Cover," *New York Times*, March 12, 2006, pp. B1, B9.
2. R. M. Kanter, "Power Failure in Management Circuits," *Harvard Business Review*, July–August 1979, p. 65.
3. J. Pfeffer, "Understanding Power in Organizations," *California Management Review*, Winter 1992, p. 35.
4. Based on B. M. Bass, *Bass & Stogdill's Handbook of Leadership*, 3rd ed. (New York: The Free Press, 1990).
5. J. R. P. French, Jr., and B. Raven, "The Bases of Social Power," in D. Cartwright (ed.), *Studies in Social Power* (Ann Arbor, MI: University of Michigan, Institute for Social Research, 1959), pp. 150–167; B. J. Raven, "The Bases of Power: Origins and Recent Developments," *Journal of Social Issues*, Winter 1993, pp. 227–251; and G. Yukl, "Use Power Effectively," in E. A. Locke (ed.), *Handbook of Principles of Organizational Behavior* (Malden, MA: Blackwell, 2004), pp. 242–247.
6. E. A. Ward, "Social Power Bases of Managers: Emergence of a New Factor," *Journal of Social Psychology*, February 2001, pp. 144–147.
7. P. M. Podsakoff and C. A. Schriesheim, "Field Studies of French and Raven's Bases of Power: Critique, Reanalysis, and Suggestions for Future Research," *Psychological Bulletin*, May 1985, pp. 387–411; T. R. Hinkin and C. A. Schriesheim, "Development and Application of New Scales to Measure the French and Raven (1959) Bases of Social Power," *Journal of Applied Psychology*, August 1989, pp. 561–567; and P. P. Carson, K. D. Carson, and C. W. Roe, "Social Power Bases: A Meta-Analytic Examination of Interrelationships and Outcomes" *Journal of Applied Social Psychology* 23, no. 14 (1993), pp. 1150–1169.
8. J. L. Roberts, "Striking a Hot Match," *Newsweek*, January 24, 2005, pp. 54–55.
9. R. E. Emerson, "Power–Dependence Relations," *American Sociological Review*, February 1962, pp. 31–41.
10. H. Mintzberg, *Power In and Around Organizations* (Upper Saddle River, NJ: Prentice Hall, 1983), p. 24.
11. R. M. Cyert and J. G. March, *A Behavioral Theory of the Firm* (Upper Saddle River, NJ: Prentice Hall, 1963).
12. C. Perrow, "Departmental Power and Perspective in Industrial Firms," in M. N. Zald (ed.), *Power in Organizations* (Nashville, TN: Vanderbilt University Press, 1970).
13. N. Foulkes, "Tractor Boy," *High Life*, October 2002, p. 90.
14. See, for example, D. Kipnis and S. M. Schmidt, "Upward-Influence Styles: Relationship with Performance Evaluations, Salary, and Stress," *Administrative Science Quarterly*, December 1988, pp. 528–542; G. Yukl and J. B. Tracey, "Consequences of Influence Tactics Used with Subordinates, Peers, and the Boss," *Journal of Applied Psychology*, August 1992, pp. 525–535; G. Blickle, "Influence Tactics Used by Subordinates: An Empirical Analysis of the Kipnis and Schmidt Subscales," *Psychological Reports*, February 2000, pp. 143–154; and G. Yukl, "Use Power Effectively," pp. 249–252.
15. G. Yukl, *Leadership in Organizations*, 5th ed. (Upper Saddle River, NJ: Prentice Hall, 2002), pp. 141–174; G. R. Ferris, W. A. Hochwarter, C. Douglas, F. R. Blass, R. W. Kolodinksy, and D. C. Treadway, "Social Influence Processes in Organizations and Human Resource Systems," in G. R. Ferris and J. J. Martocchio (eds.), *Research in Personnel and Human Resources Management*, vol. 21 (Oxford, UK: JAI Press/Elsevier, 2003), pp. 65–127; and C. A. Higgins, T. A. Judge, and G. R. Ferris, "Influence Tactics and Work Outcomes: A Meta-analysis," *Journal of Organizational Behavior*, March 2003, pp. 89–106.
16. C. M. Falbe and G. Yukl, "Consequences for Managers of Using Single Influence Tactics and Combinations of Tactics," *Academy of Management Journal*, July 1992, pp. 638–653.
17. J. Badal, "Getting a Raise from the Boss," *Wall Street Journal*, July 8, 2006, pp. B1, B5.
18. Yukl, *Leadership in Organizations*.
19. Ibid.
20. Falbe and Yukl, "Consequences for Managers of Using Single Influence Tactics and Combinations of Tactics."
21. G. R. Ferris, D. C. Treadway, P. L. Perrewé, R. L. Brouer, C. Douglas, and S. Lux, "Political Skill in Organizations," *Journal of Management*, June 2007, pp. 290–320; K. J. Harris, K. M. Kacmar, S. Zivnuska, and J. D. Shaw, "The Impact of Political Skill on Impression Management Effectiveness," *Journal of Applied Psychology* 92, no. 1 (2007), pp. 278–285; W. A. Hochwarter, G. R. Ferris, M. B. Gavin, P. L. Perrewé, A. T. Hall, and D. D. Frink," Political Skill as Neutralizer of Felt Accountability–Job Tension Effects on Job Performance Ratings: A Longitudinal Investigation," *Organizational Behavior and Human Decision Processes* 102 (2007), pp. 226–239; D. C. Treadway, G. R. Ferris, A. B. Duke, G. L. Adams, and J. B. Tatcher, "The Moderating Role of Subordinate Political Skill on Supervisors' Impressions of Subordinate Ingratiation and Ratings of Subordinate Interpersonal Facilitation," *Journal of Applied Psychology* 92, no. 3 (2007), pp. 848–855.
22. www.chicagolegalnet.com; and S. Ellison and J. S. Lublin, "Dial to Pay $10 Million to Settle a Sexual-Harassment Lawsuit," *Wall Street Journal*, April 30, 2003, p. B4.
23. L. J. Munson, C. Hulin, and F. Drasgow, "Longitudinal Analysis of Dispositional Influences and Sexual Harassment: Effects on Job and Psychological Outcomes," *Personnel Psychology*, Spring 2000, pp. 21–46; T. M. Glomb, L. J. Munson,

C. L. Hulin, M. E. Bergman, and F. Drasgow, "Structural Equation Models of Sexual Harassment: Longitudinal Explorations and Cross-Sectional Generalizations," *Journal of Applied Psychology*, February 1999, pp. 14–28; M. E. Bergman, R. D. Langhout, P. A. Palmieri, L. M. Cortina, and L. F. Fitzgerald, "The (Un)reasonableness of Reporting: Antecedents and Consequences of Reporting Sexual Harassment," *Journal of Applied Psychology*, April 2002, pp. 230–242; L. R. Offermann and A. B. Malamut, "When Leaders Harass: The Impact of Target Perceptions of Organizational Leadership and Climate on Harassment Reporting and Outcomes," *Journal of Applied Psychology*, October 2002, pp. 885–893.

24. S. Silverstein and S. Christian, "Harassment Ruling Raises Free-Speech Issues," *Los Angeles Times*, November 11, 1993, p. D2.

25. R. Ilies, N. Hauserman, S. Schwochau, and J. Stibal, "Reported Incidence Rates of Work-Related Sexual Harassment in the United States: Using Meta-analysis to Explain Reported Rate Disparities," *Personnel Psychology*, Fall 2003, pp. 607–631

26. M. Rotundo, D. Nguyen, and P. R. Sackett, "A Meta-Analytic Review of Gender Differences in Perceptions of Sexual Harassment," *Journal of Applied Psychology*, October 2001, pp. 914–922.

27. Ilies, Hauserman, Schwochau, and Stibal, "Reported Incidence Rates of Work-Related Sexual Harassment in the United States; A. B. Malamut and L. R. Offermann, "Coping with Sexual Harassment: Personal, Environmental, and Cognitive Determinants," *Journal of Applied Psychology*, December 2001, pp. 1152–1166, L. M. Cortina and S. A. Wasti, "Profiles in Coping: Responses to Sexual Harassment Across Persons, Organizations, and Cultures," *Journal of Applied Psychology*, February 2005, pp. 182–192.

28. C. R. Willness, P. Steel, and K. Lee, "A Meta-analysis of the Antecedents and Consequences of Workplace Sexual Harassment," *Personnel Psychology* 60 (2007), pp. 127–162.

29. S. A. Culbert and J. J. McDonough, *The Invisible War: Pursuing Self-Interest at Work* (New York: Wiley, 1980), p. 6.

30. Mintzberg, *Power In and Around Organizations*, p. 26. See also K. M. Kacmar and R. A. Baron, "Organizational Politics: The State of the Field, Links to Related Processes, and an Agenda for Future Research," in G. R. Ferris (ed.), *Research in Personnel and Human Resources Management*, vol. 17 (Greenwich, CT: JAI Press, 1999), pp. 1–39; and G. R. Ferris, D. C. Treadway, R. W. Kolokinsky, W. A. Hochwarter, C. J. Kacmar, and D. D. Frink, "Development and Validation of the Political Skill Inventory," *Journal of Management*, February 2005, pp. 126–152.

31. S. B. Bacharach and E. J. Lawler, "Political Alignments in Organizations," in R. M. Kramer and M. A. Neale (eds.), *Power and Influence in Organizations* (Thousand Oaks, CA: Sage, 1998, pp. 68–69.

32. D. Farrell and J. C. Petersen, "Patterns of Political Behavior in Organizations," *Academy of Management Review*, July 1982, p. 405. For analyses of the controversies underlying the definition of organizational politics, see A. Drory and T. Romm, "The Definition of Organizational Politics: A Review," *Human Relations*, November 1990, pp. 1133–1154; and R. S. Cropanzano, K. M. Kacmar, and D. P. Bozeman, "Organizational Politics, Justice, and Support: Their Differences and Similarities," in R. S. Cropanzano and K. M. Kacmar (eds.), *Organizational Politics, Justice and Support: Managing Social Climate at Work* (Westport, CT: Quorum Books, 1995), pp. 1–18.

33. Farrell and Peterson, "Patterns of Political Behavior in Organizations," pp. 406–407; and A. Drory, "Politics in Organization and Its Perception Within the Organization," *Organization Studies* 9, no. 2 (1988), pp. 165–179.

34. J. Pfeffer, *Power in Organizations* (Marshfield, MA: Pitman, 1981).

35. Drory and Romm, "The Definition of Organizational Politics."

36. S. M. Rioux and L. A. Penner, "The Causes of Organizational Citizenship Behavior: A Motivational Analysis," *Journal of Applied Psychology*, December 2001, pp. 1306–1314; and M. A. Finkelstein and L. A. Penner, "Predicting Organizational Citizenship Behavior: Integrating the Functional and Role Identity Approaches," *Social Behavior & Personality* 32, no. 4 (2004), pp. 383–398.

37. A. D. Galinsky, J. C. Magee, M. E. Inesi, and D. H. Gruenfeld, "Power and Perspectives Not Taken," *Psychological Science*, December 2006, pp. 1068–1074.

38. See, for example, G. R. Ferris, G. S. Russ, and P. M. Fandt, "Politics in Organizations," in R. A. Giacalone and P. Rosenfeld (eds.), *Impression Management in the Organization* (Hillsdale, NJ: Lawrence Erlbaum, 1989), pp. 155–156; and W. E. O'Connor and T. G. Morrison, "A Comparison of Situational and Dispositional Predictors of Perceptions of Organizational Politics," *Journal of Psychology*, May 2001, pp. 301–312.

39. Farrell and Petersen, "Patterns of Political Behavior in Organizations," p. 408.

40. G. R. Ferris and K. M. Kacmar, "Perceptions of Organizational Politics," *Journal of Management*, March 1992, pp. 93–116.

41. See, for example, P. M. Fandt and G. R. Ferris, "The Management of Information and Impressions: When Employees Behave Opportunistically," *Organizational Behavior and Human Decision Processes*, February 1990, pp. 140–158; Ferris, Russ, and Fandt, "Politics in Organizations," p. 147; and J. M. L. Poon, "Situational Antecedents and Outcomes of Organizational Politics Perceptions," *Journal of Managerial Psychology* 18, no. 2 (2003), pp. 138–155.

42. Ferris, Russ, and Fandt, "Politics in Organizations"; and K. M. Kacmar, D. P. Bozeman, D. S. Carlson, and W. P. Anthony, "An Examination of the Perceptions of Organizational Politics Model: Replication and Extension," *Human Relations*, March 1999, pp. 383–416.

43. W. A. Hochwarter, C. Kiewitz, S. L. Castro, P. L. Perrewe, and G. R. Ferris, "Positive Affectivity and Collective Efficacy as Moderators of the Relationship Between Perceived Politics and Job Satisfaction," *Journal of Applied Social Psychology*, May 2003, pp. 1009–1035; C. C. Rosen, P. E. Levy, and R. J. Hall, "Placing Perceptions of Politics in the Context of Feedback Environment, Employee Attitudes, and Job Performance," *Journal of Applied Psychology* 91, no. 1 (2006), pp. 211–230.

44. G. R. Ferris, D. D. Frink, M. C. Galang, J. Zhou, K. M. Kacmar, and J. L. Howard, "Perceptions of Organizational Politics: Prediction, Stress-Related Implications, and Outcomes," *Human Relations*, February 1996, pp. 233–266;

E. Vigoda, "Stress-Related Aftermaths to Workplace Politics: The Relationships Among Politics, Job Distress, and Aggressive Behavior in Organizations," *Journal of Organizational Behavior*, August 2002, pp. 571–591.

45. C. Kiewitz, W. A. Hochwarter, G. R. Ferris, and S. L. Castro, "The Role of Psychological Climate in Neutralizing the Effects of Organizational Politics on Work Outcomes," *Journal of Applied Social Psychology*, June 2002, pp. 1189–1207; and M. C. Andrews, L. A. Witt, and K. M. Kacmar, "The Interactive Effects of Organizational Politics and Exchange Ideology on Manager Ratings of Retention," *Journal of Vocational Behavior*, April 2003, pp. 357–369.

46. S. Aryee, Z. Chen, and P. S. Budhwar, "Exchange Fairness and Employee Performance: An Examination of the Relationship Between Organizational Politics and Procedural Justice," *Organizational Behavior & Human Decision Processes*, May 2004, pp. 1–14; and Kacmar, Bozeman, Carlson, and Anthony, "An Examination of the Perceptions of Organizational Politics Model."

47. Kacmar, Bozeman, Carlson, and Anthony, "An Examination of the Perceptions of Organizational Politics Model," p. 389.

48. Ibid., p. 409.

49. B. E. Ashforth and R. T. Lee, "Defensive Behavior in Organizations: A Preliminary Model," *Human Relations*, July 1990, pp. 621–648.

50. M. Valle and P. L. Perrewe, "Do Politics Perceptions Relate to Political Behaviors? Tests of an Implicit Assumption and Expanded Model," *Human Relations*, March 2000, pp. 359–386.

51. See T. Romm and A. Drory, "Political Behavior in Organizations: A Cross-Cultural Comparison," *International Journal of Value Based Management* 1 (1988), pp. 97–113; and E. Vigoda, "Reactions to Organizational Politics: A Cross-Cultural Examination in Israel and Britain," *Human Relations*, November 2001, pp. 1483–1518.

52. E. Vigoda, "Reactions to Organizational Politics," p. 1512.

53. Ibid., p. 1510.

54. M. R. Leary and R. M. Kowalski, "Impression Management: A Literature Review and Two-Component Model," *Psychological Bulletin*, January 1990, pp. 34–47.

55. Ibid., p. 34.

56. See, for instance, B. R. Schlenker, *Impression Management: The Self-Concept, Social Identity, and Interpersonal Relations* (Monterey, CA: Brooks/Cole, 1980); W. L. Gardner and M. J. Martinko, "Impression Management in Organizations," *Journal of Management*, June 1988, pp. 321–338; D. P. Bozeman and K. M. Kacmar, "A Cybernetic Model of Impression Management Processes in Organizations," *Organizational Behavior and Human Decision Processes*, January 1997, pp. 9–30; M. C. Bolino and W. H. Turnley, "More Than One Way to Make an Impression: Exploring Profiles of Impression Management," *Journal of Management* 29, no. 2 (2003), pp. 141–160; S. Zivnuska, K. M. Kacmar, L. A. Witt, D. S. Carlson, and V. K. Bratton, "Interactive Effects of Impression Management and Organizational Politics on Job Performance," *Journal of Organizational Behavior*, August 2004, pp. 627–640; and W.-C. Tsai, C.-C. Chen, and S.-F. Chiu, "Exploring Boundaries of the Effects of Applicant Impression Management Tactics in Job Interviews," *Journal of Management*, February 2005, pp. 108–125.

57. M. Snyder and J. Copeland, "Self-monitoring Processes in Organizational Settings," in Giacalone and Rosenfeld (eds.), *Impression Management in the Organization* (Hillsdale, NJ: Lawrence Erlbaum, 1989), p. 11; A. Montagliani and R. A. Giacalone, "Impression Management and Cross-Cultural Adaptation," *Journal of Social Psychology*, October 1998, pp. 598–608; and W. H. Turnley and M. C. Bolino, "Achieved Desired Images While Avoiding Undesired Images: Exploring the Role of Self-Monitoring in Impression Management," *Journal of Applied Psychology*, April 2001, pp. 351–360.

58. Leary and Kowalski, "Impression Management," p. 40.

59. Gardner and Martinko, "Impression Management in Organizations," p. 333.

60. R. A. Baron, "Impression Management by Applicants During Employment Interviews: The 'Too Much of a Good Thing' Effect," in R. W. Eder and G. R. Ferris (eds.), *The Employment Interview: Theory, Research, and Practice* (Newbury Park, CA: Sage Publishers, 1989), pp. 204–215.

61. Ferris, Russ, and Fandt, "Politics in Organizations."

62. A. P. J. Ellis, B. J. West, A. M. Ryan, and R. P. DeShon, "The Use of Impression Management Tactics in Structural Interviews: A Function of Question Type?" *Journal of Applied Psychology*, December 2002, pp. 1200–1208.

63. Baron, "Impression Management by Applicants During Employment Interviews"; D. C. Gilmore and G. R. Ferris, "The Effects of Applicant Impression Management Tactics on Interviewer Judgments," *Journal of Management*, December 1989, pp. 557–564; C. K. Stevens and A. L. Kristof, "Making the Right Impression: A Field Study of Applicant Impression Management During Job Interviews," *Journal of Applied Psychology* 80 (1995), pp. 587–606; and L. A. McFarland, A. M. Ryan, and S. D. Kriska, "Impression Management Use and Effectiveness Across Assessment Methods," *Journal of Management* 29, no. 5 (2003), pp. 641–661; and Tsai, Chen, and Chiu, "Exploring Boundaries of the Effects of Applicant Impression Management Tactics in Job Interviews."

64. Gilmore and Ferris, "The Effects of Applicant Impression Management Tactics on Interviewer Judgments."

65. Stevens and Kristof, "Making the Right Impression: A Field Study of Applicant Impression Management During Job Interviews."

66. C. A. Higgins, T. A. Judge, and G. R. Ferris, "Influence Tactics and Work Outcomes: A Meta-Analysis," *Journal of Organizational Behavior*, March 2003, pp. 89–106.

67. Ibid.

68. J. D. Westphal and I. Stern, "Flattery Will Get You Everywhere (Especially if You Are a Male Caucasian): How Ingratiation, Boardroom Behavior, and Demographic Minority Status Affect Additional Board Appointments of U.S. Companies," *Academy of Management Journal* 50, no. 2 (2007), pp. 267–288.

69. O. J. Labedo, "Perceptions of Organisational Politics: Examination of the Situational Antecedent and Consequences Among Nigeria's Extension Personnel," *Applied Psychology: An International Review* 55, no. 2 (2006), pp. 255–281.

70. P. P. Fu and G. Yukl, "Perceived Effectiveness of Influence Tactics in the United States and China," *Leadership Quarterly*, Summer 2000, pp. 251–266; O. Branzei, "Cultural Explanations of Individual Preferences for Influence Tactics in Cross-Cultural Encounters," *International Journal of Cross Cultural Management*, August 2002, pp. 203–218; G. Yukl, P. P. Fu, and R. McDonald, "Cross-Cultural Differences in Perceived Effectiveness of Influence Tactics for Initiating or Resisting Change," *Applied Psychology: An International Review*, January 2003, pp. 66–82; and P. P. Fu, T. K. Peng, J. C. Kennedy, and G. Yukl, "Examining the Preferences of Influence Tactics in Chinese Societies: A Comparison of Chinese Managers in Hong Kong, Taiwan, and Mainland China," *Organizational Dynamics* 33, no. 1 (2004), pp. 32–46.

71. Fu and Yukl, "Perceived Effectiveness of Influence Tactics in the United States and China."

72. S. J. Heine, "Making Sense of East Asian Self-Enhancement," *Journal of Cross-Cultural Psychology*, September 2003, pp. 596–602.

73. J. L. T. Leong, M. H. Bond, and P. P. Fu, "Perceived Effectiveness of Influence Strategies in the United States and Three Chinese Societies," *International Journal of Cross Cultural Management*, May 2006, pp. 101–120.

74. R. M. Kanter, *Men and Women of the Corporation* (New York: Basic Books, 1977).

75. See, for instance, Falbe and Yukl, "Consequences for Managers of Using Single Influence Tactics and Combinations of Tactics."

76. See J. G. Bachman, D. G. Bowers, and P. M. Marcus, "Bases of Supervisory Power: A Comparative Study in Five Organizational Settings," in A. S. Tannenbaum (ed.), *Control in Organizations* (New York: McGraw-Hill, 1968), p. 236; M. A. Rahim, "Relationships of Leader Power to Compliance and Satisfaction with Supervision: Evidence from a National Sample of Managers," *Journal of Management*, December 1989, pp. 545–556; P. A. Wilson, "The Effects of Politics and Power on the Organizational Commitment of Federal Executives," *Journal of Management*, Spring 1995, pp. 101–118; and A. R. Elangovan and J. L. Xie, "Effects of Perceived Power of Supervisor on Subordinate Stress and Motivation: The Moderating Role of Subordinate Characteristics," *Journal of Organizational Behavior*, May 1999, pp. 359–373.

77. J. Pfeffer, *Managing with Power: Politics and Influence in Organizations* (Boston: Harvard Business School Press, 1992).

78. G. R. Ferris, P. L. Perrewé, W. P. Anthony, and D. C. Gilmore, "Political Skill at Work," *Organizational Dynamics*, Spring 2000, pp. 25–37; K. K. Ahearn, G. R. Ferris, W. A. Hochwarter, C. Douglas, and A. P. Ammeter, "Leader Political Skill and Team Performance," *Journal of Management* 30, no. 3 (2004), pp. 309–327; and S. E. Seibert, M. L. Kraimer, and J. M. Crant, "What Do Proactive People Do? A Longitudinal Model Linking Proactive Personality and Career Success," *Personnel Psychology*, Winter 2001, pp. 845–874.

79. R. W. Kolodinsky, W. A. Hochwarter, and G. R. Ferris, "Nonlinearity in the Relationship Between Political Skill and Work Outcomes: Convergent Evidence from Three Studies," *Journal of Vocational Behavior*, October 2004, pp. 294–308; W. Hochwarter, "The Interactive Effects of Pro-Political Behavior and Politics Perceptions on Job Satisfaction and Affective Commitment," *Journal of Applied Social Psychology*, July 2003, pp. 1360–1378; and P. L. Perrewé, K. L. Zellars, G. R. Ferris, A. Rossi, C. J. Kacmar, and D. A. Ralston, "Neutralizing Job Stressors: Political Skill as an Antidote to the Dysfunctional Consequences of Role Conflict," *Academy of Management Journal*, February 2004, pp. 141–152.

Conflict and Negotiation

Let us never negotiate out of fear. But let us never fear to negotiate.

—Former U.S. President John F. Kennedy

LEARNING OBJECTIVES

After studying this chapter, you should be able to:

1. Define *conflict*.
2. Differentiate between the traditional, human relations, and interactionist views of conflict.
3. Outline the conflict process.
4. Define *negotiation*.
5. Contrast distributive and integrative bargaining.
6. Apply the five steps of the negotiation process.
7. Show how individual differences influence negotiations.
8. Assess the roles and functions of third-party negotiations.
9. Describe cultural differences in negotiations.

Despite a storied history and one of the best-known brand names in all of consumer products, H. J. Heinz Co. has had its share of troubles in the past decade. The company's earnings have been flat, and despite a recent upswing, Heinz's stock is well below the price at which it traded 10 years ago.

Enter Nelson Peltz, CEO and founding partner of Trian Fund Management L.P. Peltz thought Heinz's underperforming stock represented an opportunity, so

Ketchup Fight

he gradually acquired 3 percent of Heinz's shares—enough to land a seat on Heinz's board of directors, where he began lobbying for changes.

Peltz's play at Heinz is nothing new to him—he bought a 3 percent share in Kraft, a 2.98 percent stake in Cadbury Schweppes PLC, a 5.54 percent stake in Tiffany & Co., and a 5.5 percent share of Wendy's International, Inc. His goal is to buy a big enough stake to be able to lobby for changes that will raise the company's stock price, at which time he can cash in on his investment. Generally, Peltz targets high-profile consumer products companies whose stock has been underperforming.

When investors such as Peltz, Carl Icahn, or Kirk Kerkorian push for shareholder-led changes in a company, often the CEO chafes. However, in this case, the conflict became personal. Heinz CEO William R. Johnson angrily wrote to Peltz, "Now is not the time for adding a self-interested and divisive voice inside the Heinz boardroom." Peltz retorted, "Maybe they need some adult supervision." Another Heinz director entered the fight, calling Peltz "infuriating."

Like many other conflicts that turn personal, this one started out as a difference in strategies and tactics. Johnson's focus for Heinz's turnaround was on restructuring. He believed Heinz was spread too thin, and he has tried to focus the company on its best-selling brands. Peltz's goal was to cut costs even further and, at the same time, invest more in advertising to make the most of the Heinz brand.

Though it's hard to make cause-and-effect inferences for a single incident, it appears that the conflict has produced some tasty results for Heinz and its stakeholders. Since Heinz's aggressive advertising campaign last fall, the company's stock is up roughly 11 percent.

While you'd think the company's successes would ease tensions between Peltz and Johnson, personality conflicts don't often heal. Recently, when Peltz was told that Johnson claimed ownership of the idea for the advertising campaign, Peltz called that "an utter lie."[1] ■

As we see in the Heinz example, conflict can often turn personal. It can create chaotic conditions that make it nearly impossible for employees to work as a team. However, conflict also has a less-well-known positive side. We'll explain the difference between negative and positive conflicts in this chapter and provide a guide to help you understand how conflicts develop. We'll also present a topic closely akin to conflict: negotiation. But first, gauge how you handle conflict by taking the following self-assessment.

WHAT'S MY PREFERRED CONFLICT-HANDLING STYLE?

In the Self-Assessment Library (available on CD and online), take assessment II.C.5 (What's My Preferred Conflict-Handling Style?) and answer the following questions.

1. *Judging from your highest score, what's your primary conflict-handling style?*
2. *Do you think your style varies, depending on the situation?*
3. *Would you like to change any aspects of your conflict-handling style?*

A Definition of *Conflict*

1 *Define* conflict.

There has been no shortage of definitions of *conflict*.[2] Despite the divergent meanings the term has acquired, several common themes underlie most definitions. Conflict must be perceived by the parties to it; whether or not conflict exists is a perception issue. If no one is aware of a conflict, then it is generally agreed that no conflict exists. Additional commonalities in the definitions are opposition or incompatibility and some form of interaction.[3] These factors set the conditions that determine the beginning point of the conflict process.

We can define **conflict**, then, as a process that begins when one party perceives that another party has negatively affected, or is about to negatively affect, something that the first party cares about.[4] This definition is purposely broad. It describes that point in any ongoing activity when an interaction "crosses over" to become an interparty conflict. It encompasses the wide range of conflicts that people experience in organizations—incompatibility of goals, differences over interpretations of facts, disagreements based on behavioral expectations, and the like. Finally, our definition is flexible enough to cover the full range of conflict levels—from overt and violent acts to subtle forms of disagreement.

Transitions in Conflict Thought

2 *Differentiate between the traditional, human relations, and interactionist views of conflict.*

It is entirely appropriate to say there has been conflict over the role of conflict in groups and organizations. One school of thought has argued that conflict must be avoided—that it indicates a malfunctioning within the group. We call this the *traditional* view. Another school of thought, the *human relations* view, argues that conflict is a natural and inevitable outcome in any group and that it need not be evil but rather has the potential to be a positive force in determining group performance. The third, and most recent, perspective proposes not only that conflict can be a positive force in a group but explicitly argues that some conflict is *absolutely necessary* for a group to perform effectively. We label this third school the *interactionist* view. Let's take a closer look at each of these views.

The Traditional View of Conflict

The early approach to conflict assumed that all conflict was bad. Conflict was viewed negatively, and it was used synonymously with such terms as *violence, destruction*, and *irrationality* to reinforce its negative connotation. Conflict, by definition, was harmful and was to be avoided. The **traditional view of conflict** was consistent with the attitudes that prevailed about group behavior in the 1930s and 1940s. Conflict was seen as a dysfunctional outcome resulting from poor communication, a lack of openness and trust between people, and the failure of managers to be responsive to the needs and aspirations of their employees.

The view that all conflict is bad certainly offers a simple approach to looking at the behavior of people who create conflict. Because all conflict is to be avoided, we need merely direct our attention to the causes of conflict and correct those malfunctions to improve group and organizational performance. Although research studies now provide strong evidence to dispute that this approach to conflict reduction results in high group performance, many of us still evaluate conflict situations using this outmoded standard.

conflict *A process that begins when one party perceives that another party has negatively affected, or is about to negatively affect, something that the first party cares about.*

traditional view of conflict *The belief that all conflict is harmful and must be avoided.*

The Human Relations View of Conflict

The **human relations view of conflict** argued that conflict was a natural occurrence in all groups and organizations. Because conflict was inevitable, the human relations school advocated acceptance of conflict. Proponents rationalized its existence: It cannot be eliminated, and there are even times when conflict may benefit a group's performance. The human relations view dominated conflict theory from the late 1940s through the mid-1970s.

The Interactionist View of Conflict

Whereas the human relations view accepted conflict, the **interactionist view of conflict** encourages conflict on the grounds that a harmonious, peaceful, tranquil, and cooperative group is prone to becoming static, apathetic, and nonresponsive to needs for change and innovation.[5] The major contribution of the interactionist view, therefore, is encouraging group leaders to maintain an ongoing minimum level of conflict—enough to keep the group viable, self-critical, and creative.

The interactionist view does not propose that all conflicts are good. Rather, some conflicts support the goals of the group and improve its performance; these are **functional**, constructive, forms of conflict. In addition, there are conflicts that hinder group performance; these are **dysfunctional**, or destructive, forms of conflict. What differentiates functional from dysfunctional conflict? The evidence indicates that you need to look at the *type* of conflict.[6] Specifically, there are three types: task, relationship, and process.

Task conflict relates to the content and goals of the work. **Relationship conflict** focuses on interpersonal relationships. **Process conflict** relates to how the work gets done. Studies demonstrate that relationship conflicts are almost always dysfunctional.[7] Why? It appears that the friction and interpersonal hostilities inherent in relationship conflicts increase personality clashes and decrease mutual understanding, which hinders the completion of organizational tasks. Unfortunately, managers spend a lot of their time resolving personality conflicts; one survey indicated that 18 percent of managers' time is spent trying to resolve personality conflicts among staff members.[8]

Unlike with relationship conflict, low levels of process conflict and low to moderate levels of task conflict are functional. For process conflict to be productive, it must be kept low. Intense arguments about who should do what become dysfunctional when they create uncertainty about task roles, increase the time to complete tasks, and lead to members working at cross purposes. Low-to-moderate levels of task conflict consistently demonstrate a positive effect on group performance because it stimulates discussion of ideas that helps groups perform better.

The Conflict Process

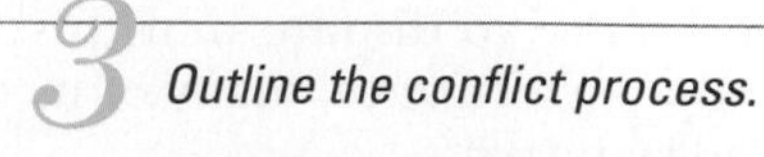

The **conflict process** has five stages: potential opposition or incompatibility, cognition and personalization, intentions, behavior, and outcomes. The process is diagrammed in Exhibit 15-1.

Stage I: Potential Opposition or Incompatibility

The first step in the conflict process is the presence of conditions that create opportunities for conflict to arise. They *need not* lead directly to conflict, but one of these conditions is necessary if conflict is to surface. For simplicity's sake, these conditions (which we can also look at as causes or sources of conflict)

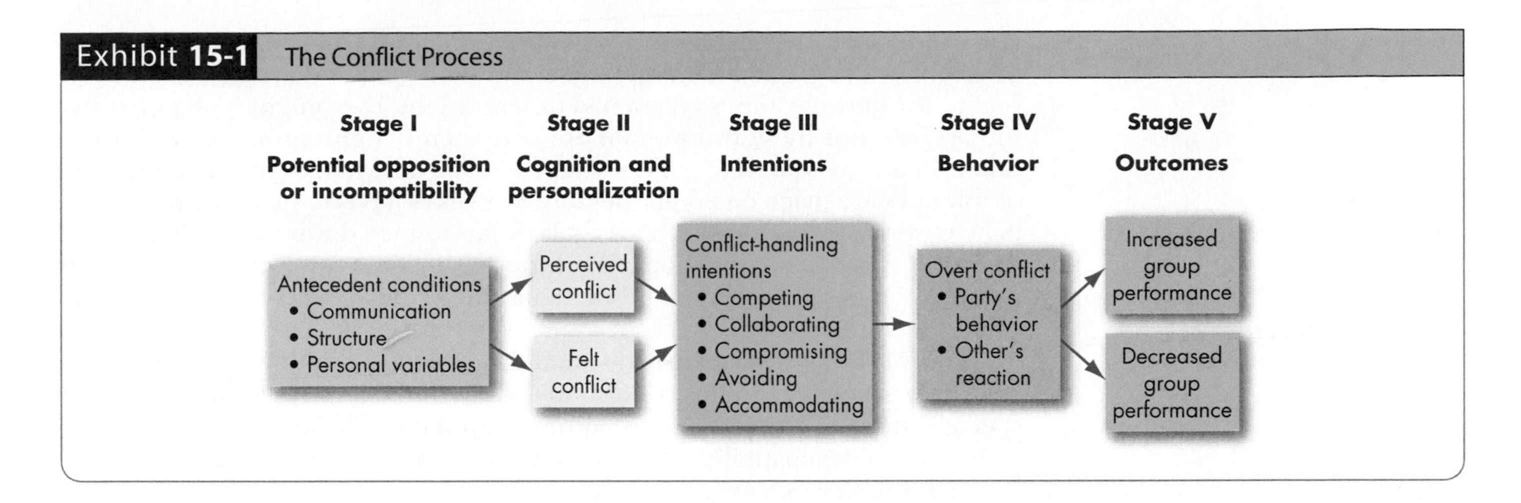

have been condensed into three general categories: communication, structure, and personal variables.

Communication Susan had worked in supply-chain management at Bristol-Myers Squibb for 3 years. She enjoyed her work in large part because her boss, Tim McGuire, was a great guy to work for. Then Tim got promoted 6 months ago, and Chuck Benson took his place. Susan says her job is a lot more frustrating now. "Tim and I were on the same wavelength. It's not that way with Chuck. He tells me something and I do it. Then he tells me I did it wrong. I think he means one thing but says something else. It's been like this since the day he arrived. I don't think a day goes by when he isn't yelling at me for something. You know, there are some people you just find it easy to communicate with. Well, Chuck isn't one of those!"

Susan's comments illustrate that communication can be a source of conflict.[9] They represent the opposing forces that arise from semantic difficulties, misunderstandings, and "noise" in the communication channels. Much of this discussion can be related to our comments on communication in Chapter 11.

A review of the research suggests that differing word connotations, jargon, insufficient exchange of information, and noise in the communication channel are all barriers to communication and potential antecedent conditions to conflict. Research has further demonstrated a surprising finding: The potential for conflict increases when either too little or too much communication takes place. Apparently, an increase in communication is functional up to a point, whereupon it is possible to overcommunicate, with a resultant increase in the potential for conflict.

Structure Charlotte and Svetlana both work at the Furniture Mart—a large discount furniture retailer. Charlotte is a salesperson on the floor, and Svetlana is the company credit manager. The two women have known each other for

human relations view of conflict *The belief that conflict is a natural and inevitable outcome in any group.*

interactionist view of conflict *The belief that conflict is not only a positive force in a group but that it is also an absolute necessity for a group to perform effectively.*

functional conflict *Conflict that supports the goals of the group and improves its performance.*

dysfunctional conflict *Conflict that hinders group performance.*

task conflict *Conflict over content and goals of the work.*

relationship conflict *Conflict based on interpersonal relationships.*

process conflict *Conflict over how work gets done.*

conflict process *A process that has five stages: potential opposition or incompatibility, cognition and personalization, intentions, behavior, and outcomes.*

years and have much in common: They live within two blocks of each other, and their oldest daughters attend the same middle school and are best friends. In reality, if Charlotte and Svetlana had different jobs, they might be best friends themselves, but these two women are consistently fighting battles with each other. Charlotte's job is to sell furniture, and she does a heck of a job. But most of her sales are made on credit. Because Svetlana's job is to make sure the company minimizes credit losses, she regularly has to turn down the credit application of a customer with whom Charlotte has just closed a sale. It's nothing personal between Charlotte and Svetlana; the requirements of their jobs just bring them into conflict.

The conflicts between Charlotte and Svetlana are structural in nature. The term *structure* is used, in this context, to include variables such as size, degree of specialization in the tasks assigned to group members, jurisdictional clarity, member-goal compatibility, leadership styles, reward systems, and the degree of dependence between groups.

Research indicates that size and specialization act as forces to stimulate conflict. The larger the group and the more specialized its activities, the greater the likelihood of conflict. Tenure and conflict have been found to be inversely related. The potential for conflict tends to be greatest when group members are younger and when turnover is high.

The greater the ambiguity in precisely defining where responsibility for actions lies, the greater the potential for conflict to emerge. Such jurisdictional ambiguities increase intergroup fighting for control of resources and territory. Diversity of goals among groups is also a major source of conflict. When groups within an organization seek diverse ends, some of which—like sales and credit at the Furniture Mart—are inherently at odds, there are increased opportunities for conflict. Reward systems, too, are found to create conflict when one member's gain is at another's expense. Finally, if a group is dependent on another group (in contrast to the two being mutually independent) or if interdependence allows one group to gain at another's expense, opposing forces are stimulated.[10]

Personal variables such as personality differences can be the source of conflict among coworkers. To reduce conflict resulting from personality differences, Vertex Pharmaceuticals teaches employees how to identify other people's personality types and then how to communicate effectively with them. At Vertex, innovation is critical to the company's mission of developing drugs that treat life-threatening diseases. By training employees to work harmoniously in spite of personality differences, Vertex hopes to eliminate unproductive conflict that impedes innovation.

Personal Variables Have you ever met someone to whom you took an immediate disliking? You disagreed with most of the opinions they expressed. Even insignificant characteristics—the sound of their voice, the smirk when they smiled, their personality—annoyed you. We've all met people like that. When you have to work with such individuals, there is often the potential for conflict.

Our last category of potential sources of conflict is personal variables, which include personality, emotions, and values. Evidence indicates that certain personality types—for example, individuals who are highly authoritarian and dogmatic—lead to potential conflict. Emotions can also cause conflict. For example, an employee who shows up to work irate from her hectic morning commute may carry that anger with her to her 9 A.M. meeting. The problem? Her anger can annoy her colleagues, which may lead to a tension-filled meeting.[11]

Stage II: Cognition and Personalization

If the conditions cited in Stage I negatively affect something that one party cares about, then the potential for opposition or incompatibility becomes actualized in the second stage.

As we noted in our definition of conflict, perception is required. Therefore, one or more of the parties must be aware of the existence of the antecedent conditions. However, because a conflict is **perceived conflict** does not mean that it is personalized. In other words, "*A* may be aware that *B* and *A* are in serious disagreement . . . but it may not make *A* tense or anxious, and it may have no effect whatsoever on *A*'s affection toward *B*."[12] It is at the **felt conflict** level, when individuals become emotionally involved, that parties experience anxiety, tension, frustration, or hostility.

Keep in mind two points. First, Stage II is important because it's where conflict issues tend to be defined. This is the place in the process where the parties decide what the conflict is about.[13] In turn, this "sense making" is critical because the way a conflict is defined goes a long way toward establishing the sort of outcomes that might settle it. For instance, if I define our salary disagreement as a zero-sum situation (that is, if you get the increase in pay you want, there will be just that amount less for me) I am going to be far less willing to compromise than if I frame the conflict as a potential win/win situation (that is, the dollars in the salary pool might be increased so that both of us could get the added pay we want). So the definition of a conflict is important because it typically delineates the set of possible settlements. Our second point is that emotions play a major role in shaping perceptions.[14] For example, negative emotions have been found to produce oversimplification of issues, reductions in trust, and negative interpretations of the other party's behavior.[15] In contrast, positive feelings have been found to increase the tendency to see potential relationships among the elements of a problem, to take a broader view of the situation, and to develop more innovative solutions.[16]

Stage III: Intentions

Intentions intervene between people's perceptions and emotions and their overt behavior. These intentions are decisions to act in a given way.[17]

Intentions are separated out as a distinct stage because you have to infer the other's intent to know how to respond to that other's behavior. A lot of conflicts

perceived conflict *Awareness by one or more parties of the existence of conditions that create opportunities for conflict to arise.*

felt conflict *Emotional involvement in a conflict that creates anxiety, tenseness, frustration, or hostility.*

intentions *Decisions to act in a given way.*

Exhibit 15-2 Dimensions of Conflict-Handling Intentions

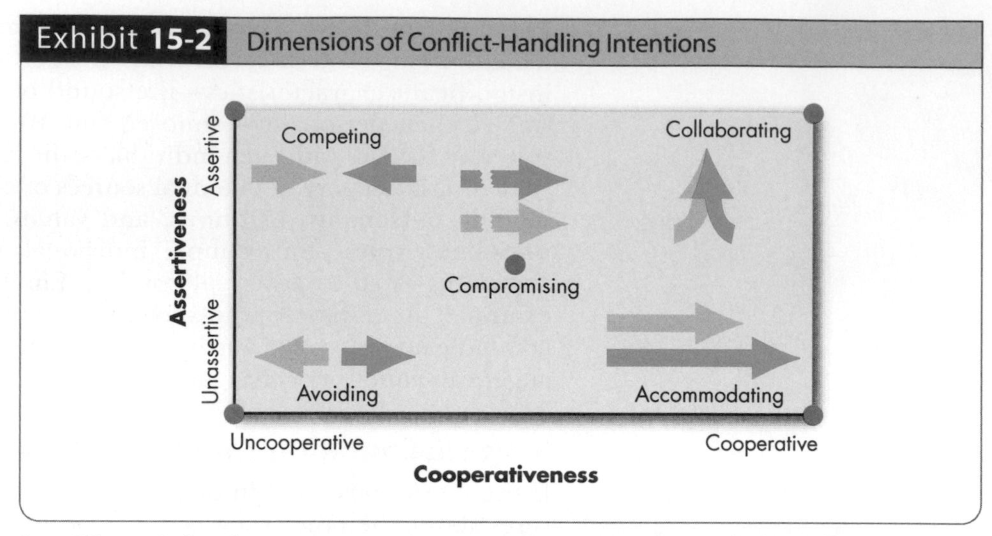

Source: K. Thomas, "Conflict and Negotiation Processes in Organizations," in M. D. Dunnette and L. M. Hough (eds.), *Handbook of Industrial and Organizational Psychology*, 2nd ed. vol. 3 (Palo Alto, CA: Consulting Psychologists Press, 1992), p. 668. Used with permission.

are escalated merely by one party attributing the wrong intentions to the other party. In addition, there is typically a great deal of slippage between intentions and behavior, so behavior does not always accurately reflect a person's intentions.

Exhibit 15-2 represents one author's effort to identify the primary conflict-handling intentions. Using two dimensions—*cooperativeness* (the degree to which one party attempts to satisfy the other party's concerns) and *assertiveness* (the degree to which one party attempts to satisfy his or her own concerns)—five conflict-handling intentions can be identified: *competing* (assertive and uncooperative), *collaborating* (assertive and cooperative), *avoiding* (unassertive and uncooperative), *accommodating* (unassertive and cooperative), and *compromising* (midrange on both assertiveness and cooperativeness).[18]

Competing When one person seeks to satisfy his or her own interests, regardless of the impact on the other parties to the conflict, that person is **competing**. Competing is when you, for example, win a bet and your opponent loses.

Collaborating When the parties to conflict each desire to fully satisfy the concerns of all parties, there is cooperation and a search for a mutually beneficial outcome. In **collaborating**, the intention of the parties is to solve a problem by clarifying differences rather than by accommodating various points of view. If you attempt to find a win/win solution that allows both parties' goals to be completely achieved, that's collaborating.

Avoiding A person may recognize that a conflict exists and want to withdraw from it or suppress it. Examples of **avoiding** include trying to just ignore a conflict and avoiding others with whom you disagree.

Accommodating When one party seeks to appease an opponent, that party may be willing to place the opponent's interests above his or her own. In other words, in order for the relationship to be maintained, one party needs to be willing to be self-sacrificing. We refer to this intention as **accommodating**. Supporting someone else's opinion despite your reservations about it, for example, would represent accommodating.

Compromising When each party to a conflict seeks to give up something, sharing occurs, resulting in a compromised outcome. In **compromising**, there is no clear winner or loser. Rather, there is a willingness to ration the object of the conflict and accept a solution that provides incomplete satisfaction of both parties' concerns. The distinguishing characteristic of compromising, therefore, is that each party intends to give up something.

Intentions are not always fixed. During the course of a conflict, they might change because of reconceptualization or because of an emotional reaction to the behavior of the other party. However, research indicates that people have an underlying disposition to handle conflicts in certain ways.[19] Specifically, individuals have preferences among the five conflict-handling intentions just described; these preferences tend to be relied on quite consistently, and a person's intentions can be predicted rather well from a combination of intellectual and personality characteristics.

Stage IV: Behavior

When most people think of conflict situations, they tend to focus on Stage IV because this is where conflicts become visible. The behavior stage includes the statements, actions, and reactions made by the conflicting parties. These conflict behaviors are usually overt attempts to implement each party's intentions. But these behaviors have a stimulus quality that is separate from intentions. As a result of miscalculations or unskilled enactments, overt behaviors sometimes deviate from original intentions.[20]

It helps to think of Stage IV as a dynamic process of interaction. For example, you make a demand on me, I respond by arguing, you threaten me, I threaten you back, and so on. Exhibit 15-3 provides a way of visualizing conflict behavior. All conflicts exist somewhere along this continuum. At the lower part of the continuum are conflicts characterized by subtle, indirect, and highly controlled forms of tension. An illustration might be a student questioning in class a point the instructor has just made. Conflict intensities escalate as they move upward along the continuum until they become highly destructive. Strikes, riots, and wars clearly fall in this upper range. For the most part, you should assume that conflicts that reach the upper ranges of the continuum are almost

Exhibit 15-3 Conflict-Intensity Continuum

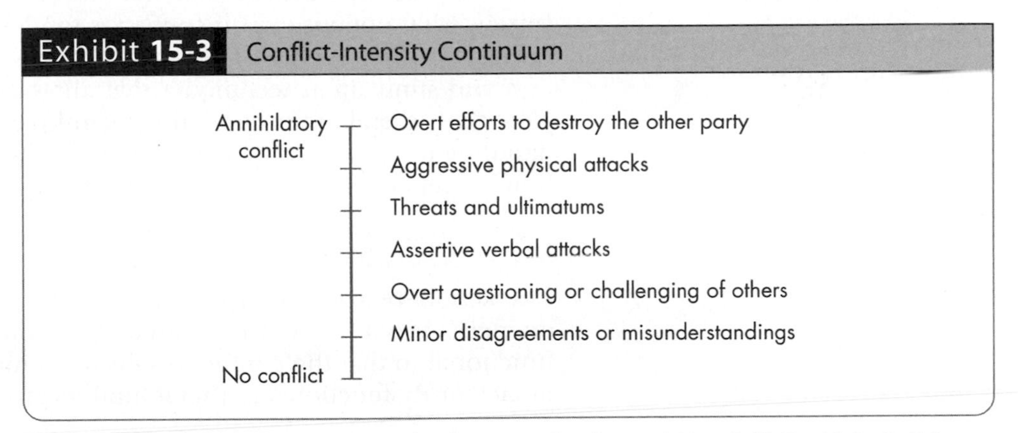

Source: Based on S. P. Robbins, *Managing Organizational Conflict: A Nontraditional Approach* (Upper Saddle River, NJ: Prentice Hall, 1974), pp. 93–97; and F. Glasi, "The Process of Conflict Escalation and the Roles of Third Parties," in G. B. J. Bomers and R. Peterson (eds.), *Conflict Management and Industrial Relations* (Boston: Kluwer-Nijhoff, 1982), pp. 119–140.

competing *A desire to satisfy one's interests, regardless of the impact on the other party to the conflict.*

collaborating *A situation in which the parties to a conflict each desire to satisfy fully the concerns of all parties.*

avoiding *The desire to withdraw from or suppress a conflict.*

accommodating *The willingness of one party in a conflict to place the opponent's interests above his or her own.*

compromising *A situation in which each party to a conflict is willing to give up something.*

Exhibit 15-4 Conflict-Management Techniques

Conflict-Resolution Techniques	
Problem solving	Face-to-face meeting of the conflicting parties for the purpose of identifying the problem and resolving it through open discusssion.
Superordinate goals	Creating a shared goal that cannot be attained without the cooperation of each of the conflicting parties.
Expansion of resources	When a conflict is caused by the scarcity of a resource—say, money, promotion, opportunities, office space—expansion of the resource can create a win/win solution.
Avoidance	Withdrawal from or suppression of the conflict.
Smoothing	Playing down differences while emphasizing common interests between the conflicting parties.
Compromise	Each party to the conflict gives up something of value.
Authoritative command	Management uses its formal authority to resolve the conflict and then communicates its desires to the parties involved.
Altering the human variable	Using behavioral change techniques such as human relations training to alter attitudes and behaviors that cause conflict.
Altering the structural variables	Changing the formal organization structure and the interaction patterns of conflicting parties through job redesign, transfers, creation of coordinating positions, and the like.
Conflict-Stimulation Techniques	
Communication	Using ambiguous or threatening messages to increase conflict levels.
Bringing in outsiders	Adding employees to a group whose backgrounds, values, attitudes, or managerial styles differ from those of present members.
Restructuring the organization	Realigning work groups, altering rules and regulations, increasing interdependence, and making similar structural changes to disrupt the status quo.
Appointing a devil's advocate	Designating a critic to purposely argue against the majority positions held by the group.

Source: Based on S. P. Robbins, *Managing Organizational Conflict: A Nontraditional Approach* (Upper Saddle River, NJ: Prentice Hall, 1974), pp. 59–89.

always dysfunctional. Functional conflicts are typically confined to the lower range of the continuum.

If a conflict is dysfunctional, what can the parties do to de-escalate it? Or, conversely, what options exist if conflict is too low and needs to be increased? This brings us to **conflict-management** techniques. Exhibit 15-4 lists the major resolution and stimulation techniques that allow managers to control conflict levels. Note that several of the resolution techniques were described earlier as conflict-handling intentions. This, of course, shouldn't be surprising. Under ideal conditions, a person's intentions should translate into comparable behaviors.

Stage V: Outcomes

The action–reaction interplay between the conflicting parties results in consequences. As our model (see Exhibit 15-1) demonstrates, these outcomes may be functional in that the conflict results in an improvement in the group's performance or dysfunctional in that it hinders group performance.

Functional Outcomes How might conflict act as a force to increase group performance? It is hard to visualize a situation in which open or violent aggression could be functional. But there are a number of instances in which it's possible to envision how low or moderate levels of conflict could improve the effectiveness of a group. Because people often find it difficult to think of instances in which conflict can be constructive, let's consider some examples and then review the research evidence. Note how all these examples focus on task and process conflicts and exclude the relationship variety.

Conflict is constructive when it improves the quality of decisions, stimulates creativity and innovation, encourages interest and curiosity among group

A lack of functional conflict among General Motors management in past decades resulted in concessions to union demands for generous health benefits and pensions. Today, burdened by health costs that GM provides to more than 1 million employees, retirees, and dependents, the automaker is eliminating jobs and closing assembly plants as part of a cost-cutting strategy. The two employees shown here embrace as the last automobile rolls off the assembly line at GM's plant in Linden, New Jersey, which GM closed after 68 years of operation.

members, provides the medium through which problems can be aired and tensions released, and fosters an environment of self-evaluation and change. The evidence suggests that conflict can improve the quality of decision making by allowing all points, particularly the ones that are unusual or held by a minority, to be weighed in important decisions.[21] Conflict is an antidote for groupthink. It doesn't allow the group to passively "rubber-stamp" decisions that may be based on weak assumptions, inadequate consideration of relevant alternatives, or other debilities. Conflict challenges the status quo and therefore furthers the creation of new ideas, promotes reassessment of group goals and activities, and increases the probability that the group will respond to change.

For an example of a company that suffered because it had too little functional conflict, you don't have to look further than automobile behemoth General Motors.[22] Many of GM's problems, from the late 1960s to the present day, can be traced to a lack of functional conflict. GM hired and promoted individuals who were yespeople, loyal to GM to the point of never questioning company actions. Many, like GM investor Kirk Kekorian, fault GM management's conflict aversion for its acceding to the UAW's demands for generous health care and pension benefits. (GM's labor costs average $73.26 per hour, which is much higher than for its Japanese competitors.) In fairness to GM, Chrysler and Ford also approved similar benefits, but they've struggled mightily as well.

Conflict aversion is not limited to the automakers. Yahoo!'s former CEO Tim Koogle was so conflict averse that a sense of complacency settled in that left managers afraid to challenge the status quo. Even though Yahoo! started out much more successful than Google, it was soon overtaken, and most now believe it will never catch up.

Research studies in diverse settings confirm the functionality of conflict. Consider the following findings. Conflict can also positively relate to productivity.

conflict management *The use of resolution and stimulation techniques to achieve the desired level of conflict.*

For instance, it was demonstrated that, among established groups, performance tended to improve more when there was conflict among members than when there was fairly close agreement. The investigators observed that when groups analyzed decisions that had been made by the individual members of that group, the average improvement among the high-conflict groups was 73 percent greater than that of those groups characterized by low-conflict conditions.[23] Others have found similar results: Groups composed of members with different interests tend to produce higher-quality solutions to a variety of problems than do homogeneous groups.[24]

The preceding leads us to predict that the increasing cultural diversity of the workforce should provide benefits to organizations. And that's what the evidence indicates. Research demonstrates that heterogeneity among group and organization members can increase creativity, improve the quality of decisions, and facilitate change by enhancing member flexibility.[25] For example, researchers compared decision-making groups composed of all-Caucasian individuals with groups that also contained members from Asian, Hispanic, and black ethnic groups. The ethnically diverse groups produced more effective and more feasible ideas and the unique ideas they generated tended to be of higher quality than the unique ideas produced by the all-Caucasian group.

Dysfunctional Outcomes The destructive consequences of conflict on a group's or an organization's performance are generally well known. A reasonable summary might state: Uncontrolled opposition breeds discontent, which acts to dissolve common ties and eventually leads to the destruction of the group. And, of course, there is a substantial body of literature to document how conflict—the dysfunctional varieties—can reduce group effectiveness.[26] Among the more undesirable consequences are a retarding of communication, reductions in group cohesiveness, and subordination of group goals to the primacy of infighting among members. At the extreme, conflict can bring group functioning to a halt and potentially threaten the group's survival.

The demise of an organization as a result of too much conflict isn't as unusual as it might first appear. For instance, one of New York's best-known law firms, Shea & Gould, closed down solely because the 80 partners just couldn't get along.[27] As one legal consultant familiar with the organization said: "This was a firm that had basic and principled differences among the partners that were basically irreconcilable." That same consultant also addressed the partners at their last meeting: "You don't have an economic problem," he said. "You have a personality problem. You hate each other!"

Creating Functional Conflict If managers accept the interactionist view toward conflict, what can they do to encourage functional conflict in their organizations?[28]

There seems to be general agreement that creating functional conflict is a tough job, particularly in large U.S. corporations. As one consultant put it, "A high proportion of people who get to the top are conflict avoiders. They don't like hearing negatives; they don't like saying or thinking negative things. They frequently make it up the ladder in part because they don't irritate people on the way up." Another suggests that at least 7 out of 10 people in U.S. business hush up when their opinions are at odds with those of their superiors, allowing bosses to make mistakes even when they know better.

Such anticonflict cultures may have been tolerable in the past but are not in today's fiercely competitive global economy. Organizations that don't encourage and support dissent may find their survival threatened. Let's look at some approaches organizations are using to encourage their people to challenge the system and develop fresh ideas.

Hewlett-Packard rewards dissenters by recognizing go-against-the-grain types, or people who stay with the ideas they believe in even when those ideas are rejected by management. Herman Miller Inc., an office furniture manufacturer, has a formal system in which employees evaluate and criticize their bosses. IBM also has a formal system that encourages dissension. Employees can question their boss with impunity. If the disagreement can't be resolved, the system provides a third party for counsel. The beermaker Anheuser-Busch builds devil's advocates into the decision process. When the policy committee considers a major move, such as getting into or out of a business or making a major capital expenditure, it often assigns teams to make the case for each side of the question. This process frequently results in decisions and alternatives that hadn't been considered previously.

One common ingredient in organizations that successfully create functional conflict is that they reward dissent and punish conflict avoiders. The real challenge for managers, however, is when they hear news they don't want to hear. The news may make their blood boil or their hopes collapse, but they can't show it. They have to learn to take the bad news without flinching. No tirades, no tight-lipped sarcasm, no eyes rolling upward, no gritting of teeth. Rather, managers should ask calm, even-tempered questions: "Can you tell me more about what happened?" "What do you think we ought to do?" A sincere "Thank you for bringing this to my attention" will probably reduce the likelihood that managers will be cut off from similar communications in the future.

Having considered conflict—its nature, causes, and consequences—we now turn to negotiation. Negotiation and conflict are closely related because negotiation often resolves conflict.

Negotiation

4 *Define* negotiation.

Negotiation permeates the interactions of almost everyone in groups and organizations. There's the obvious: Labor bargains with management. There's the not-so-obvious: Managers negotiate with employees, peers, and bosses; salespeople negotiate with customers; purchasing agents negotiate with suppliers. And there's the subtle: An employee agrees to answer a colleague's phone for a few minutes in exchange for some past or future benefit. In today's loosely structured organizations, in which members are increasingly finding themselves having to work with colleagues over whom they have no direct authority and with whom they may not even share a common boss, negotiation skills become critical.

We can define **negotiation** as a process in which two or more parties exchange goods or services and attempt to agree on the exchange rate for them.[29] Note that we use the terms *negotiation* and *bargaining* interchangeably. In this section, we contrast two bargaining strategies, provide a model of the negotiation process, ascertain the role of moods and personality traits on bargaining, review gender and cultural differences in negotiation, and take a brief look at third-party negotiations.

negotiation *A process in which two or more parties exchange goods or services and attempt to agree on the exchange rate for them.*

Bargaining Strategies

5 *Contrast distributive and integrative bargaining.*

There are two general approaches to negotiation—*distributive bargaining* and *integrative bargaining*.[30] As Exhibit 15-5 shows, distributive and integrative bargaining differ in their goal and motivation, focus, interests, information sharing, and duration of relationship. We now define distributive and integrative bargaining and illustrate the differences between these two approaches.

Distributive Bargaining You see a used car advertised for sale in the newspaper. It appears to be just what you've been looking for. You go out to see the car. It's great, and you want it. The owner tells you the asking price. You don't want to pay that much. The two of you then negotiate over the price. The negotiating strategy you're engaging in is called **distributive bargaining**. Its most identifying feature is that it operates under zero-sum conditions. That is, any gain I make is at your expense and vice versa. In the used-car example, every dollar you can get the seller to cut from the car's price is a dollar you save. Conversely, every dollar more the seller can get from you comes at your expense. So the essence of distributive bargaining is negotiating over who gets what share of a fixed pie. By **fixed pie**, we mean that the bargaining parties believe there is only a set amount of goods or services to be divvied up. Therefore, fixed pies are zero-sum games in that every dollar in one party's pocket is a dollar out of their counterpart's pocket. When parties believe the pie is fixed, they tend to bargain distributively.

Probably the most widely cited example of distributive bargaining is in labor-management negotiations over wages. Typically, labor's representatives come to the bargaining table determined to get as much money as possible out of management. Because every cent more that labor negotiates increases management's costs, each party bargains aggressively and treats the other as an opponent who must be defeated.

The essence of distributive bargaining is depicted in Exhibit 15-6. Parties *A* and *B* represent two negotiators. Each has a *target point* that defines what he or she would like to achieve. Each also has a *resistance point*, which marks the lowest outcome that is acceptable—the point below which they would break off negotiations rather than accept a less-favorable settlement. The area between these two points makes up each one's aspiration range. As long as there is some overlap between *A*'s and *B*'s aspiration ranges, there exists a settlement range in which each one's aspirations can be met.

Exhibit 15-5 Distributive Versus Integrative Bargaining

Bargaining Characteristic	Distributive Bargaining	Integrative Bargaining
Goal	Get as much of the pie as possible	Expand the pie so that both parties are satisfied
Motivation	Win/lose	Win/win
Focus	Positions ("I can't go beyond this point on this issue.")	Interests ("Can you explain why this issue is so important to you?")
Interests	Opposed	Congruent
Information sharing	Low (sharing information will only allow other party to take advantage)	High (sharing information will allow each party to find ways to satisfy interests of each party)
Duration of relationship	Short term	Long term

Exhibit 15-6 Staking Out the Bargaining Zone

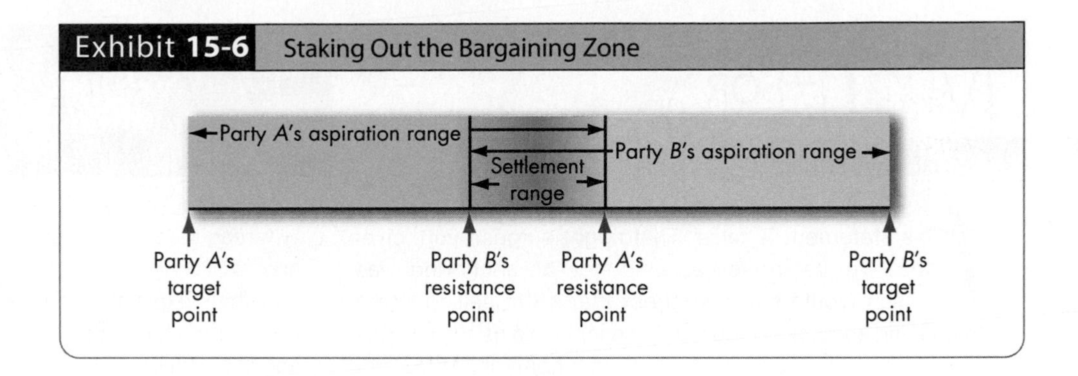

When engaged in distributive bargaining, one of the best things you can do is to make the first offer, and to make it an aggressive one. Research consistently shows that the best negotiators are those who make the first offer, and whose initial offer has very favorable terms. Why is this so? One reason is that making the first offer shows power; research shows that individuals in power are much more likely to make initial offers, speak first at meetings, and thereby gain the advantage. Another reason was mentioned in Chapter 5. Recall that we discussed the anchoring bias, which is the tendency for people to fixate on initial information. Once that anchoring point is set, people fail to adequately adjust it based on subsequent information. A savvy negotiator sets an anchor with the initial offer, and scores of negotiation studies show that such anchors greatly favor the person who sets it.[31]

For example, say you have a job offer, and your prospective employer asks you what sort of starting salary you'd be looking for. You need to realize that you've just been given a great gift—you have a chance to set the anchor, meaning that you should ask for the highest salary that you think the employer could reasonably offer. For most of us, asking for a million dollars is only going to make us look ridiculous, which is why we suggest being on the high end of what you think is reasonable. Too often, we err on the side of caution, being afraid of scaring off the employer and thus settling for too little. It *is* possible to scare off an employer, and it's true that employers don't like candidates to be assertive in salary negotiations, but liking isn't the same as respect or doing what it takes to hire or retain someone.[32] You should realize that what happens much more often is that we ask for less than what we could have gotten.

Another distributive bargaining tactic is revealing a deadline. Consider the following example. Erin is a human resources manager. She is negotiating salary with Ismail, who is a highly sought after new hire. Because Ismail knows the company needs him, he decides to play hardball and ask for an extraordinary salary and many benefits. Erin tells Ismail that the company can't meet his requirements. Ismail tells Erin he is going to have to think things over. Worried the company is going to lose Ismail to a competitor, Erin decides to tell Ismail that she is under time pressure and that she needs to reach an agreement with him immediately, or she will have to offer the job to another candidate. Would you consider Erin to be a savvy negotiator? Well, she is. Why? Negotiators who reveal deadlines speed concessions from their negotiating counterparts, making them reconsider their position. And even though negotiators don't *think* this tactic works, in reality, negotiators who reveal deadlines do better.[33]

distributive bargaining *Negotiation that seeks to divide up a fixed amount of resources; a win/lose situation.*

fixed pie *The belief that there is only a set amount of goods or services to be divvled up between the parties.*

MYTH OR SCIENCE? *"When Selling in an Auction, Start the Bidding High"*

This statement is false. That might surprise you, given that we just reviewed evidence on anchoring bias, which would seem suggest that if I'm selling something in an auction, I should set the initial bid as high as possible. Research shows that, while this generally is true, for auctions, this would be a mistake. In fact, the opposite strategy is better.

Analyzing auction results on eBay, a group of researchers found that *lower* starting bids generated higher final prices. As just one example, Nikon digital cameras with ridiculously low starting bids (one penny) sold for an average of $312, whereas those with higher starting prices went for an average of $204.[34]

What explains such a counterintuitive result? The researchers found that low starting bids attract more bidders, and the increased traffic generates more competing bidders so that in the end, the price is higher. Although this may seem irrational, negotiation and bidding behavior aren't always rational, and as you've probably experienced firsthand, once you start bidding for something, you want to "win," forgetting that for many auctions, the one with the highest bid is often the loser (the so-called winner's curse). ■

Integrative Bargaining A sales representative for a women's sportswear manufacturer has just closed a $15,000 order from a small clothing retailer. The sales rep calls in the order to her firm's credit department. She is told that the firm can't approve credit to this customer because of a past slow-payment record. The next day, the sales rep and the firm's credit manager meet to discuss the problem. The sales rep doesn't want to lose the business. Neither does the credit manager, but he also doesn't want to get stuck with an uncollectible debt. The two openly review their options. After considerable discussion, they agree on a solution that meets both their needs: The credit manager will approve the sale, but the clothing store's owner will provide a bank guarantee that will ensure payment if the bill isn't paid within 60 days. This sales-credit

United Auto Workers President Ron Gettelfinger (left) shakes hands with Ford Motor Company Executive Chairman Bill Ford at the opening of negotiations for a new union contract. Both the union and Ford say they are committed to integrative bargaining in finding mutually acceptable solutions to issues such as funding retiree health care and pensions that will boost Ford's competitiveness with Japanese automakers.

negotiation is an example of **integrative bargaining**. In contrast to distributive bargaining, integrative bargaining operates under the assumption that there are one or more settlements that can create a win/win solution.

In terms of intraorganizational behavior, all things being equal, integrative bargaining is preferable to distributive bargaining. Why? Because the former builds long-term relationships. It bonds negotiators and allows them to leave the bargaining table feeling that they have achieved a victory. Distributive bargaining, however, leaves one party a loser. It tends to build animosities and deepen divisions when people have to work together on an ongoing basis. Research shows that over repeated bargaining episodes, when the "losing" party feels positive about the negotiation outcome, he is much more likely to bargain cooperatively in subsequent negotiations. This points to the important advantage of integrative negotiations: Even when you "win," you want your opponent to feel positively about the negotiation.[35]

Why, then, don't we see more integrative bargaining in organizations? The answer lies in the conditions necessary for this type of negotiation to succeed. These include parties who are open with information and candid about their concerns, a sensitivity by both parties to the other's needs, the ability to trust one another, and a willingness by both parties to maintain flexibility.[36] Because these conditions often don't exist in organizations, it isn't surprising that negotiations often take on a win-at-any-cost dynamic.

There are some ways to achieve more integrative outcomes. For example, individuals who bargain in teams reach more integrative agreements than those who bargain individually. This happens because more ideas are generated when more people are at the bargaining table. So try bargaining in teams.[37] Another way to achieve higher joint-gain settlements is to put more issues on the table. The more negotiable issues that are introduced into a negotiation, the more opportunity there is for "logrolling" where issues are traded because of differences in preferences. This creates better outcomes for each side than if each issue were negotiated individually.[38]

Finally, you should realize that compromise may be your worst enemy in negotiating a win/win agreement. This is because compromising reduces the pressure to bargain integratively. After all, if you or your opponent caves in easily, it doesn't require anyone to be creative to reach a settlement. Thus, people end up settling for less than they could have obtained if they had been forced to consider the other party's interests, trade off issues, and be creative.[39] Think of the classic example where two sisters are arguing over who gets an orange. Unbeknownst to each other, one sister wants the orange to drink the juice, whereas the other sister wants the orange peel to bake a cake. If one sister simply capitulates and gives the other sister the orange, then they will not be forced to explore their reasons for wanting the orange, and thus they will never find the win/win solution: They could *each* have the orange because they want different parts of it!

The Negotiation Process

6 *Apply the five steps of the negotiation process.*

Exhibit 15-7 provides a simplified model of the negotiation process. It views negotiation as made up of five steps: (1) preparation and planning, (2) definition of ground rules, (3) clarification and justification, (4) bargaining and problem solving, and (5) closure and implementation.[40]

integrative bargaining *Negotiation that seeks one or more settlements that can create a win/win solution.*

Exhibit 15-7
The Negotiation

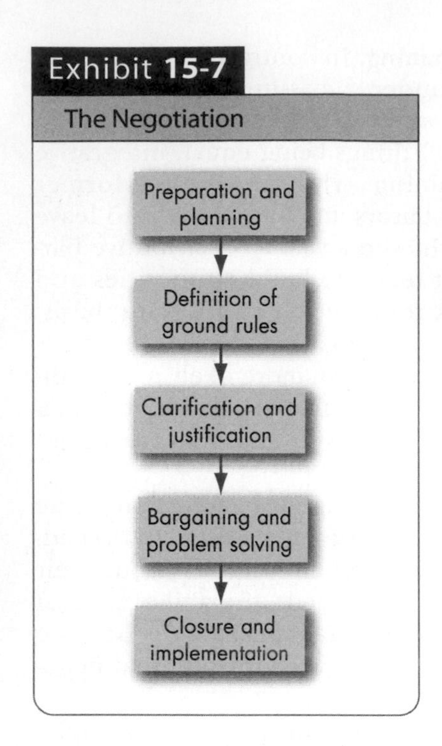

Preparation and Planning Before you start negotiating, you need to do your homework. What's the nature of the conflict? What's the history leading up to this negotiation? Who's involved and what are their perceptions of the conflict? What do you want from the negotiation? What are *your* goals? If you're a supply manager at Dell Computer, for instance, and your goal is to get a significant cost reduction from your supplier of keyboards, make sure that this goal stays paramount in your discussions and doesn't get overshadowed by other issues. It often helps to put your goals in writing and develop a range of outcomes—from "most hopeful" to "minimally acceptable"—to keep your attention focused.

You also want to prepare an assessment of what you think the other party's goals are. What are they likely to ask for? How entrenched are they likely to be in their position? What intangible or hidden interests may be important to them? What might they be willing to settle on? When you can anticipate your opponent's position, you are better equipped to counter arguments with the facts and figures that support your position.

Once you've gathered your information, use it to develop a strategy. For example, expert chess players have a strategy. They know ahead of time how they will respond to any given situation. As part of your strategy, you should determine yours and the other side's *b*est *a*lternative *t*o a *n*egotiated *a*greement (**BATNA**).[41] Your BATNA determines the lowest value acceptable to you for a negotiated agreement. Any offer you receive that is higher than your BATNA is better than an impasse. Conversely, you shouldn't expect success in your negotiation effort unless you're able to make the other side an offer they find more attractive than their BATNA. If you go into your negotiation having a good idea of what the other party's BATNA is, even if you're not able to meet theirs, you might be able to get them to change it.

Definition of Ground Rules Once you've done your planning and developed a strategy, you're ready to begin defining the ground rules and procedures with the other party over the negotiation itself. Who will do the negotiating? Where will it take place? What time constraints, if any, will apply? To what issues will negotiation be limited? Will there be a specific procedure to follow if an impasse is reached? During this phase, the parties will also exchange their initial proposals or demands.

Clarification and Justification When initial positions have been exchanged, both you and the other party will explain, amplify, clarify, bolster, and justify your original demands. This needn't be confrontational. Rather, it's an opportunity for educating and informing each other on the issues, why they are important, and how each arrived at their initial demands. This is the point at which you might want to provide the other party with any documentation that helps support your position.

Bargaining and Problem Solving The essence of the negotiation process is the actual give-and-take in trying to hash out an agreement. This is where both parties will undoubtedly need to make concessions.

Closure and Implementation The final step in the negotiation process is formalizing the agreement that has been worked out and developing any procedures that are necessary for implementation and monitoring. For major negotiations—which would include everything from labor-management negotiations to bargaining over lease terms to buying a piece of real estate to negotiating a job offer for a senior management position—this requires hammering out the specifics in a formal contract. For most cases, however, closure of the negotiation process is nothing more formal than a handshake.

Individual Differences in Negotiation Effectiveness

7 Show how individual differences influence negotiations.

Are some people better negotiators than others? Though the answer to this question might seem obvious, as it turns out the answers are more complex than you might think. Here we discuss three factors that influence how effectively individuals negotiate: personality, mood/emotions, and gender.

Personality Traits in Negotiation Can you predict an opponent's negotiating tactics if you know something about his or her personality? It's tempting to answer "yes" to this question. For instance, you might assume that high-risk takers would be more aggressive bargainers who make fewer concessions. Surprisingly, the evidence hasn't always supported this intuition.[42]

Assessments of the personality–negotiation relationship have been that personality traits have no significant direct effect on either the bargaining process or the negotiation outcomes. However, recent research has started to question the theory that personality and the negotiation process aren't connected. In fact, it appears that several of the Big Five traits are related to negotiation outcomes. For example, negotiators who are agreeable or extraverted are not very successful when it comes to distributive bargaining. Why? Because extraverts are outgoing and friendly, they tend to share more information than they should. And agreeable people are more interested in finding ways to cooperate rather than butt heads. These traits, while slightly helpful in integrative negotiations, are liabilities when interests are opposed. So the best distributive bargainer appears to be a disagreeable introvert—that is, someone who is interested in his own outcomes versus pleasing the other party and having a pleasant social exchange. Research also suggests that intelligence predicts negotiation effectiveness, but, as with personality, the effects aren't especially strong.[43]

Though personality and intelligence do appear to have some influence on negotiation, it's not a strong effect. In a sense, that's good news because it means even if you're an agreeable extrovert, you're not severely disadvantaged when it comes time to negotiate. We all can learn to be better negotiators.

Moods/Emotions in Negotiation Do moods and emotions influence negotiation? They do, but the way they do appears to depend on the type of negotiation. In distributive negotiations, it appears that negotiators who show anger negotiate better outcomes, because their anger induces concessions from their opponents. This appears to hold true even when the negotiators are instructed to show anger despite not being truly angry.

In integrative negotiations, in contrast, positive moods and emotions appear to lead to more integrative agreements (higher levels of joint gain). This may happen because, as we noted in Chapter 5, positive mood is related to creativity.[44]

Gender Differences in Negotiations Do men and women negotiate differently? And does gender affect negotiation outcomes? The answer to the first question appears to be no.[45] The answer to the second is a qualified yes.[46]

A popular stereotype is that women are more cooperative and pleasant in negotiations than are men. The evidence doesn't support this belief. However, men have been found to negotiate better outcomes than women, although the

BATNA *The best alternative to a negotiated agreement; the least the individual should accept.*

Respected for her intelligence, confident negotiating skills, and successful outcomes, Christine Lagarde was appointed by French President Nicholas Sarkozy to the powerful position of minister for the economy, finance, and employment. As the first female finance minister of a G-8 nation, Lagarde brings to her new post experience as the trade minister of France, where she used her negotiating skills in boosting French exports by 10 percent. Before that, Lagarde was a noted labor and antitrust lawyer for the global law firm Baker & McKenzie. Among her tasks, Lagarde must negotiate with France's trade unions to change the country's labor laws, including raising the 35-hour workweek, to help boost the nation's sluggish economy.

difference is relatively small. It's been postulated that this difference might be due to men and women placing divergent values on outcomes. "It is possible that a few hundred dollars more in salary or the corner office is less important to women than forming and maintaining an interpersonal relationship."[47]

The belief that women are "nicer" than men in negotiations is probably due to a confusion between gender and the lower degree of power women typically hold in most large organizations. Because women are expected to be "nice" and men "tough," research shows that, relative to men, women are penalized when they initiate negotiations.[48] What's more, when women and men actually do conform to these stereotypes—women act "nice" and men "tough"—it becomes a self-fulfilling prophecy, reinforcing the stereotypical gender differences between male and female negotiators.[49] Thus, one of the reasons why negotiations favor men is that women are "damned if they do, damned if they don't." Negotiate tough and they are penalized for violating a gender stereotype. Negotiate nice and it only reinforces the stereotype (and is taken advantage of).

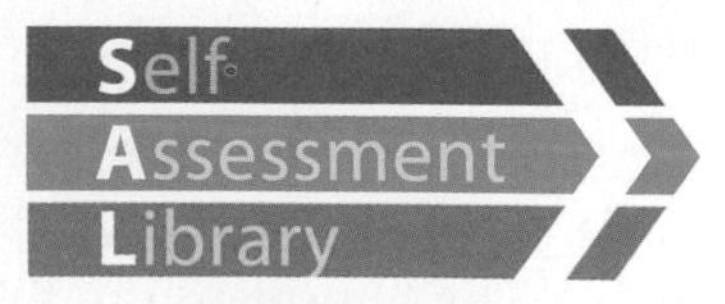

WHAT'S MY NEGOTIATING STYLE?

In the Self-Assessment Library (available on CD and online), take assessment II.C.6 (What's My Negotiating Style?).

In addition to the other party's attitudes and behaviors, the evidence also suggests that women's own attitudes and behaviors hurt them in negotiations. Managerial women demonstrate less confidence in anticipation of negotiating and are less satisfied with their performance after the process is complete, even when their performance and the outcomes they achieve are similar to those for men.[50] This latter conclusion suggests that women may unduly penalize themselves by failing to engage in negotiations when such action would be in their best interests.

International OB

Negotiating Across Cultures

Obtaining a favorable outcome in a negotiation may in part depend on the cultural characteristics of your opponent. A study of negotiators in China, Japan, and the United States found that culture plays an important role in successful negotiation. The study found that, overall, negotiators who had both a self-serving "egoistic" orientation and a high goal level fared the best overall compared with negotiators with an other-serving "prosocial" orientation and low goal level. In other words, the strategy combining a self-serving negotiation position, where one is focused only on maximizing one's own outcomes, coupled with a strong desire to obtain the best outcomes, led to the most favorable negotiation results.

However, the degree to which this particular strategy resulted in better outcomes depended on the negotiating partner. The results showed that being self-serving and having a high negotiation goal level resulted in higher outcomes (in this case, profits) only when the negotiating opponent was other-serving. Negotiators from the United States are more likely to be self-serving and have high goal levels. In China and Japan, however, there is a greater likelihood that negotiators are other-serving and thus are more concerned with others' outcomes. Consequently, negotiators from the United States are likely to obtain better outcomes for themselves when negotiating with individuals from China and Japan because American negotiators tend to be more concerned with their own outcomes, sometimes at the expense of the other party.

Though this study suggests that being self-serving can be beneficial in some situations, negotiators should be wary of being too self-serving. U.S. negotiators may benefit from a self-serving negotiation position and a high goal level when negotiating with individuals from China or Japan, but being too self-serving may result in damaged relationships, leading to less favorable outcomes in the long run.

Source: Based on Y. Chen, E. A. Mannix, and T. Okumura, "The Importance of Who You Meet: Effects of Self- Versus Other-Concerns Among Negotiators in the United States, the People's Republic of China, and Japan," *Journal of Experimental Social Psychology*, January, 2003, pp. 1–15.

Third-Party Negotiations

8 *Assess the roles and functions of third-party negotiations.*

To this point, we've discussed bargaining in terms of direct negotiations. Occasionally, however, individuals or group representatives reach a stalemate and are unable to resolve their differences through direct negotiations. In such cases, they may turn to a third party to help them find a solution. There are four basic third-party roles: mediator, arbitrator, conciliator, and consultant.[51]

A **mediator** is a neutral third party who facilitates a negotiated solution by using reasoning and persuasion, suggesting alternatives, and the like. Mediators are widely used in labor-management negotiations and in civil court disputes. The overall effectiveness of mediated negotiations is fairly impressive. The settlement rate is approximately 60 percent, with negotiator satisfaction at about 75 percent. But the situation is the key to whether or not mediation will succeed; the conflicting parties must be motivated to bargain and resolve their conflict. In addition, conflict intensity can't be too high; mediation is most effective under moderate levels of conflict. Finally, perceptions of the mediator are important; to be effective, the mediator must be perceived as neutral and noncoercive.

An **arbitrator** is a third party with the authority to dictate an agreement. Arbitration can be voluntary (requested by the parties) or compulsory (forced on the parties by law or contract). The big plus of arbitration over mediation is

mediator *A neutral third party who facilitates a negotiated solution by using reasoning, persuasion, and suggestions for alternatives.*

arbitrator *A third party to a negotiation who has the authority to dictate an agreement.*

OB In the News

"Marriage Counseling" for the Top Bosses

That the two top executives of a company conflicted with one another is no surprise. What's surprising is what they did about it.

When Watermark, a struggling maker of kayaks and car racks, brought in a new executive team, the top two executives came from very different backgrounds. CEO Jim Clark, 43, was an avid hunter and outdoorsman. COO Thomas Fumarelli, 50, was an urbane professional used to high finance in Paris and New York. Because the organization was struggling, with anxious employees who were playing them off one another, the two executives knew their differences were likely to overwhelm them. So they headed off personality conflicts at the pass with 2½ years of joint executive-coaching sessions.

Although such joint coaching sessions are highly unusual, both Clark and Fumarelli (it was his idea) credit the weekly sessions for helping them work through their differences. "It was like marriage counseling," said Clark. "You get all the issues on the table."

Early on, the coaches asked Clark and Fumarelli what they needed from another. Clark said that he needed Fumarelli to be his eyes and ears for the company and to "cover his back." Fumarelli replied that he needed Clark to support him. "I can check my ego at the door," he recalls saying, "But I need validation and support from you for the role I'm playing to support you."

The two discovered a conflict, though, when the coaches asked them separately how much time they should spend on various corporate activities. Both Clark and Fumarelli thought that development of the annual budget was his responsibility. After getting this out in the open, Clark realized the budget should primarily be Fumarelli's responsibility. "Very early on, we knew we were going to be stepping on each other's toes," Clark said.

When a private equity company bought Watermark, both left the company. But even then, the two used coaches to handle what they called their "divorce."

Source: Based on P. Dvorak, "CEO and COO Try 'Marriage Counseling,'" *Wall Street Journal*, July 31, 2006, p. B1, B3.

that it always results in a settlement. Whether or not there is a negative side depends on how "heavy-handed" the arbitrator appears. If one party is left feeling overwhelmingly defeated, that party is certain to be dissatisfied and unlikely to graciously accept the arbitrator's decision. Therefore, the conflict may resurface at a later time.

A **conciliator** is a trusted third party who provides an informal communication link between the negotiator and the opponent. This role was made famous by Robert Duval in the first *Godfather* film. As Don Corleone's adopted son and a lawyer by training, Duval acted as an intermediary between the Corleone family and the other Mafioso families. Comparing its effectiveness to mediation has proven difficult because the two overlap a great deal. In practice, conciliators typically act as more than mere communication conduits. They also engage in fact-finding, interpreting messages, and persuading disputants to develop agreements.

A **consultant** is a skilled and impartial third party who attempts to facilitate problem solving through communication and analysis, aided by a knowledge of conflict management. In contrast to the previous roles, the consultant's role is not to settle the issues, but, rather, to improve relations between the conflicting parties so that they can reach a settlement themselves. Instead of putting forward specific solutions, the consultant tries to help the parties learn to understand and work with each other. Therefore, this approach has a longer-term focus: to build new and positive perceptions and attitudes between the conflicting parties.

Global Implications

9 Describe cultural differences in negotiations.

Conflict and Culture

Although there is relatively little research on cross-cultural differences in conflict resolution strategies, some research suggests differences between Asian and U.S. managers. Some research indicates that individuals in

Japan and in the United States view conflict differently. Compared to Japanese negotiators, their U.S. counterparts are more likely to see offers from their counterparts as unfair and to reject them. Another study revealed that whereas U.S. managers were more likely to use competing tactics in the face of conflicts, compromising and avoiding are the most preferred methods of conflict management in China.[52]

Cultural Differences in Negotiations

Compared to the research on conflict, there is a lot more research on how negotiating styles vary across national cultures.[53] One study compared U.S. and Japanese negotiators. These researchers found that the Japanese negotiators tended to communicate indirectly and adapt their behaviors to the situation. A follow-up study showed that whereas among U.S. managers making early offers led to the anchoring effect we noted when discussing distributive negotiation, for Japanese negotiators, early offers led to more information sharing and better integrative outcomes.[54]

Another study compared North American, Arab, and Russian negotiators.[55] North Americans tried to persuade by relying on facts and appealing to logic. They countered opponents' arguments with objective facts. They made small concessions early in the negotiation to establish a relationship and usually reciprocated opponents' concessions. North Americans treated deadlines as very important. The Arabs tried to persuade by appealing to emotion. They countered opponents' arguments with subjective feelings. They made concessions throughout the bargaining process and almost always reciprocated opponents' concessions. Arabs approached deadlines very casually. The Russians based their arguments on asserted ideals. They made few, if any, concessions. Any concession offered by an opponent was viewed as a weakness and almost never reciprocated. Finally, the Russians tended to ignore deadlines.

Another study looked at verbal and nonverbal negotiation tactics exhibited by North Americans, Japanese, and Brazilians during half-hour bargaining sessions.[56] Some of the differences were particularly interesting. For instance, the Brazilians on average said "no" 83 times, compared to 5 times for the Japanese and 9 times for the North Americans. The Japanese displayed more than 5 periods of silence lasting longer than 10 seconds during the 30-minute sessions. North Americans averaged 3.5 such periods; the Brazilians had none. The Japanese and North Americans interrupted their opponent about the same number of times, but the Brazilians interrupted 2.5 to 3 times more often than the North Americans and the Japanese. Finally, the Japanese and the North Americans had no physical contact with their opponents during negotiations except for handshaking, but the Brazilians touched each other almost 5 times every half hour.

Summary and Implications for Managers

Many people automatically assume that conflict is related to lower group and organizational performance. This chapter has demonstrated that this assumption is frequently incorrect. Conflict can be either constructive or destructive to the functioning of a group or unit. As shown in Exhibit 15-8, levels of conflict

conciliator *A trusted third party who provides an informal communication link between the negotiator and the opponent.*

consultant *An impartial third party, skilled in conflict management, who attempts to facilitate creative problem solving through communication and analysis.*

Exhibit 15-8 Conflict and Unit Performance

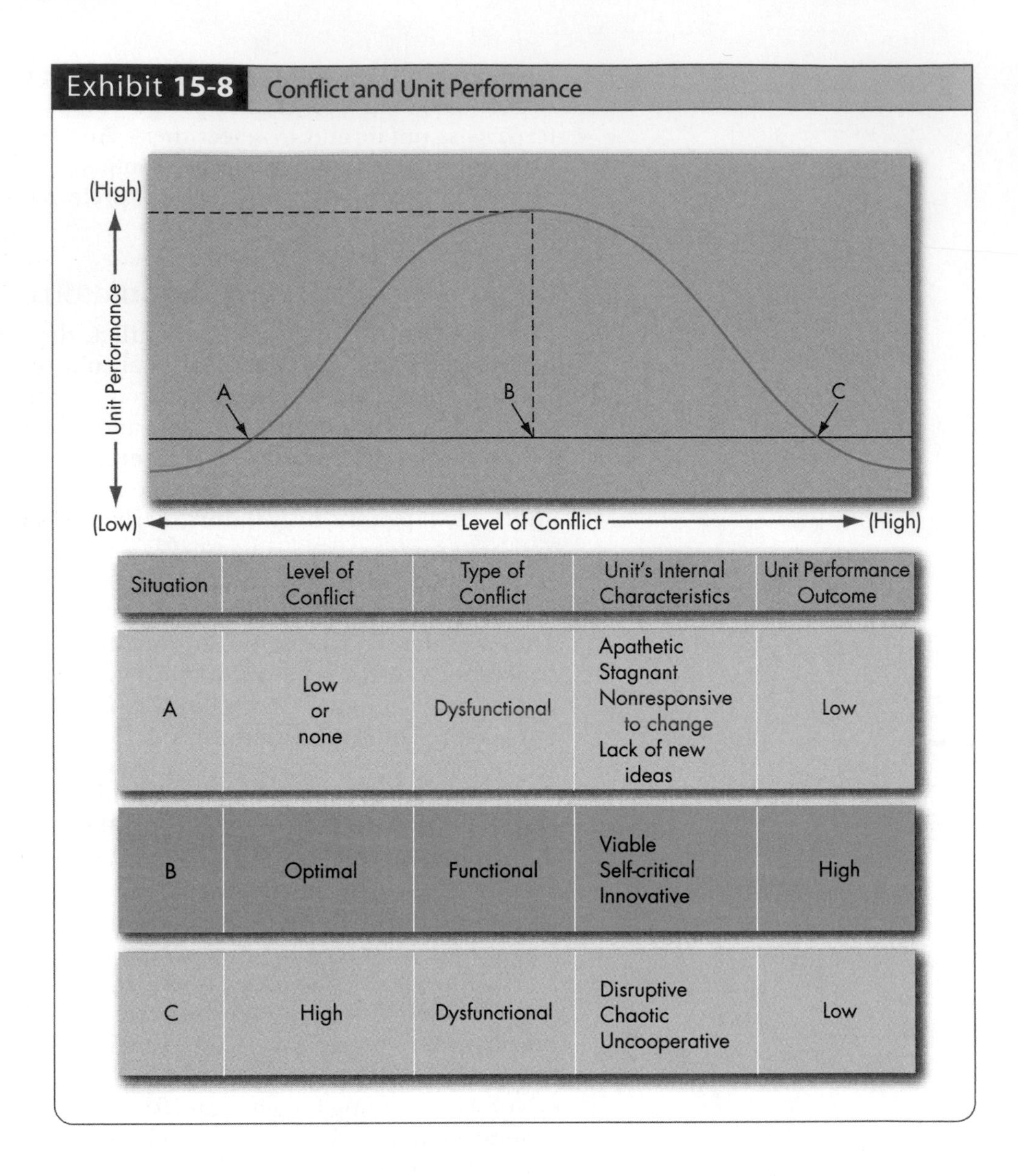

Situation	Level of Conflict	Type of Conflict	Unit's Internal Characteristics	Unit Performance Outcome
A	Low or none	Dysfunctional	Apathetic Stagnant Nonresponsive to change Lack of new ideas	Low
B	Optimal	Functional	Viable Self-critical Innovative	High
C	High	Dysfunctional	Disruptive Chaotic Uncooperative	Low

can be either too high or too low. Either extreme hinders performance. An optimal level is one at which there is enough conflict to prevent stagnation, stimulate creativity, allow tensions to be released, and initiate the seeds for change, yet not so much as to be disruptive or to deter coordination of activities.

What advice can we give managers faced with excessive conflict and the need to reduce it? Don't assume that one conflict-handling intention will always be best! You should select an intention appropriate for the situation. The following are some guidelines:[57]

- Use *competition* when quick, decisive action is vital (in emergencies), on important issues, where unpopular actions need to be implemented (in cost cutting, enforcing unpopular rules, discipline), on issues vital to the organization's welfare when you know you're right, and against people who take advantage of noncompetitive behavior.
- Use *collaboration* to find an integrative solution when both sets of concerns are too important to be compromised, when your objective is to learn, to merge insights from people with different perspectives, to gain commitment by incorporating concerns into a consensus, and to work through feelings that have interfered with a relationship.

- Use *avoidance* when an issue is trivial or when more important issues are pressing, when you perceive no chance of satisfying your concerns, when potential disruption outweighs the benefits of resolution, to let people cool down and regain perspective, when gathering information supersedes immediate decision, when others can resolve the conflict more effectively, and when issues seem tangential or symptomatic of other issues.
- Use *accommodation* when you find that you're wrong and to allow a better position to be heard, to learn, and to show your reasonableness; when issues are more important to others than to yourself and to satisfy others and maintain cooperation; to build social credits for later issues; to minimize loss when you are outmatched and losing; when harmony and stability are especially important; and to allow employees to develop by learning from mistakes.
- Use *compromise* when goals are important but not worth the effort of potential disruption of more assertive approaches; when opponents with equal power are committed to mutually exclusive goals; to achieve temporary settlements to complex issues; to arrive at expedient solutions under time pressure; and as a backup when collaboration or competition is unsuccessful.

Negotiation is an ongoing activity in groups and organizations. Distributive bargaining can resolve disputes, but it often negatively affects the satisfaction of one or more negotiators because it is focused on the short term and because it is confrontational. Integrative bargaining, in contrast, tends to provide outcomes that satisfy all parties and that build lasting relationships. When engaged in negotiation, make sure you set aggressive goals and try to find creative ways to achieve the goals of both parties, especially when you value the long-term relationship with the other party. That doesn't mean "giving in" on your self-interest; rather, it means trying to find creative solutions that give both parties what they really want.

Point | Counterpoint

CONFLICT BENEFITS ORGANIZATIONS

Let's briefly review how stimulating conflict can provide benefits to the organization:

- **Conflict is a means to solve problems and bring about radical change.** It's an effective device by which management can drastically change the existing power structure, current interaction patterns, and entrenched attitudes. If there is no conflict, it means the real problems aren't being addressed.
- **Conflict facilitates group cohesiveness.** Whereas conflict increases hostility between groups, external threats tend to cause a group to pull together as a unit. Conflict with another group brings together those within each group. Such intragroup cohesion is a critical resource that groups draw on in good and especially in bad times.
- **Conflict improves group and organizational effectiveness.** Groups or organizations devoid of conflict are likely to suffer from apathy, stagnation, groupthink, and other debilitating diseases. In fact, more organizations probably fail because they have *too little* conflict, not because they have too much. Stagnation is the biggest threat to organizations, but since it occurs slowly, its ill effects often go unnoticed until it's too late. Conflict can break complacency—though most of us don't like conflict, it often is the last best hope of saving an organization.

In general, conflicts are dysfunctional, and it is one of management's major responsibilities to keep conflict intensity as low as humanly possible. A few points support this case:

- **The negative consequences from conflict can be devastating.** The list of negatives associated with conflict is awesome. The most obvious negatives are increased turnover, decreased employee satisfaction, inefficiencies between work units, sabotage, and labor grievances and strikes. One study estimated that managing conflict at work costs the average employer nearly 450 days of management time a year.[58]
- **Effective managers build teamwork.** A good manager builds a coordinated team. Conflict works against such an objective. When a team works well, the whole becomes greater than the sum of the parts. Management creates teamwork by minimizing internal conflicts and facilitating internal coordination.
- **Conflict is avoidable.** It may be true that conflict is inevitable when an organization is in a downward spiral, but the goal of good leadership and effective management is to avoid the spiral to begin with. You don't see Warren Buffett getting into a lot of conflicts with his board of directors. It's possible they're complacent, but we think it's more likely because Berkshire Hathaway is a well-run company, doing what it should, and avoiding conflict as a result.

Questions for Review

1 What is conflict?

2 What are the differences among the traditional, human relations, and interactionist views of conflict?

3 What are the steps of the conflict process?

4 What is negotiation?

5 What are the differences between distributive and integrative bargaining?

6 What are the five steps in the negotiation process?

7 How do the individual differences of personality and gender influence negotiations?

8 What are the roles and functions of third-party negotiations?

9 How does culture influence negotiations?

Experiential Exercise

A NEGOTIATION ROLE PLAY

This role-play is designed to help you develop your negotiating skills. The class is to break into pairs. One person will play the role of Alex, the department supervisor. The other person will play C. J., Alex's boss. Both participants should read "The Situation," "The Negotiation," and then their role only.

The Situation

Alex and C. J. work for Nike in Portland, Oregon. Alex supervises a research laboratory. C.J. is the manager of research and development. Alex and C.J. are former college runners who have worked for Nike for more than 6 years. C.J. has been Alex's boss for 2 years. One of Alex's employees has greatly impressed Alex. This employee is Lisa Roland. Lisa was hired 11 months ago. She is 24 years old and holds a master's degree in mechanical engineering. Her entry-level salary was $47,500 per year. Alex told her that, in accordance with corporation policy, she would receive an initial performance evaluation at 6 months and a comprehensive review after 1 year. Based on her performance record, Lisa was told she could expect a salary adjustment at the time of the 1-year evaluation.

Alex's evaluation of Lisa after 6 months was very positive. Alex commented on the long hours Lisa was putting in, her cooperative spirit, the fact that others in the lab enjoyed working with her, and that she was making an immediate positive impact on the project she had been assigned. Now that Lisa's first anniversary is coming up, Alex has again reviewed Lisa's performance. Alex thinks Lisa may be the best new person the R&D group has ever hired. After only a year, Alex has ranked Lisa as the number-three performer in a department of 11.

Salaries in the department vary greatly. Alex, for instance, has a base salary of $76,000, plus eligibility for a bonus that might add another $7,000 to $12,000 a year. The salary range of the 11 department members is $38,400 to $66,350. The individual with the lowest salary is a recent hire with a bachelor's degree in physics. The two people whom Alex has rated above Lisa earn base salaries of $59,200 and $66,350. They're both 27 years old and have been at Nike for 3 and 4 years, respectively. The median salary in Alex's department is $54,960.

Alex's Role

You want to give Lisa a big raise. Although she's young, she has proven to be an excellent addition to the department. You don't want to lose her. More importantly, she knows in general what other people in the department are earning and she thinks she's underpaid. The company typically gives 1-year raises of 5 percent, although 10 percent is not unusual, and 20 to 30 percent increases have been approved on occasion. You'd like to get Lisa as large an increase as C.J. will approve.

C.J.'s Role

All your supervisors typically try to squeeze you for as much money as they can for their people. You understand this because you did the same thing when you were a supervisor, but your boss wants to keep a lid on costs. He wants you to keep raises for recent hires generally in the 5 to 8 percent range. In fact, he's sent a memo to all managers and supervisors saying this. He also said that managers will be evaluated on their ability to maintain budgetary control. However, your boss is also concerned with equity and paying people what they're worth. You feel assured that he will support any salary recommendation you make, as long as it can be justified. Your goal, consistent with cost reduction, is to keep salary increases as low as possible.

The Negotiation

Alex has a meeting scheduled with C.J. to discuss Lisa's performance review and salary adjustment. Take a couple minutes to think through the facts in this exercise and to prepare a strategy. Then you have up to 15 minutes to conduct your negotiation. When your negotiation is complete, the class will compare the various strategies used and pair outcomes.

Ethical Dilemma

IS IT UNETHICAL TO LIE, DECEIVE, OR COLLUDE DURING NEGOTIATIONS?

In Chapter 11, we addressed lying in the context of communication. Here we return to the topic of lying but specifically as it relates to negotiation. We think this issue is important because, for many people, there is no such thing as lying when it comes to negotiating.

It's been said that the whole notion of negotiation is built on ethical quicksand: To succeed, you must deceive. Is this true? Apparently, a lot of people think so. For instance, one study found that 28 percent of negotiators lied about at least one issue during negotiations, while another study found that 100 percent of negotiators either failed to reveal a problem or actively lied about it during negotiations if they were not directly asked about the issue. Why do you think these numbers are so high? The research on negotiation provides numerous examples of lying giving the negotiator a strategic advantage.[59]

We can probably agree that bald-faced lies during negotiation are wrong. At least most ethicists would probably agree. The universal dilemma surrounds the little lies: The omissions, evasions, and concealments that are often necessary to best an opponent.

During negotiations, when is a lie a *lie*? Is exaggerating benefits, downplaying negatives, ignoring flaws, or saying "I don't know" when in reality you do considered lying? Is declaring "this is my final offer and nonnegotiable" (even when you're posturing) a lie? Is pretending to bend over backward to make meaningful concessions lying? Rather than being considered unethical, the use of these "lies" is considered by many as an indicator that a negotiator is strong, smart, and savvy.

Or consider the issue of colluding, as when two bidders agree not to bid against one another in a (concealed) effort to keep the bids down. In some cases, such collusion is illegal, but even when it isn't illegal, is it ethical?

Questions

1. When are deception, evasiveness, or collusion out of bounds?
2. Can such tactics be legal and still be unethical?
3. Is it naive to be completely honest and bare your soul during negotiations?
4. Are the rules of negotiations unique? Is any tactic that will improve your chance of winning acceptable?

Source: Based on R. Cohen, "Bad Bidness," *New York Times Magazine*, September 2, 2006, p. 22; M. E. Schweitzer, "Deception in Negotiations," in S. J. Hoch and H. C. Kunreuther (eds.), *Wharton on Making Decisions* (New York: Wiley, 2001), pp. 187–200; and M. Diener, "Fair Enough," *Entrepreneur*, January 2002, pp. 100–102.

Case Incident 1

DAVID OUT-NEGOTIATING GOLIATH: APOTEX AND BRISTOL-MYERS SQUIBB

Peter Dolan survived many crises in his five-year tenure as CEO of drug giant Bristol-Myers Squibb. There were a corporate accounting scandal, allegations of insider trading, FBI raids of his office, and a stock price that dropped 60 percent during his tenure. But in the end, what may have done Dolan in was his negotiation performance against the head of Apotex, a Canadian drug company founded by Dr. Barry Sherman.

At its peak, Plavix—a drug to prevent heart attacks—was Bristol-Myers's best-selling drug and accounted for a staggering one-third of its profits. So when Apotex developed a generic Plavix knockoff, Dolan sought to negotiate an agreement that would pay Apotex in exchange for a delayed launch of Apotex's generic competitor. Dolan sent one of his closest lieutenants, Andrew Bodnar, to negotiate with Sherman. Bodnar and Sherman developed a good rapport, and at several points in their negotiations asked their attorneys to leave them alone. At one key point in the negotiations, Bodnar flew to Toronto alone, without Bristol-Myers's attorneys, as a "gesture of goodwill. The thinking was that the negotiations would be more effective this way."

As Dolan, Bodnar, and Bristol-Myers became increasingly concerned with reaching an agreement with Sherman and Apotex, they developed a blind spot. Privately, Sherman was betting that the Federal Trade Commission (FTC) wouldn't approve the noncompete agreement the two parties were negotiating, and his goal in the negotiation was to extract an agreement from Bristol-Myers that would position Apotex favorably should the FTC reject the deal. Indeed, he nonchalantly inserted a clause in the deal that would require Bristol-Myers to pay Apotex $60 million if the FTC rejected the deal. "I thought the FTC would turn it down, but I didn't let on that I did," Sherman said. "They seemed blind to it."

In the meantime, Apotex covertly began shipping its generic equivalent, and it quickly became the best-selling generic drug ever. Thus, Sherman also managed to launch the generic equivalent without Bristol-Myers's even considering the possibility that he would do so while still engaged in negotiations.

"It looks like a much smaller generic private company completely outmaneuvered two of the giants of the pharmaceutical industry," said Gbola Amusa, European pharmaceutical analyst for Sanford C. Bernstein & Company. "It's not clear how or why that happened. The reaction from investors and analysts has ranged from shock to outright anger." Within a few months, Dolan was out at Bristol-Myers.

Questions

1. What principles of distributive negotiation did Sherman use to gain his advantage?
2. Do you think Sherman behaved ethically? Why or why not?
3. What does this incident tell you about the role of deception in negotiation?

Source: Based on J. Carreyrou and J. S. Lublin, "How Bristol-Myers Fumbled Defense of $4 Billion Drug," *Wall Street Journal*, September 2, 2006, pp. A1, A7; and S. Saul, "Marketers of Plavix Outfoxed on a Deal," *New York Times*, August 9, 2006.

Case Incident 2

NEGOTIATION PUTS HOCKEY IN THE PENALTY BOX

Not every negotiation ends on a good note. Just ask National Hockey League (NHL) Commissioner Gary Bettman, who, on February 16, 2005, cancelled all the games remaining in the season following a 5-month lockout by the owners. Though professional sports such as hockey and baseball have had close calls with losing an entire season, Bettman's decision was a first: The whole schedule was lost. Said Bettman, "This is a sad, regrettable day."

On the other side of the dispute, Bob Goodenow, executive director of the NHL Player's Association, similarly regretted the impasse. He said, "Yes, we apologize to the fans." Though the repercussions to the league and its players are obvious, canceling the season also had ramifications on a broader level, including lost revenues for local businesses and NHL game merchandise sales.

So, why did Bettman cancel the season? The primary issue was a salary cap, but Goodenow said, "The players never asked for more money. They didn't want to be locked out. Gary owes the apology. He started the lockout. We've done an awful lot to try to get to a fair resolution." According to reports, negotiations began when the league attempted to lower the average salary from $1.8 million per year to $1.3 million per year—a 28 percent decrease. The league's reason? Although the NHL's total revenue had reached $2.1 billion a year, players were paid 75 percent of this revenue. According to the league, this high percentage kept the league from being profitable and directly contributed to the league's loss of $479 million over the past two seasons. The player's union then countered with an offer to reduce salaries by 24 percent rather than the 28 percent the league wanted. Bettman then tried an alternative solution: to persuade the union to accept a salary percentage of no more than 55 percent of league revenues. Instead of reducing pay to an average level, this proposal would link players' pay to the leagues' revenues, which could fluctuate up or down. The league's players opposed both ideas until Bettman and the NHL team owners offered a salary cap that did not link payroll and revenue. At this point, negotiations looked promising.

However, neither party could agree on an amount. The owners offered a cap of $40 million per team and then increased it to $42.5 million. But the players wanted a cap of $52 million per team and then lowered their proposal to $49 million. Although the dollar difference in this round of negotiations amounted to only 6.5 million, neither side could agree, negotiations stopped, and the season was cancelled.

Said Goodenow, "Gary gave us a final offer, a take-it-or-leave-it offer. We made a counterproposal and events ground to a halt." A reporter asked both sides whether they would have accepted a compromise of around $45 million per team. Such a compromise may have saved the season. Bettman stated, "If they wanted $45 million, I'm not saying we would have gone there, but they sure should have told us." Goodenow, however, wouldn't speculate: "The what-ifs aren't for real."

So how did the two sides eventually get the players back on the ice? They agreed to a 6-year deal that set a salary cap of $39 million per team for the 2005–2006 season. (Remember that the players wanted a cap of $49 million.) Many players were unhappy with the terms of the deal but felt that fighting the salary cap was a waste of time that did nothing but alienate the fans. Many players spoke out against Goodenow, arguing that he put the players in a no-win situation. Less than a week after the lockout ended, Goodenow resigned as executive director of the NHL Player's Association. He denied that his resignation was in response to the players' complaints. The lack of an agreement in the NHL negotiations was a loss to everyone—the league and businesses connected to the league, the owners, the players, and, of course, the fans.

Questions

1. How would you characterize the NHL negotiation—as distributive or integrative? From what perspective (distributive or integrative) did the parties approach the negotiation? How might this approach have affected the outcome?
2. What factors do you believe led to the lack of a settlement in the NHL negotiations? How might you have handled the negotiation if you were a representative of the league? of the player's union?
3. Negotiating parties are often reluctant to reveal their BATNA (best alternative to a negotiated agreement) to the opposing party. Do you believe that parties in the NHL negotiation were aware of each other's BATNA? How might this knowledge have affected the negotiation?
4. It appears that a point of compromise (a $45 million-per-team salary cap, for example) may have existed. What steps could both parties have taken to reach this point of compromise?

Source: Based on J. Lapointe, and R. Westhead, "League Cancels Hockey Season in Labor Battle," *New York Times*, February 17, 2005, p. A1.

Endnotes

1. S. Gray, "Ketchup Fight: Peltz, Heinz CEO Go at It," *Wall Street Journal*, August 4, 2006, pp. C1, C5.
2. See, for instance, C. F. Fink, "Some Conceptual Difficulties in the Theory of Social Conflict," *Journal of Conflict Resolution*, December 1968, pp. 412–460; and E. Infante, "On the Definition of Interpersonal Conflict: Cluster Analysis Applied to the Study of Semantics," *Revista de Psicologia Social* 13, no. 3 (1998), pp. 485–493.
3. L. L. Putnam and M. S. Poole, "Conflict and Negotiation," in F. M. Jablin, L. L. Putnam, K. H. Roberts, and L. W. Porter (eds.), *Handbook of Organizational Communication: An Interdisciplinary Perspective* (Newbury Park, CA: Sage, 1987), pp. 549–599.
4. K. W. Thomas, "Conflict and Negotiation Processes in Organizations," in M. D. Dunnette and L. M. Hough (eds.), *Handbook of Industrial and Organizational Psychology*, 2nd ed., vol. 3 (Palo Alto, CA: Consulting Psychologists Press, 1992), pp. 651–717.
5. For a comprehensive review of the interactionist approach, see C. De Dreu and E. Van de Vliert (eds.), *Using Conflict in Organizations* (London: Sage, 1997).
6. See K. A. Jehn, "A Multimethod Examination of the Benefits and Detriments of Intragroup Conflict," *Administrative Science Quarterly*, June 1995, pp. 256–282; K. A. Jehn, "A Qualitative Analysis of Conflict Types and Dimensions in Organizational Groups," *Administrative Science Quarterly*, September 1997, pp. 530–557; K. A. Jehn and E. A. Mannix, "The Dynamic Nature of Conflict: A Longitudinal Study of Intragroup Conflict and Group Performance," *Academy of Management Journal*, April 2001, pp. 238–251; and C. K. W. De Dreu and L. R. Weingart, "Task Versus Relationship Conflict, Team Performance, and Team Member Satisfaction: A Meta-Analysis," *Journal of Applied Psychology*, August 2003, pp. 741–749.

7. J. Yang and K. W. Mossholder, "Decoupling Task and Relationship Conflict: The Role of Intragroup Emotional Processing," *Journal of Organizational Behavior* 25, no. 5 (August 2004), pp. 589–605.
8. "Survey Shows Managers Have Their Hands Full Resolving Staff Personality Conflicts," *IPMA-HR Bulletin*, November 3, 2006.
9. R. S. Peterson and K. J. Behfar, "The Dynamic Relationship Between Performance Feedback, Trust, and Conflict in Groups: A Longitudinal Study," *Organizational Behavior & Human Decision Processes*, September–November 2003, pp. 102–112.
10. Jehn, "A Multimethod Examination of the Benefits and Detriments of Intragroup Conflict."
11. R. Friedman, C. Anderson, J. Brett, M. Olekalns, N. Goates, and C. C. Lisco, "The Positive and Negative Effects of Anger on Dispute Resolution: Evidence from Electronically Mediated Disputes," *Journal of Applied Psychology*, April 2004, pp. 369–376.
12. L. R. Pondy, "Organizational Conflict: Concepts and Models," *Administrative Science Quarterly*, September 1967, p. 302.
13. See, for instance, R. L. Pinkley, "Dimensions of Conflict Frame: Disputant Interpretations of Conflict," *Journal of Applied Psychology*, April 1990, pp. 117–126; and R. L. Pinkley and G. B. Northcraft, "Conflict Frames of Reference: Implications for Dispute Processes and Outcomes," *Academy of Management Journal*, February 1994, pp. 193–205.
14. A. M. Isen, A. A. Labroo, and P. Durlach, "An Influence of Product and Brand Name on Positive Affect: Implicit and Explicit Measures," *Motivation & Emotion*, March 2004, pp. 43–63.
15. Ibid.
16. P. J. D. Carnevale and A. M. Isen, "The Influence of Positive Affect and Visual Access on the Discovery of Integrative Solutions in Bilateral Negotiations," *Organizational Behavior and Human Decision Processes*, February 1986, pp. 1–13.
17. Thomas, "Conflict and Negotiation Processes in Organizations."
18. Ibid.
19. See R. A. Baron, "Personality and Organizational Conflict: Effects of the Type A Behavior Pattern and Self-monitoring," *Organizational Behavior and Human Decision Processes*, October 1989, pp. 281–296; R. J. Volkema and T. J. Bergmann, "Conflict Styles as Indicators of Behavioral Patterns in Interpersonal Conflicts," *Journal of Social Psychology*, February 1995, pp. 5–15; and J. A. Rhoades, J. Arnold, and C. Jay, "The Role of Affective Traits and Affective States in Disputants' Motivation and Behavior During Episodes of Organizational Conflict," *Journal of Organizational Behavior*, May 2001, pp. 329–345.
20. Thomas, "Conflict and Negotiation Processes in Organizations."
21. See, for instance, K. A. Jehn, "Enhancing Effectiveness: An Investigation of Advantages and Disadvantages of Value-Based Intragroup Conflict," *International Journal of Conflict Management*, July 1994, pp. 223–238; R. L. Priem, D. A. Harrison, and N. K. Muir, "Structured Conflict and Consensus Outcomes in Group Decision Making," *Journal of Management* 21, no. 4 (1995), pp. 691–710; and K. A. Jehn and E. A. Mannix, "The Dynamic Nature of Conflict: A Longitudinal Study of Intragroup Conflict and Group Performance," *Academy of Management Journal*, April 2001, pp. 238–251.
22. See, for instance, C. J. Loomis, "Dinosaurs?" *Fortune*, May 3, 1993, pp. 36–42.
23. J. Hall and M. S. Williams, "A Comparison of Decision-Making Performances in Established and Ad-hoc Groups," *Journal of Personality and Social Psychology*, February 1966, p. 217.
24. R. L. Hoffman, "Homogeneity of Member Personality and Its Effect on Group Problem-Solving," *Journal of Abnormal and Social Psychology*, January 1959, pp. 27–32; R. L. Hoffman and N. R. F. Maier, "Quality and Acceptance of Problem Solutions by Members of Homogeneous and Heterogeneous Groups," *Journal of Abnormal and Social Psychology*, March 1961, pp. 401–407; and P. Pitcher and A. D. Smith, "Top Management Team Heterogeneity: Personality, Power, and Proxies," *Organization Science*, January–February 2001, pp. 1–18.
25. See T. H. Cox, S. A. Lobel, and P. L. McLeod, "Effects of Ethnic Group Cultural Differences on Cooperative Behavior on a Group Task," *Academy of Management Journal*, December 1991, pp. 827–847; L. H. Pelled, K. M. Eisenhardt, and K. R. Xin, "Exploring the Black Box: An Analysis of Work Group Diversity, Conflict, and Performance," *Administrative Science Quarterly*, March 1999, pp. 1–28; and D. van Knippenberg, C. K. W. De Dreu, and A. C. Homan, "Work Group Diversity and Group Performance: An Integrative Model and Research Agenda," *Journal of Applied Psychology*, December 2004, pp. 1008–1022.
26. For example, see J. A. Wall, Jr., and R. R. Callister, "Conflict and Its Management," pp. 523–526 for evidence supporting the argument that conflict is almost uniformly dysfunctional; see also P. J. Hinds, and D. E. Bailey, "Out of Sight, Out of Sync: Understanding Conflict in Distributed Teams," *Organization Science*, November–December 2003, pp. 615–632.
27. M. Geyelin and E. Felsenthal, "Irreconcilable Differences Force Shea & Gould Closure," *Wall Street Journal*, January 31, 1994, p. B1.
28. This section is based on F. Sommerfield, "Paying the Troops to Buck the System," *Business Month*, May 1990, pp. 77–79; W. Kiechel III, "How to Escape the Echo Chamber," *Fortune*, June 18, 1990, pp. 129–130; E. Van de Vliert and C. De Dreu, "Optimizing Performance by Stimulating Conflict," *International Journal of Conflict Management*, July 1994, pp. 211–222; E. Van de Vliert, "Enhancing Performance by Conflict-Stimulating Intervention," in C. De Dreu and E. Van de Vliert (eds.), *Using Conflict in Organizations*, pp. 208–222; K. M. Eisenhardt, J. L. Kahwajy, and L. J. Bourgeois III, "How Management Teams Can Have a Good Fight," *Harvard Business Review*, July–August 1997, pp. 77–85; S. Wetlaufer, "Common Sense and Conflict," *Harvard Business Review*, January–February 2000, pp. 114–124; and G. A. Okhuysen and K. M. Eisenhardt,

"Excel Through Group Process," in E. A. Locke (ed.), *Handbook of Principles of Organizational Behavior* (Malden, MA: Blackwell, 2004), pp. 216–218.

29. J. A. Wall, Jr., *Negotiation: Theory and Practice* (Glenview, IL: Scott, Foresman, 1985).

30. R. E. Walton and R. B. McKersie, *A Behavioral Theory of Labor Negotiations: An Analysis of a Social Interaction System* (New York: McGraw-Hill, 1965).

31. J. C. Magee, A. D. Galinsky, and D. H. Gruenfeld, "Power, Propensity to Negotiate, and Moving First in Competitive Interactions," *Personality and Social Psychology Bulletin*, February 2007, pp. 200–212.

32. H. R. Bowles, L. Babcock, and L. Lei, "Social Incentives for Gender Differences in the Propensity to Initiative Negotiations: Sometimes It Does Hurt to Ask," *Organizational Behavior and Human Decision Processes* 103 (2007), pp. 84–103.

33. D. A. Moore, "Myopic Prediction, Self-Destructive Secrecy, and the Unexpected Benefits of Revealing Final Deadlines in Negotiation," *Organizational Behavior & Human Decision Processes*, July 2004, pp. 125–139.

34. G. Ku, A. D. Galinsky, and J. K. Murnighan, "Starting Low but Ending High: A Reversal of the Anchoring Effect in Auctions," *Journal of Personality and Social Psychology* 90 (June 2006), pp. 975–986.

35. J. R. Curhan, H. A. Elfenbein, and H. Xu, "What Do People Value When They Negotiate? Mapping the Domain of Subjective Value in Negotiation," *Journal of Personality and Social Psychology* 91, no. 3 (year), pp. 493–512.

36. Thomas, "Conflict and Negotiation Processes in Organizations."

37. P. M. Morgan and R. S. Tindale, "Group vs. Individual Performance in Mixed-Motive Situations: Exploring an Inconsistency," *Organizational Behavior & Human Decision Processes*, January 2002, pp. 44–65.

38. C. E. Naquin, "The Agony of Opportunity in Negotiation: Number of Negotiable Issues, Counterfactual Thinking, and Feelings of Satisfaction," *Organizational Behavior & Human Decision Processes*, May 2003, pp. 97–107.

39. C. K. W. De Dreu, L. R. Weingart, and S. Kwon, "Influence of Social Motives on Integrative Negotiation: A Meta-analytic Review and Test of Two Theories," *Journal of Personality & Social Psychology*, May 2000, pp. 889–905.

40. This model is based on R. J. Lewicki, "Bargaining and Negotiation," *Exchange: The Organizational Behavior Teaching Journal* 6, no. 2 (1981), pp. 39–40.

41. M. H. Bazerman and M. A. Neale, *Negotiating Rationally* (New York: The Free Press, 1992), pp. 67–68.

42. J. A. Wall, Jr., and M. W. Blum, "Negotiations," *Journal of Management*, June 1991, pp. 278–282.

43. B. Barry and R. A. Friedman, "Bargainer Characteristics in Distributive and Integrative Negotiation," *Journal of Personality & Social Psychology*, February 1998, pp. 345–359.

44. S. Kopelman, A. S. Rosette, and L. Thompson, "The Three Faces of Eve: Strategic Displays of Positive, Negative, and Neutral Emotions in Negotiations," *Organizational Behavior and Human Decision Processes* 99 (2006), pp. 81–101; and J. M. Brett, M. Olekalns, R. Friedman, N. Goates, C. Anderson, C. C. Lisco, "Sticks and Stones: Language, Face, and Online Dispute Resolution," *Academy of Management Journal* 50, no. 1 (2007), pp. 85–99.

45. C. Watson and L. R. Hoffman, "Managers as Negotiators: A Test of Power Versus Gender as Predictors of Feelings, Behavior, and Outcomes," *Leadership Quarterly*, Spring 1996, pp. 63–85.

46. A. E. Walters, A. F. Stuhlmacher, and L. L. Meyer, "Gender and Negotiator Competitiveness: A Meta-analysis," *Organizational Behavior and Human Decision Processes*, October 1998, pp. 1–29; and A. F. Stuhlmacher and A. E. Walters, "Gender Differences in Negotiation Outcome: A Meta-analysis," *Personnel Psychology*, Autumn 1999, pp. 653–677.

47. Stuhlmacher and Walters, "Gender Differences in Negotiation Outcome," p. 655.

48. Bowles, Babcock, and Lei, "Social Incentives for Gender Differences in the Propensity to Initiative Negotiations."

49. L. J. Kray, A. D. Galinsky, and L. Thompson, "Reversing the Gender Gap in Negotiations: An Exploration of Stereotype Regeneration," *Organizational Behavior & Human Decision Processes*, March 2002, pp. 386–409.

50. C. K. Stevens, A. G. Bavetta, and M. E. Gist, "Gender Differences in the Acquisition of Salary Negotiation Skills: The Role of Goals, Self-Efficacy, and Perceived Control," *Journal of Applied Psychology* 78, no. 5 (October 1993), pp. 723–735.

51. Wall and Blum, "Negotiations," pp. 283–287.

52. M. J. Gelfand, M. Higgins, L. H. Nishii, J. L. Raver, A. Dominguez, F. Murakami, S. Yamaguchi, and M. Toyama, "Culture and Egocentric Perceptions of Fairness in Conflict and Negotiation," *Journal of Applied Psychology*, October 2002, pp. 833–845; Z. Ma, "Chinese Conflict Management Styles and Negotiation Behaviours: An Empirical Test," *International Journal of Cross Cultural Management*, April 2007, pp. 101–119.

53. Gelfand et al., "Culture and Egocentric Perceptions of Fairness in Conflict and Negotiation," pp. 833–845; and X. Lin and S. J. Miller, "Negotiation Approaches: Direct and Indirect Effect of National Culture," *International Marketing Review* 20, no. 3 (2003), pp. 286–303.

54. W. L. Adair, T. Okumura, and J. M. Brett, "Negotiation Behavior When Cultures Collide: The United States and Japan," *Journal of Applied Psychology*, June 2001, pp. 371–385; and W. L. Adair, L. Weingart, and J. Brett, "The Timing and Function of Offers in U.S. and Japanese Negotiations," *Journal of Applied Psychology* 92, no. 4 (2007), pp. 1056–1068.

55. E. S. Glenn, D. Witmeyer, and K. A. Stevenson, "Cultural Styles of Persuasion," *Journal of Intercultural Relations*, Fall 1977, pp. 52–66.

56. J. Graham, "The Influence of Culture on Business Negotiations," *Journal of International Business Studies*, Spring 1985, pp. 81–96.

57. K. W. Thomas, "Toward Multidimensional Values in Teaching: The Example of Conflict Behaviors," *Academy of Management Review*, July 1977, p. 487.

58. Q. Reade, "Workplace Conflict Is Time-consuming Problem for Business," *PersonnelToday.com*, September 30, 2004, www.personneltoday.co.uk.

59. K. O'Connor and P. Carnevale, "A Nasty but Effective Negotiation Strategy: Misrepresentation of a Common-Value Issue," *Personality and Social Psychology Bulletin*, May 1997, pp. 504–515.

Foundations of Organization Structure

Every revolution evaporates and leaves behind only the slime of a new bureaucracy.

—Writer Franz Kafka

LEARNING OBJECTIVES

After studying this chapter, you should be able to:

1. Identify the six elements of an organization's structure.
2. Identify the characteristics of a bureaucracy.
3. Describe a matrix organization.
4. Identify the characteristics of a virtual organization.
5. Show why managers want to create boundaryless organizations.
6. Demonstrate how organizational structures differ, and contrast mechanistic and organic structural models.
7. Analyze the behavioral implications of different organizational designs.
8. Show how globalization affects organizational structure.

Fixing Ford

Ford is in trouble, and everyone knows it. It lost $12.7 billion in 2006. Its stock price plummeted from $27.63 in September 2005 to $6.97 in December 2007. There have been whispers of bankruptcy.

When Bill Ford (great-grandson of founder Henry Ford) became CEO in 2001, he started closing Ford plants at a rate of about one per year. That wasn't enough. So in 2006, Ford announced plans to close 14 more plants, at a rate of more than two per year, through 2012. When even that proved inadequate, Ford hired former Boeing executive Alan Mulally to become CEO while Ford remained as executive chairman.

Ford has come to realize, too slowly for some critics, that the new global business environment won't support Ford's current product line or organizational structure. Ford's market share has fallen steadily since 2000, when it commanded 25 percent of the market. By 2012, it may be half that. But Mulally and Ford recognize that the only way to survive is by shrinking, and Ford's painful efforts to shrink will affect every aspect of its business, including, obviously, its workforce. "Ford's always been good to me," says Dick Holland, a long-time Ford factory worker. "But things have changed."

In addition to closing plants and cutting costs, Mulally has targeted Ford's organizational structure. Mulally argues that the structure has been archaic for a long time. "We have been going out of business for 40 years," he says to every employee group he addresses. Among the structural changes Mulally wishes to make are to centralize its operations. In the past, Ford has had regional fiefdoms, where every global market has its own strategy and products. Mulally wants to break down these structural divisions and create a single worldwide organization.

While Ford was geographically decentralized, it also was highly bureaucratic within its divisions. An elaborate system of pay grades clearly established the pecking order within divisions. Managers were not encouraged to socialize with people outside their pay grade. "The bureaucracy at Ford grew, and managers took refuge in the structure when things got tough, rather than innovate or try ideas that seemed risky," said a retired Ford executive.

This decentralization also affected communication among divisions. In the past, Ford held monthly division chief meetings, during which there was little sharing of information. Mulally has changed that to weekly meetings, and he's tried to increase information sharing.

It's not clear that Mulally can transform this structure—what *BusinessWeek* called a "balkanized mess." It does seem clear, though, that without major structural changes, Ford is unlikely to survive. "There's no global company I know of that can succeed with the level of complexity we have at Ford," he says.[1] ■

Structural decisions are arguably the most fundamental ones a leader, such as Ford's Alan Mulally, has to make. Before we delve into the elements of an organization's structure and how they can affect behavior, consider how you might react to one type of organizational structure—the bureaucratic structure—by taking the following self-assessment.

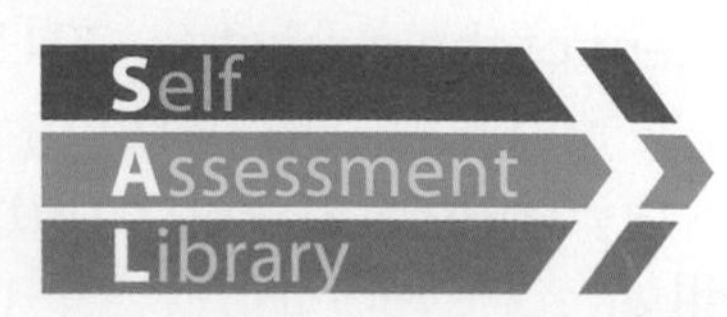

DO I LIKE BUREAUCRACY?

In the Self-Assessment Library (available on CD and online), take assessment IV.F.2 (Do I Like Bureaucracy?) and answer the following questions.

1. *Judging from the results, how willing are you to work in a bureaucratic organization?*
2. *Do you think scores on this measure matter? Why or why not?*
3. *Do you think people who score very low (or even very high) on this measure should try to adjust their preferences based on where they are working?*

What Is Organizational Structure?

1 *Identify the six elements of an organization's structure.*

An **organizational structure** defines how job tasks are formally divided, grouped, and coordinated. There are six key elements that managers need to address when they design their organization's structure: work specialization, departmentalization, chain of command, span of control, centralization and decentralization, and formalization.[2] Exhibit 16-1 presents each of these elements as answers to an important structural question. The following sections describe these six elements of structure.

Work Specialization

Early in the twentieth century, Henry Ford became rich and famous by building automobiles on an assembly line. Every Ford worker was assigned a specific, repetitive task. For instance, one person would just put on the right-front wheel, and someone else would install the right-front door. By breaking jobs up into small standardized tasks, which could be performed over and over again, Ford was able to produce cars at the rate of one every 10 seconds, while using employees who had relatively limited skills.

Ford demonstrated that work can be performed more efficiently if employees are allowed to specialize. Today we use the term **work specialization**, or *division of labor*, to describe the degree to which activities in the organization are subdivided into separate jobs. The essence of work specialization is that rather than an entire job being done by one individual, it is broken down into a number of steps, with each step being completed by a separate individual. In essence, individuals specialize in doing part of an activity rather than the entire activity.

By the late 1940s, most manufacturing jobs in industrialized countries were being done with high work specialization. Because not all employees in an organization have the same skills, management saw specialization as a means to

Exhibit 16-1 Key Design Questions and Answers for Designing the Proper Organizational Structure

The Key Question	The Answer Is Provided By
1. To what degree are activities subdivided into separate jobs?	Work specialization
2. On what basis will jobs be grouped together?	Departmentalization
3. To whom do individuals and groups report?	Chain of command
4. How many individuals can a manager efficiently and effectively direct?	Span of control
5. Where does decision-making authority lie?	Centralization and decentralization
6. To what degree will there be rules and regulations to direct employees and managers?	Formalization

organizational structure *The way in which job tasks are formally divided, grouped, and coordinated.*

work specialization *The degree to which tasks in an organization are subdivided into separate jobs.*

Work is specialized at the Russian factories that manufacture the wooden nesting dolls called matryoshkas. At this factory outside Moscow, individuals specialize in doing part of the doll production, from the craftsmen who carve the dolls to the painters who decorate them. Work specialization brings efficiency to doll production, as some 50 employees can make 100 matryoshkas every 2 days.

make the most efficient use of its employees' skills. Managers also saw other efficiencies that could be achieved through work specialization. Employee skills at performing a task successfully increase through repetition. Less time is spent in changing tasks, in putting away one's tools and equipment from a prior step in the work process, and in getting ready for another. Equally important, training for specialization is more efficient from the organization's perspective. It's easier and less costly to find and train workers to do specific and repetitive tasks. This is especially true of highly sophisticated and complex operations. For example, could Cessna produce one Citation jet a year if one person had to build the entire plane alone? Not likely! Finally, work specialization increases efficiency and productivity by encouraging the creation of special inventions and machinery.

For much of the first half of the twentieth century, managers viewed work specialization as an unending source of increased productivity. And they were probably right. Because specialization was not widely practiced, its introduction almost always generated higher productivity. But by the 1960s, there came increasing evidence that a good thing can be carried too far. The point had been reached in some jobs at which the human diseconomies from specialization—which surfaced as boredom, fatigue, stress, low productivity, poor quality, increased absenteeism, and high turnover—more than offset the economic advantages (see Exhibit 16-2). In such cases, productivity could be increased by enlarging, rather than narrowing, the scope of job activities. In addition, a number of companies found that by giving employees a variety of activities to do, allowing them to do a whole and complete job, and putting them into teams with interchangeable skills, they often achieved significantly higher output, with increased employee satisfaction.

Most managers today see work specialization as neither obsolete nor an unending source of increased productivity. Rather, managers recognize the economies it provides in certain types of jobs and the problems it creates when it's carried too far. You'll find, for example, high work specialization being used by McDonald's to efficiently make and sell hamburgers and fries and by medical specialists in most health maintenance organizations. On the other hand,

Exhibit 16-2 Economies and Diseconomies of Work Specialization

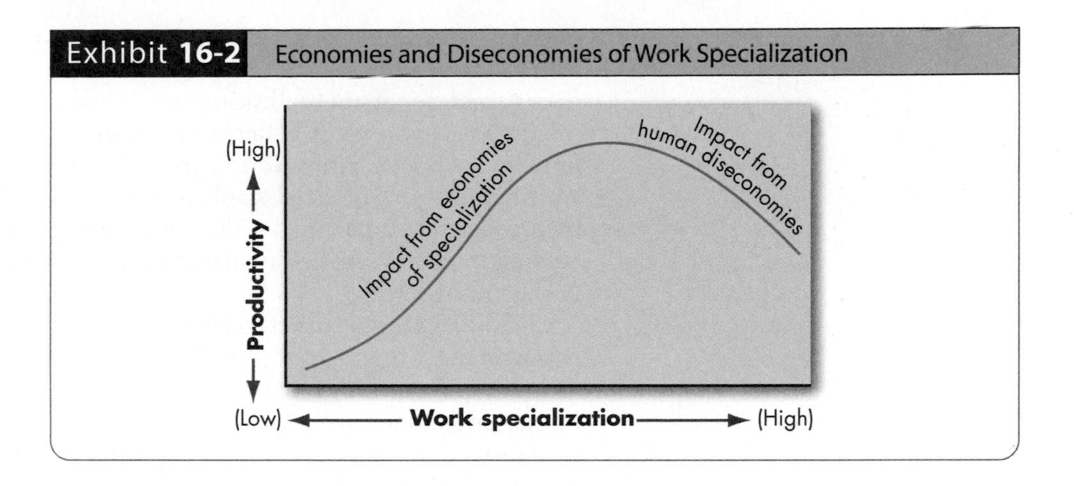

companies such as Saturn Corporation have had success by broadening the scope of jobs and reducing specialization.

Departmentalization

Once you've divided jobs up through work specialization, you need to group these jobs together so that common tasks can be coordinated. The basis by which jobs are grouped together is called **departmentalization**.

One of the most popular ways to group activities is by *functions* performed. A manufacturing manager might organize a plant by separating engineering, accounting, manufacturing, personnel, and supply specialists into common departments. Of course, departmentalization by function can be used in all types of organizations. Only the functions change to reflect the organization's objectives and activities. A hospital might have departments devoted to research, patient care, accounting, and so forth. A professional football franchise might have departments entitled Player Personnel, Ticket Sales, and Travel and Accommodations. The major advantage to this type of grouping is obtaining efficiencies from putting like specialists together. Functional departmentalization seeks to achieve economies of scale by placing people with common skills and orientations into common units.

Jobs can also be departmentalized by the type of *product* the organization produces. Procter & Gamble, for instance, is organized along these lines. Each major product—such as Tide, Pampers, Charmin, and Pringles—is placed under the authority of an executive who has complete global responsibility for that product. The major advantage to this type of grouping is increased accountability for product performance since all activities related to a specific product are under the direction of a single manager. If an organization's activities were service related rather than product related, each service would be autonomously grouped.

Another way to departmentalize is on the basis of *geography*, or territory. The sales function, for instance, may be organized by regions. Each of these regions is, in effect, a department organized around geography. If an organization's customers are scattered over a large geographic area and have similar

departmentalization *The basis by which jobs in an organization are grouped together.*

needs based on their location, then this form of departmentalization can be valuable.

Process departmentalization can be used for processing customers as well as products. If you've ever been to a state motor vehicle office to get a driver's license, you probably went through several departments before receiving your license. In one state, applicants must go through three steps, each handled by a separate department: (1) validation by motor vehicles division; (2) processing by the licensing department; and (3) payment collection by the treasury department.

A final category of departmentalization is to use the particular type of *customer* the organization seeks to reach. Microsoft, for instance, is organized around four customer markets: consumers, large corporations, software developers, and small businesses. The assumption underlying customer departmentalization is that customers in each department have a common set of problems and needs that can best be met by having specialists for each.

Large organizations may use all of the forms of departmentalization that we've described. A major Japanese electronics firm, for instance, organizes each of its divisions along functional lines and its manufacturing units around processes; it departmentalizes sales around seven geographic regions and divides each sales region into four customer groupings. Across organizations of all sizes, one strong trend has developed over the past decade. Rigid, functional departmentalization is being increasingly complemented by teams that cross over traditional departmental lines. As we described in Chapter 10, as tasks have become more complex and more diverse skills are needed to accomplish those tasks, management has turned to cross-functional teams.

Chain of Command

Thirty-five years ago, the chain-of-command concept was a basic cornerstone in the design of organizations. As you'll see, it has far less importance today.[3] But contemporary managers should still consider its implications when they decide how best to structure their organizations. The **chain of command** is an unbroken line of authority that extends from the top of the organization to the lowest echelon and clarifies who reports to whom. It answers questions for employees such as "To whom do I go if I have a problem?" and "To whom am I responsible?"

You can't discuss the chain of command without discussing two complementary concepts: *authority* and *unity of command.* **Authority** refers to the rights inherent in a managerial position to give orders and expect the orders to be obeyed. To facilitate coordination, each managerial position is given a place in the chain of command, and each manager is given a degree of authority in order to meet his or her responsibilities. The **unity-of-command** principle helps preserve the concept of an unbroken line of authority. It states that a person should have one and only one superior to whom that person is directly responsible. If the unity of command is broken, an employee might have to cope with conflicting demands or priorities from several superiors.

Times change, and so do the basic tenets of organizational design. The concepts of chain of command, authority, and unity of command have substantially less relevance today because of advancements in information technology and the trend toward empowering employees. For instance, a low-level employee today can access information in seconds that 35 years ago was available only to top managers. Similarly, networked computers increasingly allow employees anywhere in an organization to communicate with anyone else without going through formal channels. Moreover, the concepts of authority and maintaining the chain of command are increasingly less relevant as operating employees are being empowered to make decisions that previously were reserved for management. Add to this the popularity of self-managed and cross-functional teams and the creation of new structural designs that include multiple bosses, and the unity-of-command concept takes on less relevance. There are, of course, still many organizations that find they can be most productive by enforcing the chain of command. There just seem to be fewer of them today.

Span of Control

How many employees can a manager efficiently and effectively direct? This question of **span of control** is important because, to a large degree, it determines the number of levels and managers an organization has. All things being equal, the wider or larger the span, the more efficient the organization. An example can illustrate the validity of this statement.

Assume that we have two organizations, each of which has approximately 4,100 operative-level employees. As Exhibit 16-3 illustrates, if one has a uniform span of four and the other a span of eight, the wider span would have two fewer levels and approximately 800 fewer managers. If the average manager made $50,000 a year, the wider span would save $40 million a year in management salaries! Obviously, wider spans are more efficient in terms of cost. However, at some point, wider spans reduce effectiveness. That is, when the span becomes too large, employee performance suffers because supervisors no longer have the time to provide the necessary leadership and support.

Narrow, or small, spans have their advocates. By keeping the span of control to five or six employees, a manager can maintain close control.[4] But narrow spans have three major drawbacks. First, as already described, they're expensive

Exhibit 16-3 Contrasting Spans of Control

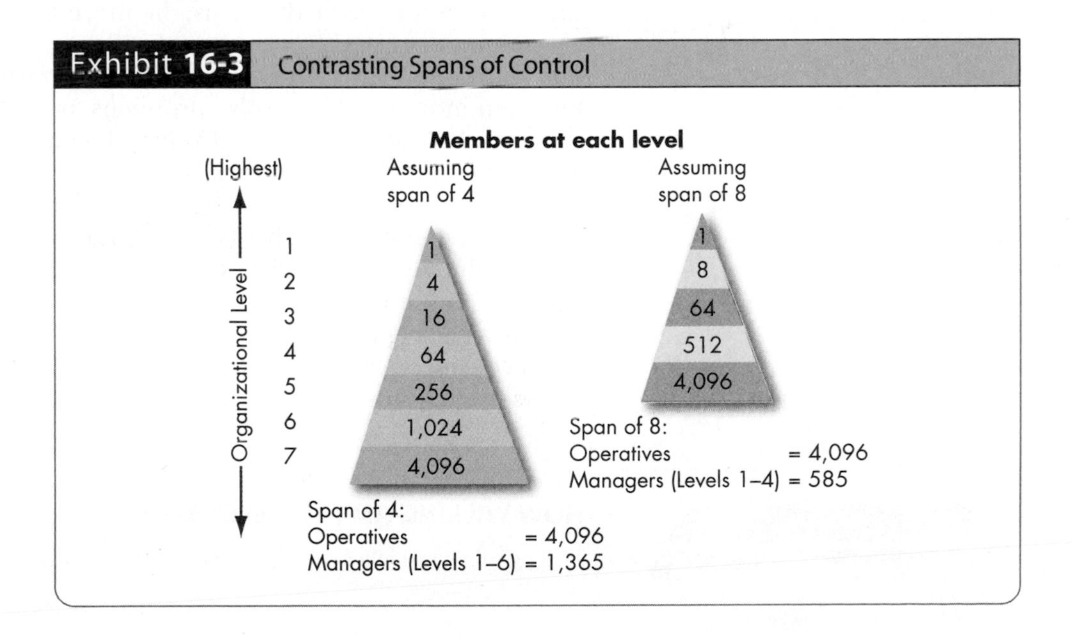

chain of command *The unbroken line of authority that extends from the top of the organization to the lowest echelon and clarifies who reports to whom.*

authority *The rights inherent in a managerial position to give orders and to expect the orders to be obeyed.*

unity of command *The idea that a subordinate should have only one superior to whom he or she is directly responsible.*

span of control *The number of subordinates a manager can efficiently and effectively direct.*

because they add levels of management. Second, they make vertical communication in the organization more complex. The added levels of hierarchy slow down decision making and tend to isolate upper management. Third, narrow spans of control encourage overly tight supervision and discourage employee autonomy.

The trend in recent years has been toward wider spans of control.[5] They're consistent with recent efforts by companies to reduce costs, cut overhead, speed up decision making, increase flexibility, get closer to customers, and empower employees. However, to ensure that performance doesn't suffer because of these wider spans, organizations have been investing heavily in employee training. Managers recognize that they can handle a wider span when employees know their jobs inside and out or can turn to their coworkers when they have questions.

Centralization and Decentralization

In some organizations, top managers make all the decisions. Lower-level managers merely carry out top management's directives. At the other extreme, there are organizations in which decision making is pushed down to the managers who are closest to the action. The former organizations are highly centralized; the latter are decentralized.

The term **centralization** refers to the degree to which decision making is concentrated at a single point in the organization. The concept includes only formal authority—that is, the rights inherent in one's position. Typically, it's said that if top management makes the organization's key decisions with little or no input from lower-level personnel, then the organization is centralized. In contrast, the more that lower-level personnel provide input or are actually given the discretion to make decisions, the more decentralization there is. An organization characterized by centralization is an inherently different structural animal from one that is decentralized. In a decentralized organization, action can be taken more quickly to solve problems, more people provide input into decisions, and employees are less likely to feel alienated from those who make the decisions that affect their work lives.

Consistent with recent management efforts to make organizations more flexible and responsive, there has been a marked trend toward decentralizing decision making. In large companies, lower-level managers are closer to "the action" and typically have more detailed knowledge about problems than do top managers. For instance, big retailers such as Sears and JCPenney have given their store managers considerably more discretion in choosing what merchandise to stock. This allows those stores to compete more effectively against local merchants.

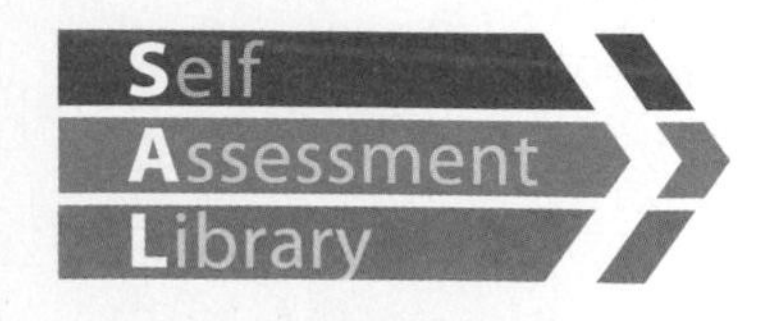

HOW WILLING AM I TO DELEGATE?

In the Self-Assessment Library (available on CD and online), take assessment III.A.2 (How Willing Am I to Delegate?).

Formalization

Formalization refers to the degree to which jobs within the organization are standardized. If a job is highly formalized, then the job incumbent has a minimum amount of discretion over what is to be done, when it is to be done, and how it is to be done. Employees can be expected always to handle the same input in exactly the same way, resulting in a consistent and uniform output. There are explicit job descriptions, lots of organizational rules, and clearly defined procedures covering work processes in organizations in which there is high formalization. Where formalization is low, job behaviors are relatively nonprogrammed, and employees have a great deal of freedom to exercise discretion in their work. Because an individual's discretion on the job is inversely related to the amount of behavior in that job that is preprogrammed by the organization, the greater the standardization, the less input the employee has into how the work is to be done. Standardization not only eliminates the possibility of employees engaging in alternative behaviors, but it even removes the need for employees to consider alternatives.

The degree of formalization can vary widely between organizations and within organizations. Certain jobs, for instance, are well known to have little formalization. College book travelers—the representatives of publishers who call on professors to inform them of their company's new publications—have a great deal of freedom in their jobs. They have no standard sales "spiel," and the extent of rules and procedures governing their behavior may be little more than the requirement that they submit a weekly sales report and some suggestions on what to emphasize for the various new titles. At the other extreme, there are clerical and editorial positions in the same publishing houses for which employees are required to be at their desks by 8:00 A.M. or be docked a half-hour's pay and, once at that desk, to follow a set of precise procedures dictated by management.

OB In the News

Siemens Simple Structure—Not

There is perhaps no tougher task for an executive than to restructure a European organization. Ask former Siemens CEO Klaus Kleinfeld.

Siemens, with $114 billion in revenues in 2006 and branches in 190 countries, is one of the largest electronics companies in the world. Although the company has long been respected for its engineering prowess, it's also derided for its sluggishness and mechanistic structure. So when Kleinfeld took over as CEO, he sought to restructure the company along the lines of what former CEO Jack Welch did at General Electric. Kleinfield has tried to make the structure less bureaucratic so that decisions are made faster. He spun off underperforming businesses. And he simplified the company's structure.

Kleinfeld's efforts drew angry protests from employee groups, with constant picket lines outside his corporate offices. One of the challenges of transforming European organizations is the active participation of employees in executive decisions. Half the seats on the Seimens board of directors are allocated to labor representatives. Not surprisingly, the labor groups did not react positively to Kleinfeld's GE-like restructuring efforts. In his efforts to speed those efforts, labor groups alleged, Kleinfeld secretly bankrolled a business-friendly workers' group to try to undermine Germany's main industrial union.

Due to this and other allegations, Kleinfeld was forced out in June 2007 and replaced by Peter Löscher. Löscher has found the same tensions between inertia and the need for restructuring. Only a month after becoming CEO, Löscher was faced with a decision whether to spin off its underperforming $14 billion auto parts unit, VDO. Löscher had to weigh the forces for stability, who wish to protect worker interests, with U.S.-style pressures for financial performance. One of VDO's possible buyers is a U.S. company, TRW, the controlling interest of which is held by U.S. private equity firm Blackstone. Private equity firms have been called "locusts" by German labor representatives, so, more than most CEOs, Löscher had to balance worker interests with pressure for financial performance. When Löscher decided to sell VDO to German tire giant Continental Corporation, Continental promptly began to downsize and restructure operations.

Source: Based on M. Esterl and D. Crawford, "Siemens CEO Put to Early Test," *Wall Street Journal,* July 23, 2007, p. A8; and J. Ewing, "Siemens' Culture Clash," *BusinessWeek,* January 29, 2007, pp. 42–46.

centralization *The degree to which decision making is concentrated at a single point in an organization.*

formalization *The degree to which jobs within an organization are standardized.*

Common Organizational Designs

We now turn to describing three of the more common organizational designs found in use: the *simple structure*, the *bureaucracy*, and the *matrix structure*.

The Simple Structure

What do a small retail store, an electronics firm run by a hard-driving entrepreneur, and an airline in the midst of a companywide pilot's strike have in common? They probably all use the **simple structure**.

The simple structure is said to be characterized most by what it is not rather than by what it is. The simple structure is not elaborate.[6] It has a low degree of departmentalization, wide spans of control, authority centralized in a single person, and little formalization. The simple structure is a "flat" organization; it usually has only two or three vertical levels, a loose body of employees, and one individual in whom the decision-making authority is centralized.

The simple structure is most widely practiced in small businesses in which the manager and the owner are one and the same. This, for example, is illustrated in Exhibit 16-4, an organization chart for a retail men's store. Jack Gold owns and manages this store. Although he employs five full-time salespeople, a cashier, and extra personnel for weekends and holidays, he "runs the show." But large companies, in times of crisis, often simplify their structures as a means of focusing their resources. For example, when Anne Mulcahy took over Xerox, its product mix and management structure were overly complex. She simplified both, cutting corporate overhead by 26 percent. In such times of crisis, she says, "It's a case of placing your bets in a few areas."[7]

The strength of the simple structure lies in its simplicity. It's fast, flexible, and inexpensive to maintain, and accountability is clear. One major weakness is that it's difficult to maintain in anything other than small organizations. It becomes increasingly inadequate as an organization grows because its low formalization and high centralization tend to create information overload at the top. As size increases, decision making typically becomes slower and can eventually come to a standstill as the single executive tries to continue making all the decisions. This often proves to be the undoing of many small businesses. When an organization begins to employ 50 or 100 people, it's very difficult for the owner-manager to make all the choices. If the structure isn't changed and made more elaborate, the firm often loses momentum and can eventually fail. The simple structure's other weakness is that it's risky—everything depends on one person. One heart attack can literally destroy the organization's information and decision-making center.

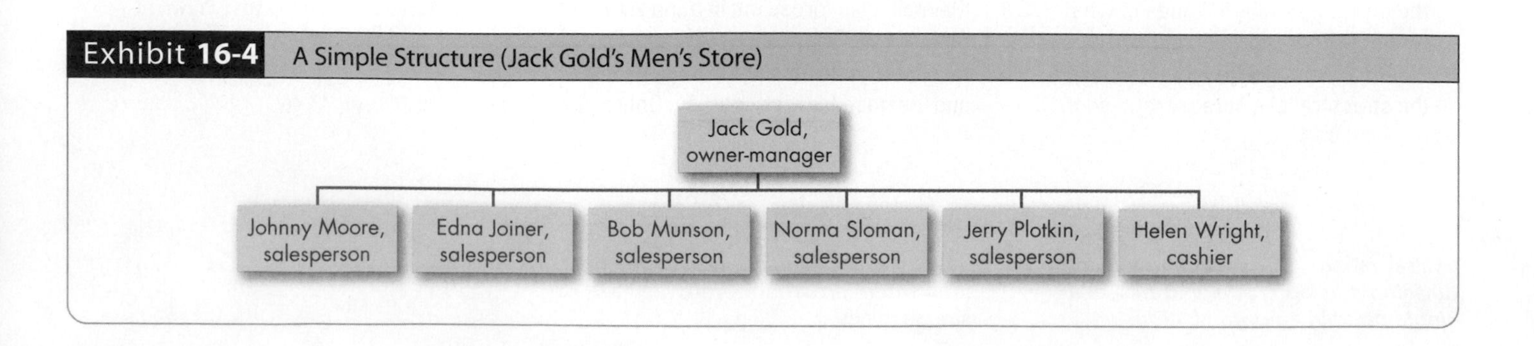

The U.S. Internal Revenue Service (IRS) relies on standardized work processes for coordination and control. IRS service-center employees follow formalized rules and regulations in performing their routine operating tasks. The bureaucracy of the IRS enables employees to perform standardized activities in an efficient way. The IRS employees shown here open about 19 million U.S. tax returns and check for missing documents or information.

The Bureaucracy

2 Identify the characteristics of a bureaucracy.

Standardization! That's the key concept that underlies all bureaucracies. Take a look at the bank where you keep your checking account, the department store where you buy your clothes, or the government offices that collect your taxes, enforce health regulations, or provide local fire protection. They all rely on standardized work processes for coordination and control.

The **bureaucracy** is characterized by highly routine operating tasks achieved through specialization, very formalized rules and regulations, tasks that are grouped into functional departments, centralized authority, narrow spans of control, and decision making that follows the chain of command. As the opening quote to this chapter attests, *bureaucracy* is a dirty word in many people's minds. However, it does have its advantages. The primary strength of the bureaucracy lies in its ability to perform standardized activities in a highly efficient manner. Putting like specialties together in functional departments results in economies of scale, minimum duplication of personnel and equipment, and employees who have the opportunity to talk "the same language" among their peers. Furthermore, bureaucracies can get by nicely with less talented—and, hence, less costly—middle- and lower-level managers. The

simple structure *A structure characterized by a low degree of departmentalization, wide spans of control, authority centralized in a single person, and little formalization.*

bureaucracy *A structure with highly routine operating tasks achieved through specialization, very formalized rules and regulations, tasks that are grouped into functional departments, centralized authority, narrow spans of control, and decision making that follows the chain of command.*

pervasiveness of rules and regulations substitutes for managerial discretion. Standardized operations, coupled with high formalization, allow decision making to be centralized. There is little need, therefore, for innovative and experienced decision makers below the level of senior executives.

One of the major weaknesses of a bureaucracy is illustrated in the following dialogue among four executives in one company: "Ya know, nothing happens in this place until we *produce* something," said the production executive. "Wrong," commented the research and development manager. "Nothing happens until we *design* something!" "What are you talking about?" asked the marketing executive. "Nothing happens here until we *sell* something!" Finally, the exasperated accounting manager responded, "It doesn't matter what you produce, design, or sell. No one knows what happens until we *tally up the results!*" This conversation points up the fact that specialization creates subunit conflicts. Functional unit goals can override the overall goals of the organization.

The other major weakness of a bureaucracy is something we've all experienced at one time or another when having to deal with people who work in these organizations: obsessive concern with following the rules. When cases arise that don't precisely fit the rules, there is no room for modification. The bureaucracy is efficient only as long as employees confront problems that they have previously encountered and for which programmed decision rules have already been established.

International OB

Structural Considerations in Multinationals

When bringing out a business innovation in any country, trudging through corporate bureaucracy can cause delays that result in a competitive disadvantage. This is especially true in China, one of the world's fastest-growing economies. Successful multinational corporations operating in China are realizing that the optimal structure is decentralized with a relatively high degree of managerial autonomy. Given that more than 1.3 billion people live in China, the opportunity for businesses is tremendous, and as a result, competition is increasing. To take advantage of this opportunity, companies must be able to respond to changes before their competitors.

For example, Tyson Foods gives its vice president and head of the company's China operations, James Rice, the freedom to build the company's business overseas. While walking past a food vendor in Shanghai, Rice got the idea for cumin-flavored chicken strips. Without the need to obtain approval from upper management, Rice and his team immediately developed the recipe, tested it, and, after receiving a 90 percent customer-approval rating, began selling the product within 2 months of coming up with the idea.

Other companies that have implemented more formalized, bureaucratic structures have fared less well. One manager of a consumer electronics company who wanted to reduce the package size of a product to lower its cost and attract lower-income Chinese customers had to send the idea to his boss. His boss, the vice president of Asian operations, then sent the idea to the vice president of international operations, who in turn sent the idea to upper management in the United States. Although the idea was approved, the process took 5 months, during which a competitor introduced a similarly packaged product.

So, when it comes to innovating in a dynamic, fast-paced economy such as China, decentralization and autonomy can be major competitive advantages for multinational companies. To gain this competitive advantage, companies like Tyson are empowering their overseas managers to make their own decisions.

Source: Based on C. Hymowitz, "Executives in China Need Both Autonomy and Fast Access to Boss," *Wall Street Journal,* May 10, 2005, p. B1.

The Matrix Structure

Another popular organizational design option is the **matrix structure**. You'll find it being used in advertising agencies, aerospace firms, research and development laboratories, construction companies, hospitals, government agencies, universities, management consulting firms, and entertainment companies.[8] Essentially, the matrix combines two forms of departmentalization: functional and product departmentalization.

3 *Describe a matrix organization.*

The strength of functional departmentalization lies in putting like specialists together, which minimizes the number necessary while allowing the pooling and sharing of specialized resources across products. Its major disadvantage is the difficulty of coordinating the tasks of diverse functional specialists so that their activities are completed on time and within budget. Product departmentalization, on the other hand, has exactly the opposite benefits and disadvantages. It facilitates coordination among specialties to achieve on-time completion and to meet budget targets. Furthermore, it provides clear responsibility for all activities related to a product, but with duplication of activities and costs. The matrix attempts to gain the strengths of each, while avoiding their weaknesses.

The most obvious structural characteristic of the matrix is that it breaks the unity-of-command concept. Employees in the matrix have two bosses—their functional department managers and their product managers. Therefore, the matrix has a dual chain of command.

Exhibit 16-5 shows the matrix form as used in a college of business administration. The academic departments of accounting, decision and information systems, marketing, and so forth are functional units. In addition, specific programs (that is, products) are overlaid on the functions. In this way, members in a matrix structure have a dual assignment—to their functional department and to their product groups. For instance, a professor of accounting who is teaching

Exhibit 16-5 Matrix Structure for a College of Business Administration

Academic Departments / Programs	Undergraduate	Master's	Ph.D.	Research	Executive Development	Community Service
Accounting						
Finance						
Decision and Information Systems						
Management						
Marketing						

matrix structure *A structure that creates dual lines of authority and combines functional and product departmentalization.*

an undergraduate course may report to the director of undergraduate programs as well as to the chairperson of the accounting department.

The strength of the matrix lies in its ability to facilitate coordination when the organization has a multiplicity of complex and interdependent activities. As an organization gets larger, its information-processing capacity can become overloaded. In a bureaucracy, complexity results in increased formalization. The direct and frequent contact between different specialties in the matrix can make for better communication and more flexibility. Information permeates the organization and more quickly reaches the people who need to take account of it. Furthermore, the matrix reduces "bureaupathologies"—the dual lines of authority reduce the tendencies of departmental members to become so busy protecting their little worlds that the organization's overall goals become secondary.

There is another advantage to the matrix. It facilitates the efficient allocation of specialists. When individuals with highly specialized skills are lodged in one functional department or product group, their talents are monopolized and underused. The matrix achieves the advantages of economies of scale by providing the organization with both the best resources and an effective way of ensuring their efficient deployment.

The major disadvantages of the matrix lie in the confusion it creates, its propensity to foster power struggles, and the stress it places on individuals.[9] When you dispense with the unity-of-command concept, ambiguity is significantly increased, and ambiguity often leads to conflict. For example, it's frequently unclear who reports to whom, and it is not unusual for product managers to fight over getting the best specialists assigned to their products. Confusion and ambiguity also create the seeds of power struggles. Bureaucracy reduces the potential for power grabs by defining the rules of the game. When those rules are "up for grabs," power struggles between functional and product managers result. For individuals who desire security and absence from ambiguity, this work climate can produce stress. Reporting to more than one boss introduces role conflict, and unclear expectations introduce role ambiguity. The comfort of bureaucracy's predictability is absent, replaced by insecurity and stress.

New Design Options

Over the past decade or two, senior managers in a number of organizations have been working to develop new structural options that can better help their firms to compete effectively. In this section, we'll describe two such structural designs: the *virtual organization* and the *boundaryless organization.*

The Virtual Organization

Why own when you can rent? That question captures the essence of the **virtual organization** (also sometimes called the *network,* or *modular,* organization), typically a small, core organization that outsources major business functions.[10] In structural terms, the virtual organization is highly centralized, with little or no departmentalization.

4 *Identify the characteristics of a virtual organization.*

The prototype of the virtual structure is today's movie-making organization. In Hollywood's golden era, movies were made by huge, vertically integrated corporations. Studios such as MGM, Warner Brothers, and 20th Century Fox owned large movie lots and employed thousands of full-time specialists—set designers, camera people, film editors, directors, and even actors.

The Boeing Company outsourced the production of about 70 percent of the components of its new 787 Dreamliner passenger jet aircraft. For example, the Italian firm Alenia Aeronautica produced the plane's rear fuselage and horizontal stabilizer, and Tokyo-based Mitsubishi Motors Corporation created the wings. Global outsourcing helped Boeing reduce the plane's development and production costs, enabling it to offer the plane at a price attractive to buyers. Before the Dreamliner's maiden flight, Boeing had a record-breaking 500 orders for the plane, many of which came from the countries that made parts for the aircraft that was assembled at Boeing's plant in the U.S. state of Washington.

Today, most movies are made by a collection of individuals and small companies who come together and make films project by project.[11] This structural form allows each project to be staffed with the talent most suited to its demands, rather than having to choose just from the people employed by the studio. It minimizes bureaucratic overhead because there is no lasting organization to maintain. And it lessens long-term risks and their costs because there is no long term—a team is assembled for a finite period and then disbanded.

Ancle Hsu and David Ji run a virtual organization. Their firm, California-based Apex Digital, is one of the world's largest producers of DVD players, yet the company neither owns a factory nor employs an engineer. They contract everything out to firms in China. With minimal investment, Apex has grown from nothing to annual sales of over $500 million in just 3 years. Similarly, actor Paul Newman's food products company, Newman's Own, sells over $120 million in food every year yet employs only 19 people. This is possible because it outsources almost everything—manufacturing, procurement, shipping, and quality control.

Almost all large organizations have increased their outsourcing. Boeing, for example, assembles all its planes in the Seattle area, but it outsources the production of many of its components. Other companies may outsource their entire information systems to organizations like EDS or IBM. Still others, such as Cingular, Dell, and Time Warner, outsource entire operations—such as customer service or technical support—to other (often overseas) organizations.

What's going on here? A quest for maximum flexibility. These virtual organizations have created networks of relationships that allow them to contract out manufacturing, distribution, marketing, or any other business function for which management feels that others can do better or more cheaply. The virtual

virtual organization *A small, core organization that outsources major business functions.*

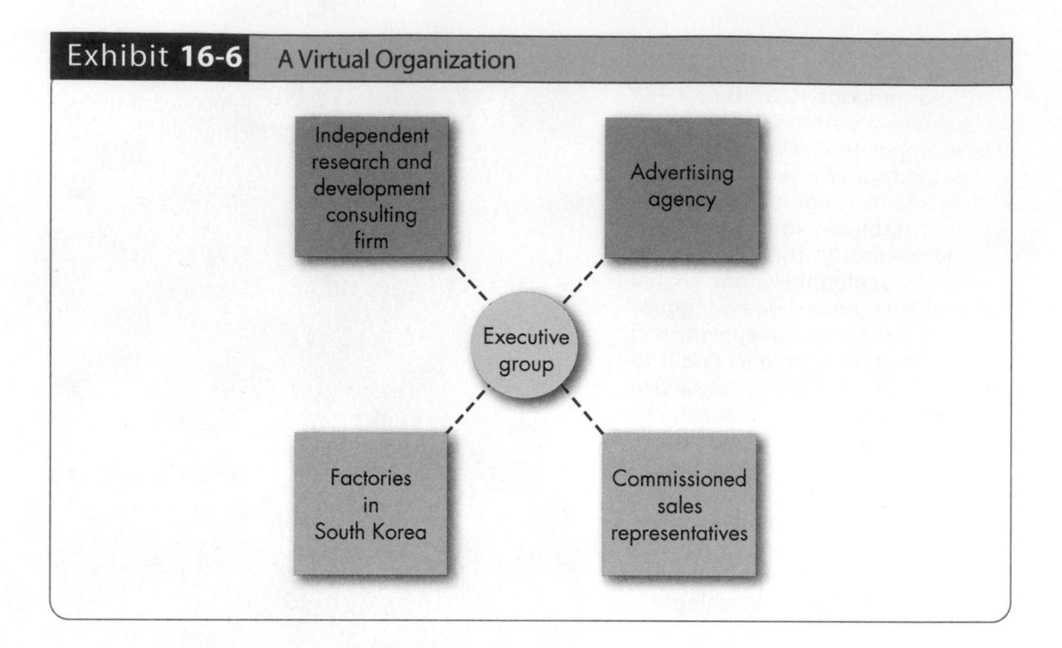

organization stands in sharp contrast to the typical bureaucracy that has many vertical levels of management and where control is sought through ownership. In such organizations, research and development are done in-house, production occurs in company-owned plants, and sales and marketing are performed by the company's own employees. To support all this, management has to employ extra staff, including accountants, human resource specialists, and lawyers. The virtual organization, however, outsources many of these functions and concentrates on what it does best. For most firms in developed countries, that means focusing on design or marketing.

Exhibit 16-6 shows a virtual organization in which management outsources all of the primary functions of the business. The core of the organization is a small group of executives whose job is to oversee directly any activities that are done in-house and to coordinate relationships with the other organizations that manufacture, distribute, and perform other crucial functions for the virtual organization. The dotted lines in Exhibit 16-6 represent the relationships typically maintained under contracts. In essence, managers in virtual structures spend most of their time coordinating and controlling external relations, typically by way of computer-network links.

The major advantage to the virtual organization is its flexibility. For instance, it allows individuals with an innovative idea and little money, such as Ancle Hsu and David Ji, to successfully compete against the likes of Sony, Hitachi, and Sharp Electronics. The primary drawback to this structure is that it reduces management's control over key parts of its business.

The Boundaryless Organization

General Electric's former chairman, Jack Welch, coined the term **boundaryless organization** to describe his idea of what he wanted GE to become. Welch wanted to turn his company into a "family grocery store."[12] That is, in spite of its monstrous size (2006 revenues were $163 billion), he wanted to eliminate *vertical* and *horizontal* boundaries within GE and break down *external* barriers between the company and its customers and suppliers. The boundaryless organization seeks to eliminate the chain of command, have limitless spans of control, and replace departments with empowered teams. And because it relies so heavily on information technology, some

5 Show why managers want to create boundaryless organizations.

Information technology is transforming hospitals from bureaucracies to boundaryless operations. At Hackensack University Medical Center, a computerized clinical information system allows multidisciplinary teams of doctors, nurses, social workers, pharmacists, nutritionists, and other medical staff members to communicate, coordinate, and implement patients' care plans. Doctors and nurses use wireless laptop computers to input patient information and medicine orders and to review lab tests and scans. The IT system improves decision making, helps ensure patient safety, and enables staff members to check patient records from remote locations.

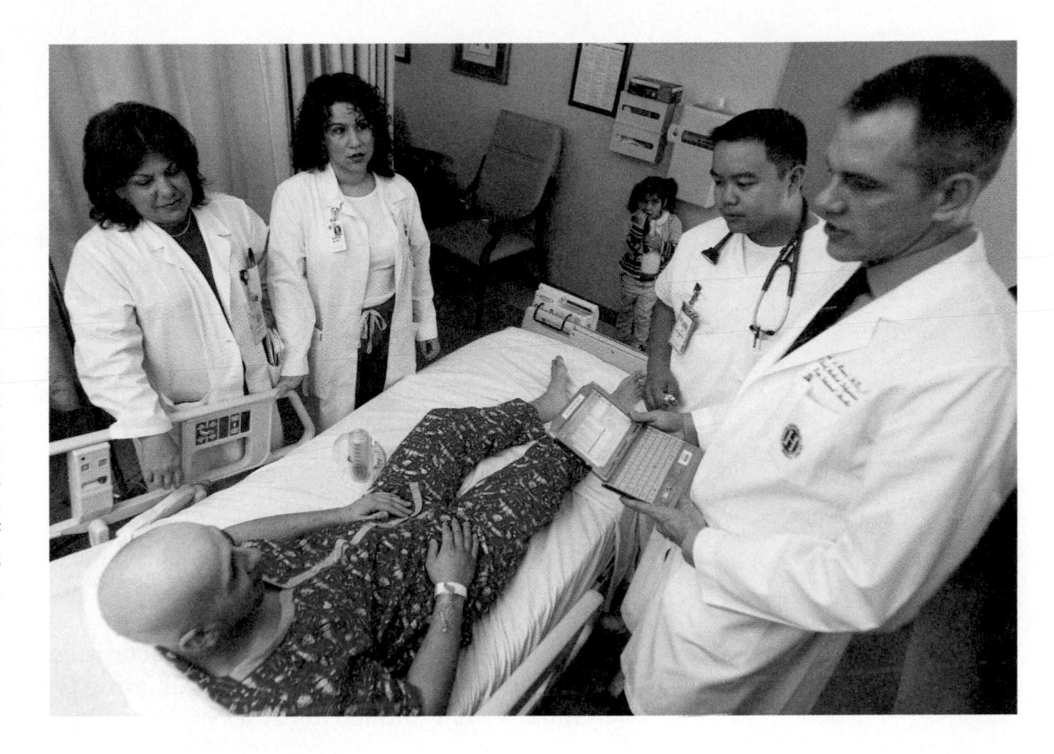

have turned to calling this structure the *T-form* (or technology-based) organization.[13] Although GE has not yet achieved this boundaryless state—and probably never will—it has made significant progress toward that end. So have other companies, such as Hewlett-Packard, AT&T, Motorola, and 3M. Let's take a look at what a boundaryless organization would look like and what some firms are doing to try to make it a reality.[14]

By removing vertical boundaries, management flattens the hierarchy. Status and rank are minimized. Cross-hierarchical teams (which include top executives, middle managers, supervisors, and operative employees), participative decision-making practices, and the use of 360-degree performance appraisals (in which peers and others above and below the employee evaluate performance) are examples of what GE is doing to break down vertical boundaries. At Oticon A/S, a $160-million-per-year Danish hearing aid manufacturer, all traces of hierarchy have disappeared. Everyone works at uniform mobile workstations. And project teams, not functions or departments, coordinate work.

Functional departments create horizontal boundaries. And these boundaries stifle interaction between functions, product lines, and units. The way to reduce these barriers is to replace functional departments with cross-functional teams and to organize activities around processes. For instance, Xerox now develops new products through multidisciplinary teams that work in a single process instead of around narrow functional tasks. Similarly, some AT&T units are now doing annual budgets based not on functions or departments but on processes such as the maintenance of a worldwide telecommunications network. Another way management can cut through horizontal barriers is to use lateral transfers, rotating people into and out of different functional areas. This approach turns specialists into generalists.

boundaryless organization *An organization that seeks to eliminate the chain of command, have limitless spans of control, and replace departments with empowered teams.*

Why Do Structures Differ?

6 Demonstrate how organizational structures differ, and contrast mechanistic and organic structural models.

In the previous sections, we described a variety of organizational designs ranging from the highly structured and standardized bureaucracy to the loose and amorphous boundaryless organization. The other designs we discussed tend to exist somewhere between these two extremes.

Exhibit 16-7 reconceptualizes our previous discussions by presenting two extreme models of organizational design. One extreme we'll call the **mechanistic model**. It's generally synonymous with the bureaucracy in that it has extensive departmentalization, high formalization, a limited information network (mostly downward communication), and little participation by low-level members in decision making. At the other extreme is the **organic model**. This model looks a lot like the boundaryless organization. It's flat, uses cross-hierarchical and cross-functional teams, has low formalization, possesses a comprehensive information network (using lateral and upward communication as well as downward), and involves high participation in decision making.[15]

With these two models in mind, we're now prepared to address a couple questions: Why are some organizations structured along more mechanistic lines whereas others follow organic characteristics? What are the forces that influence the design that is chosen? In the following pages, we present the major forces that have been identified as causes or determinants of an organization's structure.[16]

Strategy

An organization's structure is a means to help management achieve its objectives. Because objectives are derived from the organization's overall strategy, it's only logical that strategy and structure should be closely linked. More specifically, structure should follow strategy. If management makes a significant change in its organization's strategy, the structure will need to be modified to accommodate and support this change.[17]

Most current strategy frameworks focus on three strategy dimensions—innovation, cost minimization, and imitation—and the structural design that works best with each.[18]

Exhibit 16-7 Mechanistic Versus Organic Models

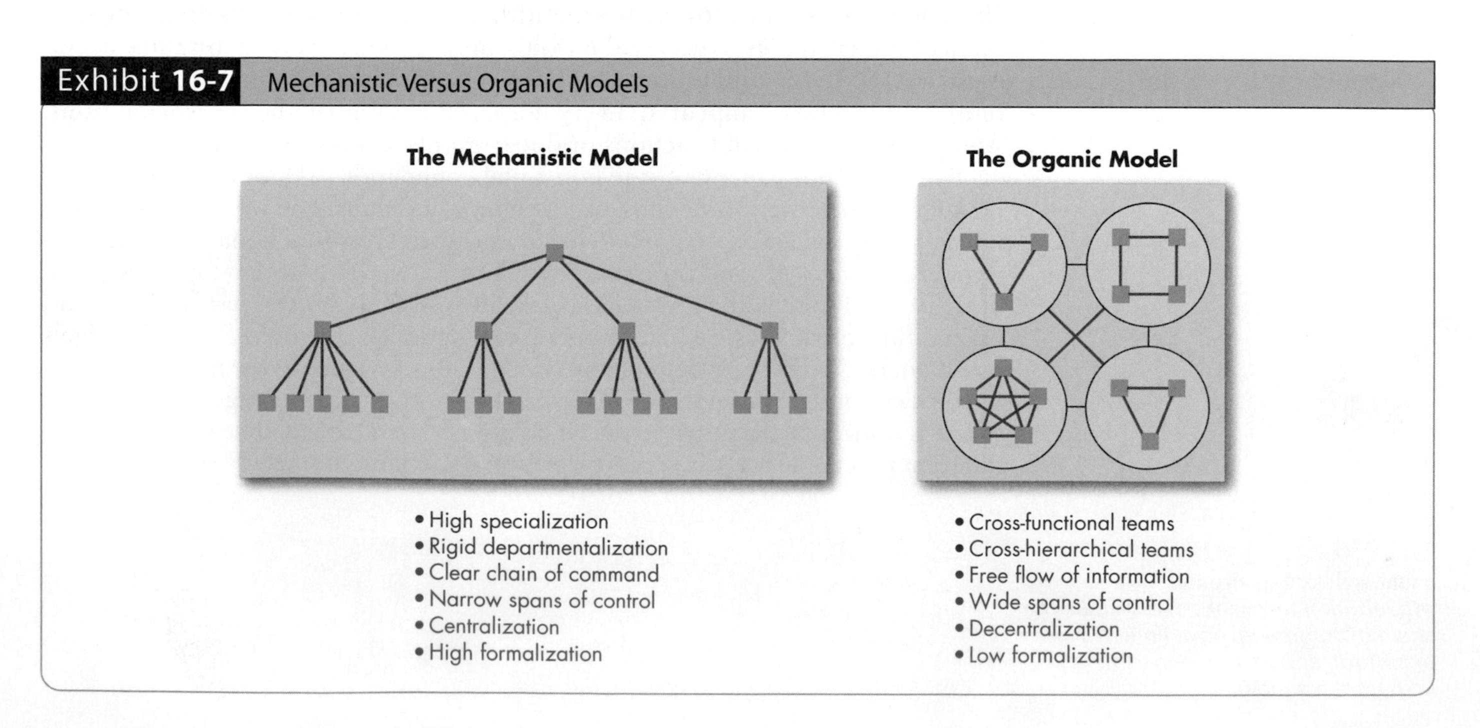

Exhibit 16-8 The Strategy–Structure Relationship

Strategy	Structural Option
Innovation	**Organic:** A loose structure; low specialization, low formalization, decentralized
Cost minimization	**Mechanistic:** Tight control; extensive work specialization, high formalization, high centralization
Imitation	**Mechanistic and organic:** Mix of loose with tight properties; tight controls over current activities and looser controls for new undertakings

To what degree does an organization introduce major new products or services? An **innovation strategy** does not mean a strategy merely for simple or cosmetic changes from previous offerings but rather one for meaningful and unique innovations. Obviously, not all firms pursue innovation. This strategy may appropriately characterize 3M and Sony, but it's not a strategy pursued by conservative retailer Marks & Spencer.

An organization that is pursuing a **cost-minimization strategy** tightly controls costs, refrains from incurring unnecessary innovation or marketing expenses, and cuts prices in selling a basic product. This would describe the strategy pursued by Wal-Mart or the makers of generic grocery products.

Organizations following an **imitation strategy** try to capitalize on the best of both of the previous strategies. They seek to minimize risk and maximize opportunity for profit. Their strategy is to move into new products or new markets only after viability has been proven by innovators. They take the successful ideas of innovators and copy them. Manufacturers of mass-marketed fashion goods that are rip-offs of designer styles follow the imitation strategy. This label probably also characterizes well-known firms such as Hewlett Packard and the Chinese PC maker Lenovo. They essentially follow their smaller and more innovative competitors with superior products, but only after their competitors have demonstrated that the market is there.

Exhibit 16-8 describes the structural option that best matches each strategy. Innovators need the flexibility of the organic structure, whereas cost minimizers seek the efficiency and stability of the mechanistic structure. Imitators combine the two structures. They use a mechanistic structure in order to maintain tight controls and low costs in their current activities, while at the same time they create organic subunits in which to pursue new undertakings.

Organization Size

There is considerable evidence to support the idea that an organization's size significantly affects its structure.[19] For instance, large organizations—those that typically employ 2,000 or more people—tend to have more specialization, more

mechanistic model *A structure characterized by extensive departmentalization, high formalization, a limited information network, and centralization.*

organic model *A structure that is flat, uses cross-hierarchical and cross-functional teams, has low formalization, possesses a comprehensive information network, and relies on participative decision making.*

innovation strategy *A strategy that emphasizes the introduction of major new products and services.*

cost-minimization strategy *A strategy that emphasizes tight cost controls, avoidance of unnecessary innovation or marketing expenses, and price cutting.*

imitation strategy *A strategy that seeks to move into new products or new markets only after their viability has already been proven.*

The degree of routineness differentiates technologies. At Wallstrip.com, nonroutineness characterizes the customized work of employees who create an entertaining daily Web video show and accompanying blog about the stock market. The show relies heavily on the knowledge of specialists such as host Lindsay Campbell and writer/producer Adam Elend, who are shown here in the production studio, where they're getting ready to film an episode of their show.

Source: Dima Gavrysh/ The New York Times

departmentalization, more vertical levels, and more rules and regulations than do small organizations. However, the relationship isn't linear. Rather, size affects structure at a decreasing rate. The impact of size becomes less important as an organization expands. Why is this? Essentially, once an organization has around 2,000 employees, it's already fairly mechanistic. An additional 500 employees will not have much impact. On the other hand, adding 500 employees to an organization that has only 300 members is likely to result in a significant shift toward a more mechanistic structure.

Technology

The term **technology** refers to how an organization transfers its inputs into outputs. Every organization has at least one technology for converting financial, human, and physical resources into products or services. The Ford Motor Co., for instance, predominantly uses an assembly-line process to make its products. On the other hand, colleges may use a number of instruction technologies—the ever-popular formal lecture method, the case-analysis method, the experiential exercise method, the programmed learning method, and so forth. In this section we want to show that organizational structures adapt to their technology.

Numerous studies have been carried out on the technology–structure relationship.[20] The details of those studies are quite complex, so we'll go straight to "the bottom line" and attempt to summarize what we know.

The common theme that differentiates technologies is their *degree of routineness.* By this we mean that technologies tend toward either routine or nonroutine activities. The former are characterized by automated and standardized operations. Nonroutine activities are customized. They include varied operations such as furniture restoring, custom shoemaking, and genetic research.

What relationships have been found between technology and structure? Although the relationship is not overwhelmingly strong, we find that routine tasks are associated with taller and more departmentalized structures. The relationship between technology and formalization, however, is stronger. Studies consistently show routineness to be associated with the presence of rule manuals, job descriptions, and other formalized documentation. Finally, an interesting relationship has been found between technology and centralization. It seems logical that routine technologies would be associated with a centralized structure, while nonroutine technologies, which rely more heavily on the knowledge of specialists, would be characterized by delegated decision authority. This position has met with some support. However, a more generalizable conclusion is that the technology-centralization relationship is moderated by the degree of formalization. Formal regulations and centralized decision making are both control mechanisms and management can substitute one for the other. Routine technologies should be associated with centralized control if there is a minimum of rules and regulations. However, if formalization is high, routine technology can be accompanied by decentralization. So we would predict that routine technology would lead to centralization, but only if formalization is low.

Environment

An organization's **environment** is composed of institutions or forces outside the organization that potentially affect the organization's performance. These typically include suppliers, customers, competitors, government regulatory agencies, public pressure groups, and the like.

Why should an organization's structure be affected by its environment? Because of environmental uncertainty. Some organizations face relatively static environments—few forces in their environment are changing. There are, for example, no new competitors, no new technological breakthroughs by current competitors, or little activity by public pressure groups to influence the organization. Other organizations face very dynamic environments—rapidly changing government regulations affecting their business, new competitors, difficulties in acquiring raw materials, continually changing product preferences by customers, and so on. Static environments create significantly less uncertainty for managers than do dynamic ones. And because uncertainty is a threat to an organization's effectiveness, management will try to minimize it. One way to reduce environmental uncertainty is through adjustments in the organization's structure.[21]

Recent research has helped clarify what is meant by environmental uncertainty. It's been found that there are three key dimensions to any organization's environment: capacity, volatility, and complexity.[22]

The *capacity* of an environment refers to the degree to which it can support growth. Rich and growing environments generate excess resources, which can buffer the organization in times of relative scarcity.

The degree of instability in an environment is captured in the *volatility* dimension. When there is a high degree of unpredictable change, the environment is dynamic. This makes it difficult for management to predict accurately the probabilities associated with various decision alternatives. Because information technology changes at such a rapid place, more organizations' environments are becoming volatile.

technology *The way in which an organization transfers its inputs into outputs.*

environment *Institutions or forces outside an organization that potentially affect the organization's performance.*

MYTH OR SCIENCE? *"People Are Our Most Important Asset"*

Though this bromide has been expressed so often it arouses a cynical smirk on the faces of many, there is evidence that for most companies, it's true.

When we separate the U.S. economy into hard or tangible (manufacturing, real estate, etc.) and soft or intangible (medical care, communications, education) sectors, the soft industries provide 79 percent of all jobs and 76 percent of all U.S. GDP. Although this separation is far from perfect, it does suggest that the so-called knowledge worker is an increasingly important part of the economy. Yet many organizational structures tend to be based on physical assets rather than intellectual resources.

For example, to return to the auto industry example, U.S. auto manufacturers focus their structure along physical assets—product lines or component systems—and outsource part-making or assembly to a small degree. Japanese auto manufacturers like Toyota or Honda, conversely, focus on developing the intellectual products in-house (design and engineering), and outsource some or most of manufacturing and assembly to the countries where they sell their products. It has been argued that these structural differences account for the intangible advantages (design, engineering) enjoyed by Japanese over U.S. automakers.

The authors of a recent study note: "While managing professional intellect is clearly the key to value creation and profitability for most companies, few have arrived at a systematic structures for developing, focusing, leveraging, and measure their intellectual capabilities."

So, even if most organizations argue that people are their most important asset, they aren't structured to make the maximum use of that asset.[23] ■

Finally, the environment needs to be assessed in terms of *complexity*—that is, the degree of heterogeneity and concentration among environmental elements. Simple environments—like in the tobacco industry—are homogeneous and concentrated. In contrast, environments characterized by heterogeneity and dispersion—think of companies in the broadband industry, such as Verizon—are called complex, meaning the environment is diverse and the competitors numerous.

Exhibit 16-9 summarizes our definition of the environment along its three dimensions. The arrows in this figure are meant to indicate movement toward higher uncertainty. So organizations that operate in environments characterized as scarce, dynamic, and complex face the greatest degree of uncertainty. Why? Because they have little room for error, high unpredictability, and a diverse set of elements in the environment to monitor constantly.

Exhibit 16-9 Three-Dimensional Model of the Environment

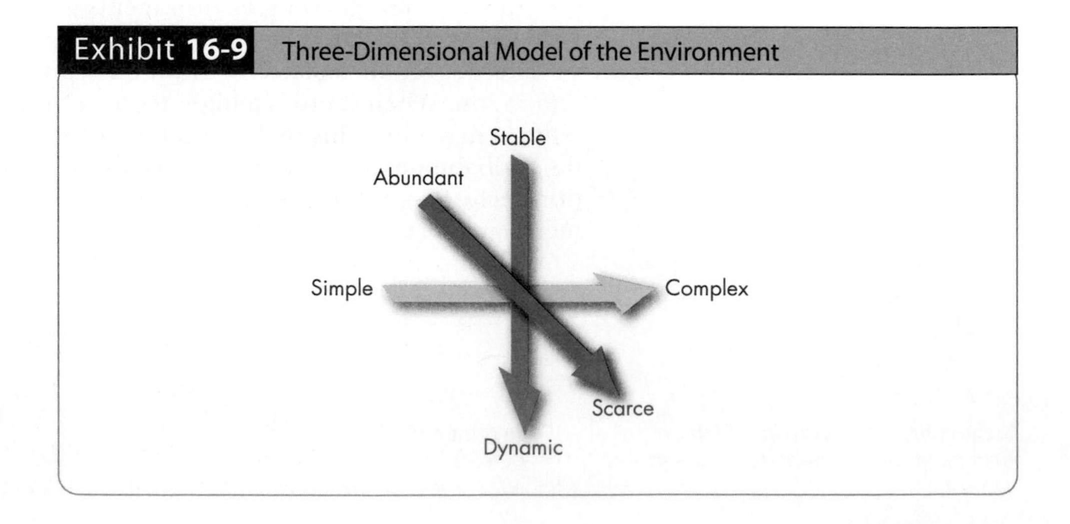

Given this three-dimensional definition of *environment*, we can offer some general conclusions. There is evidence that relates the degrees of environmental uncertainty to different structural arrangements. Specifically, the more scarce, dynamic, and complex the environment, the more organic a structure should be. The more abundant, stable, and simple the environment, the more the mechanistic structure will be preferred.

Organizational Designs and Employee Behavior

We opened this chapter by implying that an organization's structure can have significant effects on its members. In this section, we want to assess directly just what those effects might be.

7 *Analyze the behavioral implications of different organizational designs.*

A review of the evidence linking organizational structures to employee performance and satisfaction leads to a pretty clear conclusion—you can't generalize! Not everyone prefers the freedom and flexibility of organic structures. Some people are most productive and satisfied when work tasks are standardized and ambiguity is minimized—that is, in mechanistic structures. So any discussion of the effect of organizational design on employee behavior has to address individual differences. To illustrate this point, let's consider employee preferences for work specialization, span of control, and centralization.[24]

The evidence generally indicates that *work specialization* contributes to higher employee productivity but at the price of reduced job satisfaction. However, this statement ignores individual differences and the type of job tasks people do. As we noted previously, work specialization is not an unending source of higher productivity. Problems start to surface, and productivity begins to suffer, when the human diseconomies of doing repetitive and narrow tasks overtake the economies of specialization. As the workforce has become more highly educated and desirous of jobs that are intrinsically rewarding, the point at which productivity begins to decline seems to be reached more quickly than in decades past.

Although more people today are undoubtedly turned off by overly specialized jobs than were their parents or grandparents, it would be naive to ignore the reality that there is still a segment of the workforce that prefers the routine and repetitiveness of highly specialized jobs. Some individuals want work that makes minimal intellectual demands and provides the security of routine. For these people, high work specialization is a source of job satisfaction. The empirical question, of course, is whether this represents 2 percent of the workforce or 52 percent. Given that there is some self-selection operating in the choice of careers, we might conclude that negative behavioral outcomes from high specialization are most likely to surface in professional jobs occupied by individuals with high needs for personal growth and diversity.

A review of the research indicates that it is probably safe to say there is no evidence to support a relationship between *span of control* and employee performance. Although it is intuitively attractive to argue that large spans might lead to higher employee performance because they provide more distant supervision and more opportunity for personal initiative, the research fails to support this notion. At this point it's impossible to state that any particular span of control is best for producing high performance or high satisfaction among employees. Again, the reason is probably individual differences. That is, some people like to be left alone, while others prefer the security of a boss who is quickly available at

The tasks of these women making cookies at a factory in South Korea are highly standardized. Individual differences influence how these employees respond to their high work specialization. For these women, specialization may be a source of job satisfaction because it provides the security of routine and gives them the chance to socialize on the job because they work closely with coworkers.

all times. Consistent with several of the contingency theories of leadership discussed in Chapter 12, we would expect factors such as employees' experiences and abilities and the degree of structure in their tasks to explain when wide or narrow spans of control are likely to contribute to their performance and job satisfaction. However, there is some evidence indicating that a manager's job satisfaction increases as the number of employees supervised increases.

We find fairly strong evidence linking *centralization* and job satisfaction. In general, organizations that are less centralized have a greater amount of autonomy. And the evidence suggests that autonomy is positively related to job satisfaction. But, again, individual differences surface. While one employee may value her freedom, another may find autonomous environments frustratingly ambiguous.

Our conclusion: To maximize employee performance and satisfaction, individual differences, such as experience, personality, and the work task, should be taken into account. As we'll note shortly, culture needs to be taken into consideration, too.

One obvious insight needs to be made before we leave this topic: People don't select employers randomly. There is substantial evidence that individuals are attracted to, selected by, and stay with organizations that suit their personal characteristics.[25] Job candidates who prefer predictability, for instance, are likely to seek out and take employment in mechanistic structures, and those who want autonomy are more likely to end up in an organic structure. So the effect of structure on employee behavior is undoubtedly reduced when the selection process facilitates proper matching of individual characteristics with organizational characteristics.

Global Implications

8 *Show how globalization affects organizational structure.*

When we think about how culture influences how organizations are to be structured, several questions come to mind. First, does culture really matter to organizational structure? Second, do employees in different countries vary in their perceptions of different types of organizational structures? Finally, how do cultural considerations fit with our discussion of the boundaryless organization? Let's tackle each of these questions in turn.

Culture and Organizational Structure Does culture really affect organizational structure? The answer might seem obvious—yes!—but there are reasons culture may not matter as much as you think. The U.S. model of business has been very influential, so much so that the organizational structures in other countries may mirror those of U.S. organizations. Moreover, U.S. structures themselves have been influenced by structures in other countries (especially Japan, Great Britain, and Germany). However, cultural concerns still might be important. Bureaucratic structures still dominate in many parts of Europe and Asia. Moreover, one management expert argues that U.S. management often places too much emphasis on individual leadership, which may be jarring in countries where decision making is more decentralized.[26]

Culture and Employee Structure Preferences Although there isn't a great deal of research out there, it does suggest that national culture influences the preference for structure, so it, too, needs to be considered.[27] For instance, organizations that operate with people from high power distance cultures, such as those found in Greece, France, and most of Latin America, find employees much more accepting of mechanistic structures than where employees come from low power distance countries. So you need to consider cultural differences along with individual differences when making predictions on how structure will affect employee performance and satisfaction.

Culture and the Boundaryless Organization When fully operational, the boundaryless organization also breaks down barriers created by geography. Most large companies today see themselves as global corporations, and may well do as much business overseas as domestically. As a result, many companies struggle with the problem of how to incorporate geographic regions into their structure. The boundaryless organization provides one solution to this problem because geography is considered more of a tactical, logistical issue than a structural issue. In short, the goal of the boundaryless organization is to break down cultural barriers.

One way to break down barriers is through strategic alliances. Many large firms have strategic alliances or joint partnerships with other companies. These alliances blur the distinction between one organization and another as employees work on joint projects. And some companies are allowing customers to perform functions that previously were done by management. For instance, some AT&T units are receiving bonuses based on customer evaluations of the teams that serve them. Finally, telecommuting is blurring organizational boundaries. The security analyst with who does his job from his ranch in Texas or the software designer who works for a Tokyo company but does her job in the Caribbean, are just two examples of the millions of workers who are now doing their jobs outside the physical boundaries of their employers' premises.

Summary and Implications for Managers

The theme of this chapter has been that an organization's internal structure contributes to explaining and predicting behavior. That is, in addition to individual and group factors, the structural relationships in which people work has a bearing on employee attitudes and behavior.

Exhibit 16-10 Organization Structure: Its Determinants and Outcomes

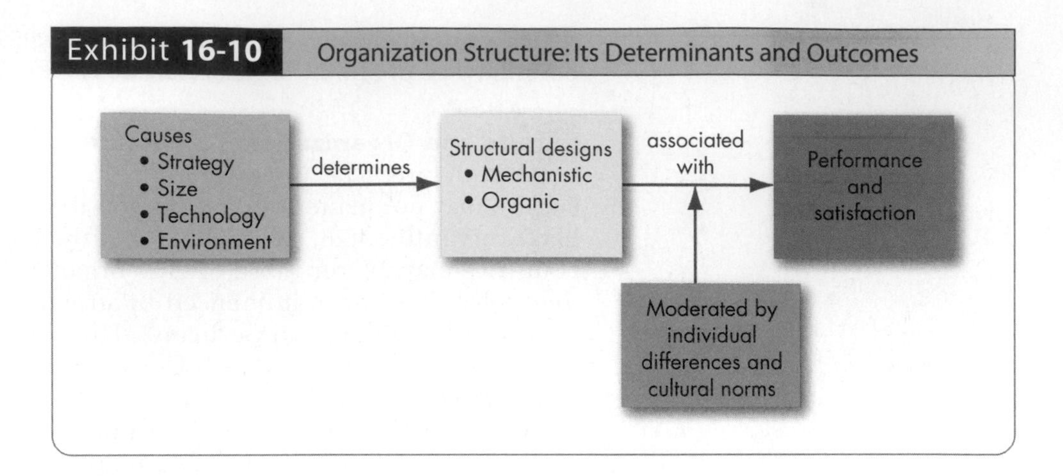

What's the basis for the argument that structure has an impact on both attitudes and behavior? To the degree that an organization's structure reduces ambiguity for employees and clarifies concerns such as "What am I supposed to do?" "How am I supposed to do it?" "To whom do I report?" and "To whom do I go if I have a problem?" it shapes their attitudes and facilitates and motivates them to higher levels of performance.

Of course, structure also constrains employees to the extent that it limits and controls what they do. For example, organizations structured around high levels of formalization and specialization, strict adherence to the chain of command, limited delegation of authority, and narrow spans of control give employees little autonomy. Controls in such organizations are tight, and behavior tends to vary within a narrow range. In contrast, organizations that are structured around limited specialization, low formalization, wide spans of control, and the like provide employees greater freedom and, thus, are characterized by greater behavioral diversity.

Exhibit 16-10 visually summarizes what we've discussed in this chapter. Strategy, size, technology, and environment determine the type of structure an organization will have. For simplicity's sake, we can classify structural designs around one of two models: mechanistic or organic. The specific effect of structural designs on performance and satisfaction is moderated by employees' individual preferences and cultural norms.

Finally, increasingly, technology is reshaping work such that organizational structures may be increasingly amorphous. This allows a manager the flexibility of taking into account things like employee preferences, experience, and culture so as to design work systems that truly motivate employees.

Point / Counterpoint

DOWNSIZING IMPROVES ORGANIZATIONAL PERFORMANCE

Point

There aren't many leaders who like to downsize. Doing so always means inflicting pain on employees and enduring attacks by politicians, labor groups, and the media. But if there is one thing we have learned in the past 20 years, it's that downsizing has been an indispensable factor in making companies more competitive.

In the 1970s and 1980s, most companies in established countries such as the United States were overstaffed. That made them vulnerable to foreign competition from companies with lower labor costs and a better ability to quickly adapt to new economic conditions and technologies. It's perhaps inevitable that companies do this: Success breeds complacency; and, when business is good, companies tend to overstaff and become bloated. Like the patient with a heart condition, they find the remedy is often painful; but fail to address it, and the eventual harm may be much worse.

Nearly all major U.S. companies that were around in the 1970s have shrunk their workforces and streamlined their operations. Look at IBM. Once one of the largest employers in the world, it often touted its no-layoff policy. But in the 1980s and 1990s, it became quite clear that IBM was too big, too complex, and spread too thin. Today, IBM is profitable again, but only after it shed nearly 100,000 jobs. Here is what former IBM CEO Lou Gerstner said about the need to restructure the company:

> It got stuck because it fell victim to what I call the success syndrome. The more successful enterprises are the more they try to replicate, duplicate, codify what makes us great. And suddenly they're inward thinking. They're thinking how can we continue to do what we've done in the past without understanding that what made them successful is to take risks, to change and to adapt and to be responsive. And so in a sense success breeds its own failure. And I think it's true of a lot of successful businesses.

Layoffs and restructuring are rarely the popular things to do. But without them, most organizations would not survive, much less remain competitive.[28]

Counterpoint

Downsizing has become a sort of rite of passage for business leaders: You're not a real leader unless you've downsized a company. However, to separate fact from myth, let's look at the evidence. Do companies that have downsized perform better as a result?

To study this, a research team looked at *Standard & Poor's 500* (S&P 500) companies over 20 years. They asked whether reductions in employment at one period of time were associated with higher levels of financial performance at a later period in time.

What did they find? In analyzing 6,418 occurrences of changes in employment among the S&P 500, they found that downsizing strategies did *not* result in improved long-term financial performance (as measured by industry-adjusted return on assets). It's important to remember that the results control for prior financial performance and reflect financial performance after the downsizing efforts occurred.

The authors of this study don't argue that downsizing is always a bad strategy. Rather, the upshot is that managers shouldn't assume layoffs are a quick fix to what ails a company. In general, downsizing does *not* improve performance, so the key is to do it only when needed and to do it in the right way.

What are some ways organizations can do this? First, they should use downsizing only as a last resort. Second, and related, they should inform employees about the problem, and give them a chance to contribute alternative restructuring solutions. Third, organizations need to bend over backward to ensure that employees see the layoff process as fair, including making sure the layoff criteria *are* fair (and ideally result from employee involvement), advance notice is given, and job relocation assistance is provided. Finally, make sure downsizing is done to good effect—not just to cut costs, but to reallocate resources to where they can be most effective.[29]

Questions for Review

1. What are the six key elements that define an organization's structure?
2. What is a bureaucracy, and how does it differ from a simple structure?
3. What is a matrix organization?
4. What are the characteristics of a virtual organization?
5. How can managers create a boundaryless organization?
6. Why do organizational structures differ, and what is the difference between a mechanistic structure and an organic structure?
7. What are the behavioral implications of different organizational designs?
8. How does globalization affect organizational structure?

Experiential Exercise

AUTHORITY FIGURES

Purpose

To learn about one's experiences with and feelings about authority.

Time

Approximately 75 minutes.

Procedure

1. Your instructor will separate class members into groups based on their birth order. Groups are formed consisting of "only children," "eldest," "middle," and "youngest," according to placement in families. Larger groups will be broken into smaller ones, with four or five members, to allow for freer conversation.
2. Each group member should talk about how he or she "typically reacts to the authority of others." Focus should be on specific situations that offer general information about how individuals deal with authority figures (for example, bosses, teachers, parents, or coaches). The group has 25 minutes to develop a written list of how the group generally deals with others' authority. Be sure to separate tendencies that group members share and those they do not.
3. Repeat step 2, except this time, discuss how group members "typically are as authority figures." Again make a list of shared characteristics.
4. Each group will share its general conclusions with the entire class.
5. Class discussion will focus on questions such as:
   a. What patterned differences have surfaced between the groups?
   b. What may account for these differences?
   c. What hypotheses might explain the connection between how individuals react to the authority of others and how they are as authority figures?

Source: This exercise is adapted from W. A. Kahn, "An Exercise of Authority," *Organizational Behavior Teaching Review* 14, no. 2 (1989–1990), pp. 28–42. Reprinted with permission.

Ethical Dilemma

HOW MUCH SHOULD DIRECTORS DIRECT?

One critical structural element of most corporations is the board of directors. Nearly any organization of appreciable size has a board of directors. And formally at least, chief executives often report to the directors. Informally, however, many boards defer to the CEO and *advise* more than *direct*.

There is some evidence, though, that this cozy relationship is starting to change. Some directors are mingling with employees to get the 411 on any problems that are brewing. Others are opening communication channels with investors to hear their complaints. Some are even taking over responsibilities that used to be handled by the CEO, such as nominating new board members.

You might think an active board is always good for an organization. However, like most structural decisions, it has downsides and risks. When directors are empowered, they can become "free agents" who pursue their own agendas, including some that may be conflict with the CEO's. Or they may make statements or disclose information that goes against company interests. For example, when the AFL-CIO union secured a meeting with Home Depot director Bonnie Hill, some executives in the company were concerned that she might disclose private information.

Though that didn't appear to be the case with Ms. Hill, one can envision some rogue board members undermining a CEO strategy they don't like through such communiqués. A final danger is the possibility that board members will micromanage a CEO's strategy. For example, when top management of one company went to the board with a proposal for executive bonuses, the board hired its own pay consultants. Such actions don't go over well with CEOs. As one said, "You don't need someone guiding your hand."

Questions

1. How active do you think boards should be?
2. Should directors mix with employees to obtain company information from the ranks? Why or why not?
3. When is the line between representing shareholders' interests and micromanaging or second-guessing the CEO?

Source: Based on K. Whitehouse, "Move Over, CEO: Here Come the Directors," *Wall Street Journal*, October 9, 2006, pp. R1, R4.

Case Incident 1

CAN A STRUCTURE BE *TOO* FLAT?

Steelmaker Nucor likes to think it has management figured out. And with good reason. It is the darling of the business press. Its management practices are often favorably reviewed in management texts. And it's been effective by nearly any business metric.

There's one fundamental management practice that Nucor doesn't appear to have mastered—how to structure itself.

Nucor has always prided itself on having just three levels of management separating the CEO from factory workers. With Nucor's structure, plant managers report directly to CEO Dan DiMicco. As Nucor continues to grow, though, DiMicco is finding it increasingly hard to maintain this simple structure. So, in 2006, DiMicco added another layer of management, creating a new layer of five executive vice presidents. "I needed to be free to make decisions on trade battles," he said.

Still, even with the new layer in its structure, Nucor is remarkably lean and simple. U.S. Steel Corp. employs 1,200 people at its corporate headquarters, compared to a scant 66 at Nucor's. At Nucor, managers still answer their own phone calls and e-mails, and the firm has no corporate jet. Even comparatively lean companies like Toyota appear fat and complicated compared to Nucor. "You're going to get at least ten layers at Toyota before you get to the president," says a former Toyota engineer.

Questions

1. How does the Nucor case illustrate the limitations of the simple organizational structure?
2. Do you think other organizations should attempt to replicate Nucor's structure? Why or why not?
3. Why do you think other organizations have developed much more complex structures than Nucor?
4. Generally, organizational structures tend to reflect the views of the CEO. As more and more "new blood" comes into Nucor, do you think the structure will begin to look like that of other organizations?

Source: P. Glader, "It's Not Easy Being Lean," *Wall Street Journal*, June 19, 2006, pp. B1, B3.

Case Incident 2

NO BOSSES AT W. L. GORE & ASSOCIATES

You've probably bought a garment made of W. L. Gore & Associates's flagship product, Gore-Tex, a fabric that blocks wind and water yet is highly breathable, thanks to Gore's patented technology. But you might not know that the company offers a host of other products, from heart patches and synthetic blood vessels to air pollution filters and fuel cells. In fact, W. L. Gore & Associates makes more than 1,000 products. Though its financial data are not publicly available, a spokesperson for the company said that Gore had double-digit revenue growth the past 3 years. With this type of performance and extensive product line, you might expect Gore to be structured like big companies such as General Electric, Microsoft, or 3M. But it's not, and it never was.

Wilbert L. Gore founded W. L. Gore & Associates in 1958. Gore believed that too much hierarchy and bureaucracy stifled creativity and adaptation, a view he formed during his 17-year career as a DuPont engineer. He stated once that "communication really happens in the car pool," meaning that informal arenas allow employees to share their ideas openly, without fear of criticism from management. So Gore decided to eliminate the hierarchy found in most organizations. Instead, he instructed everyone to communicate openly, with little regard to status differences. In fact, Gore eliminated status differences altogether.

Organizational culture guides and shapes the attitudes of employees at New Zealand Air. One of the airline's guiding principles is to champion and promote New Zealand and its national heritage both within the country and overseas. In this photo, a cabin crew member dressed in traditional Maori clothing and a pilot touch noses to represent the sharing of a single breath following a ceremony for the airline's purchase of a Boeing airplane. This expression of representing their country with pride creates a strong bond among employees.

particular interest to us.[14] As the following quote makes clear, culture defines the rules of the game:

> Culture by definition is elusive, intangible, implicit, and taken for granted. But every organization develops a core set of assumptions, understandings, and implicit rules that govern day-to-day behavior in the workplace.... Until newcomers learn the rules, they are not accepted as full-fledged members of the organization. Transgressions of the rules on the part of high-level executives or front-line employees result in universal disapproval and powerful penalties. Conformity to the rules becomes the primary basis for reward and upward mobility.[15]

The role of culture in influencing employee behavior appears to be increasingly important in today's workplace.[16] As organizations have widened spans of control, flattened structures, introduced teams, reduced formalization, and empowered employees, the *shared meaning* provided by a strong culture ensures that everyone is pointed in the same direction.

As we show later in this chapter, who receives a job offer to join the organization, who is appraised as a high performer, and who gets a promotion are strongly influenced by the individual–organization "fit"—that is, whether the applicant's or employee's attitudes and behavior are compatible with the culture. It's not a coincidence that employees at Disney theme parks appear to be almost universally attractive, clean, and wholesome looking, with bright smiles. That's the image Disney seeks. The company selects employees who will maintain that image. And once on the job, a strong culture, supported by formal rules and regulations, ensures that Disney theme-park employees will act in a relatively uniform and predictable way.

Culture as a Liability

We are treating culture in a nonjudgmental manner. We haven't said that it's good or bad, only that it exists. Many of its functions, as outlined, are valuable for both the organization and the employee. Culture enhances organizational commitment and increases the consistency of employee behavior. These are clearly benefits to an organization. From an employee's standpoint, culture is valuable because it reduces ambiguity. It tells employees how things are done and what's important. But we shouldn't ignore the potentially dysfunctional aspects of culture, especially a strong one, on an organization's effectiveness.

Barriers to Change Culture is a liability when the shared values are not in agreement with those that will further the organization's effectiveness. This is most likely to occur when an organization's environment is dynamic.[17] When an environment is undergoing rapid change, an organization's entrenched culture may no longer be appropriate. So consistency of behavior is an asset to an organization when it faces a stable environment. It may, however, burden the organization and make it difficult to respond to changes in the environment. This helps to explain the challenges that executives at organizations like Mitsubishi, Eastman Kodak, Airbus, and the U.S. Federal Bureau of Investigation have had in recent years in adapting to upheavals in their environment.[18] These organizations have strong cultures that worked well for them in the past. But these strong cultures become barriers to change when "business as usual" is no longer effective.

Barriers to Diversity Hiring new employees who, because of race, age, gender, disability, or other differences, are not like the majority of the organization's members creates a paradox.[19] Management wants new employees to accept the organization's core cultural values. Otherwise, these employees are unlikely to fit in or be accepted. But at the same time, management wants to openly acknowledge and demonstrate support for the differences that these employees bring to the workplace.

Strong cultures put considerable pressure on employees to conform. They limit the range of values and styles that are acceptable. In some instances, such as the widely publicized case involving the energy giant Texaco (which was settled on behalf of 1,400 employees for $176 million) in which senior managers made disparaging remarks about minorities, a strong culture that condones prejudice can even undermine formal corporate diversity policies.[20] Organizations seek out and hire diverse individuals because of the alternative strengths these people bring to the workplace. Yet these diverse behaviors and strengths are likely to diminish in strong cultures as people attempt to fit in. Strong cultures, therefore, can be liabilities when they effectively eliminate the unique strengths that people of different backgrounds bring to the organization. Moreover, strong cultures can also be liabilities when they support institutional bias or become insensitive to people who are different.

Barriers to Acquisitions and Mergers Historically, the key factors that management looked at in making acquisition or merger decisions were related to financial advantages or product synergy. In recent years, cultural compatibility has become the primary concern.[21] While a favorable financial statement or product line may be the initial attraction of an acquisition candidate, whether the acquisition actually works seems to have more to do with how well the two organizations' cultures match up.

Many acquisitions fail shortly after their consummation. A survey by consulting firm A.T. Kearney revealed that 58 percent of mergers failed to reach the value goals set by top managers.[22] The primary cause of failure is conflicting organizational cultures. As one expert commented, "Mergers have an unusually high failure rate, and it's always because of people issues." For instance, the 2001 $183 billion merger between America Online (AOL) and Time Warner

MYTH OR SCIENCE?

"People Socialize Themselves"

This statement is true to a significant degree. Although we generally think of socialization as the process in which a person is shaped by his environment—and indeed that is the major focus of socialization research—more evidence is accumulating that many people socialize themselves, or at least substantially mold their socialization experiences.

Research has shown that people with a proactive personality are much better at learning the ropes than are newcomers. (As we noted in Chapter 4, people with a proactive personality identify opportunities, show initiative, and take action.) That's because they are more likely to ask questions, seek out help, and solicit feedback—in short, they learn more because they seek out more information and feedback.

Research indicates that individuals with a proactive personality are also better at networking when they join an organization, and achieve a closer fit with the culture of their organizations—in short, they build their own "social capital." As a result of being more effectively socialized into the organization, proactive people tend to like their jobs more, perform them better, and show less propensity to quit. Proactive people, it seems, do a lot to socialize *themselves* into the culture of an organization.

None of this is meant to deny that socialization matters. The point is that people are not passive actors in being socialized. It may well be that how well someone is socialized into a new culture depends more on her personality than anything else.[23] ■

was the largest in corporate history. The merger has been a disaster—only 2 years later, the stock had fallen an astounding 90 percent. Culture clash is commonly argued to be one of the causes of AOL Time Warner's problems. As one expert noted, "In some ways the merger of AOL and Time Warner was like the marriage of a teenager to a middle-aged banker. The cultures were vastly different. There were open collars and jeans at AOL. Time Warner was more buttoned-down."[24]

Creating and Sustaining Culture

4 *Explain the factors that create and sustain an organization's culture.*

An organization's culture doesn't pop out of thin air. Once established, it rarely fades away. What forces influence the creation of a culture? What reinforces and sustains these forces once they're in place? We answer both of these questions in this section.

How a Culture Begins

An organization's current customs, traditions, and general way of doing things are largely due to what it has done before and the degree of success it has had with those endeavors. This leads us to the ultimate source of an organization's culture: its founders.[25]

The founders of an organization traditionally have a major impact on that organization's early culture. They have a vision of what the organization should be. They are unconstrained by previous customs or ideologies. The small size that typically characterizes new organizations further facilitates the founders' imposition of their vision on all organizational members. Culture creation occurs in three ways.[26] First, founders hire and keep only employees who think and feel the same way they do. Second, they indoctrinate and socialize these employees to their way of thinking and feeling. And finally, the founders' own behavior acts as a role model that encourages employees to identify with them

The source of Cranium's culture is co-founder and CEO Richard Tait, shown here at a toy fair demonstrating the toys and games his company makes. Tait created a culture of fun and collaboration at Cranium so employees can work in an environment that stimulates creativity and innovation in developing new products. At Cranium, employees choose their own titles. Tait chose Grand Poo Bah, and the chief financial officer selected Professor Profit. The office walls at Cranium are painted in bright primary colors, and music plays everywhere.

and thereby internalize their beliefs, values, and assumptions. When the organization succeeds, the founders' vision becomes seen as a primary determinant of that success. At this point, the founders' entire personality becomes embedded in the culture of the organization.

The culture at Hyundai, the giant Korean conglomerate, is largely a reflection of its founder Chung Ju Yung. Hyundai's fierce, competitive style and its disciplined, authoritarian nature are the same characteristics often used to describe Chung. Other contemporary examples of founders who have had an immeasurable impact on their organization's culture would include Bill Gates at Microsoft, Ingvar Kamprad at IKEA, Herb Kelleher at Southwest Airlines, Fred Smith at FedEx, and Richard Branson at the Virgin Group.

Keeping a Culture Alive

Once a culture is in place, there are practices within the organization that act to maintain it by giving employees a set of similar experiences.[27] For example, many of the human resource practices we discuss in the next chapter reinforce the organization's culture. The selection process, performance evaluation criteria, training and development activities, and promotion procedures ensure that those hired fit in with the culture, reward those who support it, and penalize (and even expel) those who challenge it. Three forces play a particularly important part in sustaining a culture: selection practices, the actions of top management, and socialization methods. Let's take a closer look at each.

Selection The explicit goal of the selection process is to identify and hire individuals who have the knowledge, skills, and abilities to perform the jobs within the organization successfully. Typically, more than one candidate will be identified who meets any given job's requirements. When that point is reached, it would be naive to ignore the fact that the final decision as to who is hired will be significantly influenced by the decision-maker's judgment of how well the candidates will fit into the organization. This attempt to ensure a proper match, whether purposely or inadvertently, results in the hiring of people who have values essentially consistent with those of the organization, or at least a good portion of those values.[28]

In addition, the selection process provides information to applicants about the organization. Candidates learn about the organization, and, if they perceive a conflict between their values and those of the organization, they can self-select themselves out of the applicant pool. Selection, therefore, becomes a two-way street, allowing employer or applicant to abrogate a marriage if there appears to be a mismatch. In this way, the selection process sustains an organization's culture by selecting out those individuals who might attack or undermine its core values.

For instance, W. L. Gore & Associates, the maker of Gore-Tex fabric used in outerwear, prides itself on its democratic culture and teamwork. There are no job titles at Gore, nor bosses nor chains of command. All work is done in teams. In Gore's selection process, teams of employees put job applicants through extensive interviews to ensure that candidates who can't deal with the level of uncertainty, flexibility, and teamwork that employees have to deal with in Gore plants are selected out.[29]

Top Management The actions of top management also have a major impact on the organization's culture.[30] Through what they say and how they behave, senior executives establish norms that filter down through the organization as to whether risk taking is desirable; how much freedom managers should give their employees; what is appropriate dress; what actions will pay off in terms of pay raises, promotions, and other rewards; and the like.

For example, Robert A. Keirlin has been called "the cheapest CEO in America."[31] Keirlin is chairman and CEO of Fastenal Co., the largest specialty retailer of nuts and bolts in the United States, with 6,500 employees. He takes a salary of only $60,000 a year. He owns only three suits, each of which he bought used. He clips grocery coupons, drives a Toyota, and stays in low-priced motels when he travels on business. Does Keirlin need to pinch pennies? No. The market value of his stock in Fastenal is worth about $300 million. But the man prefers a modest personal lifestyle. And he prefers the same for his company. Keirlin argues that his behavior should send a message to all his employees: We don't waste things in this company. Keirlin sees himself as a role model for frugality, and employees at Fastenal have learned to follow his example.

New employees at Broad Air Conditioning in Changsha, China, are indoctrinated in the company's military-style culture by going through a 10-day training session of boot camp, where they are divided into platoons and live in barracks. Boot camp prepares new hires for the military formality that prevails at Broad, where employees begin their work week standing in formation during a flag-raising ceremony of two company flags and the flag of China. All employees live in dorms on the company campus and receive free food and lodging. To motivate its workers, Broad has scattered throughout the campus 43 life-size bronze statues of inspirational leaders from Confucius to Jack Welch, the former CEO of General Electric.

Socialization No matter how good a job the organization does in recruiting and selection, new employees are not fully indoctrinated in the organization's culture. Because they are unfamiliar with the organization's culture, new employees are potentially likely to disturb the beliefs and customs that are in place. The organization will, therefore, want to help new employees adapt to its culture. This adaptation process is called **socialization**.[32]

All U.S. Marines must go through boot camp, where they "prove" their commitment. Of course, at the same time, the Marine trainers are indoctrinating new recruits in the "Marine way." All new employees at Neumann Homes in Warrenville, Illinois, go through a 40-hour orientation program.[33] They're introduced to the company's values and culture through a variety of activities—including a customer service lunch, an interactive departmental roundtable fair, and presentations made by groups of new hires to the CEO regarding the company's core values. For new incoming employees in the upper ranks, companies often put considerably more time and effort into the socialization process. At the retailer Limited Brands, newly hired vice presidents and regional directors go through an intensive 1-month program, called "onboarding," designed to immerse these executives in the culture of Limited Brands.[34] During this month, they have no direct responsibilities for tasks associated with their new positions. Instead, they spend all their work time meeting with other senior leaders and mentors, working the floors of retail stores, evaluating employee and customer habits, investigating the competition, and studying Limited Brands' past and current operations.

As we discuss socialization, keep in mind that the most critical socialization stage is at the time of entry into the organization. This is when the organization seeks to mold the outsider into an employee "in good standing." Employees who fail to learn the essential or pivotal role behaviors risk being labeled "nonconformists" or "rebels," which often leads to expulsion. But the organization will be socializing every employee, though maybe not as explicitly, throughout his or her entire career in the organization. This further contributes to sustaining the culture.

Socialization can be conceptualized as a process made up of three stages: prearrival, encounter, and metamorphosis.[35] The first stage encompasses all the learning that occurs before a new member joins the organization. In the second stage, the new employee sees what the organization is really like and confronts the possibility that expectations and reality may diverge. In the third stage, the relatively long-lasting changes take place. The new employee masters the skills required for the job, successfully performs the new roles, and makes the adjustments to the work group's values and norms.[36] This three-stage process has an impact on the new employee's work productivity, commitment to the organization's objectives, and eventual decision to stay with the organization. Exhibit 17-2 depicts this process.

The **prearrival stage** explicitly recognizes that each individual arrives with a set of values, attitudes, and expectations. These cover both the work to be done and the organization. For instance, in many jobs, particularly professional work, new members will have undergone a considerable degree of prior socialization in training and in school. One major purpose of a business school, for example, is to socialize business students to the attitudes and behaviors that business firms want. If business executives believe that successful employees value the profit ethic, are loyal, will work hard, and desire to achieve, they can hire individuals out of business schools who have been premolded in this pattern.

socialization *A process that adapts employees to the organization's culture.*

prearrival stage *The period of learning in the socialization process that occurs before a new employee joins the organization.*

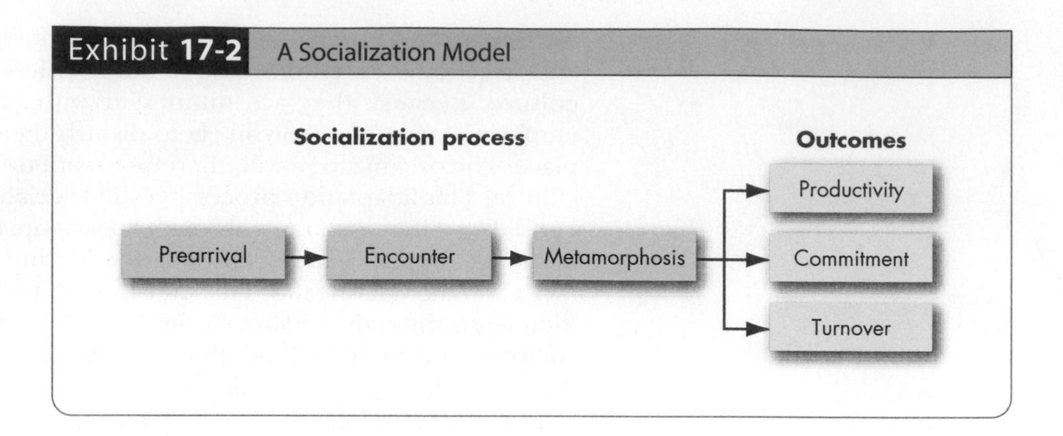

Moreover, most people in business realize that no matter how well they think they can socialize newcomers, the most important predictor of newcomers' future behavior is their past behavior. Research shows that what people know before they join the organization, and how proactive their personality is, are critical predictors of how well they adjust to a new culture.[37]

One way to capitalize on the importance of prehire characteristics in socialization is to select employees with the "right stuff" and to use the selection process to inform prospective employees about the organization as a whole. In addition, as noted previously, the selection process also acts to ensure the inclusion of the "right type"—those who will fit in. "Indeed, the ability of the individual to present the appropriate face during the selection process determines his ability to move into the organization in the first place. Thus, success depends on the degree to which the aspiring member has correctly anticipated the expectations and desires of those in the organization in charge of selection."[38]

On entry into the organization, the new member enters the **encounter stage**. Here the individual confronts the possible dichotomy between expectations—about the job, the coworkers, the boss, and the organization in general—and reality. If expectations prove to have been more or less accurate, the encounter stage merely provides a reaffirmation of the perceptions gained earlier. However, this is often not the case. Where expectations and reality differ, the new employee must undergo socialization that will detach her from her previous assumptions and replace them with another set that the organization deems desirable. At the extreme, a new member may become totally disillusioned with the actualities of the job and resign. Proper selection should significantly reduce the probability of the latter occurrence. Also, an employee's network of friends and coworkers can play a critical role in helping them "learn the ropes." Newcomers are more committed to the organization when their friendship networks are large and diverse. So organizations can help newcomers socialize by encouraging friendship ties in organizations.[39]

Finally, the new member must work out any problems discovered during the encounter stage. This may mean going through changes—hence, we call this the **metamorphosis stage**. The options presented in Exhibit 17-3 are alternatives designed to bring about the desired metamorphosis. Note, for example, that the more management relies on socialization programs that are formal, collective, fixed, serial, and emphasize divestiture, the greater the likelihood that newcomers' differences and perspectives will be stripped away and replaced by standardized and predictable behaviors. Careful selection by management of newcomers' socialization experiences can—at the extreme—create conformists who maintain traditions and customs, or inventive and creative individualists who consider no organizational practice sacred.

We can say that metamorphosis and the entry socialization process is complete when new members have become comfortable with the organization and their job.

Exhibit 17-3 Entry Socialization Options

Formal vs. Informal The more a new employee is segregated from the ongoing work setting and differentiated in some way to make explicit his or her newcomer's role, the more formal socialization is. Specific orientation and training programs are examples. Informal socialization puts the new employee directly into the job, with little or no special attention.

Individual vs. Collective New members can be socialized individually. This describes how it's done in many professional offices. They can also be grouped together and processed through an identical set of experiences, as in military boot camp.

Fixed vs. Variable This refers to the time schedule in which newcomers make the transition from outsider to insider. A fixed schedule establishes standardized stages of transition. This characterizes rotational training programs. It also includes probationary periods, such as the 8- to 10-year "associate" status used by accounting and law firms before deciding on whether or not a candidate is made a partner. Variable schedules give no advance notice of their transition timetable. Variable schedules describe the typical promotion system, in which one is not advanced to the next stage until one is "ready."

Serial vs. Random Serial socialization is characterized by the use of role models who train and encourage the newcomer. Apprenticeship and mentoring programs are examples. In random socialization, role models are deliberately withheld. New employees are left on their own to figure things out.

Investiture vs. Divestiture Investiture socialization assumes that the newcomer's qualities and qualifications are the necessary ingredients for job success, so these qualities and qualifications are confirmed and supported. Divestiture socialization tries to strip away certain characteristics of the recruit. Fraternity and sorority "pledges" go through divestiture socialization to shape them into the proper role.

They have internalized the norms of the organization and their work group, and understand and accept those norms. New members feel accepted by their peers as trusted and valued individuals. They are self-confident that they have the competence to complete the job successfully. They understand the system—not only their own tasks but the rules, procedures, and informally accepted practices as well. Finally, they know how they will be evaluated; that is, what criteria will be used to measure and appraise their work. They know what is expected of them and what constitutes a job "well done." As Exhibit 17-2 shows, successful metamorphosis should have a positive impact on new employees' productivity and their commitment to the organization and reduce their propensity to leave the organization.

Summary: How Cultures Form

Exhibit 17-4 summarizes how an organization's culture is established and sustained. The original culture is derived from the founder's philosophy. This, in turn, strongly influences the criteria used in hiring. The actions of the current top management set the general climate of what is acceptable behavior and what is not. How employees are to be socialized will depend both on the degree of success achieved in matching new employees' values to those of the organization's in the selection process and on top management's preference for socialization methods.

encounter stage *The stage in the socialization process in which a new employee sees what the organization is really like and confronts the possibility that expectations and reality may diverge.*

metamorphosis stage *The stage in the socialization process in which a new employee changes and adjusts to the job, work group, and organization.*

Exhibit 17-4 How Organization Cultures Form

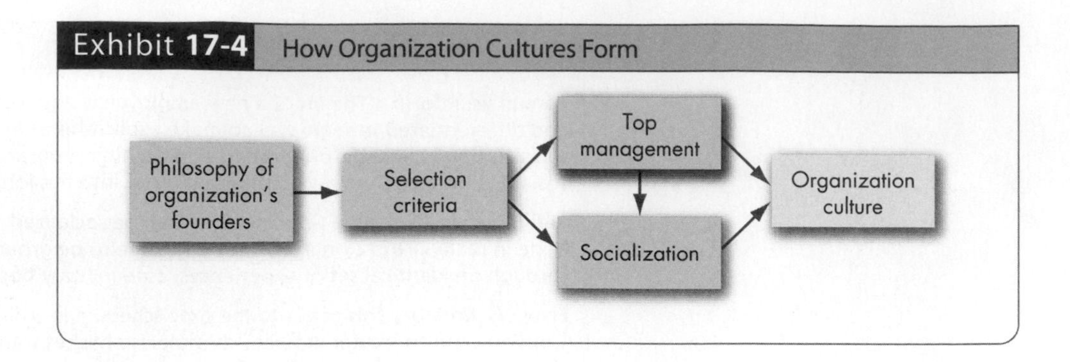

How Employees Learn Culture

5 Show how culture is transmitted to employees.

Culture is transmitted to employees in a number of forms, the most potent being stories, rituals, material symbols, and language.

Stories

During the days when Henry Ford II was chairman of the Ford Motor Co., you would have been hard pressed to find a manager who hadn't heard the story about Mr. Ford reminding his executives, when they got too arrogant, that "it's my name that's on the building." The message was clear: Henry Ford II ran the company.

Nike has a number of senior executives who spend much of their time serving as corporate storytellers. And the stories they tell are meant to convey what Nike is about.[40] When they tell the story of how co-founder (and Oregon track coach) Bill Bowerman went to his workshop and poured rubber into his wife's waffle iron to create a better running shoe, they're talking about Nike's spirit of innovation. When new hires hear tales of Oregon running star Steve Prefontaine's battles to make running a professional sport and to attain better-performance equipment, they learn of Nike's commitment to helping athletes.

Stories such as these circulate through many organizations. They typically contain a narrative of events about the organization's founders, rule breaking, rags-to-riches successes, reductions in the workforce, relocation of employees, reactions to past mistakes, and organizational coping.[41] These stories anchor the present in the past and provide explanations and legitimacy for current practices.

Rituals

Rituals are repetitive sequences of activities that express and reinforce the key values of the organization—what goals are most important, which people are important, and which people are expendable.[42] One of the better-known corporate rituals is Wal-Mart's company chant. Begun by the company's founder, Sam Walton, as a way to motivate and unite his workforce, "Gimme a W, gimme an A, gimme an L, gimme a squiggle, give me an M, A, R, T!" has become a company ritual that bonds Wal-Mart workers and reinforces Sam Walton's belief in the importance of his employees to the company's success. Similar corporate chants are used by IBM, Ericsson, Novell, Deutsche Bank, and PricewaterhouseCoopers.[43]

Material Symbols

The headquarters of Alcoa, the world's leading producer of aluminum, doesn't look like your typical head-office operation. There are few individual offices, even for senior executives. It is essentially made up of cubicles, common areas, and meeting rooms. This informal corporate headquarters conveys to employees that

At Wal-Mart, culture is transmitted to employees through the daily ritual of the "Wal-Mart cheer." Shown here is the manager of a Wal-Mart store leading employees in the motivational chant that helps preserve a small-family spirit and work environment within the world's largest retailer.

Alcoa values openness, equality, creativity, and flexibility. Some corporations provide their top executives with chauffeur-driven limousines and, when they travel by air, unlimited use of the corporate jet. Others may not get to ride in limousines or private jets, but they might still get a car and air transportation paid for by the company. Only the car is a Chevrolet (with no driver), and the jet seat is in the economy section of a commercial airliner.

The layout of corporate headquarters, the types of automobiles top executives are given, and the presence or absence of corporate aircraft are a few examples of material symbols. Others include the size of offices, the elegance of furnishings, executive perks, and attire.[44] These material symbols convey to employees who is important, the degree of egalitarianism desired by top management, and the kinds of behavior (for example, risk taking, conservative, authoritarian, participative, individualistic, social) that are appropriate.

Language

Many organizations and units within organizations use language as a way to identify members of a culture or subculture. By learning this language, members attest to their acceptance of the culture and, in so doing, help to preserve it. The following are examples of terminology used by employees at Knight-Ridder Information, a California-based data redistributor: *accession number* (a number assigned to each individual record in a database), *KWIC* (a set of key-words-in-context), and *relational operator* (searching a database for names or key terms in some order). If you're a new employee at Boeing, you'll find yourself learning a whole unique vocabulary of acronyms, including *BOLD* (Boeing online data), *CATIA* (computer-graphics-aided three-dimensional interactive application),

rituals *Repetitive sequences of activities that express and reinforce the key values of the organization, which goals are most important, which people are important, and which are expendable.*

OB In the News

Change Jobs, and You May Be in for a Culture Shock

When Lyria Charles, a project manager, changed jobs, she didn't check her e-mail on weekends. Eventually, a fellow manager pulled her aside and told her that managers were expected to read e-mail over the weekend. "I didn't know," Charles said. "No one told me."

Employees have to learn the ropes when they change jobs. But unlike many aspects of business, organizational culture has few written rules. Very often, people learn the new culture only after stumbling into barriers and violating unwritten rules. "It's like going to a different country," says Michael Kanazawa of Dissero Partners, a management consulting firm.

There are myriad ways in which one organization's culture differs from another. To paraphrase Tolstoy, in certain ways, organizations are all alike, but each develops its culture in its own way.

Some of the differences—such as dress codes—are pretty easy to detect. Others are much harder to discern. In addition to weekend e-mails, another unwritten rule Charles learned was that she shouldn't have meetings with subordinates in her own office. How did she learn that? When Charles asked to meet with them, her assistant kept scheduling the meetings in the subordinates' cubicles. When Charles asked why, her assistant told her, "That's how it's done."

One way to decode the maze is to astutely observe unwritten rules and customs and to ask lots of questions. Some learning of an organization's culture, though, is pure trial and error. When Kevin Hall started a new job as a mortgage banker, he had to make his own travel arrangements because the first person he asked said it wasn't part of her job. When he observed colleagues getting help, though, he asked someone else, who was happy to oblige. "You feel your way as you go," Hall said.

Source: Based on E. White, "Culture Shock: Learning Customs of a New Office," *Wall Street Journal*, November 28, 2006, p. B6.

MAIDS (manufacturing assembly and installation data system), *POP* (purchased outside production), and *SLO* (service-level objectives).[45]

Organizations, over time, often develop unique terms to describe equipment, offices, key personnel, suppliers, customers, or products that relate to its business. New employees are frequently overwhelmed with acronyms and jargon that, after 6 months on the job, have become fully part of their language. Once assimilated, this terminology acts as a common denominator that unites members of a given culture or subculture.

Creating an Ethical Organizational Culture

6 Demonstrate how an ethical culture can be created.

The content and strength of a culture influence an organization's ethical climate and the ethical behavior of its members.[46] An organizational culture most likely to shape high ethical standards is one that's high in risk tolerance, low to moderate in aggressiveness, and focuses on means as well as outcomes. Managers in such a culture are supported for taking risks and innovating, are discouraged from engaging in unbridled competition, and will pay attention to *how* goals are achieved as well as to *what* goals are achieved.

A strong organizational culture will exert more influence on employees than a weak one. If the culture is strong and supports high ethical standards, it should have a very powerful and positive influence on employee behavior. Johnson & Johnson, for example, has a strong culture that has long stressed corporate obligations to customers, employees, the community, and shareholders, in that order. When poisoned Tylenol (a Johnson & Johnson product) was found on store shelves, employees at Johnson & Johnson across the United States independently pulled the product from these stores before management had even issued a statement concerning the tamperings. No one had to tell these individuals what was morally right; they knew what Johnson & Johnson would expect them to do. On the other hand, a strong culture that encourages pushing the limits can be a powerful force in shaping unethical behavior. For instance, Enron's aggressive culture, with unrelenting pressure on executives to rapidly expand earnings, encouraged ethical corner-cutting and eventually contributed to the company's collapse.[47]

What can management do to create a more ethical culture? We suggest a combination of the following practices:

- *Be a visible role model.* Employees will look to the behavior of top management as a benchmark for defining appropriate behavior. When senior management is seen as taking the ethical high road, it provides a positive message for all employees.
- *Communicate ethical expectations.* Ethical ambiguities can be minimized by creating and disseminating an organizational code of ethics. It should state the organization's primary values and the ethical rules that employees are expected to follow.
- *Provide ethical training.* Set up seminars, workshops, and similar ethical training programs. Use these training sessions to reinforce the organization's standards of conduct, to clarify what practices are and are not permissible, and to address possible ethical dilemmas.
- *Visibly reward ethical acts and punish unethical ones.* Performance appraisals of managers should include a point-by-point evaluation of how his or her decisions measure up against the organization's code of ethics. Appraisals must include the means taken to achieve goals as well as the ends themselves. People who act ethically should be visibly rewarded for their behavior. Just as importantly, unethical acts should be conspicuously punished.
- *Provide protective mechanisms.* The organization needs to provide formal mechanisms so that employees can discuss ethical dilemmas and report unethical behavior without fear of reprimand. This might include creation of ethical counselors, ombudsmen, or ethical officers.

Creating a Positive Organizational Culture

7 *Describe a positive organizational culture.*

It's often difficult to separate management fads from lasting changes in management thinking, especially early. In this book, we try to keep current while staying away from fads. There is one early trend, though, that we think is here to stay: creating a positive organizational culture.

At first blush, creating a positive culture may sound hopelessly naïve, or like a Dilbert-style conspiracy. The one thing that makes us believe this trend is here to stay is that there are signs that management practice and OB research are converging.

A **positive organizational culture** is defined as a culture that emphasizes building on employee strengths, rewards more than it punishes, and emphasizes individual vitality and growth.[48] Let's consider each of these areas.

Building on Employee Strengths A lot of OB, and management practice, is concerned with how to fix employee problems. Although a positive organizational culture does not ignore problems, it does emphasize showing workers how they can capitalize on their strengths. As management guru Peter Drucker said, "Most Americans do not know what their strengths are. When you ask

positive organizational culture *A culture that emphasizes building on employee strengths, rewards more than punishes, and emphasizes individual vitality and growth.*

them, they look at you with a blank stare, or they respond in terms of subject knowledge, which is the wrong answer." Do you know what your strengths are? Wouldn't it be better to be in an organizational culture that helped you discover those, and learn ways to make the most of them?

Larry Hammond used this approach—finding and exploiting employee strengths—at a time when you'd least expect it: during the darkest days of the business. Hammond is CEO of Auglaize Provico, an agribusiness company based in the U.S. state of Ohio. The company was in the midst of its worst financial struggles and had to lay off one-quarter of its workforce. At that nadir, Hammand decided to try a different approach. Rather than dwell on what was wrong, he decided to take advantage of what was right. "If you really want to [excel], you have to know yourself—you have to know what you're good at, and you have to know what you're not so good at," says Hammond. With the help of consultant Barry Conchie, Auglaize Provico focused on discovering and using employee strengths. Hammond and Auglaize Provico turned the company around. "You ask Larry [Hammond] what the difference is, and he'll say that it's individuals using their natural talents," says Conchie.[49]

Rewarding More Than Punishing There is, of course, a time and place for punishment, but there is also a time and place for rewards. Although most organizations are sufficiently focused on extrinsic rewards like pay and promotions, they often forget about the power of smaller (and cheaper) rewards like praise. Creating a positive organizational culture means that managers "catch employees doing something right." Part of creating a positive culture is articulating praise. Many managers withhold praise either because they're afraid employees will coast, or because they think praise is not valued. Failing to praise can become a "silent killer" like escalating blood pressure. Because employees generally don't ask for praise, managers usually don't realize the costs of failing to do it.

Take the example of Elżbieta Górska-Kołodziejczyk, a plant manager for International Paper's facility in Kwidzyn, Poland. The job environment at the plant is bleak and difficult. Employees work in a windowless basement. Staffing is only roughly one-third of its prior level, while production has tripled. These challenges had done in the previous three managers. So, when Górska-Kołodziejczyk took over, she knew she had her work cut out for her. Although she had many items on her list of ways to transform the organization, at the top of her list was recognition and praise. She initially found it difficult to give praise to those who weren't used to it, especially men, but she found over time that they valued it, too. "They were like cement at the beginning," she said. "Like cement." Górska-Kołodziejczyk has found that giving praise is often reciprocated. One day a department supervisor pulled her over to tell her she was doing a good job. "This I do remember, yes," she said.[50]

Emphasizing Vitality and Growth A positive organizational culture emphasizes not only organizational effectiveness, but individuals' growth as well. No organization will get the best out of employees if the employees see themselves as mere tools or parts of the organization. A positive culture realizes the difference between a job and a career, and shows an interest not only in what the employee does to contribute to organizational effectiveness, but in what the organization does it has have assessed over thousands of organizations, fully one-third feel they are not learning and growing on their job. The figure is even higher in some industries, such as banking, manufacturing, communications, and utilities. Although it may take more creativity to encourage employee growth in some types of industries, it can happen in the fast-paced food service industry. Consider the case of Philippe Lescornez and Didier Brynaert.

Employees at Genentech, a biotechnology pioneer, work within a positive organizational culture that promotes individuals' vitality and growth. Genentech provides training opportunities and the resources and equipment needed to get work done and offers courses to help each employee develop the skills they need on their current job as well as for their future work. To discover talent within the company, Genentech allows employees to grow their careers both within departments and across them. An internal transfer program encourages employees to apply for jobs that can help them advance their careers. Scientists and engineers are also allowed to spend 20 percent of each workweek pursuing their favorite projects.

Philippe Lescornez leads a team of employees at Masterfoods in Belgium. One of his team members is Didier Brynaert, who works in Luxembourg, nearly 150 miles from Masterfoods's Belgian headquarters. Brynaert was considered a good sales promoter who was meeting expectations. Lescornez decided that Brynaert's job could be made more important if he were seen less as just another sales promoter and more as an expert on the unique features of the Luxembourg market. So Lescornez asked Brynaert for information he could share with the home office. He hoped that by raising Brynaert's profile in Brussels, he could create in him a greater sense of ownership for his remote sales territory. "I started to communicate much more what he did to other people [within the company], because there's quite some distance between the Brussels office and the section he's working in. So I started to communicate, communicate, communicate. The more I communicated, the more he started to provide material," says Lescornez. As a result, "Now he's recognized as the specialist for Luxembourg—the guy who is able to build a strong relationship with the Luxembourg clients," says Lescornez. What's good for Brynaert, of course, is also good for Lescornez, who gets credit for helping Brynaert grow and develop.[51]

Limits of Positive Culture Is a positive culture a panacea? Cynics (or should we say realists?) may be skeptical about the benefits of positive organizational culture. To be sure, even though some companies have embraced aspects of a positive organizational culture, it is a new enough area that there is some uncertainty about how and when it works best. Moreover, any OB scholar or manager needs to make sure he is objective about the benefits—and risks—of cultivating a positive organizational culture.

Not all cultures value being positive as much as U.S. culture does, and, even within U.S. culture, there surely are limits to how far we should go to preserve a positive culture. For example, Admiral, a British insurance company, has established a Ministry of Fun in its call centers to organize such events as poem writings, foosball, conker competitions (a British game involving chestnuts), and fancy dress days. When does the pursuit of a positive culture start to seem coercive? As one critic notes, "Promoting a social orthodoxy of positiveness focuses on a particular constellation of desirable states and traits but, in so doing, can stigmatize those who fail to fit the template."[52]

Our point is that there may be benefits to establishing a positive culture, but an organization also needs to be careful to be objective, and not pursue it past the point of effectiveness.

Spirituality and Organizational Culture

8 *Identify characteristics of a spiritual culture.*

What do Southwest Airlines, Avaya, The Men's Wearhouse, Ford, Wetherill Associates, and Tom's of Maine have in common? They're among a growing number of organizations that have embraced workplace spirituality.

What Is Spirituality?

Workplace spirituality is *not* about organized religious practices. It's not about God or theology. **Workplace spirituality** recognizes that people have an inner life that nourishes and is nourished by meaningful work that takes place in the context of community.[53] Organizations that promote a spiritual culture recognize that people have both a mind and a spirit, seek to find meaning and purpose in their work, and desire to connect with other human beings and be part of a community.

Why Spirituality Now?

Historical models of management and organizational behavior had no room for spirituality. As we noted in our discussion of emotions in Chapter 8, the myth of rationality assumed that the well-run organization eliminated feelings. Similarly, concern about an employee's inner life had no role in the perfectly rational model. But just as we've now come to realize that the study of emotions improves our understanding of organizational behavior, an awareness of spirituality can help you to better understand employee behavior in the twenty-first century.

Of course, employees have always had an inner life. So why has the search for meaning and purposefulness in work surfaced now? There are a number of reasons. We summarize them in Exhibit 17-5.

Characteristics of a Spiritual Organization

The concept of workplace spirituality draws on our previous discussions of topics such as values, ethics, motivation, leadership, and work/life balance. Spiritual organizations are concerned with helping people develop and reach their full

Exhibit 17-5 Reasons for the Growing Interest in Spirituality

- As a counterbalance to the pressures and stress of a turbulent pace of life. Contemporary lifestyles—single-parent families, geographic mobility, the temporary nature of jobs, new technologies that create distance between people—underscore the lack of community many people feel and increase the need for involvement and connection.
- Formalized religion hasn't worked for many people, and they continue to look for anchors to replace lack of faith and to fill a growing feeling of emptiness.
- Job demands have made the workplace dominant in many people's lives, yet they continue to question the meaning of work.
- The desire to integrate personal life values with one's professional life.
- An increasing number of people are finding that the pursuit of more material acquisitions leaves them unfulfilled.

Mark Trang, an employee of Salesforce.com, teaches business basics to fifth-grade students at an elementary school. Salesforce.com encourages every employee to donate 1 percent of his or her working time to the community. Through volunteer work, Salesforce.com gives employees the opportunity to experience the joy and satisfaction that comes from helping others. Employees give to the community by feeding the homeless, tutoring kids, gardening in community parks, lending computer expertise to nonprofit organizations, and providing disaster relief.

potential. Similarly, organizations that are concerned with spirituality are more likely to directly address problems created by work/life conflicts. What differentiates spiritual organizations from their nonspiritual counterparts? Although research on this question is only preliminary, our review identified four cultural characteristics that tend to be evident in spiritual organizations:[54]

- *Strong sense of purpose.* Spiritual organizations build their cultures around a meaningful purpose. Although profits may be important, they're not the primary values of the organization. People want to be inspired by a purpose that they believe is important and worthwhile.
- *Trust and respect.* Spiritual organizations are characterized by mutual trust, honesty, and openness. Managers aren't afraid to admit mistakes. The president of Wetherill Associates, a highly successful auto parts distribution firm, says: "We don't tell lies here, and everyone knows it. We are specific and honest about quality and suitability of the product for our customers' needs, even if we know they might not be able to detect any problem."[55]
- *Humanistic work practices.* These practices embraced by spiritual organizations include flexible work schedules, group- and organization-based rewards, narrowing of pay and status differentials, guarantees of individual worker rights, employee empowerment, and job security. Hewlett-Packard, for instance, has handled temporary downturns through voluntary attrition and shortened workweeks (shared by all), and it has handled longer-term declines through early retirements and buyouts.
- *Toleration of employee expression.* The final characteristic that differentiates spiritually based organizations is that they don't stifle employee emotions.

workplace spirituality *The recognition that people have an inner life that nourishes and is nourished by meaningful work that takes place in the context of community.*

They allow people to be themselves—to express their moods and feelings without guilt or fear of reprimand. Employees at Southwest Airlines, for instance, are encouraged to express their sense of humor on the job, to act spontaneously, and to make their work fun.

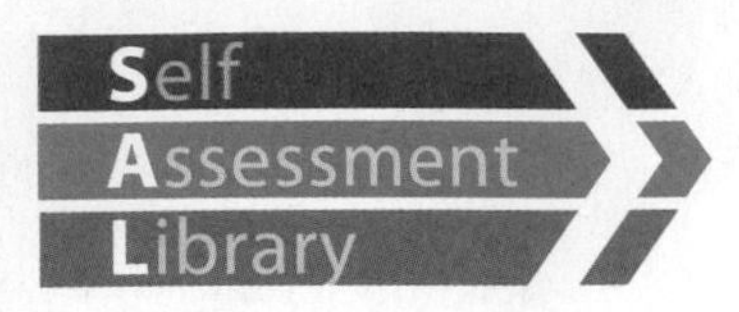

HOW SPIRITUAL AM I?

In the Self-Assessment Library (available on CD and online), take assessment IV.A.4 (How Spiritual Am I?). Note: People's scores on this measure vary from time to time, so take that into account when interpreting the results.

Criticisms of Spirituality

Critics of the spirituality movement in organizations have focused on three issues. First is the question of scientific foundation. What really is workplace spirituality? Is it just a new management buzzword? Second, are spiritual organizations legitimate? Specifically, do organizations have the right to impose spiritual values on their employees? Third is the question of economics: Are spirituality and profits compatible?

First, as you might imagine, there is very little research on workplace spirituality. We don't know whether the concept will have staying power. Do the cultural characteristics just identified really separate spiritual organizations? What is a nonspiritual organization, anyway? Do employees of so-called spiritual organizations perceive that they work in spiritual organizations? Although there is some research suggesting support for workplace spirituality (as we discuss later), before the concept of spirituality gains full credence, the questions we've just posed need to be answered.

On the second question, there is clearly the potential for an emphasis on spirituality to make some employees uneasy. Critics might argue that secular institutions, especially business firms, have no business imposing spiritual values on employees. This criticism is undoubtedly valid when spirituality is defined as bringing religion and God into the workplace.[56] However, the criticism seems less stinging when the goal is limited to helping employees find meaning in their work lives. If the concerns listed in Exhibit 17-5 truly characterize a growing segment of the workforce, then perhaps the time is right for organizations to help employees find meaning and purpose in their work and to use the workplace as a source of community.

Finally, the issue of whether spirituality and profits are compatible objectives is certainly relevant for managers and investors in business. The evidence, although limited, indicates that the two objectives may be very compatible. A recent research study by a major consulting firm found that companies that introduced spiritually based techniques improved productivity and significantly reduced turnover.[57] Another study found that organizations that provide their employees with opportunities for spiritual development outperformed those that didn't.[58] Other studies also report that spirituality in organizations was positively related to creativity, employee satisfaction, team performance, and organizational commitment.[59] And if you're looking for a single case to make the argument for spirituality, it's hard to beat Southwest Airlines. Southwest has one of the lowest employee turnover rates in the airline industry; it consistently has the lowest labor costs per miles flown of any major airline; it regularly outpaces its competitors for achieving on-time arrivals and fewest customer complaints; and it has proven itself to be the most consistently profitable airline in the United States.[60]

Global Implications

9 *Show how national culture may affect the way organizational culture is transported to a different country.*

We considered global cultural values (collectivism–individualism, power distance, and so on) in Chapter 4. Here our focus is a bit narrower: How is organizational culture affected by a global context? As the opening vignette suggests, organizational cultures are so powerful that they often transcend national boundaries. But that doesn't mean that organizations should, or could, be blissfully ignorant of local culture.

This is becoming a bigger issue. In 2007, half of GE's revenue came from outside the United States. GE even moved the headquarters of its health care division to the United Kingdom, and the number of non-U.S. citizens among GE's top 500 managers has tripled since 2001. GE is hardly alone. Large and small organizations alike are often heavily dependent on foreign product markets, labor markets, or both.

As we noted in Chapter 4, national cultures differ. Organizational cultures often reflect national culture. For example, the culture at AirAsia, a Malaysian-based airline, emphasizes informal dress so as not to create status differences. The carrier has lots of parties, participative management, and no private offices. This organizational culture reflects Malaysia's relatively collectivistic culture. However, the culture of USAirways does not reflect the same degree of informality. If USAirways were to set up operations in Malaysia, or merge with AirAsia, it would need to take these cultural differences into account. So when an organization opens up operations in another country, it ignores the local culture to its own risk.

One of the primary things U.S. managers can do is to be culturally sensitive. The United States is a dominant force in business and in culture, and with that influence comes a reputation. "We are broadly seen throughout the world as arrogant people, totally self-absorbed and loud," says one U.S. executive. Companies such as American Airlines, Lowe's, Novell, ExxonMobil, and Microsoft have implemented training programs to sensitize their managers to cultural differences. Some ways in which U.S. managers can be culturally sensitive include talking in a low tone of voice, speaking slowly, listening more, and avoiding discussions of religion and politics.

U.S. employees are not the only ones who need to be culturally sensitive. For example, three times a week, employees at the Canadian unit of Japanese video game maker Koei begin each day standing next to their desks, facing their boss, and saying in unison, "Good morning." That is followed by employees delivering short speeches on topics that range from corporate principles to 3D game engines. Koei also has employees punch a time clock. And Koei asks women to serve tea to top executive guests. Although these practices are consistent with Koei's culture, they do not fit Canadian culture very well. "It's kind of like school," says one Canadian employee.[61]

Summary and Implications for Managers

Exhibit 17-6 depicts organizational culture as an intervening variable. Employees form an overall subjective perception of the organization based on factors such as degree of risk tolerance, team emphasis, and support of people. This overall perception becomes, in effect, the organization's culture or personality. These favorable or unfavorable perceptions then affect employee performance and satisfaction, with the impact being greater for stronger cultures.

Just as people's personalities tend to be stable over time, so too do strong cultures. This makes strong cultures difficult for managers to change. When a

Exhibit 17-6 How Organizational Cultures Have an Impact on Employee Performance and Satisfaction

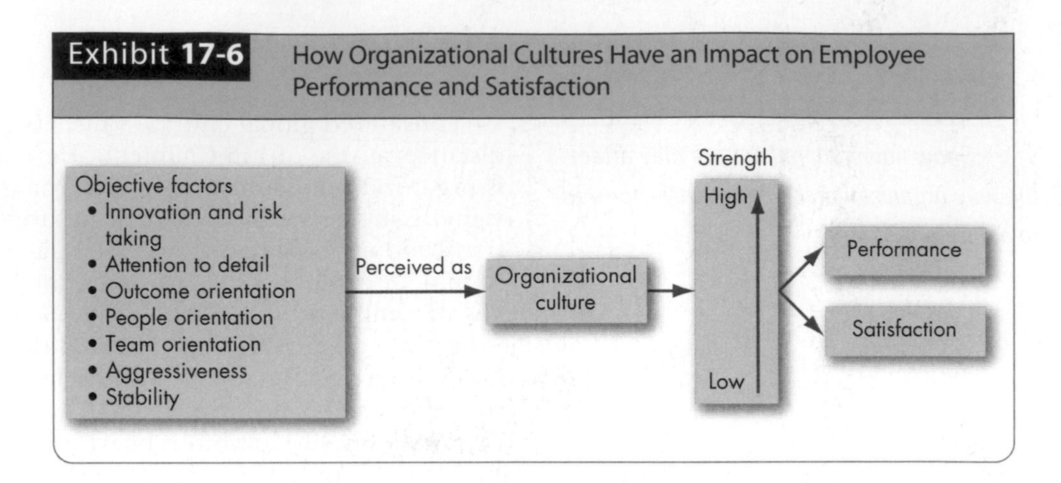

culture becomes mismatched to its environment, management will want to change it. But as the Point/Counterpoint demonstrates, changing an organization's culture is a long and difficult process. The result, at least in the short term, is that managers should treat their organization's culture as relatively fixed.

One of the most important managerial implications of organizational culture relates to selection decisions. Hiring individuals whose values don't align with those of the organization is likely to lead to employees who lack motivation and commitment and who are dissatisfied with their jobs and the organization.[62] Not surprisingly, employee "misfits" have considerably higher turnover rates than individuals who perceive a good fit.[63]

We should also not overlook the influence socialization has on employee performance. An employee's performance depends to a considerable degree on knowing what he should or should not do. Understanding the right way to do a job indicates proper socialization.

As a manager, you can shape the culture of your work environment. That is particularly the case with some of the cultural aspects we discussed in the latter part of the chapter—all managers can do their part to create an ethical culture, and spirituality and a positive organizational culture should be considered, too. Often you can do as much to shape your organizational culture as the culture of the organization shapes you.

Point | Counterpoint

ORGANIZATIONAL CULTURES CAN'T BE CHANGED

An organization's culture is made up of relatively stable characteristics. It develops over many years and is rooted in deeply held values to which employees are strongly committed. In addition, there are a number of forces continually operating to maintain a given culture. These include written statements about the organization's mission and philosophy, the design of physical spaces and buildings, the dominant leadership style, hiring criteria, past promotion practices, entrenched rituals, popular stories about key people and events, the organization's historic performance evaluation criteria, and the organization's formal structure.

Selection and promotion policies are particularly important devices that work against cultural change. Employees chose the organization because they perceived their values to be a "good fit" with the organization. They become comfortable with that fit and will strongly resist efforts to disturb the equilibrium. The terrific difficulties that organizations such as Ford, VW, and the U.S. Postal Service have had in trying to reshape their cultures attest to this dilemma. These organizations historically tended to attract individuals who desired situations that were stable and highly structured. Those in control in organizations will also select senior managers who will continue the current culture. Even attempts to change a culture by going outside the organization to hire a new chief executive are unlikely to be effective. The evidence indicates that the culture is more likely to change the executive than the other way around.

Our argument should not be viewed as saying that culture can *never* be changed. In the unusual case in which an organization confronts a survival-threatening crisis, members of the organization will be responsive to efforts at cultural change. However, anything less than that is unlikely to be effective in bringing about cultural change.

Changing an organization's culture is extremely difficult, but cultures *can* be changed. The evidence suggests that cultural change is most likely to take place when most or all of the following conditions exist:

- **A dramatic crisis.** This is a shock that undermines the status quo and calls into question the relevance of the current culture. Examples are a surprising financial setback, the loss of a major customer, and a dramatic technological breakthrough by a competitor.
- **Turnover in leadership.** New top leadership, which can provide an alternative set of key values, may be perceived as more capable of responding to the crisis (as when Mark Hurd replaced Carly Fiorina at HP).
- **Young and small organizations.** The younger the organization, the less entrenched its culture will be. Similarly, it's easier for management to communicate its new values when the organization is small.
- **Weak culture.** The more widely held a culture is and the higher the agreement among members on its values, the more difficult it will be to change. Conversely, weak cultures are more amenable to change than strong ones.

If all or most of these conditions exist, the following management actions may lead to change: initiating new stories and rituals, selecting and promoting employees who espouse the new values, changing the reward system to support the new values, and undermining current subcultures through transfers, job rotation, and terminations.

Under the best of conditions, these actions won't result in an immediate or dramatic shift in the culture. In the final analysis, cultural change is a lengthy process—measured in years rather than in months. But cultures can be changed. The success that new leadership had in turning around the cultures at companies like IBM, 3M, and GE attests to this claim.

Questions for Review

1 What is institutionalization and how does it affect organizational culture?

2 What is organizational culture and what are its common characteristics?

3 What are the functional and dysfunctional effects of organizational culture?

4 What factors create and sustain an organization's culture?

5 How is culture transmitted to employees?

6 How can an ethical culture be created?

7 What is a positive organizational culture?

8 What are the characteristics of a spiritual culture?

9 How does national culture affect how organizational culture is transported to a different country?

Experiential Exercise

RATE YOUR CLASSROOM CULTURE

Listed here are 14 statements. Using the 5-item scale (from Strongly Agree to Strongly Disagree), respond to each statement by circling the number that best represents your opinion.

	Strongly Agree	Agree	Neutral	Disagree	Strongly Disagree
1. I feel comfortable challenging statements made by my instructor.	5	4	3	2	1
2. My instructor heavily penalizes assignments that are not turned in on time.	1	2	3	4	5
3. My instructor believes that "it's final results that count."	1	2	3	4	5
4. My instructor is sensitive to my personal needs and problems.	5	4	3	2	1
5. A large portion of my grade depends on how well I work with others in the class.	5	4	3	2	1
6. I often feel nervous and tense when I come to class.	1	2	3	4	5
7. My instructor seems to prefer stability over change.	1	2	3	4	5
8. My instructor encourages me to develop new and different ideas.	5	4	3	2	1
9. My instructor has little tolerance for sloppy thinking.	1	2	3	4	5
10. My instructor is more concerned with how I came to a conclusion than with the conclusion itself.	5	4	3	2	1
11. My instructor treats all students alike.	1	2	3	4	5
12. My instructor frowns on class members helping each other with assignments.	1	2	3	4	5
13. Aggressive and competitive people have a distinct advantage in this class.	1	2	3	4	5
14. My instructor encourages me to see the world differently.	5	4	3	2	1

Calculate your total score by adding up the numbers you circled. Your score will fall between 14 and 70.

A high score (49 or above) describes an open, risk-taking, supportive, humanistic, team-oriented, easy-going, growth-oriented culture. A low score (35 or below) describes a closed, structured, task-oriented, individualistic, tense, and stability-oriented culture. Note that differences count, so a score of 60 is a more open culture than one that scores 50. Also, realize that one culture isn't preferable over another. The "right" culture depends on you and your preferences for a learning environment.

Form teams of five to seven members each. Compare your scores. How closely do they align? Discuss and resolve any discrepancies. Based on your team's analysis, what type of student do you think would perform best in this class?

Ethical Dilemma

IS THERE ROOM FOR SNOOPING IN AN ORGANIZATION'S CULTURE?

Although some of the spying Hewlett-Packard performed on some members of its board of directors appeared to violate California law, much of it was legal. Moreover, many companies spy on their employees—sometimes with and sometimes without their knowledge or consent. Organizations differ in their culture of surveillance. Some differences are due to the type of business. A Department of Defense contractor has more reason—perhaps even obligation—to spy on its employees than does an orange juice producer.

However, surveillance in most industries is on the upswing. There are several reasons for this, including the huge growth of two sectors with theft and security problems (services and information technology, respectively) and the increased availability of surveillance technology.

Consider the following surveillance actions and, for each action, decide whether it would never be ethical (mark N), would sometimes be ethical (mark S), or would always be ethical (mark A). For those you mark S, indicate on what factors your judgment would depend.

1. Sifting through an employee's trash for evidence of wrongdoing
2. Periodically reading e-mail messages for disclosure of confidential information or inappropriate use
3. Conducting video surveillance of workspace
4. Monitoring Web sites visited by employees and determining the appropriateness and work-relatedness of those visited
5. Taping phone conversations
6. Posing as a job candidate, an investor, a customer, or a colleague (when the real purpose is to solicit information)

Would you be less likely to work for an employer that engaged in some of these methods? Why or why not? Do you think use of surveillance says something about an organization's culture?

Case Incident 1

MERGERS DON'T ALWAYS LEAD TO CULTURE CLASHES

A lot of mergers lead to culture clashes and, ultimately, failure. So in 2005 when banking giant Bank of America (BOA) announced its $35 billion acquisition of credit card giant MBNA, many thought that in a few years, this merger would join for heap of those done in by cultural differences.

MBNA's culture was characterized by a free-wheeling, entrepreneurial spirit that was also quite secretive. MBNA employees also were accustomed to the high life. Their corporate headquarters in Wilmington, Delaware, could be described as lavish, and employees throughout the company enjoyed high salaries and generous perks—from the private golf course at its headquarters, to its fleet of corporate jets and private yachts.

Bank of America, in contrast, grew by thrift. It was a low-cost, no-nonsense operation. Unlike MBNA, it believed that size and smarts were more important than speed. It was an acquisition machine that some likened to *Star Trek's* relentless Borg collective.

In short, the cultures in the two companies were very, very different.

Although these cultural differences seemed a recipe for disaster, it appears, judging from the reactions of BOA and MBNA employees, that the merger has worked. How can this be?

BOA had the foresight to know which MBNA practices to attempt to change, and which to keep in place. Especially critical was BOA's appreciation and respect for MBNA's culture. "On Day 1, I was directed that this was not like the ones you are used to," said Clifford Skelton, who had helped manage BOA's acquisition of FleetBoston Financial before moving on to MBNA.

To try to manage the cultural transition, executives of both companies began by comparing thousands of practices covering everything from hiring to call-center operations. In many cases, BOA chose to keep MBNA's cultural practices in place. In other cases, BOA did impose its will on MBNA. For example, because MBNA's pay rates were well above market, many MBNA managers were forced to swallow a steep pay cut. Some MBNA employees have left, but most have remained.

In other cases, the cultures co-adapted. For example, MBNA's dress code was much more formal than BOA's business casual approach. In the end, a hybrid code was adopted, where business suits were expected in the credit-card division's corporate offices and in front of clients, but business causal was the norm otherwise.

While most believe the merger has been successful, there are tensions. Some BOA managers see MBNA managers as arrogant and autocratic. Some MBNA managers see their BOA counterparts as bureaucratic.

What about those famous MBNA perks? As you might have guessed, most of those have gone away. All but one of the corporate jets is gone. The golf course was donated t the state of Delaware. Gone too, are most of the work art that hung in MBNA's corporate offices.

Questions

1. In what ways were the cultures of Bank of America and MBNA incompatible?
2. Why do you think their cultures appeared to mesh rather than clash?
3. Do you think culture is important to the success of a merger/acquisition? Why or why not?
4. How much of the smooth transition, if any, do you think comes from both companies glossing over real differences in an effort to make the merger work?

Source: Based on E. Dash, "A Clash of Cultures, Averted," *New York Times*, February 20, 2007, pp. B1, B3.

Case Incident 2

WEGMANS

Amid corporate giants such as Microsoft, GM, and General Electric stands a relatively small grocery store that has appeared at the top (number 1 in 2005) or near the top (number 3 in 2007) of *Fortune's* "Best Companies to Work For."

Typically, grocery stores are not thought of as great places to work. Hours are anything but 9 to 5, and the pay is low compared with other occupations. The result is an industry that sees high annual turnover rates. Employees at Wegmans, however, view working for a grocer a bit differently. Instead of viewing their job as a temporary setback on the way to a more illustrious career, many employees at Wegmans view working for the grocer as their career. And given Wegmans's high profitability (it had sales in 2004 of $3.4 billion from 67 stores, giving it one of the highest profit-per-store ratios in the industry), it looks like the grocer will be around long enough to make such careers a reality for those who pursue them.

Why is Wegmans so effective? One reason is its culture. The chain began in 1930 when brothers John and Walter Wegman opened their first grocery store in Rochester, New York. One of its distinguishing features was a café that seated 300 customers. The store's immediate focus on fine foods quickly separated it from other grocers—a focus that is maintained by the company's employees, many of whom are hired based on their interest in food.

In 1950, Walter's son, Robert, became president and immediately added a generous number of employee benefits such as profit sharing and medical coverage, completely paid for by the company. What was Robert's reason for offering such great benefits? "I was no different from them," he said, referring to the company's employees. Though the benefits are still generous at Wegmans, the rising cost of health care has forced it to have all employees contribute for coverage.

Now, Robert's son, Danny, is president of the company, and he has continued the Wegmans tradition of taking care of its employees. To date, Wegmans has paid more than $54 million in college scholarships for its employees, both full time and part time. In addition to benefits, employees receive pay that is well above the market average. As a result, annual turnover at Wegmans for full-time employees is a mere 6 percent, according to the Food Marketing Institute, when is it is 24 percent in the industry overall.

The culture that has developed at Wegmans is an important part of the company's success. Employees are proud to say they work at Wegmans. For example, Sara Goggins, a 19-year-old college student who works part time at Wegmans, recalls when Danny Wegman personally complimented her on a store display that she helped set up. "I love this place," she says. "If teaching doesn't work out, I would so totally work at Wegmans." And Kelly Schoeneck, a store manager, recounts that a few years ago, her supervisor asked her to analyze a frequent-shopper program that a competitor had recently adopted. Though she assumed that her supervisor would take credit for her findings, Schoeneck's supervisor had her present her findings directly to Robert Wegman.

Maintaining a culture of driven, happy, and loyal employees who are eager to help one another is not easy. Wegmans carefully selects each employee, and growth is often slow and meticulous, with only two new stores opened each year. When a new store is opened, employees from existing stores are brought in to the new store to maintain the culture. The existing employees are then able to transmit their knowledge and the store's values to new employees.

Managers especially are ingrained in the Wegmans culture. More than half started working at Wegmans when they were teenagers. Says Edward McLaughlin, director of Cornell's Food Industry Management Program, "When you're a 16-year-old kid, the last thing you want to do is wear a geeky shirt and work for a supermarket. But at Wegman's, it's a badge of honor. You are not a geeky cashier. You are part of the social fabric."

Employees at Wegmans are not selected based on intellectual ability or experience alone. "Just about everybody in the store has some genuine interest in food," states Jeff Burris, a supervisor at the Dulles, Virginia, store. Those employees who do not express this interest may not fit in and are sometimes not hired. The result is a culture that "is bigger than Danny in the same way that Wal-Mart's became bigger than Sam [Walton]," says Darrell Rigby, a consultant at Bain & Co.

Questions

1. Would you characterize Wegmans's culture as strong or weak? Why? How is the strength of the culture at

Wegmans likely to affect its employees, particularly new hires?

2. Wegmans attempts to maintain its core cultural values by hiring individuals who are passionate about the food industry and by staffing new stores partly with existing employees. What are some advantages and disadvantages of trying to impose a similar culture throughout different areas of a company?
3. What is the primary source of Wegmans's culture, and what are some ways that it has been able to sustain itself?
4. How might stories and rituals play a role in maintaining Wegmans's corporate culture?

Source: Based on E. Iwata, "Businesses Grow More Socially Conscious," *USA Today*, June 14, 2007, p. 3B; and M. Boyle and E. F. Kratz, "The Wegman's Way," *Fortune*, January 24, 2005, pp. 62–66.

Endnotes

1. C. Ricketts, "When in London, Do as the Californians Do," *Wall Street Journal*, January 23, 2007, p. B5.
2. P. Selznick, "Foundations of the Theory of Organizations," *American Sociological Review*, February 1948, pp. 25–35.
3. See L. G. Zucker, "Organizations as Institutions," in S. B. Bacharach (ed.), *Research in the Sociology of Organizations* (Greenwich, CT: JAI Press, 1983), pp. 1–47; A. J. Richardson, "The Production of Institutional Behaviour: A Constructive Comment on the Use of Institutionalization Theory in Organizational Analysis," *Canadian Journal of Administrative Sciences*, December 1986, pp. 304–316; L. G. Zucker, *Institutional Patterns and Organizations: Culture and Environment* (Cambridge, MA: Ballinger, 1988); R. L. Jepperson, "Institutions, Institutional Effects, and Institutionalism," in W. W. Powell and P. J. DiMaggio (eds.), *The New Institutionalism in Organizational Analysis* (Chicago: University of Chicago Press, 1991), pp. 143–163; and T. B. Lawrence, M. K. Mauws, B. Dyck, and R. F. Kleysen, "The Politics of Organizational Learning: Integrating Power into the 4I Framework," *Academy of Management Review*, January 2005, pp. 180–191.
4. See, for example, H. S. Becker, "Culture: A Sociological View," *Yale Review*, Summer 1982, pp. 513–527; and E. H. Schein, *Organizational Culture and Leadership* (San Francisco: Jossey-Bass, 1985), p. 168.
5. This seven-item description is based on C. A. O'Reilly III, J. Chatman, and D. F. Caldwell, "People and Organizational Culture: A Profile Comparison Approach to Assessing Person-Organization Fit," *Academy of Management Journal*, September 1991, pp. 487–516; and J. A. Chatman and K. A. Jehn, "Assessing the Relationship between Industry Characteristics and Organizational Culture: How Different Can You Be?" *Academy of Management Journal*, June 1994, pp. 522–553.
6. The view that there will be consistency among perceptions of organizational culture has been called the "integration" perspective. For a review of this perspective and conflicting approaches, see D. Meyerson and J. Martin, "Cultural Change: An Integration of Three Different Views," *Journal of Management Studies*, November 1987, pp. 623–647; and P. J. Frost, L. F. Moore, M. R. Louis, C. C. Lundberg, and J. Martin (eds.), *Reframing Organizational Culture* (Newbury Park, CA: Sage Publications, 1991).
7. See J. M. Jermier, J. W. Slocum, Jr., L. W. Fry, and J. Gaines, "Organizational Subcultures in a Soft Bureaucracy: Resistance Behind the Myth and Facade of an Official Culture," *Organization Science*, May 1991, pp. 170–194; and S. A. Sackmann, "Culture and Subcultures: An Analysis of Organizational Knowledge," *Administrative Science Quarterly*, March 1992, pp. 140–161; G. Hofstede, "Identifying Organizational Subcultures: An Empirical Approach," *Journal of Management Studies*, January 1998, pp. 1–12.
8. T. A. Timmerman, "Do Organizations Have Personalities?" paper presented at the 1996 National Academy of Management Conference; Cincinnati, OH, August 1996.
9. S. Hamm, "No Letup—And No Apologies," *BusinessWeek*, October 26, 1998, pp. 58–64; and C. Carlson, "Former Intel Exec Slams Microsoft Culture," *eWEEK.com*, March 26, 2002, www.eweek.com/article2/0,1759,94976,00.asp.
10. See, for example, G. G. Gordon and N. DiTomaso, "Predicting Corporate Performance from Organizational Culture," *Journal of Management Studies*, November 1992, pp. 793–798; J. B. Sorensen, "The Strength of Corporate Culture and the Reliability of Firm Performance," *Administrative Science Quarterly*, March 2002, pp. 70–91; and J. Rosenthal and M. A. Masarech, "High-Performance Cultures: How Values Can Drive Business Results," *Journal of Organizational Excellence*, Spring 2003, pp. 3–18.
11. Y. Wiener, "Forms of Value Systems: A Focus on Organizational Effectiveness and Cultural Change and Maintenance," *Academy of Management Review*, October 1988, p. 536.
12. R. T. Mowday, L. W. Porter, and R. M. Steers, *Employee–Organization Linkages: The Psychology of Commitment, Absenteeism, and Turnover* (New York: Academic Press, 1982); and C. Vandenberghe, "Organizational Culture, Person-Culture Fit, and Turnover: A Replication in the Health Care Industry," *Journal of Organizational Behavior*, March 1999, pp. 175–184.
13. S. L. Dolan and S. Garcia, "Managing by Values: Cultural Redesign for Strategic Organizational Change at the Dawn of the Twenty-First Century," *Journal of Management Development* 21, no. 2 (2002), pp. 101–117.
14. See C. A. O'Reilly and J. A. Chatman, "Culture as Social Control: Corporations, Cults, and Commitment," in B. M. Staw and L. L. Cummings (eds.), *Research in Organizational Behavior*, vol. 18 (Greenwich, CT: JAI Press, 1996), pp. 157–200. See also M. Pinae Cunha, "The 'Best Place to Be': Managing Control and Employee Loyalty in a Knowledge-Intensive Company," *Journal of Applied Behavioral Science*, December 2002, pp. 481–495.
15. T. E. Deal and A. A. Kennedy, "Culture: A New Look Through Old Lenses," *Journal of Applied Behavioral Science*, November 1983, p. 501.
16. J. Case, "Corporate Culture," *INC.*, November 1996, pp. 42–53.
17. Sorensen, "The Strength of Corporate Culture and the Reliability of Firm Performance."

18. See, for instance, P. L. Moore, "She's Here to Fix the Xerox," *BusinessWeek*, August 6, 2001, pp. 47–48; and C. Ragavan, "FBI Inc.," *U.S. News & World Report*, June 18, 2001, pp. 15–21.

19. See C. Lindsay, "Paradoxes of Organizational Diversity: Living Within the Paradoxes," in L. R. Jauch and J. L. Wall (eds.), *Proceedings of the 50th Academy of Management Conference* (San Francisco, 1990), pp. 374–378; T. Cox, Jr., *Cultural Diversity in Organizations: Theory, Research & Practice* (San Francisco: Berrett-Koehler, 1993), pp. 162–170; and L. Grensing-Pophal, "Hiring to Fit Your Corporate Culture," *HRMagazine*, August 1999, pp. 50–54.

20. K. Labich, "No More Crude at Texaco," *Fortune*, September 6, 1999, pp. 205–212; and "Rooting Out Racism," *BusinessWeek*, January 10, 2000, p. 66.

21. A. F. Buono and J. L. Bowditch, *The Human Side of Mergers and Acquisitions: Managing Collisions Between People, Cultures, and Organizations* (San Francisco: Jossey-Bass, 1989); S. Cartwright and C. L. Cooper, "The Role of Culture Compatibility in Successful Organizational Marriages," *Academy of Management Executive*, May 1993, pp. 57–70; E. Krell, "Merging Corporate Cultures," *Training*, May 2001, pp. 68–78; and R. A. Weber and C. F. Camerer, "Cultural Conflict and Merger Failure: An Experimental Approach," *Management Science*, April 2003, pp. 400–412.

22. P. Gumbel, "Return of the Urge to Merge," *Time Europe Magazine*, July 13, 2003, www.time.com/time/europe/magazine/article/0,13005,901030721-464418,00.html.

23. T. A. Lambert, L. T. Eby, and M. P. Reeves, "Predictors of Networking Intensity and Network Quality Among White-Collar Job Seekers," *Journal of Career Development*, June 2006, pp. 351–365; and J. A. Thompson, "Proactive Personality and Job Performance: A Social Capital Perspective," *Journal of Applied Psychology*, September 2005, pp. 1011–1017.

24. S. F. Gale, "Memo to AOL Time Warner: Why Mergers Fail—Case Studies," *Workforce*, February 2003, www.workforce.com; and W. Bock, "Mergers, Bubbles, and Steve Case," *Wally Bock's Monday Memo*, January 20, 2003, www.mondaymemo.net/030120feature.htm.

25. E. H. Schein, "The Role of the Founder in Creating Organizational Culture," *Organizational Dynamics*, Summer 1983, pp. 13–28.

26. E. H. Schein, "Leadership and Organizational Culture," in F. Hesselbein, M. Goldsmith, and R. Beckhard (eds.), *The Leader of the Future* (San Francisco: Jossey-Bass, 1996), pp. 61–62.

27. See, for example, J. R. Harrison and G. R. Carroll, "Keeping the Faith: A Model of Cultural Transmission in Formal Organizations," *Administrative Science Quarterly*, December 1991, pp. 552–582; see also G. George, R. G. Sleeth, and M. A. Siders, "Organizational Culture: Leader Roles, Behaviors, and Reinforcement Mechanisms," *Journal of Business & Psychology*, Summer 1999, pp. 545–560.

28. B. Schneider, "The People Make the Place," *Personnel Psychology*, Autumn 1987, pp. 437–453; D. E. Bowen, G. E. Ledford, Jr., and B. R. Nathan, "Hiring for the Organization, Not the Job," *Academy of Management Executive*, November 1991, pp. 35–51; B. Schneider, H. W. Goldstein, and D. B. Smith, "The ASA Framework: An Update," *Personnel Psychology*, Winter 1995, pp. 747–773; A. L. Kristof, "Person–Organization Fit: An Integrative Review of Its Conceptualizations, Measurement, and Implications," *Personnel Psychology*, Spring 1996, pp. 1–49; D. M. Cable and T. A. Judge, "Interviewers' Perceptions of Person-Organization Fit and Organizational Selection Decisions," *Journal of Applied Psychology*, August 1997, pp. 546–561; and M. L. Verquer, T. A. Beehr, and S. H. Wagner, "A Meta-Analysis of Relations Between Person-Organization Fit and Work Attitudes," *Journal of Vocational Behavior*, December 2003, pp. 473–489.

29. L. Grensing-Pophal, "Hiring to Fit Your Corporate Culture," *HRMagazine*, August 1999, pp. 50–54.

30. D. C. Hambrick and P. A. Mason, "Upper Echelons: The Organization as a Reflection of Its Top Managers," *Academy of Management Review*, April 1984, pp. 193–206; B. P. Niehoff, C. A. Enz, and R. A. Grover, "The Impact of Top-Management Actions on Employee Attitudes and Perceptions," *Group & Organization Studies*, September 1990, pp. 337–352; and H. M. Trice and J. M. Beyer, "Cultural Leadership in Organizations," *Organization Science*, May 1991, pp. 149–169.

31. J. S. Lublin, "Cheap Talk," *Wall Street Journal*, April 11, 2002, p. B14.

32. See, for instance, J. P. Wanous, *Organizational Entry*, 2nd ed. (New York: Addison-Wesley, 1992); G. T. Chao, A. M. O'Leary-Kelly, S. Wolf, H. J. Klein, and P. D. Gardner, "Organizational Socialization: Its Content and Consequences," *Journal of Applied Psychology*, October 1994, pp. 730–743; B. E. Ashforth, A. M. Saks, and R. T. Lee, "Socialization and Newcomer Adjustment: The Role of Organizational Context," *Human Relations*, July 1998, pp. 897–926; D. A. Major, "Effective Newcomer Socialization into High-Performance Organizational Cultures," in N. M. Ashkanasy, C. P. M. Wilderom, and M. F. Peterson (eds.), *Handbook of Organizational Culture & Climate*, pp. 355–368; D. M. Cable and C. K. Parsons, "Socialization Tactics and Person-Organization Fit," *Personnel Psychology*, Spring 2001, pp. 1–23; and K. Rollag, "The Impact of Relative Tenure on Newcomer Socialization Dynamics," *Journal of Organizational Behavior*, November 2004, pp. 853–872.

33. J. Schettler, "Orientation ROI," *Training*, August 2002, p. 38.

34. K. Rhodes, "Breaking in the Top Dogs," *Training*, February 2000, pp. 67–74.

35. J. Van Maanen and E. H. Schein, "Career Development," in J. R. Hackman and J. L. Suttle (eds.), *Improving Life at Work* (Santa Monica, CA: Goodyear, 1977), pp. 58–62.

36. D. C. Feldman, "The Multiple Socialization of Organization Members," *Academy of Management Review*, April 1981, p. 310.

37. G. Chen and R. J. Klimoski, "The Impact of Expectations on Newcomer Performance in Teams as Mediated by Work Characteristics, Social Exchanges, and Empowerment," *Academy of Management Journal* 46 (2003), pp. 591–607; C. R. Wanberg and J. D. Kammeyer-Mueller, "Predictors and Outcomes of Proactivity in the Socialization Process," *Journal of Applied Psychology* 85 (2000), pp. 373–385; J. D. Kammeyer-Mueller and C. R. Wanberg, "Unwrapping the Organizational Entry Process: Disentangling Multiple Antecedents and Their Pathways to Adjustment," *Journal of Applied Psychology* 88 (2003), pp. 779–794; and E. W. Morrison, "Longitudinal Study of the Effects of Information Seeking on Newcomer Socialization," *Journal of Applied Psychology* 78 (2003), pp. 173–183.

38. Van Maanen and Schein, "Career Development," p. 59.

39. E. W. Morrison, "Newcomers' Relationships: The Role of Social Network Ties During Socialization," *Academy of Management Journal* 45 (2002), pp. 1149–1160.

40. E. Ransdell, "The Nike Story? Just Tell It!" *Fast Company*, January–February 2000, pp. 44–46.
41. D. M. Boje, "The Storytelling Organization: A Study of Story Performance in an Office-Supply Firm," *Administrative Science Quarterly*, March 1991, pp. 106–126; C. H. Deutsch, "The Parables of Corporate Culture," *New York Times*, October 13, 1991, p. F25; and M. Ricketts and J. G. Seiling, "Language, Metaphors, and Stories: Catalysts for Meaning Making in Organizations," *Organization Development Journal*, Winter 2003, pp. 33–43.
42. See K. Kamoche, "Rhetoric, Ritualism, and Totemism in Human Resource Management," *Human Relations*, April 1995, pp. 367–385.
43. V. Matthews, "Starting Every Day with a Shout and a Song," *Financial Times*, May 2, 2001, p. 11; and M. Gimein, "Sam Walton Made Us a Promise," *Fortune*, March 18, 2002, pp. 121–130.
44. A. Rafaeli and M. G. Pratt, "Tailored Meanings: On the Meaning and Impact of Organizational Dress," *Academy of Management Review*, January 1993, pp. 32–55; and J. M. Higgins and C. McAllaster, "Want Innovation? Then Use Cultural Artifacts That Support It," *Organizational Dynamics*, August 2002, pp. 74–84.
45. *DCACronyms* (Seattle: Boeing, April 1997).
46. See B. Victor and J. B. Cullen, "The Organizational Bases of Ethical Work Climates," *Administrative Science Quarterly*, March 1988, pp. 101–125; L. K. Trevino, "A Cultural Perspective on Changing and Developing Organizational Ethics," in W. A. Pasmore and R. W. Woodman (eds.), *Research in Organizational Change and Development*, vol. 4 (Greenwich, CT: JAI Press, 1990); M. W. Dickson, D. B. Smith, M. W. Grojean, and M. Ehrhart, "An Organizational Climate Regarding Ethics: The Outcome of Leader Values and the Practices That Reflect Them," *Leadership Quarterly*, Summer 2001, pp. 197–217; and R. L. Dufresne, "An Action Learning Perspective on Effective Implementation of Academic Honor Codes," *Group & Organization Management*, April 2004, pp. 201–218.
47. J. A. Byrne, "The Environment Was Ripe for Abuse," *BusinessWeek*, February 25, 2002, pp. 118–120; and A. Raghavan, K. Kranhold, and A. Barrionuevo, "How Enron Bosses Created a Culture of Pushing Limits," *Wall Street Journal*, August 26, 2002, p. A1.
48. D. L. Nelson and C. L. Cooper (eds.), *Positive Organizational Behavior* (London: Sage, 2007); K. S. Cameron, J. E. Dutton, and R. E. Quinn (eds.), *Positive Organizational Scholarship: Foundations of a New Discipline* (San Francisco: Berrett-Koehler, 2003); and F. Luthans and C. M. Youssef, "Emerging Positive Organizational Behavior," *Journal of Management*, June 2007, pp. 321–349.
49. J. Robison, "Great Leadership Under Fire," *Gallup Leadership Journal*, March 8, 2007, pp. 1–3.
50. R. Wagner and J. K. Harter, *12: The Elements of Great Managing* (New York: Gallup Press, 2006).
51. R. Wagner and J. K. Harter, "Performance Reviews Without the Anxiety," *Gallup Leadership Journal*, July 12, 2007, pp. 1–4; and Wagner and Harter, *12: The Elements of Great Managing*.
52. S. Fineman, "On Being Positive: Concerns and Counterpoints," *Academy of Management Review* 31, no. 2 (2006), pp. 270–291.
53. D. P. Ashmos and D. Duchon, "Spirituality at Work: A Conceptualization and Measure," *Journal of Management Inquiry*, June 2000, p. 139. For a comprehensive review of definitions of workplace spirituality, see R. A. Giacalone and C. L. Jurkiewicz, "Toward a Science of Workplace Spirituality," in R. A. Giacalone and C. L. Jurkiewicz (eds.), *Handbook of Workplace Spirituality and Organizational Performance* (Armonk, NY: M. E. Sharpe, 2003), pp. 6–13.
54. This section is based on C. Ichniowski, D. L. Kochan, C. Olson, and G. Strauss, "What Works at Work: Overview and Assessment," *Industrial Relations*, 1996, pp. 299–333; I. A. Mitroff and E. A. Denton, *A Spiritual Audit of Corporate America: A Hard Look at Spirituality, Religion, and Values in the Workplace* (San Francisco: Jossey-Bass, 1999); J. Milliman, J. Ferguson, D. Trickett, and B. Condemi, "Spirit and Community at Southwest Airlines: An Investigation of a Spiritual Values-Based Model," *Journal of Organizational Change Management* 12, no. 3 (1999), pp. 221–233; and E. H. Burack, "Spirituality in the Workplace," *Journal of Organizational Change Management* 12, no. 3 (1999), pp. 280–291.
55. Cited in Wagner-Marsh and Conley, "The Fourth Wave," p. 295.
56. M. Conlin, "Religion in the Workplace: The Growing Presence of Spirituality in Corporate America," *BusinessWeek*, November 1, 1999, pp. 151–158; and P. Paul, "A Holier Holiday Season," *American Demographics*, December 2001, pp. 41–45.
57. Cited in Conlin, "Religion in the Workplace," p. 153.
58. C. P. Neck and J. F. Milliman, "Thought Self-Leadership: Finding Spiritual Fulfillment in Organizational Life," *Journal of Managerial Psychology* 9, no. 8 (1994), p. 9; for a recent review, see J.-C. Garcia-Zamor, "Workplace Spirituality and Organizational Performance," *Public Administration Review*, May–June 2003, pp. 355–363.
59. D. W. McCormick, "Spirituality and Management," *Journal of Managerial Psychology* 9, no. 6 (1994), p. 5; E. Brandt, "Corporate Pioneers Explore Spiritual Peace," *HRMagazine* 41, no. 4 (1996), p. 82; P. Leigh, "The New Spirit at Work," *Training and Development* 51, no. 3 (1997), p. 26; P. H. Mirvis, "Soul Work in Organizations," *Organization Science* 8, no. 2 (1997), p. 193; and J. Milliman, A. Czaplewski, and J. Ferguson, "An Exploratory Empirical Assessment of the Relationship Between Spirituality and Employee Work Attitudes," paper presented at the National Academy of Management Meeting, Washington, DC, August 2001.
60. Cited in Milliman et al., "Spirit and Community at Southwest Airlines."
61. P. Dvorak, "A Firm's Culture Can Get Lost in Translation," *Wall Street Journal*, April 3, 2006, pp. B1, B3; K. Kranhold, "The Immelt Era, Five Years Old, Transforms GE," *Wall Street Journal*, September 11, 2006, pp. B1, B3; and S. McCartney, "Teaching Americans How to Behave Abroad," *Wall Street Journal*, April 11, 2006, pp. D1, D4.
62. J. A. Chatman, "Matching People and Organizations: Selection and Socialization in Public Accounting Firms," *Administrative Science Quarterly*, September 1991, pp. 459–484; and A. E. M. Van Vianen, "Person-Organization Fit: The Match Between Newcomers' and Recruiters Preferences for Organizational Cultures," *Personnel Psychology*, Spring 2000, pp. 113–149.
63. J. E. Sheridan, "Organizational Culture and Employee Retention," *Academy of Management Journal*, December 1992, pp. 1036–1056; and Ibid., p. 68.

Human Resource Policies and Practices

To manage people well, companies should . . . elevate HR to a position of power and primacy in the organization.
—Former General Electric CEO Jack Welch

LEARNING OBJECTIVES

After studying this chapter, you should be able to:

1 Define *initial selection* and identify the most useful methods.

2 Define *substantive selection* and identify the most useful methods.

3 Define *contingent selection* and contrast the arguments for and against drug testing.

4 Compare the four main types of training.

5 Contrast formal and informal training methods and contrast on-the-job and off-the-job training.

6 Describe the purposes of performance evaluation and list the methods by which it can be done.

7 Show how managers can improve performance evaluations.

8 Explain how diversity can be managed in organizations.

9 Show how a global context affects human resource management.

It may surprise you to learn that scores on a 12-minute paper-and-pencil test are one of the very best predictors of corporate job performance. We're talking about the Wonderlic Personnel Test, one of the most extensively validated tests ever. We first met the test in Chapter 2. Here we're going to discuss one of the most interesting things about it: It works in the United States in the National Football League (NFL).

Making the Cut in the NFL

As NFL fans know, prior to the NFL draft every year, potential draftees go through a "combine" where their skills are tested: They run, they bench press, they scrimmage—and they also take the Wonderlic. Although players and members of the media often express skepticism about the validity of the test, evidence suggests it works.

Scores on the Wonderlic range from 0 to 50, with the average being about 19. The average chemist scores 31, compared to 26 for a journalist, 22 for a bank teller, and 15 for a warehouse worker.

Wonderlic scores vary by football position. Offensive linemen and quarterbacks, on average, have much higher scores than running backs, cornerbacks, or middle linebackers.

Most NFL experts will tell you that intelligence is most important for the positions of quarterback and offensive lineman, in large part because of the extensive playbook they have to learn and remember. Here's a sample of how some quarterbacks who have recently played in the NFL have fared on the Wonderlic:*

Very Smart: 30 and Higher Alex Smith: 40, Eli Manning: 39, Charlie Frye: 38, Matt Leinart: 35, Tom Brady: 33, J.P. Losman: 31, Josh McCown: 30, Philip Rivers: 30, Tony Romo: 30, Matt Schaub: 30

Smart: 25–29 Marc Bulger: 29, Rex Grossman: 29, Matt Hasselbeck: 29, Brady Quinn: 29, Drew Brees: 28, Peyton Manning: 28, Jason Campbell: 27, Jay Cutler: 26, Carson Palmer: 26, Damon Huard: 25, Byron Leftwich: 25, Chad Pennington: 25, Ben Roethlisberger: 25

Above Average: 20–24 JaMarcus Russell: 24, Brett Favre: 22, Michael Vick: 20

It's clear that NFL quarterbacks are smart—they score well above average relative to the U.S. population. Do differences among the quarterbacks predict success? You might have your own opinion, but it doesn't appear that there is much of a relationship between how the quarterbacks scored on the Wonderlic and how they performed during the 2006-2007 season. So, it appears that a certain level of intellect is required to make it as an NFL quarterback, but after a certain point, your arm (and legs) are as important as your brains.

Some complain that the Wonderlic gets more weight than it deserves. Things have come a long way since former Harvard University player and Rhodes scholar Pat McInally's perfect score cost him in the draft because he was seen as *too* smart. McInally spent 10 years in the NFL and now works for Wonderlic.[1] ■

The message of this chapter is that human resource (HR) policies and practices—such as employee selection, training, and performance management—influence an organization's effectiveness.[2] However, studies show that many managers—even HR managers—often don't know which HR practices work and which don't. To see how much you know (before learning the right answers in the chapter!), take the self-assessment.

*Note: The players listed are 2006 starters and top picks from the 2007 draft. Some players (such as Michael Vick) did not play or start in the 2007–2008 NFL season.

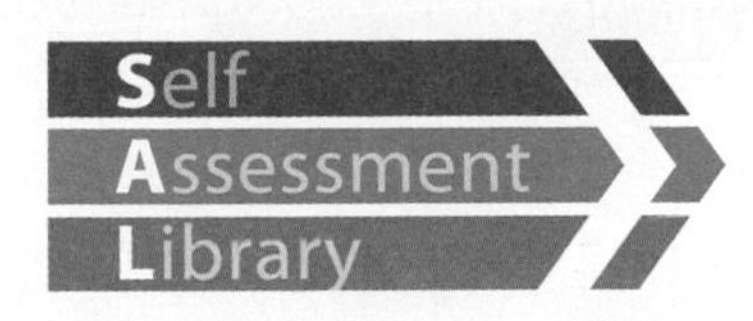

HOW MUCH DO I KNOW ABOUT HUMAN RESOURCE MANAGEMENT (HRM)?

In the Self-Assessment Library (available on CD and online), take assessment IV.G.2 (How Much Do I Know About HRM?) and answer the following questions.

1. *How did you score compared to your classmates? Did the results surprise you?*
2. *How much of effective HRM is common sense?*
3. *Do you think your score will improve after reading this chapter?*

Selection Practices

It's been said the most important HR decision you can make is who you hire. That makes sense—if you can figure out who the right people are. The objective of effective selection is to figure out who these right people are, by matching individual characteristics (ability, experience, and so on) with the requirements of the job.[3] When management fails to get a proper match, both employee performance and satisfaction suffer.

How the Selection Process Works

Exhibit 18-1 shows how the selection process works in most organizations. Having decided to apply for a job, applicants go through several stages—three are shown in the exhibit—during which they can be rejected at any time. In practice, some organizations forgo some of these steps in the interests of time. A meat-packing plant may hire someone who walks in the door (there is not a long line of people who want to "thread" a pig's intestines for a living). But most organizations follow a process that looks something like this. Let's go into a bit more detail about each of the stages.

Initial Selection

1 *Define* initial selection *and identify the most useful methods.*

Initial selection devices are the first information applicants submit and are used for preliminary "rough cuts" to decide whether an applicant meets the basic qualifications for a job. Application forms (including letters of recommendation) are initial selection devices. We list background checks as either an initial selection device or a contingent selection device, depending on how the organization does it. Some organizations prefer to check into an applicant's background right away. Others wait until the applicant is about ready to be hired, contingent on everything checking out.

Application Forms You've no doubt submitted your fair share of applications. By itself, the information submitted on an application form is not a very useful predictor of performance. However, it can be a good initial screen. For example, there's no sense in spending time interviewing an applicant for a registered nurse position if he or she doesn't have the proper credentials (education, certification, experience). More and more organizations encourage applicants to submit an application online. It takes only a few minutes, and the form can be forwarded to the people responsible for making the hiring decision. For example, the international health-care insurer Allianz Worldwide (www.allianzworldwidecare.com) has a career center page where you can search for available positions by location or job type and then apply online.

It's important that organizations be careful about the questions they ask on applications. It's pretty obvious that questions about race, gender, and nationality

Exhibit 18-1 Model of Selection Process in Organizations

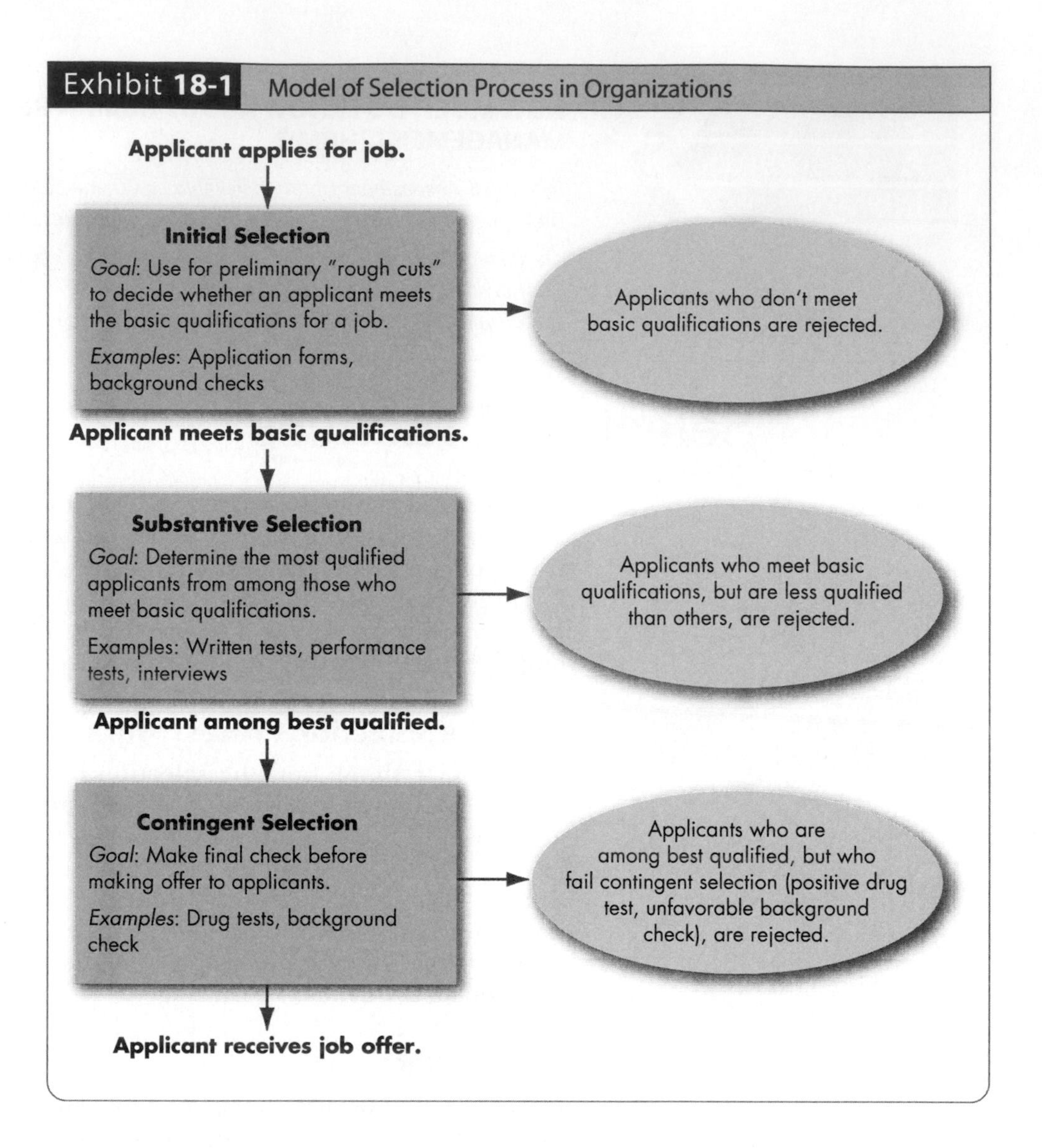

are disallowed. However, it might surprise you to learn that other questions also put companies in legal jeopardy. For example, it generally is not permissible to ask about prior arrest records or even convictions unless the answer is job related.

Background Checks More than 80 percent of employers conduct reference checks on applicants at some point in the hiring process. The reason is obvious: They want to know how an applicant did in past jobs and whether former employers would recommend hiring the person. The problem is that rarely do former employers provide useful information. In fact, nearly two-thirds of employers refuse to provide detailed reference information on applicants. Why? They are afraid of being sued for saying something bad about a former employee. Although this concern is often unfounded (employers are safe as long as they stick to documented facts), in our litigious society, most employers play it safe. The result is a paradox: Most employers want reference information, but few will give it out.

Letters of recommendation are another form of background check. These also aren't as useful as they may seem. Applicants self-select those who will write good letters, so almost all letters of recommendation are positive. In the end, readers of such letters either ignore them altogether or read "between the lines" to try to find hidden meaning there.

Finally, some employers do background checks on credit history or on criminal records. A bank hiring tellers, for example, would probably want to know about an applicant's criminal and credit histories. Because of the invasive nature of such checks, employers need to be sure there is a need for them. However, not checking can carry a legal cost. Manor Park Nursing Home in Texas failed to do a criminal background check of an employee who later sexually assaulted a resident of the nursing home. The jury awarded the plaintiff $1.1 million, concluding that the nursing home was negligent for failing to conduct a background check.[4]

Substantive Selection

2 *Define* substantive selection *and identify the most useful methods.*

If an applicant passes the initial screens, next are substantive selection methods. These are the heart of the selection process and include written tests, performance tests, and interviews.

Written Tests Long popular as selection devices, written tests ("paper-and-pencil" tests—though most are now available online) suffered a decline in use between the late 1960s and mid-1980s, especially in the United States. They were frequently characterized as discriminatory, and many organizations had not validated them as job-related. The past 20 years, however, have seen a resurgence in their use. It's been estimated that today more than 60 percent of all U.S. organizations and most of the Fortune 1000 use some type of employment test.[5] Managers have come to recognize that there are valid tests available and they can be helpful in predicting who will be successful on the job.[6] Applicants, however, tend to view written tests as less valid and fair than interviews or performance tests.[7]

Written tests are the heart of the selection process at Cabela's, a specialty retailer of hunting, fishing, camping, and other outdoor merchandise. Job applicants for the Cabela's contact center and retail stores are given a difficult 150-question test that measures the depth of their outdoor sport expertise. Cabela's management believes that the tests are helpful in determining who will succeed in providing customers with exceptional service and product knowledge.

Typical written tests include (1) intelligence or cognitive ability tests, (2) personality tests, (3) integrity tests, and (4) interest inventories.

Tests of intellectual ability, spatial and mechanical ability, perceptual accuracy, and motor ability have proven to be valid predictors for many skilled, semiskilled, and unskilled operative jobs in industrial organizations.[8] Intelligence tests have proven to be particularly good predictors for jobs that include cognitively complex tasks.[9] Many experts argue that intelligence tests are the *single best* selection measure across jobs. A recent review of the literature suggested that intelligence tests are at least as valid in European Economic Community (EEC) nations as in the United States.[10]

The use of personality tests has grown in the past decade. Japanese automakers, when staffing plants in the United States, have relied heavily on written tests to identify candidates who will be high performers.[11] Getting a job with Toyota can require up to 3 days of testing and interviewing. Organizations use numerous measures of the Big Five traits in selection decisions. The traits that best predict job performance are conscientiousness and positive self-concept.[12] This makes sense in that conscientious people tend to be motivated and dependable, and positive people are "can-do" oriented and persistent. Personality tests are relatively inexpensive and simple to use and administer.

As ethical problems have increased in organizations, integrity tests have gained popularity. These are paper-and-pencil tests that measure factors such as dependability, carefulness, responsibility, and honesty. The evidence is impressive that these tests are powerful in predicting supervisory ratings of job performance and counterproductive employee behavior on the job, such as theft, discipline problems, and excessive absenteeism.[13]

You may wonder why applicants would respond truthfully to personality and integrity tests. After all, who would answer "strongly disagree" to the question "I always show up on time," even if they were generally late? Research shows that although applicants can "fake good" if they are motivated to do so, it doesn't appear that this fakery undermines the validity of personality and integrity tests.[14] Why? One speculation is that if faking does exist, those who "fake good" on selection tests also probably continue to present themselves in a desirable light once on the job. Thus, this sort of impression management not only helps get people hired but it helps them perform better on the job, at least unless taken to pathological degrees.

Performance-Simulation Tests What better way to find out whether applicants can do a job successfully than by having them do it? That's precisely the logic of performance-simulation tests.

Although they are more complicated to develop and more difficult to administer than written tests, performance-simulation tests have increased in popularity during the past several decades. This appears to be due to the fact that they have higher "face validity" than do most written tests.

The two best-known performance-simulation tests are work samples and assessment centers. The former are suited to routine jobs, while the latter are relevant for the selection of managerial personnel.

Work sample tests are hands-on simulations of part or all of the job that must be performed by applicants. By carefully devising work samples based on specific job tasks, management determines the knowledge, skills, and abilities needed for each job. Then each work sample element is matched with a corresponding job performance element. Work samples are widely used in the hiring of skilled workers, such as welders, machinists, carpenters, and electricians. For instance, job candidates for production jobs at BMW's factory in United States have 90 minutes to perform a variety of typical work tasks on a specially built simulated assembly line.[15] Work samples yield validities superior to written aptitude and personality tests.[16]

A more elaborate set of performance-simulation tests, specifically designed to evaluate a candidate's managerial potential, are administered in **assessment centers**. In these tests, line executives, supervisors, and/or trained psychologists evaluate candidates as they go through 1 to several days of exercises that simulate real problems they would confront on the job.[17] For instance, a candidate might be required to play the role of a manager who must decide how to respond to 10 memos in an in-basket within a 2-hour period.

Interviews Of all the selection devices organizations around the globe use to differentiate candidates, the interview continues to be the most common.[18] Not only is the interview widely used, it also seems to carry a great deal of weight. That is, the results tend to have a disproportionate amount of influence on the selection decision. The candidate who performs poorly in the employment interview is likely to be cut from the applicant pool regardless of experience, test scores, or letters of recommendation. Conversely, "all too often, the person most polished in job-seeking techniques, particularly those used in the interview process, is the one hired, even though he or she may not be the best candidate for the position."[19]

These findings are important because of the unstructured manner in which the selection interview is frequently conducted.[20] The unstructured interview—short in duration, casual, and made up of random questions—is not a very effective selection device.[21] The data gathered from such interviews are typically biased and often only modestly related to future job performance. Still, managers are reluctant to use structured interviews in place of their favorite pet questions (such as "If you could be any animal, what would you be, and why?").[22]

Without structure, a number of biases can distort interview results. These biases include interviewers tending to favor applicants who share their

MYTH OR SCIENCE? "It's First Impressions That Count"

This statement is true. When we meet someone for the first time, we notice a number of things about that person: physical characteristics, clothes, firmness of handshake, gestures, tone of voice, and the like. We then use these impressions to fit the person into ready-made categories. And these first impressions tend to hold greater weight than information received later.

The best evidence about first impressions comes from research on employment interviews. Findings clearly demonstrate that first impressions count. A recent study suggested that interviewers often know whether they will hire someone soon after the opening handshake and small talk.[23]

Research on applicant appearance confirms the power of first impressions.[24] Attractive applicants fare better in interviews and overweight applicants are penalized.

Another study revealed just how superficial interviewer judgments often are. These researchers responded to employment ads in Chicago and Boston. In their responses, they submitted fake résumés of high and low quality, and used names that were traditionally African American (Kenya and Hakim) and Caucasian (Allison and Brad). The researchers found that the résumés with Caucasian names received 50 percent more callbacks than those with African American names. Moreover, while 27 percent of the high-quality résumés with Caucasian names received callbacks, only 8 percent of the high-quality résumés with African American names did.[25]

A final body of confirming research finds that interviewers' post-interview evaluations of applicants conform, to a substantial degree, to their pre-interview impressions.[26] That is, those first impressions carry considerable weight in shaping the interviewers' final evaluations, assuming that the interview elicits no highly negative information. ■

attitudes, giving unduly high weight to negative information, and allowing the order in which applicants are interviewed to influence evaluations.[27] Using a standardized set of questions, providing interviewers with a uniform method of recording information, and standardizing the rating of the applicant's qualifications reduce the variability of results across applicants and enhance the validity of the interview as a selection device. The effectiveness of the interview also improves when employers use behavioral structured interviews.[28] This interview technique requires applicants to describe how they handled specific problems and situations in previous jobs. It's built on the assumption that past behavior offers the best predictor of future behavior.

In practice, most organizations use interviews for more than a "prediction-of-performance" device.[29] Companies as diverse as Southwest Airlines, Disney, ABN-Amro Holdings, Microsoft, Unilever, and Harrah's Entertainment use the interview to assess applicant–organization fit. So in addition to specific, job-relevant skills, organizations are looking at candidates' personality characteristics, personal values, and the like to find individuals who fit with the organization's culture and image.

Contingent Selection

If applicants pass the substantive selection methods, they are basically ready to be hired, contingent on a final check. One common contingent method is a drug test. For example, Publix grocery stores make a tentative offer to

work sample test *A test that is a miniature replica of a job that is used to evaluate the performance abilities of job candidates.*

assessment centers *A set of performance-simulation tests designed to evaluate a candidate's managerial potential.*

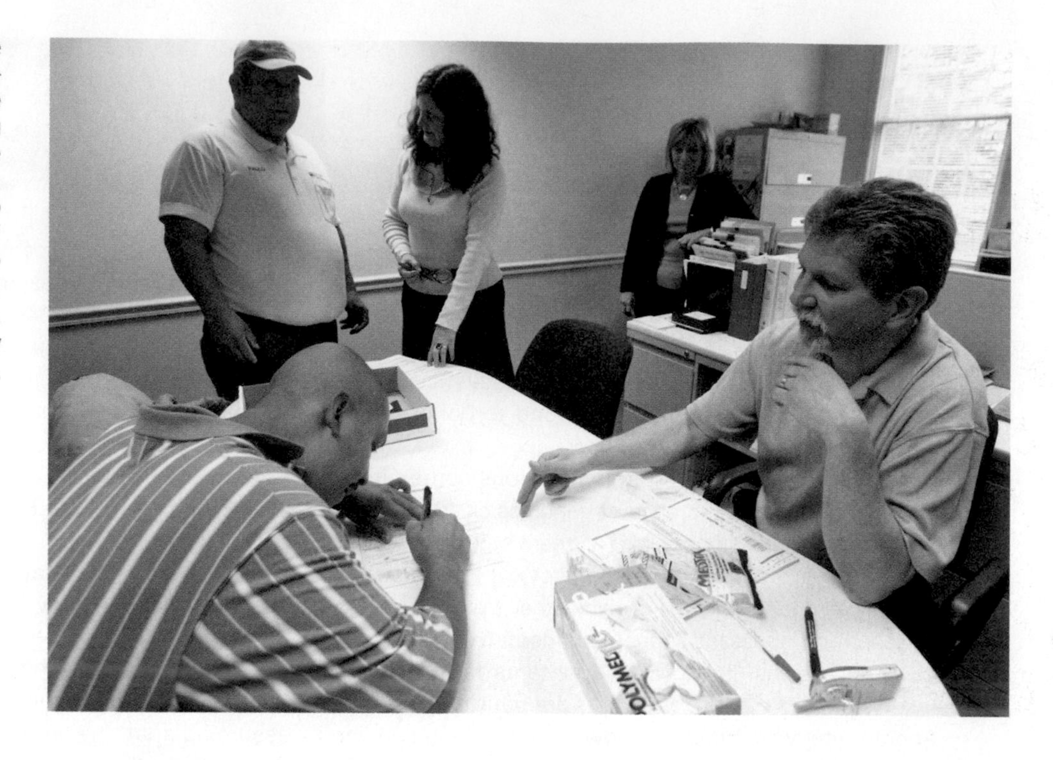

Wheeler Landscaping in the state of Ohio, uses the contingent selection method of drug testing before hiring new employees. A growing number of small businesses like Wheeler, which has 76 employees, are using drug tests to help reduce insurance costs, workers' compensation claims due to workplace accidents, absenteeism, and employee theft.

Source: Amy E. Voigt/ The New York Times

3 *Define* contingent selection *and contrast the arguments for and against drug testing.*

applicants, contingent on their passing a drug test. This means Publix is ready to make an offer to the applicant as long as the person checks out to be drug free.

Drug testing is controversial. Many applicants think it is unfair or invasive to test them without reasonable suspicion. Such individuals likely believe that drug use is a private matter and applicants should be tested on factors that directly bear on job performance, not lifestyle issues that may or may not be job relevant. Drug tests typically screen out individuals who have used marijuana but not alcohol (for both legal and practical reasons—alcohol is legal and leaves the system in 24 hours).

Employers might counter this view with the argument that drug use and abuse are extremely costly, not just in terms of financial resources but in terms of people's safety. Moreover, employers have the law on their side. The Supreme Court has concluded that drug tests are "minimally invasive" selection procedures that as a rule do not violate individuals' rights.

Drug tests are not cheap. If the first test (typically a urine test) turns up positive, then the result is reanalyzed to make sure. Contrary to popular claims, the tests generally are quite accurate, and results are not easily faked. They tend to be quite precise, telling the employer what specific kind of drug appeared to be in the applicant's system. Despite the controversy over drug testing, it's probably here to stay.

Training and Development Programs

Competent employees don't remain competent forever. Skills deteriorate and can become obsolete and new skills need to be learned. That's why organizations spend billions of dollars each year on formal training. For instance, it was reported that U.S. corporations with 100 or more employees spent more than $51 billion on formal training in a recent year.[30] For example, IBM, Accenture, Intel, and Lockheed Martin each spend in excess of $300 million per year on employee training.[31]

Types of Training

Training can include everything from teaching employees basic reading skills to conducting advanced courses in executive leadership. Here we discuss four general skill categories—basic literacy and technical, interpersonal, and problem-solving skills. In addition, we briefly discuss ethics training.

4 *Compare the four main types of training.*

Basic Literacy Skills Statistics show that nearly 40 percent of the U.S. labor force and more than 50 percent of high school graduates don't possess the basic work skills needed to perform in today's workplace.[32] The National Institute of Learning estimates that this literacy problem costs corporate America about $60 billion per year in lost productivity.[33] This problem, of course, isn't unique to the United States. It's a worldwide problem—from the most developed countries to the least.[34] For many undeveloped countries, where few workers can read or have gone beyond the equivalent of the third grade, widespread illiteracy means there is almost no hope of competing in a global economy.

Organizations increasingly have to teach basic reading and math skills to their employees. For instance, jobs at gun manufacturer Smith & Wesson have become more complex.[35] A literacy audit showed that employees needed to have at least an eighth-grade reading level to do typical workplace tasks. Yet 30 percent of the company's 676 workers with no degree scored below eighth-grade levels in either reading or math. These employees were told that they wouldn't lose their jobs, but they had to take basic skill classes, paid for by the company and provided on company time. After the first round of classes, 70 percent of attendees brought their skills up to the target level. And these improved skills allowed employees to do a better job. They displayed greater ease in writing and reading charts, graphs, and bulletin boards, increased abilities to use fractions and decimals, better overall communication, and a significant increase in confidence.

Emerging technology in the mobile-phone industry drives the need for technical-skill training at TSI Telecommunications Services. TSI trained customer-service employees to troubleshoot number-transfer orders when consumers were allowed to change their telecommunications service provider while keeping their existing telephone number. Improving employees' technical skills enables TSI to provide valuable services for its wireless carrier customers that operate in a complicated and rapidly changing industry.

Source: David Kadlubowski/ The New York Times

Technical Skills Most training is directed at upgrading and improving an employee's technical skills. Technical training has become increasingly important today for two reasons—new technology and new structural designs in the organization.

Jobs change as a result of new technologies and improved methods. For instance, many auto repair personnel have had to undergo extensive training to fix and maintain recent models with computer-monitored engines, electronic stabilizing systems, GPS, keyless remote entry, and other innovations. Similarly, computer-controlled equipment has required millions of production employees to learn a whole new set of skills.[36]

In addition, technical training has become increasingly important because of changes in organization design. As organizations flatten their structures, expand their use of teams, and break down traditional departmental barriers, employees need mastery of a wider variety of tasks and increased knowledge of how their organization operates. For instance, the restructuring of jobs at Miller Brewing Co. around empowered teams has led management to introduce a comprehensive business literacy program to help employees better understand competition, the state of the beer industry, where the company's revenues come from, how costs are calculated, and where employees fit into the company's value chain.[37]

Interpersonal Skills Almost all employees belong to a work unit, and their work performance depends to some degree on their ability to effectively interact with their coworkers and their boss. Some employees have excellent interpersonal skills, but others require training to improve theirs. This includes learning how to be a better listener, how to communicate ideas more clearly, and how to be a more effective team player.

Problem-Solving Skills Managers, as well as many employees who perform nonroutine tasks, have to solve problems on their jobs. When people require these skills but are deficient in them, they can participate in problem-solving training. This can include activities to sharpen their logic, reasoning, and problem-defining skills as well as their abilities to assess causation, develop and analyze alternatives, and select solutions. Problem-solving training has become a basic part of almost every organizational effort to introduce self-managed teams or implement quality-management programs.

What About Ethics Training? A recent survey found that about 75 percent of employees working in the 1,000 largest U.S. corporations receive ethics training.[38] This training may be included in a newly hired employee's orientation program, made part of an ongoing developmental training program, or provided to all employees as a periodic reinforcement of ethical principles.[39] But the jury is still out on whether you can actually teach ethics.[40]

Critics argue that ethics are based on values, and value systems are fixed at an early age. By the time employers hire people, their ethical values have already been established. The critics also claim that ethics cannot be formally "taught" but must be learned by example.

Supporters of ethics training argue that values can be learned and changed after early childhood. And even if they couldn't, ethics training would be effective because it helps employees to recognize ethical dilemmas and become more aware of the ethical issues underlying their actions. Another argument is that ethics training reaffirms an organization's expectations that members will act ethically.

International OB

Cultural Training

In a global economy, employee training is no longer limited to the specific tasks of the job. As more and more positions in the information technology and service industries move to India from the United States, many companies are training their Indian employees to improve their cultural skills when dealing with American clients.

For example, the Hyderabad offices of Sierra Atlantic, a California-based software company, trains its Indian employees in various aspects of U.S. culture, including addressing colleagues as Mr. or Ms., learning how to interact with others during a conference call, and even how to sip wine. According to Lu Ellen Schafer, executive director at Global Savvy, a consulting firm based in California, "The training in American culture is not to make Indian software professionals less Indian. It is to make them more globally competent."

Some companies are benefiting from cultural training. Sierra Atlantic's offices in Hyderabad, for example, won a bid with an American firm over an Indian competitor because the Sierra employees were viewed as a better cultural fit. Such successes make it likely that companies with foreign clients will either adopt or continue to use cultural training.

Source: Based on S. Rai, "Indian Companies Are Adding Western Flavor," *New York Times*, August 19, 2003, p. W1.

Training Methods

Training methods are most readily classified as formal or informal and as on-the-job or off-the-job training.

5 *Contrast formal and informal training methods and contrast on-the-job and off-the-job training.*

Historically, training meant *formal training*. It's planned in advance and has a structured format. However, recent evidence indicates that 70 percent of workplace learning is made up of *informal training*—unstructured, unplanned, and easily adapted to situations and individuals—for teaching skills and keeping employees current.[41] In reality, most informal training is nothing other than employees helping each other out. They share information and solve work-related problems with one another. Perhaps the most important outcome of this realization is that many managers are now supportive of what used to be considered "idle chatter." At a Siemens plant, for instance, management now recognizes that people needn't be on the production line to be working.[42] Discussions around the water cooler or in the cafeteria weren't, as managers thought, about nonwork topics such as sports or politics. They largely focused on solving work-related problems. So now Siemens's management encourages such casual meetings.

On-the-job training includes job rotation, apprenticeships, understudy assignments, and formal mentoring programs. But the primary drawback of these on-the-job training methods is that they often disrupt the workplace. So organizations invest in *off-the-job training*. The $51 billion figure we cited earlier for training costs was largely spent on the formal off-the-job variety. What types of training might this include? The most popular continues to be live classroom lectures. But it also encompasses videotapes, public seminars, self-study programs, Internet courses, satellite-beamed television classes, and group activities that use role-plays and case studies.

In recent years, the fastest-growing means for delivering training is probably computer-based training, or e-training.[43] Kinko's, for instance, has created an internal network that allows its 20,000 employees to take online courses covering everything from products to policies.[44] Cisco Systems provides a curriculum of

At Ito Yokado, the largest supermarket chain in Japan, week-long training for new employees includes role-playing exercises. The group of young men shown here is learning the proper techniques of guiding blind, disabled, and elderly people. This off-the-job training technique of role-playing is effective because employees become sensitive to the special needs of shoppers who require assistance.

training courses on its corporate intranet, organized by job titles, specific technologies, and products.[45] Although more than 5,000 companies now offer all or some of their employee training online, it's unclear how effective it actually is. On the positive side, e-training increases flexibility by allowing organizations to deliver materials anywhere and at any time. It also seems to be fast and efficient. On the other hand, it's expensive to design self-paced online materials, many employees miss the social interaction provided by a classroom environment, online learners are often more susceptible to distractions, and "clicking through" training is no assurance that employees have actually learned anything.[46]

Individualizing Formal Training to Fit the Employee's Learning Style

The way you process, internalize, and remember new and difficult material isn't necessarily the same way others do. This fact means that effective formal training should be individualized to reflect the learning style of the employee.[47]

Some examples of different learning styles are reading, watching, listening, and participating. Some people absorb information better when they read about it. They're the kind of people who can learn to use computers by sitting in their study and reading manuals. Some people learn best by observation. They watch others and then imitate the behaviors they've seen. Such people can watch someone use a computer for a while and then copy what they've done. Listeners rely heavily on their auditory senses to absorb information. They would prefer to learn how to use a computer, for instance, by listening to an audiotape. People who prefer a participating style learn by doing. They want to sit down, turn on the computer, and gain hands-on experience by practicing.

You can translate these styles into different learning methods. To maximize learning, readers should be given books or other reading material to review; watchers should get the opportunity to observe individuals modeling the new skills either in person or on video; listeners will benefit from hearing lectures or audiotapes; and participants will benefit most from experiential opportunities in which they can simulate and practice the new skills.

These different learning styles are obviously not mutually exclusive. In fact, good teachers recognize that their students learn differently and, therefore, provide multiple learning methods. They assign readings before class; give lectures; use visual aids to illustrate concepts; and have students participate in group projects, case analyses, role-plays, and experiential learning exercises. If you know the preferred style of an employee, you can design a formal training program to take advantage of this preference. If you don't have that information, it's probably best to design the program to use a variety of learning styles. Over-reliance on a single style places individuals who don't learn well from that style at a disadvantage.

Evaluating Effectiveness

Most training programs work rather well in that the majority of people who undergo training learn more than those who do not, react positively to the training experience, and after the training engage in the behaviors targeted by the program. Still, some factors make certain programs work better than others. For example, although lecture styles have a poor reputation, they are surprisingly effective training methods. On the other hand, conducting a needs assessment prior to training was relatively unimportant in predicting the success of a training program.[48]

The success of training also depends on the individual. If individuals are unmotivated to learn, they will benefit very little. What factors determine training motivation? Personality is important: Those with an internal locus of control, high conscientiousness, high cognitive ability, and high self-efficacy learn more in training programs. The training climate also is important: When trainees believe that there are opportunities on the job to apply their newly learned skills and enough resources to apply what they have learned, they are more motivated to learn and do better in training programs.[49]

Performance Evaluation

Would you study differently or exert a different level of effort for a college course graded on a pass–fail basis than for one that awarded letter grades from A to F? Students typically tell us they study harder when letter grades are at stake. In addition, when they take a course on a pass–fail basis, they tend to do just enough to ensure a passing grade.

This finding illustrates how performance evaluation systems influence behavior. Major determinants of your in-class behavior and out-of-class studying effort in college are the criteria and techniques your instructor uses to evaluate your performance. What applies in the college context also applies to employees at work. In this section, we show how the choice of a performance evaluation system and the way it's administered can be an important force influencing employee behavior.

Purposes of Performance Evaluation

Performance evaluation serves a number of purposes.[50] One purpose is to help management make general *human resource decisions.* Evaluations provide input into important decisions such as promotions, transfers, and terminations. Evaluations also *identify training and development needs.* They pinpoint employee skills and competencies that are currently inadequate but for which remedial programs can be developed. Evaluations also fulfill the purpose of *providing feedback to employees* on how the organization views their performance. Furthermore, performance evaluations are the *basis for reward allocations.* Decisions as to who gets merit pay increases and other rewards are frequently determined by performance evaluations.

6 *Describe the purposes of performance evaluation and list the methods by which it can be done.*

Each of these functions of performance evaluation is valuable. Yet their importance to us depends on the perspective we're taking. Several are clearly relevant to human resource management decisions. But our interest is in organizational behavior. As a result, we shall be emphasizing performance evaluation as a mechanism for providing feedback and as a determinant of reward allocations.

What Do We Evaluate?

The criteria that management chooses to evaluate when appraising employee performance will have a major influence on what employees do. The three most popular sets of criteria are individual task outcomes, behaviors, and traits.

Individual Task Outcomes If ends count, rather than means, then management should evaluate an employee's task outcomes. Using task outcomes, a plant manager could be judged on criteria such as quantity produced, scrap generated, and cost per unit of production. Similarly, a salesperson could be assessed on overall sales volume in the territory, dollar increase in sales, and number of new accounts established.

General Electric Company evaluates the performance of its corporate managers, including the group of GE's top executives in India shown here, on five "growth traits." The traits are inclusiveness, imagination/courage, expertise, external focus, and clear thinking/decisiveness. By evaluating its 5,000 top managers on these traits, GE believes it will generate corporate leaders who will help the company achieve its goal of building the revenue growth of its business units that operate throughout the world.

Behaviors In many cases, it's difficult to identify specific outcomes that can be directly attributed to an employee's actions. This is particularly true of personnel in advisory or support positions and individuals whose work assignments are intrinsically part of a group effort. We may readily evaluate the group's performance but have difficulty distinguishing clearly the contribution of each group member. In such instances, it's not unusual for management to evaluate the employee's behavior. Using the previous examples, behaviors of a plant manager that could be used for performance evaluation purposes might include promptness in submitting monthly reports or the leadership style the manager exhibits. Pertinent salesperson behaviors could be the average number of contact calls made per day or sick days used per year.

Note that these behaviors needn't be limited to those directly related to individual productivity.[51] As we pointed out in our previous discussion on organizational citizenship behavior (see specifically Chapters 1 and 4), helping others, making suggestions for improvements, and volunteering for extra duties make work groups and organizations more effective and often are incorporated into evaluations of employee performance.

Traits The weakest set of criteria, yet one that is still widely used by organizations, is individual traits.[52] We say they're weaker than either task outcomes or behaviors because they're farthest removed from the actual performance of the job itself. Traits such as having a good attitude, showing confidence, being dependable, looking busy, or possessing a wealth of experience may or may not be highly correlated with positive task outcomes, but only the naive would ignore the reality that such traits are frequently used as criteria for assessing an employee's level of performance.

Who Should Do the Evaluating?

Who should evaluate an employee's performance? By tradition, the task has fallen to the manager, on the grounds that managers are held responsible for their employees' performance. But that logic may be flawed. Others may actually be able to do the job better.

With many of today's organizations using self-managed teams, telecommuting, and other organizing devices that distance bosses from their employees, an employee's immediate superior may not be the most reliable judge of that employee's performance. Thus, in more and more cases, peers and even subordinates are being asked to participate in the performance evaluation process. Also, increasingly, employees are participating in their own performance evaluation. For instance, a recent survey found that about half of executives and 53 percent of employees now have input into their performance evaluations.[53] As you might surmise, self-evaluations often suffer from overinflated assessment and self-serving bias. Moreover, self-evaluations are often low in agreement with superiors' ratings.[54] Because of these drawbacks, self-evaluations are probably better suited to developmental than evaluative purposes and should be combined with other sources of information to reduce rating errors.

In most situations, in fact, it is highly advisable to use multiple sources of ratings. Any individual performance rating may say as much about the rater as about the person being evaluated. By averaging across raters, we can obtain a more reliable, unbiased, and accurate performance evaluation.

The latest approach to performance evaluation is the use of 360-degree evaluations.[55] It provides for performance feedback from the full circle of daily contacts that an employee might have, ranging from mailroom personnel to customers to bosses to peers (see Exhibit 18-2). The number of appraisals can be as few as 3 or 4 or as many as 25, with most organizations collecting 5 to 10 per employee.

More and more employers are using 360-degree programs. What's their appeal? By relying on feedback from coworkers, customers, and subordinates, these organizations are hoping to give everyone more of a sense of participation in the review process and gain more accurate readings on employee performance.

Exhibit 18-2 360-Degree Evaluations

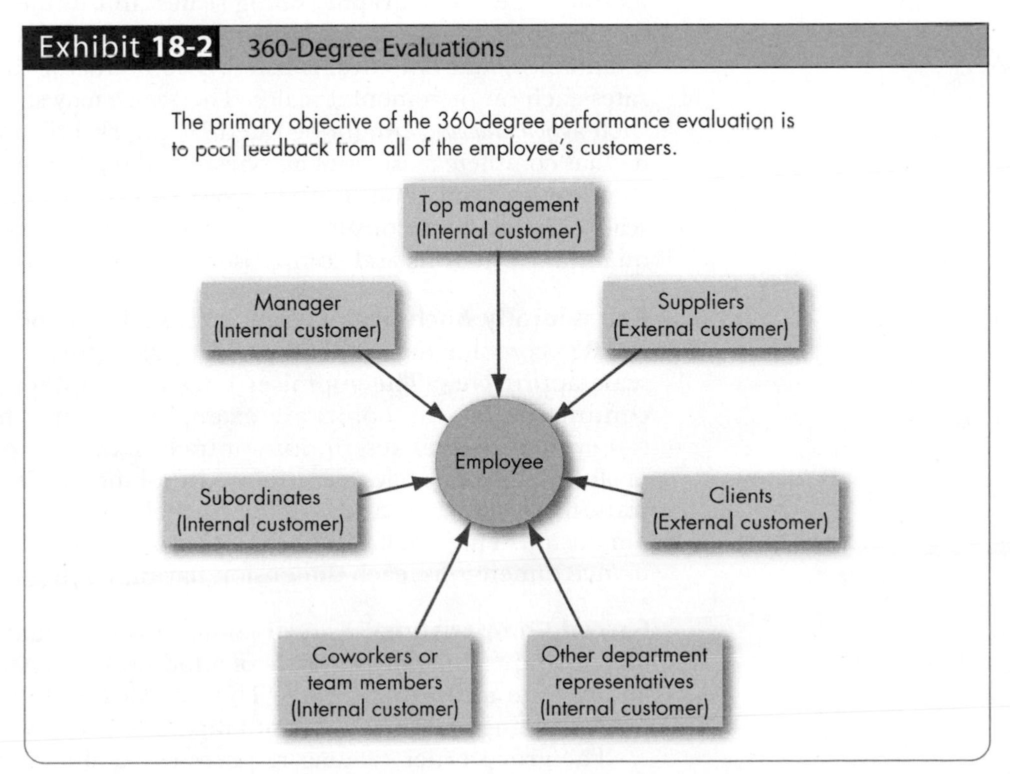

Source: Adapted from *Personnel Journal*, November 1994, p. 100.

The evidence on the effectiveness of 360-degree evaluations, however, is mixed.[56] It provides employees with a wider perspective of their performance. But it also has the potential for being misused. For instance, to minimize costs, many organizations don't spend the time to train evaluators in giving constructive criticism. Some organizations allow employees to choose the peers and subordinates who evaluate them, which can artificially inflate feedback. Problems also arise from the difficulty of reconciling disagreements and contradictions between rater groups.

Methods of Performance Evaluation

The previous sections explained *what* we evaluate and *who* should do the evaluating. Now we ask: *How* do we evaluate an employee's performance? That is, what are the specific techniques for evaluation?

Written Essays Probably the simplest method of evaluation is to write a narrative describing an employee's strengths, weaknesses, past performance, potential, and suggestions for improvement. The written essay requires no complex forms or extensive training to complete. But in this method a good or bad appraisal may be determined as much by the evaluator's writing skill as by the employee's actual level of performance.

Critical Incidents **Critical incidents** focus the evaluator's attention on the behaviors that are key in making the difference between executing a job effectively and executing it ineffectively. That is, the appraiser writes down anecdotes that describe what the employee did that was especially effective or ineffective. The key here is to cite only specific behaviors, not vaguely defined personality traits. A list of critical incidents provides a rich set of examples from which the employee can be shown the behaviors that are desirable and those that call for improvement.

Graphic Rating Scales One of the oldest and most popular methods of evaluation is the use of **graphic rating scales**. In this method, a set of performance factors, such as quantity and quality of work, depth of knowledge, cooperation, attendance, and initiative, is listed. The evaluator then goes down the list and rates each on incremental scales. The scales may specify five points, so a factor such as *job knowledge* might be rated 1 ("poorly informed about work duties") to 5 ("has complete mastery of all phases of the job"). Although they don't provide the depth of information that essays or critical incidents do, graphic rating scales are less time-consuming to develop and administer. They also allow for quantitative analysis and comparison.

Behaviorally Anchored Rating Scales **Behaviorally anchored rating scales (BARS)** combine major elements from the critical incident and graphic rating scale approaches: The appraiser rates the employees based on items along a continuum, but the points are examples of actual behavior on the given job rather than general descriptions or traits. Examples of job-related behavior and performance dimensions are found by asking participants to give specific illustrations of effective and ineffective behavior regarding each performance dimension. These behavioral examples are then translated into a set of performance dimensions, each dimension having varying levels of performance.

Forced Comparisons Forced comparisons evaluate one individual's performance against the performance of another or others. It is a relative rather than an absolute measuring device. The two most popular comparisons are group order ranking and individual ranking.

The **group order ranking** requires the evaluator to place employees into a particular classification, such as top one-fifth or second one-fifth. This method is often used in recommending students to graduate schools. Evaluators are asked whether the student ranks in the top 5 percent of the class, the next 5 percent, the next 15 percent, and so forth. But in this type of performance appraisal, managers deal with all their subordinates. Therefore, if a rater has 20 employees, only 4 can be in the top fifth and, of course, 4 must also be relegated to the bottom fifth. The **individual ranking** approach rank-orders employees from best to worst. If the manager is required to appraise 30 employees, this approach assumes that the difference between the first and second employee is the same as that between the twenty-first and twenty-second. Even though some of the employees may be closely grouped, no ties are permitted. The result is a clear ordering of employees, from the highest performer down to the lowest.

One parallel to the use of forced ranking systems is a forced distribution in the giving of college grades. Why would universities do this?

As shown in Exhibit 18-3, the average GPA of a Princeton University undergraduate has gotten much higher over time.[57]

It's not just Princeton. For example, the average student GPA at Wheaton College was 2.75 in 1962. Now it's 3.40. At Pomona College, the average GPA was 3.06 in 1970. Now it's 3.43. About half the grades at Duke, Harvard, and Columbia Universities are in the "A" range. At Harvard, 91 percent of seniors graduated with some sort of honors in 2001. These are just randomly selected

Exhibit 18-3 Grade Inflation at Princeton University

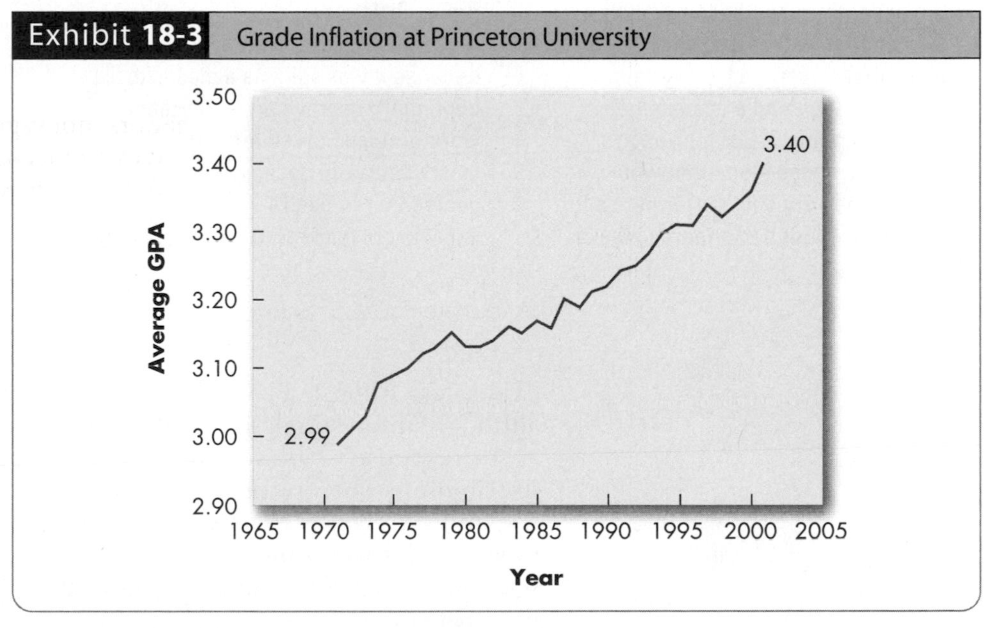

Source: www.gradeinflation.com.

critical incidents *A way of evaluating the behaviors that are key in making the difference between executing a job effectively and executing it ineffectively.*

graphic rating scales *An evaluation method in which the evaluator rates performance factors on an incremental scale.*

behaviorally anchored rating scales (BARS) *Scales that combine major elements from the critical incident and graphic rating scale approaches: The appraiser rates the employees based on items along a continuum, but the points are examples of actual behavior on the given job rather than general descriptions or traits.*

group order ranking *An evaluation method that places employees into a particular classification, such as quartiles.*

individual ranking *An evaluation method that rank-orders employees from best to worst.*

OB *In the News*

The Rise and Fall of Forced Ranking

Forced ranking was once one of the fastest-growing trends in performance evaluation. Companies like Ford, GE, Microsoft, Sun Microsystems, H&R Block, and Sprint were among the 33 percent of U.S. companies that were ranking their employees from best to worst and then using those rankings to compensate, manage, and fire.

Forced ranking, or what has derisively been called "rank and yank" by its critics, was created because many top executives had become frustrated by managers who rated all their employees "above average." In addition, executives wanted a system that would increase the organization's competitiveness—one that would reward the very best performers and encourage poor performers to leave.

For instance, all 18,000 of Ford Motor's managers underwent the forced ranking process. These managers were divided into groups of 30 to 50 and then rated. For each group, 10 percent had to get an A, 80 percent a B, and 10 percent a C. Anyone receiving a C was barred from a pay raise, and 2 consecutive years of a C rating resulted in either a demotion or a termination.

The best-known "rank and yank" program is GE's "20–70–10 plan." The company forces the heads of each of its divisions to review all managers and professional employees and to identify their top 20 percent, middle 70 percent, and bottom 10 percent. GE then does everything possible to keep and reward its top performers and fires all bottom-group performers.

Forced ranking grew in popularity because it was seen as a means to continually improve an organization's workforce and to reward those who are most deserving. Research has suggested that forced ranking systems yield initial improvements in productivity, but that their benefits diminished over time as the poor performers are weeded out.

Although forced ranking systems are still in use, many companies that adopted the system, like Hallmark Cards, have recently dropped it. They found it undermined employee morale and created a "zero-sum game" that discouraged cooperation and teamwork. In addition, several companies have been hit with age discrimination suits by older workers who claim the system has adversely affected them. Several large companies, including Ford and Capital One, settled class-action suits in which former employees claimed that forced ranking systems discriminated against employees based on sex, age, or race.

Sources: Based on K. Holland, "Performance Reviews: Many Need Improvement," *New York Times*, September 10, 2006, www.nytimes.com/2006/09/10/business/yourmoney/10mgmt.html; D. Stafford, "Forced Rankings Are No Cure," *Kansas City Star*, January 27, 2005; and S. E. Scullen, P. K. Bergey, and L. Aiman-Smith, "Forced Distribution Rating Systems and the Improvement of Workforce Potential: A Baseline Simulation," *Personnel Psychology*, Spring 2005, pp. 1–32.

examples. Almost all universities have seen considerable grade inflation, although, interestingly, it may be more severe at prestigious institutions.

In response to grade inflation, some colleges have instituted forced grade distributions whereby professors must give a certain percentage of students A's, B's, and C's. This is exactly what Princeton recently did; each department can now give A's to no more than 35 percent of its students. Natasha Gopaul, a senior at Princeton, commented, "You do feel you might be one of the ones they just cut off."

Suggestions for Improving Performance Evaluations

7 *Show how managers can improve performance evaluations.*

The performance evaluation process is a potential minefield of problems. For instance, evaluators can unconsciously inflate evaluations (positive leniency), understate performance (negative leniency), or allow the assessment of one characteristic to unduly influence the assessment of others (the halo error). Some appraisers bias their evaluations by unconsciously favoring people who have qualities and traits similar to their own (the similarity error). And, of course, some evaluators see the evaluation process as a political opportunity to overtly reward or punish employees they like or dislike. Although there are no protections that will *guarantee* accurate performance evaluations, the following suggestions can significantly help to make the process more objective and fair.

Use Multiple Evaluators As the number of evaluators increases, the probability of attaining more accurate information increases. If rater error tends to follow a normal curve, an increase in the number of appraisers will tend to find the majority congregating about the middle. We often see multiple evaluators in competitions in such sports as diving and gymnastics. A set of evaluators judges a performance, the highest and lowest scores are dropped, and the final evaluation is made up of those remaining. The logic of multiple evaluators applies to organizations as well.

If an employee has had 10 supervisors, 9 having rated her excellent and 1 poor, we can safely discount the one poor evaluation. Therefore, by moving employees about within the organization so as to gain a number of evaluations or by using multiple assessors (as provided in 360-degree appraisals), we increase the probability of achieving more valid and reliable evaluations.

Evaluate Selectively Appraisers should evaluate only in areas in which they have some expertise.[58] This precaution increases the interrater agreement and makes the evaluation a more valid process. It also recognizes that different organizational levels often have different orientations toward those being rated and observe them in different settings. In general, therefore, appraisers should be as close as possible, in terms of organizational level, to the individual being evaluated. Conversely, the more levels that separate the evaluator and the person being evaluated, the less opportunity the evaluator has to observe the individual's behavior and, not surprisingly, the greater the possibility for inaccuracies.

Train Evaluators If you can't *find* good evaluators, the alternative is to *make* good evaluators. There is substantial evidence that training evaluators can make them more accurate raters.[59]

Common errors such as halo and leniency have been minimized or eliminated in workshops where managers practice observing and rating behaviors. These workshops typically run from 1 to 3 days, but allocating many hours to training may not always be necessary. One case has been cited in which both halo and leniency errors were decreased immediately after exposing evaluators to explanatory training sessions lasting only 5 minutes.[60] But the effects of training appear to diminish over time.[61] This suggests the need for regular refresher sessions.

Provide Employees with Due Process The concept of *due process* can be applied to appraisals to increase the perception that employees are being treated fairly.[62] Three features characterize due process systems: (1) Individuals are provided with adequate notice of what is expected of them; (2) all evidence relevant to a proposed violation is aired in a fair hearing so the individuals affected can respond; and (3) the final decision is based on the evidence and free of bias.

There is considerable evidence that evaluation systems often violate employees' due process by providing them with infrequent and relatively general performance feedback, allowing them little input into the appraisal process, and knowingly introducing bias into performance ratings. However, when due process has been part of the evaluation system, employees report positive reactions to the appraisal process, perceive the evaluation results as more accurate, and express increased intent to remain with the organization.

Providing Performance Feedback

For many managers, few activities are more unpleasant than providing performance feedback to employees.[63] In fact, unless pressured by organizational policies and controls, managers are likely to ignore this responsibility.[64]

Why the reluctance to give performance feedback? There seem to be at least three reasons. First, managers are often uncomfortable discussing performance weaknesses directly with employees. Even though almost every employee could stand to improve in some areas, managers fear a confrontation when presenting negative feedback. This apprehension apparently applies even when people give negative feedback to a computer! Bill Gates reports that Microsoft conducted a project requiring users to rate their experience with a computer. "When we had the computer the users had worked with ask for an evaluation of its performance, the responses tended to be positive. But when we had a second computer ask the same people to evaluate their encounters with the first machine, the people were significantly more critical. Their reluctance to criticize the first computer 'to its face' suggested that they didn't want to hurt its feelings, even though they knew it was only a machine."[65]

Second, many employees tend to become defensive when their weaknesses are pointed out. Instead of accepting the feedback as constructive and a basis for improving performance, some employees challenge the evaluation by criticizing the manager or redirecting blame to someone else. A survey of 151 area managers in Philadelphia, for instance, found that 98 percent encountered some type of aggression after giving employees negative appraisals.[66]

Finally, employees tend to have an inflated assessment of their own performance. Statistically speaking, half of all employees must be below-average performers. But the evidence indicates that the average employee's estimate of his or her own performance level generally falls around the 75th percentile.[67] So even when managers are providing good news, employees are likely to perceive it as not good enough.

The solution to the performance feedback problem is not to ignore it, but to train managers to conduct constructive feedback sessions. An effective review—one in which the employee perceives the appraisal as fair, the manager as sincere, and the climate as constructive—can result in the employee's leaving the interview in an upbeat mood, informed about the performance areas needing improvement, and determined to correct the deficiencies.[68] In addition, the performance review should be designed more as a counseling activity than a judgment process. This can best be accomplished by allowing the review to evolve out of the employee's own self-evaluation.

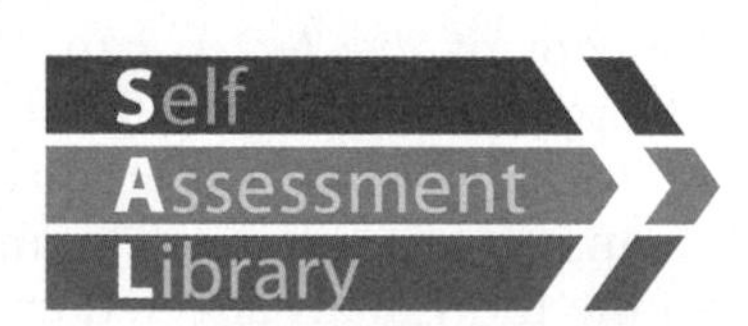

HOW GOOD AM I AT GIVING PERFORMANCE FEEDBACK?

In the Self-Assessment Library (available on CD and online), take assessment III.A.3 (How Good Am I at Giving Performance Feedback?).

Managing Diversity in Organizations

8 Explain how diversity can be managed in organizations.

David Morris and his father, Saul, started Habitat International in 1981. Located in Rossville, Georgia, the company manufactures a grasslike indoor/outdoor carpet. From the beginning, the Morrises hired refugees from Cambodia, Bosnia, and Laos, many of whom didn't speak English. But when a social-service worker suggested in 1984 that the company hire mentally challenged people, Saul balked. Hiring someone with a condition such as Down syndrome seemed too chancy. But David thought otherwise. He talked his dad into giving it a try.[69]

Diversity training for police officers in Miami, Florida, includes a program called Building Cultural Competency. Designed to improve police–citizen relationships, the training focuses on developing interpersonal skills such as active listening and understanding the differences in the cultural, religious, and ethnic population in the community.

The first group of eight mentally disabled workers came in with their job coach from the social-services agency and went straight to work boxing mats. Two weeks later, says Saul, employees were coming to him and wondering why the company couldn't "hire more people like this, who care, do their work with pride, and smile?"

Today, 75 percent of Habitat's employees have some kind of disability. People with schizophrenia, for instance, are driving forklifts next to employees with autism or cerebral palsy. Meanwhile, the Morris father-and-son team is doing good things both for these people and for themselves. The disabled employees have enhanced self-esteem and are now self-sufficient enough to be off government aid, and the Morrises enjoy the benefits of a dedicated, hard-working labor force. "We have practically zero absenteeism and very little turnover," says David.

Habitat International illustrates the role of employee selection in increasing diversity. But effective diversity programs go well beyond merely hiring a diverse workforce. They also include managing work–life conflicts and providing diversity training. These seem to be common characteristics among major organizations that have developed reputations as diversity leaders—including Avon, McDonald's, Pfizer, PepsiCo, GlaxoSmithKline, Xerox, and UBS Investment Bank.[70]

Work–Life Conflicts

We introduced work–life balance in Chapter 1 and discussed the forces that are blurring the lines between work life and personal life. In this section we want to elaborate on this issue—specifically focusing on what organizations can do to help employees reduce conflicts.

Work–life conflicts grabbed management's attention in the 1980s, largely as a result of the growing number of women with dependent children entering the workforce. In response, most major organizations took actions to make their workplaces more family friendly.[71] They introduced programs such as on-site child care, summer day camps, flextime, job sharing, leaves for school functions, telecommuting, and part-time employment. But organizations quickly realized that work–life conflicts were not experienced only by female employees with children. Male workers and women without children were also facing this problem. Heavy work loads and increased travel demands, for instance, were making it increasingly hard for a wide range of employees to meet both work and personal responsibilities. A Harvard University study found that 82 percent of men between the ages of 20 and 39 said a "family-friendly" schedule was their most important job criterion.[72]

Organizations are modifying their workplaces to accommodate the varied needs of a diverse workforce. This includes providing a wide range of scheduling options and benefits that allow employees more flexibility at work and permit them to better balance or integrate their work and personal lives. For instance, employees at the corporate office of retailer Eddie Bauer are provided with flexible scheduling, plus a full array of on-site services, including dry cleaning pick-up and delivery, an ATM, a gym with personal trainers, flu shots, Weight Watchers classes, and financial seminars.[73] Exhibit 18-4 lists some

Exhibit 18-4 Work–Life Initiatives

Strategy	Program or Policy	Example
Time-based strategies	Flextime Job sharing Part-time work Leave for new parents Telecommuting Closing plants/offices for special occasions	At Mentor Graphics, 98 percent of employees use flextime IBM; gives parents three years of job-guaranteed leave following childbirth J. M. Smuckers shuts down plants in deer country for first day of hunting season
Information-based strategies	Intranet work/life Web site Relocation assistance Eldercare resources	Ernst & Young provides intranet work/life Web sites that include information on how to write flexible work arrangements proposals, find a job share partner, etc.
Money-based strategies	Vouchers for child care Flexible benefits Adoption assistance Discounts for child-care tuition Leave with pay	At Lucent Technologies, employees with 6 months of service receive 52 weeks of childbirth leave at half pay
Direct services	On-site child care Emergency back-up care On-site health/beauty services Concierge services Takeout dinners	S. C. Johnson offers its employees subsidized concierge services for car maintenance, shopping, etc. AFLAC has two on-site child-care centers Genentech has an on-site hair salon Stratus Technologies provides on-site mammograms and skin-cancer testing Every major location of Johnson & Johnson has a fitness center
Culture-change strategies	Training for managers to help employees deal with work/life conflicts Tie manager pay to employee satisfaction Focus on employees' actual performance, not "face time"	Lucent, Marriott, Merck, Pfizer, Prudential, and Xerox, among others, tie manager pay to employee satisfaction

Source: Based on C. A. Thompson, "Managing the Work–Life Balance Act: An Introductory Exercise," *Journal of Management Education*, April 2002, p. 210; and R. Levering and M. Maskowitz, "The Best in the Worst of Times," *Fortune*, February 4, 2002, pp. 60–90.

broader examples of initiatives that organizations provide to help their employees reduce work–life conflicts.

Recent research on work–life conflicts has provided new insights for managers into what works and when. For instance, evidence indicates that time pressures aren't the primary problem underlying work–life conflicts.[74] It's the psychological incursion of work into the family domain and vice versa. People are worrying about personal problems at work and thinking about work problems at home. So dad may physically make it home in time for dinner, but his mind is elsewhere while he's at the dinner table. This suggests that organizations should spend less effort helping employees with time-management issues and more helping them clearly segment their lives. Keeping work loads reasonable, reducing work-related travel, and offering on-site quality child care are examples of practices that can help in this endeavor.

Also, not surprisingly, people have been found to differ in their preference for scheduling options and benefits.[75] Some people prefer organizational initiatives that better segment work from their personal lives. Others prefer initiatives that facilitate integration. For instance, flextime segments because it allows employees to schedule work hours that are less likely to conflict with personal responsibilities. On the other hand, on-site child care integrates by blurring the boundaries between work and family responsibilities. People who prefer segmentation are more likely to be satisfied and committed to their work when offered options such as flextime, job sharing, and part-time hours. People who prefer integration are more likely to respond positively to options such as on-site child care, gym facilities, and company-sponsored family picnics.

Diversity Training

The centerpiece of most diversity programs is training. For instance, a relatively recent survey found that 93 percent of companies with diversity initiatives used training as part of their programs.[76] Diversity training programs are generally intended to provide a vehicle for increasing awareness and examining stereotypes. Participants learn to value individual differences, increase their cross-cultural understanding, and confront stereotypes.[77]

Global Implications

9 *Show how a global context affects human resource management.*

Many of the human resource policies and practices discussed in this chapter have to be modified to reflect cultural differences.[78] To illustrate this point, let's briefly look at the universality of selection practices and the importance of performance evaluation in different cultures.

Selection

A recent study of 300 large organizations in 22 countries demonstrated that selection practices differ by nation.[79] A few common procedures were found. For instance, the use of educational qualifications in screening candidates seems to be a universal practice. For the most part, however, different countries tend to emphasize different selection techniques. Structured interviews, as a case in point, were popular in some countries and nonexistent in others. The authors of the study suggested that "certain cultures may find structured interviews antithetical to beliefs about how one should conduct an interpersonal interaction or the extent to which one should trust the judgment of the interviewer."[80]

noteworthy not because he's leading a successful company but because he's leading a company that's fighting for its survival.

Any drug company is one launch away from instant success—think Viagra or Prozac—or financial ruin. Sometimes they're both, like Merck. When Merck launched the anti-arthritis drug Vioxx in 1999, it quickly rose to sales of $2.5 billion per year. However, problems with the drug soon became apparent, and lawsuits started to accumulate. In 2004, Merck pulled Vioxx from the market, and it now budgets $1 billion per year to fight lawsuits against the product.

Clark's predecessor shrugged off Merck's problems. Not Clark. He's trying to make changes in the company that reach well beyond the Vioxx debacle. He argues to employees that without dramatic changes, Merck will not survive.

Clark's vision for transforming Merck includes streamlining the company—eliminating its hierarchical organizational structure, which he felt worked against innovation—and gathering more input from patients, doctors, and employees. He also set new goals for bringing drugs to market as well as establishing other markers of performance. Increased accountability is a big part of how Clark hopes to change the culture at Merck.

Many analysts have applauded his efforts. "At least we can measure whether the company is meeting its goals or not," said one industry analyst. "It's very important for us to be able to respond and say, 'Here's our scorecard of how we're doing,' vs. saying, 'Trust me, in 2010 we'll be there,'" Clark says.

In addition to setting high aspirations, and transforming Merck's structure, Clark has also attacked the complacency that, he argues, has put the entire industry in a rut. "If you ever feel comfortable that your model is the right model, you end up where the industry is today," he says. "It's always going to be continuous improvement. We will never declare victory."

It's not clear whether Clark and Merck will be successful. But it is clear that Clark does not see the status quo as an option. "A crisis is a terrible thing to waste," says the CEO.[1] ■

This chapter is about change and stress. We describe environmental forces that require managers to implement comprehensive change programs. We also consider why people and organizations often resist change and how this resistance can be overcome. We review various processes for managing organizational change. We also discuss contemporary change issues for today's managers. Then we move to the topic of stress. We elaborate on the sources and consequences of stress. Finally, we conclude this chapter with a discussion of what individuals and organizations can do to better manage stress levels.

Before we delve into the subject of change, see how well you handle change by taking the following self-assessment.

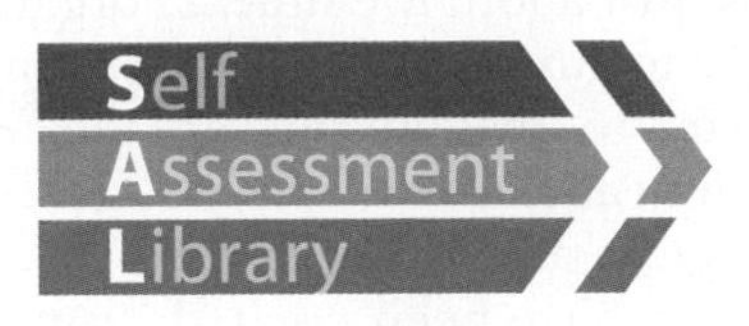

HOW WELL DO I RESPOND TO TURBULENT CHANGE?

In the Self-Assessment Library (available on CD and online), take assessment III.C.1 (How Well Do I Respond to Turbulent Change?) and answer the following questions.

1. *How did you score? Are you surprised by your score?*
2. *During what time of your life have you experienced the most change? How did you deal with it? Would you handle these changes in the same way today? Why or why not?*
3. *Are there ways you might reduce your resistance to change?*

Forces for Change

1 *Identify forces that act as stimulants to change and contrast planned and unplanned change.*

No company today is in a particularly stable environment. Even traditionally stable industries such as energy and utilities have witnessed—and will continue to experience—turbulent change. Companies that occupy a dominant market share in their industries must change, sometimes radically. While Microsoft is struggling with launching its controversial new operating system—Vista—it also is trying to outflank smaller companies such as Google that are increasingly offering free, Web-based software packages. How well Microsoft performs is not simply a function of managing one change but a matter of how well it can manage both short-term and long-term changes.

Thus, the dynamic and changing environments that organizations face today require adaptation, sometimes calling for deep and rapid responses. "Change or die!" is the rallying cry among today's managers worldwide. Exhibit 19-1 summarizes six specific forces that are acting as stimulants for change.

Exhibit 19-1 Forces for Change

Force	Examples
Nature of the workforce	More cultural diversity Aging population Many new entrants with inadequate skills
Technology	Faster, cheaper, and more mobile computers Online music sharing Deciphering of the human genetic code
Economic shocks	Rise and fall of dot-com stocks 2000–2002 stock market collapse Record low interest rates
Competition	Global competitors Mergers and consolidations Growth of e-commerce
Social trends	Internet chat rooms Retirement of baby boomers Rise in discount and "big box" retailers
World politics	Iraq–U.S. war Opening of markets in China War on terrorism following 9/11/01

In a number of places in this book, we've discussed the *changing nature of the workforce.* For instance, almost every organization is having to adjust to a multicultural environment. Demographic changes, immigration, and outsourcing also have transformed the nature of the workforce.

Technology is changing jobs and organizations. Just about the time an organization adapts to one technological change, other technological challenges and opportunities come to the forefront. It is not hard to imagine the very idea of an office becoming an antiquated concept in the near future.

Economic shocks have continued to impose changes on organizations. In recent years, for instance, new dot-com businesses have been created, turned tens of thousands of investors into overnight millionaires, then crashed, and others rose in their wake. And record low interest rates first stimulated a rapid rise in home values in the United States, helped sustain consumer spending, and benefited many industries, especially construction and banking. But when the bubble burst, businesses in these same industries suffered.

Competition is changing. The global economy means that competitors are as likely to come from across the ocean as from across town. Heightened competition means that successful organizations will be the ones that can change in response to the competition. They'll be fast on their feet, capable of developing new products rapidly and getting them to market quickly. They'll rely on short production runs, short product cycles, and an ongoing stream of new products. In other words, they'll be flexible. They will require an equally flexible and responsive workforce that can adapt to rapidly and even radically changing conditions.

Social trends don't remain static. For instance, in contrast to just 15 years ago, people are meeting and sharing information in Internet chat rooms; Baby Boomers have begun to retire; and consumers are increasingly doing their shopping at "big box" retailers and online. A company like the fashion merchandiser Liz Claiborne needs to continually adjust its product and marketing strategies to be sensitive to changing social trends, as it did when it sold off brands (like Ellen Tracy), de-emphasized large department stores like Macy's as vendors, and streamlined its operations and cut staff.

Throughout this book we have argued strongly for the importance of seeing OB in a global context. Business schools have been preaching a global perspective since the early 1980s, but no one—not even the strongest proponents of globalization—could have imagined how *world politics* would change in recent years. We've seen the breakup of the Soviet Union; the opening up of China and Southeast Asia; political instability in many parts of the world; and, of course, the rise of Muslim fundamentalism. The invasion of Iraq by the United States has led to an expensive postwar rebuilding and an increase in anti-American attitudes in much of the world. The attacks on New York and Washington, DC, on September 11, 2001, and the subsequent war on terrorism have led to changes in business practices related to the creation of backup systems, employee security, employee stereotyping and profiling, and post-terrorist-attack anxiety.

Planned Change

A group of housekeeping employees who work for a small hotel confronted the owner: "It's very hard for most of us to maintain rigid 7-to-4 work hours," said their spokeswoman. "Each of us has significant family and personal responsibilities. And rigid hours don't work for us. We're going to begin looking for someplace else to work if you don't set up flexible work hours." The owner listened thoughtfully to the group's ultimatum and agreed to its request. The next day, the owner introduced a flextime plan for these employees.

A major automobile manufacturer spent several billion dollars to install state-of-the-art robotics. One area that would receive the new equipment was quality control. Sophisticated computer-controlled equipment would be put in place to significantly improve the company's ability to find and correct defects. Because the new equipment would dramatically change the jobs of the people working in the quality-control area, and because management anticipated considerable employee resistance to the new equipment, executives were developing a program to help people become familiar with the equipment and to deal with any anxieties they might be feeling.

Fiat Group Automobiles hired an outsider as a change agent to return the ailing company to profitability. As Fiat's new CEO, Sergio Marchionne led a turnaround by changing a hierarchical, status-driven firm into a market-driven one. Marchionne reduced the layers of Fiat's management and fired 10 percent of its 20,000 white-collar employees. He improved relationships with union employees, reduced car-development time, and introduced new car designs. Marchionne is shown here with the redesigned version of the compact Fiat 500, which he hopes will be for the company what the iPod was for Apple.

Both of the previous scenarios are examples of **change**. That is, both are concerned with making things different. However, only the second scenario describes a **planned change**. Many changes in organizations are like the one that occurred at the hotel—they just happen. Some organizations treat all change as an accidental occurrence. We're concerned with change activities that are proactive and purposeful. In this chapter, we address change as an intentional, goal-oriented activity.

What are the goals of planned change? Essentially there are two. First, it seeks to improve the ability of the organization to adapt to changes in its environment. Second, it seeks to change employee behavior.

If an organization is to survive, it must respond to changes in its environment. When competitors introduce new products or services, government agencies enact new laws, important sources of supplies go out of business, or similar environmental changes take place, the organization needs to adapt. Efforts to stimulate innovation, empower employees, and introduce work teams are examples of planned-change activities directed at responding to changes in the environment.

Because an organization's success or failure is essentially due to the things that its employees do or fail to do, planned change also is concerned with changing the behavior of individuals and groups within the organization. Later in this chapter, we review a number of techniques that organizations can use to get people to behave differently in the tasks they perform and in their interactions with others.

Who in organizations is responsible for managing change activities? The answer is **change agents**.[2] Change agents can be managers or nonmanagers, current employees of the organization, newly hired employees, or outside consultants. A contemporary example of a change agent is Lawrence Summers, former president of Harvard University.[3] When he accepted the presidency in 2001, Summers aggressively sought to shake up the complacent institution by, among other things, leading the battle to reshape the undergraduate curriculum, proposing that the university be more directly engaged with problems in education and public health, and reorganizing to consolidate more power in the president's office. His change efforts generated tremendous resistance, particularly among Harvard faculty. Finally, in 2006, when Summers made comments suggesting that women were less able to excel in science than men, the Harvard faculty revolted, and in a few weeks, Summers was forced to resign. Despite Summer's support among students—a poll shortly before his resignation showed

change *Making things different.*

planned change *Change activities that are intentional and goal oriented.*

change agents *Persons who act as catalysts and assume the responsibility for managing change activities.*

that students supported him by a 3:1 ratio—his efforts at change had ruffled one too many feathers. In 2007, he was replaced with Drew Gilpin Faust, Harvard's first female president, who promised to be less aggressive in instituting changes.[4]

Summers's case shows that many change agents fail because organizational members resist change. In the next section, we discuss resistance to change and what can be done about it.

Resistance to Change

One of the most well-documented findings from studies of individual and organizational behavior is that organizations and their members resist change. One recent study showed that even when employees are shown data that suggests they need to change, they latch onto whatever data they can find that suggests they are okay and don't need to change. Our egos are fragile, and we often see change as threatening.[5]

2 *List the sources for resistance to change.*

In some ways, resistance to change is positive. It provides a degree of stability and predictability to behavior. If there weren't some resistance, organizational behavior would take on the characteristics of chaotic randomness. Resistance to change can also be a source of functional conflict. For example, resistance to a reorganization plan or a change in a product line can stimulate a healthy debate over the merits of the idea and result in a better decision. But there is a definite downside to resistance to change. It hinders adaptation and progress.

Resistance to change doesn't necessarily surface in standardized ways. Resistance can be overt, implicit, immediate, or deferred. It's easiest for management to deal with resistance when it is overt and immediate. For instance, a change is proposed and employees quickly respond by voicing complaints, engaging in a work slowdown, threatening to go on strike, or the like. The greater challenge is managing resistance that is implicit or deferred. Implicit resistance efforts are more subtle—loss of loyalty to the organization, loss of motivation to work, increased errors or mistakes, increased absenteeism due to "sickness"—and hence are more difficult to recognize. Similarly, deferred actions cloud the link between the source of the resistance and the reaction to it. A change may produce what appears to be only a minimal reaction at the time it is initiated, but then resistance surfaces weeks, months, or even years later. Or a single change that in and of itself might have little impact becomes the straw that breaks the camel's back. Reactions to change can build up and then explode in some response that seems totally out of proportion to the change action it follows. The resistance, of course, has merely been deferred and stockpiled. What surfaces is a response to an accumulation of previous changes.

Exhibit 19-2 summarizes major forces for resistance to change, categorized by individual and organizational sources. Individual sources of resistance reside in basic human characteristics such as perceptions, personalities, and needs. Organizational sources reside in the structural makeup of organizations themselves.

Before we move on to ways to overcome resistance to change, it's important to note that not all change is good. Research has shown that sometimes an emphasis on making speedy decisions can lead to bad decisions. Sometimes the line between resisting needed change and falling into a "speed trap" is a fine one indeed. What's more, sometimes in the "fog of change," those who are initiating change fail to realize the full magnitude of the effects they are causing or to estimate their true costs to the organization. Thus, although the perspective generally taken is that rapid, transformational change is good, this is not always

Exhibit 19-2 Sources of Resistance to Change

Individual Sources

Habit—To copy with life's complexities, we rely on habits or programmed responses. But when confronted with change, this tendency to respond in our accustomed ways becomes a source of resistance.

Security—People with a high need for security are likely to resist change because it threatens their feelings of safety.

Economic factors—Changes in job tasks or established work routines can arouse economic fears if people are concerned that they won't be able to perform the new tasks or routines to their previous standards, especially when pay is closely tied to productivity.

Fear of the unknown—Change substitutes ambiguity and uncertainty for the unknown.

Selective information processing—Individuals are guilty of selectively processing information in order to keep their perceptions intact. They hear what they want to hear and they ignore information that challenges the world they've created.

Organizational Sources

Structural inertia—Organizations have built-in mechanisms—like their selection processes and formalized regulations—to produce stability. When an organization is confronted with change, this structural inertia acts as a counterbalance to sustain stability.

Limited focus of change—Organizations are made up of a number of interdependent subsystems. One can't be changed without affecting the others. So limited changes in subsystems tend to be nullified by the larger system.

Group inertia—Even if individuals want to change their behavior, group norms may act as a constraint.

Threat to expertise—Changes in organizational patterns may threaten the expertise of specialized groups.

Threat to established power relationships—Any redistribution of decision-making authority can threaten long-established power relationships within the organization.

Threat to established resource allocations—Groups in the organization that control sizable resources often see change as a threat. They tend to be content with the way things are.

the case. Some organizations, such as Baring Brothers Bank in the United Kingdom, have collapsed for this reason.[6] Change agents need to carefully think through the full implications.

Overcoming Resistance to Change

Seven tactics have been suggested for use by change agents in dealing with resistance to change.[7] Let's review them briefly.

Education and Communication Resistance can be reduced through communicating with employees to help them see the logic of a change. Communication can reduce resistance on two levels. First, it fights the effects of misinformation and poor communication: If employees receive the full facts and get any misunderstandings cleared up, resistance should subside. Second, communication can be helpful in "selling" the need for change. Indeed, research shows that the way the need for change is sold matters—change is more likely when the necessity of changing is packaged properly.[8] A study of German companies revealed that changes are most effective when a company communicates its rationale balancing various stakeholder (shareholders, employees, community, customers) interests versus a rationale based on shareholder interests only.[9]

Participation It's difficult for individuals to resist a change decision in which they participated. Prior to making a change, those opposed can be brought into the decision process. Assuming that the participants have the expertise to make a meaningful contribution, their involvement can reduce resistance, obtain commitment, and increase the quality of the change decision. However, against these advantages are the negatives: potential for a poor solution and great consumption of time.

Building Support and Commitment Change agents can offer a range of supportive efforts to reduce resistance. When employees' fear and anxiety are high, employee counseling and therapy, new-skills training, or a short paid leave of absence may facilitate adjustment. Research on middle managers has shown that when managers or employees have low emotional commitment to change, they favor the status quo and resist it.[10] So firing up employees can also help them emotionally commit to the change rather than embrace the status quo.

Implementing Changes Fairly Try as managers might to have employees see change positively, most workers tend to react negatively. Most people simply don't like change. But one way organizations can minimize the negative impact of change, even when employees frame it as a negative, is to makes sure the change is implemented fairly. As we learned in Chapter 6, procedural fairness becomes especially important when employees perceive an outcome as negative, so when implementing changes, it's crucial that organizations bend over backwards to make sure employees see the reason for the change, and perceive that the changes are being implemented consistently and fairly.[11]

Manipulation and Cooptation *Manipulation* refers to covert influence attempts. Twisting and distorting facts to make them appear more attractive, withholding undesirable information, and creating false rumors to get employees to accept a change are all examples of manipulation. If corporate management threatens to close down a particular manufacturing plant if that plant's employees fail to accept an across-the-board pay cut, and if the threat is actually untrue, management is using manipulation. *Cooptation*, on the other hand, is a form of both manipulation and participation. It seeks to "buy off" the leaders of a resistance group by giving them a key role in the change decision. The leaders' advice is sought, not to seek a better decision, but to get their endorsement. Both manipulation and cooptation are relatively inexpensive and easy ways to gain the support of adversaries, but the tactics can backfire if the targets become aware that they are being tricked or used. Once discovered, the change agent's credibility may drop to zero.

Selecting People Who Accept Change Research suggests that the ability to easily accept and adapt to change is related to personality—some people simply have more positive attitudes about change than others.[12] It appears that people who adjust best to change are those who are open to experience, take a positive attitude toward change, are willing to take risks, and are flexible in their behavior. One study of managers in the United States, Europe, and Asia found that those with a positive self-concept and high risk tolerance coped better with organizational change. The study authors suggested that organizations could facilitate the change process by selecting people who score high on these characteristics. Another study found that selecting people based on a resistance-to-change scale worked well in winnowing out those who tended to react emotionally to change or to be rigid.[13]

Coercion Last on the list of tactics is coercion; that is, the application of direct threats or force on the resisters. If the corporate management mentioned in the previous discussion really is determined to close a manufacturing plant if employees don't acquiesce to a pay cut, then coercion would be the label attached to its change tactic. Other examples of coercion are threats of transfer, loss of promotions, negative performance evaluations, and a poor letter of recommendation. The advantages and drawbacks of coercion are approximately the same as those mentioned for manipulation and cooptation.

The Politics of Change

No discussion of resistance to change would be complete without a brief mention of the politics of change. Because change invariably threatens the status quo, it inherently implies political activity.[14]

Internal change agents typically are individuals high in the organization who have a lot to lose from change. They have, in fact, risen to their positions of authority by developing skills and behavioral patterns that are favored by the organization. Change is a threat to those skills and patterns. What if they are no longer the ones the organization values? Change creates the potential for others in the organization to gain power at their expense.

Politics suggests that the impetus for change is more likely to come from outside change agents, employees who are new to the organization (and have less invested in the status quo), or from managers slightly removed from the main power structure. Managers who have spent their entire careers with a single organization and eventually achieve a senior position in the hierarchy are often major impediments to change. Change, itself, is a very real threat to their status and position. Yet they may be expected to implement changes to demonstrate that they're not merely caretakers. By acting as change agents, they can symbolically convey to various constituencies—stockholders, suppliers, employees, customers—that they are on top of problems and adapting to a dynamic environment. Of course, as you might guess, when forced to introduce change, these long-time power holders tend to implement incremental changes. Radical change is too threatening.

Power struggles within the organization will determine, to a large degree, the speed and quantity of change. You should expect that long-time career executives will be sources of resistance. This, incidentally, explains why boards of directors that recognize the imperative for the rapid introduction of radical change in their organizations frequently turn to outside candidates for new leadership.[15]

Approaches to Managing Organizational Change

Now we turn to several approaches to managing change: Lewin's classic three-step model of the change process, Kotter's eight-step plan, action research, and organizational development.

Lewin's Three-Step Model

Kurt Lewin argued that successful change in organizations should follow three steps: **unfreezing** the status quo, **movement** to a desired end state, and **refreezing** the new change to make it permanent.[16] (See Exhibit 19-3.) The value of this model can be seen in the following example, when the management of a large oil company decided to reorganize its marketing function in the Western United States.

3 Compare the four main approaches to managing organizational change.

unfreezing *Changing to overcome the pressures of both individual resistance and group conformity.*

movement *A change process that transforms the organization from the status quo to a desired end state.*

refreezing *Stabilizing a change intervention by balancing driving and restraining forces.*

Exhibit 19-3 Lewin's Three-Step Change Model

Unfreezing → Movement → Refreezing

The oil company had three divisional offices in the western United States, located in Seattle, San Francisco, and Los Angeles. The decision was made to consolidate the divisions into a single regional office to be located in San Francisco. The reorganization meant transferring more than 150 employees, eliminating some duplicate managerial positions, and instituting a new hierarchy of command. As you might guess, a move of this magnitude was difficult to keep secret. The rumor of its occurrence preceded the announcement by several months. The decision itself was made unilaterally. It came from the executive offices in New York. The people affected had no say whatsoever in the choice. For those in Seattle or Los Angeles, who may have disliked the decision and its consequences—the problems inherent in transferring to another city, pulling youngsters out of school, making new friends, having new coworkers, undergoing the reassignment of responsibilities—their only recourse was to quit. In actuality, fewer than 10 percent did.

The status quo can be considered to be an equilibrium state. To move from this equilibrium—to overcome the pressures of both individual resistance and group conformity—unfreezing is necessary. It can be achieved in one of three ways. (See Exhibit 19-4.) The **driving forces**, which direct behavior away from the status quo, can be increased. The **restraining forces**, which hinder movement from the existing equilibrium, can be decreased. A third alternative is to combine the first two approaches. Companies that have been successful in the past are likely to encounter restraining forces because people question the need for change.[17] Similarly, research shows that companies with strong cultures excel at incremental change but are overcome by restraining forces against radical change.[18]

The oil company's management could expect employee resistance to the consolidation. To deal with that resistance, management could use positive incentives to encourage employees to accept the change. For instance, increases in pay can be offered to those who accept the transfer. Very liberal moving expenses can be paid by the company. Management might offer low-cost mortgage funds to allow employees to buy new homes in San Francisco. Of course, management might also consider unfreezing acceptance of the status quo by removing restraining forces. Employees could be counseled individually. Each employee's concerns and apprehensions could be heard and specifically clarified. Assuming that most

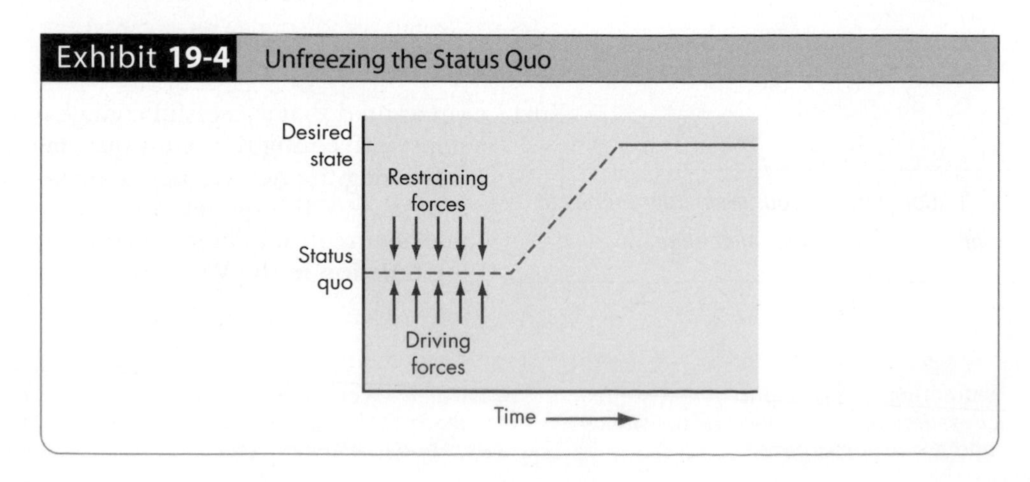

of the fears are unjustified, the counselor could assure the employees tha was nothing to fear and then demonstrate, through tangible evidenc restraining forces are unwarranted. If resistance is extremely high, mana may have to resort to both reducing resistance and increasing the attrac of the alternative if the unfreezing is to be successful.

Research on organizational change has shown that, to be effective, has to happen quickly.[19] Organizations that build up to change do less we those that get to and through the movement stage quickly.

Once the consolidation change has been implemented, if it is to be succe ful, the new situation needs to be refrozen so that it can be sustained over time. Unless this last step is taken, there is a very high chance that the change will be short-lived and that employees will attempt to revert to the previous equilibrium state. The objective of refreezing, then, is to stabilize the new situation by balancing the driving and restraining forces.

How could the oil company's management refreeze its consolidation change? By systematically replacing temporary forces with permanent ones. For instance, management might impose a permanent upward adjustment of salaries. The formal rules and regulations governing behavior of those affected by the change should also be revised to reinforce the new situation. Over time, of course, the work group's own norms will evolve to sustain the new equilibrium. But until that point is reached, management will have to rely on more formal mechanisms.

Kotter's Eight-Step Plan for Implementing Change

John Kotter of the Harvard Business School built on Lewin's three-step model to create a more detailed approach for implementing change.[20] Kotter began by listing common failures that managers make when trying to initiate change. These included the inability to create a sense of urgency about the need for change, failure to create a coalition for managing the change process, the absence of a vision for change and to effectively communicate that vision, not removing obstacles that could impede the achievement of the vision, failure to provide short-term and achievable goals, the tendency to declare victory too soon, and not anchoring the changes into the organization's culture.

Kotter then established eight sequential steps to overcome these problems. They're listed in Exhibit 19-5.

Exhibit 19-5 Kotter's Eight-Step Plan for Implementing Change

1. Establish a sense of urgency by creating a compelling reason for why change is needed.
2. Form a coalition with enough power to lead the change.
3. Create a new vision to direct the change and strategies for achieving the vision.
4. Communicate the vision throughout the organization.
5. Empower others to act on the vision by removing barriers to change and encouraging risk taking and creative problem solving.
6. Plan for, create, and reward short-term "wins" that move the organization toward the new vision.
7. Consolidate improvements, reassess changes, and make necessary adjustments in the new programs.
8. Reinforce the changes by demonstrating the relationship between new behaviors and organizational success.

Source: Based on J. P. Kotter, *Leading Change* (Boston: Harvard Business School Press, 1996).

driving forces *Forces that direct behavior away from the status quo.*

restraining forces *Forces that hinder movement from the existing equilibrium.*

Notice how Exhibit 19-5 builds on Lewin's model. Kotter's first four steps essentially extrapolate on the "unfreezing" stage. Steps 5 through 7 represent "movement." And the final step works on "refreezing." So Kotter's contribution lies in providing managers and change agents with a more detailed guide for successfully implementing change.

Action Research

Action research refers to a change process based on the systematic collection of data and then selection of a change action based on what the analyzed data indicate.[21] Its importance lies in providing a scientific methodology for managing planned change. The process of action research consists of five steps: diagnosis, analysis, feedback, action, and evaluation. You'll note that these steps closely parallel the scientific method.

The change agent, often an outside consultant in action research, begins by gathering information about problems, concerns, and needed changes from members of the organization. This *diagnosis* is analogous to the physician's search to find specifically what ails a patient. In action research, the change agent asks questions, interviews employees, reviews records, and listens to the concerns of employees.

Diagnosis is followed by *analysis*. What problems do people key in on? What patterns do these problems seem to take? The change agent synthesizes this information into primary concerns, problem areas, and possible actions.

Action research includes extensive involvement of the change targets. That is, the people who will be involved in any change program must be actively involved in determining what the problem is and participating in creating the solution. So the third step—*feedback*—requires sharing with employees what has been found from steps one and two. The employees, with the help of the change agent, develop action plans for bringing about any needed change.

Now the *action* part of action research is set in motion. The employees and the change agent carry out the specific actions to correct the problems that have been identified.

The final step, consistent with the scientific underpinnings of action research, is *evaluation* of the action plan's effectiveness. Using the initial data gathered as a benchmark, any subsequent changes can be compared and evaluated.

Action research provides at least two specific benefits for an organization. First, it's problem focused. The change agent objectively looks for problems, and the type of problem determines the type of change action. Although this may seem intuitively obvious, a lot of change activities aren't done this way. Rather, they're solution centered. The change agent has a favorite solution—for example, implementing flextime, teams, or a process reengineering program—and then seeks out problems that the solution fits. Second, because action research so heavily involves employees in the process, resistance to change is reduced. In fact, once employees have actively participated in the feedback stage, the change process typically takes on a momentum of its own. The employees and groups that have been involved become an internal source of sustained pressure to bring about the change.

Organizational Development

No discussion of managing change would be complete without including organizational development. **Organizational development (OD)** is not an easily defined single concept. Rather, it's a term used to encompass a collection of planned-change interventions built on humanistic-democratic values that seek to improve organizational effectiveness and employee well-being.[22]

Organizational development at Wal-Mart includes a new voluntary program called the Personal Sustainability Project that seeks to improve employee well-being and organizational effectiveness. Through workshops, retreats, and seminars, Wal-Mart informs employees about the benefits of issues ranging from physical fitness to energy conservation and then gives them the freedom to make positive changes in their personal lives and in their workplace. Wal-Mart employees in this photo sample healthy food as part of a seminar promoting the benefits of fitness and lifestyle improvements.

Source: Michael Stravato/ The New York Times

The OD paradigm values human and organizational growth, collaborative and participative processes, and a spirit of inquiry.[23] The change agent may be directive in OD; however, there is a strong emphasis on collaboration. The following briefly identifies the underlying values in most OD efforts:

1. *Respect for people.* Individuals are perceived as being responsible, conscientious, and caring. They should be treated with dignity and respect.
2. *Trust and support.* An effective and healthy organization is characterized by trust, authenticity, openness, and a supportive climate.
3. *Power equalization.* Effective organizations deemphasize hierarchical authority and control.
4. *Confrontation.* Problems shouldn't be swept under the rug. They should be openly confronted.
5. *Participation.* The more that people who will be affected by a change are involved in the decisions surrounding that change, the more they will be committed to implementing those decisions.

What are some of the OD techniques or interventions for bringing about change? In the following pages, we present six interventions that change agents might consider using.

Sensitivity Training It can go by a variety of names—**sensitivity training**, laboratory training, encounter groups, or T-groups (training groups)—but all refer to a method of changing behavior through unstructured group interaction.[24]

action research *A change process based on systematic collection of data and then selection of a change action based on what the analyzed data indicate.*

organizational development (OD) *A collection of planned change interventions, built on humanistic-democratic values, that seeks to improve organizational effectiveness and employee well-being.*

sensitivity training *Training groups that seek to change behavior through unstructured group interaction.*

Members are brought together in a free and open environment in which participants discuss themselves and their interactive processes, loosely directed by a professional behavioral scientist. The group is process oriented, which means that individuals learn through observing and participating rather than being told. The professional creates the opportunity for participants to express their ideas, beliefs, and attitudes and does not accept—in fact, overtly rejects—any leadership role.

The objectives of the T-groups are to provide the subjects with increased awareness of their own behavior and how others perceive them, greater sensitivity to the behavior of others, and increased understanding of group processes. Specific results sought include increased ability to empathize with others, improved listening skills, greater openness, increased tolerance of individual differences, and improved conflict-resolution skills.

Survey Feedback One tool for assessing attitudes held by organizational members, identifying discrepancies among member perceptions, and solving these differences is the **survey feedback** approach.[25]

Everyone in an organization can participate in survey feedback, but of key importance is the organizational family—the manager of any given unit and the employees who report directly to him or her. A questionnaire is usually completed by all members in the organization or unit. Organization members may be asked to suggest questions or may be interviewed to determine what issues are relevant. The questionnaire typically asks members for their perceptions and attitudes on a broad range of topics, including decision-making practices; communication effectiveness; coordination between units; and satisfaction with the organization, job, peers, and their immediate supervisor.

The data from this questionnaire are tabulated with data pertaining to an individual's specific "family" and to the entire organization and then distributed to employees. These data then become the springboard for identifying problems and clarifying issues that may be creating difficulties for people. Particular attention is given to the importance of encouraging discussion and ensuring that discussions focus on issues and ideas and not on attacking individuals.

Finally, group discussion in the survey feedback approach should result in members identifying possible implications of the questionnaire's findings. Are people listening? Are new ideas being generated? Can decision making, interpersonal relations, or job assignments be improved? Answers to questions like these, it is hoped, will result in the group agreeing on commitments to various actions that will remedy the problems that are identified.

Process Consultation No organization operates perfectly. Managers often sense that their unit's performance can be improved, but they're unable to identify what can be improved and how it can be improved. The purpose of **process consultation (PC)** is for an outside consultant to assist a client, usually a manager, "to perceive, understand, and act upon process events" with which the manager must deal.[26] These might include work flow, informal relationships among unit members, and formal communication channels.

PC is similar to sensitivity training in its assumption that organizational effectiveness can be improved by dealing with interpersonal problems and in its emphasis on involvement. But PC is more task-directed than is sensitivity training. Consultants in PC are there to "give the client 'insight' into what is going on around him, within him, and between him and other people."[27] They do not solve the organization's problems. Rather, the consultant is a guide or coach who advises on the process to help the client solve his or her own problems. The consultant works with the client in *jointly* diagnosing what processes need

To improve dysfunctional relationships between management and union employees, American Airlines CEO Gerard Arpey (right in photo) formed problem-solving teams to find new ways to compete on efficiency and service. A joint leadership team of senior managers and union officials meets monthly to discuss strategy and finances, another team communicates with employees through American's and union Web sites, and other teams of flight attendants and airport workers are trying to improve customer service. To resolve the problem of funding pensions, Arpey is shown here joining pilots and flight attendants in lobbying Congress for support of pension reform legislation.

improvement. The emphasis is on "jointly" because the client develops a skill at analyzing processes within his or her unit that can be continually called on long after the consultant is gone. In addition, by having the client actively participate in both the diagnosis and the development of alternatives, there will be greater understanding of the process and the remedy and less resistance to the action plan chosen.

Team Building As we've noted in numerous places throughout this book, organizations are increasingly relying on teams to accomplish work tasks. **Team building** uses high-interaction group activities to increase trust and openness among team members.[28] Team building can be applied within groups or at the intergroup level, at which activities are interdependent. For our discussion, we emphasize the intragroup level and leave intergroup development to the next section. As a result, our interest concerns applications to organizational families (command groups) as well as to committees, project teams, self-managed teams, and task groups. Team building is applicable where group activities are interdependent. The objective is to improve coordinative efforts of members, which will result in increasing the team's performance.

The activities considered in team building typically include goal setting, development of interpersonal relations among team members, role analysis to clarify each member's role and responsibilities, and team process analysis. Of course, team building may emphasize or exclude certain activities, depending on the purpose of the development effort and the specific problems with which

survey feedback *The use of questionnaires to identify discrepancies among member perceptions; discussion follows, and remedies are suggested.*

process consultation (PC) *A meeting in which a consultant assists a client in understanding process events with which he or she must deal and identifying processes that need improvement.*

team building *High interaction among team members to increase trust and openness.*

the team is confronted. Basically, however, team building attempts to use high interaction among members to increase trust and openness.

It may be beneficial to begin by having members attempt to define the goals and priorities of the team. This will bring to the surface different perceptions of what the team's purpose may be. Following this, members can evaluate the team's performance—how effective is the team in structuring priorities and achieving its goals? This should identify potential problem areas. This self-critique discussion of means and ends can be done with members of the total team present or, when large size impinges on a free interchange of views, may initially take place in smaller groups followed by the sharing of their findings with the total team.

Team building can also address itself to clarifying each member's role on the team. Each role can be identified and clarified. Previous ambiguities can be brought to the surface. For some individuals, it may offer one of the few opportunities they have had to think through thoroughly what their job is all about and what specific tasks they are expected to carry out if the team is to optimize its effectiveness.

Intergroup Development A major area of concern in OD is the dysfunctional conflict that exists between groups. As a result, this has been a subject to which change efforts have been directed.

Intergroup development seeks to change the attitudes, stereotypes, and perceptions that groups have of each other. For example, in one company, the engineers saw the accounting department as composed of shy and conservative types, and the human resources department as having a bunch of "ultra-liberals who are more concerned that some protected group of employees might get their feelings hurt than with the company making a profit." Such stereotypes can have an obvious negative impact on the coordination efforts between the departments.

Although there are several approaches for improving intergroup relations,[29] a popular method emphasizes problem solving.[30] In this method, each group meets independently to develop lists of its perception of itself, the other group, and how it believes the other group perceives it. The groups then share their lists, after which similarities and differences are discussed. Differences are clearly articulated, and the groups look for the causes of the disparities.

Are the groups' goals at odds? Were perceptions distorted? On what basis were stereotypes formulated? Have some differences been caused by misunderstandings of intentions? Have words and concepts been defined differently by each group? Answers to questions like these clarify the exact nature of the conflict. Once the causes of the difficulty have been identified, the groups can move to the integration phase—working to develop solutions that will improve relations between the groups. Subgroups, with members from each of the conflicting groups, can now be created for further diagnosis and to begin to formulate possible alternative actions that will improve relations.

Appreciative Inquiry Most OD approaches are problem-centered. They identify a problem or set of problems, then look for a solution. **Appreciative inquiry (AI)** accentuates the positive.[31] Rather than looking for problems to fix, this approach seeks to identify the unique qualities and special strengths of an organization, which can then be built on to improve performance. That is, it focuses on an organization's successes rather than on its problems.

Advocates of AI argue that problem-solving approaches always ask people to look backward at yesterday's failures, to focus on shortcomings, and rarely result in new visions. Instead of creating a climate for positive change, action research and OD techniques such as survey feedback and process consultation end up placing blame and generating defensiveness. AI proponents claim it makes more sense to refine and enhance what the organization is already doing well. This allows the organization to change by playing to its strengths and competitive advantages.

The AI process essentially consists of four steps, often played out in a large-group meeting over a 2- or 3-day time period and overseen by a trained change agent. The first step is *discovery*. The idea is to find out what people think are the strengths of the organization. For instance, employees are asked to recount times they felt the organization worked best or when they specifically felt most satisfied with their jobs. The second step is *dreaming*. The information from the discovery phase is used to speculate on possible futures for the organization. For instance, people are asked to envision the organization in 5 years and to describe what's different. The third step is *design*. Based on the dream articulation, participants focus on finding a common vision of how the organization will look and agree on its unique qualities. The fourth stage seeks to define the organization's *destiny*. In this final step, participants discuss how the organization is going to fulfill its dream. This typically includes the writing of action plans and development of implementation strategies.

AI has proven to be an effective change strategy in organizations such as GTE, Roadway Express, and the U.S. Navy. For instance, during a recent 3-day AI seminar with Roadway employees, workers were asked to recall ideal work experiences—when they were treated with respect, when trucks were loaded to capacity or arrived on time. Assembled into nine groups, the workers were then encouraged to devise money-saving ideas. A team of short-haul drivers came up with 12 cost-cutting and revenue-generating ideas, one of which could alone generate $1 million in additional profits.[32]

Creating a Culture for Change

4 Demonstrate two ways of creating a culture for change.

We've considered how organizations can adapt to change. Recently, some OB scholars have focused on a more proactive approach to change—how organizations can embrace change by transforming their cultures. In this section we review two such approaches: stimulating an innovative culture and creating a learning organization.

Stimulating a Culture of Innovation

How can an organization become more innovative? An excellent model is W. L. Gore, the $1.4-billion-per-year company best known as the maker of Gore-Tex fabric.[33] Gore has developed a reputation as one of America's most innovative companies by developing a stream of diverse products—including guitar strings, dental floss, medical devices, and fuel cells.

What's the secret of Gore's success? What can other organizations do to duplicate its track record for innovation? Although there is no guaranteed formula, certain characteristics surface again and again when researchers study

intergroup development *OD efforts to change the attitudes, stereotypes, and perceptions that groups have of each other.*

appreciative inquiry (AI) *An approach that seeks to identify the unique qualities and special strengths of an organization, which can then be built on to improve performance.*

Respected as one of the world's most innovative companies, Starbucks turned a commodity product that was declining in sales and invented specialty coffees as a major new product category. Starbucks relies on its employees to share customer insights with managers and takes product development teams on inspirational field trips to view customer behavior, local cultures, and fashion trends. Starbucks has extended its coffee shops from American college campuses and urban sites to locations throughout the world, including the shop shown here at a shopping center in Ramadan, Dubai.

innovative organizations. We've grouped them into structural, cultural, and human resource categories. Our message to change agents is that they should consider introducing these characteristics into their organization if they want to create an innovative climate. Before we look at these characteristics, however, let's clarify what we mean by innovation.

Definition of *Innovation* We said change refers to making things different. **Innovation** is a more specialized kind of change. Innovation is a new idea applied to initiating or improving a product, process, or service.[34] So all innovations involve change, but not all changes necessarily involve new ideas or lead to significant improvements. Innovations in organizations can range from small incremental improvements, such as Nabisco's extension of the Oreo product line to include double-stuffed cookies and chocolate-covered Oreos, up to radical breakthroughs, such as Toyota's battery-powered Prius.

Sources of Innovation *Structural variables* have been the most studied potential source of innovation.[35] A comprehensive review of the structure–innovation relationship leads to the following conclusions.[36] First, organic structures positively influence innovation. Because they're lower in vertical differentiation, formalization, and centralization, organic organizations facilitate the flexibility, adaptation, and cross-fertilization that make the adoption of innovations easier. Second, long tenure in management is associated with innovation. Managerial tenure apparently provides legitimacy and knowledge of how to accomplish tasks and obtain desired outcomes. Third, innovation is nurtured when there are slack resources. Having an abundance of resources allows an organization to afford to purchase innovations, bear the cost of instituting innovations, and absorb failures. Finally, interunit communication is high in innovative organizations.[37] These organizations are high users of committees, task forces, cross-functional teams, and other mechanisms that facilitate interaction across departmental lines.

Innovative organizations tend to have similar *cultures*. They encourage experimentation. They reward both successes and failures. They celebrate mistakes. Unfortunately, in too many organizations, people are rewarded for the absence of failures rather than for the presence of successes. Such cultures extinguish risk taking and innovation. People will suggest and try new ideas only when they feel such behaviors exact no penalties. Managers in innovative organizations recognize that failures are a natural byproduct of venturing into the unknown. When Barry Bonds set the Major League Baseball record for home runs (73), he also had more strikeouts (93). And he is remembered (and paid $20 million per year) for the former, not the latter.

Within the *human resources* category, we find that innovative organizations actively promote the training and development of their members so that they keep current, offer high job security so employees don't fear getting fired for making mistakes, and encourage individuals to become champions of change. Once a new idea is developed, **idea champions** actively and enthusiastically promote the idea, build support, overcome resistance, and ensure that the innovation is implemented.[38] The evidence indicates that champions have common personality characteristics: extremely high self-confidence, persistence, energy, and a tendency to take risks. Idea champions also display characteristics associated with transformational leadership. They inspire and energize others with their vision of the potential of an innovation and through their strong personal conviction in their mission. They are also good at gaining the commitment of others to support their mission. In addition, idea champions have jobs that provide considerable decision-making discretion. This autonomy helps them introduce and implement innovations in organizations.[39]

Creating a Learning Organization

Another way organizations can proactively manage change is to make continuous growth part of its culture—to become a learning organization.[40] In this section, we describe what a learning organization looks like and methods for managing learning.

What's a Learning Organization? A **learning organization** is an organization that has developed the continuous capacity to adapt and change. Just as individuals learn, so too do organizations. "All organizations learn, whether they consciously choose to or not—it is a fundamental requirement for their sustained existence."[41] However, some organizations just do it better than others.

Most organizations engage in what has been called **single-loop learning.**[42] When errors are detected, the correction process relies on past routines and present policies. In contrast, learning organizations use **double-loop learning**. When an error is detected, it's corrected in ways that involve the modification of the organization's objectives, policies, and standard routines. Double-loop learning challenges deeply rooted assumptions and norms within an organization. In this way, it provides opportunities for radically different solutions to problems and dramatic jumps in improvement.

innovation *A new idea applied to initiating or improving a product, process, or service.*

idea champions *Individuals who take an innovation and actively and enthusiastically promote the idea, build support, overcome resistance, and ensure that the idea is implemented.*

learning organization *An organization that has developed the continuous capacity to adapt and change.*

single-loop learning *A process of correcting errors using past routines and present policies.*

double-loop learning *A process of correcting errors by modifying the organization's objectives, policies, and standard routines.*

Exhibit 19-6 Characteristics of a Learning Organization

1. There exists a shared vision that everyone agrees on.
2. People discard their old ways of thinking and the standard routines they use for solving problems or doing their jobs.
3. Members think of all organizational processes, activities, functions, and interactions with the environment as part of a system of interrelationships.
4. People openly communicate with each other (across vertical and horizontal boundaries) without fear of criticism or punishment.
5. People sublimate their personal self-interest and fragmented departmental interests to work together to achieve the organization's shared vision.

Source: Based on P. M. Senge, *The Fifth Discipline* (New York: Doubleday, 1990).

Exhibit 19-6 summarizes the five basic characteristics of a learning organization. It's an organization in which people put aside their old ways of thinking, learn to be open with each other, understand how their organization really works, form a plan or vision that everyone can agree on, and then work together to achieve that vision.[43]

Proponents of the learning organization envision it as a remedy for three fundamental problems inherent in traditional organizations: fragmentation, competition, and reactiveness.[44] First, *fragmentation* based on specialization creates "walls" and "chimneys" that separate different functions into independent and often warring fiefdoms. Second, an overemphasis on *competition* often undermines collaboration. Members of the management team compete with one another to show who is right, who knows more, or who is more persuasive. Divisions compete with one another when they ought to cooperate and share knowledge. Team project leaders compete to show who the best manager is. And third, *reactiveness* misdirects management's attention to problem solving rather than creation. The problem solver tries to make something go away, while a creator tries to bring something new into being. An emphasis on reactiveness pushes out innovation and continuous improvement and, in its place, encourages people to run around "putting out fires."

Managing Learning How do you change an organization to make it into a continual learner? What can managers do to make their firms learning organizations? The following are some suggestions:

- *Establish a strategy.* Management needs to make explicit its commitment to change, innovation, and continuous improvement.
- *Redesign the organization's structure.* The formal structure can be a serious impediment to learning. By flattening the structure, eliminating or combining departments, and increasing the use of cross-functional teams, interdependence is reinforced and boundaries between people are reduced.
- *Reshape the organization's culture.* To become a learning organization, managers need to demonstrate by their actions that taking risks and admitting failures are desirable traits. That means rewarding people who take chances and make mistakes. And management needs to encourage functional conflict. "The key to unlocking real openness at work," says one expert on learning organizations, "is to teach people to give up having to be in agreement. We think agreement is so important. Who cares? You have to bring paradoxes, conflicts, and dilemmas out in the open, so collectively we can be more intelligent than we can be individually."[45]

An excellent illustration of a learning organization is what Richard Clark is trying to do at Merck. In addition to changing Merck's structure so that innovation can come from customers (patients and doctors), Merck is also trying to reward researchers for taking risks, even if their risky ideas end in failure. Merck's transformed strategy, structure, and culture may or may not succeed, but that's part of the risk of stimulating change through creating a learning organization.

Work Stress and Its Management

Most of us are aware that employee stress is an increasing problem in organizations. Friends tell us they're stressed out from greater work loads and having to work longer hours because of downsizing at their companies (see Exhibit 19-7). Parents talk about the lack of job stability in today's world and reminisce about a time when a job with a large company implied lifetime security. We read surveys in which employees complain about the stress created in trying to balance work and family responsibilities.[46] In this section we'll look at the causes and consequences of stress, and then consider what individuals and organizations can do to reduce it.

5 *Define* stress *and identify its potential sources.*

What Is Stress?

Stress is a dynamic condition in which an individual is confronted with an opportunity, demand, or resource related to what the individual desires and for which the outcome is perceived to be both uncertain and important.[47] This is a complicated definition. Let's look at its components more closely.

Stress is not necessarily bad in and of itself. Although stress is typically discussed in a negative context, it also has a positive value.[48] It's an opportunity when it offers potential gain. Consider, for example, the superior performance that an athlete or stage performer gives in "clutch" situations. Such individuals often use stress positively to rise to the occasion and perform at or near their maximum. Similarly, many professionals see the pressures of heavy work loads and deadlines as positive challenges that enhance the quality of their work and the satisfaction they get from their job.

Exhibit 19-7 Too Much Work, Too Little Time

With companies downsizing workers, those who remain find their jobs are demanding increasing amounts of time and energy. A national sample of U.S. employees finds that they:

Feel overworked	54%
Are overwhelmed by workload	55%
Lack time for reflection	59%
Don't have time to complete tasks	56%
Must multitask too much	45%

Source: BusinessWeek, July 16, 2001, p. 12.

stress *A dynamic condition in which an individual is confronted with an opportunity, a demand, or a resource related to what the individual desires and for which the outcome is perceived to be both uncertain and important.*

In short, some stress can be good, and some can be bad. Recently, researchers have argued that **challenge stressors**—or stressors associated with work load, pressure to complete tasks, and time urgency—operate quite differently from **hindrance stressors**—or stressors that keep you from reaching your goals (red tape, office politics, confusion over job responsibilities). Although research on challenge and hindrance stress is just starting to accumulate, early evidence suggests that challenge stressors are less harmful (produce less strain) than hindrance stressors.[49]

More typically, stress is associated with **demands** and **resources**. Demands are responsibilities, pressures, obligations, and even uncertainties that individuals face in the workplace. Resources are things within an individual's control that can be used to resolve the demands. This demands–resources model has received increasing support in the literature.[50] Let's discuss what it means.

When you take a test at school or you undergo your annual performance review at work, you feel stress because you confront opportunities and performance pressures. A good performance review may lead to a promotion, greater responsibilities, and a higher salary. A poor review may prevent you from getting a promotion. An extremely poor review might even result in your being fired. In such a situation, to the extent that you can apply resources to the demands—such as being prepared, placing the exam or review in perspective, or obtaining social support—you will feel less stress.

Research suggests that adequate resources help reduce the stressful nature of demands when demands and resources match. For example, if emotional demands are stressing you, then having emotional resources in the form of social support is especially important. Conversely, if the demands are cognitive—say, information overload—then job resources in the form of computer support or information are more important. Thus, under the demands and resources perspective on stress, having resources to cope with stress is just as important in offsetting stress as demands are in increasing it.[51]

Potential Sources of Stress

What causes stress? As the model in Exhibit 19-8 shows, there are three categories of potential stressors: environmental, organizational, and personal. Let's take a look at each.[52]

Exhibit 19-8 A Model of Stress

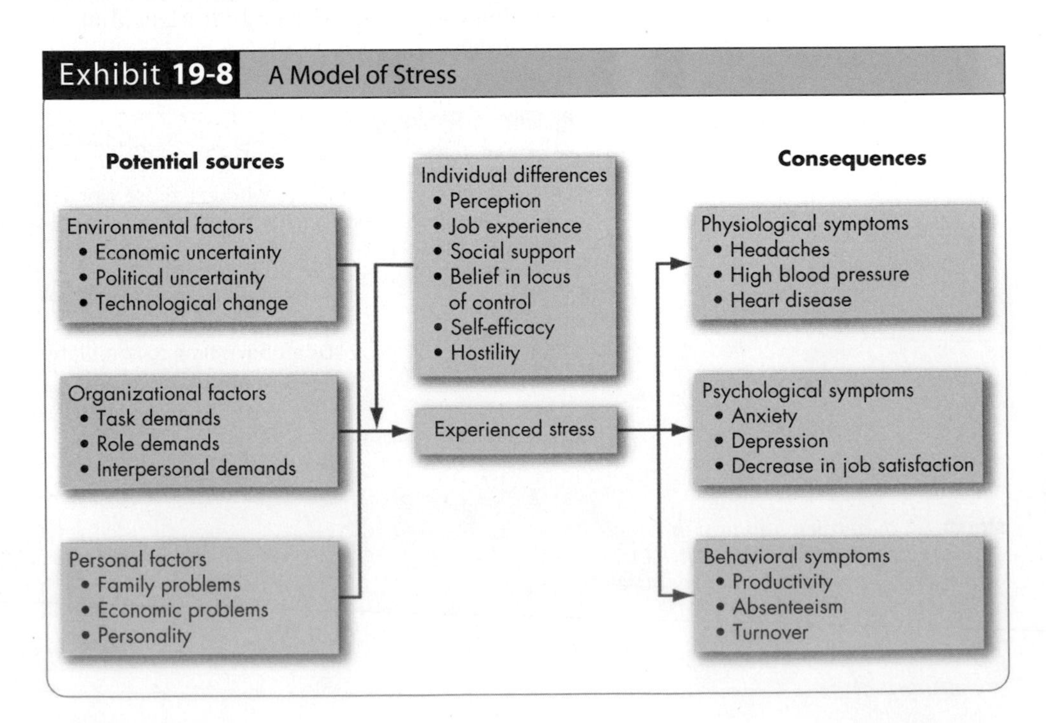

MYTH OR SCIENCE? "Meetings Stress People Out"

As a general rule, this statement is false. A recent investigation revealed that whether you love or hate meetings depends on your work environment, your personality, and your attitude about meetings.[53]

In one study of 676 employees, the researchers found that time spent in meetings led to positive reactions (higher job satisfaction, lower depression and intentions to quit) for people whose work was interdependent, but negative reactions for those whose work was independent. This result makes sense in that if you rely on other people to get your work done, meetings are a productive way to exchange information and coordinate efforts. If you do your work independently, however, meetings are likely to simply be interruptions to getting your work done.

Even more interesting were the results of the second study, of 304 employees in the United Kingdom and United States. The researchers found that for accomplishment-oriented people—those who were goal oriented and hard driving—meetings led to negative reactions. However, for people who scored low on this measure, time spent in meetings was positive.

Finally, the researchers also found in the second study that people's attitudes toward meetings mattered. If people had positive attitudes about meetings, then meetings were more enjoyable and less stressful. For people with negative attitudes, the opposite was true. So your attitude toward meetings is a bit of a self-fulfilling prophecy: If you think they're a waste of time, they will be. ■

Environmental Factors Just as environmental uncertainty influences the design of an organization's structure, it also influences stress levels among employees in that organization. Indeed, evidence indicates that uncertainty is the biggest reason people have trouble coping with organizational changes.[54] There are three main types of environmental uncertainty: economic, political, and technological.

Changes in the business cycle create *economic uncertainties.* When the economy is contracting, for example, people become increasingly anxious about their job security. *Political uncertainties* don't tend to create stress among North Americans as they do for employees in countries like Haiti or Venezuela. The obvious reason is that Canada and the United States have stable political systems, in which change is typically implemented in an orderly manner. Yet political threats and changes, even in these countries can induce stress. For instance, the threats by Quebec to separate from Canada, or the difficulties of East Germany integrating with West Germany, lead to political uncertainty that becomes stressful to people in these countries.[55] *Technological change* is a third type of environmental factor that can cause stress. Because new innovations can make an employee's skills and experience obsolete in a very short time, computers, robotics, automation, and similar forms of technological innovation are a threat to many people and cause them stress.

challenge stressors *Stressors associated with work load, pressure to complete tasks, and time urgency.*

hindrance stressors *Stressors that keep you from reaching your goals (red tape, office politics, confusion over job responsibilities).*

demands *Responsibilities, pressures, obligations, and even uncertainties that individuals face in the workplace.*

resources *Things within an individual's control that can be used to resolve demands.*

Organizational Factors There is no shortage of factors within an organization that can cause stress. Pressures to avoid errors or complete tasks in a limited time, work overload, a demanding and insensitive boss, and unpleasant coworkers are a few examples. We've categorized these factors around task, role, and interpersonal demands.[56]

Task demands are factors related to a person's job. They include the design of the individual's job (autonomy, task variety, degree of automation), working conditions, and the physical work layout. Assembly lines, for instance, can put pressure on people when the line's speed is perceived as excessive. Similarly, working in an overcrowded room or in a visible location where noise and interruptions are constant can increase anxiety and stress.[57] Increasingly, as customer service becomes ever more important, emotional labor is a source of stress.[58] Imagine being a flight attendant for Southwest Airlines or a cashier at Tesco. Do you think you could put on a happy face when you're having a bad day?

Role demands relate to pressures placed on a person as a function of the particular role she plays in the organization. Role conflicts create expectations that may be hard to reconcile or satisfy. Role overload is experienced when the employee is expected to do more than time permits. Role ambiguity is created when role expectations are not clearly understood and the employee is not sure what he or she is to do.

Interpersonal demands are pressures created by other employees. Lack of social support from colleagues and poor interpersonal relationships can cause stress, especially among employees with a high social need.

Personal Factors The typical individual works about 40 to 50 hours a week. But the experiences and problems that people encounter in the other 120-plus nonwork hours each week can spill over to the job. Our final category, then, encompasses factors in the employee's personal life. Primarily, these factors are family issues, personal economic problems, and inherent personality characteristics.

National surveys consistently show that people hold *family* and personal relationships dear. Marital difficulties, the breaking off of a relationship, and discipline troubles with children are examples of relationship problems that create stress for employees that aren't left at the front door when they arrive at work.[59]

Economic problems created by individuals overextending their financial resources is another set of personal troubles that can create stress for employees and distract their attention from their work. Regardless of income level—people who make $80,000 per year seem to have as much trouble handling their finances as those who earn $18,000—some people are poor money managers or have wants that always seem to exceed their earning capacity.

Studies in three diverse organizations found that stress symptoms reported prior to beginning a job accounted for most of the variance in stress symptoms reported 9 months later.[60] This led the researchers to conclude that some people may have an inherent tendency to accentuate negative aspects of the world in general. If this is true, then a significant individual factor that influences stress is a person's basic disposition. That is, stress symptoms expressed on the job may actually originate in the person's *personality*.

Stressors Are Additive A fact that tends to be overlooked when stressors are reviewed individually is that stress is an additive phenomenon.[61] Stress builds up. Each new and persistent stressor adds to an individual's stress level. So a single stressor may be relatively unimportant in and of itself, but if it's added to an already high level of stress, it can be "the straw that breaks the camel's back." If we want to appraise the total amount of stress an individual is under, we have to sum up his or her opportunity stresses, constraint stresses, and demand stresses.

Individual Differences

Some people thrive on stressful situations, while others are overwhelmed by them. What is it that differentiates people in terms of their ability to handle stress? What individual difference variables moderate the relationship between *potential* stressors and *experienced* stress? At least four variables—perception, job experience, social support, and personality—have been found to be relevant moderators.

In Chapter 5, we demonstrated that employees react in response to their perception of reality rather than to reality itself. *Perception*, therefore, will moderate the relationship between a potential stress condition and an employee's reaction to it. For example, one person's fear that he'll lose his job because his company is laying off personnel may be perceived by another as an opportunity to get a large severance allowance and start his own business. So stress potential doesn't lie in objective conditions; it lies in an employee's interpretation of those conditions.

The evidence indicates that *experience* on the job tends to be negatively related to work stress. Why? Two explanations have been offered.[62] First is the idea of selective withdrawal. Voluntary turnover is more probable among people who experience more stress. Therefore, people who remain with an organization longer are those with more stress-resistant traits or those who are more resistant to the stress characteristics of their organization. Second, people eventually develop coping mechanisms to deal with stress. Because this takes time, senior members of the organization are more likely to be fully adapted and should experience less stress.

There is increasing evidence that *social support*—that is, collegial relationships with coworkers or supervisors—can buffer the impact of stress.[63] The logic underlying this moderating variable is that social support acts as a palliative, mitigating the negative effects of even high-strain jobs.

Personality also affects the degree to which people experience stress and how they cope with it. Perhaps the most widely studied personality trait in stress is *Type A personality*, which we discussed in Chapter 4. Type A—particularly that aspect of

The Wieden & Kennedy advertising agency creates a socially supportive atmosphere that reduces the negative effects of employees' high-stress jobs. Open workspaces emphasize teamwork and neighborliness as employees collaborate on creating ad campaigns for the company's clients. The employees in this photo cheer on coworkers during a company basketball game.

Source: Leah Nash/ The New York Times

Type A that manifests itself in hostility and anger—is associated with increased levels of stress and risk for heart disease.[64] More specifically, people who are quick to anger, maintain a persistently hostile outlook, and project a cynical mistrust of others are at increased risk of experiencing stress in situations.

HOW STRESSFUL IS MY LIFE?

In the Self-Assessment Library (available on CD and online), take assessment III.C.2 (How Stressful Is My Life?).

Consequences of Stress

6 *Identify the consequences of stress.*

Stress shows itself in a number of ways. For instance, an individual who is experiencing a high level of stress may develop high blood pressure, ulcers, irritability, difficulty making routine decisions, loss of appetite, accident-proneness, and the like. These symptoms can be subsumed under three general categories: physiological, psychological, and behavioral symptoms.[65]

Physiological Symptoms Most of the early concern with stress was directed at physiological symptoms. This was predominantly due to the fact that the topic was researched by specialists in the health and medical sciences. This research led to the conclusion that stress could create changes in metabolism, increase heart and breathing rates, increase blood pressure, bring on headaches, and induce heart attacks.

The link between stress and particular physiological symptoms is not clear. Traditionally, researchers concluded that there were few, if any, consistent relationships.[66] This is attributed to the complexity of the symptoms and the difficulty of objectively measuring them. More recently, some evidence suggests that stress may have harmful physiological effects. For example, one recent study linked stressful job demands to increase susceptibility to upper respiratory illnesses and poor immune system functioning, especially for individuals who had low self-efficacy.[67]

Psychological Symptoms Stress can cause dissatisfaction. Job-related stress can cause job-related dissatisfaction. Job dissatisfaction, in fact, is "the simplest and most obvious psychological effect" of stress.[68] But stress shows itself in other psychological states—for instance, tension, anxiety, irritability, boredom, and procrastination.

The evidence indicates that when people are placed in jobs that make multiple and conflicting demands or in which there is a lack of clarity about the incumbent's duties, authority, and responsibilities, both stress and dissatisfaction are increased.[69] Similarly, the less control people have over the pace of their work, the greater the stress and dissatisfaction. Although more research is needed to clarify the relationship, the evidence suggests that jobs that provide a low level of variety, significance, autonomy, feedback, and identity to incumbents create stress and reduce satisfaction and involvement in the job.[70]

Behavioral Symptoms Behavior-related stress symptoms include changes in productivity, absence, and turnover, as well as changes in eating habits, increased smoking or consumption of alcohol, rapid speech, fidgeting, and sleep disorders.[71]

OB In the News

The Ten Most Stressful Jobs—And One More That Didn't Make the List

According to the U.S. Centers for Disease Control and Prevention (CDC) and *Health* magazine, the top 10 most and least stressful jobs are:

10 Most Stressful Jobs	10 Least Stressful Jobs
1. Inner-city high school teacher	1. Forester
2. Police officer	2. Bookbinder
3. Miner	3. Telephone line worker
4. Air traffic controller	4. Toolmaker
5. Medical intern	5. Millwright
6. Stockbroker	6. Repairperson
7. Journalist	7. Civil engineer
8. Customer service/complaint worker	8. Therapist
9. Secretary	9. Natural scientist
10. Waiter	10. Sales representative

One job that certainly seems like it should be on the list is flight attendant. Planes are more full than ever, passengers are grumpier than ever (due to full planes, smaller seats, fewer perks, and more delays), and the pay and job security seems to decline with every passing year.

Of these factors, perhaps none is more stressful than the increasingly tense relationship between passengers and flight attendant. Lori Sheridan—a Northwest flight attendant since 1968—said her job description used to be all about providing "whatever the passenger wanted." Now, she said, "It's all about telling them what they can and can't do."

"It's one more level of stress on top of several years of pretty severe stress," said Patricia Friend, president of the largest flight attendant's union.

Sources: Based on *Helicobacter pylori and Peptic Ulcer Disease*, Centers for Disease Control and Prevention, U.S. Department of Health and Human Services; and M. Maynard, "Maybe the Toughest Job Aloft," *New York Times*, August 15, 2006, pp. C1, C6.

There has been a significant amount of research investigating the stress–performance relationship. The most widely studied pattern in the stress–performance literature is the inverted-U relationship.[72] This is shown in Exhibit 19-9.

The logic underlying the inverted U is that low to moderate levels of stress stimulate the body and increase its ability to react. Individuals then often perform their tasks better, more intensely, or more rapidly. But too much stress places unattainable demands on a person, which result in lower performance. This inverted-U pattern may also describe the reaction to stress over time as well as to changes in stress intensity. That is, even moderate levels of stress can have a negative influence on performance over the long term as the continued intensity of the stress wears down the individual and saps energy resources. An athlete may be able to use the positive effects of stress to obtain higher performance during every Saturday's game in the fall season, or a sales executive may be able to psych herself up for her presentation at the annual national meeting. But moderate levels of stress experienced continually over long periods, as

Exhibit 19-9 The Inverted-U Relationship Between Stress and Job Performance

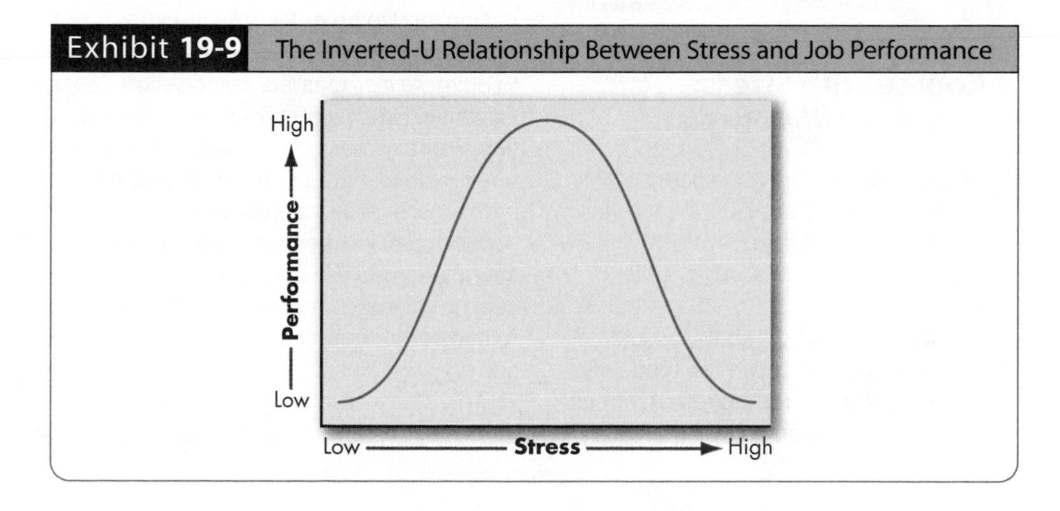

typified by the emergency room staff in a large urban hospital, can result in lower performance. This may explain why emergency room staffs at such hospitals are frequently rotated and why it is unusual to find individuals who have spent the bulk of their career in such an environment. In effect, to do so would expose the individual to the risk of "career burnout."

In spite of the popularity and intuitive appeal of the inverted-U model, it doesn't get a lot of empirical support.[73] At this time, managers should be careful in assuming that this model accurately depicts the stress–performance relationship.

Managing Stress

From the organization's standpoint, management may not be concerned when employees experience low to moderate levels of stress. The reason, as we showed earlier, is that such levels of stress may be functional and lead to higher employee performance. But high levels of stress, or even low levels sustained over long periods, can lead to reduced employee performance and, thus, require action by management.

7 *Contrast the individual and organizational approaches to managing stress.*

Although a limited amount of stress may benefit an employee's performance, don't expect employees to see it that way. From the individual's standpoint, even low levels of stress are likely to be perceived as undesirable. It's not unlikely, therefore, for employees and management to have different notions of what constitutes an acceptable level of stress on the job. What management may consider to be "a positive stimulus that keeps the adrenalin running" is very likely to be seen as "excessive pressure" by the employee. Keep this in mind as we discuss individual and organizational approaches toward managing stress.[74]

Individual Approaches An employee can take personal responsibility for reducing stress levels. Individual strategies that have proven effective include implementing time-management techniques, increasing physical exercise, relaxation training, and expanding the social support network.

Many people manage their time poorly. The well-organized employee, like the well-organized student, can often accomplish twice as much as the person

International OB

Coping with Stress: Cultural Differences

Stress is a common complaint of workers worldwide. But how workers manage that stress, and whether they seek social support for relief, varies from one culture to another. A recent study examined this issue.

The study compared the tendency to seek social support to relieve stress among some Asian groups (Koreans and Asian Americans) to that of European Americans. Given that Asians tend to be more collectivist than European Americans (who tend to be more individualist), two possibilities arise. First, a collectivist orientation might increase the likelihood that one would want to talk about stressful problems, in essence seeking social support. Second, because collectivists strive for group harmony, they may keep problems to themselves and fail to use social support as a means of coping with stress.

The study found support for the latter suggestion: Koreans, Asians, and Asian Americans reported using social support less often than European Americans because they were concerned about maintaining group harmony. What's the upshot? Collectivists experiencing stress may be limiting themselves in terms of coping mechanisms and may need to find other means of coping with work-related stress.

Source: Based on S. Taylor, D. K. Sherman, H. S. Kim, J. Jarcho, K. Takagi, and M. Dunagan, "Culture and Social Support: Who Seeks It and Why?" *Journal of Personality and Social Psychology,* September 2004, pp. 354–362.

Cross-functional support for innovation efforts appeals to people in collectivist cultures like Finland. Hannu Nieminen, head of Insight and Innovation of Nokia Design, leads a global team of more than 300 people representing 34 different nationalities in developing cellular phones for the Finland-based company. The team includes designers, psychologists, researchers, anthropologists, engineers, and technology specialists who are based in major cities around the world. They collaborate by blending macro trends with insights from local cultures in designing products that appeal to country-specific customer needs and tastes.

who is poorly organized. So an understanding and utilization of basic *time-management* principles can help individuals better cope with tensions created by job demands.[75] A few of the most well-known time-management principles are (1) making daily lists of activities to be accomplished, (2) prioritizing activities by importance and urgency, (3) scheduling activities according to the priorities set, and (4) knowing your daily cycle and handling the most demanding parts of your job during the high part of your cycle, when you are most alert and productive.[76]

Physicians have recommended noncompetitive physical exercise, such as aerobics, walking, jogging, swimming, and riding a bicycle, as a way to deal with excessive stress levels. These forms of *physical exercise* increase heart capacity, lower the at-rest heart rate, provide a mental diversion from work pressures, and offer a means to "let off steam."[77]

Individuals can teach themselves to reduce tension through *relaxation techniques* such as meditation, hypnosis, and biofeedback. The objective is to reach a state of deep relaxation, in which one feels physically relaxed, somewhat detached from the immediate environment, and detached from body sensations.[78] Deep relaxation for 15 or 20 minutes a day releases tension and provides a person with a pronounced sense of peacefulness. Importantly, significant changes in heart rate, blood pressure, and other physiological factors result from achieving the condition of deep relaxation.

As we noted earlier in this chapter, having friends, family, or work colleagues to talk to provides an outlet when stress levels become excessive. Expanding your *social support network*, therefore, can be a means for tension reduction. It provides you with someone to hear your problems and to offer a more objective perspective on the situation.

Organizational Approaches Several of the factors that cause stress—particularly task and role demands—are controlled by management. As such, they can be modified or changed. Strategies that management might want to consider include improved personnel selection and job placement, training, use of realistic goal setting, redesigning of jobs, increased employee involvement, improved organizational communication, offering employee sabbaticals, and establishment of corporate wellness programs.

Certain jobs are more stressful than others but, as we learned earlier in this chapter, individuals differ in their response to stressful situations. We know, for example, that individuals with little experience or an external locus of control tend to be more prone to stress. *Selection and placement* decisions should take these facts into consideration. Obviously, management shouldn't restrict hiring to only experienced individuals with an internal locus, but such individuals may adapt better to high-stress jobs and perform those jobs more effectively. Similarly, *training* can increase an individual's self-efficacy and thus lessen job strain.

We discussed *goal setting* in Chapter 6. Based on an extensive amount of research, we concluded that individuals perform better when they have specific and challenging goals and receive feedback on how well they are progressing toward these goals. The use of goals can reduce stress as well as provide motivation. Specific goals that are perceived as attainable clarify performance expectations. In addition, goal feedback reduces uncertainties about actual job performance. The result is less employee frustration, role ambiguity, and stress.

Redesigning jobs to give employees more responsibility, more meaningful work, more autonomy, and increased feedback can reduce stress because these factors give the employee greater control over work activities and lessen dependence on others. But as we noted in our discussion of work design, not all

Xerox Corporation employee Joanne Belknap took a four-month sabbatical to work as a volunteer for the American Cancer Society, where she visited businesses and informed managers and employees about the society's programs. Xerox grants employees fully paid sabbaticals to work on community service projects. Sabbaticals are one way that organizations can rejuvenate employees by allowing them to work on meaningful projects in the community.

employees want enriched jobs. The right redesign, then, for employees with a low need for growth might be less responsibility and increased specialization. If individuals prefer structure and routine, reducing skill variety should also reduce uncertainties and stress levels.

Role stress is detrimental to a large extent because employees feel uncertain about goals, expectations, how they'll be evaluated, and the like. By giving these employees a voice in the decisions that directly affect their job performance, management can increase employee control and reduce this role stress. So managers should consider *increasing employee involvement* in decision making.[79]

Increasing formal *organizational communication* with employees reduces uncertainty by lessening role ambiguity and role conflict. Given the importance that perceptions play in moderating the stress–response relationship, management can also use effective communications as a means to shape employee perceptions. Remember that what employees categorize as demands, threats, or opportunities are merely an interpretation, and that interpretation can be affected by the symbols and actions communicated by management.

What some employees need is an occasional escape from the frenetic pace of their work. In recent years, companies such as Charles Schwab, DuPont, L.L.Bean, Nike, and 3Com have begun to provide extended voluntary leaves.[80] These *sabbaticals*—ranging in length from a few weeks to several months—allow employees to travel, relax, or pursue personal projects that consume time beyond normal vacation weeks. Proponents argue that these sabbaticals can revive and rejuvenate workers who might be headed for burnout.

Our final suggestion is to offer organizationally supported **wellness programs.** These programs focus on the employee's total physical and mental condition.[81] For example, they typically provide workshops to help people quit smoking, control alcohol use, lose weight, eat better, and develop a regular exercise program. The assumption underlying most wellness programs is that employees need to take personal responsibility for their physical and mental health. The organization is merely a vehicle to facilitate this end.

Organizations can expect a payoff from their investment in wellness programs. And most of those firms that have introduced wellness programs have found significant benefits. For instance, a study of eight Canadian organizations found that every dollar spent on their comprehensive wellness programs generated a return of $1.64, and for high-risk employees, such as smokers, the return was nearly $4.00.[82]

Global Implications

8 *Explain global differences in organizational change and work stress.*

Organizational Change A number of change issues we've discussed in this chapter are culture bound. To illustrate, let's briefly look at five questions: (1) Do people believe change is possible? (2) If it's possible, how long will it take to bring it about? (3) Is resistance to change greater in some cultures than in others? (4) Does culture influence how change efforts will be implemented? (5) Do successful idea champions do things differently in different cultures?

Do people believe change is possible? Remember that cultures vary in terms of beliefs about their ability to control their environment. In cultures in which people believe that they can dominate their environment, individuals will take a proactive view of change. This, for example, would describe the United States and Canada. In many other countries, such as Iran and Saudi Arabia, people see themselves as subjugated to their environment and thus will tend to take a passive approach toward change.

If change is possible, how long will it take to bring it about? A culture's time orientation can help us answer this question. Societies that focus on the long term, such as Japan, will demonstrate considerable patience while waiting for positive outcomes from change efforts. In societies with a short-term focus, such as Canada and the United States, people expect quick improvements and will seek change programs that promise fast results.

Is resistance to change greater in some cultures than in others? Resistance to change will be influenced by a society's reliance on tradition. Italians, as an example, focus on the past, whereas U.S. adults emphasize the present. Italians, therefore, should generally be more resistant to change efforts than their U.S. counterparts.

Does culture influence how change efforts will be implemented? Power distance can help with this issue. In high–power distance cultures, such as Spain or Thailand, change efforts will tend to be autocratically implemented by top management. In contrast, low–power distance cultures value democratic methods. We'd predict, therefore, a greater use of participation in countries such as Denmark and the Netherlands.

Finally, do successful idea champions do things differently in different cultures? Yes.[83] People in collectivist cultures prefer appeals for cross-functional support for innovation efforts; people in high-power-distance cultures prefer champions to work closely with those in authority to approve innovative activities before work is begun; and the higher the uncertainty avoidance of a society, the more champions should work within the organization's rules and procedures to develop the innovation. These findings suggest that effective managers will alter their organization's championing strategies to reflect cultural values.

wellness programs *Organizationally supported programs that focus on the employee's total physical and mental condition.*

So, for instance, although idea champions in Russia might succeed by ignoring budgetary limitations and working around confining procedures, champions in Austria, Denmark, Germany, or other cultures high in uncertainty avoidance will be more effective by closely following budgets and procedures.

Stress In considering global differences in stress, there are three questions to answer: (1) Do the causes of stress vary across countries? (2) Do the outcomes of stress vary across cultures? and (3) Do the factors that lessen the effects of stress vary by culture? Let's deal with each of these questions in turn.

First, research suggests that the job conditions that cause stress show some differences across cultures. One study of Chinese and U.S. employees revealed that whereas U.S. employees were stressed by a lack of control, Chinese employees were stressed by job evaluations and lack of training. While the job conditions that lead to stress may differ across countries, it doesn't appear that personality effects on stress are different across cultures. One study of employees in Hungary, Italy, the United Kingdom, Israel, and the United States found that Type A personality traits (see Chapter 4) predicted stress equally well across countries.[84]

Second, evidence tends to suggest that stressors are associated with perceived stress and strains among employees in different countries. In other words, stress is equally bad for employees of all cultures.[85]

Third, although not all factors that reduce stress have been compared across cultures, research does suggest that, whereas the demand to work long hours leads to stress, this stress can be reduced by the resource of social support such as having friends or family to talk to. A recent study found this to be true of workers in a diverse set of countries (Australia, Canada, England, New Zealand, the United States, China, Taiwan, Argentina, Brazil, Colombia, Ecuador, Mexico, Peru, and Uruguay).[86]

Summary and Implications for Managers

The need for change has been implied throughout this text. "A casual reflection on change should indicate that it encompasses almost all of our concepts in the organizational behavior literature."[87] For instance, think about attitudes, motivation, work teams, communication, leadership, organizational structures, human resource practices, and organizational cultures. Change was an integral part in the discussion of each.

If environments were perfectly static, if employees' skills and abilities were always up-to-date and incapable of deteriorating, and if tomorrow were always exactly the same as today, organizational change would have little or no relevance to managers. But the real world is turbulent, requiring organizations and their members to undergo dynamic change if they are to perform at competitive levels.

Managers are the primary change agents in most organizations. By the decisions they make and their role-modeling behaviors, they shape the organization's change culture. For instance, management decisions related to structural design, cultural factors, and human resource policies largely determine the level of innovation within the organization. Similarly, management decisions, policies, and practices will determine the degree to which the organization learns and adapts to changing environmental factors.

We found that the existence of work stress, in and of itself, need not imply lower performance. The evidence indicates that stress can be either a positive or a negative influence on employee performance. For many people, low to moderate amounts of stress enable them to perform their jobs better by increasing their work intensity, alertness, and ability to react. However, a high level of stress, or even a moderate amount sustained over a long period, eventually takes its toll, and performance declines. The impact of stress on satisfaction is far more straightforward. Job-related tension tends to decrease general job satisfaction.[88] Even though low to moderate levels of stress may improve job performance, employees find stress dissatisfying.

Point / Counterpoint

MANAGING CHANGE IS AN EPISODIC ACTIVITY

Organizational change is an episodic activity. That is, it starts at some point, proceeds through a series of steps, and culminates in some outcome that those involved hope is an improvement over the starting point. It has a beginning, a middle, and an end.

Lewin's three-step model represents a classic illustration of this perspective. Change is seen as a break in the organization's equilibrium. The status quo has been disturbed, and change is necessary to establish a new equilibrium state. The objective of refreezing is to stabilize the new situation by balancing the driving and restraining forces.

Some experts have argued that organizational change should be thought of as balancing a system made up of five interacting variables within the organization—people, tasks, technology, structure, and strategy. A change in any one variable has repercussions on one or more of the others. This perspective is episodic in that it treats organizational change as essentially an effort to sustain equilibrium. A change in one variable begins a chain of events that, if properly managed, requires adjustments in the other variables to achieve a new state of equilibrium.

Another way to conceptualize the episodic view of looking at change is to think of managing change as analogous to captaining a ship. The organization is like a large ship traveling across the calm Mediterranean Sea to a specific port. The ship's captain has made this exact trip hundreds of times before with the same crew. Every once in a while, however, a storm will appear, and the crew has to respond. The captain will make the appropriate adjustments—that is, implement changes—and, having maneuvered through the storm, will return the ship to calm waters. Like this ship's voyage, managing an organization should be seen as a journey with a beginning and an end, and implementing change as a response to a break in the status quo and needed only occasionally.

The episodic approach may be the dominant paradigm for handling organizational change, but it has become obsolete. It applies to a world of certainty and predictability. The episodic approach was developed in the 1950s and 1960s, and it reflects the environment of those times. It treats change as the occasional disturbance in an otherwise peaceful world. However, it bears little resemblance to today's environment of constant and chaotic change.[89]

If you want to understand what it's like to manage change in today's organizations, think of it as equivalent to permanent white-water rafting.[90] The organization is not a large ship, but more akin to a 40-foot raft. Rather than sailing a calm sea, this raft must traverse a raging river made up of an uninterrupted flow of permanent white-water rapids. To make things worse, the raft is manned by 10 people who have never worked together or traveled the river before, much of the trip is in the dark, the river is dotted by unexpected turns and obstacles, the exact destination is not clear, and at irregular intervals the raft needs to pull to shore, where some new crew members are added and others leave. Change is a natural state and managing change is a continual process. That is, managers never get the luxury of escaping the white-water rapids.

The stability and predictability characterized by the episodic perspective no longer captures the world we live in. Disruptions in the status quo are not occasional, temporary, and followed by a return to an equilibrium state. There is, in fact, no equilibrium state. Managers today face constant change, bordering on chaos. They're being forced to play a game they've never played before, governed by rules that are created as the game progresses.

Questions for Review

1 What forces act as stimulants to change, and what is the difference between planned and unplanned change?

2 What forces act as sources of resistance to change?

3 What are the four main approaches to managing organizational change?

4 How can managers create a culture for change?

5 What is stress and what are the possible sources of stress?

6 What are the consequences of stress?

7 What are the individual and organizational approaches to managing stress?

8 What does research tell us about global differences in organizational change and work stress?

Experiential Exercise

POWER AND THE CHANGING ENVIRONMENT

Objectives

1. To describe the forces for change influencing power differentials in organizational and interpersonal relationships.
2. To understand the effect of technological, legal/political, economic, and social changes on the power of individuals within an organization.

The Situation

Your organization manufactures golf carts and sells them to country clubs, golf courses, and consumers. Your team is faced with the task of assessing how environmental changes will affect individuals' organizational power. Read each of the five scenarios and then, for each, identify the five members in the organization whose power will increase most in light of the environmental condition(s).

(m) = male (f) = female

Advertising expert (m)	Accountant-CPA (m)
Chief financial officer (f)	General manager (m)
Securities analyst (m)	Marketing manager (f)
Operations manager (f)	Computer programmer (f)
Industrial engineer (m)	Chemist (m)
Product designer (m)	In-house counsel (m)
Public relations expert (m)	Human resource manager (f)
Corporate trainer (m)	

1. New computer-aided manufacturing technologies are being introduced in the workplace during the upcoming 2 to 18 months.
2. New federal emission standards are being legislated by the government that will essentially make gas-powered golf carts (40 percent of your current business) obsolete.
3. Sales are way down for two reasons: (a) a decline in the number of individuals playing golf and (b) your competitor was faster to embrace lithium batteries, which allow golf carts to go longer with a charge.
4. Given the growth of golf courses in other countries (especially India, China, and Southeast Asia), the company is planning to go international in the next 12 to 18 months.
5. The U.S. Equal Employment Opportunity Commission is applying pressure to balance the male–female population in the organization's upper hierarchy by threatening to publicize the predominance of men in upper management.

The Procedure

1. Divide the class into teams of three to four students each.
2. Teams should read each scenario and identify the five members whose power will increase most in light of the external environmental condition described.
3. Teams should then address the question: Assuming that the five environmental changes are taking place at once, which five members of the organization will now have the most power?
4. After 20 to 30 minutes, representatives of each team will be selected to present and justify their conclusions to the entire class. Discussion will begin with scenario 1 and proceed through to scenario 5 and the "all at once" scenario.

Source: Adapted from J. E. Barbuto, Jr., "Power and the Changing Environment," *Journal of Management Education*, April 2000, pp. 288–296.

Ethical Dilemma

STRESSING OUT EMPLOYEES IS YOUR JOB

Some of the most admired business leaders argue that the only way to get the most out of people is to stretch them. This view would seem to be backed by both business anecdotes and research evidence. "If you do know how to get there, it's not a stretch target," former GE CEO Jack Welch has said. "We have found that by reaching for what appears to be the impossible, we often actually do the impossible; and even when we don't quite make it, we inevitably wind up doing much better than we would have done."[91]

As for the research evidence, we noted in Chapter 6 that goal-setting theory—whereby managers set the most difficult goals to which employees will commit—is perhaps the best-supported theory of motivation.

The implication is that to be the most effective manager you need to push, push, and push more.

But does this pose an ethical dilemma for managers? What if you learned that pushing employees to the brink came at the expense of their health or their family life? While it seems true that managers get the performance they expect, it also seems likely that some people push themselves too hard. When Kathie Nunley, who travels more than 100 days a year, had to miss her son winning an art competition, the only person she could share her news with was the Delta ticket agent. "It hit me how sad it was that I was sharing this moment with an airline agent rather than my son," she said.

On the one hand, you may argue that employees should be responsible for their own welfare, and that it would be paternalistic, and encourage mediocrity, to "care for" employees. On the other hand, if your stretch goals mean that your best employees are those who give it all for the organization—even putting aside their own personal or family interests—is that what you wish to be as a manager?

Questions

1. Do you think there is a trade-off between the positive (higher performance) and negative (increased stress) effects of stretch goals?
2. Do you think a manager should consider stress when setting stretch goals for employees? If you answered no, then what should a manager do if a valued employee complains of too much stress? If you answered yes, then how might this be done?
3. How do you think you would respond to stretch goals? Would they increase your performance? Would they stress you?

Case Incident 1

INNOVATING INNOVATION

Executives at Procter & Gamble (P&G) are pretty happy these days. P&G's stock has nearly doubled over the past 5 years, and the company's performance has been unusually resistant to the myriad changes that affect all companies.

Many at P&G might point to chief technology officer Gil Cloyd as one of the sources of this success. Although short-term performance is obviously important, Cloyd has been more focused on long-term change, specifically how P&G approaches research and development (R&D). Given the enormous variety of products that P&G offers, including toilet paper, laundry detergents, personal care products, and pet food, the ability to sustain a competitive level of innovation is a tremendous challenge. Says Cloyd, "One of the challenges we have is serving the needs of a very diverse consumer population, but yet be able to do that quickly and very cost effectively. In the consumer products world we estimate that the required pace of innovation has doubled in the last three years. That means we have less time to benefit from any innovation that we bring into the marketplace." Cloyd's approach is simple yet complex: Innovate innovation.

What is innovating innovation? As Cloyd explains, "What we've done is refine our thinking on how we conduct and evaluate research and development. We've made some changes. For example, historically, we tended to put the evaluation emphasis on technical product performance, patents, and other indicators of internal R&D efforts. Now there is more emphasis on perceived customer value." Cloyd describes P&G's innovation process as holistic, meaning it touches every department of an organization. Holistic innovation includes first setting appropriate financial goals and then implementing an innovation program for all aspects of the product—from its manufacturing technology to those aspects that the customer experiences directly, such as the product's packaging and appearance.

One of Cloyd's major goals at P&G is to acquire most product ideas from sources external to the organization, which it is close to doing. As a result, P&G has doubled the number of new products with elements that originated outside the company.

Though P&G is enjoying enormous success due in part to its innovation program, Cloyd is not resting on his laurels. He emphasizes learning as a critical element to continued innovation success. One area he's exploring is computer modeling and simulation. Previously, manufacturing was the main user of computer modeling. Now, Cloyd is using it in the product design process. Explains Cloyd, "A computational model helps us more quickly to understand what's going on. The simulation capabilities are also allowing us to interact with consumers much more quickly on design options. For example, Internet panels can engage consumers in as little as 24 hours. Digital technology is very important in helping us learn faster. Not only will it accelerate innovation, but the approach will greatly enhance the creativity of our people." By continually looking for new ways to design, produce, and market products, Cloyd and P&G are indeed "innovating innovation."

Questions

1. This book covers the notion of "idea champions." What characteristics of Gil Cloyd make him an idea champion?
2. Would you consider P&G to be a "learning organization"? What aspects of P&G lead you to your answer?
3. Although Cloyd is a major reason for P&G's innovation success, what are some structural features of P&G that might contribute to its ability to innovate so well?
4. The benefits of technological innovations for companies are often short lived because other companies adopt the same technology soon after. What factors do you believe contribute to P&G's ability to continually innovate at such a competitive level?

Source: Based on A. Markels, "Turning the Tide at P&G," *U.S. News & World Report*, October 22, 2006, pp. 1–3; and J. Teresko, "P&G's Secret: Innovating Innovation," *IndustryWeek*, December 2004, pp. 26–34.

Case Incident 2

THE RISE OF EXTREME JOBS

Before Barbara Agoglia left her job at American Express, she was spending 13 hours a day working and commuting. She also had to be available via cell phone 24/7. The last straw came when she didn't have time to wait with her son at his bus stop. Carolyn Buck also has an extreme job. She usually works more than 60 hours a week for Ernst & Young and often has to travel to India and China.

Agoglia and Buck are not alone. Most U.S. adults are working more hours than ever, but one group in particular stands out: those with extreme jobs—people who spend more than half their time working and commuting to and from work. More than 1.7 million people consider their jobs *too* extreme, according to a recent study.

What accounts for the rise in extreme jobs? It's not entirely clear, but the usual suspects of globalization, technology, and competitiveness are high on everyone's lists.

As extreme as Agoglia and Buck's jobs may seem, U.S. workers may have it comparatively easy. Most surveys indicate that extreme jobs are worse in developing counties. A 2006 *Harvard Business Review* study of managers in 33 global companies indicated that, compared to U.S. managers, managers in developing countries were more than twice as likely to have extreme jobs.

For those who hold extreme jobs, a personal life often takes a back seat. Among extreme job holders, 44 percent take fewer than 10 vacation days per year. Many individuals with extreme jobs see society changing into a "winner takes all" mode, where those who are willing to go the extra mile will reap a disproportionate share of the intrinsic and extrinsic rewards.

Why do people take extreme jobs (or allow their jobs to become extreme)? A 2006 study suggested that, for both men and women, the number 1 reason they work long, stressful hours is not pay. Rather, it's that the stimulating or challenging work gives them a rush. As one Asian manager said, "Building this business in markets where no one has done anything like this before is enormously exciting. And important. We've built distribution centers that are vital to China's growth—they contribute to the overall prospects of our economy."

Although this sounds all good, the situation is more complicated when you ask holders of extreme jobs about what their jobs cost them. Among such job holders, 66 percent of men and 77 percent of women say their job interferes with their ability to maintain a home. For those with extreme jobs who have children, 65 percent of men and 33 percent of women say it keeps them from having a relationship with their children. And 46 percent of male and female extreme job holders say their jobs interfere with having a strong relationship with their spouse. About half of each group say it interferes with their sex life. "I can't even fathom having a boyfriend," says one extreme job holder. Another extreme job holder, Chris Cicchinelli, was so concerned about being out of touch with work during his honeymoon that he got a satellite phone. Even that didn't help. He ended up cutting his 10-day honeymoon to 5 days. "I had major anxiety," he said.

Questions

1. Do you think you will ever have an extreme job? Are you sure? Explain.

2. Why do you think the number of extreme jobs has risen?
3. Do you think organizations should encourage extreme jobs, discourage them, or completely leave them to an employee's discretion?
4. Why do you think people take extreme jobs in the first place?

Sources: T. Weiss, "How Extreme Is Your Job?" *Forbes*, February 1, 2007, p. 1; S. A. Hewlett and C. B. Luce, "Extreme Jobs," *Harvard Business Review*, December 2006, pp. 49–58; and S. Armour, "Hi, I'm Joan, and I'm a Workaholic," *USA Today*, May 23, 2007, pp. 1B, 2B.

Endnotes

1. Based on "Is Merck's Medicine Working?" *BusinessWeek*, June 30, 2007, pp. 1–3; K. McKay, "Merck CEO Sets Sights on Change," *USA Today*, February 27, 2006, pp. 1B, 2B.
2. See, for instance, K. H. Hammonds, "Practical Radicals," *Fast Company*, September 2000, pp. 162–174; and P. C. Judge, "Change Agents," *Fast Company*, November 2000, pp. 216–226.
3. J. Taub, "Harvard Radical," *New York Times Magazine*, August 24, 2003, pp. 28–45+.
4. A. Finder, P. D. Healy, and K. Zernike, "President of Harvard Resigns, Ending Stormy 5-Year Tenure," *New York Times*, February 22, 2006, pp. A1, A19.
5. P. G. Audia and S. Brion, "Reluctant to Change: Self-Enhancing Responses to Diverging Performance Measures," *Organizational Behavior and Human Decision Processes* 102 (2007), pp. 255–269.
6. M. T. Hannan, L. Pólos, and G. R. Carroll, "The Fog of Change: Opacity and Asperity in Organizations," *Administrative Science Quarterly*, September 2003. pp. 399–432.
7. J. P. Kotter and L. A. Schlesinger, "Choosing Strategies for Change," *Harvard Business Review*, March–April 1979, pp. 106–114.
8. J. E. Dutton, S. J. Ashford, R. M. O'Neill, and K. A. Lawrence, "Moves That Matter: Issue Selling and Organizational Change," *Academy of Management Journal*, August 2001, pp. 716–736.
9. P. C. Fiss and E. J. Zajac, "The Symbolic Management of Strategic Change: Sensegiving via Framing and Decoupling," *Academy of Management Journal* 49, no. 6 (2006), pp. 1173–1193.
10. Q. N. Huy, "Emotional Balancing of Organizational Continuity and Radical Change: The Contribution of Middle Managers," *Administrative Science Quarterly*, March 2002, pp. 31–69; D. M. Herold, D. B. Fedor, and S. D. Caldwell, "Beyond Change Management: A Multilevel Investigation of Contextual and Personal Influences on Employees' Commitment to Change," *Journal of Applied Psychology* 92, no. 4 (2007), pp. 942–951; and G. B. Cunningham, "The Relationships Among Commitment to Change, Coping with Change, and Turnover Intentions," *European Journal of Work and Organizational Psychology* 15, no. 1 (2006), pp. 29–45.
11. D. B. Fedor, S. Caldwell, and D. M. Herold, "The Effects of Organizational Changes on Employee Commitment: A Multilevel Investigation," *Personnel Psychology* 59 (2006), pp. 1–29.
12. S. Oreg, "Personality, Context, and Resistance to Organizational Change," *European Journal of Work and Organizational Psychology* 15, no. 1 (2006), pp. 73–101.
13. J. A. LePine, J. A. Colquitt, and A. Erez, "Adaptability to Changing Task Contexts: Effects of General Cognitive Ability, Conscientiousness, and Openness to Experience," *Personnel Psychology*, Fall, 2000, pp. 563–593; T. A. Judge, C. J. Thoresen, V. Pucik, and T. M. Welbourne, "Managerial Coping with Organizational Change: A Dispositional Perspective," *Journal of Applied Psychology*, February 1999, pp. 107–122; and S. Oreg, "Resistance to Change: Developing an Individual Differences Measure," *Journal of Applied Psychology*, August 2003, pp. 680–693.
14. See J. Pfeffer, *Managing with Power: Politics and Influence in Organizations* (Boston: Harvard Business School Press, 1992), pp. 7, and 318–320.
15. See, for instance, W. Ocasio, "Political Dynamics and the Circulation of Power: CEO Succession in U.S. Industrial Corporations, 1960–1990," *Administrative Science Quarterly*, June 1994, pp. 285–312.
16. K. Lewin, *Field Theory in Social Science* (New York: Harper & Row, 1951).
17. P. G. Audia, E. A. Locke, and K. G. Smith, "The Paradox of Success: An Archival and a Laboratory Study of Strategic Persistence Following Radical Environmental Change," *Academy of Management Journal*, October 2000, pp. 837–853.
18. J. B. Sorensen, "The Strength of Corporate Culture and the Reliability of Firm Performance," *Administrative Science Quarterly*, March 2002, pp. 70–91.
19. J. Amis, T. Slack, and C. R. Hinings, "The Pace, Sequence, and Linearity of Radical Change," *Academy of Management Journal*, February 2004, pp. 15–39; and E. Autio, H. J. Sapienza, and J. G. Almeida, "Effects of Age at Entry, Knowledge Intensity, and Imitability on International Growth," *Academy of Management Journal*, October 2000, pp. 909–924.
20. J. P. Kotter, "Leading Changes: Why Transformation Efforts Fail," *Harvard Business Review*, March–April 1995, pp. 59–67; and J. P. Kotter, *Leading Change* (Harvard Business School Press, 1996).
21. See, for example, C. Eden and C. Huxham, "Action Research for the Study of Organizations," in S. R. Clegg, C. Hardy, and W. R. Nord (eds.), *Handbook of Organization Studies* (London: Sage, 1996).
22. For a sampling of various OD definitions, see N. Nicholson (ed.), *Encyclopedic Dictionary of Organizational Behavior* (Malden, MA: Blackwell, 1998), pp. 359–361; H. K. Sinangil and F. Avallone, "Organizational Development and

Change," in N. Anderson, D. S. Ones, H. K. Sinangil, and C. Viswesvaran (eds.), *Handbook of Industrial, Work and Organizational Psychology*, vol. 2 (Thousand Oaks, CA: Sage, 2001), pp. 332–335.

23. See, for instance, R. Lines, "Influence of Participation in Strategic Change: Resistance, Organizational Commitment and Change Goal Achievement," *Journal of Change Management*, September 2004, pp. 193–215.
24. S. Highhouse, "A History of the T-Group and Its Early Application in Management Development," *Group Dynamics: Theory, Research, & Practice*, December 2002, pp. 277–290.
25. J. E. Edwards and M. D. Thomas, "The Organizational Survey Process: General Steps and Practical Considerations," in P. Rosenfeld, J. E. Edwards, and M. D. Thomas (eds.), *Improving Organizational Surveys: New Directions, Methods, and Applications* (Newbury Park, CA: Sage, 1993), pp. 3–28.
26. E. H. Schein, *Process Consultation: Its Role in Organizational Development*, 2nd ed. (Reading, MA: Addison-Wesley, 1988), p. 9. See also E. H. Schein, *Process Consultation Revisited: Building Helpful Relationships* (Reading, MA: Addison-Wesley, 1999).
27. Schein, *Process Consultation.*
28. W. Dyer, *Team Building: Issues and Alternatives* (Reading, MA: Addison-Wesley, 1994).
29. See, for example, E. H. Neilsen, "Understanding and Managing Intergroup Conflict," in J. W. Lorsch and P. R. Lawrence (eds.), *Managing Group and Intergroup Relations* (Homewood, IL: Irwin-Dorsey, 1972), pp. 329–343.
30. R. R. Blake, J. S. Mouton, and R. L. Sloma, "The Union–Management Intergroup Laboratory: Strategy for Resolving Intergroup Conflict," *Journal of Applied Behavioral Science*, no. 1 (1965), pp. 25–57.
31. See, for example, R. Fry, F. Barrett, J. Seiling, and D. Whitney (eds.), *Appreciative Inquiry & Organizational Transformation: Reports From the Field* (Westport, CT: Quorum, 2002); J. K. Barge and C. Oliver, "Working with Appreciation in Managerial Practice," *Academy of Management Review*, January 2003, pp. 124–142; and D. van der Haar and D. M. Hosking, "Evaluating Appreciative Inquiry: A Relational Constructionist Perspective," *Human Relations*, August 2004, pp. 1017–1036.
32. J. Gordon, "Meet the Freight Fairy," *Forbes*, January 20, 2003, p. 65.
33. D. Anfuso, "Core Values Shape W. L. Gore's Innovative Culture," *Workforce*, March 1999, pp. 48–51; and A. Harrington, "Who's Afraid of a New Product?" *Fortune*, November 10, 2003, pp. 189–192.
34. See, for instance, R. M. Kanter, "When a Thousand Flowers Bloom: Structural, Collective and Social Conditions for Innovation in Organizations," in B. M. Staw and L. L. Cummings (eds.), *Research in Organizational Behavior*, vol. 10 (Greenwich, CT: JAI Press, 1988), pp. 169–211.
35. F. Damanpour, "Organizational Innovation: A Meta-Analysis of Effects of Determinants and Moderators," *Academy of Management Journal*, September 1991, p. 557.
36. Ibid., pp. 555–590.
37. See P. R. Monge, M. D. Cozzens, and N. S. Contractor, "Communication and Motivational Predictors of the Dynamics of Organizational Innovation," *Organization Science*, May 1992, pp. 250–274.
38. J. M. Howell and C. A. Higgins, "Champions of Change," *Business Quarterly*, Spring 1990, pp. 31–32; and D. L. Day, "Raising Radicals: Different Processes for Championing Innovative Corporate Ventures," *Organization Science*, May 1994, pp. 148–172.
39. Howell and Higgins, "Champions of Change."
40. See, for example, T. B. Lawrence, M. K. Mauws, B. Dyck, and R. F. Kleysen, "The Politics of Organizational Learning: Integrating Power into the 4I Framework," *Academy of Management Review*, January 2005, pp. 180–191.
41. D. H. Kim, "The Link Between Individual and Organizational Learning," *Sloan Management Review*, Fall 1993, p. 37.
42. C. Argyris and D. A. Schon, *Organizational Learning* (Reading, MA: Addison-Wesley, 1978).
43. B. Dumaine, "Mr. Learning Organization," *Fortune*, October 17, 1994, p. 148.
44. F. Kofman and P. M. Senge, "Communities of Commitment: The Heart of Learning Organizations," *Organizational Dynamics*, Autumn 1993, pp. 5–23.
45. Dumaine, "Mr. Learning Organization," p. 154.
46. See, for instance, K. Slobogin, "Many U.S. Employees Feel Overworked, Stressed, Study Says," *CNN.com*, May 16, 2001, www.cnn.com; and S. Armour, "Rising Job Stress Could Affect Bottom Line," *USA Today*, July 29, 2003, p. 1B.
47. Adapted from R. S. Schuler, "Definition and Conceptualization of Stress in Organizations," *Organizational Behavior and Human Performance*, April 1980, p. 189. For an updated review of definitions, see C. L. Cooper, P. J. Dewe, and M. P. O'Driscoll, *Organizational Stress: A Review and Critique of Theory, Research, and Applications* (Thousand Oaks, CA: Sage, 2002).
48. See, for instance, M. A. Cavanaugh, W. R. Boswell, M. V. Roehling, and J. W. Boudreau, "An Empirical Examination of Self-Reported Work Stress Among U.S. Managers," *Journal of Applied Psychology*, February 2000, pp. 65–74.
49. N. P. Podsakoff, J. A. LePine, and M. A. LePine, "Differential Challenge-Hindrance Stressor Relationships with Job Attitudes, Turnover Intentions, Turnover, and Withdrawal Behavior: A Meta-analysis," *Journal of Applied Psychology* 92, no. 2 (2007), pp. 438–454; J. A. LePine, M. A. LePine, and C. L. Jackson, "Challenge and Hindrance Stress: Relationships with Exhaustion, Motivation to Learn, and Learning Performance," *Journal of Applied Psychology*, October 2004, pp. 883–891.
50. N. W. Van Yperen and O. Janssen, "Fatigued and Dissatisfied or Fatigued but Satisfied? Goal Orientations and Responses to High Job Demands," *Academy of Management Journal*, December 2002, pp. 1161–1171; and N. W. Van Yperen and M. Hagedoorn, "Do High Job Demands Increase Intrinsic Motivation or Fatigue or Both? The Role of Job Control and Job Social Support," *Academy of Management Journal*, June 2003, pp. 339–348.
51. J. de Jonge and C. Dormann, "Stressors, Resources, and Strain at Work: A Longitudinal Test of the Triple-Match Principle," *Journal of Applied Psychology* 91, no. 5 (2006), pp. 1359–1374.
52. This section is adapted from C. L. Cooper and R. Payne, *Stress at Work* (London: Wiley, 1978); S. Parasuraman and J. A. Alutto, "Sources and Outcomes of Stress in Organizational Settings: Toward the Development of a Structural Model," *Academy of Management Journal* 27, no. 2 (June 1984), pp. 330–350; and P. M. Hart and C. L. Cooper, "Occupational

Stress: Toward a More Integrated Framework," in N. Anderson, D. S. Ones, H. K. Sinangil, and C. Viswesvaran (eds.), *Handbook of Industrial, Work and Organizational Psychology*, vol. 2 (London: Sage, 2001), pp. 93–114.

53. S. G. Rogelberg, D. J. Leach, and P. B. Warr, and J. L. Burnfield, "'Not Another Meeting!' Are Meeting Time Demands Related to Employee Well-Being?" *Journal of Applied Psychology* 91, no. 1 (2006), pp. 86–96.

54. A. E. Rafferty and M. A. Griffin, "Perceptions of Organizational Change: A Stress and Coping Perspective," *Journal of Applied Psychology* 71, no. 5 (2007), pp. 1154–1162.

55. H. Garst, M. Frese, and P. C. M. Molenaar, "The Temporal Factor of Change in Stressor-Strain Relationships: A Growth Curve Model on a Longitudinal Study in East Germany," *Journal of Applied Psychology*, June 2000, pp. 417–438.

56. See, for example, M. L. Fox, D. J. Dwyer, and D. C. Ganster, "Effects of Stressful Job Demands and Control of Physiological and Attitudinal Outcomes in a Hospital Setting," *Academy of Management Journal*, April 1993, pp. 289–318.

57. G. W. Evans and D. Johnson, "Stress and Open-Office Noise," *Journal of Applied Psychology*, October 2000, pp. 779–783.

58. T. M. Glomb, J. D. Kammeyer-Mueller, and M. Rotundo, "Emotional Labor Demands and Compensating Wage Differentials," *Journal of Applied Psychology*, August 2004. pp. 700–714; A. A. Grandey, "When 'The Show Must Go On': Surface Acting and Deep Acting as Determinants of Emotional Exhaustion and Peer-Rated Service Delivery," *Academy of Management Journal*, February 2003, pp. 86–96.

59. V. S. Major, K. J. Klein, and M. G. Ehrhart, "Work Time, Work Interference with Family, and Psychological Distress," *Journal of Applied Psychology*, June 2002, pp. 427–436; see also P. E. Spector, C. L. Cooper, S. Poelmans, T. D. Allen, M. O'Driscoll, J. I. Sanchez, O. L. Siu, P. Dewe, P. Hart, L. Lu, L. F. R. De Moreas, G. M. Ostrognay, K. Sparks, P. Wong, and S. Yu, "A Cross-National Comparative Study of Work-Family Stressors, Working Hours, and Well-Being: China and Latin America Versus the Anglo World," *Personnel Psychology*, Spring 2004, pp. 119–142.

60. D. L. Nelson and C. Sutton, "Chronic Work Stress and Coping: A Longitudinal Study and Suggested New Directions," *Academy of Management Journal*, December 1990, pp. 859–869.

61. H. Selye, *The Stress of Life*, rev. ed. (New York: McGraw-Hill, 1956).

62. S. J. Motowidlo, J. S. Packard, and M. R. Manning, "Occupational Stress: Its Causes and Consequences for Job Performance," *Journal of Applied Psychology*, November 1987, pp. 619–620.

63. See, J. B. Halbesleben, "Sources of Social Support and Burnout: A Meta-Analytic Test of the Conservation of Resources Model," *Journal of Applied Psychology* 91, no. 5 (2006), pp. 1134–1145; N. Bolger and D. Amarel, "Effects of Social Support Visibility on Adjustment to Stress: Experimental Evidence," *Journal of Applied Psychology* 92, no. 3 (2007), pp. 458–475; and N. A. Bowling, T. A. Beehr, and W. M. Swader, "Giving and Receiving Social Support at Work: The Roles of Personality and Reciprocity," *Journal of Vocational Behavior* 67 (2005), pp. 476–489.

64. R. Williams, *The Trusting Heart: Great News About Type A Behavior* (New York: Times Books, 1989).

65. Schuler, "Definition and Conceptualization of Stress," pp. 200–205; and R. L. Kahn and M. Byosiere, "Stress in Organizations," in M. D. Dunnette and L. M. Hough (eds.), *Handbook of Industrial and Organizational Psychology*, 2nd ed., vol. 3 (Palo Alto, CA: Consulting Psychologists Press, 1992), pp. 604–610.

66. See T. A. Beehr and J. E. Newman, "Job Stress, Employee Health, and Organizational Effectiveness: A Facet Analysis, Model, and Literature Review," *Personnel Psychology*, Winter 1978, pp. 665–699; and B. D. Steffy and J. W. Jones, "Workplace Stress and Indicators of Coronary-Disease Risk," *Academy of Management Journal*, September 1988, pp. 686–698.

67. J. Schaubroeck, J. R. Jones, and J. L. Xie, "Individual Differences in Utilizing Control to Cope with Job Demands: Effects on Susceptibility to Infectious Disease," *Journal of Applied Psychology*, April 2001, pp. 265–278.

68. Steffy and Jones, "Workplace Stress and Indicators of Coronary-Disease Risk," p. 687.

69. C. L. Cooper and J. Marshall, "Occupational Sources of Stress: A Review of the Literature Relating to Coronary Heart Disease and Mental Ill Health," *Journal of Occupational Psychology* 49, no. 1 (1976), pp. 11–28.

70. J. R. Hackman and G. R. Oldham, "Development of the Job Diagnostic Survey," *Journal of Applied Psychology*, April 1975, pp. 159–170.

71. E. M. de Croon, J. K. Sluiter, R. W. B. Blonk, J. P. J. Broersen, and M. H. W. Frings-Dresen, "Stressful Work, Psychological Job Strain, and Turnover: A 2-Year Prospective Cohort Study of Truck Drivers," *Journal of Applied Psychology*, June 2004, pp. 442–454; and R. Cropanzano, D. E. Rupp, and Z. S. Byrne, "The Relationship of Emotional Exhaustion to Work Attitudes, Job Performance, and Organizational Citizenship Behaviors," *Journal of Applied Psychology*, February 2003. pp. 160–169.

72. See, for instance, S. Zivnuska, C. Kiewitz, W. A. Hochwarter, P. L. Perrewe, and K. L. Zellars, "What Is Too Much or Too Little? The Curvilinear Effects of Job Tension on Turnover Intent, Value Attainment, and Job Satisfaction," *Journal of Applied Social Psychology*, July 2002, pp. 1344–1360.

73. L. A. Muse, S. G. Harris, and H. S. Field, "Has the Inverted-U Theory of Stress and Job Performance Had a Fair Test?" *Human Performance* 16, no. 4 (2003), pp. 349–364.

74. The following discussion has been influenced by J. E. Newman and T. A. Beehr, "Personal and Organizational Strategies for Handling Job Stress," *Personnel Psychology*, Spring 1979, pp. 1–38; J. M. Ivancevich and M. T. Matteson, "Organizational Level Stress Management Interventions: A Review and Recommendations," *Journal of Organizational Behavior Management*, Fall–Winter 1986, pp. 229–248; M. T. Matteson and J. M. Ivancevich, "Individual Stress Management Interventions: Evaluation of Techniques," *Journal of Management Psychology*, January 1987, pp. 24–30; J. M. Ivancevich, M. T. Matteson, S. M. Freedman, and J. S. Phillips, "Worksite Stress Management Interventions," *American Psychologist*, February 1990, pp. 252–261; and R. Schwarzer, "Manage Stress at Work Through Preventive and Proactive Coping," in E. A. Locke (ed.), *Handbook of Principles of Organizational Behavior* (Malden, MA: Blackwell, 2004), pp. 342–355.

75. T. H. Macan, "Time Management: Test of a Process Model," *Journal of Applied Psychology*, June 1994, pp. 381–391; and B. J. C. Claessens, W. Van Eerde, C. G. Rutte, and R. A. Roe, "Planning Behavior and Perceived Control of Time at Work," *Journal of Organizational Behavior*, December 2004, pp. 937–950.

76. See, for example, G. Lawrence-Ell, *The Invisible Clock: A Practical Revolution in Finding Time for Everyone and Everything* (Seaside Park, NJ: Kingsland Hall, 2002); and B. Tracy, *Time Power* (New York: AMACOM, 2004).

77. J. Kiely and G. Hodgson, "Stress in the Prison Service: The Benefits of Exercise Programs," *Human Relations*, June 1990, pp. 551–572.

78. E. J. Forbes and R. J. Pekala, "Psychophysiological Effects of Several Stress Management Techniques," *Psychological Reports*, February 1993, pp. 19–27; and M. Der Hovanesian, "Zen and the Art of Corporate Productivity," *BusinessWeek*, July 28, 2003, p. 56.

79. S. E. Jackson, "Participation in Decision Making as a Strategy for Reducing Job-Related Strain," *Journal of Applied Psychology*, February 1983, pp. 3–19.

80. S. Greengard, "It's About Time," *Industry Week*, February 7, 2000, pp. 47–50; and S. Nayyar, "Gimme a Break," *American Demographics*, June 2002, p. 6.S. Greengard, "It's About Time," *IndustryWeek*, February 7, 2000, pp. 47–50; and S. Nayyar, "Gimme a Break," *American Demographics*, June 2002, p. 6.

81. See, for instance, B. Leonard, "Health Care Costs Increase Interest in Wellness Programs," *HRMagazine*, September 2001, pp. 35–36; and "Healthy, Happy and Productive," *Training*, February 2003, p. 16.

82. D. Brown, "Wellness Programs Bring Healthy Bottom Line," *Canadian HR Reporter*, December 17, 2001, pp. 1+.

83. See S. Shane, S. Venkataraman, and I. MacMillan, "Cultural Differences in Innovation Championing Strategies," *Journal of Management* 21, no. 5 (1995), pp. 931–952.

84. J. Chen, C. Silverthorne, and J. Hung, "Organization Communication, Job Stress, Organizational Commitment, and Job Performance of Accounting Professionals in Taiwan and America," *Leadership & Organization Development Journal* 27, no. 4 (2006), pp. 242–249; C. Liu, P. E. Spector, and L. Shi, "Cross-National Job Stress: A Quantitative and Qualitative Study," *Journal of Organizational Behavior*, February 2007, pp. 209–239.

85. H. M. Addae and X. Wang, "Stress at Work: Linear and Curvilinear Effects of Psychological-, Job-, and Organization-Related Factors: An Exploratory Study of Trinidad and Tobago," *International Journal of Stress Management*, November 2006, pp. 476–493.

86. P. E. Spector et al., "A Cross-National Comparative Study of Work-Family Stressors, Working Hours, and Well-Being: China and Latin America Versus the Anglo World," *Personnel Psychology*, Spring 2004, pp. 119–142.

87. P. S. Goodman and L. B. Kurke, "Studies of Change in Organizations: A Status Report," in P. S. Goodman (ed.), *Change in Organizations* (San Francisco: Jossey-Bass, 1982), p. 1.

88. Kahn and Byosiere, "Stress in Organizations," pp. 605–608.

89. For contrasting views on episodic and continuous change, see K. E. Weick and R. E. Quinn, "Organizational Change and Development," in J. T. Spence, J. M. Darley, and D. J. Foss (eds.), *Annual Review of Psychology*, vol. 50 (Palo Alto, CA: Annual Reviews, 1999), pp. 361–386.

90. This perspective is based on P. B. Vaill, *Managing as a Performing Art: New Ideas for a World of Chaotic Change* (San Francisco: Jossey-Bass, 1989).

91. J. D. Breul, "Setting Stretch Goals Helps Agencies Exceed Their Reach," *Government Leader 1*, no. 9 (September/October 2006), www.governmentleader.com/issues/1_9/commentary/205-1.html); G. Stoller, "Frequent Business Travelers Pack Guilt, *USA Today*, June 22, 2006, www.usatoday.com/money/biztravel/2006-06-21-road-warriors-usat_x. htm.

Appendix A

Research in Organizational Behavior

For every complex problem, there is a solution that is simple, neat, and wrong.
—H.L. Mencken

A number of years ago, a friend of mine was excited because he had read about the findings from a research study that finally, once and for all, resolved the question of what it takes to make it to the top in a large corporation. I doubted there was any simple answer to this question but, not wanting to dampen his enthusiasm, I asked him to tell me of what he had read. The answer, according to my friend, was *participation in college athletics.* To say I was skeptical of his claim is a gross understatement, so I asked him to tell me more.

The study encompassed 1,700 successful senior executives at the 500 largest U.S. corporations. The researchers found that half of these executives had played varsity-level college sports.[1] My friend, who happens to be good with statistics, informed me that since fewer than 2 percent of all college students participate in intercollegiate athletics, the probability of this finding occurring by mere chance is less than 1 in 10 million! He concluded his analysis by telling me that, based on this research, I should encourage my management students to get into shape and to make one of the varsity teams.

My friend was somewhat perturbed when I suggested that his conclusions were likely to be flawed. These executives were all males who attended college in the 1940s and 1950s. Would his advice be meaningful to females in the twenty-first century? These executives also weren't your typical college students. For the most part, they had attended elite private colleges such as Princeton and Amherst, where a large proportion of the student body participates in intercollegiate sports. And these "jocks" hadn't necessarily played football or basketball; many had participated in golf, tennis, baseball, cross-country running, crew, rugby, and similar minor sports. Moreover, maybe the researchers had confused the direction of causality. That is, maybe individuals with the motivation and ability to make it to the top of a large corporation are drawn to competitive activities like college athletics.

My friend was guilty of misusing research data. Of course, he is not alone. We are all continually bombarded with reports of experiments that link certain substances to cancer in mice and surveys that show changing attitudes toward sex among college students, for example. Many of these studies are carefully designed, with great caution taken to note the implications and limitations of the findings. But some studies are poorly designed, making their conclusions at best suspect, and at worst meaningless.

Rather than attempting to make you a researcher, the purpose of this appendix is to increase your awareness as a consumer of behavioral research. A knowledge of research methods will allow you to appreciate more fully the care in data collection that underlies the information and conclusions presented in this text. Moreover, an understanding of research methods will make you a more skilled evaluator of the OB studies you will encounter in business and professional journals. So an appreciation of behavioral research is important because (1) it's the foundation on which the theories in this text are built, and (2) it will benefit you in future years when you read reports of research and attempt to assess their value.

Purposes of Research

Research is concerned with the systematic gathering of information. Its purpose is to help us in our search for the truth. Although we will never find ultimate truth—in our case, that would be to know precisely how any person or group would behave in any organizational context—ongoing research adds to our body of OB knowledge by supporting some theories, contradicting others, and suggesting new theories to replace those that fail to gain support.

Research Terminology

Researchers have their own vocabulary for communicating among themselves and with outsiders. The following briefly defines some of the more popular terms you're likely to encounter in behavioral science studies.[2]

Variable

A *variable* is any general characteristic that can be measured and that changes in amplitude, intensity, or both. Some examples of OB variables found in this textbook are job satisfaction, employee productivity, work stress, ability, personality, and group norms.

Hypothesis

A tentative explanation of the relationship between two or more variables is called a *hypothesis.* My friend's statement that participation in college athletics leads to a top executive position in a large corporation is an example of a hypothesis. Until confirmed by empirical research, a hypothesis remains only a tentative explanation.

Dependent Variable

A *dependent variable* is a response that is affected by an independent variable. In terms of the hypothesis, it is the variable that the researcher is interested in explaining. Referring back to our opening example, the dependent variable in my friend's hypothesis was executive succession. In organizational behavior research, the most popular dependent variables are productivity, absenteeism, turnover, job satisfaction, and organizational commitment.[3]

Independent Variable

An *independent variable* is the presumed cause of some change in the dependent variable. Participating in varsity athletics was the independent variable in my friend's hypothesis. Popular independent variables studied by OB researchers include intelligence, personality, job satisfaction, experience, motivation, reinforcement patterns, leadership style, reward allocations, selection methods, and organization design.

You may have noticed we said that job satisfaction is frequently used by OB researchers as both a dependent and an independent variable. This is not an error. It merely reflects that the label given to a variable depends on its place in the hypothesis. In the statement "Increases in job satisfaction lead to reduced turnover," job satisfaction is an independent variable. However, in the statement "Increases in money lead to higher job satisfaction," job satisfaction becomes a dependent variable.

Moderating Variable

A *moderating variable* abates the effect of the independent variable on the dependent variable. It might also be thought of as the contingency variable: If X (independent variable), then Y (dependent variable) will occur, but only under conditions Z (moderating variable). To translate this into a real-life example, we might say that if we increase the amount of direct supervision in the work area (X), then there will be a change in worker productivity (Y), but this effect will be moderated by the complexity of the tasks being performed (Z).

Causality

A hypothesis, by definition, implies a relationship. That is, it implies a presumed cause and effect. This direction of cause and effect is called *causality.* Changes in the independent variable are assumed to cause changes in the dependent variable. However, in behavioral research, it's possible to make an incorrect assumption of causality when relationships are found. For example, early behavioral scientists found a relationship between employee satisfaction and productivity. They concluded that a happy worker was a productive worker. Follow-up research has supported the relationship, but disconfirmed the direction of the arrow. The evidence more correctly suggests that high productivity leads to satisfaction rather than the other way around.

Correlation Coefficient

It's one thing to know that there is a relationship between two or more variables. It's another to know the *strength* of that relationship. The term *correlation coefficient* is used to indicate that strength, and is expressed as a number between −1.00 (a perfect negative relationship) and +1.00 (a perfect positive correlation).

When two variables vary directly with one another, the correlation will be expressed as a positive number. When they vary inversely—that is, one increases as the other decreases—the correlation will be expressed as a negative number. If the two variables vary independently of each other, we say that the correlation between them is zero.

For example, a researcher might survey a group of employees to determine the satisfaction of each with his or her job. Then, using company absenteeism reports, the researcher could correlate the job satisfaction scores against individual attendance records to determine whether employees who are more satisfied with their jobs have better attendance records than their counterparts who indicated lower job satisfaction. Let's suppose the researcher found a correlation coefficient of +0.50 between satisfaction and attendance. Would that be a strong association? There is, unfortunately, no precise numerical cutoff separating strong and weak relationships. A standard statistical test would need to be applied to determine whether the relationship was a significant one.

A final point needs to be made before we move on: A correlation coefficient measures only the strength of association between two variables. A high value does *not* imply causality. The length of women's skirts and stock market prices, for instance, have long been noted to be highly correlated, but one should be careful not to infer that a causal relationship between the two exists. In this instance, the high correlation is more happenstance than predictive.

Theory

The final term we introduce in this section is *theory*. Theory describes a set of systematically interrelated concepts or hypotheses that purports to explain and predict phenomena. In OB, theories are also frequently referred to as *models*. We use the two terms interchangeably.

There are no shortages of theories in OB. For instance, we have theories to describe what motivates people, the most effective leadership styles, the best way to resolve conflicts, and how people acquire power. In some cases, we have half a dozen or more separate theories that purport to explain and predict a given phenomenon. In such cases, is one right and the others wrong? No! They tend to reflect science at work—researchers testing previous theories, modifying them, and, when appropriate, proposing new models that may prove to have higher explanatory and predictive powers. Multiple theories attempting to explain common phenomena merely attest that OB is an active discipline, still growing and evolving.

Evaluating Research

As a potential consumer of behavioral research, you should follow the dictum of *caveat emptor*—let the buyer beware! In evaluating any research study, you need to ask three questions.[4]

Is it valid? Is the study actually measuring what it claims to be measuring? A number of psychological tests have been discarded by employers in recent years because they have not been found to be valid measures of the applicants' ability to do a given job successfully. But the validity issue is relevant to all research studies. So, if you find a study that links cohesive work teams with higher productivity, you want to know how each of these variables was measured and whether it is actually measuring what it is supposed to be measuring.

Is it reliable? Reliability refers to consistency of measurement. If you were to have your height measured every day with a wooden yardstick, you'd get highly reliable results. On the other hand, if you were measured each day by an elastic tape measure, there would probably be considerable disparity between your height measurements from one day to the next. Your height, of course, doesn't change from day to day. The variability is due to the unreliability of the measuring device. So if a company asked a group of its employees to complete a reliable job satisfaction questionnaire, and then repeat the questionnaire six months later, we'd expect the results to be very similar—provided nothing changed in the interim that might significantly affect employee satisfaction.

Is it generalizable? Are the results of the research study generalizable to groups of individuals other than those who participated in the original study? Be aware, for example, of the limitations that might exist in research that uses college students as subjects. Are the findings in such studies generalizable to full-time employees in real jobs? Similarly, how generalizable to the overall work population are the results from a study that assesses job stress among 10 nuclear power plant engineers in the hamlet of Mahone Bay, Nova Scotia?

Research Design

Doing research is an exercise in trade-offs. Richness of information typically comes with reduced generalizability. The more a researcher seeks to control for confounding variables, the less realistic his or her results are likely to be. High precision, generalizability, and control almost always translate into higher costs. When researchers make choices about whom they'll study, where their research will be done, the methods they'll use to collect data, and so on, they must make some concessions. Good research designs are not perfect, but they do carefully reflect the questions being addressed. Keep these facts in mind as we review the strengths and weaknesses of five popular research designs: case studies, field surveys, laboratory experiments, field experiments, and aggregate quantitative reviews.

Case Study

You pick up a copy of Soichiro Honda's autobiography. In it he describes his impoverished childhood; his decisions to open a small garage, assemble motorcycles, and eventually build automobiles; and how this led to the creation of one of the largest and most successful corporations in the world. Or you're in a business class and the instructor distributes a 50-page handout covering two companies: Wal-Mart and Kmart. The handout details the two firms' histories; describes their corporate strategies, management philosophies, and merchandising plans; and includes copies of their recent balance sheets and income statements. The instructor asks the class members to read the handout, analyze the data, and determine why Wal-Mart has been so much more successful than Kmart in recent years.

Soichiro Honda's autobiography and the Wal-Mart and Kmart handouts are case studies. Drawn from real-life situations, case studies present an in-depth analysis of one setting. They are thorough descriptions, rich in details about an individual, a group, or an organization. The primary source of information in case studies is obtained through observation, occasionally backed up by interviews and a review of records and documents.

Case studies have their drawbacks. They're open to the perceptual bias and subjective interpretations of the observer. The reader of a case is captive to what the observer/case writer chooses to include and exclude. Cases also trade off generalizability for depth of information and richness of detail. Because it's always dangerous to generalize from a sample of one, case studies make it difficult to prove or reject a hypothesis. On the other hand, you can't ignore the in-depth analysis that cases often provide. They are an excellent device for initial exploratory research and for evaluating real-life problems in organizations.

Field Survey

A lengthy questionnaire was created to assess the use of ethics policies, formal ethics structures, formalized activities such as ethics training, and executive involvement in ethics programs among billion-dollar corporations. The public affairs or corporate communications office of all *Fortune* 500 industrial firms and 500 service corporations were contacted to get the name and address of the "officer most responsible for dealing with ethics and conduct issues" in each firm. The questionnaire, with a cover letter explaining the nature of the study, was mailed to these 1,000 officers. Of the total, 254 returned a completed questionnaire, for a response rate just above 25 percent. The results of the survey found, among other things, that 77 percent had formal codes of ethics and 54 percent had a single officer specifically assigned to deal with ethics and conduct issues.[5]

The preceding study illustrates a typical field survey. A sample of respondents (in this case, 1,000 corporate officers in the largest U.S. publicly held corporations) was selected to represent a larger group that was under examination (billion-dollar U.S. business firms). The respondents were then surveyed using a questionnaire or interviewed to collect data on particular characteristics (the content and structure of ethics programs and practices) of interest to the researchers. The standardization of response items allows for data to be easily quantified, analyzed, and summarized, and for the researchers to make inferences from the representative sample about the larger population.

The field survey provides economies for doing research. It's less costly to sample a population than to obtain data from every member of that population. (There are, for instance, more than 5,000 U.S. business firms with sales in excess of a billion dollars; and since some of these are privately held and don't release financial data to the public, they are excluded from the *Fortune* list). Moreover, as the ethics study illustrates, field surveys provide an efficient way to find out how people feel about issues or how they say they behave. These data can then be easily quantified.

But the field survey has a number of potential weaknesses. First, mailed questionnaires rarely obtain 100 percent returns. Low response rates call into question whether conclusions based on respondents' answers are generalizable to nonrespondents. Second, the format is better at tapping respondents' attitudes and perceptions than behaviors. Third, responses can suffer from social desirability; that is, people saying what they think the researcher wants to hear. Fourth, since field surveys are designed to focus on specific issues, they're a relatively poor means of acquiring depth of information. Finally, the quality of the generalizations is largely a factor of the population chosen. Responses from executives at *Fortune* 500 firms, for instance, tell us nothing about small- or medium-sized firms or not-for-profit organizations. In summary, even a well-designed field survey trades off depth of information for breadth, generalizability, and economic efficiencies.

Laboratory Experiment

The following study is a classic example of the laboratory experiment. A researcher, Stanley Milgram, wondered how far individuals would go in following commands. If subjects were placed in the role of a teacher in a learning experiment and told by an experimenter to administer a shock to a learner each time that learner made a mistake, would the subjects follow the commands of the experimenter? Would their willingness to comply decrease as the intensity of the shock was increased?

To test these hypotheses, Milgram hired a set of subjects. Each was led to believe that the experiment was to investigate the effect of punishment on memory. Their job was to act as teachers and administer punishment whenever the learner made a mistake on the learning test.

Punishment was administered by an electric shock. The subject sat in front of a shock generator with 30 levels of shock—beginning at zero and progressing in 15-volt increments to a high of 450 volts. The demarcations of these positions ranged from "Slight Shock" at 15 volts to "Danger: Severe Shock" at 450 volts. To increase the realism of the experiment, the subjects received a sample shock of 45 volts and saw the learner—a pleasant, mild-mannered man about 50 years old—strapped into an "electric chair" in an adjacent room. Of course, the learner was an actor, and the electric shocks were phony, but the subjects didn't know this.

Taking his seat in front of the shock generator, the subject was directed to begin at the lowest shock level and to increase the shock intensity to the next level each time the learner made a mistake or failed to respond.

When the test began, the shock intensity rose rapidly because the learner made many errors. The subject got verbal feedback from the learner: At 75 volts, the learner began to grunt and moan; at 150 volts, he demanded to be released from the experiment; at 180 volts, he cried out that he could no longer stand the pain; and at 300 volts, he insisted that he be let out, yelled about his heart condition, screamed, and then failed to respond to further questions.

Most subjects protested and, fearful they might kill the learner if the increased shocks were to bring on a heart attack, insisted they could not go on with their job. Hesitations or protests by the subject were met by the experimenter's statement, "You have no choice, you must go on! Your job is to punish the learner's mistakes." Of course, the subjects did have a choice. All they had to do was stand up and walk out.

The majority of the subjects dissented. But dissension isn't synonymous with disobedience. Sixty-two percent of the subjects increased the shock level to the maximum of 450 volts. The average level of shock administered by the remaining 38 percent was nearly 370 volts.[6]

In a laboratory experiment such as that conducted by Milgram, an artificial environment is created by the researcher. Then the researcher manipulates an independent variable under controlled conditions. Finally, since all other things are held equal, the researcher is able to conclude that any change in the dependent variable is due to the manipulation or change imposed on the independent variable. Note that, because of the controlled conditions, the researcher is able to imply causation between the independent and dependent variables.

The laboratory experiment trades off realism and generalizability for precision and control. It provides a high degree of control over variables and precise measurement of those variables. But findings from laboratory studies are often difficult to generalize to the real world of work. This is because the artificial laboratory rarely duplicates the intricacies and nuances of real organizations. In addition, many laboratory experiments deal with phenomena that cannot be reproduced or applied to real-life situations.

Field Experiment

The following is an example of a field experiment. The management of a large company is interested in determining the impact that a four-day workweek would have on employee absenteeism. be more specific, management wants to know if employees working four 10-hour days have lower absence rates than similar employees working the traditional five-day week of 8 hours each day. Because the company is large, it has a number of manufacturing plants that employ essentially similar workforces. Two of these are chosen for the experiment, both located in the greater Cleveland area. Obviously, it would not be appropriate to compare two similar-sized plants if one is in rural Mississippi and the other is in urban Copenhagen because factors such as national culture, transportation, and weather might be more likely to explain any differences found than changes in the number of days worked per week.

In one plant, the experiment was put into place—workers began the four-day week. At the other plant, which became the control group, no changes were made in the employees' five-day week. Absence data were gathered from the company's records at both locations for a period of 18 months. This extended time period lessened the possibility that any results would be distorted by the mere novelty of changes being implemented in the experimental plant. After 18 months, management found that absenteeism had dropped by 40 percent at the experimental plant, and by only 6 percent in the control plant. Because of the design of this study, management believed that the larger drop in absences at the experimental plant was due to the introduction of the compressed workweek.

The field experiment is similar to the laboratory experiment, except it is conducted in a real organization. The natural setting is more realistic than the laboratory setting, and this enhances validity but hinders control. In addition, unless control groups are maintained, there can be a loss of control if extraneous forces intervene—for example, an employee strike, a major layoff, or a corporate restructuring. Maybe the greatest concern with field studies has to do with organizational selection bias. Not all organizations are going to allow outside researchers to come in and study their employees and operations. This is especially true of organizations that have serious problems. Therefore, since most published studies in OB are done by outside researchers, the selection bias might work toward the publication of studies conducted almost exclusively at successful and well-managed organizations.

Our general conclusion is that, of the four research designs we've discussed to this point, the field experiment typically provides the most valid and generalizable findings and, except for its high cost, trades off the least to get the most.[7]

Aggregate Quantitative Reviews

What's the overall effect of organizational behavior modification (OB Mod) on task performance? There have been a number of field experiments that have sought to throw light on this question. Unfortunately, the wide range of effects from these various studies makes it hard to generalize.

To try to reconcile these diverse findings, two researchers reviewed all the empirical studies they could find on the impact of OB Mod on task performance over a 20-year period.[8] After discarding reports that had inadequate information, had nonquantitative data, or didn't meet all conditions associated with principles of behavioral modification, the researchers narrowed their set to 19 studies that included data on 2,818 individuals. Using an aggregating technique called *meta-analysis*, the researchers were able to synthesize the studies quantitatively and to conclude that the average person's task performance will rise from the 50th percentile to the 67th percentile after an OB Mod intervention.

The OB Mod–task performance review done by these researchers illustrates the use of meta-analysis, a quantitative form of literature review that enables researchers to look at validity findings from a comprehensive set of individual studies, and then apply a formula to them to determine if they consistently produced similar results.[9] If results prove to be consistent, it allows researchers to conclude more confidently that validity is generalizable. Meta-analysis is a means for overcoming the potentially imprecise interpretations of qualitative reviews and to synthesize variations in quantitative studies. In addition, the technique enables researchers to identify potential moderating variables between an independent and a dependent variable.

In the past 25 years, there's been a surge in the popularity of this research method. Why? It appears to offer a more objective means for doing traditional literature reviews. Although the use of meta-analysis requires researchers to make a number of judgment calls, which can introduce a considerable amount of subjectivity into the process, there is no arguing that meta-analysis reviews have now become widespread in the OB literature.

Ethics in Research

Researchers are not always tactful or candid with subjects when they do their studies. For instance, questions in field surveys may be perceived as embarrassing by respondents or as an invasion of privacy. Also, researchers in laboratory studies have been known to deceive participants about the true purpose of their experiment "because they felt deception was necessary to get honest responses."[10]

The "learning experiments" conducted by Stanley Milgram, which were conducted more than 30 years ago, have been widely criticized by psychologists on ethical grounds. He lied to subjects, telling them his study was investigating learning, when, in fact, he was concerned with obedience. The shock machine he used was a fake. Even the "learner" was an accomplice of Milgram's who had been trained to act as if he were hurt and in pain. Yet ethical lapses continue. For instance, in 2001, a professor of organizational behavior at Columbia University sent out a common letter on university letterhead to 240 New York City restaurants in which he detailed how he had eaten at this restaurant with his wife in celebration of their wedding anniversary, how he had gotten food poisoning, and that he had spent the night in his bathroom throwing up.[11] The letter closed with: "Although it is not my intention to file any reports with the Better Business Bureau or the Department of Health, I want you to understand what I went through in anticipation that you will respond accordingly. I await your response." The fictitious letter was part of the professor's study to determine how restaurants responded to complaints. But it created culinary chaos among many of the restaurant owners, managers, and chefs as they reviewed menus and produce deliveries for possibly spoiled food, and questioned kitchen workers about possible lapses. A follow-up letter of apology from the university for "an egregious error in judgment by a junior faculty member" did little to offset the distress it created for those affected.

Professional associations like the American Psychological Association, the American Sociological Association, and the Academy of Management have published formal guidelines for the conduct of research. Yet the ethical debate continues. On one side are those who argue that strict ethical controls can damage the scientific validity of an experiment and cripple future research. Deception, for example, is often necessary to avoid contaminating results. Moreover, proponents of minimizing ethical controls note that few subjects have been appreciably harmed by deceptive experiments. Even in Milgram's highly manipulative experiment, only 1.3 percent of the subjects reported negative feelings about their experience. The other side of this debate focuses on the rights of participants. Those favoring strict ethical controls argue that no procedure should ever be emotionally or physically distressing to subjects, and that, as professionals, researchers are obliged to be completely honest with their subjects and to protect the subjects' privacy at all costs.

Summary

The subject of organizational behavior is composed of a large number of theories that are research based. Research studies, when cumulatively integrated, become theories, and theories are proposed and followed by research studies designed to validate them. The concepts that make up OB, therefore, are only as valid as the research that supports them.

The topics and issues in this book are for the most part research-derived. They represent the result of systematic information gathering rather than merely hunch, intuition, or opinion. This doesn't mean, of course, that we have all the answers to OB issues. Many require far more corroborating evidence. The generalizability of others is limited by the research methods used. But new information is being created and published at an accelerated rate. To keep up with the latest findings, we strongly encourage you to regularly review the latest research in organizational behavior. The more academic work can be found in journals such as the *Academy of Management Journal, Academy of Management Review, Administrative Science Quarterly, Human Relations, Journal of Applied Psychology, Journal of Management, Journal of Organizational Behavior,* and *Leadership Quarterly.* For more practical interpretations of OB research findings, you may want to read the *Academy of Management Execuive, California Management Review, Harvard Business Review, Organizational Dynamics,* and the *Sloan Management Review.*

Endnotes

1. J. A. Byrne, "Executive Sweat," *Forbes,* May 20, 1985, pp. 198–200.
2. See D. P. Schwab, *Research Methods for Organizational Behavior* (Mahwah, NJ: Lawrence Erlbaum Associates, 1999); and S. G. Rogelberg (ed.), *Blackwell Handbook of Research Methods in Industrial and Organizational Psychology* (Malden, MA: Blackwell, 2002).
3. B. M. Staw and G. R. Oldham, "Reconsidering Our Dependent Variables: A Critique and Empirical Study," *Academy of Management Journal,* December 1978, pp. 539–559; and B. M. Staw, "Organizational Behavior: A Review and Reformulation of the Field's Outcome Variables," in M. R. Rosenzweig and L. W. Porter (eds.), *Annual Review of Psychology,* vol. 35 (Palo Alto, CA: Annual Reviews, 1984), pp. 627–666.
4. R. S. Blackburn, "Experimental Design in Organizational Settings," in J. W. Lorsch (ed.), *Handbook of Organizational Behavior* (Upper Saddle River, NJ: Prentice Hall, 1987), pp. 127–128; and F. L. Schmidt, C. Viswesvaran, D. S. Ones, "Reliability Is Not Validity and Validity Is Not Reliability," *Personnel Psychology,* Winter 2000, pp. 901–912.
5. G. R. Weaver, L. K. Trevino, and P. L. Cochran, "Corporate Ethics Practices in the Mid-1990's: An Empirical Study of the Fortune 1000," *Journal of Business Ethics,* February 1999, pp. 283–294.
6. S. Milgram, *Obedience to Authority* (New York: Harper & Row, 1974). For a critique of this research, see T. Blass, "Understanding Behavior in the Milgram Obedience Experiment: The Role of Personality, Situations, and Their Interactions," *Journal of Personality and Social Psychology,* March 1991, pp. 398–413.
7. See, for example, W. N. Kaghan, A. L. Strauss, S. R. Barley, M. Y. Brannen, and R. J. Thomas, "The Practice and Uses of Field Research in the 21st Century Organization," *Journal of Management Inquiry,* March 1999, pp. 67–81.
8. A. D. Stajkovic and F. Luthans, "A Meta-Analysis of the Effects of Organizational Behavior Modification on Task Performance, 1975–1995," *Academy of Management Journal,* October 1997, pp. 1122–1149.
9. See, for example, K. Zakzanis, "The Reliability of Meta Analytic Review," *Psychological Reports,* August 1998, pp. 215–222; C. Ostroff and D. A. Harrison, "Meta-Analysis, Level of Analysis, and Best Estimates of Population Correlations: Cautions for Interpreting Meta-Analytic Results in Organizational Behavior," *Journal of Applied Psychology,* April 1999, pp. 260–270; R. Rosenthal and M. R. DiMatteo, "Meta-Analysis: Recent Developments in Quantitative Methods for Literature Reviews," in S. T. Fiske, D. L. Schacter, and C. Zahn-Wacher (eds.), *Annual Review of Psychology,* vol. 52 (Palo Alto, CA: Annual Reviews, 2001), pp. 59–82; and F. L. Schmidt and J. E. Hunter, "Meta-Analysis," in N. Anderson, D. S. Ones, H. K. Sinangil, and C. Viswesvaran (eds.), *Handbook of Industrial, Work & Organizational Psychology,* vol. 1 (Thousand Oaks, CA: Sage, 2001), pp. 51–70.
10. For more on ethical issues in research, see T. L. Beauchamp, R. R. Faden, R. J. Wallace, Jr., and L. Walters (eds.), *Ethical Issues in Social Science Research* (Baltimore, MD: Johns Hopkins University Press, 1982); and J. G. Adair, "Ethics of Psychological Research: New Policies, Continuing Issues, New Concerns," *Canadian Psychology,* February 2001, pp. 25–37.
11. J. Kifner, "Scholar Sets Off Gastronomic False Alarm," *New York Times,* September 8, 2001, p. A1.

Comprehensive Cases

Case 1 Arnold Schwarzenegger: Leader of California?

The governor of California, Arnold Schwarzenegger, or "Arnold" as the state's residents like to call him, is arguably playing the biggest role of his career. Elected in the October 2003 recall election that featured a hodgepodge of 135 candidates, including U.S. celebrities Gary Coleman, Larry Flint, and Mary "Mary Carey" Cook, Schwarzenegger replaced incumbent Gray Davis as the governor of the most populous state in the country by raking in 48.1 percent of the popular vote. Californians, weary of Gray Davis's lack of progress, decided to put their trust in a man best known for his roles in action movies such as the *The Terminator* and *Total Recall*.

Schwarzenegger's ascent to the governor's seat is impressive when one considers his background. Born in the small town of Thal, Austria, on July 30, 1947, Schwarzenegger was the product of a modest and harsh upbringing. His parents strictly disciplined him—treatment that he says "would be called child abuse" today. Schwarzenegger explains, "My hair was pulled. I was hit with belts. So was the kid next door, and so was the kid next door. It was just the way it was. Many of the children I've seen were broken by their parents, which was the German-Austrian mentality. Break the will. They didn't want to create an individual . . . It was all about conforming. I was the one who did not conform and whose will could not be broken. Therefore I became a rebel. Every time I got hit, and every time someone said, 'You can't do this,' I said, 'This is not going to be for much longer, because I'm going to move out of here. I want to be rich. I want to be somebody.' "

Determined to leave Austria, Schwarzenegger began to search for a way out, a way to become "somebody." He found that way out through bodybuilding. As a child, he idolized bodybuilder Reg Park, a former Mr. Universe. Though his parents objected, Schwarzenegger pursued bodybuilding so vehemently that at one point he was able to bench-press 520 pounds (for comparison, physical fitness experts typically say that it is good to be able to bench press one's own body weight).

At age 19, Schwarzenegger was crowned Mr. Universe. He continued to win championships, and, in 1970, he even defeated his idol, Reg Park, for the Mr. Universe title. Schwarzenegger now says that bodybuilding was instrumental to his success as an actor and as a politician. "I know it from my bodybuilding—that I can see my goals very clearly . . . It takes the confidence to ignore critics and naysayers," he states.

Having accomplished his goal of becoming Mr. Universe, Schwarzenegger set his sights on America to pursue acting and moved to the United States at age 21. Although he attended acting school, his odd last name and thick accent at first kept him from acquiring roles. He eventually landed a small role in the film *Hercules in New York* and continued to appear in other films such as *Stay Hungry* and *Pumping Iron*. In 1982, however, Schwarzenegger made his mark in the film *Conan the Barbarian*, which grossed more than $100 million worldwide. His on-screen charisma, massive physique, and uniqueness compared to American actors made him a standout. Since moving to the United States, Schwarzenegger has made 33 movies and has become one of the most highly paid actors in the world. For *Terminator 3*, Schwarzenegger earned an astounding $33 million—a record sum at the time.

After succeeding as a bodybuilder and an actor, Schwarzenegger began eyeing a bigger prize: the California governor's seat. During his acting career, Schwarzenegger had formed a strong network of powerful friends and advisors, including investor Warren Buffet, economist Milton Friedman, and Israeli Prime Minister Benjamin Netanyahu. As the recall election neared, Schwarzenegger consulted with his network of allies. Buffet told Schwarzenegger that California needed strong leadership, and Friedman gave him advice on how to improve California's dismal economy. All of this advice gave Schwarzenegger the vision he needed to propel himself to the rank of governor. Running as a moderate Republican, he sought to unite Democrats and Republicans, pass a balanced budget, reduce government spending, and resuscitate the business community. Once he accomplished these goals, Schwarzenegger would confidently state to the rest of the world that California was *back*. Schwarzenegger's vision came at a perfect time: Governor Davis witnessed the rise and fall of the tech boom. When the tech bubble burst, revenue plummeted. In 2001 and 2002, state revenue from the income tax fell 27 percent, yet spending remained the same. Although Davis was not solely responsible for the resulting Californian debt, Californians were eager to place blame.

Hungry for someone to take the reins from Gray Davis and steer California away from its troubles, many Californians embraced Schwarzenegger as he campaigned across the state. His name recognition and charismatic personality made him a leading candidate. Schwarzenegger's style is vastly different from other politicians. His wit, honesty, and lack of concern for political correctness struck a chord with voters. (As he told one interviewer at *Fortune* magazine following the election, "I love smart women. I have no patience for bimbos.") It was perhaps this larger-than-life persona that led him to "terminate" Gray Davis in the recall election.

Following the election, Schwarzenegger immediately began making policy for California. Within only a few days of his swearing in, Schwarzenegger had a viable economic recovery plan. To the praise of the state's residents, he repealed the car-tax increase, which would have raised almost $4 billion in revenue but was hated by Californians. He continued his strong push for reform, passing propositions that made a $15 billion bond offering possible and that paved the way for a balanced budget. In April 2004, he persuaded the state's legislature to pass a bill overhauling workers' compensation, a victory for businesses trying to reduce costs but a defeat for workers.

A testament to his approachable personality was the fact that he broke tradition by actually going from his office on the first floor to the upstairs offices of the legislators to meet with them. Schwarzenegger's chief of staff, Pat Clarey, can't remember the previous four governors doing that. All in all, the newly elected "governator," using his charisma and network of powerful friends, inched closer each day to his vision.

Even the Republican party took notice. Though more moderate than the Republican Party would like, Schwarzenegger knew that his popularity and charisma were an asset to the Republican convention during President George W. Bush's 2004 reelection campaign. While the Republican party convention organizers were debating whether to invite the moderate Schwarzenegger to speak, Schwarzenegger told the *New York Times*, "If they're smart, they'll have me obviously in prime time." Schwarzenegger got his wish. Two days after the interview, he was invited to speak during his requested time. Republican operatives weren't disappointed with quips such as "This is like winning an Oscar. As if I would know! Speaking of acting, one of my movies was called *True Lies*. And that's what the Democrats should have called their convention." Schwarzenegger's speech at the convention electrified the crowd, further solidifying his role as a charismatic leader.

Not everything has been rosy. One of his major goals was to pass a $103 billion budget plan that he believed would be a tremendous step toward economic recovery. He set an optimistic timeline of passing the budget by June 30, 2004. Schwarzenegger worked tirelessly, negotiating budget reductions with state-affiliated organizations such as universities, prisons, and the teacher's union. However, negotiations began to fall apart when he made conflicting promises to the opposing parties on state and local budget linkages. Instead of victoriously passing his budget on time, the state legislature recessed for the July 4th weekend, leaving Schwarzenegger and his budget on hold.

Not to be dissuaded, Schwarzenegger began campaigning to the public to garner support for his budget. He even went so far as to call opponents "girlie men" at a public rally—an incident that infuriated his critics. Though eventually he was able to pass a revised version of his original budget, Schwarzenegger continued to attempt to fix California's financial crisis through various cost-cutting initiatives. He took on the California teachers' union, trying to persuade it to revamp entirely the way it hires, pays, and fires teachers. During this time, his approval rating fell to 55 percent. Though still high, his approval rating was down from a staggering 65 percent. Many of his ideas are abhorrent to the teachers' union. For example, Schwarzenegger wants to tie teachers' pay to test scores. Many teachers feel that this undermines their ability to teach what they think are important topics and will result in a narrow curriculum.

Some believe Arnold Schwarzenegger is a powerful politician, but he says that he really doesn't like the word *power* because it tends to have a negative connotation. Schwarzenegger says, "Power is basically influence. That's the way I see it. It's being able to have the influence to make changes to improve things." Schwarzenegger has a clear vision of how he wants to improve things; the question is not only whether he can create beneficial policies but also whether he has the ability and support to implement those policies. Although he realizes that his charisma helped him to become governor, Schwarzenegger also knows the importance of vision to a leader. As he puts it, "There is no one, and when I say no one, I mean no one, who will back me off my vision. I will go over burning coals for that."

Questions for Discussion

1. What words would you use to describe Arnold Schwarzenegger's personality? Do any of these fit into the Big Five taxonomy of personality? How might these personality traits influence Schwarzenegger's leadership skills? How might these traits have helped Schwarzenegger get to where he is now?
2. Based on the case, as governor of California, what types of power is Schwarzenegger likely to have? What types of influence tactics does Schwarzenegger appear to use?
3. How would you describe Schwarzenegger's leadership style using the leadership theories covered in this textbook? What details of the case lead you to these conclusions? Is Schwarzenegger's leadership style likely to be effective? Why or why not?
4. Applying concepts from goal-setting theory, explain how goals have influenced Schwarzenegger's progression to the governor's seat. What aspects of the case suggest that Schwarzenegger is committed to the goals that he has set for himself?
5. Are there any "dark sides" to Schwarzenegger's charisma and leadership skills? What might these be, and how might they affect his relationships with others and his ability to govern?
6. How might Schwarzenegger's personality and leadership style help or hinder his ability to effectively negotiate with other parties such as the teachers' union?

Source: Based on B. Morris, A. Gil, P. Neering, and O. Ryan, "Arnold Power," *Fortune,* August 9, 2004, 77–87; and R. Grover and A. Bernstein, "Arnold Gets Strict with the Teachers," *Business Week,* May 2, 2005, 84–85.

Case 2 *What Customers Don't Know Won't Hurt Them, or Will It?*

Sitting at her desk at the car rental shop where she worked, Elena couldn't believe what she was hearing. Gripping the phone tightly, Elena listened as the head manager of the company's legal department told her that a car that she had recently rented to a customer had blown a tire while the customer was driving on a nearby highway. Although the customer, Jim Reynolds, tried to maintain control of the vehicle, he crashed into another car, seriously injuring himself and the other driver. Apparently, the tire had noticeable structural damage that caused it to blow. Elena stared at her desk in shock as the legal department manager asked whether she was aware of the tire's condition before renting the car to Mr. Reynolds.

"I . . . I'm sorry, what did you say?" asked Elena.

"I asked whether you were aware that the tire was damaged before renting the car to Mr. Reynolds," repeated the manager.

Elena paused, thinking back to when she had rented the car to Mr. Reynolds. Unfortunately, she knew the answer to the manager's question, but she did not know whether she wanted to answer it. Her mind raced with worried thoughts about how she let herself get into this position, and then she remembered when her supervisor first told her to lie to a customer.

Elena had started working for the rental car company 2 years ago. Fresh out of college, she was intrigued by the possibilities of joining a company and moving up the ranks into management. She worked hard, sometimes putting in 50 or more hours a week. And she was good at her job, too. Customers would frequently tell her supervisor of Elena's great service and courtesy. Within no time, the supervisor began telling her that she was a strong candidate for management and would probably be running her own rental office within the next year.

Intrigued with becoming a manager, Elena began to work even harder. She was the first one at the office each morning and the last one to leave. Things were going well, until one particularly busy day, when the rental office had more business than it could handle. The office typically had a few vehicles left for walk-in customers, but on this day the lot was empty except for one SUV, which a couple had reserved for their vacation. The couple's reservation was for 1 P.M., and it was now 12 noon. Proactive as usual, Elena decided to go check the SUV to make sure it was ready for the couple. As she got up from her desk, the door to the rental office flew open, and a man rushed toward the counter.

"Do you have anything to rent?" he quickly asked. "I don't have a reservation, but I really need a car right now for the rest of the week."

Elena apologized and explained that the only vehicle they had at the moment was reserved, but that he could wait at the office until another car was returned. In fact, she said, they expected to have two vehicles returned around 3 P.M.

"That's not good enough," the man replied. "I need a car now."

"Again, I do apologize sir, but it wouldn't be fair to those with a reservation to rent the only car that is available," said Elena.

With a frown, the man turned to leave. As he did, Elena's supervisor, who had been listening to the conversation, chimed in. "So you really need a car, huh?" he asked the man.

The man whirled around. "Yes, I do."

"I'll rent it to you for $150 a day," said Elena's supervisor. One hundred and fifty dollars a day was much more than the rental company's usual fee.

The man paused for a moment and then said, "Fine, I'll take it."

As he left with the only vehicle left on the lot, a stunned Elena asked her supervisor why he had rented the SUV when he knew that it was reserved—and at such a high price.

"That guy would have paid anything, and he ended up paying twice as much as we would have gotten out of it," her supervisor said, laughing. "Look, if you're going to be a manager, you need to know how to make money. Always take the best deal you can get."

"Even if it means losing another customer?" Elena asked. "What are we going to tell the couple who had a reservation for that SUV?"

"*You're* going to tell them that it broke down unexpectedly and it's at the shop. If you want to be a manager, start acting like one."

Soon after, the couple with the reservation walked into the rental office. Elena didn't want to lie to them, but she also didn't want to jeopardize her chances of obtaining a management position. She also figured that the couple would be more understanding if she told them that the SUV had broken down than if she told them that she had rented it to another customer. So Elena followed her manager's advice and lied to the couple.

In the months that followed, Elena encountered several more instances where her supervisor asked her to lie to customers because her office had reserved too many vehicles. Pretty soon, it became second nature, as she found herself lying to customers without pressure from her supervisor. To date, however, her lies hadn't caused any serious harm to anyone, at least as far as she knew. That track record changed, however, the day Jim Reynolds rented a car from her.

The day was routine in that the rental office was very busy. There were only two vehicles on the lot—a compact car and a new luxury sedan. Mr. Reynolds had reserved the less expensive compact car. However, when checking the car over before Mr. Reynolds arrived, Elena noticed a large lump on the outside well of the passenger-side front tire. From her training, she knew that this lump could be dangerous. But Elena also knew that she would have to give Mr. Reynolds the luxury sedan for the same price as the compact car if she decided not to rent him the compact car. She thought about what her supervisor had told her and knew that he probably would be upset if she didn't get a high rate out of their new luxury sedan. Besides, she reasoned, the car will be fine and Mr. Reynolds would have it for only a day. So Elena went through the routine. With a smile and a handshake, she rented the compact car to Mr. Reynolds, who didn't notice the tire because it was on the passenger side, and Elena didn't walk Mr. Reynolds around the car—a routine practice at the rental company.

Fast-forward one day and Elena's world had completely changed. Now, Elena was on the phone with the manager of the company's legal department, wondering how she ever thought it would be safe to rent the car to Mr. Reynolds. She could admit that she knew about the tire and decided to rent the car anyway, or she could lie and say that the tire looked fine when she rented the car. If she told the truth, becoming a manager would probably be out of the question, at least for a long while. Anger welled up inside her. She had worked hard to get where she was. She regretted not having told her supervisor that she wasn't going to lie to customers, even if it meant getting a better rate. But that moment had passed. She could tell the legal department manager that her supervisor had told her to lie to customers, but she knew that her manager would deny it. Either way, the options weren't too appealing.

"Hello? . . . hello?" asked the legal department manager.

Elena returned to the conversation. "Sorry, I lost you for a moment," she said. "Yeah . . . about Mr. Reynolds . . . "

Questions for Discussion

1. Using concepts from reinforcement theory, explain why Elena might be motivated to lie to customers. With reinforcement theory in mind, do you think that Elena will confess to the legal representative? Why or why not?
2. How might the rental office's climate influence Elena's behavior? What factors contribute to the current climate? What steps could you take to improve the ethics at this office?
3. Do you blame Elena for her behavior or do you attribute her behavior to external factors? How do concepts from attribution theory fit in?
4. Consider Elena's personality. Would you predict that escalation of commitment will occur (and she will lie to the legal representative), or will she decide to come clean? Explain your answer.
5. Do you think Elena would make a good leader some day? Why or why not? What factors might this depend on?
6. What emotions might Elena be experiencing? How might Elena's emotions affect her decision to tell the legal department manager about the incident with Mr. Reynolds?

Are Five Heads Better Than One?

Evan, Conner, Alexis, Derek, and Judy had been team members for only one week, but they felt that they were already working well together. Upper management at their company, Advert, a medium-sized marketing firm, picked the five employees for a special project: the development of a commercial promoting the launch of a client's 60-inch plasma flat-screen television. The project was especially critical because the television company was one of Advert's most important clients, and the firm's revenues had been slipping lately due to a few poor ad campaigns. Needless to say, upper management at Advert wanted the team to hit a home run with the project.

Upper management didn't have any trouble picking the five employees. All were bright, talented individuals who came up with creative ideas. More important, reasoned the top managers, the employees were similar on a number of characteristics. Evan, Conner, Alexis, Derek, and Judy were around the same age, had worked for the company for about the same amount of time, and because they all tended to be sociable, friendly, and valued getting along with others, their personalities seemed to mesh as well.

To give the team creative room, management allowed them as much autonomy as possible. It gave the team the freedom to see the project through from start to finish—coming up with their own ideas, hiring someone to film the commercial once the idea was in place, creating and maintaining a budget, and presenting the final commercial to the client. Advert's top managers had already met with and assured the client that it was in good hands with this team.

Excited to begin working, the team decided to meet in person to discuss ideas for the commercial. Conner, who was used to leading others in his previous work groups, took the head seat at the group's table. Immediately, he told the group his idea for the commercial.

"I've been thinking about this a lot since I was first told about the project," he said. "I know our client well, and I think they want us to do something out of the box—something that will grab people's attention."

Conner proceeded to explain his idea for the commercial, which centered on a college student "loser" trying to get a date. After one particular attractive female turns him down, and she and her friends ridicule him, the student returns sullenly to his dorm, plunks down on an old sofa, and turns on his small, black-and-white "loser" television. But in the next shot, the student is setting up a 60-inch plasma television in his dorm room, door ajar. While he's doing this, the group of attractive females walks by. In the final shot, the student is in his dorm room watching his new television, with the group of attractive females around him.

Following his explanation, Conner leaned back in his seat and folded his arms across his chest. Grinning proudly, he asked, "Well, what do you think?"

Alexis was the first to speak up. "Um, I don't know." She paused. "I think it's a pretty good start." Hesitantly, she added, "The only thing that I worry about is that our client won't like it. They pride themselves on being more sophisticated than their competitors. To them, this television is both an electronics device and a work of art." But then Alexis quickly added, "But I don't know, maybe you're right that we need to do something different."

Conner, with a slight frown on his face, asked the other group members, "What do the rest of you think?"

Evan responded, "Yeah, I think it's a pretty good idea."

"Judy?" asked Conner.

"I agree. It has potential."

"Well, everyone else seems to agree with me. What do you think Derek?" Conner asked, with the other three members staring at Derek.

Derek paused for a moment. He had his own ideas as well, and because he had worked with the client, perhaps more than any of the other team members, he wasn't sure about Conner's idea. Derek had pictured a commercial that placed the television in a stylish, contemporary Manhattan apartment, with a couple in their 30s enjoying a classic movie, a bottle of red wine on the coffee table.

Feeling the heat from his teammates' gazes, reluctantly Derek said, "Yeah, that sounds good."

"Great, it's settled then," beamed Conner. "We'll have this commercial to them in no time if we stay at this pace."

So the team fleshed out the commercial over the next month. Everyone got along, and the feeling of camaraderie strengthened. Once on board with Conner's idea, the team members became more confident that they would be successful, so much so that they made the commercial even racier than the original idea. The attractive girls would be dressed provocatively, and instead of watching the television, the student and the girls would be laughing and drinking, with the television on in the background. There were a few hesitations here and there as members expressed other ideas, but each team member, enjoying the group's solidarity, decided that it would be better to keep the team in good spirits rather than risk losing the team's morale.

The team quickly decided on a company to shoot the commercial and approved the actors. In a short time, they had completed their commercial. The next step was to present the commercial to their client. Conner took it upon himself to alert management that the team was ready to present the commercial.

"Impressive. Your team is a month ahead of the deadline," said one of the top managers. "We have a lot riding on this, so I hope that it's good. I presume everything went well then?"

Conner nodded. "Yes, very well. No problems or disagreements at all. I think we worked really well together."

On the day of the presentation, the team waited anxiously in a meeting room for their client to arrive. Advert's top managers took their seats in the meeting room. Soon after, three of the client's managers, dressed in professional attire, walked into the meeting room and sat down quietly. After welcoming the clients to the presentation, Conner and his teammates began the presentation, with Conner leading the way. He explained that the idea had come to the team almost instantly, and that given that everyone thought it was a good idea, he was sure that their company would feel the same. Then he dimmed the lights, pressed play, and let the commercial run.

It did not take long for the team to realize that the commercial was not having the effect they had wanted on their clients or their managers. The clients exchanged several sideways glances with one another, and the managers shifted nervously in their seats. After what seemed like an eternity, the commercial ended and the lights came back on. An awkward silence filled the room. The clients began murmuring among themselves.

"That was, um, interesting," said one of the clients, finally.

Conner replied that he thought the idea was "out of the box," and that, therefore, audiences would easily remember it.

"Oh, they'll remember it all right," smirked one of the clients. She then turned to Advert's top managers and stated, "This is not at all what we were looking for. The commercial doesn't fit our needs and doesn't portray the image that we are trying to obtain. Given that you told us that we would be in good hands with this team, my colleagues and I fear that your company will not be able to meet our goals. We appreciate the time that this took, but we will likely employ another advertising firm to film our commercial." With that, she and her colleagues left the room.

After a thorough lecturing from Advert's top managers, the team was disbanded. One month later, Derek was at home watching television when a commercial came on. Classical music played in the background as the camera swept through a modern home. The camera slowly rose up behind a tan leather sofa seating a couple enjoying a bottle of wine and watching a new 60-inch plasma television. In the bottom corner of the screen, in small writing, was the name of one of Advert's competitors. Apparently, Advert's former clients got what they were looking for in the end, but from a competitor. Derek shook his head and vowed to speak up next time he had an idea.

Questions for Discussion

1. What factors contributed to the poor performance of the Advert team? As a manager, what could you have done to help the team perform better?
2. According to the case, the Advert team was given a relatively high degree of autonomy. How might this autonomy have contributed to the presence of groupthink?
3. Teams can be either homogeneous or heterogeneous. How would you characterize the Advert team, and how did this affect the team's creativity and performance?
4. What are some group decision-making techniques that could have helped reduce conformity pressures and groupthink among the Advert team?
5. What different forms of communication could have been employed to improve the sharing of ideas among the Advert team? How might this have affected its performance and satisfaction?
6. How would you describe Conner's leadership style? Why do you think his style wasn't effective? In what situations might Conner be an effective leader?

Case 4 *Wal-Mart's World*

Just how does Wal-Mart, the world's largest retailer, maintain its corporate culture across all of its 4,000 stores? How does this giant, with sales a staggering $288 billion in fiscal year 2004, promote and preserve its image as a small-town store where the customer is king? Part of the answer lies in Wal-Mart's legendary Saturday Morning Meeting.

The Saturday Meeting started with Wal-Mart founder Sam Walton, who thought it unfair that he could take off on the weekends while his employees worked. So, in 1962, Sam Walton began arriving at his store, Walton's Five & Dime, in Bentonville, Arkansas, each Saturday between two and three in the morning. There, he would scrutinize the previous week's records to determine which merchandise was selling and which was not, as well as how sales were faring. However, Mr. Walton didn't stop there. When his store's "associates" (Walton called all his workers associates to emphasize that they were his colleagues as well as his employees) arrived, he would hold a quick morning meeting to openly share the store's information with them. He would also ask for their opinions on matters such as what items he should put on sale and how he should display certain products. Such meetings served not only to use the store's employees in multiple ways but also to convey to his employees that he valued their input and wanted them to learn the business.

Even as Wal-Mart grew into a multibillion-dollar company, the Saturday Morning Meeting continued. Ever since, Wal-Mart has held them at the home office in Bentonville. Each Saturday morning, some 600 managers, many of whom live in Bentonville and make weekly trips to their respective territories, pack the 400-seat auditorium, waiting for their fearless leader to arrive. First, it was Sam Walton. Then, it was CEO David Glass. Now, at 7:00 A.M. sharp, current CEO Lee Scott heads the meeting. As usual, Scott starts off the meeting by leading the crowd in a Wal-Mart cheer: "Give me a W! Give me an A! Give me an L! Give me a Squiggly! . . . "

Though Saturday Morning Meeting topics typically include the company's financial performance, merchandising, and areas of improvement, the meeting is, above all else, a means to keep the company and its employees as close-knit as possible. Such solidarity is imperative to Wal-Mart's strategy of quick market response. When new ideas or problems surface, managers are comfortable sharing them with others. Decisions are made quickly, and action is taken.

For example, while discussing merchandising mistakes during a meeting, Paul Busby, regional vice president for the Northeastern United States, was concerned about a particular item that Wal-Mart was not carrying. "I went into a Kmart near one of my stores to look around and found an item that made me wonder why we don't have it." With a Kmart bag next to him, Busby pulls out a poker table cover and chip set that Kmart is selling for $9.99. "We should really have this product because it's a much better value than ours."

In response to Busby's concern, Scott McCall, the divisional merchandise manager for toys, replied, "We've got a pretty nice poker set in our stores, but I'll check with our sources and get back to you."

A mere 10 minutes passed before McCall asked for the microphone again. With cheers from the crowd, McCall stated, "Paul, I just wanted you to know that I've arranged for those Kmart poker sets to be acquired and be on the trucks rolling out to all the stores next week." Examples such as this illustrate the trust that Sam Walton had in his staff to make decisions. Instead of going through layers of red tape, Wal-Mart's managers can have their ideas implemented quickly. Of course, not all decisions are beneficial; however, those that are can result in immediate gains.

Such quick responses are difficult, if not impossible, for other large companies to execute. As former CEO David Glass explains, "The Saturday Morning Meeting was always a decision-making meeting to take corrective action, and the rule of thumb was that by noon we wanted all the corrections made in the stores." Glass clarifies, "Noon on Saturday." Glass further explains that since no other companies could even come close to the speed at which Wal-Mart executes strategy and change, Wal-Mart developed and sustains a competitive advantage. Wal-Mart's vast distribution network and purchasing power allow it to move products efficiently and sell them at a low price. For example, following the devastation of hurricane Katrina, Wal-Mart, rather than former U.S. FEMA (Federal Emergency Management Agency), was one of the first organizations to distribute food and other goods to hurricane victims.

The Saturday Morning Meeting serves other purposes as well. Perhaps due to Wal-Mart's culture of retail fanaticism and continuous improvement of efficiency, the culture of Wal-Mart has been described as "neurotic." According to one Wal-Mart insider, "Mechanisms like these meetings keep that neurotic tension alive even at this enormous scale."

In fact, the Saturday Morning Meeting is not the only meeting Wal-Mart uses to maintain company culture. On Friday there is a merchandising meeting, where regional vice presidents get together to discuss what products are selling well. And not all meetings are for managers. Consistent with Sam Walton's emphasis on employee involvement, every Wal-Mart store has a 15-minute shift-change meeting three times a day. During these meetings, managers go over the store's performance numbers as well as ask their associates whether they have specific ideas that might improve sales. Managers send what they think are good ideas up to the regional vice president, who then proposes the ideas at the Saturday-morning meeting. The Wal-Mart greeter was one such idea, which a rank-and-file employee suggested. The greeter helped to put a friendly face on what might be viewed as a large, impersonal organization. Such structure helps to ensure that Wal-Mart's upper managers, who oftentimes are responsible for 100 or more stores, keep in touch with the daily happenings of their business.

One other aspect of Wal-Mart's culture is its frugality, a characteristic of Sam Walton that has endured even through Wal-Mart's tremendous growth and financial success. Walton began his strict focus on keeping costs low early on to gain an advantage over competitors such as Sears and Kmart. Walton was known to make executives sleep eight to a room on company trips. He himself drove a modest old pick-up truck and flew coach whenever he traveled. Amazingly, these characteristics have remained ingrained in Wal-Mart's culture. The current CEO, Lee Scott, drives a Volkswagen Beetle and has also shared hotel rooms to reduce costs.

But maintaining Wal-Mart's culture has not always been easy. In the late 1980s and early 1990s, attendance at the Saturday Morning Meetings grew tremendously, which made it impossible for everyone to speak. David Glass, CEO during that time, recalls complaints of boredom. So some of Wal-Mart's suppliers (who often attend the Saturday Morning Meetings), eager to impress and ingratiate themselves with the top brass, began bringing in entertainers such as singer Garth Brooks and former football player Joe Montana. However, the meetings began to lose focus. As Glass recalls of the entertainment, "You had to be careful how you did that because it becomes more fun to do that than fix the problems." By the late 1990s, the company began inviting guests who had more educational value, such as former U.S. President Bill Clinton and CEOs Jack Welch and Warren Buffet. These speakers were able to share their success stories with Wal-Mart's managers, giving them new ideas on how to conduct business and run the organization.

Perhaps the biggest obstacle to Wal-Mart is the increased public scrutiny that comes with being the world's largest company. In the past, the company had more tolerance for employee mistakes. It would strongly reprimand an employee who made an offhand sexist remark, for example, but if the employee altered his or her behavior, then the company let the employee stay. Today, however, Wal-Mart adheres to a stricter policy. As Mr. Scott explains, Wal-Mart is "not mean but less kind. Today, when you find somebody doing something wrong, you not only have to let them go, you have to document it so it is covered and people understand. That is a bit of a culture change. It's a company that operates in a different context than when Sam Walton was alive and when David Glass ran the company. Management cannot allow extraneous issues to bleed over. My role has to be, besides focusing on driving sales, to eliminate the constant barrage of negatives that causes people to wonder if Wal-Mart will be allowed to grow."

Indeed, Wal-Mart frequently finds itself in the news, though lately in stories that paint the company in a negative light. Controversies over Wal-Mart's anti-union position, its hiring and promotion practices (such as outsourcing the cleaning of its stores to illegal immigrants and working them seven days a week), and its treatment of employees (including accusations of discrimination and underpayment of employees) all make it increasingly difficult for Wal-Mart to maintain the image of a friendly, affordable retailer that Sam Walton had in mind when he founded the company. On this topic, Scott says, "Over the last couple of years I've been spending much of the time talking about all the negative publicity we've been getting, not from the standpoint that we hate the press, but by asking our people what we are doing that allows people to perpetuate these kinds of negative discussions about Wal-Mart."

If Wal-Mart is to enjoy continued success, it will have to find solutions to the above problems and the negative publicity that results. Perhaps the company should go back to its Walton roots? Or maybe it should alter its culture and market position to match its growth. For a company that has over 4,000 stores operating in the United States, Mexico, Canada, South America, Korea, China, and Europe; 1.5 million employees; and over 100,000 different products for sale, sustaining or changing the company's culture is a tremendous challenge. Thus far, however, Wal-Mart appears to be handling the challenge well.

Questions for Discussion

1. According to the textbook, there are seven primary characteristics that capture the essence of an organization's culture. How would you describe Wal-Mart's culture using these seven characteristics?
2. Based on this case, would you characterize Wal-Mart's culture as strong or weak? Why? How might Wal-Mart's culture contribute to its long-term performance?
3. As an upper manager of Wal-Mart, what steps could you take to either maintain or enhance the culture of Wal-Mart?
4. What are some aspects of Wal-Mart's culture that have persevered, but yet may be disadvantageous in today's economy?
5. How might Wal-Mart's negative press affect employee morale, job satisfaction, and organizational commitment? As a manager, what steps would you take to improve employee attitudes?
6. Characterize Wal-Mart's organizational structure. Is it mechanistic or organic? Does it have a high degree of centralization or decentralization? How might Wal-Mart's structure affect its employees in terms of their productivity and job attitudes?

Source: Based on D. Garbato, "Wal-Mart's Scott Concedes Size Impacts Corporate Culture," *Retail Merchandiser*, October 2004, p. 12; B. Schlender, "Wal-Mart's $288 Billion Meeting," *Fortune*, April 18, 2005, 90–99; and "Wal Around the World," *The Economist*, December 8, 2001, pp. 55–57.

Apple's Beethoven

Management guru Jim Collins calls him the "Beethoven of business," Wall Street loves him, and Bill Gates was once his nemesis. Who is this powerful man? It's Steve Jobs, cofounder and current chief executive officer of Apple Computer. But despite its trailblazing start, Apple has suffered in recent years, losing sales and market share to big companies such as IBM and Microsoft. The slide even caused many analysts to question whether Apple had anything innovative left to offer. But Jobs, in characteristic fashion, has once again cornered a market, thanks to a small device—with big musical power—called the iPod.

Although Apple competed with computer giant Microsoft during the early 1980s, it soon found itself on the fringes of the computer industry because its computer, the Mac, wasn't compatible with many software programs that businesses needed. Personal computers (PCs), along with Microsoft's Windows operating system, began to dominate, sending the Mac to niche markets. By 1986, Apple's board of directors forced Steve Jobs out of the company. By the late 1990s, even the most fanatic Apple users were turning to different products because of the Mac's compatibility issues and Microsoft's ever-increasing dominance. Apple's share in the computer industry continued to decline, bottoming out at a mere 2 percent in the mid-1990s.

Apple knew it had to improve its operating system, so it bought the computer company Next in 1997, which, as circumstances would have it, Jobs himself was running. Along with Next came Jobs, who eventually returned to the forefront of Apple. Jobs's plan was simple: Rather than focus on hardware, Apple should focus on software. Create the right software, he reasoned, and the hardware sales would follow.

So Jobs began making moves that at first seemed risky but in the end paid off. One of the first things he did was to partner with his former rival, Bill Gates. Gates agreed to supply Apple with its popular Office and Internet Explorer programs as well as buy $150 million of Apple stock. Though this deal was good for Microsoft, it was even better for Apple, whose future was now tied to the more successful Microsoft in that Microsoft now had an interest in maintaining Apple's survival. Apple was no longer a competitor in a strict sense.

Because developing software is a costly undertaking, Jobs tried to keep the company afloat by offering computer hardware, which was simply a means to get into the software business. He pushed the company's managers for innovative thinking, which led to the introduction of the iMac in 1998. The iMac immediately stood out from its competitors for its odd, colorful styling, but compatibility issues with some widely used programs still remained. Though the iMac was not the innovative success that Jobs had hoped for, it bought him time to continue developing software.

During this time, Apple developed a new operating system that Jobs thought would revolutionize the computer industry: Mac OS X. The system was based on the operating system Unix and was superior to Windows in several areas, including stability and security. Now that he had the operating system, Jobs needed exciting software to go along with it. Knowing that he already had a deal with Microsoft, Jobs headed to Adobe Systems to ask them to develop a video editing program for his new operating system. Jobs recalled, "They said flat-out no. We were shocked, because they had been a big supporter in the early days of the Mac. But we said, 'Okay, if nobody wants to help us, we're just going to have to do this ourselves.' "

Adobe's rejection may have been a blessing in disguise for Apple. Jobs quickened the pace on software development, and in less than a year released two video editing programs, one for professionals and one for consumers. The software helped keep the buzz alive for Apple's innovative reputation. Feeling confident, Jobs knew that Apple needed to develop more software applications if it were to thrive, but he still hadn't noticed a phenomenon taking place on the Internet: the birth of online music.

In 2000, music lovers the world over, particularly young adults and teenagers, were downloading MP3s (digital music files) by the thousands from what were then illegal online music services, Napster being the company most in the news at that time. Online music delivery was an exciting product for consumers in that they could easily pick and choose what songs to buy and create their own music libraries on their computers. It was also a controversial issue in that there was no way (yet) to compensate artists and their record companies for the sales.

But for Jobs, the opportunity to deliver music to online consumers in a legitimate, user-friendly way was right up his alley. "I felt like a dope," he said. "I thought we had missed it. We had to work hard to catch up." He set out to develop the best "customer experience" possible.

So Apple began to install CD-ROM burners as a standard feature on all of its computers, hoping that it hadn't missed an opportunity. The burners allowed users to save electronic files, such as digital music files, onto a CD. The addition of burners as a standard feature was a crucial first step in marketing digital music because it offered a way to play digital music on devices other than a computer.

But Apple still needed to offer software that allowed users to manage their digital music files. Microsoft already sold several computer programs of this sort. For Apple, developing software that could easily manage and navigate through thousands of songs and allow a user to call up a song on a whim was no easy task. Jobs didn't have the answer himself, but he found it in a company called SoundStep. Jeff Robbin, the founder of SoundStep, teamed with several engineers and developed the program iTunes in just over three months. Not only was iTunes Apple's answer to comparable Windows jukeboxes, but many consumers found it a superior program with great search and sorting capabilities.

Jobs then hit on his big, Apple-saving idea: Develop a small, portable device, like the Sony Walkman, that could hold a user's entire digital music library. Jobs turned to Robbin again. In November 2001—a mere nine months later—Robbin and his team had developed the iPod, which is basically a small, handheld computer the size of a deck of cards (now, some are even smaller) with a simple interface for navigating through one's digital library and a set of earphones for easy listening. Music could be taken from a user's existing CD collection and "ripped" to the iPod via the user's computer, or online music file-sharing services such as Napster could be used to download songs onto the iPod.

Though Jobs believed that the iPod would be a success, he kept at his goal of developing the best "customer experience" possible. Napster, as well as other online music file-sharing services, was in the midst of lawsuits, leaving the door open for more legitimate, licensed services to emerge. By April 2003, Apple debuted its online iTunes Music store, allowing customers to legitimately buy songs for 99 cents that they could then download and store on their Mac computers and iPods. Major recording companies, such as Sony and Universal, agreed to sell their songs on iTunes, and the result was a tremendous success. As Eddy Cue, vice president for applications at Apple recalled, "We had hoped to sell a million songs in the first six months, but we did that in the first six days." While the iTunes store was busy selling digital music, Robbin and his team developed a Windows version of the iTunes store, further broadening Apple's market.

To say that Apple has done well with the iPod is an understatement. By January 2005, the company had sold more than 10 million iPods and 250 million songs. As a result, its stock price hit a record high of almost $80 per share in February 2005, and analysts estimated that Apple would earn $13 billion in revenues in 2005.

Jobs credits Apple's success to maintaining its core values of innovation and a continuous focus on the consumer. "The great thing is that Apple's DNA hasn't changed. The place where Apple has been standing for the last two decades is exactly where computer technology and the consumer electronics markets are converging. So it's not like we're having to cross the river to go somewhere else; the other side of the river is coming to us." Jobs further stated, "At Apple we come at everything asking, 'How easy is this going to be for the user? How great is it going to be for the user?' "

Though it appears that Apple is on a roll, its competitors are beginning to catch up. Not only has Microsoft entered the online music market but companies such as Wal-Mart and Napster (Napster is now on legal footing) are trying to capture some of the market share. As of the latest look, Wal-Mart was offering songs at 88 cents each, undercutting Apple's iTunes. Indeed, Apple's first-mover advantage will erode as competitors mimic Apple's product. Because they can copy Apple's online music store instead of creating it from scratch, start-up costs are lower for new entrants. What, then, will be the next move for Steve Jobs and Apple?

Questions for Discussion

1. Using the three-component model of creativity, describe what makes Steve Jobs, and by extension, Apple Computer, successful. Based on the case, which components does Jobs seem to possess in the highest degree? What aspects of the case led you to this conclusion?
2. What leadership theories are most applicable to Steve Jobs and why? How can these theories explain Jobs's recent successes?
3. Based on the case's description of Jobs, what can you infer about his personality? In other words, how would you describe his personality using terms from the book?
4. Are situational factors solely responsible for Apple's success, or is it due to the traits and leadership skills of Steve Jobs? If both contribute, which do you believe is more important and why?
5. Using Lewin's Three-Step Model of organizational change, explain Apple's development of and success with the iPod.
6. Would you characterize Apple as a learning organization? Why or why not? As a manager, what could you do to ensure that Apple continues to be innovative?

Source: Based on B. Schendler, "How Big Can Apple Get?" *Fortune*, February 21, 2005, 66–73.

GM and the UAW: A One-Sided Negotiation?

From 1947 through 1977, General Motors (GM) dominated the automobile industry, capturing an average of 45 percent of the auto market. Of the "Big Three" U.S. automakers (GM, Ford, and Chrysler), GM ranked first in sales in every year during this time frame and ranked first in profits for 16 of the 20 years. Needless to say, GM sat comfortably atop the automobile industry.

Now, decades later, GM's share of the U.S. automobile market is down to 25.4 percent, its lowest level since it competed with Henry Ford's Model T. Rumors of bankruptcy abound. In March of 2005, GM lowered its earnings forecast, which sent its stock price to its worst one-day fall since October 19, 1987, when the stock market crashed. Following this, GM announced that it had lost a staggering 1 billion dollars during its first quarter alone. Finally, adding insult to injury, GM disclosed that its sales were plummeting, and for this its stock earned Standard & Poor's grade of junk-bond status. What once was the world's largest and most profitable auto manufacturer is now puttering along in the slow lane.

So who or what is responsible for GM's decline? Though there are numerous factors that are hurting the company, one major factor has been the United Auto Workers (UAW) union and its long relationship with GM over the years.

The relationship first took shape during the Depression, when demand for cars overall fell sharply and almost half of all autoworkers lost their jobs as a result. Those autoworkers that did keep their jobs received greatly reduced pay because the major auto companies could barely afford to stay in business. However, GM, through the leadership of Alfred Sloan, remained competitive and profitable. But working conditions paled in comparison to today's standards. It was not typical for companies, including GM, to provide benefits such as health insurance, and pension plans were unheard of.

All of this began to change for GM in 1936, when two major players in the UAW, Walter and Victor Reuther, staged a sit-down strike at one of GM's primary plants, Fisher Body Plant No. 1, in GM's hometown of Flint, Michigan. Though the governor at the time, Frank Murphy, instructed over 4,000 guardsmen to maintain peace at the strike, he did not give them the authority to evict the strikers, forcing Sloan to negotiate with the UAW (though Sloan later stated that "we would not negotiate with the union while its agents forcibly held possession of our properties . . . we finally felt obliged to do so"). As a result of the strike, GM formally recognized the UAW as a legal organization in 1937. Shortly after, in 1941, Ford formally recognized the UAW, giving the union even greater power.

What followed was a relationship that endured over the years, giving the UAW and its members some of the best benefits in the country. Indeed, the UAW was a powerful negotiator. Victor Reuther, believing strongly that all workers should have health insurance, tried first to bargain with the federal government. After several failed attempts, he turned to Sloan at GM. Although Sloan initially viewed Reuther's request for health insurance and pension plans as "extravagant beyond reason," one of Reuther's proposals eventually persuaded him. Previously, GM and the UAW engaged in contract renegotiations each year, which made it difficult for GM's managers and workers to plan ahead because they were unsure what the costs would be for the following year. Reuther, capitalizing on this problem, offered to agree to longer contracts. As Sloan later stated, "Longer intervals gave the corporation more assurance that it could meet its long-range production schedules." What was the catch to the UAW's concession? In return for longer contracts, the UAW insisted that each and every contract be better for the UAW than the one before it. Sloan agreed to the terms of the negotiation, setting the stage for health insurance, pension plans, and other employee benefits.

During the economic boom following World War II, demand soared, leaving the auto industry rich with profit. As Reuther stated to the auto industry during these times, "It's a growing market—we have nothing to fight over." So, at first, contract renegotiations went smoothly and costs of employee benefits stayed at a minimum. But little by little, the UAW negotiated better benefits for its members. In 1943, GM allowed workers to purchase health insurance; however, GM did not incur any of the cost because workers put their money into a pool. Five years later, the union successfully negotiated two powerful benefits. The first, an "escalator clause," stipulated that GM give raises based on the cost of living. The second, the "improvement factor," rewarded workers for increasing efficiency. As a plant increased in efficiency, and lowered costs as a result, workers at the plant received raises. Then, in 1950, GM agreed to pay 50 percent of all its workers' health care premiums, including workers' families, and it also agreed to develop and pay for a pension plan. Three years later, GM extended these benefits to its retired workers.

Business was still booming in 1959, when the UAW persuaded GM to guarantee workers' wages—even for those workers the company had laid off. Thus, workers could be assured that they would receive no less than what GM had promised to pay them, even during economic hardship. The UAW continued to push GM to further sweeten its benefits—per their original deal—and in 1961, GM agreed to pay 100 percent of all health care premiums, again for workers and their families. Three years later, GM extended this benefit to its retirees.

GM's market share around that time peaked at 50.7 percent, but in 1966, the same year that Alfred Sloan died, a little-known company called Datsun exported a car to the United States, marking the entry of Japanese automakers in the U.S. market. During this time, Japan's influence was minimal, and GM continued to agree to increase benefits to its workers. In 1970, for instance, the UAW persuaded GM to provide full retirement benefits after 30 years of service. In addition, GM agreed to extend health insurance benefits to cover mental and prenatal and postnatal conditions. As UAW negotiator Douglas Fraser recalls, "We had a lot of arguments over mental health. I don't believe we had any arguments over full premiums."

From GM's standpoint, the concessions it made over the years may be relatively minor when considered in isolation, but their cumulative impact is now taking its toll. As the company has lost market share to increased competition from both domestic and foreign producers, particularly Japanese producers, more and more workers have retired, leaving GM with huge expenses. GM anticipates health care costs to top $5.6 billion in 2005 alone, and it is estimated that GM's long-term health care liabilities are $77 billion. To fund its pension plans, GM has long-term liabilities of $89 billion—a tremendous amount when one considers that GM's revenues in 2004 were $193 billion.

And costs continue to soar as baby boomers retire in droves, leaving younger workers to support retirees and causing large discrepancies in the number of current and retired workers. GM now employs 150,000 people, yet it funds health care for 1.1 million people. And because of the ever-increasing benefits packages that the UAW negotiated with GM over the years, GM's health care plan is far better than what the average U.S. company provides. While average U.S. citizens pay 32 percent of their medical costs, GM workers and members of the UAW pay only 7 percent. In fact, GM now spends more than double on health care what it spends on steel to produce its automobiles. As one former GM investor quipped, "When you invest in GM, you are not investing in a car company. You are investing in a money-management firm and an HMO."

All of these rising costs have caused GM considerable financial problems. Although some analysts suggest that GM should streamline operations, Thomas Kowaleski, a spokesperson for GM, said, regarding the enormous cost of benefits, "We cannot be profitable at 20 percent market share because legacy costs won't go away." Even closing a plant is no longer under GM's discretion—the UAW must approve it. To make matters worse, even if GM halts production at a given plant, it still has to pay its workers 95 percent of their regular wages, even though GM's wages are 60 percent more than the industry average.

All in all, GM may have negotiated itself into a stranglehold with the UAW. But there are two sides to consider. On the one hand, offering great employee benefits is a goal that all organizations should have, as workers should receive the best treatment possible and companies want to attract the best workers possible. On the other hand, if the UAW continues to press GM for improvements, and GM concedes, the company may no longer exist to provide those benefits.

Questions for Discussion

1. How would you characterize the type of conflict that exits between GM and the UAW using the various conflict-handling interventions described in Chapter 15?
2. Based on the case, would you conclude that GM and the UAW have engaged in distributive or integrative bargaining? Which type would be better for the two parties in the long term, and why?
3. What types of power does the UAW hold over GM? How has this power influenced its ability to negotiate with GM?
4. Based on the case, what decision-making errors with the union might have led GM to its current financial position? What can GM do to eliminate these errors in the future?
5. Although benefits such as a "guaranteed wage" likely are appealing to workers, how might such benefits affect employee motivation? How might they affect job satisfaction and organizational commitment? Could this be a case where management engages in the "folly of rewarding A, while hoping for B?"
6. As a manager of a large company such as GM that operates in a highly competitive environment, how would you attempt to strike an appropriate balance between employee treatment and company profitability?

Source: Based on R. Lowenstein, "What Went Wrong at GM," *Smart Money*, July 2005, 78–82.

Case 7 *A Question of Motivation*

Alex and Katrien have a few things in common. Both are students at the same university, and both work full-time at a local supermarket to make ends meet and help pay for college. Though the pay isn't great, it's a steady job that allows them some flexibility, which helps when scheduling classes. Both students joined the supermarket two years ago, and, given their similar situations, became friends quickly.

Although Katrien seems to enjoy her job, arriving and leaving work each day with a smile on her face, Alex often grumbles and complains about his work. Much of the time, Alex complains about his boss, Jacque, who oversees the produce department. Katrien works for Jonathan, a 10-year veteran who everyone generally admires for his friendly demeanor and relaxed management style.

Most employees want to work for Jonathan, as he often assigns his employees different duties each week so workers don't get bored. Katrien, for instance, can be working at the checkout counter one week, stocking shelves the next, and the store's culinary center the following week.

The culinary center is a new service that the store is test-marketing. Employees show customers how to create exciting recipes from start to finish. It is Katrien's favorite place in the store to work. She is also responsible for taking customers around the store to locate ingredients for a culinary center recipe, many of the ingredients being some of the store's finest. And she enjoys allowing customers to sample what she cooks. So far, the culinary center is a success, and many of the store's more expensive ingredients are becoming difficult to keep in stock. To help with this issue, Jonathan encourages his employees to notify him immediately when an item is running low and even empowers employees to reorder items from vendors. By doing this, Katrien has quickly grasped how the supermarket operates.

Alex's supervisor, in contrast, prefers most of his employees to work in the same area each day—Alex is one of those employees. Jacque believes that the best way to master a job is to do it over and over again. This means that Alex has to stock the same produce areas each day. As boxes of produce are delivered to the store's supply room, Alex unloads their contents onto the shelves. Alex also must constantly reorganize the produce already on the shelves to make them look as orderly as possible. Most of the time, though, he doesn't feel inclined to do either task.

After a particularly boring morning of restocking apples (the store had apples on sale that day), Alex met Katrien for lunch in the break room. After sitting down, Alex reached into his lunchbox and pulled out an apple, a look of disgust on his face. "Ugh . . . If I have to look at another apple, I'm going to be sick."

"Bad day again?" asked Katrien as Alex stuffed the apple back into his lunchbox.

"I stocked apples all morning—what do you think?" Alex retorted.

"Why don't you tell Jacque you want to do something else?" Katrien inquired. "I see that he lets Denise work in other areas." Katrien leaned closer. "I've even heard that she gets paid more than you. Is that true?" she whispered.

"Apparently, she gets paid $2.00 more an hour, but I do the same things that she does. Oh, that's right. One thing I don't do is tell Jacque what a cool shirt he has on or how awesome his car is. They're both pathetic if you ask me," frowned Alex.

"Two dollars more an hour, but she's been here for only 3 months!" Katrien exclaimed. "And I know that you work just as hard as she does. No wonder you're so irritated all the time."

"I don't even care any more. What's the point? If I stock more apples, or something meaningless like that, what does it get me—another sticker that says 'good job'? Oooh, that's really great. Thanks a bunch Jacque!" replied Alex, punctuating his last sentence with a sarcastic thumbs-up. "Anyway, enough about my day. How's yours going?"

"Pretty good, actually. Jonathan and I met earlier today, and we both set a goal for me to sell 10 bottles of truffle oil next week."

"Wow. That stuff is pretty expensive, isn't it?" asked Alex.

"Thirty-five dollars for four ounces," replied Katrien. "It'll be tough, but I found a pretty good recipe that I'll be making for customers who stop by the culinary center." She paused, then said, "I think I'll be able to do it. I've made quite a few similar recipes before, and even though this one is more difficult, it shouldn't be too bad. Besides, if I sell the oil Jonathan said that he'll give me a $75 bonus. So I'm definitely going to give it a shot. The nice thing is that I'll be able to do this on my own, without someone breathing down my neck."

"Well that's certainly more than I'll be making this week," said Alex. "This job is okay, but I'd probably leave if I could. It's too risky right now to just quit. If I can't find something, then I'll be in trouble when that next tuition bill comes around."

"Look on the bright side. At least you make more than Jean. She's been here for 7 years, still working in the deli," replied Katrien.

"That's true," sighed Alex as he returned to his lunch. He looked up at the clock. They had been at lunch for a half hour already. Jacque was quite the stickler about keeping lunch to a minimum. Although store policy allowed employees 45 minutes for lunch, Jacque often pushed his employees to keep it to 30 minutes. As Alex quickened his chewing, Jacque strolled into the break room and opened the refrigerator, his back to Alex and Katrien.

Wheeling around with a soda in hand, Jacque commented, "Bit of a long lunch, hey Alex?"

Alex could feel the blood rising to his face. "It's been exactly a half hour, and I'm almost finished," he said.

"Well, we're running low on apples again. So quit lying around and get back to work." Jacque walked toward the door, stopped, and turned around. "I thought that college students were supposed to be smarter than this. At the very least I would hope that they could tell time." He added, "I guess the university must have glossed over your application." And with that, Jacque left.

"What a jerk," said Katrien after Jacque was out of earshot.

"What else is new," said Alex. "I'd guess I'd better get back to work." Alex got up and returned what was left of his lunch to the refrigerator. When he opened the door, he noticed a sandwich labeled with a post-it note that read "Jacque's." After glancing quickly to the door, he casually swept the sandwich onto the floor. Katrien turned around at the sound.

"Oops," smirked Alex. He paused, staring down at the sandwich. "Five-second rule!" he said as he picked up the sandwich, being sure to smear the underside of it on the floor. After putting it neatly back on the shelf, Alex turned to Katrien. "Well Katrien, have a good one. I think maybe I'll take my time on those apples."

Questions for Discussion

1. How can expectancy theory be used to explain the differences in motivation between Alex and Katrien? What specifics from the case apply to expectancy theory?
2. Alex states that he is underpaid for the work he does. What motivational theory does this apply to, and how would it explain Alex's behavior?
3. Using concepts from organizational justice, explain why Alex knocks his boss's lunch to the floor. What should Alex's boss do to improve the fairness of his treatment?
4. Using concepts from the emotions and moods chapter, explain why Alex retaliates toward his supervisor. Was his behavior driven purely by emotion, or did cognition also play a role? How so?
5. Compare and contrast Alex and Katrien in terms of each person's level of work stress. How might stress affect their attitudes and behaviors within their work environment?
6. Discuss Alex and Katrien in terms of each person's job attitudes (for example, job satisfaction, organizational commitment). What factors might be responsible for any differences?

The Big Promotion

Devon and Isabella arrived outside their boss's office at the same time and took a seat. Both exchanged a cordial "hello," but they didn't say much else as they waited outside. Fidgeting nervously in their seats, the two knew that only one of them was going to receive what would be the biggest promotion of their careers.

Devon and Isabella worked for a large software company and each was responsible for managing one of the company's largest divisions. Both had been in their current position for years, hoping that a spot at the company's corporate headquarters would open up. That time had arrived a month earlier when one of the company's senior executives retired. Such positions did not open frequently, so Devon and Isabella knew that this was a tremendous opportunity.

For the past month, they had prepared for their meeting with the company's CEO, Paul McAllister. Although Paul already knew Devon and Isabella well, he wanted to meet with them at the same time to see how they handled the pressure of being interviewed in front of each other.

After waiting for what seemed like an eternity, Devon and Isabella looked up simultaneously as Paul opened the door to his office.

"Isabella. Devon. Good to see you. Come on in," said Paul.

Devon and Isabella entered Paul's office and took the chairs ready for them at the front of his desk.

Paul broke the silence by saying, "Well, you both know why you are here, so there's no need to waste time. I already know your resumes backwards and forwards, and I've gathered as much information as possible from those who know you best, so now it comes down to hearing it, 'straight from the horses' mouths.' I'm going to ask you both one question only, and it's the same question for both of you. Let me flip a coin to see who will respond first." He flipped the coin. "Devon, you're up."

Devon sat up with confidence, eyeing Paul.

Paul began. "To function effectively in an executive position requires strong leadership skills. Both of you have gained valuable experience as managers of your respective divisions, making decisions that have resulted in strong performances from those divisions. But you have also, as managers, followed directives that this corporate office has handed down. As an executive, this will change. You will no longer take directives—you will give them. In short, you will be responsible for guiding the future of this company, and its success will depend greatly on you. So my question to you both is: How do you plan to succeed as a leader if you are offered this position?"

"Well Paul," responded Devon, "That is an excellent question. I believe that, to be a successful leader, one must be able to exert influence. When you get down to it, that is what leadership is all about—the ability to influence others. I have demonstrated that I have this ability since I joined the ranks of management." Devon paused, collecting his thoughts. "It is my opinion that leadership boils down to what actions you take with your employees. For me, leadership is all about rewarding and punishing appropriately. I try to make my employees' jobs less complicated by stating exactly what they need to do, assigning particular tasks, setting appropriate goals, and ensuring that my subordinates have the resources they need."

Paul listened carefully as Devon continued. "Basically, I am an organizer. When employees accomplish a given task or goal, I reward them appropriately for their work. When employees fail to accomplish an assignment, an appropriate response from me is needed. If it is clear that the employee did not try to accomplish the task, then punishment is necessary, and this punishment could range from a verbal reprimand to termination, depending, of course, on the circumstances. If the employee did not have the necessary skills or resources to complete a task, then my job is to provide those skills and resources. By rewarding and punishing employees based on their performance, I am able not only to influence employee behavior to match the goals of the organization but also to send a clear message as to what I expect."

Devon added, "I also want to note that a strong sense of fairness guides all of my decisions—I reward and punish justly. As a result, my employees are satisfied with their work and perform at high levels. So I will bring my ability to influence behavior with me if I am offered this position, and in doing so will be able to shape the future of our company."

"Thank you, Devon," responded Paul. "Isabella, how would you answer this question?"

"Well, Paul," said Isabella, "I think you'll find that my perspective on leadership is different from Devon's. Although I certainly agree with Devon that giving clear guidance to employees, setting appropriate goals, and rewarding employees for accomplishing tasks is a fundamental leadership quality, I believe that it takes more than that to be a successful leader. You see, I do not believe that just anyone can be a leader. To be a leader requires a certain 'something' that not all people possess."

"And you believe that you possess that certain something?" interrupted Paul.

Isabella grinned. "I think you'll find that my record suggests that I do, in fact. You see, successful leadership is about motivating people beyond the formal requirements of their jobs. It is not enough in today's global economy to simply ensure that employees are completing their tasks. To survive, and moreover, grow, leaders must challenge employees to look ahead, to contribute ideas, and to make sacrifices for the good of the company. My job as a leader of this company is to create a vision of where we will be 5, 10, and 15 years from now. I see us creating new technologies, as well as merging existing technologies, to give our company the competitive advantage it needs to sustain growth in the long term. By sharing this vision with my employees, we will all be able to pursue the same goals."

Isabella continued, "I inspire my subordinates to see the company as their own, rather than as a means to a paycheck. I consider employee input and the different needs of each worker, and I challenge each and every one of them to think outside the box and develop innovative solutions to the problems facing us. The end result is, in my opinion, a highly motivated workforce with a common goal—to make sure our company is the industry leader."

Paul nodded, thinking about both answers. He had scrutinized each person's record carefully, and both were qualified for the job. However, the two candidates differed in important ways. Devon had built a strong reputation for being a traditional, straightforward leader, motivating his employees well, setting appropriate goals, and ensuring that employees accomplished tasks on time—even ahead of schedule. However, Devon was not known for developing the most creative solutions, and he lacked the vision that Paul knew was an important competency to have as an executive.

Isabella, in contrast, had built a reputation as being a visionary leader. Though her ideas were a bit unconventional at times, in many cases they were directly responsible for getting the company out of a jam. In addition, her magnetic personality made her a favorite among employees. However, Isabella often revealed a somewhat egotistical personality, and Paul was unsure whether this egoism would be amplified if she were in a more authoritative position.

Paul had to make a tough decision. He thought about his company's future. Things were relatively stable now, and business was good, but he knew that stability was not always certain.

"I would like to thank you both for coming today. You're making this a tough decision for me," said Paul. "I need to think about this a bit more, but I'll be getting back to you soon." He paused, then added, "You'll have my answer tomorrow morning."

Questions for Discussion

1. Using terms from the text, how would you describe Devon's leadership style? How would you describe Isabella's leadership style?
2. Whose leadership style do you believe would be more effective, Isabella's or Devon's? Why? What, if any, situational factors might their effectiveness depend on?
3. If you were Paul, who would you hire and why?
4. What are some potential downsides to each candidate's leadership style?
5. Whose employees do you think are likely to be more motivated, Devon's or Isabella's? Whose employees are likely to have higher job satisfaction, trust in leadership, and organizational commitment? Why?
6. Based on their leadership styles, in what type of organizational structure would Devon be most effective? What about Isabella? Why?

ILLUSTRATION CREDITS

Chapter 1
37. Mark Crosse/AP Wide World Photos
39. Matt Rourke/AP Wide World Photos
44. Elaine Thompson/AP Wide World Photos
51. Getty Images, Inc.
54. Melanie Stetson Freeman/The Christian Science Monitor/Getty Images, Inc.
56. AP Wide World Photos
58. Jessica Kourkounis/The New York Times
62. Greg Ruffing/Redux Pictures

Chapter 2
77. Dave Yoder/The New York Times
82. Douglas Healey/The New York Times
84. © Ed Kashi/Corbis
88. Mario Villafuerte/Redux Pictures
91. Toru Yamanaka/Agence France Presse/Getty Images
96. Joe Raedle/Getty Images, Inc.

Chapter 3
107. Eros Hoagland/Redux Pictures
111. © Jodi Hilton/Corbis
112. Aynsley Floyd/AP Wide World Photos
116. Kim Kyung-Hoon/Corbis/Reuters America LLC
122. Katsumi Kasahara/AP Wide World Photos
123. STR/Agence France Presse/Getty Images

Chapter 4
137. Fred R. Conrad/The New York Times
140. AP Wide World Photos
141. Manish Swarup/AP Wide World Photos
142. Chris Pizzello/AP Wide World Photos
145. Charles Rex Arbogast/AP Wide World Photos
148. Ben Baker/Redux Pictures

Chapter 5
171. Joyce Dopkeen/The New York Times
178. Misha Erwitt/The New York Times
181. © Kim Kulish/Corbis
182. © Ferran Paredes/Reuters/Corbis
190. Toshifumi Kitamura/Agence France Presse/Getty Images
192. © Darryl Bush/San Francisco Chronicle/CORBIS All Rights Reserved

Chapter 6
207. Christopher Gardner Media
214. AP Wide World Photos
221. Ralph Orlowski/Corbis/Reuters America LLC
224. Julia Cumes/AP Wide World Photos
226. Justin Sullivan/Getty Images, Inc.
235. CLARO CORTES IV/Reuters/Corbis/Bettmann

Chapter 7
247. Thomas Strand Studio
252. Thomas Broening Photography
255. Enzo/AGE Fotostock American, Inc.
258. Lawrence Bartlett/Agence France Presse/Getty Images
260. Chris Mueller/Chris Mueller/Redux Pictures
263. Ben Garvin/The New York Times
266. Pat Sullivan/AP Wide World Photos
268. Paul Sakuma/AP Wide World Photos

Chapter 8
283. Aijaz Rahi/AP Wide World Photos
288. Doug Mindell Photography
293. Beaver County Times, Lucy Schaly/AP Wide World Photos
295. © James Leynse/CORBIS All Rights Reserved
299. © Kimberly White/Reuters/Corbis
301. Stephen Chernin/Getty Images, Inc.
303. STR/Agence France Presse/Getty Images

Chapter 9
317. Ryanstock/Taxi/Getty Images
321. © Bob Daemmrich/CORBIS All Rights Reserved
323. Chris Graythen/Getty Images, Inc.
327. Courtesy of AT&T Archives and History Center, Warren, NJ
332. Tom Wagner/Redux Pictures
334. © Redlink/CORBIS All Rights Reserved

Chapter 10
355. Optimus Solutions
359. Alexandra Boulat/VII/AP Wide World Photos
364. Ruth Fremson/The New York Times
367. Jim Wilson/The New York Times
369. AP Wide World Photos
372. Harry Cabluck/AP Wide World Photos

Chapter 11
383. Cheryl Senter/AP Wide World Photos
386. Shizuo Kambayashi/AP Wide World Photos
388. Erik S. Lesser/The New York Times
397. Noah Berger/The New York Times
400. Alyson Aliano/Alyson Aliano Photography
403. Alyssa Banta/Redux Pictures

Chapter 12
417. Charles Rex Arbogast/AP Wide World Photos
419. Jason Kempin/FilmMagic/Getty Images, Inc.
424. Scott Cohen/AP Wide World Photos
425. Carlos Osorio/AP Wide World Photos
430. Patrick Allard/REA/Redux Pictures

Chapter 13
445. Ben Baker/Redux Pictures
448. Paul Sakuma/AP Wide World Photos
450. Koji Sasahara/AP Wide World Photos
452. © Michele Asselin/Corbis Outline
456. Mel Evans/AP Wide World Photos
460. Thaddeus Harden/Corbis/Outline
463. STRDEL/Agence France Presse/Getty Images
470. Djamilla Rosa Cochran/WireImage for CHANEL/Getty Images, Inc.

Chapter 14
483. © Alan Schein Photography/CORBIS All Rights Reserved
486. John Bazemore/AP Wide World Photos
489. Christopher LaMarca/Redux Pictures
493. Charles Bennett/AP Wide World Photos
496. AP Wide World Photos
499. George Frey/AP Wide World Photos

Chapter 15
517. Gene J. Puskar/AP Wide World Photos
522. Michele McDonald/The Boston Globe/Redux Pictures

527. © Ed Murray/The Star Ledger/CORBIS All Rights Reserved
532. Carlos Osorio/AP Wide World Photos
536. Jacques Demarthon/Agence France Presse/Getty Images

Chapter 16

551. M. Spencer Green/AP Wide World Photos
554. © Shen Bohan/Xinhua Press/CORBIS All Rights Reserved
561. Melanie Stetson Freeman/Getty Images, Inc./Christian Science Monitor
565. Robert Sorbo/Corbis/Reuters America LLC
567. © Ed Kashi/CORBIS All Rights Reserved
570. Dima Gavrysh/The New York Times
574. © epa/CORBIS All Rights Reserved

Chapter 17

583. Kirsty Wigglesworth/AP Wide World Photos
586. William Thomas Cain/Getty Images, Inc.
589. Elaine Thompson/AP Wide World Photos
593. Spencer Platt/Getty Images, Inc.
594. © Michael Brown/CORBIS All Rights Reserved
599. Gilles Mingasson/Getty Images, Inc.
603. © Kim Kulish/CORBIS All Rights Reserved
605. Jakub Mosur/AP Wide World Photos

Chapter 18

617. Rob Tringali/Sportschrome/Allsport Concepts/Getty Images
621. William Thomas Cain/Getty Images, Inc.
624. Amy E. Voigt/The New York Times
625. David Kadlubowski/The New York Times
627. Yoshikazu Tsuno/Agence France Presse/Getty Images
630. Mustafa Quraishi/AP Wide World Photos
637. Yesikka Vivancos/AP Wide World Photos
640. Yuriko Nakao/Corbis/Reuters America LLC

Chapter 19

651. Mel Evans/AP Wide World Photos
655. Antonio Calanni/AP Wide World Photos
663. Michael Stravato/The New York Times
665. Joe Raedle/Getty Images, Inc.
668. Richard Allenby-Pratt/arabianEye/Redux Pictures
675. Leah Nash/The New York Times
679. Kevin Rivoli/AP Wide World Photos
680. Aijaz Rahi/AP Wide World Photos

Name Index

A

B

C

M

N

O

P

Q

R

Organization Index

GLINDEX

A Combined Glossary/Subject Index

References followed by b indicate boxes; e, exhibits

F

G

H

I

J

M

N

Q

R

S